# A BIBLIOGRAPHY OF STEPHEN LEACOCK

# A Bibliography of
# Stephen Leacock

CARL SPADONI

ECW PRESS

CANADIAN CATALOGUING IN PUBLICATION DATA

Spadoni, Carl
    A bibliography of Stephen Leacock

Includes bibliographical references and index.
ISBN 1-55022-365-8

1. Leacock, Stephen, 1869–1944 – Bibliography. 1. Title.

PS8523.E15Z991 1998      016.818'5209      C98-931406-5
PR9199.3.L367Z868 1998

This book has been published with the assistance of grants from the Social Sciences and Humanities Research Council of Canada, The Canada Council, and the Ontario Arts Council.

Design and imaging by ECW Type & Art, Oakville, Ontario.
Printed and bound by Data Reproductions, Ann Arbor, Michigan.

Distributed by General Distribution Services,
30 Lesmill Road, Don Mills, Ontario M3B 2T6.

Published by ECW PRESS,
2120 Queen Street East,
Toronto, Ontario M4E 1E2.

http://www.ecw.ca/press

PRINTED AND BOUND IN CANADA

# Table of Contents

*Book [illegible]*

# TABLE OF CONTENTS

7

# TABLE OF CONTENTS

TABLE OF CONTENTS

# *Acknowledgments*

A descriptive bibliography of this scope and size cannot be carried out without the cooperation and industry of many persons and institutions. In search of elusive imprints, a bibliographer must necessarily strain the limits of good will of even the most gracious and accommodating individuals.

My first thanks go to my research assistant, Sheila Turcon. I have known Sheila since 1980 when she and I were hired at McMaster University. She has worked at a number of research-related jobs in the humanities at McMaster, and I am indeed fortunate to have had her as an assistant throughout this bibliographical project. My admiration for her diligence and accuracy has remained undiminished throughout these years. I readily acknowledge her contribution to sections C to F and H to K. Although I have provided her with verified entries and leads to countless others, she has drafted the entries as required, arranged them appropriately, rendered them consistent in terms of format, pursued many leads on her own initiative, and pointed out errors, inconsistencies, and omissions in the final draft of the book. The scanning of many journals and newspapers for leads is largely due to her meticulous efforts.

Several other research assistants also worked on this project. At an initial stage my friend and colleague, Judy Donnelly, checked drafts of many descriptions from the A and B sections. She corrected transcriptions and offered constructive criticism. At McGill University Mita Sen-Roy hunted for Leacock's contributions in the *McGill Daily* and Montreal newspapers; Marjorie Gagnon also verified data for me in Montreal-related newspapers. In England Colin Davey tracked down Leacock's contributions to British serials at the Cambridge University Library and the British Library Newspaper Archives at Colindale.

A major debt is owed to previous bibliographers. A casual reader might have the impression that in my survey of previous bibliographies of Leacock (see pp. 33-6), I relish pointing out defects and omissions in these bibliographies. In point of fact, the opposite is the case. I place great importance on this previous work. I never had the pleasure of Gerhard R. Lomer's company. However, I have looked at his own papers at McGill, in particular his interesting correspondence with W. Kaye Lamb, and have the highest admiration for his pioneering efforts undertaken before the age of electronic resources and the availability of Leacock's papers at the Stephen Leacock Museum. Although I have not collaborated with Ralph L. Curry, I am grateful for his commitment and hard work in organizing Leacock's papers and in searching for new writings. Curry's enormous contribution to Leacock studies should not be forgotten.

Antiquarian book dealers have contributed to this bibliography significantly by finding and selling me books. They have known of my collecting of Leacock's books, and have generously given me first refusal of books which could have been sold quite easily to other customers. I have also benefited by their bibliographical observations and musings.

McMaster University Library deserves particular thanks. In 1995 the Library provided me with a research leave to pursue my bibliographical work. The Department of Interlending and Document Supply (Anne Pottier and Valerie Thomas) attended to my many requests. Grazyna Ziolkowski assisted me in the translation of Russian titles (A111); Ruby Chan offered similar assistance for Chinese titles (A130). I also made extensive use of the important publishers' archives at McMaster in the William Ready Division of Archives and Research Collections; acknowledgment is made to McMaster as owners of these archives.

Many librarians, archivists, and curators answered my numerous queries and gave me direction. Two individuals merit special mention. The Director of the Stephen Leacock Museum, Daphne Mainprize, has shared my enthusiasm for Leacock's work. She and her staff allowed me access to Leacock's papers and library and even permitted me the use of the Museum's word processor and photocopier. I have enjoyed our many conversations together about Leacock's life and lore. Bruce Whiteman, formerly the Head of Rare Books and Special Collections at McGill University and now Head Librarian of the William Andrews Clark Memorial Library, UCLA, gave me access to McGill's Friedman collection and other papers. He and his family opened up their home to me during my many visits to Montreal. His advice about bibliographical problems is much appreciated. In an age when researchers regard electronic technology as a panacea, his connoisseurship is a reminder that there is no quick route to textual scholarship.

Staff from institutions who assisted me in my work include the following: John Burtniak, Special Collections Librarian, Brock University Library; Victoria Owen, Director, Library Services, The Canadian National Institute for the Blind; Anne Dondertman (especially with respect to encyclopedia articles), Sandra Alston, Edna Hajnal, and Garron Wells, Thomas Fisher Rare Book Library, University of Toronto; George F. Henderson, Queen's University Archives; Richard Virr, Department of Rare Books and Special Collections, McGill University; Apollonia Steele, Special Colections Librarian, University of Calgary; Michel Brisebois and Peter Rochon, National Library of Canada; Anne Goddard, National Archives of Canada; John Jakobson and Patricia Stone, North York Public Library; Phoebe Chartrand and Rob Michel, McGill University Archives; Pamela Miller, McCord Museum, McGill University (for the records of the Pen and Pencil Club); Marian Spence, Archivist, Upper Canada College; Cheryl Ennals, University Archivist, Mount Allison University; Cheryl Avery, University Archives, University of Saskatchewan; Leslie A. Morris, Curator of Manuscripts, The Houghton Library, Harvard University; Nancy M. Deromedi, Reference Assistant, Bentley Historical Library, The University of Michigan; Gene DeGruson, Curator of Special Collections, Leonard H. Axe Library, Pittsburgh State University; Bernard R. Crystal, Curator of Manuscripts, Rare Book and Manuscript Library, Columbia University in the City of New York; Margaret R. Goostray, Mugar Memorial Library, Boston University; Maynard Brichford, University Archivist, University of Illinois at Urbana-Champaign; Rachel Howarth and Will Goodwin, Harry Ransom Humanities Research Center, The University of Texas at Austin; Kimberly King Zea, Special Collections, Dartmouth College Library; Margaret M. Sherry, Department of Rare Books and Special Collections, Princeton University Libraries; Craig A. Wilson, University of Delaware Libraries; Rebecca Campbell Cape, Lilly Library, Indiana University; Robin Anne O'Sullivan, The University of Chicago Library; Vincent Giroud, Curator of Modern Books and Manuscripts, The Beinecke Rare Book and Manuscript Library, Yale University Library; Lars Mahinske and Shanta Uddin, *Encyclopaedia Britannica*; James Roan, Museum of American History at the Smithsonian Institutions; Nicholas Smith, Under-Librarian, Rare Books Department, Cambridge University Library; Julie Anne Lambert, The Bodleian Library; Sir Anthony Kenny, The Rhodes House; Frances Miller, The Library, University of Reading; Robert R.L. Arpots, Curator of Rare Books, University Library, Katholieke Universiteit Nijmegen; and Diane Woods, Alexander Turnbull Library, National Library of New Zealand.

Information was also obtained from publishers: Gail Stewart, Assistant to the Publisher, McClelland & Stewart Inc., for information on books published by M&S since 1989; Glenn Clever of Borealis / Tecumseh Presses Limited for A11k; David B. Noxon of Canadiana House for A117; Peter Sibbald Brown for A13b and A131; Barry L. Penhale of Natural Heritage / Natural History

Inc. for A126; John Robert Colombo for A132; Gaye Poulton, Contracts Department, Random House UK Limited (for John Lane The Bodley Head).

In addition to professional staff, a number of individuals either provided me with information or allowed me to examine their collections of Leacock material: J.A. "Pete" McGarvey; Reta Burrows; Jack McClelland for access to his correspondence in the McClelland and Stewart fonds at OHM; David Staines, University of Ottawa; Janet Friskney for information on the McClelland and Stewart's New Canadian Library and for searching microfilms of newspapers; Peter E. Greig for A60; William H. Latimer; John F. Evans; and Chris R. Tame, the Director of the Libertarian Alliance, for A127.

In the Introduction I have briefly listed archives and libraries where Leacock's papers, correspondence, and books are located. Acknowledgement in terms of ownership of material is made to these many repositories. For permission to quote from the papers of John Lane The Bodley Head, I am grateful to Random House UK Limited. Nancy Winthrop, Leacock's grandniece, has generously permitted me to quote from Leacock's unpublished writings.

In terms of funding, the Bibliographical Society of America awarded me a research fellowship in 1993. This fellowship allowed me to begin the bibliography in earnest, to map it out, and to travel to various libraries and archives. The Social Sciences and Humanities Research Council of Canada awarded me a strategic research grant from 1994 to 1997, and permitted me to extend the project to the end of March 1998. Funding from SSHRC has paid for the work of my research assistants, travel, and incidental expenses. Part of the SSHRC grant has also been used to subsidize publication.

I dedicate this bibliography to my friend and colleague, Richard Landon, the Director of the Thomas Fisher Rare Book Library at the University of Toronto. In 1979–80 when I completed a library science degree at Toronto's Faculty of Library and Information Science, I was fortunate to take his courses in rare books and bibliography. Richard's formidable knowledge and infectious enthusiasm instilled in me the love of books. He has inspired a generation of bibliographers and rare book librarians. In some measure this bibliography is a reflection of his enduring influence.

Carl Spadoni
William Ready Divison of Archives and Research Collections
McMaster University Library

# Chronology

1869     Birth of Leacock on 30 December at Swanmore, Hampshire, England.

1876     In the spring Leacock's family joins his father, Peter, in Canada, and sails from Liverpool for Montreal. The family lives on a farm in the hamlet of Egypt in Ontario, situated near the village of Sutton in the Township of Georgina.

1882     In January Leacock is enrolled at Upper Canada College in Toronto.

1886     He is appointed joint editor of the school paper, the *College Times* (vol. 6). Thirteen issues appear between 4 November 1886 and 9 June 1887.

1887     On 7 April Leacock's first signed article, "The Vision of Mirza (New Edition)" (C87.1), is published in the *College Times*. In the spring he graduates as head boy from Upper Canada College. In June he writes the matriculation examinations at the University of Toronto, and wins a scholarship. In the summer Leacock's father leaves his family forever. Leacock begins his studies at the University of Toronto in November.

1888     Due to family exigencies Leacock withdraws from the University of Toronto, goes to the Strathroy Collegiate Institute in September, and obtains his teacher's certificate as a specialist in Latin, Greek, French, German, and English.

1889     In February he is hired as a modern language teacher at Uxbridge High School. In the fall he joins the staff of Upper Canada College as junior master, and resumes his studies at the University of Toronto.

1890     From October to December Leacock is associate editor of the University of Toronto's paper, the *Varsity*. He contributes a column entitled "The Sanctum Philosopher" (see C90.1). He wins the Julius Rossin Scholarship.

1891    Leacock graduates with an honours degree from the University of Toronto, and is appointed Assistant House Master at Upper Canada College.

1894    On 19 May he makes his debut as a professional humorist with the publication of "ABC: or, The Human Element in Mathematics" (see C94.1).

1895    The entire teaching staff of Upper Canada College is dismissed. Leacock is re-hired by the new Principal, George Parkin, as senior housemaster.

1899    Leacock resigns from Upper Canada College, borrows $1,500 from his mother, and on 25 September begins graduate studies at the University of Chicago.

1900    At the end of his first academic year at Chicago, Leacock earns a fellowship. In June he is offered the position of sessional lecturer in political science and history at McGill University. On 7 August in New York City, he marries Beatrix Hamilton, a granddaughter of Sir Henry Pellatt.

1901    On 7 January he gives his first lecture at McGill University.

1903    On 11 May Leacock defends his doctoral thesis, "The Doctrine of *Laissez Faire*" (see A134). His Ph.D. in political economy and political science is conferred on 16 June *magnum cum laude*. He is appointed as a lecturer in political economy at McGill.

1906    From 12 January to 23 March, Leacock delivers a series of lectures on the British Empire at the Queen's Hall in Ottawa (see A1). *Elements of Political Science* (A2) is published in June. He is promoted to the rank of Associate Professor at McGill.

1907    During February and April, he is a member of the editorial board of the *University Magazine* (vol. 6, two issues) under the editorship of Andrew Macphail. From 23 April to 5 March 1908, Leacock tours the British Empire as a Cecil Rhodes lecturer on "Imperial Organization." On 8 July *Baldwin, Lafontaine, Hincks: Responsible Government* (A4) is published in The Makers of Canada Series.

1908    On 15 April Leacock purchases property at Old Brewery Bay on Lake Couchiching in the Township of South Orillia. At McGill he is appointed William Dow Professor of Political Economy, and becomes Chairman of the Department of Economics and Political Science.

1910    At his own instigation Leacock arranges for the vanity publication of his first book of humour, *Literary Lapses* (A5). It is published on 9 April in an edition of 3,000 copies. John Lane becomes Leacock's English publisher, and promotes him as "The Canadian Mark Twain."

1911 The first English edition of *Nonsense Novels* (A7a) is published in May. Leacock writes articles against free trade with the United States, and in the federal election he campaigns for the Conservatives in Montreal and Simcoe County.

1912 In January and February the Musson Book Co. temporarily obtains the agency for the Canadian sales of Leacock's humorous books. The Publishers' Press, which had arranged the newspaper syndication of Leacock's articles and had published the Canadian issue of *Nonsense Novels* (A7a.1), goes bankrupt in April. Between 17 February and 22 June, *Sunshine Sketches of a Little Town* (A11) is published serially in the *Montreal Star*. In February and March arrangements are made so that Bell and Cockburn handle Canadian sales of the book. The first English edition is published on 9 August.

1913 The American edition of *Behind the Beyond and Other Contributions to Human Knowledge* (A12a) is published on 31 October. At McGill Leacock establishes the Political Economy Club.

1914 In July Leacock is feted by The Bodley Head at an afternoon tea-party attended by a number of literary celebrities, including Wyndham Lewis, H.H. Munro, and Ezra Pound. The first four chapters (C14.9, C14.13-5, C14.17) of *Arcadian Adventures with the Idle Rich* (A16) are published in the *American Magazine* between July and November. The book is published on 2 November. Volumes 1 (*The Dawn of Canadian History*, A17), 2 (*The Mariner of St. Malo*, A18), and 20 (*Adventurers of the Far North*, A19) of The Chronicles of Canada series are published. Bell and Cockburn goes bankrupt in December. S.B. Gundy assumes the agency for Leacock's books in Canada.

1915 Beginning on 15 February, and on many other occasions throughout the duration of the First World War, Leacock gives readings from his humorous work in aid of the Belgian Relief Fund. Between April and December, with Sir William Peterson, C.W. Colby, and P.T. Lafleur, he edits three issues of the *University Magazine* (vol. 14). On 19 August, Leacock's son, Stephen Lushington, is born. The American edition of *Moonbeams from the Larger Lunacy* (A21) is published on 22 October.

1916 On 14 or 20 April the American edition of *Essays and Literary*

*Studies* (A22a) is published. The American edition of *Further Foolishness* (A24a) is published on 1 December.

1917 On 20 June Leacock receives an honorary LL.D. from Brown University. On 15 December the American edition of *Frenzied Fiction* (A26a) is published.

1919 On 12 April the American edition of *The Hohenzollerns in America with the Bolsheviks in Berlin and Other Impossibilities* (A29a) is published. Leacock is elected as a Fellow of Royal Society of Canada. He receives an honorary LL.D. from Queen's University. He serves as the first chairman of the editorial board of the *McGill News* (the organ of the Graduates' Society of McGill University).

1920 On 16 January the American edition of *The Unsolved Riddle of Social Justice* (A31a) is published. Leacock receives an honorary Litt.D. degree from Dartmouth College on 23 June. The American edition of *Winsome Winnie and Other New Nonsense Novels* (A32a) is published on 24 November.

1921 On 14 September Leacock sails for England. From 4 October to 23 December, he embarks on a lecture tour of England and Scotland. Leacock is a charter member of the Canadian Authors Association.

1922 On 3 January John Lane sells the American branch of his publishing company, the John Lane Company, to Dodd, Mead. Thereafter, Dodd, Mead becomes Leacock's chief publisher in the United States. The American edition of *My Discovery of England* (A37a) is published on 17 June.

1923 On 22 June the English edition of *Over the Footlights and Other Fancies* (A39a) is published. The American edition of *College Days* (A40a) is published on 20 October.

1924 The English edition of *The Garden of Folly* (A43a) is published at the end of July.

1925 On 15 December Leacock's wife dies of cancer.

1926 After 6 February S.B. Gundy is no longer Leacock's Canadian publisher. Leacock approaches the Macmillan Company of Canada to take over Canadian sales. On 26 April he drafts an agreement with the Macmillan Company of Canada for a monographic series, the McGill University Economic Studies in the National Problems of Canada; the series is intended as a venue for the publication of theses written by graduate students from McGill's Department of Economics and Political Science. The

English edition of *Winnowed Wisdom* (A44a) is published in June.

1927     On 7 October Leacock is awarded an honorary D.Litt. degree from the University of Toronto.

1928     In May the Orillia contractors, E. Webb and Son, rebuild Leacock's country home at Old Brewery Bay. The American edition of *Short Circuits* (A52a) is published on 15 June.

1929     On 15 November the English edition of *The Iron Man and the Tin Woman and Other Futurities* (A53a) is published.

1930     On 24 July the English edition of *Economic Prosperity in the British Empire* (A54b) is published. In late August *The Leacock Book* (A55) is published. The first American edition of *Laugh with Leacock* (A56a) is published on 3 October.

1931     On 23 January McClelland and Stewart acquires the Canadian rights to most of Leacock's previously published books. *Wet Wit & Dry Humour* (A57) is published on 8 May.

1932     In early January the Canadian edition of *Back to Prosperity* (A58a) is published. *The Dry Pickwick and Other Incongruities* (A59) is published on 19 February. Although some copies of Leacock's edition of *Lahontan's Voyages* (A60) are released to the public in April, the book's publisher, Graphic Publishers, goes bankrupt at the time of publication. Leacock resigns from the Royal Society of Canada in May. On 23 September the American edition of *Afternoons in Utopia* (A61) is published. The English edition of *Mark Twain* (A62) is published on 17 November.

1933     The English edition of *Charles Dickens: His Life and Work* (A65a) is published on 28 November. Sir Arthur Currie, the Principal of McGill, dies on 30 November; Leacock's tribute (C33.10) to him is reprinted in many Canadian newspapers.

1934     On 23 February the American edition of *Lincoln Frees the Slaves* (A67a) is published. Beginning on 27 March, Leacock gives a series of radio broadcasts of his humorous works; although he agrees to deliver twenty-six talks over the radio, only sixteen are actually given. On 21 June Bishop's College confers a Doctor of Civil Laws on Leacock in recognition of his contribution to Canadian letters. *The Greatest Pages of Charles Dickens* (A69) is published on 11 July. On 24 August *The Pursuit of Knowledge* (A70) is published.

1935     On 16 January Leacock is awarded the Mark Twain Medal. The American edition of *Humor, Its Theory and Technique* (A73a) is published on 10 April.

1936   In early March the first American edition of *The Greatest Pages of American Humor* (A77a) is published. *Hellements of Hickonomics in Hiccoughs of Verse Done in Our Social Planning Mill* (A78) is published on 31 March. On 31 May Leacock is forced into retirement at McGill University. McGill confers on him an honorary LL.D., and makes him Professor Emeritus. Leacock is appointed to the Advisory Board of the Encyclopaedia Britannica Foundation on 26 August. The Canadian edition of *The Gathering Financial Crisis in Canada* (A79a) is published in October. On 28 October the American edition of *Funny Pieces: A Book of Random Sketches* (A80) is published. On 25 November Leacock embarks on a lecture tour of western Canada, his first stop being in Port Arthur, ON, on 27 November. The University of Michigan grants him a Litt.D. degree.

1937   The Bodley Head experiences financial problems. In January the company is sold to P.P. Howe, who forms a new company with the assistance of other publishers. These problems cause delays in the publication of the English editions of Leacock's books. In June the Canadian edition of *My Discovery of the West* (A82a) is published. The American edition of *Here Are My Lectures and Stories* (A83a) is published on 15 November. The English edition of *Humour and Humanity* (A84) is also published on 15 November in The Home University Library of Modern Knowledge series. The Royal Society of Canada awards Leacock the Lorne Pierce Medal for his contribution to Canadian letters.

1938   In March Leacock is admitted to Montreal's Royal Victoria Hospital for prostrate surgery. The American edition of *Model Memoirs and Other Sketches from Simple to Serious* (A86a) is published on 23 November. Leacock is awarded the Governor-General's Prize for *My Discovery of the West* in the non-fiction category.

1939   On 16 June, at Kitchener to the McGill Association of Ontario, with his friend René du Roure in attendance, Leacock delivers his last public speech. On 27 October the Canadian edition of *All Right, Mr. Roosevelt* (A87a) is published in the Oxford Pamphlets on World Affairs series. The American edition of *Too Much College* (A88a) is published on 10 November.

1940   On 14 May the American edition of *The British Empire* (A89a) is published. *Stephen Leacock's Laugh Parade* (A91) is published on 15 October.

1941     At the end of November *Canada: The Foundations of Its Future* (A92) is printed by the Gazette Printing Company, and is ready for distribution to the public.

1942     On 24 February the first American edition of *My Remarkable Uncle and Other Sketches* (A93a) is published. The English edition of *Our Heritage of Liberty* (A94a) is published on 5 June. On 8 September Leacock agrees to revise or rewrite completely all the entries related to Canada in the *Encyclopaedia Britannica*. On 13 November the American edition of *Montreal, Seaport and City* (A94b) is published in the Seaport Series.

1943     On 5 January the American edition of *How to Write* (A96a) is published. The American edition of *Happy Stories Just to Laugh at* (A99) is published on 12 November.

1944     On 16 March Leacock undergoes an operation for cancer of the throat. On 28 March he dies at Toronto General Hospital.

1947     Harry Symons is awarded the Leacock Memorial Medal for Humour for *Ojibway Melody*. Thereafter, the medal is awarded annually for the best book of humour written by a Canadian.

1958     On 5 July Leacock's home at Old Brewery Bay is declared by the Canadian government to be a national historic site.

# Introduction

SCOPE AND ARRANGEMENT OF THE BIBLIOGRAPHY

This descriptive bibliography records Stephen Leacock's published work from his first known venture into print (C87.1) until the cut-off date of 1998. All his publications are included — his many books, pamphlets, and broadsides, his humorous sketches and stories, his social, political, and economic commentaries, his scholarly accomplishments as an historian, his diatribes against prohibition, his syndicated articles, his doggerel verse, letters to editors, his reminiscences, translations of his work, interviews, reports of his speeches, and so on. The only exceptions to this all-encompassing approach are the following: the unsigned course descriptions that he wrote or may have edited annually for the Department of Economics and Political Science found in McGill University's academic calendars; quotations from manuscripts, letters, and other archival documents in antiquarian or auction catalogues; extracts of less than a few hundred words such as "A Leacock Sampler" in Leslie F. Hannon, ed., *Maclean's Canada: Portrait of a Country* (Toronto: McClelland and Stewart, 1960), pp. 94–9.

In view of the fact that new editions of Leacock's work have continued to appear after his death, it seems eminently sensible to include his posthumous publications as well as those that were published during his lifetime. The bibliography is limited to published work rather than archival documents, although the latter are often cited. Leacock's papers are held at several repositories; to describe these documents in a comprehensive way would require a separate volume. Also excluded is secondary literature, that is to say, commentaries by critics and others on Leacock's work, life, and times. The only exception to the citation of secondary literature is when a publication includes something substantial that Leacock wrote himself (see section K).

Although I have aimed at completeness, I fully realize that with a writer of Leacock's stature and prolific pen, this pursuit is a will-o'-the-wisp. A hundred years hence, bibliographers and other scholars will be reporting newly discovered writings of Leacock. His publications often appear not just in mainstream magazines such as *Vanity Fair* or *Collier's* but in obscure newspapers and journals devoted to fishing, mining, and a host of other subjects. If an editor of a college magazine in Winnipeg or Providence, Rhode Island, asked Leacock to write a short piece on a particular subject, he often complied even when he had a pressing deadline to finish several books. If the editor offered him a nominal fee, that spurred him on to do the job. He certainly wrote for money, and he took pride in the accumulation of his royalties. However, he sometimes dashed off or revised an article without a fee because the magazine editor had praised his work.

It may be of some interest to note Leacock's annual earnings during the heyday of his writing career. In 1914–5 he earned $10,103.87. By 1922–3, one of his most successful years financially, his total earnings were $40,988.33. His salary at McGill during that time had increased from $3,500 to $5,500. In 1914–5 he made almost $240 from his magazine articles and more than $2,500 from his book royalties; his speaking engagements outside of McGill only earned him $100. In 1922–3 his articles, including those from syndication, earned $9,429, his lectures earned more than $3,200, and his royalties from books amounted to slightly more than $8,400 (information based on Leacock's notebook of royalty payments at SLM).

Leacock's major articles often appeared on both sides of the Atlantic. His literary agents such as Paul R. Reynolds maximized his earnings. Reprintings seemingly go on and on. After his humorous articles were published in serial form, Leacock usually gathered them together into a book. In the preface to *Moonbeams from the Larger Lunacy*, he speaks of the prudent husbandman who repeatedly rakes his fields for more straw and of the child who squeezes the lemons in a water jug to produce more lemonade: "So does the sagacious author, after having sold his material to the magazines and been paid for it, clap it into book-covers and give it another squeeze." Even so, there are many instances of Leacock's serial publications that have never been reprinted.

The monographic republication of his serial contributions was a pattern that Leacock established practically on an annual basis. But he also reversed that process, so to speak. This is especially in evidence with respect to his short syndicated articles in the 1920s. He used the services of syndication agencies on several occasions: Max Joseph Epstein of the Publishers' Press in 1910 and 1911; Max Elser, Jr. of the Metropolitan Newspaper Service from 1921 to 1930; the Dominion News Syndicate during the 1920s; the Bell

Syndicate in the 1930s; and Andrew Miller of Miller Services Limited in 1937–8. Leacock's weekly syndicated articles for the Metropolitan Newspaper Service appeared in dozens of newspapers in North America, England, India, and China (see A38). I have reported Leacock's Metropolitan syndicated articles, but in doing so, I have selected a representative newspaper such as the *Montreal Standard*. No attempt has been made to track down the multiple reprintings of these syndicated articles. Many of the syndicated articles, it should be noted, are taken from sketches or articles in Leacock's previously published books. With respect to these syndicated extracts, he often shortened the piece or added a sentence or paragraph to suit his purposes.

The bibliography not only attempts to record all of Leacock's publications, but it does so physically and intellectually by following the protocols of descriptive bibliography. This bibliographical approach makes certain assumptions. To begin with, Leacock's publications are grouped together into various traditional categories, organized chronologically within each category — his separate publications (A section), his contributions to books (B section), his contributions to periodicals (section C), and so on. The extent of description varies according to the significance or nature of the publication. A entries, for example, are described in depth, and are accompanied by publishing history. To qualify for the A section, a publication must have appeared separately and have been distributed to the public; in a few instances an imprint distributed to a small audience has been included (for example, advertisement brochures from his publishers). B entries are described in a manner similar to the A entries but without a complete description of the book's contents. For C entries description is limited to title of the article, name of the periodical, volume and issue number, date, and pagination.

With the exception of sections H (translations) and I (recordings by Leacock, Braille, talking books, and films), all items have been examined. The reasons for these exceptions are the following: (1) Many translations are cited in national bibliographies and tools such as *Index Translationum*. Unfortunately, most of these translations are especially difficult to locate in North American libraries, and often can only found in their country of origin. To examine copies of these translations would have necessitated travelling to distant places at great expense. (2) Audio recordings and items in Braille are similarly difficult to locate. They are often housed in national centers for the visually handicapped, are intended for a special clientele, and are generally not available through interlibrary loan.

I have added several new categories to those that are commonly found in descriptive bibliographies such as section E (Lectures Given) and section J

(Encyclopedia Articles). These sections reflect Leacock's career as a writer and lecturer. During the 1920s, the heyday of Leacock's time on the lecture circuit, he thought nothing of taking a train from Montreal at mid-week, travelling to an American city such as Chicago or Boston, speaking at various cities along the way, and returning to Montreal for his lectures at McGill University on the next Monday. In the preface to *Sunshine Sketches of a Little Town*, Leacock remarked that he ". . . would sooner have written 'Alice in Wonderland' than the whole Encyclopaedia Britannica." In point of fact, he was a busy contributor to encyclopedias. Almost a year before his death, for example, he agreed to revise or rewrite all the entries in the *Encyclopaedia Britannica* relating to Canada. He wrote to every town and city in Canada listed in the *Encyclopaedia Britannica* for demographic and other statistical information. For many of these entries he merely updated the information, but for others he completely rewrote the entry.

Bibliographies ordinarily report only recorded publications of an author in spite of the fact that there are often leads to publications that simply cannot be found. Section L (Lost Leads) constitutes a nebulous class of potential publications — a list of imprints and articles not located. These consist of genuine leads to items which I have been unable to verify. The lead may have been cited in a previous bibliography or by Leacock himself in his correspondence or notebooks. The item in question cannot be located because the citation is simply wrong or incomplete, the item may been published at an earlier or later date or in a different publication, the publication in question no longer appears to be extant, or the item for whatever reason never appeared in print. I am hopeful that some of the items in this section will be found by scholars in the future. Not included in section L are Leacock's incomplete or unrealized projects. An author such as Leacock dreams of many books, but only a finite number of them are finished in a lifetime. He proposed many ideas to his publishers — for example, "My Discovery of Europe: Summer Time Sketches of the Casinos & Watering Places on the Continent" (leaflet at SLM, 4 pp., 50 copies printed by the Beaver Hall Press of Montreal on 26 February 1927). I regret to say that however interesting these unfinished ventures may appear, they lie outside the scope of the bibliography.

Collectors of Leacock's books, antiquarian dealers, and librarians will undoubtedly benefit from this bibliography. They will be able to identify editions, issues, variants, and reprintings. Although I greatly admire collectors of books, the primary audience for this bibliography ultimately is the scholar and reader who wishes to examine, enjoy, and discover Leacock's work. Leacock's writings will continue to be published, and undoubtedly they will eventually appear in critical or collected editions. My basic assumption is that one cannot gather, study, or judge Leacock's texts for a scholarly edition unless one knows what they are, where they have occurred, and how they have evolved in the context of his life and publishing career. This bibliography, when combined with a union list of Leacock's manuscripts, will provide the groundwork for a collected edition or for a series of individual critical editions.

With respect to the collecting of books, I am mindful of Leacock's own caveat. He argued that the market value of a first edition is no indication of the literary or intellectual significance of the work itself or of the eminence of the author. He regarded bibliomania as a harmless activity, bordering on lunacy, in which collectors are deceived by the preciousness of pristine editions: "Indeed the 'first edition hobby' is one of the minor forms of mental derangement, seldom ending in homicide and outside the scope of the law" (A65a, p. 257). I partly agree with this criticism, especially when collectors (and I am among them) go to extraordinary lengths to acquire fine copies of books. Fussiness of this kind wrongly leads the collector to desire the object (the physical book) for its own sake without regard to the object's critical importance (the text of the book). In an essay in which he lampooned the classics and the study of Latin and Greek, Leacock satirized book collecting in the following way:

> The first edition will be an *édition de luxe*, bound in vellum or perhaps in buckskin, and sold at five hundred dollars. It will be limited to five hundred copies, and, of course, sold only to the feeble minded. The next edition will be the Literary Edition, and sold to artists, authors, actors, and contractors. After that will come the Boarding House Edition, bound in board and paid for in the same way. ("Homer and Humbug, an Academic Discussion," in A12a, p. 190)

## DESCRIPTIVE ELEMENTS

By necessity a descriptive bibliography employs bibliographical terms and other words and phrases from the book arts. These terms, words and phrases (for example, edition, issue, state, quasi-facsimile transcription, etc.) have a precise meaning, and I have tried to be clear and consistent in my employment of them. In lieu of a glossary of terms, I refer the reader to Roy Stokes's *A Bibliographical Companion* (Metuchen, N.J.: Scarecrow Press, 1989) and Geoffrey Ashall Glaister's *Glossary of the Book* (London: George Allen and Unwin, 1960).

Each entry in the bibliography is numbered. Minimally, an item number consists of an alphabetical letter in capitals followed by a numeric. A11, for example, signifies Leacock's eleventh separate publication, *Sunshine Sketches of a Little Town*. For the A and B sections, in order to individuate and differentiate editions and issues, item numbers are often more complex (for example, A11b.1), and feature a lower case alphabetical letter and a decimal number. Brief descriptions and usually a date are provided after the item number in the A and B sections for clarity — for example, "*first Canadian issue of the first American edition* (1931)." Numbering in the C, D, E, F, J, K, and L sections includes the year of publication accompanied by a decimal number. For example, C12.2 means that the article in question is the second serial article by Leacock published in 1912.

In addition to the item number, descriptions in the A section are comprised of the following fields of information: quasi-facsimile transcription of the title page; collation; pagination; foliation; measurement of the trimmed leaf in millimetres (height × width); contents; text; binding and dust jacket; notes; and copies examined. In certain cases, when issues are being described and the issue is almost the same as the derivative edition, some fields of information have been eliminated or information related to these fields has been compressed.

Title-page transcription, collation, pagination, foliation, and measurement conform to the bibliographical principles enunciated by Fredson Bowers and Philip Gaskell. The kind of typeface found on the title page is specified only if it is distinctive or unusual. My source for the style of typefaces is J. Lieberman's *Type and Typefaces: A Treasury of Typography Book*, 2nd ed. (New Rochelle, New York: The Myriade Press, 1978).

The contents field records each separate section or part of a book, including the half-title page, the copyright page, the preface, the table of contents, the text, advertisements, and all blank leaves. The text field is similar to the table of contents of a book, and specifically refers to Leacock's text. For example, if the book in question is a collection of stories, then each story will be listed. All binding variants and dust jackets are described. With respect to the type of binding and its colour, I have tried to keep things as simple as possible. I have not employed the *ISCC-NBS Centroid Color Charts*; these charts unfortunately only became available to me at a late stage of my bibliographical work. The notes concern publishing history and are based largely on primary sources — they relate to the genesis and development of the book, Leacock's interaction with his publishers, the publication of the book (printing, distribution, and sales), and the book's price. The extent of the notes varies considerably. When little or practically no notes are provided, the reader can assume that I have been unable to locate relevant information from primary sources. All publications, except the entries in the H and I sections, have been examined, and locations are cited for copies examined. In all cases the copy examined is the "ideal copy" (ordinarily the first printing and in the condition described). For copies at Canadian libraries, the location symbols have been taken from the twelfth edition of *Symbols of Canadian Libraries / Sigles des bibliothèques canadiennes* (Ottawa: National Library of Canada, 1987).

Citations in the C, D, F, J, K, and L sections follow the fourteenth edition of *The Chicago Style Manual* (1993). Annotations have been provided to the entries in certain sections such as D and F in order to convey the importance of Leacock's literary or publishing activity. Items in section G (Authorized Adaptations, Separately Published) have ordinarily been attributed to Leacock as a joint author because his name appears on the title page. Archival evidence shows quite clearly, however, that he did not participate as an author in these adaptations but only authorized them. Consequently, for entries in section G, description has been curtailed somewhat and does not wholly follow the protocols of descriptive bibliography. Other adaptations of Leacock's work — for example, Mavor Moore's *Sunshine Town* or one man shows such as those by John Stark — are not recorded.

## PREVIOUS BIBLIOGRAPHIES OF LEACOCK

Peter McArthur's *Stephen Leacock* (A41) contained the first comprehensive bibliography of Stephen Leacock's publications. At the time Leacock was fifty-three years of age and in mid-career. As a humorist he had established himself internationally as a successor to Mark Twain. He was renowned as a platform speaker, and was respected as a social critic. His sketches and stories, much sought after by editors, appeared regularly in magazines in North America and in Great Britain. In addition, he was a household name to newspaper readers who enjoyed his amusing articles, syndicated on a weekly basis throughout the world.

On 28 July and 3 October 1923, Lorne Pierce, the Book Editor and Literary Advisor to The Ryerson Press, inquired on McArthur's behalf about Leacock's publications. Pierce sent Leacock a checklist. Leacock crossed out four pages of magazine articles attributed to him, and he hurriedly appended another three pages of "Longer Magazine articles (other than those reprinted in books)." The bibliography in *Stephen Leacock* was divided into six parts: I Historical Works; II Works on Economics; III Essays; IV Humorous Works;

v Magazine Articles; and vi Magazine References. Part v was in fact revised according to Leacock's direction with his proviso duly noted.

In 1935, a year prior to Leacock's retirement from McGill University, the McGill University Library School Class of 1935 undertook the first separately published bibliography of his work, *A Bibliography of Stephen Butler Leacock*, under the direction of Marion Villiers Higgins, Instructor of Bibliography. Enumerative and classified, the McGill bibliography was divided into published works by Leacock and works about him. The former category was subdivided into twelve sections: biography, economics, education, history, humour, journalism, literary criticism, political science, sociology, sports, syndicated articles, and translations. Higgins acknowledged ". . . the complete cooperation of Dr. Leacock without which the compilation of this bibliography would have been impossible" (p. 4). At the same time she admitted:

> It was with much regret that the idea of a complete bibliography had to be abandoned, due to the fact that lists of syndicated articles are not available and that un-indexed magazines and newspapers require a page by page search, a service which many libraries were naturally unable to give. (p. 4)

Leacock told McGill University's Librarian, Gerhard R. Lomer, that he was ". . . deeply sensible of the honour done to me in the preparation of a bibliography" (4 March 1935, QMMRB). As a sign of his gratitude Leacock even promised to donate the manuscripts of his books to McGill, although he did not make the first installment of his gift until 1942.

In contrast to the pamphlet produced under Higgins's direction, Lomer's *Stephen Leacock: A Check-List and Index of His Writings* (Ottawa: National Library, 1954) is a more sustained effort, compiled several years after Leacock's death. Lomer knew Leacock personally, and he was quite aware of the scope and complexity of Leacock's canon. A supplement to Higgins's bibliography, covering the period from April 1935 to April 1942, had been compiled by H.L. Macdonald. Lomer availed himself of Macdonald's unpublished typescript, located in the files of McGill's Library School. He also checked another typescript "put together from printed lists but apparently not from an examination of the works, by a student in one of the English classes at McGill" (Lomer, p. 11). Lomer's checklist is comprised of three sections: a description in alphabetical order of Leacock's books, pamphlets, translations, prefaces, and introductions; a list of his essays, sketches, and articles in alphabetical order, excluding syndicated pieces; and a list of the manuscripts that Leacock donated to McGill University.

In 1946 Norman H. Friedman, a former student of Leacock, donated his impressive collection of Leacock's books to his alma mater. Most of the items in Friedman's collection were in fine condition as issued, and many had been inscribed by Leacock with revealing remarks as to publishing history (often quoted by Lomer). Although Lomer scrutinized Friedman's collection and tried, "in so far as this was practicable," to examine the first edition of each of Leacock's works, he indicated by an asterisk after each entry the editions that he had personally examined. Unfortunately, many editions cited by Lomer did not have an asterisk after the entry in question. In carrying out his bibliography, Lomer acknowledged the assistance of Leacock's secretary, Grace Reynolds, librarians from many libraries, and the publishing houses at The Bodley Head and Dodd, Mead. W. Kaye Lamb, the newly appointed Dominion Archivist and Librarian of the National Library of Canada, assisted Lomer greatly by examining copies of Leacock's books housed at the British Museum. In the compilation of his checklist, Lomer scoured national bibliographies and available indexes to periodicals.

In spite of such cooperation, Lomer admitted: "This reference aid to librarians and amateurs of Canadian writing is called a *Check-list* because unfortunately it cannot, at this present time, achieve the technical completeness strictly required by a *Bibliography*" (p. 11). The simultaneous publication of editions and issues in London, New York, and Toronto troubled Lomer. Which place of publication had priority? The records of English publishers, apparently destroyed ". . . in the War, occasionally raise bibliographical problems that at the moment cannot be definitely settled," he maintained (p. 13). Translations of Leacock's work also eluded Lomer.

"A comprehensive list of all of Leacock's publications, chronologically arranged, may appropriately appear as an appendix to a future definitive biography of the Canadian writer," Lomer suggested (p. 11). Ralph L. Curry's *Stephen Leacock: Humorist and Humanist* (New York: Doubleday, 1959) was the first biography of Leacock. Prior to the publication of his biography in September 1959, Curry had compiled an update to 1956 of Lomer's *Check-list*: "Stephen Butler Leacock: A Check-list," *Bulletin of Bibliography* 22, no. 5 (January–April 1958): 106–9. Shortly after completing his doctoral dissertation on the literary aspects of Leacock's humour, Curry journeyed to Orillia, ON, in July 1955 from Georgetown, Kentucky. He befriended people such as J.A. "Pete" McGarvey who wished to turn Leacock's home at Old Brewery Bay into an historic site. Curry charmed Leacock's son, Stephen Lushington, into getting access to Leacock's papers. "As exhaustive as Dr. Lomer's research was, there are some incomplete or erroneous entries, and there are some items his book lacks," Curry pointed out in his update.

He added that this was "largely because he [Lomer] did not have access to Leacock's correspondence and personal files." In his update Curry listed newly found editions, works in Braille, contributions to books and periodicals, encyclopedia articles, syndicated articles placed by Miller Services Limited (titles only), and translations.

Curry was hired as the curator of the Stephen Leacock Memorial Home (later called the Stephen Leacock Museum). He remained in that position until 1977, travelling each summer to Orillia where he arranged and described Leacock's papers and oversaw the museum's active programme to an increasing number of visitors. Curry also compiled a chronological checklist, "Stephen Leacock: The Writer and His Writings," which appeared in the proceedings of a Leacock symposium, *Stephen Leacock: A Reappraisal* (Ottawa: University of Ottawa, 1986). Although the editor of this volume, David Staines, referred to Curry's checklist as "the first complete bibliography of Leacock's publications" (p. 4), Curry's checklist was in fact not an advance over Lomer's previous compilation. Curry neglected to describe different editions, translations, and posthumous publications. He listed a few titles of syndicated articles but added the caveat: "These syndicated pieces have no proof of publication, although there are references to them in Leacock's correspondence; Leacock was paid for publication on these dates" (p. 160). Bibliographical errors and tantalizing incomplete descriptions were introduced into Leacock's canon by Curry. The greatest fault of Curry's checklist was that most of the cited publications had simply not been physically examined and verified.

## SOURCES CONSULTED

This descriptive bibliography of Leacock's publications has been constructed from a wide variety of sources: bibliographies, reference tools, periodical and book collections, archives (fonds and collections), databases, on-line catalogues, biographies, and other secondary literature. Entries found in previous bibliographies of Leacock have been searched. In addition to the bibliographies discussed in the previous section, many other bibliographies have been examined. These include: bibliographies devoted to Canadian literature and history such as Helen Hoy's *Modern English-Canadian Prose: A Guide to Information Sources* (Detroit: Gale Research Co., 1983), R.E. Watters's *A Checklist of Canadian Literature and Background Materials, 1628–1960*, 2nd ed., rev. and enl. (Toronto: University of Toronto Press, 1972), and

Paul Aubin, Paul-André Linteau, and Louis-Marie Côté's *Bibliographie de l'histoire du Québec et du Canada / Bibliography of the History of Quebec and Canada*, 8 vols. (Québec: Institut québecois de recherche sur la culture, 1981–90); and national bibliographies, including *Canadiana* and its predecessors, *The British Library General Catalogue*, *The English Catalogue of Books*, and the *National Union Catalog*. Entries in the *Cumulated Book Index* and the *United States Catalog, Books Published* were also perused, although the data in such entries appears dubious. Reference tools that have been examined include *Canadian Books in Print*, its American and British counterparts, the *Canadian Periodical Index*, and *Index Translationum*. Indexes that have been consulted include the *Personal Name Index to the New York Times*, *The Times Index*, Grace F. Heggie and Anne McGaughey's *Index to Canadian Bookman*, Heggie and Gordon R. Adhead's *An Index to Saturday Night: The First Fifty Years, 1887–1937*, and Heggie and McGaughey's *The University Magazine 19101–1920: An Annotated Index*.

Leacock's papers and library at the Stephen Leacock Museum contain a wealth of information about Leacock's publishing career: his correspondence, manuscripts, magazine publications, notebooks, royalty payments, income tax returns, and other financial documents. I have read or looked at all of this material. When publishing history is given in the notes of an A or B entry and a source has not been cited, the reader should assume that information has been obtained from the Leacock fonds at the Leacock Museum. An important document at the Leacock Museum is Leacock's notebook of royalty payments (1910–25) of his books of humour; books and pamphlets for which Leacock received a flat fee (such as the three books that Leacock wrote for The Chronicles of Canada series) are not listed in the notebook. The payments begin with *Literary Lapses* (A5) and end with *The Garden of Folly* (A43). In this notebook he usually recorded the date of publication, the number of copies sold annually (rather than the number of copies printed of an edition or impression), and the amount of royalty paid. In addition to the Leacock fonds, I have also examined J.A. "Pete" McGarvey's collection of Leacockiana that McGarvey donated to the Museum.

At McGill University there are two major holdings of Leacock's papers (see Marcel Caya, ed. et al., *Guide to Archival Resources at McGill University / Guide des sources d'archives à l'Université McGill* (Montreal: McGill University Archives, 1985). Leacock donated many of his manuscripts to McGill. These are located in the Department of Rare Books and Special Collections along with the Friedman book collection. Both the Leacock fonds and the book collection have been added to and enlarged since Leacock and Friedman made their donations. Among the items in the Department of Rare Books and

Special Collections is a notebook (1901–25) in which Leacock recorded his publications (see K94.2, pp. 12–3, for sample entries). The notebook lists the title of a work, its date of completion, and usually the place of publication. In spite of this methodical and meticulous appearance of record keeping, Leacock was quite vague about where and when his articles were published. Often the notebook neglects to state where a piece appeared, and sometimes the word, "syndicated," is the only clue as to publication.

The second location of Leacock material at McGill is in the McGill University Archives, which contain the administrative papers of McGill's Principals (RG32, Sir William Peterson and his successors), the Dean of Arts (RG32), Leacock's papers as Chairman of the Department of Economics and Political Science, the Gerhard R. Lomer fonds, the university's annual reports, and so on. The annual reports list faculty publications, but Leacock recorded his own publications on a hit-and-miss basis; none of his humorous or syndicated articles is reported in these reports perhaps because they were not sufficiently academic in nature. An important resource at the McGill University Archives is a large collection of photocopied news clippings related to events and developments at the university.

Between 1991 and 1994 Leacock's niece, Barbara Nimmo, sold the papers that she had inherited from her uncle to the National Archives of Canada; Mrs. Nimmo had sold the manuscript of *Sunshine Sketches of a Little Town* to the Montreal Standard Publishing Company (donated to the Leacock Museum) in 1966 and the manuscript of Leacock's thesis, "The Doctrine of *Laissez Faire*," to the University of Chicago in 1964. Section E (Lectures Given) is based mainly on Leacock's lecture notebooks at the National Archives. The lecture notebooks, which begin on 7 January 1915 and end on 9 March 1937, include the date of a specific lecture, place, subject or title, and Leacock's comments. In transcribing these notebooks, I have edited them considerably in order to compress entries and render them consistent, added lectures not recorded by Leacock, and altered entries with see-references and the exact title of a lecture. In addition to the Leacock collection acquired from Mrs. Nimmo, the National Archives contain many other archives that include Leacock-related material.

Many other archives have been perused in order to provide a complete story of Leacock's publishing career. Some of these archives are as follows: the John Lane The Bodley Head fonds at the University of Texas at Austin and at the University of Reading; the Paul R. Reynolds fonds, the Marie M. Meloney fonds, the John W. Cunliffe fonds, and the Carnegie Endowment fonds at the Special Collections, Columbia University Libraries; the Houghton Mifflin fonds at the Houghton Library, Harvard University; the Clarke Irwin fonds, the Macmillan Company of Canada fonds, the Dodd, Mead fonds, and the McClelland and Stewart fonds at McMaster University Library; the George Lindsey fonds at the Archives of Ontario; the W.C. Bell fonds at the Thomas Fisher Rare Book Library, University of Toronto; the Methuen ledgers at the Lilly Library, Indiana University; the Seagram Ltd. fonds at the Hagley Museum and Library; the Lorne Pierce fonds at Queen's University; and the records of the Copyright Office at the Library of Congress.

Whenever possible I have tried to examine at least two copies of each particular edition or issue; if only one copy has been cited (for example, *The Case Against Prohibition*, A36a, and *Foggy Finance*, A85), the reader can assume, at least for the A section, that I have been unable to find another copy. In certain instances such as *Six Lectures on the British Empire* (A1) and *Xmas Convivial and Pleasant at No. 19 Redpath Crescent* (A51a), all known extant copies have been examined.

My own book and periodical collection has served as a physical basis of the bibliography. I have collected Leacock's work fastidiously since 1979 (see my article, "Collecting Leacock," *Canadian Notes & Queries* no. 45 (autumn 1991): 9–12). The collection is one of the largest of its kind, containing, for example, over fifty different editions, issues, variants, and printings of *Sunshine Sketches of a Little Town*. Besides my own book and periodical collection, major collections of Leacock's works can be found at McGill University (Friedman collection), Orillia Public Library, North York Public Library, the Thomas Fisher Rare Book Library, and the National Library of Canada. The range of collections that have been examined is reflected in the list of locations.

In terms of electronic resources I have benefited enormously from the OCLC WorldCat, RLIN, and the Dialog databases. At the Library of Congress I have used the Eureka database which provides access to talking books and books in Braille. On-line public access catalogues have been searched through the Internet via Gopher and later on with the Web. The Web site version of books in print (amazon.com) has also been examined. For a number of items in the C section, URLs have been cited for electronic reprints.

Many serials have been searched either to verify a specific item or to search for vague citations. The following magazines, journals, and newspapers have been searched systematically for Leacock's articles: *American Aviation*, May 1942–May 1943; *American Magazine*, 1913–4; *Banking*; *Canadian Banker*; *Canadian Journal of Economics*; *Good Housekeeping*, 1939–June 1940, January–June 1943; *Goblin*; *Hamilton Spectator*, April 1924–31 July 1925; *Harpers*, vols. 132 (1915–16) to 168 (1933–4); *Hearst's Magazine*, June–December 1917 (except October), January–June 1918; *Hunting and Fishing*,

1940–1; *Journal of Political Economy*; *Judge*, 1919–31; *Leslies*, early 1920s; *McGill Daily*, 1911–36; *McGill Fortnightly Review*; *McGill Martlet*; *McGill's Old Annual*; *Manchester Guardian*, November 1905; *Montreal Standard*, May–August 1910, 1921–9; *Montreal Star*, January–August 1912; *Macleans*; *New York Herald Tribune*, 1 February 1944 to 31 March 1944, magazine section only; *New York Times*; *New Yorker*; *Orillia News-Letter*, 5 August 1925 to 25 May 1927; *Orillia Packet*, 1895–6, 1899–24; *Orillia Times*, 1900 to 1930 May 1901, 9 November 1905 to 21 August 1913, 15 October 1914 to 11 October 1917; *Orillia Packet and Times*, 5 January 1928 to 16 October 1941, 30 March to 27 April 1944; *Ottawa Evening Journal*, 1910–2; *Puck*, 13 February 1901 to 25 July 1906 to December 1916; *Rod and Gun in Canada*, 1944–October 1945; *Rotarian*, 1915–44; *Saturday Night Magazine*, up to 1944; *Sunday Times* (London), July to December 1919; *Scholastic*, 1923, 1926–1936; *Toronto Star Weekly*, 1923–October 1925; *Toronto World*, December 1920 to 9 April 1921; *The Trail* (Colorado), 1910 to May 1911; *Queen's Quarterly*; *The Times* (London); *University Magazine* (McGill University); *University Monthly* (University of Toronto); *Vancouver Province*, 20 January–8 February 1908; *Vancouver Sunday Sun* 1923–April 1924; and *Vanity Fair*, May 1914–June 1927.

With regard to Leacock's lecture tour of Great Britain from October to December 1921, the following newspapers were examined for specific dates of lectures: *Manchester Guardian*; *Glasgow Herald*; and from London, the *Times, Pall Mall Gazette, Daily Telegraph, Observer, Daily Express, Daily Herald, Daily Mail*, and the *Citizen*. With respect to Leacock's lectures in Canada such as his tour of western Canada in 1936–7, practically all relevant newspapers have been searched.

## LEACOCK AS A JOURNAL EDITOR

Leacock served as an editor for a number of journals and was on several editorial boards. In the C section his editorial activity is often referred at the end of an entry. However, in view of the fact that a separate section of the bibliography is not devoted to his editorial association with journals, it is perhaps worthwhile to list them in this introduction. The following journals and boards are the ones in question: (1) joint editor of Upper Canada College's journal, *College Times*, with F.J. Davidson, and chairman of the Publications Committee for the academic year, 1886–7. (2) Associate editor of the University of Toronto's *Varsity* during the autumn term of 1890. He resigned from that position on 2 December 1890. (3) Member of the editorial board of two issues of the *University Magazine*, vol. 6 (February and April 1907). When the editor of the journal, Andrew Macphail, served overseas during the First World War, Leacock edited three issues of the journal (vol. 14, April to December 1915) with Sir William Peterson, C.W. Colby, and P.T. Lafleur. (4) According to Legate (K70.2, p. 101), Leacock was the first chairman of the editorial board of the *McGill News*, the organ of the Graduates' Society of McGill University, which began in 1919. (5) Leacock was a charter member of the Canadian Authors' Association and a member of the editorial board of *Canadian Bookman*. (6) On 26 August 1936 Leacock was appointed to the Advisory Board of the Encyclopaedia Britannica Foundation.

## INDEX

A cumulative index provides access to names (the names of authors, editors, translators, and publishers) and the titles of articles and books. To a limited extent subject access is also given to Leacock's works of non-fiction. Citations in the index are keyed to item numbers, not pages. In addition to the index, there are see-references in the descriptions at appropriate places to link entries.

# Location Symbols

| | |
|---|---|
| AEU | University of Alberta, Edmonton, AB |
| ALU | University of Lethbridge, Lethbridge, AB |
| BOD | Bodleian Library (John Johnson collection), Oxford University, Oxford, England |
| BUFF | Buffalo and Erie County Public Library, Buffalo, NY |
| BVIV | University of Victoria, Victoria, BC |
| CHAR | Geauga County Public Library, Chardon, OH |
| CNIB | The Canadian National Insitute for the Blind, Library for the Blind, Toronto, ON |
| COL | Special Collections, Columbia University Libraries, New York, NY |
| CON | Walter A. Maier Library, Concordia Collegiate Institute, Bronxville, NY |
| CS | Carl Spadoni (personal collection), Hamilton, ON |
| CUL | Cambridge University Library, England |
| DEL | University of Delaware Library, Newark, DE |
| DLC | Library of Congress, Washingston, DC |
| EVANS | John F. Evans, 454 Queen St. South, Hamilton, ON |
| FREE | Free Library of Philadelphia, Philadelpia, PA |
| GPM | Georgia Southern College Library, Statesboro, GA |
| GZD | Public Library System, Milwaukee, WI |
| GZQ | Marquette University Memorial Library, Milwaukee, WI |
| GZM | University of Wisconsin-Madison Memorial Library, Madison, WI |
| HAG | Hagley Museum and Library, Wilmington, DE |

| | |
|---|---|
| HLS | Harvard College Library, Harvard University, Cambridge, MA |
| HOUGHT | The Houghton Library, Harvard University, Cambridge, MA |
| IEN | Northwestern University, Chicago, ILL |
| IOL | Wahlert Memorial Library, Loras College, Dubuque, IO |
| KKU | University of Kansas Libraries, Lawrence, KS |
| LAT | William H. Latimer, 8 Burkston Place, Islington, ON |
| LILLY | The Lilly Library, Indiana University, Bloomington, IND |
| MOSTJMW | Missouri Western State College Library, St. Joseph, MO |
| NFSM | Queen Elizabeth II Library, Memorial University of Newfoundland, St. John's, NF |
| NSDAL | Killam Library, Dalhousie University, NS |
| OBER | Oberlin College Library, Oberlin, OH |
| OH | Hamilton Public Library, Hamilton, ON |
| OHM | McMaster University Library, Hamilton, ON |
| OKQ | Queen's University, Kingston, ON |
| OONL | National Library of Canada, Ottawa, ON |
| OORI | Orillia Public Library, Orillia, ON |
| OPET | Trent University, Peterborough, ON |
| OSTCB | Brock University, St. Catharines, ON |
| OTAR | Archives of Ontario, Toronto, ON |
| OTMCL | Metropolitan Library of Toronto, Toronto, ON |
| OTNY | North York Public Library, North York, ON |
| OTU | Robarts Library, University of Toronto, ON |
| OTUT | Trinity College, University of Toronto, Toronto, ON |
| OTUTF | Thomas Fisher Rare Book Library, University of Toronto, Toronto, ON |
| OTV | E.J. Pratt Library, Victoria University in the University of Toronto, Toronto, ON |
| OTY | York University, Toronto, ON |
| OWA | University of Windsor Libraries, Assumption University of Windsor, Windsor, ON |
| OWTU | University of Waterloo, Waterloo, ON |
| OWU | Beegly Library, Ohio Wesleyan University, Delaware, OH |
| PHOEN | Phoenix Public Library, Phoenix, AZ |

| | |
|---|---|
| PITT | Leonard H. Axe Library, Pittsburgh State University, Pittsburg, KS |
| QMG | Webster Library, Concordia University, Montreal, PQ |
| QMM | McLennan Library, McGill University, Montreal, PQ |
| QMM Archives | McGill University Archives, Montreal, PQ |
| QMMED | Education Library, McGill University, Montreal, PQ |
| QMMRB | Department of Rare Books and Special Collections, McGill University, Montreal, PQ |
| RB | Reta Burrows, 109 Collegiate Drive, Orillia, ON |
| READ | The Library, The University of Reading, Reading, England |
| RED | University of Redlands Library, Redlands, CA |
| SLM | Stephen Leacock Museum, Orillia, ON |
| SRU | University of Regina, SK |
| SUNY | State University of New York, Buffalo, NY |
| SYR | Syracuse University, Syracuse, NY |
| TEX | Harry Ransom Humanities Research Center, The University of Texas at Austin, Austin, TX |
| UCLA | Library, University of California, Los Angeles, CA |
| UWO | The University of Western Ontario, London, ON |
| VA | University of Virginia Library, Charlottesville, VA |
| VCTEX | Victoria College and University of Houston-Victoria, Library, Victoria, TX |
| WIH | The State Historical Society of Wisconsin, WI |
| YALE | The Beinecke Rare Book and Manuscript Library, Yale University Library, New Haven, CT |

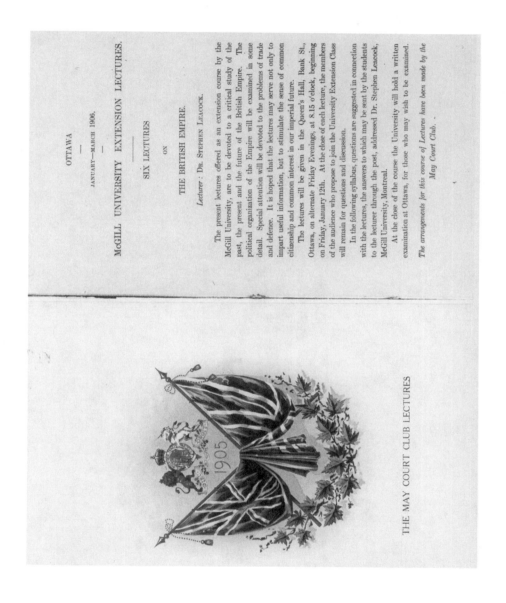

1. *Six Lectures on the British Empire* (A1), Leacock's first separate publication, the syllabus of his lectures delivered in early 1906 at the Queen's Hall in Ottawa. Photograph courtesy of the National Library of Canada.

# ELEMENTS OF
# POLITICAL SCIENCE

BY

## STEPHEN LEACOCK, B.A., Ph.D.

ASSOCIATE PROFESSOR OF POLITICAL SCIENCE
McGILL UNIVERSITY, MONTREAL

BOSTON AND NEW YORK
HOUGHTON, MIFFLIN AND COMPANY
The Riverside Press, Cambridge
1906

2. Leacock's first book, the first American edition (A2a) of his textbook, *Elements of Political Science*, published in June 1906.

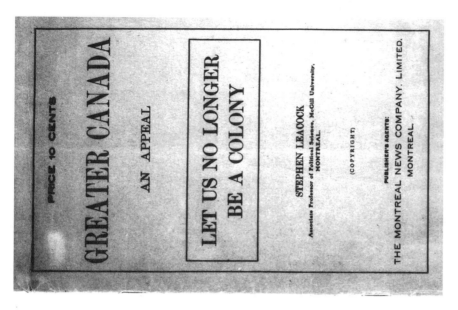

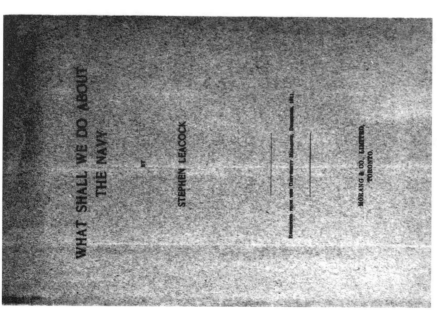

3. Two early political pamphlets: *What Shall We Do About the Navy* (A9) published in December 1911; and *Greater Canada, An Appeal. Let Us No Longer Be a Colony* (A3) published on 20 March 1907.

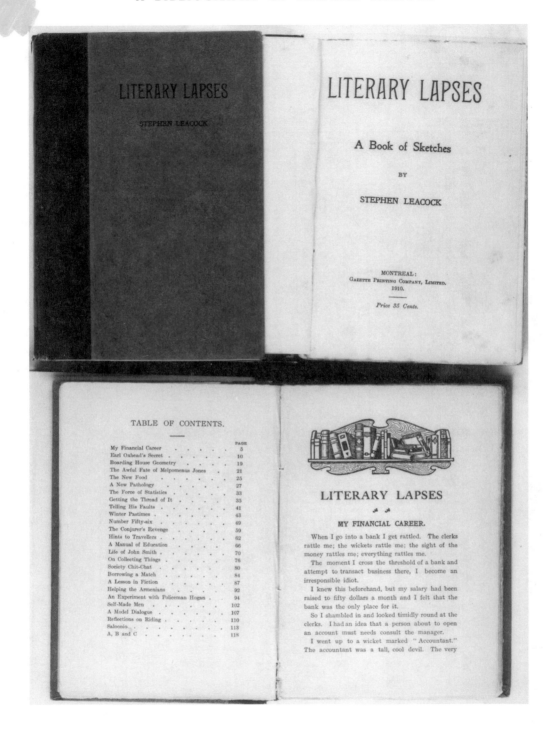

4. The first Canadian edition of Leacock's first book of humour, *Literary Lapses* (A5a). He arranged for its publication in an edition of 3,000 copies on 9 April 1910.

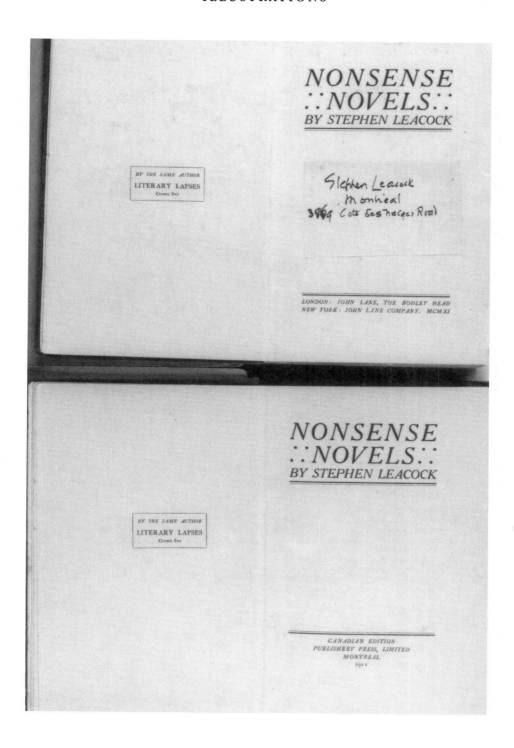

5. The first English edition and the first Canadian issue of Leacock's second book of humour, *Nonsense Novels* (A7a and A7a.1), both probably published in May 1911.

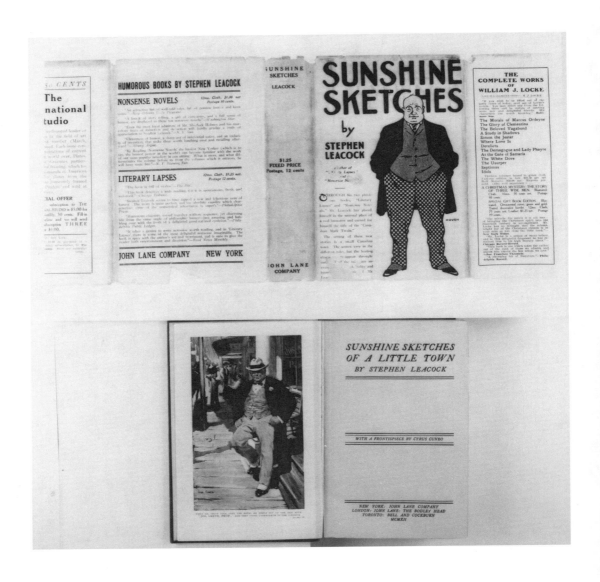

6. The first American issue of *Sunshine Sketches of a Little Town* (A11a.1) published on 20 September 1912.

7. The American and English editions of *Behind the Beyond and Other Contributions to Human Knowledge* (A12a and A12b) published on 31 October 1913 and November 1913, respectively.

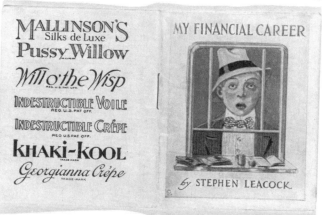

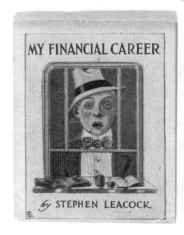

8. The first, second, and fourth issues of *My Financial Career and How to Make a Million Dollars* (A14a, A14a.1, and A14a.3), a miniature book published on 17 September 1914. Photograph courtesy of the Department of Rare Books and Special Collections, McGill University.

9. The first Canadian issue of *Arcadian Adventures with the Idle Rich* (A16a.1) published on 31 October 1914.

10. *The Marionettes' Calendar 1916* (A20), twelve poems written by Leacock with drawings by A.H. Fish, published in September 1915.

11. The Canadian issue of *Moonbeams from the Larger Lunacy* (A21a.1) published on 20 October 1915.

12. The introduction and the first page of Leacock's essay, "The Amazing Genius of O. Henry," in *Bagdad on the Subway* (A23), a promotional pamphlet written by Leacock for O. Henry's *Complete Works*, published in 1916 or sometime thereafter.

13. The first and second editions of Leacock's pamphlet, *National Organization for War* (A25a and A25b), published in December 1916 and March 1917, respectively. Photograph courtesy of the National Library of Canada.

14. "Stephen Leacock's Own Story of His Life," which appeared in a leaflet (A30b) issued by John Lane The Bodley Head to promote his lecture tour of Britain in 1921.

LIBERTY      MODERATION

# "The Case Against Prohibition"

### By DR. STEPHEN LEACOCK
Professor of Economics, McGill University, Montreal

Being an Address delivered at the opening of the Toronto campaign held at Foresters' Hall under the auspices of the Citizens' Liberty League

As this address is applicable to the Manitoba Temperance Act it is re-published by

**THE MODERATION LEAGUE OF MANITOBA**
By courtesy of
The Citizens' Liberty League of Ontario

15. The Canadian edition of *The Case Against Prohibition* (A36a) published in April 1921.

16. The Canadian, American, and English editions of *College Days* (A40b, A40a, A40c), published on 1 November, 20 October, and 15 November 1923, respectively.

17. Two pamphlets, both published by the Macmillan Company of Canada, written by Leacock, addressing the problems of the Depression: *Stephen Leacock's Plan to Relieve the Depression in 6 Days to Remove it in 6 Months to Eradicate it in 6 Years* (A64), published on 28 February 1933; and *The Gathering Financial Crisis in Canada: A Survey of the Present Critical Situation* (A79), published on 8 October 1936.

18. The English edition (A84a), the American issue (A84a.1), the American edition (A84b), and the Japanese abridged edition (A84c) of *Humour and Humanity: An Introduction to the Study of Humour*, first published on 15 November 1937.

# FOGGY FINANCE

### by *STEPHEN LEACOCK*

**REPRINTED BY**

## THE CONNECTICUT SOCIETY
## OF ALBERTURNIANS

**DECEMBER, 1937**

19. *Foggy Finance* (A85), a pamphlet published the
Connecticut Society of Alberturnians in December 1937.

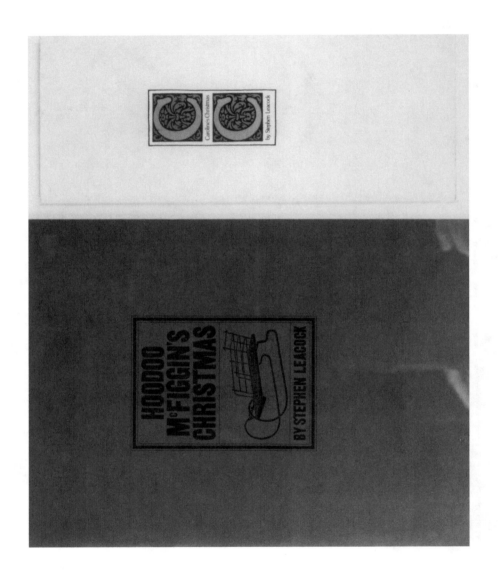

20. Two publications issued as Christmas keepsakes by Cooper & Beatty, Limited: *Caroline's Christmas; or, The Inexplicable Infant* (A113b), 1969; and *Hoodoo McFiggin's Christmas* (A122), 1970.

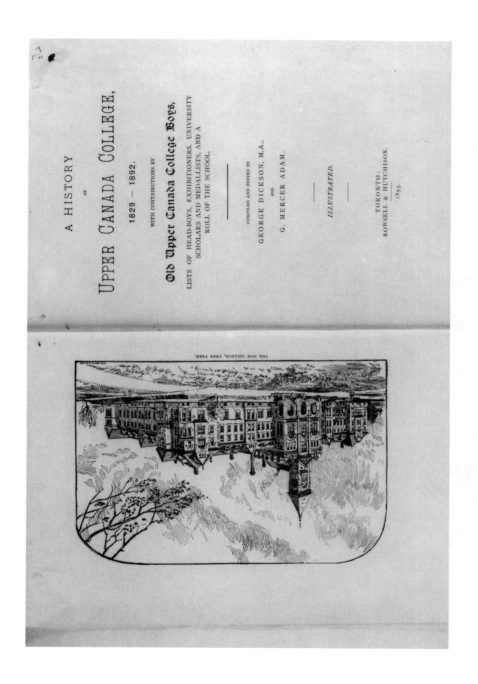

21. *A History of Upper Canada College, 1829–1892* (B1), published in 1893. Leacock either "contributed to the volume or furnished materials for it. . . ."

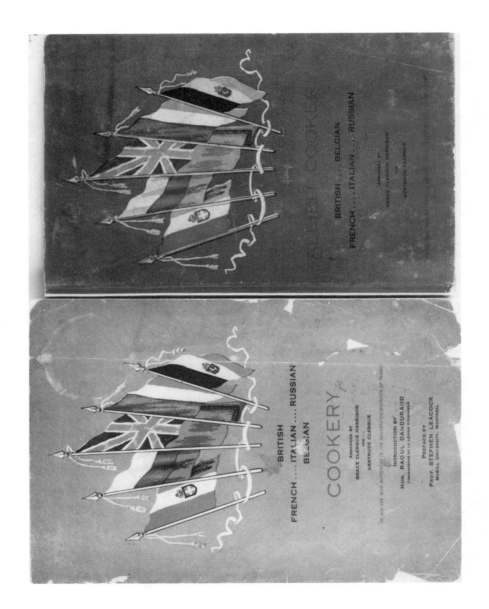

22. The Canadian and American editions of a cookery book (B4), both published in 1916. Leacock contributed a humorous preface entitled "Allied Food."

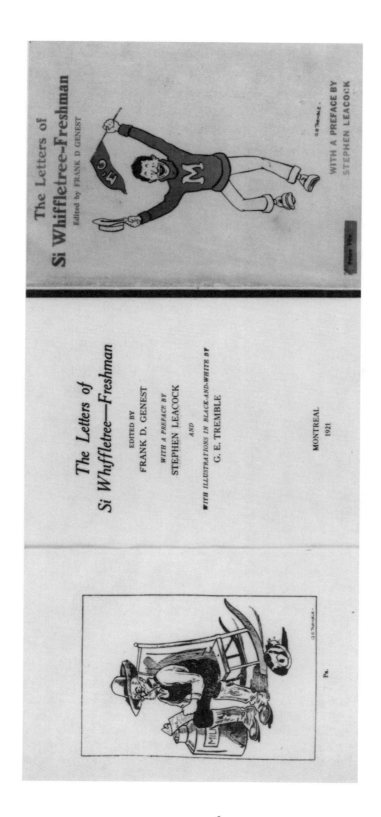

23. Frank D. Genest's *The Letters of Si Whiffletree — Freshman* (B9), published in March 1921. Leacock wrote a preface to it.

24. Theses written by graduate students in the Department of Economics and Political Science at McGill University. Nos. 1 (B11), 2 (B12), 4 (B13), 6 (B14), 9 (B16), and 14 (B18) of the McGill University Economic Studies in the National Problems of Canada (series xv). Leacock wrote prefaces to them and arranged for their publication. Published between 1925 and 1930.

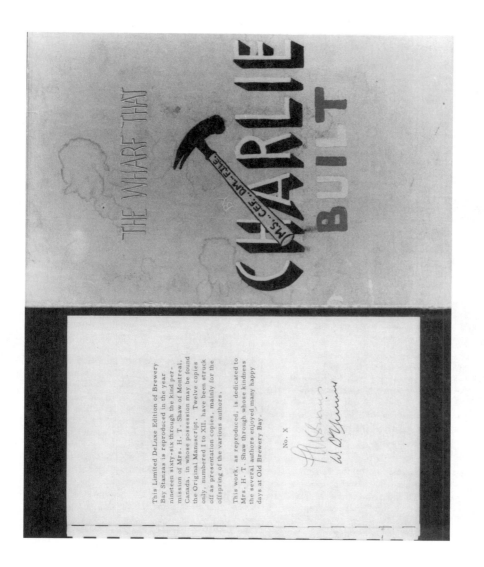

25. *The Wharf That Charlie Built* (B32), a book of verse accompanied by illustrations, written in August 1943 and published in April 1966. Leacock's contribution is entitled "Epilogue to These Stanzas."

### Poetry.

O'er the glassy floor implastic
Did we trip the light fantastic,
Whirling swift in giddy mazes round the room ;
And I felt her breath come faster,
Through her teeth of alabaster,
Sweet perfumed as a rose in summer bloom.

Swift we glided o'er the waxy
Floor, amid the bright galaxy,
To the music of Waldteufel's latest waltz ;
By Jove ! she'd nearly mashed me,
When some one sudden passed me—
"Take care, old boy ! those pearly teeth are false."

BEESWAX.

### TAM O' SHANTER.

#### A RECOLLECTION.

'Tis nought but a faded, worn out hat,
Yet I treasure it still with care,—
'Tis not for its beauty—I think not of that—
But for maid so passing fair,

Whose small hands made me that hat so dear,
Whose bright eyes smiled on me then,
Whose voice and whose steps were wont to cheer
Me. But ne'er shall we speak again,

For she has gone to the Continent,
To Berlin, to *finish* there,
And, while I o'er lesson books am bent,
She shines, a radiant star,

And men, not boys, are now at her feet,
And yet—do you think I'm a fool ?
Why ! I don't give a rip for the maiden sweet,
And the Tam's worn while carrying coal.

D. F.

### THE VISION OF MIRZA.

#### (*New Edition.*)

\* \* \* \* \* \* \*

The genius then led me to the top of a lofty building, situated within pleasing gardens, and surmounted with a turret on which waved an antique flag. On examining its waving folds I saw there cabalistic writing, executed in dull green, upon the surface of the flag. The writing appeared to be Arabic, for I was able to distinctly make out the words "U. C. C. Palmam qui," though the rest was hidden from mine eyes. While I was meditating on this curious relic of the past the genius touched my arm. "Cast thine eyes westward," said he, "and tell me what thou seest." I looked as directed. "I see," said I, "numerous youth armed with harquebuses, and girt with white bands about their loins. In front march several who blow fiercely on horns, and one of more mature age walking alone and striking sadly upon a drum." "Thou sayest well," said the genius, "they are members of the lost tribes of Judea, and wander round incessantly after the manner you have described. He that beateth upon the drum is the last remnant of a dissipated life, and must soon go to his account." "Who," said I, "is that man of noble bearing, with eagle eye and tight trousers, who accompanies and directs the tribes in their wanderings ?" "The dwellers in Goschen call him 'Bull,' for short," answered the genius sadly. "Who," I again queried, "is that short dissip——" "Hush-sh," said the genius, "I see of whom thou wouldst speak. Slander him not, lest ill befall thee. But now," said he, "cast thine eyes more to the northward, and again tell me what thou seest." "I see," said I, "a vast prison, with closely-barred windows, and filled with prisoners of youthful age and appearance." "They are not prisoners," said the genius sternly, "they go out on Saturdays." "What," said I, "causeth their extreme thinness and the gauntness of their faces ?" "They are not thin," said the genius coldly ; "thy tongue runneth too freely. Moreover," he added musingly, "they come from Hamilton." "And who," said I, "is the damsel, leaning from an upper window, and exceeding beautiful ?" "It is Bedelia," said the genius, with a quick blush of shame, "heed her not. But," said he, "look down below us on the broad stones and gravel that lie beneath." "I see," said I, after some minutes of observation, "a group of Roman philosophers." The genius smiled bitterly. "You could not have chosen a more fitting name for them," said he. "They are clad," I continued, "in black togas of light material with the exception of one——" "Ah," said the genius, "he is well known to the dwellers in Goschen for his rich baritone appetite." "Their heads,"

26. Leacock's first publication (C87.1), "The Vision of Mirza (New Edition.),"
which appeared in *College Times* (Upper Canada College) on 7 April 1887.

# "Q"

## A FARCE IN ONE ACT

By

STEPHEN LEACOCK and
BASIL MACDONALD HASTINGS

LONDON
SAMUEL FRENCH, LTD.
PUBLISHERS
26 SOUTHAMPTON STREET
STRAND, W.C.2

NEW YORK
SAMUEL FRENCH
PUBLISHER
25 WEST 45TH STREET

27. *"Q": A Farce in One Act* (G1), published on 30 December 1915, adapted by Basil Macdonald Hastings, and based on Leacock's short story, "'Q' A Psychic Pstory of the Psupernatural."

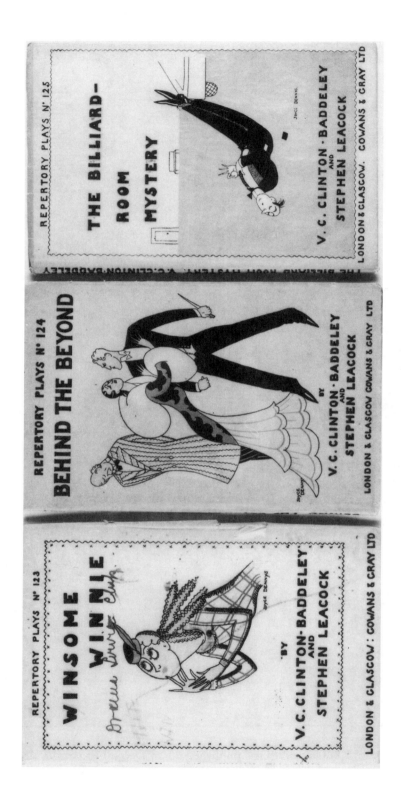

28. Three plays (G2, G3, and G4) written and adapted by V.C. Clinton-Baddeley from Leacock's stories, published in 1932 and 1934.

29. Two German translations of Leacock's work, *Die Abenteuer der armen Reichen* (H29) and *Humor und Humbug* (H30), both published in 1925.

A BIBLIOGRAPHY OF
*Stephen Leacock*

# A Section: SEPARATE PUBLICATIONS

## A1 SIX LECTURES ON THE BRITISH EMPIRE 1906

[caption title] OTTAWA | [rule] | JANUARY—MARCH 1906. | [rule] | McGILL UNIVERSITY EXTENSION LECTURES. | [rule] | SIX LECTURES | ON | THE BRITISH EMPIRE. | *Lecturer :* DR. STEPHEN LEACOCK.

◆ 1⁶. 1–12 pp. (6 leaves). 232 × 151 mm.

CONTENTS: pp. *1–2* caption title, brief introduction to the lecture series, and list of recommended readings; pp. *3–8* summaries of leacock's lectures; pp. *9–11* questions for students; p. *12* list of dates and times of the lectures, price of admission ($1 for the whole course, 50¢ for a single lecture), and names of individuals where admission tickets can be obtained.

TEXT: Syllabus of Leacock's lectures with questions: lecture no. 1 The Making of the Empire: The Lessons of Its History, 12 January 1906; lecture no. 2 The Constituents of the Empire: A Study of the Self Governing Colonies, 26 January 1906; lecture no. 3 The Economics of Empire, 9 February 1906; lecture no. 4 Imperial Defence, 23 February 1906; lecture no. 5 Imperial Federation, 9 March 1906; lecture no. 6 The Imperial Dependencies, 23 March 1906.

BINDING: Bound in a glossy white wrapper, sewn signature. The front of the wrapper has a colour illustration featuring the British coat of arms, 1905 in light brown, two British flags crossed, and maple leaves. Beneath the illustration is the following: MAY COURT CLUB LECTURES. On the back of the wrapper is the following: THE MORTIMER CO., Limited | Printers, Etc.

NOTES: From 12 January to 23 March 1906, on alternate Friday evenings at the Queen's Hall in Ottawa, Leacock gave six lectures as an extension course arranged by the May Court Club under the auspices of McGill University. One of the Club's sponsors was Lady Evelyn Grey, the Governor General's wife. The choice of Leacock as the speaker was, in fact, arranged by the Governor General, Earl Grey. When Grey wrote to Sir William Peterson, the Principal of McGill University, and inquired about a suitable speaker, Peterson heartily recommended Leacock on 4 November 1905 (see Alan Bowker, Introduction to *The Social Criticism of Stephen Leacock* (A124), p. xii).

The course was "devoted to a critical study of the past, the present and the future of the British Empire" (p. *1* of the pamphlet). At the end of each lecture members of the audience were invited to partake in a question-and-answer period. There was also an examination for students at the close of the course.

The text of Leacock's first lecture was published on 20 January 1906 by the *Ottawa Evening Journal* and the *Ottawa Citizen* (see C6.1 and also C6.2, C6.3 and D6.2–3). At the fifth and six lectures the Governor General and a party from Government House attended. According to a report of the last lecture published in the *Ottawa Citizen* ("May Court Lectures. An Excellent Course Concluded. Prof. Leacock. . . . ," 24 March 1906, p. 10), Leacock's lectures were ". . . thoroughly inspiring and entertaining." Grey was so impressed by Leacock's imperial zeal, that he used his influence with the Cecil Rhodes Trust so that Leacock could lecture in England, New Zealand, Australia, and South Africa on "Imperial Development and Organization" (see E7.7).

This pamphlet was obviously given to members of the public and students who purchased an admission ticket to Leacock's lecture series in Ottawa. Given the large attendance at the lectures, it is probable that at least 500 copies of the pamphlet were printed.

COPIES EXAMINED: OONL (two copies).

## A2 ELEMENTS OF POLITICAL SCIENCE 1906

**A2a** *first American edition*:

ELEMENTS OF | POLITICAL SCIENCE | BY | STEPHEN LEACOCK, B.A., PH.D. | ASSOCIATE PROFESSOR OF POLITICAL SCIENCE | McGILL UNIVERSITY, MONTREAL | [publisher's device of Houghton, Mifflin and Co.: person in swaddling clothes playing a pipe near a tree, a candle in the foreground, with motto "Tout bien ou rien" on a banner, 𝕿𝖍𝖊 𝕽𝖎𝖛𝖊𝖗𝖘𝖎𝖉𝖊 𝕻𝖗𝖊𝖘𝖘 at the bottom on a banner, and publisher's initials on a shield] | BOSTON AND NEW YORK | HOUGHTON, MIFFLIN AND COMPANY | 𝕿𝖍𝖊 𝕽𝖎𝖛𝖊𝖗𝖘𝖎𝖉𝖊 𝕻𝖗𝖊𝖘𝖘, 𝕮𝖆𝖒𝖇𝖗𝖎𝖉𝖌𝖊 | 1906

• $1^4$ $2^{10}$ $3^6$ $4^{10}$ $5^6$ $6^{10}$ $7^6$ $8^{10}$ $9^6$ $10^{10}$ $11^6$ $12^{10}$ $13^6$ $14^{10}$ $15^6$ $16^{10}$ $17^6$ $18^{10}$ $19^6$ $20^{10}$ $21^6$ $22^{10}$ $23^6$ $24^{10}$ $(242 + \chi 1)$ $25^6$ $26^{10}$ $27^6$ $28^2$. *i–v*, vi–ix, *1–4*, 4–21, *22*, 23–40, *41*, 42–51, *52*, 53–70, *71*, 72–88, *89*, 90–109, *110*, 111–137, *138–141*, 142–153, *154*, 155–180, *181*, 182–206, *207*, 208–232, *233*, 234–257, *258*, 259–291, *292*, 293–331, *332*, 333–354, *355–357*, 358–370, *371*, 372–385, *386*, 387–409, *410–411*, 412–417, *1* pp. (215 leaves). Folded leaf (table of legislatures) tipped in between pp. 354 and *355*. 192 × 122 mm.

CONTENTS: p. *i* half title; p. *ii* blank; p. *iii* title; p. *iv* COPYRIGHT 1906 BY STEPHEN LEACOCK | ALL RIGHTS RESERVED; pp. *v*, vi–ix table of contents; p. *1* blank; pp. 2–4, 4–409 text (pp. *3, 138, 140,* and *356* blank); p. *410* blank; pp. *411–417* index; p. *1* 𝕿𝖍𝖊 𝕽𝖎𝖛𝖊𝖗𝖘𝖎𝖉𝖊 𝕻𝖗𝖊𝖘𝖘 | *Electrotyped and printed by H. O. Houghton & Co.* | *Cambridge, Mass., U.S.A.*

TEXT: There are three parts: I The Nature of the State; II The Structure of the Government; III The Province of Government. In the table of contents chapters are further subdivided into numbered sections.

Part I consists of the following: chapter I Political Science, the Theory of the State; chapter II The Origin of the State; Fallacious Theories; chapter III The True Origin of the State; chapter IV The Sovereignty of the State; chapter V The Liberty of the Individual; chapter VI Relation of States to One Another; chapter VII The Form of the State.

Part II consists of the following: chapter I The Separation of Powers; chapter II The Legislature; chapter III The Executive; chapter IV The Judiciary and the Electorate; chapter V Federal Government; chapter VI Colonial Government; chapter VII Local Government; chapter VIII Party Government.

Part III consists of the following: chapter I Individualism; chapter II Socialism; chapter III The Modern State.

BINDING: Bound in dark blue vertically ribbed cloth. A rectangle is blind-stamped on the upper and lower boards. Stamped on the spine in gilt: ELEMENTS | OF | POLITICAL | SCIENCE | LEACOCK | HOUGHTON | MIFFLIN [Greek-styled ampersand] CO.

NOTES: In the preface to *How to Write*, Leacock recollected in a humorous vein about the composition of his textbook and its impact:

> So I took my pick and shovel to the college library and in three years I completed my *Elements of Political Science*. This book had an outstanding, indeed an ominous, success. It was no sooner adopted as the text book by the renovated government of China, than the anti-Manchu rebellion swept the former Empire. The Khedive of Egypt's attempt to use it as the text book of the Egyptian schools, was followed by the nationalist outbreak.

See also Leacock's holograph inscription in Friedman's copy at QMMRB: "At one time it was used in 35 American universities and many British. It was, I understand, the first textbook used in China after the establishment of the Republic and in Egypt before the war ... not quite dead in 1937. I still receive small cheques" (quoted by Lomer, p. 26). According to Curry's *Stephen Leacock: Humorist and Humanist* (p. 71), Leacock's textbook was translated into nineteen languages; no evidence has been found to substantiate such a claim, however.

Leacock gave lectures to students at McGill University as early as 1901–02 under the title "Elements of Political Science." His notebook for these lectures along with teaching notes for related courses survives in the Barbara Nimmo collection at NAC. He actually began the writing of *Elements of Political Science* in September 1903, approximately three months after he obtained his Ph.D. from the University of Chicago. He received an encouraging letter from Houghton, Mifflin (William S. Booth) on 22 April 1904, and on 2 May 1904, he informed Booth that he hoped to submit a part of the manuscript to him, possibly before Christmas of that year (HOUGHT).

Leacock completed the manuscript in March 1905. Houghton, Mifflin accepted the book for publication with minor revisions on 13 October 1905, having received a favourable report from an outside reader. The contract is dated 25 October 1905. Leacock received a royalty of 10% on all copies sold. He agreed to a 5% royalty if the price was reduced. On 30 December 1905 he was requested to prepare a summary of 300 to 500 words for Houghton, Mifflin's spring announcement list. He finished correcting the proofs by 10 April 1906. The book was published in June 1906 at $1.75. Leacock registered the copyright with the Copyright Office at DLC on 8 June 1906 (Class A, XXc, no. 147799). He received a cheque for $76.90 for sales up to 1 October 1906. "Considering the scope of the book, this seems very satisfactory," he remarked on 2 November 1906. The first printing of 1,000 copies was completed on 31 May 1906. Other reprintings are as follows (each one 1,000 copies unless indicated otherwise): 9 November 1906; 23 May 1907 (270 copies); 2 October 1908; July 1909; December 1910; July 1911; and June 1912 (500 copies). This would indicate that 6,770 copies were printed altogether (information from Book showings.

U: books published October 1905 to December 1906, and editorial department, pressed letter books (223 and 224), MS Am 2030, Houghton Mifflin papers, HOUGHT).

COPIES EXAMINED: CS (three copies, two with 1906 on the title page); OORI; OTNY; OTUTF; QMMRB (without 1906 on title page); SLM (copy belonging to Leacock's mother).

**A2a.1** *English issue*:

ELEMENTS OF | POLITICAL SCIENCE | BY | STEPHEN LEACOCK, B.A., PH.D. | ASSOCIATE PROFESSOR OF POLITICAL SCIENCE | McGILL UNIVERSITY, MONTREAL | London | ARCHIBALD CONSTABLE & CO. LTD. | BOSTON AND NEW YORK | HOUGHTON, MIFFLIN & CO. | 1906

Cancel title. Otherwise, the English issue is identical to the American edition. 198 × 125 mm. Bound in greyish green cloth with lines blind-stamped on the top and bottom of both boards and the spine. Stamped on the spine in gilt as follows: ELEMENTS | OF | POLITICAL | SCIENCE | LEACOCK | CONSTABLE | LONDON.

NOTES: *The English Catalogue of Books* records the date of publication of the Constable edition on September 1906 at 7s. 6d. Cr. 8vo. The ledger books at HOUGHT record the following: "162/150" on 1 April 1907; 100 copies in January 1908; and 250 copies on 29 August 1910. Leacock's royalty reports at SLM record that between that 1 April and 1 October 1910, 250 copies sold in England. On 1 October 1911, 600 copies in sheets were sent to England. 250 copies of the English issue were sold according to Houghton Mifflin's royalty report of 30 April 1913.

COPIES EXAMINED: CUL (date-stamped 12 October 1906).

**A2b** *Second American edition* (1913):

ELEMENTS OF | POLITICAL SCIENCE | BY | STEPHEN LEACOCK, B.A., PH.D. | HEAD OF THE DEPARTMENT OF ECONOMICS AND POLITICAL | SCIENCE, McGILL UNIVERSITY, MONTREAL | *REVISED EDITION* | [publisher's device of Houghton, Mifflin and Co.: person in swaddling clothes playing a pipe near a tree, a candle in the foreground, with motto "Tout bien ou rien" on a banner, The Riverside Press at the bottom on a banner, and publisher's initials on a shield] | BOSTON, NEW YORK, AND CHICAGO | HOUGHTON MIFFLIN COMPANY | The Riverside Press Cambridge

This revised edition is mainly from the same setting of type as the first edition. In addition to the title leaf, the following pages have either been altered or inserted: 106–109, 109a–109b, 136–137, 172–180, 180a–180d, 206, 223–224, 226, 231–232, 273, 279–281, 288–289, 306–307, 347–354, tipped-in leaf, 354a, 415–417. The copyright page reads: COPYRIGHT, 1906 AND 1913, BY STEPHEN LEACOCK | ALL RIGHTS RESERVED. Two issues were examined. The leaves for both measure 192 × 122 mm. In the first issue the last page following p. 417 is blank. The binding is identical to that of A2a with stamping in gilt on the spine as follows: ELEMENTS | OF | POLITICAL | SCIENCE | REVISED | EDITION | LEACOCK | HOUGHTON | MIFFLIN CO. In the second issue the verso of p. 417 reads: The Riverside Press Cambridge | CAMBRIDGE . MASSACHUSETTS | U . S . A. At the end of the book there are six leaves of advertisements for books published by Houghton Mifflin. The binding of the second issue is dark blue cloth (neither ribbed nor blind-stamped). Stamped in gilt on the spine as follows: ELEMENTS | OF | POLITICAL |

SCIENCE | *REVISED* | *EDITION* | LEACOCK | HOUGHTON | MIFFLIN CO.

NOTES: The first printing of 1,000 copies occurred in February 1913. Published 9 June 1913 at $1.75. Leacock received a royalty of 10%. He registered the copyright with the Copyright Office at DLC on 23 June 1913 (ClA350145). Other reprintings are as follows (each one 1,000 copies unless indicated otherwise): October 1913; March 1914; October 1914; January 1916 (1,302 copies); October 1916 (1,317 copies); September 1917; and September 1918; May 1919. This would indicate that 6,770 copies were printed altogether (printing information from Book showings. U: books published October 1905 to December 1906, MS Am 2030, Houghton Mifflin fonds, HOUGHT).

COPIES EXAMINED: CS (first issue); OORI (second issue); QMMRB (first issue).

## A2b.1 *English issue* [1913?]:

ELEMENTS OF | POLITICAL SCIENCE | BY | STEPHEN LEACOCK, B.A., PH.D. | ASSOCIATE PROFESSOR OF POLITICAL SCIENCE | McGILL UNIVERSITY, MONTREAL | 𝕷𝖔𝖓𝖉𝖔𝖓 | CONSTABLE & CO. LIMITED | BOSTON AND NEW YORK | HOUGHTON MIFFLIN COMPANY | 1912

With the exception of the title leaf, the sheets of this issue are identical to those of A2b. The title leaf is a cancel, and its verso reads: COPYRIGHT 1906 BY STEPHEN LEACOCK | ALL RIGHTS RESERVED | [rubber-stamped in blue] *Printed in Great Britain*. This would suggest that the plates for this issue were sent to England by Houghton, Mifflin, that the issue was printed there, and that Constable substituted their own title leaf in place of the American one. See the notes below, however, in which royalty reports state that copies in sheets were sent to England. The title leaf, in fact, is almost the same as Constable's 1911 printing of A2a.1. The date of 1912, however, is a curiosity since *The English Catalogue of Books* has a publication date of September 1913. Also examined was a copy with 1913 as the date on the title page.

BINDING: Bound in dark green cloth. A rectangle is blind-stamped on the upper and lower boards. Stamped on the spine in gilt as follows: [rule blind-stamped] | ELEMENTS | OF | POLITICAL | SCIENCE | LEACOCK | CONSTABLE | LONDON | [rule blind-stamped].

NOTES: Houghton, Mifflin's royalty reports at SLM record the following number of copies that were sent to England in sheets: 500 copies when the issue first appeared; between October 1913 and April 1914, 1,000 copies; between October 1914 and April 1915, 252 copies; between 1 April and October 1917, 500 copies; between 1 October 1918 and 1 Apr 1919, 550 copies; between April 1919 and April 1920, 510 copies; between 30 April and 20 October 1920, 500 copies. These reports would indicate that at least 3,812 copies sold of this issue.

COPIES EXAMINED: CS (1912); LAT (1913).

## A2c *first English edition* (1921):

ELEMENTS OF | POLITICAL SCIENCE | BY | STEPHEN LEACOCK, B.A. | PH.D., LITT.D., LL.D, F.R.S.C. | HEAD OF THE DEPARTMENT OF ECONOMICS AND POLITICAL SCIENCE | McGILL UNIVERSITY, MONTREAL | *NEW AND ENLARGED EDITION* | LONDON | CONSTABLE & COMPANY LTD. | 1921

◆ A⁴ B–K⁸ L⁸ (L1 + χ1) M–2C⁸ [$1 signed]. *1–6, v–vi, 1–2, 3–116, 117, 118–132, 133–134, 135–195, 196, 197–333, 334–336, 337–397, 1–3* pp. (204 leaves). Folded leaf (table of legislatures 1921) tipped in between pp. 146 and 147. 188 × 123 mm.

CONTENTS: pp. *1–2* blank; p. *3* half title; p. *4* blank; p. *5* title; p. *6* blank; pp. *v–vi* table of contents; pp. *1–386* text (pp. *2, 134, 334,* and *336* blank); pp. *387–397* index; p. *1* PRINTED IN GREAT BRITAIN BY | RICHARD CLAY & SONS, LIMITED, | BUNGAY, SUFFOLK.; pp. *2–3* advertisements for books on politics published by Constable.

TEXT: The same as A2d.

BINDING: Bound in olive green cloth. A rectangle is blind-stamped on the upper board. Stamped on the spine as follows: [rule blind-stamped] | ELEMENTS | OF | POLITICAL | SCIENCE | LEACOCK | CONSTABLE | LONDON | [rule blind-stamped].

NOTES: The arrangements for Leacock to revise his textbook were made through Houghton, Mifflin. See the notes to A2d. Constable inquired about the revisions to the book several times. Houghton, Mifflin informed Leacock on 23 November 1920: "We have sent them [Constable] the galley proofs of the revised edition. They now write to ascertain whether it would be safe for them to begin setting from these galley proofs" (HOUGHT). Once the costs of plates were paid for, Leacock received a royalty of 10%. According to *The English Catalogue of Books*, Constable published this edition in June 1921 at 12s. At least 2,921 copies were sold up to October 1939.

COPIES EXAMINED: CS (first impression and 1924 reprint).

## A2d *third American edition* (1921):

ELEMENTS OF | POLITICAL SCIENCE | BY | STEPHEN LEACOCK, B.A., PH.D. | LITT.D., LL.D, F.R.S.C. | HEAD OF THE DEPARTMENT OF ECONOMICS AND POLITICAL | SCIENCE, McGILL UNIVERSITY, MONTREAL | *NEW AND ENLARGED EDITION* | [illustration within an oval of a nude man who is sitting and playing a pipe] | HOUGHTON MIFFLIN COMPANY | BOSTON • NEW YORK • CHICAGO • SAN FRANCISCO | 𝕿𝖍𝖊 𝕽𝖎𝖛𝖊𝖗𝖘𝖎𝖉𝖊 𝕻𝖗𝖊𝖘𝖘 𝕮𝖆𝖒𝖇𝖗𝖎𝖉𝖌𝖊

Two states were examined: (1) copy as transcribed in the quasi-facsimile; (2) probably a later reprinting where the last three lines on the title page are: BOSTON • NEW YORK • CHICAGO • DALLAS | SAN FRANCISCO | 𝕿𝖍𝖊 𝕽𝖎𝖛𝖊𝖗𝖘𝖎𝖉𝖊 𝕻𝖗𝖊𝖘𝖘 𝕮𝖆𝖒𝖇𝖗𝖎𝖉𝖌𝖊. Information on the copyright page (p. *iv*) is also slightly different.

◆ 1–23⁸ 24⁸ (241 + χ1) 25–27⁸. *i–v, vi–vii, viii–ix, x–xiii, 1–4, 4–20, 21, 22–37, 38, 39–48, 49, 50–68, 69, 70–85, 86, 87–111, 112, 113–120, 121, 122–138, 139–141, 142–152, 153, 154–182, 183, 184–206, 207–208, 209–231, 232, 233–254, 255, 256–287, 288, 289–325, 326, 327–349, 350–353, 354–365, 366, 367–380, 381, 382–402, 403–405, 406–415, 1–3* pp. (217 leaves). Folded leaf (table of legislatures 1921) tipped in between pp. 354 and 355. 184 × 121 mm.

CONTENTS: p. *i* half title; p. *ii* blank; p. *iii* title; p. *iv Revised, February 1921* | COPYRIGHT, 1921, BY STEPHEN LEACOCK | Copyright, 1906 and 1913, by Stephen Leacock | ALL RIGHTS RESERVED | 𝕿𝖍𝖊 𝕽𝖎𝖛𝖊𝖗𝖘𝖎𝖉𝖊 𝕻𝖗𝖊𝖘𝖘 | CAMBRIDGE • MASSACHUSETTS | U•S•A; pp. *v,* v–vii preface dated "*June,* 1921"; p. *viii* blank; pp. *ix,* x–xiii table of contents; p. *1* blank; pp. *2–4, 4–402* text (p. *3* blank); p. *403* INDEX; p. *404* blank; pp. *405, 406–415* index; pp. *1–3* blank.

TEXT: The table of contents is basically the same as A2a. The following has been added: part I chapter IV section 7 Recent Criticism of the Doctrine of Sovereignty; parts I chapter VI section 6 The League of Nations. The following has been deleted: part II chapter IV section 5 Criticism of Existing Systems; the Case of Women, of Negroes, etc. The text has been updated throughout, particularly statistical information and the endings of chapters with suggested readings and further authorities.

BINDING AND DUST JACKET: Bound in dark green cloth with the following stamped in gilt on the spine: ELEMENTS | OF | POLITICAL | SCIENCE | REVISED | AND | ENLARGED | EDITION | LEACOCK | HOUGHTON | MIFFLIN CO. The jacket is tan coloured without any lettering.

NOTES: Leacock completed the revisions to his textbook on 29 May 1920. He received the first set of galleys on 4 August 1920, and he sent a statement for a circular about the revisions to the book sometime before 12 August 1920. The circular was not printed before 4 March 1921, however, because Leacock failed to return the proof of it (copy of circular not extant). Houghton, Mifflin informed Leacock on 9 August 1920 about publication:

> As soon as the manuscript reached us we sent it at once to the Press, asking them to begin work on it immediately. First, however, we had to study the manuscript to see whether it would be feasible to use part of the present plates. We found that it would be necessary to reset the entire book because of the numerous changes. Having decided upon an attractive new type page, we then proceeded to set the book and the galleys went forward to you as fast they could be set, read by our proof reading department and "cleaned up". We regret that you have not returned any of these galley proofs because as soon as they begin to come back to us we can immediately begin to make up the pages, cast and finish the plates which, as you doubtless know, requires some little time.

Leacock finished reading all the galleys on 29 December 1920 ". . . except the lists of books at the ends of the chapters in parts II & III." The index was prepared by Houghton, Mifflin at for a fee of $30. Leacock examined the page proofs in January and February 1921. Houghton, Mifflin complained on 16 March 1921 that Leacock had still not written the preface to the revised edition. Although the circular and newspaper advertising announced publication of the revised edition in August 1921, it did not go on sale until 1 January 1922. Leacock received an advance copy just before Christmas 1921. Published on 21 December 1921 at $2.25. Leacock received a royalty of 10%. He registered the copyright with the Copyright Office at DLC on 17 January 1922 (ClA653570). The copyright was renewed by Leacock on 16 December 1940. The copyright was renewed again by George Leacock, Barbara Nimmo, and Frank Chauvin on 16 October 1950 (R68516).

Houghton, Mifflin told Leacock on 9 December 1921 that it would probably be necessary to destroy some stock of the previous edition. It would appear that this was not done, however; copies of the previous edition sold until October 1923. The first printing of A2d consisted of 2,500 copies according to a requisition of 29 June 1920 (HOUGHT). Up to 30 April 1942, at least 6,638 copies sold. Between 30 April 1940 and 30 April 1942, only 29 copies sold.

COPIES EXAMINED: CS (both states, the first in jacket); QMMRB (second state, rebound).

## A3 GREATER CANADA 1907

[cover title: all lines within a rectangle] PRICE 10 CENTS | GREATER CANADA | AN APPEAL | [the next two lines within another rectangle] LET US NO LONGER | BE A COLONY | STEPHEN LEACOCK | Associate Professor of Political Science, McGill University, | MONTREAL, | (COPYRIGHT) | PUBLISHER'S AGENTS: | THE MONTREAL NEWS COMPANY, LIMITED. | MONTREAL.

♦ $1^6$. *1*, *2–10*, *1–2* pp. (6 leaves). 256 × 170 mm.

CONTENTS: pp. *1–10* text; pp. *1–2* blank.

BINDING: Bound in stiff wrappers, wire-stitched. The wrapper has two variant colours: light green and red. On the verso of the front of the wrapper is the following: Entered according to Act of the Parliament of Canada, in the year Nineteen | Hundred and Seven by STEPHEN LEACOCK, in the Department of Agriculture. Printed on the inside of the back wrapper is the contents of the April 1907 issue of the *University Magazine*, listing Leacock's article with the same title as this pamphlet.

NOTES: Leacock's pamphlet was published on 20 March 1907. It sold for 10¢ and at a trade price of 7½¢. Number of copies printed not known. This pamphlet is from the same sheets as Leacock's article, which appeared simultaneously in the *University Magazine* (see C7.5). On the day of publication the wholesale agents, the Montreal News Co. Ltd. and the Toronto News Co. Ltd., issued a small, yellow display poster (275 × 213 mm.) for bookstores. The first four lines of the poster state: THIS OUGHT TO HOLD US FOR A WHILE | Prof. Leacock Scolds Canadians for their Poor Spirit. | *I WILL NOT BE A COLONIAL* | CANADIAN SNOWS vs. ENGLISH COAL. The poster claims: "This appeal for the consideration of the Statesmen and Public Spirited People | of Canada has special reference to the Colonial Conference shortly to be held in | London, and is one that will be read with wide interest by all. Every Bookseller should be familiar with it." It is distinctly possible that Leacock designed and wrote the poster and arranged for its printing. See also "'Greater Canada,' an Appeal for a Higher and More Real Imperialism by Prof. Leacock. . . . ," *Montreal Gazette*, 20 March 1907, p. 5

According to an editorial in the *Vancouver Daily Province* ("Leacock to the Rescue," 27 March 1907), Leacock's pamphlet was given as a speech at the annual banquet of the Insurance Institute of Montreal (25 February 1907). The editorial questioned the wisdom of publishing the speech. ". . . Professor Leacock is a comparatively young man, if not an exceedingly youthful one, so that his pamphlet demands not only post-prandial leniency, but . . . good-humored forbearance. . . ." The editorial compared Leacock's style to a "diluted compound of Carlyle and the Prophet Downie, with a dash of epic poetry thrown in." The editorial went further and said that "while the orator runs amok at nearly everything in Canada, he propounds no better way and offers no solution."

COPIES EXAMINED: CS (both variant wrappers); OONL (three copies with the light green wrapper, two copies with the red wrapper); OTNY (red wrapper); OTUTF (red wrapper); QMMRB (both variant wrappers); SLM (poster).

## A4 BALDWIN LAFONTAINE HINCKS 1907

A4a *first Canadian edition, edition de luxe*:

THE MAKERS OF CANADA | [rule; the next three lines in red] | BALDWIN | LAFONTAINE | HINCKS | RESPONSIBLE GOVERNMENT | BY | STEPHEN LEACOCK | [in red] *EDITION DE LUXE* | TORONTO | MORANG & CO., LIMITED | 1907

◆ $1-24^8$. *i–viii*, ix–xii, *1–21*, 22, *23–71*, 72, *73–153*, 154, *155–197*, 198, *199–247*, 248, *249–279*, 280, *281–303*, 304, *305–360*, *361–362*, *363–371*, 1 pp. (192 leaves). 231 × 151 mm.

CONTENTS: p. *i* series title and names of editors; p. *ii* blank; p. *iii* half title; p. *iv* blank; p. *v* limitation statement, signed by George Morang, and numbered individually; p. *vi* blank; p. *vii* title; p. *viii Entered according to Act of Parliament of Canada | in the year 1907 by Morang & Co., Limited, in the | Department of Agriculture*; pp. ix–x preface dated "*July 31st, 1906.*"; *pp. xi–xii table of contents; pp. 1–360 text (pp. 24, 72, 154, 198, 248, 280, and 304 blank)*; p. *361* INDEX; p. *362* blank; pp. *363–371* index; p. *1* blank. The frontispiece (with tissue guard) has a black-and-white reproduction of an oval portrait of Baldwin with his signature in facsimile.

TEXT: chapter I Introductory; chapter II The Moderate Reformers and the Canadian Rebellion; chapter III The Unions of the Canadas; chapter IV Lord Sydenham and Responsible Government; chapter V The First LaFontaine-Baldwin Ministry; chapter VI The Coming of Metcalfe; chapter VII The Metcalfe Crisis; chapter VIII In Opposition; chapter IX The Second Lafontaine-Baldwin Ministry; chapter X The Rebellion Losses Bill; chapter XI The End of the Ministry.

BINDING: Bound in cream-coloured buckram, top edge gilt, with a paper label affixed to the spine. Printed on the label as follows: [two rules; the next two lines in red] | *THE MAKERS OF | CANADA* | [rule] | BALDWIN | LAFONTAINE | HINCKS | BY | STEPHEN LEACOCK | [rule] | [in red] 𝔈𝔡𝔦𝔱𝔦𝔬𝔫 𝔡𝔢 𝔏𝔲𝔵𝔢 | [two rules]. Paper with watermark of the publisher and series name. An extra paper label is tipped in at the end of the book.

NOTES: Leacock's book was the fourteenth volume of The Makers of Canada series. Published by Morang & Co. Limited between 1904 and 1911, the series consists of twenty-one volumes on the history of Canada. An Index volume appeared in 1911, and a supplementary volume on Sir Charles Tupper was published in 1916. Initially, the volumes appeared in an edition de luxe, limited to 400 numbered sets, signed by George N. Morang and sold by subscription. The editors of the series were Pelham Edgar and Duncan Campbell Scott; William Dawson Le Sueur joined the editorial board afterwards. Le Sueur, who wrote the second volume of the series, *Count Frontenac*, and would later become embroiled in legal suits with Morang and George Lindsey concerning Le Sueur's projected biography of William Lyon Mackenzie, acted as Leacock's editor.

Leacock completed his manuscript on 1 August 1906. Le Sueur's editing of Leacock's manuscript did not go well practically from the start. Le Sueur sent Leacock extensive criticisms in September 1906 (the criticisms of chapters V and VI are extant in Lindsey's papers, F37, at OTAR). According to Le Sueur's biographer, Clifford G. Holland, Le Sueur "was appalled to find him [Leacock] adopting a partisan liberal slant in the volume, while knowing him to actually hold very conservative views" (see *William Dawson LeSueur (1840–1917) A Canadian Man of Letters: The Sage of Ottawa* (San Francisco: Mellen

Research University Press, 1993), p. 244; and A.B. McKillop, ed., *A Critical Spirit: The Thought of William LeSueur* (Toronto: McClelland and Stewart in association with the Institute of Canadian Studies, Carleton University, 1977), pp. 250–1, 272).

Initially, Leacock was receptive to "putting more *Hincks* into my book," he told Morang on 26 October 1906. Extra information was placed into the footnotes in order "not to disturb the proportions of the book by shoving it into the text."

Leacock wrote to Edgar about Le Sueur's "*grossest* alterations." Scott told Edgar on 26 October 1906 that Leacock had no grounds for complaint (Edgar fonds, file 41, OTV). "LeSueur where he made alterations made them lightly in pencil so that they could be easily rubbed out, and where he suggested modifications in the wording, put them on separate slips in the form of a memorandum, and said that the whole of his suggestions were made for the author's consideration." On 2 November 1906, Leacock informed his American publisher, Houghton, Mifflin, that he was ". . . busily engaged in proof reading, note making, index making etc. . . . It seems to involve such a lot of odd work that it may keep me busy till the end of the winter" (HOUGHT). A day later, Leacock complained to Morang:

> I do not think it proper for him [Le Sueur] to make changes in the proof without my sanction. It is I who have to sign the book. I do not agree with Mr. LeSueur's views, and do not wish to put my name to them, not to have them reflected in a book written by me, and for which I am responsible. I can hardly be expected to state in detail by correspondence my reasons for not accepting such suggestions of Mr. LeSueurs as I do not accept. It would involve discussing the whole history of Canada. . . . Who is writing this book, Mr. LeSueur or I? If I am to state in full in writing my reason for every phrase I use there is no end of the thing. I think Mr. LeSueur's views on Responsible government quite wrong. I want to keep them out of my book.

Morang was caught in the middle of this difference in professional opinion. He hoped that Leacock would be accommodating, and would see his way to making some alterations. Le Sueur did suggest to Morang that Edgar could assume editorial responsibilities for the book. Le Sueur then wrote a somewhat conciliatory letter (14 November 1906) to Leacock, but Leacock did not acknowledge it. "I much doubt whether he [Leacock] intends to take any notice of it," Le Sueur wrote to Morang on 20 December 1906. "The fact is he [Leacock] is in a false position and does not see how to get out of it. He knows that I did *not* take gross liberties, to say nothing of 'the grossest,' with his manuscript. . ." On 3 January 1907 Morang sent Le Sueur and Leacock a separate set of "five more gallies." Ten or twelve "more gallies" were promised from the printer the next day. Le Sueur was asked to proofread and correct the galleys and to send them to Leacock for his consideration. Leacock visited Morang on 20 March 1907, and was asked by Morang to see Edgar with respect to the book's index. More proofs (pp. 318–359) were sent to Le Sueur and Leacock on 1 May 1907, although it would appear that Leacock still did not reply to Le Sueur's letters. The book was published on 8 July 1907. According to W.L. Grant in his general introduction to volume one of the Anniversary edition, the type ". . . was cast in Scotland for the first edition, and from which it was printed in Toronto by the Murray Printing Company."

COPIES EXAMINED: OTNY (no. 64); QMMRB (two copies — no. 17, and the other rebound in red leather, not signed by the publisher and not numbered).

**A4a.1** *first Canadian edition, "Parkman edition"* (1907):

THE MAKERS OF CANADA | [rule] | BALDWIN | LAFONTAINE | HINCKS | RESPONSIBLE GOVERNMENT | BY | STEPHEN LEACOCK | TORONTO | MORANG & CO., LIMITED | 1907

◆ $1^2$ $2-25^8$ $26^2$. *1–10*, ix–xii, 1–21, 22, 23–71, 72, 73–153, *154*, 155–197, *198*, 199–247, 248, 249–279, 280, 281–303, 304, 305–360, 361–362, 363–371, 1–7 pp. (196 leaves). 219 × 151 mm.

The Parkman edition is in fact an issue from the same setting of type as A4a. It has additional blank leaves at the beginning and end. The recto of the leaf before the half title reads: 𝔓𝔞𝔯𝔨𝔪𝔞𝔫 𝔈𝔡𝔦𝔱𝔦𝔬𝔫 | THE MAKERS OF CANADA | VOL. VIX.

BINDING: Bound in half maroon leather and half pink and gold marbled paper boards. The endpapers are in matching marbled paper, top edge stained gilt. Stamped in gilt on the spine: [rule] | [maple leaf] | [rule] | THE | MAKERS | OF | CANADA | [rule] | VOL.XIV | [rule] | [maple leaf] | [rule] | BALDWIN | [rule] | LAFONTAINE | [rule] | HINCKS | BY | S.B.LEACOCK | [rule] | [maple leaf] | [rule] | [maple leaf] | MORANG | [rule].

NOTES: In advertising the Parkman edition, Morang stated that "every detail of this publication" has been "given careful and zealous attention." The type used is "large and clear" with ample spacing in the margins. The paper is of the highest quality, "antique finish, opaque and durable. The illustrations are faithful reproductions of authentic originals, executed in photogravure and printed on Japan vellum. The bindings are artistic and strong" (advertising booklet, *The Makers of Canada* (Toronto: Morang, 1909)). Number of copies printed not known.

Reprinted in 1909 and 1910 with stamping in gilt on the spine.

COPIES EXAMINED: CS (1907, 1909, 1910).

**A4a.2** *English issue* (1907):

THE MAKERS OF CANADA | [rule; the next three lines in red] | BALDWIN | LAFONTAINE | HINCKS | RESPONSIBLE GOVERNMENT | BY | STEPHEN LEACOCK | [in red] LONDON: T. C. & E. C. JACK | TORONTO: MORANG & CO., LIMITED | 1907

The English issue is similar to A4a. The limitation statement after the half-title reads: *This work is limited to One Hundred and | Twenty Sets for the United Kingdom, | Signed and Numbered. | Number* [number hand-written]. The verso of the title leaf is blank. Two binding variants were examined: (1) brown quarter leather with light brown buckram sides; (2) light brown buckram with dark brown buckram sides. Stamped in gilt on the spine: THE MAKERS OF | CANADA | BALDWIN | LAFONTAINE | HINCKS | BY | STEPHEN | LEACOCK | [coat of arms of Canada] | T.C.&.E.C.JACK. Price 21s.

COPIES EXAMINED: CUL (variant (1)); FREE (rebound, lacking preliminary leaves); UCLA (no. 60, variant (2)).

**A4a.3** *first edition, "University edition"* (1912):

In this issue Leacock's book (dated 1912 on the title page) has been bound with two other volumes of The Makers of Canada series: Nathanael Burwash's *Egerton Ryerson* and Sir John George Bourinot's *Lord Elgin*. Two binding variants were examined: (1) green cloth with stamping on the spine in gilt as follows: THE MAKERS OF | CANADA VOL 8 | [maple leaves]; (2) brown leather, top edge stained gilt, multi-coloured brown endpapers. Blind-stamped on the upper and lower boards within a rectangle, with maples leaves at the corners, is the Canadian coat of arms inside a compartment and laurel leaves. The spine identifies this issue as volume VIII of the University edition.

In all likelihood, the "University edition" was a marketing attempt by Morang to dispose of unbound sheets of Leacock's book and other books of the Makers series. The OCLC WorldCat database records a printing in 1910, but the copy in question is in fact dated 1912.

COPIES EXAMINED: BVIV (rebound, erroneously dated 1910 by OCLC WorldCat); CS (brown leather).

**A4b** *"Anniversary" revised edition* entitled *Mackenzie Baldwin LaFontaine Hincks* and bound with Alfred D. DeCelles's *Papineau Cartier* (1926):

THE MAKERS OF CANADA SERIES | [rule] | *Anniversary Edition* | [rule] | [the next four lines in red] MACKENZIE | BALDWIN | LAFONTAINE | HINCKS | BY | STEPHEN LEACOCK | *Illustrated under the direction of A. G. Doughty, C.M.G., Litt.D.* | *Deputy Minister, Public Archives of Canada* | LONDON AND TORONTO | [in red] OXFORD UNIVERSITY PRESS | 1926

◆ 1–23$^{16}$ 24$^{14}$. i–viii, ix–x, 1–2, 1–33, 34, 35–67, 68, 69–89, 90, 91–131, 132, 133–221, 222, 223–271, 272, 273–327, 328, 329–384, 385–386, 387–395, 1–11, 1–17, 18, 19–25, 26, 27–53, 54, 55–73, 74, 75–97, 98, 99–141, 142, 143–161, 162, 163–183, 184, 185–203, 1–5, 1–19, 20, 21–65, 66, 67–93, 94, 95–103, 104, 105–136, 1–2 pp. (382 leaves). 199 × 127 mm.

CONTENTS: p. *i* THE MAKERS OF CANADA SERIES | FOUNDED BY GEORGE N. MORANG | W. L. GRANT, M.A. (OXON.), LL.D., EDITOR-IN-CHIEF; p. *ii* blank; p. *iii* VOL. V. | MACKENZIE | BALDWIN LAFONTAINE HINCKS | PAPINEAU CARTIER; p. *iv* blank; p. *5* title; p. *6* COPYRIGHT, CANADA, 1926 | BY THE MAKERS OF CANADA, LIMITED | PRINTED IN CANADA; p. *v* editor's preface (by W.P.M. Kennedy) dated "September 1st, 1925"; p. *vi* blank; pp. ix–x table of contents; pp. *1* list of illustrations; p. 2 blank; pp. 1–384 text (pp. *34, 68, 90, 132, 222, 272,* and *328* blank); p. *385* INDEX; p. *386* blank; pp. 387–395. The rest of the volume pertains to DeCelles's *Papineau Cartier*. Illustrations include the frontispiece and those facing pp. 26, 36, 50, 60, 86, 170, 348, and 374.

TEXT: Although the chapter titles are identical to those of A4a, the text has been altered in many respects. In his preface Kennedy states that he has ". . . extended the account of William Lyon Mackenzie. . . .; secondly, the survey of the earlier part of Bagot's régime has been completely changed in order to present his constitutional experiment from a detailed study of his correspondence. . . ." Leacock's preface has been deleted.

BINDING: Bound in red pebble-grained cloth with red signet and top edge in gilt. A series of floral compartments and rules along with the volume number, titles, and publisher's name are stamped in gilt on the spine; blind-stamped on the upper board is a banner with Oxford University Press and its coat of arms.

NOTES: In the general introduction to volume 1 of the Anniversary edition of The Makers of Canada series, W.L. Grant states that Oxford University Press acquired the plates of the

original edition from Morang. Grant took over the duties of editor of the series, arranged
for revisions to the texts, and in some cases replaced them altogether (Sir John Bourinot's

by Kennedy). The new edition of the enlarged Makers
ith individual volumes containing more than one text.
nks Leacock ". . . for his courteous permission to deal
s kindness during the process of revision." Number of
on not known.

copies).

Magazine edition" (1928):

ERIES | [rule] | MacLean's Magazine
| BALDWIN | LAFONTAINE | HINCKS | BY |
ed under the direction of A. G. Doughty,
r, Public Archives of Canada | LONDON AND
RSITY PRESS | 1928

and the binding, this issue is identical to A4b. Bound
spine gilt identical to A4b. A rectangle is blind-stamped
on the upper and lower boards.

COPIES EXAMINED: CS.

## A5 LITERARY LAPSES 1910

**A5a** *first Canadian edition* (1910):

LITERARY LAPSES | A Book of Sketches | BY | STEPHEN LEACOCK |
MONTREAL: | Gazette Printing Company, Limited. | 1910. | [rule] |
*Price 35 Cents.*

◆ $1-8^8$. *1–5, 6–9, 10, 11–18, 19, 20, 21, 22–24, 25, 26, 27, 28–32, 33, 34–40, 41, 42, 43, 44–48,
49, 50–58, 59, 60–69, 70, 71–75, 76, 77–79, 80, 81–86, 87, 88–109, 110, 111–112, 113, 114–117,
118, 119–125, 1–3* pp. (64 leaves). 179 × 121 mm.

CONTENTS: p. *1* title; p. *2* Copyright, Canada, 1910 | by STEPHEN LEACOCK.; p. *3* preface;
p. *4* table of contents; pp. *5–125* text; pp. *1–3* blank.

TEXT: My Financial Career; Lord Oxhead's Secret: A Romance in One Chapter; Boarding
House Geometry; The Awful Fate of Melpomenus Jones; The New Food; A New Pathology;
The Force of Statistics; Getting the Thread of It; Telling His Faults; Winter Pastimes;
Number Fifty-Six; The Conjurer's Revenge; Hints to Travellers; A Manual of Education;
The Life of John Smith; On Collecting Things; Society Chit-Chat As It Should Be Written;
Borrowing a Match; A Lesson in Fiction; Helping the Armenians; An Experiment with
Policeman Hogan; Self-Made Men; A Model Dialogue; Reflections on Riding; Saloonio: A
Study in Shakespearean Criticism; A, B and C: The Human Element in Mathematics.

BINDING AND DUST JACKET: Bound in pale green paper boards, quarter-bound with dark
green cloth, with a paper label mounted near the top of the spine. Stamped on the upper
board: LITERARY LAPSES | STEPHEN LEACOCK. Printed on the paper label: LITERARY
| LAPSES | [rule] | A BOOK | OF | SKETCHES | [rule] | STEPHEN | LEACOCK. Dust jacket

not seen, but apparently issued in jacket. In the late 1980s, at a book fair in California, Richard Shu of Alphabet Books saw a copy in jacket for sale, but the whereabouts of that copy is not known.

NOTES: Prompted by his wife, Beatrix, and by Mrs. B.K. Sandwell, Leacock sent a collection of his humorous sketches, some of which had been previously published in magazines (for example, *Puck*, *Life*, and *Truth*), to Houghton, Mifflin and Company, the American publisher of *Elements of Political Science* (A2). He told William S. Booth of Houghton, Mifflin on 31 December 1906:

> The dignified kind of humour which these sketches are supposed to represent is perhaps better without illustration. But I leave that to you. One might suggest that a photogravure of an Equestrian Statue of the author surrounded by the Houghton Mifflin firm might be inserted at the back of the book. (HOUGHT)

Houghton, Mifflin rejected the manuscript much to their regret thereafter. On 15 December 1921, when Houghton, Mifflin failed to purchase the John Lane Company from John Lane, they informed Leacock that there was ". . . no living author that we would take over with more pleasure than yourself. . . ." (HOUGHT).

Leacock and his brother George together decided that they would privately arrange for the book's publication. B.K. Sandwell opposed the scheme because he thought that the publication of humorous stories would tarnish Leacock's academic reputation. In the end Leacock thought it was unfair to place his brother at financial risk. He arranged for the distribution of the book with the Montreal News Company on 3 February 1910 and for its printing with the Gazette Printing Company on 4 April 1910. It cost him 15 1/3¢ per copy to have the books bound and printed. According to Leacock's calculation of 5 February [1910], the total costs for printing and binding were $461.16, including $109.20 for composition and $66.96 for paper. He promised to furnish the Montreal News Company with 300 advertising placards. The book was published on 9 April 1910. The edition consisted of 3,000 copies. Leacock took 100 copies for himself. The book "sold like hot pop corn," Leacock wrote in the inscribed copy in the Friedman collection at QMMRB (see Lomer, p. 39). Copies sold for 35¢ apiece, with Leacock receiving 23¢ on each copy sold. By 9 August 1910 only a few hundred copies were available, and on 11 October 1910 Leacock told John Lane: "My Canadian Edition is sold out" (information based on archives at SLM and TEX).

Reprint of "Society Chit-Chat" in *Answers* 61, no. 1,582 (21 September 1918): 221; *Vancouver Sunday Sun*, 8 April 1923, ("Magazine"), p. 5. Syndicated by Metropolitan Newspaper Service, New York. Reprint of "Number Fifty-Six" in Bert Case Diltz, ed., *Frontiers of Wonder Book II* (Toronto: McClelland and Stewart, 1968), pp. 42–47. Reprint of "A Christmas Letter" in *A Canadian Yuletide Treasury* (Toronto: Clarke, Irwin, 1982), pp. 96–7.

COPIES EXAMINED: CS (three copies); OTNY (four copies); QMMRB (three copies).

## A5b *first English edition* [1910]:

*LITERARY LAPSES | BY STEPHEN LEACOCK |* [thick-thin rule] *|* [thin-thick rule] *| LONDON: JOHN LANE, THE BODLEY HEAD | NEW YORK: JOHN LANE COMPANY. MCMXI*

◆ $A^8$ B–$P^8$ $Q^4$ [$1 signed]. 1–4, 5–6, 7–8, 9–245, 246, 247–248 pp. (124 leaves). 183 × 122 mm.

CONTENTS: p. 1 half title; p. 2 blank; p. 3 title; p. 4 WILLIAM BRENDON AND SON, LTD., PRINTERS, PLYMOUTH; pp. 5–6 contents; p. 7 fly title; p. 8 blank; pp. 9–245 text; p. 246 blank; pp. 247–248 acknowledgments.

TEXT: My Financial Career; Lord Oxhead's Secret: A Romance in One Chapter; Boarding-House Geometry; The Awful Fate of Melpomenus Jones; A Christmas Letter; How to Make a Million Dollars; How to Live to Be 200; How to Avoid Getting Married; How to Be a Doctor; The New Food; A New Pathology; The Poet Answered; The Force of Statistics; Men Who Have Shaved Me; Getting the Thread of It; Telling His Faults; Winter Pastimes; Number Fifty-Six; Aristocratic Education; The Conjurer's Revenge; Hints to Travellers; A Manual of Education; Hoodoo McFiggin's Christmas; The Life of John Smith; On Collecting Things; Society Chit-Chat As It Should Be Written; Insurance Up to Date; Borrowing a Match; A Lesson in Fiction; Helping the Armenians; A Study in Still Life. — The Country Hotel; An Experiment with Policeman Hogan; The Passing of the Poet; Self-Made Men; A Model Dialogue; Back to the Bush; Reflections on Riding; Saloonio: A Study in Shakespearean Criticism; Half-Hours with the Poets; A, B, and C: The Human Element in Mathematics.

BINDING AND DUST JACKET: Bound in orange cloth, top edge stained gilt. Stamped on the upper board in gilt: *LITERARY LAPSES | By STEPHEN LEACOCK*. Stamped on the spine in gilt: *LITERARY | LAPSES | By | STEPHEN | LEACOCK*.

The front and spine panels of the jacket are similar to the stamping on the upper board and spine with the following exceptions: printing is in black; the lines on the front panel are within three rectangles; the spine panel has the publisher's name along with two rules at the top and bottom. The only known copy of the jacket was missing the back panel and the flaps.

NOTES: John Lane was the first publisher to approach Leacock about the book's English rights (5 July 1910). T. Fisher Unwin had read reviews of the book in the *Spectator* and tried to arrange publication on 11 July 1910. Similarly, Thomas B. Wells of Harper & Brothers made inquiries for an American edition on 18 August 1910.

Leacock accepted Lane's offer of 15% royalty on 17 July 1910. In July, August and September of that year he sent Lane additional sketches and poems for an enlarged edition. In the English edition fourteen new humorous sketches were added to the twenty-six sketches published in the first Canadian edition. The poems that were sent to Lane were deemed unsuitable for inclusion, however. On 5 October 1910 Lane told Leacock that the Gazette Printing Company's estimate for printing was too high. (Lane had written to the Gazette Printing Company sometime in July of that year). Publication in England would be cheaper and preferable, Lane informed Leacock. On 11 October 1910 Leacock returned "revised proofs of 39 sketches as indicated in the table of contents shewing the order to place them." He noted: "The sketch *Back to the Bush* is in your hands. I don't think I need [to] read the proof of it, nor see any further revision or page proof." On 3 November 1910 he signed and sent Lane the contract for the book, and he remarked: "I must congratulate you upon the excellent appearance of the type that you are using." In the contract at READ, dated 7 November 1910, Leacock received 15% royalty on the English edition (thirteen copies being reckoned as twelve).

Notwithstanding the publication date of 1911 on the title page, publication occurred in November 1910 according to *The English Catalogue of Books*. The book sold for 3s 6d.

The number of copies printed of the first impression is not known. By 30 June 1911 (the date of the first royalty report cited in Leacock's notebook of royalty payments at SLM), 1,262 copies had sold of the English edition ($148.69 royalty earned).

Information on copyright pages of later printings indicates that the book was reprinted in 1911, 1912 (three times), 1914, 1915, 1916, 1917 (twice), 1919, 1920, 1922, 1924, 1926, 1927 ("cheap edition"), 1930 (twice), 1931, 1937, and 1941. There was obviously a reprinting in 1913 (see notes to A5b.6).

From the date of publication to the end of 1 August 1925, 34,051 copies sold of the English edition (3,015 copies sold to the Australasian market and 1,669 to the colonial market).

One of the stories in the book, "How to Live to Be 200," was pirated and reprinted with slight alterations as "How to Die a Natural Death" by Douglas Lloyd Jr. in *Saucy Stories*, an American journal bound up and published in England. B.W. Willett of The Bodley Head reported the piracy on 22 November 1922. Although Willett informed Leacock that no further legal steps would be taken due to a flaw in the 1921 Copyright Act, the publisher of *Saucy Stories* agreed to pay £20 for the piracy on 8 January 1923.

COPIES EXAMINED: BOD (partial jacket, John Johnson collection); CS (first printing; reprints in 1914 ("sixth edition"), 1919 in jacket ("eleventh edition"), and 1930 in jacket); QMMRB (first printing).

## A5b.1 *first American issue* [1910]:

The title leaf and the contents are identical to A5b, except that sixteen unnumbered pages of ads for books published by the John Lane Company have been added after p. 248. Bound in dark green cloth. Within a solid cream rectangle on the upper board is stamped (the letters and rectangle are green): LITERARY | LAPSES [shamrock] | STEPHEN LEACOCK. Printed on the spine in cream: LITERARY | LAPSES | [rule] | LEACOCK. Dust jacket not seen.

NOTES: When Leacock accepted John Lane's offer for an English edition on 17 July 1910, he presumed ". . . that you will put the book in the United States market as well." According to Lomer (p. 39), the American issue was published on 8 November 1910 at $1.25 (postage 12¢ extra). On 29 November 1911 Leacock pointed out to Lane: "I note according to my account that I am credited with Royalties on 940 (equal 868), Literary Lapses sold in America: the price is put at 3/6 and the royalty at 10 per cent, Is this correct? The price is put at $1.25, and the royalty 10 per cent. This would make $108.50, due to me. . . ." Reprints of A5b.1 probably occurred with the same frequency as A5b. Reprints examined include "fourth edition" (1912 reprint), "fifth edition" (1913 reprint), "sixth edition" (1914 reprint), and 1918 (printed by the Press of J.J. Little & Ives Co.). According to an advertising brochure issued by the John Lane Company, the book was into its 27th edition ("i.e. printing) by 1920 ($1.50 cloth).

Leacock's notebook of royalty payments at SLM records that 18,850 copies sold up to the end of 1921. Thereafter, the American rights were transferred to Dodd, Mead.

COPIES EXAMINED: CS (first printing; reprints in 1912, 1913, 1914, 1919 (in jacket)); OORI (first printing); OTNY.

## A5b.2 *first Canadian issue* (1911):

LITERARY LAPSES | BY STEPHEN LEACOCK | [thick-thin rule] | CANADIAN EDITION | MONTREAL NEWS COMPANY LIMITED | MONTREAL | 1911

Leaves measure 186 × 123 mm. The contents of this issue are identical to A5b, except that eight unnumbered pages of ads for books published by John Lane The Bodley Head have been added after p. 248. Bound in dark green vertically ribbed cloth. Rectangular compartments are blind-stamped on the upper board with floral ornaments on the top compartment. Stamped in white on the upper board: LITERARY LAPSES | STEPHEN LEACOCK. Stamped in white on the spine: LITERARY | LAPSES | STEPHEN | LEACOCK | THE | MONTREAL NEWS | COMPANY. Dust jacket not seen.

NOTES: In his contract with The Bodley Head, Leacock stipulated: "The author reserves the exclusive right of publication in Canada and the publisher undertakes not to offer his edition or editions of the book for sale in Canada" (The Bodley Head fonds, READ). However, on 3 November 1910, Leacock asked John Lane about copies to be sold in Canada:

> My present Canadian Edition [A5a] is sold out and as the booksellers are asking for more copies, I should like to know how soon and at what price you could send me either the sheets of the book, with price quoted per thousand, or copies of your edition itself (I to pay the Canadian Customs) with price quoted per five hundred. It would not be necessary to print a special title page for me as I would have a slip of paper inserted here with the imprint of the Canadian seller, which would probably be the Montreal News Company.

On 10 April 1911 Lane arranged with the Montreal News Company to buy 1,000 copies of the English edition in flat sheets from Leacock. According to Leacock's notebook of royalty payments at SLM, he received a royalty of $250 for this issue. With the exception of the ads, the sheets were printed from the same set of plates as A5b (second impression). The first two pages of ads are for the "*Second* [English] *Edition*" (i.e. printing), and feature excerpts from British reviews of the book.

COPIES EXAMINED: CS.

## A5b.3 *second Canadian issue* (1911):

This issue is identical to the second printing of A5b. The title page is the same as A5b, and the verso of the title leaf reads: SECOND EDITION | WILLIAM BRENDON AND SON, LTD., PRINTERS, PLYMOUTH. There are eight pages of advertisements after p. 248 (identical to those of A5b.2). The binding is the same as A5b.2 except on the spine where MUSSON has replaced the Montreal News Company as publisher. Dust jacket not seen.

NOTES: On 31 October 1911 Lane told Leacock that the Musson Book Co. wanted to purchase 200 copies in sheets of the English edition. The copies were charged to Leacock at 8 pence apiece, and then he was to charge Musson for the incurred costs. The arrangement with Musson was formalized on 6 January 1912, and on 8 January the Musson Book Co. (J.H. Charles) sent Leacock a cheque for $37.50 in royalties. The book sold at a retail price of $1.25.

According to Leacock's notebook of royalty payments at SLM, the Musson Book Co. sold 3,329 copies of in all (3,116 copies up to the end of 1915, and thirteen further copies sold at the end of December 1919). Three other Musson issues were also examined.

COPIES EXAMINED: CS.

## A5b.4  *third Canadian issue* [1912]:

*LITERARY LAPSES | BY STEPHEN LEACOCK* | [thick-thin rule] | [in overlapping, swash letters] MBCo. | [thin-thick rule] | TORONTO | THE MUSSON BOOK CO., LIMITED

Identical to A5b.2, except the title leaf is a cancel and the verso of this leaf is blank. Also the verso of the half title (p. 2), which is blank in a5b.2, has the following printed on it: [both lines within a rectangle] | *BY THE SAME AUTHOR* | NONSENSE NOVELS. The binding is identical to a5b.3. Dust jacket not seen.

NOTES:  On 28 November 1912 Lane told Leacock that he was sending the Musson Book Co. "1,000 copies with the Publisher's Press imprint and invoicing them at the same time, and am accordingly crediting your account with the number." This probably accounts for the cancel leaf on this Musson issue. The Publishers' Press went bankrupt earlier in that year, and as a result the original title leaf with the Publishers' Press imprint would have been excised by Musson before publication in Canada. On Leacock's difficulties with the Publishers' Press, see the notes to A7a.1.

Also examined are two variant bindings, undoubtedly from a later reprinting in 1912. For both these variants, the title leaf is a cancel identical to A5b.4. However, this reprinting lacks publisher's ads, and on p. 2, lists *Sunshine Sketches of a Little Town* in addition to *Nonsense Novels*. One variant is in full green leather with LITERARY LAPSES stamped in gilt on the upper board within a floral rectangular compartment and stamping in gilt of a floral design, the title, Leacock's name, and MUSSON on the spine. The other variant is bound in half brown leather and half light brown cloth with the title, Leacock's name, rules, a floral rectangular compartment, and MUSSON stamped in gilt on the spine.

COPIES EXAMINED: CS (first printing; later printing in brown leather and light brown cloth); LAT (later printing in green leather); QMMRB (first printing).

## A5b.5  *fourth Canadian issue* [1912?]:

*LITERARY LAPSES | BY STEPHEN LEACOCK* | [thick-thin rule] | TORONTO | THE MUSSON BOOK COMPANY | LIMITED

This issue has four blank leaves after p. 248. *Nonsense Novels* and *Sunshine Sketches of a Little Town* are listed on p. 2. This would indicate that it is probably from a later printing in 1912 (after 9 August 1912). The title leaf is integral, and its verso (p. 4) reads: WILLIAM BRENDON AND SON, LTD., PRINTERS, PLYMOUTH, ENGLAND.

The binding is the same as A5b.3. The dust jacket is light beige with printing in blue. Printed on the front panel of the jacket: [all lines within a rectangle] Literary Lapses | [two rules] | [three paragraphs about the book and Leacock as a humorist] | [two rules] | BY STEPHEN LEACOCK. Printed on the spine: Literary | Lapses | BY | STEPHEN | LEACOCK | [in overlapping, swash letters] MBCo. | MUSSON. On the back panel within a rectangle are press opinions of *Nonsense Novels*. The flaps are blank.

NOTES:  On 18 March 1913 J.H. Charles of the Musson Book Co. informed Leacock that the 1,000 copies obtained from Lane had all been sold (987 sold and 13 for review and presentation). This may refer to the sale of this issue or possibly A5b.4. In any event it is likely that this issue consisted of 1,000 copies.

COPIES EXAMINED: CS (two copies, one in jacket); OORI; OTNY; OTUTF.

## A5b.6 *fifth Canadian issue* (1913):

*LITERARY LAPSES* | *BY STEPHEN LEACOCK* | [thick-thin rule] | [thin-thick rule] | *TORONTO: THE MUSSON BOOK CO. LTD.* | *NEW YORK:JOHN LANE COMPANY::LONDON* | JOHN LANE, THE BODLEY HEAD. MCMXIII

Cancel title. The copyright page reads: FIFTH EDITION | WILLIAM BRENDON AND SON, LTD., PRINTERS, PLYMOUTH | ENGLAND. There are four leaves of advertisements after p. 248. *Nonsense Novels* and *Sunshine Sketches of a Little Town* are listed on p. 2. The binding is the same as A5b.3.

NOTES: Another 1,000 copies were obtained by the Musson Book Co. from John Lane on 31 January 1913. These were all sold by 24 March 1914. These copies were perhaps from the "FIFTH EDITION" (i.e. printing) or possibly from A5b.5. The print run for this issue was probably 1,000 copies.

COPIES EXAMINED: CS; LAT; OTNY; OTUTF (two copies).

## A5b.7 *sixth Canadian issue* (1915):

*LITERARY LAPSES* | *BY STEPHEN LEACOCK* | [thick-thin rule] | [thin-thick rule] | *LONDON: JOHN LANE THE BODLEY HEAD* | *NEW YORK: JOHN LANE COMPANY* | *TORONTO: S. B. GUNDY MCMXV* | *Published in Canada for Humphrey Milford*

Leaves measure 188 × 126 mm. Identical to A5b with the following exceptions: the title leaf is a cancel, and the verso identifies this issue as the "SEVENTH EDITION" [i.e. impression]; the verso of the half title (p. 2) has the following printed on it: [all lines within a rectangle] | *BY THE SAME AUTHOR* | NONSENSE NOVELS | SUNSHINE SKETCHES | OF A LITTLE TOWN | BEHIND THE BEYOND | ARCADIAN ADVEN- | TURES WITH THE | IDLE RICH. Bound in orange cloth, top edge stained orange. Stamped on the upper board in gilt within three blind-stamped rectangles: *LITERARY LAPSES* | *By STEPHEN LEA-COCK*. Stamped on the spine in gilt: [two rules blind-stamped] | *LITERARY* | LAPSES | *By* | *STEPHEN* | *LEACOCK* | *GUNDY* | [two rules blind-stamped]. Dust jacket not seen.

NOTES: When Leacock's Canadian publisher, Bell and Cockburn, went bankrupt at the end of 1914, Leacock arranged a contract with S.B. Gundy for four new books of humour in February 1915. Gundy also took control over the Canadian market of Leacock's previous published books of humour. By the end of 1915 Gundy sold 248 copies of this issue ($62 royalty). Until the end of 1923 Gundy sold 1,724 copies of this issue.

COPIES EXAMINED: CS; QMMRB.

## A5b.8 *Second American issue* (1922):

*LITERARY LAPSES* | *BY STEPHEN LEACOCK* | [thick-thin rule] | [thin-thick rule] | *NEW YORK: DODD, MEAD AND COMPANY* | *1922*

The verso of the title leaf of this issue reads: PRINTED IN U. S. A. On p. 2 seven books are listed as by the same author, the first being *Behind the Beyond* and the last *Further Foolishness*. Bound in green cloth. The upper board is blind-stamped and is similar to A5b.1. Stamped on the spine in gilt: LITERARY | LAPSES | [rule] | LEACOCK | DODD, MEAD | & COMPANY. The dust jacket is similar to those for later reprints of the John Lane Company. The front panel has a colour illustration in art-nouveau style by A.H. Fish of a couple on a couch looking at a book. The spine panel is printed in blue as follows: LITERARY | LAPSES | *By* | STEPHEN | LEACOCK | DODD, MEAD | AND COMPANY. The back panel is blank. On the front flap are excerpts from press opinions of the book; the back flap has a list of Leacock's other books published by Dodd, Mead with press opinions.

NOTES: According to Leacock's notebook of royalty payments at SLM, Dodd, Mead sold 571 copies in its first royalty statement of 1 August 1922. 3,817 copies sold up to 1 August 1925. Lomer (p. 40) records reprints in 1923, 1927, 1943, and 1944. The OCLC WorldCat database also records reprints in 1924, 1925, 1931, 1936, and 1937. There was also a reprint arranged on 23 February 1934 (250 copies) and reprints in 1939 and 1942. Royalty reports from Dodd, Mead indicate that the book approximately sold 150 to 400 copies annually.

COPIES EXAMINED: CS (1942 printing in jacket); LAT (1923, red leather); NFSM (1939); OTNY (1922 and 1924 printings in jacket).

### A5b.9 *third American issue* (1970):

*LITERARY LAPSES | BY STEPHEN LEACOCK*| [thick-thin rule] | *Short Story Index Reprint Series* | [publisher's device, almost three lines in height, to the left of the next three lines: abstract design of building with four columns] | BOOKS FOR LIBRARIES PRESS | A Division of Arno Press, Inc. | New York, New York

The verso of the title leaf reads as follows: First Published 1911 | Reprinted 1970 | STANDARD BOOK NUMBER: | 8369-3561-6 | LIBRARY OF CONGRESS CATALOG CARD NUMBER: | 70-122728 | PRINTED IN THE UNITED STATES OF AMERICA. Pagination is the same as A5b, except that the last leaf of this issue is blank and unpaginated. Leaves measure 202 × 130 mm. Bound in dark brown paper boards with stamping on the spine in gilt as follows: Leacock LITERARY LAPSES.

NOTES: Number of copies printed and date of publication not known.

COPIES EXAMINED: NSDAL.

### A5c *second English edition* (1939):

LITERARY LAPSES | BY | STEPHEN LEACOCK | [publisher's device: illustration of a penguin] | PENGUIN BOOKS LIMITED | HARMONDSWORTH MIDDLESEX ENGLAND

◆ $A^{16}$ B–$F^{16}$ [$1 signed]. *1–4*, 5, 6, *7–182*, *1–10* pp. (96 leaves). 180 × 112 mm.

CONTENTS: p. *1* half title; p. *2* information on the author and publisher's note; p. *3* title; p. *4* First published 1910 | Published in Penguin Books 1939 | MADE AND PRINTED IN GREAT BRITAIN FOR PENGUIN BOOKS LTD., BY | WYMAN & SONS LIMITED,

LONDON, READING AND FAKENHAM.; pp. 5–6 table of contents; pp. 7–181 text; p. 182 acknowledgments; pp. 1–10 ads (complete list of Penguin publications up to June 1939, extract from H.C. Armstrong's *Grey Wolf (Mustafa Kemal)*, etc.).

TEXT: Identical to A5b.

BINDING AND DUST JACKET: Paperback, sewn signatures. The spine and front cover consist of three sections, orange at the top and bottom and white in the middle. The front cover is as follows: [the first two lines within a rounded compartment outlined in black within the top orange section] PENGUIN | BOOKS | [the next four lines are within the white section, are flanked by the word FICTION vertically in orange on both sides] LITERARY | LAPSES | STEPHEN LEACOCK | [the next line and illustration within the bottom orange section] COMPLETE [illustration of penguin] UNABRIDGED. The spine records the author, title, and series number (212). The back cover, in orange, lists within two rectangles the latest additions to the Penguin publications for May and July 1939 and those of the Pelican publications for September 1939.

The front, spine, and back panels of the jacket are identical to the cover. On the front flap are quotations from A.P. Herbert and the *Evening Standard* along with the price (6d). The back flap has a black-and-white photograph of Leacock, biographical information about him, and information about the reading-case label.

NOTES: Allen Lane of John Lane The Bodley Head inquired about a Penguin edition on 22 August 1936. The royalty was 1/4d per copy sold. Leacock agreed to these terms on 17 September 1936. According to *The English Catalogue of Books* and copyright pages, publication occurred in July 1939, reprinted December 1939. The book sold for 6d. According to the first royalty report (dated 26 November 1940), between 28 July and 31 December 1939, the book sold 34,964 copies in "ordinary sales" and 11,654 in export sales. Leacock earned £34 17s 8d in royalty. Owing to a rise in production costs during the Second World War, the price of the book was raised to 9d on 19 March 1942, and Leacock received a pro rata increase in royalty to 30s per 1,000 copies sold.

COPIES EXAMINED: CS (first and second printings); QMMRB (first printing).

## A5c.1 *Canadian issue of the second English edition* (1945):

LITERARY LAPSES | *by* | STEPHEN LEACOCK | [illustration of fountain] | COLLINS | 70 BOND STREET, TORONTO

♦ 1–6$^{16}$ [with the exception of the first gathering, the recto of the first leaf of each gathering is signed 213, which is the series number]. 1–10, 11–186, 1–6 pp. (96 leaves). 178 × 110 mm.

CONTENTS: p. 1 [circle] | COLLINS | WHITE CIRCLE | POCKET EDITION; p. 2 frontispiece photograph by Karsh with quotation from A.P. Herbert; p. 3 title; p. 4 COPYRIGHT CANADA 1910 | By STEPHEN LEACOCK | PUBLISHED IN WHITE CIRCLE EDITION 1945 | INTRODUCTION COPYRIGHT CANADA 1945 | *By* WM. COLLINS SONS & CO. CANADA LTD. | PRINTED IN CANADA FOR WM. COLLINS SONS & CO. LTD. | BY THE BRYANT PRESS LIMITED, TORONTO; pp. 5–8 introduction by B.K. Sandwell (photo by Karsh of Leacock with child feeding chickens on p. 7); pp. 9–10 contents; pp. 11–185 text; p. 186 acknowledgments; pp. 1–6 ads for Collins White Circle Pocket Novels.

TEXT: Identical to A5b but see the note.

BINDING: Paperback, all edges stained red. The upper wrapper is a reproduction of a coloured drawing signed by M. Paull of various buildings (a bank, a laundry, and newspaper), signs, and people (a woman shaking out a rug, a policeman, a man lifting small weights, etc). Printed on the upper wrapper: [the first two lines in yellow calligraphy] Literary | Lapses | [remaining lines in white] STEPHEN | LEACOCK | [printed in a circular pattern] .A COLLINS WHITE CIRCLE POCKET NOVEL | [within the circle] 25¢. The lower wrapper, coloured yellow, discusses the people found in Leacock's sketches. Printed on the spine: [vertically in white] LITERARY LAPSES • LEACOCK | [within a solid white circle] 213.

NOTES: On 25 August 1939 John McClelland informed Frank Appleton of Wm. Collins Sons & Co. Canada Ltd. that McClelland and Stewart Limited held the Canadian rights to *Literary Lapses*. The book was advertised by Collins "for fall publication in the Penguin Series." McClelland asked Appleton to withdraw the title from their list. Appleton wrote to Leacock on 10 November 1939 and inquired about Canadian rights.

The Canadian issue appeared after Leacock's death, however. Number of copies printed and date of publication not known.

Although the pagination of Leacock's stories in A5c.1 differs from A5c, the setting of type is in fact the same. The prelims (pages prior to p. 11) and the ads are new.

COPIES EXAMINED: CS (three copies); QMMRB (three copies).

## A5d  *third English edition* (1948):

*LITERARY LAPSES* | *by* | Stephen Leacock | *London* | John Lane The Bodley Head

◆  A–F$^{16}$ [$1 signed (–A1), fifth leaf signed *]. *1–4, 5–6, 7–8, 9–189, 1–3* pp. (96 leaves). 186 × 122 mm.

CONTENTS: p. *1* half title; p. *2* list of thirty-three books by the same author, the first being *Recollections and Reflections* [no such book exists as such] and the last *The Boy I Left Behind Me*; p. *3* title; p. *4* [nineteen lines listing previous printings] *Reprinted 1948* | Printed in Great Britain by | BUTLER AND TANNER LTD., FROME, SOMERSET | for JOHN LANE THE BODLEY HEAD LTD. | 8 Bury Place, London, W.C.1; pp. *5–6* table of contents; p. *7* fly title; p. *8* blank; pp. *9–188* text; p. *189* acknowledgments; pp. *1–3* blank.

TEXT:  Identical to A5b.

BINDING AND DUST JACKET: Bound in green cloth with Leacock's name and the title stamped down the spine and The | Bodley | Head at the foot of the spine. The jacket is green. Leacock name appears twice in capitals on the front panel with the title at an angle in block capitals inside a solid black ornamental oval. The spine of the jacket is similar to the spine of the book except that the title appears within a solid black ornamental oval. The back panel has an advertisement for the 23rd large impression of *Nonsense Novels*. On the front flap are press opinions of *Literary Lapses*, the price (6d) and the printing (20th large impression); also on the front flap are two paragraphs stating that The Bodley Head is pleased to have this book and *Nonsense Novels* in print again. Printed on the back flap: Printed in Great Britain for | John Lane The Bodley Head Ltd.

NOTES: Although this edition is listed as a reprint (20th large impression), it is in fact a new setting of type.

According to Lomer (p. 40), the book was published on 28 September 1948. The OCLC WorldCat database records reprintings in 1952 and 1956. Number of copies printed not known.

COPIES EXAMINED: CS (1950 reprint in jacket); OTUTF (1948 printing in jacket); VCTEX (1948 printing, no jacket, rebound).

## A5e  *New Canadian Library edition* (1957):

*Stephen Leacock* | LITERARY | *Introduction by Robertson Davies* | LAPSES | *General Editor* • *Malcolm Ross* | *New Canadian Library* • *No. 3* | McCLELLAND & STEWART LIMITED | Toronto

♦  *i–v*, vi, *vii*, viii–xi, *1–2*, 2–15, *16*, 17–21, *22*, 23–25, *26*, 27–29, *30*, 31–41, *42*, 43–53, *54*, 55–75, *76*, 77–83, *84*, 85–86, *87*, 88–107, *108*, 109–113, *114*, 115–127, *128*, 129–131, *132*, 133–146, *1–2* pp. (80 leaves). 183 × 112 mm.

CONTENTS: p. *i* half title; p. *ii* blank; p. *iii* title; p. *iv* Copyright, Canada, 1910 | Copyright © Canada, 1957 | by | McClelland & Stewart Limited | [four lines concerning copyright] | PRINTED AND BOUND IN ENGLAND BY | HAZELL WATSON AND VINEY LTD | AYLESBURY AND LONDON; pp. *v*–vi table of contents; pp. *vi*, viii–xi introduction by Robertson Davies dated May, 1957; p. *1* blank; pp. 2, 2–146 text; p. *1* note about the author; p. 2 blank.

BINDING: Paperback, perfect bound. The front cover has a black-and-white sketch of Leacock's face with an irregular, brown vertical band on the left side. On the back cover are two brown bands and information about the book. Cover design by Frank Newfeld. Price: $1.00. N3 of the NCL series.

NOTES: Published on 17 January 1958. The first impression consisted of 5,000 copies. By the end of the spring 1958, 3,921 copies had sold; 5,883 copies sold by the end of the year. By the end of 1979 51,563 copies had sold (information based on file 14, "New Canadian Library," box 93, and file 7, box Ca2, series A, part I, McClelland and Stewart fonds, OHM).

COPIES EXAMINED: CS (1960, 1982, 1989); OORI (first printing); QMMRB (first printing, 1965).

## A5e.1  NCL *edition, second issue* (1989):

STEPHEN LEACOCK | Literary Lapses | *With an afterword by Robertson Davies* | [wavy block, short wavy rule] | M&S | [rule]

The pagination for this issue is: *1–7*, 8–21, *22*, 23–31, *32*, 33–35, *36*, 37–47, *48*, 49–59, *60*, 61–81, *82*, 83–89, *90*, 91–92, *93*, 94–113, *114*, 115–119, *120*, 121–133, *134*, 135–137, *138*, 139–157, *1–3*. Although the pagination differs considerably from A5e, the text is in fact from the same setting of type. The preliminary pages and the table of contents have been reset. Davies's introduction appears as an afterword at pp. 153–157. The latter is followed by a list of books written by Leacock. Paperback, perfect bound. A reproduction of David B. Milne's "Billboards" is on the front cover. Price $4.95. ISBN 0-7710-9983-5. Series design by T.M. Craan.

NOTES: Published on 1 April 1989 in a print run of 7,875 copies. There was a reprinting of 3,850 copies on 2 May 1991. By the end of 1996 11,196 copies had sold.

COPIES EXAMINED: CS.

## A6 EXTENSION LECTURES ON THE ELEMENTS OF POLITICAL ECONOMY 1910

### A6a *first syllabus*:

[cover title] 𝔐𝔠𝔊𝔦𝔩𝔩 𝔘𝔫𝔦𝔳𝔢𝔯𝔰𝔦𝔱𝔶. | [rule] | SESSION 1910–1911 | [rule] | EXTENSION LECTURES | ON THE | ELEMENTS OF POLITICAL ECONOMY | BY | Dr. STEPHEN LEACOCK | Head of the Department of Economics and Political Science | McGill University.

• Leaflet folded once to form four unnumbered pages. 215 × 140 mm.

In addition to this leaflet abstracts of various extension lectures have survived. Leacock arranged for the printing of these abstracts either for this course or for the same course a year or two later. They are as follows: II Some Fundamental Economic Concepts (276 × 202 mm.); IV Money (226 × 150 mm.); chapter V Bi-Metalism [sic] and Paper Money (243 × 151 mm.); VI The Movement of Prices (224 × 152 mm.); VI The Theory of Free Trade (240 × 152 mm.); X Free Trade in Great Britain (140 × 135 mm.); XI The Tariff Policy of the German Empire (216 × 137 mm.); XI The Economic Basis of Protection (216 × 137 mm.). With the exception of II and X which are broadsides, these abstracts are also in leaflet form, folded once with text on pp. *1* and *3* and pp. *2* and *4* blank. On one of the abstracts (XI The Economic Basis of Protection), Leacock wrote the following on p. *4*: "I Introd[uction] (not printed) II. Fundam[ental] Econ[omic] Concepts III Value IV Money [crossed out: V Monop[oly] Prices of Trust VI R[ailwa]y Rates] V Bi Met[allism] Pap[er] Money VI. Mon[opoly] of Prices VII. Theory of Free Trade VIII. Free Trade of G[reat]B[ritain]. IX. Ec[onomic] Basis of Prot[ection] X Tariff Policy [crossed out: Protection] of Germany XI."

CONTENTS: p. *1* cover title; pp. *2–4* text.

TEXT: A general statement about the lectures and a preliminary syllabus, the latter with the following topics: 1 Production; 2 The Theory of Value; 3 Law of Monopoly Price; 4 Money; 5 Bimetallism; 6 Paper Money; 7 Foreign Trade and Tariff Policy; 8 The Foreign Exchanges; 9 Banking; 10 Corporation Finance; 11 Labour and Wages; 12 Taxation.

BINDING: Off-white paper stock, no wrapper.

NOTES: This syllabus along with the abstracts of Leacock's lectures was handed out to students who were enrolled in this extension course, one of several such courses extending over a period of two years and leading to a Diploma in Commerce at McGill University. The syllabus was also ". . . sent out to the heads of business firms, bankers, etc., in the hope that they will see fit to bring it to the attention of young men in their employ." The course, which ran from 10 October 1910 to the middle of April 1911, was open to the public for a fee of $5. 125 students took the course. Leacock lectured on each Monday evening. According to his notebook at SLM (J84) he was paid $500 to teach the course.

In the syllabus Leacock states: "The precise scope of the lectures cannot be exactly determined until it is possible to form some judgment of the number and capacities of the students who are to take the course." The syllabus reflects the substance of Leacock's twenty-five articles published from 12 November 1910 to 29 April 1911 in *Saturday Night* and elsewhere under the general heading, "Practical Political Economy" (see C10.34). He even signed a contract with Houghton, Mifflin on 1 March 1911 (10% royalty) for a book with such a title. The book was never published, however.

COPIES EXAMINED: SLM (two copies of the syllabus; one copy of II; one copy of IV; twenty-three copies of V; two copies of VI (The Movement of Prices); three copies of VI (The Theory of Free Trade); thirty copies of X; three copies of XI (The Economic Basis of Protection); one copy of XI (The Tariff Policy of the German Empire).

## A6b  *second syllabus* [1917?]:

[cover title; all lines within two rectangles] 𝕸𝖈𝕲𝖎𝖑𝖑 𝖀𝖓𝖎𝖛𝖊𝖗𝖘𝖎𝖙𝖞 | EXTENSION DEPARTMENT | [rule] | Elements of | Political | Economy | A COURSE OF TWENTY-FIVE | LECTURES *by* | PROF. STEPHEN LEACOCK | [nine lines about the time and location of the lectures, payment ($5), and registration]

♦ Leaflet folded once to form four unnumbered pages. 228 × 151 mm.

In addition to this syllabus several abstracts of Leacock's extension lectures at McGill University have survived at SLM. Some of these may have been abstracts of lectures for this specific course. Others were undoubtedly issued by Leacock to students for other years when he gave this extension course on political economy. Their dating is uncertain. They are as follows: The Theory of Wages (leaflet, 4 pp., pp. 2 and 4 blank, 216 × 139 mm.); Taxation in the United Kingdom and the United States (leaflet, 4 pp., pp. 2 and 4 blank, 215 × 136 mm.); The International Movement of Money and the Foreign Exchanges (broadside, 254 × 140 mm.); The Tariff System of the United States (broadside, 215 × 141 mm.); Industrial Legislation (leaflet, 4 pp., pp. 2 and 4 blank, 213 × 140 mm.).

CONTENTS: p. *1* cover title; pp. *2–3* syllabus with recommended readings; p. *4* list of other extension courses available to students.

TEXT: I Wealth and Its Production; II The Theory of Value; III The Theory of Monopoly Price; IV Money; V Index Numbers and the Rise in the Cost of Living; VI International Trade and the Foreign Exchanges; VII Free Trade and Protection; VIII Distribution — Rent Wages, Interest, Profits and the Theory of Population; IX Taxation and Public Finance; X Social Legislation and Socialism; XI The Economic Aspect of the War. On p. 2, Leacock notes: "Some of the chapters below represent more than one lecture."

BINDING: Off-white paper stock, no wrapper.

NOTES: Leacock gave extension lectures on an annual basis for a number of years. In addition to 1910 (see above), his notebook (J84) records payments of $500 for extension lectures in 1911–14. Undoubtedly, he continued to deliver these lectures during the First World War. Like A6a, the lectures for this course would have run from October to April. In this case Leacock lectured every Thursday evening in the Arts Building at McGill. This syllabus is undated, but references in chapters X and XI of the syllabus suggest that the course occurred during the late stages of the war, perhaps before the onset of the Russian Revolution.

COPIES EXAMINED: SLM (three copies of the syllabus; nine copies of The Theory of Wages; two copies of Taxation in the United Kingdom and the United States; four copies of The International Movement of Money and the Foreign System of the United States; two copies of Industrial Legislation).

## A7 NONSENSE NOVELS 1911

### A7a *first English edition*:

NONSENSE | ::NOVELS:: | BY STEPHEN LEACOCK | [thick-thin rule] | [thin-thick rule] | LONDON: JOHN LANE, THE BODLEY HEAD | NEW YORK: JOHN LANE COMPANY. MCMXI

◆ $A^8$ B–$P^8$ $Q^8$ [$1 signed]. *1–6, 7, 8, 9, 10–12, 13–29, 30–32, 33–53, 54–56, 57–69, 70–72, 73–92, 93–94, 95–111, 112–114, 115–133, 134–136, 137–156, 157–158, 159–178, 179–180, 181–203, 204–206, 207–230, 1–10, 1–16* pp. (128 leaves). 183 × 123 mm.

CONTENTS: pp. *1–2* blank; p. *3* half title; p. *4* [all lines within a rectangle] *BY THE SAME AUTHOR* | LITERARY LAPSES | Crown 8vo; p. *5* title; p. *6* WILLIAM BRENDON AND SON, LTD. PRINTERS, PLYMOUTH; p. *7–8* preface; p. *9* table of contents; p. *10* blank; pp. *11–230, 1* text (pp. *12, 30, 32, 54, 56, 70, 72, 94, 112, 114, 134, 136, 158, 180, 204,* and *206* blank); p. *2* blank; pp. *3–10* advertisements for books published by John Lane, including the second "edition" (i.e. printing) of *Literary Lapses*; pp. *1–16* John Lane's list of fiction.

TEXT: I Maddened by Mystery; or, The Defective Detective; II 'Q.' A Psychic Pstory of the Psupernatural; III Guido the Gimlet of Ghent: A Romance of Chivalry; IV Gertrude the Governess; or, Simple Seventeen; V A Hero in Homespun; or, The Life Struggle of Hezekiah Hayloft; VI Sorrows of a Super Soul; or, The Memoirs of Marie Mushenough; VII Hannah of the Highlands; or, The Laird of Loch Aucherlocherty; VII Soaked in Seaweed; or, Upset in the Ocean; IX Caroline's Christmas; or, The Inexplicable Infant; X The Man in Asbestos: An Allegory of the Future.

BINDING: Bound in green cloth, top edge gilt. Stamped in gilt on the upper board within two blind-stamped rectangles: *NONSENSE NOVELS* | *By STEPHEN LEACOCK*. Stamped in gilt on the spine: [blind-stamped rule] | *NONSENSE* | *NOVELS* | *By* | *STEPHEN* | *LEACOCK* | *THE* | *BODLEY HEAD* | [blind-stamped rule]. Dust jacket not seen.

NOTES: This collection of ten parodies was published serially in *Saturday Night* and elsewhere from 10 December 1910 to 11 February 1911 under the generic title, "Novels in Nutshells" (see C10.39). The draft table of contents in Leacock's notebook at SLM (J84) also lists ten stories. Eight of them are the same as they appeared in publication, although the titles vary somewhat — "Hannah of the Highlands; or, The Laird of Loch Aucherlocherty," for example, was first entitled "Hannah of the Hebrides; or, The Highlander with the Hiccoughs." The two titles that Leacock did not develop were entitled "Wow-Wow the Wingless; or, Animal Life at Its Very Crudest" and "Mabel the Man Trap; or, The Sins of Society." A few pages later in J84 he added several possibilities for other "Novels in Nutshells." These included: "Court Society: The Prince" and "A War Story (Mixed Up Evolutions)." The latter apparently were also not completed.

In his notebook of royalty payments at SLM, Leacock recorded 30 June 1911 as the first royalty statement for the English edition (887 copies sold). The book was probably published in May 1911 since the Canadian issue was arranged at that time. Stephen Franklin (see A120) has 24 May 1911 as the date of publication. The contract with John Lane The Bodley Head at READ is dated 8 March 1911. Leacock was paid a royalty of 15% (thirteen copies being reckoned as twelve, raised to 20% at the end of 1919). The book sold for 3s

6d. Number of copies of the first printing not known. Up to 1 February 1924 Leacock recorded that 72,322 copies had sold on all editions and issues. This includes approximately 33,463 copies of printings of this edition; some of these copies were sold to the colonial (1,435 copies) and Australasian markets (2,675 copies).

Between January 1925 and December 1932, approximately 4,685 copies sold (more than 3,000 copies at a reduced royalty of 10%). There were also 537 copies in foreign sales, 426 in colonial sales, and twenty-five in Australasian sales.

Other printings examined: fifth 1913, twelfth 1919, thirteenth 1920, 1926 ("Cheap Edition"), and 1932 ("*Popular Cro. 8vo Edition*"). The latter lists reprints in 1911, 1912 (three times), 1914, 1915, 1916 (twice), 1918, 1919, 1920, 1922, 1925, 1927; reference is also made in the 1932 "edition" to a *Cheap Edition* printed twice in 1926 (presumably this is also a reprint of A7a). The copyright page of A7b provides the following information: first edition, May 1911; reprinted June 1911, February 1912, October 1912, December 1912, January 1914, February 1915, April 1916, December 1916, September 1918, September 1919, September 1921. Lomer (p. 46) also records a reprint in 1937. The OCLC WorldCat database lists a reprint in 1958.

Three of the stories in the book ("Soaked in Seaweed; or, Upset in the Ocean," "Gertrude the Governess; or, Simple Seventeen," and "Guido the Gimlet of Ghent: A Romance of Chivalry") were published in *Good Humour* [no. 1] (1913): 43–60 under the title "Nonsense Novels: Three Potted Parodies."

COPIES EXAMINED: CS (first and fifth printings, no jacket; twelfth, thirteenth, and 1932 reprints in jacket); QMMRB (twelfth printing, no jacket); SLM (1926, Leacock's copy).

## A7a.1 *first Canadian issue*:

NONSENSE | ::NOVELS:: | BY STEPHEN LEACOCK | [thick-thin rule] | [thin-thick rule] | CANADIAN EDITION | PUBLISHERS' PRESS, LIMITED | MONTREAL | 1911

The first Canadian issue is identical to A7a with the exceptions of the title leaf, the spine of the binding (lacking a publisher's imprint), and the absence of publisher's ads. The verso of the title leaf of the Canadian issue (p. 6) reads: *Copyright by John Lane*, 1911 | *All rights reserved* | WILLIAM BRENDON AND SON, LTD. PRINTERS, PLYMOUTH | ENGLAND. Dust jacket not seen.

NOTES: As early as August 1910 the Publishers' Press arranged for the syndication of Leacock's sketches and poems (75% of the gross receipts went to Leacock) in Canadian and American magazines and newspapers. Leacock and many of his colleagues became directors of the company. But Leacock severed his connection with the management of the Publishers' Press in August 1911 when he learned that his name had been used without his authority as president of the company. Unfortunately, the company's manager, Max Joseph Epstein, was involved in a number of fraudulent activities, including stealing stereotype plates from a rival agency.

Publication of the first Canadian issue probably occurred simultaneously with A7a. In his contract with The Bodley Head Leacock reserved the exclusive right of publication in Canada. Nonetheless, on 3–4 April 1911, John Lane arranged to supply Leacock with 3,000 copies of the Canadian issue in sheets. Leacock himself records, however, that the print run consisted of 2,000 copies. (The extra 1,000 copies with the imprint of the Publishers' Press went to the Musson Book Co. in January 1912 — see A7a.3). Lane charged Leacock directly, who in turn charged all costs to the Publishers' Press. In February 1912, however, there were insufficient funds to cover the cheque ($222) sent to Lane by Epstein. In addition to paying Epstein's outstanding bill to Lane, Leacock received no royalty for the first Canadian issue, and his stock in the Publishers' Press proved worthless when the company went bankrupt in April 1912. For further information, see Carl Spadoni, "The Publishers Press of Montreal," *Papers of the Bibliographical Society of Canada* 24 (1985): 38–50.

COPIES EXAMINED: CS (two copies); QMMRB.

## A7a.2 *first American issue*:

With the exception of the binding and the publisher's ads, the first American issue is identical to A7a. After the last page of the text, there are eight leaves of ads for books published by the John Lane Company. The collation for this issue is: $A^8$ B–O$^8$ P$^4$ Q$^8$ [$1 signed]. Bound in brown cloth (apparently with cream lettering; copy examined was faded). Stamped on the upper board in raised characters inside a solid cream rectangle: [the solid rectangle is itself within a cream rectangle] NONSENSE | NOVELS [shamrock illustration] | STEPHEN LEACOCK. Stamped on the spine: NONSENSE | NOVELS | [rule] | LEACOCK | JOHN LANE | COMPANY.

Dust jacket for the first printing not seen. The dust jacket of the fifth "edition" (i.e. printing) of 1913 is cream coloured with brown lettering. The upper portion of the front panel of the jacket is similar to the stamping on the upper board. The lower portion of the front panel has a paragraph within a rectangle that describes Leacock in "full bloom as a finished humorist." The back of the jacket has an advertisement for the books of Julian Street. The front flap carries an advertisement for the complete works of William J. Locke. On the back flap is an advertisement for *The International Studio*. Also examined in jacket was the 1920 impression printed by the Press of J.J. Little & Ives Co., bound in green cloth with a reset preface, altered pagination, but the same setting of type.

NOTES: Publication of the American issue was probably simultaneous with the English edition. The royalty was 10%. The book initially sold for $1 (postage 10¢ extra). The print run of the first impression is not known. On 19 August 1911, Leacock thanked Lane "for your good works in connection with my *Nonsense Novels*, and for much else." He informed Lane that he had recently travelled to New York where he had made the acquaintance of the managers of the John Lane Company: "They were extremely kind to me," Leacock stated, "and I was delighted to find that you have such energetic and able men in charge of your American house."

According to an advertising brochure issued by the John Lane Company, the book was into its thirtieth "edition" (i.e. printing) by 1920 ($1.50 cloth). Leacock received an increase in royalty to 20% on 31 December 1919. The first two royalty reports of John Lane The Bodley Head (confirmed by Leacock's own royalty records) indicate the following: up to 30 June 1912, 1,608 copies sold (counted as 1,485 copies), $148.50 earned; up to 30 June 1912 3,179 (counted as 2,934 copies), $293.40 earned. The John Lane Company continued to market the book until the end of 1921 when the house was sold to Dodd, Mead. In all 26,430 copies were sold on all printings of the first American issue. Up to 1 July 1920 Leacock received a royalty of $1,861.91. For the period thereafter (until the end of 1921), royalty earnings are not extant.

COPIES EXAMINED: CS (1913 (fifth printing) and 1920 impressions, both in jacket); QMMRB (1918 impression); RB (first printing).

### A7a.3 *second Canadian issue* [1912]:

Although the title leaf of this issue is identical to A7a.1, there are four leaves of ads from John Lane after the text (identical to the first four leaves of ads in A7a). Moreover, the binding is green ribbed cloth. Two connected compartments are blind-stamped on the upper board. Within the upper compartment is another compartment with leafy acorn ornaments at the left and right sides and within the compartment stamped in white: NONSENSE NOVELS. Stamped in white inside the lower compartment: STEPHEN LEACOCK. Stamped in white on the spine: [rule] | NONSENSE | NOVELS | STEPHEN | LEACOCK | MUSSON | [rule]. Dust jacket not seen.

NOTES: On 8 January 1912 Leacock informed Lane that owing to the financial and legal problems with the Publishers' Press, he had asked the Musson Book Co. to take ". . . over the 1000 copies of Nonsense Novels which you have with the imprint of the Publishers Press." Leacock told Lane on 27 February 1912 that the Musson Book Co. had also assumed the agency for the Canadian sales of the book. Musson paid Lane eleven pence apiece for sets of the sheets. Leacock instructed Lane to deliver the sheets to Musson's London agents, who would forward them to Canada. Leacock received 12½% royalty on these books. The book sold for $1.25 (information based on the archives of John Lane The Bodley Head, TEX). On 18 March 1913 J.H. Charles of the Musson Book Co. sent Leacock a cheque for $331.31 for combined royalties on this book and *Literary Lapses* (767 copies sold of *Nonsense Novels* of 1,000 obtained, presumably copies of this issue).

There are four other Musson issues. See A7a.4–7. According to Leacock's notebook of royalty payments at SLM, the Musson Book Co. sold 2,275 copies between 18 March 1913 and 31 December 1919; between 31 December 1915 and 31 December 1919, only 154 copies sold.

COPY EXAMINED: CS.

### A7a.4 *third Canadian issue* (1912):

*NONSENSE* | *::NOVELS::* | *BY STEPHEN LEACOCK* | [thick-thin rule] | [thin-thick rule] | *LONDON: JOHN LANE, THE BODLEY HEAD* | *NEW YORK: JOHN LANE COMPANY. MCMXII*

The verso of the title leaf of this issue reads: *THIRD EDITION* | WILLIAM BRENDON AND SON, LTD. PRINTERS, PLYMOUTH. In other words this is the third printing from John Lane The Bodley Head. There are four leaves of Lane ads, the first ad of the third "edition" of the book (priced at 3s 6d). The binding is identical to A7a.3. Dust jacket not seen.

NOTES: When B.W. Willett of John Lane The Bodley Head informed Leacock's lawyer, Warwick Chipman, on 21 February 1912 that the cheque sent by the manager of the Publishers' Press was bad, Willett also told Leacock that 500 copies had gone to the Musson Book Co. for the Canadian issue. Leacock himself wrote to the Musson Book Co. on 2 March 1912: "I learn from Mr. Lane," Leacock wrote, "that . . . he has delivered to you 500 copies of Nonsense Novels. I presume not with Publishers Press imprint. . . ." (information based on the archives at SLM and TEX).

COPIES EXAMINED: CS.

**A7a.5** *fourth Canadian issue* (1913):

*NONSENSE* | *::NOVELS::* | *BY STEPHEN LEACOCK* | [thick-thin rule] | [thin-thick rule] | *TORONTO: THE MUSSON BOOK CO. LTD.* | *NEW YORK:JOHN LANE COMPANY::LONDON* | *JOHN LANE, THE BODLEY HEAD. MCMXIII*

Cancel title. The verso of the title leaf of this issue reads: FIFTH EDITION | WILLIAM BRENDON AND SON, LTD., PRINTERS, PLYMOUTH | ENGLAND. Although this would indicate that this issue is taken from the sheets of The Bodley Head's fifth printing, there are four leaves of Lane ads after the text, the first ad for the fourth "edition" of the book. The following is found on p. 4: [all lines within a rectangle] *BY THE SAME AUTHOR* | LITERARY LAPSES | SUNSHINE SKETCHES | OF A LITTLE TOWN. The binding is identical to A7a.3. Dust jacket not seen.

NOTES: On 18 March 1913 J.H. Charles of the Musson Book Co. pointed out to Leacock that although their contract called for a royalty of 12½%, he was willing to increase the royalty to 15% in view of the book's continuing sales. Number of copies of this issue not known, but 500 copies appears likely.

COPIES EXAMINED: OHM.

**A7a.6** *fifth Canadian issue* [1913?]:

*NONSENSE NOVELS* | *BY STEPHEN LEACOCK* | [thick-thin rule] | [in overlapping, swash letters] MBCo. | [thin-thick rule] | TORONTO | THE MUSSON BOOK CO., LIMITED

Cancel title. The verso of the title leaf is blank. The leaves measure 188 × 123 mm. There are no advertisements. Pages 229–230, 1–2 are cancels. The binding is identical to A7a.3. Dust jacket not seen. Published in late 1913 or possibly 1914 since *Behind the Beyond* is listed on p. 4 as having been published.

COPIES EXAMINED: OTNY.

**A7a.7** *sixth Canadian issue* (1914?):

*NONSENSE* | *::NOVELS::* | *BY STEPHEN LEACOCK* | [thick-thin rule] | TORONTO | THE MUSSON BOOK COMPANY | LIMITED

Cancel title. The verso of the title leaf is blank. There are four leaves of Lane ads after the text, the first ad for the fifth "edition" of the book. The following is found on p. 4: [all lines within a rectangle] *BY THE SAME AUTHOR* | LITERARY LAPSES | SUNSHINE SKETCHES | OF A LITTLE TOWN | BEHIND THE BEYOND. The binding is identical to A7a.3. Dust jacket not seen.

NOTES: On 24 March 1914 J.H. Charles of the Musson Book Co. informed Leacock that on 31 January of that year, 233 copies were in stock and 500 more were ordered. The copies that were ordered apparently refer to this issue.

COPIES EXAMINED: CS.

**A7a.8** *seventh Canadian issue* (1915):

*NONSENSE* | *::NOVELS::* | *BY STEPHEN LEACOCK* | [thick-thin rule] |

[thin-thick rule] | *LONDON: JOHN LANE THE BODLEY HEAD* | *NEW YORK: JOHN LANE COMPANY* | *TORONTO: S. B. GUNDY MCMXV* | *Published in Canada for Humphrey Milford*

Cancel title. The verso of the title leaf of this issue reads: *EIGHTH EDITION* | WILLIAM BRENDON AND SON, LTD., PRINTERS, PLYMOUTH, ENGLAND. There are no publisher's advertisements after the text. On p. 4 within a rectangle is a list of four other books by Leacock, the last being *Arcadian Adventures with the Idle Rich*. The sheets are, therefore, identical to the Bodley Head's eighth impression of the book. The binding is the same as A7a with *GUNDY* stamped at the foot of the spine. Dust jacket not seen.

NOTES: Although the Musson Book Co. took over the Canadian publication of *Nonsense Novels* in January 1912, Leacock arranged a contract with S.B. Gundy for four books in February 1915. The contract came about when Leacock's Canadian publisher, Bell & Cockburn, went bankrupt at the end of December 1914 and W.C. Bell joined Gundy's staff. Gundy was the head of the Canadian branch of Oxford University Press. John Lane The Bodley Head supplied Gundy with copies of *Nonsense Novels* for the Canadian market. According to Leacock's notebook of royalty payments at SLM, Oxford University Press sold 218 copies in Canada by 31 December 1915 ($54.50 royalty). Between 31 December 1915 and 1 July 1923, Leacock's notebook records that Gundy sold 1,379 copies. See also A7a.9 and A7a.10 for other Gundy issues.

COPIES EXAMINED: QMMRB.

## A7a.9 *eighth Canadian issue* (1916):

*NONSENSE* | *::NOVELS::* | *BY STEPHEN LEACOCK* | [thick-thin rule] | [thin-thick rule] | *LONDON: JOHN LANE, THE BODLEY HEAD* | *NEW YORK: JOHN LANE COMPANY. MCMXVI*

The verso of the title leaf of this issue reads: *NINTH EDITION* | WILLIAM BRENDON AND SON, LTD., PRINTERS, PLYMOUTH, ENGLAND. There are no publisher's advertisements after the text. On p. 4 within a rectangle is a list of six books by Leacock, the last being *Essays and Literary Studies*. The sheets are, therefore, identical to the Bodley Head's ninth impression of the book. The binding is in green leather. A rectangle is blind-stamped on both the upper and lower boards. Stamped in gilt on the upper board within the rectangle: NONSENSE NOVELS. The spine features a series of rectangular floral designs, rules (some blind-stamped), the title, and Leacock's name. The imprint at the bottom of the spine is OXFORD; in other words, S.B. Gundy of Oxford University Press sold copies of this issue.

COPIES EXAMINED: CS.

## A7a.10 *ninth Canadian issue* (1916):

*NONSENSE* | *::NOVELS::* | *BY STEPHEN LEACOCK* | [thick-thin rule] | [thin-thick rule] | *LONDON: JOHN LANE, THE BODLEY HEAD* | *NEW YORK: JOHN LANE COMPANY* | *TORONTO: S. B. GUNDY MCMXVI*

Cancel title. The verso of the title leaf of this issue reads: WILLIAM BRENDON AND SON, LTD., PRINTERS, PLYMOUTH, ENGLAND. The binding is the same as A7a.8. Dust jacket not seen. In other respects, this issue is identical to A7a.9.

COPIES EXAMINED: CS.

**A7a.11** *second American issue* (1922):

*NONSENSE* | *::NOVELS::* | *BY STEPHEN LEACOCK* | [thick-thin rule] | [thin-thick rule] | *NEW YORK: DODD, MEAD AND COMPANY* | *MCMXXII*

Pagination for this issue is: *1–6, 5, 6, 7, 8–10, 11–27, 28–30, 31–51, 52–54, 55–67, 68–70, 71–90, 91–92, 93–109, 110–112, 113–131, 132–134, 135–154, 155–156, 157–176, 177–178, 179–201, 202–204, 205–229, 1*. The preface has been reset, and there are no advertisements after the text. It is nevertheless from the setting of type as A7a. The verso of the title leaf reads: Published in U. S. A. | BY DODD, MEAD AND COMPANY, INC. | PRINTED IN U. S. A. On p. 4 within a rectangle is a list of seven books by Leacock, the first being *Behind the Beyond* and the last *Moonbeams from the Larger Lunacy*. Bound in green cloth. Blind-stamped on the upper board in raised characters inside a solid rectangle: [all lines within a raised rectangle] NONSENSE | NOVELS [shamrock illustration] | STEPHEN LEACOCK. Stamped on the spine in gilt: NONSENSE | NOVELS | [rule] | LEACOCK | DODD, MEAD | & COMPANY. Dust jacket not seen but apparently illustrated by John Kettelwell.

NOTES: This issue was published several months after The Bodley Head sold their American branch to Dodd, Mead. Leacock received a royalty of 20%. The number of copies printed of the first impression is not known. Leacock's notebook of royalty payments at SLM records the following: 1 August 1922 815 copies sold; 1 February 1923 799 copies; 1 August 1923 807 copies sold; 1 February 1924 1,776 copies sold. The book was obviously a very good seller. In 1923 Dodd, Mead also issued the book in leather. Frank Dodd proposed an "edition" in limp red leather at $2.50 retail, 30¢ royalty to Leacock. The records of Dodd, Mead at OHM indicate that reprintings occurred in August 1948 (500 copies), December 1950 (500 copies, $50 royalty), November 1958 (1,000 copies, royalty $100), and February 1961.

Of some note is the 1923 illustrated reprint (203 × 141 mm.), which employs John Kettelwell's illustrations from The Bodley Head's second edition (see A7b). On 7 February 1923, Frank Dodd arranged with John Lane to print 1,000 sets in a smaller size than A7b, so that ". . . they fit with our own text plates and make a book somewhat larger than the regular edition, to sell for $2.50 or $3.00 retail." Dodd offered Leacock a royalty of 30¢ on these copies. This illustrated reprint is in dark green cloth, top edge stained orange. The upper board incorporates design features from Dodd, Mead's standard binding and the binding of A7b. Colour plates: frontispiece, facing p. 12, facing p. 60, facing p. 74, facing p. 100, facing p. 120, and facing p. 192. The endpapers are orange with Kettelwell's illustrations in silhouette, which in A7b are found at the end of each sketch.

In addition to the first impression published in 1922, the following impressions were also examined: 1924, 1927, 1929, 1941, 1943, 1944, 1945, and 1959. Lomer (p. 47) cites an impression in 1948. The OCLC WorldCat database lists reprints in 1925, 1926, and 1935.

COPIES EXAMINED: CS (1927, 1929, 1943, 1944, 1945, and 1959 printings, all in jacket; 1923 illustrated, 1924 and 1941 printings without jackets); OHM (1922 and 1943 printings, no jackets); QMMRB (1923 illustrated printing).

**A7a.12** *third American issue* [1928]:

NONSENSE NOVELS | STEPHEN LEACOCK | [rule] | [the next two lines within an oval which contains an illustration of a sundial and an open book]

The SUN DIAL | [ornament] *Library* [ornament] | [rule] | GARDEN CITY PUBLISHING COMPANY, INC. | GARDEN CITY, NEW YORK

This issue is similar to A7a.11. There is a blank leaf after the text. The endpapers feature an illustration (initialled WAD) in brown within a zig-zag rectangular compartment of a sundial in a garden setting. Bound in black cloth, top edge stained black, with the title and Leacock's name stamped in pink on the upper board within a green compartment (flowers at the edges of the compartment in pink). The title and Leacock's name are also stamped in pink on the spine with rules, decorations, and the imprint stamped in green. The dust jacket is light green with an illustration in green and pink on the front panel by Rick Spencer of a couple (the man with a book in his hand). The back panel has the following heading in pink: THE VOGUE | OF THE SMALL BOOK. Below this heading are two paragraphs on the Sun Dial Library in green with the logo (as on the title page) in pink. The front flap has information on *Nonsense Novels*; the back flap has information on the Star Series ($1 each). The verso of the jacket is light yellow with a list of books published by the Sun Dial Library.

NOTES:   In June 1928 Dodd, Mead supplied plates to the Sundial Library for an edition of 2,500 copies retailing at $1. It was described as "a handy volume limp leather library," although no copy in leather was examined.

COPIES EXAMINED:   LAT (in jacket); SYR (no jacket).

## A7b   *second English edition* (1921):

NONSENSE | ::NOVELS:: | BY STEPHEN LEACOCK | ILLUSTRATED BY JOHN KETTELWELL | [concentric circles having a caricature of two faces of a smiling girl in pigtails and two faces of an unhappy professor wearing a mortar board and glasses; in the centre of the circles is •SL•] | LONDON: JOHN LANE THE BODLEY HEAD | NEW YORK: JOHN LANE COMPANY MCMXXI

♦   A⁸ B–L⁸ [$1 signed]. *1–4*, 5, 6, 7, *8–10*, 11–23, *24–26*, 27–41, *42–44*, 45–54, *55–56*, 57–70, 71–74. 75–87, *88–90*, 91–104, *105–106*, 107–120, *121–122*, 123–137, *138–140*, 141–156, *157–158*, 159–176 pp. (88 leaves). 215 × 172 mm.

CONTENTS:   p. *1* half title; p. *2* list of twelve books within a rectangle by Leacock published by The Bodley Head, the first being *Literary Lapses* and the last *The Unsolved Riddle of Social Justice*; p. *3* title; p. *4* [twelve lines dealing with previous printings of the book] | *Illustrated Edition . September 1921* | *The Mayflower Press, Plymouth, England*. William Brendon & Son, Ltd.; p. *5* preface; p. *6* blank; p. *7* table of contents and list of coloured plates; p. *8* blank; p. *9–176* text (pp. *10, 24, 26, 42, 44, 56, 71, 74, 88, 90, 106, 122, 138,* and *140* blank).

Colour plates: frontispiece, facing p. 12, facing p. 58, facing p. 80, facing p. 96, facing p. 124, and facing p. 150. Black illustrations in silhouette found at the end of each sketch (full page illustration on p. *71*).

TEXT:   Identical to A7a.

BINDING:   Three binding variants were examined: (1) greyish blue cloth, top edge stained greyish blue, with stamping on the upper board in blue and on the spine in gilt; (2) olive green cloth; (3) orangish red leather. Issued without a jacket

A thick rectangle is stamped on the upper board of (1), and within the rectangle is the following: NONSENSE NOVELS | STEPHEN LEACOCK | [right-angled rule, folded at the ends, with an illustration of a man wearing a deerstalker and pince-nez (illustration identical to p. 87)] | [thick band]. Stamped on the spine of (1): [two rules, two rules] | NON | SENSE | NOVELS | STEPHEN | LEACOCK | ILLUSTRATED BY | J. KETTELWELL | THE BODLEY HEAD | [two rules, two rules]. The endpapers for this binding feature a caricature in blue of a smiling boy.

(2) appears to be a later binding with sheets measuring 211 × 166 mm. Stamped on the spine in black: NON | SENSE | NOVELS | STEPHEN | LEACOCK | ILLUSTRATED BY | J. KETTELWELL | THE | BODLEY HEAD.

A floral compartment is blind-stamped on the upper board of (3). The following is stamped on the spine: [rule blind-stamped] | [the next four lines in gilt] NONSENSE | NOVELS | STEPHEN | LEACOCK | [ornamental rectangle blind-stamped].

NOTES: On 15 March 1921 B.W. Willett of John Lane The Bodley proposed to publish an illustrated edition of *Nonsense Novels* in the autumn with illustrations by John Kettelwell. He offered Leacock a royalty of 10% on the assumption that the book would sell for 7s 6d. He could not offer Leacock his standard royalty rate of 20% because the edition would require a new setting of type, blocks, and illustrations. He hoped that the company's travelling salesmen could show off blocks and samples by July of that year. Leacock in fact had championed Kettelwell's art work and had introduced him to John Lane on 6 January 1914 (see Leacock's letter of that date at YALE). Leacock accepted Willett's offer on 8 April 1921: "I am delighted to hear that John Kettelwell is to do a set of pictures for 'NONSENSE NOVELS.' I am sure that he is just the man." He suggested a royalty of one shilling if the price were 10s 6d (less than 10%) or 7s 6d. Willett agreed to Leacock's terms on 22 April 1921. Later, during his lecture tour of England in the autumn of 1921, Leacock complained that he was not receiving 20% on the illustrated edition. This prompted a 3–page letter from Willett (3 November 1921):

> . . . with regard to the illustrated edition of "NONSENSE NOVELS", I think that we may take some credit for our enterprise in getting this out in time for your visit, when it was evident that we should not get a new book from you for this autumn. Please remember that this was entirely our own idea and our own speculation, and that the royalties you will get from this publication will be in addition to those you get on the ordinary edition.

According to *The English Catalogue of Books*, the illustrated edition was published in October 1921 at 10 s 6d. The number of copies printed is not known. In his notebook of royalty payments at SLM, Leacock recorded that 1,254 copies sold by 31 December 1921. By the end of 1923 1,912 copies had sold. Willett told Leacock that S.B. Gundy took 250 copies for the Canadian market. See also the notes to A7a.9 for Dodd, Mead's illustrated reprint in 1923.

COPIES EXAMINED: CS (the first two variant bindings; two copies of the first binding, one with a small broadside issued on the occasion of *Laugh with Leacock* with Leacock's comment: "My favorite among my works is: *Nonsense Novels*."); OTNY (two copies of (1), one of (3)); QMMRB (two copies of (1), one copy having proofs of six of the eight plates).

**A7c** *third English edition* (1948):

NONSENSE NOVELS | *by* | Stephen Leacock | *London* | John Lane The Bodley Head

◆ A–F$^{16}$ [$1 signed (–A1), fifth leaf of each gathering signed*]. *1–4, 5, 6, 7, 8–10*, 11–24, *25–26*, 27–43, *44–46*, 47–57, *58–60*, 61–76, *77–78*, 79–92, *93–94*, 95–110, *111–112*, 113–128, *129–130*, 131–147, *148–150*, 151–168, *169–170*, 171–189, *1–3* pp. (96 leaves). 186 × 123 mm.

CONTENTS: p. *1* half title; p. *2* list of thirty-three books by the same author, the first being *Recollections and Reflections* (no such book exists as such) and the last *The Boy I Left Behind Me*; p. *3* title; p. *4* [twenty-two lines listing previous printings] *Reprinted 1948* | Printed in Great Britain by | BUTLER AND TANNER LTD., FROME, SOMERSET | for JOHN LANE THE BODLEY HEAD LTD. | 8 Bury Place, London, W.C.1; p. *5* table of contents; p. *6* blank; p. *7* preface; p. *8* blank; pp. 9–189, *1* text (pp. *10, 26, 44, 46, 58, 60, 78, 94, 112, 130, 148, 150*, and *170* blank); p. *2* advertisement for six of Leacock's books; p. *3* list of fiction classics.

TEXT: Identical to A7a.

BINDING AND DUST JACKET: Presumably bound in green cloth with Leacock's name and the title stamped down the spine and The | Bodley | Head at the foot of the spine.

NOTES: According to Lomer (p. 46), this edition was published on 28 September 1948. Price: 6s. Number of copies printed not known. The copy examined was the 1952 reprint, whose copyright page indicates that there was also a reprint in 1950.

COPIES EXAMINED: CS (1952 reprint in jacket, 25th large impression); OORI (1958, 27th impression).

**A7d** *first Canadian edition* (1963):

Stephen Leacock | [swelled rule] | NONSENSE | NOVELS | [swelled rule] | Introduction: S. Ross Beharriell | General Editor: Malcolm Ross | New Canadian Library No. 35 | [publisher's device: abstract design within an oval of a person on a horse-drawn chariot, taking aim with a bow and arrow] | MCCLELLAND AND STEWART LIMITED

◆ *i–vi*, vii–xiii, *1–2, 16–40, 41, 42–50, 51, 52–64, 65, 66–77, 78–79, 80–92, 93, 94–106, 107*, 108–120, *121*, 122–136, *137*, 138–153, *154, 155, 1–5* pp. (80 leaves). 184 × 111 mm.

CONTENTS: p. *i* half title; p. *ii* blank; p. *iii* title; p. *iv* First published in 1911 by John Lane, the Bodley Head | © McClelland and Stewart Limited, 1963 | [six lines concerning copyright] | *The Canadian Publishers* | McClelland and Stewart Limited | 25 Hollinger Road, Toronto 16 | PRINTED AND BOUND BY | HAZELL WATSON AND VINEY LTD | AYLESBURY AND SLOUGH, ENGLAND; p. *v* table of contents; p. *vi* blank; pp. vii–xii Beharriell's introduction; p. xiii preface; p. *1* blank; pp. *2, 16–153* text (p. *78* blank): p. *154* blank; p. *155* information about Leacock; p. *1* blank; p. *2–3* list of titles in the New Canadian Library Series; pp. *4–5* blank.

TEXT: Identical to A7a.

BINDING: Perfect bound in red, orange, and white stiff pictorial wrappers. The front cover has a black-and-white sketch of Leacock with an an irregular, orange vertical band on the left side. On the back cover are two orange bands and information about the book. Cover design by Donald Grant and Frank Newfeld. Price: $1.25. N35 of the NCL series.

NOTES: S. Ross Beharriell, who was paid $100 for his introduction to the New Canadian Library edition, read and returned his proofs on 12 March 1963. The Editorial Department of McClelland and Stewart actually wrote to the Boston Public Library in October 1962 in order to obtain a first edition of the book. (Boston Public Library had in fact disposed of their copy). Published on 20 July 1963 or thereabouts. The first impression consisted of 5,000 copies. By the end of 1963 2,397 copies had sold. By the end of 1979 29,187 had sold. Reprinted 1965, 1968, and 1969 (information based on file 14, "New Canadian Library," box 93; file 29, box Ca6; file 9, box Ca11; file 13, box Ca25 — McClelland and Stewart fonds, OHM).

COPIES EXAMINED: CS (1968 reprint); OORI (first printing); SLM (1969 reprint).

A7e *first American edition* (1971):

*NONSENSE* | *::NOVELS::* | *BY STEPHEN LEACOCK* | [thick-thin rule] | [thin-thick rule] | DOVER PUBLICATIONS, INC. | NEW YORK

♦ $1-4^{16}$. 1-13, 2-9, 10-11, 12-20, 21, 22-27, 28-29, 30-38, 39, 40-47, 48-49, 50-58, 59, 60-68, 69, 70-78, 79, 80-89, 90-91, 92-102, 1-14 pp. (64 leaves). 202 × 138 mm.

CONTENTS: pp. 1-2 blank; p. 3 half title; p. 4 blank; p. 5 title; p. 6 This Dover edition, first published in 1971, is an | unabridged and unaltered republication of the work | originally published by the John Lane Company in | 1912. | *International Standard Book Number:* 0-486-22759-6 | *Library of Congress Catalog Card Number: 78-166423* | Manufactured in the United States of America | Dover Publications, Inc. | 180 Varick Street | New York, N.Y. 10014; p. 7 preface; p. 8 blank; p. 9 table of contents; p. 10 blank; p. 11 fly title; p. 12 blank; pp. 13, 2-102 text (pp. 10, 28, 48, and 90 blank); pp. 1-2 blank; pp. 3-13 a catalogue of selected Dover books in all fields of interest; p. 14 blank.

TEXT: Identical to A7a.

BINDING: Bound in glossy stiff paper covers protected within clear plastic, sewn signatures glued to covers. The top part of the front cover is pink, the bottom orange; it has a multi-coloured collage of the title, the price ($1.75), and the title and Leacock's name in yellow. The spine is orange with the following down it: Leacock NONSENSE NOVELS Dover 0-486-22759-6. The back cover, which is pale yellow with a large orange, rectangular border, has information about Leacock, the book, and Dover's book design. On the verso of the front and back covers is a list of Dover Humor Books. Cover designed by Theodore Menten.

NOTES: Date of publication and number of copies printed not known.

There appears to have been another American edition published by Peter Smith (6 Lexington Ave., Magnolia MA 01930, ISBN 0-8446-0176-4) sometime in 1970s. See Margery Fee and Ruth Cawker, *Canadian Fiction: An Annotated Bibliography* (Toronto: Peter Martin Associates, 1976), p. 66. No copy of this edition was located, however.

COPIES EXAMINED: CS.

## A8 THE GREAT VICTORY IN CANADA 1911

[all lines within a rectangle; the first four lines within another rectangle, which has a leafy, floral ornament at its base] The Great Victory | [two heavy rules] in

Canada [two heavy rules] | by Prof. Stephen Leacock | McGill University, Montreal | [the remaining lines within another separate rectangle] | [two rules] Reprint from [two rules] | The National Review, – London, Eng.

* $I^8$. *1–3, 2–12, 1–2* pp. (8 leaves). 237 × 163 mm.

CONTENTS: p. *1* title; p. *2* blank; pp. *3, 2–12* text (the final line on the last page is: STEPHEN LEACOCK.); pp. *1–2* blank.

BINDING: Bound in tan wrappers, wire-stitched, with blue lettering on the front of the wrapper as follows: THE | NATIONAL | REVIEW | EDITED BY L. J. MAXSE | November 1911 | [the next six lines within two rectangles] The Great Victory | [two heavy rules] in Canada [two heavy rules] | [two rules] | By Prof. Stephen Leacock | McGill University, Montreal | (Reprint) | PUBLISHED BY THE PROPRIETOR AT | 23 RYDER STREET, ST. JAMES'S, LONDON, S.W. | Registered at the G.P.O. for | transmission to Canada at | the special rate of 1d. per lb. | [the next line to the right of the previous three lines:] Price 2s. 6d. net. The back of the wrapper is blank.

NOTES: From the same setting of type (except page numbers) as Leacock's article in the *National Review* (see C11.33). Number of copies printed not known.

COPIES EXAMINED: OONL (lacking the wrapper); QMMRB.

## A9 WHAT SHALL WE DO ABOUT THE NAVY 1911

[cover title] WHAT SHALL WE DO ABOUT | THE NAVY | BY | STEPHEN LEACOCK | [rule] | REPRINTED FROM THE UNIVERSITY MAGAZINE, DECEMBER, 1911. | [rule] | MORANG & CO., LIMITED, | TORONTO

* $I^{10}$. *1, 2–19, 1* pp. (10 leaves). 256 × 172 mm.

CONTENTS: pp. *1, 2–19* text; p. *1* blank.

BINDING: Bound in grey wrappers, wire-stitched.

NOTES: The full title of Leacock's pamphlet is *What Shall We Do About the Navy: The Policy of a United Front*. It is from the same setting of type as its serial publication in the *University Magazine* (see C11.37). The publisher of this journal was George Morang & Co. Number of copies printed and price not known.

COPIES EXAMINED: CS (an extra first and last leaf (conjugate leaves, pp. *1, 2, 19, 1*) mistakenly inserted).

## A10 THE UNIVERSITY SCHOOL OF COMMERCE 1912

[caption title] McGill University. | [rule] | The University School of Commerce. | [rule] | GENERAL ANNOUNCEMENT. | [rule]

* Leaflet folded once. *1–4* pp. (2 leaves). 213 × 140 mm.

TEXT: Announcement that McGill University has established the University School of Commerce; programme of studies for diploma course; evening extension classes; regulations regarding admission; diplomas and degrees; fees; prizes, scholarships, etc.; direction and management; list of members of the Advisory Committee; instruction.

BINDING: Printed on off-white paper stock, no wrapper.

NOTES: Leacock was authorized by the Faculty of Arts at McGill University to publicize the activities of the School of Commerce. The School was established the previous autumn to meet the needs of young men intent on a business career. Leacock was a member of the School's Advisory Committee, and he also taught an extension course on political economy for students of the School. He prepared this circular and had 2,500 copies printed. They were sent to all principals of schools in Quebec and eastern Ontario, to major companies in Montreal, and some 400 business men. In June and September 1911 Leacock also took out advertisements in the English newspapers in Montreal, and he also wrote articles about the School in these newspapers (see C11.32, information based on Leacock's "Report of the School of Commerce," February 1912, QMM Archives, RG 32, container 3, file 41).

COPY EXAMINED: QMM Archives.


AII SUNSHINE SKETCHES OF A LITTLE TOWN 1912

AIIa *first English edition*:

*SUNSHINE SKETCHES | OF A LITTLE TOWN | BY STEPHEN LEACOCK |* [thick-thin rule] | [thick-thin rule] | *WITH A FRONTISPIECE BY CYRUS CUNEO |* [thin-thick rule] | [thin-thick rule] | *LONDON: JOHN LANE THE BODLEY HEAD | NEW YORK: JOHN LANE COMPANY. MCMXII | TORONTO: BELL AND COCKBURN.*

◆ $A^8$ B–$R^8$ $S^6$ $T^8$ [$1 signed]. i–vi, vii–xii, 1–4, 1–61, 62, 63–93, 94, 95–131, 132, 133–211, 212, 213–253, 254, 255–264, i–iv, 1–16 pp. (150 leaves). 184 × 127 mm.

CONTENTS: pp. *i–ii* blank; p. *iii* half title; p. *iv* [all lines within a rectangle] *BY THE SAME AUTHOR* | [rule] | LITERARY LAPSES | THIRD EDITION. | NONSENSE NOVELS | THIRD EDITION; p. *v* title; p. *vi* THE ANCHOR PRESS, LTD., TIPTREE ESSEX; pp. vii–xii dated "*McGill University,* | *June,* 1912."; p. *1* table of contents; p. 2 blank; p. *3* fly title; p. 4 blank; pp. 1–264 text (pp. *62, 94, 132, 212,* and *254* blank); pp. i–iv advertisements; pp. 1–16 John Lane's list of fiction. Colour frontispiece of Jos. Smith standing by his hotel.

TEXT: chapter I The Hostelry of Mr. Smith; chapter II The Speculations of Jefferson Thorpe; chapter III The Marine Excursion of the Knights of Pythias; chapter IV The Ministrations of the Rev. Mr. Drone; chapter V The Whirlwind Campaign in Mariposa; chapter VI The Beacon on the Hill; chapter VII The Extraordinary Entanglement of Mr. Pupkin; chapter VIII The Fore-ordained Attachment of Zena Pepperleigh and Peter Pupkin; chapter IX The Mariposa Bank Mystery; chapter X The Great Election in Missinaba County; chapter XI The Candidacy of Mr. Smith; chapter XII L'Envoi. The Train to Mariposa.

BINDING AND DUST JACKET: Bound in maroon cloth, top edge stained maroon. Stamped on the upper board in gilt within two blind-stamped rectangles: *SUNSHINE SKETCHES | OF A LITTLE TOWN | By STEPHEN LEACOCK.* Stamped on the spine in gilt: [two rules blind-stamped] | *SUNSHINE | SKETCHES | OF | A LITTLE | TOWN | By | STEPHEN | LEACOCK* | THE BODLEY HEAD | [two rules blind-stamped].

The dust jacket is white with lettering in blue. The illustration by Cyrus Cuneo appears on the front panel but is yellower there than the frontispiece. Printed above the illustration: SUNSHINE SKETCHES | *By* STEPHEN LEACOCK. The spine panel has the following:

an ornament above a rectangle (containing the title and Leacock's name); an ornamental rectangular compartment; and THE BODLEY HEAD within another rectangle. The other sections of the jacket were clipped in the only known surviving copy.

NOTES: Between 17 February and 22 June 1912, *Sunshine Sketches of a Little Town* appeared serially in twelve instalments in the *Montreal Daily Star* (see C12.6–17). According to B.K. Sandwell ("Stephen Leacock, Worst Dressed Writer, Made Fun Respectable," *Orillia Packet and Times*, 6 April 1944, p. 16; "How the 'Sketches' Started," *Saturday Night* (August 1951): 7), the idea for the series originated with the *Star*'s managing editor, Edward Beck. Prior to its publication in this book, Leacock's autobiographical preface also appeared in a journal (see C11.38), although he added several paragraphs to it at the end. The earliest surviving notes for the book (2 pages, photocopy at SLM, see K66.2), dated 7 January 1912, are entitled "Plan and Ideas for a series of sketches about a little country town & the people in it: Each sketch about 4000 words." A draft of the manuscript has also survived at SLM (purchased on 24 August 1966 from Leacock's niece, Barbara Nimmo, with funds ($20,000) from John G. McConnell, president of the Montreal Standard Publishing Company, Ltd.).

Leacock told his publisher, John Lane, about the sketches on 24 February 1912. He sent several of them to him under separate cover. "I hope to do ten or twelve of these and to make a book of about 50,000 words," he informed Lane in the hope that Lane would arrange serialization of the stories in England and the United States and then publish them in book form. The sketches were not serialized outside of Canada. Leacock sent further instalments to Lane on 2 March, 11 March, and 20 March 1912. By the latter date he had written 35,000 words (the first five chapters). Practically from the start, Leacock wanted The Bodley Head to set the type for the book in order to take advantage of the Canadian market immediately after serial publication. On 3 April 1912, however, he told Lane that the chapters that had been sent were not good enough and that he would be keeping the rest of the manuscript. He promised to send ". . . the whole copy *from the start* in a revised and corrected form so as to minimize proof reading."

Leacock left for France on 12 May 1912. Upon his arrival there he told Lane that he had completed the entire manuscript (62,500 words). He sent the manuscript from Paris, and he apparently read the proofs before his departure on 15 June 1912 from Le Havre back to Canada. The contract with The Bodley Head at READ is dated 30 May 1913. Leacock received 15% royalty on the English edition (thirteen copies being reckoned as twelve). According to Leacock's notebook of recorded publications and speeches at QMMRB, the English edition was published on 9 August 1912.

The dramatic and moving picture rights to the book were sold on 10 August 1915 to Hughes Massie & Co. (2% royalty, £50 advance, minus 10% for Lane's commission), who acted on behalf of Michael Morton. Morton's play, called "Jeff," had a French-Canadian barber as the central character. The play was performed at His Majesty's Theatre in Montreal for a week (see "Prof. Leacock to Make His Debut as Playwright," *Montreal Star*, 15 June 1916, p. 2). Leacock did not think well of Morton's play, however. He wrote his own play of the book (see C17.10), and he wanted to be released from Morton's contract. For his part Morton placed an injunction against Leacock to stop any dramatization of the book except his own. He planned to revise his play after the war for production in the United States. As late as 6 February 1923, he refused to let Leacock regain the dramatic rights to the book (information from Leacock's correspondence with John Lane at TEX).

In his notebook of royalty payments at SLM, Leacock recorded 31 December 1912 as the first royalty statement for the English edition (3,209 copies sold of which 563 were for the colonial and 500 for the Australasian markets). Up to the end of 1923, 14,794 copies sold of the English edition. A further 3,549 copies were colonial sales, and another 2,603 copies were Australasian sales. Up the end of 1923 43,644 copies sold for all editions. According to the verso of A11f, there were impressions in 1912 (three times), 1913, 1914, 1917, 1918 (twice), 1920, 1923, 1925, and 1933 ("cheap edition"). This information conflicts somewhat with the copyright pages of the examined copies. According to *The English Catalogue of Books*, the "cheaper ed." was published in September 1933 at 3s 6d; Lomer (p. 52) has 8 September 1933 as the date of publication.

During the 1930s sales of the English edition, including those to the colonial and foreign markets, varied from approximately 300 copies to less than 100 copies per year.

COPIES EXAMINED: BOD (jacket, John Johnson collection); CS (first, fourth (one copy in green suede, one in cloth), fifth printings, 1912; seventh [1916]; eighth [1918]; and ninth [1920] (in jacket)); OTUTF (third impression, 1912); SLM (first printing, no jacket).


## A11a.1 *first American issue*:

*SUNSHINE SKETCHES | OF A LITTLE TOWN | BY STEPHEN LEACOCK |* [thick-thin rule] | [thick-thin rule] | *WITH A FRONTISPIECE BY CYRUS CUNEO* | [thin-thick rule] | [thin-thick rule] | *NEW YORK: JOHN LANE COMPANY | LONDON: JOHN LANE: THE BODLEY HEAD | TORONTO: BELL AND COCKBURN | MCMXII*

Cancel title. The first leaf of the preface (pp. vii–viii) is also a cancel. The preface has been reset, and is dated September 1912. The verso of the title leaf reads: *All Rights Reserved*. After the last page of the text, there are eight leaves of ads for books published by the John Lane Company. The collation is: $A^8$ (+/–A3.4) B–R$^8$ S$^4$ T$^8$ [$1 signed]. The leaves measure 187 × 120 mm.

BINDING AND DUST JACKET: Bound in brown cloth with cream lettering. Stamped on the upper board in brown raised characters inside a solid cream rectangle: [the solid rectangle is itself within a cream rectangle] SUNSHINE | SKETCHES | STEPHEN LEACOCK. Stamped on the spine: SUNSHINE | SKETCHES | [rule] | LEACOCK | JOHN LANE | COMPANY.

The dust jacket is cream-coloured with a colour illustration (by Hovsh) of Jos. Smith on the front panel. To the left of the illustration are two paragraphs on Leacock and his book; Leacock is said to have ". . . earned for himself the title of the 'Canadian Mark Twain.'" Printed on the spine: SUNSHINE | SKETCHES | [rule] | LEACOCK | $1.25 | FIXED PRICE | Postage, 12 cents | JOHN LANE | COMPANY. On the back panel are advertisements with excerpts from reviews of *Literary Lapses* and *Nonsense Novels*. The front flap has an advertisement for the complete works of William J. Locke. On the back flap is an advertisement for the *International Studio*.

NOTES: Published on 20 September 1912. The rights to the American issue were included in Leacock's contract with The Bodley Head. He received 15% royalty (raised to 20% in 1919). In his notebook of royalty payments at SLM, Leacock recorded 31 December 1912 as the first royalty statement for this issue (1,226 copies sold, $169 royalty). Up to the end of 1921, 7,805 copies sold. According to an advertising brochure issued by the John Lane Company, the book was into its fifteenth "edition" (i.e. printing) by 1920 ($1.50 cloth).

COPIES EXAMINED: CS (first printing, no jacket); OTNY (first printing, no jacket); QMMRB (eighth impression [1918]). Copy of jacket obtained from Robert Dagg Rare Books, catalogue 24 (October 1996), item 230.

### A11a.2 *first Canadian issue*:

The first Canadian issue is the same as A11a with the following exceptions: there are no advertisements after the text; the binding is dark red, and has BELL & COCKBURN as the imprint on the spine; the top edge is not stained. Leaves measure 182 × 122 mm. Dust jacket not seen.

NOTES: When Leacock and John Lane corresponded about the book's progress in February and March 1912, they had agreed that Bell and Cockburn would handle Canadian sales. The Canadian company had acted as Lane's agent. Leacock hoped that Bell and Cockburn would order 1,500 copies. On 23 May 1912 W.C. Bell agreed to pay Leacock a royalty of 15% on the retail price ($1.25). The Canadian issue appeared simultaneously with the American issue (20 September 1912). It consisted of 4,500 copies. On 13 December 1912 Bell sent Leacock an advance royalty cheque of $750. At the beginning, sales were so quick that deliveries of copies did not come fast enough. Bell hoped to sell 10,000 copies by mid-1913, although he stated: "Montreal has been a great disappointment to us as we have received very few repeats . . . and presume that they will come with a rush at the last moment." By 9 January [1913] Bell sent Leacock another cheque for $79.25. Another 500 copies had been received from Lane, and a further 1,000 were are on the way.

In his notebook of royalty payments at SLM, Leacock recorded that 4,095 copies had sold by the end of 1912 ($829.25 royalty), and another 1,300 copies by 30 June 1913 ($243.75 royalty).

In an undated, unpublished reminiscence entitled "The Human Side. Thumbnail Sketches," Bell recalled: "For many years I was Leacock's Canadian agent. . . . [In his company at his home in Orillia] Stephen never gave expression to his professional humor, but nevertheless always found a way to provoke a humorous situation" (Bell fonds, OTUTF).

COPIES EXAMINED: CS (two copies of the first printing; fourth impression 1912); OORI; QMMRB (three copies of the first printing; third impression 1912; fourth impression in rust-coloured suede binding).

### A11a.3 *second Canadian issue* (1915):

*SUNSHINE SKETCHES | OF A LITTLE TOWN | BY STEPHEN LEACOCK |* [thick-thin rule] | [thick-thin rule] | *WITH A FRONTISPIECE BY CYRUS CUNEO |* [thin-thick rule] | [thin-thick rule] | *LONDON: JOHN LANE THE BODLEY HEAD | NEW YORK: JOHN LANE COMPANY | TORONTO: S. B. GUNDY MCMXV | Published in Canada for Humphrey Milford.*

Cancel title. The verso of the title leaf reads: THE ANCHOR PRESS, LTD., TIPTREE ESSEX, ENGLAND. The sheets measure 190 × 131 mm., but are otherwise identical to A11.2. Bound in reddish purple cloth with stamping as in A11a.2 except with *GUNDY* in gilt at the foot of the spine. Dust jacket not seen.

NOTES: When Bell and Cockburn went bankrupt at the end of 1914 and Bell joined the firm of S.B. Gundy, Leacock told Bell on [12 December 1914] that he did not think that the future sales of *Sunshine Sketches of a Little Town* and *Behind the Beyond* would be very large. He requested 20% royalty on *Sunshine Sketches*, but left it to Bell's judgment as to terms (Bell fonds, OTUTF). In the first royalty statement to the end of June 1915, Leacock earned $56.50 on 226 copies sold. Up to the end of December 1923, 2,978 copies sold. Gundy continued to sell the book until February 1926 when Leacock severed his connection with Gundy. Lomer (p. 51) mistakenly records an edition published by Gundy in 1912.

Also examined was a copy in a similar binding but with a variant, integral title leaf. The latter is undated (sixth impression), and makes no reference to Cuneo's frontispiece. The imprint of The Bodley Head is on the spine, and there are four pages of Bodley Head advertisements after p. 264. This would suggest that it is simply a reprint from The Bodley Head rather than an issue designed specifically for Gundy.

COPIES EXAMINED: CS; OTUTF (Thoreau MacDonald collection; and copy with integral title leaf).

## A11a.4 *second American issue* (1970):

SUNSHINE SKETCHES | OF A LITTLE TOWN | BY STEPHEN LEACOCK | [thick-thin rule] | [thick-thin rule] | *WITH A FRONTISPIECE BY CYRUS CUNEO* | [thin-thick rule] | *Short Story Index Reprint Series* | [publisher's device to the left of the next two lines: abstract design of building with four columns] | BOOKS FOR LIBRARIES PRESS | FREEPORT, NEW YORK

This is a photographic reprint of A11a.2. Pagination is the same as A11a.2 with the following exceptions: there is no preliminary blank leaf; the last leaf of this issue is blank; the first leaf of this issue has the half title of A11a.2 on the recto and the photocopied image of the frontispiece on the verso. The verso of the title leaf reads as follows: First Published 1912 | Reprinted 1970 | STANDARD BOOK NUMBER: | 8369-3595-0 | LIBRARY OF CONGRESS CATALOG CARD NUMBER: | 71-125228 | PRINTED IN THE UNITED STATES OF AMERICA. Leaves measure 195 × 127 mm. Bound in red cloth with publisher's device blind-stamped on the upper board and stamping in silver down the spine as follows: [dark red ornament] | [the next two lines within a solid dark red rectangle] SUNSHIME SKETCHES | [below the previous line] LEACOCK | [dark red ornament] | [within an oval] B*f*L.

Also examined was a copy (with leaves measuring 202 × 133 mm., perhaps a later printing) with three lines to the right of the publisher's device on the title page as follows: BOOKS FOR LIBRARIES PRESS | A Division of Arno Press, Inc. | New York, New York. This copy is bound is in dark blue simulated leather (paper boards) with stamping down the spine in gilt as follows: Leacock SUNSHINE SKETCHES [within an oval] B*f*L.

NOTES: Published in June 1970. Number of copies printed not known. The book was still in print in 1997 (at $24.95).

COPIES EXAMINED: CS (dark blue simulated leather); OONL (red cloth).

## A11a.5 *third American issue* (1984):

SUNSHINE SKETCHES | OF A LITTLE TOWN | BY STEPHEN LEACOCK | [thick-thin rule] | [thick-thin rule] | *WITH A FRONTISPIECE BY CYRUS*

*CUNEO* | [thin-thick rule] | AYER COMPANY, PUBLISHERS, INC. | SALEM, NEW HAMPSHIRE 03079

Like A11.4, this issue is also a photographic reprint of A11a.2. The verso of the title leaf reads as follows: First Published 1912 | Reprint Edition 1984 | AYER Company, Publishing, Inc. | 47 Pelham Road | Salem, New Hampshire 03079 | [remaining five lines identical to that of A11.4]. The paper stock is thicker than that of A11a.4. There is an additional blank, preliminary leaf and another blank leaf at the end, but otherwise, pagination of this issue is the same as A11.4. Bound in dark blue paper boards resembling buckram with stamping down the spine in silver as follows: Leacock SUNSHINE SKETCHES [copy examined had book label at the foot of the spine].

NOTES: Number of copies printed and date of publication not known.

COPY EXAMINED: ALU.

A11b *first American edition* (1922):

SUNSHINE SKETCHES | OF A LITTLE TOWN | [thick-thin rule] | BY STEPHEN LEACOCK | [thin-thick rule] | [publisher's device: ornamental oval compartment with leaves at the corners and within the oval a woman's face and two open books] | [thick-thin rule] | NEW YORK: DODD, MEAD AND COMPANY | 1922 | [thin-thick rule]

♦ 1–16⁸. *i–iv*, v–xi, *xii*, xiii, *1–3*, 1–269, *1–3* pp. (144 leaves). 186 × 130 mm.

CONTENTS: p. *i* half title; p. *ii* nine books by the same author, the first being *Literary Lapses* and the last *My Discovery of England*; p. *iii* title; p. *iv* PUBLISHED IN U. S. A. 1922 | BY DODD, MEAD AND COMPANY, INC. | 𝕿𝖍𝖊 𝕼𝖚𝖎𝖓𝖓 & 𝕭𝖔𝖉𝖊𝖓 𝕮𝖔𝖒𝖕𝖆𝖓𝖞 | [rule] | BOOK MANUFACTURERS | RAHWAY NEW JERSEY; pp. v–xi preface; p. *xii* blank; p. xiii table of contents; p. *1* blank; p. *2* fly title; p. *3* blank; pp. 1–269 text; pp. *1–3* blank.

TEXT: Identical to A11a.

BINDING AND DUST JACKET: Bound in green cloth. On the upper board is a black rectangle and within it a solid black rectangle containing the following in green: SUNSHINE | SKETCHES | STEPHEN LEACOCK. Stamped on the spine in black: SUNSHINE | SKETCHES | [rule] | LEACOCK | DODD, MEAD | & COMPANY.

The dust jacket is white with printing in blue. An illustration in white, green, blue, and yellow (signed VAA) of a hill town is on the front, back, and spine panels. Also on the back panel are a paragraph about the setting of the book and a quotation from the *Boston Transcript*. The flaps are blank.

NOTES: A few months after the John Lane Company was sold to Dodd, Mead, Jefferson Jones asked Leacock on 18 May 1922 if Dodd, Mead could make a set of their own plates for a new American edition. Jefferson suggested that Leacock could also update the preface, but the only change to the preface was the reference to Dodd, Mead on p. ix. The book sold for $1.50. Dodd, Mead proposed an "edition" in red limp leather on 9 February 1923 (uniform with four other works of Leacock published by Dodd, Mead in red leather — *Literary Lapses, Nonsense Novels, Behind the Beyond*, and *My Discovery of England*). It sold for $2.50, and Leacock received a royalty of 30¢ on each copy sold. This is fact a reprint (186 × 119 mm.). In 1923 there was also a reprint in maroon cloth, the sheets being the same size as those of the reprint in red leather. Also examined were impressions of the regular edition reprinted in 1925 and 1941.

In the first royalty edition dated 1 August 1922, Dodd, Mead sold 210 copies of its edition. Up to the end of 1 February 1924, 1,194 copies sold. Approximately 100 copies sold annually thereafter.

COPIES EXAMINED: CS (first printing, 1923 printing in red leather and cloth, impressions of 1925 and 1941; all in jackets except the copy in leather).

A11b.1 *first Canadian issue of the first American edition* (1931):

SUNSHINE SKETCHES | OF A LITTLE TOWN | [thick-thin rule] | BY STEPHEN LEACOCK | [thin-thick rule] | [illustration of a quill in an inkwell] | [thick-thin rule] | McCLELLAND & STEWART, LIMITED | PUBLISHERS TORONTO | 1931 | [thin-thick rule]

The verso of the title leaf of this issue reads: COPYRIGHT CANADA, 1931 | BY McCLELLAND & STEWART, LIMITED | PRINTED IN CANADA | Press of | The Hunter-Rose Co., Limited | Toronto. The page (p. *ii*) facing the title page lists fifteen other books by Leacock, the first being *Literary Lapses* and the last *College Days*. In other respects the sheets of this issue are identical to those of A11b.

BINDING AND DUST JACKET: There are at least three binding variants: red cloth similar to that of A11b with McCLELLAND | & STEWART at the foot of the spine; pink cloth without a solid black rectangle on the upper board and the imprint McLELLAND [sic] | & STEWART | LIMITED at the foot of the spine; light red cloth without a solid black rectangle on the upper board and McCLELLAND | & STEWART | LIMITED at the foot of the spine.

The dust jacket is similar to that of A11b. In the illustration red replaces yellow in a number of places. The front flap has an excerpt from *Highways of Canadian Literature* pertaining to *Sunshine Sketches*. On the back flap is a list of books published by McClelland and Stewart.

NOTES: In December 1930 when the Macmillan Company of Canada failed to obtain the Canadian agency to Leacock's previously published books, McClelland and Stewart inquired about the publication of *Sunshine Sketches of a Little Town*. Leacock signed a contract with McClelland and Stewart on 23 January 1931. In return for 10% royalty and an advance of $300 against royalties, he gave McClelland and Stewart the Canadian rights to the following books: *Sunshine Sketches*; *Literary Lapses*; *Nonsense Novels*; *Behind the Beyond*; *Arcadian Adventures with the Idle Rich*; *Moonbeams from the Larger Lunacy*; *Essays and Literary Studies*; *Further Foolishness*; *Frenzied Fiction*; *The Hohenzollerns in America*; *The Unsolved Riddle of Social Justice*; *Winsome Winnie*; and *My Discovery of England*.

On 12 May 1931, with the exception of *Sunshine Sketches*, McClelland and Stewart placed an order for fifty copies of each book from The Bodley Head. In other words, McClelland and Stewart sold and distributed copies of the English edition of these books.

2,500 copies of this issue of *Sunshine Sketches* were printed in April 1931 from plates supplied by Dodd, Mead. Approximately 2,000 copies had been bound by May 1933, and the rest were still in sheets at that time (information on print run from George L. Parker's notes of the McClelland and Stewart fonds, OHM).

COPIES EXAMINED: CS (first two variant bindings, red cloth in jacket); QMMRB (third variant without jacket).

**A11b.2** *second Canadian issue of the first American edition* (1947):

SUNSHINE SKETCHES | OF A LITTLE TOWN | [thick-thin rule] | BY STEPHEN LEACOCK | [thin-thick rule] | [illustration of a floral arrangement and a burning lamp on a book] | [thick-thin rule] | REPRINT SOCIETY OF CANADA, LIMITED | MONTREAL | [thin-thick rule]

The collation of this issue is $1-9^{16}$. Pagination is the same as A11b. The sheets measure 182 × 125 mm. The verso of the title leaf reads: COPYRIGHT CANADA, 1931 | BY McCLELLAND & STEWART, LIMITED | REPRINTED 1947 | PRINTED IN CANADA.

BINDING AND DUST JACKET: Bound in maroon paper boards. A solid black rectangle is at the top of the spine. Within this rectangle is the following: [all lines in gilt within two rectangles, the inner one wavy] SUNSHINE | SKETCHES | [rule] | LEACOCK.

The front and spine panels of the jacket are dark brown. The rest of the jacket is beige with printing in brown. The back panel has a photo of Leacock in brown by Karsh and biographical information on Leacock. On the front flap is a list of future books issued by the Reprint Society, premium books for introducing new members, and a gift book on joining the Society. The back panel is blank.

NOTES: The Reprint Society of Canada, Limited was incorporated by letters patent on 29 May 1947 (NAC, microfilm reel C-4125, Liber #422, folio #289). This book was apparently issued by the Reprint Society for its members sometime before November 1947 since the front flap has a list of future Reprint Society selections. The first book that is listed is Phillip Guedalla's *The Duke* for November [1947]. Printed by Richardson, Bond & Wright in Toronto. Number of copies printed not known.

COPIES EXAMINED: CS.

**A11b.3** *third Canadian issue of the first American edition* (1953):

SUNSHINE SKETCHES | OF A LITTLE TOWN | [thick-thin rule] | BY STEPHEN LEACOCK | [thin-thick rule] | [publisher's device: abstract design within an oval of a person on a horse-drawn chariot, taking aim with a bow and arrow] | [thick-thin rule] | McCLELLAND & STEWART, LIMITED | Publishers Toronto | [thin-thick rule]

Cancel title. The other differences in this issue from that of A11b.2 are the following: the first leaf; a leaf with a photo by Karsh has been inserted before the title leaf; and there is no blank leaf at the end. The copyright page reads: COPYRIGHT CANADA, 1931 | BY McCLELLAND & STEWART, LIMITED | Reissued, 1953 | PRINTED IN CANADA.

BINDING AND DUST JACKET: The binding is the same as that of A11b.2, top edge stained black. The jacket is red with an illustration on the front panel of a couple (Zena Pepperleigh and Peter Pupkin) seated on rocking chairs. The back panel refers to the CBC television programme based on the book. The flaps are white with printing in black and red. In addition to biographical information on Leacock, the front flap advertises "A beautiful Gift Edition of *Sunshine Sketches* with original drawings by Grant MacDonald." On the back flap is a quotation from Arthur L. Phelps's *Canadian Writers*.

NOTES: Phelps's *Canadian Writers* was published by McClelland and Stewart in 1951. Shortly thereafter, Mavor Moore adapted *Sunshine Sketches* for radio, and the Canadian Broadcasting Corporation televised his musical version of the book (Moore's play *Sunshine Town* premiered at the Royal Alexandra Theatre in Toronto on 10–22 January 1955).

Hugh P. Kane of McClelland and Stewart obtained an estimate for printing 5,000 copies of this issue with the T.H. Best Printing Co. Ltd. on 22 December 1952. However, Fred Whitcombe of the Reprint Society of Canada Limited informed McClelland and Stewart on 19 January 1953 that Richardson, Bond & Wright held the plates and would not ". . . permit a transfer in ownership of offset negatives or plates if they are to be used outside of their plant." Whitcombe allowed Kane the use of the Society's plates for $225.00 (half the cost of creating them). In March 1953 Best printed new jackets and "repaired" 5,099 copies at a cost of $254.95. The illustration on the front panel of the jacket (prepared by Bomac Engravers for $120 and set on to plates by Howlett & Smith for $51.09) was based on a photograph of the "Porch Proposal" supplied by the CBC. The book sold for $1.50 to the trade and $1 to schools. See also A11b.4 and A11b.5 for related issues (information based on file 36, DK2, McClelland and Stewart fonds, OHM).

COPIES EXAMINED: CS (in jacket).

## A11b.4 *fourth Canadian issue of the first American edition* [1955]:

This issue is a reprint of A11b.3. The title leaf is integral, however, and its verso reads: This edition published in Canada, 1947, by | THE REPRINT SOCIETY OF CANADA LIMITED | by arrangement with McClelland & Stewart, Limited. | PRINTED IN CANADA. The binding is identical to A11b.3, except that McCLELLAND | & STEWART is stamped in gilt at the foot of the spine (top edge stained red). Otherwise, this issue is the same as A11b.3.

Reprints by Richardson, Bond & Wright were ordered in June 1955 (5,000 copies), August 1957 (5,000 copies), and April 1958 (2,500 copies) (information based on file 36, DK2, McClelland and Stewart fonds, OHM).

COPIES EXAMINED: CS (two copies in jacket).

## A11b.5 *fifth Canadian issue of the first American edition* [1958]:

This issue is the same as A11b.4 except that there is a gathering of eight additional leaves (pp. 271–286) after the text. These consist of a biographical note about Leacock and questions about the book. Bound in red pictorial cloth, resembling the front, spine, and back panels of the dust jacket of A11b.3. D.H. Carr prepared a set of notes and questions for this issue in 1958 (he sold the rights for $200 on 11 June 1958). Printings of 2,500 copies of this "educational edition" were ordered in April 1958 and March 1959 (information based on file 36, DK2, McClelland and Stewart fonds, OHM).

COPIES PRINTED: EVANS; OTUTF.

## A11c *second English edition* (1941):

SUNSHINE SKETCHES OF A | LITTLE TOWN | BY | STEPHEN LEACOCK | [publisher's device: illustration of a penguin] | ALLEN LANE: PENGUIN BOOKS | HARMONDSWORTH MIDDLESEX ENGLAND | 41 EAST 28TH STREET NEW YORK U.S.A.

♦ $A^{16}$ B–$E^{16}$ [\$1 signed]. *i–v*, vi–viii, *1–3*, 12–*158*, *1–2* pp. (80 leaves). 179 × 110 mm.

CONTENTS: p. *i* half title with a quotation from Richard King in *The Tatler*; p. *ii* black-and-white photograph of Leacock with biographical information about him and a publisher's note; p. *iii* title; p. 4 First published 1912 | [eleven lines listing reprintings] | Published in Penguin Books 1941 | MADE AND PRINTED IN GREAT BRITAIN FOR PENGUIN BOOKS LIMITED | BY WYMAN AND SONS, LTD., LONDON FAKENHAM AND READING; pp. *v*–viii preface; p. *1* table of contents; p. *2* blank; pp. *3*, 12–*158* text; p. *1* advertisement for Cadbury's of Bournville; p. *2* advertisements for the Penguin editions of *Literary Lapses* and *Selected Short Stories of Saki* and for the special reading-case label.

TEXT: Identical to A11a.

BINDING: Paperback, sewn signatures. The spine and front of the wrapper consist of three sections, orange at the top and bottom and white in the middle. The upper wrapper is as follows: [the first two lines within a rounded oval compartment outlined in black within the top orange section] PENGUIN | BOOKS | [the next four lines are within the white section, are flanked by the word FICTION vertically in orange on both sides] | SUNSHINE SKETCHES | OF A LITTLE TOWN | STEPHEN | LEACOCK | [illustration of a penguin within the bottom orange section]. The spine records the author, title, and series number (320). The back of the wrapper has an advertisement for Greys Cigarettes.

NOTES: The Penguin edition was arranged from 10 June and 3 September 1940 between C.J. Greenwood of The Bodley Head and Allen Lane. Lane paid The Bodley Head an advance of £60 (£30 on signature of the contract and the remainder sixty days from signature) on account of royalties of 1/4d per copy. Leacock probably split the advance with The Bodley Head. The book sold for 6d. Number of copies sold and exact date of publication not known. In all likelihood the book sold as many copies as the Penguin edition of *Literary Lapses* (A5c). The price of the book was raised to 9d after 19 March 1942, and Leacock received a pro rata increase in royalty to 30s per 1,000 copies sold. Reprinted in September 1942 (information based on the Penguin Books fonds, University Library, Bristol University).

COPIES EXAMINED: CUL (date-stamped 30 July 1941); GZQ (rebound copy, September 1942).

## A11d  *third English edition* (1942):

SUNSHINE SKETCHES | OF A LITTLE TOWN | *By* | STEPHEN LEACOCK | [illustration of a fountain] | LONDON 48 PALL MALL | WM. COLLINS SONS & CO. LTD. | GLASGOW, TORONTO, SYDNEY, AUCKLAND

♦ *1–6*$^{16}$. *1–12*, 13–*191*, *1* pp. (96 leaves). 180 × 102 mm.

CONTENTS: p. *1* COLLINS | POPULAR | NOVEL; p. *2* list of twenty-five books by the same author, the first being *Literary Lapses* and the last *Stephen Leacock's Laugh Parade*; p. *3* title; p. 4 COPYRIGHT CANADA 1942 BY | McCLELLAND AND STEWART LIMITED | [rule] | PUBLISHED BY ARRANGEMENT | [rule] | PRINTED IN CANADA; pp. *5–10* preface; p. *11* preface; p. *12* blank; pp. 13–*191* text; p. *1* advertisement for the books of Ngaio Marsh.

TEXT: Identical to A11a.

BINDING: Paperback, sewn signatures. The front cover and spine are in dark orange, light orange, and black. The illustration of a fountain is on the front cover within a solid white circle. On the back cover are descriptions of four Collins White Circle Pocket Editions which are contained within a white solid rectangle, outlined by a dark orange rectangular frame. Series title: White Circle Pocket Novel.

NOTES: This edition was apparently arranged for the English market by the Toronto branch of William Collins Sons. According to the bottom of p. 191, it was printed by the Bryant Press Ltd. in Toronto. Date of publication, number of copies printed, and price not known. See the notes to A11d.1 for further information.

COPIES EXAMINED: CS; QMMRB.

**A11d.1** *Canadian issue of the third English edition* (1944):

SUNSHINE SKETCHES | OF A LITTLE TOWN | *By* | STEPHEN LEACOCK | [illustration of a fountain] | COLLINS | 70 BOND STREET, TORONTO

The verso of the title leaf has 1944 as date of publication, but is otherwise the same as A11d. The recto of the first leaf (p. *1*) reads: [circle] | COLLINS | WHITE CIRCLE | POCKET NOVELS. The verso of the last leaf is blank.

BINDING: Paperback, sewn signatures, all edges stained red. The front cover and spine have a colour illustration of a small community, railroad, lake, steamer, and so on. The back cover is yellow with a list of the main characters of the book. Price 25¢. Series number 223.

NOTES: On 15 April 1942 White Circle Books through John McClelland of McClelland and Stewart arranged for an edition in paper to sell for 25¢ with a royalty of 1¢ per copy. McClelland proposed to split the royalty with Leacock and offered to send him a cheque for $125 on the first 25,000 copies sold. Leacock accepted McClelland's proposal on 18 April 1942. McClelland sent Leacock this amount as an advance royalty on 22 October 1942. According to the bottom of p. 191, this issue was printed by Advocate Printers Ltd. in Winnipeg. Number of copies printed not known.

COPIES EXAMINED: CS; OORI; QMMRB.

**A11e** *first Canadian edition, first illustrated edition* (1948):

*Sunshine Sketches | of | A Little Town | by | Stephen Leacock | McClelland & Stewart Limited | Toronto*

◆ 1¹⁰ 2–4⁸ 5¹⁰ 6–18⁸. i–vi, vii–xiii, 1–9, 3–36, 37–38, 39–62, 63–64, 65–94, 95–96, 97–120, 121–122, 123–134, 135–136, 137–151, 152–154, 155–171, 172–174, 175–193, 194–196, 197–220, 221–222, 223–239, 240–242, 243–264, 265–266, 267–275, 1 pp. (148 leaves). 215 × 143 mm.

CONTENTS: p. *i* half title; p. *ii* blank; p. *iii* title; p. *iv* Copyright in Canada, 1948, *by* | MCCLELLAND & STEWART LIMITED | *Printed in Canada by* | THE HUGH HEATON PRINTING HOUSE LIMITED | Toronto; p. *v* preface title; p. *vi* blank; pp. vii–xiii preface; p. *1* blank; pp. 2 table of contents; p. *3* blank; p. *4* list of illustrations; p. *5* blank; p. 6 fly title; p. *7* blank; pp. 8–9, 3–275 text (pp. *9, 38, 64, 96, 122, 136, 152, 154, 172, 174, 194, 196, 222, 240, 242,* and *266* blank); p. *1* blank. Colour illustrations (half tones): frontispiece; facing pp. 16, 33, 49, 68, 85, 100, 132, 149, 165, 180, 228, and 245.

TEXT: Identical to A11a.

BINDING AND DUST JACKET: Bound in orangish brown cloth with a reproduction of the Stephen Leacock Memorial Medal embossed on the upper board. Stamped in gilt on the spine: [first six lines in script] *sunshine | sketches | of a | little | town | Leacock |* McClelland | and | Stewart. Also examined was a copy in purple simulated leather.

The front and spine panels are red with an illustration by Grant Macdonald of a fire engine pulled by three horses. On the back panel is a black-and-white photograph of Leacock by Karsh. The flaps have paragraphs about Leacock and his book. Emanuel Hahn's permission for the reproduction of the Stephen Leacock Memorial Medal is acknowledged on the front flap.

NOTES: The specifications for an edition of 5,000 copies were prepared by the Hugh Heaton Printing House Ltd. on 11 February 1948 at 86.2¢ per copy. In January and February of that year Hugh P. Kane of McClelland and Stewart corresponded with Mary Sheridan of the Orillia Public Library and with C.H. Hale of the *Orillia Packet and Times*. The former sent a first edition of the book for the setting of type. Hale provided historical information. He also sent photographs of places in Orillia that relate to *Sunshine Sketches* and a newsclipping of a photograph of the Stephen Leacock Memorial Medal designed by Emanuel Hahn (see *Orillia Packet and Times*, 18 September 1947, p. 1). Kane and Grant Macdonald, who was engaged to do the illustrations in February, visited Hale in Orillia on 15 April 1948. An order for an edition of 3,000 copies (2,994 copies received; total cost for printing, binding, etc. $3,223.80) was placed with the Hugh Heaton Printing House Ltd. on 29 June 1948. Macdonald completed all of his drawings except for the colour tints on 24 July, and on 21 August, he posted his drawing of the jacket. On 20 September Kane arranged with John Pinches (Medalists) Ltd. for the die of Hahn's medal to be made of brass in the negative for embossing on the upper board of the book. Macdonald was delighted to receive the second proofs of his illustrations on 29 September. The book was published on 30 November 1948 (at $4.50), although there had been problems in production: the editorial department neglected to give Hahn credit on the jacket; and Macdonald's name was omitted from the title page. The former was corrected, but Macdonald's name only appeared on the title page of subsequent impressions. Macdonald was initially disconcerted by the reception of his drawings, but this was dispelled by B.K. Sandwell who heaped praise on the new edition for its typography and illustrations (see "Leacock for Canadians," *Saturday Night*, 1 February 1949, p. 2) (information based on file 37, DK2, McClelland and Stewart fonds, OHM).

McCorquodale & Blades (Canada) Ltd. reprinted the book in June 1955 (2,500 copies, 2,078 copies bound by T.H. Best Printing Co., Ltd. on 30 June 1955), February 1962 (1,500 copies), 1965, 1967, and 1974. The latter is bound in black paper boards and has a matching cardboard box.

COPIES EXAMINED: CS (1948 (also in simulated leather), 1955, 1965, and 1967 in jacket; 1974 in box); QMMRB (two copies of the first printing, one in jacket).

## A11e.1 *American issue of the first Canadian edition* (1949):

*Sunshine Sketches | of | A Little Town | by | Stephen Leacock | Illustrations | by Grant Macdonald | 1949 | Dodd, Mead & Company | New York*

Cancel title. In other respects this issue is identical to A11e. Dust jacket not seen. Date of publication not known. The print run was undoubtedly quite small (500 copies or less) since only one copy is known to be extant.

COPIES EXAMINED: DEL.

**A11f** *fourth English edition* (1952):

*SUNSHINE SKETCHES | OF A LITTLE TOWN | by | Stephen Leacock | London | JOHN LANE THE BODLEY HEAD*

♦ $1^{16}$ $2-6^{16}$. 1–4, 5, 6, 7–192 pp. (96 leaves). 184 × 125 mm.

CONTENTS: p. *1* half title; p. *2* list of thirty-three books by the same author, the first being *Recollections and Reflections* [no such book exists as such] and the last *The Boy I Left Behind Me*; p. *3* title; p. *4* [eleven lines listing previous printings] | *Cheap edition* 1933 | *Reprinted* 1952 | [three lines about copyright] | Printed in Great Britain by | THE PITMAN PRESS, BATH | for JOHN LANE THE BODLEY HEAD LTD. | 28, Little Russell St., London, W.C.1; p. *5* table of contents; p. *6* blank; pp. *7–192* text.

TEXT: Identical to A11a.

BINDING AND DUST JACKET: Bound in orange paper boards; Stamped on the spine: Stephen | LEACOCK | [rule with a diamond in the center] | SUNSHINE | SKETCHES | OF A | LITTLE | TOWN | THE | BODLEY | HEAD.

The front panel of the jacket has a colour illustration of a frontier town (Glovers Hardware, a bank, farmers, a minister with a fishing pole, a dog, etc.) with the title on a banner. On the back panel is a list of Bodley Head Cheap Editions. The front flap has a paragraph on the book and Leacock, noting that this is the cheap edition (6s). On the back flap is a list of The Bodley Head's other cheap editions by Leacock (also at 6s).

NOTES: Although this edition is cited on the copyright page as a reprint of the 1933 cheap edition, it is in fact a new setting of type and the 1933 cheap edition is a reprint of A11a. According to *The English Catalogue of Books*, this edition was published on 23 June 1952. Number of copies printed not known.

COPIES EXAMINED: CS.

**A11g** *second Canadian edition* (1960):

*Stephen Leacock* | [two rows of leafy ornaments] | [the next five lines in open type] SUNSHINE | SKETCHES | OF A | LITTLE | TOWN | *Preface by Malcolm Ross* | *New Canadian Library. No. 15* | *McClelland & Stewart Limited*

♦ *i–viii*, ix–xi, *xii*, xiii–xvi, 1–153, *1–7* pp. (88 leaves). 184 × 110 mm.

CONTENTS: pp. *i–ii* blank; p. *iii* half title; p. *iv* blank; p. *v* title; p. *vi* Copyright in Canada, 1931, 1960 | by | McClelland & Stewart Limited | [four lines concerning copyright] | PRINTED AND BOUND IN ENGLAND BY | HAZELL WATSON AND VINEY LTD | AYLESBURY AND SLOUGH ENGLAND; p. *vii* table of contents; p. *viii* blank; pp. ix–xi editor's preface (by Ross); p. *xii* blank; pp. xiii–xvi Leacock's preface; pp. 1–153 text; p. *1* blank; p. *2* note about the author; p. *3* blank; p. *4* list of books in New Canadian Library series; pp. *5–7* blank.

TEXT: Identical to A11a.

BINDING: Paperback, perfect bound. The front cover has a brown sketch of Leacock's face with an irregular, yellow vertical band on the left side. On the back cover are two yellow bands and information about the book. Cover design by Frank Newfeld. Price: $1. N13 of the NCL series.

NOTES: Planning for the NCL edition began in February 1960. Claire Pratt of McClelland and Stewart commented on Ross's introduction on 8 March, and a few revisions were made to it. Although the proposed publication date was 22 October, the book was available on 19 November and published on 5 December 1960. Number of copies printed of the first impression not known. By the end of 1960 730 copies had sold. By the end of 1979 142,332 copies had sold (information based on file 1, box 47, and file 14, "New Canadian Library," box 93, series A, part I, McClelland and Stewart fonds, OHM). This number of copies sold undoubtedly includes the educational issue as well (A11g.1).

Reprinted in 1961, 1964, 1965, 1970 (by T.H. Best Printing Company Ltd.). There was also a reprinting on 7 February 1963 of 7,000 copies (information based on Ca4, McClelland and Stewart fonds, OHM).

COPIES EXAMINED: CS (1960, 1965, 1970); OORI (1960); QMMRB (1960).

## A11g.1 *second Canadian edition, educational issue* (1960):

*Stephen Leacock* | [two rows of leafy ornaments] | [the next five lines in open type] SUNSHINE | SKETCHES | OF A | LITTLE | TOWN | *Notes and questions by D. H. Carr,* | *Head of the English Department,* | *Central Collegiate, London, Ontario* | *McClelland & Stewart Limited*

This issue omits Ross's introduction but has eighteen pages of notes and questions after the text (last numbered page is 172). Bound in blue, yellow, and orange paper boards with an illustration of some of the characters of the book on the upper board.

NOTES: This issue was published simultaneously as the regular NCL edition. There was a reprint of 6,000 copies of on 31 October 1961 (cost of $2,148.30) (information from file 37, DK2, McClelland and Stewart fonds, OHM). According to the copyright page of the 1970 reprint (Chariot Literature Text), there were reprints in 1961, 1963, 1964, 1965, 1966, 1967, and 1969.

COPIES EXAMINED: CS (1960 and 1970); OORI (1967, Chariot Literature Text).

## A11g.2 *second Canadian edition, New Canadian Library Classic* (1982):

Stephen Leacock | Sunshine Sketches | of a Little Town | of a Little Town | New Canadian Library N15 | Introduction by: John Stevens | McClelland and Stewart

◆ *1–18, 1–153, 1–5* pp. (88 leaves). 178 × 108 mm.

In this issue the first fourteen pages and the pages after the text have been reset. A new introduction by John Stevens replaces Ross's introduction. ISBN 0-7710-9115-X. The copyright page indicates: NCL Classic Edition published 1982. Paperback with New Canadian Library Classic designation and a black-and-white photograph of a steam boat on the front cover. On the back cover are the lines: "Indispensable for the appreciation of Canadian literature." | THE CANADIAN CLASSICS COMMITTEE.

NOTES: At the Calgary Conference on the Canadian Novel held in February 1978, Jack McClelland and Malcolm Ross arranged for various academics to designate certain Canadian books as classics. *Sunshine Sketches* was so designated. See Robert Lecker's *Making It Real: The Canonization of English-Canadian Literature* (Concord, Ont.: Anansi, 1995), pp. 167–72.

Reprinted in 1984.

COPIES EXAMINED: CS (1984).

**A11h** *third Canadian edition* (1987):

STEPHEN LEACOCK | Sunshine Sketches | of a Little Town | *With an Afterword by Jack Hodgins* | [wavy block, short wavy rule] | M&S | [rule]

◆ *i–vi*, vii–xi, *1*, 13–35, *36*, 37–97, *98*, 99–133, *134*, 135–151, *152*, 153–179, *180*, 181–191, *1–9* pp. (100 leaves). 178 × 108 mm.

CONTENTS: p. *i* biographical information about Leacock; p. *ii* THE NEW CANADIAN LIBRARY | General Editor: David Staines | ADVISORY BOARD | Alice Munro | W.H. New | Guy Vanderhaeghe; p. *iii* title; p. *iv* Copyright © 1931, 1960 by McClelland and Stewart Limited | Afterword copyright © by Jack Hodgins | [five lines about copyright] | [nine lines of Canadian Cataloguing in Publication Data] | Typesetting by Pickwick | Printed and bound in Canada | [five lines of the publisher's name and address]; p. *v* table of contents; p. *vi* blank; pp. vii–xi preface; p. *1* blank; pp. 13–186 text (pp. *36, 98, 134, 152,* and *180* blank); pp. 187–191 Hodgins's afterword; p. *1* blank; pp. *2–4* list of Leacock's books; p. *5* blank; p. *6* titles by Leacock in the NCL Library with an order form; pp. *7–9* blank.

TEXT: Identical to A11a.

BINDING: Paperback, perfect bound. A reproduction of A.J. Casson's "Early Morning" is on the front cover. Price $5.95. ISBN 0-7710-9984. Series design by T.M. Craan.

NOTES: Published on 5 October 1987 in an edition of 10,407 copies (received on 5 September 1987). Reprints are as follows: 29 March 1989 10,414 copies; 20 August 1990 6,600 copies; 1 May 1991 11,000 copies; 9 July 1991 9,833 copies; 13 January 1994 16,317 copies. By the end of 1996 46,547 copies had sold.

COPIES EXAMINED: CS.

**A11i** *fourth Canadian edition* (1996):

Sunshine Sketches | of a Little Town | *by* Stephen Leacock | RP | REFERENCE PRESS

◆ 1–17⁸. *i–vi*, vii–xii, *1*, 1–253, *1–6* pp. (136 leaves). 222 × 152 mm.

CONTENTS: p. *i* half title; p. *ii* blank; p. *iii* title; p. *iv* [three lines about copyright] | Published in Canada by Reference Press | with the financial assistance of | the National Library of Canada. | First published in Canada in 1912 by Bell and Cockburn. | Set in 16/18 Plantin. | [five lines about the cover illustration; eight lines of Canadian Cataloguing in Publication Data]; p. *v* table of contents; p. *vi* blank; pp. vii–xii, *1* preface; pp. 1–253 text; pp. *1–6* blank.

TEXT: Identical to A11a.

BINDING: Casebound in laminated, flesh-tone paper boards. Printed on the upper board: *Sunshine Sketches* | [white rule] | STEPHEN LEACOCK | [colour illustration (outlined in white) of Jos. Smith by Cyrus Cuneo] | Large Print. The author's surname and title are printed down the spine, and at the foot of the spine within a white square are the lines: RP | LP. A paragraph about the book appears on the lower board along with the bar code and ISBN number (0-919981-43-7).

NOTES: This edition is the seventh title in the Large Print Title series published by Reference Press (P.O. Box 70, Teeswater, ON, N0G 2S0) with the financial assistance of the National Library of Canada. The illustration on the upper board was supplied by Carl Spadoni and taken from the frontispiece of A11a. Published in mid-February 1996 or slightly thereafter in an edition of 250 copies at $28.50 a copy.

COPIES EXAMINED: CS (two copies).

### A11j *fifth Canadian edition, second illustrated edition* (1996):

STEPHEN LEACOCK | [sun rays in brown] | [the next three lines in open type] *Sunshine Sketches | of a | Little Town* | ILLUSTRATED BY WESLEY BATES | [wavy block, short wavy rule] | M&S | [rule]

◆ 1–23⁴. i–vii, viii–x, 1–3, 14–35, 36, 37–51, 52, 53–72, 73, 74–88, 89, 90–97, 98, 99–108, 109, 110–120, 121, 122–133, 134, 135–150, 151, 152–162, 163, 164–177, 178, 179–184 pp. (92 leaves). 254 × 210 mm.

CONTENTS: p. *i* half title; p. *ii* engraving of Leacock; p. *iii* title; p. *iv* Copyright © 1996 by McClelland & Stewart Inc. | Illustrations copyright © Wesley Bates 1996 | First published in Canada in 1912 by Bell and Cockburn, Toronto. | This illustrated edition first published in 1996 | [six lines about copyright; six lines of Canadian Cataloguing Publication Data] | Typesetting by M&S, Toronto | Printed and bound in Canada | [five lines with the address of McClelland and Stewart] | 1 2 3 4 5 00 99 98 97 96; p. *v* table of contents; p. *vi* blank; pp. *vii*, viii–x, *1* preface; p. 2 blank; pp. 3, 14–184 text. Scraperboard engravings on pp. 18, 29, 37, 44, 61, 68–69, 74, 80, 92, 94, 104–105, 114, 118, 124, 127, 141, 147, 154, 157, 167, 176, and 182–183. Decorative initials begin each chapter.

TEXT: Identical to A11a.

BINDING: Bound in light blue cloth. Printed down the spine in silver: LEACOCK *Sunshine Sketches of a Little Town* | [wavy block, short wavy rule] | M&S | [rule].

The front panel of the jacket has a colour scraperboard engraving of the Mariposa Belle moored to a pier in the foreground, a couple in a canoe, and the town of Mariposa in the background. The back panel has the same illustration but in reverse. Also on the back panel are four lines about this edition and the ISBN number (0-7710-5001-1). The spine panel is printed in black and is similar to the spine of the book. The front flap has information about the book and the price ($30, $26.95 US). On the back panel are engravings of Leacock and Bates with biographical information on both of them. Jacket design by Sari Ginsberg.

NOTES: Wesley Bates began the illustrations to this edition in late June 1996. He finished them in early August. The book was published on 16 October 1996 in an edition of 8,810 copies (received on 16 September 1996). A book launch sponsored by Bryan Prince, Book-seller, and McClelland & Stewart was held on 24 November 1996 at the Gallery on the Bay in Hamilton, ON. See Jeff Mahoney, "Hamilton Artist Tackles Leacock's Classic," *Hamilton Spectator*, 23 November 1996, p. W6. By the end of 1996 6,625 copies had sold. For information on Bates, see his book *The Point of the Graver* (Erin, ON: Porcupine's Quill, 1994).

COPIES EXAMINED: CS; numerous other copies at Bryan Prince's bookstore.

### A11k *sixth Canadian edition* (1996):

[all lines within two rectangles] Sunshine Sketches of a | Little Town | by | Stephen Leacock | A Critical Edition | Edited by | Gerald Lynch | [publisher's device: calligraphic T within a partial oval] | *The Tecumseh Press Ltd.* | Ottawa, *Canada* | 1996

◆ 1–12, ix–xii, 1–4, xv–xviii, 1–3, 2–20, 21, 22–34, 35, 36–52, 53, 54–66, 67, 68–73, 74, 75–82, 83, 84–92, 93, 94–103, 104, 105–117, 118, 119–127, 128, 129–140, 141, 142–145, 146–147, 148–161, 162, 163–175, 176, 177–222, 223, 224–225, 1 pp. (126 leaves). 216 × 140 mm.

CONTENTS: p. 1 blank; pp. 2–3 map of Mariposa by Darrel A. Norris; p. 4 blank; p. 5 half title; p. 6 information on the Canadian Critical Editions series edited by John Moss and Gerald Lynch; p. 7 title; p. 8 Copyright © by The Tecumseh Press Ltd., 1996 | [four lines concerning copyright permission] | [three lines acknowledging the financial assistance of the Department of Canadian Heritage and the Ontario Arts Council] | [ten lines of Canadian Cataloguing data] | [three lines indicating that copyright has been obtained for articles reprinted in the Documentary and Criticism sections] | Cover art from the frontispiece by Cyrus Cuneo | to the first edition of 1912. | [three lines acknowledging permission to use Norris's map] | *Printed and bound in Canada*; p. 9 dedication to David Bentley; p. 10 blank; p. 11–12 table of contents; pp. ix–xi editor's preface; p. xii biographical information about Leacock; p. 1 photograph by V. Tetley-Miller of Richard Jack's portrait of Leacock; p. 2 blank; p. 3 fly title; p. 4 blank; pp. xv–xviii Leacock's preface; pp. 1–2 blank; p. 3, 2–145 text; p. 146 blank; pp. 147–161 Biography (James Doyle's "Deeps and Shallows: The Elusive Life of Stephen Leacock"); pp. 162–175 Documentary (B.K. Sandwell's "How the 'Sketches' Started," Arthur Lower's "The Mariposa Belle," and Douglas Bush's "Small-Town Ontario"); pp. 176–222 Criticism (Peter McArthur's "Praise and Caution," Desmond Pacey's "The Eighteenth-Century Tory," R.E. Watters's "Leacock's Canadian Humour," Silver Donald Cameron's "The Ironist," Robertson Davies's "The Satirist," Alan Bowker's "The Social Scientist," William H. Magee's "The Local Colourist," and Gerald Lynch's "The Train to Mariposa"); pp. 223–225 bibliography; p. 1 logo of printer, AGMV L'imprimeur.

TEXT: Identical to A11a. However, the editor has made a "few silent changes of inarguable errors ('devices' for 'advices'; missing end punctuation, and similar typos)" (p. xi).

BINDING: There are two binding variants, both of which are perfect bound. (1) Casebound in black cloth with the following stamped in gilt down the spine: Sunshine Sketches of a Little Town | [below the previous line] Stephen Leacock | [publisher's device of Tecumseh Press]. The dust jacket is dark forest green with printing in white. On the front of the jacket is a reproduction of Cyrus Cuneo's frontispiece to A11a. The back of the jacket has a paragraph comparing Leacock's book to Mark Twain's *The Adventures of Huckleberry Finn*, the names of the twelve contributors who comment on the book, biographical information about Gerald Lynch, and the ISBN number. The flaps are blank. (2) Paperback, identical to the dust jacket of the cloth-bound variant, except for the ISBN number.

NOTES: This edition of *Sunshine Sketches* is the first volume in a series of critical editions of Canadian literary texts. Gerald Lynch, who teaches English at the University of Ottawa, is the author of *Stephen Leacock: Humour and Humanity* (1988) and several works of fiction. Although A11k claims to be a critical edition, readers should note that Lynch has not compared the copy-text of A11k with competing texts (e.g. C12.6–17). Published on 8 September 1996. Price $29.95 cloth (100 copies printed), $14.95 paperback (660 copies).

COPIES EXAMINED: CS (both binding variants); OONL (paperback).

## A12 BEHIND THE BEYOND 1913

### A12a *American edition*:

*BEHIND THE* | ::: *BEYOND* ::: | *AND OTHER CONTRIBUTIONS* | *TO HUMAN KNOWLEDGE* | [thick-thin rule] | *BY STEPHEN LEACOCK* | *AUTHOR OF "NONSENSE NOVELS," "LITERARY* | : : : *LAPSES," "SUNSHINE SKETCHES," ETC.* : : : | [thin-thick rule] | *ILLUSTRATED BY A. H. FISH* | [illustration of a woman from the back sitting on a divan, a fan in one of her hands and a mask in the other] | [thick-thin rule] | *NEW YORK: JOHN LANE COMPANY* | *LONDON: JOHN LANE, THE BODLEY HEAD* | *TORONTO: BELL & COCKBURN. MCMXIII*

◆ $1-12^8$ $13^2$. $1-10$, $11-50$, $51-52$, $53-90$, $91-92$, $93-156$, $157-158$, $159-166$, $167-168$, $169-182$, $183-184$, $185-195$, $1$ pp. (98 leaves). $185 \times 126$ mm.

CONTENTS: p. *1* half title; p. *2* list of three other books by Leacock, *Nonsense Novels*, *Literary Lapses*, and *Sunshine Sketches of Little Town*, published by the John Lane Company; p. *3* title; p. *4* COPYRIGHT, 1913, BY | THE CROWELL PUBLISHING COMPANY | COPYRIGHT, 1913, BY | THE CENTURY COMPANY | COPYRIGHT, 1913, BY | JOHN LANE COMPANY; p. *5* table of contents; p. *6* blank; p. *7* list of illustrations; p. *8* blank; pp. *9-195* text (pp. *52, 92, 158, 168*, and *184* blank); p. *1* illustration of a woman holding a fan. Colour frontispiece, "The Prologue"; black-and-white illustrations facing pp. *12, 28, 30, 50, 58, 66, 72, 84, 88, 98, 114, 120, 142, 146, 166*, and *174*.

TEXT: Behind the Beyond: A Modern Problem Play.

Familiar Incidents consists of: I With the Photographer; II The Dentist and the Gas; III My Lost Opportunities; IV My Unknown Friend; V Under the Barber's Knife

Parisian Pastimes consists of: I The Advantages of a Polite Education; II The Joys of Philanthropy; III The Simple Life in Paris; IV A Visit to Versailles; V Paris at Night.

The Retroactive Existence of Mr. Juggins; Making a Magazine: The Dream of a Contributor; Homer and Humbug, an Academic Discussion.

BINDING AND DUST JACKET: Bound in green cloth, top edge stained green. Stamped on the upper board: [gold rectangle and within it, a solid gold rectangle, which contains a raised green rectangle and the following in raised green characters] BEHIND THE | [cross] BEYOND [cross] | [rule] | STEPHEN LEACOCK. Stamped in gilt on the spine: BEHIND | THE | BEYOND | [rule] | LEACOCK | JOHN LANE | COMPANY.

The jacket is white with printing and the illustration in brown. On the front panel is an illustration by Fish similar to that facing p. *12* (which is entitled "The Curtain Rises"). Printing on the spine is similar to that of the spine with the addition of the price, $1. The back panel has the heading: HUMOROUS BOOKS BY STEPHEN LEACOCK. The front flap has information on the book and Leacock (referred to as the "Canadian Mark Twain"). On the back flap is an advertisement for *The International Studio*.

Also examined was an advance copy in light green wrappers. The front of the wrapper has the heading: *TO BOOKSELLERS*. Leacock is praised as "the natural successor to Mark Twain." The book is said to be published on 24 October 1913. The day in question is crossed out, and 31 is hand-written above 24.

NOTES: Leacock's book of sketches gathers together a number of humorous articles that were first published in various magazines such as *Saturday Night*, *American Magazine*, and

*Century Magazine*. On 5 November 1912, for example, Leacock sent W.A. Johnson of the John Lane Company "Familiar Incidents with the Photographs [Photographer]," the first of a series of articles that he had promised to "a new paper [*Saturday Mirror*] that is being founded here; they start to print these articles in December and pay me 2½ cents a word for the Canadian Serial Rights (note book rights)." Leacock wanted Johnson to sell the series in the United States (The Bodley Head fonds, TEX). Leacock sold the opening sketch of the book to Albert A. Bryden of the *American Magazine* on 1 January 1913, and Bryden informed him on 23 July 1913 that "Behind the Beyond" is very successful (now out four days)."

The American edition was published on 31 October 1913 at $1. The copyright was registered with the Copyright Office at DLC on 6 November 1913 (ClA358127). The copyright was renewed on 16 January 1941.

By the end of 1913, 3,909 copies (thirteen copies reckoned as twelve, 3,609 sold at 15% royalty) had sold, earning Leacock a royalty of $541.35. According to an advertising brochure issued by the John Lane Company, the book was into its tenth "edition" (i.e. printing) by 1920 ($1.50 cloth). The previous year the royalty rate had been raised to 20%. By the end of 1921, when John Lane sold the American branch of his company to Dodd, Mead, 14,204 copies had sold of the American edition. In his notebook of royalty payments at SLM, Leacock recorded that 44,799 copies had sold of all editions by 1 February 1925.

On 17 November 1913 James L. Ford asked Leacock's permission to dramatize "Behind the Beyond" for an amateur production of the New York Stage Society (Ford and Leacock split the royalties). Ford's production premiered in New York on 2 February 1914 in New York. The Yale Dramatic Association also produced a dramatization of this sketch sometime before 13 November 1922. See also G3 for the dramatization by Clinton-Baddeley.

COPIES EXAMINED: CS (two copies in jacket of the first printing; advance copy; 1913 [1916], 1917, 1920, 1921 printings, none in jacket except the latter printing); OORI (1917 and 1918 printings, neither in jacket).

## A12a.1 *American issue* [1922?]):

BEHIND THE | ::: BEYOND ::: | AND OTHER CONTRIBUTIONS | TO HUMAN KNOWLEDGE | [thick-thin rule] | BY STEPHEN LEACOCK | AUTHOR OF "NONSENSE NOVELS," "LITERARY | : : : LAPSES," "SUNSHINE SKETCHES," ETC. : : : | [thin-thick rule] | ILLUSTRATED BY A. H. FISH | [illustration of a woman from the back sitting on a divan, a fan in one of her hands and a mask in the other] | [thick-thin rule] | NEW YORK | DODD, MEAD & COMPANY | 1923

Although this issue (185 × 132 mm.) is from the same setting of type as A12a, it lacks the frontispiece and other illustrations. The leaf with the list of illustrations has been deleted, and a blank leaf has been added at the end. The verso of the half title (p. 2) is blank. The copyright page reads: COPYRIGHT, 1913, BY | THE CROWELL PUBLISHING COMPANY | COPYRIGHT, 1913, BY | THE CENTURY COMPANY | COPYRIGHT, 1913, BY | DODD, MEAD & COMPANY | PRINTED IN U. S. A.

The binding is similar to A12a, but the upper board is blind-stamped and the Dodd, Mead imprint is stamped in gilt on the spine. The jacket is light blue with printing in dark blue, and is similar to that of A12a. Dodd, Mead's imprint replaces that of the John Lane Company. There is no price on the spine panel. A list of Leacock's books appears on the back panel of the jacket within three ornamental rectangles with the heading *LAUGH with LEACOCK*. On the front flap is an advertisement for the book (stating mistakenly that it comes with illustrations). The back flap has an advertisement for *My Discovery of England*.

The transcribed copy is the 1923 reprint. In all likelihood there was a printing in 1922, but no copy of that printing could be located. Also examined was a copy in maroon cloth (180 × 114 mm.) with Leacock's signature in facsimile stamped on the upper board. The sheets of this copy are the same as the transcribed copy except the verso of the half title has a list of books by Leacock. The jacket is cream-coloured with black lettering, rules and rectangles in red, and advertisements of the leather edition of Leacock's works.

NOTES: From the beginning of 1922 to February 1925, 1,852 copies sold. Between 1 February 1927 and 1 August 1933, 445 more copies sold. On 9 February 1923, Dodd, Mead proposed an "edition" in limp red leather at $2.50 retail, 30¢ royalty to Leacock. The OCLC WorldCat database records reprintings in 1926 and 1931.

COPIES EXAMINED: CS (1923 reprint, both variants).

## A12b *English edition* [1913]:

*BEHIND THE | :: BEYOND :: | & OTHER CONTRIBUTIONS | TO HUMAN KNOWLEDGE | BY STEPHEN LEACOCK | ILLUSTRATED BY A. H. FISH* | [illustration of a woman from the back sitting on a divan, a fan in one of her hands and a mask in the other] | *LONDON: JOHN LANE, THE BODLEY HEAD | NEW YORK: JOHN LANE COMPANY | TORONTO: BELL AND COCKBURN MCMXIV*

♦ $A^8$ B–M$^8$ N$^4$. *1–10, 11–52, 53–54, 55–92, 93–94, 95–158, 159–160, 161–168, 169–170, 171–184, 185–186, 187–196, 1–4* pp. (100 leaves). 189 × 29 mm.

CONTENTS: p. *1* half title; p. *2* list of three books by the same author within a rectangle (the fifth "edition" of *Literary Lapses*, the fifth "edition" of *Nonsense Novels*, and the fourth "edition" of *Sunshine Sketches of a Little Town*); p. *3* title; p. *4* WILLIAM BRENDON AND SON LTD, PRINTERS, PLYMOUTH; p. *5* table of contents; p. *6* blank; p. *7* list of illustrations; p. *8* blank; pp. *9–196, 1* text (pp. *10, 54, 94, 160, 170,* and *186* blank); pp. *2–4* advertisements with press opinions of Leacock's three other books published by The Bodley Head. Colour frontispiece with black-and-white illustrations facing pp. 11, 28, 32, 52, 60, 68, 74, 84, 90, 100, 116, 122, 144, 148, 166, and 174.

TEXT: Identical to A12a.

BINDING AND DUST JACKET: Bound in red cloth. Stamped on the upper board in gilt within two blind-stamped rectangles: *BEHIND THE BEYOND | By STEPHEN LEACOCK.* Stamped on the spine in gilt: [two rules blind-stamped] | *BEHIND | THE | BEYOND | By | STEPHEN | LEACOCK | THE | BODLEY HEAD* | [two rules blind-stamped].

The dust jacket is white with Fish's frontispiece illustration on the front panel. Printed on the spine panel: *BEHIND | THE | BEYOND | By | STEPHEN | LEACOCK* | THE BODLEY HEAD. On the back panel within a rectangle is new and forthcoming fiction. The front flap has the book's blurb; the back flap is blank.

Also examined was a copy bound in rust suede with pale marbled endpapers, top edge stained gilt. Stamped on the upper board in gilt within a green wreath of red flowers as follows: BEHIND | THE BEYOND | [rule] | LEACOCK. This variant lacks the final leaf of advertisements. This copy probably originated from sheets supplied to Bell and Cockburn since the final leaf was excised from the Canadian issue.

NOTES: In late April and May 1913 Leacock sent manuscripts or printed texts of his sketches for *Behind the Beyond* to B.W. Willett of The Bodley Head. He received page proofs on 9 September 1913. At that time he discussed the choice of illustration for the jacket, his favourite being "The Curtain Rises." He apparently also sent ". . . some extra copy to bring the book up to a better length" (The Bodley Head fonds, TEX). He returned the contract to John Lane on 9 December 1913, and informed him: "I am delighted with *Behind the Beyond* and am awfully glad to see that it is getting such a good reception. The booksellers here tell me that they are doing very well with it" (YALE). The contract with John Lane The Bodley Head at READ is dated 20 December 1913. Leacock received 15% on the English and American editions (thirteen copies reckoned as twelve) and 10% on the Canadian issue (to be paid by Bell & Cockburn). The book was published in November 1913 according to Leacock's notebooks of recorded publications, speeches, royalty payments at QMMRB and SLM. *The English Catalogue of Books* also has November 1913 at 3s 6d. By the end of 1913 3,903 had sold, 1,000 copies being for the Australasian market. Up to the end of February 1925, 21,709 copies sold of the English edition; of this number approximately 1,882 were sold to the Australasian market and 2,340 copies to the colonial market.

According to the 1931 reprint ("cheaper ed." published in June 1931 at 3s 6d), there were two reprints apiece in 1917 and 1919 and a reprinting in 1920.

In November 1921 The Bodley Head stopped the performance of "Behind the Beyond" in Australia and South Africa. It ". . . cost us a great deal of time and correspondence," Willett told Leacock on 3 November 1921. In Barbara Nimmo's papers at NAC, there is a brochure of a play based on the sketch by Marcus St. John and Mlle. La Roche. The brochure is printed in blue by William Brooks & Co. Ltd. The brochure describes Leacock's work, has excerpts from the press related to the dramatic recitation of the two actors, and pirates the illustrations from the book.

COPIES EXAMINED: CS (first printing in jacket and suede binding; fifth "edition," 1919 in jacket; fifth "edition," 1920, not in jacket; 1931 in jacket); QMMRB (fifth "edition," 1919, not in jacket).

## A12b.1 *first Canadian issue* [1913]:

The Canadian issue is identical to A12b with the following exceptions: the last leaf has been removed (the stub is present); BELL & COCKBURN is at the foot of the spine; the jacket also has the Canadian imprint on the spine panel, but otherwise is the same as that of the English edition.

Also examined were two copies in leather: black leather with floral designs stamped in gilt on the upper board and spine; green leather with floral compartments stamped in gilt on the spine. Both copies have OXFORD stamped on the spine. This would indicate that they were sold by the Canadian branch of Oxford University Press, which was managed by S.B. Gundy (see also A12b.3).

NOTES: Leacock arranged for publication of the Canadian issue with W.C. Bell. He informed Bell on 3 April 1913:

But meantime I have other stuff: The American Magazine is to publish in a month or so an imitation play of mine called *Behind the Beyond*. It is a satire on the modern problem play. It contains 7500 words. Mr. Johnson [of the John Lane Company] is going to publish it either all by itself or as a 50 cent book like those of Julian Street — or as a more expensive book, putting with it other fugitive writings that I have ready. But I feel sure that the separate small book is best. I presume that you would like to take this is on for Canada. . . . (Bell fonds, OTUTF)

Leacock asked Bell to get in touch with Johnson about publication in Canada. He also referred to another possible book entitled "A Holiday in Paris." Leacock and Bell corresponded on 11 June 1913 and 9 September [1913] about publication plans. Leacock also originally conceived "Familiar Incidents" as a separate book. By September of that year he decided to amalgamate these three separate projects into one book.

According to Leacock's notebook of royalty payments at SLM, 5,150 copies of the Canadian issue (price $1.25) sold by the end of December 1913 ($965.62 royalty). 615 further copies were reported as having been sold by Bell and Cockburn on 7 December 1914 just before the company went bankrupt.

COPIES EXAMINED: CS (cloth, not in jacket; copies in leather with OXFORD on the spine); QMMRB (in jacket).

## A12b.2 *Australasian issue* [1913]:

The copyright page of this issue reads: AUSTRALASIAN EDITION | WILLIAM BRENDON AND SON, LTD. PRINTERS, PLYMOUTH. The last leaf (advertisements) has been excised. In other respects this issue is the same as 12b. The copy that was examined was rebound. Leacock received 10% royalty for Australasian issue. See the notes to 12b for number of copies sold.

COPIES EXAMINED: RED.

## A12b.3 *second Canadian issue* (1915):

*BEHIND THE | :: BEYOND :: | & OTHER CONTRIBUTIONS | TO HUMAN KNOWLEDGE | BY STEPHEN LEACOCK | ILLUSTRATED BY A. H. FISH |* [illustration of a woman from the back sitting on a divan, a fan in one of her hands and a mask in the other] *| LONDON: JOHN LANE, THE BODLEY HEAD | NEW YORK: JOHN LANE COMPANY | TORONTO: S. B. GUNDY MCMXV | Published in Canada for Humphrey Milford.*

Cancel title. The verso of the title leaf reads: WILLIAM BRENDON AND SON, LTD., PRINTERS, PLYMOUTH, ENGLAND. *GUNDY* is stamped in gilt at the foot of the spine. Otherwise, this issue is identical to 12b.1. Dust jacket not examined.

Two variant bindings were examined: a copy bound in half brown leather with pink boards, top edge stained gilt, rules and floral ornaments stamped on the spine in gilt. There is a black label on the spine stamped in gilt as follows: BEHIND | THE | BEYOND | [rule] | STEPHEN | LEACOCK. The other variant binding is identical to the one described in A12b.1 (green leather with floral compartments and OXFORD stamped in gilt on the spine).

NOTES: See the notes to A11a.3 for the transfer of the Canadian rights in *Behind the Beyond* to S.B. Gundy. In his notebook of royalty payments at SLM, Leacock recorded that Oxford University Press sold 144 copies by 30 June 1915. Undoubtedly, some of these copies were from Bell and Cockburn's sheets. Leacock noted that on 1 July 1920 Oxford University

Press did not have any stock left of the Canadian issue. By 1 January 1925 Gundy had sold 1,270 copies.

COPIES: OORI (half brown leather with pink boards); QMMRB (no jacket); SLM (green leather, Leacock's copy).

### A12c *second English edition* (1928):

[all lines within two rectangles; between the rectangles is a series of small squares] BEHIND THE BEYOND | and other contributions | to human knowledge | *by* | STEPHEN LEACOCK | JOHN LANE | THE BODLEY HEAD LTD

◆ $A^4 B–G^{16} H^{12}$ [$1 signed]. *i–vi*, vii, *1–3, 3–50, 51–52, 53–94, 95–96, 97–168, 169–170, 171–179, 180–182, 183–198, 199–200, 201–213, 1–3* pp. (112 leaves). 170 × 113 mm.

CONTENTS: pp. *i–ii* blank; p. *iii* half title (with series name); p. *iv* blank; p. *v* title; p. *vi First published in . . . . . 1913* | [five lines listing reprints] | *First published in The Week-End Library. 1928* | Made and Printed in Great Britain by Butler & Tanner Ltd., Frome and London; p. vii table of contents; p. *1* blank; pp. *2–3, 3–213* text (pp. *3, 52, 96, 170, 180, 182,* and *200* blank); p. *1* blank; pp. *2–3* advertisement for the Week-End Library series.

TEXT: Identical to A12a.

BINDING AND DUST JACKET: Bound in dark red cloth, top edge stained dark red. Blind-stamped along the edges of the upper board is a series of small squares; also stamped on the upper board in gilt is Leacock's signature in facsimile. The title, author's name, and ornamental rules are stamped in gilt on the spine.

The jacket is light blue with printing in black. On the front panel of the jacket is the title, Leacock's name, price (3s 6d), and an illustration of the front door of The Bodley Head's building (with the series title in the top right-hand corner). The back panel has a list of titles in the Week-End Library series within a rectangle. Printed on the spine panel are ornamental rules, the title, Leacock's name, and the price. The front flap has quotations from the *Spectator* and *Punch*. The back flap is blank.

Also examined was a 1937 reprint in pink cloth, no. 12 in The Bodley Head Library series.

NOTES: Number of copies printed not known. Price 3s 6d. Lomer (p. 22) has 9 March 1928 as the date of publication. According to *The English Catalogue of Books*, this edition was published in the Week-End Library series in March 1928; the same source records that the 1937 impression was reprinted in November of that year.

COPIES EXAMINED: CS (1937 reprint); GZM (first printing, no jacket); SLM (Leacock's copy in jacket).

### A12d *first Canadian edition* (1969):

[all lines within three rectangles, the outer one thick; the rectangles are inside an ornamental rectangular border] *Stephen Leacock* | BEHIND | THE BEYOND | *and* | *Other Contributions* | *to Human Knowledge* | INTRODUCTION: DONALD CAMERON | GENERAL EDITOR: MALCOLM ROSS | NEW CANADIAN LIBRARY NO. 67 | [publisher's device: abstract design within an oval of a person on a horse-drawn chariot, taking aim with a bow and arrow] |

## MCCLELLAND AND STEWART LIMITED | TORONTO/MONTREAL

♦ *i–v*, vi–viii, *ix*, x, *1–5*, 16–22, *23*, 24, 25, 26, 27, *28–33*, 34, *35–37*, *38*, 39, *40–42*, 43–45, 46, 47–49, *50*, 51, *52*, 53, 54, *55–57*, *58*, 59, *60*, *61–63*, 64–66, 67, 68, *69–72*, 73, *74–76*, 77, *78–79*, *80*, 81, 82, *83–86*, 87, *88–92*, 93, 94, *95*, 96, 97, *98–102*, *103–104*, 105–106, *107*, 108, *109–110*, *111–112*, *113*, 114–117, *118–120*, 121–125, *1–3* pp. (114 leaves). 184 × 111 mm.

CONTENTS: p. *i* half title; p. *ii* frontispiece; p. *iii* Copyright © 1916 by John Lane Company | Introduction copyright © 1969 by McClelland and Stewart, Limited | Illustrations, from the original edition, by A. H. Fish | ALL RIGHTS RESERVED | *The Canadian Publishers* | McClelland and Stewart Limited | 25 Hollinger Road, Toronto 16 | PRINTED AND BOUND IN ENGLAND BY | HAZELL WATSON AND VINEY LTD | AYLESBURY, BUCKS; pp. *v*, vi–viii Donald Cameron's introduction; pp. *ix–x* table of contents; pp. *1–2* list of illustrations; pp. *3–5*, 16–125 text (pp. *40, 64,* and *118* blank); p. *1* biographical information about the author; pp. *2–3* list of books in the New Canadian Library series. Illustrations on pp. *4, 23, 27, 38, 52, 58, 68, 77, 82, 93, 97, 107,* and *113*.

TEXT: Identical to A12a.

BINDING: Perfect bound in pink, white, and black stiff pictorial wrappers. The front cover has a black-and-white sketch of Leacock with an irregular, pink vertical band on the left side. On the back cover are two pink bands and information about the book. Cover design by William Henry. Price: $1.50. N67 of the NCL series.

NOTES: By the end of the spring 1969, 938 copies sold; 1,419 copies sold by the end of the year. By the end of 1979 8,749 copies had sold (information based on file 14, "New Canadian Library," box 93, series A, part I, McClelland and Stewart fonds, OHM).

Lomer (p. 22) records a "reprint" published by McClelland and Stewart in 1937, but no such copy was located.

COPIES EXAMINED: CS (first and second impressions, the latter printed by T.H. Best Printing Company Limited); OORI (first printing).

## A13 THE METHODS OF MR. SELLYER 1914

### A13a *American edition*:

[all lines within two light brown rectangles] THE METHODS | [two light brown rules] *of* [two light brown rules] | MR. SELLYER | [two light brown rules touching the inner rectangle] | *A Book Store Study* | BY | STEPHEN LEACOCK | AUTHOR OF | *"Behind the Beyond"* | *"Nonsense Novels"* | *"Literary Lapses,"* etc. | [two light brown rules touching the inner rectangle] | NEW YORK | JOHN LANE COMPANY | MCMXIV

♦ *1–5⁴*. *1–40* pp. (20 leaves). 174 × 98 mm.

CONTENTS: p. *1* THE METHODS OF | MR. SELLYER | [rule] | WRITTEN BY | STEPHEN LEACOCK | ESPECIALLY FOR | THE ANNUAL CONVENTION | OF THE | AMERI-CAN BOOKSELLERS' | ASSOCIATION | MAY FOURTEENTH | 1914 | PRESENTED BY | JOHN LANE COMPANY, NEW YORK | PRINTED AND BOUND BY | J. J. LITTLE & IVES COMPANY | NEW YORK; p. 2 blank; p. 3 half title; p. 4 blank; p. *5* title; p. 6 Copyright, 1914, by | JOHN LANE COMPANY: p. dedication: TO | THE BOOKSELLERS | OF | THE UNITED STATES AND CANADA; p. 8 blank; pp. *9–37* text; pp. *38–40* blank.

BINDING: Bound in camel cloth, quarter-bound in brown leather, top edge stained in gilt. Stamped in gilt on the upper board: [all lines with two rectangles] | THE METHODS | of | MR. SELLYER | STEPHEN LEACOCK. All type in the book is dark brown. The text features rules and illustrations of books in light brown.

NOTES: According to Leacock's notebook of recorded publications and speeches at QMMRB, *The Methods of Mr. Sellyer* was "Published as Presentation Booklet. J.L. Co. N.Y." on 11 April 1914. Number of copies printed not known. However, according to Raymond T. Bond's letter to Gerhard R. Lomer of 7 September 1950 (Lomer fonds at QMM Archives), the book was published on 13 May 1914. The latter date of publication is confirmed by the Copyright Office at DLC. The copyright was registered on 16 May 1914 (ClA374103). The book sold for 50¢. The copyright was renewed by Leacock on 23 January 1942. Lomer (p. 41) cites an English edition: "London, Lane, 1914. 37 p." No copy of an English edition is known to be extant. Leacock's sketch was later retitled "The Reading Public: A Book Store Study" when it appeared in *Moonbeams from the Larger Lunacy* (A15). Reprinted in the *Bodleian* 6, no. 63 (June 1914): 811–5.

COPIES EXAMINED: CS; LAT (three copies); OONL; OTUTF; QMMRB.


**A13b** *Canadian edition* entitled *The Reading Public: A Bookstore Study* (1995):

THE READING | PUBLIC | [silhouette in red of a person wearing a broad-brimmed hat] | *A Bookstore Study by* | STEPHEN LEACOCK | *with an Afterword by* | TIMOTHY FINDLEY | LAKE SIMCOE ONTARIO CANADA 1995

♦ $1^{12}$. *1*–6, 7–14, *15*–16, *17*–20, *1*–4 pp. (12 leaves). 216 × 138 mm.

CONTENTS: p. *1* half title; p. *2* *Issued* | *in celebration of* | *the tenth anniversary of* | PETER GZOWSKI'S | INVITATIONALS | *for Canadian literacy* | *7 June 1995.* | *Publication* | *has been made possible* | *by a generous donation from* | SUPERIOR PROPANE INC. | *through its international For Literacy project*; p. *3* title; p. *4* THE READING PUBLIC | Printed in Canada | This edition | Copyright © 1995 | Hedge Road Press Ltd. | Post Office Box 488 | Sutton West | Ontario | LoE 1Ro | AFTERWORD | Copyright © 1995 | Timothy Findley | SUPERIOR PROPANE INC. | 75 Tiverton Court | Unionville | Ontario | L3R 9S3; p. *5* Gzowski' foreword; p. *6* blank; pp. 7–14 text; p. *15* fly title for Findley's afterword; p. *16* blank; pp. *17*–20 Findley's afterword; p. *1* information on Leacock, Findley, and Peter Sibbald Brown; p. *2* blank; p. *3* colophon; p. *4* blank.

BINDING AND DUST JACKET: Bound in flecked orange, stiff paper, wire-stitched. The jacket is from the same paper stock as the wrapper. Printed on the front panel of the jacket: THE READING | PUBLIC | [silhouette in red of a person wearing a broad-brimmed hat] | STEPHEN | LEACOCK | *with an Afterword by* | TIMOTHY FINDLEY.

NOTES: In his foreword Gzowksi states that this publication is "... the second example of Peter Sibbald Brown's typographic artistry to adorn one of our evenings at the Red Barn." See the notes to A132 which provide background information. According to the colophon, this pamphlet was designed by Brown and printed with Bembo type at Toronto for the Hedge Road Press.

Published on 7 June 1995 in an edition of 500 copies. Distributed free to people who attended the festivities at the Red Barn Theatre on Jackson's Point the night before

Gzowksi's golf tournament, the Peter Gzowski Invitational. See also "Rallying Round Literacy," *Maclean's* 108, no. 25 (19 June 1995): 6.

COPIES EXAMINED: CS; OTNY; SLM.

## A14 MY FINANCIAL CAREER AND HOW TO MAKE A MILLION DOLLARS 1914

### A14a *first issue*:

[all lines and illustrations in green unless otherwise indicated] MY FINANCIAL CAREER | *and* | HOW TO MAKE A MILLION DOLLARS | [illustration, primarily in orange, of a bank teller's window with a stack of money, coins, and a passbook] | Stephen Leacock | COPYRIGHT 1914 | [diamond-shaped ornament] THE [diamond-shaped ornament] | WINTHROP PRESS | NEW [illustration of a bird with its wings spread] YORK

◆ $1^{16}$. The title leaf and its conjugate, which are from a glossy paper stock, are not part of the collation. 1–2, 1–13, 14, 15–32, 1–2 pp. (18 leaves counting the title leaf and its conjugate). 71 × 56 mm.

CONTENTS: p. *1* title; p. *2* colour illustration of four men in suits, three seated smoking cigars, one standing smoking a cigarette, with caption: What I love to do is walk up and | down among them.; pp. *1*–*13* text; p. *14* blank; pp. *15*–*32* text; p. *1* blank; p. *2* twenty lines in green within an orange, ornamental rectangle; the lines begin: It is our intention to present to | our friends many of the best short | stories ever published. The last ten lines list names of authors whose stories will be published by The Winthrop Press.

TEXT: My Financial Career; How to Make a Million Dollars.

BINDING: Bound in pictorial wrappers, wire-stitched. The wrapper and the title leaf (and its conjugate) are from the same glossy paper stock. The front of the wrapper features a colour illustration within a rectangle of a man's head and shoulders; he is wearing a hat, jacket, and bow-tie, and is behind the wicket of a bank. Above the illustration: MY FINANCIAL CAREER. Below the illustration: *by* STEPHEN LEACOCK | [the next two lines in the lower left-hand corner of the rectangle] © | W.R.

On the inside of the front wrapper are twenty-one lines in green within an orange, ornamental rectangle; the first eleven lines are a quotation (in italics) from Edgar Allan Poe, and the last ten lines give the source of the two sketches (*Literary Lapses*) and acknowledge permission from John Lane Company, Publishers, N.Y. The first issue has a diamond-shaped design on the back wrapper in blue. At the top of the design is a lion standing on two legs with ornaments on either side. At the bottom of the design are ornaments and a bird with wings outstretched. In the centre of the design are the following three lines: BOOKS SHOULD TO ONE OF | THESE FOUR ENDS CONDUCE: | FOR WISDOM, PIETY, DELIGHT OR USE. The inside of the back wrapper has the following lines in green within an orange, ornamental rectangle: The World's Best | Short Stories | now presented with | [the next line curved and in shadowed type] OMAR | TURKISH BLEND | CIGARETTES | One Story accompanying | each package | 100 Titles ready-more | in preparation.

NOTES: This miniature, which reprints C95.1 and C10.14, was distributed in different promotional ways: within a package of cigarettes (first issue); given to customers buying silk products (second issue); given to customers of a piano company (third issue); for the use of troops in the American military (fourth issue). Published on 17 September 1914. The copyright was registered with the Copyright Office at DLC on 23 September 1914 (Entry, Cl. A, XXc, No. A386054). The number of copies printed of each issue is not known. There is no apparent priority in the first three issues. Reference is made in the fourth issue to the American participation in the First World War. This would indicate that the fourth issue was published after April 1917, when the United States declared war on Germany.

The transcription of the title page, the collation, the illustration on p. 2, and the text are the same in all issues. The pagination is also identical, except that p. 32 is paginated in the first issue and not paginated in the other issues.

The Winthrop Press (and later John H. Eggers Co.) published at least sixty different titles of these miniatures. The first issue states that 100 titles are "in preparation." See, for example, the miniatures authored by Edgar Allan Poe described in *BAL*: items 16246, 16247, and 16248.

COPIES EXAMINED: CS; OTUTF.

## A14a.1 *second issue*:

The leaves of the second issue measure 70 × 54 mm. In the second issue the conjugate of the title leaf, which is not paginated, has information on buying a silk dress; the names of various fabrics are provided such as Mallinson's Silks de Luxe, Pussy Willow, etc. In the copy examined of the second issue, the printing of the text is too high on the pages, almost to the point of cropping the ascenders of letters.

BINDING: The front of the wrapper is identical to the first issue, but the colouring is more vibrant in the second issue. On the inside of the front wrapper are eighteen lines in green within an orange, ornamental rectangle. The first eight lines are a quotation in italics; the ninth line reads: — COWPER: Retirement.; the remaining nine lines give the source of the sketches (*Literary Lapses*). On the back of the wrapper of the second issue are seven different Mallinson trade-mark names in varying typefaces (screened, outline, etc.). The information on how to buy a silk dress from the conjugate of the title leaf is continued on the inside of the back of the wrapper.

COPY EXAMINED: CS.

## A14a.2 *third issue*:

The leaves of the third issue measure 73 × 55 mm. In the third issue the conjugate of the title leaf, which is not paginated, has information about the Mansfield Piano Co.

BINDING: The front of the wrapper is identical to the first issue. The verso of the front wrapper is identical to that of the second issue. On the back of the wrapper of the third issue is the following: Mansfield Piano Co. | [rule] MANUFACTURERS OF [rule] | PIANOS AND PLAYER PIANOS | 135TH ST. AND WILLOW AVE., NEW YORK | [two rules]. The verso of the back wrapper is as follows: The . . . | Mansfield | [two rules] | Piano | AND | Concertone | [two rules] | Player Piano | [ornament] | ARE SOLD FROM COAST TO COAST.

COPY EXAMINED: LAT.

**A14a.3** *fourth issue* [1917?]:

The conjugate of the title leaf is blank.

BINDING AND SLEEVE: The front of the wrapper, including its verso, is identical to the second issue, although the colouring is somewhat blurry. On the back of the wrapper of the fourth issue: 𝕶𝖓𝖎𝖌𝖍𝖙𝖘 𝖔𝖋 𝕮𝖔𝖑𝖚𝖒𝖇𝖚𝖘 | *Committee on War Activities* | [rule] | [three paragraphs, consisting of seventeen lines, stating that the Knights of Columbus "have aided the Nation in every war since the Knights have been established . . . [and] are ready now and always to lend a helping hand to every boy in the American uniform." The inside of the back wrapper, printed in green, has a statement from John H. Eggers Co., Inc., The House of Little Books, New York, indicating that the company is publishing "in this form some of the World's Best Short Stories. Twelve sets of five titles each are now ready and additional titles are now ready, and will be issued shortly." Seventeen authors are mentioned whose works will be published "and many more."

Enclosed in a cardboard sleeve with three miniature imprints by Maurice Brown Kirby and Philip E. Curtiss's *The Bow-Legs of Destiny*. The front of the sleeve is in green, orange, and white with a vignette of a sailing ship, two vertical rules, and the title Short Stories. The back of the sleeve has a solid green rectangle and inside it an orange rectangle. Inside the rectangles are paragraphs similar to the back wrapper. The additional lines are: There are twelve different sets | of Stories similar to those inclosed | in this package. This is set No. 3 | [rule] | Presented with Compliments of | KNIGHTS OF COLUMBUS | Committee on War Activities.

COPY EXAMINED: QMMRB.

## A15  NUMBER FIFTY-SIX  1914

**A15a** *first issue*:

[all lines and illustrations in green unless otherwise indicated; the first two lines in a rectangular compartment with the letters resembling chopsticks and N, F, and S in orange] Number | Fifty-Six | [illustration of the head and shoulders of a Chinese man with Chinese letters on small orange posters on either side; the next two lines within a rectangle and with angled letters] | by | Stephen Leacock | [illustration of a green and orange vase containing reeds with wispy lines extending to the poster on the left side of the Chinese man; to the left of the vase is the following:] COPYRIGHT 1914 | [ornament] THE [ornament] | WINTHROP PRESS | NEW YORK | [illustration in the shape of an inverted pyramid consisting of ornaments and a bird with its wings spread]

◆ $1^{16}$. The title leaf and its conjugate, which are from a glossy paper stock, are not part of the collation. 1–2, 1–31, 1–3 pp. (18 leaves counting the title leaf and its conjugate). 71 × 56 mm.

CONTENTS: p. *1* title; p. *2* colour illustration of two men, one of a Chinese person holding a candlestick and pointing to a picture and the other man in a suit with a pipe in his mouth. Caption: "The picture is, of course, an ideal one."; pp. 1–31, *1* text; p. *1* blank; p. *2* twenty-two lines in green within an orange, ornamental rectangle; the first three lines are: It is our intention to present to | our friends many of the best short | stories ever published. . . . The last eleven lines list names of authors whose stories will be published by The Winthrop Press.

BINDING: Bound in pictorial wrappers, wire-stitched. The wrapper and the title leaf (and its conjugate) are from the same glossy paper stock. The front of the wrapper features a colour illustration within a rectangle of a Chinese man at a laundry who is holding up a shirt with a red stain on it. At the top of the illustration in red: NUMBER | FIFTY-SIX | [in blackish red] *by Stephen Leacock.*

On the inside of the front wrapper are nineteen lines in green. The first eight lines are a quotation in italics. The next line is: — Cowper — Retirement. The remaining lines give the source of the story (*Literary Lapses*) and acknowledge permission from John Lane Company, Publishers, N.Y. The back of the wrapper (including its verso) is identical to that of A14a, but the blue is darker on the back wrapper.

NOTES: Published on 8 October 1914. The copyright was registered with the Copyright Office at DLC on 19 October 1914 (Entry, Cl. A, XXc, No. A389081). For information on the publication of this miniature, see the notes to A14a.

COPY EXAMINED: OTUTF.

## A15a.1 *second issue*:

The leaves of the second issue measure 71 × 55 mm. In the second issue the conjugate of the title leaf has information on buying a silk dress; the names of various fabrics are provided such as Mallinson's Silks de Luxe, Pussy Willow, etc. On the copy examined (pp. 23–24), the title is partially printed on the outer margin.

BINDING: The front of the wrapper is identical to the first issue. On the inside of the front wrapper are eighteen lines in green within an orange, ornamental rectangle. The first eight lines are a quotation in italics; the ninth line reads: — COWPER: Retirement.; the remaining nine lines give the source of the sketches (*Literary Lapses*). On the back of the wrapper of the second issue are seven different Mallinson trade-mark names in varying typefaces (screened, outline, etc.). The information on how to buy a silk dress from the conjugate of the title leaf is continued on the inside of the back of the wrapper.

COPY EXAMINED: CS.

*Signed.*

## A16 ARCADIAN ADVENTURES WITH THE IDLE RICH 1914

### A16a *American edition*:

ARCADIAN | ADVENTURES | WITH THE IDLE RICH | [thick-thin rule] | BY STEPHEN LEACOCK | AUTHOR OF "BEHIND THE BEYOND" | "NONSENSE NOVELS," "LITERARY LAPSES," ETC. | [thin-thick rule] | [thick-thin rule] | NEW YORK : JOHN LANE COMPANY | LONDON : JOHN LANE, THE BODLEY HEAD | TORONTO : BELL & COCKBURN : MCMXIV | [thin-thick rule]

◆ *1–19*[8] *20*[6]. *1–8, 9–310, 1–6* pp. (158 leaves). 184 × 126 mm.

CONTENTS: p. *1* half title; p. *2* list of four other books by the same author; p. *3* title; p. *4* COPYRIGHT, 1914, BY | THE CROWELL PUBLISHING COMPANY | [rule] | COPY-RIGHT, 1914, BY | JOHN LANE COMPANY; p. *5* table of contents; p. *6* blank; p. *7* fly title; p. *8* blank; pp. *9–310* text; pp. *1–6* blank.

TEXT: chapter I A Little Dinner with Mr. Lucullus Fyshe; chapter II The Wizard of Finance; chapter III The Arrested Philanthropy of Mr. Tomlinson; chapter IV The Yahi-Bahi Oriental Society of Mrs. Rasselyer-Brown; chapter V The Love Story of Mr. Peter Spillikins; chapter VI The Rival Churches of St. Asaph and St. Osoph; chapter VII The Ministrations of the Rev. Uttermust Dumfarthing; chapter VIII The Great Fight for Clean Government.

BINDING AND DUST JACKET: Bound in red cloth. Stamped on the upper board: [within two gold rectangles is a solid gold rectangle, which contains raised red characters] ARCAD-IAN ADVENTURES | WITH THE IDLE RICH | [rule] | STEPHEN LEACOCK. Stamped in gilt on the spine: ARCADIAN | ADVENTURES | WITH THE | IDLE RICH | [rule] | LEACOCK | JOHN LANE | COMPANY.

The jacket is white with a colour illustration on the front panel of a woman in an evening gown who is standing on a set of stairs between two columns draped in garlands. She is carrying a lamb and a shepherd's crook. A young person, wearing a grass skirt and holding a top hat, offers her a plate of coins. Printing on the other panels is in blue. Printed on the spine panel: ARCADIAN | ADVENTURES | *with the* | IDLE RICH | [rule] | *STEPHEN* | *LEACOCK* | Author of | "Nonsense Novels," | "Behind the Beyond," | etc. | *$1.25* Net | JOHN LANE | COMPANY. On the back panel is a list of the latest fiction. The front flap features an advertisement of the book with a quotation from the *American Magazine*. An advertisement for the *International Studio* is found on the back flap.

NOTES: On 5 November 1912 Leacock wrote to W.A. Johnson of the John Lane Company:

> It is very likely that my next book will deal with the *Idle Rich* and will be called *Arcadian Adventures* with the *Idle Rich*. It will probably be in about 12 instalments of 5000 words each (thats [sic] only a guess, none of it is written). I can easily dispose of the serial rights here. But perhaps I'D [sic] better wait till I have some chapters of it done before I discuss it further with you." (The Bodley Head fonds, TEX)

According to his notebook of recorded publications and speeches at QMMRB, Leacock completed chapter I on 19 February 1914, chapter II on 10 March, chapter III on 24 March, chapter IV on 20 April, chapter V on 6 May, chapter VI on 12 July, chapter VII on 1 August, and chapter VIII on 5 August. See also Leacock's notebook at SLM (J84) which has outlines of various tables of contents and tentative chapters. Manuscripts of chapters 1, 4, 5, and 7 are at QMMRB.

"I am awfully pleased that you like the opening pages of *Arcadian Adventures*," Leacock told Johnson on 28 April 1913. "I hope to send along more but it may be rather slow work — or perhaps very fast. I don't know" (TEX). The first five chapters appeared in the *American Magazine* between July and November 1914 (see C14.9, C14.13-5, C14.17, and C14.21). The remaining chapters were not published prior to their appearance in book form. The American edition was published on 31 October 1914 (date confirmed by the Copyright Office at DLC and R.T. Bond's letter to Gerhard R. Lomer, 7 September 1950, Lomer fonds at QMM Archives). The copyright was registered on 6 November 1914 (ClA388252). The copyright was renewed on 4 February 1942.

When he received his six author's copies of the American edition, Leacock conveyed his appreciation to John Lane on 11 November 1914. Yet he was pessimistic about the book's chances of success: "Unfortunately there is every sign here that the market will be a dull one. Nobody reads anything. But I hope that the book will do well sooner or later." On the next day, 12 November 1914, upon reading the "most glowing reviews . . . from all over the United States, longer & better than I ever had before," his mood was buoyant (TEX). With regard to the contract for this edition, see the notes to A16b.

By the end of 1914 3,403 copies had sold of the American edition, earning Leacock a royalty of $588.93. Up to the end of 1922, when the John Lane Company was sold to Dodd, Mead, 7,767 copies had been sold (Leacock's notebook of royalty payments at SLM). According to an advertising brochure, the book was into its "Fourth Edition" by 1920 ($1.50 cloth).

Leacock recorded that up 1 February 1925, 37,990 copies had sold for all editions.

Chapter VI reprinted in Carl F. Klinck and Reginald E. Watters, eds., *Canadian Anthology* (Toronto: Gage, 1974), pp. 170–83; Michael Benazon, ed., *Montreal Mon Amour Short Stories form Montreal* (Toronto: Deneau, 1989), pp. 2–18.

COPIES EXAMINED: CS (three copies, one in jacket); LAT (in jacket); QMMRB (in jacket).

## A16a.1 *first Canadian issue:*

The Canadian issue is identical to A16a with the following exceptions: BELL | AND | COCKBURN is at the foot of the spine; the jacket has the Canadian imprint on the spine panel, has an advertisement for BOOKS BY STEPHEN LEACOCK on the back panel, and is blank on the back flap.

NOTES: On 3 April 1913 Leacock informed W.C. Bell that *Arcadian Adventures* ". . . has not yet reached the advertising stage. Hardly any of it is written and in any case it is likely that Mr. Walter Johnson (John Lane Co) will arrange to serialise it before book publication. This would take a long time" (Bell fonds, OTUTF). On 10 August 1914 Bell agreed to pay Leacock a royalty of 20% on "stock from New York." The edition consisted of 4,000 copies (price $1.25), and Leacock received a royalty of $1,000. By 12 November 1914 Leacock complained to John Lane that Bell and Cockburn had not yet paid the royalties due on 1 July 1914. The company was in financial difficulty, and Leacock was unable to get any definite assurance of payment at that time. "Under these circumstances I am quite sure that you will understand my point of view when I say that I should not wish to have any royalties paid by you through an order on them," Leacock told Lane (The Bodley Head fonds, TEX).

For the second and third issues, see A16b.2 and A16b.3.

COPIES EXAMINED: CS (two copies, one in jacket); QMMRB (not in jacket).

## A16a.2 *fourth Canadian issue* (1920):

ARCADIAN | ADVENTURES | WITH THE IDLE RICH | [thick-thin rule] | BY STEPHEN LEACOCK | AUTHOR OF "BEHIND THE BEYOND" | "NONSENSE NOVELS," "LITERARY LAPSES," ETC. | [thin-thick rule] | [thick-thin rule] | NEW YORK: JOHN LANE COMPANY | LONDON: JOHN LANE, THE BODLEY HEAD | MCMXXX | [thin-thick rule]

Bound in red cloth with stamping on the boards in black as in A16a but with GUNDY on the spine. Dust jacket not seen. This is the 1920 impression of the American edition; two extra blank leaves are at the beginning. Although Gundy obtained copies of the book through The Bodley Head, it would appear that Gundy ran out of stock sometime in 1920 and received a small number of copies from the John Lane Company. For sales by Gundy, see the notes to A16b.3.

COPIES EXAMINED: CS.

**A16a.3**  *American issue* (1922):

ARCADIAN | ADVENTURES | WITH THE IDLE RICH | [thick-thin rule] | BY STEPHEN LEACOCK | AUTHOR OF "BEHIND THE BEYOND" | "NONSENSE NOVELS," "LITERARY LAPSES," ETC. | [thin-thick rule] | [thick-thin rule] | NEW YORK | DODD, MEAD AND COMPANY | 1922

* $1-20^8$ $20^2$. *1–12, 9–310, 1–10* pp. (162 leaves). 189 × 135 mm.

The first two leaves and the last four leaves are blank. The copyright page reads: COPYRIGHT, 1914, BY | THE CROWELL PUBLISHING COMPANY | [rule] | COPYRIGHT, 1914, BY | JOHN LANE COMPANY | PRINTED IN U. S. A. The page facing the title leaf lists seven other books by the same author. In other respects the sheets of this issue are identical to those of A16a.

The binding is similar to A16a, but the upper board is blind-stamped and the Dodd, Mead imprint is stamped in gilt on the spine. Dust jacket not seen.

NOTES: According to Leacock's notebook of royalty payments at SLM, Dodd, Mead sold 143 copies of this issue up to 1 August 1922 after the company had purchased the American branch of John Lane. By February 1925 746 copies had been sold. Thereafter, sales were negligible. Between 1 February and 1 August 1927, for example, twenty-five copies sold; only four copies sold between 1 February and 1 August 1928.

On 10 January 1925 Grosset & Dunlap approached Dodd, Mead to reprint "some of the slower titles": 75¢ apiece, print run of 5000 copies, at 10¢ royalty (half to Leacock, half to Dodd, Mead). When Leacock gave his assent to this proposal, Frank Dodd informed Leacock on 9 February 1925 that Grosset & Dunlap was planning to reprint *Arcadian Adventures* in the fall of that year. Dodd assured Leacock on 18 February 1925: "You may be sure we shall not consider reprint editions of LITERARY LAPSES and NONSENSE NOVELS for the present anyway. I shall insist on Grosset taking only the books which have a small sale in the regular edition, or none at all." No copies of the projected issue by Grosset & Dunlap have been located.

COPIES EXAMINED: BUFF.

**A16b**  *English edition* [1914]:

*ARCADIAN ADVENTURES | WITH THE IDLE RICH | BY STEPHEN LEACOCK | [thick-thin rule] | [thin-thick rule] | LONDON: JOHN LANE THE BODLEY HEAD | NEW YORK: JOHN LANE COMPANY | TORONTO: BELL & COCKBURN MCMXV*

* $A^4$ $B-U^8$ $X^2$ $Y^8$ [$1 signed]. *1–8, 1–303, 1–21* pp. (166 leaves). 191 × 128 mm.

CONTENTS: p. *1* half title; p. *2* list of four other books by the same author; p. *3* title; p. *4* THE ANCHOR PRESS, LTD., TIPTREE ESSEX.; p. *5* table of contents; p. *6* blank; p. *7* fly title; p. *8* blank; pp. *1–303, 1* text; pp. *2–5* advertisements with press opinion for *Nonsense Novels* ("seventh edition"), *Literary Lapses* ("seventh edition"), *Behind the Beyond*, and *Sunshine Sketches of a Little Town* ("fifth edition"); pp. *6–21* John Lane's list of fiction; p. *21* advertisement for the New Pocket Library.

TEXT: Identical to A16a.

BINDING AND DUST JACKET: Bound in dark blue cloth, top edge stained blue. Stamped on the upper board in light blue within two blind-stamped rectangles: *ARCADIAN ADVEN-*

*TURES | WITH THE IDLE RICH | By STEPHEN LEACOCK*. Stamped on the spine in light blue: [two rules blind-stamped] | *ARCADIAN | ADVENTURES | WITH THE | IDLE RICH | By | STEPHEN | LEACOCK | THE | BODLEY HEAD |* [two rules blind-stamped].

The dust jacket has the same illustration as A16a on the front panel, although the title and Leacock's name appear in italics and in blue. Printed on the spine panel in red: *ARCADIAN | ADVENTURES | WITH THE | IDLE RICH | by | STEPHEN | LEACOCK | 3/6 | NET | THE BODLEY HEAD.* On the back panel in blue is a list of new and forthcoming novels. The flaps were clipped on the only known extant jacket of the book.

NOTES: On 2 February 1914 Leacock informed B.W. Willett of The Bodley Head that "I expect to have the whole MSS of my *Arcadian Adventures with the Idle Rich* ready by Sep 1st." By 6 May 1914 he had written 43,000 words. He left for France shortly thereafter. While in Paris on 6 July 1914, Leacock was unable to find a typist who understood English. He proposed sending the manuscript to Willett so that it could be typed there with a copy provided to the John Lane Company. He asked Willett to begin printing so that he could read galley proofs during his stay in Europe. Leacock dropped off the remaining manuscript for typing in London before he sailed back to Canada on 18 July. He kept Willett informed of his plans on 9 July 1914:

> . . . I think it likely that when I leave there will still be a few thousand words to finish, but very little. We can now take it for granted that the book will contain from *sixty* to *sixty five* thousand words. As the original date assigned in our correspondence (I think via Jefferson Jones [of the John Lane Co.]) was September 1st, I presume it will be alright if the small part that will be unfinished when I sail is sent back from Canada within a week of my landing. I must of course read *galley proofs* but if these come out pretty well I imagine that I can dispense with reading the page proofs. I should like with your approval to see the book bound in blue of the colour of the enclosed piece of card. My own opinion inclines to three & six as the price, which makes it uniform with the others; but in this of course your judgment is better than mine.

The contract with The Bodley Head for rights in the United Kingdom, the colonies, India, and the United States is dated 20 June 1914. It committed John Lane to publish Leacock's next four works of fiction (*Moonbeams from a Larger Lunacy, Further Foolishness, Frenzied Fiction,* and *The Hohenzollerns in America*). Leacock received a royalty of 20% on the first 7,000 copies sold and 25% royalty on subsequent copies sold with an advance of £100, thirteen copies being reckoned as twelve. For the American edition, Leacock received a royalty of 15% on the first 10,000 copies sold, 20% thereafter (copies of contracts at READ and SLM). The book sold for 3s 6d. Lomer (p. 19) has 25 November 1914 as the date of publication of the English edition.

By the end of 1914 3,317 copies had sold of the English edition, 1,000 for the Australasian market and 166 being colonial copies. By the end of 1924, 22,008 copies had sold. Of this number approximately 2,592 were Australasian and 2,699 colonial. The book continued to sell thereafter, annual sales being approximately 150 to 300 copies. Reprinted in 1918, 1919 ("third edition"), 1920 ("fourth edition"), and 1930 (cited by the OCLC WorldCat database). According to the copyright page of A16c, reprintings occurred in 1917, 1918, 1920, 1925, and 1930 ("cheap edition").

COPIES EXAMINED: CS (first printing, 1918, 1919, and 1920, only 1919 in jacket); BOD (first printing in jacket, flaps clipped).

**A16b.1** *Australasian issue* [1914]:

The verso of the title leaf reads: *AUSTRALASIAN EDITION.* | THE ANCHOR PRESS, LTD., TIPTREE ESSEX. The leaves measure 189 × 125 mm. There are no advertisements after the text. Otherwise, this issue is identical to A16b. Dust jacket not seen. For sales of this issue, see the notes to A16b.

COPIES EXAMINED: CS; QMMRB.

**A16b.2** *second Canadian issue* (1915):

This Canadian issue is identical to A16b with the following exceptions: the ten leaves of advertisements have been deleted; the binding is in green leather with floral compartments and OXFORD stamped in gilt on the spine. This would indicate that copies were sold by the Canadian branch of Oxford University Press, which was managed by S.B. Gundy.

COPIES EXAMINED: CS; SLM.

**A16b.3** *third Canadian issue* (1915):

*ARCADIAN ADVENTURES* | *WITH THE IDLE RICH* | *BY STEPHEN LEACOCK* | [thick-thin rule] | [thin-thick rule] | *LONDON: JOHN LANE THE BODLEY HEAD* | *NEW YORK: JOHN LANE COMPANY* | *TORONTO: S. B. GUNDY MCMXV* | *Published in Canada for Humphrey Milford.*

Cancel title. The verso of the title leaf reads: THE ANCHOR PRESS, LTD., TIPTREE ESSEX, ENGLAND. The ten leaves of advertisements, which appear in the English edition, have been omitted. Two binding variants were examined: the first is identical to A16b, except that *GUNDY* is at the foot of the spine (dust jacket not seen); the second binding variant is in half blue leather and half grey moiré cloth. The spine of the second binding variant is stamped in gilt with rules, floral compartments, and GUNDY at the foot of the spine; the title and Leacock's name are stamped in gilt on a red label.

NOTES: See the notes to A11a.3 for the transfer of the Canadian rights of Leacock's books from Bell and Cockburn to S.B. Gundy. In his notebook of royalty payments at SLM, Leacock recorded that Oxford University Press sold 290 copies by 30 June 1915 (royalty to Leacock of $72.50). Undoubtedly, some of these copies were from sheets from Bell and Cockburn (A16b.2) and the John Lane Company (A16a.2). By 1 January 1925 Oxford University Press had sold 2,018 copies in all. Sales for the last six months of 1924 amounted to 512 copies ("Cheap Edn"); this would suggest that these copies may not have had a Gundy imprint.

COPIES EXAMINED: CS (two copies of the first variant, one copy of the second); QMMRB (first variant binding).

**A16c** *second English edition* (1952):

*ARCADIAN ADVENTURES* | *WITH THE IDLE RICH* | *by* | Stephen Leacock | *London* | JOHN LANE THE BODLEY HEAD

◆ 1¹⁶ 2–4¹⁶ 5¹⁶ [$1 signed]. 1–4, 5, 6, 7–192 pp. (96 leaves). 184 × 122 mm.

CONTENTS: p. 1 half title; p. 2 list of thirty-three books by the same author, the first being *Recollections and Reflections* [no such book exists as such] and the last *The Boy I Left*

*Behind Me*; p. *3* title; p. *4* [six lines listing previous printings] | *Reprinted* 1952 | [three lines about copyright] | Printed in Great Britain by | THE PITMAN PRESS, BATH | for JOHN LANE THE BODLEY HEAD LTD. | 28, Little Russell St., London, W.C.1; p. *5* table of contents; p. *6* blank; pp. *7–192* text.

TEXT: Identical to A5b.

BINDING AND DUST JACKET: Bound in orange paper boards with stamping on the spine as follows: Stephen | LEACOCK | [rule with a solid diamond in the centre] | ARCADIAN | ADVENTURES | WITH THE | IDLE RICH | THE | BODLEY | HEAD.

On the front panel of the dust jacket is a colour illustration of four men in tuxedos, one seated, another standing against a fireplace, another with a crown on his head, and the remaining man with his glasses on his forehead. The back panel has a list of the Bodley Head Cheap Editions. The title is printed vertically on the spine within an elongated oval, the latter within a solid brown rectangular compartment. On the front flap is a quotation from J.B. Priestley about the book and the price (6s). A list of other cheap editions by Leacock is on the back flap.

NOTES: According to *The English Catalogue of Books*, this edition was published on 23 June 1952. Number of copies printed not known.

COPIES EXAMINED: QMMRB.

## A16d *first Canadian edition* [1960]:

[title page consists of two pages; on left-hand page:] *New Canadian Library* • *No.*10 | [on right-hand page:] STEPHEN LEACOCK | [on left-hand page:] ARCADIAN ADVENTURES [on right-hand page:] with the Idle Rich | *Introduction : Ralph L. Curry* | *General Editor : Malcolm Ross* | [on left-hand page:] McCLELLAND & | STEWART LIMITED | Toronto

♦ *i–vii*, viii–xi, *1–4*, 2–21, *22*, 23–36, *37*, 38–56, *57*, 58–77, *78*, 79–100, *101*, 102–117, *118*, 119–138, *139*, 140–157, *1–5* pp. (88 leaves). 185 × 112 mm.

CONTENTS: p. *i* half title; pp. *ii–iii* title; p. *iv* Copyright, 1914, The Crowell Publishing Company and John Lane Company | Copyright, Canada, 1959, McClelland & Stewart Limited | [four lines concerning copyright]; p. *v* table of contents; p. *vi* blank; pp. *vii*–xi Curry's introduction; p. *1* blank; p. *2* fly title; p. *3* blank; pp. *4*, 2–157 text; p. *1* blank; p. *2* note about the author; p. *3* list of books in the New Canadian Library series; p. *4* blank; p. *5* PRINTED AND BOUND BY | HAZELL WATSON AND VINEY LTD | AYLESBURY AND SLOUGH, ENGLAND.

TEXT: Identical to A16a.

BINDING: Paperback, perfect bound. The front cover has a grey sketch of Leacock's face with an irregular, blue vertical band on the left side. On the back cover are two blue bands and information about the book. Cover design by Frank Newfeld. Price: $1. N10 of the NCL series.

NOTES: Ralph L. Curry was asked to write an introduction to this edition in December 1958. He sent Ross the introduction on 19 January 1959. He was paid $100 for his introduction on 10 August 1959. A proof copy of the book was available on 29 September 1959. Curry returned the page proofs to Claire Pratt of McClelland and Stewart on 12 October 1959. The Editorial Department gave specifications to the Production Department on 26 October 1959.

Although the copyright page has the date of publication as 1959, publication actually occurred in late April 1960. By the spring of 1960 3,285 copies had sold. By the end of 1979 44,847 had sold. Reprinted 1965, 1968, and 1969 (information based on file 8, box 36, file 1; "New Canadian Library," box 47; and file 14, "New Canadian Library," box 93, series A, part I, McClelland and Stewart fonds, OHM).

COPIES EXAMINED: CS (first printing); OHM (third reprint 1965, tenth and eleventh printings 1969); QMMRB (first printing); SLM (twelfth reprint, 1969).

### A16e *second Canadian edition* (1989):

STEPHEN LEACOCK | Arcadian Adventures | with the Idle Rich | *With an Afterword by Gerald Lynch* | [wavy block, short wavy rule] | M&S | [rule]

◆ *1–6, 7–203, 204, 205–211, 1–5* pp. (108 leaves). 178 × 108 mm.

CONTENTS: p. *1* biographical information about Leacock; p. *2* THE NEW CANADIAN LIBRARY | General Editor: David Staines | ADVISORY BOARD | Alice Munro | W.H. New | Guy Vanderhaeghe; p. *3* title; p. *4* Copyright © 1914 by The Crowell Publishing Company and | John Lane Company | Copyright © Canada 1959 McClelland and Stewart Limited | Afterword copyright © by Gerald Lynch | Reprinted 1989 | [five lines about copyright] | [nine lines of Canadian Cataloguing in Publication Data] | Typesetting by Pickwick | Printed and bound in Canada | [five lines of the publisher's name and address]; p. *5* table of contents; p. *6* blank; pp. *7–203* text; p. *204* blank; pp. *205–211* Lynch's afterword; p. *1* blank; pp. *2–4* list of Leacock's books; p. *5* titles by Leacock in the NCL Library with an order form.

TEXT: Identical to A16a.

BINDING: Paperback, perfect bound. A reproduction of Paul Lemieux's "The Country Club" is on the front cover. Price $5.95. ISBN 0-7710-9966-5. Series design by T.M. Craan.

NOTES: Published in May 1989. 5,000 copies were ordered, but the actual number of copies received on 1 April 1989 was not recorded. By the end of 1989 2,930 copies had sold. Reprintings are as follows: 25 March 1991 5,079 copies; 2 June 1993 4,400 copies; 15 February 1996 3,264 copies. By the end of 1996 14,108 copies had sold.

COPIES EXAMINED: CS.

### A17 THE DAWN OF CANADIAN HISTORY 1914

### A17a *first issue*:

THE DAWN OF | CANADIAN HISTORY | A Chronicle of Aboriginal Canada and | the coming of the White Man | BY | STEPHEN LEACOCK | [illustration of a sailing ship inside a floral rectangular compartment with the motto EX UNO | DISCE OMNES] | TORONTO | GLASGOW, BROOK & COMPANY | 1914

◆ π⁶ A-G⁸ [$1 signed; with initials, D.C.H.]. *i–vii*, ix, x, xi–xii, *1*, 2–105, *106*, 107–112 pp. (62 leaves). 179 × 123 mm.

CONTENTS: pp. *i–iv* list of thirty-two volumes in the Chronicles of Canada series (divided into eight parts), edited by George M. Wrong and H.H. Langton, a number of volumes published and others in preparation; p. *v* half title; p. *vi* blank; p. *vii* title; p. *viii* Copyright *in all Countries subscribing to | the Berne Convention*; p. ix table of contents; p. *x* blank;

pp. xi–xii list of illustrations; pp. *1–105* text; p. *106* blank; pp. *107–109* bibliographical note; pp. *110–112* index. The last two lines on p. *112* are: Printed by T. and A. Constable, Printers to His Majesty | at the Edinburgh University Press. Colour frontispiece "The Mystery of the New Land" from a colour drawing by C.W. Jefferys. Other illustrations facing pp. 28, 30, 36, 42, 66, 68, 70, 74, 78, 80, 98, and 100.

TEXT: chapter I Before the Dawn; chapter II Man in America; chapter III The Aborigines of Canada; chapter IV The Legend of the Norsemen; chapter V The Bristol Voyages; chapter VI Forerunners of Jacques Cartier.

BINDING: Bound in maroon cloth with an oval crest blind-stamped on the upper board. On the inside of the crest in an oval pattern are the shields of the Canadian provinces and within that the shield of Canada. Also on the crest are the name of series, a crown, lion, and leaves. Stamped in gilt on the spine as follows: [dotted rule, flower and leaves, dotted rule] | THE | DAWN OF | CANADIAN | HISTORY | [flower] | STEPHEN | LEACOCK | [dotted rule, flowers and leaves, dotted rule] | GLASGOW | BROOK *&* Co | [dotted rule].

This volume of the series undoubtedly appeared uniformly with other volumes of the series in different binding variants.

NOTES: The Chronicles of Canada series consists of thirty-two volumes. The series was initiated by the Morang and Co. Limited under the title the Chronicles of Canada for Boys and Girls, and authors were contracted as early as September 1910 to write individual volumes. The rights to the series were transferred to the Macmillan Company of Canada on 26 September 1912. On 1 October 1912, the Macmillan Company sold these rights to The Publishers Association of Canada, Limited, whose first Vice-President was Arthur Brook (information based on file 9, box 223, Macmillan Company of Canada fonds, OHM).

Leacock wrote three volumes of the series (volumes 1, 2, and 20 — see also A18 and A19). *The Dawn of Canadian History* (volume 1) and *The Mariner of St. Malo* (volume 2) comprise part I of the series entitled "The First European Visitors." Leacock's contract with Morang, dated 8 February 1912, is not extant. In his notebook of recorded publications and speeches at QMMRB, Leacock wrote: "Dec 4 [1912]. Completed 'Dawn of Canadian History' (begun Oct 1 [1912])." Leacock received $200 to write the book. His notebook at SLM (J84) records that two instalments of $100 each were paid to him on 1 May 1913 and 31 July 1913. The section dealing with John Cabot was reprinted in C.L. Bennet and Lorne Pierce, eds., *Argosy to Adventure* (Toronto: Ryerson Press / Macmillan Company of Canada, 1935), pp. 9–12.

Also examined were the following reprints: 1920 (green cloth and wine cloth), 1921 (wine cloth and blue cloth). The 1920 impression was printed by the Hunter-Rose Co., Limited. Number of copies printed not known. Lomer (p. 25) also records a reprint in 1915. Although the reprints are from the same setting of type, the listing of the series in the preliminary section has been shifted to the end of the book (titles and authors differ somewhat from the first listing and the series has nine parts, rather than eight). Pagination is *i–iv*, v, *vi*, vii–viii, 1, 2–105, *106*, 107–112, *1–4*. The title in the reprints has also been shortened to *The Dawn of Canadian History: A Chronicle of Aboriginal Canada*.

COPIES EXAMINED: CS (impressions of 1914, 1920 (green cloth), and 1921); OH (1920, wine cloth); QMMRB (1914 and 1920, the latter rebound).

**A17a.1** *second issue* (1964):

THE DAWN OF | CANADIAN HISTORY | A Chronicle of Aboriginal Canada | BY | STEPHEN LEACOCK | [illustration of a sailing ship inside a floral rectangular compartment with the motto EX UNO | DISCE OMNES] | TORONTO | UNIVERSITY OF TORONTO PRESS

According to the verso of the title leaf the University of Toronto Press purchased unbound stock of the series, and the series was published *"in a limited edition in 1964."* The set sold for $65. Pagination is similar to the reprints of the first edition: *i–iv*, v, *vi*, vii–viii, *1*, 2–105, *106*, 107–112. The list of the volumes of the series does not appear at the end of the book. Collation is: $\pi^4$ A–G$^8$ [$1 signed; with compositor's initials, D.C.H.]. Bound in maroon cloth similar to the cloth of A17a, except that the upper board is blank, the stamping on the spine is in silver, the volume number (I) has been added to the spine, and TORONTO replaces the name of the original publisher.

In all liklihood this edition consisted of approximately 1,000 copies. In 1959 Arthur H. Brook of the United States Publishers Association attempted to sell the remaining stock (1,031 sets in sheets at the warehouse of the Edinburgh University Press) to McClelland and Stewart. The United States Publishers Association owned the Canadian subsidiary, United Editors Limited, which in turn owned Glasgow, Brook and Co. Although the deal failed to materialize at that time, it would appear that the same stock was sold to the University of Toronto Press some five years later (information based on file 4, box 12, series A, part I, McClelland and Stewart fonds, OHM).

COPIES EXAMINED: CS.

## A18 THE MARINER OF ST MALO 1914

**A18a** *first issue*:

THE MARINER | OF ST MALO | A Chronicle of the Voyages | of Jacques Cartier | BY | STEPHEN LEACOCK | [illustration of a sailing ship inside a floral rectangular compartment with the motto EX UNO | DISCE OMNES] | TORONTO | GLASGOW, BROOK & COMPANY | 1914

♦ $\pi^6$ A–H$^8$ [$1 signed; with initials, M.St.M.]. *i–viii*, ix, *x*, xi, *1–2*, 2–112, *113*, 114–125, *1–3* pp. (70 leaves). 179 × 122 mm.

CONTENTS: p. *i* series title and names of editors (George M. Wrong and H.H. Langton); pp. *ii–iv* list of thirty-two volumes in the Chronicles of Canada series (divided into eight parts); p. *v* half title; p. *vi* blank; p. *vii* title; p. *viii Copyright in all Countries subscribing to | the Berne Convention*; p. ix table of contents; p. x blank; p. xi list of illustrations; p. *1* blank; pp. 2, 2–120 text; pp. 121–122 bibliographical note; pp. 123–125 index; pp. *1–3* blank. The last two lines on p. 125 are: Printed by T. and A. Constable, Printers to His Majesty | at the Edinburgh University Press. Colour frontispiece "Jacques Cartier at Hochelaga, 1535" from a colour drawing by C.W. Jefferys. Other illustrations facing pp. 2, 4, 16 (folded map), 54, 70, 90, and 110.

TEXT: chapter I Early Life; chapter II The First Voyage — Newfoundland and Labrador; chapter III The First Voyage — The Gulf of St. Lawrence; chapter IV The Second Voyage — St. Lawrence; chapter V The Second Voyage — Stadacona; chapter VI The Second Voyage

— Hochelaga; chapter VII The Second Voyage — Winter at Stadacona; chapter VIII The Third Voyage; chapter IX The Close of Cartier's Career. Itinerary of Cartier's Voyages.

BINDING: Two binding variants were examined: (1) wine flexible leather with wine endpapers, top edge gilt, and signet. The upper cover has the same crest as A17a, except it is stamped in gilt within two blind-stamped rectangles. Stamped in gilt on the spine as follows: [dotted rule, three flowers, dotted rule] | THE | MARINER | +OF+ | STMALO | [flower] | STEPHEN | LEACOCK | [dotted rule, flowers and leaves, dotted rule] | GLASGOW | BROOK & Co | TORONTO | [dotted rule]. (2) wine cloth, top edge stained gilt, with signet. Leaves measure 174 × 120 mm. The upper board has a series of floral compartments and dotted rules at the top and bottom in white. Stamped in gilt inside the top compartment: THE • MARINER | OF • ST • MALO | + + + | STEPHEN•LEACOCK. Beneath this top compartment and on the left side within another compartment is the series title in white and on the right side within two rectangles and an oval wreath is the crest in gilt of the shields of the Canadian provinces and within that the shield of Canada. The publisher's name is in white at the bottom of the upper board. Stamped in gilt on the spine as follows: [dotted rule, flower, dotted rule] | THE | MARINER | +OF+ | ST•MALO | [flower] | STEPHEN | LEACOCK | [dotted rule, flowers and leaves, dotted rule] | GLASGOW | BROOK & Co | [dotted rule].

NOTES: For information on The Chronicles of Canada series, see the notes section of A17a. Leacock contracted with the Morang & Co. to write "Voyages of Jacques Cartier" on 3 November 1910. In his notebook of recorded publications and speeches at QMMRB, Leacock itemized: "Nov [1911] – wrote 'Voyages of Jacques Cartier' (Morang & Co)." The contract (1 October 1912) which transferred the rights of the series from the Macmillan Company of Canada to The Publishers Association of Canada Limited states that Leacock was paid $100 for writing the book "in part payment of amount." In his notebook at SLM (J84) Leacock recorded that the final instalment of $200 was paid in February 1913. It would appear, therefore, that he received $300 in all. Exact date of publication and number of copies printed not known.

Also examined were impressions in 1915, 1920 (printed by Hunter-Rose Co.), and 1921. Although the reprints are from the same setting of type, the listing of the series in the preliminary section has been shifted to the end of the book (titles and authors differ somewhat from the first listing and the series has nine parts, rather than eight). Pagination is *i–iv*, v, *vi*, vii, *1–2*, 2–112, *113*, 114–125, *1–7*.

COPIES EXAMINED: CS (impressions of 1915 (wine flexible leather), 1920 (green cloth and wine cloth), and 1921 (maroon cloth) ; LAT (1914 second variant); QMMRB (impressions of 1914 first variant, 1915 (wine cloth), and 1920 (rebound).

## A18a.1 *second issue* (1964):

THE MARINER | OF ST MALO | A Chronicle of the Voyages | of Jacques Cartier | BY | STEPHEN LEACOCK | [illustration of a sailing ship inside a floral rectangular compartment with the motto EX UNO | DISCE OMNES] | TORONTO | UNIVERSITY OF TORONTO PRESS

For information about this issue, see A17a.1. Pagination is similar to A18a: *1–9*, 2–125, *1–3*. The list of the volumes of the series does not appear at the end of the book. The list of illustrations has been omitted. Collation is: $\pi^4$ A–H$^8$ [$1 signed; with compositor's initials, M.St.M.]. Bound in maroon cloth. The upper board is blank. Stamping on the spine in silver as follows: [dotted rule, flower with leaves, dotted rule] | 2 | THE | MARINER | +OF+ | ST•MALO | [flower] | STEPHEN | LEACOCK | [dotted rule, flowers and leaves, dotted rule] | TORONTO | [dotted rule].

COPIES EXAMINED: OH.

## A19 ADVENTURERS OF THE FAR NORTH 1914

### A19a *first issue*:

ADVENTURERS | OF THE FAR NORTH | A Chronicle of the Frozen Seas | BY | STEPHEN LEACOCK | [illustration of a sailing ship inside a floral rectangular compartment with the motto EX UNO | DISCE OMNES] | TORONTO | GLASGOW, BROOK & COMPANY | 1914

♦ $\pi^6$ A–I$^8$ K$^4$ [$1 signed; with initials, A.F.N.]. *i–viii*, ix, *x*, xi, *1–2*, 2–152 pp. (82 leaves). 176 × 121 mm.

CONTENTS: p. *i* CHRONICLES OF CANADA SERIES | THIRTY-TWO VOLUMES ILLUSTRATED | Edited by GEORGE M. WRONG and H. H. LANGTON | [rule]; p. *ii–iv* list of thirty-two volumes in the Chronicles of Canada series (divided into eight parts), this book being volume 20; p. *v* half title; p. *vi* blank; p. *vii* title; p. *viii Copyright in all Countries subscribing to | the Berne Convention*; p. ix table of contents; p. *x* blank; p. xi list of illustrations; p. *1* blank; pp. 2, 2–146 text; pp. 147–148 bibliographical note; pp. 149–152 index. The last two lines on p. 152 are: Printed by T. and A. Constable, Printers to His Majesty | at the Edinburgh University Press. Colour frontispiece "The Arctic Council Discussing a Plan of Search for Sir John Franklin" from the National Portrait Gallery. Other illustrations facing pp. *1* (folded map), 42, 50, 70, and 112.

TEXT: chapter I The Great Elizabethan Navigators; chapter II Hearne's Overland Journey to the Northern Ocean; chapter III Mackenzie Descends the Great River of the North; chapter IV The Memorable Exploits of Sir John Franklin; chapter V The Tragedy of Franklin's Fate; chapter VI Epilogue. The Conquest of the Pole.

BINDING: There are at least two binding variants.

The first variant is bound in blue cloth, top edge stained gilt, with signet. The upper board has a series of floral compartments and dotted rules at the top and bottom in dark blue. Stamped in gilt inside the top compartment: ADVENTURERS • OF | THE • FAR • NORTH | + + + | STEPHEN•LEACOCK. Beneath this top compartment and on the left side within another compartment is the series title in dark blue, and on the right side within two rectangles and an oval wreath is the crest in gilt of the shields of the Canadian provinces and within that the shield of Canada. The publisher's name is stamped in dark blue at the bottom of the upper board. Stamped in gilt on the spine as follows: [dotted rule, flower, dotted rule] | ADVENT= | =URERS• | OF•THE• | FAR•NORTH | [flower] | STEPHEN | LEACOCK | [dotted rule, flowers and leaves, dotted rule] | GLASGOW | BROOK & C<u>o</u> | [dotted rule].

The second variant is bound in wine flexible leather, with wine endpapers, top edge gilt, and signet. The upper cover has the same crest as the first variant, except it is stamped in gilt within two blind-stamped rectangles. Stamped in gilt on the spine as follows: [dotted rule, three flowers, dotted rule] | 20 | ADVEN= | TURERS | +OF+ | THE•FAR | NORTH | [flower] | STEPHEN | LEACOCK | [dotted rule, flowers and leaves, dotted rule] | GLASGOW | BROOK & Co | TORONTO | [dotted rule].

NOTES: For information on The Chronicles of Canada series, see the notes section of A17a. In his notebook of recorded publications and speeches at QMMRB, Leacock wrote: "Sep 1 [1913]. Book. Adventurers of the Far North." According to his notebook at SLM (J84) he was paid $250 by the Publishers Association on 6 September 1913 for writing the book. Exact date of publication and number of copies printed not known.

   Along with other chapters selected from two other books in the series, chapters IV and V (pp. 89–135) were reprinted by the publishers in *Six Chapters from the Chronicles of Canada* ([1915?]) for private distribution as "a literary sample-book." An excerpt from chapter II is reprinted with the title "Search for the Coppermine" in *Great Canadian Adventures* (Montreal: The Reader's Digest Association (Canada) Ltd., 1976), 464–71.

COPIES EXAMINED: LAT (first variant); QMMRB (second variant).

## A19a.1 *second issue*:

ADVENTURERS | OF THE FAR NORTH | A Chronicle of the Arctic Seas | BY | STEPHEN LEACOCK | [illustration of a sailing ship inside a floral rectangular compartment with the motto EX UNO | DISCE OMNES] | TORONTO | GLASGOW, BROOK & COMPANY | 1914

◆ $\pi^4$ A–I$^8$ K$^4$ L$^2$ [$1 signed; with initials, A.F.N.]. *i–iv*, v, *vi*, vii, *1–2*, 2–152, *1–4* pp. (82 leaves). 179 × 122 mm.

CONTENTS: p. *i* series title, editors' names, volume number (20), title, author's name, and part (*Part VI* | *Pioneers of the North and West*); p. *ii* blank; p. *iii* title; p. *iv* *Copyright in all Countries subscribing to* | *the Berne Convention*; p. v table of contents; p. *vi* blank; p. vii list of illustrations; p. *1* blank; pp. 2, 2–146 text; pp. 147–148 bibliographical note; pp. 149–152 index; pp. *1–4* list of thirty-two volumes in the Chronicles of Canada series (divided into nine parts), edited by George M. Wrong and H.H. Langton.

BINDING: Bound in blue flexible leather, with wine endpapers, top edge gilt, and signet. Stamping is the same as the second variant of A17a.

NOTES: This issue is from the same setting of type as the first issue. The printer (as indicated on p. 152) and the illustrations are the same as well. The subtitle has been altered slightly. The series list has been moved to the back of the book. The number of parts in the series has been expanded to nine parts.

COPIES EXAMINED: CS (impressions of 1914, 1920 (wine cloth), and 1921 (wine cloth)); QMMRB (1922 maroon cloth).

## A19a.2 *third issue* (1964):

ADVENTURERS | OF THE FAR NORTH | A Chronicle of the Arctic Seas | BY | STEPHEN LEACOCK | [illustration of a sailing ship inside a floral rectangular compartment with the motto EX UNO | DISCE OMNES] | TORONTO | UNIVERSITY OF TORONTO PRESS

For information about this issue, see A17a.1. Pagination is similar to A19a: *1–6, v, 1–2, 2–152*. The list of the volumes of the series does not appear at the end of the book. The list of illustrations and the folded map have been removed; the illustrations have been repositioned. Collation is: $\pi^4$ A–I$^8$ K$^4$ [$1 signed; with initials, A.F.N.]. Bound in maroon cloth. The upper board is blank. Stamping on the spine in silver as follows: [dotted rule, flower with leaves, dotted rule] | 20 | ADVENT= | =URERS• | •OF•THE• | FAR•NORTH | [flower] | STEPHEN | LEACOCK | [dotted rule, flowers and leaves, dotted rule] | TORONTO | [dotted rule].

COPIES EXAMINED: OH.

## A20 THE MARIONETTES' CALENDAR 1916 1915

[the first five lines hand-written; the first three lines in outline characters] THE | MARIONETTES' CALENDAR | [in red] 1916. | *Rhymes by Stephen Leacock.* | *Drawings by A.H. Fish.* | [illustration of a cuckoo clock in red and black, the hands pointing to one o'clock] | LONDON: JOHN LANE, THE BODLEY HEAD | NEW YORK: JOHN LANE COMPANY

♦ 1$^6$ 2–3$^4$. *1–28* pp. (14 leaves). 241 × 173 mm.

CONTENTS: p. *1* illustration of a shield containing a rooster (a cock, i.e. Leacock) on one side and a fish (i.e. the illustrator, A.H. Fish) on the other, separated by a vertical line with a star at the top of the line; p. *2* table of contents; p. *3* title; pp. *4, 6, 8, 10, 12, 14, 16, 18, 20, 22, 24,* and *26* text of Leacock's poems with Fish's illustrations; pp. *5, 7, 9, 11, 13, 15, 17, 19, 21, 23, 25,* and *27* engagement calendar for each month of the year; p. *28* illustration of Pierrette bowing and below the illustration in the right corner in a calligraphic hand: W•W•CURTIS L•T•D [•T•D raised and with two dots underneath the characters] | Cheylesmore Press | Coventry | Printers *&* Engravers.

TEXT: I Rencontre; II Pas joyeux; III L'aveu; IV Promenade fatale; V Jalousie; VI Trahison; VII Le complot; VIII Pas passioné; IX La fuite; X Coeur brisé; XI Pauvre Pierrot; XII La fin.

BINDING: Bound in cream-coloured thick paper wrappers, glued to the signatures. The paper is of the same paper stock as the rest of the book. On the front of the wrapper the first five lines are identical to those on the title page, except the first three lines are red. Below these lines is a drawing by Fish of Pierrot and Pierrette and another Harlequin puppet (an adversary of Pierrot). The back wrapper features an illustration of Pierrette bowing (identical to p. *28*). The verso of the back cover has an advertisement for Leacock's books published by John Lane, The Bodley Head. *Arcadian Adventures with the Idle Rich* is said to be: JUST OUT — A NEW VOLUME BY STEPHEN LEACOCK. In one copy (CS), the English prices are blocked out in black, and American prices are stamped underneath these.

NOTES: *The Marionettes' Calendar 1916* is an engagement calendar. It consists of rhyming verse concerning the ill-fated love story of the Harlequin puppets, Pierrot and Pierrette. There are twelve poems by Leacock, one for each month of the year. These are accompanied by stylish drawings by A.H. Fish and with facing pages, also by Fish, of a monthly calendar. Anne Harriet Fish (d. 1964), who studied under John Hassall and at the London School of Art and in Paris, contributed drawings and caricatures to a wide variety of periodicals in the 1920s and 1930s, including *Cosmopolitan*, the *Tatler*, and *Vogue*. Leacock recalled on 29 October 1937: "She [Fish] & I at Mr. Lane's suggestion made a little picture book of 12 scenes called A Marionettes Calendar (about 1920 or 1921 — The pictures were made first and I wrote the poetry. I lost my few copies & could never get others" (inscribed in Norman Friedman's copy of the second Canadian issue of *Behind the Beyond* (1915) at QMMRB, quoted by Lomer, p. 22).

According to Leacock's notebook of recorded publications at QMMRB, he completed his verses in June 1914. A manuscript entitled "A Calendar of Marionettes" (13 pp.) is located at SLM. He acknowledged payment of £20 for his verses from The Bodley Head on 25 August 1914. *The English Catalogue of Books* has a publication date of September 1915 (price 1s 6d). Lomer (p. 41) gives 17 September 1915 as the date of publication. On 6 October 1915, Leacock thanked Lane ". . . for the copies of the Marionettes' Calendar which have just reached me — It is beautifully put together & most artistic. Couldn't we plan some further work of this sort that Miss Fish and I might do together" (The Bodley Head fonds, TEX). Number of copies printed not known.

Leacock and Fish first met at a Saturday afternoon tea party held for Leacock and his wife at The Bodley Head offices (see the *Bodleian* 6, no. 64 (July 1914): 832). Fish herself would later tell Friedman on 7 March [1938] that she ". . . had entirely forgotten the 'Marionettes Calendar.'. . . Please give my very best respects to Professor Leacock. It seems quite sometime ago — we met in the gold old days of John Lane."

Leacock's verses and Fish's drawings were also published in the form of a hanging calendar (also at 1s 6d). However, no copy of the hanging calendar is known to be extant. See also the *Bodleian* 7, no. 79 (October 1915): 1057, which advertises the calendar and engagement book and reprints the first stanza, "Rencontre."

COPIES EXAMINED: CS; HLS; QMMRB (containing correspondence with Fish).

## A21 MOONBEAMS FROM THE LARGER LUNACY 1915

### A21a *American edition*:

MOONBEAMS | FROM THE | LARGER LUNACY | [thick-thin rule] | BY STEPHEN LEACOCK | AUTHOR OF "NONSENSE NOVELS," "ARCADIAN ADVENTURES WITH | THE IDLE RICH," "BEHIND THE BEYOND," ETC. . . . | [thin-thick rule] | [thick-thin rule] | NEW YORK: JOHN LANE COMPANY | LONDON: JOHN LANE, THE BODLEY HEAD | TORONTO: S. B. GUNDY: MCMXV | [thin-thick rule]

◆ $1-18^8$. *1–4, 5, 6, 7–8, 9–10, 11–34, 35–36, 37–51, 52–54, 55–132, 133–134, 135–143, 144–146, 147–152, 153–154, 155–164, 165–166, 167–169, 170–172, 173–179, 180–182, 183–192, 193–194, 195–205, 206–208, 209–213, 214–216, 217–218, 219–220, 221–226, 227–228, 229–240, 241–242, 243–250, 251–252, 253–271, 272–274, 275–282, 1–6* pp. (144 leaves). 187 × 130 mm.

CONTENTS: p. *1* half title; p. *2* list of six other books by the same author, the first being *Behind the Beyond* and the last *The Marionettes' Calendar and Engagement Book 1916*; p. *3* title; p. *4* Copyright, 1915, | BY JOHN LANE COMPANY | Press of | J. J. Little & Ives Company | New York, U. S. A.; p. *5* Leacock's preface dated "McGill University | Montreal. | Oct. 1, 1915."; p. *6* blank; pp. *7–8* table of contents; p. *9–282* text (pp. *10, 36, 52, 64, 134, 144, 146, 154, 166, 170, 172, 180, 182, 194, 206, 208, 214, 216, 220, 228, 242, 252, 272,* and *274* blank); pp. *1–3* advertisements for Leacock's books with excerpts from reviews; p. *4* advertisement for the *International Studio*; pp. *5–6* blank.

TEXT: chapter I Spoof: A Thousand-Guinea Novel; chapter II The Reading Public; chapter III Afternoons at My Club — 1 The Anecdotes of Dr. So and So — 2 The Shattered Health of Mr. Podge — 3 The Amazing Travels of Mr. Yarner — 4 The Spiritual Outlook of Mr. Doomer — 5 The Reminiscences of Mr. Apricot — 6 The Last Man Out of Europe — 7 The War Mania of Mr. Jinks and Mr. Blinks — 8 The Ground Floor — 9 The Hallucination of Mr. Butt; chapter IV Ram Spudd; chapter V Aristocratic Anecdotes; chapter VI Education Made Agreeable; chapter VII An Every-Day Experience; chapter VIII Truthful Oratory; chapter IX Our Literary Bureau; chapter X Speeding Up Business; chapter XI Who Is Also Who; chapter XII The Passionate Paragraphs; chapter XIII Weejee the Pet Dog; chapter XIV Sidelights on the Supermen; chapter XV The Survival of the Fittest; chapter XVI The First Newspaper; chapter XVII In the Good Time After the War.

BINDING: Bound in dark blue cloth. Stamped on the upper board: [within two gold rectangles is a solid gold rectangle, which contains raised dark blue characters] MOON-BEAMS | FROM THE | LARGER LUNACY | [rule] | STEPHEN LEACOCK. Stamped in gilt on the spine: MOONBEAMS | FROM THE | LARGER | LUNACY | [rule] | LEACOCK | JOHN LANE | COMPANY. Dust jacket not seen.

NOTES: *Moonbeams from the Larger Lunacy* gathers together a number of Leacock's humorous sketches that first appeared in *Vanity Fair*, the *American Magazine*, the *Popular Magazine*, and other magazines. In his preface Leacock compares the republication of his sketches to the prudent husbandman who repeatedly rakes straw from a field and to the child who squeezes the lemons in an empty lemonade jug. Sometime between 5 October 1913 and 3 February 1914, in his notebook at SLM (J84), Leacock indicated: "this is the title of a book of collected sketches for 1915."

By 10 July 1915 Leacock had 40,000 words in hand (about twenty sketches). He had suggested to Jeff Jones of the John Lane Company that the manuscript would be sent to him and that corrected galley proofs would then be supplied to The Bodley Head. "Jeff Jones thinks that my short stuff (suitable for reading out loud) always finds a good reception and he is most hopeful of the book," Leacock informed John Lane on 20 July 1915. The manuscript was sent to Jones a few days later. Leacock received proofs of the book on 10 September (information based on The Bodley Head fonds, TEX). According to his notebook of recorded publications and speeches at QMMRB, the American edition was published on 20 October 1915. Price $1.25. In his letter to Gerhard R. Lomer of 7 September 1950, R.T. Bond of Dodd, Mead recorded 22 October 1915 as the date of publication (Lomer fonds at QMM Archives). The latter date of publication is confirmed by the Copyright Office at DLC. The copyright was registered on 26 October 1915 (ClA416089). The copyright was renewed by Leacock on 31 December 1942. For information on the contract for the book, see A21b.

By the end of 1915 4,436 copies (counted as 4,095 copies at 15% royalty) had sold of the American edition, earning Leacock a royalty of $767.82. 11,249 copies sold in all up to the end of 1921. Leacock recorded that 39,340 copies had sold of all editions by 1 February 1925. The OCLC WorldCat database lists impressions in 1916 and 1917. A brochure issued by the John Lane Company in 1920 advertises the "Sixth Edition" at $1.50 cloth.

COPIES EXAMINED: CS (two copies of the first impression; 1917 impression); QMMRB (1917 not in jacket).

**A21a.1** *Canadian issue*:

MOONBEAMS | FROM THE | LARGER LUNACY | [thick-thin rule] | BY
STEPHEN LEACOCK | AUTHOR OF "NONSENSE NOVELS," "ARCADIAN
ADVENTURES WITH | THE IDLE RICH," "BEHIND THE BEYOND,"
ETC. . . . | [thin-thick rule] | [thick-thin rule] | TORONTO: S. B. GUNDY |
NEW YORK: JOHN LANE COMPANY | LONDON: JOHN LANE, THE
BODLEY HEAD | MCMXV | [thin-thick rule]

Copies were examined both with a cancel title and an integral title; their priority is unknown.
GUNDY is stamped in gilt on the spine. In other respects this issue is the same as A21a.

On the front panel of the dust jacket is an illustration in yellow against a light blue
background of the man in the moon who is sitting on a broom and reading a book (entitled
"Leacock's Works"). The rest of the jacket is white with black lettering. Printed on the spine
panel: MOONBEAMS | FROM THE | LARGER | LUNACY | [star] | STEPHEN | LEAC-
OCK | *Author of* | "*Nonsense Novels,*" | "*Literary Lapses,*" | "*Behind the* | *Beyond,*" | *etc.*
| $1.25 | NET | GUNDY. The back panel has an advertisement for William J. Locke's *Jaffery*.
The front flap has the book blurb, quotations from *Vanity Fair* and the *Boston Transcript*,
and the price ($1.25). On the back flap is an advertisement for Frances Fenwick Williams's
*A Soul on Fire*.

NOTES: On 4 February 1915 Leacock told John Lane that he had signed with S.B. Gundy
for four future books. W.C. Bell, who had been hired by Gundy when his own company
went bankrupt, began taking advance orders for *Moonbeams from the Larger Lunacy* on
20 July 1915. Publication of the Canadian issue was undoubtedly simultaneous with the
American edition. 3,874 copies sold by the end of the year, earning Leacock a royalty of
$968.50. In all 5,005 copies sold by the end of 1924.

See also A21b.2.

COPIES EXAMINED: CS (five copies in all, four with integral title, two copies in jacket);
QMMRB (two copies, both with cancels, one in jacket).

**A21a.2** *American issue* (1922):

MOONBEAMS | FROM THE | LARGER LUNACY | [thick-thin rule] | BY
STEPHEN LEACOCK | AUTHOR OF "NONSENSE NOVELS," "ARCADIAN
ADVENTURES WITH | THE IDLE RICH," "BEHIND THE BEYOND,"
ETC. . . . | [thin-thick rule] | [thick-thin rule] | NEW YORK | DODD, MEAD
AND COMPANY | 1922

The verso of the half title is blank. The copyright page reads: Copyright, 1915, | BY JOHN
LANE COMPANY | PRINTED IN U. S. A. There is a blank leaf after the text (p. 282), and
the advertisements found in A21a have been deleted. Otherwise, the sheets of this issue are
identical to those of A21a.

BINDING AND DUST JACKET: The copy that was examined was rebound. The 1925 reprint
of this issue is in brownish red cloth. Lettering on the upper board is blind-stamped but in
other respects is the same as A21a. Stamping on the spine is in gilt similar to A21a except
that the last two lines are: DODD, MEAD | & COMPANY. The dust jacket is similar to
that of A21a.1. The illustration on the front panel is blue and white. The back panel is
blank. On the front flap is a list of other books by Leacock published by Dodd, Mead with

excerpts from reviews. The back flap has an advertisement for *Arcadian Adventures with the Idle Rich*.

NOTES: According to Leacock's notebook of royalty payments at SLM, Dodd, Mead sold 242 copies of this issue up to 1 August 1922 after the company had purchased the American branch of John Lane. By 1 February 1925 1,083 copies had been sold. Thereafter, approximately fifty copies sold annually.

COPIES EXAMINED: CS (1925 printing in jacket); OWA (1922).

## A21b *first English edition* [1915]:

*MOONBEAMS FROM THE* | *LARGER LUNACY* | *BY STEPHEN LEACOCK* | [thick-thin rule] | [thin-thick rule] | *LONDON: JOHN LANE, THE BODLEY HEAD* | *NEW YORK: JOHN LANE COMPANY. MCMVI*

◆ A⁴ B–P⁸ [$1 signed]. *i–iv*, v–vi, 1–3, *2*–21, *22*, 23–35, *36*, 37–101, *102*, 103–111, *112*, 113–131, *132*, 133–159, *160*, 161–171, *172*, 173–183, *184*, 185–191, *192*, 193–209, *210*, 211–216, *1–8* pp. (116 leaves). 183 × 125 mm.

CONTENTS: p. *i* half title; p. *ii* list of six other books by the same author, the first being *Arcadian Adventures with the Idle Rich* and the last *A Marionette's Calendar* [*The Marionettes' Calendar 1916*]; p. *iii* title; p. *iv* WILLIAM BRENDON AND SON, LTD., PRINTERS, PLYMOUTH, ENGLAND; pp. v–vi table of contents; p. *1* fly title; p. *2* blank; pp. 3, *2*–216, *1* text (pp. *22, 36, 102, 112, 132, 160, 172, 184, 192,* and *210* blank); p. *2* blank; pp. *3–8* advertisements for Leacock's books with excerpts from reviews.

TEXT: Identical to A21a, although many of the titles have subtitles — for example, "Ram Spudd: The New-World Singer."

BINDING AND DUST JACKET: Bound in greenish blue cloth with lettering in yellow. Stamped on the upper board within two blind-stamped rectangles: *MOONBEAMS FROM THE* | *LARGER LUNACY* | *By STEPHEN LEACOCK*. Stamped on the spine: [two rules blind-stamped] | *MOONBEAMS* | *FROM THE* | *LARGER* | *LUNACY* | *By* | *STEPHEN* | *LEACOCK* | *THE* | *BODLEY HEAD* | [two rules blind-stamped].

   The front panel of the jacket is identical to that of A21a.1. The rest of the jacket is white with black printing. Printed on the spine panel: MOONBEAMS | FROM | THE LARGER | LUNACY | BY | STEPHEN | LEACOCK | 3/6 | Net. | THE BODLEY HEAD. On the back panel is a list of new and forthcoming novels. The flaps were clipped on the only known extant jacket of the book.

NOTES: Leacock sent a corrected set of proofs of the American edition to John Lane on 10 September 1915. Although one of the sketches, "In Good Times After the War," had been sold to the *Tatler*, Leacock instructed Lane on 30 September to stop its publication in that magazine (serial publication was too close to the book's publication). According to *The English Catalogue of Books*, the English edition was published in December 1915. Lomer (p. 43) has 3 December 1915 as the date of publication. On 23 December 1915 Leacock told Lane: "Am glad to hear that Moonbeams is out and is doing so well, all things considered" (The Bodley Head fonds, TEX).

   The contract with The Bodley Head for rights in the United Kingdom, the colonies, India, and the United States is dated 20 June 1914 (see the notes to A16b). At that time Leacock signed a contract for *Arcadian Adventures with the Idle Rich*, and *Moonbeams from the*

*Larger Lunacy* was the second work of fiction which was promised to John Lane in a multi-book deal. Leacock received a royalty of 20% on the first 7,000 copies sold, 25% on subsequent copies sold, with an advance of £100.

The print run of the first impression was 10,000 copies. In its royalty statement of 5 April 1916, The Bodley Head reported that to the end of 1915, Leacock earned £329.16 (minus expenses of £110.10): 4,209 copies had sold in all — 2,841 counted as 2,2650 copies in England at 20%, 1,000 copies for the Australasian market at 10%, and 338 copies for the colonial market at 10% In addition, there were 133 review and presentation copies. By the end of 1925 23,850 copies had sold; of this number, 2,957 copies went to Australasian market and 2,530 to the colonial market. During the rest of Leacock's lifetime, the book sold less than 100 copies annually.

According to the copyright page of the "cheap edition" of 1933, there were reprints in 1917, 1918, 1920, and 1925. The third printing occurred in 1919.

COPIES EXAMINED: BOD (first printing in partial jacket); CS (first printing, 1920 "fourth edition"); QMMRB (first printing; 1917 "second edition"; 1919 "third edition" in jacket; 1933, "cheap edition" printed by Western Printing Services, Ltd., Bristol).

## A21b.1 *Australasian issue* [1915]:

The verso of the title leaf reads: *AUSTRALASIAN EDITION* | WILLIAM BRENDON AND SON, LTD., PRINTERS, PLYMOUTH, ENGLAND. The leaves measure 191 × 127 mm. Otherwise, this issue is identical to A21b. Dust jacket not seen. For sales of this issue, see the notes to A21b.

COPIES EXAMINED: CS.

## A21b.2 *Canadian issue* [1915?]:

This Canadian issue (180 × 122 mm.) is identical to A21b with the following exceptions: the three leaves of advertisements have been deleted; all edges gilt; marbled endpapers; signet; the binding is in black leather with floral designs and rectangles stamped in gilt on the upper board and the spine; OXFORD is stamped in gilt at the foot of the spine. This would indicate that copies were sold by the Canadian branch of Oxford University Press, which was managed by S.B. Gundy. Copies were perhaps supplied to Gundy by The Bodley Head when Gundy ran out of copies of A21a.1.

COPIES EXAMINED: CS.

## A21c *Canadian edition* (1964):

Stephen Leacock | [open swelled rule] | MOONBEAMS | FROM | THE LARGER | LUNACY | [open swelled rule] | Introduction: Robertson Davies | General Editor: Malcolm Ross | New Canadian Library No. 43 | [publisher's device: abstract design within an oval of a person on a horse-drawn chariot, taking aim with a bow and arrow] | MCCLELLAND AND STEWART LIMITED

♦ *i–iv, v–x, 11–137, 138, 139, 140, 141–142, 1–2* pp. (72 leaves). 184 × 112 mm.

CONTENTS: p. *i* half title; p. *ii* blank; p. *iii* title; p. *iv* * | First published in 1916 by John Lane the Bodley Head | © McClelland and Stewart Limited, 1964 | * | [six lines concerning copyright] | * | *The Canadian Publishers* | McClelland and Stewart Limited | 25 Hollinger Road, Toronto 16 | * | PRINTED AND BOUND BY | HAZELL WATSON AND VINEY

LTD | AYLESBURY, BUCKS, ENGLAND; pp. v–vi table of contents; pp. vii–x introduction by Davies; pp. 11–137 text; p. *138* blank; p. *139* biographical information about the author; p. *140* blank; pp. *141–142* list of books in the New Canadian Library series; pp. *1–2* blank.

TEXT: Identical to A21a.

BINDING: Paperback, perfect bound. The covers are white with the design and lettering in green, brown, and red. A drawing of Leacock's face and shoulders in brown is on the front cover. with an irregular, green vertical band on the left side. On the back cover are two green bands, information about the book in brown type. and the book's price ($1.25). Covers designed by Donald Grant and John Zehethofer.

NOTES: On 26 November 1963 Robertson Davies sent a copy of the first English edition to McClelland and Stewart for photocopying and the setting of type. Published on 5 September 1964. S.J. Totton complimented Davies for his introduction on 16 September 1964: "Seldom does one encounter in a few brief pages so profound and sympathetic an introduction to an author's work." By the end of that year 1,360 copies had sold. By the end of 1979 14,740 had sold (information based on file 14, "New Canadian Library," box 93, series A, file 34, box Ca6, and file 13, box Cae12, McClelland and Stewart fonds, OHM). Reprinted by T.H. Best Printing Company Limited in 1971. Number of copies of each impression not known.

COPIES EXAMINED: CS (two copies of the first printing; second printing); SLM (second printing).

## A21d *second English edition* (1984):

Moonbeams | from the | Larger Lunacy | Stephen Leacock | ALAN SUTTON | 1984

♦ *i–iv*, v, *vi*, vii–viii, 1–119, *1* pp. (64 leaves). 198 × 128 mm.

CONTENTS: p. *i* half title; p. *ii* blank; p. *iii* title; p. *iv* Alan Sutton Publishing | 17a Brunswick Road | Gloucester GL1 1HG | First published by John Lane, | The Bodley Head 1915 | All rights reserved | This edition published 1984 | [six lines of British Library Cataloguing in Publication Data] | ISBN 0-86299-158-7 | *Cover picture supplied by Bookworms, Evesham* | Printed and bound in Great Britain by | The Guernsey Press Company Limited, | Guernsey, Channel Islands.; p. v preface; p. *vi* blank; pp. vii–viii table of contents; pp. 1–119 text; p. *1* blank.

TEXT: Identical to A21a.

BINDING: Paperback, perfect bound. The covers are cream-coloured. On the front cover is a colour illustration of a man dressed in a formal long jacket and top hat, who is smoking a pipe, reading a newspaper, and pushing an old-fashioned baby carriage; the carriage is stuck against the trunk of a slender tree. The title and Leacock's name on the front cover are in blue. The title and Leacock's name are printed down the spine in blue; at the foot of the spine are a publishing logo (small illustration of a ram) and the publisher's name. On the back cover are some excerpts from reviews, a paragraph on the book's contents, the ISBN number, and price (£2.95).

NOTES: Published in June 1984 according to *Books in Print*. The book was out of print before January 1988.

COPIES EXAMINED: OONL.

## A21α STEPHEN LEACOCK [1915]

[cover title: all lines printed in dark green within a rectangle] "A GREAT AND CONTAGIOUS HUMOURIST [sic]" | — *Vanity Fair* | [rule] | STEPHEN LEACOCK | *Author of* | *"Behind the Beyond," "Sunshine Sketches,"* | *"Nonsense Novels," "Literary Lapses,"* | *"Moonbeams from the Larger Lunacy," etc.* | [photograph of Leacock in green with vertical rules on each side of the photograph attached to longer horizontal rules at the top and bottom] | [five lines quoting the *Boston Evening Transcript*] | [rule] | JOHN LANE COMPANY | [the next two lines to the right of the previous line] PUBLISHERS | NEW YORK

◆ $1^8$. *1*, 2–16 pp. (8 leaves). 185 × 122 mm.

CONTENTS: pp. *1–7, 9, 11, 13, 15* text ; pp. *8, 10, 12, 14, 16* "What Others Think of Him" (extracts of reviews of Leacock's books).

TEXT: pp. *1–4* What He Thinks of Himself (excerpt from the preface to *Sunshine Sketches of a Little Town*); pp. *5–7* A Book Full of Smiles: My Financial Career (taken from *Literary Lapses*); p. *9* Leacock at His Funniest: An Extract from "Soaked in Seaweed" (taken from *Nonsense Novels*); Sunshine and Humour: Regarding Mariposa (remainder of the preface to *Sunshine Sketches of a Little Town*); p. *13* One Long, Heavy Laugh: An Extract from "Parisian Pastimes" (taken from *Behind the Beyond*); p. *15* Fun with the Idle Rich: The Yahi-Bahi Oriental Society of Mrs. Rasselyer-Brown (taken from *Arcadian Adventures with the Idle Rich*).

BINDING: Issued in a light green paper wrapper, wire-stitched. On the verso of the front cover is a reproduction of a drawing of Leacock by Vernon Hill. On the back cover is a list of "THE BOOKS OF STEPHEN LEACOCK."

NOTES: This pamphlet was issued by the John Lane Company as an advertisement brochure sometime after reviews appeared in American newspapers and periodicals of *Moonbeams from the Larger Lunacy* (A21a). Consequently, its date of publication is probably November or December 1915. The pamphlet consists of excerpts from Leacock's humorous books and extracts of reviews.

COPIES EXAMINED: CS.

## A22 ESSAYS AND LITERARY STUDIES 1916

### A22a *American edition*:

ESSAYS | AND | LITERARY STUDIES | [thick-thin rule] | BY STEPHEN LEACOCK | AUTHOR OF "MOONBEAMS FROM THE LARGER LUNACY," | "NONSENSE NOVELS," "LITERARY LAPSES," ETC. | [thin-thick rule] | [thick-thin rule] | NEW YORK: JOHN LANE COMPANY | LONDON: JOHN LANE, THE BODLEY HEAD | TORONTO: [three triangular shapes, each consisting of three dots] S. B. GUNDY | [four triangular shapes, each consisting of three dots] MCMXVI [four triangular shapes, each consisting of three dots] | [thin-thick rule]

◆ $1–19^8$ $20^6$. *1–8, 9–37, 38–40, 41–61, 62–64, 65–95, 96–98, 99–136, 137–138, 139–159,*

160–162, 163–189, 190–192, 193–230, 231–232, 233–266, 267–268, 269–310, 1–6 pp. (158 leaves). 187 × 125 mm.

CONTENTS: p. *1* half title; p. *2* list of six books (with prices) by the same author, the first being *Moonbeams from the Larger Lunacy* and the last *Arcadian Adventures with the Idle Rich*; p. *3* title; p. *4* Copyright, 1916, | BY JOHN LANE COMPANY | Press of | J.J. Little & Ives Company | New York, U.S.A.; p. *5* table of contents; p. *6* blank; pp. *7–310* text (pp. *8, 38, 40, 62, 64, 96, 98, 138, 160, 162, 190, 192, 232,* and *268* blank); pp. *1–5* advertisements by the John Lane of Leacock's books and of *The International Studio*; p. *6* blank.

TEXT: chapter I The Apology of a Professor: An Essay on Modern Learning; chapter II The Devil and the Deep Sea: A Discussion of Modern Morality; chapter III Literature and Education in America; chapter IV American Humour; chapter V The Woman Question; chapter VI The Lot of the Schoolmaster; chapter VII Fiction and Reality: A Study of the Art of Charles Dickens; chapter VIII The Amazing Genius of O. Henry; chapter IX A Rehabilitation of Charles II.

BINDING AND DUST JACKET: Bound in red ribbed cloth. Stamped in gilt on the upper board are two rectangles, the outer one thick. Within these rectangles is a solid gilt rectangle with lettering highlighted in red as follows: ESSAYS AND | LITERARY STUDIES | [rule] | STEPHEN LEACOCK. Stamped in gilt on the spine as follows: ESSAYS | AND | LITERARY | STUDIES | [rule] | LEACOCK.

The jacket is light yellow with printing in brown. The front panel features a photograph of Leacock at his writing desk. Below the photograph within a rectangle are two short paragraphs that praise this "collection of brilliant essays . . . illuminated throughout by Professor Leacock's singular gift of humour and his characteristic originality of thought." The spine of the jacket is similar to the book's spine with the addition of the price ($1.25). On the back panel are a list of books by Gilbert K. Chesterton published by the John Lane Company with excerpts from reviews. The front flap has an advertisement of Leacock's other books published by the John Lane Company. On the back flap is an advertisement of *The International Studio*.

NOTES: The earliest mention of this book is in a letter that Leacock wrote to W.C. Bell on 1 January 1915. Bell's firm, Bell and Cockburn, had gone bankrupt the previous month, and Bell had joined the staff of S.B. Gundy, the Canadian branch of Oxford University Press. Leacock informed Bell that he had just sent Jeff Jones of the John Lane Company a manuscript of 6,000 words entitled "The Mind of the Master Fiction & Reality in the Art of Charles Dickens A Fireside Fantasy." Leacock hoped to have this published as a small book. He added: "Later on if we ever come to publish a set of my works this and other stuff would go into a volume called *Literary Studies* or *Essays and Literary Studies*." (Bell fonds, OTUTF).

The rights to the American edition were arranged through John Lane. On 28 November 1915 Leacock told Lane: "I am sending to Jefferson Jones the copy for the book, — *ESSAYS AND LITERARY STUDIES* of which both he and I have written to you. By this means he can send it on to you in galley proof which is simpler & saves time." The manuscript was sent to Jones on 23 December 1915. The book was published on 14 April 1916. The copyright was registered with the Copyright Office at DLC on 15–16 April 1916 (ClA427736). The copyright was renewed by Mrs. Mary [May] Shaw (claimed to be the executor of the Leacock estate) on 13 April 1944.

"The American edition is out and is admirably made," Leacock wrote enthusiastically to Lane on 22 April 1916 (The Bodley Head fonds, TEX). Lomer (p. 27) has 6 July 1916 as the date of publication, which in all likelihood is the date of publication of the English edition.

A draft of the table of contents, "Notes for Contents of Book (1916)," exists in Leacock's notebook at SLM (J84). It lists the titles of five chapters with insertions. The only chapter not listed in this draft that was later included in the book is "A Rehabilitation of Charles II." In addition, this draft has the following chapters as possibilities: "Also. Revised *College & Business* (Univ. Magazine): rewritten under the Theory & Practice without reference to commercial classes specifically." "also. Shakespeare — (what I think about Shakespeare," and "The Peacemakers." Leacock, in fact, wanted to publish the "Peace Makers" as a 50¢ book in time for the Christmas market. Although he sold this essay to *Maclean's*, both Jones and Lane opposed its publication as a small book. Leacock accepted Lane's verdict on 28 November 1915. The essay was included in *Further Foolishness*.

The print run of the first impression is not known. According to Leacock's notebook of royalty payments at SLM, the first royalty statement occurred on 1 July 1916. 1,564 copies had sold, earning a royalty of $270.75. Up to the end of 1921 3,591 copies sold in all. The OCLC WorldCat database records reprintings as follows: second and third impressions in 1916, fourth impression in 1920, sixth impression in 1921, and seventh impression in 1922. The 1922 impression is, in fact, a reprinting of the English edition. Leacock recorded that 15,502 copies had sold by 1 February 1925.

"Amazing Genius of O. Henry" is reprinted in O. Henry's *Waifs and Strays* (Garden City, New York: Doubleday, 1919), pp. 171–194; and in *The Complete Works of O. Henry* (Garden City, New York: Doubleday, Page, 1926), pp. 1339–48. See also A23.

COPIES EXAMINED: CS (two copies, one in jacket); QMMRB ("THIRD EDITION" on copyright page, not in jacket).

### A22a.1 *Canadian issue*:

ESSAYS | AND | LITERARY STUDIES | [thick-thin rule] | BY STEPHEN LEACOCK | AUTHOR OF "MOONBEAMS FROM THE LARGER LUNACY," | "NONSENSE NOVELS," "LITERARY LAPSES," ETC. | [thin-thick rule] | [thick-thin rule] | S. B. GUNDY [three triangular shapes, each consisting of three dots] TORONTO | [four triangular shapes, each consisting of three dots] MCMXVI [four triangular shapes, each consisting of three dots] | [thin-thick rule]

With the exception of the title page and the foot of the spine (GUNDY replaces JOHN LANE | COMPANY), the Canadian issue is identical to the American edition. Dust jacket not seen.

NOTES: Leacock gave Lane the authority to arrange for publication of the book in Canada. The royalty for the Canadian market was presumably 15%, the same as the American and English editions. Publication of the Canadian issue probably occurred simultaneously with the American edition. According to Leacock's notebook of recorded publications at QMMRB, the first royalty statement occurred on 1 July 1916. 937 copies had sold, earning a royalty of $175.69. Up to the end of 1 January 1925 1,605 copies sold in all.

COPIES EXAMINED: CS; QMMRB.

**A22a.2** *American issue* [1922?]:

ESSAYS | AND | LITERARY STUDIES | [thick-thin rule] | BY STEPHEN LEACOCK | AUTHOR OF "MOONBEAMS FROM THE LARGER LUNACY," | "NONSENSE NOVELS," "LITERARY LAPSES," ETC. | [thin-thick rule] | [publisher's device: rectangular floral compartment containing an illustration of a woman's head, two open books, and initials D M *&* Co] | [thick-thin rule] | NEW YORK | DODD, MEAD AND COMPANY | 1924 | [thin-thick rule]

This issue is virtually the same as A22a. There are two blank leaves after p. 310. The verso of the title leaf reads: Copyright, 1916, | By DODD, MEAD & COMPANY, INC. | *Printed in U. S. A.* Bound in green cloth. The leaves measure 187 × 130 mm. Lettering on the upper board is blind-stamped but in other respects is the same as A22a. Stamping on the spine is in gilt similar to A22a except that the last two lines are: DODD, MEAD | *&* COMPANY. Dust jacket not examined. The dust jacket of the 1927 impression is similar to that of A22a. The publisher's name has been replaced, and the price is not on the spine panel. The back panel and flap are blank. The front flap has an advertisement of Leacock's other books published by Dodd, Mead.

NOTES: According to Leacock's notebook of royalty payments at SLM, Dodd, Mead sold ninety-two copies of this book from the beginning of 1922 to 1 August 1922. This would indicate that Dodd, Mead printed the book in 1922 when it took over the rights to Leacock's books from the John Lane Company. However, a 1922 printing was not located. It is possible that Dodd, Mead did not publish the book with its imprint but sold the John Lane Company's stock instead. Leacock's notebook records that another 351 copies sold up to 1 February 1925. Royalty statements issued by Dodd, Mead in the late 1920s and early 1930s show that the book sold at a slow rate — no more than seventy copies in a six-month period. Between 1 February 1933 and 1 August 1933, for example, sixteen copies had sold, earning a royalty of $3.20.

COPIES EXAMINED: CS (1927 printing in jacket); OHM (1924, no jacket).

**A22b** *English edition*:

*ESSAYS AND | LITERARY STUDIES | BY STEPHEN LEACOCK | [thick-thin rule] | [thin-thick rule] | LONDON: JOHN LANE, THE BODLEY HEAD | NEW YORK: JOHN LANE COMPANY. MCMXVI*

◆ $A^8$ B–P$^8$ Q$^{10}$ R$^{12}$ [$1 signed; Q5 signed Q2]. *1–10,* 11–33, *34–36,* 37–52, *53–54,* 55–78, *79–80,* 81–111, *112–114,* 115–131, *132–134,* 135–155, *156–158,* 159–188, *189–190,* 191–217, *218–220,* 221–253, *1–31* pp. (142 leaves). 190 × 125 mm.

CONTENTS: pp. *1–2* blank; p. *3* half title; p. *4* six books by the same author, the first *Literary Lapses* and the last *Moonbeams from the Larger Lunacy*; p. *5* title; p. *6* WILLIAM BRENDON AND SON, LTD., PRINTERS, PLYMOUTH, ENGLAND; p. *7* table of contents; p. *8* blank; pp. 9–253 text (pp. *10, 34, 36, 54, 80, 112, 114, 132, 134, 156, 158, 190, 218,* and *220* blank); p. *1* blank; pp. *2–6* advertisements with excepts of press opinions of Leacock's books; pp. *7–30* John Lane's List of Fiction; p. *31* advertisement for the New Pocket Library.

TEXT: Identical to A22a.

BINDING: Bound in green cloth, top edge stained green. Blind-stamped on the upper board as follows: [all lines within two rectangles] *ESSAYS AND | LITERARY STUDIES | By STEPHEN LEACOCK*. Stamped in gilt on the spine as follows: [blind-stamped rule] | *ESSAYS | AND | LITERARY | STUDIES | By | STEPHEN | LEACOCK | THE | BODLEY HEAD* | [blind-stamped rule].

The dust jacket is white with black lettering and a black-and-white photograph of Leacock on the front panel. The price on the spine is 3s 6d. On the back panel within a rectangle is a list of Leacock's books published by the Bodley Head, some with excerpts from reviews. The only copy with a jacket had the flaps cut.

NOTES: On 20 July 1915 Leacock told Lane: "I also want to bring out as soon as the market is suitable a book called — *ESSAYS AND LITERARY STUDIES*. It consists of magazine articles (not political) & I am *sure* it will do well enough." He assured Lane that the book would not count as one of the "works of fiction" specified in previous contracts. Leacock sent the contract back unsigned on 24 January 1916. He placed such confidence in Lane that he told him: "Make the *Essays* contract any way you like. I know that I am always safe in your hands" (The Bodley Head fonds, TEX). The contract with John Lane The Bodley Head at READ is dated 12 April 1916: 15% on the English and American editions up to 3,000 copies, 20% thereafter (thirteen copies reckoned as twelve). According to *The English Catalogue of Books*, the English edition was published in July 1916 at 3s 6d.

According to Leacock's notebook of royalty payments at SLM, the first royalty statement occurred on 1 July 1916. It indicates that at that time 775 copies were sold to the Australasian market. By the end of 1916 another 2,722 copies had sold in England. In all 9,464 copies sold of the English edition up to the end of 1 February 1925. Of this number, 1,385 were sold to Australasia and 278 to the colonies. There was a reprinting in September 1927 of 500 copies for which Leacock received 10% royalty. The book was selling approximately 100 copies per year at that time. Also examined was the second printing (1916), fifth printing (1919), the sixth printing (1921), the seventh printing (1922), and the eight printing. The OCLC WorldCat database records the third impression in 1917 and the fourth in 1918. The prices of the 1921 and 1925 printings are 6s and 5s respectively.

According to Leacock the photograph used on the jacket was taken by Mr. Alexander "with a high power (for the time) moving picture camera." Leacock recalled meeting him in Orillia in 1920, although this date is too late by several years. Leacock took him out fishing, and even purchased a fish at a butcher's shop so that it could be included in the photographs. Initially Alexander was very careful about his camera, but once he started fishing, he forgot all about it and said "To hell with it" (story told by Leacock in the Friedman copy of the Canadian issue at QMMRB, see Lomer, p. 27).

COPIES EXAMINED: CS (first printing no jacket; 1921 no jacket; 1922 in jacket); BOD (first printing, partial jacket); OHM (1919 and 1922, neither in jacket); QMMRB (second printing 1916, no jacket; 1921 and 1925 printings, both in jacket).

## A23 BAGDAD ON THE SUBWAY [1916?]

[cover title: within a rectangular compartment is an illustration in grey, yellow, black, white, and flesh-tone; at the top of the illustration is a woman who is weeping and below that is a man in Arabian dress, a hookah, and a vase; below the weeping woman and to the right of the vase is the following, the first and third lines outlined in white:] Bagdad | on the | [swash y] Subway | by | *Stephen* | *Leacock*

◆ $1^{12}$. *1–2, 3–21, 1–3* pp. (12 leaves including the wrapper). 229 × 159 mm.

CONTENTS: p. *1* front of the wrapper; p. *2* Leacock's introduction entitled "Why People Should Own and Read Books," signed in facsimile by him and with an oval portrait of Leacock; pp. *3–21* text; pp. *1–2* advertising for twelve volumes of O. Henry's works, entreating readers to send in a card for a free book by Kipling; p. *3* back of the wrapper. Illustrations depicting various scenes in O. Henry's stories occur frequently throughout the text.

TEXT: "The Amazing Genius of O. Henry."

BINDING: Bound in pictorial wrappers, wire-stitched. The paper stock of the wrapper is the same as that used for other leaves. The back of the wrapper has a rectangular compartment in grey, black, and flesh-tone. The heading is: Finish This Story | for Yourself —. Below the heading is a paragraph written by O. Henry followed by a few lines indicating how he tells the story in an engaging manner.

NOTES: On 26 April 1916, C.D. Morley of Doubleday Page & Co. wrote to Jefferson Jones of the John Lane Company as follows:

> I want to say how very keenly I have enjoyed reading Professor Leacock's magnificent essay on O. Henry. With the permission of your house we would like very much to quote some extracts from the essay in our O. Henry advertising. June 12th, has been fixed as 'O. Henry Day', and in Chickering and Hall at Lord and Taylor's we are planning a special celebration honoring his memory. Mr. Page is trying to get Mr. Leacock here for that occasion. . . .

Leacock apparently did not attend this celebration.

The number of copies printed, the date of publication, and the issuing body of this pamphlet are not known. The *National Union Catalog*, for example, has [New York: n.p. 192–]. On p. 3 of the pamphlet, Leacock's *Essays and Literary Studies* is credited as the first appearance of "The Amazing Genius of O. Henry." According to his notebook of recorded publications at QMMRB, he wrote this essay on 14 April 1915, one year prior to its publication in book form.

Leacock's pamphlet was probably used for promotional purposes by Doubleday, Page and Co. in 1916 or somewhat later. The authorized edition of O. Henry's *Complete Works* was published in twelve volumes between 1904 and 1910 by Doubleday, Page and Co. Reprintings of these volumes occurred in 1912, 1916, 1919, and 1920. The verso of the back of the wrapper of this pamphlet refers to 130,000 people who have purchased these volumes.

The pamphlet's title, *Bagdad on the Subway*, refers to O. Henry's creative ability to transform New York into "a city of mystery and romance." In particular, Leacock's reference is to O. Henry's stories in *The Four Million* (1906) about everyday life in New York. "It has become, as O. Henry loves to call it, Bagdad upon the Subway," Leacock wrote (p. 8). See also A22a.

COPIES EXAMINED: CS; OTNY; VA.

## A24 FURTHER FOOLISHNESS 1916

### A24a *American edition*:

FURTHER | FOOLISHNESS | SKETCHES AND SATIRES | ON THE FOLLIES OF THE DAY | [thick-thin rule] | BY STEPHEN LEACOCK | AUTHOR OF "NONSENSE NOVELS," "MOONBEAMS FROM | THE LARGER LUNACY," "BEHIND THE BEYOND," ETC. | [thin-thick rule] | [thick-thin rule] | [NEW YORK: JOHN LANE COMPANY | LONDON: JOHN LANE, THE BODLEY HEAD | TORONTO: S. B. GUNDY : MXMXVI | [thin-thick rule]

◆ $1-19^8\,20^4$. *1-4*, 5, 6, 7, *8-10*, 11-129, *130-132*, 133-220, *221-222*, 223-280, *281-282*, 283-312 pp. (156 leaves). 187 × 125 mm.

CONTENTS: p. *1* half title; p. *2* list of seven books by Leacock published by the John Lane Company, the first being *Behind the Beyond* the last *Moonbeams from the Larger Lunacy*; p. *3* title; p. *4* Copyright, 1916, | BY JOHN LANE COMPANY | Press of | Little & Ives Company | New York, U.S.A.; p. *5* Leacock's preface, dated "Nov. 1, 1916."; p. *6* blank; p. *7* table of contents; p. *8* blank; p. *9-312* text (pp. *102*, *130*, *132*, *222*, and *282* blank).

TEXT: The book is comprised of four chapters, each of which contains separate sketches or satires. I Peace, War and Politics; II Movies and Motors, Men and Women; III Follies in Fiction; and IV Timid Thoughts on Timely Topics.

I consists of: 1 Germany from within out; 2 Abdul Aziz Has His: An Adventure in the Yildiz Kiosk; 3 In Merry Mexico; 4 Over the Grape Juice, or, The Peace Makers; 5 The White House from without in.

II consists of: 6 Madeline of the Movies: A Photoplay Done Back into the Words; 7 The Call of the Carbureter, or, Mr. Blinks and His Friends; 8 The Two Sexes, in Fives or Sixes: A Dinner Party Study; 9 The Grass Bachelor's Guide; 10 Every Man and His Friend. Mr. Grunch's Portrait Gallery; 11 More Than Twice Told Tales, or, Every Man His Own Hero; 12 A Study in Still Life: My Tailor.

III consists of: 13 Stories Shorter Still; 14 The Snoopopaths, or, Fifty Stories in One; 15 Foreign Fiction in Imported Instalments: Serge the Superman, a Russian Novel.

IV consists of: 16 Are the Rich Happy?; 17 Humor as I See It.

BINDING AND DUST JACKET: Bound in red cloth with stamping on the boards in gilt. A solid rectangle (enclosed within two rectangles) is stamped on the upper board. Within this solid rectangle is the following: [jester's symbol] FURTHER [jester's symbol] | FOOLISH-NESS | [rule] | STEPHEN LEACOCK. Stamped on the spine: FURTHER | FOOLISH | NESS | [jester's symbol] | LEACOCK | JOHN LANE | COMPANY.

On the front panel of the jacket is a colour illustration (signed M.B.A.) in orange, white, blue, yellow, and red with hand lettering. In the foreground of the illustration are two harlequin puppets (holding a sign) and in the background a tent filled with people. Above the illustration within a separate rectangle is: FURTHER ● FOOLISHNESS. Written on the sign: WALK IN! WALK IN! | [rule] | ALL THE FOLLIES | OF THE DAY! Below the illustration within a rectangle is the following: [yellow flower] STEPHEN LEACOCK [yellow flower]. The rest of the jacket is white with blue lettering. Printed on the spine panel: FURTHER | FOOLISHNESS | By | STEPHEN | LEACOCK | Author of | "Nonsense Novels" | "Behind the Beyond" | "Moonbeams from the | Larger Lunacy," etc. | $1.25 | NET | JOHN

LANE | COMPANY. The back panel of the jacket has A ROUSING LIST OF RECENT FICTION. The front flap has a synopsis of the book with the heading: UP-TO-DATE FUN. The book is described as "*Cloth, 12mo, $1.25 net*". The back flap has a list of OTHER BOOKS BY | Stephen Leacock published by the John Lane Company.

NOTES: The sketches for this book were gathered together by Leacock from his publications in magazines such as *Vanity Fair*, *Maclean's*, *Puck*, and *Century Magazine*. He records, for example, that "Madeline of the Movies" was completed on 8 November 1915 for *Puck*, "The Snoopopaths" on 21 December 1915 for *Vanity Fair*, and "Humour as I See It" on 19 March 1916 and "Abdul Aziz Has His" on 8 October 1916, both for *Maclean's*. "In Merry Mexico" was finished on 14 October 1916 "for book only". The American edition was published on 1 December 1916 at $1.25. For the contract and rights concerning the American edition, see the notes to the English edition (A24b).

By the end of 1916 4,891 copies were sold. Up to the end of 1921 (when the John Lane Company was sold to Dodd, Mead), another 6,321 copies were sold. According to advertising brochure issued by the John Lane Company, the book was into its sixth edition (i.e printing) by 1920 ($1.50 cloth).

Leacock himself recorded that by the end of 1921, 38,673 copies had sold for all editions and up to 1 February 1925, 42,484 copies.

Reprint: "Every Man and His Friends," *Answers* 61, no. 1,589 (9 November 1918): 337.

COPIES EXAMINED: CS (in jacket); QMMRB (first printing and 1917 reprint, neither in jacket).


## A24a.1 *Canadian issue*:

FURTHER | FOOLISHNESS | SKETCHES AND SATIRES | ON THE FOLLIES OF THE DAY | [thick-thin rule] | BY STEPHEN LEACOCK | AUTHOR OF "NONSENSE NOVELS," "MOONBEAMS FROM | THE LARGER LUNACY," "BEHIND THE BEYOND," ETC. | [thin-thick rule] | [thick-thin rule] | TORONTO: [three sets of three dots, each in the shape of a triangle] S. B. GUNDY : NEW YORK: JOHN LANE COMPANY | LONDON: JOHN LANE, THE BODLEY HEAD | [four sets of three dots, each in the shape of a triangle] MCMXVI [four sets of three dots, each in the shape of a triangle] | [thin-thick rule]

The Canadian issue is identical to the American edition with the exceptions of the title page, the boards (GUNDY on the spine), and the dust jacket. The jacket of the Canadian issue is similar to that of A24a. GUNDY replaces JOHN LANE | COMPANY on the spine panel. The back panel is almost the same as the front flap of A24a, and the front flap is almost the same as the back flap of A24a. On the back flap of the Canadian jacket is an advertisement for William J. Locke's *The Wonderful Year*.

NOTES: The Canadian issue was undoubtedly published simultaneously with the American edition in order to protect the latter's international copyright. Publication was announced in *Bookseller and Stationer* 33, no. 1 (January 1917): 32. By the end of 1916 2,468 copies had sold (royalty of $617). Between 1917 and 1 August 1924 1,159 more copies were sold. At this point, according to Leacock's records, 180 further copies were sold up to 1 February 1925 as a "Cheap Edn" (probably sold at a reduced price). Although this record keeping indicates that slightly more than 3,800 copies were sold in all, it is likely that the print run of the Canadian issue consisted of 4,000 copies.

COPIES EXAMINED: CS (two copies, one in jacket); QMMRB (not in jacket).

## A24a.2 *American issue* [1922?]:

FURTHER | FOOLISHNESS | SKETCHES AND SATIRES | ON THE FOLLIES OF THE DAY | [thick-thin rule] | BY STEPHEN LEACOCK | AUTHOR OF "NONSENSE NOVELS," "MOONBEAMS FROM | THE LARGER LUNACY," "BEHIND THE BEYOND" ETC. | [thin-thick rule] | [thick-thin rule] | NEW YORK | DODD, MEAD & COMPANY | MCMXXIII | [thin-thick rule]

The verso of the title leaf of the Dodd, Mead issue reads as follows: Copyright, 1916, | BY DODD, MEAD & COMPANY, INC. | *Printed in U. S. A.* Bound in green cloth. The boards are blind-stamped similar to the stamping of A24a, except the following is at the foot of the spine: DODD, MEAD | & COMPANY. The dust jacket (1925 printing examined) is also similar to that of A24a. DODD, MEAD | AND COMPANY is at the foot of the jacket's spine. The flaps of the Dodd, Mead issue and A24a are similar, the former with updated information. The back panel of the Dodd, Mead issue is blank. Priced at $2.

Leacock recorded that Dodd, Mead sold 173 copies of *Further Foolishness* in its first royalty statement (1 August 1922). A copy of this issue with 1922 on the title page could not be located. 990 further copies sold between that date and 1 February 1933.

COPIES EXAMINED: CS (1925 printing in jacket); OTY (1923 printing without jacket).

## A24b *English edition* (1917):

FURTHER | FOOLISHNESS | SKETCHES AND SATIRES | ON THE FOLLIES OF THE DAY | BY STEPHEN LEACOCK | [thin-thick rule] | [thick-thin rule] | LONDON: JOHN LANE, THE BODLEY HEAD | NEW YORK: JOHN LANE COMPANY. MCMXVII

◆ A⁶ B–I⁸ K-P⁸ Q¹⁰ [$1 signed; Q5 signed Q2]. *i–vi*, vii, *viii*, ix–xi, *1–4*, 3–45, *46–48*, 49–79,*80*, 81–97, *98*, 99–111, *112*, 113–117, *118–120*, 121–159, *160*, 161–181, *182*, 183–201, *202*, 203–209, *210–212*, 213–234, *1–10* pp. (128 leaves). 182 × 122 mm.

CONTENTS: p. *i–ii* blank; p. *iii* half title; p. *iv* list of seven books by Leacock published by The Bodley Head, the first being *Behind the Beyond* and the last *Moonbeams from the Larger Lunacy*; p. *v* title; p.*vi* PRINTED BY WILLIAM BRENDON AND SON, LTD., PLYMOUTH, ENGLAND; p. vii preface dated "*November 1, 1916*"; p. *viii* blank; pp. ix–x table of contents; p. xi list of illustrations; p. *1* blank; pp. 2–3, 3–234 text (pp. *46, 48, 80, 98, 112, 118, 120, 160, 182, 202, 210,* and *212* blank); pp. *1–4* advertisements of Leacock's books published by The Bodley Head with press opinions; pp. *5–8* advertisements of new novels, popular novels, etc. published by The Bodley Head; pp. *9–10* blank. Colour frontispiece by A.H. Fish. Other illustrations (facing pp. 121, 122, 124, 128, and 130) by M. Blood.

TEXT: Identical to A24a. However, the order of the sections (called "chapters" in A24a) is different. The order in the English edition is as follows: Follies in Fiction; Movies and Motors. Men and Women; Peace, War, and Politics; Timid Thoughts on Timely Topics.

BINDING AND DUST JACKET: Bound in green cloth, top edge stained light blue with lettering on the boards in light blue. Stamped on the upper board as follows: [all lines within two blind-stamped rectangles] *FURTHER FOOLISHNESS* | *By STEPHEN LEACOCK*. Stamped on the spine as follows: [two blind-stamped rules] | *FURTHER* | *FOOLISHNESS* | *By* | *STEPHEN* | *LEACOCK* | *THE* | *BODLEY HEAD* | [two blind-stamped rules].

The jacket is white with blue lettering. The front panel has the same colour illustration by A.H. Fish that is used as the frontispiece — a man in a kimono with a bird in a cage, scissors, and a plant. The caption on the frontispiece is: A PRETTY COSTUME DESIGNED BY "FISH" FOR A GRASS BACHELOR. Above the illustration on the front panel is the following (the F in the first two lines below the line level; several letters swash): FURTHER | FOOLISHNESS | By | Stephen | Leacock. Printed on the spine of the jacket: FURTHER | FOOLISHNESS | BY | STEPHEN | LEACOCK | 3/6 | Net. | THE BODLEY HEAD. The back panel has a list of seven other books by Leacock published by The Bodley Head (with press opinions). The flaps are blank.

NOTES: Leacock originally planned this book of sketches on 12 October 1915. He was hoping to ". . . catch the Xmas sale." "I shall *not* put in the *Peacemakers* but will include *Germany from Within*," Leacock told John Lane. But Leacock's proposal was premature. On 27 June 1916, he informed Lane that he had written to Jeff Jones of the American branch of the company about lengthening the book — "including other things with it, all war studies." He mentioned "A Diary of the President" (from *Vanity Fair*), a revised version of the "Peace Makers," and ". . . a new piece, still to be written to called *In Merry Mexico* All of this under an attractive title & with a gay jacket will sell like a hot bun." The book was uppermost in his mind on 25 August 1916, although he still had no title yet. On 22 September 1916, he reported to Lane that he had 35,000 to 40,000 words ready. The book appeared too thin, however, and he considered including his play of *Sunshine Sketches of a Little Town* to add another 25,000 words. Two days later, he came up with the title of the book. Leacock apologized to Lane about the delay in publication of the English edition on 24 December 1916. He had neglected to send Lane a manuscript or galleys of the American edition. By this time Leacock had seen Fish's drawing of the frontispiece. It ". . . is simply delightful," he told Lane. "What a wonderful high standard she keeps up (I see her pictures in the illustrated papers each week)" (information based on The Bodley Head fonds, TEX).

The contract with John Lane The Bodley Head for rights in the United Kingdom, the colonies, India and the United States is dated 20 June 1914. At that time Leacock signed the contract for *Arcadian Adventures with the Idle Rich*, and *Further Foolishness* was the third work of fiction which was promised to Lane in a multi-book deal. Leacock received a royalty of 20% on first 7,000 copies sold, 25% on subsequent copies sold, with an advance of £100.

According to *The English Catalogue of Books*, the English edition was published in February 1917. By 1 July 1917 (the first royalty statement), 6,906 had sold in England, 2,525 copies in Australasia, and 979 copies as colonial. Up to the end of 1929, 12,307 further copies had sold in England, 1,150 further copies in Australasia, 1,551 further copies as colonial, and 387 further copies Australasian / colonial.

According to the copyright page of the 1931 reprint, there were reprints in 1917, 1918, 1919, 1921, and 1924.

COPIES EXAMINED: CS (first and fourth printings in jacket, the latter 1919 "*FOURTH*

*EDITION*"; first and third printings not in jacket, the latter 1917 "*THIRD EDITION*"); QMMRB (first, 1919, and 1931 printings, none in jacket).

### A24b.1 *Australasian issue* (1917):

The Australasian issue is the same as A24b with the following exceptions: the verso of the title leaf reads *AUSTRALASIAN EDITION* | PRINTED BY WILLIAM BRENDON AND SON, LTD., PLYMOUTH, ENGLAND; the sheets measure 183 × 120 mm. Dust jacket not seen. For the sales of this issue, see the notes to A24b.

COPIES EXAMINED: CS; QMMRB.

### A24c *Canadian edition* (1968):

[all lines within three rectangles; the rectangles are enclosed within a wavy rectangular frame] *Stephen Leacock* | FURTHER | FOOLISHNESS | *Sketches and Satires* | *On* | *The Follies of The Day* | INTRODUCTION : D. W. COLE | GENERAL EDITOR : MALCOLM ROSS | NEW CANADIAN LIBRARY NO. 60 | [publisher's device: abstract design of a person on a horse-drawn chariot, taking aim with a bow and arrow] | MCCLELLAND AND STEWART | LIMITED

♦ *i–v*, vi–xii, 1–5, 18–91, 92–93, 94–148, 149, 150–164, 1–4 pp. (84 leaves). 182 × 110 mm.

CONTENTS: p. *i* half title; p. *ii* blank; p. *iii* title; p. *iv* Copyright, 1916, by John Lane Company | Introduction © 1968, McClelland and Stewart Limited | *The Canadian Publishers* | McClelland and Stewart Limited | 25 Hollinger Road, Toronto 16 | PRINTED AND BOUND BY | HAZELL WATSON AND VINEY LTD | AYLESBURY, BUCKS; pp. *v–xii* D.W. Cole's introduction, dated August, 1967; p. *1* Leacock's preface; p. *2* blank; pp. *3–4* table of contents; pp. *5, 18–164* text (p. *92* blank); p. *1* biographical information on Leacock; p. *2* blank; pp. *3–4* list of titles in the New Canadian Library series.

TEXT: Identical to A24b.

BINDING: Bound in stiff paper, perfect bound. The covers are white, gold, purple, and black. A drawing of Leacock's face in black is on the front cover. The back cover has a paragraph on the book's contents and the book's price ($1.25). Covers designed by William Henry.

NOTES: By the end of 1968 1,350 copies had sold. By the end of 1979 11,286 had sold (information based on file 14, "New Canadian Library," box 93, series A, McClelland and Stewart fonds, OHM). Date of publication and number of copies of the first printing not known.

COPIES EXAMINED: CS; QMMRB.

### A25 NATIONAL ORGANIZATION FOR WAR 1916

### A25a *first Canadian edition*:

[cover title: all lines within two ornamental rectangles which are composed of solid and empty dots] FOR FREE DISTRIBUTION | [rule] | NATIONAL | ORGANIZATION | FOR WAR [swash Rs] | [ornamental sprocket] | By STEPHEN LEACOCK

♦ 1⁴. 1, 2–7, 1 pp. (4 leaves). 224 × 130 mm.

CONTENTS: p. *1* cover title; pp. 2–7 text; p. *1* [all lines within two ornamental rectangles which are composed of solid and empty dots; the next six lines within a rectangle that has a floral ornament at its base] NATIONAL | THRIFT | NATIONAL | SAVING | NATIONAL | INVESTMENT | This pamphlet is printed for free distribution. WILL | YOU HELP to circulate it? If so, send one dollar | for fifty copies or any larger sum, for copies at two | cents each, to the PHILIP DAVIS PRINTING CO., | LIMITED, Hamilton, Ontario. The copies will | either be sent to you to distribute or if you prefer it, | either be sent out free to bookstores and news-stands, | without further trouble to yourself.

BINDING. Issued without wrappers or boards, off-white paper stock, wire-stitched.

NOTES: The following entry occurs in Leacock's notebook of recorded publications and speeches at QMMRB: "Dec 10 [1916] National Organisation for War. Star — Pamphlet." This would suggest that this publication appeared in the *Montreal Star* before it was printed as a pamphlet. A search in that newspaper, however, failed to locate such an article.

Leacock told John Lane on 24 December 1916 that he had arranged to print 2,000 copies of this pamphlet at his own expense for free distribution. He then asked Lane to ". . . get it copied in English papers (no pay to me, of course), I also want Lord Northcliffe to take it up. I hear that he reads my books: that will do an introduction. Do *you* know him — or can you, through friends, get my pamphlet before him." He thanked Lane on 16 March 1917: "I am very glad that Lord Northcliffe is printing the pamphlet." No copy of the English edition has been located, however (The Bodley Head fonds, TEX).

Reprinted in B6.

COPIES EXAMINED: OONL (three copies); SLM (three copies).

## A25b *second Canadian edition* (1917):

[cover title] FOR FREE DISTRIBUTION | [rule] | [ornament] | NATIONAL | ORGANIZATION | FOR | WAR | BY | STEPHEN | LEACOCK | [ornament] | REPRINTED FOR | THE NATIONAL SERVICE BOARD | OF CANADA | [rule] | OTTAWA: Printed by J. de L. Taché, | Printer to the King's Most Excellent Majesty, 1917.

◆   $1^6$. *1*–2, *3*–11, *1* pp. (6 leaves). 227 × 100 mm.

CONTENTS: p. *1* cover title; pp. 2–11 text; p. *1* [the first nine lines within a rectangle] | NATIONAL | SERVICE | BY | NATIONAL | THRIFT | NATIONAL | SAVING | NATIONAL | INVESTMENT | *What are* | *You Doing* | *to Win* | *the War?*

BINDING. Issued without wrappers or boards, off-white paper stock, wire-stitched.

NOTES: Leacock told Lane on 16 March 1917: "The government here, — I think I told you, — are circulating a quarter of a million [copies of my pamphlet]." The copy at OONL was received on 20 April 1917.

COPIES EXAMINED: OONL; OTAR (Miscellaneous Military Records #57, MU2061); OTNY; QMMRB.

## A26  FRENZIED FICTION  1917

### A26a *American edition* [1917]:

FRENZIED | [three dots in the shape of a triangle] FICTION [three dots in the shape of a triangle] | [thick-thin rule] | BY STEPHEN LEACOCK | AUTHOR

OF "FURTHER FOOLISHNESS," | "NONSENSE NOVELS," "LITERARY LAPSES," ETC. | [thin-thick rule] | [thick-thin rule] | NEW YORK: JOHN LANE COMPANY | LONDON: JOHN LANE, THE BODLEY HEAD | TORONTO: S. B. GUNDY : MCMXVIII | [thin-thick rule]

◆  $1-18^8$ $19^4$. $1-4$, 5, $6-8$, $9-294$, $1-2$ pp. (148 leaves). 186 × 123 mm.

CONTENTS: p. *1* half title; p. *2* list of eight books by Leacock published by the John Lane Company, the first being *Further Foolishness* and the last *Moonbeams from the Larger Lunacy*; p. *3* title; p. *4* Copyright, 1917, | BY JOHN LANE COMPANY | Printed by | Prospect Press | New York, U.S.A.; p. *5* table of contents; p. *6* blank; p. *7* fly title; p. *8* blank; pp. *9–294* text; pp. *1–2* blank.

TEXT: I My Revelations As a Spy; II Father Knickerbocker: A Fantasy; III The Prophet in Our Midst; IV Personal Adventures in the Spirit World; V The Sorrows of a Summer Guest; VI To Nature and Back Again; VII The Cave Man As He Is; VIII Ideal Interviews — I With a European Prince, II With Our Greatest Actor, III With Our Greatest Scientist, IV With Our Typical Novelists; IX The New Education; X The Errors of Santa Claus; XI Lost in New York: A Visitor's Soliloquy; XII This Strenuous Age; XIII The Old, Old Story of How Five Men Went Fishing; XIV Back from the Land; XV The Perplexity Column As Done by the Jaded Journalist; XVI Simple Stories of Success or How to Succeed in Life; XVII In Dry Toronto: A Local Study of a Universal Topic; XVIII Merry Christmas.

BINDING AND DUST JACKET: Two binding variants were examined: one in green cloth with stamping on the boards in dark green; the other in red ribbed cloth with stamping on the boards in gilt. A solid rectangle (enclosed within two rectangles) is stamped on the upper board. Within this solid rectangle is the following in raised letters: FRENZIED | [jester's stick] FICTION [jester's stick] | [rule] | STEPHEN LEACOCK. Stamped on the spine: FRENZIED | FICTION | [jester's stick] | LEACOCK | JOHN LANE | COMPANY. Dust jacket not seen.

NOTES: The sketches for this book were gathered together by Leacock from his publications in magazines such as *Vanity Fair*, *Maclean's*, and *Puck*. In his notebook at QMMRB, he records, for example, that "Simple Stories of Success" was completed on 27 December 1915 for *Maclean's*. A few sketches such as sections III ("With Our Greatest Scientist," completed 23 September 1917) and IV ("With Our Typical Novelists," completed 7 October 1917) of "Ideal Interviews" were written specifically for inclusion in the book. On 30 July 1917 Leacock told Miss Fetherstonhaugh, his typist at McGill University, that he would have to ". . . to patch up a book of sketches, as usual, instead of a novel of anything sustained, this autumn." He asked her to estimate the number of words for several sketches: "Errors of Santa Claus" (completed 21 October 1916), "Lost in New York" (completed 26 November 1916), "Are Schoolboys Happy?" (completed 25 January 1917), "Father Knickerbocker" (completed 17 April 1917), and "Personal Adventures in the Spirit World" (completed 10 May 1917). He instructed her on 2 September 1917 to find other sketches that she had apparently typed for him and to send these to Jeff Jones at the John Lane Company. Leacock had already written 33,000 words and another 17,000 words were wanting by 10 October 1917 (RG 32, container 4, file 43, QMM Archives).

The American edition was published on 15 December 1917 at $1.25. No copy was examined with the date of 1917 on the title page. The copyright was registered with the Copyright Office at DLC on 17 and 19 December 1917 (ClA479691). For the contract and rights concerning the American edition, see the notes to the English edition (A26b).

By the end of 1917 4,339 copies were sold. A further 5,757 copies were sold up to the end of 1921 before the John Lane Company was sold to Dodd, Mead. According to an advertising brochure issued by the John Lane Company, the book was into its "Fifth Edition" [i.e. printing] by 1920, selling at $1.50.

Leacock recorded that for all editions and issues, 39,234 copies were sold up to 1 February 1925. The book continued to sell at a reduced rate thereafter.

"With Our Greatest Scientist" was reprinted as "Simple as Day," in *Defenders of Democracy: Contributions from the Representative Men and Women of Letters and Other Arts from Our Allies and Our Own Country* (New York: John Lane Company, 1918), pp. 111–117.

COPIES EXAMINED: CS (both binding variants, neither in jacket).

### A26a.1 *Canadian issue*:

FRENZIED | [three dots in the shape of a triangle] FICTION [three dots in the shape of a triangle] | [thick-thin rule] | BY STEPHEN LEACOCK | AUTHOR OF "FURTHER FOOLISHNESS," | "NONSENSE NOVELS," "LITERARY LAPSES," ETC. | [thin-thick rule] | [thick-thin rule] | TORONTO: S. B. GUNDY | NEW YORK: JOHN LANE COMPANY | LONDON: JOHN LANE, THE BODLEY HEAD | MCMXVIII | [thin-thick rule]

The Canadian issue is identical to the American edition with the exception of the title page and the imprint on the spine (in red cloth with GUNDY stamped in gilt at the foot of the spine). The jacket is cream-coloured. The front panel has a colour illustration of three harlequin clowns who are sitting on a bench and are looking at a large book or newspaper inscribed with Leacock's name. "A ROUSING LIST OF RECENT FICTION" is on the back panel. Printed on the spine panel: FRENZIED | FICTION | *By* | STEPHEN | LEACOCK | Author of | "Nonsense Novels" | "Behind the Beyond" | "Moonbeams from the | Larger Lunacy," etc | [next two lines in red] $1.25 | NET | GUNDY. A list of other books by Leacock with excerpts from reviews is on the front flap. The back flap has an advertisement for William J. Locke's *The Red Planet*.

NOTES: The Canadian issue was undoubtedly published simultaneously with the American edition in order to protect the latter's international copyright. By the end of 1917 2,059 copies had sold (royalty of 25¢ per copy, $514.75 royalty). Between 1918 and 1 July 1924, 1,318 were sold. At this point, according to Leacock's records, 230 further copies were sold until 1 March 1925 as a "cheap Ed" (probably sold at a reduced price). Although this record keeping indicates that slightly more than 3,600 copies sold, it is more than likely that the edition consisted of 4,000 copies.

COPIES EXAMINED: CS (in jacket); QMMRB (two copies, neither in jacket).

### A26a.2 *first American issue* [1922?]:

FRENZIED | [three dots in the shape of a triangle] FICTION [three dots in the shape of a triangle] | [thick-thin rule] | BY STEPHEN LEACOCK | AUTHOR OF "FURTHER FOOLISHNESS," | "NONSENSE NOVELS," "LITERARY LAPSES," ETC. | [thin-thick rule] | [thick-thin rule] | NEW YORK | DODD, MEAD & COMPANY | MCMXXIII | [thin-thick rule]

According to Leacock's notebook of royalty payments at SLM, Dodd, Mead sold 385 copies from the beginning of 1922 to 1 August of that year. However, no copy of this issue could be found with the date of 1922 on the title page.

The verso of the title leaf of the 1923 reprint reads as follows: Copyright, 1917, | By DODD, MEAD & COMPANY, INC. | *Printed in U. S. A.*. The copy examined at OWU was rebound and not in jacket. Information on the binding and jacket is based on the 1924 printing.

Bound in bright red cloth, the texture different from that of A26a. Stamping on the boards is similar to that to that of A26a. Stamping on the front board is blind-stamped within a blind-stamped rectangle. Stamping on the spine is in gilt, the publisher's name at the foot of the spine: DODD, MEAD | & COMPANY.

The dust jacket is similar to that of A26a.1. The Dodd, Mead jacket is white with lettering in blue. The illustration on the front panel is the same as that of A26a.1. On the back panel within a broken, ornamental rectangle is the heading "Laugh with Leacock," advertising Leacock's books published by Dodd, Mead. The front panel has an advertisement for *Literary Lapses*, and the back panel has a similar advertisement for *Nonsense Novels*.

NOTES: 1,200 copies sold of this issue up to 1 February 1925. Price $2.00. Thereafter, in the 1930s, the book sold from approximately 150 to less than 100 copies annually.

COPIES EXAMINED: CS (1924 printing in jacket); OWU (1923 printing).

### A26a.3 *second American issue, photographic reprint* (1970)

FRENZIED | [three dots in shape of a triangle] FICTION [three dots in shape of a triangle] | [thick-thin rule] | BY STEPHEN LEACOCK | *Short Story Index Reprint Series* | [publisher's device, two lines in height, to the left of the next two lines: abstract design of a building with four columns] | BOOKS FOR LIBRARIES PRESS | FREEPORT, NEW YORK

The verso of the title leaf reads as follows: First Published 1917 | Reprinted 1970 | STANDARD BOOK NUMBER: | 8369-3594-2 | LIBRARY OF CONGRESS CATALOG CARD NUMBER: | 78-125227 | PRINTED IN THE UNITED STATES OF AMERICA. Pagination is the same as A26a. The page opposite the title page is blank. Leaves measure 196 × 124 mm. Bound in light orangish red cloth. Stamped on the spine as follows: [red crossing lines] | [the next two lines in silver stamped vertically within a solid red rectangle] FRENZIED FICTION | LEACOCK | [red crossing lines].

COPIES EXAMINED: ALU.

### A26a.4 *third American issue, photographic reprint* (1992)

FRENZIED | [three dots in shape of a triangle] FICTION [three dots in shape of a triangle] | [thick-thin rule] | BY STEPHEN LEACOCK | AYER COMPANY, PUBLISHERS, INC. | SALEM, NEW HAMPSHIRE 03079

The verso of the title leaf reads as follows: First Published 1917 | Reprinted 1970 | Reprint Edition, 1992 | Ayer Company, Publishers, Inc. | Salem, New Hampshire 03079 | [remaining five lines identical to those of A26a.3]. Pagination is the same as A26a, except that there is an additional blank leaf at the beginning and at the end. The page opposite the title page is blank. Leaves measure 196 × 124 mm. Bound in red laminated plastic over paper boards with white lettering on the upper board and spine. Stamped on the upper board: FRENZIED | FICTION | [thick-thin rule] | BY STEPHEN LEACOCK. Stamped on the spine: LEACOCK | [the next line stamped vertically] FRENZIED FICTION | AYER.

COPIES EXAMINED: CS.

## A26b *English edition* (1918):

FRENZIED FICTION | BY STEPHEN LEACOCK | [thick-thin rule] | [thin-thick rule] | *LONDON: JOHN LANE, THE BODLEY HEAD* | *NEW YORK: JOHN LANE COMPANY, MCMXVIII*

◆ A⁴ B–I⁸ K-Q⁸ *⁴ [$1 signed]. *1*–8, *1*–239, *1*–9 pp. (128 leaves). 188 × 125 mm.

CONTENTS: p. *1* half title; p. *2* list of eight books by Leacock published by The Bodley Head, the first being *Literary Lapses* and the last *Further Foolishness*; p. *3* title; p. *4* WILLIAM BRENDON AND SON, LTD., PRINTERS, PLYMOUTH, ENGLAND.; pp. *5*–6 table of contents; p. *7* fly title; p. *8* blank; pp. *1*–239, *1* text; pp. *2*–9 advertisements of Leacock's books published by The Bodley Head with press opinions.

TEXT: Identical to 26a.

BINDING AND DUST JACKET: Bound in blue cloth, top edge stained blue, with stamping in dark blue. Stamped on the upper board within two blind-stamped rectangles as follows: *FRENZIED FICTION* | *By STEPHEN LEACOCK*. Stamped on the spine as follows: [blind-stamped rule] | *FRENZIED* | *FICTION* | *By* | *STEPHEN* | *LEACOCK* | *THE* | *BODLEY HEAD* | [blind-stamped rule].

The front panel of the jacket has a white background, lettering in green stencil type, and a colour illustration by John Kettelwell of two men in Oriental dress. One man, blond and curly-haired, is smoking a cigar, is seated with his feet resting on a cushioned foot-stool, and has a quill pen in one hand and a scroll in the other. The other man appears to be his black servant who is carrying an inkwell. The rest of the jacket is white with black lettering. Printed on the spine panel of the jacket: FRENZIED | FICTION | STEPHEN | LEACOCK | THE | BODLEY HEAD. The back panel of the jacket has a list of THE WORKS OF STEPHEN LEACOCK within a rectangle. The front flap features an advertisement of Cecil Sommers's *Temporary Heroes*. Similar advertisements are on the back flap for *A Diary of the Great Warr* and *A Second Diary of the Great Warr*, both by Samuel Pepys, Jr.

NOTES: The contract with John Lane The Bodley Head for rights in the United Kingdom, the colonies, India and the United States is dated 20 June 1914. At that time Leacock signed a contract for *Arcadian Adventures with the Idle Rich*, and *Frenzied Fiction* was the fourth work of fiction which was promised to Lane in a multi-book deal. Leacock received a royalty of 20% on the first 7,000 copies sold, 25% on subsequent copies sold, with £100 advance. According to *The English Catalogue of Books*, the English edition was published in June 1918 at 4s ("Cr. 8vo"). There were five printings by 1921. Lomer (p. 28) notes further printings in 1924 and 1931.

By 1 July 1918 (the first royalty statement), Leacock recorded that 7,354 copies had sold in Great Britain, 1,780 copies to Australasia, and 1,166 copies to the colonies. Between 1 July 1918 and the end of December 1929, sales were as follows: 13,949 copies in Great Britain, 2,802 copies to the colonies, 750 copies to Australasia, and 121 copies to the colonies / Australasia.

COPIES EXAMINED: CS (first printing in jacket; "*Second Edition*" (i.e. second printing), 1920, in jacket; "*Fourth Edition*" (i.e. fourth printing), 1919, in jacket; "*Fifth Edition*" (i.e. fifth printing), 1921, no jacket); QMMRB (first printing, not in jacket).

### A26b.1 *Australasian issue* (1918):

The Australasian issue is identical with A26b with the following exceptions: the verso of the title reads *Australasian Edition* | WILLIAM BRENDON AND SON, LTD., PRINTERS, PLYMOUTH, ENGLAND.; the final gathering (advertisements) is absent; the leaves measure 185 × 123 mm. In all liklihood the jacket is the same as A26b but trimmed slightly (only a portion of the front panel of the jacket exists in the copy examined). For number of copies sold of this issue, see the notes to A26b.

COPY EXAMINED: QMMRB.

### A26c *first Canadian edition* (1965):

Stephen Leacock | [open swelled rule] | FRENZIED | FICTION | [open swelled rule] | Introduction: David Dooley | General Editor: Malcolm Ross | New Canadian Library No. 48 | [publisher's device: abstract design of a person on a horse-drawn chariot, taking aim with a bow and arrow] | MCCLELLAND AND STEWART LIMITED

♦ *i–iv*, v–xiii, *1*, 15–157, *158*, 159–160 pp. (80 leaves). 185 × 111 mm.

CONTENTS: p. *i* half title; p. *ii* blank; p. *iii* title; p. *iv* First published in 1919 [sic] by John Lane, the Bodley Head | © McClelland and Stewart Limited, 1965 | [six lines concerning copyright] | *The Canadian Publishers* | McClelland and Stewart Limited | 25 Hollinger Road, Toronto 16 | PRINTED AND BOUND BY | HAZELL WATSON AND VINEY LTD | AYLESBURY BUCKS ENGLAND; pp. v–vi table of contents; pp. vii–xiii D.J. Dooley's introduction; p. *1.* blank; pp. 15–156 text; p. 157 biographical information on Leacock; p. *158* blank; pp. 159–160 list of titles in the New Canadian Library series.

TEXT: Identical to A26a.

BINDING: Bound in stiff paper, perfect bound. The covers are white and green with lettering primarily in black. A drawing of Leacock's face in green is on the front cover. The back cover has a paragraph on the book's contents and the book's price ($1.25). Covers designed by Frank Newfeld.

NOTES: The setting of type for this edition came from the 1919 reprint of the English edition (a26b). McClelland and Stewart acknowledged receipt of Dooley's introduction on 27 April 1964. He returned the page proofs to M&S on 20 August 1964. By the end of 1965 1,667 copies had sold. By the end of 1979 16,754 had sold. Reprinted in 1984 (information based on file 14, "New Canadian Library," box 93, series A, and file 12, box Cae12, McClelland and Stewart fonds, OHM). Date of publication and number of copies printed for each impression not known.

COPIES EXAMINED: CS (two copies; proof copy owned by Malcolm Ross); SLM (1984 reprint manufactured by Webcom Limited).

## A27 MERRY CHRISTMAS 1917

### A27a *first edition*:

MERRY CHRISTMAS | *By* STEPHEN LEACOCK | *Courtesy of Hearst's Magazine*

◆ 1–3⁴. 1–7, 2–15, 1–3 pp. (12 leaves). 206 × 145 mm.

CONTENTS: pp. *1–2* blank; p. *3* half title; p. *4* blank; p. *5* title; p. *6* blank; pp. *7, 2–15* text; p. *1* Two hundred copies printed in the | shop of WILLIAM EDWIN RUDGE | for his friends. *Christmas, 1917.*; pp. *2–3* blank.

BINDING: Bound in pale blue paper boards with silver flecks, quarter-bound in white paper boards, with matching endpapers stained blue also flecked with silver, deckle edges. Three rectangles are blind-stamped on the upper board. Blind-stamped within these rectangles is a series of eleven Christmas toys or objects (a wooden horse, a chicken, a moose, a toy soldier, a jack-in-the-box, etc.). Two smaller rectangles are also blind-stamped within the three rectangles. The following is stamped in blue within the two rectangles: MERRY | CHRISTMAS. Apparently issued without a jacket.

NOTES: Leacock's story, "Merry Christmas," first appeared in *Hearst's Magazine* in December 1917 (see C17.23).

COPIES EXAMINED: OTNY; SLM (Leacock's copy).

### A27b *second edition* (1967):

A | MERRY | CHRISTMAS | by STEPHEN LEACOCK | Illustrated by Thomas R. Lubbock | LEDERER, STREET & ZEUS CO. | Berkeley, California | 1967

◆ 1¹⁶. 1–32 pp. (16 leaves). 222 × 126 mm.

CONTENTS: pp. *1–2* blank; p. *3* half title; p. *4* drawing in black ink of sad Santa Claus p. *5* title; p. *6* Grateful acknowledgement is extended to | Dodd, Mead Co., Inc. for permission to reprint | this story.; p. *7 Greetings and Best Wishes | from* | WALTER AND KATHARINE KOLASA: p. *8* drawing in black ink of Father Time; *9–11* foreword, signed F.A.K., with a list of other volumes issued at Christmas by the same publisher; p. *12* blank; p. *13 A Prayer for Christmas*; p. *14* blank; pp. *15–28* text; p. *29* drawing in black ink of Santa Claus holding a toy horse; pp. *30–32* blank.

BINDING: Bound in stiff white wrappers with flaps, wire-stitched. Printed on the front cover, all lines hand-written: [swash and in red] *A* | [first letter swash and in red, the line at an angle] *Merry* | [the first letter swash and in green, the line at an angle] *Christmas* | *by Stephen Leacock*.

NOTES: This publisher issued a booklet at Christmas from 1937 to 1940 and then again from 1946 onward. According to the foreword, the publication of Leacock's story marked "the thirthieth anniversary of the first edition in our series of commemorative booklets, one each year, except for those omitted during World War II." Probably distributed to friends at no charge. Number of copies printed not known.

COPIES EXAMINED: CS.

## A28 WET OR DRY? 1918

### A28a *Canadian edition*:

[caption title; four lines enclosed within two zig-zag rectangles] *Wet or Dry?* |
[rule] | By STEPHEN LEACOCK | (Copyright, 1918)

◆ Leaflet folded once to form four unnumbered pages. 217 × 140 mm.

CONTENTS: The leaflet consists of the transcribed lines (noted above) and the text of
Leacock's address. After the text are the following: STEPHEN LEACOCK. | [urn ornament].

TEXT: The text begins directly after the lines enclosed within the zig-zag rectangles. The
first line of the text is: "There can be little doubt that all of North America — or all of it
that lies between the Mexicans and the Esquimaux — is going dry." The last several lines
of the text on p. 4 are: "The editor of this paper will receive perhaps threatening letters
from Mothers' Meetings and Children's Blue Ribbon Societies for daring to print it. And
for myself, the lawyers and judges and doctors whom I have quoted will say that they never
heard of me, and that they never took anything stronger in their lives than raspberry vinegar.
Never mind. Perhaps I shall be able to work in Hayti or in Dutch Borneo or some sensible
country."

BINDING: Off-white paper stock.

NOTES: In his notebook of recorded publications at QMMRB, Leacock wrote: "December
13 [1918] Montreal Star". His article first appeared in *Saturday Night* on 22 November
1918 (see C18.27). He undoubtedly arranged for the printing of this leaflet himself. Number
of copies printed not known.

COPIES EXAMINED: SLM (five copies, only one being in perfect condition).

### A28b *American edition* entitled *The Truth about Prohibition from the Viewpoint of an Eminent Professor*:

[cover title; all lines within three rectangles, the two outside ones ornamental]
The Truth About | Prohibition from | the Viewpoint of an | Eminent Professor |
[two ornamental rules] | By Stephen Leacock | Department of Political Economy
| McGill University | [oval with linked compartments, the first line curved]
ALLIED PRINTING | [the next word in a compartment] TRADE [the next two
words in a compartment] UNION [under the previous word] LABEL [the next
word in a compartment] COUNCIL | [in a compartment with curved lines]
NEW YORK CITY] | [to the right of the oval] 287

◆ $1^4$. 1–2, 3–8 pp. (4 leaves). 152 × 90 mm.

CONTENTS: p. *1* title; p. 2 blank; pp. 3–8 text.

TEXT: Identical to 25a.

BINDING: Issued on off-white paper stock, no wrapper. The copy examined was resown.

NOTES: According to the *National Union Catalog*, this pamphlet was published in [1915?]
by the Allied Printing Trades Council. This dating is doubtful, however, since the text was
written by Leacock in 1918 (see the notes to the above entry). Neither the sponsorship of
the pamphlet nor the number of copies printed is known. The number, 287, on the cover
may be the copy number, which would indicate that the edition consisted of at least that

number of copies. In all likelihood the pamphlet appeared sometime after its serial appearance. Leacock lectured several times in New York City between February and April 1919, and it may have been at that time that the pamphlet was published.

COPIES EXAMINED: HLS.

## A29 THE HOHENZOLLERNS IN AMERICA 1919

### A29a *American edition*:

[thick-thin rule] | THE | HOHENZOLLERNS | [three dots in the shape of a triangle] IN AMERICA [three dots in the shape of a triangle] | WITH THE BOLSHEVIKS IN BERLIN | AND OTHER IMPOSSIBILITIES | [rule] | BY STEPHEN LEACOCK | [rule] | NEW YORK: JOHN LANE COMPANY | LONDON: JOHN LANE, THE BODLEY HEAD | TORONTO: S. B. GUNDY: MCMXIX | [thin-thick rule]

♦ $1-17^8$. *1-4*, 5, *6-8*, 9-72, *73-74*, 75-99, *100-102*, 103-114, *115-116*, 117-179, *180-182*, *183-269*, *1-3* pp. (136 leaves). 186 × 123 mm.

CONTENTS: p. *1* half title; p. 2 list of nine books by Leacock published by the John Lane Company, the first being *Frenzied Fiction* and the last *Moonbeams from the Larger Lunacy*; p. *3* title; p. 4 [two thick rules] | COPYRIGHT, 1919 | BY JOHN LANE COMPANY | THE • PLIMPTON • PRESS | NORWOOD•MASS•U•S•A; p. 5 table of contents; p. 6 blank; pp. 8-269 text (pp. 8, *74*, *100*, *102*, *116*, *180*, and *182* are blank); pp. *1-3* blank.

TEXT: I The Hohenzollerns in America (comprised of six chapters); II With the Bolsheviks in Berlin; III Afternoon Tea with the Sultan: A Study of Reconstruction in Turkey; IV Echoes of the War; V Other Impossibilities.

IV consists of the following sketches: 1 The Boy Who Came Back; 2 The War Sacrifices of Mr. Spugg; 3 If Germany Had Won; 4 War and Peace at the Galaxy Club; 5 The War News As I Remember It; 6 Some Just Complaints about the War; 7 Some Startling Side Effects of the War.

V consists of the following sketches: 1 The Art of Conversation; 2 Heroes and Heroines; 3 The Discovery of America Being Done into Moving Pictures and out Again; 4 Politics from within; 5 The Lost Illusions of Mr. Sims; 6 Fetching the Doctor: From Recollections of Childhood in the Canadian Countryside.

BINDING AND DUST JACKET: Bound in green cloth, top edge stained green. A dark green solid rectangle (enclosed within two dark green rectangles) is stamped on the upper board. Within this solid rectangle is the following in raised letters: *The* HOHENZOLLERNS | [jester's stick] IN AMERICA [jester's stick] | [rule] | STEPHEN LEACOCK. Stamped on the spine in dark green: *The* | HOHEN- | ZOLLERNS | *in* | AMERICA | [solid oval] | LEACOCK | JOHN LANE | COMPANY.

The front panel of the jacket is white with a blue, red and black illustration within two black rectangles. The illustration by Carlton Ellinger features three people (one with a box on his back bearing the name W. HOHEN) carrying luggage and walking on a ship's gangplank. Above the illustration are three lines in red: *The* | Hohenzollerns | in America. Below the illustration are two lines in red: by Stephen Leacock | *Author of "Nonsense Novels," "Behind the Beyond," etc.* The rest of the jacket is white with black lettering, except for the price of the book in red. Printed on the spine panel of the jacket: THE | HOHEN- | ZOLLERNS | IN | AMERICA | [rule] *By* [rule] | STEPHEN | LEACOCK | [the next two lines in red] | $1.25 | NET | JOHN LANE | COMPANY. The back panel has a list of LATEST FICTION SUCCESSES. The front flap has a synopsis of the book with the heading *Leacock | Solves the Kaiser Problem!* The back flap has a list of Leacock's other books (with press opinions) published by the John Lane Company. Also examined was the dust jacket in a second state with $1.50 price sticker affixed to the spine panel.

NOTES: In his notebook of recorded publications at QMMRB, Leacock wrote: "Jan 30 [1919] Hohenzollerns Finished." In the same notebook he indicated that he completed "Ch.I.' on 1 November 1918 for *Vanity Fair*, "Chap II" at the beginning of December 1918, and "Chap III" on 29 December 1918. Leacock told B.W. Willett on 28 January 1919 (The Bodley Head fonds, TEX):

> I had asked Jefferson Jones [of the John Lane Company] to forward my correspondence in the new book to save writing it all out twice. . . . He hopes to have the book in type in about a month & published by March 15: I am sending you the copy & he will be sending you the galley proofs. This, you will remember, is what we have been doing for some years.

The American edition was published on 12 April 1919. The copyright was registered with the Copyright Office at DLC on 19 April 1919 (ClA515282). The copyright was renewed by Stephen Lushington Leacock on 8 April 1970 (R482733).

By 1 July 1919 6,114 copies had been sold (royalty to Leacock of $949.46). Another 567 copies sold by the end of year ($141.75 royalty). According to an advertising brochure issued by the John Lane Company, the book was into its 25th Thousand by 1920. This number of copies printed may refer to total number of copies printed for all editions, although Leacock himself recorded 22,780 copies for all editions by the end of 1920. Another 436 copies were sold of the American edition before Dodd, Mead purchased the John Lane Company (up to the end of 1921).

Between 1922 and 1 August 1933 Dodd, Mead sold a total of 222 copies of the American edition. The American edition was still in print as of 1 June 1944. In a three-year period between 1 February 1941 and 1 February 1944, Dodd, Mead reported that the book had earned $5.80 royalty in American sales. No copy of an issue with Dodd, Mead as publisher was examined, however.

COPIES EXAMINED: CS (in jacket); EVANS (in jacket); QMMRB (in jacket).

## A29a.1 *Canadian issue*:

[thick-thin rule] | THE | HOHENZOLLERNS | [three dots in the shape of a triangle] IN AMERICA [three dots in the shape of a triangle] | WITH THE BOLSHEVIKS IN BERLIN | AND OTHER IMPOSSIBILITIES | [rule] | BY STEPHEN LEACOCK | [rule] | TORONTO: S. B. GUNDY : NEW YORK: JOHN LANE COMPANY | LONDON: JOHN LANE, THE BODLEY HEAD | MCMXIX | [thin-thick rule]

The Canadian issue is identical to the American edition except for the following: the title page (see above transcription); JOHN LANE | COMPANY is replaced by GUNDY on the book's spine; and the dust jacket — Gundy's name throughout, an ad for Sergeant Ralph

S. Kendall's *Benton of the Royal Mounted* on the back flap, and a list of other books by Leacock (with press opinions) on the back panel.

NOTES: Leacock told B.W. Willett on 28 January 1919:

> As to Gundy, he has only the contract that I made with him some years ago giving him the *Canadian sale* of the books contracted for with Mr. Lane in 1914. This new book is the last of them. I presume therefore that your arrangements with Gundy will be similar to those of past years: I think he buys his books from your New York company. (The Bodley Head fonds, TEX)

The Canadian issue was undoubtedly published simultaneously with the American edition. By 1 July 1919 2,375 had sold ($593 royalty). Another 170 copies ($42.50 royalty) sold by the end of 1919. Between 1920 and 1 July 1924 212 more copies were sold. According to Leacock's record of royalty payments, 141 copies were sold between July 1924 and January 1925. He refers to the latter as the "Cheap Edn". Ordinarily, this would imply a re-issue of the book, but it is more likely that Oxford University Press (for which Gundy acted as agent) reduced the price of the remaining copies at this time.

COPIES EXAMINED: CS (two copies, one in jacket); QMMRB (two copies, one in jacket).

## A29b *English edition*:

THE HOHENZOLLERNS | IN AMERICA [four floral illustrations] | *AND OTHER IMPOSSIBILITIES* | *BY STEPHEN LEACOCK* | [thin-thick rule] | [thick-thin rule] | *LONDON: JOHN LANE, THE BODLEY HEAD* | *NEW YORK: JOHN LANE COMPANY, MCMXIX*

◆ A⁴ B–R⁸ [$1 signed]. *1–10, 3–65, 66–68, 69–92, 93–94, 95–106, 107–108, 109–168, 169–170, 171–254, 1–2* pp. (132 leaves). 189 × 127 mm.

CONTENTS: pp. *1–2* blank; p. *3* half title; p. *4* list of nine books by Leacock published by The Bodley Head, the first being *Literary Lapses* and the last *Frenzied Fiction*; p. *5* title; p. *6* WILLIAM BRENDON AND SON, LTD., PRINTERS, PLYMOUTH, ENGLAND; pp. *7–8* table of contents; pp. *9–10, 3–254* text (pp. *10, 66, 68, 94, 108,* and *170* are blank); pp. *1–2* advertisements of Leacock's books published by The Bodley Head with press opinions.

TEXT: The same as the American edition, although the third sketch of V is entitled The Discovery of America by Cinematograph Being Done in Moving Pictures and out Again.

BINDING AND DUST JACKET: Bound in camel-coloured buckram with lettering in dark brown. Stamped on the upper board within two blind-stamped rectangles: *THE HOHENZOLLERNS | IN AMERICA and | OTHER IMPOSSIBILITIES | By STEPHEN LEACOCK.* Stamped on the spine: *The | HOHEN- | ZOLLERNS | IN | AMERICA | By | STEPHEN | LEACOCK.*

The front panel of the jacket has a colour illustration within a green rectangle as follows: [the first three lines hand-written in green] THE HOHENZOLLERNS IN | AMERICA AND OTHER IMPOSSIBILITIES | [the next line in script] By Stephen Leacock. | [green rule] | [illustration of a fat, bald, grey bearded man with a large nose, who is dressed in mismatched trousers, vest, and jacket; clothes with price tags in the background]. The rest of the jacket is white with blue lettering. Printed on the spine panel of the jacket: THE | HOHEN- |

ZOLLERNS | IN | AMERICA | BY | STEPHEN | LEACOCK | THE | BODLEY HEAD. The back panel of the jacket lists THE WORKS OF STEPHEN LEACOCK (nine books listed with press opinions, 5s each volume, all crown 8vo). The front flap has advertisements for Samuel Pepys, Junr.'s *A Last Diary of the Great Warr* and Muriel Hine's *The Hidden Valley*. The back flap has an advertisement with press opinions of the *"Third Edition"* (i.e. printing) of *Frenzied Fiction*.

NOTES: The contract with John Lane The Bodley Head for rights in the United Kingdom, the colonies, India and the United States is dated 20 June 1914. At that time Leacock signed a contract for *Arcadian Adventures with the Idle Rich*, and *The Hohenzollerns in America* was the fifth book which was promised to Lane in a multi-book deal. Leacock received 20% royalty on the first 7,000 copies sold, 25% on subsequent copies sold. He was also paid an advance of £100. The title of the English edition differs slightly from that of the American edition. Both John Lane and B.W. Willett did not like Leacock's title. Leacock told Willett [date stamped 27 March 1919, The Bodley Head fonds, TEX]:

> What you say is quite true: the Kaiser might be shot at any minute but in that case it is not the *title* that is queried it is the book itself. Jones & I have agreed that it shall not be published if anything of that sort happens while it is in the press. But as 75 or 80 pages deal with the Hohenzollerns in America we think that the book had better stand or fall in that.

According to *The English Catalogue of Books*, the English edition was published in July 1919 ("Cr. 8vo") at 5s. By the end of 1919 9,098 copies were sold, 3,231 further copies to the colonies and Australasia. From 1920 to June 1931, another 1,516 copies sold, 618 further copies to the colonies, and 150 further copies to Australasia.

COPIES EXAMINED: CS (two copies, one in jacket); QMMRB (two copies, one in jacket).

## A30 DOCTOR STEPHEN LEACOCK WILL DELIVER A LECTURE 1920

### A30a *American edition*:

[cover title: all lines within two rectangles with corner ornaments and ornaments midway lengthwise between the two rectangles] DOCTOR | [two rules] | STEPHEN B. LEACOCK | [two rules] | WILL DELIVER A LECTURE | "THE PROBLEM OF | SOCIAL JUSTICE" | AT THE | AUDITORIUM | (MAIN HALL) | THURSDAY, JANUARY 15TH | AT 8 P.M. | UNDER THE AUSPICES OF THE | CITY CLUB

◆ $1^4$. *1–8* pp. (4 leaves). 157 × 84 mm.

CONTENTS: p. *1* title; p. *2* poem entitled "To Stephen Leacock" reprinted from *Punch* (London); pp. *3–7* text; p. *8* back of wrapper: [ornamental rule] | *Mr. Leacock's Books* | [ornament] | IN A SERIOUS VEIN: | [six lines listing four books, one being "The Problem of Social Justice"] | IN A LIGHT VEIN: | [eight lines listing eight six books] | [ornamental rule].

TEXT: The text is entitled "Stephen Leacock's Own Story of His Life."

BINDING: Issued in wire-stitched wrappers, off-white paper.

NOTES: According to his lecture notebooks at NAC, Leacock spoke at the Quadrangle Club in Chicago on 15 January 1920 and at Milwaukee, Wisconsin on 17 January 1920. On the latter date his topic was "The Problem of Social Justice." This pamphlet, however, indicates that he spoke at Wisconsin on 15 January 1920. The basis of his lecture would be expanded for more extensive treatment in his book, *The Unsolved Riddle of Social Justice* (A31). This promotional pamphlet was probably handed out to people who attended the lecture. The text first appeared in *Canada: An Illustrated Weekly for All Interested in the Dominion* (see C11.38) in a slightly altered form, and was later published as part of the preface to *Sunshine Sketches of a Little Town* (see A11). Only one copy of the pamphlet is known to be extant.

COPY EXAMINED: WIH.

## A30b *English edition* (1921):

[transcription of the first page] ÆOLIAN HALL NEW BOND STREET, W. | [rule] | FOUR LECTURES *By* | STEPHEN LEACOCK | *The Master Humorist* | [rectangle advertising Leacock's talks, "Frenzied Fiction" and "The Drama as I See It," between 17–21 October 1921] | [black-and-white photograph of Leacock at his writing desk and to the left of the photograph sixteen lines about Leacock as a humorist] | [five lines concerning the purchase of tickets and the arrangement of Leacock's lecture tour by Mr. Gerald Christy, The Lecture Agency, Ltd.]

♦ Leaflet folded once to make four unnumbered pages. 259 × 208 mm.

CONTENTS: p. *1* described in quasi-facsimile; p. *2* poem entitled "To Stephen Leacock" reprinted from *Punch* (London); pp. 2–3 text; p. *4* advertisement by John Lane The Bodley Head of "The Books of Stephen Leacock."

TEXT: Identical to A30a.

BINDING: Plain white paper stock.

NOTES: This leaflet which contains "Stephen Leacock's Own Story of His Life" was apparently issued by John Lane The Bodley Head to promote Leacock's lecture tour of Britain. Copies printed not known. See also A120.

COPIES EXAMINED: CS; SLM.

## A31 THE UNSOLVED RIDDLE OF SOCIAL JUSTICE 1920

### A31a *first American edition*:

[thick-thin rule] | THE | UNSOLVED RIDDLE | OF | SOCIAL JUSTICE | [thick-thin rule] | BY STEPHEN LEACOCK | B. A., PH. D., LITT. D., F. R. C. S. | *Professor of Political Economy at McGill University,* | *Montreal* | AUTHOR OF "ESSAYS AND LITERARY STUDIES," ETC. | [thin-thick rule] | [thick-thin rule] | NEW YORK: JOHN LANE COMPANY | LONDON: JOHN LANE, THE BODLEY HEAD | TORONTO: S. B. GUNDY: MCMXX | [thin-thick rule]

♦ 1–6$^{12}$ 7$^4$. 1–8, 9–152 pp. (76 leaves). 184 × 123 mm.

CONTENTS: p. *1* half title; p. *2* list of ten books by Leacock within a rectangle, the first being *Frenzied Fiction* and the last *The Hohenzollerns in America*; p. *3* title; p. *4* Copyright, 1920, | BY JOHN LANE COMPANY | p. *5* table of contents; p. *6* blank; p. *7* fly title; p. *8* blank; pp. *9–152* text.

TEXT: chapter I The Troubled Outlook of the Present Hour; chapter II Life, Liberty and the Pursuit of Happiness; chapter III The Failures and Fallacies of Natural Liberty; chapter IV Work and Wages; chapter V The Land of Dreams: The Utopia of the Socialist; chapter VI How Mr. Bellamy Looked Backward; chapter VII What is Possible and What Is Not.

BINDING AND DUST JACKET: There are two binding variants. (1) Red cloth, stamped on the upper board is a solid black rectangle. Outside of this solid rectangle are a thin rectangle and a thick rectangle. Red raised lettering within the solid rectangle is as follows: THE | UNSOLVED RIDDLE | OF SOCIAL JUSTICE | [rule] | STEPHEN LEACOCK. Stamped on the spine: THE | UNSOLVED | RIDDLE | OF | SOCIAL | JUSTICE | [rule] | LEACOCK | JOHN LANE | COMPANY. (2) Red cloth, with blind-stamping on the upper board and stamping in gilt on the spine, the stamping being similar to the first variant. The leaves for this variant measure 187 × 130 mm., and the copyright page has been rubber-stamped: PRINTED IN U. S. A.

The jacket is cream coloured with red lettering. Printed on the front panel of the jacket: *THE BOOK OF THE HOUR* | [thick-thin rectangle] | The UNSOLVED RIDDLE | OF SOCIAL JUSTICE | [rule] | By STEPHEN LEACOCK, B.A., Ph.D. | Professor of Political Economy at McGill University, Montreal | *Author of "Essays and Literary Studies," etc.* | [thin-thick rule] | [five paragraphs which summarize the book's contents] | [thick-thin rule] | JOHN LANE COMPANY, *Publishers*, NEW YORK. Printed on the spine panel: THE | UNSOLVED | RIDDLE | OF | SOCIAL | JUSTICE | [rule] | LEACOCK | $1.25 | NET | JOHN LANE | COMPANY. On the back panel of the jacket is an advertisement for *Essays and Literary Studies*. The front flap has an advertisement for *The Hohenzollerns in America and Other Impossibilities*. An advertisement for eight other books by Leacock appears on the back flap.

NOTES: The contract (copies at SLM and READ) with John Lane The Bodley Head and the John Lane Company is dated 15 October 1919. Leacock received 20% royalty with an advance of £50 on the English edition and $250 on the American edition one month prior to publication. Leacock retained control of the Canadian rights on the basis of a minimum of 5,000 copies. The contract also raised Leacock's royalties on his previous books to 20%. He promised his next three books of fiction to The Bodley Head (£125 advance for the English edition and $625 advance for the American, 20% royalty).

According to Leacock's notebook of recorded publications and speeches at QMMRB, he wrote three chapters in June 1919. In fact, he finished chapter II on 18 June 1919, and then sent it to Miss Fetherstonaugh at McGill University for typing. At the time he was also in touch with an agent called Crandall who was attempting to have the chapters syndicated in *the New York Times* (see file 59, container 4, RG 32, QMM Archives). Leacock finished writing the book on 2 August 1919. In addition to the *New York Times*, the chapters were syndicated in the *Montreal Star*, the *Toronto Star*, and the *London Express* (see C19.14–8 and C19.21–2).

Published on 16 January 1920. The copyright was registered with the Copyright Office at DLC on 19 January 1920 (ClA561512). Leacock told John Lane on 29 January 1920:

"Jeff Jones has just got out *The Unsolved Riddle*. I think it will do pretty well" (The Bodley Head fonds, TEX). By 1 July 1920 2,261 copies had sold of the American edition. By the end of 1921, when the John Lane Company was sold to Dodd, Mead, 2,637 copies had been sold in all. Leacock recorded that by February 1925, 8,539 copies had sold of all editions.

No copy of an issue with Dodd, Mead as publisher was located. Up to February 1925, Dodd, Mead sold 312 copies. Thereafter, Dodd, Mead sold approximately ten copies annually. The book was still in print as of 1 February 1944 when Dodd, Mead reported to Leacock's niece, Barbara Nimmo, that during the 1940s the book had earned a royalty of $63.60 in American sales.

Chapter VI was reprinted in part in a composite pamphlet entitled *How Mr. Bellamy Looked Backward* (Milwaukee: American Constitutional League of Wisconsin, 1920), pp. 1–17. The pamphlet also includes Alvin M. Higgins's *The Class Struggle*. The publication in pamphlet form omits the first six paragraphs of chapter VI, and begins with two paragraphs taken from the end of chapter V. The pamphlet was published on 9 July 1920, and the copyright registered at DLC on 21 July 1920 by the American Constitutional League of Wisconsin, Milwaukee.

See also Alan Bowker's edition of *The Social Criticism of Stephen Leacock: The Unsolved Riddle of Social Justice and Other Essays* (A124).

COPIES EXAMINED: CS (two copies of the first variant binding, one in jacket); GZD (composite pamphlet, *How Mr. Bellamy Looked Backward*); QMMRB (both variant bindings, neither in jacket).

## A31a.1 *Canadian issue*:

[thick-thin rule] | THE | UNSOLVED RIDDLE | OF | SOCIAL JUSTICE | [thick-thin rule] | BY STEPHEN LEACOCK | B. A., PH. D., LITT. D., F. R. C. S. | *Professor of Political Economy at McGill University* | *Montreal* | AUTHOR OF "ESSAYS AND LITERARY STUDIES," ETC. | [thin-thick rule] | [thick-thin rule] | TORONTO: S. B. GUNDY | NEW YORK: JOHN LANE COMPANY | LONDON: JOHN LANE, THE BODLEY HEAD | MCMXX | [thin-thick rule]

The Canadian issue is identical to the American edition except for the title page and the imprint on the spine where JOHN LANE | COMPANY has been replaced by GUNDY (as in first variant of the American edition). The jacket of the Canadian issue is similar to that of the American edition. The front panel, spine, and front flap are the same except for the substitution of Gundy's name. The back panel and back flap are blank.

NOTES: Leacock gave S.B. Gundy and Oxford University Press the Canadian rights on 11 February 1920. He received a royalty of 20% and an advance $500. The agreement gave Gundy the Canadian rights to Leacock's ten published books of humour for four years. The books were to sell for $1.25 apiece, and Leacock was guaranteed a minimum royalty of $1,600. By the end of 1920 872 copies sold the Canadian issue. No further copies are recorded by Leacock as having been sold thereafter.

COPIES EXAMINED: CS (without jacket); OORI (in jacket); QMMRB (without jacket).

**A31b** *first English edition*:

THE UNSOLVED RIDDLE | :: OF SOCIAL JUSTICE :: | BY STEPHEN
LEACOCK | [thick-thin rule] | [thin-thick rule] | LONDON: JOHN LANE,
THE BODLEY HEAD | NEW YORK: JOHN LANE COMPANY. MCMXX

◆ A⁴ B⁸ K⁸ *⁴ [$1 signed]. 1–10, 3–22, 23–24, 25–37, 38–40, 41–56, 57–58, 59–77, 78–80, 81–93, 94–96, 97–114, 115–116, 117–139, 1–13 pp. (80 leaves). 187 × 125 mm.

CONTENTS: p. *1–2* blank; p. *3* half title; p. *4* list of ten books by Leacock published by The Bodley Head, the first being *Essays and Literary Studies* and the last *The Hohenzollerns in America*; p. *5* title; p. *6* WILLIAM BRENDON AND SON, LTD., PRINTERS, PLYMOUTH, ENGLAND; p. *7* table of contents; p. *8* blank; p. *9* title of first chapter; p. *10* blank; pp. *3–139, 1* text (pp. *24, 38, 40, 58, 78, 80, 94, 96,* and *115* blank); pp. *2–12* advertisements with press opinions of ten books by Leacock published by The Bodley Head; p. *13* advertisement for the humorous novels of Harry Leon Wilson.

TEXT: Identical to A31a.

BINDING AND DUST JACKET: Bound in green cloth with maroon lettering. Stamped on the upper board within three blind-stamped rectangles: *THE UNSOLVED RIDDLE | OF SOCIAL JUSTICE | By STEPHEN LEACOCK.* Stamped on the spine: [two rules blind-stamped] | *THE | UNSOLVED | RIDDLE | OF | SOCIAL | JUSTICE | By | STEPHEN | LEACOCK | THE | BODLEY HEAD* | [two rules blind-stamped].

The dust jacket is light greenish blue. Printed on the front panel of the jacket: THE UNSOLVED RIDDLE | OF SOCIAL JUSTICE | BY | STEPHEN LEACOCK | Professor of Political Economy at McGill University, | Montreal and Author of | "Essays and Literary Studies," etc. | [twenty-three lines within a rectangle — two paragraphs about Leacock and his work with a listing of the contents]. Printed on the spine panel: The | Unsolved | Riddle | of Social | Justice | Stephen | Leacock | THE | BODLEY | HEAD. On the back panel is an advertisement for *My Discovery of England*; this advertisement would indicate that the examined jacket is a later printing. The front flap has an advertisement for William J. Locke's *The Tale of Triona*. On the back flap are advertisements for Robert Benchley's *Of All Things* (with a quotation from Leacock's introduction) and R.S. Hooper's *And the Next*.

NOTES: On 20 November 1919, Leacock instructed Lane: "If you have not received the MS of *The Unsolved Riddle of Social Justice* please cable me at once as it was sent to you long ago" (TEX). According to *The English Catalogue of Books*, the English edition sold for 5s and was published in March 1920. By 1 July 1920 3,387 copies had sold (379 to the colonies and 770 Australasian). Up to February 1925, 4,728 copies had sold (860 to the colonies and 895 Australasian). Thereafter, approximately fifty copies sold annually.

COPIES EXAMINED: CS (two copies, one in jacket); QMMRB (first and second printings, neither in jacket, the second rebound).

## A32 WINSOME WINNIE 1920

**A32a** *first American edition*:

WINSOME | WINNIE | [the next two lines in smaller size type and to the right of the previous line] AND | OTHER | New Nonsense Novels | BY STEPHEN

*LEACOCK* | [thick-thin rule] | [thin-thick rule] | *NEW YORK: JOHN LANE COMPANY* | *LONDON: JOHN LANE, THE BODLEY HEAD* | *TORONTO: S.B. GUNDY* [three dots in the shape of a triangle] *MCMXX*

◆ $1-15^8$ $16^4$. 1–4, 5, 6–8, 9–42, 43–44, 45–63, 64–66, 67–93, 94–96, 97–141, 142–144, 145–176, 177–178, 179–203, 204–206, 207–223, 224–226, 227–243, 1–5 pp. (124 leaves). 185 × 125 mm.

CONTENTS: pp. *1* half title; p. *2* list of eleven books by Leacock, the first being *Frenzied Fiction* and the last *Essays and Literary Studies*; p. *3* title; p. *4* COPYRIGHT, 1920, | BY HARPER & BROTHERS | COPYRIGHT, 1920, | BY JOHN LANE COMPANY | *Printed in the United States of America*; p. *5* table of contents; p. *6* blank; pp. *7–243* text (pp. *8, 44, 64, 66, 94, 96, 142, 144, 178, 204, 206, 224,* and *226* are blank); pp. *1–5* blank.

TEXT: I Winsome Winnie; or, Trial and Temptation; II John and I; or, How I Nearly Lost My Husband; III The Split in the Cabinet; or, The Fate of England; IV Who Do You Think Did It? or, The Mixed-Up Murder Mystery; V Broken Barriers; or, Red Love on a Blue Island; VI The Kidnapped Plumber: A Tale of the New Time; VII The Blue and the Grey: A Pre-War War Story; VIII Buggam Grange: A Good Old Ghost Story.

I and IV are comprised of the following chapters. For I — chapter I Thrown on the World; chapter II A Rencounter; chapter III Friends in Distress; chapter IV A Gambling Party in St. James's Close; chapter V The Abduction; chapter VI The Unknown; chapter VII The Proposal; chapter IX [i.e. VIII] Wedded at Last. For IV — chapter I He Dined with Me Last Night; chapter II I Must Save Her Life; chapter III I Must Buy a Book on Billiards; chapter IV That Is Not Billiard Chalk; chapter V Has Anybody Seen Kelly? chapter VI Show Me the Man Who Wore Those Boots; chapter VII Oh, Mr. Kent, Save Me! chapter VIII You Are Peter Kelly; chapter IX Let Me Tell You the Story of My Life; chapter X So Do I.

BINDING AND DUST JACKET: Bound in green cloth, top edge stained green. A dark green solid rectangle is stamped on the upper board. Within this solid rectangle is the following: [all lines within a rectangle] WINSOME WINNIE | [leafy ornament] AND OTHER [leafy ornament] | NEW NONSENSE NOVELS | STEPHEN LEACOCK. Stamped on the spine in dark green: WINSOME | WINNIE | . [rule] . | LEACOCK | JOHN LANE | COMPANY.

The jacket is white with printing in blue. The front panel has a colour illustration of a man with mutton chops kneeling by a woman who is wearing blue gloves, a blue hat, and a blue and pink long dress. The following is printed above and to the left of the illustration: WINSOME WINNIE | *And other new Nonsense Novels* | By | STEPHEN | LEACOCK. On the spine panel is the following: WINSOME | WINNIE | *and other* | NEW | NONSENSE | NOVELS | [ornament] | *STEPHEN* | *LEACOCK* | JOHN LANE | COMPANY. Within two rectangles on the back panel of the jacket is a list of AUTUMN FICTION SUCCESSES. The front flap has a synopsis of *Winsome Winnie* with the heading *Delicious Travesties*. The back flap lists other books (with press opinions) by Leacock published by the John Lane Company.

NOTES: The rights to the American edition were arranged by John Lane The Bodley Head as part of a three-book deal on 15 October 1919 (see the notes to A32b). Leacock completed the manuscript in its entirety on 20 August 1920. He told B.W. Willett of The Bodley Head on 4 October 1920 that ". . . Jeff Jones's [American] printers were very slow" (The Bodley Head fonds, TEX). The American edition was published on 19 November 1920, ten days prior to that of the English edition. Leacock himself records this date in his notebook of royalty payments at SLM and directly underneath that date "Eng 29". This would suggest that the English edition appeared on 29 November 1920. However, correspondence between Leacock and the John Lane Company indicates that 4,500 copies of advance sales occurred by 24 November 1920, the best ever in terms of advance sales for an American edition of one of his books. $500 was spent on publicity. The copyright was registered with the Copyright Office at DLC on 24 November 1920 (ClA604327). Prior to publication, the book was listed at $1.25. It rose to $1.50 on 1 August 1920 but eventually sold at $1.75. The reference to Harper & Brothers on the verso of the title leaf occurs because four stories under the series title "New Nonsense Novels" were published in *Harper's Monthly Magazine* (see C20.11, C20.15, C20.19, and C20.20).

By the end of 1920 5,924 copies had been sold. On 4 November 1921 John Lane decided to sell the American branch. He wrote to Leacock on that date and complained that 20% royalty was simply too high: "No one in this country can afford to give 20% royalty unless 20,000 or 25,000 are subscribed." He sold the American branch of his company to Dodd, Mead done on 3 January 1922. In fact, Lane and Leacock met each other in New York at the National Arts Club at the end of that month when Leacock returned from his speaking tour of England. Leacock records that a further 2,833 copies sold in 1921 before the American branch was sold.

36,693 copies were sold for all editions up to February 1925.

COPIES EXAMINED: CS (no jacket); QMMRB (two copies, one in jacket).

## A32a.1 *Canadian issue*

WINSOME | WINNIE | [the next two lines in smaller size type and to the right of the previous line] AND | OTHER | *New Nonsense Novels* | BY STEPHEN LEACOCK | [thick-thin rule] | [thin-thick rule] | *TORONTO:* [two sets of three dots in the shape of a triangle] *S. B. GUNDY* | *LONDON: JOHN LANE, THE BODLEY HEAD* | *NEW YORK: JOHN LANE COMPANY* | *MCMXX*

The binding of the Canadian issue is identical to that of the American issue except that JOHN LANE | COMPANY has been replaced by GUNDY. The Canadian dust jacket is also similar to that of the American edition. S.B. Gundy's name occurs as the publisher, the back panel has a list of other books by Leacock (with press opinions) published by Gundy, and the back flap has an advertisement for Sergeant Ralph S. Kendall's *The Luck of the Mounted*.

NOTES: Although the contract with John Lane The Bodley Head required Gundy to pay Leacock 20% royalty on all copies sold of the Canadian issue, the advance that Gundy paid Leacock is not known (probably $500). The date of publication of the Canadian issue was undoubtedly the same date as that of the American edition since the sheets from the Canadian issue are the same as those of the American edition with the exception of the title page. 4,000 copies were printed of the Canadian issue. 2,638 were sold by the end of 1920, and the remaining copies (1,362) by 1 July 1922. In his notebook at SLM, Leacock added "to complete 4000 covered by adv. royalty."

COPIES EXAMINED: CS (3 copies, all in jacket); QMMRB (in jacket).

## A32a.2 *first American issue* [1922?]:

WINSOME | WINNIE | [the next two lines in smaller size type and to the right of the previous line] AND | OTHER | *New Nonsense Novels* | BY STEPHEN

*LEACOCK* | [thick-thin rule] | [thin-thick rule] | *NEW YORK* | *DODD, MEAD AND COMPANY* | *1923*

The sheets (187 × 126 mm.) for this issue are the same as A32a, with the exception of the title leaf. On the verso of the title leaf, the line BY JOHN LANE COMPANY has been replaced by BY DODD, MEAD AND COMPANY INC.. Bound in red cloth. The upper board is similar to that of a32a except that the former has blind-stamping. Stamping on the spine of the Dodd, Mead issue is in gilt, identical to that of a32a, except that JOHN LANE | COMPANY is replaced by DODD, MEAD | & COMPANY. The jacket of the Dodd, Mead issue is also similar to that of 29a. Beside the change of the publisher's name, the Dodd, Mead jacket is cream coloured, the illustration on the front panel is pink and blue, and the back flap and the back panel are blank.

NOTES: Leacock recorded that Dodd, Mead sold 362 copies of the American edition of *Winsome Winnie* up to 1 August 1922 and a further 184 copies to 1 February 1923. This would indicate either that a printing of the Dodd, Mead issue occurred in 1922 or else that Dodd, Mead sold copies printed by the John Lane Company. The earliest known printing of the Dodd, Mead issue is 1923. Neither the exact date of this issue nor the number of copies printed is known, however. Between 1 February 1923 and 1 February 1925, 576 copies sold. Another printing occurred in 1926. Sales of the 1926 printing were very slow. Only 191 copies sold between February 1927 and August 1933 ($2 apiece, $.40 royalty per copy, $76.40 total royalty).

COPIES EXAMINED: CS (1926 printing in jacket); EVANS (1926 printing in jacket); IOL (1923 printing, no jacket).

### A32a.3 *second American issue* (1970):

*WINSOME* | *WINNIE* | [the next two lines in smaller size type and to the right of the previous line] *AND OTHER* | *New Nonsense Novels* | *BY STEPHEN LEACOCK* | [thick-thin rule] | *Short Story Index Reprint Series* | [publisher's device, two lines in height, to the left of the next two lines: abstract design of building with four columns] | BOOKS FOR LIBRARIES PRESS | FREEPORT, NEW YORK

The verso of the title leaf reads as follows: First Published 1920 | Reprinted 1970 | INTERNATIONAL STANDARD BOOK NUMBER: | 0-8369-3725-2 | LIBRARY OF CONGRESS CATALOG CARD NUMBER: | 74-140333 | PRINTED IN THE UNITED STATES OF AMERICA. Pagination is the same as A32a. The page opposite the title page is blank. Leaves measure 197 × 123 mm. Bound in light blue cloth with the publisher's device blind-stamped on the upper board. Stamping on the spine is as follows: [all rules dark blue; vertical rule crossed by two zig-zag rules] | [the next two lines vertically in silver within a dark blue solid rectangle] | *WINSOME WINNIE* | *LEACOCK* | [vertical rule crossed by two zig-zag rules] | [the next three lines within a silver oval] | B | *f* | L.

COPIES EXAMINED: SRU.

### A32b *English edition* [1920]:

*WINSOME WINNIE* | *AND OTHER NEW* | *NONSENSE NOVELS* | *BY STEPHEN LEACOCK* | [thin-thick rule] | [thick-thin rule] | *LONDON: JOHN*

## LANE, THE BODLEY HEAD | NEW YORK: JOHN LANE COMPANY MCMXXI

◆ A⁸ B–Q⁸ [$1 signed]. *1–8, 9–42, 43–44, 45–63, 64–66, 67–93, 94–96, 97–141, 142–144, 145–176, 177–178, 179–203, 204–206, 207–223, 224–226, 227–242, 1–14* pp. (*128* leaves). *188* × *125* mm.

CONTENTS: p. *1* half title; p. *2* list of eleven other books by Leacock, the first being *The Hohenzollerns in America and Other Impossibilities* and the last *The Unsolved Riddle of Social Justice*; p. *3* title; p. *4 Printed in Great Britain by R. Clay & Sons, Ltd., London and Bungay*; pp. *5–6* table of contents; pp. *7–242, 1* text (pp. *8, 44, 64, 66, 94, 96, 142, 144, 178, 204, 206, 224,* and *226* are blank); p. *2* blank; p. *3–13* advertisements, with press opinions, of Leacock's books; p. *14* advertisement, with press opinion, of Harry Leon Wilson's humorous novels.

TEXT: Identical to the American edition.

BINDING AND DUST JACKET: Bound in dark green buckram, top edge stained green, with stamping on the boards in blue. Stamped on the upper board: [all lines within two blind-stamped rectangles] WINSOME WINNIE | AND OTHER | NEW NONSENSE NOVELS | By STEPHEN LEACOCK. Stamped on the spine as follows: WINSOME | WINNIE | AND OTHER | NEW NONSENSE | NOVELS | By | STEPHEN | LEACOCK | The | Bodley Head.

The jacket of the English edition is similar to that of the American edition. The printing is bluer, and the illustration on the front panel has more vivid contrast in colour. On the spine panel of the jacket is the following: WINSOME | WINNIE | AND OTHER | NEW | NONSENSE | NOVELS | STEPHEN | LEACOCK | 5/- | NET | THE | BODLEY | HEAD. Within a rectangle on the back panel of the jacket is a list of THE WORKS OF STEPHEN LEACOCK. The front flap lists NEW FICTION (five books) published by The Bodley Head. The back flap advertises Pamela Glenconner's *The Earthen Vessel* and Richard King's *Over the Fire-Side*.

NOTES: The contract with John Lane The Bodley Head and the John Lane Company for the rights in Great Britain, the colonies and the United States for "three further works of fiction" is dated 15 October 1919. *Winsome Winnie* was the first book under this contract. Leacock received 20% royalty on all copies sold of these editions. The advance was £125 on the English edition, $625 on the American edition, both to be paid one month prior to publication.

On 5 May 1920, Leacock asked B.W. Willett of The Bodley Head to arrange for the serial publication of a series of stories from his forthcoming collection of humour. He informed Willett that *Harper's* had paid him $500 for the American serial rights to the series. Leacock was dissatisfied with *Harper's* collective title, *New Nonsense Novels*. By the time that Leacock sent the second story in the series, "John and I," on 28 May 1920, Willett had arranged for their publication in the *Bystander*. Leacock sent the third article of the series, "The Split in the Cabinet," to Willett on 26 June 1920 . He informed Willett: "Manuscript (8 or 10 stories in all) will be all complete on *Aug 15*. Each story will come to you as finished. Let us try to make date of publication about October 15th — we are doing that here." By this time he had finally settled on the book's title. On 28 June 1920, Leacock asked Willett to arrange for John Kettelwell to do the jacket for the book. By 7 July 1920, Leacock had written 22,000 words.

According to Lomer (p. 56), the English edition was published on 24 November 1920. He records reprints in 1920, 1921, and 1922. A later entry in Lomer's bibliography for the "popular crown 8vo. edition, 1929," however, has a conflicting date of [3 May] 1920 for the first printing. Leacock has 29 November 1920 as the date of publication in his notebook of royalty payments at SLM. Notwithstanding this date, no copy was found with a 1920 date on the title page.

12,071 copies sold by the end of 1920. From 1921 to February 1925 another 9,743 copies were sold (of these, 2,404 copies sold to the colonies and 500 to Australasia). According to the copyright page of the 1929 reprint, the book was reprinted in 1921 and 1922).

COPIES EXAMINED: CS (two copies of the first impression, one in jacket; one copy of the second impression).


## A33 THE NEED FOR DORMITORIES AT MCGILL 1920

[cover title; colour illustration of trees, buildings, and three young men, one holding a tennis racket with McG on his sweater; black rule, white rule; the next two lines in red within a solid black rectangular compartment] | [c raised] McGILL STUDENTS' | RESIDENCES | [white rule, black rule]

◆  *1⁴. 1–2, 3–7, 8 pp. (4 leaves, including wrappers). 163 × 115 mm.*

CONTENTS: p. *1* front of wrapper; p. *2* statement from the Booklet Editor, McGill Endowment Centennial; pp. *3–7* text; p. *8* back of wrapper. The Booklet Editor's statement and text are printed within red rectangles with running head: *McGILL CENTENNIAL ENDOWMENT.*

TEXT: Leacock's text begins on p. *3*. Transcription of the first six lines, which precede the text, is as follows: [all lines within a red rectangle] THE NEED | FOR DORMITORIES | AT McGILL | By STEPHEN LEACOCK | Professor of Political Economy, McGill University | [diamond containing a solid diamond].

BINDING. Pictorial wrapper, wire-stitched. The front of the wrapper is described above in the quasi-facsimile transcription. The back of the wrapper continues the scenic view of the McGill campus — buildings, bleachers, and a track and field area. Beneath the illustration is the following: [black rule, white rule; shield of McGill University set within a solid, black rectangular compartment; white rule, black rule].

NOTES: This pamphlet was commissioned by the Publicity Committee of the McGill Centennial Endowment Campaign in order to raise money for the university. According to the Booklet Editor, "a series of small booklets" would "be mailed to a selected list of 10,00 names, previous to the actual Campaign for subscriptions, which starts November 15th, for a total objective of $5,000,000." In his notebook of publications and speeches, Leacock recorded that his "campaign pamphlet" was written on 20 October 1920. Publication of the pamphlet probably occurred shortly thereafter. See also C20.23.

In his pamphlet Leacock recalls his days at the University of Toronto when he lived in different boarding houses. He theorizes about the nature of university education and states: "To my mind the greatest of all our needs is the building of college dormitories to supply to our students a wider college life than we can given them now."

Leacock's text is reprinted in *Fontanus* 7 (1994): 7–8. The wrapper of the pamphlet is also reproduced in this issue of *Fontanus* on p. 32.

COPIES EXAMINED: CS; QMMRB.

## A34 MY MEMORIES AND MISERIES AS A SCHOOLMASTER [19?]

MY MEMORIES | AND MISERIES AS A | SCHOOLMASTER | BY | STEPHEN LEACOCK | Illustrated by | C. W. JEFFERYS | WITH THE COMPLIMENTS OF THE AUTHOR | UPPER CANADA COLLEGE | ENDOWMENT AND EXTENSION FUND | Head Office, Gooderham Building | TORONTO, CANADA

• $1^8$. *1–3*, 4–15, pp. (8 leaves including the wrappers). 188 × 134 mm.

CONTENTS: p. *1* front of wrapper; p. *2* *Published by permission MacLean's Magazine*; p. *3* title; p. *4* illustration by C.W. Jefferys of two schoolmasters near a fence and a tree, with caption: He takes him out to a deserted corner of the playground; pp. *5–6* text; p. *7* illustration by Jefferys of Leacock in evening dress shaking hands with a person in a military uniform, with caption: "You licked me at Upper Canada College"; pp. *8–11* text; p. *12* illustration by Jefferys of an older man holding a cigar, with caption: I've just given Jimmy fifty dollars; pp. *13* text; p. *14* illustration by Jefferys of a student, with caption: Jimmy can be led, if led gently; p. *15* text; p. *1* back of wrapper.

BINDING: Bound in off-white wrappers, wire-stitched. The paper used for the wrappers is the same as that of the other leaves. On the front of the wrapper: MY MEMORIES | AND MISERIES AS | A SCHOOLMASTER | [thick-thin rule] | *By STEPHEN LEACOCK* | [coat of arms of Upper Canada College — crown, leaves in a circular design, and a scroll with the motto PALMAM QUI MERUIT FERAT]. On the back of the wrapper: PRINTED BY | SOUTHAM PRESS, LIMITED, TORONTO.

NOTES: This essay, accompanied by Jefferys's illustrations, originally appeared in *Maclean's Magazine* in November 1919 (see C19.23). However, it is not known when Upper Canada College issued the pamphlet for publicity purposes.

COPIES EXAMINED: CS; OBER; OTNY; QMMRB.

## A35 THE ECONOMIC THEORY OF MONEY 1921

[cover title] McGILL UNIVERSITY | *Session 1920–21* | BANKERS' EXTENSION COURSE | [small ornament] | THE ECONOMIC THEORY | OF MONEY | *A Course of Six Lectures* | by | PROFESSOR STEPHEN LEACOCK, | B.A., Ph.D., Litt.D., LL.D., F.R.S.C. | 1. ECONOMIC SCIENCE AND THE THEORY OF VALUE. | 2. THE VALUE OF GOLD MONEY. | 3. SILVER AS MONEY. | 4. PAPER MONEY. | 5. BANK DEPOSITS AND CHEQUES AS A MEDIUM OF EXCHANGE. | 6. WAR CREDIT AND INFLATION. | [small ornament] | [eight lines in italics in which Leacock states that he cannot lecture "*at a pace slow enough to permit of anything like dictation, or even the taking of complete and final notes in the class room.*" He advises students to "*avail themselves of this abstract,*" to jot down notes rapidly, and then to write out the whole lecture.]

- Each leaflet folded once to form four unnumbered pages. 202 × 127 mm. There are five separate leaflets for the first five lectures.

CONTENTS: Each leaflet has the same cover title with pp. 2–4 containing an abstract for the lecture in question.

BINDING: Off-white paper stock, no wrapper.

TEXTS: The following describes the major headings that Leacock employed in his abstracts: (1) Abstract of Lecture No. 1 Economic Science and the Theory of Value: Meaning of the Theory of Money and Its Place in Economic Science; The Data of the Theory of Value; Forces Behind the Market Price; The Theory of Value — Controversial Ground. On p. 4 is a Banker's Library of Books on Economics.
(2) Abstract of Lecture No. 2 The Value of Gold Money: Definition of Money; Origin of Money; Requisite Qualities in Money; What Then Regulates the Value (Purchasing Power) of a Standard Gold Coin?; Analysis of the Demand and Supply of Money; statistical tables on monetary stocks (gold) of the principal countries of the world (1919), mint par of exchange in terms of Canadian and U.S. dollar, and production of gold in the world since the discovery of America.
(3) Abstract of Lecture No. 3 Silver as Money: Silver as the Single Standard; The Price of Silver 1910–1920; Bimetallism.
(4) Abstract of Lecture No. 4 Paper Money: Chapters in the History of Paper Money; Rapid Multiplication and Depreciation of Continental Dollars; table on the fluctuating value of the greenback 1860–1878; The Pure Theory of Paper Money; statistical tables on paper money in circulation at the end of 1919 and world paper currency, 1914 to 1920.
(5) Abstract of Lecture No. 5 Bank Deposits and Cheques as a Medium of Exchange: Bank Deposits; The Gold Points; Clearing House Statistics; Trade Balances.

NOTES: Leacock's lectures began circa 14 January 1921. According to the report in the *Financial Post* of the first lecture, "Six hundred bank men followed the lecturer with intense interest as he gave them a glimpse — to many the first — of the fundamental attitude of the economist" (see D21.1). A leaflet for the sixth lecture is not extant.

COPIES EXAMINED: NAC (Barbara Nimmo collection), one copy of Lecture No. 2; SLM, three copies of Lecture No. 1, one copy of Lecture No. 2, one copy of Lecture No. 3, one copy of Lecture No. 4, one copy of Lecture No. 5.

## A36 THE CASE AGAINST PROHIBITION [1921]

### A36a *Canadian edition*:

[cover title; all lines within two rectangles, the outer one thick] LIBERTY MODERATION | "The Case Against | Prohibition" | By DR. STEPHEN LEACOCK | Professor of Economics, McGill University, Montreal | Being an Address delivered at | the opening of the Toronto cam- | paign held at Foresters' Hall | under the auspices of the Citi- | zens' Liberty League | As this address is applicable to | the Manitoba Temperance Act it | is re-published by | THE MODERATION LEAGUE OF MANITOBA | By courtesy of | The Citizens' Liberty League of | Ontario

- Leaflet folded once to form four unnumbered pages. 233 × 152 mm.

CONTENTS: p. *1* cover title; pp. 2–4 text.

BINDING: Printed on off-white paper stock, no wrapper.

NOTES: In his biography, *Stephen Leacock: Humorist and Humanist* (p. 147), Curry states:

> In 1921 he gave a public address, "The Case Against Prohibition," for the Citizens' Liberty League of Toronto, in which he made it clear that he was opposed on both theoretical and practical grounds. Theoretically, it was an invasion of private rights; the law could not declare two million people criminals. Practically, since the law would not be obeyed — witness the United States — it would breed crime.

Leacock's address was reported in several Toronto newspapers: see "Leacock Scores 'Drys' in Address Defending 'Wets' Says Fanatical Minority Has Captured Public's Ear and Legislatures," *Toronto Star*, 4 April 1921, p. 2; and "Professor Leacock Is Opposed to Prohibition as a Matter of Principle," *Toronto World*, 4 April 1921 (see D21.3 and F21.2). Number of copies printed not known. In his checklist, "Stephen Leacock: The Writer and His Writings," in David Staines's *Stephen Leacock: A Reappraisal* (Ottawa: Ottawa University Press, 1986), Curry cites this leaflet as having been published in London by The Freedom Association. No English edition was located, however.

COPIES EXAMINED: CS.

## A36b *American edition*:

[cover title; thick-thin rule] | LIBERTY MODERATION | *"The Case Against | Prohibition"* | FROM AN ADDRESS | By DR. STEPHEN LEACOCK | Professor of Economics, McGill University | [floral ornament] | FREEDOM TEMPERANCE | [thin-thick rule]

♦ Leaflet folded once to form four unnumbered pages. 218 × 95 mm.

CONTENTS: p. *1* cover title; pp. 2–4 text.

BINDING: Printed on off-white paper stock, no wrapper.

NOTES: Although nothing is known about this leaflet's issuing body, it was undoubtedly published in the United States. The copy at QMMRB came from the American Antiquarian Society. In addition, the first paragraph and eight paragraphs from the middle of A36a have been omitted in this edition; the missing paragraphs concern the temperance movement in Canada and Britain. A new paragraph has been added at the end: "The sharper the tyranny the quicker the cure. But this I do know: that a law based upon a lie shall sooner or later be dashed to pieces against the impregnable power of truth." Number of copies printed not known.

COPIES EXAMINED: HLS; QMMRB.

## A37 MY DISCOVERY OF ENGLAND 1922

### A37a *American edition*:

MY DISCOVERY | OF ENGLAND | [thick-thin rule] | BY STEPHEN LEACOCK | [thin-thick rule] | [publisher's device: illustration of a woman's face and two open books within an oval, ornamental, leafy frame] | [thick-thin rule] | NEW YORK | DODD, MEAD AND COMPANY | 1922 | [thin-thick rule]

♦ 1–16⁸ 17¹⁰. *i–iv*, v–viii, 1–4, 3–16, 17–18, 19–26, 27–28, 29–47, 48–50, 51–76, 77–78, 79–115, 116–118, 119–150, 151–152, 153–165, 166–168, 169–187, 188–190, 191–219, 220–222, 223–264, 1–2 pp. (138 leaves). 186 × 129 mm.

CONTENTS: p. *i* half title; p. *ii* list of thirteen books by Leacock, the first *Winsome Winnie* the last and *Essays and Literary Studies*; p. *iii* title; p. *iv* COPYRIGHT, 1922, | BY DODD, MEAD AND COMPANY, INC. | PRINTED IN THE U. S. A. BY | 𝕿𝖍𝖊 𝕼𝖚𝖎𝖓𝖓 & 𝕭𝖔𝖉𝖊𝖓 𝕮𝖔𝖒𝖕𝖆𝖓𝖞 | [rule] | BOOK MANUFACTURERS | RAHWAY NEW JERSEY; pp. v–viii, "Introduction of Mr. Stephen Leacock Given by Sir Owen Seaman on the Occasion of His First Lecture in London"; p. *1* table of contents; p. 2 blank; pp. *3–4*, 3–264 text (pp. 4, *18, 28, 48, 78, 116, 152, 166, 188, 190, 220,* and *222* blank); pp. *1–2* blank.

TEXT: I The Balance of Trade in Impressions; II I Am Interviewed by the Press; III Impressions of London; IV A Clear View of the Government and Politics of England; V Oxford As I See It; VI The British and the American Press; VII Business in England. Wanted — More Profiteers; VIII Is Prohibition Coming to England?; IX "We Have with Us To-night"; X Have the English Any Sense of Humour?.

BINDING AND DUST JACKET: Bound in red cloth. A solid rectangle is blind-stamped on the upper board. Within this solid rectangle are two raised rectangles, which contain the following in raised characters: MY DISCOVERY | OF ENGLAND | [rule] | STEPHEN LEACOCK. Stamped in gold on the spine: MY | DISCOVERY | OF | ENGLAND | [rule] | LEACOCK | DODD, MEAD | & COMPANY.

The front panel of the jacket has a caricature of a man in a tuxedo with a pointer in his right hand aimed at a map of Great Britain, the word ENGLAND in red and curved. The background of the illustration is light blue with the title and Leacock's name in white. The rest of the jacket is white with light blue lettering. Printed on the spine panel as follows: MY | DISCOVERY | OF | ENGLAND | *By* | STEPHEN | LEACOCK | Author of | "Nonsense Novels," | etc. | DODD, MEAD | & COMPANY. The back panel has a list of Leacock's books, within three ornamental rectangles, available from Dodd, Mead, having the general heading, *LAUGH with LEACOCK*. The front flap has a synopsis of the book and the price ($1.50). The back flap has an advertisement for *Nonsense Novels*.

NOTES: *My Discovery of England* was the first new book by Leacock published by Dodd, Mead and Company after Dodd, Mead purchased the John Lane Company of New York. The rights for the book had already been established by John Lane The Bodley Head on 15 October 1919 (see the notes to A37b). Although Dodd, Mead inherited Leacock as one of John Lane's authors, initially Leacock was wary of the new relationship. Frank Dodd visited Leacock at Montreal in early February 1922. Leacock was impressed by Dodd's enthusiasm, but he did not immediately engage in any long-term contracts for future books.

On 6 February 1922 Dodd wrote to Leacock: "Your letter and the initial chapter of MY DISCOVERY OF ENGLAND has just arrived. We are planning a dummy at once." On 6 April 1922, Jefferson Jones, who had been the manager of the John Lane Company and had found employment with Dodd, Mead, informed Leacock: "The complete manuscript of MY DISCOVERY OF ENGLAND, arrived Wednesday afternoon and went to the printers Thursday to be typeset. We expect galley proofs shortly and will send you a set for correction." Galleys were sent to Leacock on 26 April 1922. Publication of the American edition occurred on 17 June 1922. The copyright was registered with the Copyright Office at DLC on 20 June 1922 (ClA674656).

By 1 August 1922 6,459 copies had sold. On 11 January 1923, Dodd reported to Leacock:

We have sold the book with the greatest enthusiasm and have spent much money in advertising it energetically, and special efforts with the trade, throughout the entire season from June to January, never for one minute relaxing our efforts. The results have been eminently satisfactory to us and I feel sure to you also. The American sale, exclusive to Canada, will run approximately by the 1st of February to 15,000 copies, and we have printed the book six times.

By 1 February 1935, 19,785 copies sold. Up to this same period of time, Leacock recorded in his notebook of royalty payments at SLM that 45,807 copies had sold for all editions. In the late 1920s and early 1930s, 150 to 100 copies of the American edition sold annually. Sales declined considerably thereafter. It would appear that the book was still in print on 1 June 1944. For the period 1 February 1941 to 1 February 1944, Dodd, Mead reported that the book had not accrued any "regular" book earnings but had $50 in "perm. earnings."

On 9 February 1923, Dodd proposed an "edition" in limp red leather at $2.50 retail, 30¢ royalty per copy to Leacock. Copies examined reveal reprintings as follows: second printing, July 1922; third printing, August 1922; and fourth printing, November 1922; fifth printing, December 1922; and sixth printing, January 1923.

See also A127.

COPIES EXAMINED: CS (first and sixth printings in jacket; fourth printing without jacket); QMMRB (first and six printings, neither in jacket).

## A37a.1 *Canadian issue*:

MY DISCOVERY | OF ENGLAND | [thick-thin rule] | BY STEPHEN LEACOCK | [thin-thick rule] | [thick-thin rule] | TORONTO: S. B. GUNDY | MCMXXII | [thin-thick rule]

Besides the title page, the Canadian issue differs from the American edition in two other respects: the spine has GUNDY in the place of DODD, MEAD | & COMPANY; similar replacement of the publisher's name occurs on the spine panel of the jacket and on the front flap.

NOTES: S.B. Gundy expressed his concern to Leacock as to the nature of the book in early March 1922. Gundy felt that the book was not a work of "fiction," did not fall within the confines of the established contract (15 October 1919), and might be difficult to sell as a profitable venture. On 25 April 1922, after having obtained Leacock's authorization, Gundy ordered 4,000 copies from Dodd, Mead for the Canadian issue. Publication was simultaneous with the American edition and at the same price ($1.50). By 9 December 1922, Gundy had sold 4,000 copies of the Canadian issue, and he asked Dodd, Mead to provide another 1,000 copies. He told Leacock: "I sent a draft to Lane for 6¢ per copy on the 4000 books, as per our agreement." On 1 April 1924, Gundy reported: "My Discovery of England had exceptional pull, and we sold 5000 copies within a reasonable time. . . ." Leacock's notebook of royalty payments at SLM indicates that all copies of the Canadian issue had sold by 1 July 1923.

COPIES EXAMINED: CS (in jacket); QMMRB (in jacket).

**A37b** *English edition:*

MY DISCOVERY | OF ENGLAND | BY STEPHEN LEACOCK | [thick-thin rule] | [thin-thick rule] | *LONDON: JOHN LANE THE BODLEY HEAD LTD* | *MCMXXII*

◆ A⁸ B–O⁸ [$1 signed]. *1–4, 5–7, 8,, 9, 10–12, 13–219, 1–5* pp. (112 leaves). 185 × 123 mm.

CONTENTS: pp. *1* half title; p. *2* list of twelve other books by Leacock, the first being *Literary Lapses* and the last *Essays and Literary Studies*; p. *3* title; p. *4* Printed in Great Britain at | *The Mayflower, Press, Plymouth*. William Brendon & Son, Ltd.; pp. *5–7* preface ("Introduction of Mr. Stephen Leacock given by Sir Owen Seaman on the occasion of his first Lecture in London."); p. *8* blank; p. *9* table of contents; p. *10* blank; p. *11* fly title; p. *12* blank; pp. *13–219* text; p. *1* advertisement, including quotation from Leacock's introduction, of Robert Benchley's *Of All Things*; pp. *2–5* advertisements, with press opinions, of Leacock's books.

TEXT: Identical to the American edition.

BINDING AND DUST JACKET: Bound in green cloth with stamping on the boards in blue, top edge stained blue. Stamped on the upper board within two blind-stamped rectangles as follows: *MY DISCOVERY | OF ENGLAND | By STEPHEN LEACOCK*. Stamped on the spine as follows: *MY | DISCOVERY | OF | ENGLAND | By | STEPHEN | LEACOCK | The | Bodley Head.*

The front panel of the jacket has a colour illustration of an elderly couple in nineteenth-century dress who are standing on a cliff and looking out at the ocean. The rest of the jacket is white with blue lettering. Printed on the spine panel: MY | DISCOVERY | OF | ENGLAND | STEPHEN | LEACOCK | 5/– | NET | THE | BODLEY | HEAD. The back panel and the flaps have an advertisement with excerpts from reviews for Ben Travers's *A Cuckoo in the Nest*.

NOTES: From October to December 1921 Leacock made a lecture tour of Britain (see section E for specific dates and places). He earned a profit of $543 for the tour (receipts $6,028; expenses including purchases of $900 and a trip to Paris, $1,350, amounted to $5,485). *My Discovery of England* recounts in a humorous fashion some of the incidents that occurred during the tour along with Leacock's opinions of English customs and manners. Sir Owen Seaman, the editor of *Punch*, acted as chairman of Leacock's talk in London on 17 October 1921 at the Aeolian Hall. The book was written between 8 January and 31 March 1922, shortly after Leacock's return to Canada.

The contract with John Lane The Bodley Head and John Lane Company for the rights in Great Britain, the colonies and the United States for "three further works of fiction" is dated 15 October 1919. *My Discovery of England* was the second book under this contract. Leacock received 20% royalty on all copies sold of the British, American and Canadian editions. The advance was £125 on the British edition, $625 on the American edition, both one month prior to publication. Leacock apparently received an advance on the Canadian issue as well. Some discussion ensued between Leacock and The Bodley Head in March 1922 as to whether the book really fell within the boundaries of a work of fiction.

Leacock informed B.W. Willett of his intention to write the book on 8 January 1922. He planned to serialize the articles in *Harper's Magazine* and to complete the manuscript within two months. On 19 January 1922, Willett told Leacock: "As for the title of the new book I have gone to liking 'My Discovery of England' & [John] Kettelwell is doing the wrapper for this title." By the beginning of the next month, on 4 February, Leacock sent Willett two chapters, which enabled The Bodley Head to make up a dummy of his new book. A few days later, on 9 February, Willett observed:

> With regard to your new book, there are signs that we ought to do pretty well with this, but I know that it will be difficult for you to find time to write it. Still, I hope you will be able to, as it really is important from everybody's point of view to get it out this Spring, before the memory of your lecture tour has had time to die out.

On 18 February Seaman sent Leacock a revised version of his chairman's remarks for the preface; he requested Leacock to send him a proof before publication. Leacock informed Willett on 25 February that he was working on the book every spare minute in the hope of completing the manuscript by 1 April. Although he had already written half of the book, some 20,000 words, university commitments and other engagements delayed his progress. Leacock, in fact, posted the manuscript to John Lane on 31 March 1922. He did not read proofs, but engaged Miss Grant Cook to read the proofs in The Bodley Head's offices.

By 13 June 1922 the book was being delivered to booksellers. It was published on 17 June 1922. Leacock was sent a proof of the advertising. Willett sent a royalty cheque to Leacock on 29 September 1922 for £540.5.6. By 1 July 1922 9,224 copies had sold (856 to the colonies and 1,750 to Australasia). By the end of 1925, 21,555 copies sold of the English edition (1,983 to the colonies and 3,100 to Australasia). The book was reprinted in 1922, 1925, and 1931. The latter reprinting sold for 3s 6d.

COPIES EXAMINED: CS (first printing, 1925, and 1931 printings, all in jacket; second "edition" i.e. printing not in jacket); QMMRB (first printing in jacket).

### A37c  *Canadian edition* (1961):

Stephen Leacock | [open, swelled rule] | MY | DISCOVERY | OF | ENGLAND | [open, swelled rule] | Introduction : George Whalley | General Editor : Malcolm Ross | New Canadian Library No. 28 | [publisher's device: abstract design of a person on a horse-drawn chariot, taking aim with a bow and arrow] | MCCLELLAND AND STEWART LIMITED

◆  *i–vi*, vii–xiv, *xv*, 16–26, *27*, 28–34, *35*, 36–49, *50–51*, 52–70, *71*, 72–96, *97*, 98–120, *121*, 122–130, *131*, 132–145, *146–147*, 148–168, *169*, 170–197, *1–3* pp. (100 leaves). 183 × 110 mm.

CONTENTS:  p. *i* half title; p. *ii* blank; p. *iii* title; p. *iv* Copyright, Canada, 1922 | Copyright, Canada, 1961 | by | McClelland & Stewart Limited | [six lines concerning copyright] | PRINTED AND BOUND BY | HAZELL WATSON AND VINEY LTD | AYLESBURY AND SLOUGH, ENGLAND; p. *v* table of contents; p. *vi* blank; pp. vii–xiv George Whalley's introduction; pp. *xv*–197 text; p. *1* blank; p. 2 biographical information on Leacock; p. *3* list of titles in the New Canadian Library series.

TEXT:  Identical to A37a.

BINDING:  Bound in stiff paper, perfect bound. The covers are white and pale blue with lettering in purple. A drawing of Leacock's face in red is on the front cover. The back cover has a paragraph on the book's contents and the book's price ($1). Covers designed by Frank Newfeld.

NOTES:  By the end of 1961 1,603 copies had sold. By the end of 1979, 21,157 copies had sold (information based on file 14, "New Canadian Library," box 93, series A, part I, McClelland and Stewart fonds, OHM). Reprinted in 1963 ($1.25) and 1968 ($1.50).

COPIES EXAMINED: CS (first, second, and third printings).

## A38 A BANNER OFFERING TO NEWSPAPERS 1923

[all lines within two rectangles] A BANNER OFFERING | TO NEWSPAPERS | [the next lines within two separate rectangles, the outer one thick] STEPHEN | LEACOCK | ACE OF HUMORISTS | ONCE A WEEK | METROPOLITAN NEWSPAPER SERVICE | MAXIMILIAN ELSER, JR., General Manager | 150 NASSAU STREET NEW YORK CITY

◆ 9 unnumbered leaves printed on the rectos only. 335 × 258 mm. White paper stock, leaves not bound together.

CONTENTS: folio 1 title; folio 2 announcement (with heading "Laugh With Leacock") by the Metropolitan Newspaper Service that it is offering a series of Leacock's weekly illustrated articles; folio 3 photo of Leacock with biographical information about him; folios 4–9 text.

TEXT: "The Balance of Trade in Impressions," "Impressions of London," "My Financial Career," and "The Kidnapped Plumber." Each article is accompanied by illustrations done by Kessler.

NOTES: Leacock's weekly stories of humour were syndicated throughout the world by the Metropolitan Newspaper Service. The series began in January 1921. Many stories were written by Leacock expressly for this series, and many were reprinted or taken from sketches found in his books. When an article had been previously published, Leacock shortened or altered the article to the required number of words.

On 24 February 1923, Max Elser, Jr. informed Harold Ober, who worked with Leacock's literary agent, Paul R. Reynolds, that the Metropolitan Newspaper Service had printed and distributed 600 copies of a small circular (printing cost $15.50), 1,000 copies of a large circular (printing cost $159.50), fifty copies of one syndicated story, and 150 copies of three other stories (printing cost $80). These circulars and stories were used for the purpose of promotion so that newspapers would buy and syndicate Leacock's articles. "I personally presented Leacock in a dozen towns as far west as Omaha," Elser told Ober. Mr. Sharp, an agent, promoted Leacock to newspapers in the south and southwest parts of the United States, and another agent, Mr. Hadley, did the same on the west coast.

COPIES EXAMINED: SLM.

## A39 OVER THE FOOTLIGHTS 1923

### A39a English edition:

OVER THE | FOOTLIGHTS | AND OTHER FANCIES | BY STEPHEN LEACOCK | [thick-thin rule] | [thin-thick rule] | LONDON: JOHN LANE THE BODLEY HEAD LTD | MCMXXIII

◆ A$^{16}$ B–I$^{16}$ [$1 signed, fifth leaf signed *]. i–iv, v–vi, 1, 2, 3–193, 194, 195–278, 1–4 pp. (144 leaves). 189 × 128 mm.

CONTENTS: p. *i* half title; p. *ii* list of other books by Leacock published by The Bodley Head; p. *iii* title; p. *iv* *First Published in 1923* | MADE AND PRINTED IN GREAT BRITAIN BY MORRISON AND GIBB LTD., EDINBURGH; pp. v–vi contents; p. 1 [thick-thin rule] | *OVER THE FOOTLIGHTS* | [thin-thick rule]; p. 2 blank; pp. 3–192 text; p. 193 [thick-thin rule] | *OTHER FANCIES* [thin-thick rule]; p. *194* blank; pp. 195–278, 1 text; p. 2 blank; pp. *3–4* some press opinions.

TEXT: The text consists of two parts: Over the Footlights, the first ten sketches; and Other Fancies, sketches XI to XXII.

I Cast Up by the Sea, a Seacoast Melodrama; II Dead Men's Gold, a Film of the Great Nevada Desert; III The Soul Call, an Up-to-Date Piffle-Play; IV Oroastus, a Greek Tragedy; V The Sub-Contractor, an Ibsen Play; VI The Historic Drama; VII The Russian Drama (A, Old Style, Basilisk Vangorod — B, New Style, Damned Souls); VIII The Platter of Life; IX The Vampire Woman; X The Raft, an Interlude; XI First Call for Spring; or, Oh, Listen to the Birds!; XII How I Succeeded in My Business; XIII The Dry Banquet; XIV My Lost Dollar; XV Radio, a New Form of Trouble; XVI Roughing It in the Bush; XVII Abolishing the Heroine; XVIII My Affair with My Landlord; or, Did I Dream It?; XIX Why I Refuse to Play Golf; XX The Approach of the Comet: Do You Really Care If It Hits You?; XXI Personal Experiments with the Black Bass; XXII L'Envoi: To a Faded Actor.

BINDING AND DUST JACKET: Bound in blue cloth, top edge stained blue. Stamped on the upper board within three blind-stamped rectangles: *OVER THE FOOTLIGHTS* | *AND OTHER FANCIES* | *by STEPHEN LEACOCK*. Stamped on the spine: *OVER THE* | *FOOTLIGHTS* | *AND OTHER* | *FANCIES* | *By* | *STEPHEN* | *LEACOCK* | *The* | *Bodley Head*.

On the front panel of the jacket is a drawing in black, orange, and yellow by Christopher Hassall. The drawing is of a bald man (a conductor) whose back is to the reader. He carries "EXPLANATORY | NOTES" and apparently stands before a stage. Printed on the spine panel of the jacket: OVER THE | FOOTLIGHTS | 5/– | NET | THE | BODLEY | HEAD. The back panel has some press opinions of the work of Ben Travers. The front flap of the jacket has advertisements of James Branch Cabell's *Jurgen* and *The Cream of the Jest*. The back flap has advertisements of Harry Leon Wilson's *Merton of the Movies* and Robert Benchley's *Love Conquers All*.

Also examined was a copy in orange cloth (not seen in jacket, however) with smaller sheets measuring 183 × 121 mm. This appears to be the cheaper "edition," which according to *The English Catalogue of Books* was issued in June 1932 and sold for 3s 6d. The lettering on the boards of the cheap edition is the same as that of the first printing in blue cloth, except there is no blind-stamping on the upper board. The orange cloth has a smooth finish, and is not stained on the top edge. The only textual difference is on the verso of the first leaf which lists Leacock's books published by The Bodley Head. With respect to *Further Foolishness: Sketches and Satires on the Follies of the Day*, the description in the first printing has: With coloured Frontis- | piece by "FISH" and 5 other Plates by | M. BLOOD. In the cheaper edition, the description does not mention the plates by Blood.

NOTES: The contract with John Lane The Bodley Head and the John Lane Company for the rights in Great Britain, the colonies, and the United States for "three further works of fiction" is dated 15 October 1919. *Over the Footlights and Other Fancies* was the third book under this contract. Leacock received 20% royalty on all copies sold for all editions.

The advance on the English edition was £125, which was to be paid to Leacock one month prior to publication.

Leacock made a false start on this book on 21 August 1921. He told John Lane that he had been working on ". . . a book of burlesque plays & films (moving pictures) under the title THE DRAMA AS I SEE IT" (The Bodley Head fonds, TEX). Leacock promised to send Lane a table of contents, but his plans were delayed when he embarked on a lecture tour of England.

On 24 December 1922 Leacock informed B.W. Willett that he made a good start on his book, "The Drama as I See It": "It is a set of 7 or 8 plays & films done on the model of *Behind the Beyond*, as if one sat in the audience, not in dramatic form" (TEX). Leacock mentioned that the first American serial rights were to appear in *Harper's Magazine*, and he hoped for similar arrangements in England through his agents Christy and Moore. Willett replied positively on 8 January 1923 about Leacock's progress, but thought the title unattractive. Leacock shared Willett's qualm about the title of his new book in a letter of 20 January 1923, and ten days later, on 30 January 1923, he told Willett:

> I enclose a title page with the book title as I now propose it. WHERE THESPIS WALKS Studies in the Plays and Films of Yesterday and Today. I think I see a very good cover, with Thespis leading a little procession of actors of different actors and types, down to the chorus-girl and the Vamp.

> The new proposed title did not appeal to Willett, however. He believed that few would understand the classical allusions which Leacock intended (13 February 1923).

By 2 March Leacock had written 22,000 words, and on 31 March he told Willett that he would mail the manuscript on 12 April:

> The reason why I am able to send this stuff along so soon is that I have decided to take what Drama pieces I have finished (30,000 words) and add 15,000 words of mixed sketches. If I delay we miss the market & the year & I might not get any good stuff done anyway. Please rush this book along fast. It will be far better to have it simultaneous in U.S. Canada & England (TEX).

Willett received the typescript on 23 April 1923. Leacock sent him another sketch, "The Historic Drama," for inclusion on 2 May 1933 and a revised version of "Cast Up by the Sea" on 8 May. He also asked Willett to remove a sketch entitled "Sack the Lot" on 6 May. The English edition was set in type by 15 May 1923. Leacock did not read the proofs, but he sent Willett instructions for the proof reader. The English edition was published on 22 June 1923. The copyright was registered at the Copyright Office of DLC by Dodd, Mead on 12 July 1923 (ClAint.5179). On 25 June 1923 Willett mailed Leacock the advance royalty. On 29 September 1923 Willett remarked that due to Hassall's dust jacket, Leacock's book was prominently displayed "in every bookseller's window."

By 1 July 1923 8,552 copies had sold, including 832 copies to the colonies and 1,750 to Australasia. By the end of 1925 12,733 copies had sold (1,052 to the colonies and 1,750 to Australasia). It would appear that approximately fifty copies sold annually thereafter.

Leacock's notebook at SLM, J104, has a preliminary table of contents, the manuscript of "Personal Experiments with the Black Bass" (19 pp.), and tearsheets of various stories taken from *Harper's Weekly*, *Maclean's Magazine*, and the *Montreal Standard*.

"The Raft, an Interlude" is reprinted in John Stevens, ed., *Ten Canadian Short Plays* (Toronto: Dell, 1975), pp. [13]–22.

COPIES EXAMINED: CS (two copies in blue cloth, one in jacket; orange cloth not in jacket); QMMRB (not in jacket).

## A39b *American edition* (1923):

OVER THE | FOOTLIGHTS | [thick-thin rule] | BY STEPHEN LEACOCK | [thin-thick rule] | [publisher's device: illustration of a woman's face and two open books within an oval, ornamental frame] | [thick-thin rule] | NEW YORK | DODD, MEAD AND COMPANY | 1923 | [thin-thick rule]

◆ $1-17^8$ $18^{10}$. *1*–8, 3–195, *196–198*, 199–285, *1* pp. (146 leaves). 186 × 129 mm.

CONTENTS: p. *1* half title; p. *2* list of other books by Leacock (*BY THE SAME AUTHOR*) published by Dodd, Mead; p. *3* title; p. *4* COPYRIGHT, 1923, | BY DODD, MEAD AND COMPANY, INC. | PRINTED IN U. S. A. | VAIL-BALLOU COMPANY | BINGHAMTON AND NEW YORK; pp. *5*–6 contents; p. *7* [thick-thin rule] | *OVER THE FOOTLIGHTS* | [thin-thick rule]; p. *8* blank; pp. 3–195 text; p. *196* blank; p. *197* [thick-thin rule] | *OTHER FANCIES* | [thin-thick rule]; p. *198* blank; pp. 199–285 text; p. *1* blank.

Text: The book is divided into two sections as in the English edition: the first section, entitled Over the Footlights, has chapters I–X; the second section, entitled Other Fancies (chapters I–XII). In the American edition the second and third sketches have traded places.

BINDING AND DUST JACKET: Bound in red cloth. Blind-stamped with raised letters on the upper board within two rectangles: OVER THE | FOOTLIGHTS | [rule] | STEPHEN LEACOCK. Stamped in gold on the spine: OVER | THE | FOOTLIGHTS| [rule] | LEAC-OCK | DODD, MEAD | & COMPANY.

The front panel of the jacket (designed by John Held Jr.) is mainly black with white lettering. A man in a tuxedo, holding a mask, stands on top of five proscenium arches. The back panel has an advertisement (titled Laugh with Leacock and within an ornamental rectangle) of Leacock's other books published by Dodd, Mead. The front flap of the jacket has a synopsis of the book. The back flap is blank. The following is printed on the spine panel: [three ornamental rules] | OVER THE | FOOTLIGHTS | *By* | STEPHEN | LEACOCK | *Author of* | *"Nonsense Novels"* | *"My Discovery* | *of England"* | *Etc.* | $1.50 | DODD, MEAD | AND COMPANY | [three ornamental rules].

NOTES: In his correspondence with Leacock on 11 January 1923, Frank Dodd referred to the new book as "Nonsense Plays." But Leacock questioned Dodd's title on 1 February 1923:

> I wired you today that I am still perplexed about the title of my book. I don't like to call the book NONSENSE PLAYS or BURLESQUE PLAYS or any general thing of this sort meaning a comic collection. The book is *not* that. It is really like a view or picture of the modern drama, as seen always from the point of view of the immediate spectator sitting in the theatre.

With respect to Leacock's proposed title "Where Thespis Walks," Dodd told Leacock on 23 February 1923 that "we all feel that this would be a mistake." He suggested three alternatives: "Footlights and Films"; "Footlights and Flashes"; or "Across the Footlights".

Leacock mailed "the entire manuscript of Over the Footlights (note title) on Apr. 12." with the exception of "nos. V and VI.," and he included extra sketches, "Sub Contractor, an Ibsen Play," "Basilisk Vangorod, a Russian Play," and "Damned Souls, a (New Style) Russian Play". The typescript was sent to the printer a few days later on 16 April 1923. Leacock inspected the proofs prior to 7 May, and on that date, he remarked to B.W. Willett of The Bodley Head: "On Dodd Meads [sic] galleys I find a good many things to change. The copy was evidently not in good shape."

Leacock received an advance of $625 on the American edition one month prior to publication. Published on 21 July 1924. On 24 July 1923, Dodd informed Leacock: "OVER THE FOOTLIGHTS has started out exceedingly well and our advance orders are far in excess of the book last year." The copyright was registered at the Copyright Office of DLC on 26 July 1923 (ClA711332). The copyright was renewed by George Leacock on 8 September 1950 (R66922).

By 1 August 1923 7,750 copies had sold, and by 1 February 1925 13,236 copies had sold. By the mid-1930 sales had declined to less than fifty copies annually.

COPIES EXAMINED: CS (in jacket).

## A39b.1 *Canadian issue* (1923):

OVER THE | FOOTLIGHTS | [thick-thin rule] | BY STEPHEN LEACOCK | [thin-thick rule] | [publisher's device of Dodd, Mead] | [thick-thin rule] | TORONTO | S. B. GUNDY | 1923 | [thin-thick rule]

On the spine of the Canadian issue DODD, MEAD | & COMPANY is replaced by GUNDY. The dust jackets are quite similar. The Canadian dust jacket differs in the following respects from that of the American edition: on the spine panel there is no price and DODD, MEAD | AND COMPANY is replaced by S. B. GUNDY; the back panel is blank; and on the bottom of the back flap, DODD, MEAD AND COMPANY | Publishers New York has been replaced by S. B. GUNDY | TORONTO.

NOTES: On 2 December 1922, S.B. Gundy told Leacock: "I shall be delighted to take your book 'THE DRAMA AS I SEE IT' on the basis of our contract." Gundy informed Frank Dodd on 13 March 1923 that he wanted to publish " 'Across the Footlights" by end of May of that year. Publication was undoubtedly simultaneous with the American edition. The print run of the Canadian issue consisted of 5,000 copies. On 1 April 1924 2,300 copies were still in stock and had not been sold.

COPIES EXAMINED: CS (in jacket); QMMRB (two copies, neither in jacket).

## A40 COLLEGE DAYS 1923

### A40a *American edition*:

COLLEGE DAYS | [thick-thin rule] | BY STEPHEN LEACOCK | [thin-thick rule] | [publisher's device: illustration of a woman's face and two open books within an oval, ornamental, leafy frame] | [thick-thin rule] | NEW YORK | DODD, MEAD AND COMPANY | 1923 | [thin-thick rule]

♦ $1-11^8 \ 12^4$. 1–6, v–vi, 1–4, 3–6, 7–8, 9–23, 24–26, 27–35, 36–38, 39–42, 43–44, 45–56, 57–58, 59–62, 63–64, 65–69, 70–72, 73–77, 78–80, 81–86, 87–88, 89–100, 101–102, 103–109, 110–112,

113–121, 122–124, 125–132, 133–134, 135–161, 162–164, 165–169, 1–5 pp. (92 leaves). 188 × 129 mm.

CONTENTS: pp.1–2 blank; p. 3 half title; p. 4 blank; p. 5 title; p. 6 COPYRIGHT, 1923, | BY DODD, MEAD AND COMPANY, INC. | PRINTED IN THE U. S. A. BY | The Quinn & Boden Company | [rule] | BOOK MANUFACTURERS | RAHWAY NEW JERSEY; pp. v–vi preface; p. 1 table of contents; p. 2 blank; p. 3–4, 3–169 text (pp. 8, 24, 26, 36, 38, 44, 58, 64, 70, 72, 78, 80, 88, 110, 112, 122, 124, 134, 162, and 164 blank); pp. 1–5 blank.

TEXT: My College Days: A Retrospect; My Memories and Miseries as a Schoolmaster; Laus Varsitatis: A Song in Praise of the University of Toronto; The Oldest Living Graduate; The Faculty of Arts; English As She Is Taught at College; A Little Glimpse into the College Future [The preceding leaf has the title "The Lengthening of the College Course," and the running heads for this sketch are "Lengthening the Course."]; A Subscription with Reflections; Toronto and McGill; The Children's Corner; A Sermon on College Humour; A Christmas Examination; Idleness: A Song for the Long Vacation; The Diversions of a Professor of History; The Old College and the New University.

The section entitled "The Diversions of a Professor of History" consists of an explanatory note and the following individual poems: To-Day in History, August 4, 1778 (Victory of Gwalior); August 2, 1704 (Battle of Blenheim); August 5, 1809 (Birth of Alfred Tennyson); August 8, 1843 (The Annexation of Natal); August 9, 1902 (King Edward VII Crowned); August 10, 1866 (The Straits Settlements Founded); August 12, 1905 (Anglo-Japanese Alliance); August 14, 1763 (Admiral Albemarle Took Havana); August 11, 1535 (Jacques Cartier Discovered the St. Lawrence); August 15, 1870 (Manitoba Becomes a Province); August 16, 1713 (New Brunswick Founded); August 17, 1896 (Gold Discovered in the Yukon); August 18, 1577 (Birth of Rubens); August 19, 1897 (Introduction of the Horseless Cab); August 20, 1896 (Fridtjof Nansen's Ship "The Fram" Returns Safely to Skjervoe); August 22, 1903 (Expedition of the "Neptune" Under Commander Low to Hudson Straits); August 26, 1346 (Great Slaughter of the French by the English at Crecy); and August 27, 1870 (Invention of the Gramophone).

BINDING AND DUST JACKET: Bound in red cloth. A solid rectangle is blind-stamped on the upper board. Within this solid rectangle are two raised rectangles, which contain the following in raised characters: COLLEGE DAYS | [rule] | STEPHEN LEACOCK. Stamped in gold on the spine: COLLEGE | DAYS | [rule] | LEACOCK | DODD, MEAD | & COMPANY.

The dust jacket is light tan-coloured, featuring the same design employed on the title page of the illustrated edition of *Nonsense Novels* (see A7b) a circular design of two laughing girls in pigtails, two professors with mortar boards, moustaches, and glasses, and .SL. in the centre. On the front panel of the jacket within two red rectangles, the outer one thick: COLLEGE | DAYS | [small design to the right of the previous two lines] | [design in a larger size] | [small design; the next two lines to the right of the design] | STEPHEN | LEACOCK. The back panel has the design within two red squares (situated in the left-hand corner of two red rectangles). Within the rectangles is a paragraph highlighting the book's contents. On the spine panel: [thick-thin rule] | COLLEGE | DAYS | STEPHEN | LEACOCK | $1.25 | DODD, MEAD | & COMPANY | [thin-thick rule]. The flaps are blank.

NOTES: *College Days* incorporates essays, sketches, and poems written by Leacock over a period of twenty years, primarily in university-based magazines. The contract with Dodd,

Mead is dated 23 February 1923. It specifies a royalty of 10% on the first 10,000 copies sold and 20% thereafter. On 26 February 1923, Leacock sent a chapter of the book to Dodd, Mead. The complete typescript probably was received by Dodd, Mead a few days later. On 13 March 1923, A.M. Chase of Dodd, Mead sent Leacock a set of the proofs by registered post. Published on 20 October 1923. The copyright was registered with the Copyright Record Office at DLC on 25 October 1923 (ClA759584). The copyright was renewed by George Leacock on 8 December 1950 (R71373).

By 1 February 1924 3,781 copies had sold. Up to 1 February 1925 4,392 copies had sold. Thereafter, sales declined considerably. For example, between 1 February and 1 August 1927, thirteen copies were sold. Between 1 February and 1 August 1928, thirty-two copies sold. Between 1 August 1929 and 1 February 1930, twenty-one copies sold. Between 1 August 1930 and 1 Feb 1931, five copies sold.

Also examined was the second printing, which is identical to the first, except for the additional lines on the copyright page: First Printing, October, 1923 | Second Printing, December, 1923.

COPIES EXAMINED: CS (both printings in jacket).

## A40b *Canadian edition*:

[all lines within an ornamental, rectangular border (with leaves at the corners)] *College Days* | *By* Stephen Leacock | [ornament] | S. B. GUNDY | PUBLISHER – TORONTO

• $1^8$ $2-10^8$ [$1 signed]. *1*–8, 7–8, 9–*10*, 11–14, *15*–*16*, 17–32, *33*–*34*, 35–*41*, *42*–*44*, 45–*48*, 49–*50*, 51–60, *61*–*62*, 63–*66*, 67–*68*, 69–*73*, 74–*76*, 77–*81*, 82–*84*, 85–*111*, *112*–*114*, 115–*126*, *127*–*128*, 129–*138*, *139*–*140*, 141–*146*, *147*–*148*, 149–*153*, *1*–5 pp. (80 leaves). 187 × 125 mm.

CONTENTS: pp. *1*–*2* blank; p. *3* half title; p. *4* blank; p. *5* title; p. 6 Copyright, Canada, 1923 | by S. B. Gundy, Toronto | Printed in Canada; pp. 7–8 table of contents; pp. 7–8 preface dated "McGill University, October 1st, 1923."; pp. 9–*151* text; p. [*1*] logo of Warwick Bros. & Rutter Limited Toronto Printers & Bookbinders; pp. 2–5 blank.

TEXT: I My College Days: A Retrospect; II My Memories and Miseries As a Schoolmaster; III Laus Varsitatis: A Poem in Praise of the University of Toronto; IV The Oldest Living Graduate; V The Dean's Dinner; VI English As She Is Taught at College; VII Glimpses of the College Future; VIII Toronto and McGill; IX The Diversions of a Professor of History; X Children's Corner (1902); XI A Christmas Examination; XII Idleness: A Song for the Long Vacation; XIII The Old College and the New University.

Section IX has an additional poem, "August 7, 1657. Death of Admiral Blake," not included in A40a and A40c.

BINDING AND DUST JACKET: Bound in bright orange cloth. Stamped on the upper board: [the first three lines within two rectangles, the outer one thick] COLLEGE DAYS | by | STEPHEN LEACOCK | [below the rectangles are five rows of two kinds of alternating ornaments (twenty-five ornaments in all, five per row)]. Stamped on the spine: College | Days | [rule] | Leacock | GUNDY.

The dust jacket is also orange but not as bright as the colour of the boards. The front and spine panels are identical to the stamping and decoration on the upper board and spine, although the printing on the jacket is somewhat fainter. On the back panel of the jacket: [all lines within two rectangles; the first fifteen lines within another rectangle] Stephen

Leacock's Works | [fourteen numbered titles of Leacock's books, each on a separate line, the first being 1. Frenzied Fiction and the last 14. Over the Footlights] | S. B. GUNDY | PUBLISHER – – TORONTO. The front flap features a summary of *College Days* within two rectangles. The back flap has a similar summary for *My Discovery of England*.

NOTES: In his notebook of royalty payments at SLM, Leacock has 1 November 1923 as the date of publication of the Canadian edition. 2,000 copies were printed. On 17 December 1923, unaware that Gundy had published a separate edition, B.W. Willett of The Bodley Head complained to Leacock: "By the way we cabled Gundy our price for the wrapper blocks of 'College Days' but we have heard nothing from him." Willett believed that Gundy had a grudge against The Bodley Head. It may have been for this reason that Gundy published his own edition without consulting The Bodley Head. Galley proofs of the Canadian edition with Leacock's holograph annotations and corrections, marked up for the printer, are located at OTUTF (W.C. Bell fonds). The Canadian edition omits two essays published in A40a (A Subscription with Reflections and A Sermon on College Humour).

COPIES EXAMINED: CS (in jacket).

## A40c *English edition*:

*COLLEGE DAYS* | BY | *STEPHEN LEACOCK* | [thick-thin rule] | [thin-thick rule] | *LONDON: JOHN LANE THE BODLEY HEAD LTD* | *MCMXXIII*

◆ $A^8$ B-L$^8$ [$1 signed]. *1–4, 5–7, 8–10, 11–14, 15–16, 17–30, 31–32, 33–39, 40–42, 43–46, 47–48, 49–57, 58–60, 61–63, 64–66, 67–71, 72–74, 75–78, 79–80, 81–85, 86–88, 89–100, 101–102, 103–109, 110–112, 113–121, 122–124, 125–130, 131–132, 133–136, 137–138, 139–164, 1–12* pp. (88 leaves). 189 × 127 mm.

CONTENTS: p. *1* half title; p. *2* list of other books by Leacock published by The Bodley Head; p. *3* title; p. *4* Made and Printed in Great Britain at | *The Mayflower Press, Plymouth*. William Brendon & Son, Ltd.; pp. *5–6* Leacock's preface dated October, 1923; p. *7* table of contents; p. *8* blank; pp. *9–164* text; pp. *1–7* advertisements of Leacock's books published by The Bodley Head with press opinions; pp. *8–12* advertisements (with press opinions) of other authors' books published by The Bodley Head — Ben Travers's *Rookery Nook*, *A Cuckoo in the Nest*, and *The Dippers*, a number of books by Harry Leon Wilson, H.H. Munro's *The Square Egg and Other Stories*, and Robert Benchley's *Of All Things* and *Love Conquers All*.

TEXT: Identical to A40a. The essays and poems are numbered I to XV. "The Old College and the New University" is printed before "The Diversions of a Professor of History."

BINDING AND DUST JACKET: Bound in dark blue cloth with yellow lettering and top edge stained yellow. On the upper board within blind–stamped rectangles: *COLLEGE DAYS* | *By STEPHEN LEACOCK*. Stamped on the spine: *COLLEGE* | *DAYS* | *By* | *STEPHEN* | *LEACOCK* | *The* | *Bodley Head*.

The front panel of the jacket is a coloured illustration by Christopher Hassall of a professor in academic garb, apparently laughing, holding a hand to his mouth. Printed on the front panel: COLLEGE DAYS | STEPHEN LEACOCK | [signed by Hassall in left–hand corner below his illustration]. The back panel of the jacket features advertisements of R.S. Hooper's *One at a Time* and *And the Next*. The front flap has an advertisement of William J. Locke's *Moordius & Co.* The back flap has advertisements of Muriel Hine's *The Spell of*

*Siris* and *Stories of Love and Laughter*. Printed on the spine panel: COLLEGE | DAYS | STEPHEN | LEACOCK | 5/– | NET | THE | BODLEY | HEAD.

NOTES: On 2 March 1923 B.W. Willett wrote to Leacock: "With regard to 'College Days' this has not yet come to hand, but we will of course consider it as soon as we receive it, and send you a cable at once." Although he was obviously receptive to the publication of another book by Leacock, Willett was worried by the fact that his travellers were already advertising *Over the Footlights and Other Fancies* (as "The Drama as I See It"). The publication of two books by Leacock, one right after the other, might cause confusion in the booktrade, Willett thought. He suggested that the publication of *College Days* could be delayed until Christmas, thereby generating greater sales. A few days later, on 8 March 1923, the typescript arrived at the offices of The Bodley Head. ". . . I cannot write you anything very definite about it," Willett informed Leacock, "but the terms you mention seem all right." The timing of the book's publication still caused Willett some concern. A week after receiving the typescript, on 15 March 1923, Willett stated: "There seems to be some awfully good stuff in this, though of course a lot of it, especially the poetry, is rather local in interest. Still we shall be delighted to publish it on the terms you suggested, viz: 10% on the first 10,000 copies, 20% afterwards and the usual 10% on Colonies." There may not have been an advance royalty since none is specified in the terms of Willett's letter. Christopher Hassall's design of the dust jacket was almost finished by 29 September 1923.

On 15 November 1923, Willett told Leacock: "I have pleasure in sending you herewith account of 'College Days' on publication, together with cheque for £114.3.9, the amount due in royalties." A week before Christmas on 17 December 1923, Willett reported that 5,000 copies had been sold.

By the end of 1923 5,699 copies had sold (733 copies to the colonies and 1,000 copies to Australasia). Up to 1 January 1925, 9,710 copies had sold (1,007 to the colonies and 1,200 copies to Australasia). Royalty reports from The Bodley Head indicate that the book continued to sell at a much slower rate thereafter: for example, between July and December 1925, 105 copies at 20%, twenty–eight colonial copies at 10%, 100 Australasian copies at 10%. According to *The English Catalogue of Books*, there was also a "New ed. Cr. 8vo . . . 164 p.," which appeared on the market in September 1932 and sold for 3s. 6d. It would appear that the latter is a "cheaper edition" (a reprint with a reduced royalty).

COPIES EXAMINED: CS (in jacket).

## A41 STEPHEN LEACOCK 1923

### A41a *first issue, Haliburton edition*:

STEPHEN LEACOCK | *by* | PETER McARTHUR | [publisher's device: floral compartment containing a plaque with Egerton Ryerson's portrait and below the plaque: RYERSON | FOVNDED | 1829] | TORONTO | THE RYERSON PRESS

♦ *S.L.* — 1⁸ S.L. — 2–S.L. — 12⁸ [$1 signed]. *1–10, 1–19,* 20–22, *23–28,* 29–30, *31–32,* 33–34, *35–45,* 46–48, *49–63,* 64–66, *67–81,* 82–84, *85–93,* 94–96, *97–114,* 115–116, *117–123,* 124–126, *127–163,* 164–166, *167–176, 1–6* pp. (96 leaves). 177 × 117 mm. There is an extra leaf at the beginning and end, but these appear to be attached to the endpapers and are not part of the gatherings.

CONTENTS: p. *1* half title with series statement; p. *2* blank; p. *3 HALIBURTON EDITION*

| *This edition is limited to Two Hundred and Fifty* | *Numbered Sets, being the first* | *printing, of which this is* | *Number* [number stamped in red]; p. *4* series statement with names of the editors and dedication to the writers of Canada; p. *5* title; p. *6* COPYRIGHT IN ALL COUNTRIES | SUBSCRIBING TO THE BERNE CONVENTION; p. *7* table of contents; p. *8* blank; p. *9* BIOGRAPHICAL | [two rules]; p. *10* blank; pp. *1–19* biography of Leacock by McArthur; p. *20* blank; pp. *21–123* anthology (i.e. text, with pp. *22, 30, 34, 46, 48, 64, 66, 82, 84, 94, 96,* and *116* blank); p. *124* blank; pp. *125–163* appreciation by McArthur (p. *126* blank); p. *164* blank; p. *165* BIBLIOGRAPHY | [two rules]; p. *166* blank; pp. *167–173* bibliography; pp. *174–176* index; p. *1* THIS BOOK IS A | PRODUCTION OF | [plaque with Ryerson's portrait and below the portrait: Ryerson | Press | Founded | 1829] | TORONTO. CANADA; pp. *2–6* blank. Between pp. *6* and *7* are: a leaf on glossy paper with Leacock's photo and his signature in facsimile; and a tissue guard.

TEXT: My Financial Career and Boarding-House Geometry from *Literary Lapses*; L'Envoi: The Train to Mariposa from *Sunshine Sketches of a Little Town*; The Little Girl in Green from *Arcadian Adventures with the Idle Rich*; A Hero in Homespun; or, The Life Struggle of Hezekiah Hayloft from *Nonsense Novels*; The Spiritual Outlook of Mr. Doomer from *Moonbeams from the Larger Lunacy*; The Sorrows of a Summer Guest from *Frenzied Fiction*; Oxford Smoking from *My Discovery of England*.

BINDING: Bound in dark brown leather with brown signet. The paper has a watermark and ragged edges, except for the top edge which is stained in gilt. Stamped in gilt on the upper board is Leacock's signature in facsimile within two joined rectangles. Stamped in gilt on the spine: MAKERS | CANADIAN | LITERATURE | [ornament] | STEPHEN | LEACOCK | [rule] | McARTHUR | [floral, rectangular compartment] | [plaque with Ryerson's portrait and below the portrait: Ryerson | Press | Founded | 1829]. The endpapers are marbled dark brown.

NOTES: In the fall of 1922 Lorne Pierce, the Book Editor and Literary Advisor to The Ryerson Press, conceived of a series, The Makers of Canadian Literature, that would be a tribute to Canadian authors. Each volume would consist of a portrait of the "Maker," a biography, an anthology of the Maker's work, a critical appreciation, a bibliography, and an index. Pierce was the series editor; Victor Morin was the associate editor responsible for the volumes in French. Thirteen volumes of the series appeared, although many more were planned and some were actually written and never published.

Leacock was flattered that he was to be included in the Makers series and that Peter McArthur had been commissioned to compile the book. In a letter of 11 January 1923 (addressed to "Mr. Ryerson"), he told Pierce that ". . . Peter MacArthur [sic] . . . helped me to bring out my first book. Up to the time of meeting him I had really only done short, casual stuff." Pierce asked Leacock for copies of his books on 14 May 1923. He inquired about bibliographical data on 28 July and 3 October 1923. Pierce sent Leacock a checklist of his publications. Leacock crossed out a number of them, and he wrote out three pages of "Longer Magazine articles (other than those reprinted in books)." A photograph of Leacock was obtained from Notman and Sons in late October 1923 just before the book went to press.

McArthur apparently received a flat fee of $500 for the book. He did not receive much help from Leacock by way of biographical information. He had to rely on the morgue of the *Toronto Globe*. McArthur informed Pierce on 19 November 1923 that "Stephen has come out of the silence. He seems to be entirely satisfied with the appreciation." In an undated note Leacock told McArthur: "First rate. Fine. Excellent. Of course it is too flattering but I don't object to that at all." Leacock asked for six copies of the book to be sent to him at his expense on 7 December 1923 (information based on the Lorne Pierce fonds at OKQ).

For general information on the Makers series, see Margery Fee, "Lorne Pierce, Ryerson Press, and The Makers of Canadian Literature Series," *Papers of the Bibliographical Society of Canada* 24 (1985): 51–71.

COPIES EXAMINED: OKQ (copy no. 3).

### A41a.1 *second issue, Fréchette edition*:

Transcription identical to A41.

This issue is almost identical to A41 with the following exceptions. (1) The limitation statement on p. 3 reads: *FRÉCHETTE EDITION | This edition is limited to One Thousand | Numbered Sets, being the first | printing, of which this is | Number* [number stamped in red]. (2) The paper is not watermarked. (3) There is no tissue guard for Leacock's photograph.

BINDING: Bound in black imitation flexible leather with black signet, top edge stained gilt and matching black endpapers.
Stamping on the boards in gilt is the same as A41a.

COPIES EXAMINED: EVANS (copy no. 3).

### A41a.2 *third issue*:

[all lines within a leafy, rectangular compartment, initialed JP at the right-hand corner of the compartment; the leaf design extends to the facing page] STEPHEN LEACOCK | *by* | PETER McARTHUR | [floral ornament] | TORONTO | THE RYERSON PRESS

◆ $\pi^4$ S.L. — $1^8$ S.L. — 2-S.L. — $11^8$ S.L. — $12^2$ [\$1 signed]. *1–8*, 1–19, *20–22*, 23–28, *29–30*, 31–32, *33–34*, 35–45, *46–48*, 49–63, *64–66*, 67–81, *82–84*, 85–93, *94–96*, 97–114, *115–116*, 117–123, *124–126*, 127–163, *164–166*, 167–176, *1–4* pp. (94 leaves). 165 × 108 mm.

CONTENTS: p. *1* half title with series statement; p. *2* series statement with names of the editors and dedication to the writers of Canada; p. *3* title; p. *4* COPYRIGHT, CANADA, 1923, BY | THE RYERSON PRESS; p. *5* table of contents; p. *6* blank; p. *7* BIOGRAPHICAL | [two rules]; p. *8* blank; pp. 1–176 identical to A41; p. *1* THIS BOOK IS A | PRODUCTION OF | [plaque with Ryerson's portrait and below the portrait: Ryerson | Press | Founded | 1829]; pp. *2–4* blank. Between pp. *6* and *7* is a leaf with a tipped-in photo of Leacock and his signature in facsimile.

BINDING: Bound in blue cloth with blue signet, top edge stained blue, light blue flecked endpapers with name of The Ryerson Press, its founding, and portrait of Ryerson. Stamping in gilt on the boards is similar to A41a.

COPIES EXAMINED: CS.

**A41a.3** *fourth issue, Library edition*:

[all lines within a leafy, rectangular compartment, initialed JP at the right-hand corner of the compartment; the leaf design extends to the facing page] STEPHEN LEACOCK | *by* | PETER McARTHUR | [publisher's device: floral compartment containing a plaque with Egerton Ryerson's portrait and below the plaque: RYERSON | FOVNDED | 1829] | TORONTO | THE RYERSON PRESS

♦ *S.L.* — 1⁸ S.L. — 2–S.L. — 12⁸ [$1 signed]. *1–10, 1–19,* 20–22, *23–28,* 29–30, *31–32, 33–34,* 35–45, *46–48,* 49–63, *64–66,* 67–81, *82–84, 85–93,* 94–96, *97–114, 115–116,* 117–123, *124–126,* 127–163, *164–166,* 167–176, *1–6* pp. (96 leaves). 163 × 112 m.

CONTENTS: p. *1* half title with series statement; p. *2* blank; p. *3* LIBRARY EDITION; p. *4* series statement with names of the editors and dedication to the writers of Canada; p. *5* title; p. *6* COPYRIGHT IN ALL COUNTRIES | SUBSCRIBING TO THE BERNE CONVENTION; p. *7* table of contents; p. *8* blank; p. *9* BIOGRAPHICAL | [two rules]; p. *10* blank; pp. *1–176* identical to A41; p. *1* THIS BOOK IS A | PRODUCTION OF | [plaque with Ryerson's portrait and below the portrait: Ryerson | Press | Founded | 1829] | TORONTO. CANADA; pp. *2–6* blank. Between pp. *8* and *9* is a leaf with a photo of Leacock and his signature in facsimile.

BINDING: Bound in blue cloth. Leacock's signature in facsimile is blind-stamped on the upper board within a blind-stamped rectangle. Stamping in gilt on the spine is similar to A41a.

COPIES EXAMINED: CS.

**A41a.4** *first American issue* (1969):

[all lines within a leafy, rectangular compartment, initialed JP at the right-hand corner of the compartment] STEPHEN LEACOCK | *by* | PETER McARTHUR | [floral ornament] | THE FOLCROFT PRESS, INC. | FOLCROFT, PA.

This issue (216 × 151 mm.) is a photographic reprint of A41a.2. The verso of the title leaf reads as follows: First Published 1923 | Reprinted 1969. The title leaf of A41a.2 is also present. The preliminary pages have been re-arranged slightly; the book ends at p. 176. Price $10.

BINDING: Bound in blue laminated plastic over paper boards. Stamped in gilt down the spine: STEPHEN LEACOCK [open diamond containing a solid diamond] McARTHUR | [two horizontal rules; two horizontal rules].

COPIES EXAMINED: AEU.

**A41a.5** *second American issue* (1976):

[all lines within a leafy, rectangular compartment, initialed JP at the right-hand corner of the compartment] STEPHEN LEACOCK | *by* | PETER McARTHUR | [floral ornament] | NORWOOD EDITIONS | 1976

This issue (216 × 146 mm.) is also a photographic reprint of A41a.2. The verso of the title leaf reads as follows: [eleven lines of Library of Congress in Publication Data, including

ISBN 0-842-1662-8] | *LIMITED TO 100 COPIES* | Manufactured in the United States of America | NORWOOD EDITIONS BOX 38 NORWOOD, PA. 19074. In spite of the limitation statement on the title leaf, this issue was reprinted in 1977; the versos of the title leaves are blank in the 1977 reprint.

The OCLC WorldCat database also records an edition published by R. West in Philadelphia in 1977 (176 pp.; 23 cm.). ISBN 0849217067 at $20. No copy of the book could be located, although DLC is given as a location.

BINDING: Bound in green laminated plastic over paper boards. Stamped in silver down the spine: [open diamond containing a solid diamond] STEPHEN LEACOCK [open diamond containing a solid diamond] McARTHUR [open diamond containing a solid diamond].

COPIES EXAMINED: CS; NFSM (1977 reprint).


## A42 THE GOLD STANDARD 1924

[cover title: all lines within a rectangle; the first two lines within two separate rectangles] The | Gold Standard | By | Professor Stephen Leacock | Professor of Economics, McGill University | Montreal. | [ornament] | An Address delivered before the 1924 | Life Insurance Educational Congress, | held at Toronto, Ont.

◆ 1⁶. *1-2*, 3-11, *1* pp. (6 leaves). 228 × 155 mm.

CONTENTS: p. *1* title; p. *2* blank; pp. 3-11 text; p. *1* blank.

BINDING: Printed on off-white paper stock, no wrapper, wire-stitched.

NOTES: Leacock spoke on the restoration of the gold standard at the Life Insurance Educational Congress in Toronto on 1 February 1924 (see D24.1). On 5 February 1924 William May, Jr., the assistant manager of the Sun Life Assurance Company of Canada, told Sir Arthur Currie, the Principal of McGill University:

> Permit me to thank you for sending Professor Leacock to address the Educational Congress of Life Underwriters at Toronto. His address was simply magnificent, and made a tremendous impression upon his audience. I have heard the address praised on every hand, both for its material and for the splendid manner in which it was delivered. (file 955, container 59, RG2, QMM Archives).

On one copy of this pamphlet at SLM, Leacock wrote: "unfortunately not revised: a shorthand report full of omissions & errors." Number of copies printed not known.

COPIES EXAMINED: QMMRB; SLM (two copies, one inscribed as indicated).


## A43 THE GARDEN OF FOLLY 1924

**A43a** *English edition:*

THE GARDEN | : OF FOLLY : | A PICTURE OF THE WORLD WE LIVE IN | BY STEPHEN LEACOCK | [thick-thin rule] | *"This poor old world works hard and gets no richer; thinks hard and | gets no wiser; worries much and gets no happier. It casts off old | errors to take on new ones; laughs at ancient superstitions and shivers | over modern ones. It is at best but a Garden of Folly, whose chattering | gardeners move a moment among the flowers, waiting for the sunset."* | *(Confucius ,[sic] or Tutankhamen — I forget which.)* | [thin-thick rule] | *LONDON: JOHN LANE THE BODLEY HEAD LTD | MCMXXIV*

◆ A–I$^{16}$ [$1 signed (–A1), fifth leaf signed * (e.g. A*)]. *1–4*, 5–11, *12–14*, 15–40, *41–42*, 43–76, *77–78*, 79–103, *104–106*, 107–134, *135–136*, 137–168, *169–170*, 171–200, *201–202*, 203–219, *220–222*, 223–233, *234–236*, 237–246, *247–248*, 249–276, *1–12* pp. (144 leaves). 190 × 127 mm.

CONTENTS: p. *1* half title; p. *2* list of fifteen other books by Leacock, the first being *Literary Lapses* and the last *College Days*; p. *3* title; p. *4* Made and printed in Great Britain at | *The Mayflower Press, Plymouth*. William Brendon & Son, Ltd.; pp. *5–10* preface, Concerning Humour and Humorists; p. *11* table of contents; p. *12* blank; pp. *13–276*, *1* text (pp. *14*, *42*, *78*, *104*, *106*, *136*, *170*, *202*, *204*, *220*, *222*, *234*, *236*, and *248* blank); p. *2* blank; pp. *3–10* advertisements of Leacock's books published by The Bodley Head with press opinions; pp. *11–12* advertisements, with press opinions, of Ben Travers's *Rookery Nook*, *The Dippers*, and *A Cuckoo in the Nest*.

TEXT: I The Secrets of Success; II The Human Mind Up to Date; III The Human Body: Its Care and Prevention; IV The Perfect Salesman: A Complete Guide to Business; V Romances of Business — 1 Alfred of the Advertisements: A Romance of the Back Pages; 2 Tom Lachford, Promoter; 3 Our Business Benefactors; VI The Perfect Lover's Guide; or, How to Select a Mate, on Sea or on Shore; VII The Progress of Human Knowledge — 1 The Restoration of Whiskers: A Neglected Factor in the Decline of Knowledge; 2 Then and Now; VIII Glimpses of the Future in America — 1 Resumption of the Mail Coach Service; 2 Form of Application to Be Used in the Not-Very-Far Future in Trying to Secure a Hotel Room; 3 List of Honour: Pullman Company Announcement for March; 4 The Immigration Laws Keep on Improving; 5 The Socialization of the Church; IX My Unposted Correspondence; X Letters to the New Rulers of the World — 1 To the Secretary of the League of Nations; 2 To a Disconsolate King; 3 To a Plumber; 4 To a Hotel Manager; 5 To a Prohibitionist; 6 To a Spiritualist.

BINDING AND DUST JACKET: Bound in greenish blue cloth, top edge stained blue, lettering on the boards in green. Stamped on the upper board within three blind-stamped rectangles as follows: *THE GARDEN OF FOLLY | By STEPHEN LEACOCK*. Stamped on the spine as follows: [two rules blind-stamped] | *THE | GARDEN | OF | FOLLY | By | STEPHEN | LEACOCK | The | Bodley Head*.

The front panel of the jacket has an illustration by Christopher Hassall in red, yellow, and white of a jester holding a magnifying glass in one hand and a globe of the world in the other. The rest of the jacket is white with black lettering. Printed on the spine panel: THE GARDEN | OF FOLLY | STEPHEN | LEACOCK | 5/– | NET | THE | BODLEY | HEAD. The back panel has advertisements, with press opinions, of books by Ben Travers. The flaps also carry similar advertisements. On the front flap are ads of H.H. Munro's *The Square Egg and Other Stories*, Harry Leon Wilson's *So This Is Golf*, and R.S. Hooper's *One at a Time*. The back flap has ads of Robert Benchley's *Of All Things* and *Love Conquers All*.

Also examined is a re-issue in orange cloth, which *The English Catalogue of Books* describes as a "new edition" published in October 1932 at 3s 6d. In fact, this re-issue is a reprint with trimmed sheets (184 × 124 mm). The jacket is the same as that of the regular edition except that 3/6 replaces 5/– on the spine panel.

NOTES: When Leacock informed B.W. Willett of The Bodley Head on 21 January 1923 about his new book of humour, he stated: "I want to sell book rights only for Britain Dominions except Canada. I want to keep all second serial rights, picture rights, dramatic rights, etc. I want as now on my other books twenty per cent and I think my advance royalty ought to be higher than on the other books; and I want to count thirteen books sold as thirteen and not as twelve."

On this basis Leacock was willing to give The Bodley Head rights to *The Garden of Folly* and to his next two books of humour. If these terms were not agreeable, however, he told Willett that further books would each have to be negotiated separately, in spite of their cordial relations. Willett repled positively on 11 February 1924, and he agreed to Leacock's terms a few days later on 15 February 1924: £250 advance; twelve books counted as twelve; and contracts on the same terms for Leacock's next two books of humour. The contract at READ is dated 29 April 1924. Chapters 1 to 6 apparently sold to the Bombay, Baroda and Central India *Railway Magazine*.

Christopher Hassall finished his design of the book's dust jacket on 1 April 1924, although he found it difficult to complete it without seeing more of the actual manuscript. Proofs of the jacket were sent to Dodd, Mead and to S.B. Gundy on that date. Willett received Leacock's manuscript on 28 April 1924. He received corrections to the manuscript on 24 June 14 1924, the same day in fact that the proofs were ready. The proofs were not read by Leacock. On 31 July 1924 Willett sent Leacock the advance due on the date of publication: "It is early days yet to say how it is likely to go, but we are doing our best to boost it," he wrote by way of encouragement. A few months later, on 10 October 1924, Willett reported that the book was getting good press and selling very well. By the end of 1925 12,343 copies had sold (1,818 copies to the colonies and 2,250 copies to Australasia). 789 copies sold in 1925 (188 copies to the colonies and 200 copies to Australasia). Sales declined thereafter to less than 100 copies annually.

"The Perfect Salesman: A Complete Guide to Business" reprinted in Allen Churchill, ed., *A Treasury of Modern Humor* (New York: Tudor, 1940), pp. 330–44; in *Strictly on the Funny Side* (Toronto: Royce Publishers (Canada) Ltd., [194?]), pp. 57–89.

COPIES EXAMINED: CS (first printing and re-issue, both in jacket).


## A43b *American edition*:

THE GARDEN | OF FOLLY | [thick-thin rule] | BY STEPHEN LEACOCK | [thin-thick rule] | *"This poor old world works hard and gets | no richer: thinks hard and gets no wiser: | worries much and gets no happier. It casts off | old errors to take on new ones: laughs at | ancient superstitions and shivers over modern | ones. It is at best but a Garden of Folly, | whose chattering gardeners move a moment | among the flowers, waiting for the sunset."* | (*Confucius* — or *Tutankhamen* — I forget which) | [thick-thin rule] | NEW YORK | DODD, MEAD AND COMPANY | 1924 | [thin-thick rule]

♦ 1–16⁸ 17⁴ 18–19⁸. *i–iv*, v–xi, 1–4, 3–30, 31–32, 33–68, 69–70, 71–97, 98–100, 101–131, 132–134, 135–168, 169–170, 171–202, 203–204, 205–222, 223–224, 225–236, 237–238, 239–249, 250–252, 253–282, 1–2 pp. (148 leaves). 192 × 129 mm.

CONTENTS: p. *i* half title; p. *ii* list of fifteen other books by Leacock, the first being *Literary Lapses* and the last *College Days*; p. *iii* title; p. *iv* COPYRIGHT, 1924 | BY DODD, MEAD

AND COMPANY, INC. | PRINTED IN U. S. A. | VAIL-BALLOU, INC. | BINGHAMTON AND NEW YORK; pp. v–x preface, Concerning Humour and Homourists [sic]; p. xi table of contents; p. *1* blank; pp. 2–3, 3–282 text (pp. *3, 32, 70, 98, 100, 132, 134, 170, 204, 224, 238, 250,* and *252* blank); pp. *1–2* blank.

TEXT: Identical to A43a.

BINDING AND DUST JACKET: Bound in red cloth. A solid rectangle is blind-stamped on the upper board. Within this solid rectangle are two raised rectangles, which contain the following in raised characters: THE GARDEN | OF FOLLY | [rule] | STEPHEN LEACOCK. Stamped in gold on the spine: THE | GARDEN | OF | FOLLY | [rule] | LEACOCK | DODD, MEAD | *&* COMPANY.

The front panel of the jacket in red, black, and white features an illustration of a jester seated in a swivel chair, his feet perched on a desk. The remainder of the jacket is white with black lettering. On the spine panel of the jacket: [thick-thin rule] | THE | GARDEN | OF | FOLLY | [rule] | STEPHEN | LEACOCK | *Author of* | "OVER THE | FOOTLIGHTS," | *etc.* | DODD, MEAD | AND COMPANY | [thin-thick rule]. On the back panel within an ornamental rectangle is a list of Leacock's books for sale by Dodd, Mead. The general heading preceding the list is: Laugh with Leacock. The front flap has a synopsis of *The Garden of Folly* with the price, $2. A similar description for *Over the Footlights*, but without the price, is on the back flap.

NOTES: On 19 January 1924, Leacock told Frank Dodd: "I send you herewith the advance note on my further book. I shall do my utmost to have the copy all ready by the end of May." The contract with Dodd, Mead is dated 28 February 1924 (copies in Dodd, Mead files at OHM and the Barbara Nimmo collection at NAC). Leacock agreed to deliver the manuscript by 1 July 1924. He received 20% royalty on all copies sold with an advance of $1,000. The manuscript arrived at the Dodd, Mead offices on 28 April 1924, and was sent to the printer by 2 May 1924. Parts of chapter 2 were missing, and Leacock supplied another copy of it. At this time he also had requested deletions of various portions of the manuscript. The book was published on 2 August 1924. The copyright registered with the Copyright Office at DLC on 7 August 1924 (ClA800367). The copyright was renewed by George Leacock on 27 August 1951 (R82637).

On 12 August 1924 Dodd informed Leacock: "I meant to write you when we sent your check for the advance royalty and tell you that THE GARDEN OF FOLLY has started out very well." Dodd was enthusiastic that this would prove to be Leacock's best-selling book. On 6 November 1924 Dodd told Leacock:

> . . . the first sale of THE GARDEN OF FOLLY is approximately the same as the first sale of OVER THE FOOTLIGHTS to date. There is no evidence that there will be any falling-off during the balance of the season. In going over the figures don't lose sight of the fact also that you are receiving 10 cents a copy more per book than formerly and therefore the total returns should be considerably more than past years.

By February 1925 12,123 copies had sold. Sales declined considerably in the 1930s, less than twenty-five copies annually. The book was still in print on 1 June 1944, although it had only earned a royalty of $8.80 in a three-year period between 1 February 1941 and 1 February 1944.

The Barbara Nimmo collection at NAC also has another contract with Dodd, Mead dated

24 April 1925 for Leacock's next two volumes of humorous works following *The Garden of Folly* (each manuscript to consist of not less than 50,000 words). Leacock was to receive 20% royalty of the published retail price with an advance on publication of $1,000.

Also examined were the second (August 1924) and third printings (November 1924).

COPIES EXAMINED: CS (first and second printings, both in jacket); QMMRB (third printing, rebound).

### A43b.1 *Canadian issue:*

THE GARDEN | OF FOLLY | [thick-thin rule] | BY STEPHEN LEACOCK | [thin-thick rule] | *"This poor old world works hard and gets | no richer: thinks hard and gets no wiser: | worries much and gets no happier. It casts off | old errors to take on new ones: laughs at | ancient superstitions and shivers over modern | ones. It is at best but a Garden of Folly, | whose chattering gardeners move a moment | among the flowers, waiting for the sunset." | (Confucius — or Tutankhamen — I forget which)* | [thick-thin rule] | TORONTO | S. B. GUNDY | 1924 | [thin-thick rule]

The Canadian issue is identical to A43b with the following exceptions: the verso of the title leaf of the Canadian issue reads PRINTED IN THE U. S. A.; GUNDY in gilt is at the foot of the spine; S.B. Gundy and Toronto replace the American publisher's name and place of publication on the jacket.

NOTES: On 1 April 1924, S.B. Gundy wrote to Leacock: "Under present conditions of the book market in Canada 5000 copies of almost any book is too big a bite. . . . I will buy from Dodd Mead the Canadian Edition and will endeavour to arrange with Lane for the English jacket. I will pay you $750.00 on day of publication on account of Royalty, at the rate of 25¢ a copy, for all copies sold in Canada."

Although The Bodley Head sent a proof of Christopher Hassall's jacket to Gundy in early April 1924, Gundy did not use the English jacket for the Canadian issue. The book sold for $2 in Canada, and was apparently published on the same day as the American edition. The print run consisted of 3,000 copies.

COPIES EXAMINED: CS (three copies, one in jacket); QMMRB (not in jacket).

## A44 WINNOWED WISDOM 1926

### A44a *English edition:*

*WINNOWED | : WISDOM : | BY STEPHEN LEACOCK | [thick-thin rule] | thin-thick rule] | LONDON: JOHN LANE THE BODLEY HEAD LTD | MCMXXVI*

• A–I$^{16}$ [$1 signed (–A1), A5 signed *]. *i–vi*, vii–xiv, *1–2*, 1–25, *26–28*, 29–69, *70–72*, 73–107, *108–110*, 111–164, *165–166*, 167–195, *196–198*, 199–224, *225–226*, 227–254, *255–256*, 257–264, *1–8* pp. (144 leaves). 183 × 122 mm.

CONTENTS: pp. *i–ii* blank; p. *iii* half title; p. *iv* list of sixteen books by Leacock, the first being *Literary Lapses* and the last *The Garden of Folly*; p. *v* title; p. *vi First published in 1926* | Made and printed in Great Britain by Butler & Tanner Ltd., Frome and London; pp.

vii–xii preface, An Appeal to the Average Man, dated: *February* 1, *1926*; pp. xiii–xiv table of contents; pp. *1–2*, *1–264* text (pp. *26*, *28*, *70*, *72*, *108*, *110*, *166*, *196*, *198*, *226*, and *256* blank); pp. *1–4* advertisements of Leacock's books published by The Bodley Head with press opinions; pp. *5–7* advertisements, with press opinions, of Ben Travers's *Rookery Nook*, *A Cuckoo in the Nest*, *Mischief*, and *The Dippers*; p. *8* advertisement, with press opinions, of Ward Muir's *Jones in Paris*.

TEXT: The text is comprised of eight parts.

I The Outlines of Everything Designed for Busy People at Their Busiest — Volume One. The Outline of Shakespeare; Volume Two. The Outline of Evolution; Volume Three. The Business Outline of Astronomy; Volume Four. Outline of Recent Advances in Science.

II Brotherly Love Among the Nations — The Next War; International Amenities: Can We Wonder That It's Hard to Keep Friends?; The Mother of Parliaments; An Advance Cable Service: International News a Month Ahead; Back from Europe: Does Travel Derange the Mind?

III Studies in the Newer Culture — The New Attaboy Language: A Little Study in Culture from Below Up; The Cross-Word Puzzle Craze; Information While You Eat; The Children's Column As Brought-Up-to-Date; Old Proverbs Made New.

IV In the Good Old Summer Time — The Merry Month of May As Treated in the Bygone Almanac; How We Kept Mother's Birthday As Related by a Member of the Family; Summer Sorrows of the Super-Rich, or Does This Happen Only in America?; How My Wife and I Built Our Home for £1 2s. 6d.; The Everlasting Angler; Have We Got the Year Backwards?, or Is Not Autumn Spring?; Our Summer Convention As Described by One of Its Members.

V Travel and Movement — All Aboard for Europe: Some Humble Advice for Travellers; The Gasolene Good-Bye; Complete Guide and History of the South Based on the Best Novels of "Travellers' Impressions"; The Give-and-Take of Travel: A Study in Petty Larceny.

VI Great National Problems — The Laundry Problem: A Yearning for the Vanished Washerwoman; The Questionnaire Nuisance: A Plan to Curb Zealous Investigators in Their Thirst for Knowledge; This Expiring World; Are We Fascinated with Crime?

VII Round Our City — At the Ladies' Culture Club: A Lecture on the Fourth Dimension; Our Business Barometer for Use in the Stock Exchanges and Stock Yards; My Pink Suit: A Study in the New Fashions for Men; Why I Left Our Social Workers' Guild.

VIII The Christmas Ghost: Unemployment in One of Our Oldest Industries.

BINDING AND DUST JACKET: Bound in grey cloth with stamping in blue, top edge stained blue. Stamped on the upper board within two rectangles: WINNOWED WISDOM | STEPHEN | LEACOCK. Stamped on the spine: [rule] | STEPHEN | LEACOCK | [rule] | WINNOWED | WISDOM | [rule] | THE BODLEY HEAD | [rule].

The front panel of the jacket features an illustration in green, brown, white, and black, done by Christopher Hassall, of an older man, possibly a monk, sitting on a pile of books at a desk and cutting clippings with a pair of scissors. The rest of the jacket is white with black lettering. Printed on the spine panel: WINNOWED | WISDOM | STEPHEN | LEACOCK | 5/- | NET | THE | BODLEY | HEAD. The back panel has an advertisement for the complete works of "Saki" (H.H. Munro). On the front flap is an advertisement of J. Storer Clouston's *The Lunatic in Charge*. Advertisements, with press opinions, of books by Ben Travers are on the back flap.

Also examined was a later state of the jacket with a floral ornament on the spine panel and the price 3s 6d. According to *The English Catalogue of Books*, this is the cheap edition issued in September 1938.

In addition to the cloth binding, there is also a binding in stiff paper. The latter may be an advance copy, however. The front and back covers have the same illustration and ad for Saki's works as found on the dust jacket of the cloth binding. The spine of the stiff paper copy is the same as the spine portion of the jacket, except there is no price present.

NOTES: The terms for *Winnowed Wisdom* were established on 15 February 1924 when B.W. Willett of The Bodley Head agreed to Leacock's terms for *The Garden of Folly* — namely, 20% on all copies sold and £250 royalty on the day of publication. The contract for *The Garden of Folly* gave The Bodley Head rights to Leacock's next two books of humour.

Leacock sent the manuscript to Willett on 25 January 1926. On 21 March 1926, Willett told Leacock:

> I am sending you to-day the page proofs of "WINNOWED WISDOM". As you will see, we have considerably altered the typography from the slip proofs, I think for the better, and we have also made a number of obvious corrections in the text. I hope, therefore, that you will find it all right and will be able to cable us your 'O.K.'

By this time Hassall had finished his design for the jacket. Leacock thanked Willett for the cheque of £250 on 3 June 1926. This would indicate that book was published several days prior to that date. However, according to *The English Catalogue of Books*, *Winnowed Wisdom* was published in June 1926.

The number of copies printed is not known. The extant royalty reports at SLM indicate that 145 copies sold between January and June 1927 (46 colonial copies); 68 copies between January and June 1928 (10 foreign, 9 colonial, and 25 Australasian). Sales declined thereafter to less than fifty copies annually.

See also *Laughter & Wisdom of Stephen Leacock* (A75), which includes the sheets of this book along with *The Dry Pickwick*.

COPIES EXAMINED: CS (both binding variants, cloth copies with different states of the jacket); OTNY.

## A44a.1 *Canadian issue*:

*WINNOWED | : WISDOM : | BY STEPHEN LEACOCK | [thick-thin rule] | thin-thick rule] | THE MACMILLAN COMPANY OF CANADA LTD | AT ST. MARTIN'S HOUSE TORONTO*

The Canadian issue is identical to the English edition in practically all respects. The binding is the same as that of the English edition, except that the name of The Bodley Head has been replaced by that of Macmillan. The dust jacket of the Canadian issue has the same illustration by Hassall. The spine panel of the Canadian issue's jacket reads: WINNOWED | WISDOM | STEPHEN | LEACOCK | MACMILLAN. The back panel and flaps of the Canadian issue's jacket are blank.

NOTES: On 6 February 1926, Leacock advised Willett and Frank Dodd that he was severing his connection with his Canadian publisher, S.B. Gundy. Although there was no official contract for the Canadian issue, Leacock and Hugh Eayrs of the Macmillan Company of Canada exchanged letters in early February 1926, giving Macmillan the Canadian book rights to *Winnowed Wisdom* and to Leacock's next two books of humour. In return, the Macmillan Company agreed to pay Leacock 30¢ a copy on all copies sold and an advance royalty of $500 per title on the date of publication. Eayrs had the option of buying sheets from Leacock's London or New York publishers or of manufacturing a Canadian edition.

The number of copies printed of this issue is not known. Royalty reports from the Macmillan Company of Canada Ltd. at SLM show that the book sold poorly a few years after publication: between 1 April 1928 and 31 March 1929, 10 copies; between 1 August 1932 and 1 February 1933, 15 copies; between 1 February 1933 and 1 August 1933, 9 copies.

COPIES EXAMINED: CS (in jacket); QMMRB (no jacket).

### A44a.2 *Australasian issue*:

The title page of the Australasian issue is identical to that of A44b. The copyright pages are also the same, except that the Australasian issue has the additional line: AUSTRALASIAN EDITION. The binding of the Australasian issue is identical to A44b.1. Dust jacket not seen.

COPIES EXAMINED: CS.

### A44b *American edition*:

WINNOWED | WISDOM | A NEW BOOK OF HUMOUR | [thick-thin rule] | BY STEPHEN LEACOCK | [thin-thick rule] | [publisher's device: inverted triangle with D • M • & • Co at the base and below this an illustration of a face, two open books, and two burning torches in the shape of a V] | [thick-thin rule] | NEW YORK | DODD, MEAD AND COMPANY | 1926 | [thin-thick rule]

• 1–19$^8$. 1–6, v–xii, 1–2, 3–28, 29–30, 31–85, 86–88, 89–125, 126–128, 129–184, 185–186, 187–216, 217–218, 219–245, 246–248, 249–278, 279–280, 281–288, 1–2 pp. (152 leaves). 187 × 130 mm.

CONTENTS: pp. 1–2 blank; p. 3 half title; p. 4 list of seventeen books by Leacock, the first being *Literary Lapses* and the last *Winnowed Wisdom*; p. 5 title; p. 6 COPYRIGHT, 1924, 1925, 1926 | BY DODD, MEAD AND COMPANY, INC. | PRINTED IN U. S. A. | THE VAIL-BALLOU, INC. | BINGHAMTON AND NEW YORK; pp. v–x preface, An Appeal to the Average Man; pp. xi–xii table of contents; pp. 1–288 text (pp. 2, 30, 86, 88, 126, 128, 186, 218, 246, 248, and 280 blank); pp. 1–2 blank.

TEXT: The American edition also has eight parts like the English edition. There are two new stories in part II of the American edition: French Politics for Beginners; and New Light from New Minds. The titles of several stories have been altered slightly: "The New Attaboy Language: A Little Study in Culture from Below Up" as "A Little Study in Culture from Below Up"; "How My Wife and I Built Our Home for £1 2s. 6d" as "How My Wife and I Built Our Home for $4.90"; "The Gasolene Good-Bye" as "The Gasoline Goodbye". Several stories in the American edition lack subtitles: for example, "Summer Sorrows of the Super-Rich" and "The Laundry Problem." The two final paragraphs from "An Advance Cable Service" in the English edition have been placed in the middle of the story in the American edition (see pp. 73–4). The preface in the American edition is also slightly different than its English counterpart. References to American and Canadian place names replace English ones.

BINDING AND DUST JACKET: Bound in red cloth. A solid rectangle is blind-stamped on the upper board. Within this solid rectangle are two raised rectangles, which contain the following in raised characters: WINNOWED | WISDOM | [rule] | STEPHEN LEACOCK. Stamped in black on the spine: WINNOWED | WISDOM | [rule] | LEACOCK | DODD, MEAD | & COMPANY.

The front panel of the jacket in red, black, grey,and white features an illustration, signed by John Held Jr., of a jester standing beside a machine with a pulley. The remainder of the jacket is white with black lettering. On the spine panel of the jacket: [thick-thin rule] | WINNOWED | WISDOM | By | STEPHEN | LEACOCK | Author of | "Literary Lapses" | "Over the Footlights" | "The Garden of Folly" | etc. | DODD, MEAD | AND COMPANY | [thin-thick rule]. On the back panel within an ornamental rectangle is a list of Leacock's books for sale by Dodd, Mead. The general heading preceding the list is: Laugh with Leacock. The front flap has a synopsis of Winnowed Wisdom with the price, $2. A similar description for The Garden of Folly is on the back flap.

NOTES: The contract with Dodd, Mead is dated 24 April 1925 but without a specified title. When Leacock arranged for the contract of The Garden of Folly, the contract for that book also included the rights to Leacock's next two books of humour on the same basis — namely, 20% on all copies sold and an advance of $1,000 on the day of publication. The "press copy" at DEL is dated 26 June 1926, the day of publication. The copyright was registered with the Copyright Office at DLC on 30 June and 1 July 1926 (ClA891988). The copyright was renewed by George Leacock on 2 July 1953 (R114338).

Number of copies printed not known. Between 1 February and 1 August 1927, 261 copies sold. Between 1 February and 1 August 1928, 62 copies sold. Between 1 August 1929 and 1 February 1930, 51 copies sold. Between 1 February 1931 and 1 February 1932, 41 copies sold.

Also examined was the second printing, which is identical to the first, except for the additional lines on the copyright page: First Printing, June, 1926 | Second Printing, August, 1926.

COPIES EXAMINED: CS (second printing in jacket); HLS (first and second printings, neither in jacket); OTNY (advance proof copy in paper wrappers; front of the wrapper and spine panel identical to the front of the jacket, back of the wrapper blank); QMMRB (second printing in jacket).

## A44c Canadian edition:

Stephen Leacock | Winnowed | Wisdom | General Editor: Malcolm Ross | New Canadian Library No. 74 | [publisher's device: abstract design within an oval of a person on a horse-drawn chariot, taking aim with a bow and arrow] | McClelland and Stewart Limited | Toronto/Montreal

◆  i–vi, vii–ix, 1–2, 2–13, 14, 15–89, 90, 91–117, 118, 119–133, 134, 135–139, 140, 141, 1 pp. (76 leaves). 183 × 109 mm.

CONTENTS: p. i half title; p. ii blank; p. iii title; p. iv © McClelland and Stewart Limited 1971 | ALL RIGHTS RESERVED | The Canadian Publishers | McClelland and Stewart Limited | 25 Hollinger Road, Toronto 374 | Printed and bound in Canada by | T. H. Best Printing Company Limited; pp. v–vi table of contents; pp. vii–ix preface, An Appeal to the Average Man; p. 1 blank; p. 2, 2–139 text (pp. 14, 90, 118, and 134 blank); p. 140 blank; p. 141 information about Leacock; p. 1 blank.

TEXT: Identical to A44a.

BINDING: Bound in stiff paper, perfect bound. The covers are greyish green, white, red, and black. The front cover consists of three solid, rectangular compartments, outlined in greyish green. Stamped on the front cover: National Canadian Library N 74 | [the next two lines within a red compartment] | An exhilarating potpourri of Leacock | at his funniest | [the next two lines within a white compartment] | Stephen Leacock | Winnowed Wisdom | [white and red abstract design within a black compartment]. On the back cover is a solid red, rectangular compartment, outlined in greyish green. Within the compartment on the back cover is the price ($2.35), name of the series, publisher's name, a black silhouette of Leacock's head and shoulders, and three paragraphs that highlight the book's contents. On the back cover is the line: First New Canadian Library Edition 1971. The spine has the author's name, the logo of the series, title, and series number.

NOTES: By the end of 1971 1,849 copies had sold. By the end of 1979 6,832 had sold (information based on file 14, "New Canadian Library," box 93, series A, McClelland and Stewart fonds, OHM). Date of publication and number of copies of each impression not known.

Also examined was the "second reprint," so stated on the back cover, and a reprint in 1982.

COPIES EXAMINED: CS (first printing and 1982 reprint); OHM (first and second printings).

## A45 FOLLIES IN FICTION [1926]

LITTLE BLUE BOOK NO. | [the next line two lines in height and to the right of the previous line and of the third transcribed line] 1119 | Edited by E. Haldeman-Julius | Follies in Fiction | Stephen Leacock | HALDEMAN-JULIUS COMPANY | GIRARD, KANSAS

◆ $1^{32}$. 1–5, 6–63, 1 pp. (32 leaves). 126 × 88 mm.

CONTENTS: p. 1 title; p. 2 Reprinted from "Further Foolishness," by arrangement with the publisher | Copyright 1916 by Dodd, Mead and Company, Inc.; p. 3 table of contents; p. 4 blank; pp. 5, 6–63 text; p. 64 advertisement.

TEXT: Stories Shorter Still (An Irreducible Detective Story, A Compressed Old English Novel, and A Condensed Interminable Novel); The Snoopopaths; or, Fifty Stories in One; Foreign Fiction in Imported Instalments; Serge the Superman; My Revelations as a Spy; Lost in New York — A Visitor's Soliloquy.

BINDING: Bound in a light, greyish blue stiff-paper wrapper, wire-stitched. Printing on the front cover is identical to the first six lines of the title page. The last two lines of the title page, the name of the publisher and the place of publication, are not on the front cover.

NOTES: Published on 30 October 1926 according to E. Haldeman-Julius's *My Second 25 Years: Instead of a Footnote an Autobiography*, Big Blue Book No. B–814 (Girard, Kansas: Haldeman-Julius Publications, 1949), p. 116. 12,500 copies were printed. First advertised in "Last Call! More Than 900 Little Blue Books at 4¢ Each Until Nov. 30 1926," *Haldeman-Julius Weekly*, 20 November 1926, p. 5.

COPIES EXAMINED: DLC.

## A46 A BOOK OF FUNNY DRAMATICS [1926]

LITTLE BLUE BOOK NO. | [the next line two lines in height and to the right of the previous line and of the third transcribed line] 1116 | Edited by E. Haldeman-Julius | A Book of | Funny Dramatics | Stephen Leacock | HALDEMAN-JULIUS COMPANY | GIRARD, KANSAS

◆ $1^{32}$. 1–5, 6–64 pp. (32 leaves). 126 × 87 mm.

CONTENTS: p. 1 title; p. 2 Reprinted from "Over the Footlights," by | arrangement with the publisher | Copyright, 1923, | By Dodd, Mead and Company, Inc. | PRINTED IN THE UNITED STATES OF AMERICA; p. 3 table of contents; p. 4 blank; pp. 5, 6–61 text; pp. 62–64 list of other Little Blue Books published by the Haldeman-Julius Company.

TEXT: The Soul Call; Dead Men's Gold; Historical Drama (which consists of three plays — Des deux choses l'une: A Drama of the First Empire; Mettawamkeag: An Indian Tragedy; and Forging the Fifteenth Amendment: A Drama of the Civil War).

BINDING: Bound in a light, greyish blue stiff-paper wrapper, wire-stitched. Printing on the front cover is identical to the first six lines of the title page. The last two lines of the title page, the name of the publisher and the place of publication, are not on the front cover.

NOTES: Published on 10 November 1926 according to E. Haldeman-Julius's *My Second 25 Years: Instead of a Footnote an Autobiography*, Big Blue Book No. B–814 (Girard, Kansas: Haldeman-Julius Publications, 1949), p. 116. 20,000 copies were printed. First advertised in "Last Call! More Than 900 Little Blue Books at 4¢ Each Until Nov. 30 1926," *Haldeman-Julius Weekly*, 20 November 1926, p. 5.

On 9 April 1969, Henry J. Haldeman, son and heir of Julius, assigned the copyright in this little book to Norman E. and Lenore Tanis.

COPIES EXAMINED: CS; OTUTF; PITT (two different printings); QMMRB.

## A47 ESSAYS OF SERIOUS SPOOFING [1926]

LITTLE BLUE BOOK NO. | [the next line two lines in height and to the right of the previous line and of the third transcribed line] 1120 | Edited by E. Haldeman-Julius | Essays of Serious | Spoofing | Stephen Leacock | HALDEMAN-JULIUS COMPANY | GIRARD, KANSAS

◆ $1^{32}$. 1–3, 4–64 pp. (32 leaves). 125 × 85 mm.

CONTENTS: p. 1 title; p. 2 Reprinted from | "Essays and Literary Studies," | by arrangement with the publisher. | Copyright, 1916, | Dodd, Mead & Co., Inc. | PRINTED IN THE UNITED STATES OF AMERICA; pp. 3, 4–64 text.

TEXT: The Devil and the Deep Sea: A Discussion of Modern Morality; The Woman Question; Literature and Education in America.

BINDING: Two variant wrappers were examined, both wire-stitched: (1) light, greyish blue stiff paper; (2) tan stiff paper. Printing on the front cover of each wrapper is identical to the first six lines of the title page. The last two lines of the title page, the name of the publisher and the place of publication, are not on the front cover. On the bottom of the back cover of the copy examined in tan stiff paper is an oval-shaped logo with the following words:

[curved] TYPOGRAPHICAL | UNION [ornament] LABEL | [curved] GIRARD.

NOTES: Published on 10 November 1926 according to E. Haldeman-Julius's *My Second 25 Years: Instead of a Footnote an Autobiography*, Big Blue Book No. B–814 (Girard, Kansas: Haldeman-Julius Publications, 1949), p. 116. 14,000 copies were printed. First advertised in "Last Call! More Than 900 Little Blue Books at 4¢ Each Until Nov. 30 1926," *Haldeman-Julius Weekly*, 20 November 1926, p. 5.

COPIES EXAMINED: CS (both variant wrappers); PITT (three printings, the last after 1947); OTUTF (tan); QMMRB (light, greyish blue).

## A48 THE HUMAN ANIMAL AND ITS FOLLY [1926]

LITTLE BLUE BOOK NO. | [the next line two lines in height and to the right of the previous line and of the third transcribed line] 1117 | Edited by E. Haldeman-Julius | The Human Animal | and Its Folly | Stephen Leacock | HALDEMAN-JULIUS COMPANY | GIRARD, KANSAS

◆ $1^{32}$. *1–5*, 6–62, *63*, 64 pp. (32 leaves).

CONTENTS: p. *1* title; p. 2 Reprinted from "The Garden of Folly" | by arrangement with the Publisher | Copyright, 1924, by | Dodd, Mead and Company, Inc. | PRINTED IN THE UNITED STATES OF AMERICA; p. *3* fly title; p. *4* blank; pp. *5*, 6–62 text; pp. 63–64 list of other Little Blue Books of wit and humor published by the Haldeman-Julius Company.

TEXT: The Human Mind Up to Date; The Human Body — Its Care and Prevention; The Restoration of Whiskers — A Neglected Factor in the Decline of Knowledge; Then and Now: The College News of Forty Years Ago and the College News of Today.

BINDING: Three variant wrappers were examined, all wire-stitched: (1) light, greyish blue stiff paper (127 × 88 mm.); (2) tan stiff paper (127 × 85 mm.); (3) tan stiff paper (128 × 88 mm.). Printing on the front cover of each wrapper is identical to the first six lines of the title page. The last two lines of the title page, the name of the publisher and the place of publication, are not on the front cover.

An oval is printed on the back cover of (2), but the printing is too dark as to distinguish characters. On the back cover of the copy of (3) is the following: [engraving of Haldeman-Julius] | E. HALDEMAN-JULIUS | Editor | LITTLE BLUE BOOKS | [circle with illustration of a globe with glasses reading a book labelled "LITTLE | BLUE BOOKS" and the following words inside the top half of the circle:] ★ A UNIVERSITY IN PRINT ★ [inside the bottom half of the circle] READ THE WORLD OVER | [solid oval].

NOTES: Published on 11 November 1926 according to E. Haldeman-Julius's *My Second 25 Years: Instead of a Footnote an Autobiography*, Big Blue Book No. B–814 (Girard, Kansas: Haldeman-Julius Publications, 1949), p. 116. 19,000 copies were printed. First advertised in "Last Call! More Than 900 Little Blue Books at 4¢ Each Until Nov. 30 1926," *Haldeman-Julius Weekly*, 20 November 1926, p. 5.

COPIES EXAMINED: CS (light, greyish blue stiff paper); EVANS (tan stiff paper, second variant binding); PITT (two printings, the last *ca.* 1949); QMMRB (tan stiff paper, second variant binding); RB (tan stiff paper, third variant binding).

## A49 THIS LIFE AS I SEE IT [1926]

LITTLE BLUE BOOK NO. | [the next line two lines in height and to the right of the previous line and of the third transcribed line] 1118 | Edited by E. Haldeman-Julius | This Life As I See It | Stephen Leacock | HALDEMAN-JULIUS COMPANY | GIRARD, KANSAS

♦ $1^{32}$. $1$–$3$, $4$–$64$ pp. ($32$ leaves). $126 \times 87$ mm.

CONTENTS: p. $1$ title; p. $2$ Reprinted from "Literary Lapses," | by arrangement with the publisher. | Published in U. S. A. by Dodd, Mead & Co., Inc. | PRINTED IN THE UNITED STATES OF AMERICA; p. $3$, $4$–$64$ text.

TEXT: My Financial Career; Boarding-House Geometry; The Awful Fate of Melpomenus Jones; How to Make a Million Dollars; How to Live to Be 200; How to Avoid Getting Married; How to Be a Doctor; The New Food; Men Who Have Shaved Me; Hints to Travelers; A Manual of Education; On Collecting Things; Society Chit-Chat As It Should Be Written; Borrowing a Match; A Lesson in Fiction.

BINDING: Bound in light, greyish blue stiff-paper wrappers, wire-stitched. Printing on the front cover is identical to the first six lines of the title page. The last two lines of the title page, the name of the publisher and the place of publication, are not on the front cover.

NOTES: Published on 11 November 1926 according to E. Haldeman-Julius's *My Second 25 Years: Instead of a Footnote an Autobiography*, Big Blue Book No. B–814 (Girard, Kansas: Haldeman-Julius Publications, 1949), p. 116. 15,000 copies were printed. First advertised in "Last Call! More Than 900 Little Blue Books at 4¢ Each Until Nov. 30 1926," *Haldeman-Julius Weekly*, 20 November 1926, p. 5.

The Haldeman-Julius Collection at PITT has examples of three printings. The last printing, 1,000 copies produced after 1951 by Henry J. Haldeman, son and heir of Julius, was published without a wrapper.

COPIES EXAMINED: OTUTF; PITT.

## A50 A BOOK OF RIDICULOUS STORIES [1926]

LITTLE BLUE BOOK NO. | [the next line two lines in height and to the right of the previous line and of the third transcribed line] 1115 | Edited by E. Haldeman-Julius | A Book of Ridiculous | Stories | Stephen Leacock | HALDEMAN-JULIUS COMPANY | GIRARD, KANSAS

♦ $1^{32}$. $1$–$5$, $6$–$64$ pp. ($32$ leaves). $126 \times 86$ mm. for variants ($1$) and ($2$), $126 \times 89$ mm. for variant ($3$).

CONTENTS: p. $1$ title; p. $2$ Reprinted from "Nonsense Novels," | by arrangement with the publisher. | Published in U. S. A. by | Dodd, Mead and Company, Inc. | PRINTED IN THE UNITED STATES OF AMERICA; p. $3$ table of contents; p. $4$ blank; pp. $5$, $6$–$64$ text.

TEXT: Maddened by Mystery; or, the Defective Detective; "Q": A Psychic Pstory of the Psupernatural; Gertrude the Governess; or, Simple Seventeen; A Hero in Homespun; or, The Life Struggle of Hezekiah Hayloft; and Guido the Gimlet of Ghent: A Romance of Chivalry.

BINDING: Four variant wrappers were examined, all wire-stitched: (1) grey stiff paper; (2)

glossy white paper; (3) blue stiff paper; (4) green stiff paper. Printing on the front cover of each wrapper is identical to the first six lines of the title page. The last two lines of the title page, the name of the publisher and the place of publication, are not on the front cover. In the case of (3) the following, additional lines are also the front cover: [all lines within a ribboned rectangle except for the logo] | *Published for* | Automatic Libraries | A Division of O. D. Jennings & Company | 4309 West Lake St., Chicago, Ill. | A NATIONAL INSTITUTION | [oval-shaped logo as follows:] [curved] TYPOGRAPHICAL | UNION [ornament] LABEL | [curved] GIRARD. The logo that is found on the front cover of (3) is printed on the back cover of (2), although it is printed too heavily as to be legible. On the back of the wrapper of (4) is the following: [black pen-ink sketch of Haldeman-Julius] | E. HALDEMAN-JULIUS | Editor | LITTLE BLUE BOOK | [blurred, illegible logo].

NOTES: Published on 13 November 1926 according to E. Haldeman-Julius's *My Second 25 Years: Instead of a Footnote an Autobiography*, Big Blue Book No. B–814 (Girard, Kansas: Haldeman-Julius Publications, 1949), p. 116. 53,000 copies were printed. First advertised in "Last Call! More Than 900 Little Blue Books at 4¢ Each Until Nov. 30 1926," *Haldeman-Julius Weekly*, 20 November 1926, p. 5.

The Haldeman-Julius Collection at PITT has examples of five printings (the last *ca.* 1949).

COPIES EXAMINED: CS (first three variants); OTUTF (green wrappers); PITT; QMMRB (grey stiff paper).

## A51 XMAS CONVIVIAL AND PLEASANT [1927?]

A51a *first edition*:

[cover title: illustration in dark green of two bells with sprigs of holly; the holly berries and the bell clangers in red] | XMAS | CONVIVIAL and PLEASANT | AT | No. 19 | REDPATH CRESCENT | [snowflake ornament]

♦ $1^6$. *1–12* pp. (6 leaves). 167 × 123 mm.

CONTENTS: p. *1* cover title; p. *2–12* text.

TEXT: Poems addressed to various individuals: Our Host, Herbert [Shaw]; Our Sister, Ness [Agnes Fairweather, née Fitzgerald, sister of May Shaw]; Our Sister, Gerry [Geraldine Hutchison, née Fitzgerald, sister of May Shaw]; Our Brother, Fergus [Hutchison]; Our Brother, Charlie [Fairweather]; René [du Roure]; My Brother George [Leacock]; Our Harold [Morrow, married to one of May Shaw's sister]; Our Little Lambs at the Side Table [Stevie Leacock, June and Donnie Fairweather, Rowan Hutchison, David Ulrichsen, and Peggy Shaw]; Our Hostess, Fitz [May Shaw, née Fitzgerald]; The Poet Himself.

BINDING: Issued without wrappers, white paper stock, with two perforations for a red ribbon tying the leaves together.

NOTES: In 1927 or thereabouts, Herbert and May Shaw hosted a Christmas dinner party in Montreal to which Leacock and other friends and family were invited. Among the people present were Leacock's best friend, René du Roure (the head of the French Department at McGill University), and Leacock's brother, George. May Shaw ("Fitz") was a close friend of Leacock's wife, Beatrix. The Shaws lived nearby Leacock in Montreal, and they also had a cottage close to Leacock's home in Orillia. Mrs. Shaw was often in Leacock's company, and from time to time she assisted him in his research and writing (see, for example, A95).

Leacock wrote this pamphlet of playful poems on this occasion. He undoubtedly arranged for its printing in Montreal. Number of copies printed not known but probably less than twenty-five copies since they were intended for distribution to those attending the dinner party and perhaps to members of Leacock's family.

The last page (p. *12*) is as follows: [illustration of red wreath] | THE POET HIMSELF | [rule] | Here sit I, proud as any Peacock | And sign myself, | Yours, | [copies examined bear Leacock's signature].

Two of the poems, "My Brother George" and "Our Hostess, Fitz," are reproduced in facsimile in K83.1, pp. 20, 36.

COPIES EXAMINED: LAT (red ribbon disintegrated; copy formerly belonging to Leacock's sister, Daisy Burrows, with people identified by Leacock); NAC (without the red ribbon, Barbara Nimmo collection); OTNY.

## A51b *second edition* (1990):

XMAS | Convivial and Pleasant | at No. 19 | Redpath Crescent | *By* | STEPHEN LEACOCK | *Reprinted, with an introduction, by* | JOHN N. MAPPIN | [illustration in red of holly and a lantern] | MONTREAL | Printed for John N. Mappin by William Poole | at the Poole Hall Press, Grimsby, Ontario | for Christmas 1990

◆ $1^{12}$. *1*–24 pp. (12 leaves). 200 × 145 mm.

CONTENTS: p. *1* title; p. 2 blue ornament resembling a snowflake; pp. *3–11* John Mappin's introduction; pp. *12–22* text (p. 22 has Leacock's signature in facsimile and also includes a short poem by Mappin); p. 23 blue ornament resembling a snowflake (but different from the ornament on p. 2); p. 24 colophon.

TEXT: Identical to A51a.

BINDING: Bound in a beige wrapper with two perforations for a red ribbon tying the leaves together. Printed on the front of the wrapper: [illustration of a green sprig of holly and two red bells] | XMAS | CONVIVIAL and PLEASANT | AT | No. 19 | REDPATH CRESCENT | [greenish blue floral ornament].

NOTES: John N. Mappin is a Montreal antiquarian bookseller. He has issued a number of Christmas booklets on an annual basis. One of these, for example, is *The Goblin: A Brief History of Canada's Humour Magazine of the 1920s* (1988), which reprints Leacock's "A Sermon on Humour" (see C21.7).

According to the colophon this edition consists of 175 signed copies ". . . *set by hand in Century Schoolbook roman & italic, and printed on Noranda Antique Recycled Book Paper using a 10x15 Chandler & Price*." It was printed in September 1990 and available in early October of the same year. Copies were given away by Mappin to his friends and acquaintances. Only a few copies were sold by way of Mappin's antiquarian catalogues at $35 apiece.

Following Leacock's poem "The Poet Himself" on p. 22 is the following: "The best to You, | May only Good Things happen, | A Christmas Greeting from | Your Friend, [Mappin's signature]." See also Walter Buchignani, "A Feast of Stephen," *Montreal Gazette*, 23 December 1990, p. B7, which reproduces several pages from Mappin's edition and discusses the origins of Leacock's pamphlet and its republication.

COPIES EXAMINED: CS (no. 16).

## A52 SHORT CIRCUITS 1928

### A52a *American edition*:

SHORT CIRCUITS | [thick-thin rule] | BY STEPHEN LEACOCK | [thin-thick rule] | [publisher's device: inverted triangle with D • M • & • Co at the base and below this an illustration of a face, two open books, and two burning torches in the shape of a V] | [thick-thin rule] | NEW YORK | DODD, MEAD AND COMPANY | 1928 | [thin-thick rule]

◆ $1$–$24^8$. $i$–$iv$, v–vii, $1$–$3$, $1$–$372$, $1$–$2$ pp. (192 leaves). 188 × 130 mm.

CONTENTS: p. *i* half title; p. *ii* list of eighteen books by Leacock, the first being *Literary Lapses* and the last *Short Circuits*; p. *iii* title; p. *iv* COPYRIGHT, 1928, | BY DODD, MEAD AND COMPANY, INC. | PRINTED IN THE U. S. A. BY | Quinn & Boden Company, Inc. | [rule] | BOOK MANUFACTURERS | RAHWAY NEW JERSEY; pp. v–vii table of contents; p. *1* blank; p. *2* fly title; p. 2 blank; pp. 1–372 text; pp. *1*–*2* blank.

TEXT: The text is comprised of ten sections: I Short Circuits in the Social Current; II Short Circuits in the Open Air; III Save Me from My Friends; IV People We Know; V Short Circuits in Education; VI Short Circuits by Radio and Cinema; VII Short Circuits in International Relations; VIII Bygone Currents; IX Short Circuits in Current Literature; X The Epilogue of This Book: An Elegy Near a City Freight Yard.

Part I: Old Junk and New Money: A Little Study in the Latest Antiques; "Speaking of India —"; How to Borrow Money; Life's Minor Contradictions; A Great Life in Our Midst; The Perfect Gift: A Little Study in the Art of Tactful Giving; Scenery and Signboards; The Life of John Mutation Smith; Inference As an Art; Our Get-Together Movement.

Part II: A Lesson on the Links: The Application of Mathematics to Golf; The Family at Football; Life in the Open.

Part III: From My Friend the Deadbeat; From My Friend the Reporter; From My Friend with a Speech to Make; From My Friend the Guide.

Part IV: The Man in the Pullman Car; The Criminal by Proxy; The People Just Back from Europe Who Never Should Have Left Home; The Man with the Adventure Story.

Part V: A Year at College As Revealed in the Newer Comic Journalism; The Unintelligence Test; Easy Ways to Success; Fun As an Aid to Business: Is a Sense of Humor a Financial Asset?; The Stamp-Album World.

Part VI: If Only We Had the Radio Sooner; What the Radio Overhead; One Crowded Quarter Second; Done into Movies.

Part VII: Things I Hardly Dare Whisper; Hands Across the Seas; If They Go on Swimming; If Mussolini Comes; This World Championship Stuff and Why I Am Out of It; Get Off the Earth.

Part VIII: The Lost World of Yesterday: A Pen Picture of the Vanished Past — The Horse and Buggy; Come Back to School and Let Us See What the Dear Old Days Felt Like; The Fall Fair and the Autumn Exposition; Extinct Monsters; The Passing of the Back Yard: Another Social Revolution Coming Straight at Us.

Part IX: The Literary Sensations of 1929: A Confidential Guide to the New Books; Children's Poetry Revised: How the Dear Old Poems of Our Childhood Need to Be Brought Up to Date; Illustrations I Can Do without: Some Gentle Suggestions for the Contemporary Illustrated Magazines; Our Summer Pets As Presented by Our Enthusiastic Nature Writers;

The Old Men's Page: A Brand New Feature in Journalism; A Guide to the Underworld: A Little Unsocial Register for the Use of Readers of Up-to-Date Fiction; Love Me, Love My Letters: The Use of Ink for the First Inklings of Love; With the Authorities Showing How Easily They Excel at Their Own Games; Literature and the Eighteenth Amendment; The Hunt for a Heroine; Bed-time Stories for Grown-Up People; Softening the Stories for the Children; The Great Detective.

Part X has only one story. It has the same title as the heading of the part itself.

BINDING AND DUST JACKET: There are two binding variants: red cloth and beige cloth, both with the same black stamping. Stamped on the upper board as follows: SHORT | [rule resembling a lightning bolt] | [at a slight angle] CIRCUITS | [rule resembling a lightning bolt] | [vertical rule resembling a lightning bolt to the left of the next two lines] | STEPHEN | LEACOCK. Stamped on the spine as follows: SHORT | CIRCUITS | [rule resembling a lightning bolt] | STEPHEN | LEACOCK | [rule resembling a lightning bolt] | DODD [small solid, inverted triangle] MEAD | & COMPANY.

The front panel of the jacket has a colour illustration (against a green background) of a man looking at a woman, sparks emanating from their held hands. The green background of the illustration extends to the spine panel of the jacket. The rest of the jacket is beige with black lettering. The back panel has two paragraphs by Leacock, taken from his preface to *Sunshine Sketches of a Little Town*, along with a list of "*Popular Leacock Titles: Each $2.00*". The front flap has a synopsis of the book and the price ($2). The back flap has similar information for *The Garden of Folly*.

NOTES: The contract with Dodd, Mead is dated 24 April 1925. The title is unspecified in the contract because it was part of a multi-book deal with Leacock. The royalty was 20% on all copies sold with an advance of $1,000 on the day of publication against accrued royalties.

On 31 January 1928, Frank Dodd told Leacock that he was delighted to hear that Leacock had gathered together a new collection of his humorous sketches: "We would like to bring the book out in June, as that is the month in which we have published a number of the other books, and it seems to have a double advantage of getting some of the late spring sale and a carry-over through the autumn season." On 7 February 1928, Dodd expressed his enthusiasm for Leacock's suggested title: "SHORT CIRCUITS is a bully title, and I am glad you can squeeze it out to 50,000 words. The more, the merrier."

Leacock sent the manuscript on 27 February 1928. A.M. Chase acknowledged receipt of it on 2 March: "We have already looked it over and are enthusiastic. I am sending the manuscript to the printer, with orders to follow in general the style of the other books, leaving separate pages for the chapter titles as you suggested. We shall have galley proofs for you in two weeks." Published on 15 June 1928. On 18 June 1928, Leacock received his cash advance of $1,000. The copyright was registered with the Copyright Office at DLC on 21 June 1928 (ClA1082159). The copyright was renewed by George Leacock on 31 August 1955 (R155062).

Number of copies printed not known. By 1 August 1928, 4,984 copies had sold, earning a royalty of $1,993.60 (in addition 7 copies "spec. sales"). Between 1 August 1928 and 1 February 1929, 697 copies sold. After 1931, sales declined to less than fifty copies annually.

COPIES EXAMINED: CS (two copies in red cloth, one in jacket; one copy in beige cloth without the jacket); QMMRB (red cloth in jacket).

**A52b** *English edition*:

SHORT | CIRCUITS | BY STEPHEN LEACOCK | [thick-thin rule] | [thin-thick rule] | *LONDON : JOHN LANE THE BODLEY HEAD LTD*

◆ A⁶ B–L¹⁶ M¹⁴ [$1 signed]. i–vi, vii–ix, 1–3, 1–95, 96, 97–143, 144, 145–336, 1–12 pp. (180 leaves). 185 × 122 mm.

CONTENTS: pp. *i–ii* blank; p. *iii* half title; p. *iv* list of seventeen other books by Leacock, the first being *Literary Lapses* and the last *Winnowed Wisdom*; p. *v* title; p. *vi First published in 1928* | Made and Printed in Great Britain by Butler & Tanner Ltd., Frome and London; pp. vii–ix table of contents; p. *1* blank; pp. 2–3, 1–336 text (pp. *3, 96,* and *144* blank); p. *1–8* advertisements, with press opinions, of Leacock's books; pp. *9–12* advertisements, with press opinions, of books by other authors (Ben Travers, H.H. Munro, and recent fiction) published by The Bodley Head.

TEXT: The text of the English edition is the same as that of the American edition except the English edition is lacking one sketch from part VIII: The Fall Fair and the Autumn Exposition.

BINDING AND DUST JACKET: Bound in orange cloth, top edge stained orange, with blue lettering on the boards. Stamped on the upper board as follows: *SHORT CIRCUITS* | [rule] | *STEPHEN LEACOCK*. Stamped on the spine as follows: *SHORT* | *CIRCUITS* | [rule] | *STEPHEN* | *LEACOCK* | *THE* | *BODLEY HEAD*.

The front panel of the jacket has a colour illustration against a green background, signed by Christopher Hassall, of a portly man who has stepped on a live electrical cord. The man is in mid-air, his mouth is wide open, his shoes have left his feet, and his shirt collar has popped open. The rest of the jacket is white with blue lettering. Printed on the spine panel: SHORT | CIRCUITS | STEPHEN | LEACOCK | 7/6 | NET | THE | BODLEY | HEAD. The back panel lists seventeen books by Leacock published by The Bodley Head: "*Uniform Edition. Crown 8vo. Cloth. 5s. net each.*" The front flap advertises the collected works of "Saki" (H.H. Munro). A similar advertisement for books by Ben Travers is on the back flap.

NOTES: On 30 January 1928 Leacock proposed a new book to B.W. Willett of The Bodley Head, similar in Leacock's opinion to *Literary Lapses* and *Winnowed Wisdom*. Almost a month later, on 26 March 1928, Willett asked Leacock to supply "the missing pages in the manuscript." He told Leacock on 17 April 1928:

> "Short Circuits" is a very much longer book than any of your others. We had, therefore, to decide to publish it at 7/6d. . . . The proofs will be ready in about ten days or a fortnight. As most of the matter is reprint matter we could, I think, quite well read and correct the proofs here, as we have done before, sending you at the same time two sets of proofs for you to look through in case of any serious mistakes.

By this time Christopher Hassall was designing the book's dust jacket.

According to *The English Catalogue of Books*, the English edition was published in June 1928. Leacock was sent his advance of £250 (less £50 income tax) on 5 July 1928. Eight articles from the book were apparently sold to a Scottish serial shortly after publication, Willett informed Leacock. By the end of the year on 20 December 1928, Willett reported:

"'Short Circuits' is going along steadily though I daresay the sales have been to a certain extent affected by the fact that being double the ordinary length of your books we had to make the price higher."

Number of copies printed not known. Between July and December 1929, 23 copies sold (11 colonial). Similar sales of the book occurred in the early 1930s.

On 22 January 1936, the book in sheets was still available in the warehouse of The Bodley Head. Surplus sheet stock was disposed of at 4d per copy. See also *The Leacock Laughter Book* (A76), which includes the sheets of this book along with *Afternoons in Utopia*.

COPIES EXAMINED: CS (in jacket); QMMRB (not in jacket).

## A52b.1 *Canadian issue*:

SHORT | CIRCUITS | BY STEPHEN LEACOCK | [thick-thin rule] | [thin-thick rule] | *THE MACMILLAN COMPANY OF CANADA LTD.* | *AT ST. MARTIN'S HOUSE TORONTO*

Aside from the title page, the only other difference between the English edition and the Canadian issue is the book's spine where *THE* | *BODLEY HEAD* has been replaced by THE MACMILLAN Co. [. under o]. Dust jacket not seen.

NOTES: On 7 February 1928, Frank Dodd asked Leacock about the Canadian rights to *Short Circuits*. He suggested that McClelland and Stewart handle the Canadian market (since M&S represented Dodd, Mead in Canada), but the Canadian rights had already been determined in favour of the Macmillan Company of Canada in February 1926 when Hugh Eayrs obtained the rights to *Winnowed Wisdom* and to Leacock's next two books of humour. On 29 June 1928, Eayrs sent Leacock an advance royalty of $500, and he informed him: "Stock of this book has just been received from England and already we are receiving calls for it." In the Macmillan Company's royalty report of 31 March 1929, 1,021 copies had sold at $2.50 apiece (30¢ per copy royalty, $306.30). Between 1 April 1929 and 31 March 1930, 90 copies sold ($27.00 royalty).

COPIES EXAMINED: OHM; QMMRB.

## A52c *Canadian edition* [1967]:

Stephen Leacock | SHORT CIRCUITS | Introduction: D. J. Dooley | General Editor: Malcolm Ross | New Canadian Library No. 57 | [publisher's device: abstract design of a person on a horse-drawn chariot, taking aim with a bow and arrow] | MCCLELLAND AND STEWART LIMITED

◆ *i–iv*, v–vii, *viii*, ix–xiv, *1–2*, 3–7, *8*, 9–23, *24*, 25–35, *36–38*, 39–41, *42*, 43–49, *50–52*, 53–62, 63–64, 65–74, 75–76, 77–79, *80*, 81–82, *83*, 84–89, *90*, 91–92, *93–94*, 95–97, *98*, 99–111, *112–114*, 115–120, *121*, 122–133, *134–136*, 137–141, *142*, 143–152, *153–154*, 155–163, *164*, 165–216, *217–218*, 219–220, *1–6* pp. (120 leaves). 184 × 111 mm.

CONTENTS: p. *i* half title; p. *ii* blank; p. *iii* title; p. *iv* First published 1928 | Introduction © McClelland and Stewart Limited | All Rights Reserved | *The Canadian Publishers* | McClelland and Stewart Limited | 25 Hollinger Road, Toronto 16 | PRINTED AND BOUND IN CANADA BY | T. H. BEST PRINTING COMPANY LIMITED; p. v–vii table of contents; p. *viii* blank; pp. ix–xiv D.J. Dooley's introduction; pp. *1*–220 text (pp. *36*, *50*, *112*, and *134* are blank); p. *1* biographical information about Leacock; p. 2 blank; pp. 3–4 list of books publication in the New Canadian Library series; pp. *5–6* blank.

TEXT: Identical to A52a.

BINDING: Paperback, perfect bound. The covers are white with lettering and illustration is blue, brown, and red. A drawing of Leacock's face in brown is on the front cover. The back cover has two paragraphs in brown type on the book's contents and the book's price ($1.65). Cover designed by Frank Newfeld.

NOTES: Published in 1967 according to *Canadiana*. By the end of the spring 1967, 1,053 copies had sold; 1,692 copies sold by the end of the year. By the end of 1979 8,075 copies had sold (information based on file 14, "New Canadian Library," box 93, series A, part I, McClelland and Stewart fonds, OHM).

COPIES EXAMINED: CS.

## A53 THE IRON MAN AND THE TIN WOMAN 1929

A53a *English edition*:

THE IRON MAN | AND | THE TIN WOMAN | AND OTHER FUTURITIES | *By* STEPHEN LEACOCK | LONDON | JOHN LANE THE BODLEY HEAD LIMITED

◆ A–K$^{16}$ L$^4$ [$1 signed (–A1), fifth leaf signed * (e.g. A*)]. *i–vi*, vii–ix, *1–3*, 1–44, *45–46*, 47–98, *99–100*, 101–163, *164–166*, 167–190, *191–192*, 193–209, *210–212*, 213–262, *263–264*, 265–307, *1–9* pp. (164 leaves). 185 × 122 mm.

CONTENTS: pp. *i–ii* blank; p. *iii* half title; p. *iv* list of seventeen other books by Leacock, the first being *Literary Lapses* and the last *Short Circuits*; p. *v* title; p. *vi First published in 1929 | Made and Printed in Great Britain by | Tonbridge Printers, Peach Hall Works, Tonbridge*; pp. vii–ix table of contents; p. *1* blank; pp. 2–3, *1*–307 text (pp. *3, 46, 100, 164, 166, 192, 210, 212,* and *264* blank); p. *1* blank; pp. *2–7* advertisements, with press opinions, of Leacock's books; pp. *8–9* advertisements, with press opinions, of books by other authors published by The Bodley Head.

TEXT: The text is comprised of seven parts: I Pictures of the Bright Time to Come; II Great Lives in Our Midst; III To-Day and To-Morrow; IV College Now and College Then; V In the Golf Stream; VI Futurity in Fiction; VII Also —.

Part I: The Iron Man and the Tin Woman; Further Progress in Specialization; When Social Regulation Is Complete; Isn't It Just Wonderful?; The Last of the Rubber Necks; Athletics for 1950; The Criminal Face; Astronomical Alarms.

Part II: Memoirs of an Iceman; The Memoirs of a Night-Watchman; Confessions of a Super-Extra Criminal; The Life of J. Correspondence Smith; Eddie the Bar-Tender: The Ghost of the Bygone Past; Janus and the Janitor; The Intimate Disclosures of a Wronged Woman.

Part III: Little Conversations of the Hour; Travel Is So Broadening; Tommy and Milly at the Farm; Uninvented Inventions; Life's Little Inconsistencies; New World — New Things; The Repatriation of the Minstrel; More Messages from Mars; Portents of the Future; Rural Urbanity; Potter's Corners.

Part IV: All Up!; Willie Nut Tries to Enter College; Graduation Day at the Barbers' College; Correspondence Manual Number One.

Part V: The Golfomaniac; The Golfer's Pocket Guide; The Golf Season in Retrospect.

Part VI: Long after Bedtime; The Newer Truthfulness; Little Lessons in Journalism; More Literary Scandals; Who Reads What; Overhauling the Encyclopaedia; Jazzled Journalism; This Heart-to-Heart Stuff.

Part VII: Forty Years of Billiards; The Hero of Home Week; Conversations I Can Do without; Speculative Credit; "Mr. Chairman, I Beg to Move —"; The Early Rising of Primus Jones; Fifty Cents' Worth.

BINDING AND DUST JACKET: Bound in dark yellow cloth, top edge stained dark yellow. Stamped on the upper board in black as follows: *THE IRON MAN &* | *THE TIN WOMAN* | [rule] | *STEPHEN LEACOCK*. Stamped on the spine in gilt as follows: *THE* | *IRON MAN* | *AND* | *THE TIN* | *WOMAN* | [rule] | *STEPHEN* | *LEACOCK* | *THE* | *BODLEY HEAD*.

On the front and spine panels of the jacket is a colour illustration. In the foreground are three men and two women in formal attire (one woman is seated); they are all looking at a man and a woman who are mechanical robots. The rest of the jacket is white with blue lettering. The back panel lists other books by Leacock published by The Bodley Head, the last being *Short Circuits* with press opinions. The front flap has a synopsis of *The Iron Man and the Tin Woman*. On the back flap is a list of some recent fiction published by The Bodley Head.

NOTES: On 20 December 1928 B.W. Willett of The Bodley Head asked Leacock whether his new book of humour would be available in time for advertisement in the spring catalogue. Leacock sent the manuscript by registered mail on 9 September 1929. He enclosed ". . . a list of articles that may be omitted if necessary, and the order in which they may be chucked out" (The Bodley Head fonds, READ). The text of two or three articles was lacking; these were sent on 18 September. Leacock asked Willett to proceed with publication — "no time for proofs." The agreement for the book is dated 9 October 1929 (copy of the contract at READ and the Barbara Nimmo collection at NAC). According to the contract The Bodley Head was to pay Leacock 20% royalty on the English edition and £250 on the day of publication. The agreement also gave the publisher the rights to Leacock's next two volumes of humour on the same basis. On 15 November 1929, the day of publication, Willett sent Leacock the promised advance (minus £50 for income tax). Leacock received a copy of the book and payment on 20 November. "The *Iron Man* is excellently put together & the jacket most amusing," he told Willett (READ). 2,844 copies sold by 31 December 1929 at 7s 6d, earning £1,066 10s (Leacock earned 20% of this amount, although he received no payment since it was less than the advance). Another 995 copies sold by this date to the colonial market at 3 s. 3d. royalty apiece (earning Leacock 20% of £161 13s. 9d.).

COPIES EXAMINED: CS (first and second printings, the first in jacket); QMMRB (second printing, no jacket).

## A53b *American edition*:

THE IRON MAN & | THE TIN WOMAN | *With Other Such Futurities* | A BOOK OF LITTLE SKETCHES OF | TO-DAY AND TO-MORROW | [thick-thin rule] | BY STEPHEN LEACOCK | [thin-thick rule] | [publisher's device: inverted triangle with D • M • & • Co at the base and below this an illustration of a face, two open books, and two burning torches in the shape of a V] | [thick-thin rule] | NEW YORK | DODD, MEAD AND COMPANY | 1929 | [thin-thick rule]

◆ 1–20⁸. i–iv, v–vi, 1–2, 1–309, 1–3 pp. (160 leaves). 187 × 130 mm.

CONTENTS: p. *i* half title; p. *ii* list of nineteen books by Leacock, the first being *Literary Lapses* and the last *The Iron Man and the Tin Woman*; p. *iii* title; p. *iv* COPYRIGHT, 1929, | BY DODD, MEAD AND COMPANY, INC. | PRINTED IN THE U. S. A. BY | Quinn & Boden Company, Inc. | [rule] | BOOK MANUFACTURERS | RAHWAY, NEW JERSEY; pp. v–vi table of contents; p. *1* fly title; p. *2* blank; pp. *1–309* text; pp. *1–3* blank.

TEXT: Several stories from parts III and VII of the English edition are missing from the American edition. Missing from part III: Uninvented Inventions; The Repatriation of the Minstrel; Potters's Corners. Missing from part VII: Speculative Credit; The Early Rising of Primus Jones. However, the American edition has an additional story in part VI: A Midsummer Detective Mystery. In other respects the text of the American edition is the same as that of the English edition.

BINDING AND DUST JACKET: Bound in red cloth. Lettering on the upper board stamped in black and outlined in silver as follows: THE IRON MAN AND | THE TIN WOMAN | STEPHEN [the second E at a slight angle] LEACOCK. Stamping on the spine in black as follows: THE | IRON MAN | AND THE | TIN | WOMAN | ■ | STEPHEN | LEACOCK | DODD [small, solid inverted triangle] MEAD | & COMPANY.

The front panel of the jacket has an illustration, signed by John Held, Jr., in orange, yellow, and black of male and female mechanical robots. Lettering on the front panel is yellow, outlined in black, and similar to that of the stamping on the upper board. The rest of the jacket is yellow with black lettering. Printing on the spine panel is as follows: THE IRON | MAN AND | THE TIN | WOMAN | By | STEPHEN | LEACOCK | Author of | "Nonsense | Novels," | "Literary | Lapses" | etc. | DODD, MEAD | AND COMPANY. The back panel of the jacket has two paragraphs by Leacock, taken from his preface to *Sunshine Sketches of a Little Town*, along with a list of "*Popular Leacock Titles: Each $2.00*". The front flap has a synopsis of the book and the price ($2). The back flap has similar information for *Short Circuits*.

NOTES: On 13 February 1929, Frank Dodd wrote to Leacock:: "I am delighted to hear that there is a prospect of having a volume of sketches this year. We ought to have at least 60,000 words to make a book of respectable bulk — 70,00 would be better." He requested Leacock to send the manuscript as soon as possible for publication in the autumn (1 September). Although Leacock was prepared to send Dodd 30,000 words in March 1929, it was not until 21 August 1929 that he informed him:

> I am glad to say that I have now plenty of sketches from which to choose the book (same terms as before I understand). . . . For the title I propose to use a title of one of the sketches. The Iron Man & The Tin Woman And Other Such Futurities. It sounds to me a good selling title and would illustrate well. The only objection is that it is only a title [of] one sketch but that is even done and the subtitle shows that the sketches hang together.

A few days later, on 28 August 1929, Dodd replied that he liked the title and that he planned publication in the spring of the next year or sooner if he could receive the manuscript in October. He had one reservation, however:

The only point that I am a little disturbed about is the 20 percent royalty, as we find it in these days of high cost of manufacture, advertising and overhead in general, pretty difficult indeed to show a profit and pay that rate, especially on a $2.00 book. It certainly gives a publisher very little room.

He asked Leacock to reconsider the royalty rate, 15% being more equitable from the publisher's point of view. He added that he would abide by Leacock's decision on the matter: "We are proud to have your books on our list and I certainly would go a long way before losing you."

Leacock replied on 3 September 1929, telling Dodd that he still wanted 20% royalty. If Dodd lost money on the book, he vowed to take 15% on the next book. The contract is dated 6 September 1929: 20% on all copies sold with an advance of $1,000 to be paid on the day of publication. Clause 20 of the contract gave Dodd, Mead the rights to Leacock's next book of humour. On 20 Sept 1929, Dodd informed Leacock that we are "going ahead with it [the printing of the manuscript] as fast as possible. John Held, Jr., has been engaged to do the jacket as he is without peer in this field, in our opinion." The first batch of proofs were sent to Leacock on 25 September. By this time Held had finished the design of the jacket. "The rest of the book, including the four chapters which arrived about a week ago, will be on the way to you within a day or so," Dodd told Leacock. The book was published on 22 November 1929. The copyright was registered with the Copyright Office at DLC on 27 November 1929 (ClA17060). The copyright was renewed by George Leacock on 6 February 1957 (R185930).

By 1 February 1930, 5,259 copies had been sold at $.40 royalty per copy for Leacock ($2,103.60 earned). Another thirteen copies at reduced royalty of $.20 had also sold up to that time. Between 1 August 1930 and 1 August 1932 135 copies sold ($54.40 royalty).

COPIES EXAMINED: CS (in jacket); QMMRB (two copies, neither in jacket, one rebound).

## A53b.1 *Canadian issue*:

THE IRON MAN & | THE TIN WOMAN | *With Other Such Futurities* | A BOOK OF LITTLE SKETCHES OF | TO-DAY AND TO-MORROW | [thick-thin rule] | BY STEPHEN LEACOCK | [thin-thick rule] | [publisher's device: inverted triangle with D • M • & • Co at the base and below this an illustration of a face, two open books, and two burning torches in the shape of a V] | [thick-thin rule] | TORONTO: THE MACMILLAN COMPANY OF | CANADA LIMITED, AT ST. MARTIN'S HOUSE | 1929 | [thin-thick rule]

The Canadian issue is identical to A53b. Two variant bindings were examined: one where MACMILLAN replaces that of Dodd, Mead; the other with the American publisher's name on the spine. Dust jacket of the Canadian issue not seen.

NOTES: On 25 November 1929, the Macmillan Company of Canada sent Leacock an advance of $500 against royalties. Up to 31 March 1930, 797 copies sold at $.30 royalty per copy ($239.10). Between 1 August 1932 and 1 February 1933, 5 copies sold at $.40 royalty per copy. Between 1 February 1933 and 1 August 1933, 3 copies sold ($1.20 royalty).

COPIES EXAMINED: CS (Macmillan on spine); QMMRB (Dodd, Mead on spine).

## A54 ECONOMIC PROSPERITY IN THE BRITISH EMPIRE 1930

**A54a** *The Economic Integration of the Empire*, circular:

[cover title: row of ornaments; thick-thin rule] | NOW IN THE PRESS | [thin-thick rule] | *The. . . . . . . . . . . . . . . .Co-Announce for Publication* | *in the Spring of 1930* | [small ornament] | [the next four lines apparently in red] THE | ECONOMIC INTEGRATION | *of the* | BRITISH EMPIRE | *By* | STEPHEN LEACOCK | B.A., Ph.D., LL.D., Litt.D., F.R.S.C. | Head of the Department of Economics and Political Science | McGill University, Montreal. | [small ornament] | *The Book of the Season* | [paragraph which begins: Professor Leacock's brilliant and fascinating presentation. . . .] | [thick-thin rule; row of ornaments]

Leaflet folded once to form four unnumbered pages. Only a proof copy has survived. Galleys measure 358 × 216 mm.

TEXT: The text is on pp. 2–4. The general heading on p. 2 is: *An Undeveloped Empire*. This is followed by a paragraph and then by sub-headings in bold type, each with a paragraph or two of explanation. The sub-headings are: THE PARTITION OF OUR ESTATE; RESOURCES, CAPITAL, MIGRATION; AN INTEGRATED RECIPROCAL TRADE; A COLOSSUS WITH FEET OF CLAY; AMERICA DEPENDS ON EXPORT TRADE; BUT CAN CONCEDE NOTHING; AN IMPERIAL RECIPROCAL SYSTEM; THE CRY OF THE CONSUMER.

The circular concludes with a list of the CENTRAL IDEAS OF THE BOOK. The last two lines are: The Economic Integration of the British Empire is an- | nounced for publication at the end of May, 1930.

NOTES: On 24 January 1930, when Leacock was writing "The Economic Integration of the Empire," later entitled *Economic Prosperity in the British Empire*, he informed his publisher, Hugh Eayrs of the Macmillan Company of Canada, that he wanted "to get started on publicity." Leacock's intention was to have "1,000 4 page circulars . . . quite enough I known to sell this book in thousands." According to Leacock, the printing estimate was $20. Although the Macmillan Company's name was not on the galley proof, Leacock told Eayrs that he could insert it as need be. Eayrs requested to see the proof on 1 February. Leacock sent it on 13 February. On 10 March Eayrs sent back the proof with alterations. He instructed Leacock to have 2,000 copies printed, to keep the type standing in case of a reprinting, and to charge all costs to the Macmillan Company. Leacock kept 100 copies of the circular for himself. On 12 April 1930, Eayrs informed Leacock that most of the 1,900 circulars had been dispatched, "one, to the important and larger trade and public libraries in this country, two, to the heads of banks, trust companies, loan companies, insurance offices, and so on, and three, to a hand-picked list of influential men, some members of parliament, some not, but all who are likely to be interested in the book."

The first page of the proof copy is reproduced in K83.2 (at p. 62).

COPY EXAMINED: OHM (file 15, box 113, Macmillan Company of Canada fonds).

**A54b** *English edition*:

ECONOMIC PROSPERITY | IN THE BRITISH EMPIRE | *by* | STEPHEN LEACOCK | B. A., PH.D., LL.D., LITT.D., F.R.S.C. | HEAD OF THE

## DEPARTMENT OF ECONOMICS AND POLITICAL | SCIENCE, McGILL UNIVERSITY MONTREAL | CONSTABLE & CO LTD | LONDON

◆  A⁴ B–Q⁸ R⁴ [$1 signed]. *i–vi, vii, 1–3, 3–146, 147–148, 149–245, 1–3* pp. (128 leaves). 187 × 123 mm.

CONTENTS: p. *i* half title; p. *ii* list of books by the same author (*The Elements of Political Science*) and on the same subject; p. *iii* title; p. *iv* PUBLISHED BY | *Constable & Company Limited* | *London W.C.2* | • | BOMBAY | CALCUTTA MADRAS | *Oxford University* | *Press* | • | First Published 1930 | Printed in Great Britain by Butler & Tanner Ltd., Frome and London; p. *v* explanation that the title of the book was changed too late for an alteration of the running heads (ECONOMIC INTEGRATION OF THE BRITISH EMPIRE); p. *vi* blank; p. vii table of contents; p. *1* blank; pp. 2–3, 3–245, *1* text (pp. *3* and *148* blank); pp. 2–3 blank. Maps on pp. 35, 51, 59

TEXT: There are two parts: I Until Now; II From Now on.

Part I: chapter I The Empire As a Proprietary Asset; chapter II The Possible Expansion of the White Race within the British Empire; chapter III The Historical Development of Economic Relations within the Empire; chapter IV The Migration of Population in the Past; chapter V The Export and Investment of British Capital.

Part II: chapter I A Proposal for an Integrated Tariff System within the Empire; chapter II A Proposal of Policy for the Settlement of New Country; chapter III The Integration of Credit, Currency, and Capital; chapter IV The Intellectual Unity of the Empire; chapter V What to Do and How to Do It: The Work of an Economic Conference.

BINDING: Bound in red cloth. A rectangle is blind-stamped on the upper board. Stamped in gilt on the spine: [rule blind-stamped] | ECONOMIC | PROSPERITY | IN THE | BRITISH | EMPIRE | LEACOCK | CONSTABLE | LONDON | [rule blind-stamped]. Dust jacket not seen.

NOTES: Leacock authorized Eayrs to arrange the publication of the English edition. Eayrs approached the English branch of the Macmillans. He informed Leacock on 26 February 1930 that the English branch could not consider publication without seeing the manuscript. Eayrs wanted the English branch to pay an advance of $1,000 on publication. Much to Eayrs's astonishment, the English branch declined publication on 6 March 1930. Their reader, the distinguished economist, John Maynard Keynes, characterized Leacock's book as "extraordinarily commonplace" (see lot 192K, Sotheby's auction catalogue of *The Archive of Macmillan Publishers Ltd. (1905–1969)*, 19 July 1990). Several months after the book had been published, on 2 January 1931, Leacock complained to Eayrs:

> The Macmillan Co of London refused my Empire book, the first publishers to refuse anything of mine since Houghton Mifflin after accepting my Political Science refused my Literary Lapses in 1909 . . . that's 21 years ago . . . your house was the first . . . they are the only ones who can say, "we could have published Leacock's books but we don't want to".

Eayrs tried to reassure Leacock on 10 January 1931 that he had tried his "damndest to sell the idea" to the other branches of the Macmillan Company. During this period Eayrs was attempting to secure the Canadian market for Leacock's previously published books. The negative decision by the London Macmillans — in addition to the fact that Eayrs was unwilling to pay advance royalties for these Leacock's older titles — spelled the end of their cozy relationship.

Eayrs arranged publication of the English edition with Constable & Co. Ltd. On 15 June 1930, Leacock cabled Constable: "Appreciate your interest call the book ECONOMIC PROSPERITY IN THE BRITISH EMPIRE but please hurry greatly concerned with delay." Constable replied on 27 June 1930 that the book would be published on 24 July 1930 but that it was too late to change the running heads. The book sold for 7s 6d. Leacock received his author's copies on 7 August 1930. He requested Constable to send him word about sales and a "formal contract as based on arrangements made by the good offices of Mr. Eayrs." By 30 December 1930, 2,890 copies had been sold, but 1,000 of these were by agreement, free of royalty, since they were sent out by the Orillia Board of Trade (see A54a.1). Consequently, Leacock earned $341.82 (less $76.90 for income tax) on 1,890 copies sold (at 10% royalty). 206 copies sold in 1931 ($31.28 royalty). On 4 February 1932, Eayrs gave Constable permission to reduce the list price from 7s 6d to 3s 6d, the customary British list price reduction after first publication. Approximately 298 further copies sold from 1 July 1931 till the end of 1932.

Leacock informed B.W. Willett of The Bodley Head on 4 October 1930:

> You may have observed perhaps that *Constable & Co* have a book of mine on Empire politics & if so I hope you will realize that this involves no disloyalty to the Bodley Head. Constable & Co published work of mine of that class long before my connection with Mr Lane: indeed they have sold my work for 25 years. (The Bodley Head fonds, READ).

COPIES EXAMINED: CUL.

## A54b.1  *English edition*, issue of the Orillia Board of Trade:

This issue differs from the English edition in two respects. The upper board is blind-stamped as follows: WITH THE COMPLIMENTS | OF THE | BOARD OF TRADE | ORILLIA | ONTARIO CANADA. A leaf has been tipped in opposite the title leaf. The recto of the tipped-in leaf is blank. The verso has a foreword consisting of three paragraphs that endorses Leacock's proposal for economic unity within the Empire and draws ". . . attention to the opportunities for investment of British capital in the industries of Canada."

NOTES:  On 9 April 1930, Leacock spoke at the Orillia Board of Trade on "The Integration of the Empire." The president of the Board wrote to him ". . . that the members would be glad to help to circulate . . . [the] book as soon as it came out" (Leacock to Eayrs, 14 April 1930, Macmillan fonds, OHM). In October 1930 the Board of Trade purchased and mailed 1,000 copies abroad to English newspapers and to important men in public life. The mailing list of 611 members of the House of Commons, 142 newspapers, and 247 other individuals is at OORI.

Eayrs asked Leacock on 18 October 1930 why the copies were not ordered from the Macmillan Company of Canada Ltd. He pointed out to Leacock that "you get no royalty on this particular order and Constable's no profit." In fact, when the Macmillan Company calculated Leacock's royalties from Constable, Leacock received an overpayment of $255.48. He repaid this amount to Eayrs on 28 March 1932. Eayrs told Leacock a day later: "The whole trouble [with the overpayment] arose I may say, in the first place, because you arranged the Orillia Board of Trade sale with Constable and we knew nothing about it until afterwards."

COPIES EXAMINED: CS; OORI.

**A54b.2** *Canadian issue:*

ECONOMIC PROSPERITY | IN THE BRITISH EMPIRE | *by* | STEPHEN LEACOCK | B.A., Ph.D., LL.D., Litt.D., F.R.S.C. | HEAD OF THE DEPARTMENT OF ECONOMICS AND POLITICAL | SCIENCE, McGILL UNIVERSITY MONTREAL | THE MACMILLAN COMPANY | OF CANADA LTD | TORONTO | 1930

With the exceptions of the title page, the verso of the half title (being blank), and the binding and jacket, the Canadian issue is the same as the English edition.

BINDING AND DUST JACKET: There are two binding variants. (1) red ribbed cloth with stamping on the spine in gilt as follows: ECONOMIC | PROSPERITY | IN THE | BRITISH | EMPIRE | [rule] | LEACOCK | MACMILLAN. (2) pink cloth with stamping on the spine as in (1) but in black. (1) has priority.

The dust jacket is beige with lettering in red. On the front panel within a red rectangle is the title, Leacock's name, some of his degrees, and a paragraph about the book. On the back panel within two rectangles is a list of recent Canadian titles from Macmillan's list. Printed on the spine panel: ECONOMIC | PROSPERITY | in the | BRITISH | EMPIRE | [diamond] | STEPHEN | LEACOCK | MACMILLAN. The front flap lists the book's table of contents. The back flap has an advertisement for *The Fuel Problem of Canada*.

NOTES: In late 1929 Leacock decided to curtail his lectures outside of McGill University and to stop writing syndicated humour. He hoped to finish a book entitled "Chapters in Political Economy." However, he told Eayrs on 22 November 1929 that he was keen on a new book, "The Economic Integration of the British Empire": "I began it some time ago & now the development of politics in England is throwing a tremendous change in its way. I think I'd like to do it first" (Macmillan fonds, OHM).

Eayrs told Leacock on 28 November that he was "vastly interested" in the new book. He already written to the Macmillans in New York about an American edition. On 5 December 1929 Leacock informed Eayrs that the manuscript would be between 80 to 100 thousand words with about twenty maps. He hoped to complete all writing by 24 May. He had engaged one of his younger colleagues, Professor John Culliton, to work on the statistical matter. He was optimistic about his progress and the book's reception:

> I have written so far a good many thousand words & am writing it every day.
> There will be no difficulty whatever in our arranging terms of publication. But what I am anxious for is that the book should have a good appearance & be put on the market with a "hurrah".

Almost two months later on 24 January 1930, Leacock was "driving ahead" on his book. A stenographer was kept busy typing the manuscript. He proposed the following terms to Eayrs:

> As I said in conversation I want 10 per cent on the first 5000 in Canada and then 20% and 10% on the first five thousand in England and then 20% and ditto in the U.S. and advance royalty in a lump sum of $25000. I am sure from what you said that this will suit you.

Eayrs agreed to the royalty percentages on 14 February, but he found the advance royalty too steep: ". . . it predicates sales running to the scores of thousands." He advised Leacock that although the English edition could prove lucrative, the American end would not be worth a great deal. Leacock backed down on his request for an advance royalty on 3 March in spite of his belief that without such an advance a publisher would have no incentive to promote a book. Eayrs suggested on 4 March that he would handle all markets and would pay an advance royalty ". . . consistent with the situation at the time we receive the manuscript, and we shall make this as adequate as possible from your point of view." On 5 March Leacock agreed to Eayrs's overall responsibility for publication with the exception of the American market. On the next day he let Eayrs handle everything, allowing the royalty in the United States to be reduced to 15% after 4,000 copies sold.

Leacock mailed three copies of the typescript to Eayrs on 14 April 1930. Eayrs requested the maps to be drawn by Thoreau Macdonald on 15 April. A few weeks after the English edition had been secured with Constable, Eayrs travelled to England at the end of June 1930 to oversee arrangements. He cabled his secretary, E. Elliott Booth, on 7 July 7: "SHIPPING LEACOCK FOLDED COLLATED SEWN THIS WEEK." She wrote to Leacock on the next day, and inquired about his preference for the colour of the binding and the jacket. The sheets arrived from England on 6 August, and were then sent to the bindery. But on 9 August Leacock grew impatient with the apparent delay in publication of the book in Canada. The English edition had already received wide publicity in English periodicals and newspapers. He also lamented the lack of progress in the American edition. Eayrs replied to Leacock's letter on 12 August: "I may tell you that the speed with which the book was put through the press in England was due to me and my appearance there." He had arranged for reviews in the *Express*, the *Times*, the *Morning Post*, the *Spectator*, and other newspapers. At his own expense Eayrs had printed and distributed 5,000 circulars (no copy extant) to promote Constable's edition. "The Canadian edition will be finished binding and issued on Thursday," he informed Leacock. "We shall use one advertisement on its appearance and then lay off for a bit since this is the summer season and Toronto, Montreal and Ottawa are pretty empty. This book is our big book for Fall and if it does not go across it will not be for want of trying."

The Macmillan Company of Canada formally registered the copyright in Leacock's book on 30 August 1930. The production card at OHM indicates that 519 copies were bound by T.H. Best Printing Co. on 15 August 1930, 507 copies on 21 October 1930, and 250 copies on 28 May 1931. Another 540 copies were delivered to the Macmillans on 30 January 1934, and another 255 copies the next day. In all the Canadian issue consisted of 2,071 copies. T.H. Best Printing Co. printed 2,000 jackets in August 1930. The issue cost $1,027.55 ($679.95 for the production of the sheets, folding, sewing, and shipment to Canada).

By 13 December 1930, 845 copies of the Canadian issue had sold ($.20 per copy, $169 royalty). There were 52 presentation copies. Up to 31 March 1933, another 174 copies were sold. The book was reduced in price from $2 to $1.25 on 17 November 1931. The remaining stock was sold off in January 1934. 145 copies, for example, were remaindered or sold as part of a lot to Simpsons at 20¢ apiece or even less.

There was no American edition. Dodd, Mead was quite lukewarm to publication in March 1930, and Leacock did not press them to take the book. The New York branch of the Macmillans did not think there was sufficient interest in the United States to merit manufacturing. A former employee from Dodd, Mead who established his own publishing company, Richard R. Smith Inc., was initially enthusiastic but eventually became wary of publication. In the end these publishers were only willing to import sheets (250 copies) from Eayrs.

See also the notes to A58c.

COPIES EXAMINED: CS (both binding variants in jacket plus another copy of the first binding variant without jacket); OORI (first binding variant in jacket); QMMRB (first binding variant in jacket; second binding variant without jacket).

## A55 THE LEACOCK BOOK 1930

THE | LEACOCK BOOK | Being Selections from the works of Stephen | Leacock arranged with an Introduction by | Ben Travers | LONDON | JOHN LANE THE BODLEY HEAD

• $A^8$ $B^4$ B–R$^8$ [$1 signed]. *1–6, v–ix, x, xi–xiii, xiv, xv–xx, 1–2, 1–248, 1–8* pp. (140 leaves). 185 × 122 mm.

CONTENTS: pp. *1–2* blank; p. *3* half title; p. *4* list of nineteen books by Leacock published by The Bodley Head, the first being *Literary Lapses* and the last *The Iron Man and the Tin Woman*; p. *5* title; p. *6 First Published in 1930* | Made and Printed in Great Britain by Butler & Tanner Ltd., Frome and London; pp. *v–ix* introduction by Ben Travers, dated June, 1930; p. *x* blank; pp. *xi–xiii* Leacock's preface from *Sunshine Sketches of a Little Town*; p. *xiv* blank; pp. *xv–xx* table of contents; p. *1* fly title; p. *2* blank; pp. *1–248* text; p. *1* ads with excerpts from reviews of Leacock's *The Iron Man and the Tin Woman* and *Short Circuits*; p. *2* list of other books by Leacock published by The Bodley Head; p. *3* ads with excerpts from reviews of five books written by Travers published by The Bodley Head; pp. *5–8* list of other books, some with ads, published by The Bodley Head (including The Bodley Head Mysteries, the Week-End Library, and books by Lady Kitty Vincent).

CONTENTS: This anthology is comprised of five parts: Personal Adventures; Nonsense Novels; General Contributions to Human Knowledge; Narrative; and A Chapter of Philosophy. The contributions to each part, some of which are reprinted in full, are taken primarily from Leacock's books of humour (which are identified in parentheses in the table of contents).

Personal Adventures consists of the following: My Financial Career; The Anecdotes of Dr. So and So; The Spiritual Outlook of Mr. Doomer; Under the Barber's Knife; With the Photographer; The Advantages of a Polite Education; The Simple Life in Paris; A Visit to Versailles; Paris at Night; The Prophet in Our Midst; Personal Adventures in the Spirit World; The Sorrows of a Summer Guest; Ideal Interviews; My Unposted Correspondence; and "We Have with Us To-Night."

Nonsense Novels consists of the following: Gertrude the Governess; or, Simple Seventeen; A Hero in Homespun; or, The Life Struggle of Hezekiah Hayloft; Sorrows of a Super Soul; or, The Memoirs of Marie Mushenough; Hannah of the Highlands; or, The Laird of Loch Aucherlocherty; Soaked in Seaweed; or, Upset in the Ocean; Caroline's Christmas; or, The Inexplicable Infant; Foreign Fiction in Imported Instalments; Winsome Winnie; or, Trial and Temptation; John and I; or, How I Nearly Lost My Husband; The Split in the Cabinet; or, The Fate of England; Who You Think Did It?; or, The Mixed up Murder Mystery; The Kidnapped Plumber; or, A Tale of the New Life; The Blue and the Grey: A Pre-War Story; Buggam Grange: A Good Old Ghost Story.

General Contributions to Human Knowledge consists of the following: Boarding-House Geometry; A New Pathology; Society Chit-Chat As It Should Happen; A, B, and C: The

Human Element in Mathematics; Homer and Humbug; Education made Agreeable; or, The Diversions of a Professor; The Art of Conversation; The Restoration of Whiskers; Brotherly Love among the Nations; Back from Europe: Does Travel Derange the Mind?; Studies in the Newer Culture; In the Good Old Summer Time; Travel and Movement; The Laundry Problem: A Yearning for the Vanished Washerwoman; The Snoopopaths; or, Fifty Stories in One; The Call of the Carburettor; Every Man and His Friends: Mr. Crunch's Portrait Gallery; The British and the American Press; The Strenuous Age; The First Newspaper; Behind the Beyond: A Modern Problem Play; Oroastus; A Greek Tragedy; The Sub-Contractor: An Ibsen Play; and The Fram.

Narrative consists of the following: The Speculations of Jefferson Thorpe; The Marine Excursions of the Knights of Pythias; The Ministrations of the Rev. Mr. Drone; The Whirlwind Campaign; The Beacon on the Hill; The Extraordinary Entanglement of Mr. Pupkin; The Mariposa Bank Mystery; The Great Election in Missinaba County; The Candidacy of Mr. Smith; A Little Dinner with Mr. Lucullus Fyshe; The Wizard of Finance; The Arrested Philanthropy of Mr. Tomlinson; The Yahi-Bahi Oriental Society of Mrs. Rasselyer-Brown; The Love Story of Mr. Peter Spillikins; The Rival Churches of St. Asaph and St. Osoph; The Ministrations of the Rev. Uttermust Dumfarthing; The Great Fight for Clean Government; The Survival of the Fittest.

A Chapter of Philosophy consists of the following: The Apology of a Professor; My Memories and Miseries As a Schoolmaster; My College Days: A Retrospect; Humour as I See It; The Woman Question; The Human Mind Up to Date; The Balance of Trade in Impressions; I Am Interviewed by the Press; Oxford As I See It; Simple Stories of Success; or, How to Succeed in Life; The Devil and the Deep Sea: A Discussion of Modern Morality; How Mr. Bellamy Looked Backward; Philosophies in Brief.

BINDING AND DUST JACKET: Bound in brown cloth with yellow lettering, top edge stained yellow. Stamped on the upper board: THE LEACOCK BOOK. Stamped on the spine as follows: THE | LEACOCK | BOOK | EDITED | BY | BEN TRAVERS | THE BODLEY HEAD.

The dust jacket is white with a colour design by Christopher Hassall on the front panel as follows: [three lines hand-written in brown to the left of a drawing] | The | Leacock | Book | [drawing of a man in eighteenth-century dress, presumably Ben Travers, with puppets of smaller people in front of him and a hat near his feet; in his left hand Travers holds a puppet of a professor (presumably Leacock) who is dressed in academic garb and mortar board] | [to the left of the drawing is Hassall's signature in facsimile]. All other lettering on the jacket is blue. On the spine panel of the jacket: THE | LEACOCK | BOOK | Selected, with an | Introduction | By | BEN TRAVERS | 5s. net. | THE | BODLEY | HEAD. On the back panel (within a rectangle) is a list of books by Leacock published by John Lane The Bodley Head. The front flap features three paragraphs on The Leacock Book. Listed on the back flap are five books written by Travers published by The Bodley Head with excerpts from reviews.

NOTES: Ben Travers began working for John Lane in 1911. He eventually edited the firm's in-house magazine, The Bodleian, and after the First World War, he wrote a series of comic novels, which The Bodley Head published. Travers and Leacock first met at this time with mutual admiration of each other's work.

Leacock cabled his acceptance of the terms for the book on 18 February 1930. B.W. Willett asked Leacock to sign the agreement on 25 February. The contract at READ (undated copy in the Barbara Nimmo collection at NAC) is dated 11 April 1930: 10% royalty up to 4,000 copies, 20% thereafter. Canada and the United States were excluded from the contract for two main reasons: at the time Frank C. Dodd was arranging to prepare his own anthology of Leacock's works, *Laugh with Leacock* (A56a), selected by Raymond T. Bond; Dodd, Mead was represented in Canada by McClelland and Stewart whereas The Bodley Head tended to place their books with the Macmillan Company of Canada. *The Leacock Book* was published in late August 1930 according to a notice in the *Bookman* (confirmed by *The English Catalogue of Books*).

When Dodd appealed to Leacock to shut out *The Leacock Book* from Canada, Leacock replied on 10 September 1930: "Both books are now made up. They are done in form in matter in editing and the content. Both seem to me excellent. I do not see how I can use my legal rights to have one of these shut out of Canada. . . ."

Number of copies printed not known. Between January and June 1931 70 copies sold, 3 to the foreign and 43 to the colonial markets. The Macmillan Company of Canada sold 229 copies between 3 October 1930 and 31 March 1931 (royalty of $25.85). The Macmillans sold 23 more copies sold between 1 April 1931 and 31 March 1932.

Leacock told Willett on 1 October 1930: "*The Leacock Book* is first rate. I wrote to Ben Travers. . . . I am afraid (this only to you and me as Hassall's pictures before were always so delightful) the cover, the *face*, will be a handicap. . . ." (The Bodley Head fonds, READ).

COPIES EXAMINED: CS (in jacket); QMMRB (no jacket).

## A56 LAUGH WITH LEACOCK 1930

### A56a *first American edition*:

LAUGH | *with* | LEACOCK | [ornament] | *An Anthology* | *of the Best Work of* | STEPHEN LEACOCK | [ornament] *New York* | DODD, MEAD & COMPANY | 1930

◆ 1–22$^8$. i–ii, iii–x, 1–2, 1–339, 1 pp. (176 leaves). 187 × 129 mm.

CONTENTS: p. *i* title; p. *ii* COPYRIGHT, 1913, 1915 | By DODD, MEAD & COMPANY | COPYRIGHT, 1916, 1917, 1920, 1922, 1923, 1924, 1925, | 1926, 1928, 1929, 1930 | By DODD, MEAD & COMPANY, INC. | COPYRIGHT, 1913 | By THE CROWELL PUBLISHING COMPANY | COPYRIGHT, 1913 | THE CENTURY COMPANY | COPYRIGHT, 1920 | By HARPER & BROTHERS | [three lines about copyright] | PRINTED IN THE U. S. A. BY | Quinn & Boden Company, Inc. | [rule] | BOOK MANUFACTURERS | RAHWAY, NEW JERSEY; pp. iii–viii preface with an introductory note from the editor addressed to Professor Leacock and tributes from fourteen other humorists; pp. ix–x table of contents; p. *1* half title; p. 2 blank; pp. 1–339 text; p. *1* blank.

TEXT: My Financial Career; Buggam Grange: A Good Old Ghost Story; How We Kept Mother's Day As Related by a Member of the Family; The Laundry Problem; The Great Detective; The Old, Old Story of How Five Men Went Fishing; Guido the Gimlet of Ghent: A Romance of Chivalry; The Hallucination of Mr. Butt; Cast Up by the Sea; How My Wife and I Built Our Home for $4.90; Softening the Stories for Children; The Everlasting Angler; Love Me, Love My Letters; The Golfomaniac; Gertrude the Governess: or, Simple Seventeen; Letters to the New Rulers of the World; The Marine Excursion of the Knights of Pythias; My Lost Dollar; Personal Experiments with the Black Bass; The Restoration of Whiskers a

Neglected Factor in the Decline of Knowledge; Then and Now: The College News of Forty Years Ago and the College News of Today; Old Junk and New Money; Oxford As I See It; The Snoopopaths or Fifty Stories in One; My Affair with My Landlord; The Give and Take of Travel; The Retroactive Existence of Mr. Juggins; Homer and Humbug, an Academic Discussion; "We Have with Us To-night"; Caroline's Christmas: or, The Inexplicable Infant; Father Knickerbocker — A Fantasy; Simple Stories of Success or How to Succeed in Life; Historical Drama; Humour as I See It; L'Envoi: The Faded Actor.

BINDING: Bound in red moiré cloth, top edge stained red. Stamped in gilt on the upper within a blind-stamped rectangle: LAUGH WITH | LEACOCK | *by* STEPHEN LEACOCK. Stamped in gilt on the spine as follows: LAUGH | WITH | LEACOCK | DODD, MEAD | & COMPANY. The endpapers are light yellow with a series of joined and intersecting green rectangles in various designs. Dust jacket not seen.

There is apparently a variant binding in red ribbed cloth.

NOTES: While in London Frank C. Dodd suggested to The Bodley Head that both companies should publish an anthology of Leacock's best and most popular sketches. Although the Bodley Head published its own anthology under the title *The Leacock Book* (A55), the contents of the two anthologies are dissimilar. A book with the title *Laugh with Leacock* (see A108) was later published in London by Transworld Publishers, but its contents also differ from A56. Consequently, there is no English edition of this book.

Dodd proposed the idea to Leacock on 20 February 1930, and on 28 February 1930, Leacock authorized him to make a selection of suitable sketches. He accepted a royalty of 10% up to 4,000 copies and 15% thereafter. The selection was made by Raymond T. Bond who acted as the book's editor. The book sold for $2.50. On 20 August 1930, Dodd sent Leacock his author's copies under separate cover. Published on 3 October 1930. The copyright was registered with the Copyright Office at DLC on 10–11 October 1930 (ClA28829). The copyright was renewed by George Leacock on 12 July 1958 (R217198).

Dodd, Mead & Company (Canada) Ltd. handled the Canadian market through John McClelland of McClelland and Stewart. Dodd shipped 1,000 copies to McClelland shortly after publication.

On 14 November 1930, Dodd wrote to Leacock: "You will be glad to know that LAUGH WITH LEACOCK is selling along nicely, and I am quite sure has fully justified our confidence in it." 2,839 copies had sold by 1 February 1931 ($.25 per copy royalty, earning $709.75). In addition, by that date, there had been six copies on "Spec Sales" and 661 copies sold to foreign countries ($132.75 royalty). By 26 January 1934 Dodd informed Leacock that 3,900 copies had sold and that the stock was virtually exhausted. Dodd wanted to reprint 250 copies, but did not want to pay Leacock an increased royalty of 15% according to their agreement. On 1 February 1934, he even suggested that instead of reprinting the book, it could be sold at $1 with Leacock receiving 5¢ a copy. Leacock agreed to a royalty of 10% on all copies sold.

The book was reprinted in small quantities thereafter, sometimes in print runs of 500 or 1,000. A quality reprint series in paper, Apollo editions, was inaugurated in the spring of 1961. The Leacock estate received a royalty of 5% on these copies.

Printing information on the copyright page of the twenty-third printing is as follows: Published, October 1930; second printing, October 1930; third printing, December 1930; fourth printing, August 1931; fifth printing, January 1934; sixth printing, November 1934; seventh printing, July 1935; eighth printing, December 1935; ninth printing, February 1937;

tenth printing, January 1938; eleventh printing, December 1938; twelfth printing, January 1940; thirteenth printing, December 1940; fourteenth printing, December 1941; fifteenth printing, November 1942; sixteenth printing, December 1943; seventeenth printing, December 1943; eighteenth printing, November 1944; nineteenth printing, April 1945; twentieth printing, February 1946; twentieth-first printing, June 1952; twenty-second printing, November 1953; twenty-third printing, August 1955. There also was a twenty-fourth printing in November 1956.

COPIES EXAMINED: CS (first printing; 1946, 1953, 1955, all in jacket; Apollo edition series; 1981 in paper); OTNY (first printing, no jacket; 1946, no jacket); (QMMRB (first printing, no jacket).

## A56a.1  *first Canadian issue* (1956):

LAUGH | *with* | LEACOCK | [ornament] | *An Anthology* | *of the Best* Work *of* | STEPHEN LEACOCK | [ornament] | McCLELLAND & STEWART LTD. | TORONTO CANADA

The verso of the title leaf indicates that this issue was published from the sheets of Dodd, Mead's twenty-fourth printing of November 1956. Bound in orange cloth with stamping in black as in the Dodd, Mead edition, except that McCLELLAND | & STEWART is at the foot of the spine. The dust jacket is also similar to Dodd, Mead's jacket. On the front, spine, and back panels is a colour collage of various dust jackets of Leacock's previously published books. The first two lines on the front panel are: The cream of Leacock's humor | in one volume! The last two lines are: Selected from fourteen popular | books by Stephen Leacock. On the top and bottom of the back panel are quotations from Irvin Cobb and Charles (Chic) Sale. The front and back flaps feature advertisements for *Laugh with Leacock* and *The Leacock Roundabout*, respectively.

COPIES EXAMINED: CS (twenty-fourth and twenty-seventh printings in jacket).

## A56a.2  *second Canadian issue* (1968):

Laugh | with | Leacock | [leafy ornament] | *An Anthology of the Best* Work | of *Stephen Leacock* | [publisher's device: abstract design within an oval of a person on a horse-drawn chariot, taking aim with a bow and arrow] | McClelland and Stewart Limited | *Toronto/Montreal*

This issue is a photographic reprint of A56a published by McClelland and Stewart in the Canadian Best-Seller Library Series (CBL 41). The copyright page is as follows: [seven lines concerning copyright holders] | ALL RIGHTS RESERVED | First paperback publication in Canadian | Best Seller Library, 1968 | *The Canadian Publishers* | McClelland and Stewart Limited | 25 Hollinger Road, Toronto 16 | Printed and bound in Canada. The leaves measure 176 × 109 mm. Perfect bound in pictorial stiff paper. The front cover has a colour illustration of a smiling mouth in the clouds above a town. The back cover is mainly gold, and has quotations from the *Financial Post*, J.B. Priestley, and the *Kingston Whig Standard* along with two paragraphs about the book. Price 95¢.

NOTES: Published in January 1968 in an edition of 25,585 copies. The Leacock estate received a royalty of 6% (information from the McClelland and Stewart fonds, OHM).

COPIES EXAMINED: CS (two copies); QMMRB.

**A56a.3** *third Canadian issue* (1983):

Stephen Leacock | Laugh with Leacock | New Canadian Library N176 | McClelland and Stewart

This issue is a photographic reprint of A56a published by McClelland and Stewart in the New Canadian Library Series (N176). The verso of the title is as follows: [six lines concerning copyright holders] | First paperback edition 1968 | NCL Edition published 1983 | [six lines about copyright] | 0-7710-9331-4 | *The Canadian Publishers* | McClelland and Stewart Limited | 25 Hollinger Road, Toronto. The verso of the last leaf has a list of selected New Canadian Library titles. An extra leaf (the recto has quotations from the *Financial Post*, J.B. Priestley, and the *Kingston Whig Standard*; the verso biographical information about Leacock) has been added at the beginning. The leaves measure 177 × 106 mm. Perfect bound in white stiff paper with the title in green and a black silhouette of Leacock on the front cover.

COPIES EXAMINED: CS.

**A56b** *second American edition* [1944]:

[all lines within two rectangles in two columns separated by a vertical rule; to the right of the vertical rule] LAUGH | *with* LEACOCK | *An Anthology* | *of the Best Work of* | STEPHEN LEACOCK | *Editions for the Armed Services, Inc.* | A NON-PROFIT ORGANIZATION SPONSORED BY THE | COUNCIL ON BOOKS IN WARTIME, NEW YORK | [remaining lines to the left of the vertical rule] PUBLISHED BY ARRANGEMENT WITH | DODD, MEAD & COMPANY, NEW YORK | *Manufactured in the United States of America*

◆ 1–9$^{16}$. *1–11*, 12–287, *1* pp. (144 leaves). 112 × 166 mm.

CONTENTS: p. *1* title; p. *2* [eleven lines about copyright] | *All rights reserved — no part of this book may | be reproduced in any form without permission in | writing from the publisher.*; pp. *3–4* preface by the editor addressed to Professor Leacock; pp. *5–7* tributes from other humorists; pp. *8–9* table of contents; p. *10* blank; pp. *11*, 12–287 text; p. *1* biographical information about Leacock.

TEXT: Identical to A56a.

BINDING: Bound in stiff paper, wire stabbed. The front cover is divided into two sections, black on the left side and yellow on the right, with a red band across the bottom extending over to the spine. A photograph of the Dodd, Mead edition is at an angle, and to the bottom left of the photograph within a solid light blue circle is the following in white: ARMED | SERVICES | EDITION. In the top left-hand corner in white is the series number G–197. To the right of the photo in the yellow section is the following: [the first two lines in red] LAUGH WITH | LEACOCK | [the next two lines in black] WIT AND HUMOR BY | STEPHEN LEACOCK | [seven lines in red about the Editions for the Armed Services]. Printed on the red band in white: THIS IS THE COMPLETE BOOK — NOT A DIGEST. The verso of the front cover has information on the Armed Services Editions with their logo.

   The title and Leacock's name are printed in white down the spine against a light blue background. Printed at the bottom of the spine in the red band is the series number in white. On the back of the wrapper is a red rectangular border with stars inside the border. Printed within the border against a yellow background is a paragraph in two columns about

Leacock's book and four lines about this edition. On the verso of the back cover is a list of books published by the Editions for the Armed Services, Inc. (G–181 to G–210).

NOTES: On 1 February 1944, Dodd, Mead allowed the Council on Books in Wartime to publish an edition. The royalty was 1¢ per copy printed (minimum quantity 50,000 copies). Published in April 1944 according to the copyright page of the Pocket Books' edition (A56c). See also *Editions for the Armed Services, Inc.: A History Together with the Complete List of 1324 Books Published for American Armed Forces Overseas* (New York: Editions for the Armed Services, Inc., [1948]).

COPIES EXAMINED: DLC; TEX.


## A56c  *third American edition* (1947):

LAUGH | WITH | LEACOCK | *An Anthology* | *of the Best Work of* | STEPHEN LEACOCK | [publisher's device: illustration of an encircled kangaroo, reading a book and with a book in its pouch] | *POCKET BOOKS, INC.* | *Rockefeller Center, New York*

♦  *i–ix*, x, 1–3, 4, 5–324, 1–2 pp. (168 leaves). 162 × 102 mm.

CONTENTS: p. *i* title; p. *ii* THE PRINTING HISTORY OF | Laugh with Leacock | [twenty-three lines within a rectangle giving a list of twenty previous printings by Dodd, Mead and the printing of the Armed Services edition] | Pocket Books edition published January, 1947 | 1st printing . . . . . . . . . . . . December, 1946 | [five lines stating that this new edition is complete, from a new set of plates, and easy to read] | PRINTED IN THE U. S. A. | [six lines concerning copyright]; pp. *iii–viii* preface with an introductory note from the editor addressed to Professor Leacock and tributes from fourteen other humorists; pp. *ix–x* table of contents; pp. 1–324 text; pp. *1–2* a selected list of Pocket Books, dated January 1947. Leacock's is no. 396.

TEXT: Identical to A56a.

BINDING: Perfect bound in coloured, glossy, pictorial stiff paper, all edges and endpapers stained red. The front cover has an illustration of a man (probably the Great Detective) in a green overcoat who comes out of the rain into a room and greets a couple in their bed clothes. The front cover also has the publisher's device (the circle in solid yellowish orange) and a unique number in red at the top, indicating the number of copies sold of the Pocket Book editions. The back cover has the heading A Pocketful of Laughs.

COPIES EXAMINED: CS (four copies).


## A56c.1  *Canadian issue of third American edition* (1947):

LAUGH | WITH | LEACOCK | *An Anthology* | *of the Best Work of* | STEPHEN LEACOCK | [publisher's device: illustration of an encircled kangaroo, reading a book and with a book in its pouch] | POCKET BOOKS OF CANADA LTD. | MONTREAL

According to the copyright page, this issue is from the second printing of this edition, December 1946, published in January 1947. The last leaf, dated January 1947, lists Pocket Book Best Sellers issued by Pocket Books of Canada, Ltd. The binding is almost the same as A56c; orange colours on A56c are red, the yellow circle on the spine of A56c is orange, and instead of having a unique number at the top of the front cover, the following lines appear in red: More than 152,000,000 | Pocket Books have been sold.

COPIES EXAMINED: CS.

## A56d *Japanese abridged edition* (1986):

Stephen Leacock | Laugh with Leacock | *edited with notes* | *by* | Akira Nishio | SANSYUSYA

◆ *i–iii*, iv–v, *1–3*, 1–46, 47, 48–66, *1–2* pp. (38 leaves). 210 × 149 mm.

CONTENTS: p. *i* title; p. *ii Laugh with Leacock | An Anthology of the Best Work of Stephen Leacock | by Stephen Leacock* | copyright © 1958 by Stephen Leacock | English reprint rights arranged with the Bodley Head Ltd. through | Japan UNI Agency, Inc. Tokyo; pp. *iii*–v editor's introduction in Japanese dated 1986; p. *1* blank; p. 2 table of contents; p. *3* blank; pp. 1–46 text; pp. 47–66 explanatory notes in Japanese; p. *1* copyright information in Japanese; p. 2 blank.

TEXT: My Financial Career; The Hallucination of Mr. Butt; Old Junk and New Money: A Study in the Latest Antiques; Simple Stories of Success; How to Succeed in Life; "We Have with Us To-night."

BINDING: Paperback, perfect bound with pictorial covers.

COPIES EXAMINED: OONL.

## A57 WET WIT & DRY HUMOUR 1931

[the first word of the first two lines in Egyptian type; the remaining words of the first two lines in an ornamental typeface] WET WIT & | DRY HUMOUR | DISTILLED FROM THE | PAGES OF | STEPHEN LEACOCK | [illustration of a waiter with a mustache standing behind a counter] | DODD • MEAD & COMPANY | NEW YORK MCMXXXI

◆ 1–17[8]. *i–vi*, vii–viii, *1–2*, 1–260, *1–2* pp. (136 leaves). 187 × 130 mm.

CONTENTS: p. *i* half-title; p. *ii* blank; p. *iii* title; p. *iv* COPYRIGHT, 1917, 1919, 1922, 1923, 1924, 1925, 1926, 1928, 1929, 1931 | BY DODD, MEAD AND COMPANY, INC. | All rights reserved — no part of this book may be | reproduced in any form without permission in | writing from the publisher. | PRINTED IN THE U. S. A. BY | Quinn & Boden Company, Inc. | [rule] | BOOK MANUFACTURERS | RAHWAY, NEW JERSEY; p. *v* This book is compiled in friendly appreciation of | Prohibition in the United States, the greatest thing | that ever happened — to Canada; p. *vi* blank; pp. vii–viii table of contents; p. *1* fly-title; p. 2 blank; pp. 1–260 text; pp. *1–2* blank.

TEXT: The Dry Pickwick: England's Greatest Writer Adapted to America's Greatest Legislation; The Revised or Dry Pickwick; A Mediaeval Hole in One: Wet Golf in Dry History; A Guide to the Province of Quebec for the Use of American Tourists; A Butler of the Old School As Transformed and Enlarged Under the Eighteenth Amendment; Confessions of a Soda Fiend Written from a Condemned Cell; Children's Poetry Revised with One Eye on the Eighteenth Amendment; Eddie the Bartender: A Ghost of the Bygone Past; First Call for Spring; or Oh, Listen to the Birds; An Experiment with Policeman Hogan; How to Be a

Doctor; A Study in Still Life. — The Country Hotel; The Lost Illusions of Mr. Sims; Cool Drinks for the Merry Month of May As Treated in the Bygone Almanacs; Literature and the Eighteenth Amendment; More Messages from Mars: A Personal Encounter with the First Martian Across; Conversations I Can Do without: Enough of Some People's Talk to Explain Why; The Errors of Santa Claus; This Strenuous Age; In Dry Toronto: A Local Study of a Universal Topic; Letters to a Prohibitionist; The Dry Banquet; Is Prohibition Coming to England?; Why I Refuse to Play Golf; L'Envoi: In Praise of the Americans.

BINDING AND DUST JACKET: The binding is in camel buckram with printing in blue, top edge stained blue. Stamped on the upper board: [the first word of the first two lines in Egyptian type; the remaining words of the first two lines in an ornamental typeface] WET WIT & | DRY HUMOUR | [illustration of a bottle] | STEPHEN LEACOCK. Stamped on the spine: WET | WIT | & | DRY | HU- | MOUR | [ornamental rule and above the right side of the rule:] • | [the next line hand-written] | *Leacock* | [illustration of goblet with 5¢ on it] | DODD, MEAD | *&* COMPANY.

The dust jacket is in camel and blue with printing in both colours. On the front panel: [the first two lines in blue as on title page and upper board; below the first two lines is the same illustration as on the title page, but the background is filled in with bottles, and is signed "arthur hawkins" in brown; below the illustration in blue:] STEPHEN LEACOCK. The spine panel of the jacket is blue with printing in brown and white, and is similar to the spine of the book. The back panel is as follows: [the first two lines in blue] "Not Many but Good Books" | — BAYARD TAYLOR | [the next line in brown] | A distinguished group of new novels from the Dodd, Mead spring list | [three blue rules; the next twenty-seven lines describe six new books published by Dodd, Mead (*Wet Wit and Dry Humour* being the fifth book described); three blue rules] | [the next line in blue] DODD, MEAD AND COMPANY • Publishers Since 1839 | [the remaining three lines in the lower left corner in brown, the first and third lines curved] | PRINTED | IN | U.S.A. The flaps are printed in brown. The front flap has the price, title, author's name, blurb, and publisher's name, and the back flap provides similar information for *Laugh with Leacock* priced at $2.50.

The endpapers are cream-coloured, and have the same illustration as the illustration on the front of the jacket.

NOTES: On 19 October 1930, Frank Dodd wrote to Leacock:

> Mr. [Raymond T.] Bond of our staff, who compiled the anthology [*Laugh with Leacock*] (which by the way is starting off very well) suggests that if you have no new book for 1931, we might bring out a collection of your essays dealing with prohibition. He tells me that there are enough of them to make a small book, and it ought to be very amusing. Would you have any objection to this?

Leacock gave his assent to the idea on 21 November 1930, but he did not think that his English publisher would be interested in the book. On 8 December 1930, Dodd advised Leacock: "If you can send us the new material for the Prohibition book promptly, I am inclined to bring this out in the spring, the earlier the better. Would February be too soon for you? It all depends on when the extra 10,000 words will be available, and the selection of a good title." Leacock replied that he could easily write another 10,000 words in time, and he suggested the title: *Wet and Dry Humour from the Pages of Stephen Leacock*.

The contract with Dodd, Mead is dated 15 December 1930 (copies in the Dodd, Mead fonds at OHM and the Barbara Nimmo collection at NAC). Leacock received 10% royalty on the first 4,000 copies sold and 15% thereafter. There was a 10% royalty on copies sold in Canada. On 14 January 1931, Leacock informed Dodd that he had written "an opening piece called Dry Pickwick. It runs well over 6,000 words. . . ." He suggested a change of title. Dodd (16 January 1931) reacted negatively to this suggestion: "I am rather sorry that you are so steamed up about the new title, as we all feel here that the original title, WET WIT AND DRY HUMOR, fits the book perfectly, is shorter, and stamps the book for exactly what it is, without raising the question which might be raised as to what is a 'Dry Pickwick.' " By this time the jacket and plates had already been made. On 17 March 1931, Dodd, Mead requested Leacock to return the corrected proofs. Leacock complied on 25 March.

According to Bond's letter to Gerhard Lomer (7 September 1950 in Lomer's papers at QMM Archives), the book was published on 8 May 1931; this date of publication is the same at the one at the Copyright Office at DLC. Price $2. According to the copyright page of the second reprinting, printings occurred in April of that year. The copyright was registered on 13–14 May 1931 (ClA37314). The copyright was renewed by Stephen Lushington Leacock on 12 March 1959 (R232746). Curtis Brown Ltd. informed Frank Dodd on 16 June 1931: "[B.W.] Willett [of The Bodley Head] is not agreeable to 'WET WIT AND DRY HUMOUR' being published in England in this form."

By 1 February 1931, 2,284 copies had sold in the United States ($.20 per book, $456.80 royalty). In addition, one copy ("Spec Sale"), 265 copies in Canada ($.20 per copy, $53 royalty), and 34 copies sold in foreign countries ($3.20 royalty). Between 1 August 1931 and 1 August 1933, 343 copies sold (116 copies in Canada) The book was still in print as of 1 February 1944 when Dodd, Mead reported to Leacock's niece, Barbara Nimmo, that for the previous three years the book had earned a royalty of $22.21 on American and Canadian sales.

COPIES EXAMINED: CS (first and second printings in jacket); QMMRB (first printing in jacket).

## A58 BACK TO PROSPERITY 1932

### A58a *Canadian edition*:

BACK TO PROSPERITY | The Great Opportunity of | The Empire Conference | *By* | STEPHEN LEACOCK | B.A., Ph.D., LL.D., Litt. D., F.R.S.C. | Head of the Department of Economics and Political Science, McGill University, Montreal | [publisher's device: rectangle containing leaves, three open books, shield, motto on a banner (FOLIA INTER FOLIA), and publisher's name] | TORONTO: THE MACMILLAN COMPANY OF | CANADA LIMITED, AT ST. MARTIN'S HOUSE | 1932

◆ $1-4^8 5^8 (+/-57) 6^8 7^{10}$. 1–8, 108 pp. (58 leaves). 190 × 124 mm. There was a printing error on p. 69. As a result, the original leaf, which was lacking the final line, was replaced with a cancellans. In some copies, however, the original leaf was not cancelled.

CONTENTS: p. *1* half title; p. *2* blank; p. *3* title; p. *4* Copyright, Canada, 1932 | by | THE MACMILLAN COMPANY OF CANADA LIMITED | [three lines concerning copyright] | PRINTED IN CANADA; p. *5* table of contents; p. *6* blank; p. *7* fly title; p. *8* blank; pp. *1*–108 text.

TEXT: chapter I The Background of the Conference; chapter II Empire Trade; chapter III Currency and the Gold Standard; chapter IV Can Silver Come Back?; chapter V Summary and Conclusion.

BINDING AND DUST JACKET: There are two variant bindings, one in dark blue cloth and the other in light blue cloth, both with lettering in black. The upper board is stamped as follows: BACK TO | PROSPERITY | [rule] | STEPHEN LEACOCK. Stamped down the spine: BACK TO PROSPERITY [diamond containing a solid diamond] Leacock MAC-MILLAN.

The dust jacket is beige with printing in blue. On the front panel: BACK | TO | [arrow pointing diagonally to the next line, which is printed diagonally to the left of the first two lines] | PROSPERITY | [remaining lines to the left of the previous line] THE GREAT | OPPORTUNITY | OF THE | EMPIRE CONFERENCE | by | STEPHEN LEACOCK. On the back panel of the jacket, within two rectangles, the outer one thick, are excerpts from reviews of *Economic Prosperity in the British Empire*. Printing on the spine panel repeats the same line found on the spine of the book.

NOTES: In November 1931 Leacock informed Hugh Eayrs of the Macmillan Company of Canada that he was working on another book, a successor to *Economic Prosperity in the British Empire* (A54). The Imperial Economic Conference was meeting in Ottawa during the summer of 1932, and Leacock saw it as an opportunity once again to present his case of reduced trade barriers within the Empire. He had "recently been writing a lot of stuff (syndicated) on current economics affecting the empire (gold standard, prosperity, silver, etc.). . . ." His plan was to reformulate these writings into a more coherent package. He promised to finish the book in twenty-five days or less on the understanding that the Macmillan Company of Canada would rush it into print. He suggested "ten per cent royalty with a suitable advance or guarantee." He received an advance of $300 for all editions. On 8 December 1931 he announced that with the exception of some awkward figures, the book was finished. A few days later three copies of the typescript were sent to the Macmillan Company. Eayrs was instructed to handle all markets and to issue advance publicity in the press. A review article on the front page of the *Toronto Daily Star* (Frederick Griffin, "Thomas Hit Nail on the Head When He Cried 'Humbug', Stephen Leacock Says 25,000,000 Unemployed Could Stage a War with Benefit, Cancel War Debts," 21 December 1931, pp. 1–2) was arranged by Eayrs several weeks prior to publication. The book underwent several title changes. On the draft of the circular used for promotional purposes (no copy extant), the title is recorded as "The Coming Imperial Conference and the Return to Prosperity". Leacock cabled the final title on 9 December 1931.

The galley proofs bearing editorial corrections were sent to Leacock on 28 December 1931. He returned them two days later. His own alterations to the proofs cost $10.50. Printing (on Old Vale Antique Laid paper) and binding were done by the Hunter Rose Co. Six copies were apparently finished by 4 January 1932, but the major printing job was undertaken by 8 January when 494 copies were delivered to the Macmillan Company. The production card for the book at OHM records a total of 2,014 copies delivered (6 copies on 7 January 1932, 494 copies on 8 January 1932, 250 copies on 25 February 1932, 250 copies on 13 May 13 1932, and 1,014 copies on 15 January 1934). The total cost for printing and binding for an edition of 2,000 copies was $539.60 (26.76¢ per copy). The type was ordered distributed on 27 August 1932. On 5 January 1932, Eayrs arranged for Leacock to receive his advance of $300. The book was published on 9 January 1932. The Macmillan Company of Canada registered the copyright at the Copyright Office of DLC on 27 January 1932 (ClAint.16012). The book sold for $1.

On 9 February 1932 Eayrs informed Leacock that some 4,000 circulars for the book had gone to members of the Toronto Board of Trade, the Empire Club, and the Montreal Board of Trade. He added: "The book is getting interesting attention. So far its sales have been light, but then frankly there isn't one book of any sort or kind that is selling. In all my years in the game I have never known the book business quite so bad." In a royalty report of sales up to 31 March 1932, 801 copies had sold.

COPIES EXAMINED: CS (both variant bindings in jacket); QMMRB (light blue cloth with cancel; dark blue cloth, one in jacket, neither with a cancel).

## A58a.1 *American issue*:

BACK TO PROSPERITY | The Great Opportunity of | The Empire Conference | *By* | STEPHEN LEACOCK | B.A., Ph.D., LL.D., Litt. D., F.R.S.C. | Head of the Department of Economics and Political Science, McGill University, Montreal | NEW YORK | THE MACMILLAN COMPANY | 1932

♦ $1-6^8 \ 7^{10}$. *1–8*, 1–108 pp. (58 leaves). 187 × 125 mm.

The sheets of the American issue are identical to those of the Canadian edition with the exceptions of the title leaf and p. 69. In the American issue the following line is missing from the bottom of p. 69: "Here there was a dilemma. One way the". The copyright page in the American issue reads as follows: Copyright, 1932 | by THE MACMILLAN COMPANY | [rule] | [six lines regarding copyright] | [rule] | Printed and published, February, 1932. | Printed in the United States of America.

BINDING AND DUST JACKET: Bound in dark blue cloth with the following stamped in gold on the spine: BACK | TO | PROSPERITY | [rule] | LEACOCK | MACMILLAN | ._.

The dust jacket is pink with printing in blue. Printed on the front panel of the jacket: [all lines within five rectangles, the outer ones thick, the middle one ornamental; the first two lines in rimmed type] BACK TO | PROSPERITY | The Great Opportunity of | the Empire Conference | [the next line in rimmed type] BY STEPHEN LEACOCK | Head of the Department of Political Economy | in McGill University, Montreal. Printed vertically up the spine panel of the jacket: Macmillan [open bar] BACK TO PROSPERITY [open bar] Leacock. On the front flap is the title, Leacock's name, his academic position, blurb, publisher's name, and price. The back panel and the back flap are blank.

NOTES: Eayrs told Leacock on 7 December 1931: "You will also like to hear that I have arranged with The Macmillan Company, New York, to manufacture the book there." The American branch of the Macmillans paid Leacock 12½% royalty with an advance of $100. Eayrs sent the manuscript to H.S. Latham on 17 December 1931. Published on 8 February 1932, the American issue was printed from offset plates using photographs of the page proofs of the Canadian edition. "New York are doing a rather unusual thing," Eayrs informed Leacock on 5 January 1932. "We are sending our forms down as they come off the press and they are photographing them and plating from photographs instead of setting type and going through the whole business of author's corrections. They expect to be out on Saturday also." Published on 16 February 1932. The copyright was registered at the Copyright Office of DLC on 17–18 February 1932 (ClA48551). The number of copies printed is not known. The book sold for $1. In a royalty report of sales up to 31 March 1932, 326 copies had sold.

COPIES EXAMINED: CS (price clipped on jacket).


**A58b** *English edition*:

BACK TO PROSPERITY | THE GREAT OPPORTUNITY OF | THE EMPIRE CONFERENCE | *by* | STEPHEN LEACOCK | B.A., PH.D., LL.D., LITT.D., F.R.S.C. | *Head of the Department of Economics* | *and Political Science, McGill University,* | *Montreal* | CONSTABLE & CO LTD | LONDON | 1932

♦ A⁴ B–G⁸ H⁴ [$1 signed]. *1–6*, v, *1–3, 3–24, 25–26, 27–53, 54–56, 57–78, 79–80, 81–98, 99–100, 101–102, 1–2* pp. (56 leaves). 183 × 123 mm.

CONTENTS: pp. *1–2* blank; p. *3* half title; p. *4 Also by Stephen Leacock* | ECONOMIC PROSPERITY IN THE | BRITISH EMPIRE | [26 lines of excerpts from reviews] | THE ELEMENTS | OF POLITICAL SCIENCE; p. *5* title; p. *6* PUBLISHED BY | *Constable and Company Ltd.* | LONDON | • | *Oxford University Press* | BOMBAY CALCUTTA MADRAS | • | *The Macmillan Company* | *of Canada, Limited* | TORONTO | Printed in Great Britain by Butler & Tanner Ltd., Frome and London; p. v table of contents; p. *1* blank; p. *2* blank; pp. *3–4, 3–102, 1* text (pp. *4, 26, 54, 56, 80,* and *100* blank); pp. *2* blank.

BINDING AND DUST JACKET: Bound in green cloth with a black rectangle stamped on the upper board and the following stamped in black on the spine: [rule] | BACK | TO | PROSPERITY | LEACOCK | CONSTABLE | [rule].

The dust jacket is pale yellow with lettering printed in green. Printed on the front panel: [all lines within two rectangles, the outer one thick; the first ten lines within a separate rectangle] BACK TO | PROSPERITY | The | Great Opportunities | of the Empire Conference | by | STEPHEN LEACOCK | author of | Economic Prosperity in the | British Empire | [remaining lines within a separate rectangle] The Background of | the Conference | Empire Trade | [the next three lines are to the right of the previous three lines divided by a vertical rule] | Currency and the | Gold Standard | Can Silver come back | Summary and Conclusion. Printed on the spine panel of the jacket: BACK TO | PROS- | PERITY | [ornament] | STEPHEN | LEACOCK | [vertical rule] | 3/6 | net | [ornament] | CONSTABLE. On the back panel within two rectangles, the outer one thick, is an ad for *Economic Prosperity in the British Empire* (with excerpts from reviews), which is said to be "Uniform with this volume". The flaps provide a summary of the book with the price.

NOTES: Eayrs arranged the publication of the English edition. On 21 November 1931, Constable and Company Ltd. indicated its agreement to publish an English edition. Leacock received a royalty of 10% (15% after 10,000 copies) with an advance of £50. The memorandum of agreement between the Macmillan Company of Canada and Constable is dated 31 December 1931. On 15 February 1932, Eayrs told Leacock that the manuscript had been sent to Constable on 17 December 1931. Constable received the manuscript on 2 January 1932. They informed Leacock on 17 February 1932: "Unfortunately the signing of the contract was delayed: we did not, in fact, get it back here signed until the 11th of January. We then immediately put the manuscript in hand." The delay in publication upset both Leacock and Eayrs. On 18 February 1932, Eayrs complained to O. Kyllmann of Constable: "Leacock has been extremely troubled because you have not yet published BACK

TO PROSPERITY. . . . The book was published here on January 8th, and has been published by Macmillan in New York for some ten days, yet the British market which Leacock is very concerned about is not yet served." On 21 February 1932, Leacock wrote to Eayrs:

> It seems to me that Constable's have been guilty of a breach of contract which has had for me very serious financial consequences. But apart from money I can't conceal from you my disappointment and indignation that the publication of the book should have been delayed till after the great tariff debate on the introduction of protection in Eng. The whole purpose of my hurried & desperate work on this book for the sake of which I threw aside everything else was to get it before the public in plenty of time in the hope it might contribute to influence public opinion.

Coupled with the overpayment problem that Leacock incurred with respect to *Economic Prosperity in the British Empire*, Constable's publication delay resulted in a lack of faith on Leacock's part about Eayrs's publishing acumen. He wrote to Eayrs on 14 March 1932: "If Constable had got the book out in January by this time they would have sold thousands & I would have had the money. What am I to do about that? What redress have I got for that? Is that claim against you, or against Constable?" He suggested an alternative to Eayrs: that either the claim for overpaid royalties on *Economic Prosperity in the British Empire* would remain outstanding until sufficient royalties had accumulated on *Back to Prosperity* or that all relevant documents would be submitted to his Toronto lawyer, M.G.L. Smith of Smith, Rae & Greer. Eayrs was sympathetic to Leacock's grievance. On 17 March 1932, he offered to meet with Leacock and his lawyer to discuss the contracts. With regard to the overpayment problem he informed Leacock that the auditors were putting pressure on him to have it repaid (Leacock had agreed to do so the previous summer) and that also Leacock had already been paid an advance on the Canadian edition of *Back to Prosperity*: "There is no fuss between you and me," he told Leacock. "I should dislike it even more than you. As I say above, I shall be delighted to talk with Mr. Smith, but what the devil two friends want to refer a matter of this kind to an attorney, despite the excellence of that attorney, for, I don't know." Leacock's lawyer advised him to make good the overpayment to the Macmillan Company of Canada because no court would award him damages for delay in publication unless an actual loss in revenue could be proven. Leacock followed his lawyer's advice. "I grant that I cannot prove likely what I would have done and would not have done as there was no contract with the penalty clause in it and there no provable damages," Leacock admitted on 20 March 1932. In a five-page letter to Leacock Eayrs pleaded: "You know how I feel about Constable's delay in publishing BACK TO PROSPERITY. Everything was done here to get them to bring it out swiftly, just as the Toronto and New York editions came out swiftly. I have only to add that I have acted from beginning to end in complete good faith, as you know I would act." The English edition was published on 21 March 1932. Eayrs sent Leacock an author's copy of the Constable edition on 11 April 1932. The number of copies printed is not known. In a royalty report of sales up to 31 March 1932, 941 copies had sold.

COPIES EXAMINED: CS (in jacket); QMMRB (in jacket).

## A59 THE DRY PICKWICK 1932

THE | DRY PICKWICK | AND OTHER INCONGRUITIES | by | STEPHEN LEACOCK | LONDON | JOHN LANE THE BODLEY HEAD LIMITED

◆ A⁴ B–I¹⁶ K⁸ L⁴ [$1 signed]. *i–iv*, v, *1–3*, 1–36, *37–38*, 39–46, *47–48*, 49–63, *64–66*, 67–76, *77–78*, 79–85, *86–88*, 89–93, *94–96*, 97–104, *105–106*, 107–119, *120–122*, 123–137, *138–140*, 141–148, *149–150*, 151–156, *157–158*, 159–164, *165–166*, 167–172, *173–174*, 175–179, *180–182*, 183–193, *194–196*, 197–203, *204–206*, 207–213, *214–216*, 217–227, *228–230*, 231–238, *239–240*, 241–247, *248–250*, 251–260, *261–262*, 263–271, *1–9* pp. (144 leaves). 185 × 121 mm.

CONTENTS: p. *i* half-title; p. *ii* list of twenty books by Leacock published by The Bodley Head, the first being *Literary Lapses* and the last *The Leacock Book*; p. *iii* title; p. *iv* First *Published in 1932* | Made and Printed in Great Britain by Butler & Tanner Ltd., Frome and London; p. v table of contents; p. *1* blank; pp. 2–3, *1–271* text (pp. *3, 38, 48, 64, 66, 78, 86, 88, 93, 96, 106, 120, 122, 138, 140, 150, 158, 166, 174, 180, 182, 194, 196, 204, 206, 214, 216, 228, 230, 240, 248, 250,* and *262* blank); p. *1* blank; pp. 2–9 advertisements, the first three for Leacock's books.

TEXT: The Dry Pickwick: England's Greatest Writer Adapted to America's Greatest Legislation; Ratification of the New Naval Disagreement (An Extract from the Annual Register of 1933); A Mediæval Hole in One: Wet Golf in Dry History; The Great War As Recorded by Mr. William Shakespeare; If the Gandhi Habit Spreads; In Praise of the Americans; Once to Everyman; Confessions of a Soda Fiend Written from a Condemned Cell; A Guide to the Province of Quebec for the Use of American Tourists; Why the Next War Didn't Happen; A, B, and C After Twenty Years; Breakfast at the Smiths': A Little Study in the Beauty of Cheerfulness; The Perfect Optimist or Day-Dreams in a Dental Chair; Children's Poetry Revised with One Eye on the Eighteenth Amendment; "Tum and Play Dolf"; Ho for Happiness: A Plea for Lighter and Brighter Literature; Tennis at the Smiths': A Simple Statement of the Facts; A Butler of the Old School; The Flying Carpet; Come and See Our Town: How the Visitor Feels When Shown Around; Inflation and Deflation or Flation in and de; L'Envoi: What Next? A Glimpse into Our Ultimate Future.

BINDING AND DUST JACKET: Bound in purple cloth with stamping in white, top edge stained purple. Stamped on the upper board: [the first line in ornamental type] STEPHEN LEACOCK | [the remaining lines in rustic type] THE | DRY PICKWICK. Stamped on the spine: [the first three lines in rustic type] THE | DRY | PICKWICK | [the next three lines in ornamental type] STEPHEN | LEACOCK | *THE BODLEY HEAD*.

The dust jacket is pale green with printing in black. On the front panel: [the first three lines in rustic type] THE | DRY PICKWICK | BY STEPHEN LEACOCK | [below all lines within a rectangular compartment is an illustration (apparently signed MC) of four men in Victorian dress being held up by a thief in more contemporary dress who is carrying a gun and a bottle]. On the spine panel of the jacket: [the first four lines in rustic type] THE DRY | PICKWICK | STEPHEN | LEACOCK | 5/– | net | THE BODLEY HEAD. On the back panel within a rectangle is a list of Leacock's books and within another rectangle are extracts from reviews of *The Iron Man and the Tin Woman*. On the front flap is a synopsis of *The Dry Pickwick*. The back flap has extracts from reviews of *The Leacock Book*.

Notes: The contract for the book was sent to Leacock in March 1931, although he had not returned it to The Bodley Head as of 29 February 1932. He returned it in April 1932, but

B.W. Willett sent it back to him because Leacock had forgotten to sign it. The copy at SLM is dated 9 October 1929, the copy in the Barbara Nimmo collection at NAC is undated, and the one at READ is dated 18 April 1932. Leacock received a royalty of 15% on the first 4,000 copies sold and 20% thereafter. Willett wrote to Leacock on 6 October 1931: "I am very glad to get your letter of the 26th September and to know that there is really a chance of 'The Dry Pickwick' coming along." On 26 October 1931, Leacock cabled: "If forty thousand words enough could send Dry Pickwick Dec First even Nov fifteenth if Xmas market Possible. Cable." It was in fact too late for the Christmas market since at least six weeks were needed to print, bind, and publish the book. Moreover, booksellers were not keen to take on extra books after the first week of December. Willett suggested that Leacock send the manuscript for publication in January or February. The manuscript arrived at The Bodley Head on 16 November 1931. Willett mailed two sets of proofs to Leacock on 11 December 1931. "I know that you don't care about correcting your own proofs so I am having them done here," Willett added. On 1 January 1932, Willett told Leacock: "With regard to the date of publication, we shall not be able to publish 'Dry Pickwick' until February and we ought to give that a run for at least two or three months before we do another one of yours." Willett sent Leacock a proof of the "first rate wrapper" by this time. Leacock sent a cable in which he pointed out a "misprint in the Mediaeval story." Willett informed him on 8 January 1932: "However, though the book is printed, it is not yet bound so I am able to put in a cancel page in which it will be all right." In point of fact, the offending page was not replaced by a cancel.

Leacock wrote to Willett on 9 January 1932:

> I am so glad to hear such good news of *Dry Pickwick*. You will recall that this book as originally proposed was to be partly reprinted from others, as was *Wet Wit & Dry Humour*, the American sister book. On that account I put the royalty low & cut out all advance royalty.
>
> As it turns out, the book is all new stuff just the same as any other.
>
> I ask no change in the amount (percentage) of the royalty but would you perhaps send me an advance on publication of whatever you feel the sales justify. . . . Like all people here I fought this hard winter, — dividends cut & capital unsaleable [sic], heavy taxes & low receipts. Hence these tears. (The Bodley Head fonds, READ)

Willett replied on 21 January, and promised to pay a subscription advance within a week of publication. He hoped that Leacock would be able to ". . . sell a Canadian edition of this to McClelland [and Stewart]." But there was no Canadian edition or issue. The book was published on 19 February 1932.

In their royalty report of 25 February 1932, The Bodley Head recorded that 1,852 copies had sold in England at 15% royalty (£69 9s, less income tax of £17 7s 3d, earning £52 1s 9d) and that a further 1,037 copies had sold to the colonies at 10% royalty (£15 11s 1d). Willett informed Leacock on 29 February 1932: "With regard to the sales of 'The Dry Pickwick', the subscription was a little disappointing but both the booksellers and circulating libraries are very cautious in their buying at the present time and our travellers are confident that the book will do well, so I shall hope to let you have better news shortly."

On 22 January 1936 surplus sheet stock was disposed of at 4d per copy. This stock was presumably used in the composite volume, *Laughter & Wisdom of Stephen Leacock* (see A75).

COPIES EXAMINED: CS.

## A60 LAHONTAN'S VOYAGES 1932

LAHONTAN'S | VOYAGES | Edited with Introduction and Notes | *by* | STEPHEN LEACOCK, B.A. Ph. D. | [publisher's device: Thunder Bird within a circle (designed by Alan Beddoe)] | 1932 | GRAPHIC PUBLISHERS LIMITED | OTTAWA CANADA

♦ 1–23$^8$. i–iv, v–xvi, 1–337, *338*, 339–348, *1–4* pp. (184 leaves). 198 × 121 mm.

CONTENTS: p. *i* THE CANADA SERIES | GENERAL EDITOR, LAWRENCE J. BURPEE | [two rules] | VOLUME THREE | [rule] | LAHONTAN'S VOYAGES; p. *ii* photographic reproduction of title page of volume II of the 1703 edition of Lahontan's *New Voyages to North-America*; p. *iii* title; p. *iv* THE CANADA SERIES | *Copyright in Canada, 1932* | PRODUCED ENTIRELY IN CANADA | *At the Printing House of* | GRAPHIC PUBLISHERS LIMITED; pp. v–xvi Introduction: Lahontan and His Times; pp. 1–337 text of Lahontan's book; p. *338* blank; pp. 339–348 editorial notes; pp. *1–4* blank.

BINDING: There are two binding variants. One is in black cloth with LAHONTAN'S | VOYAGES stamped in gilt on the upper board and LAHON- | TAN'S | VOYAGES on the spine. The other variant is in black limp cloth. On the upper board stamping is as follows: [all lines within an ornamental compartment] LAHONTAN'S | VOYAGES. Stamped on the spine: LAHON- | TAN'S | VOYAGES | [floral ornament] | [publisher's device] | GRAPHIC | [ornament].

NOTES: Graphic Publishers, a small commercial publishing house in Ottawa devoted exclusively to the publication of Canadian books, issued its first book in 1925 and went bankrupt in 1932. Leacock's edition of *Lahontan's Voyages* was the third volume of Graphic's Canada Series and the last book published by Graphic.

In the copy of this book at the Friedman collection in QMMRB, there is a lengthy inscription by Leacock:

> I received, through Dr. Burpee c/ Ottawa, a contract with the Graphic Co to do an introduction to Lahontan's journal with notes. . . The company failed & paid nothing. . . But I found out long afterwards that some copies of the book had gone through the press though it was never in the market. I was never able to get a copy.
>
> Lahontan was in my opinion not a liar but a great explorer the first in upper Minnesota. His opposition to the church occasioned his exile and defaced his reputation.
>
> See my paper to & printed by the Minnesota historical society about ? 1927 ? (see D33.9)

On 26 September 1931, Leacock informed the editor of the series, Lawrence J. Burpee, that he had already finished his preface (5,000 words). He wondered whether the Graphic Publishers would set it into type and advertise the book as forthcoming. By 14 October Leacock had started on the editorial notes.

During the period that he was editing the book, Leacock also sent Burpee "Baron de Lahontan, Explorer" for publication in the *Canadian Geographical Journal* (see C32.7). Burpee was the journal's editor, and on 23 October 1931, he told Leacock that he offered "no editorial dissent to your conclusions which are the result of careful study." Burpee added in a postscript: "The Lahontan you have been editing is a reprint of the English edition of 1703, edited by Reuben G. Thwaites and published in Chicago, 1905."

Leacock sent the proofs of the book back to Burpee on 1 February [1932], although he regarded the small type as unfortunate. A few copies were sent out for review (see William Hoffer's List no. 58 (September 1984), item 101, which offered a review copy dated 26 April 1932). Graphic's catalogue for 1931–32 indicates that the book was in fact published ($2.50). Number of copies printed not known.

In his last letter to Burpee (20 May 1932), however, Leacock stated that the copyright in the preface belonged to him, not with Graphic, and that Graphic was not entitled to sell the book without having acquired such copyright. On 15 May 1932, Leacock transferred the rights in the book to the Macmillan Company of Canada on the condition that the edition would be reset completely. The Macmillan Company never issued the book. Leacock also inquired about the book's publication with Houghton, Mifflin Co. in November 1932, but the American publisher informed him on 11 January 1933 ". . . that under present publishing conditions it seems inadvisable for us to undertake the book."

In her autobiography *The Side Door: Twenty-Six Years in My Book Room* (Toronto: Ryerson, 1958, pp. 78–79), the antiquarian bookseller, Dora Hood, relates that in 1935 a copy of the book was advertised in one of her catalogues (catalogue 15, item no. 242). Leacock apparently sent her a letter by special delivery and ordered the book. On 26 March 1936, he asked Hood who the publisher was, and he raised concern about the copyright and "the legality of selling it" (information based on Leacock's letters to Burpee in the possession of Peter E. Greig; Burpee and Hood's letters to Leacock at SLM; and Houghton, Mifflin fonds at HOUGHT).

COPIES EXAMINED: CS (both variant bindings); OORI (black cloth); QMMRB (black cloth).

## A61 AFTERNOONS IN UTOPIA 1932

### A61a *American edition*:

[the first three lines hand-lettered at different angles] AFTERNOONS | [the next line interspersed with three stars and two planets] IN UTOPIA | STEPHEN LEACOCK | [ribbon rule] | Tales of the New Time | [ribbon rule] | DODD, MEAD & COMPANY | NEW YORK MCMXXXII

♦ 1–14$^8$ 15$^2$. i–iv, v–vi, 1–2, 3–36, 37–38, 39–77, 78–80, 81–99, 100–102, 103–161, 162–164, 165–205, 206–208, 209–221, 1 pp. (114 leaves). 187 × 130 mm.

CONTENTS: p. *i* half title; p. *ii* list of nineteen books by Leacock, the first being *Literary Lapses* and the last *Wet Wit and Dry Humour*; p. *iii* title; p. *iv* COPYRIGHT, 1932, | BY DODD, MEAD AND COMPANY, INC. | [three lines about copyright] | PRINTED IN THE U. S. A. BY | Quinn & Boden Company, Inc. | [rule] | BOOK MANUFACTURERS | RAHWAY, NEW JERSEY; pp. *v–vi* table of contents; pp. *1–221* text (pp. *2, 38, 78, 80, 100, 102, 162, 164, 206,* and *208* blank); p. *1* blank.

TEXT: The text consists of six parts: I Utopia Old and New; II Grandfather Goes to War; III The Doctor and the Contraption; IV Rah! Rah! College or, Tom Buncom at Shucksford: A Picture of the College of the Future; V The Band of Brothers: Being the Memoirs of a Future Communist; VI A Fragment from Utopia: The Fifty-Fifty Sexes. Each part consists of chapters.

Part I: chapter I Dear Old Utopia; chapter II Ten Seconds for Refreshments; chapter III The Real Utopia.

Part II: chapter I War Stuff; chapter II He Goes in A.D. 1810; chapter III He Goes in 1950; chapter IV With the League of Nations, A.D. 2000 or So; chapter V War in Utopia, Later Still; chapter VI War Extracts from the Press of A.D. 2050.

Part III: chapter I Medicine As It Was; chapter II Medicine Year, 1932: The Doctor and the Contraption; chapter III The Walrus and the Carpenter.

Part IV chapter I Introduction — Anno Domini 1880; chapter II A First Day at College; chapter III The Rah Rah Life; chapter IV Danger Ahead; chapter V Sunk and Saved!; chapter VI College in Utopia; chapter VII The Dissolution of Shucksford College A.D. 2000.

Part V: chapter I Reflections on the Fall of Capitalism Written A.D. 2020; chapter II Our Courts of Justice; chapter III Our System in Operation; chapter IV Lights and Shadows; chapter V Revolution.

Part VI: chapter I The Fifty-Fifty Sexes.

BINDING AND DUST JACKET: Bound in pale green cloth. The first three lines on the upper board are the same as those on the title page. Stamped on the spine: [the first four lines and the sixth line hand-lettered at different angles] AFTER- | NOONS | IN | UTOPIA | [illustration of jester's stick] | LEACOCK | DODD, MEAD | & COMPANY.

On the front and spine panels of the jacket is an illustration in blue, brown, and black by Eldon Kelley of Leacock in an overcoat, suit, and hat standing on top of the globe with a pile of books stacked near his feet and planets and stars in the firmament. The back panel in blue and black against a white background has a list of seven fiction leaders from the fall list of Dodd, Mead. On the front flap is a synopsis of the book with the price ($2). The back flap advertises *Laugh with Leacock* with adulatory comments by George Ade, Robert Benchley, and Ellis Parker Butler.

NOTES: When Frank Dodd asked Leacock on 16 December 1931 whether he wanted to announce a new volume of essays, Leacock enthusiastically replied on 20 December 1931:

> Your letter just came at the right time. I plan for the spring a new book Afternoons in Utopia, to be made up of stories and sketches all turning on our economic and political future. I send you a blurb herewith which will show you just what was intended. Not one of the stories is written so there will hardly be time to get more than 1 or 2 of them in magazines. But I won't wait. Life is too short. . . .

Dodd was immediately receptive, but he did not want to publish the book during the period between April and June 1932, since, generally, that was "the slackest season of the year" (22 December 1931). The contract with Dodd, Mead is dated 23 December 1931 (copies at OHM and the Barbara Nimmo collection at NAC). Leacock agreed to deliver the manuscript by 1 April 1932. He received 15% royalty on all copies sold, 20% after 10,000 copies, with an advance of $1,000 to be paid on the day of publication. Leacock was asked to send another blurb on 9 February to advertise the book. By 22 June 1932 he had sent the manuscript to Dodd, Mead. On 23 September 1932, the day of publication, Dodd, Mead sent Leacock an advance of $920 ($1,000 minus 8% alien tax). Copies were received by the Copyright Office at DLC on 26 September 1932, and the copyright was registered two days later (ClA56110). The copyright was renewed by Stephen Lushington Leacock on 7 June 1960 (R257893).

It was Leacock's opinion on 16 December 1932 that the dust jacket of the book hampered sales. R.T. Bond wrote a memo to Dodd on 21 December 1932 that was passed to Leacock. Bond could not agree with Leacock's judgment: "When we discussed a jacket early last summer, it was decided not use the old John Held style, as we felt there was too much of that particular type of drawing on the market and its appeal had been blunted." Bond pointed out that *Afternoons in Utopia* had been widely circulated and reviewed, but unfortunately, times were tough and people generally were just not buying books at Christmas. On 9 February [1933] Leacock told his English publisher, Allan Lane: "I liked immensely the jacket on the Utopia book. The American one was awful but as it was meant as a picture of me I ought not to complain" (The Bodley Head fonds, READ).

Up to 1 February 1933 1,875 copies sold at a royalty of 30¢ per copy ($562.50 royalty). Dodd reported to Leacock on 11 February 1933: ". . . AFTERNOONS IN UTOPIA did rather badly, as you know, and the figures computed as of today indicate that there is still over $400 unearned [from the advance of $1,000] . . . . I hasten to say that we did our best to sell it, and it had its full share of our advertising campaign." Between 1 February 1933 and 1 August 1933, 98 copies were sold (earning a royalty of $29.40 royalty). By this latter date there was still $403.95 unearned from the advance of $1,000.

COPIES EXAMINED: CS (in jacket); QMMRB (rebound).

## A61b *English edition*:

AFTERNOONS | IN UTOPIA | TALES OF THE NEW TIME | *by* | STEPHEN LEACOCK | LONDON | JOHN LANE THE BODLEY HEAD LIMITED

◆ A⁴ B–Q⁸ [$1 signed (also having compositor's initials A.U.), Q2a signed Q*]. *i–iv*, v–vi, *1–2*, 1–37, *38–40*, 41–83, *84–86*, 87–107, *108–110*, 111–175, *176–178*, 179–192, *193–194*, 195–240 pp. (124 leaves). 182 × 124 mm.

CONTENTS: p. *i* half title; p. *ii* list of books written by Leacock published by The Bodley Head, the first being *Literary Lapses* and the last *The Dry Pickwick*; p. *iii* title; p. *iv First published in 1932* | Made and printed in Great Britain by Butler & Tanner Ltd., Frome and London; pp. v–vi table of contents; pp. *1–2*, 1–240 text (pp. *2, 38, 40, 84, 86, 108, 110, 176, 178,* and *194* blank).

TEXT: The text of the English edition is the same as that of the American edition with the following exceptions. Chapter headings for the sketches are used in two parts of the English edition only. Chapter I of part I of the American edition ("Dear Old Utopia") is split into two sketches in the English edition: "Utopia, Old and New" and "Dear Old Utopia." Part VI in the American edition appears at the end of the English edition. "The Dissolution of Shucksford College A.D. 2000" is absorbed into "College in Utopia" in the English edition. There are minor title changes as well: "Ten Seconds for Refreshments" as "Ten Seconds for Refreshment"; "He Goes in A.D. 1810" as "He Goes in 1810"; "War Extracts from the Press of A.D. 2050" as "War Extracts from the Press of A.D. 2500."

BINDING AND DUST JACKET: Bound in orange cloth, top edge stained green. On the upper board black ornamental tooled lettering is stamped over a red geometric design resembling sun rays. Lettering is slanted upwards towards the upper right-hand corner as follows: *Afternoons* | *in Utopia - by* | *Stephen* | *Leacock* | [blind-stamped on the bottom left-hand-corner is a diamond containing a stylized number 8]. Stamped on the spine, the first six lines in ornamental tooled lettering: After- | noons | in Utopia | Stephen | Leacock | THE BODLEY | HEAD.

The dust jacket is white with a colour drawing on the front panel by Joyce Dennys. The drawing is of a young man, dressed as a dandy, resting on a cloud, surrounded by angelic cherubs. On the spine panel: AFTERNOONS | IN UTOPIA | [fleur-de-lis] | 5/– | NET | THE | BODLEY | HEAD. The back panel of the jacket highlights sections of *Afternoons in Utopia*. The front flap lists Leacock's books (and prices) published by The Bodley Head. The back flap is blank.

NOTES: The first mention by Leacock that he was working on a book with this title occurs in his correspondence with John Lane on 5 November 1913. On that occasion he told Lane that he was uncertain of his progress on *Arcadian Adventures with the Idle Rich* because he had ". . . started some different stuff called *Afternoons in Utopia* which may develop into something. If it begins to do so, I'll send along a bit of it" (The Bodley Head fonds, TEX). This, however, was a false start, and the book did not manifest itself as a serious project until the early 1930s.

On 27 March 1931, John Lane The Bodley Head cabled: "EXTREMELY INTERESTED IN UTOPIA PREFER TO ARRANGE WITH CANADIAN DISTRIBUTOR RE PAYMENT OF ROYALTIES ON CANADIAN EDITION OWING TO ABNORMAL EXCHANGE CONDITIONS." Leacock was apparently silent about the book's progress until 20 December 1931, when he wrote similar letters to Frank Dodd and B.W. Willett. Leacock received a royalty of 20% on all copies sold with an advance of £250. Willett informed Leacock on 1 January 1932 that in spite of his enthusiasm for *Afternoons in Utopia*, he did not want to publish it until May or June at the earliest, however, because he first wanted to give *The Dry Pickwick* a good run. But Leacock had sent the manuscript of the book to The Bodley Head on 20 June 1932. Upon reading it, Ronald Boswell assured Leacock on 14 July 1932: "AFTERNOONS IN UTOPIA is very good stuff and I am putting it in hand at once for publication in the autumn."

A set of corrected page proofs was sent to Leacock on 18 August 1932. Leacock cabled his corrections on 12 September 1932, giving his permission to start printing. The book was advertised as being published on 4 November 1932 at 5 s. Boswell sent Leacock £187 10s, being the £250 advance due on the date of publication minus income tax: "The book is going along quite nicely and is getting some excellent notices," he told Leacock. In the royalty report of 23 January 1933 (from the date of publication until the end of the year), there was a negative balance of £133 4s 11d. This would indicate that slightly more than 2,500 copies sold by this time. In 1933 200 copies sold in England, twenty-nine copies to the foreign market, and 161 to the colonial market.

Surplus sheet stock was disposed of at 4d per copy on 22 January 1936. This stock was presumably used in the composite volume, *The Leacock Laughter Book* (see A76).

COPIES EXAMINED: CS (2 copies, 1 in jacket).


## A61b.1 *Canadian issue*:

AFTERNOONS | IN UTOPIA | TALES OF THE NEW TIME | *by* | STEPHEN LEACOCK | THE MACMILLAN COMPANY OF CANADA LTD. | AT ST. MARTIN'S HOUSE TORONTO

The Canadian issue is the same as the English edition with the following exceptions: the imprint on the spine and jacket; the omission of a price on the Canadian jacket; and the flaps of the Canadian jacket being blank.

NOTES: Frank Dodd inquired about the Canadian rights on 14 January 1932. Expressing his preference for his Canadian agent, McClelland and Stewart, he offered to supply the Canadian publisher with a set of plates or stock. Leacock broached the subject of the book with Hugh Eayrs of the Macmillan Company of Canada on 20 January 1932. He bluntly told Eayrs: "Your firm had rather hard luck with my other funny books . . . but I can't let this go without a substantial consideration. Are you interested or rather leave it alone S.L." Eayrs cabled his interest on 2 February 1932 and offered an advance of $250 on publication. Leacock, however, had second thoughts about Eayrs's offer. On 9 February Eayrs voiced his disappointment in not having the book, and he complained that the public was confused about publishing arrangements when "A New Leacock" was announced in the press — was the publisher Macmillan or McClelland and Stewart?

B.W. Willett and Leacock exchanged letters in early March 1932 about the Canadian rights. Leacock was concerned that if a Canadian edition used American sheets, the retail price at $2.25 would be ". . . too high altogether to reach a wide market" (9 March 1932). He hoped that Willett could supply 1,000 sets of sheets to a Canadian distributor.

On 22 June 1932, Leacock attempted to make arrangements for a Canadian issue with W.C. Bell of Oxford University Press. He informed him about Eayrs's offer. McClelland and Stewart had also offered a 20% royalty, an advance of $300, and a retail price of $2.25. Leacock suggested to Bell that they jointly purchase sheets from The Bodley Head, for Bell to make publishing arrangements, to sell the book at $1.50, and to split the profits fifty-fifty between Bell and himself. Bell, however, did not accept Leacock's offer, and on 25 July 1932 Leacock asked Bell to act on his behalf with Eayrs (Bell fonds, OTUTF).

Allen Lane of The Bodley Head was still confused about the status of the Canadian edition on 19 August 1932. Bell visited Eayrs on 30 August 1932 to settle arrangements for Leacock. On 6 September 1932 Eayrs reported: "I finally arranged to buy Lane's edition of AFTERNOONS IN UTOPIA. I cannot get a very good price. However, we are prepared to go ahead on the basis of paying you 25¢ a copy. We shall probably list the book at $1.75." Once final arrangements had been made, it took more than two months for The Bodley Head to supply Eayrs with sheets. 230 copies of the Canadian issue had sold by 10 December 1932. Eayrs expressed his frustration to Leacock on that date: "It seems too bad, particularly in a difficult season. However the book is reacting pretty well and we are going hard after it both by advertising and travelling it." Between 18 November 1932 and 31 March 1933, 514 copies sold of the Canadian issue.

The book was reviewed unfavourably in the *London Advertiser* on 10 December 1932. Leacock wrote to the *Mail and Empire* on 14 January 1933 since he believed that the review had originated there, apparently written by W.A. Deacon. He complained to the editor that the review embodied personal malice instead of literary criticism. The Executive Editor of the *Mail and Empire*, Vernon Knowles, assured Leacock on 31 January 1933 that the review was not written by Deacon and that the *Mail and Empire* had no connection with the review at all. But Eayrs informed Leacock on 2 February 1933 that Deacon had indeed written the review. Leacock wrote back to the *Mail and Empire* on 6 February, this time with a letter directed to Deacon. Knowles replied on 9 February 1933, stating that he would not pass on Leacock's letter and that he was a bit perturbed that Leacock had not taken his word on the matter as to the review's authorship. Leacock wrote back again saying that his publisher had ascertained that Deacon had written the review.

COPIES EXAMINED: CS (in jacket); QMMRB (in jacket).

## A62 MARK TWAIN 1932

**A62a** *first English edition*:

MARK TWAIN | BY | STEPHEN LEACOCK | WITH A FRONTISPIECE | PETER DAVIES LIMITED | 1932

♦ $A^8$ B–$K^8$ $L^4$ [$1 signed]. *1–6, 7–153, 154, 155–161, 162, 163–167, 1* pp. (84 leaves plus frontispiece photograph of Twain taken in *1870* signed *Rischgitz*). 191 × 127 mm.

CONTENTS: p. *1* half title; p. *2* blank; p. *3* title; p. *4 First published in November 1932* | Printed in Great Britain for PETER DAVIES LTD. by T. and A. CONSTABLE LTD. | at the University Press, Edinburgh; p. *5* table of contents; p. *6* blank; pp. *7–153* text; p. *154* blank; pp. *155–161* chronology and bibliography; p. *162* blank; pp. *163–167* index; p. *1* blank.

TEXT: chapter I Childhood and Youth — Mark Twain As Tom Sawyer 1835–1857; chapter II Life on the Mississippi 1857–1861; chapter III Roughing It in the West 1861–1866; chapter IV Innocents Abroad and at Home 1867–1870; chapter V The Flood-Tide of Success 1870–1877; chapter VI Mark Twain As a National Asset 1877–1894; chapter VII Disaster 1894–1900; chapter VIII The Evening of a Long Day 1900–1910; chronology of the Life and Work of Mark Twain [Samuel Langhorne Clemens]; bibliography; index.

BINDING AND DUST JACKET: Bound in black cloth, top edge stained light green. No lettering on the boards. Stamping on the spine in gilt as follows: [two rules] | [two rules] | [the spine for the next five lines is stained green] MARK | TWAIN | * | STEPHEN | LEACOCK | [two rules] | [rule] | [the next line within a solid, green rectangle] DAVIES | [two rules].

   The front and spine panels of the jacket are light green with white lettering. On the front panel: MARK TWAIN | STEPHEN LEACOCK. On the spine panel: MARK | TWAIN | STEPHEN | LEACOCK | 5/– | NET | PETER DAVIES. The back panel is white with light green lettering as follows: [four rules] | UNIFORM WITH THIS VOLUME | 5/– | EACH | NET | [seventeen lines, each line listing the title of the biography and author joined by a line] | [four rules] | PETER DAVIES LTD., 30 HENRIETTA STREET, W.C.2 | [five rules]. The flaps are blank.

NOTES: Leacock's biography of Mark Twain was one of a series of short biographies on prominent individuals published by Peter Davies in England and by D. Appleton in the United States. The English edition was published on 17 November 1932. The copyright was registered at the Copyright Office of DLC by D. Appleton & Co. on 26 November 1932 (ClAint.17135). Number of copies printed not known. *The English Catalogue of Books* also records a cheap edition (not seen), probably a reprint, published in November 1935 at 3s 6d. The book was reprinted without the chronology, bibliography, and index in J. Hooper Wise, J.E. Congleton, Alton C. Morris, and John C. Hodges, *College English: The First Year* (New York: Harcourt, Brace, 1956), rev. ed., pp. 237–76.

COPIES EXAMINED: CS (2 copies, one in dust jacket; one stamped EXPORT EDITION on the front free endpaper and the other COLONIAL EDITION); QMMRB (in jacket).

**A62a.1** *American issue* (1974);

MARK TWAIN | BY | STEPHEN LEACOCK | WITH A FRONTISPIECE | [publisher's device: initials, *HH*, in two overlapping lines within a broken circle]

| HASKELL HOUSE PUBLISHERS Ltd. | *Publishers of Scarce Scholarly Books* |
NEW YORK, N. Y. 10012 | 1974

This American issue is a photographic reprint of the first English edition. The frontispiece appears on p. 2 (that is, the verso of the half title). The verso of the title leaf reads: First Published in 1905 [sic] | HASKELL HOUSE PUBLISHERS Ltd. | *Publishers of Scarce Scholarly Books* | 280 LAFAYETTE STREET | NEW YORK, N. Y. 10012 | [eight lines within a rectangle of Library of Congress Cataloguing in Publication Data] | Printed in the United States of America. Bound in orange cloth with black stamping down the spine as follows: MARK TWAIN STEPHEN LEACOCK. Leaves measure 186 × 127 mm. Yellow endpapers. Published in May 1974. Number of copies printed not known.

COPIES EXAMINED: OTY.

**A62b** *American edition* (1933):

MARK TWAIN | By | STEPHEN LEACOCK | [publisher's device of D. Appleton and Company: tree and open book within a banner having motto INTER FOLIA FRUCTUS ] | NEW YORK | D. APPLETON AND COMPANY | 1933

◆ $1-10^8$ $11^4$. *1–6, 1–19, 20, 21–26, 27, 28–42, 43, 44–54, 55, 56–75, 76, 77–113, 114, 115–134, 135, 136–150, 151, 152–155, 156–158, 159–161, 1* pp. (84 leaves plus frontispiece, identical to the English edition but without attribution to Rischgitz). 190 × 130 mm.

CONTENTS: p. *1* half title; p. *2* list of twelve books in the Appleton Biographies Series; p. *3* title; p. *4* COPYRIGHT, 1933, BY D. APPLETON AND COMPANY | *All rights reserved. This book, or parts | thereof, must not be reproduced in any | form without permission of the publisher.* | PRINTED IN THE UNITED STATES OF AMERICA; p. *5* table of contents; p. *6* blank; pp. *1–161, 1* text.

TEXT: Identical to A62a.

BINDING AND DUST JACKET: Bound in black cloth, top edge stained red. No lettering on the boards. Stamping on the spine in gilt as follows: [two rules] | [two rules] | [the spine for the next five lines is stained red] | MARK | TWAIN | * | STEPHEN | LEACOCK | [two rules] | [rule] | [the next line within a solid, red rectangle] | APPLETON | [two rules].

The dust jacket is tan coloured with black and red lettering. The front panel of the jacket is as follows: MARK TWAIN | [thick red rule] | [rule] BY STEPHEN LEACOCK | [oval portrait (engraving) of Twain signed BA] | [in red] APPLETON BIOGRAPHIES. The back panel is as follows: APPLETON BIOGRAPHIES | [twelve lines in red listing books in the series] | Other Distinguished Volumes are to Follow | [rule] | [thick red rule] | | [the next two lines in red] | D. APPLETON AND COMPANY — NEW YORK | $2.00 per volume | 2519****. On the spine panel of the jacket: MARK | TWAIN | STEPHEN | LEACOCK | [thick red rule from the front of the jacket] | [red, leafy design with black, wavy rules] | [thick red rule from the back of the jacket] | [red seal with the words:] | *THIS IS | AN* | [curved] *APPLETON* | BOOK. The front flap has a quote from the *London Evening Standard*, title and author, a synopsis of Leacock's biography, the price ($2), the publisher's name, and the last line — 2547****. On the back flap are two paragraphs on Leacock himself, the publisher's name, and the last line — 2548****.

NOTES: The American edition was published on 3 February 1933. The copyright was registered at the Copyright Office of DLC on 6 February 1933 (ClA59305). The copyright was renewed by Stephen Lushington Leacock on 15 November 1960 (R266001). Number of copies printed not known.

COPIES EXAMINED: CS (in jacket); QMMRB (1935 reprint, rebound).

## A62c *second English edition* (1938):

MARK TWAIN | BY | STEPHEN LEACOCK | THOMAS NELSON & SONS LTD | LONDON EDINBURGH PARIS MELBOURNE | TORONTO AND NEW YORK

◆ $1^8$ $2$–$10^8$ $11^4$ [$1 signed, also signed (4,607); eighth leaf of the first gathering signed (4,607); fifth leaf of the fifth gathering signed (4,607) and K]. 1–4, 5, 6, 7–153, *154*, 155–161, *162*, 163–167, *1* pp. (84 leaves). 168 × 110 mm.

CONTENTS: p. *1* Short Biographies — No. 4 | MARK TWAIN; p. *2* blank; p. *3* title; p. *4* *All rights reserved* | THOMAS NELSON & SONS LTD | [five lines listing addresses of the publisher in various cities] | [rule] | *First published, November 1932* | *First published in this Series, March 1938*; p. *5* table of contents; p. *6* blank; pp. 7–153 text; p. *154* blank; pp. 155–161 chronology and bibliography; p. *162* blank; pp. 163–167 index (last two lines of p. 167: PRINTED IN GREAT BRITAIN AT | THE PRESS OF THE PUBLISHERS); p. *1* blank.

TEXT: Identical to A62a.

BINDING AND DUST JACKET: Bound in light grey cloth, top edge stained grey. No lettering on the boards. Stamped in red on the spine: MARK | TWAIN | STEPHEN | LEACOCK | NELSON.

The front and spine panels of the jacket are bluish purple with white lettering. The remaining sections of the jacket are white with bluish purple lettering. On the front panel: [on each side, four vertical rules] | MARK | TWAIN | Stephen Leacock | Short Biographies. No. 4. On the spine panel from bottom to top: Nelson | [vertically] MARK TWAIN [cross] Stephen Leacock. Printed on the back panel: [thick-thin rule] | Short Biographies | [ten lines listing series number, title, and author] | NELSON | [thin-thick rule]. On the front flap: STEPHEN LEACOCK'S | MARK TWAIN | [five lines quoting an excerpt from a review in the *Times*]. The back flap is blank.

NOTES: Number of copies printed not known. Price 1s 6d.

COPIES EXAMINED: CS (one copy in jacket; two copies reprinted March 1938, one in jacket).

## A63 STEPHEN LEACOCK'S PUBLIC LECTURES [1932?]

[caption title] *Stephen Leacock's Public Lectures* | [rule] | A Memorandum for the use of Lecture Committees | [rule]

◆ Broadside. 216 × 140 mm. Printed on off-white paper.

NOTES: This broadside was sent to people who inquired whether Leacock was available as a lecturer. Leacock states that his lectures are of two kinds: "serious lectures on Educational, Political and Literary topics" and "lectures . . . of a purely humorous and amusing character. . . ." He describes the latter as consisting ". . . of literary and dramatic burlesques, with a running comment." Under each category he provides examples of talks that he has given in recent years. The variety of lecture topics ranges from education and democracy, the social teachings of the greater humorists, and frenzied fiction. The suggested date of the broadside is in keeping with the subjects of lectures that Leacock delivered at this time.

COPIES EXAMINED: SLM (many copies).

## A64 STEPHEN LEACOCK'S PLAN 1933

STEPHEN LEACOCK'S | PLAN | To Relieve the Depression in 6 Days | To Remove it in 6 Months | To Eradicate it in 6 Years | [publisher's device: rectangle containing leaves, three open books, shield, motto on a banner (FOLIA INTER FOLIA), and publisher's name] | ■ IN CANADA ■ at the bottom)] | TORONTO: THE MACMILLAN COMPANY OF | CANADA LIMITED, AT ST. MARTIN'S HOUSE | 1933

♦ 1¹⁰. 1–2, 1–18 pp. (10 leaves). 229 × 152 mm.

CONTENTS: p. 1 title; p. 2 Copyright, Canada, 1933 | by | THE MACMILLAN COMPANY OF CANADA LIMITED | All rights reserved — no part of this book | may be reproduced in any form without | permission in writing from the publishers. | PRINTED IN CANADA | PRESS OF THE HUNTER-ROSE COMPANY, LIMITED; pp. 1–18 text.

BINDING: Bound in a yellow wrapper with red lettering, wire-stitched. On the front of the wrapper: [six rectangles connect the middle of the first and third lines] STEPHEN | LEACOCK'S | PLAN | TO RELIEVE | the Depression in | 6 DAYS | TO REMOVE it in | 6 MONTHS | TO ERADICATE it in | 6 YEARS | [rule] | PRICE 25 CENTS. On the back of the wrapper: Also by STEPHEN LEACOCK | "BACK TO PROSPERITY" | [rule] | [excerpts of eight reviews from journals or newspapers] | STEPHEN LEACOCK'S PLAN (25c.) | and | BACK TO PROSPERITY ($1.00) | are both published by | THE MACMILLANS IN CANADA : TORONTO.

NOTES: On 30 January 1933, Hugh Eayrs of the Macmillan Company of Canada wrote to Leacock: ". . . why don't you do a brief book on 'Inflation.' Despite Bennett's absolutely doggone stand everybody here feels that some move in this direction is bound to come. A short book 'What about Inflation' — or some better title — would in my opinion do very well." Leacock indicated his willingness to undertake the pamphlet on 1 February 1933. He agreed to no royalty up to 5,000 copies and 5¢ for every copy above 5,000. Leacock informed Eayrs on 6 February: "I shall have all the MS complete when I go to Toronto Feb 15th — It's only a matter of printing. I should think that if you announced it in the heels of the speech [to the Empire Club] — or *no* to announce it *now* — to the trade & get orders & announce it *with* a splash right after the Toronto speech." Leacock's only concern was the lack of an American publisher. On 14 February 1933, Eayrs had sent out notices to all the newspapers in Toronto, Montreal, Ottawa, Winnipeg, and Vancouver about Leacock's forthcoming pamphlet. With respect to American publication, Eayrs stated: "As to [the Macmillans in] New York, between you and me as friends, I am so damned fed up that it isn't any good bothering. But Frank Dodd or the Appleton crowd or anybody else, I should think, would be tickled to get it." Five days later on 19 February, Leacock sent Eayrs the manuscript: "Copy finished & posted. Naturally not possible to type it. But I think they can read it. As to proofs better send me one by rush special delivery & I'll telegraph if any real error gets in . . . my part is done: your act comes now." A day later Leacock asked Frank Dodd if he would publish an American edition of the pamphlet on the same terms as the Canadian edition. "Will send you a Canadian book in three or four days," he told Dodd. ". . . no need to buy [a] pig in a poke. It might go over big." Dodd was somewhat doubtful about publication, but he was receptive to the idea: ". . . I will let you know quickly. But if you have got the real formula, it ought to sell a million copies!" There was no American edition, however.

By 28 February, 200 copies had already been distributed to important Canadian newspapers and to politicians. Another 100 copies were sent to Leacock himself. George Drew told Eayrs on 4 March 1933 that the substance of Leacock's pamphlet was basically the same as his speech to the Empire Club of Canada ("The Riddle of the Depression," delivered by Leacock on 16 February 1933). Drew, who had introduced Leacock as the speaker to the members of the Club on that occasion, was shocked at "the cavalier attitude adopted by the local press" to Leacock's proposals. On 6 March 1933, Eayrs had placed Leacock's pamphlet ". . . in every store large and small where books can be sold from coast to coast, the American News Company having taken 4,000 copies on consignment." Although the pamphlet was already published, the copyright was registered on 14 March 1933. Eayrs's secretary, E. Elliott Booth, informed Leacock on 13 May 1933 that "The sales for The Leacock Plan stand around five thousand copies, but this figure includes those copies which are out on consignment. I have discussed the matter with the Trade Department here, and we all feel that Mr. Eayrs would take the view that it had better be left on consignment until the time of the London Conference." The number of copies sold of Leacock's pamphlet was confirmed by Eayrs a few months later on 19 July 1933: "As to the PLAN, there is nothing coming to you yet, our net outright sales to date being 4434. There are still some we understand with the American News — though not many — to come back from our consignment sales of them. In other words, we have not yet reached 5000 sales mark, but are at the moment around 570 short of it."

Leacock himself admitted to Jim Eakins on 20 December 1934: "My pamphlet called *Stephen Leacock's Plan*, sold, I think, just over 5,000. This is not good enough for publisher and author." When Barbara Nimmo, Leacock's executrix, wrote to the Macmillan Company of Canada about the status of Leacock's copyrights, Ellen Elliot wrote an internal memo to Robert Huckvale on 1 May 1944 in which she referred to *Stephen Leacock's Plan* as "a spectacular flop" (information based on Macmillan Company of Canada fonds at OHM and Leacock fonds at SLM).

COPIES EXAMINED: CS (two copies); QMMRB (three copies).

## A65 CHARLES DICKENS 1933

A65a *English edition*:

CHARLES DICKENS | *His Life and Work* | BY | STEPHEN LEACOCK | LONDON | PETER DAVIES | 1933

◆ $\pi^4$ A–Q$^8$ R$^{10}$ [$1 signed (+R2)]. *i–vi*, vii–viii, 1–258, 259–260, 261–267, 268, 269–275, 1 pp. (142 leaves). 216 × 136 mm.

CONTENTS: pp. *i–ii* blank; p. *iii* half title; p. *iv* blank; p. *v* title; p. *vi Published in November*

1933 | PRINTED IN GREAT BRITAIN BY ROBERT MACLEHOSE AND CO. LTD. | THE UNIVERSITY PRESS, GLASGOW; pp. vii–viii table of contents; pp. 1–258, 259 text; p. 260 blank; pp. 261–267 Chronology; p. 268 blank; pp. 269–275, 1 index.

TEXT: chapter I The Childhood and Youth of Charles Dickens; chapter II Mr. Pickwick Takes the World by Storm; chapter III "Boz" Conquers England; chapter IV "Boz" Visits America 1842; chapter V Years of Success 1842–1847; chapter VI Flood Tide (1845–1850); chapter VII *Bleak House* and Social Reform (1850–1854); chapter VIII Dickens as an Editor (1854–1857); chapter IX Dickens Separates from His Wife (1858); chapter X Dickens Takes the Platform (1858–1865); chapter XI The Second Visit to America; chapter XII Closing in — The Close (1870); chapter XIII The Mystery of More Than Edwin Drood. Epilogue.

BINDING AND DUST JACKET: There are two binding variants, each with a different coloured dust jacket: maroon cloth with the top edge stained maroon and stamping in gilt; light blue cloth with stamping in dark blue. Both are stamped on the spine as follows: CHARLES | DICKENS | ★ | *Stephen* | *Leacock* | DAVIES.

The dust jacket for copies in maroon cloth is cream-coloured with the illustration in brown and printing on the spine in brown. The front panel has a reproduction of a photograph of Dickens seated in a chair. Above the photograph in white: CHARLES | DICKENS. Beneath the photograph in white: STEPHEN LEACOCK. Printed on the spine panel: CHARLES | DICKENS | [rule] | LEACOCK | 10s. 6d. | NET | DAVIES. On the back panel of the jacket is an advertisement, with excerpts from reviews, for Leacock's *Mark Twain*. The flaps are blank. The dust jacket for copies in light blue cloth is cream-coloured with printing and the illustration in blue. The second jacket has 5s as the price on the spine, but is otherwise the same as the first jacket. The price reduction would indicate that the copies in light blue cloth were bound up at a later date after publication when sales were diminishing.

NOTES: On 3 August 1933, Russell Doubleday cabled Peter Davies, "accepting his offer for publication of your Charles Dickens book, based upon terms mentioned in your letter to me." Leacock received an advance royalty of $750. The royalty percentage is not known. Leacock was billed $10.50 on 16 November 1933 for the preparation of the index. The English edition was published on 28 November 1933. The copyright was registered at the Copyright Office of DLC on 12 December 1933 (ClAint.18471). In its royalty statement of 2 January 1934, Davies reported a royalty of $371, leaving an unearned balance of $379. Number of copies printed not known.

COPIES EXAMINED: CS (both binding variants in jacket); OORI (maroon cloth in jacket, presentation copy signed and dated by Leacock January 1934); OTNY (light blue cloth in jacket); QMMRB (light blue cloth in jacket).

### A65b *American edition* (1934):

[all lines within a brownish orange compartment, which is comprised of illustrations reproduced from the title page of *The Posthumous Papers of the Pickwick Club*: a man shooting his rifle; a sleeping man fishing on a boat; a fishing pole, fish, net, and quiver; and a rifle, net, and fishing pole. The first two lines in curved, rustic type:] CHARLES | DICKENS | [the next two lines in script with swash letters] *His Life and Work* | *by* | [in shaded type] STEPHEN LEACOCK | [rule with a solid diamond in the centre] | [in script with swash capitals] *Doubleday Doran and Company Inc.* | GARDEN CITY NEW YORK | *1934*

♦  $1^8$ ($11 + \chi^1$) $2$–$21^8$. i–vi, vii–ix, x, xi–xii, 1–3, 2–315, 316, 317–322, 1–2 pp. (169 leaves). 228 × 153 mm. The title leaf is tipped in.

CONTENTS: p. *i* half title; p. *ii* list of twenty-six books by Leacock, the first being *Charles Dickens* and the last *Elements of Political Science*; p. *iii* title; p. *iv* PRINTED AT THE *Country Life Press*, GARDEN CITY, N. Y., U. S. A. | COPYRIGHT, 1933, 1934 | BY DOUBLEDAY, DORAN & COMPANY, INC. | ALL RIGHTS RESERVED | FIRST EDITION; pp. *v* note regarding the sources of the illustrations; p. *vi* blank; pp. vii–ix table of contents; p. *x* blank; pp. *xi–xii* list of illustrations; p. *1* fly title; p. 2 blank; p. 3, 2–315 text; p. 316 blank; pp. 317–322 index; pp. *1–2* blank.

Text illustrations are on pp. 106, 118, 157, 227, 251, and 270. Halftone illustrations on glossy white paper are tipped in facing pp. *3* (frontispiece), 12, 24, 32. 44, 52. 92, 93, 100, 160, 236, 272, and 292.

TEXT: Identical to the English edition.

BINDING AND DUST JACKET: Bound in brownish orange cloth with an oval portrait of Dickens's head and shoulders (with leaves at the top and bottom of the oval) blind-stamped on the upper board. On the spine is a solid black rectangle, and stamped in gilt within the rectangle is the following: CHARLES | DICKENS | STEPHEN | LEACOCK | DOUBLEDAY | DORAN. Blind-stamped beneath the rectangle is a series of rules and leaves. Top edge stained brownish orange.

The jacket is white. The front panel is similar to the title page except that the illustration is enlarged and in colour. The publisher's name has been deleted and in its stead is the following: A vivid, human portrait of the | most prodigious figure in | modern literature. Printed on the spine of the jacket: [the first two lines in yellow, curved, rustic characters] CHARLES | DICKENS | [the next two lines in script with swash letters] *His Life and Work* | *by* | STEPHEN LEACOCK | [rule with a solid diamond in the centre] | [illustration in colour of a fishing pole, fish, leaves, net, and quiver] | Doubleday | Doran. On the back panel is a black-and-white illustration of a Dickensian scene and an excerpt from the beginning paragraphs of Leacock's book. The last three lines on the back panel are: [the first three lines in pink] STEPHEN LEACOCK *brings to life the prodigious legendary* | *figure behind Mr. Pickwick and Little Nell and Oliver Twist in* | CHARLES DICKENS: His Life and Work | 219. The front flap has the price ($3), two excerpts from the book, and a very brief summary. The last line on the front flap is: 2034. The back flap features an advertisement for Nella Braddy's biography of Anne Sullivan Macy.

NOTES: In Barbara Nimmo's collection of her uncle's papers at NAC, there is a memorandum of agreement between Leacock and Doubleday, Page & Company dated 13 March 1926. Leacock apparently returned the contract on 15 April 1926. He agreed to deliver the manuscript by 1 October 1926. The work was entitled *Life of Charles Dickens*, Benefactors of Mankind series. Leacock was to receive "ten per cent. on the retail price, cloth style, on the first 3,000 copies," 15% thereafter, with an advance of $1,000 two months after the receipt of the completed manuscript. This was obviously a false start because nothing further came of Leacock's attempted biography of Dickens in 1926.

On 28 July 1933, Russell Doubleday of Doubleday, Doran and Company told Leacock that he was delighted to receive "the chronology for the Dickens book. We can get right to work now on setting and publishing plans." Although the American edition was available and on sale before Christmas 1933, it was not officially published until 3 January 1934.

The copyright was registered at the Copyright Office of DLC on 4 January 1934 (ClA68877). The copyright was renewed by Stephen Lushington Leacock on 4 January 1961 (R268769). Leacock was paid an advance of $250 on 16 March 1934, author's alterations to the galleys cost $54.75, and there was a charge for the index of $10.50 (done on 16 November 1933).

In the first royalty report dated 2 July 1934, 5,455 copies had sold: 3,000 copies at 10% ($.30 per copy), 1,899 copies at 15% ($.45 per copy), 175 copies for Canada at $.15 per copy, 350 copies for Canada $.225 per copy, six copies of foreign sales at $.15 per copy, seventeen copies of foreign sales at $.225 per copy, and eight copies via mail order at $.06 per copy. The total royalty was $1,864.76. Up to 2 January 1936, another 819 copies sold, twenty copies of which sold to Canada ($359.06 total royalty). Thereafter, copies of the regular edition continued to sell in very low numbers (by 1 July 1936, twenty-five copies, one to Canada, two in foreign sales, five by mail order).

In January 1935 a number of misprints and minor mistakes were noted in Leacock's account — for example, p. 190 Dickens began *Little Dorrit* in June 1857, not 1858; p. 191 William Dorrit, not Edward Dorrit; p. 170 Mr. Bounderby, not Mr. Bounderly. These, however, were never corrected in subsequent impressions or issues.

Leacock's biography was chosen by the Doubleday Dollar Book Club on 10 February 1936 as their May selection. The Doubleday Book Club printing is not readily identifiable as such, but the sheet size was reduced to 206 × 139 mm. and the jacket was altered on the back panel and the flaps. Although the royalty was reduced to 5¢ a copy, 46,823 copies of the Dollar Book Club printing sold by 1 July 1936, earning Leacock $2,341.15 in royalty. Another 1,608 copies sold of this printing by 2 January 1937 ($80.40 royalty). By 2 May 1938, however, only seventy-three copies sold.

On 16 April 1942 T.B. Costain's secretary, Ethel Hulse, informed Leacock that the book was out of print.

COPIES EXAMINED: CS (later impression not in jacket; 1936 reprint in jacket); OTNY (first printing in jacket); QMMRB (two copies of first impression, both in jacket, one a presentation copy, dated by Leacock 15 February 1934).

## A65b.1 *American issue* (1938):

[all lines within a compartment, which is comprised of illustrations reproduced from the title page of *The Posthumous Papers of the Pickwick Club*: a man shooting his rifle; a sleeping man fishing on a boat; a fishing pole, fish, net, and quiver; and a rifle, net, and fishing pole. The first two lines in curved, rustic type:] CHARLES | DICKENS | [the next two lines in script with swash letters] *His Life and Work* | by | [in shaded type] STEPHEN LEACOCK | [rule with a solid diamond in the centre] | [with swash capitals] *The Sun Dial Press, Inc.* | GARDEN CITY NEW YORK

This issue bears a close resemblance to the 1936 reprint of A65b. The verso of the title leaf reads: PRINTED AT THE *Country Life Press*, GARDEN CITY, N. Y., U. S. A. | 1938 | THE SUN DIAL PRESS, INC. | COPYRIGHT, 1933, 1934 | BY DOUBLEDAY, DORAN & COMPANY, INC. | ALL RIGHTS RESERVED.

BINDING AND DUST JACKET: Bound in light brown cloth, top edge stained brown, with the logo of the Sun Dial Press blind-stamped on the bottom right-hand corner of the lower board. Stamped on the spine: [two rules blind-stamped] | [the next five lines in gilt]

CHARLES DICKENS | STEPHEN | LEACOCK | SUN DIAL PRESS | [series of rules and leaves blind-stamped]. The imprint on the jacket's spine is that of the Sun Dial Press. In other respects the binding and jacket are the same as the 1936 reprint of A65b.

NOTES: The exact date of publication of this issue is not known. The first royalty statement, dated 2 May 1938, notes that the book sold for 98¢ and that 543 copies sold at 5¢ royalty per copy ($27.15 total royalty). Another 2,784 copies sold up to 1 May 1941 ($139.20 total royalty).

COPIES EXAMINED: CS.

## A66 GENERAL CURRIE 1933

[cover title: row of ornaments] | GENERAL CURRIE | *An Appreciation* | *by* | STEPHEN LEACOCK | *Reprinted from* | "*The Montreal Daily Herald*," | *December 6th, 1933* | [ornament] | *A WORD OF EXPLANATION* | [twelve lines in italics in reference to Leacock's obituary tribute and its distribution] | [signature in facsimile] *JEMacpherson*

◆ Leaflet folded once to form four unnumbered pages. 222 × 100 mm.

CONTENTS: p. *1* title; pp. *2–3* text; p. *4* blank.

BINDING: Issued without wrappers, off-white paper stock.

NOTES: After having served as Commander of the Canadian Corps during the First World War, Sir Arthur Currie was appointed principal and vice-chancellor of McGill University in 1920. He remained in that position until his death on 30 November 1933. Leacock taught Currie at Strathroy Collegiate Institute in 1888, and he developed an abiding friendship with him at McGill. See *The Boy I Left Behind Me* (A104a), pp. 160–1.

Leacock's tribute was reprinted in many newspapers across Canada (see C33.10). According to the word of explanation on the cover title, Macpherson considered the tribute to be a literary treasure. He arranged for the printing of the leaflet and its distribution to ex-service men. The manuscript at SLM is 8 pp. Number of copies printed not known.

COPIES EXAMINED: OTUTF; SLM.

## A67 LINCOLN FREES THE SLAVES 1934

### A67a *American edition*:

LINCOLN | FREES THE SLAVES | | BY | STEPHEN LEACOCK | ILLUSTRATED | G•P•PUTNAM'S SONS | NEW YORK | MCMXXXIV

◆ *1–11*⁸. *1–10, 13–178* pp. (88 leaves). 190 × 130 mm.

CONTENTS: p. *1* half title with series statement (Great Occasions); p. *2* frontispiece photograph of Lincoln at the time of the Douglas debates (reproduced courtesy of Amos Pinchot, Esq.); p. *3* title; p. *4* COPYRIGHT, 1934, BY STEPHEN LEACOCK | All rights reserved. This book, or parts thereof, must | not be reproduced in any form without permission. | MANUFACTURED | IN THE UNITED STATES OF AMERICA | AT THE VAN PRESS; p. *5* table of contents; p. *6* blank; p. *7* list of illustrations; p. *8* blank; p. *9* fly title; p. 10 blank; pp. 13–172 text; pp. 173–178 index. Illustrations on pp. 53, 77, 103, 137, 155, 165, and 169.

TEXT: chapter I Slavery in America; chapter II The Irrepressible Conflict; chapter III Lincoln in Illinois; chapter IV Towards the Abyss; chapter V Secession; chapter VI War; chapter VII Emancipation; chapter VIII Epilogue; Appendix — Final Emancipation Proclamation.

BINDING AND DUST JACKET: Bound in light brownish yellow cloth, top edge stained blue. Stamping on the spine in gilt as follows: [two rules] | [the spine for the next six lines is stained black] | LINCOLN | FREES | THE | SLAVES | * | LEACOCK | PUTNAM | [two rules]. A variant binding in grey cloth has black lettering on the spine and no staining on the top edge. The stamping on the spine is similar to that of the spine on the standard binding except that there are no rules or staining.

The front and spine panels of the jacket are blue with white lettering. The front panel is as follows: LINCOLN FREES | THE SLAVES | [oval portrait of Lincoln within a rectangular frame, identical to the frontispiece but smaller, with a border around the frame and two vertical bars on each side] | STEPHEN LEACOCK. Printed on the spine panel: LEACOCK | ■ | [the next line down the spine] | LINCOLN FREES THE SLAVES | ■ | PUTNAM. The remainder of the jacket is white with black lettering. The back panel has an excerpt from the book. The front flap of the jacket gives a synopsis of the book with the author's name, title, and price ($1.50). On the back flap is a list of other books in the Great Occasions Series.

NOTES: The contract in the Barbara Nimmo collection at NAC is dated 13 July 1933. Leacock agreed to deliver the manuscript on 1 November 1933. The contract gave G.P. Putnam's Sons exclusive rights of publication in the United States and Canada. Leacock was to receive 10% on the first 10,000 copies sold, 15% thereafter (5% on reprint editions), and an advance of $125 against royalties on the delivery of the manuscript, and a further advance of $125 on the date of publication.

The American edition was published on 23 February 1934. Leacock registered the copyright at the Copyright Office of DLC on 2 March 1934 (ClA70688). The copyright was renewed by Stephen Lushington Leacock on 23 June 1961 (R278088).

Earle H. Balch of Putnam's sent Leacock $105 on 1 March 1934 (deduction of 8% tax on foreign authors). The advance on receipt of the manuscript had already been sent several months before that date. Thomas Allen distributed the book in Canada and was charging $1.75 for other volumes of the series. Number of copies printed not known. By 31 July 1935, 791 copies had sold (571 within the U.S., 213 to Canada, 6 to the Orient, and 1 special order).

COPIES EXAMINED: CS (two copies in light brownish yellow cloth, one in dust jacket; variant binding in dust jacket); QMMRB (three copies in light brownish yellow cloth, two copies in jacket).

## A67b *first English edition* (1935):

LINCOLN FREES | THE SLAVES | | BY | STEPHEN LEACOCK | WITH A FRONTISPIECE | LONDON | PETER DAVIES

♦ $A^8 B-K^8$. 1–6, 9–161, 1 pp. (80 leaves, plus frontispiece photograph of Lincoln by Rischgitz). 191 × 131 mm.

CONTENTS: p. *1* half title with series statement (Great Occasions); p. *2* blank; p. *3* title; p. *4* *First published in October* 1935 | Printed in Great Britain for PETER DAVIES LTD. | by SHERRATT & HUGHES, at St. Ann's Press | Manchester.; p. *5* table of contents; p. *6* blank; pp. 9–161, *1* text.

TEXT: The English edition is shorter than the American edition (see the notes). A bibliography (list of works consulted) has been added; the appendix has been deleted. With the exception of the frontispiece, there are no illustrations.

BINDING AND DUST JACKET: Bound in light yellow cloth, top edge stained reddish brown. Stamping on the spine in gilt as follows: [two rules] | [two rules] | [the spine for the next seven lines is stained reddish brown] | LINCOLN | FREES | THE | SLAVES | * | STEPHEN | LEACOCK | [two rules] | [rule] | [the next line within a solid reddish brown rectangle] | DAVIES | [two rules]. A variant binding is in blue cloth, top edge stained blue. Stamping on the spine of the variant binding is identical to that of the standard cloth's spine except that the former is not stained.

The jacket is green and white. The front panel of the jacket has a series of green rules of varied heaviness and two solid, green rectangles. Within the first rectangle in white: LINCOLN FREES | THE SLAVES. Within the second rectangle in white: STEPHEN LEACOCK. The pattern of rules and solid rectangles is carried over to the spine panel of the jacket. Within the first rectangle on the spine panel: LINCOLN | FREES | THE SLAVES. Within the second rectangle on the spine panel: STEPHEN | LEACOCK. On the bottom of the spine panel is a white circle which contains: 5/– | NET. The last line in white at the bottom of the jacket's spine is: PETER DAVIES. The back panel is comprised of rules of varied heaviness, a list of other volumes in the same series, the price, and the publisher's name and address. The flaps of the jacket are blank.

NOTES: A.E. Grant of Peter Davies Ltd. wrote enthusiastically to Leacock on 11 July 1933:

> I cannot tell you how pleased I was to get your letter, and to hear that you may abandon Lafayette for Lincoln. As you know, this is the book which has attracted me immensely from the first moment that you suggested it, and sent me your picture of Lincoln as a man . . . we shall be delighted to offer you the same terms as Putnam's — as advance of £100 (£50 on delivery of the manuscript and £50 on publication) on a royalty of 10% up to 10,000, and 15% thereafter.

Leacock apparently informed Grant on 12 December 1933 that he had finished the manuscript. He posted the manuscript on 8 January 1934. By 9 February 1934, Grant had received a set of proofs of the American edition. Although he told Leacock that he had "drawn a wonderful and moving picture of the man," Grant estimated that the book was nearer 40,000 words than 30,000. As such, it was one-third longer than the others in the series, and production costs would escalate. He asked Leacock to compress the manuscript. Leacock had intended to include appendices. Grant requested Leacock to omit them altogether. He also suggested that the few references to British inhumanity should be eliminated and that Leacock forward a checklist of sources consulted.

On 20 February 1934, Leacock marked up the American proofs for Grant and cut 7,500 words from the book. But Leacock wanted to see the proofs of the English edition in view of the drastic cuts that he had made. ". . . We have now sent the book to press, and are having galleys printed to forward to you for correction. . . . ," Grant told Leacock.

He anticipated publication in the early autumn.

On 4 April 1934, Grant asked Leacock to think about illustrations for the book. The illustrations in the American edition, Grant maintained, were inadequate. Aside from the frontispiece, no illustrations were used in English edition, however. Leacock received the galleys by 6 June 1934. He told Grant on 26 June 1934 that he was correcting them. Grant acknowledged receiving the corrected proofs from Leacock on 6 September 1934. He told Leacock that in view of "the unavoidable delay about getting hold of the illustrations," publication would have to wait until January 1935.

On 22 February 1935, Leacock sent a copy of the American edition to Frank and Alice Hett: "It is published in England also but in a badly reduced form as they could only use 30,000 words for matters of economy & uniformity . . . So I had to cut out almost 8000." According to *The English Catalogue of Books* (and the copyright page), the English edition was published in October 1935. Number of copies printed not known.

COPIES EXAMINED: CS (binding in light yellow cloth in dust jacket; variant binding without the jacket); QMMRB (light yellow cloth in jacket).

## A67c *second English edition* (1941):

*Great* | [rule] *Occasions* [rule] | THE SPANISH ARMADA | *by Lorna Rea* | MARATHON SALAMIS | *by Compton Mackenzie* | LINCOLN FREES THE SLAVES | *by Stephen Leacock* | GORDON AT KHARTOUM | *by John Buchan* | *London 1941* | READERS UNION LIMITED | *by arrangement with* | [rule] PETER DAVIES LIMITED [rule]

♦ $\pi^{12}$ A$^2$ B–K$^{16}$ L$^6$ [\$1 signed, fifth leaf signed * except the preliminary, unsigned gathering and the L gathering]. *1*–*8*, *9*–*88*, *89*–*90*, *91*–*169*, *170*–*172*, *173*–*255*, *256*–*258*, *259*–*328* pp. (164 leaves). 195 × 130 mm.

CONTENTS: p. *1* half title; p. *2* blank; p. *3* title; p. *4* [rule] THIS EDITION FIRST PUBLISHED 1941 [rule] | *Made 1941 in Great Britain* | PRINTED AT THE WINDMILL PRESS, KINGSWOOD | AND PUBLISHED BY READERS UNION LIMITED | CHANDOS PLACE, CHARING CROSS, LONDON | *Administrative Address:* | [rule] DUNHAMS LANE, LETCHWORTH, HERTFORDSHIRE [rule]; p. *5* table of contents; p. 6 blank; pp. 7–88 text of Rea's book; pp. 89–169 text of Mackenzie's book; p. *170* blank; pp. *171*–*255* text of Leacock's book; p. *256* blank; pp. *257*–*328* text of Buchan's book.

TEXT: Leacock's text is identical to A67b. The bibliography and index have been deleted.

BINDING: Bound in light blue cloth with matching stain on the top edge and lettering in silver. Stamped on the upper board: GREAT OCCASIONS | [heavy rule] | REA • MAC-KENZIE • LEACOCK • BUCHAN. Stamped on the spine: [wavy rule] | *Great* | *Occasions* | [wavy rule] | [wavy rule] | [within a circle] RU. Dust jacket not seen.

The front endpaper has a map of the world by Thomas Derrick for Hakluyt's *Voyages*; on the rear endpaper are maps of Marathon and Salamis.

NOTES: This composite volume was published for the members of a book club, the Readers Union. Number of copies printed not known.

COPIES EXAMINED: CS.

## A68 STEPHEN LEACOCK 1934

### A68a *English edition*:

[all lines within an ornamental, ribbon rectangle] Methuen's | Library of Humour | Edited by E. V. Knox | STEPHEN | LEACOCK | [illustration of mask of humour] | Methuen & Co. Ltd. | 36 Essex Street, W.C.2 | LONDON

◆ π⁴ 1–9⁸ 10⁴ [$1 signed]. i–iv, v, vi, vii, 1, 1–151, 1 pp. (80 leaves). 166 × 103 mm.

CONTENTS: p. *i* half title; p. *ii* series title, series editor's name, price (2s 6d), and authors in the series (Leacock being the tenth listed); p. *iii* title; p. *iv First Published in 1934* | [illustration of the front of a building with columns and arched entrance] | PRINTED IN GREAT BRITAIN; p. v acknowledgement to John Lane The Bodley Head, for permission to reprint the stories.; p. *vi* blank; p. vii table of contents; p. *1* blank; pp. 1–151 text; p. *1* PRINTED BY | JARROLD AND SONS LTD. | NORWICH.

TEXT: I The Split in the Cabinet; or, The Fate of England; II Broken Barriers; or, Red Love on a Blue Island; III Back from the Land; IV The Sorrows of a Summer Guest; V The Perfect Salesman: A Complete Guide to Business; VI Oroastus: A Greek Tragedy; VII Caroline's Christmas; or, The Inexplicable Infant; VII Buggam Grange: A Good Old Ghost Story.

BINDING AND DUST JACKET: Bound in orangish brown cloth with illustration of jester's face and ornaments blind-stamped on the upper board. Stamped in gilt on the spine: *Library* | *of* | *Humour* | [open diamond] | *Stephen* | *Leacock* | *Methuen.*

The dust jacket is tan yellow. On the front panel of the jacket is an illustration in pink and black, signed Hendy, of vines, a mask of humour, grass, flowers, and several people (a golfer, a policeman, a king, etc.). Within the illustration are the following lines: METHUEN'S | LIBRARY OF | HUMOUR | Edited by E.V.KNOX | *Editor of "Punch"* | STEPHEN | LEACOCK | [heavy rule outside of illustration]. On the spine panel of the jacket: METHUEN'S | LIBRARY | OF | HUMOUR | EDITED BY | E.V.KNOX | [illustration of a person slumped over a pink sofa reading a book] | STEPHEN | LEACOCK | 2'6 | net | METHUEN | [heavy rule extending front the front panel of jacket]. The back panel has an advertisement, within a rectangle, of Methuen's Library of Humour. On the front flap are: the series title, editor's name, title of the book, quotation from E.V. Lucas's *Reading, Writing and Remembering* regarding Leacock as a humorist, and the name of the publisher. The back flap of the jacket is blank.

NOTES: On 31 July 1933, Ronald Boswell of John Lane The Bodley Head informed Leacock that Methuen & Co. Ltd. wanted to publish "a volume of extracts from your humorous books about 30,000 words long" in a Library of Humour edited by E.V. Knox. The terms were the following: the book to sell for 2s 6d, an advance of £50 on account of a royalty of 12.5% on all copies sold of the British edition, including foreign and colonial sales. Boswell suggested that The Bodley Head and Leacock would split the advance and any accruing royalties. Leacock gave his assent to Methuen's proposal on 13 August [1933]. The contract with Methuen is dated 12 September 1933. On 27 January 1934, Leacock apparently wrote to Methuen, and inquired about publication. The company replied on 8 February, stating that publication was slated for July 1934. On 7 February 1934, Boswell wrote to Leacock: "Methuens have not yet published the volume of selections from your books so we have not yet received the money from them, but as soon as it comes, we will send you your half." On 20 June 1934, Methuen & Co. Ltd. sent Leacock £50, care of

The Bodley Head. *The English Catalogue of Books* reports that the book was published in June 1934.

According to the Methuen ledgers at LILLY, 4,000 copies in quires were initially printed by Jarrold and Sons Ltd. on 23 April 1934. 2,000 copies in quires were delivered to Methuen on 16 May and 2,059 copies on 8 October. This would indicate that in fact, the total number of unbound copies printed appears to have been slightly more than 4,000 copies (4,059). 4,300 dust jackets were printed by Jarrold on 21 April 1934. 2,000 copies were bound on 16 May 1934 and the remaining 2,059 copies on 8 October 1934 (the type was also distributed on 8 October). The mould for the jacket was destroyed on 14 October 1941.

In its royalty statement of November 1934 (up to the end of June 1934), Methuen & Co. Ltd. reported selling 317 copies (291 in Britain and 26 copies in colonial and foreign sales). Between 30 June 1934 and 31 December 1937, another 604 copies sold (361 copies in Britain and 243 copies in colonial and foreign sales). Leacock did not earn anything beyond his advance royalty, and on the basis of the Methuen ledgers and correspondence at SLM, it appears that less than 1,000 copies were sold of the entire edition.

COPIES EXAMINED: CS (in jacket); QMMRB (no jacket); SLM (Leacock's copy in jacket, autographed "To Stephen Leacock from Stephen Leacock Jan 5 1935").

**A68a.1** *American issue* (entitled *The Perfect Salesman*):

*The | PERFECT SALESMAN | By | STEPHEN LEACOCK | Edited by E. V. Knox | New York | ROBERT M. McBRIDE & COMPANY*

◆ $1-10^8$. Identical pagination and foliation as the English edition. 171 × 133 mm.

CONTENTS: p. *i* half title; p. *ii* blank; p. *iii* title; p. *iv* THE PERFECT SALESMAN | COPYRIGHT | BY DODD, MEAD & COMPANY | COPYRIGHT, 1934 | ROBERT M. McBRIDE & COMPANY | PRINTED IN THE UNITED STATES | OF AMERICA | FIRST EDITION; p. *v* Reprinted through the courtesy of | Dodd, Mead & Company | New York; p. *vi* blank; p. vii table of contents; p. *1* blank; pp. 1–151 text; p. *1* blank.

TEXT: Identical to the English edition.

BINDING AND DUST JACKET: Bound in royal blue cloth with a white label pasted on to the upper board. On the label in red lettering: ★ | THE | PERFECT | SALESMAN | ★ | *Stephen Leacock*.

The dust jacket is white. On the front panel of the jacket: *STEPHEN LEACOCK* | [in red] ★ | *The | Perfect | Salesman* | [in red] ★ | *EDITED BY E. V. KNOX*. On the spine panel: *LEACOCK* | [in red] ★ | *The | Perfect | Salesman* | [in red] ★ | *McBRIDE*. The back panel advertises McBRIDE NEW FICTION, Joseph Hilton Smyth's *The Nuder Gender* (priced at $2 with a photo of Smyth) and Ralph Aiken's *The Ghost Hunters* (priced at $2). The front flap briefly describes the contents of *The Perfect Salesman* (priced at $1), "as selected by E. V. Knox, editor of the world's most famous periodical, 'Punch.'" On the back flap is a "coupon" for readers to fill in and to mail to the publisher for "announcements and descriptive folders" of important publications.

NOTES: In May and June 1934 Robert M. McBride & Co. arranged with Dodd, Mead to publish an anthology of Leacock's stories in The Library of Humour, jointly published with Methuen. McBride made the selection of stories, and offered the same arrangement as they did for the G.K. Chesterton volume in that series: $100 down against 10% royalty.

Frank Dodd wrote to Leacock on 1 June 1934, stating that if Leacock was agreeable to the proposal, they would divide the advance and royalties equally: "Robert McBride & Company, publishers, are pestering us to give them permission to use selections from your work in a series which they are publishing in conjunction with Methuen of London, called The Library of Humor." Leacock gave his permission to McBride to proceed on the understanding that the American edition would not circulate in England since the English edition had already been arranged independently. McBride signed a contract with Dodd, Mead on 19 June 1934 with intended publication in August or September of that year. Although the American issue was printed in the United States, it would appear that Methuen shipped a set of plates to McBride for the printing. Frank Dodd sent Leacock a copy of the book on the day of publication, 24 August 1934. Number of copies printed not known. The copyright was registered with the Copyright Office at DLC on 29 September 1934 (ClA76197). The copyright was renewed by Crown Publishers, Inc. on 16 August 1962 (R300123).

COPIES EXAMINED: CS (in jacket); QMMRB (no jacket).

## A69 THE GREATEST PAGES OF CHARLES DICKENS 1934

[all lines within a compartment, which is comprised of illustrations reproduced from the title page of *The Posthumous Papers of the Pickwick Club*: a man shooting his rifle; a man asleep fishing on a boat; a fishing pole, fish, net, and quiver; and a rifle, net, and fishing pole. The first four lines curved; the first two lines in open type, the next two in rustic type:] THE | GREATEST PAGES OF | CHARLES | DICKENS | [ornamental rule] | [the next five lines in outline type] A Biographical Reader and a | Chronological Selection from | the Works of Dickens with a | Commentary on his | Life and Art. | [in shaded type] STEPHEN LEACOCK | [ornamental rule] | [in script with swash capitals] *Doubleday Doran and Company Inc.* | GARDEN CITY NEW YORK | 1934

♦  1–16⁸. i–iv, v–viii, 1–6, 3–4, 5–6, 7–24, 25–26, 27–30, 31–32, 33–55, 56–58, 59–60, 61–62, 63–76, 77–78, 79–197, 108–110, 111–114, 115–116, 117–128, 129–130, 131–141, 142–144, 145–146, 147–148, 149–166, 167–168, 169–191, 192–194, 195–196, 197–198, 199–218, 219–220, 221–224, 225–226, 227–233, 1–3 pp. (128 leaves). 228 × 152 mm.

CONTENTS: p. *i* half title; p. *ii* list of twenty-seven books by Leacock, the first *The Greatest Pages of Charles Dickens* and the last *Elements of Political Science*; p. *iii* title; p. *iv* PRINTED AT THE *Country Life Press*, GARDEN CITY, N. Y., U. S. A. | COPYRIGHT, 1934 | BY DOUBLEDAY, DORAN & COMPANY, INC. | ALL RIGHTS RESERVED | FIRST EDITION; pp. v–vi preface dated "*May 1, 1934*"; pp. vii–viii table of contents; p. *1* list of halftone illustrations; p. *2* blank; p. *3* list of text illustrations; p. *4* blank; pp. *5–6, 3–223* text (pp. 2, 6, 26, 32, 56, 58, 62, 78, 108, 110, 116, 130, 142, 144, 148, 168, 192, 194, 198, 220, and 226 blank); p. *1–3* blank. Text illustrations are on pp. *5, 31, 61, 115, 147, 197,* and *225.* Halftone illustrations on glossy white paper are tipped in facing pp. 44, 68, 104, and 136.

TEXT: chapter one Childhood and Youth of Dickens 1812–1836; chapter two Mr. Pickwick Takes the World by Storm 1836–1838; chapter three Boz Conquers England 1838–1841;

chapter four America Conquers "Boz" 1842; chapter five Dickens Invades Europe 1842–1846; chapter six The Flood Tide of Success 1846–1850; chapter seven Dickens Reforms the World 1850–1854; chapter eight The Falling Shadow of the Prison Wall 1854–1858; chapter nine The Ashes Burn Out on the Hearth 1858–1868; chapter ten And After That the Dark 1868–1870. Each chapter consists of introductory commentary by Leacock with selected excerpts from Dickens's work.

BINDING AND DUST JACKET: Bound in green cloth with an oval portrait of Dickens's head and shoulders (with leaves at the top and bottom of the oval) blind-stamped on the upper board. On the spine is a solid black rectangle, and stamped in gilt within the rectangle is the following: THE | GREATEST | PAGES OF | CHARLES | DICKENS | STEPHEN | LEACOCK | DOUBLEDAY | DORAN. Blind-stamped beneath the rectangle is a series of rules and leaves. Top edge stained yellowish green.

The dust jacket is tan coloured. On the front panel of the jacket within a red rectangle is the following: [the first three lines in open type] THE | GREATEST PAGES | OF | [the next two lines in red rustic type] CHARLES | DICKENS | [the next four lines in red outline type against a background in red of a street scene of nineteenth-century England] A chronological selection | from the WORKS of Dickens | with a commentary on his | LIFE and ART | [in red] STEPHEN LEACOCK. The spine panel has the title, the copyright date, initials of the publisher, Leacock's name, the series (The Greatest Pages Series), and the name of the publisher. On the front flap is the price ($2.50) with the heading in red: THE BEST OF | Charles Dickens. This is followed by a summary of the book; the last line after the summary is 2121. The back flap features excerpts from reviews of Leacock's *Charles Dickens: His Life and Work*. On the back panel is a list of "BOOKS OF | ENDURING VALUE" published by Doubleday Doran.

NOTES: On 10 March 1934, less than three months after the publication of Leacock's biography of Dickens (A65), Russell Doubleday of Doubleday, Doran and Company wrote to Leacock: "I am delighted to know that you are interested in the idea of compiling a Dickens Reader." Doubleday suggested that Leacock could compile a large anthology of 1,200 to 1,500 pages. When Leacock sent excerpts of Dickens's works to Doubleday, Doubleday replied on 16 March 1934 that he was ". . . very much pleased with the Dickens material that arrived this morning, and after reading it and seeing your layout and title, and visualizing your plan, we all agree that your scheme is the right one to follow." He asked Leacock to hurry so that they could publish in May while ". . . the Dickens iron is very hot." Doubleday posted Leacock a check for $250 ". . . on account of whatever contract we make." He acknowledged receipt of Leacock's manuscript on 31 March 1934. He told Leacock: It ". . . looks grand. We have immediately put it in hand for setting, and we are studying it at the same time for illustrations."

The contract, dated 4 April 1934, is for world rights on a profit-sharing basis (taking into account expenses for production and profits from sales) — "60% to you and 40% to us," with advance payment to Leacock of $250. The edition consisted of 2,671 copies. Published on 11 July 1934. The copyright was registered with the Copyright Office at DLC on 27 July 1934 (ClA73624). The copyright was renewed by Stephen Lushington Leacock on 13 July 1961 (R278988).

On 20 July 1934, Doubleday told Leacock: "I am so glad that you liked the style of THE GREATEST PAGES OF CHARLES DICKENS. The book has started out fairly well and I hope it will have the success it deserves." By 8 October, according to Doubleday, the book had ". . . already earned its keep and will show black figures for both of us next period." The royalty report ending on 2 January 1935 indicates that 1,595 copies were sold with revenues of $2,255.63. The expenses for the book (plant account $705.63, paper, printing and binding $591.07, and operating costs $789.47) were $2,086.17. The gross profit at that time was $169.46 ($101.68 to Leacock). Since Leacock received an advance of $250, there was still an unearned balance of $148.32. Leacock never received any recompense beyond his advance royalty. The edition was exhausted by 2 May 1938. The semi-annual royalty reports appear to be conflicting as to the actual number of copies sold: another seventy-two copies sold up to 1 July 1935 and another 751 copies up to 2 January 1936. But the report of 1 July 1936 states that of the entire edition, there were sales of 1,551 copies, 1,081 (?) sent out as review copies, with thirty-nine copies in stock. The plates for the book were reclaimed for their metal content in June 1943 (government request during the war).

Despite limited sales, Leacock wanted to do similar books in the Greatest Pages series for Mark Twain and Samuel Pepys. The former, he was informed by Doubleday, was not possible because Harper and Brothers jealously guarded Twain's copyright. In fact, on 14 October 1934, Harper and Brothers denied Leacock's request to reprint selections from Twain's works. Doubleday and his editorial staff vetoed the idea of a Pepys reader on the grounds that Pepys had already been anthologized sufficiently. Leacock told his friend, J.A.T. Lloyd, on 8 April 1935: "I invented the series (Greatest Pages of) — & Mr. D[oubleday] is very appreciative. . . ."

COPIES EXAMINED: CS (two copies, one in jacket); LAT (in jacket); OORI (in jacket); QMMRB (in jacket).

## A70 THE PURSUIT OF KNOWLEDGE 1934

THE PURSUIT | OF KNOWLEDGE | * | A DISCUSSION OF | FREEDOM AND COMPULSION | IN EDUCATION | * | by STEPHEN LEACOCK | DEPARTMENT OF | ECONOMICS AND POLITICAL SCIENCE | MCGILL UNIVERSITY | [swelled rule] | LIVERIGHT PUBLISHING Corporation | NEW YORK

◆ $1-3^8$. *1-12, 13-48* pp. (24 leaves). 183 × 115 mm.

CONTENTS: p. *1* half title; p. *2 KAPPA DELTA PI LECTURE SERIES* | * | [list of five books, Leacock's book being no. 5 of the series]; p. *3* title; p. *4* COPYRIGHT, 1934, BY STEPHEN LEACOCK | PRINTED | IN THE UNITED STATES | OF AMERICA; pp. *5–6* introduction by the editor, Alfred L. Hall-Quest; p. *7* table of contents; p. *8* blank; pp. *9–10* Leacock's preface dated "August 20th, 1934"; p. *11* fly title; p. *12* blank; pp. *13–48* text.

TEXT: Chapter I Two Rival Principles; chapter II The Organization of Education; chapter III Educational Method; chapter IV The Examination; chapter V College and Professional Requirements.

BINDING AND DUST JACKET: Two binding variants were examined: dark blue cloth; and dark blue cloth (but slightly lighter in colour and not as grainy in texture). Stamped on the upper board in gold: THE PURSUIT OF KNOWLEDGE | [rule] | STEPHEN LEACOCK | [rule] | THE KAPPA DELTA PI LECTURE SERIES. Stamped in gold down the spine: THE PURSUIT OF KNOWLEDGE.

The dust jacket is greenish yellow with green lettering. On the front panel of the jacket are three vertical rules (one wavy), the title, author's name, and a short paragraph on Leacock's lectures (the fifth volume in the series). The back panel lists and briefly describes (prices given) the first four volumes of the series. The information on the front flap has the price $1.20, the title of the book, Leacock's name, and a summary of the book's contents. The back flap is blank.

NOTES: On 28 June 1934, Alfred L. Quest-Hall of New York University's Institute of Education asked Leacock to write a brief preface to *The Pursuit of Knowledge*. "The manuscript is now in press," he informed Leacock. Published on 24 August 1934. The copyright was registered by Leacock at the Copyright Office of DLC on 8 September 1934 (ClA75569). The copyright was renewed by Stephen Lushington Leacock on 24 August 1961 (R280900). On 11 October 1934, Arthur Pell of the Liveright Publishing Corporation sent Leacock six complimentary copies of the book. Neither the royalty arrangements nor the number of copies printed is known.

COPIES EXAMINED: CS (both variant bindings, each in jacket with the price clipped on the front flap); QMMRB (dark blue cloth).

## A71 SUGGESTIONS FOR ECONOMY AT MCGILL 1935

[cover title:] Confidential | Not for Circulation | SUGGESTIONS FOR | ECONOMY AT | Mc GILL | Stephen Leacock | January 1935

◆ Leaflet folded once to form four unnumbered pages. 140 × 110 mm.

CONTENTS: p. *1* cover title; pp. 2–4 text, the last page dated "Jan. 21, 1935." All copies examined had an insertion in Leacock's hand ("9–11 am and") on the last page concerning the hours of the Arts Building for a McGill Matriculation class.

TEXT: On p. 2 of this leaflet Leacock addresses the members of the Faculty of Arts on how to save money at McGill University. He suggests six measures, and ends by saying: "7. These savings will amount to $40,000."

BINDING: Printed on plain off-white paper stock, no wrapper.

NOTES: This leaflet apparently was privately printed by Leacock for distribution to his colleagues in the Faculty of Arts at McGill University — "The Governors of the University having invited us to consider ways of economy." He proposes the following: (1) not to replace Faculty when they die, resign or retire; (2) to offer one professor in each department a year's absence on two fifths pay; (3) to stop sending student delegates to Washington D.C.; (4) to stop subsidizing athletics; (5) to suppress a department that teaches subjects of doubtful value; and (6) to open a McGill Matriculation class.

Leacock regarded his proposals as tentative because he added "Confidential | Not for Circulation" to the cover title. The very fact that he issued another leaflet a month or so later (A72) indicates that his ideas on this subject were in a state of flux. Number of copies printed not known.

COPIES EXAMINED: QMMRB; SLM (approximately seventy copies).

## A72 THE RESTORATION OF FINANCES OF MCGILL UNIVERSITY 1935

[cover title] COPYRIGHT AND CONFIDENTIAL | THE RESTORATION OF THE FINANCES | OF McGILL UNIVERSITY | [ornament] | Suggestions submitted to the Consideration of my Fellow | Members of the University. | I.TO DIMINISH THE DEFICIT. | II.TO CARRY THE DEFICIT. | III.TO REMOVE THE DEFICIT. | Stephen Leacock, | February 28, 1935. | [eight rules, the first seven identical, and the last one thick]

◆ Leaflet folded once to form four unnumbered pages. 260 × 185 mm.

CONTENTS: p. *1* cover title; pp. 2–4 text. The last two lines of p. *4* are: STEPHEN LEACOCK. | Copyright, Ottawa, 1935.

TEXT: The text consists of two preliminary sections: The Present Situation; and The Mode of Approach. Section I, Ways to Reduce the Deficit, has two parts: A By Economizing; and B By Making Money. Sections II and III are entitled: To Carry the Deficit; and Removing the Deficit.

BINDING: Issued on off-white paper stock, no wrapper.

NOTES: This leaflet is a complete revision of Leacock's leaflet (A71) that he issued in January 1935. In his earlier leaflet he proposed six measures to reduce the deficit of McGill University. Here he has developed and expanded his ideas. Part A of section I puts forward five measures to economize university finances: (1) contract the staff; (2) drop "all departments and academic functions of few students and of doubtful value"; (3) cut out the School of Physical Education; (4) cut out the museums; and (5) stop subsidies from fees to athletics. Part B of section I has six further suggestions on how the university can make money: (6) open a McGill Matriculation School; (7) establish a university press; (8) open a university book room; (9) begin a university journal (in particular, the *McGill Fortnightly Review*); (10) establish a graduate subscription lottery; and (11) "Farm out the *Franchise of the Stadium.*"

Leacock sent a copy of this leaflet to A.E. Morgan, the Principal of McGill University, on 14 February 1935. At about the same time he asked Professor Harold Hibbert of the Department of Industrial and Cellulose Chemistry for his comments. Hibbert read the leaflet with much interest, and replied on 27 March 1935. He commented on the two sections dealing with ways to reduce the deficit and to carry the deficit. He disagreed with Leacock's proposals to abolish the School of Physical Education and to have a graduate subscription lottery. The most valuable part of leaflet, Hibbert thought, was Leacock's suggestion for "a five year issue of bonds for $1,000,000 secured on the McGill Campus (south end) in individual lots and carrying interest at 2½% with repayment in terms of the Dominion of Canada general index number to secure it against loss by the coming rose of prices." (information based on file 955, container 59, RG2, QMM Archives; and file at QMMRB).

Number of copies printed not known.

COPIES EXAMINED: CS; QMM Archives; QMMRB; SLM (four copies).

## A73 HUMOR: ITS THEORY AND TECHNIQUE 1935

### A73a *American edition*:

[all lines within a rectangle; the left and right sides of the rectangle with bevelled edges] HUMOR | ITS THEORY AND TECHNIQUE | WITH | EXAMPLES AND SAMPLES | *A Book of Discovery* | *by* | STEPHEN LEACOCK | [illustration of a jester] | DODD, MEAD & COMPANY | NEW YORK 1935

◆ 1–16⁸ 17¹⁰. i–iv, v, 1–3, 1–268 pp. (138 leaves). 197 × 140 mm.

CONTENTS: p. *i* half title; p. *ii* list of eighteen books by Leacock, the first *Literary Lapses* and the last *Afternoons in Utopia*; p. *iii* title; p. *iv* COPYRIGHT, 1935 | BY DODD, MEAD AND COMPANY, INC. | ALL RIGHTS RESERVED | NO PART OF THIS BOOK MAY BE REPRODUCED IN ANY FORM | WITHOUT PERMISSION IN WRITING FROM THE PUBLISHER | PRINTED IN THE UNITED STATES OF AMERICA | BY THE VAIL-BALLOU PRESS, INC., BINGHAMTON, N. Y.; p. v table of contents; p. *1* blank; p. 2 fly title; p. 3 blank; pp. 1–268 text.

TEXT: chapter I An Analysis of Humor; chapter II Fun with Words; chapter III Parody, Burlesque and Mistranslation; chapter IV Technique of the Greater Humorists: Charles Dickens and Mark Twain; chapter V Comic and Super-Comic Verse; chapter VI An Appended Sample; chapter VII Story Tellers and Story Killers; chapter VIII National Characteristics; chapter IX Humor Through the Ages; chapter X This Very Minute; chapter XI Epilogue: From the Ridiculous to the Sublime. Chapter VI reprints Leacock's poem, "The Lost Anatomist" (C34.15).

BINDING AND DUST JACKET: Bound in light brownish grey cloth with stamping in blue. Stamped on the upper board: ~HUMOR~ | ITS THEORY AND TECHNIQUE | STEPHEN LEACOCK. Stamped on the spine: HUMOR | [illustration of jester's stick] | LEACOCK | DODD, MEAD | & COMPANY.

The front and spine panels of the jacket are turquoise with lettering and illustration in white and red. Both these panels have zig-zag rules and an illustration of a jester's stick. The remainder of the jacket is cream-coloured with lettering in red. The back panel features an advertisement for the Silver Jubilee edition of *The Need of Change*. The front flap has a synopsis of Leacock's book. The back flap has an advertisement for *Laugh with Leacock* with the book's price ($2.50) and quotations from George Ade, Robert Benchley, and Ellis Parker Butler.

NOTES: On 9 February 1933, Leacock wrote to Dodd, Mead: "Herewith enclosed I send you the outline of the new book *Humour* which I propose to do next spring or next summer. . . . I wish to make it an easy and pleasant book suitable for adverse times." Two days later Frank Dodd replied that he was "delighted to hear that a new book is in the offing for next summer." He offered Leacock an advance of $500 instead of the usual $1,000 because the previous book of humour, *Afternoons in Utopia*, had not sold as they had hoped. He offered Leacock 15% royalty but found this "pretty stiff, in view of the record on the last book." Leacock agreed to these terms on 20 February for a book of forty to fifty thousand words. The initial contract with Dodd, Mead is dated 21 February 1933. Leacock was to deliver the manuscript by 1 June 1933. On 17 March 1933 he contemplated a book of 60,000 words and asked Dodd to make the contract 1 January 1934. He added: ". . . if I can get it done by Sept. 15, 1933, we would get it out as a Xmas market book." Although

Dodd was keen to advertise the book in the press, he advised Leacock on 22 March 1933 to "leave the question as to publication in abeyance for the time being. . . ." A second contract for the book is dated 29 March 1933.

On 9 May 1933, E.H. Dodd, Jr. sent Leacock a colour sketch of his proposed book titled "Why Laugh?". Leacock suggested the subtitle "The Theory and Technique of Humour" on 13 May. With respect to the design of the jacket he remarked that the face depicted was "sardonic and unattractive": "At best it is but a formula figured like a gargoyle. How would you like to substitute a picture of Bacchus Launching Mona Lisa. — Such a design as that I think would have more bounce to it."

In anticipation of an announcement of publication in the company's spring catalogue, Frank Dodd inquired about the book's progress on 8 November 1933. On 12 November Leacock stated that he would finish the manuscript by the summer of 1934. He had lectured at the University of Minnesota (19 October 1933, E33.26) on "The Technique of Humor." Dodd replied on 14 November, however: "I think it would be just as well to postpone publication until next summer, as that will give you ample time, and by then we can at least hope that it will have a better chance of success." Dodd asked about Leacock's progress several times thereafter (on 27 March and 2 April 1934, for example). On 24 August 1934, exasperated by the delays, he wrote to Leacock: "Where, oh where, is the manuscript of WHY LAUGH? We need it badly." Leacock replied on 6 September 1934: "I am sorry to say that hot weather in August knocked me right out of work, though I wasn't ill and so I am away behind with *Why Laugh*. Working hard now." On 12 October [1934], he told Dodd that "My Why Laugh book is going ahead now in good shape." On 21 November he reported: "Book nearly done: will be all right for the end of year. I've been lecturing on American humour with a fine response. The book is all right but I still very much doubt your title. In England the book will be called the Theory & Technique of Humour." Leacock mailed the manuscript to Dodd, Mead just before Christmas 1934.

Leacock continued to voice his displeasure with the title, "Why Laugh?". He regarded the book's potential market to be in the colleges and universities. Dodd finally saw Leacock's point of view about the title on 29 January 1935. The proofs (labelled *Why Laugh?*) were sent to Leacock on 13 February 1935, and he corrected and returned them on 26 February 1935. He disapproved of the font of type because it did not sufficiently distinguish paragraphs. Initially, there was also a problem of serialization rights with chapter X, which used material from "Sex, Sex, Sex — I'm Sick of It." Luckily, the article appeared in the *Rotarian* on 24 March 1935, two weeks prior to the book's publication on 10 April 1935 (price $2.50). The copyright was registered with the Copyright Office at DLC on 12 April 1935 (ClA82746). The copyright was renewed by Stephen Lushington Leacock on 15 October 1962 (R302963).

On 2 July 1935 Dodd informed Leacock:

> HUMOR is selling along steadily, but certainly it has not done anything like as well as your DICKENS. I can only attribute this to the very different subject matter of the two books and the fact that a first class biography is always in demand. . . . I have just had a computation made of the sales if HUMOR to date. The total is certainly disappointing, but after all, it is too early to judge yet. It is between fifteen and sixteen hundred.

According to the royalty report of 1 August 1935, 1,329 copies (44 special sale) sold of the

American edition ($542.66 royalty before taxes, including Canadian sales). The book was still in print at the time of Leacock's death. For the period between 1 February 1941 to 1 February 1944, Dodd, Mead reported a royalty of $37.51 in American sales and $9.90 royalty in Canadian sales.

COPIES EXAMINED: CS (in jacket); OHM (Dodd, Mead house library copy in the company's archives).

### A73a.1 *Canadian issue*:

[all lines within a rectangle; the left and right sides of the rectangle with bevelled edges] HUMOR | ITS THEORY AND TECHNIQUE | WITH | EXAMPLES AND SAMPLES | *A Book of Discovery* | *by* | STEPHEN LEACOCK | [illustration of a jester] | Canadian Edition | For Sale in Canada Only | DODD, MEAD & COMPANY | (CANADA) LIMITED TORONTO

NOTES: On 5 April 1935, Dodd, Mead arranged to bind 500 copies of the American edition with a Canadian imprint to be published by Dodd, Mead & Co. (Canada) Ltd. The Canadian issue was sold by McClelland and Stewart, Dodd, Mead's Canadian agents. Leacock received a royalty of 15% on sales of this issue. According to Dodd, Mead's royalty report, 104 copies of the Canadian issue sold by 1 August 1935. With the exception of the title page, the Canadian issue is identical to A73a (price $2.50).

COPIES EXAMINED: CS (in jacket); QMMRB (two copies, one in jacket, the other rebound).

### A73b *advertising leaflet*:

[cover title] | [black-and-white photograph of Leacock's head; red rule, remaining lines in red against a black background; the next three lines in script] | *By* | [the next two lines at an angle] *Stephen* | *Leacock* | [the next line with black inline] HUMOR | Its Theory and Technique

♦ Leaflet folded once to form four unnumbered pages. 159 × 86 mm.

On p. 2 are: two introductory paragraphs with the heading, *Humor in a Distressed World*; an illustration of a jester's stick in red; and Leacock's signature in facsimile. The remaining pages have the table of contents with a perforated section on the last page for sending an order of the book to Dodd, Mead. Apparently distributed to bookstores and other venues near the date of publication of the American edition. Number of copies printed not known.

COPIES EXAMINED: CS; SLM (many copies).

### A73c *English edition*:

HUMOUR | ITS THEORY *&* TECHNIQUE | *with* | *Examples and Samples* | *A Book of Discovery* | *By* | *Stephen Leacock* | LONDON | JOHN LANE THE BODLEY HEAD

♦ A$^8$ B–S$^8$ T$^4$ [$1 signed]. *i–iv*, v, *1–3*, 1–288 pp. (148 leaves). 174 × 113 mm.

CONTENTS: p. *i* half title; p. *ii* list of twenty-one books by Leacock, the first being *Literary Lapses* and the last *The Dry Pickwick*; p. *iii* title; p. *iv* PRINTED IN GREAT BRITAIN | BY WESTERN PRINTING SERVICES LTD., BRISTOL; p. v table of contents; p. *1* blank; p. 2 fly title; p. *3* blank; pp. 1–288 text.

TEXT: Identical to A73a. Titles of chapters have been altered somewhat — for example, chapter I is entitled Why Laugh? An Analysis of Humour.

BINDING AND DUST JACKET: Bound in orange cloth with red lettering, top edge stained orange. Stamped on the upper board: *HUMOUR* | *STEPHEN* | *LEACOCK*. Stamped on the spine: *HUMOUR* | [ornamental rule] | *STEPHEN* | *LEACOCK* | [publisher's device: oval portrait of John Bodley with initials JL] | THE BODLEY HEAD. Dust jacket not seen.

NOTES: On the same day that he wrote to Dodd, Mead (9 February 1933), Leacock sent a similar letter to his English publisher. To Leacock's proposal Allen Lane replied that although he was glad to hear that a new book was in the offing, he could only offer £100 advance instead of the usual £250 because the sales would be lower than for a book of humorous sketches. Leacock agreed to Lane's terms on 17 March [1933]. On 24 April Leacock agreed to accept "15% [royalty] up to 4,000 in view of hard times." He added: "I should not care to let my future books go under 20% but with things being so bad this one doesn't matter." He asked Lane about the Canadian edition and suggested $200 Canadian, 15% royalty up to 4,000 copies sold, and 20% thereafter: "The Canadian sales of my books have always been reserved and so I insert a clause to that effect." Lane told Leacock on 2 May 1933 to take care of the Canadian edition himself. Copies of the contract, dated 2 May 1933, are extant at READ and in Leacock's papers at SLM.

On 31 July 1933, Leacock decided to postpone the book till after the New Year, informing Ronald Boswell that it would be difficult to write it in a hurry and that the market was poor. On 7 February 1934, Boswell inquired: "Can you g[i]ve me any news of your book on HUMOUR and let me know when can we expect the material?" Leacock finally told Lane on 25 November 1934 that "my book *Theory & Technique of Humour* will be posted to you in M.S. on Dec 24." Leacock hoped for simultaneous publication in England and America. Published before 15 September 1935 (review in the *Sunday Times* (London) on that date). Price 7s 6d. Number of copies printed or sold not known.

COPIES EXAMINED: OTNY (no jacket); QMMRB (proof copy).


## A74 A MEMORANDUM ON SOCIAL RESEARCH 1935

[cover title] A | MEMORANDUM | ON | SOCIAL RESEARCH | AT | McGILL UNIVERSITY | STEPHEN LEACOCK | Oct. 7, 1935.

◆ $1^4$. 1–8 pp. (4 leaves). 144 × 112 mm.

CONTENTS: p. *1* cover title; p. *2* blank; p. *3* fly title (identical to cover title); p. *4* paragraph entitled SCOPE; p. *5–8* list of six volumes, with an explanation of the contents of the first three volumes, for a series entitled SOCIAL RESEARCH SERIES.

TEXT: There is really no text to this pamphlet. The section entitled SCOPE consists of five paragraphs of a proposal for a series of studies by McGill students.

BINDING: Issued without a wrapper on off-white paper stock, wire-stitched.

NOTES: Leacock apparently prepared this pamphlet for various administrators at McGill University. His proposal called for the publication by McGill University of interdisciplinary studies written by students. He wanted to avoid "the field admirably covered by the Canadian Department of Statistics, the Reports in the Sessional Papers, and the Special

Reports of Commissions." The field of study that he had in mind "involves cultural elements outside of tabulation and statistical measurement," which is shared by "various college departments and not exclusively in any" (p. 4). The titles that he proposed as possible publications are the following: vol. I Interchange of Population between Canada and the United States; vol. II Persistence and Absorbtion [sic] of Languages in the Settlement of Canada; vol. III Motion Pictures in Canada; vol. IV Radio in Canada; vol. V The Mechanization of Agriculture in Its Economic and Cultural Effect; and vol. VI British and American Culture in Canada: A Study of Relative Impact. It would appear that nothing came of Leacock's proposal. Privately printed. Number of copies printed not known.

COPIES EXAMINED: SLM (six copies).

## A75 LAUGHTER & WISDOM OF STEPHEN LEACOCK 1936

*LAUGHTER & | : WISDOM : | OF STEPHEN LEACOCK | [thick-thin rule] | BEING TWO VOLUMES | IN ONE | 'THE DRY PICKWICK' | AND | 'WINNOWED WISDOM' | JL | JOHN LANE THE BODLEY HEAD | LONDON*

♦ $A^4$ (–A4) B–I$^{16}$ K$^8$ A$^{16}$ (–A1.2) B–I$^{16}$ [\$1 signed]. *1–6, 1–36, 37–38*, 39–46, 47–48, 49–63, 64–66, *67–76, 77–78, 79–85, 86–88, 89–93, 94–96, 97–104, 105–106, 107–119, 120–122, 123–137, 138–140, 141–148, 149–150, 151–156, 157–158, 159–164, 165–166, 167–172, 173–174, 175–179, 180–182, 183–193, 194–196, 197–203, 204–206, 207–213, 214–216, 217–227, 228–230, 231–238, 239–240, 241–247, 248–250, 251–260, 261–262, 263–271, 1–3, vii–xiv, 1–2, 1–25, 26–28, 29–69, 70–72, 73–107, 108–110, 111–164, 165–166, 167–195, 196–198, 199–224, 225–226, 227–254, 255–256, 257–264, 1–8* pp. (281 leaves). 185 × 121 mm.

CONTENTS: p. *1* half title; p. *2* THE DRY PICKWICK | [rule] | *First published* 1932 | WINNOWED WISDOM | [rule] | *First published* 1926; p. *3* title; p. *4* First published in one volume | 1936 | Made and Printed in Great Britain by Butler & Tanner, Ltd., Frome and London; p. *5* half title of *The Dry Pickwick*; p. *6* blank; pp. *1–271* text of *The Dry Pickwick* pp. (pp. *38, 48, 64, 66, 78, 86, 88, 94, 96, 106, 120, 122, 138, 140, 150, 158, 166, 174, 180, 182, 194, 196, 204, 206, 214, 216, 228, 230, 240, 248,* and *262* blank; p. *1* blank; p. *2* title of *Winnowed Wisdom*; p. *3* copyright page; pp. vii–xii preface to *Winnowed Wisdom*; pp. xiii–xiv table of contents to *Winnowed Wisdom*; pp. *1–2, 1–264* text of *Winnowed Wisdom* (pp. *2, 108, 110, 166, 196, 198, 226,* and *256* blank); pp. *1–8* advertisements.

TEXT: Identical to the texts of A59 and A44a.

BINDING: Bound in orange cloth with stamping on the spine as follows: LAUGHTER | AND | WISDOM | [rule] | STEPHEN | LEACOCK | THE BODLEY HEAD. Apparently issued without a jacket.

NOTES: On 22 January 1936, surplus sheet stock of *The Dry Pickwick* was disposed of at 4d per copy. This stock was presumably used in this composite volume — in other words, instead of remaindering the books or disposing of the sheets, The Bodley Head used unsold stock of both books for a new Leacock title.

Number of copies printed not known.

COPIES EXAMINED: LAT; OTUTF; QMMRB.

## A76 THE LEACOCK LAUGHTER BOOK 1936

THE | LEACOCK LAUGHTER | BOOK | *containing* | SHORT CIRCUITS | AFTERNOONS IN UTOPIA | LONDON | JOHN LANE THE BODLEY HEAD LIMITED

♦ $A^4$ ($A3+\chi1,2$) $B-L^{16}$ $M^{14}$ ($-M9$ to $M14$) $A^4$ ($-A1$, $+/-A2$) $B-Q^8$ [$1 signed ($B-Q^8$ having compositor's initials A.U.), Q2a signed Q*]. *i–vi*, vii–ix, *1–3*, 1–95, *96*, 97–143, *144*, 145–336, *1–2*, v–vi, *1–2*, 1–37, *38–40*, 41–83, *84–86*, 87–107, *108–110*, 111–175, *176–178*, 179–192, *193–194*, 195–240 pp. (297 leaves). 183 × 126 mm.

CONTENTS: pp. *i–ii* blank; p. *iii* half title; p. *iv* SHORT CIRCUITS | *First published 1928* | AFTERNOONS IN UTOPIA | *First published 1932*; p. *v* title; p. *vi* THIS EDITION first published 1936 | Made and Printed in Great Britain by | BUTLER & TANNER, FROME, SOMERSET.; pp. vii–ix table of contents of *Short Circuits*; p. *1* blank; pp. *1–2*, 1–336 text of *Short Circuits* (pp. *2, 96*, and *144* blank); pp. *1–2* title leaf of *Afternoons in Utopia*; pp. v–vi table of contents of *Afternoons in Utopia*; pp. *1–2*, 1–240 text of *Afternoons in Utopia* (pp. *2, 38, 40, 84, 86, 108, 110, 176, 178*, and *194* blank). The title leaf of *Afternoons in Utopia* is a cancel.

TEXT: Identical to the texts of A52b and A61b.

BINDING: Bound in orange cloth with stamping on the spine as follows: THE | LEACOCK | LAUGHTER | BOOK | THE BODLEY HEAD. Apparently issued without a jacket.

NOTES: On 22 January 1936, surplus sheet stock of *Afternoons in Utopia* was disposed of at 4d per copy. This stock was presumably used in this composite volume — in other words, instead of remaindering the two books or disposing of the sheets, The Bodley Head used unsold stock of both books for a new Leacock title.

Exact publication and number of copies printed not known.

COPIES EXAMINED: CS; OORI; OTMCL.

## A77 THE GREATEST PAGES OF AMERICAN HUMOR 1936

### A77a *first American edition*:

[rule; row of ornaments; rule] | THE GREATEST PAGES OF | American Humor | SELECTED AND DISCUSSED BY | Stephen Leacock | [rule] | A Study of the Rise and Development of HUMOROUS | WRITINGS IN AMERICA with Selections from | the most notable of the HUMORISTS. | [rule] | [publisher's device — ship, anchor, netting, land, and two people in eighteenth-century dress, one pointing to letters DD] | [rule] | DOUBLEDAY, DORAN & COMPANY, INC. | GARDEN CITY 1936 NEW YORK | [rule; row of ornaments; rule]

♦ $1-19^8$. *i–iv*, v–vii, *1–3*, 2–293, *1* pp. (152 leaves). 199 × 140 mm.

CONTENTS: p. *i* half title; p. *ii* Some Books By | STEPHEN LEACOCK | [twenty-eight books listed in twenty-three lines]; p. *iv* title; p. *v* PRINTED AT THE *Country Life Press*, GARDEN CITY, N.Y., U.S.A. | COPYRIGHT, 1936 | BY DOUBLEDAY, DORAN & COMPANY, INC. | ALL RIGHTS RESERVED | FIRST EDITION; pp. v–vii table of contents; p. *1* fly title; p. *2* blank; pp. *3*, 2–293 text; p. *1* blank.

TEXT: Generally speaking, the text alternates between chapters of Leacock's discussion and chapters of selections from the works of the humorists discussed.

Chapter I The Origins of American Humor; chapter II Selections from Benjamin Franklin's Works (Poor Richard's Almanac, Sending Felons to America, Petition of the Letter Z); chapter III Classic America Smiles; chapter IV Selections from Irving and Hawthorne (Rip Van Winkle, The Celestial Railroad); chapter V Democracy Starts a Laugh of Its Own; chapter VI Selections from Crockett, Major Downing and Josh Billings (Colonel Crockett Snubs Harvard, Crockett Finds Philadelphia Too Fast, Captain Downing Defies the British, Billings on the Mule, Billings on the Hen, Josh Rebukes Billings); chapter VII Artemus Ward: His Life, His Book, His Death (High-Handed Outrage in Utica, Artemus Ward in the Egyptian Hall); chapter VIII Sunrise in the West; chapter IX Bret Harte's "Lothaw"; chapter X Mark Twain; chapter XI Selections from Mark Twain (from *The Innocents Abroad*, from *Huckleberry Finn*, Mark Twain Roughs It Across the Plains); chapter XII The "After-Mark" of American Humor; chapter XIII Selections from Max Adler, Uncle Remus and Oliver Wendell Holmes (An Accident in a Newspaper Office, Uncle Remus Initiates the Little Boy, Thoughts at the Breakfast Table); chapter XIV The Century Runs Out; chapter XV Selections from Mr. Dooley, John Kendrick Bangs, Hashimura, Togo (Wallace Irwin), and George Ade's Fables (Mr. Dunne Presents Mr. Dooley, Mr. Dooley on the Philippines, from *A Houseboat on the Styx*, from *Letters of a Japanese Schoolboy*, The Fable of Springfield's Fairest Flower and Lonesome Agnes Who Was Crafty); chapter XVI The Enchanted World of O. Henry; chapter XVII Selections from O. Henry (A Municipal Report, Jeff Peters as a Personal Magnet); chapter XVIII Humor in a Changing World; chapter XIX Selections from Benchley, Cobb and Lardner (from *Of All Things*, from *Here Comes the Bride — and So Forth*, Haircut); chapter XX L'Envoi: Our Present Need of Humor — Our Brilliant Contemporaries (from *Life*, from *Vanity Fair*, from the *New Yorker*, Syndicated Laughter, The Columnist, A Wreath for Will Rogers).

BINDING AND DUST JACKET: Bound in red cloth except for a black rectangular compartment on the spine, top edge stained red. Blind-stamped on the upper board is an illustration of a candle, books, and a writing quill. Stamped on the black compartment on the spine in gilt: THE | GREATEST | PAGES OF | AMERICAN | HUMOR | STEPHEN | LEACOCK | DOUBLEDAY | DORAN. A series of double rules and vines are blind-stamped above and below the black compartment.

The front and spine panels of the dust jacket are red with white lettering and illustrations and rules in dull gilt. On the front panel: [heavy rule extending from the spine] | GREATEST PAGES | OF | AMERICAN | HUMOR | [caricature of the head and shoulders of a jester with six rules on either side] | STEPHEN LEACOCK | [heavy rule extending from the spine]. On the spine panel of the jacket: [heavy rule] | THE | GREATEST | PAGES | OF | AMERICAN | HUMOR | STEPHEN | LEACOCK | [caricature (but smaller in size than the front panel) of the head and shoulders of a jester] | DOUBLEDAY | DORAN | [heavy rule]. The back panel of the jacket and the flaps are white with red lettering. On the back panel is an advertisement for Don Marquis's *Three Masterpieces of Mirth*. The flaps have a synopsis of the book, information on Leacock's writing career, and the price ($2.50).

NOTES: When Harper and Brothers refused to allow Leacock to annotate and edit an edition of Mark Twain's selected works for the Greatest Pages series of Doubleday, Doran and Company, Leacock wrote to Russell Doubleday on 3 November [1934]:

Yes — or we might alter the idea to Greatest Pages of American Humour. Benjamin Franklin to Mark Twain.

That would give us the use on *Innocents Abroad Roughing It* & Tom Sawyer — and if successful leave room for a second (later) volume. *Mark Twain till Today*. I only first thought of this & send it for what it's worth.

Doubleday was receptive to the idea, but on 8 November 1934, he advised Leacock "that it would be better to carry it from Benjamin Franklin to Mark Twain and beyond, because it is some time since Mark Twain died, and there are a good many people who have reached some distinction in humor since his time." Doubleday requested Leacock to prepare an outline. A day later Leacock replied enthusiastically: "I let no grass grow under my feet. Herewith a (tentative) abstract." Only Twain's work, Leacock reckoned, would require payment for copyright. "The others are either dead and out of copyright or don't matter *individually* enough to count. They ought to be glad to get in: if not they can stay out." Doubleday was almost as enthusiastic about the project as Leacock, although he expressed reservations about copyright permission on 22 November 1934. He planned to make Leacock's edition on American humorists "less elaborate" and "less expensive" than *The Greatest Pages of Charles Dickens*.

On 4 January 1935, Leacock wrote similar letters to Irvin Cobb, George Ade, and Robert Benchley in which he asked them if he could use 2,000 words of their funniest works without a fee. On the same day he suggested to Doubleday that the contract for the book would be the same as *The Greatest Pages of Charles Dickens* (a profit-sharing basis, 60% to Leacock, 40% to Doubleday, Doran). On 10 January 1935, Harper and Brothers gave Leacock authorization to reprint selections from Twain's *Connecticut Yankee* and *Huckleberry Finn* for a fee of $200. Doubleday agreed to the same terms as *The Greatest Pages of Charles Dickens* on 16 January 1935. Doubleday, Doran paid the copyright fee on the Twain selections (only *Huckleberry Finn* required payment), but Doubleday suggested to Leacock that he should receive no "advance in this case, unless you must have the money." Leacock was amenable to Doubleday's suggestion, but he added on 21 January [1935]: "But I think you might guarantee a royalty of $250 six months after publication. Otherwise, the contract looks a little vague." In his telegram to Leacock of 11 February 1935, Benchley told Leacock: "ANYTHING OF MINE THAT YOU MIGHT WANT TO USE IN YOUR BOOK WAS YOURS IN THE FIRST PLACE." Ade gave his assent on 12 February 1935 and so did Cobb on 15 February.

On 14 March 1935, Leacock sent Doubleday the table of contents and the chapter on Artemus Ward. He informed Doubleday that the book would be completed by 15 May 1935. But, on 20 March 1935, Doubleday expressed his concerns again about copyright problems: "In looking over your table of contents, I note that you wish to include extracts from a good many writers whose work is in copyright and whose publishers will certainly exact permission fees. . . ." The contract could not be drawn up unless the question of fees was settled, Doubleday pointed out. Nevertheless, he told Leacock: "With the material in hand I am sure we can get up a dummy description, design for wrapper and cover, and so forth, for our salesmen." Leacock tried to assuage Doubleday's qualms about copyright in a letter of 26 March 1935. He had looked at the *World Almanac* and had ascertained that American copyright expires after fifty-six years:

This means that there is no copyright on Mark Twain's Tom Sawyer, Roughing It or Innocents Abroad. There is no copyright on the work of Bret Harte which I need: etc.

As to O. Henry, I understand your firm has the copyright. I have already permission from Irvin Cobb, Bob Benchley, and George Ade. . . . I am writing to the publishers of Ring Lardner, Montegue Glass, . . . who are all dead. No[t] one of them is indispensable. Therefore the whole cost of copyright is the small sum paid for Huck Finn [$100]. I am therefore going ahead at full speed; will make the book full length and cut it as required.

On 8 April 1935, Charles Scribner's Sons stipulated a payment of $50 for the use of Ring Lardner's "Hair Cut." Leacock asked them to reconsider (Scribner's said $30 on 22 May 1935). Doubleday inquired about the book's progress on 27 April 1935. He also inquired about possible illustrations and the wrapper. He sent Leacock a contract for the book on 29 April 1935 on the same basis as *The Greatest Pages of Charles Dickens* with the understanding that the only permission fee would be for the use of the Mark Twain selection and that Leacock would receive $250 royalties within six months after publication.

Doubleday acknowledged the "final copy" of Leacock's manuscript on 29 July 1935. On 13 August 1935, he asked Leacock to devote a chapter to "comparatively current humor as it has appeared in periodicals, including such people as Ring Lardner, Ogden Nash, some of the New Yorker crowd and others." Leacock replied by telegram on [19 August 1935]: "FINE IDEA ACTING ON IT AT ONCE." Leacock wrote to John Wheeler of the North America Newspaper Alliance for a selection of works of contemporary, popular syndicated authors.

Proofs were sent to Leacock on 9 January 1936; he returned them on 28 January 1936. The book was published in early March 1936 (probably 6 March). The edition consisted of 2,008 copies. By 1 July 1936 1,570 copies had sold, and 181 were sent out as review copies. The cost of sales and operating costs amounted to $1,313.25, but revenue amounted to $2,274.29 ($961.04 profit, 60% of which was Leacock's share — $576.62). By 2 May 1938 only three copies were left in stock, 1,802 had sold, and 213 had been sent out for review copies. No copies were in stock by 1 May 1939.

COPIES EXAMINED: CS (in jacket); QMMRB (two copies, neither in jacket, one rebound).

A77a.1 *first American issue* (1936):

[rule; row of ornaments; rule] | THE GREATEST PAGES OF | American Humor | SELECTED AND DISCUSSED BY | Stephen Leacock | [rule] | A Study of the Rise and Development of HUMOROUS | WRITINGS IN AMERICA with Selections from | the most notable of the HUMORISTS. | [rule] | [publisher's device — illustration of a sun dial with words SUN DIAL | [curved] PRESS] | [rule] | THE SUN DIAL PRESS | Garden City New York | [rule; row of ornaments; rule]

With the exception of the title leaf, the sheets of this issue are identical to the those of the edition published by Doubleday, Doran. Two states of this issue were examined: one where the last line of the verso of the title leaf lacks the last line of the Doubleday, Doran edition (i.e. the line FIRST EDITION); and the other where the line reads: CL.

BINDING AND DUST JACKET: Bound in red buckram, top edge stained red. The binding is very similar to that of the Doubleday, Doran edition with the following exceptions: the illustration on the upper board is stamped in black; printing on the spine is also in black without a black, rectangular compartment; the lines, DOUBLEDAY | DORAN, are not on the spine, and at the bottom of the spine is the imprint and logo of the Sun Dial Press.

The front panel of the dust jacket is orange. All lines (in black) on the front panel are within a gold compartment, comprised of two rectangles joined with leafy fronds: THE | GREATEST PAGES | OF | AMERICAN | HUMOR | FROM BENJAMIN FRANKLIN | TO THE RADIO WITS OF TODAY. | *Including* | The most delightful selections from HAW-THORNE, IRVING, | HOLMES, MARK TWAIN, O. HENRY, IRVIN COBB, RING LARD- | NER, ROBERT BENCHLEY, WILL ROGERS, GEORGE ADE, etc. | *Edited by that master of drollery and satire* | STEPHEN LEACOCK. The spine panel of the jacket is dull gold with the title, the author's name, and the publisher's imprint and logo. The back panel and the flaps are white. "*An Announcement | of vital interest to every Book-Lover*" is on the back panel in red and black (Sun Dial imprints at a 60% reduction of the original price). With minor modifications (no price, printing in black), the flaps have the same lines of print as those on the flaps of the Doubleday, Doran jacket.

NOTES: The date of publication of the Sun Dial Press issue is not known. Royalty statements indicate that the book initially sold for $.89 (later increased to $1). Between 2 January 1937 and 1 May 1942, 8,187 copies sold, earning Leacock a royalty of 5¢ a copy ($409.35).

COPIES EXAMINED: CS (both states — copy in jacket; copy not in jacket with CL on the copyright page); QMMRB (both states in jacket).

## A77a.2 *second American issue* (1942):

[rule; row of ornaments] | [rule] | THE GREATEST PAGES OF | American Humor | SELECTED AND DISCUSSED BY | Stephen Leacock | [rule] | A Study of the Rise and Development of HUMOROUS | WRITINGS IN AMERICA with Selections from | the most notable of the HUMORISTS. | [rule] | [illustration of a target with an arrow pointing downward through the bull's-eye with the words CENTER BOOKS curved] | [rule] | THE SUN DIAL PRESS | NEW YORK | [rule; row of ornaments; rule]

The sheets of this issue (185 × 125 mm.) are smaller in size than those of the Doubleday, Doran edition. With the exception of the title leaf, however, the issue was printed from the same set of plates. The verso of the title leaf reads: COPYRIGHT, 1936, BY DOUBLEDAY, DORAN AND COMPANY, INC. | *All rights reserved* | CENTER BOOKS EDITION PUB-LISHED SEPTEMBER 1942 | CENTER BOOKS is a new series published by | The Sun Dial Press, Time and Life Building, | Rockefeller Center, New York, N. Y. | PRINTED AND BOUND IN THE UNITED STATES OF AMERICA | BY THE AMERICAN BOOK-STRATFORD PRESS, INC., N. Y. C.

BINDING AND DUST JACKET: Bound in reddish purple cloth, all edges yellow, with yellow stamping on the spine as follows: [rule; leafy rule; rule] | THE | GREATEST | PAGES OF | AMERICAN | HUMOR | [rule] | *Stephen Leacock* | [rule; leafy rule; rule] | [illustration of target similar to that on the title page] | SUN DIAL PRESS.

The front and spine panels of the jacket are red. The front panel has the title, a paragraph describing the American humorists selected, Leacock's name, and caricatures of Huckle-berry Finn, Rip Van Winkle, a knight in armour, and a man in a plaid jacket and hat who is smoking a cigarette. Printed on the spine panel: The Greatest | Pages of | American | [in white] HUMOR | [illustration of Huckleberry Finn] | Edited by that master | of drollery and satire | [the next three lines and illustration in white] Stephen | Leacock | 10 | [illustration of target similar to that on the title page] | Sun Dial Press. The back panel and the flaps are white with black lettering and some red lettering. On the back panel is an advertisement for the Center Books series with a photograph of sample books. The front flap has a synopsis of the book. The back flap has further information on the Center Books series (Leacock's book, no. 10 of the series, appears at an angle, separated by a dotted line).

NOTES: On 17 July 1942, Lillian F. Robins of Doubleday, Doran informed Leacock that the firm wanted to issue "a new reprint line in the same manner as the Triangle book." The royalty was 1½¢ per copy with a minimum guarantee of 10,000 copies. Leacock received a royalty of $150 on 1 March 1943 (minus copies returned and U.S. tax, $119.05 royalty).

COPIES EXAMINED: CS (two copies — one without a jacket and the other in jacket but lacking the first leaf); SLM (in jacket).

## A77b  *English edition* (1937):

THE GREATEST PAGES OF | AMERICAN HUMOUR | *Selected and discussed* | *by* | STEPHEN LEACOCK | A STUDY OF THE RISE AND DEVELOPMENT | OF HUMOROUS WRITINGS IN AMERICA WITH | SELECTIONS FROM THE MOST NOTABLE | OF THE HUMORISTS | [publisher's device — illustration of arch and bare tree] | METHUEN *&* CO. LTD. LONDON | *36 Essex Street, Strand, W.C.*2

* $A^8$ B–$T^8$ [$1 signed]. *i–iv*, v–ix, 1–3, 3–293, 1 pp. (152 leaves). 197 × 135 mm.

CONTENTS: p. *i* half title; p. *ii* blank; p. *iii* title; p. *iv* First published in Great Britain in 1937 | PRINTED IN GREAT BRITAIN; pp. v–viii table of contents; p. ix acknowledgment; p. *1* blank; p. *2* fly title; p. *3* blank; pp. 3–293 text; p. *1 Printed in Great Britain | by Turnbull & Spears, Edinburgh.*

TEXT: Identical to the American edition.

BINDING AND DUST JACKET: Bound in orange cloth with blue lettering on the spine as follows: AMERICAN | HUMOUR | SELECTED AND | DISCUSSED BY | [the next two lines and rule at an angle and in script] *Stephen* | *Leacock* | [ornamental rule] | METHUEN.

The jacket is pale yellow with lettering in black. At the top and bottom of the front and spine panels is a solid orange area with a zig-zag edge. The back panel has a list of books of humour published by Methuen. The front flap has two paragraphs about the book and the price (7s 6d). The back flap indicates that this is a Methuen book and that further information about Methuen imprints can be located in *Zigzag*, the company's literary magazine, or directly from the company itself.

NOTES: Tegan Harris of Methuen & Co. Ltd. inquired about an English edition on 28 February 1936. Although the arrangement between Leacock and Doubleday, Doran and Company had no reference to world rights, Russell Doubleday informed Leacock on 17 March 1936 that for any income secured abroad, Leacock would receive 75% of royalties and Doubleday, Doran 25%. Leacock gave his approval for an English edition on 23 March 1936.

According to the Methuen ledgers at LILLY, 2,000 copies in quires were initially printed on 1 January 1937. Another 2,000 copies in quires were delivered to Methuen on 23 February 1937. In fact, the total number of unbound copies printed appears to have been slightly more than 4,000 copies (4,034). On 1 February 1937, 1,000 copies were bound.

Copies were apparently bound on demand thereafter. 2,250 dust jackets were manufactured by Stoddart & Malcolm on 8 February 1937. The type was distributed on 16 June 1937. The jacket blocks were destroyed on 22 July 1942. The book was out of print sometime after 1 February 1940 (the remaining 172 copies were bound on that date).

COPIES EXAMINED: CS (no dust jacket); CUL (in jacket); QMMRB (no jacket).

## A78 HELLEMENTS OF HICKONOMICS 1936

[with the exception of the lines in italics, all lines are in tooled type] HELLEMENTS | OF HICKONOMICS | in | HICCOUGHS of VERSE | DONE IN OUR SOCIAL PLANNING MILL | STEPHEN LEACOCK | *Ph.D. Chicago, Litt.D. Brown, Litt.D. Dartmouth, L.L.D. Queens,* | *Litt.D. Toronto, D.C.L. Bishop's* | [floral ornament] | DODD, MEAD & COMPANY | New York Mcmxxxvi

◆ 1–6$^8$. *i–iv, v–xi, xii, 1–2, 3–4, 5–6, 7–13, 14–16, 17–24, 25–26, 27–35, 36–38, 39–54, 55–56, 57–71, 72–74, 75–76, 77–78, 79–84* pp. (48 leaves). 203 × 137 mm.

CONTENTS: p. *i* half title; p. *ii* blank; p. *iii* title; p. *iv* COPYRIGHT, 1936 | BY DODD, MEAD AND COMPANY, INC. | ALL RIGHTS RESERVED | NO PART OF THIS BOOK MAY BE REPRODUCED IN ANY FORM | WITHOUT PERMISSION IN WRITING FROM THE PUBLISHER | PRINTED IN THE UNITED STATES OF AMERICA | BY THE VAIL-BALLOU PRESS, INC., BINGHAMTON, N. Y.; pp. *v–x* preface by Leacock dated April Fool's Day, 1936; p. *xi* table of contents; p. *xii* blank; pp. *1–84* text.

TEXT: I The Social Plan; II Dead Certainty: The Hickonomics of Insurance; III The Ranchman's Reverie: The Hickonomics of Planned Production; IV Happy Jim, the Consumer; V Oh! Mr. Malthus! The Hickonomics of Hearth and Heart; VI Meet Mr. Wegg, Banker: The Hickonomic Theory of Banking; VII Finale: A Resurrection of Adam Smith; VII An Educational Appendix: For Those Who Can Read It and Care to.

BINDING AND DUST JACKET: Bound in salmon cloth, top edge stained salmon. Stamped on the upper board: HELLEMENTS | OF | HICKONOMICS | STEPHEN | LEACOCK. Stamped on the spine: LEACOCK | [the next line down the spine] HELLEMENTS of HICKONOMICS | DODD, MEAD | & COMPANY.

The front and spine panels of the jacket are in salmon with blue lettering. On the front panel of the jacket: H*ellements* | OF | *Hickonomics* | [illustration in yellow and blue, signed RL, of a jester wearing glasses and a mortar board and balancing numbers on a pencil] | STEPHEN LEACOCK. On the spine panel: STEPHEN | LEACOCK | ☆ | [the next line down the spine] H*ellements* OF H*ickonomics* | ☆ | DODD, MEAD | & COMPANY. The remaining sections of the jacket are in dark yellow with blue lettering. The back panel has an advertisement for William S. Mudd's *The Old Boat Rocker* (110th printing, priced at $1.50). On the front flap is a description of *Hellements of Hickonomics* (priced at $1.50). The back flap carries an advertisement for *Laugh with Leacock* with quotations from George Ade, Robert Benchley, and Ellis Parker Butler.

NOTES: On 29 November 1935, Leacock suggested to Wambly Bald of the *New York American* that the newspaper could run "a series of 10 sets of verses, for use in 10 successive weeks, to be called *Hickonomics* or Hiccoughs of Verse, Done in Our Social Planning Mill.

The idea is to present a lot of the economic discussions and problems and perplexities of to-day in this form of verse, – half mocking and half serious, at times even pathetic."
He informed Bald that he had already written a few of them; the rest were written in his head, ". . . all done in a few days." Leacock made a similar proposal to Marie M. Meloney of the *New York Herald Tribune.* "I have been doing some wonderful stuff," he told Meloney on 19 December 1935: "These poems are worth either big money or nothing. But that doesn't worry the Herald[.] I want to offer first U.S. Serial Rights with no antecedent release." Both newspaper editors declined to publish Leacock's satiric poems. Leacock's agent, Paul R. Reynolds, also sent the poems to the *New Yorker,* the *New York Post,* and the Bell Syndicate. Reynolds (24 February 1936) was hopeful of serial publication but confessed ". . . to being somewhat stumped partly by the length of the poems. . . . humorous verses of this kind, as far as they are published here, are apt to be much shorter." On 28 February 1936, Leacock instructed Reynolds not to ". . . bother with the *Hickonomics* any more, as the date for book publication is so near that there's no time for serializing it & I don't want to delay" (information based on Meloney fonds and Reynolds fonds, COL; and SLM).

Frank Dodd's opinion about Leacock's verses on 19 December 1935 was not overly optimistic: "Quite frankly, we are not as excited over the possibilities in book form of HICKONOMICS as you seem to be, but very likely I am wrong, and certainly we would like to publish the book and see what can be done to put it over." The contract with Dodd, Mead is dated 17 December 1935. Leacock agreed to deliver the manuscript by 15 February 1936. It arrived in New York on 12 February. He received 10% royalty, 12½% after 5,000 copies sold, 20% after 20,000. On copies sold in Canada which were distributed by Dodd, Mead & Company (Canada), Limited, there was a royalty of 10%, 20% after 10,000 sold. The dust jacket was sent for Leacock's approval on 4 February 1936. But he disliked it, and on 8 February [1935], he suggested that Gluyas Williams do the jacket instead. Dodd, Mead was not receptive to Williams as the artist, however, because he was too expensive. Instead Kurt Wiese was employed to do the illustrative work (including head pieces at the beginning of each chapter). The proofs were sent to Leacock on 27 February 1936. Leacock was quite pleased with Wiese's illustrations, but he requested two of them (Jimmy the Consumer and Malthus) be redrawn.

On 8 January [1936], Leacock had failed to arrange syndication of his verses with the British American Newspaper Services. He offered the book to John Lane The Bodley Head on 5 February [1936] on the same basis as was offered to Dodd, Mead. Leacock took it for granted that the book would be published by The Bodley Head: "I think it will make a big hit," he remarked (The Bodley Head fonds, READ). The typescript arrived at The Bodley Head on 26 February 1936. Leacock urged publication in England shortly after publication in the United States. The reader's report of 29 February [1936] was not encouraging, however: "This is by no means Stephen Leacock at his best. . . . Up to a point they [the verses] are amusing & stimulating, but I found them *all* too long. I suppose we will have to publish it, but I am very doubtful of its success" (READ). The Bodley Head tried to buy 250 copies in sheets from Dodd, Mead on 18 May 1936, but by this time the entire American edition was already bound up. Leacock inquired again about an English edition on 17 June 1936. The Bodley Head apparently took and sold 100 copies of the American edition on 19 November 1936.

Aside from the fact that The Bodley Head was unimpressed with Leacock's verses, the major reason why there was no English edition was due to the firm's financial problems. In

January 1937 the company was sold to P.P. Howe, who formed a new company with the assistance of George Allen & Unwin Ltd., Jonathan Cape Ltd., and J.M. Dent & Sons Ltd. In view of these developments Leacock withdrew his offer of publication on 18 January 1937. Leacock's friend, Frank Paget Hett, met with Howe and informed Leacock on [4 February 1937]: "The M.S. is with the firm & consideration of its publication will take place if & when you agree." On 15 February 1938, Leacock even proposed publication to Peter Davies Ltd. on a 10% royalty basis. Howe told Leacock on 19 March 1937 that the book would ". . . have doubtful prospects here." On 2 April 1937, Leacock gave Howe an ultimatum: "You publish it on a 10% basis, or don't publish it all." As late as 4 March 1938, Howe declined publication: "I do not feel the book is saleable here, and I don't think the change of title [*Happy Jim the Consumer*] would make much difference."

The American edition was published on 31 March 1936. The copyright was registered with the Copyright Office at DLC on 3, 14 April 1936 (ClA93681). The copyright was renewed by Stephen Lushington Leacock on 15 May 1963 (R315599). There was a second printing in May 1936. 1,007 copies sold ($.15 royalty per copy, $151.05) up to 1 August 1936. The book was still in print on 1 June 1944. In the three-year period between 1 February 1941 and 1 February 1944, the book earned $12.38 in royalty. In retrospect Leacock admitted that "The sales were poor . . . [and] the title . . . unfortunate" (letter to Peter Davies Ltd., 15 February 1938).

COPIES EXAMINED: CS (two copies of first printing in jacket; second printing in jacket; QMMRB (three copies of first printing, all in jacket; Friedman copy with a page of the manuscript dated 15 April 1936 — see Lomer, p. 32).

## A79 THE GATHERING FINANCIAL CRISIS 1936

### A79a *Canadian edition*:

THE GATHERING | FINANCIAL CRISIS | IN | CANADA | [ornament] | A Survey of the Present Critical Situation | By | STEPHEN LEACOCK | *Ph.D., Litt.D., LL.D., D.C.L.* | *Sometime Head of the Department of Economics and Political* | *Science and now Professor Emeritus, of McGill University,* | *Montreal.* | [publisher's device of the Macmillan Company of Canada: large leaf, containing THE MACMILLANS IN CANADA printed in a semi-circle; inside the large leaf is a smaller leaf laid on an open book, and on a scroll attached to the stem of the large leaf is the motto FOLIA INTER FOLIA] | TORONTO: THE MACMILLAN COMPANY OF | CANADA LIMITED, AT ST. MARTIN'S HOUSE | 1936

◆ $1^{16}$. 1–8, 1–24 pp. (16 leaves). 228 × 152 mm.

CONTENTS: p. *1* half title; p. *2* NOTE | [six lines in which Leacock credits the London *Morning Post* (July 1936) for publishing his articles and for allowing them to be reprinted] | STEPHEN LEACOCK. | The Old Brewery Bay, | Lake Couchiching | August, 1936; p. *3* title; p. *4* COPYRIGHT, CANADA, 1936 | BY | THE MACMILLAN COMPANY OF CANADA LIMITED | [six lines stating that except for brief passages in reviews, no part of the book can be reproduced without written permission from the publishers] | Printed in Canada; pp. *5–6* preface extracted from the editorial columns of the London *Morning Post*, 6 July 1936; p. *7* fly title; p. *8* blank; pp. *1–24* text.

TEXT: I The Dominion; II The Provinces and Municipalities; III The Railway System; IV Summing Up.

BINDING: Bound in pictorial wrappers, wire-stitched. The back of the wrapper is white. The front has a black-and-white photograph of Leacock's head and shoulders. Above Leacock's head, hand-written in white: *Stephen Leacock*. Across the bottom of the photograph on a diagonal is a white, horizontal band with the following on it: [the first word hand-written] *The GATHERING FINANCIAL | • CRISIS IN CANADA •*.

NOTES: This pamphlet reprints Leacock's articles that were first published in the *Morning Post* on 6–9 July 1936 (see C36.15–8). Hugh Eayrs of the Macmillan Company of Canada Limited agreed to publish the articles on 10 August 1936, and on the same day Leacock posted the manuscript to him. Both Eayrs and his editor, Ellen Elliott, expressed concern about the brevity of the work (8,200 words). Leacock replied to their concern on 25 August 1936, telling Eayrs that ". . . a new book of 25,000 words would be an entirely different thing, less readable, less saleable and would need several months work, during which the market would be gone." Leacock suggested publication as a pamphlet selling for 50 or 55¢ with a royalty of 5¢. Eayrs agreed to these terms on 27 August 1936 (price 50¢) with 10% royalty.

The design for the front wrapper was sent to Leacock for his approval on 18 September and was then forwarded to Reliance Engravers on 30 September. Composition and printing were completed by C.W. Press on 2 October. The total cost of manufacturing the Canadian edition and the English issue was $118.61. Although 750 copies were printed of the Canadian edition, 735 copies were delivered to the Macmillan Company on 8 October. Elliott told Leacock on 14 October 1936: "Our travelling salesmen are all on the road at the moment, and equipped with copies of the booklet." Copyright registration occurred a day later. A royalty statement, dated 26 January 1937, records that Leacock earned $8.75 on 175 copies sold. The type was ordered distributed on 5 May 1937.

The manuscript entitled "The Financial Position of Canada: A Survey of the Present Critical Situation" (25 pages with insertions) along with a typescript (27 pp.) and a final carbon typescript (28 pp.) is at NAC.

COPIES EXAMINED: CS; OONL (three copies).

## A79a.1 *English issue*:

THE GATHERING | FINANCIAL CRISIS | IN | CANADA | [ornament] | A Survey of the Present Critical Situation | By | STEPHEN LEACOCK | *Ph.D., Litt.D., LL.D., D.C.L. | Sometime Head of the Department of Economics and Political | Science and now Professor Emeritus, of McGill University, | Montreal.* | [publisher's device of Lovat Dickson: a deer with letters L and D on each side encircled with leaves] | LOVAT DICKSON LIMITED | PUBLISHERS | LONDON

NOTES: When Eayrs agreed to publish Leacock's pamphlet on 27 August 1936, he cabled Lovat Dickson to accept similar terms for the English issue. A memorandum of agreement (dated 1936) between the Macmillan Company of Canada and Lovat Dickson Limited stipulates that Leacock was to deliver the manuscript to Dickson by 15 September 1936. For the English issue Leacock received 10% royalty on all copies sold up to 5,000 copies and 15% thereafter. The manuscript was not sent to Dickson, however. Eayrs arranged the production of the English issue from the same setting of type (750 copies printed, 735 delivered on 8 October 1936). Besides the title page, the English issue has a slightly different wrapper than its Canadian counterpart: the price, 6d, is over-printed in red within a circle on the front of the wrapper; the back of the wrapper features an advertisement for Alan Sullivan's *The Great Divide*.

COPIES EXAMINED: CUL.

## A80 FUNNY PIECES 1936

### A80a *American edition* (1936):

[all lines within a rectangle; the left and right sides of the rectangle having bevelled edges] FUNNY | PIECES | A BOOK OF | RANDOM | SKETCHES | *by* | STEPHEN LEACOCK | DODD, MEAD & COMPANY | NEW YORK MCMXXXVI

◆ *1–19*[8]. i–iv, v–viii, *1–2, 3–56, 57–58, 59–128, 129–130, 131–165, 166–168, 169–208, 209–210, 211–227, 228–230, 231–248, 249–250, 251–292, 1–4* pp. (152 leaves). 187 × 131 mm.

CONTENTS: p. *i* half title; p. *ii* list of nineteen books by Leacock, the first being *Literary Lapses* and the last *Hellements of Hickonomics*; p. *iii* title; p. *iv* COPYRIGHT, 1936, | BY DODD, MEAD AND COMPANY, INC. | All rights reserved — no part of this book may be | reproduced in any form without permission in | writing from the publisher. | PRINTED IN THE U. S. A. BY | Quinn & Boden Company, Inc. | [rule] | BOOK MANUFACTURERS | RAHWAY, NEW JERSEY; p. *v–vi* preface; p. *vii–viii* table of contents; pp. *1–292* text; pp. *1–4* blank.

TEXT: Part I The School Section — Getting by at College: A Study in How to Elude the Examiner; Bygone Schoolbooks (I Mrs. Magnall and Mrs. Marcett; II Ciphers and Sentiment — The Arithmetic That Was; III Parlez-Vous Français?); Opening Day at College: An Autumn Study; Recovery After Graduation: How Fatal Is a College Course?; History Revisited: Famous Old Stories Restored to Their Proper Setting (I Columbus and the Egg; II Wolfe and Gray's "Elegy"; III King Alfred and the Cakes); The Merit of the Young: If Only Our Teachers Could Discern It; Campus Notes: When the Methods of Commerce and Athletics Obtain a Still Further Hold on the Colleges.

Part II The Literary Section — What the Reviewers Missed: If They Had Only Had a Chance at the Masterpieces of the Past!; The Invasion of Human Thought by Mathematical Symbols: For Economics, Mathematical Symbolism Is the Means Adopted; Imaginary Persons: From John Doe to John Bull: From Punch and Judy to Brother Jonathan; Adventures in Torts: How to Make Laughter Out of Dust; Words and How to Use Them: A Wise-Crack about the Beans of Most Guys; Mythical Men and What They Are Really Like; Interviews as They Were and Are; What Happened Next?: The Sequel to Some Famous World Stories.

Part III Brain Stuff in General — Life and Laughter: How to Infuse Our Life with the Spirit of Merriment; The Hidden Secret of the City: That It Still Dreams of the Farm; New Light from Bright Minds; The Personal Habits and Sayings of the Emperor Napoleon as Advertised.

Part IV Nation and Nation — The International Stuff: For Men Like Myself; Ways of Diplomacy: How the Noble Fellows Saved the World (I: Finding a Formula; II: The

Brown-Jones Embroglio); The Barber's Outline of History: One of Its Many Faces; How Nations Write Their History.

Part V Papers of the Ignoramus Club — I How We Organized; II The Club Gives a Luncheon to Disarm Europe; III The Ignoramus Club Starts a Camp for Overfed Boys.

Part VI Drama Section — Red Riding Hood Up-to-Date; Beauty and the Boss; or, The Sacrifice of a Stenographer.

Part VII Personalia — Looking Back on College; The End of the Senility Gang: An Episode at McGill University; My Ideas on Academic Freedom; I'll Stay in Canada.

BINDING AND DUST JACKET: Bound in red cloth, top edge stained blue. Blind-stamped on the upper board is a solid rectangle. Within this rectangle are two raised rectangles which contain the following in raised characters: FUNNY | PIECES | [rule] | STEPHEN LEAC-OCK. Stamped on the spine in gilt: FUNNY | PIECES | [rule] | LEACOCK | DODD, MEAD | & COMPANY.

The jacket is red, beige, and black. On the front panel of the jacket: [all lines and illustrations within a red rectangle] FUNNY | PIECES | [two intersecting, solid red circles, outlined in black, one containing an illustration of a lamb and a butterfly, the other containing an illustration of an owl wearing a mortar board, the latter signed R.W.] | [remaining lines in red] STEPHEN | LEACOCK. On the spine panel of the jacket: [all lines and illustrations within a red rectangle] FUNNY | PIECES | [the next two lines in red] STEPHEN | LEACOCK | [two intersecting, solid red circles, outlined in black, the top one containing an illustration of an owl wearing a mortar board, the lower with the following:] | DODD, MEAD | & COMPANY. The back panel advertises New AUTUMN Fiction. The front flap has a description of Funny Pieces. The back flap is an advertisement for Cornelia Otis Skinner's Excuse It, Please! (at $2).

NOTES: On 20 November 1935, Frank Dodd told Leacock: "I am delighted that we [will] have FUNNY PIECES for next autumn, and I take pleasure in enclosing herewith a contract on the same terms as the last book, which I hope will be satisfactory." The contract (copies at Macmillan fonds, OHM and at SLM) is dated 19 December 1935. Leacock agreed to deliver the manuscript by 1 June 1936. He received 15% royalty on all copies sold (including Canada) with an advance of $500 on publication.

Dodd, Mead received the blurb for the book from Leacock on 24 April 1936. The first batch of proofs was sent to Leacock on 21 August 1936; the remaining proofs were mailed to him a week later. Leacock was sent six author's copies on 20 October 1936. Published 28 October 1936. The copyright was registered at the Copyright Office of DLC on 31 October 1936 (ClA1001163). When he sent Leacock the advance, E.H. Dodd, Jr. observed: "We all feel that this is an unusually interesting and sparkling collection of your work and are looking forward with enthusiasm to a successful career for it." Number of copies printed not known. The book was still in print as of 1 June 1944 when Dodd, Mead informed Leacock's niece, Barbara Nimmo, that in a three-year period between 1 February 1941 and 1 February 1944, the book had earned a royalty of $2.44 in American and Canadian sales.

Some of the articles were syndicated by the Bell Syndicate in a number of newspapers in early February 1937 (Detroit News, Milwaukee Journal, Chicago Daily News, Kansas City Star, Toronto Telegram, St. Louis Globe Democrat, and Philadelphia Bulletin).

Lomer (pp. 28–29) records a reprint in 1937. He also lists a Canadian issue: "Toronto, McClelland & Stewart, ltd., 1936. viii, 292 p." However, no copy of a Canadian issue has ever been located.

"Interview with a Movie Queen" in the section, "Interviews as They Were and Are," is written by Leacock's son.

COPIES EXAMINED: CS (price clipped on jacket); QMMRB (in jacket).

## A80b  *English edition* (1937):

*FUNNY PIECES | A BOOK OF | RANDOM | SKETCHES | By | Stephen Leacock | LONDON | JOHN LANE THE BODLEY HEAD*

◆  $A^4$ $B^{12}$ $C^4$ $D^{12}$ $E^4$ $F^{12}$ $G^4$ $H^{12}$ $I^4$ $K^{12}$ $L^4$ $M^{12}$ $N^4$ $O^{12}$ $P^4$ $Q^{12}$ $R^4$ $S^{12}$ $T^4$ $U^{12}$ $X^{10}$ [$1 signed, X2 signed]. *i–vi, vii–ix, x, xi–xii, 1–2, 3–62, 63–64, 65–140, 141–142, 143–182, 183–184, 185–230, 231–232, 233–253, 254–256, 257–276, 277–278, 279–326, 1–2* pp. (170 leaves). 182 × 119 mm.

CONTENTS: pp. *i–ii* blank; p. *iii* half title; p. *iv* list of twenty-two books by Leacock, the first being *Literary Lapses* and the last *Humour: Its Theory and Technique*; p. *v* title; p. *vi* FIRST PUBLISHED IN 1937 | PRINTED IN GREAT BRITAIN | BY WESTERN PRINTING SERVICES LTD., BRISTOL; pp. vii–ix preface; p. x blank; pp. xi–xii table of contents; pp. 1–326 text; p. *1* advertisement with excerpts from reviews for *Humour: Its Theory and Technique* (priced at 7s 6d); p. 2 blank.

TEXT: Identical to the American edition, although a few words in the titles of two essays have been spelled slightly differently: "Bygone Schoolbooks" as "By-Gone School Books," "The Brown-Jones Embroglio" as "The Brown-Jones Imbroglio."

BINDING AND DUST JACKET: Bound in orange cloth with blue lettering. Stamped on the upper board: *FUNNY | PIECES | STEPHEN | LEACOCK*. Stamped on the spine: *FUNNY | PIECES |* [ornamental, looping line] *| STEPHEN | LEACOCK |* THE BODLEY HEAD.

The jacket is white with red and blue lettering. The front, spine, and back panels have a pattern in red that is repeated, consisting of Leacock's name and the title: fun | ny | pie | ces | [the next two lines to the left of the previous two lines] step | hen | lea | cock. On the front of the jacket in blue: funny | pieces | stephen | leacock. On the spine panel of the jacket: funny | pieces | stephen | leacock | the | bodley | head. Printing on the flaps of the jacket is in blue. The front flap describes the book (priced at 7s 6d), and begins: *"before the advent of* . . . ." The back flap has excerpts from reviews, attesting to Leacock's skills as a humorist.

NOTES: A contract for the English edition was sent to Leacock on 27 February 1936. The extant contract at READ is dated 14 April 1936. The terms were the same as Leacock's previous book (advance royalty of £100 on the date of publication, 15% royalty up to 4,000 copies sold, 20% thereafter). Lindsay Drummond of John Lane The Bodley Head inquired about Leacock's progress on 22 June 1936 (the contract specified delivery of the manuscript (60,000 words) before 30 June 1936). The Bodley Head wanted to announce publication in the autumn. Leacock promised that the book would be finished by 13 July 1936. The Bodley Head sent him a set of proofs on 27 October 1936.

Publication was delayed, however, when the company experienced financial problems and was sold to P.P. Howe in January 1937 (see the notes to A78). On 18 January 1937, Leacock pointed out that the contract had lapsed, although he did not ask for damages. Howe assured Leacock on 2 February that the company was solvent: "As you will have concluded the publication of this [*Funny Pieces*] was held up on the entry of the Receiver, but your corrected proofs are safely in my possession." According to Leacock's friend, Frank Paget Hett, the book had been listed in The Bodley Head's catalogue at 7s 6d by [4 February

1937]. Howe sought Leacock's permission to print the book on 19 March 1937. He sent the corrected proofs to the printer on 7 April 1937 in the hope of publication by the end of the month. He informed Leacock on 4 June 1937: "FUNNY PIECES will make its appearance on the 15th, and advance copies will be posted to you next week. We are planning a small definite campaign to place your name on record again, and I hope we shall be successful in securing for the book the sales which it deserves." By 17 June 1937 405 copies had sold in England, 2 foreign, and 386 colonial (£24 8s 9d royalty). These sales figures were not encouraging. Howe maintained on 18 June that the book was ". . . not an altogether easy one to get the trade to accept in full quantity on subscription, as it falls between the two trade stools of fiction and non-fiction." He reported on 10 August 1937: " 'Funny Pieces' continue to make sales in an unsensational fashion."

Lomer dates the English edition as [1937] but erroneously records the date of publication as 15 June 1939. He also lists a reprint published 5 September 1939. According to *The English Catalogue of Books*, the English edition was published in June 1937, and the "cheaper edition" (a reprint) appeared in September 1939 (at 3s 6d).

COPIES EXAMINED: CS (in jacket).

## A81 WHAT NICKEL MEANS TO THE WORLD 1937

WHAT NICKEL MEANS | TO THE | WORLD | *By* | STEPHEN LEACOCK | *Professor Emeritus of Political Economy* | *McGill University* | *Montreal* | *Copyright 1937* | *Johnson, Ring & Company* | *Limited* | [floral ornament] | PREPARED EXPRESSLY FOR | JOHNSON, RING & COMPANY | LIMITED | *Investment Securities* | 38 KING ST. W. TORONTO, CANADA

◆ $11^4$. *1–2, 3–25, 1–3* pp. (14 leaves). 235 × 99 mm.

CONTENTS: p. *1* title; p. *2* *NOTE OF INTRODUCTION* | [four paragraphs in italics in which Leacock states that his pamphlet "*represents an* | *expanded form of the discussion of the same* | *topic in a series of articles contributed by me* | *to the press under the title of* '*My Discovery* | *of the West,*' *and shortly to appear in book* | *form.*" He thanks the Canadian Institute of Mining and Metallurgy and the Ontario Nickel Corporation, Limited for providing him with statistical and documentary information. He tells the reader that he cannot speak with the authority of a metallurgist but will approach the subject from an economic standpoint.] | STEPHEN LEACOCK. | *April, 1937.*; pp. *3–25* text; pp. *1–3* blank.

BINDING: Issued in a stiff, cream-coloured paper wrapper, wire-stitched. On the front of the wrapper: [all lines within three rectangles, the outer rectangle is blue, the two inner rectangles are greyish blue; all lines in blue except the second line which is in greyish blue outlined with blue] What | NICKEL [with the N as a capital n] | means to | the World | [Leacock's signature in facsimile at an angle partially underlined]. On the lower right-hand corner of the back of the wrapper in blue: PRINTED IN CANADA. The copy at OONL is enclosed in a grey and blue slipcase, but it would appear that this was not issued with the pamphlet.

NOTES: On 10 March 1937, Salter A. Hayden of the legal firm McCarthy & McCarthy wrote to Leacock on behalf of the Ontario Nickel Corporation and Johnson, Ring & Co. of Toronto with the proposal that Leacock write ". . . for them an article on the subject of Base Metals, their value, and use, devoting particular attention to nickel." Leacock telegraphed back asking about the length of the article and compensation. Hayden and Leacock discussed the matter further on the telephone. Hayden reaffirmed his invitation to Leacock on 13 March 1937. According to Hayden, the purpose of the publication would be ". . . to furnish information to those members of the public who may become interested in nickel and through a more complete understanding of the uses and future of nickel in the purchase of stock in a nickel company." Two days later, on 15 March 1937, G.H. Johnson confirmed that his company would pay Leacock $500 for "a pamphlet of approximately 3,500 words." He sent Leacock an advance of $250. Leacock telegraphed that he would write the piece one week after receiving research and statistical information from Johnson. Johnson's secretary, Jo Barger, sent Leacock the remaining $250 on 31 March 1937. Barger corrected a few figures in Leacock's manuscript and requested him to supply a missing page (supplied on 2 April). Advertisements about the pamphlet's publication were released to newspapers at this time. Galley proofs were sent to Leacock on 5 April. Number of copies printed not known.

COPIES EXAMINED: CS; OONL; QMMRB; SLM (six copies).

## A82 MY DISCOVERY OF THE WEST 1937

### A82a *poster*:

MY DISCOVERY OF THE WEST | [two rules] | A series of twelve articles, dealing with the relations of East and West in Canada. The articles are based on a | lecture tour just completed by Professor Stephen Leacock from Fort William to the Pacific coast. The main | purpose of the articles is serious discussion but they are expressed in the vigorous and humorous style which has | given to Stephen Leacock an international reputation. The length of the articles is from 3,500 to about 4,500 | words each. The extracts and digests of the various chapters as given below indicates their character. The first | weekly article is to be released on Saturday, March 6, 1937. The material on this sheet is copyright and cannot | without permission be used in whole or in part | [two rules] | [seven columns (along with a black-and-white photograph of Leacock in the columns) which summarize the first eleven chapters of Leacock's book; the title of chapter XII, Dominion and Provinces, is given but not summarized] | [rule] | Sales agents and distributors: MILLER SERVICES LIMITED, 302–303 McKinnon Bldg., Toronto, Canada

♦ Broadside. 610 × 465 mm. Off-white wove paper, no water mark.

NOTES: Leacock's tour of western Canada (from 25 November 1936 to 18 January 1937) was sponsored by the Canadian Bankers' Association. He accepted an honorarium of $10,000 plus expenses, which came to approximately $3,000. The deal was arranged through the advertising agency Cockfield Brown & Co. Apparently Leacock was completely unaware of his sponsors. See Robert MacIntosh, *Different Drummers: Banking and Politics in Canada* (Toronto: Macmillan Canada, 1991), pp. 90–1.

On 8 December 1936, Andrew Miller of Miller Services Limited wrote to Leacock and offered to syndicate his articles in Canadian newspapers on a commission basis — 60% to Leacock and 40% to himself. The articles would concern Leacock's impressions of the West, which later would be gathered together as a book. When Leacock agreed to Miller's proposal, Miller advised him on 30 December 1936: "Don't fail to interest editors as you meet them at Victoria, Vancouver and other points homeward bound by telling them about the coming series. . . . We will stand behind any arrangement you make. . . ." He requested Leacock to send the first and second instalments not later than 20 January 1937. Miller was able to syndicate the articles in newspapers in Toronto, Montreal, Vancouver, Edmonton, Ottawa, and elsewhere (see C37.7).

Miller's first intention was to produce a large broadside which would entice newspaper editors to subscribe to the syndicated series of articles. On 22 January 1937, he wrote to Leacock: "I expected dummy for broadside here this morning. Printers were set to go at it and make a quick job of the printing." Three days later, he informed Leacock: "I have arranged for a battery of six or more expert stencil cutters to be ready at 8.30 Friday morning to cut stencils of as much of your story as will be ready. Each cutter will take a chapter and six chapters will be cut by 3 pm when they will be turned over to machines and be printed by Saturday noon." By 27 January 1937, in anticipation of their meeting in Toronto, Leacock had completed chapters 1 and 2, and he had mapped out and written parts of ten other chapters: chapter 3 200 words; chapter 4 200 words; chapter 5 1,000 words; chapter 6 100 words; chapter 7 1,000 words; chapter 8 200 words; chapter 9 600 words; chapter 10 100 words; chapter 11 1,000 words; and chapter 12 100 words. "*Print* is the thing," Leacock remarked in encouragement of Miller's hopes for syndication. "I will give you 10% on what I get in England if you will give me printed copies [of the broadside], — that, with luck *pays* for the printing for all. I shall not have more than 2 chapters ready — there is no need to. I don't want mimeographing for this broadside sheet — it's no good — can't be seen and read." Leacock sent ten copies of the broadside to the *Evening Standard* (London) in early February 1937. However, the articles failed to generate interest abroad, and they were not serialized in England or in the United States. Miller received proofs of chapters 13 to 17 of the Canadian edition from Thomas Allen on 20 May 1937. These chapters were not syndicated originally by him in Canadian newspapers. Miller attempted to get them syndicated before the Canadian edition was published but to no avail. Newspaper editors thought that the series was interesting, but not enough to warrant further articles.

COPIES EXAMINED: SLM (six copies).

## A82b *Canadian edition*:

MY DISCOVERY | OF THE WEST | [ornamental rule] | *A Discussion of East and West in Canada* | [ornamental rule] | STEPHEN LEACOCK | B.A., PH.D., LL.D., LITT.D., D.C.L. | PROFESSOR EMERITUS, McGILL UNIVERSITY | [ornamental rule] | 1937 | THOMAS ALLEN [two ornamental hyphens] *PUBLISHER* | TORONTO

◆ $1-9^8$ $10^4$ $11-18^8$. $1-8$, $1-272$ pp. (140 leaves). 204 × 130 mm.

CONTENTS: p. *1* half title; p. *2* blank; p. *3* title; p. *4* COPYRIGHT, CANADA, 1937, | BY | STEPHEN LEACOCK. | PRINTED IN CANADA | T. H. BEST PRINTING CO., LIMITED | TORONTO, ONT.; p. *5* preface (My Claim on the West: A Prophecy That Came True); p. *6* blank; p. *7* table of contents; p. *8* blank; pp. *1–272* text.

TEXT: chapter I My Proposal of Discovery; chapter II Fort William and the Waterway; chapter III So This Is Winnipeg; chapter IV Winnipeg and the East; chapter V Saskatchewan and Wheat; chapter VI Our Eldorado in the Wilderness; chapter VII Debit and Credit in

Alberta; chapter VIII The Pure Theory of Social Credit; chapter IX Monarchy in the West; chapter X British Columbia: Empire Province; chapter XI The Island of the Blest; chapter XII Provinces and Dominion; chapter XIII Our Railway Muddle; chapter XIV Immigration and Land Settlement; chapter XV The Land of Dreams; chapter XVI Ways and Means of Salvation; chapter XVII No Vote of Thanks.

BINDING AND DUST JACKET: Bound in blue cloth with black lettering, top edge stained blue. Stamped on the upper board: *My* DISCOVERY | *of the* WEST | [ornament] | *STEPHEN LEACOCK*. Stamped on the spine: *My* | DISCOVERY | *of the* | WEST | * | STEPHEN | LEACOCK | ALLEN.

On the front, back, and spine panels of the jacket is a partial map of Canada in white, blue, red, and black. A caricature of Leacock (in academic garb, wearing a mortar board, and peering through binoculars) is on the front panel of the jacket. His itinerary across Western Canada is outlined in red. On the back panel at the outer edge of the Pacific Ocean are a partial sun, the face and shoulders of an Oriental man in uniform, and the word NIPPON. The front flap has a synopsis of the book and its price ($2). On the back flap are a list of BOOKS OF MERIT (*FICTION* and *GENERAL*) published by Thomas Allen.

NOTES: Leacock gave Thomas Allen the authority to publish a Canadian edition and to negotiate the American market (see the notes to A82b.1). The proofs of the Canadian edition were ready for Leacock's inspection shortly after 15 May 1937. Allen sent Leacock a contract during the summer of 1937, but Leacock apparently never returned it. The book was published prior to 15 June 1937 because Leacock sent P.P. Howe of The Bodley Head a copy of the Canadian edition on that date. The Canadian edition consisted of 2,488 copies. By the end of 1937 1,125 copies had been sold, 100 had been sent out for review, and 1,263 were still in stock ($337.50 royalty to Leacock at 30¢ a copy). In spite of the fact that the book would win the Governor General's award for non-fiction, Allen told Leacock on 14 January 1938:

> I regret your book did not go over as well as we thought it would and unfortunately we bound up the whole edition. . . . If MY DISCOVERY OF THE WEST doesn't show much life this spring we will have to remainder it — but before doing so we will give it every chance. My opinion is that running it in the newspapers first hurt the sale in the bookstores.

On 8 November 1938, Allen informed Leacock that he had ". . . offered it at $50 per hundred and still have about 700 copies." The royalty report of 31 December 1938 indicates that of the 1,263 copies in stock, 268 were sold (earning Leacock $80.40, 30¢ per copy) and 995 copies were remaindered.

COPIES EXAMINED: CS (in jacket); QMMRB (two copies, one in jacket).

## A82b.1 *American issue*:

MY DISCOVERY | OF THE WEST | [ornamental rule] | *A Discussion of East and West in Canada* | [ornamental rule] | STEPHEN LEACOCK | B.A., PH.D., LL.D., LITT.D., D.C.L. | PROFESSOR EMERITUS, McGILL UNIVERSITY | [publisher's device of Hale, Cushman & Flint: anchor and open book with initials H C F] | [ornamental rule] | BOSTON AND NEW YORK | HALE, CUSHMAN & FLINT

◆  $1–17^8$ $18^4$. $1–8$, $1–272$ pp. (140 leaves). $200 \times 137$ mm.

CONTENTS:  p. *1* half title; p. *2* blank; p. *3* title; p. *4* COPYRIGHT 1937, BY | STEPHEN LEACOCK | [four lines concerning copyright and permission to reproduce or quote passages] | *First printing, August 1937* | PRINTED IN THE UNITED STATES OF AMER-ICA | BY THE POLYGRAPHIC COMPANY OF AMERICA, N.Y.; p. *5* table of contents; p. *6* blank; p. *7* preface (My Claim on the West: A Prophecy That Came True); p. *8* blank; pp. *1–272* text.

BINDING AND DUST JACKET:  Bound in grey cloth with red lettering. Stamped on the upper board: MY DISCOVERY | OF THE WEST | STEPHEN LEACOCK. Stamped on the spine: MY | DISCOVERY | OF THE | WEST | [rule] | LEACOCK | HALE | CUSHMAN | & | FLINT.

On the front, back, and spine panels of the dust jacket is a partial map of Canada (Ontario through to British Columbia) in brown, blue, and black with a caricature of Leacock wearing a mortar board on the front of the jacket. The flaps of the jacket in white with black lettering feature a brief discussion of Leacock's career and his odyssey across western Canada. The front flap also lists the price of the book, $2.

TEXT:  Identical to A82b.

NOTES:  On 23 November 1936, Leacock wrote to his American publisher, Frank Dodd, about his proposed lecture tour of western Canada. His experiences during the tour would be recorded, and would result in a book tentatively entitled "My Western Excursion: A Study of East and West in Canada." Initially, he planned serialization of the book in eight instalments of 5,000 words, each to be released weekly between 1 March and 1 May 1937. "I propose to publish it as a book on April 1, 1937. It ought, with proper salesmanship, to sell easily up to 5000 in Canada . . . . in the United States it wouldn't sell much but as a combined U.S. and Canada it should be all right." He did not expect an advance or guaranteed royalty. He requested 10% royalty up to 10,000 copies sold (retail price $1.50, 15% if $2 or more) and 20% thereafter. Dodd was receptive, although he admitted that "the book you describe would not find any great market here." He was willing to manufacture an American edition or to import sheets from a Canadian publisher, preferably the Macmillans in Canada, he informed Leacock on 27 November 1936. Dodd suggested 10% royalty, even if the book sold for $2 or more. Despite Dodd's willingness to proceed with an edition, Leacock was unconvinced of Dodd's full participation. A royalty of 10% on a book selling at $2 or more was unacceptable to Leacock. "I shall therefore see if any first class publisher will take it on those terms and if not I will publish it myself," he told Dodd on 5 December 1936. Their inability to reach a compromise in conjunction with Dodd, Mead's apparent lack of interest prompted a stinging letter from Leacock, written on 2 January 1937, in which he took Dodd, Mead to task for failing to capitalize on his lecture tour: "*Never, never* once have I seen an advertisement of my books in a paper. When the front page was all filled up with my pictures and interviews and report the opportunity was obvious to put in an advertisement for my books. I am sure I need not dot the i's and cross the t's of all this."

On the same day that he angrily wrote to Dodd, Mead, Leacock offered the book to Thomas Allen, requesting him to take care of the American market with Houghton Mifflin. Frank Dodd attempted to placate Leacock on 11 January 1937. He agreed to 15% royalty at $2. At the same time he informed Leacock that with the exception of Leacock's last three books, Dodd, Mead had no rights in Canada at all. Moreover, the Toronto branch of Dodd, Mead had not received a schedule of Leacock's itinerary. If anything, the fault of publicity lay at the doorstep of Leacock's Canadian distributors. "My Western Excursion" had, in fact, been announced in Dodd, Mead's spring list. In his reply of [18 January 1937], Leacock was somewhat apologetic that he had acted hastily, but by this time it was too late for Dodd, Mead to publish the American edition.

Houghton Mifflin expressed its interest in the book on 4 January 1937, but turned down the book on 8 February 1937. John S. Clapp of Hale, Cushman & Flint agreed to terms on 28 April 1937 — 15% royalty on all copies sold at a retail price of $2 for an edition of not less than 3,000 copies. Clapp informed Leacock, however, that although manufacture and promotion of the book could proceed as soon as Leacock gave the signal, publication would not be possible before 15 August 1937. A contract was sent to Leacock on 7 May 1937. Thomas Allen undoubtedly arranged for T.H. Best to send a set of plates to Hale, Cushman & Flint for printing in the United States. Notwithstanding the date of the first printing (August 1937) on the verso of the title leaf, the American issue was published on 30 October 1937. Copies were received by the Copyright Office at DLC on 20 November 1937, and the copyright was registered on 19 November 1937 (A112191). The copyright was renewed by George Leacock on 10 August 1949 (R50923).

797 copies sold in October 1937, 166 copies in November, and 63 in December (1,026 total number up to end of 1937, at 15%, 30¢ a copy, $307.60 royalty (–$15.39, 5% taken for tax). 151 copies sold between 1938 and June 1941. The book was remaindered on 31 July 1941.

COPIES EXAMINED: CS (three copies, two in jacket); QMMRB (in jacket).

## A82c *English edition*:

MY DISCOVERY OF | THE WEST | *A Discussion of East and West in Canada* | STEPHEN LEACOCK | B.A., PH.D., LITT.D., LL.D., D.C.L. | PROFESSOR EMERITUS | MCGILL UNIVERSITY, MONTREAL | LONDON | JOHN LANE THE BODLEY HEAD

◆ $A^8$ B–U$^8$ X$^4$ [$1 signed]. *1–12*, 13–325, *1–3* pp. (164 leaves). 215 × 136 mm.

CONTENTS: pp. *1–2* blank; p. *3* half title; p. *4* list of books by the same author, the first being *Literary Lapses* and the last *Funny Pieces;* p. *5* title; p. 6 FIRST PUBLISHED IN 1937 | PRINTED IN GREAT BRITAIN BY | UNWIN BROTHERS LIMITED, LONDON AND WOKING; p. 7 preface; p. *8* blank; p. 9 table of contents; p. *10* blank; p. *11* fly title; p. *12* blank; pp. 13–325 text; p. *1* blank; p. *2* advertisement with excerpts from reviews for *Funny Pieces*; p. *3* blank.

TEXT: Identical to A82b.

BINDING AND DUST JACKET: Bound in dark red cloth, top edge stained red, with lettering on the spine in gilt as follows: MY | DISCOVERY | OF THE | WEST | STEPHEN | LEACOCK | THE | BODLEY HEAD.

The front and spine panels of the jacket are dark red with white lettering. On the front panel: STEPHEN | LEACOCK | MY | DISCOVERY | OF THE | WEST | A DISCUSSION OF EAST | AND WEST IN CANADA. On the spine panel: MY | DISCOVERY | OF THE | WEST | [down the spine] LEACOCK | THE | BODLEY | HEAD. The back panel, which is white with black lettering, features advertisements with excerpts for *Funny Pieces* and *Humour: Its Theory and Technique* (PROFESSOR STEPHEN LEACOCK'S | *most recent humorous works*). On the front flap are three paragraphs about Leacock and the ideas he discusses in his book (with the price at the bottom of the flap, 12s 6d). The back flap is blank.

NOTES: On 19 March 1937, P.P. Howe of The Bodley Head informed Leacock that although *My Discovery of the West* was not to be published by Dodd, Mead, ". . . we should be very pleased to have the opportunity of carrying out your wishes with regard to this book." Leacock offered Howe the same terms as Thomas Allen: 15% on the first 10,000, 20% thereafter. "This book might do well in England as the political and financial people will be interested in the serious side." Leacock sent the manuscript to The Bodley Head on 19 April 1937. He asked the company to pay him a royalty on the book ". . . after publication, anything or nothing, justified by opening sale." He added: "Please rush this book. Please don't sell it as *funny*. It is the very thing for English investing, reading and political public. Look it over and you'll see." Howe sent Leacock a contract on 4 June 1937 (copy at The Bodley Head fonds, READ). He was hoping to arrange for Lord Tweedsmuir (John Buchan) to write a foreword to the book, but on 14 June 1937, Leacock scotched the idea: "That would never do. My friends would all think it . . . a great mistake for me to solicit a preface from the Governor General or allow one to be solicited in my name. I once met Lord Tweedsmuir about 15 years ago or rather I went to see him on business, he being then with Nelsons publishing firm." The typescript was sent to the printers on 30 June 1937, although there was a delay in printing due to the arrival of the Canadian edition (which contained differences in the text) and the annual holiday of the printers at that time. On 10 August 1937, Howe told Leacock that the proofs were being read carefully with a view to publication on 21 September 1937. Lomer (p. 44) records 23 September 1937 as the date of publication. The first royalty report, 27 September 1937, indicates that 166 copies had sold in England and 41 as foreign sales (royalty to Leacock £15 10s 3d). "The book has had a friendly reception and will no doubt make sales daily," Howe assured Leacock on 28 September 1937.

COPIES EXAMINED: CS (price clipped from front flap of jacket); QMMRB (no jacket).

## A83 HERE ARE MY LECTURES AND STORIES 1937

### A83a *American edition*:

[rule, ornamental rule] | HERE ARE MY LECTURES | AND | STORIES | STEPHEN LEACOCK | [publisher's device of Dodd, Mead: oval containing open book and portrait of classical figure with leaves and company name] | DODD, MEAD & COMPANY | NEW YORK 1937 | [ornamental rule, rule]

◆ *1–16*[8] *17*[4]. *i–iv*, v–vii, *viii*, ix–x, *1–2* 3–27, *28–32*, 33–65, *66–70*, 71–95, *96–100*, 101–115, *116–120*, 121–137, *138–142*, 143–167, *168–172*, 173–183, *184–186*, 187–196, *197–198*, 199–203, *204–206*, 207–212, *213–214*, 215–219, *220–222*, 223–227, *228–230*, 231–239, *240*, 241–242, *243–244*, 245–251, *1–3* pp. (132 leaves). 187 × 130 mm.

CONTENTS: p. *i* half title; p. *ii* list of twenty books by Leacock, the first being *Literary Lapses* and the last *Funny Pieces*; p. *iii* title; p. *iv* COPYRIGHT, 1937, | BY DODD, MEAD AND COMPANY, INC. | All rights reserved — no part of this book may be | reproduced in any form without permission in | writing from the publisher. | PRINTED IN THE U. S. A. BY | Quinn & Boden Company, Inc. | [rule] | BOOK MANUFACTURERS | RAHWAY. NEW JERSEY; pp. v–vii preface by Leacock dated Nov. 1, 1937; p. *viii* blank; pp. ix–x table of contents; pp. *1–251* text (pp. *2, 28, 30, 32, 66, 68, 70, 96, 98, 100, 116, 118, 120, 138, 140, 142, 168, 170, 172, 184, 186, 198, 204, 206, 214, 220, 222, 228, 230, 240,* and *244* blank); pp. *1–3* blank.

TEXT: Chapter I Lecture. How Soon Can We Start the Next War; Interleaf Story. Mutual Esteem.

Chapter II Lecture. Recovery After Graduation; or, Looking Back on College; Interleaf Story. Which Was It?

Chapter III Lecture. What I Don't Know about the Drama; Interleaf Story. Ominous Outlook.

Chapter IV Lecture. Frenzied Fiction: First Lecture. Murder at $2.50 a Crime; Interleaf Story. All Present.

Chapter V Frenzied Fiction: Second Lecture. Love at $1.25 a Throb; Interleaf Story. The Time That Doesn't Fly.

Chapter VI Lecture. Frenzied Fiction: Third Lecture. Passion at 25 Cents a Gasp; Interleaf Story. Technical Terms.

Chapter VII My Fishing Pond; Interleaf Fish Stories. (1) Poor Luck; (2) Open Opportunity; (3) Lines to a Fellow Fisherman.

Chapter VIII The Two Milords. Prologue: A Little Causerie on the Foolishness of Foreign Languages.

Chapter IX My Newspaper and How I Read It. A Press Club Talk with Apologies.

Chapter X Why I Am Leaving My Farm. A Lunch Club Talk to Stop the Back to the Land Movement.

Chapter XI While You're at It. Expert Advice on Knocking Your House into Shape.

Chapter XII The Sit-Down Strike in My Parlour, They Came and They Wouldn't Go.

Chapter XIII The Advancement of Learning. A Talk to Graduate Students; Interleaf Story. Tubes Out of Order.

Chapter XIV Looking Back from Retirement.

BINDING AND DUST JACKET: Bound in red cloth, top edge stained blue. Blind-stamped on the upper board is a solid rectangle. Within this rectangle are two raised rectangles, which contain the following lines in raised characters: HERE ARE MY | LECTURES | [rule] | STEPHEN LEACOCK. Stamped on the spine in gilt: HERE | ARE MY | LECTURES | [rule] | LEACOCK | DODD, MEAD | & COMPANY.

The top, bottom, and sides of the front panel of the jacket are in orange. On the front panel: [the first and last lines in white] | STEPHEN | [the next three lines hand-written and in orange within a solid black rectangle, which itself is outlined several times in white, orange, and black] | *Here* | [to the right of the previous line is a caricature of Leacock, who is dressed in a suit, coat, and hat, with a walking stick] | *Are My* | *Lectures!* | LEACOCK. The spine panel is black with orange lettering: *Here Are* | *My* | *Lectures!* | • | LEACOCK | • | DODD, MEAD | & COMPANY. Remaining sections of the jacket are white with black lettering. The back panel has an advertisement for Cornelia Otis Skinner's *Excuse It, Please!* (13th printing). On the front flap is a description of *Here Are My Lectures and Stories* (price $2). The back flap has an advertisement for Wolcott Gibbs's *Bed of Neuroses*. The letter T is in the bottom left corner of the back flap.

NOTES: On the same day [18 January 1937] that Leacock informed Frank Dodd that he had offered *My Discovery of the West* to Thomas Allen and Houghton Mifflin, he told Dodd: "I have no[w] finished & done with lecturing forever (except that I have 3 engagements to fill in the next six weeks). . . . *so* I propose to publish lectures under a fair title. . . . *HERE ARE MY LECTURES* or *LECTURES THEY LAUGHED AT.*" The contract with Dodd, Mead for the American and Canadian rights is dated 20 January 1937. Leacock received 10% royalty up to 5,000 copies, 15% thereafter.

Dodd inquired about the book's progress on 21 April 1937 in the hope that the book could be scheduled for publication in the autumn. On 27 May 1937, Leacock told Dodd that he hoped to complete the book by 15 August 1937. Leacock wrote a blurb for the book in May. Dodd acknowledged receipt of Leacock's manuscript on 4 October 1937. The manuscript had to be sent to an editor because it ". . . was not in very good shape. . . ." Dodd sent the manuscript to the printers with a view to publication on 10 November 1937. Author's copies were sent to Leacock on 8 November 1937, and the book was published on 15 November. "We all think this is an usually bright and amusing book and are hoping that it will meet with the success it deserves," E.H. Dodd, Jr. remarked. Copies were received by the Copyright Office at DLC on 17 November 1937, and the copyright was registered a day later (A112127). The copyright was renewed by Stephen Lushington Leacock on 27 November 1964 (R349936).

Number of copies printed not known. The book was still in print as of 1 June 1944. Between 1 February 1941 and 1 February 1944, the book had earned a royalty of $4.90.

COPIES EXAMINED: QMMRB (two copies, both in jacket).

## A83a.1 *Canadian issue*:

Identical to the American edition except that the verso of the title leaf has been rubber-stamped in red as follows: CANADIAN EDITION | FOR SALE IN | CANADA ONLY. John McClelland, who acted as the director of Dodd, Mead & Company (Canada), Ltd., told Leacock on 16 November 1937 ". . . that supplies of the book have been sent to each of the Book Stores in Montreal. We have already arranged that a supply will be on hand at the Book Store operated in connection with the Book Fair and it will be on display at our stand with our other books." Lomer (p. 32) records a Canadian edition: Toronto, McClelland & Stewart, limited, 1937. However, no copy of this edition has ever been seen.

COPIES EXAMINED: CS (price clipped from front flap of dust jacket); QMMRB (price clipped front flap).

## A83a.2 *American issue, photographic reprint* (1973):

[rule, ornamental rule] | HERE ARE MY LECTURES | AND | STORIES | STEPHEN LEACOCK | *Essay Index Reprint Series* | BOOKS FOR LIBRARIES PRESS | PLAINVIEW, NEW YORK | [ornamental rule, rule]

The verso of the title leaf of this issue reads as follows: COPYRIGHT, 1937, | BY DODD, MEAD AND COMPANY, INC. | Copyright © Renewed 1964 by Stephen Leacock | Reprinted 1973 by arrangement with Dodd, Mead & | Company, Inc. | [seven lines of Library of Congress Cataloging in Publication Data] | PRINTED IN THE UNITED STATES OF AMERICA. The only other difference between this issue and A83a is p. *ii*, which is blank in this issue. Bound in greyish blue buckram with lettering stamped on the spine in gilt as follows: [thick rule] | [the next line down the spine] | Here Are My Lectures and Stories | LEACOCK | [thick rule]. Leaves measure 188 × 123 mm.

COPIES EXAMINED: OTUT.

## A83b  *English edition* (1938):

HERE ARE MY | LECTURES | *By* | *Stephen Leacock* | LONDON | JOHN LANE THE BODLEY HEAD

◆ A¹⁶ B–I¹⁶ K⁸ L⁴ [$1 signed, fifth leaf signed * for B–I gatherings (e.g. B*)]. *i–vi*, vii–xii, *13–14*, 15–45, *46–50*, 51–92, *93–96*, 97–128, *129–132*, 133–151, *152–156*, 157–177, *178–182*, 183–213, *214–218*, 219–232, *233–234*, 235–245, *246–248*, 249–255, *256–258*, 259–266, *267–268*, 269–274, *275–276*, 277–283, *284–286*, 287–297, *298*, 299–300, *301–302*, 303–311, *312* pp. (156 leaves); 183 × 124 mm.

CONTENTS:  pp. *i–ii* blank; p. *iii* half title; p. *iv By the same Author* | [list of twenty-four books by Leacock, the first being *Literary Lapses* and the last *My Discovery of the West*] | THE BODLEY HEAD; p. *v* title; p. *vi* FIRST PUBLISHED IN 1938 | PRINTED IN GREAT BRITAIN BY | UNWIN BROTHERS LIMITED, LONDON AND WOKING; pp. vii–x preface by Leacock dated November 1, 1937; p. xi–xii table of contents; pp. *13–311* text; p. *312* blank.

TEXT:  Identical to the American edition.

BINDING AND DUST JACKET:  Bound in dark yellow cloth with lettering in red. Stamped on the upper board: *HERE ARE MY* | LECTURES | *STEPHEN* | *LEACOCK*. Stamped on the spine: *HERE* | *ARE MY* | *LECTURES* | [ornamental, looping line] | *STEPHEN* | *LEACOCK* | *THE* | *BODLEY HEAD*.

The front, spine, and back panels of the jacket are yellow with the title in white in a repeating line pattern. All other lettering on these panels is in red. The front and back panels are the same, as follows: Stephen | Leacock | HERE | ARE MY | LECTURES. On the spine panel of the jacket: Here | Are My | Lectures | [the next line vertically down the spine] LEACOCK | THE | BODLEY | HEAD. All lettering on the flaps is in red against a white background. The first two paragraphs of the front flap are a revision of the paragraphs from Leacock's preface (p. x); the last paragraph on the front flap compares Leacock to Mark Twain who "doubled the roles of humorous writer and lecturer." The price on the front flap is 7s 6d. On the back flap is an advertisement for Leacock's *Funny Pieces* with excerpts of reviews from five magazines and newspapers.

NOTES:  On 19 March 1937, P.P. Howe of John Lane The Bodley Head offered Leacock a contract for the book on the same basis as *Funny Pieces*, but the contract was not signed at that time. Howe wrote to Leacock on 24 December 1937: "I am now rather anxious to receive the copy of Frank Dodd's edition of 'Here Are My Lectures' as the title is overdue for inclusion in our Spring list." Howe received a copy of the American edition on 25 January 1938. He sent Leacock a contract for the book, and arranged for the printing of the English edition with a view to publication in March 1938. Leacock sent back the contract for reconsideration on 15 February 1938. He wanted a royalty of 15% on the English edition, not 10% as in the American edition: "When I offered it to you, as I did to Dodd, it looked an uncertain book. He accepted right away: you didn't. By the time you accepted the book was not uncertain, being already published here and a success. But as

I never withdraw the offer you are of course free to go ahead at 10 per cent and I won't grumble." Howe relented on 4 March, and offered Leacock 15%, the same terms as *Funny Pieces*. He told him: ". . . We shall publish early in April, in time for Easter." The contract (copies at SLM and READ) is dated 22 March 1938. The English edition appeared circa 11 April 1938 (the date of the first royalty statement, 309 copies sold in England, 2 foreign, 257 colonial, £26 7s 3d royalty). On 29 July 1939, Howe reported that the book was "jogging along rather quietly to the near-thousand point. . . ." A critic on the *Sunday Times* "discovered" the book, resulting "in immediate sales of two hundred copies."

Lomer (p. 32) gives 5 April 1938 as the date of publication. He also records what appears to be a reprint on 18 April 1940. According to *The English Catalogue of Books*, publication occurred in April 1938.

COPIES EXAMINED: CS (price clipped from front flap); QMMRB (in jacket).


## A84 HUMOUR AND HUMANITY 1937

### A84a *English edition*:

HUMOUR | AND HUMANITY | *An Introduction to the Study* | *of Humour* | *By* | STEPHEN LEACOCK | PROFESSOR EMERITUS, MCGILL UNIVERSITY | [publisher's device (silhouette of a wall of a gothic building)] | LONDON | Thornton Butterworth Ltd

◆ $A^{16}$ B–$H^{16}$ $I^2$ (+$I$1.2) [$1 signed]. *1*–6, 7, 8, 9, *10*, 11–247, 248, *249*–254, *1*–6 pp. (130 leaves). 164 × 103 mm.

CONTENTS: p. *1*–2 blank; p. *3* half-title HUMOUR AND | HUMANITY | THE | HOME UNIVERSITY LIBRARY | OF MODERN KNOWLEDGE; p. *4* list of editors of the Home University Library (H.A.L. Fisher, Gilbert Murray, and Julian Huxley); p. *5* title; p. *6 First Published . . . . 1937* | *All Rights Reserved* | MADE AND PRINTED IN GREAT BRITAIN; p. 7 table of contents; p. 8 blank; p. 9 preface; p. *10* blank; pp. 11–247 text; p. 248 blank; pp. *249*–250 bibliography; pp. 251–254 index; p. *1* blank; p. 2 Printed in Great Britain by | Butler & Tanner Ltd., | Frome and London; pp. *3*–6 list of books up to December 1937 arranged by category in the Home University Library of Modern Knowledge series (Leacock's book, no. 184, listed under Political and Social Science).

TEXT: chapter I On the Nature of Humour; chapter II The Expression of Humour: Words; chapter III The Expression of Humour: Ideas; chapter IV The Humour of Situation; chapter V The Humour of Character; chapter VI Comic Verse: The Lighter Notes; chapter VII Humorous Poetry: The Undertones; chapter VIII Humour and Craftsmanship; chapter IX Humour and Sublimity.

BINDING AND DUST JACKET: Bound in light blue cloth, top edge stained blue. Stamped in blue on the upper board: [heavy rule] | THE | HOME UNIVERSITY LIBRARY | [person and rays of the sun within a circle] | [heavy rule]. Stamped in blue on the spine: [heavy rule] | HUMOUR | AND | HUMANITY | STEPHEN | LEACOCK | THORNTON | BUTTERWORTH | [heavy rule].

There are two variant dust jackets. The one that apparently was first issued has a red front panel with black lettering as follows: THE | HOME UNIVERSITY | LIBRARY | [the next two lines within a solid white rectangle] | HUMOUR AND HUMANITY | STEPHEN

LEACOCK | [black and white illustration of an open book and a gothic cathedral surrounded by laurel leaves] | THORNTON BUTTERWORTH LIMITED. The jacket's spine panel is also red with the series title, series number (184), Leacock's name, the title, an illustration of an open book within laurel leaves, and the publisher's name. The remainder of the jacket is white with black lettering. The back panel has the series title, the names of the three editors, two prospectuses (1. list of titles with contents and 2. courses of study with the aid of the library), and the name and address of Thornton Butterworth. The front flap has excerpts from reviews about the series and the book's price (2s 6d). The back flap states the purpose of the series, and lists the chief subjects of the series.

The second dust jacket is dark yellow with printing in black. The front panel has the series title, the title of book, Leacock's name and position at McGill (similar to the title page), a silhouette of a gothic building and grounds, and the publisher's name and address. The back panel lists the series, the names of the editors, three available prospectuses (1. list of titles, 2. list of titles with contents, and 3. courses of study with the aid of the library), a silhouette of a gothic building and grounds, and the publisher's name and address. On the spine of the jacket: [heavy rule] | The | Home | University | Library | 184 | [rule] | HUMOUR | AND | HUMANITY | STEPHEN | LEACOCK | [silhouette of a wall of a gothic building] | THORNTON | BUTTERWORTH | [heavy rule]. The front flap has excerpts from reviews about the series (no price stated). The back flap is similar to the back flap of the first dust jacket.

NOTES: Leacock apparently wrote letters of inquiry to Thornton Butterworth and Henry Holt and Company on 20 March 1936. He asked them to invite him to write a book on humour for the Home University Library series. He pointed out: "I hope I may with modesty take for granted that you know who I am and what I claim I may have to look upon humour as my business." Butterworth complied with Leacock's request on 14 April 1936. He sent Leacock a memorandum of agreement, although he expressed a concern of overlapping content with Leacock's *Humour: Its Theory and Technique*. Leacock did not reply to this overture, and on 23 June 1936, Butterworth mistakenly interpreted Leacock's silence as a sign of his unwillingness to proceed any further. Leacock finally replied on 20 August 1936, indicating his intention to write the book under the title, *Humour and Humanity*. The agreement is dated 22 August 1936. He agreed to deliver the manuscript by 1 January 1937 (later changed to 1 July 1937). The agreement called for an advance of £50 on the day of publication, 1d on copies sold of the English edition, 1½d on copies on any American edition, ½d on any trade discount, and one third of the net amount on any foreign translations. To the agreement Leacock appended a note about "the freedom of my judgment," in which he stated his preference for modern humour over the humour of the ancient world and classical literature.

Butterworth could not accept this proviso to the contract, however, because ultimately, it meant that Leacock's work would be beyond editorial scrutiny. A compromise was reached in October 1936. In particular, Leacock worried about the views of one of the editors of the Home University Library series, the classical scholar, Gilbert Murray. ". . . The Greeks were not very funny men," Leacock observed in spite of Murray's opinion to the contrary. He would not write the book if Murray's opinions prevailed in such matters. He added: "I will go to work on it. In any case it is complimentary to be asked to write a book for a house which I have admired for years." Sir Tresham Lever inquired about Leacock's progress on 13 April 1937. On 21 June 1937, Leacock informed Tresham:

> My book for the Home University Series, *Humour and Humanity*, is finished. I am sure you will be well pleased with it. It runs to 50,000 words as exactly as can be. I expect to post the manuscript to you by the end of the week. There will be no need to send proofs to me. . . . The book is written in a vein to give no offence to anyone in religion, literary or political grounds. It brings in plenty of American interest as is natural since I live in America. . . . It has been to me a great pleasure in the doing. . . .

Tresham received Leacock's manuscript on 19 July 1937, and the editors approved its publication on 10 August 1937. Published on 15 November 1937. Copies of the English edition were received by the Copyright Office at DLC on 11 January 1938; the copyright was registered on 11 January 1938 (Aint.23505). Leacock was sent £37 10s (his advance minus tax) as advance on 25 November 1937. 500 copies were sent to Thomas Nelson's in Toronto on 1 December 1937 for distribution in Canada. By the end of 1937 1,649 copies sold. Another 450 copies sold by 31 December 1938, but Leacock still had an unearned balance of £20 4s 6d. 1,217 further copies (326 copies colonial) were sold to the end of 1943 (unearned balance of £2 19s 2d including American sales).

COPIES EXAMINED: CS (two copies with the variant jackets); LAT (in dark yellow jacket); QMMRB (three copies — proof copy, in dark yellow jacket, rebound).

## A84a.1 *American issue* (1938):

HUMOUR | AND HUMANITY | *An Introduction to the Study* | *of Humour* | *By* | STEPHEN LEACOCK | PROFESSOR EMERITUS, MCGILL UNIVERSITY | NEW YORK | Henry Holt and Company | LONDON | Thornton Butterworth Ltd

The American issue is identical to the English edition, except that the title leaf is a cancel. The copyright page reads: *First Published* . . . . *1938* | *All Rights Reserved* | MADE AND PRINTED IN GREAT BRITAIN.

BINDING AND DUST JACKET: Bound in black cloth with stamping in orange. The upper board has two rectangles, one inside another, the smaller one containing the lines: HOME | UNIVERSITY | LIBRARY. Stamped on the spine: [rule] | HUMOUR | AND | HUMANITY | LEACOCK | HENRY HOLT | AND COMPANY | [rule].

The American issue has a glassine wrapper and also a dust jacket in white with green and purple lettering and illustration. The front and spine panels have a repeating, green oval pattern, with laurel leaves, of an owl on a book (Holt's logo) and of the initials of the company. On the front panel are three white compartments with purple lettering as follows: [within the first compartment] | HUMOUR AND | HUMANITY | [rule] | STEPHEN LEACOCK | [within the second compartment] | This is one of the volumes of the | Home University Library | of Modern Knowledge | [eight lines stating the names of the editors, the fact that the books are written by authorities, and that they cover educational and cultural subjects] | [within the third compartment] | HENRY HOLT AND COMPANY. The spine panel has two solid white rectangles amid the oval pattern with purple lettering as follows: [within the first rectangle] | Humour | and Humanity | [rule] | LEACOCK | 153 | [within the second rectangle] | Henry Holt | and Company. The back panel and the flaps are printed in green, and list volumes of the series.

NOTES: As early as 31 January 1933, Gilbert Loveland of Henry Holt and Company wrote to Leacock: "It happens that our president, Mr. Richard H. Thornton, is now in London, and I am sending him your letter of the twenty-fifth with all possible speed." Leacock made inquiries about the Home University Library series at that time. He wrote again three years later on 21 March 1936, this time in reference to a book about the nature of humour. Thornton informed him on 27 March 1936 that "editorial matters for the Library are settled on the other side" of the Atlantic.

The American issue was published on 2 March 1938 and sold for $1.25. The copyright was registered with the Copyright Office at DLC on 10 March 1938 (A115350). The copyright was renewed by Stephen Lushington Leacock on 3 March 1965 (R356944). On 30 August 1938, Thornton informed Leacock that 1,200 copies had sold. Another twenty-five copies had sold in 1939. 24 copies sold to 31 July 1941.

COPIES EXAMINED: CS (two copies, one with the glassine wrapper and dust jacket).

## A84b  *American edition* (1938):

[the first word in open type] HUMOR AND | [the next word in open type] HUMANITY | *An Introduction to the Study* | *of Humor* | BY | STEPHEN LEACOCK | NEW YORK | HENRY HOLT AND COMPANY

♦  1–15$^8$. *1*–*10*, 3–225, 226, 227–232 pp. (120 leaves). 214 × 138 mm.

CONTENTS: p. *1* half title; p. *2* blank; p. *3* title; p. *4* *This book was written originally for the* | *Home University Library.* | COPYRIGHT, 1938, | BY | STEPHEN LEACOCK | PRINTED IN THE | UNITED STATES OF AMERICA; p. *5* table of contents; p. 6 blank; p. 7 preface; p. 8 blank; p. 9 fly title; p. *10* blank; pp. 3–225 text; p. 226 blank; pp. 227–228 bibliography; pp. 229–232 index.

TEXT:  Identical to A84a.

BINDING AND DUST JACKET:  Bound in dark blue cloth with gilt lettering, top edge stained greyish blue. Stamped on the upper board, hand-written and at an angle: *Humor* | *and* | *Humanity*. The same three lines appear on the top of the spine, although considerably smaller in size, followed by two other lines on the spine: LEACOCK | HOLT.

The dust jacket is dark blue, red, and white. The top third of the front panel is red, containing three lines in white: [hand-written] *The New Book by* | STEPHEN | LEACOCK | [white rule extending to the spine panel of the jacket]. The remainder of the front panel is dark blue with three lines in white, identical to the lines on the upper board but smaller. The top third of the spine panel is dark blue with the same three lines as on the upper board but smaller and in white. A white rule separates the remaining portion of the spine panel, which is dark blue with lines in white as follows: STEPHEN | LEACOCK | HOLT. The back panel and the flaps are white with dark blue lettering. The back panel lists important new books published by Holt. The front flap hints at the contents of Leacock's book, gives the price ($2), and the publisher's name and address. The back flap has an advertisement for George Duhamel's *The Pasquier Chronicles*.

There is a later variant binding and jacket. The later binding is practically the same colour as the earlier one, but the cloth appears somewhat grainier in texture. The front and spine panels are orange with white lettering. The back panel and flaps of the later jacket are white with orange lettering. The lines on the front and spine of the later jacket are the same as the earlier jacket, except that the line *The New Book by* has been deleted from the front of the jacket. The back panel of the later jacket has advertisements for George Herriman's *Krazy Kat* and Corey Ford's *The Horse of Another Color*. The front flap of the later jacket provides a synopsis of the book with the price and publisher's name and address. The back flap has an advertisement for Crockett Johnson's *Barnaby* and *Barnaby & Mr. O'Malley*.

NOTES: On 30 August 1938, Richard T. Thornton informed Leacock that he would be publishing a "library edition" of *Humor and Humanity* ". . . because booksellers and librarians do not like the smaller size" of the volumes in the Home University Library. This apparently refers to this American edition. But the autographed copy at QMMRB of this edition is dated 2 March 1938, and a copy inscribed by Leacock to his sister is dated 10 July 1938 (sold by Steven Temple Books). By the end of 1938 1,195 copies of this edition had been sold (1½d per copy, £7 9s 4d), but Leacock did not receive a penny because the edition was covered in the contract with the Home University Library and there was still an unearned balance of £20 4s 6d. In an undated letter written in shorthand at this time, Leacock complained that although the contract was legal, ". . . the 3 cents and a fine U.S. edition to sell for $2.00 and over . . . is not cricket. . . ." He suggested that a normal royalty should be paid, and the proceeds given "to a British War Charity." Almost two years later, on 8 August 1940, Leacock told his American agent, Paul R. Reynolds:

> I did a book for Thornton Butterworth (Home Univ. Lib.) 10% royalty with 2½d on 2 sh[illings] & did not notice (my own fault) that the contract cut the U.S. royalty to 1½d. Nor did I notice that the U.S. book could be, under the contract, be brought out at more than 2 shillings. Result — Henry Holt took over the U.S. rights, brought out the book at [$]2.00, & paid Butterworth 20 cents a book royalty of which they gave me three cents. Again, my own fault, but sharp business. (Reynolds fonds, COL)

Also note that the Web site Amazon.com lists an edition (possibly a photographic reprint) published by Century Bookbinding in June 1980. This later edition was out of print by 1997.

COPIES EXAMINED: CS (both variant bindings and jackets); LAT (later variant binding in jacket).

## A84c *Japanese abridged edition* (1965):

Stephen Leacock | HUMOUR AND HUMANITY | EDITED WITH INTRODUCTION AND NOTES | *BY* | N. UYAMA | *Professor at Shizuoka University* | SEIBIDO | *1965*

◆ *1–3*, ii–iii, *1–3*, *1–101*, *1–3* pp. (56 leaves). 82 × 127 mm.

CONTENTS: p. *1* title; p. *2* HUMOUR AND HUMANITY | Oxford University Press | London | Copyright by Stephen Leacock | *This book is published in Japan* | *by arrangement with Oxford University Press*; pp. *3*, ii–iii editor's introduction in Japanese; p. *1* blank; p. *2* table of contents; p. *3* blank; pp. *1–62* text; pp. *63–101* notes in Japanese explaining the meaning of words and phrases in Leacock's text; p. *1* blank; p. *2* copyright page in Japanese; p. *3* list of books in Seibido's English Texts series.

TEXT: chapter I On the Nature of Humour; chapter II Humour and Craftsmanship; chapter III Humour and Sublimity.

BINDING: Perfect bound in white and green stiff paper with a plastic jacket. Heavy black rules run across the top and bottom of the covers. On the back cover is a list of books in Seibido's English Texts series. Price 200 yen.

NOTES: This abridged edition, which includes chapters I, VIII, and IX of A84, belongs to a series of texts intended for Japanese students who are learning English. Date of publication and number of copies printed not known.

COPIES EXAMINED: EVANS.

## A85 FOGGY FINANCE 1937

[cover title; all lines within an ornamental, ribbon rectangle; the first letters in the next two lines are above and below the line levels] FOGGY | FINANCE | *by* STEPHEN LEACOCK | REPRINTED BY | THE CONNECTICUT SOCIETY | OF ALBERTURNIANS | DECEMBER, 1937

♦ $1^8$. *1–2, 1–13, 1* pp. (8 leaves). 135 × 90 mm.

CONTENTS: p. *1* statement by the Connecticut Society of Alberturnians; p. *2* blank; pp. *1–13* text; p. *1* blank.

TEXT: Foggy Finance: Be a Fiscal Expert and Learn Less Than You Know.

BINDING: Orange tan paper wrapper, with a grainy finish on the outside of the wrapper, smooth surface on the inside; wire-stitched.

NOTES: On the first page (p. *1*) of this pamphlet, the Connecticut Society of Alberturnians expresses its pleasure in publishing the essay by Leacock: ". . . to whom we can only bow in profound admiration." Reprinted from the *Commentator* 2 (November 1937): 17–21 (C37.54), "by special permission of the Magazine and Author." Neither the Connecticut Historical Society nor the University of Connecticut at Hartford were able to shed any light on the aims of this Society. Only one known copy of the pamphlet is known to be extant. Number of copies printed not known.

COPIES EXAMINED: CS.

## A86 MODEL MEMOIRS 1938

### A86a *American edition*:

[thick-thin rule] | MODEL MEMOIRS | AND OTHER SKETCHES FROM | SIMPLE TO SERIOUS | By | STEPHEN LEACOCK | [publisher's device of Dodd, Mead: oval containing open book and portrait of classical figure with leaves and company name] | DODD, MEAD & COMPANY | NEW YORK 1938 | [thin-thick rule]

♦ $1–19^8$ $20^{10}$. *i–vi*, vii–viii, *1–2*, 3–17, *18–20*, 21–46, *47–48*, 49–57, *58–60*, 61–79, *80–82*, 83–89, *90–92*, 93–100, *101–102*, 103–109, *110–112*, 113–120, *121–122*, 123–131, *132–134*, 135–143, *144*, 145–146, *147–148*, 149–151, *152–154*, 155–158, *159–160*, 161–165, *166–168*, 169–177, *178–182*, 183–187, *188–192*, 193–207, *208–210*, 211–219, *220*, 221–222, *223–224*, 225–230, *231–232*, 233–243, *244*, 245–246, *247–248*, 249–254 *255–256*, 257–268, *269–270*, 271–284, *285–286*, 287–295, *296–298*, 299–305, *306–308*, 309–316 pp. (162 leaves). 187 × 130 mm.

CONTENTS: p. *i* half title; p. *ii* list of twenty-one books by Leacock, the first being *Literary Lapses* and the last *Here Are My Lectures*; p. *iii* title; p. *iv* COPYRIGHT, 1938, | BY DODD, MEAD AND COMPANY, INC. | All rights reserved — no part of this book may be | reproduced in any form without permission in | writing from the publisher. | PRINTED IN

THE UNITED STATES OF AMERICA; p. *v* preface by Leacock dated October 1938; p. *vi* blank; pp. vii–viii table of contents; pp. *1–316* text (pp. *2, 18, 20, 48, 58, 60, 80, 82, 90, 92, 102, 110, 112, 122, 132, 134, 144, 148, 150, 154, 160, 166, 168, 178, 180, 182, 188, 190, 192, 208, 210, 220, 224, 232, 244, 248, 256, 270, 286, 296, 298, 306*, and *308* blank).

TEXT: I Model Memoirs: (1) My Victorian Girlhood by Lady Nearleigh Slopover; (2) Through Arabia on a Mule by Major Allhell Late Pindilwani Field Force (Third Base); (3) Up and Down Downing Street; or, Who Started the Great War?: Memoirs of a War Diplomat (The One Hundredth Set of Such); (4) So This Is the United States: A Six Weeks' Thorough Survey As Made by a Lecturer from England; (5) The Criminal Memoirs of Napoleon Bonaparte. II Model Monologues: (1) Mrs. Uplift Betters Society; (2) Mrs. Newrich Buys Antiques; (3) Mrs. Eiderdown Roughs It in the Bush; (4) Mrs. Easy Has Her Fortune Told; III The Dissolution of Our Dinner Club. Interleaf Story — How Teachers Swim. IV How to Lose Money (for Amateurs). V The Familiar Magic of Fishing: A Pullman Car Transformed into a Trout Stream. VI Overworking the Alphabet. VII On the Need for a Quiet College. Interleaf Story — Truck Problem Solved. VIII Turn Back the Clock; or, at Least, Make It Slower. Interleaf Story — Quality Does It. IX Come Out into the Garden. Interleaf Story — All Nice People. X The Anatomy of Gloom: An Appeal to Bankers. Interleaf Story — A Dip into Psychology. XI Then and Now: Were We Happier Fifty Years Ago? Interleaf Story — Thrown Out. XII What I Read Then — What You Read Now: An Essay for the Young. Interleaf Story — Feeding Time. XIII Hand Me Down That Book. XIV Who Knows It?: Our Passion for Information. XV How Much Does Language Change? XVI How Far Can We Plan?: An Excursion into Economics. XVII College as Comic Stuff. XVIII All Is Not Lost! A Recollection.

BINDING AND DUST JACKET: Bound in red cloth. A solid rectangle is blind-stamped on the upper board. Within this rectangle are two raised rectangles which contain the following in raised characters: [jester's stick] MODEL [jester's stick] | MEMOIRS | [rule] | STEPHEN LEACOCK. Stamped on the spine in gilt: MODEL | MEMOIRS | [jester's stick] | LEACOCK | DODD, MEAD | & COMPANY.

The front and spine panels of the jacket are brownish orange. On the front panel: [two rules extending to the spine] | [the next two lines in white] | Model | Memoirs | [sketch of Leacock with zig-zag lines on both sides of the sketch; the next three lines to the left of the sketch:] | and | Other | Sketches | [the next three lines to the right of the sketch:] from | Simple to | Solemn | [the next line hand-written] *by Stephen Leacock*. On the spine panel: [two rules extending over from the front panel] | [the next two lines in white:] Model | Memoirs | LEACOCK | [four crossed lines in x-shapes] | [the remaining lines on the spine in white:] DODD MEAD | *&* COMPANY. The back panel is printed in brownish orange and black. A black-and-white photo of Leacock appears in the upper left corner. To the right of the photo in brownish orange is *Books by* | Stephen | Leacock. Two quotations from reviews are printed under the photo with the heading in brownish orange: LAUGH WITH LEACOCK. Seventeen other titles by Leacock are also listed on the back panel. On the front flap of the jacket is a description of *Model Memoirs* (price $2). The back flap carries an ad for Cornelia Otis Skinner's *Dithers and Jitters* (priced at $2); the letter T is printed by itself under the description of Skinner's book.

In the copies examined the paper stock up to p. *122* is white, but the remaining leaves are somewhat embrowned. This would indicate that two different paper stocks were used, and that one is more acidic in nature, causing foxing over time.

NOTES: On 25 February 1938, Leacock proposed a book to Dodd, Mead entitled "Idle Hours for Vacant Minds." The contract at SLM is dated 1 March 1938; Leacock was to complete the book by 1 August 1938. Included in Leacock's book was a section on "Model Memoirs," which was intended as a satire on the genre of autobiography. This part of the book greatly appealed to Howard C. Lewis of Dodd, Mead and to Frank Dodd. Dodd told Leacock on 21 March 1938: "We both like the latest title, MODEL MEMOIRS, somewhat better than IDLE HOURS, although they are both good. As you say, IDLE HOURS can be used later perhaps." The jacket was designed on 28 April 1938.

On 6 June 1938, Dodd asked about Leacock's progress. The contract sent in March had not been signed, and Dodd wondered whether Leacock would finish the book as scheduled. The contract with Dodd, Mead for *Model Memoirs* is dated 22 August 1938. Leacock agreed to deliver the manuscript by 1 September 1938. He received 15% royalty on all copies sold and "an advance on publication date equal to the accrued royalties earned up to that date." The contract also covered the book rights in Canada.

By 9 June 1938 Leacock had completed 11,000 words; he planned to write another 20,000 by 15 August. Leacock sent the manuscript on 26 August 1938; it arrived at Dodd, Mead's offices on 29 August. Proofs were sent to Leacock at Old Brewery Bay on 16 September 1938, and he returned them on 25 September. One short sketch was left out and had to be inserted at this point. Publication was delayed because Leacock's article, "Model Memoirs: My Victorian Girlhood by Lady Nearleigh Slopover," was due to appear in *Saturday Evening Post* on 12 November (on the newsstands on 9 November 1938). The book was finally published on 23 November 1938. On that date Leacock was sent $380 ($400 less 5% alien tax) in accrued royalty. Copies were received by the Copyright Office on 28 November 1938, and the copyright was registered on 26 November 1938 (A122840). Number of copies printed not known.

On 20 February 1939, M.M. Geffen of *Omnibook* signed a contract with Dodd, Mead to issue an abridgement of approximately 30,000 words in the April 1939 issue of their magazine. They paid $500 royalty for this one-time use with the proviso that further payment would be made if circulation exceeded 50,000 copies.

Sometime shortly after 23 May 1940, another 250 copies were printed (these were referred to as an "edition of 250 copies"). Leacock received an advance of $25 for this "edition" instead of the regular royalty because of the excessive expense in manufacturing and selling such a small "edition" (no copy found). Lomer (p. 42) also records a reprinting in 1939.

One of Leacock's notebooks at SLM (J60) has several tables of contents for the book: one for "Idle Hours for Vacant Minds" dated 20 February 1938; one for *Model Memoirs* dated 7 June 1938 ("Done July 2 = 35,000 [words]"); and another dated 14 August 1938.

"Mrs. Newrich Buys Antiques" reprinted in Guy Pocock and M.M. Bozman, eds., *Modern Humour* (London: J.M. Dent & Sons, 1940), pp. 29–34. "Come Out into the Garden" reprinted in *Peter Gzowski's Spring Tonic* (Edmonton: Hurtig, 1979), pp. 47–50.

COPIES EXAMINED: CS (in jacket); QMMRB (two copies, one in jacket).

A86a.1 *first American issue, photographic reprint* (1971):

[thick-thin rule] | MODEL MEMOIRS | AND OTHER SKETCHES FROM | SIMPLE TO SERIOUS | By | STEPHEN LEACOCK | *Essay Index Reprint Series* | [publisher's device, two lines in height, to the left of the next two lines: abstract design of building with four columns] | BOOKS FOR LIBRARIES PRESS | FREEPORT, NEW YORK

The verso of the title leaf reads as follows: First Published 1938 | Reprinted 1971 | INTERNATIONAL STANDARD BOOK NUMBER: | 0-8369-2434-7 | LIBRARY OF CONGRESS CATALOG CARD NUMBER: | 77-156678 | PRINTED IN THE UNITED STATES OF AMERICA | BY | NEW WORLD BOOK MANUFACTURING CO., INC. | HALLANDALE, FLORIDA 33009. Pagination is the same as A86a, except that the leaf containing Leacock's preface is omitted and three blank leaves have been added at the end. The page opposite the title page is blank. Leaves measure 216 × 135 mm. Bound in blue buckram with stamping on the spine in silver as follows: LEACOCK | [rule] | [the next two lines within a solid maroon rectangle] | MODEL | MEMOIRS | [rule] | [the next three lines within an oval] | B | *f* | L.

COPIES EXAMINED: OTMCL.

**A86a.2** *second American issue, photographic reprint* (1992):

[thick-thin rule] | MODEL MEMOIRS | AND OTHER SKETCHES FROM | SIMPLE TO SERIOUS | By | STEPHEN LEACOCK | AYER COMPANY, PUBLISHERS, INC. | SALEM, NEW HAMPSHIRE 03079

The verso of the title leaf records that the book was reprinted in 1971, but then adds: Reprint Edition, 1992 | Ayer Company, Publishers, Inc. | Salem, New Hampshire 03079. The last eight lines on the copyright page are identical to A86a.1. Pagination is the same as A86a.1, except there is a blank leaf at the beginning and four blank leaves at the end. Leaves measure 209 × 137 mm. Bound in reddish brown laminated plastic over paper boards with white lettering on the upper board and spine. Stamped on the upper board: Model Memoirs | By Stephen Leacock. Stamped on the spine: Leacock | [the next line stamped vertically] Model Memoirs | Ayer.

COPIES EXAMINED: CS; SLM (many copies for sale).

**A86b** *English edition* (1939):

MODEL MEMOIRS | AND OTHER SKETCHES FROM | SIMPLE TO SERIOUS | By | Stephen Leacock | LONDON | JOHN LANE THE BODLEY HEAD

◆ $A^{16}$ B–$L^{16}$ $M^4$ [\$1 signed, fifth leaf signed * ]. *1–6, 7, 8, 9–10, 11–12, 13–29, 30–32, 33–61, 62–64, 65–74, 75–76, 77–98, 99–100, 101–108, 109–110, 111–119, 120–122, 123–130, 131–132, 133–141, 142–144, 145–154, 155–156, 157–168, 169–170, 171–174, 175–176, 177–181, 182–184, 185–190, 191–192, 193–203, 204–206, 207–213, 214–216, 217–235, 236–238, 239–250, 251–252, 253–257, 258, 259–260, 261–262, 263–277, 278–280, 281–286, 287–288, 289–301, 302–304, 305–320, 321–322, 323–335, 336–338, 339–347, 348–350, 351–359, 360* pp. (180 leaves). 183 × 121 mm.

CONTENTS: p. *1–2* blank; p. *3* half title; p. *4* list of twenty-five books by Leacock, the first being *Literary Lapses* and the last *Here Are My Lectures*; p. *5* title; p. *6* FIRST PUBLISHED IN 1939 | PRINTED IN GREAT BRITAIN BY | UNWIN BROTHERS LIMITED, LONDON AND WOKING; p. *7* preface by Leacock dated November 1938; p. *8* blank; pp. *9–10* table of contents; pp. *1–359* text (pp. *12, 30, 32, 62, 64, 76, 100, 110, 120, 122, 132, 140,*

*144, 156, 170, 176, 182, 184, 192, 204, 206, 214, 216, 236, 238, 252, 258, 262, 278, 280, 288, 302, 304, 322, 336, 338, 348,* and *350* blank); p. *360* blank.

TEXT: Identical to the American edition, except for the "interleaf story" in section VII which has the title "Removal Problem Solved" instead of "Truck Problem Solved." The stories are virtually the same in both editions. In the English edition the phrases, "trucking company" and "truck," have been replaced by "removal company" and "removal van," respectively. Note also that the preface in the English edition is a condensation of the preface in the American edition. The latter refers to American magazines where some of Leacock's sketches first appeared in print.

BINDING AND DUST JACKET: Bound in reddish maroon cloth with blue lettering on the upper board and spine. Stamped on the upper board: *MODEL MEMOIRS* | *STEPHEN* | *LEACOCK*. Stamped on the spine: *MODEL* | *MEMOIRS* | [ornamental, looping line] | *STEPHEN* | *LEACOCK* | *THE* | *BODLEY HEAD*.

The front and spine panels of the dust jacket are similar to the American edition with the following exceptions: a thick-thin rule is at the top and a thin-thick rule at the bottom; and "and Other Sketches" and "from Simple to Solemn" is missing from each side of the sketch of Leacock on the front panel; and Dodd, Mead has been replaced by THE | BODLEY HEAD on the spine portion. The back panel employs the same photo of Leacock as the American edition. The photo is centered, however, on the English jacket. Under the photo is: STEPHEN | LEACOCK | [twelve lines of excerpts from three reviews] | THE BODLEY HEAD. The front flap describes the contents of *Model Memoirs*, and provides the price of the book (7s 6d). The back flap has ads for *My Discovery of the West* ("Canadian Prize for | Literature" at 12s 6d) and *Here Are My Lectures* (at 7s 6d).

NOTES: On 24 February 1938, Leacock informed Curtis Brown, Ltd. that he was "planning a series of twelve (burlesque) articles under the heading of *Model Memoirs*." By this time he was intent on their syndication in England. P.P. Howe of John Lane The Bodley Head told Leacock on 1 April 1938: "I am delighted to know that this book has a name 'Model Memoirs', and shall much look forward to the receipt of an early copy." Leacock was grateful for Howe's positive reaction. He told Howe on 24 April 1938 that he had already written about a quarter of the book and that it was too late for serialization of the sketches. The blurb for the book was sent to Howe on 25 May 1938. The manuscript was sent to the printer by 30 September 1938. The contract, which is dated 1 November 1938 (copy at READ and SLM), gave Leacock a royalty of 15% on all copies sold with an advance on publication earned by subscription sales. Price 7s 6d. Howe received Leacock's proofs on 10 January 1939. The book was published on 11 March 1939 (595 copies sold in England, 408 copies colonial, royalty of £29 7s 4d). By 7 June 1939 1,800 copies had sold.

Lomer (p. 42) states that English edition was published on 10 March 1939. The copy used for transcription is dated "Xmas 1938," however. *The English Catalogue of Books* records publication in March 1939.

The English edition employs Dodd, Mead's design for the jacket. When the latter company saw the Bodley Head edition on 21 September 1939, they requested that the Bodley Head pay half of the artist's fee.

COPIES EXAMINED: CS (in jacket).

## A87 ALL RIGHT, MR. ROOSEVELT 1939

### A87a *Canadian edition*:

OXFORD PAMPHLETS ON WORLD AFFAIRS | No. C.1 | [rule] | ALL RIGHT, | MR. ROOSEVELT | (*Canada and the United States*) | BY | STEPHEN LEACOCK | TORONTO | OXFORD UNIVERSITY PRESS | 1939

♦ $1^{20}$. *1–2, 3–40* pp. (20 leaves). 183 × 120 mm.

CONTENTS: p. *1* title; p. *2* three paragraphs in which Leacock explains the purpose of his pamphlet — "to stress the value, both to the British Empire and to all the world, of the continuance in despite of wars abroad, of that international peace and good will which now unites all of English-speaking North America." After the paragraphs the following lines are present: STEPHEN LEACOCK | *McGill University,* | *October, 1939.* | PRINTED IN CANADA AND PUBLISHED BY | THE OXFORD UNIVERSITY PRESS, AMEN HOUSE, TORONTO; pp. *3–40* text, including four statistical tables on pp. *38–40*.

BINDING: Bound in pink paper wrappers, wire-stitched. On the front of the wrapper: No. C.1 Price 10c. | [rule] | ALL RIGHT, | MR. ROOSEVELT | (*Canada and the United States*) | By STEPHEN LEACOCK | [coat of arms of Oxford University Press (ornamental shield with two crowns above an open book and another crown below the book with the following words across the book: DOMIMINA | NUSTIO | ILLUMEA)] | [the bottom part of the wrapper is black with lettering in pink] OXFORD PAMPHLETS | ON WORLD AFFAIRS. The back of the wrapper advertises the Oxford Pamphlets on World Affairs. "A SERIES of short accounts of current international topics | written by expert historians, economists, lawyers, and scientists. | Average length 32 pages, price 10c. each." Nos. 1–16, C.1 (Leacock's pamphlet), and C.2 are listed. Also listed, *To be published shortly*, are three other works, the first one being W. Arnold-Forster's *The Blockade in the Last War*. The back of the wrapper also states that *Other Pamphlets are in active preparation*. This line is followed by a rule, and the last two lines are: PRINTED IN CANADA FOR OXFORD UNIVERSITY PRESS, AMEN HOUSE | 480 UNIVERSITY AVENUE, TORONTO, CANADA.

NOTES: On 27 September 1939, the manager of the Canadian branch of Oxford University Press, W.H. Clarke, asked Leacock if he had ". . . seen references in the press to the Oxford University Pamphlets on World Affairs. . . ." Clarke suggested: "I am persuaded also that we ought immediately to initiate a series of our own — a series written by Canadians on subjects of particular interest to us, and to Americans, as we should have in mind a sale both in Canada and in the United States." He invited Leacock to prepare a pamphlet on "Canada and United States Neutrality." Oxford University Press would pay a reasonable honorarium, he assured Leacock. Although he questioned Clarke's vague reference to an honorarium, Leacock told Clarke that he would donate the honorarium to a charity. Clarke received the manuscript on 17 October 1939, and sent proofs to Leacock on the next day. He asked Leacock to write ". . . a paragraph or two — about one hundred words in all — to serve as a sort of preface to be inserted on the reverse of the title page." The proofs were returned to Oxford University Press on 20 October 1939. The pamphlet was published on 27 October 1939. A copy was received by the Copyright Office at DLC on 3 November 1939; copyright registration occurred on 17 November 1939 (Aint25552). By 14 November 1939 5,000 copies had sold in Canada.

There were two reprintings, the second in November 1939 and the third in February 1940.

In the reprints the wrapper is orange. On the wrapper of the second reprinting the back of the wrapper lists nos. 1–17 (no. 17 being W. Arnold-Forster's *The Blockade, 1914–1919*), C.1, and C.2. Only two works are said *To be published shortly*. Otherwise, the second reprint is identical to the first printing. The title page of the third reprint has the additional lines: *Any profits to the Author from this pamphlet | will be given to War Charities.* Reprinting information is also found on p. 2. The back of the wrapper on the third reprint lists nos. 1–24, C.1, C.2, C.4 (also available in the original French), and C.5. On p. 26 of the third reprint (nine lines from the bottom), "that" has been changed to "than," and also, figures are corrected in one of the tables.

By 25 April 1940 12,204 copies had sold to the trade, 199 to schools, and 2,040 to news companies. Expenses (typesetting, paper, etc.) amounted to $687.04. The total sales in Canada and the United States realized $910.69. Leacock's honorarium was $50.

Reprinted in A103.

COPIES EXAMINED: CS (all three printings); OONL (first printing; two copies of the second printing); QMMRB (two copies of first printing); SLM (two copies of first printing, one of the second, Leacock's copies).

**A87a.1** *American issue*:

PAMPHLETS ON WORLD AFFAIRS | No. C.1 | [rule] | ALL RIGHT, | MR. ROOSEVELT | (*Canada and the United States*) | BY | STEPHEN LEACOCK | FARRAR & RINEHART, INC. | NEW YORK | 1939

The American issue is identical to the first impression of the Canadian edition with the exception of the title leaf. On the verso of the title leaf (i.e. p. 2), the same three paragraphs in which Leacock explains the purpose of his pamphlet are present. However, after these paragraphs the following lines are present: STEPHEN LEACOCK | *McGill University,* | *October, 1939.* | PRINTED IN CANADA.

BINDING: Bound in pink paper wrappers, wire-stitched. On the front of the wrapper: No. C.1 Price 15c. | [rule] | ALL RIGHT, | MR. ROOSEVELT | (*Canada and the United States*) | By STEPHEN LEACOCK | [solid black rectangle with a pink rectangle outlined inside it and with the letters fr in pink] | [the bottom part of the front wrapper is black with lettering in pink] | PAMPHLETS ON | WORLD AFFAIRS. The back of the wrapper advertises the Pamphlets on World Affairs. "A SERIES of short accounts of current international topics | written by expert historians, economists, lawyers, and scientists. | Average length 32 pages, price 15c. each, 8 for $1.00." Nos. 1–17, C.1 (Leacock's pamphlet), and C.2 are listed. Also listed, *To be published shortly*, are two other works, the first one being Nathaniel Micklem's *National Socialism and Christianity* and the second D. McLachlan's *Education under the Nazis*. The back of the wrapper also states that *Other Pamphlets are in active preparation.* This line is followed by a rule, and the last line is: PRINTED IN CANADA. The wrapper of the American issue is consequently patterned off of the second printing of the Canadian edition.

NOTES: W.H. Clarke arranged for the pamphlet's publication in the United States. He informed Leacock on 15 November 1939: "May I now confirm our arrangement to pay a royalty of three-quarters of a cent per copy on the American sales. Actually there was no need for a discussion of this point with Farrar and Rinehart, as my price to them (4¢) is inclusive of the 3/4¢ to you." 1,000 copies had sold of the American issue by 15 November 1939. By 29 April 1940 Clarke reported that in spite of his best efforts at promotion, only 1,025 copies had sold of the American issue.

COPY EXAMINED: IEN.

## A88 TOO MUCH COLLEGE 1939

### A88a *American edition*:

Stephen Leacock | [ornamental rule] | [in open type] Too Much College | OR | [in open type] Education Eating Up Life | *With Kindred Essays in* | *Education and Humour* | [publisher's device of Dodd, Mead: oval containing open book and portrait of classical figure with leaves and company name] | [ornamental rule] | [remaining lines in open type] Dodd, Mead & Company | New York 1939

◆ 1–20⁸. *i–iv*, v–ix, *1–5*, 3–20, 21–22, 23–44, 45–46, 47–59, 60–62, 63–78, 79–80, 81–105, 106–108, 109–120, 121–122, 123–133, 134–136, 137–148, 149–150, 151–164, 165–168, 169–175, 176–178, 179–180, 181–182, 183–188, 189–190, 191–194, 195–196, 197–236, 237–240, 241–255, 1–5 pp. (136 leaves). 187 × 131 mm.

CONTENTS: p. *i* half title; p. *ii* list of twenty-two books by Leacock, the first being *Literary Lapses* and the last *Model Memoirs*; p. *iii* title; p. *iv* COPYRIGHT, 1939 | BY DODD, MEAD AND COMPANY, INC. | All rights reserved — no part of this book may be | reproduced in any form without permission in | writing from the publisher. | PRINTED IN THE U. S. A. BY | Quinn & Boden Company, Inc. | [rule] | BOOK MANUFACTURERS | RAHWAY, NEW JERSEY; pp. v–vi table of contents; pp. vii–ix preface dated "October 1, 1939"; p. *1–5*, 3–255 text (pp. *1, 3, 4, 22, 46, 60, 62, 80, 106, 108, 122, 134, 136, 150, 166, 168, 176, 178, 190, 196, 238,* and *240* blank); pp. *1–5* blank. The frontispiece is a half-tone illustration of a drawing by Peggy Shaw with the caption, "College Calling."

TEXT: There are four sections. Only the first section has numbered chapters.

Too Much College is comprised of the following: chapter I Education Eating Up Life; chapter II The Machine at Work; chapter III What Good Is Latin?; chapter IV Mathematics Versus Puzzles; chapter V Parlez-vous français? or Why We Can't Learn Modern Languages?; chapter VI Has Economics Gone to Seed?; chapter VII Psychology: The Black Art of the College; chapter VIII Teaching the Unteachable; chapter IX Rah! Rah! College!

Kindred Essays in Education and Humour is comprised of the following: When Men Retire; As History Grows Dim; Twenty Cents's Worth of Murder; Reader's Junk.

Little Stories for Good Luck is comprised of the following: Three on Each; Nothing Missing; Thinking of Tomorrow; Information While You Drink; No Place for Gentlemen; "We Have with Us Tonight"; A Humble Lover; The Magic of Finance; He Guessed Right; Electric Service; Our Vanished Industries; Couldn't Sleep a Wink; Go to Mother; Five Dollars, Right Now; Are Professors Absent-Minded?; Wanted: A Goldfish; Mushrooms; Help Wanted; Atmosphere; Freedom of Thought; His Better Self; Oh, Sleep! Oh, Gentle, Sleep!

Epilogue consists of one sketch, Bass Fishing on Lake Simcoe with Jake Gaudaur.

BINDING AND DUST JACKET: Bound in red cloth. A solid rectangle is blind-stamped on the upper board. Within this rectangle are two raised rectangles which contain the following in raised characters: TOO MUCH | COLLEGE | [rule] | STEPHEN LEACOCK. Stamped on the spine in gilt: TOO MUCH | COLLEGE | [illustration of a mortar board] | LEACOCK | DODD, MEAD | & COMPANY.

The front panel of the jacket, which is mainly bluish purple with a pink band at the bottom, has a caricature by Eldon Kelley of Leacock manipulating marionettes (made of professors and students) above a pile of books. The spine panel is also mainly bluish purple, having a silhouette of Leacock's face. The remainder of the jacket is white, primarily with bluish purple lettering. A photo of Leacock appears in the upper left corner of the back panel. To the right of the photo in pink is *Books by* | Stephen | Leacock. Two quotations from reviews are printed under the photo with the heading in pink: LAUGH WITH LEACOCK. Seventeen other titles by Leacock are also listed on the back panel. On the front flap of the jacket is a description of *Too Much College* with the price ($2.50). The back flap has an advertisement for *Laugh with Leacock* (last line: B 24C–10–39).

NOTES: Leacock made a false start on this book in 1933. On 13 February 1933, he suggested to his agent, Paul R. Reynolds, that he should approach *Harper's Magazine* for a series of articles on education:

> I propose to publish about a year from now a book called *The Wasted Spaces of Modern Education*. It is essentially a discussion of the waste of time in education, — waste in learning to spell with our silly alphabet, — waste in the attempt to teach "literature" (a thing about as teachable as an appetite for dinner), — waste of time in mechanical examinations. . . . I can't do this as a book for a year because I have first i to finish a book on Dickens nearly done ii write a book called "Humour," not begun and other things.

Leacock's proposal for the book included a draft of the table of contents (Reynolds fonds, COL)

In writing to Leacock on 3 November 1938, Frank Dodd observed:

> I ran across one or two articles of yours on modern education in the *Times Magazine Supplement* [see C38.21–2] recently which are excellent. I wonder whether you are going to continue to do more in this vein, and whether there might not be a book in it eventually.

Leacock reacted enthusiastically to Dodd's suggestion, and Dodd told him on 9 November 1938: "We would like very much to publish the book and I am counting on you to have it ready for late spring or early autumn of next year."

The contract (for a book entitled "Education Eating Up Life") with Dodd, Mead is dated 28 February 1939. Leacock agreed to deliver the manuscript by 1 June 1939. He received 15% on all copies sold (including Canada), 10% if the book was less than 50,000 words. Dodd, Mead & Co. (Canada) Ltd. was to handle sales in Canada. On 13 March 1939, Dodd informed Leacock that the proposed title was not to his liking: ". . . the wording makes the book sound like something pretty strictly for school teachers and librarians." On 15 March 1939, Leacock came up with the final title. He sent a blurb at this time for an announcement in the press.

On 30 August 1939, Leacock sent the manuscript to Dodd. He informed him the previous day that the manuscript was 50,000 words ". . . of which a little over 37,000 words are *Too Much College* proper and the rest supplementary essays in education and humour. . . . If I remember rightly you are to pay me on publication such royalty as you feel your sales justifies [sic]." Leacock completed his reading of the galley proofs by 18 October 1939. The book was published on 10 November 1939. Six author's copies were mailed to him on 3 November 1939. He also received a cheque for $190 (earnings up to the date of publication). Dodd told Leacock: "We are all keen about this book and feel that in it you have said some of the most important things that have come from your pen in a long time."

Two copies were received by the Copyright Office at DLC on 14 November 1939; the copyright registered was on 14 November 1939 (A135329). The copyright was renewed by Stephen Lushington Leacock on 8 August 1967 (R415485).

On 31 January 1940, Edward Dodd reported that the book had sold ". . . 4,500 to date and it seems to be gaining momentum right along." Dodd, Mead's royalty report of 1 February 1940 indicates, however, that from the date of publication, 3,016 copies had sold in America and 862 in Canada. Leacock received another $855.62 for American sales and another $284.97 for Canada. Another 1,000 copies sold by 25 June 1940. By 28 August 1940 total sales were 6,800 copies in the United States and 1,500 in Canada. For the period 1 February 1940 to 1 August 1940, 3,860 copies sold in the United States (at 30¢ per copy, $1,158. royalty), 689 copies sold in Canada ($.3375 per copy, $232.54 royalty), 13 copies in foreign sales, and 2 special copies sold. In their report of 1 June 1944 to Leacock's niece, Barbara Nimmo, Dodd, Mead recorded that between 1 February 1941 and 1 February 1944, the book had earned a royalty of $1,206.27 in American and Canadian sales.

At SLM there is a notebook (J95) devoted to the book. There are several tables of contents, one dated 15 March 1939 with eighteen chapters. The notebook has many inserted pages (for example, a copy of Leacock's article, "A Note on Latin," from the *Classical Outlook* and a typescript entitled "Teaching of French in Ontario").

The copyright page of the sixteenth printing records the following information: Published, November 1939 | Second printing, December, 1939 | Third printing, January, 1940 | Fourth printing, January, 1940 | Fifth printing, February, 1940 | Sixth printing, March 1940 | Seventh printing, April, 1940 | Eighth printing, June, 1940 | Ninth printing, November, 1940 | Tenth printing, January, 1941 | Eleventh printing, March, 1941 | Twelfth printing, May, 1941 | Thirteenth printing, October, 1941 | Fourteenth printing, January, 1942 | Fifteenth printing, February, 1942 | Sixteenth printing, June 1945.

"Bass Fishing on Lake Simcoe" reprinted in Brita Mickleburgh, ed., *Canadian Literature: Two Centuries In Prose* (Toronto: McClelland and Stewart, 1973, reprinted 1975), pp. 129–37.

COPIES EXAMINED: CS (first, fifth, sixth, twelfth, fourteenth, and sixteenth printings, all in jacket except the sixth); QMMRB (three copies of the first printing, one copy in jacket; fourth printing not in jacket).

## A88b *English edition* (1940):

TO0 MUCH COLLEGE | OR | EDUCATION EATING UP LIFE | With *Kindred Essays in Education | and Humour | by | Stephen Leacock* | LONDON | JOHN LANE THE BODLEY HEAD

♦ *A⁸ B–S⁸* [$1 signed]. *1–6, 7–9, 10, 11–12, 13–14, 15–34, 35–36, 37–60, 61–62, 63–77, 78–80,*

81–97, 98–100, 101–127, 128–130, 131–144, 145–146, 147–158, 159–160, 161–173, 174–176, 177–191, 192–194, 195–202, 203–204, 205–206, 207–208, 209–215, 216–218, 219–223, 224–226, 227–270, 271–272, 273–288 pp. (144 leaves). 182 × 120 mm.

CONTENTS: pp. *1–2* blank; p. *3* half title; p. *4* list of twenty-seven books by Leacock, the first being *Literary Lapses* and the last *Our British Empire*; p. *3* title; p. *4* FIRST PUBLISHED 1940 | PRINTED IN GREAT BRITAIN BY | UNWIN BROTHERS LIMITED, LONDON AND WOKING; pp. *7–9* preface dated "*October 1, 1939*"; p. *10* blank; pp. *11–12* table of contents; pp. *13–288* text (pp. *14, 36, 62, 78, 80, 98, 100, 128, 130, 146, 160, 174, 176, 192, 194, 204, 208, 216, 218, 224, 226, 272* blank).

TEXT: Identical to the American edition.

BINDING AND DUST JACKET: Bound in yellow cloth. Stamped on the upper board: *TOO MUCH COLLEGE | STEPHEN | LEACOCK*. Stamped on the spine: *TOO | MUCH | COLLEGE* | [ornamental rule] | *STEPHEN | LEACOCK | THE | BODLEY HEAD*.

The front and spine panels of the jacket are dark brown. The remainder of the jacket is yellow. At the top of the front and spine panels are four white rules; three white rules are at the bottom. Printed on the front panel: [the first three lines are cream-coloured with swash capitals] *Too | Much | College* | [in brown within a solid, cream-coloured rectangular compartment] STEPHEN LEACOCK. Printed on the spine panel: [the first three lines in white] *Too | Much | College* | [the next two lines in brown within a white rectangular compartment] STEPHEN | LEACOCK | the next two lines in white] *the | bodley head*. The remaining panels of the jacket are printed in brown. The back panel has quotations about Leacock from A.P. Herbert, the *Sunday Times*, and the *Evening Standard*. On the front flap is a synopsis of the book with the price, 7s 6d. The back flap has a list of twenty-seven other books by Leacock.

NOTES: The contract for the English edition is dated 1939 only. Leacock received a royalty of 15% with an advance on publication of the amount earned by subscription sales. He cabled The Bodley Head on 27 August 1939. "BOOK FINISHED POSTING THIS WEEK DODD PUBLISHING OCTOBER FIRST." On 29 August 1939, Leacock asked P.P. Howe of The Bodley Head not to "anglicize the edition. It would be too difficult." The first batch of proofs (pp. 1–59) were sent to Leacock on 20 November 1939. The English edition was published on 7 March 1940. At that time 393 copies had sold, 247 copies in colonial sales, for a royalty of £17 9s 1d. Number of copies printed not known.

COPIES EXAMINED: CS (in jacket); OORI (in jacket).

## A89 THE BRITISH EMPIRE 1940

### A89a *American edition*:

THE | BRITISH EMPIRE | *Its Structure, Its Unity, Its Strength* | BY | STEPHEN LEACOCK | DODD, MEAD & COMPANY | NEW YORK 1940

♦ 1–17$^8$ 18$^4$. *i–iv*, *v–vi*, *1–6*, *1–245*, *246–258*, *259–263*, *1–5* pp. (140 leaves). 187 × 130 mm.

CONTENTS: p. *i* half title; p. *ii* list of twenty–three books by Leacock, the first *Literary Lapses* and the last *Too Much College*; p. *iii* title; p. *iv* COPYRIGHT, 1938, | BY DODD, MEAD AND COMPANY, INC. | All rights reserved — no part of this book may be | reproduced in any form without permission in | writing from the publisher. | PRINTED IN

THE U. S. A. BY | Quinn & Boden Company, Inc. | [rule] | BOOK MANUFACTURERS | RAHWAY, NEW JERSEY; pp. v–vi preface dated April 1940; p. *1* table of contents; p. *2* blank; p. *3* list of maps; p. *4* blank; p. *5* fly title; p. *6* blank; pp. *1–245* text; p. *246* blank; pp. *247–257* Appendix: Table of the British Empire (five tables printed in columns); p. *258* blank; pp. *259–263* index; pp. *1–3* blank. Maps tipped in between pp. 44 and 45, 70 and 71, 110 and 111, 150 and 151, 190 and 191, and 230 and 231.

TEXT: Chapter I The Story of the Empire; Chapter II The Geographical and Maritime Aspect of the Empire; Chapter III The Wealth and Resources of the Empire; Chapter IV Imperial Government; Chapter V The Dominions; Chapter VI The Economics of the Empire; Chapter VII Bonds of Empire.

BINDING AND DUST JACKET: Bound in red cloth, top edge stained blue. A solid rectangle is blind-stamped on the upper board. Within this rectangle are two raised rectangles which contain the following in raised characters: THE BRITISH | EMPIRE | [rule] | STEPHEN LEACOCK. Stamped on the spine in gilt: THE | BRITISH | EMPIRE | [rule] | LEACOCK | DODD, MEAD | & COMPANY.

The front and spine panels of the jacket are red, white, and blue. The front panel has a map of the world with the British Empire in red. The rest of the jacket is white. The back panel has a black-and-white photograph of Leacock in the upper left-hand corner. To the right of this photograph are three lines in red: *Books by* | Stephen | Leacock. Quotations from reviews are printed below the photograph in blue with the heading in red, LAUGH WITH LEACOCK. Seventeen other titles in two columns are also listed on the back panel. Lettering on the flaps is printed in blue. The front flap has a synopsis of the book. The back flap has a similar descriptive advertisement for *Laugh with Leacock*. The last line on the back flap: C–4–40–25C.

NOTES: On 23 October 1939, Frank Dodd assured Leacock that Dodd, Mead would publish "A Presentation of the British Empire." Dodd assumed that in view of the audience for the book in the United States, the American edition would differ slightly from its English counterpart. (In fact, the text for both editions is identical except for certain corrections made in the English edition.) There are two surviving contracts with Dodd, Mead, one dated 23 October 1939 and another dated 8 February 1940. The latter contract has a proviso regarding Canadian sales. The royalty was 10% up to 2,500 copies, 15% thereafter, with an advance on publication date equal to the accrued royalties. On copies sold in Canada, Leacock received 10% on the first 1,000 copies and 15% thereafter. He agreed to deliver the manuscript by 15 February 1940.

On 22 February 1940, Leacock informed Edward H. Dodd, Jr.: "I am working hard but the Empire is large." He was doing the footnotes at that time, and suggested that he could add them at the foot of the page proofs. Dodd, Mead requested Leacock to add the notes to the galleys, not to page proofs. Dodd, Mead received Leacock's manuscript (without footnotes) on 26 March 1940 and Leacock's drawings of the maps for the book on 8 April 1940. The maps were redrawn by a professional draftsman and engraved the following week. A set of electroplates of these maps was sent to The Bodley Head. The first batch of galleys was sent to Leacock on 12 April 1940, the last batch on 17 April.

The American edition was published on 14 May 1940. Price $2. Copies were received by the Copyright Office on 8 May 1940; the copyright was registered on 16 May 1940 (A140312). The copyright was renewed by Stephen Lushington Leacock on 22 January

1968 (R427942). Dodd, Mead & Company (Canada), Ltd. registered the Canadian copyright with the Copyright Office on 11 May 1940.

Leacock was sent a royalty of $118.75, one day after the book's publication. Up to 1 August 1940, 999 copies sold in the United States (royalty at 20¢ per copy, $199.80), 628 copies in Canada ($141.30 royalty), 3 special sales, and 13 copies to foreign markets. Between February 1, 1941 and February 1, 1944 the book had earned $78.70 royalty in American sales and $177.91 royalty in Canadian sales.

COPIES EXAMINED: CS (two copies, one in jacket); OONL (in jacket); OORI (in jacket); QMMRB (three copies, one in jacket); SLM (in jacket).

## A89b *advertising leaflet for the Canadian market*:

[cover title: greyish black-and-white photo of Leacock; the remaining lines in white against a red background] THE | BRITISH EMPIRE | ITS UNITY — ITS STRUCTURE — ITS STRENGTH | [in script] *By* Stephen Leacock

◆ Leaflet on cream-coloured paper stock folded once to form four unnumbered pages. 230 × 153 mm.

CONTENTS: This leaflet consists of introductory paragraphs and three excerpts from Leacock's book. The excerpts have headings in red: *Reaction of America on England*, *Mysteries of British Government*, and *National Character: The Briton and His Bath*. At the bottom right-hand corner on p. *3* is a photo of the American edition. On p. *4* is a perforated order form to purchase the book from Dodd, Mead & Company (Canada), Ltd. at $2.25. Last line: PRINTED IN U. S. A.

NOTES: On 4 April 1940 Leacock told C.J. Greenwood of The Bodley Head: "I have prepared with the publishers [Dodd, Mead] a circular of about 2000 words of extracts. I propose to send these all over with letters. No American publisher would think of arresting all of this on the threshold." The circular was prepared by Raymond T. Bond and distributed after publication of the American edition. Although this leaflet was prepared for the Canadian market, it is possible that a similar one was distributed in the United States for the American market.

COPIES EXAMINED: NAC (Barbara Nimmo collection, Publicity for Book (8–2), SLM.

## A89c *first English edition* (advertisement):

ADVANCE | ANNOUNCEMENT | JOHN LANE THE BODLEY HEAD | LTD | [swelled rule] | Our British Empire | Stephen Leacock | [four paragraphs of text] | *Cr. 8vo 5s. (approx.)*

◆ Broadside on pale yellow paper. 222 × 143 mm.

NOTES: This promotional broadside was issued sometime prior to the publication of the English edition. The text (begins "Stephen Leacock's new book is a sweeping presentation. . . .") is identical to the text on the front flap of A89a. The front flap of A89d begins: "Stephen Leacock's new book, and undoubtedly his greatest, is a sweeping presentation. . . ."

COPY EXAMINED: SLM.

**A89d** *first English edition*:

STEPHEN LEACOCK | Our British Empire | ITS STRUCTURE • ITS HISTORY | ITS STRENGTH | LONDON | John Lane The Bodley Head

◆ A–H$^{16}$ I$^{12}$ [$1 signed (–A1); A5 signed A*]. *1–5*, 6, *7–13*, *14–15*, *16–17*, *18–59*, 60, *61–79*, *80–81*, *82–89*, *80*, *91–131*, *132*, *133–143*, *144–145*, *146–172*, *173*, *174–207*, *208*, *209–214*, *215*, *216–255*, *256*, *257–275*, *276*, *277–280* pp. (140 leaves). 187 × 130 mm.

CONTENTS: p. *1* half title; p. *2* list of twenty-seven books by Leacock, the first being *Literary Lapses* and the last *Too Much College*; p. *3* title; p. *4* First published 1940 | Printed in Great Britain by | UNWIN BROTHERS LIMITED, LONDON AND WOKING | in *12–Point Perpetua Type* | for John Lane The Bodley Head Limited | 8 Bury Place, London, W.C.1; pp. *5–6* preface dated April 1940; p. *7* table of contents; p. *8* blank; p. *9* list of maps; p. *10* blank; p. *11* fly title; p. *12* blank; pp. *13–265* text; pp. *266–275* Appendix: Table of the British Empire; pp. *276–280* index. Text includes maps: pp. *16–17, 80–81,* 112, *144–145, 208,* and 235.

TEXT: Identical to A89a.

BINDING AND DUST JACKET: Bound in black, grey, and white patterned cloth with red lettering stamped on the spine as follows: [three rules] | OUR | BRITISH | EMPIRE | [three rules] | THE | BODLEY HEAD. Top stained red; endpapers feature a map of the world with a legend showing British possessions, the League of Nations mandate, and the British sphere of influence.

The front and spine panels of the jacket are greyish black with curved and rectangular lines and lettering in red and white at various angles. The front panel has an illustration of a globe. The remainder of the jacket is white with lettering primarily in black, a few lines in red. On the back panel of the jacket is an advertisement for André Maurois's *The Battle of France*. The front flap carries a synopsis of Leacock's book and the price, 7s 6d. The back flap is blank, except for the line, *Printed in Great Britain*.

NOTES: On 6 June 1939, the Director of J.M. Dent & Sons Ltd., W.G. Taylor, wrote to P.P. Howe of John Lane The Bodley Head with respect to Leacock 's article "Canada and the Monarchy," which had appeared in the *Atlantic Monthly* in June 1939 (see C39.35). Taylor suggested to Howe that Leacock should write a stimulating "account of the British Empire for children." When Howe passed on Taylor's suggestion, Leacock replied by telegram that the proposed Empire book is "just right." Taylor, who also served as one of the directors of The Bodley Head, sent Leacock a draft contract on 10 July 1939, which stipulated that Leacock would be paid an advance royalty of £125. A few months later on 3 October [1939], Leacock informed Taylor that he would finish the manuscript by the new year: "As to the tone not juvenile not academic not boring and yet with information." On 29 November 1939, Leacock reported that he would have the manuscript ready by 15 February 1940. He requested that The Bodley Head not use the Dodd, Mead jacket as it was unsuitable for the English market. He also inquired whether The Bodley Head could supply 3,000 copies with a Canadian imprint. By the end of the year, however, he decided not to pursue a Canadian edition and to let Dodd, Mead handle the Canadian rights. On 18 March 1940, both Taylor and C.J. Greenwood tried to dissuade Leacock from letting Dodd, Mead control the Canadian market.

Leacock sent his manuscript (with footnotes) on 4 April 1940. He told Greenwood that since Dodd, Mead would be publishing the book several months prior to the appearance of the English edition, it did not make sense to delay distribution in Canada:

> I have the most eager hope for the value of this book in helping to hold American sympathy. It is more important in the States than at home, because with most of us it is preaching to the converted. There it may call sinners to repentance or at least keep converts from sin, and strengthens faith already there. I have written it at great speed under a great strain.

On receipt of the manuscript, Greenwood enthusiastically told Leacock on 8 May 1940: "What an excellent book this is! Surely one of your most important works — perhaps *the* most important." Proofs were sent to Leacock on 4 June 1940. The Ministry of Information reviewed the galleys, and on 18 June 1940, Greenwood sent Leacock seven pages of suggested changes made by "a prominent historian." Leacock gave Greenwood *carte blanche* in the question of corrections. On 26 August 1940, the Ministry of Information also requested The Bodley Head to send about 200 copies of the English edition "to certain professors of history and Colonial relations etc. at American Universities." Although technically this was a violation of the American copyright, Dodd, Mead did not object to this free distribution. On 14 November 1940, the free books were sent to Thomas Nelson & Sons Ltd. in Toronto. The British Library of Information in New York supplied Leacock with a mailing list. The book was such a hit with the British government that Leacock was invited to England on 6 December 1940 to deliver a series of lectures.

Lomer (p. 47) has a publication date of 3 September 1940. *The English Catalogue of Books* records publication in September 1940. Reprinted in 1941. An excerpt from chapter VII was reprinted in Christian Mawson's *Portrait of England: An Anthology* (Harmondsworth, England: Penguin Books, 1942), pp. 201–2 (entitled "The Barrier").

COPIES EXAMINED: CS (in jacket); OORI (in jacket); QMMRB (in jacket).

## A89d.1 *English issue* (1941):

STEPHEN LEACOCK | Our British Empire | ITS STRUCTURE • ITS HISTORY | ITS STRENGTH | THE RIGHT BOOK CLUB | 121 CHARING CROSS ROAD | LONDON, W.C.2

This issue is from the same setting of type as A89d. However, the collation is $A^{12} \chi^2 B-H^{16} I^{12} K^2$ [\$1 signed (–A1); fifth leaf signed * (e.g. B*) (–A1, I gathering signed * rather than I*); A3 signed A*]. Several of the maps are positioned elsewhere throughout the text, altering the sequence of pagination. The verso of the title leaf of this issue reads: This edition 1941 | Printed in Great Britain by | UNWIN BROTHERS LIMITED, LONDON AND WOKING.

BINDING AND DUST JACKET: Bound in blue cloth, top edge stained blue. Stamped on the spine as follows: [the first six lines within a solid, dark blue rectangle, which itself is outlined by a dark blue rectangle] *Our* | *British* | *Empire* | • | STEPHEN | LEACOCK | [the remaining three lines at the foot of the spine within another solid, dark blue rectangle, which is outlined by a dark blue rectangle] THE | RIGHT | BOOK CLUB.

The front and spine panels of the jacket have a purple background. On the front panel in red, white, and purple are coats of arms of countries of the British Empire. The rest of the jacket is white with purple lettering (except the first two words of the front flap which are in red). On the back panel within three rectangles is a notice informing the reader that the book is a Book Club edition (price 2s 6d). The front flap has a synopsis of the book. On the back flap is a list of members of the Right Book Club (secretary, selection committee, and patrons).

NOTES: On 14 November 1940, C.J. Greenwood of John Lane The Bodley Head informed Leacock:

> You will be pleased to hear that the book is selling very steadily here, and there is every indication that it will continue; furthermore, I have sold an edition of 7,000 sheets to one of the 2/6d. Book Clubs, and we shall be accounting this to you as on previous occasions.

COPIES EXAMINED: CS (in jacket).

## A89e *second English edition* (1941):

STEPHEN LEACOCK | (*Of McGill University, Toronto* [sic], *Canada*) | Our British Empire | ITS STRUCTURE • ITS HISTORY | ITS STRENGTH | LONDON | John Lane The Bodley Head

◆ $A^{12} \chi^2$ B–H$^{16}$ I$^{12}$ K$^2$ [\$1 signed (–A1); fifth leaf signed * (–A5, I5); A3 signed A*; I5 signed I★]. *1–5*, 6, *7–13*, 14–43, *44–45*, 46–58, *59*, 60–75, *76–77*, 78–88, *89*, 90–130, *131*, 132–139, *140–141*, 142–170, *171*, 172–207, *208*, 209–211, *212*, 213–251, *252*, 253–271, *272*, 273–276, *1–4* pp. (140 leaves). 184 × 123 mm.

CONTENTS: p. *1* half title; p. *2* list of twenty-seven books by Leacock, the first being *Literary Lapses* and the last *Too Much College*; p. *3* title; p. *4* First published . . . . 1940 | Second Impression . . . . 1941 | Second Edition . . . . 1941 | Printed in Great Britain by | UNWIN BROTHERS LIMITED, LONDON AND WOKING | for John Lane The Bodley Head Limited | 8 Bury Place, London, W.C.1; pp. *5–6* preface dated April 1940 but with preceding line, *McGill University, Toronto* [sic], *Canada*; p. *7* table of contents; p. *8* blank; p. *9* list of maps; p. *10* blank; p. *11* fly title; p. *12* blank; pp. *13–261* text; p. *262–271* Appendix: Table of the British Empire; pp. *272–276* index; pp. *1–4* blank. Text includes maps: pp. 44–45, 76–77, 111, 140–141, 208, and 235.

TEXT: Identical to A89d but several passages and sentences have been either deleted or rewritten in this edition. See, for example, p. 22 of A89c versus p. 20 of A89e (re the Pope), pp. 47–48 of A89d versus pp. 46–47 of A89e (re the Falkland Islands), p. 49 of A89d versus p. 48 of A89e (re China and Japan), p. 64 of A89e versus p. 63 of A89d (re the German island of Nauru), and p. 218 of A89d versus p. 214 of A89e (re socialism).

BINDING AND DUST JACKET: The binding is the same as A89d except that the stamping on the spine is in blue. Top edge stained blue; endpapers are the same as A89d. The jacket is the same as that of A89d except for the back panel of the jacket, which has an advertisement for André Maurois's *Why France Fell* (6th impression) and *The Battle of France* (2nd impression).

NOTES: Number of copies printed and exact date of publication not known.

COPIES EXAMINED: LAT.

## A89e.1 *English issue of the second edition* (1941):

STEPHEN LEACOCK | (*Of McGill University, Toronto* [sic], *Canada*) | Our

British Empire | ITS STRUCTURE • ITS HISTORY | ITS STRENGTH |
LONDON 1941 | Readers Union Limited | *by arrangement with* | John Lane The
Bodley Head

◆ Collation identical to A89e except I5 is not signed. *1–5, 6, 7–13, 14–43, 44–45, 46–58, 59, 60–75,
76–77, 78–88, 89, 90–139, 140–141, 142–171, 172, 173–207, 208, 209–213, 214, 215–254, 255,
256–264, 265, 266–275, 276, 277–280* pp. (140 leaves). 185 × 122 mm.

CONTENTS: pp. *1–2* identical to A89e; p. *3* title; p. *4 Made 1941 in Great Britain* |
PRINTED BY UNWIN BROTHERS LIMITED WOKING | *and published by* | READERS
UNION LIMITED | CHANDOS PLACE CHARING CROSS WC2 | & DUNHAMS LANE
LETCHWORTH HERTS; pp. *5–12* identical to A89e; pp. *13–264* text; p. *265* blank; pp.
*266–275* Appendix: Table of the British Empire; pp. *276–280* index. Maps identical to A89e
on the same pages.

TEXT: This issue is basically from the same setting of type as A89e. There are at least three
instances, however, where this issue has several sentences or passages that are not present
in A89e: p. *37* (on French settlers); p. *167* (concerning Amritsar); p. *203* of A89e and pp.
*204–205* of A89e.1 (on the uses of the Dutch language in South Africa and Gaelic in Ireland).
These additions have resulted in minor changes to the index as well.

BINDING: Bound in blue cloth with stamping on the spine as follows: [three white wavy
rules: the next three lines in white] | Our | British | Empire | [three white wavy rules] | [three
red wavy rules; the next line in red] | *Leacock* | [three red wavy rules]. Endpapers identical
to A89b. Dust jacket not seen.

NOTES: On 17 January 1941 C.J. Greenwood told Leacock:

> The British Council is delighted with your book OUR BRITISH EMPIRE, and when
> we have made some trifling amendments in it, and above all in the maps, to meet the
> susceptibilities of Government Departments (at home and abroad!) they will probably
> purchase a substantial number of copies.

The British Council's interest may have resulted in this edition issued by the Readers Union
Limited.

COPIES EXAMINED: CS.


## A90 THE BABES IN THE WOODS 1940

[play bill in green with all lettering in green on both sides] The Babes in the
Woods | Written by Stephen Leacock for the Occasion. | [ornament] | [five lines
in italics setting the scene of the play — two Babes, a brother and a sister, emerge
from a forest looking for a safe haven; thirty seven lines of dialogue between the
two Babes, SHE and THE BOY; the last line on this side is:] | STEPHEN
LEACOCK. | [on the other side:] *Souvenir Programme Sold for the Red Cross –
– 10 cents* | [rule] | The Old Brewery Players | Third Annual Mid-Summer
Entertainment | Friday, August 16, 1940 | [rule] | PROGRAMME | [rule] | A
WORD OF WELCOME. – – – The Master of Ceremonies | [Four plays are listed
with their cast of characters: Leacock's "A Discovery of the Play by the Babes in
the Woods," Peggy Shaw's "Leap Year Lapses," Michael O'Mara's "The

Intelligence Service; or, One More Reason Why There'll Always Be an England," and Leacock's "Courage: A Dramatic Interlude of the South Coast." An intermission of ten minutes occurs after the first two plays.] | GOD SAVE THE KING | [rule] | All Proceeds with no Deductions for Expenses to be Given to the Red Cross | [nine lines in two columns giving names of the stage crew and others assisting in the production of the plays] | The Refreshment Booths will open immediately after the singing of God Save the King. | *Souvenir Programme Sold for the Red Cross – – 10 cents* | [rule]

◆ Broadside. 372 × 210 mm.

NOTES: In his biography, *Stephen Leacock: Humorist and Humanist* (pp. 191–2), Ralph L. Curry notes that Leacock liked to write plays for children, staging them in his living room or on his lawn at Old Brewery Bay, his home in Orillia, Ontario. Frequently, the plays were also staged at the home of Leacock's close friend, Mrs. H.T. Shaw, who lived nearby around the bay of Lake Couchiching. Leacock's son, Stevie, and Mrs. Shaw's daughter, Peggy, along with their friends acted in the plays, but the adults were also involved in the acting and production. Leacock had programmes printed for a number of them, apparently at the *Orillia Packet and Times* office. See also the reminiscences of Dode Spencer, Marge Carter, and Elizabeth Burrows Langdon in K83.1, pp. 114–7.

Several of these programmes have survived in Leacock's papers at SLM: "Red Riding Hood," 17 August 1929; "Beauty and the Boss," New Year's Eve, 1929 (playbill reproduced in A120) — for a report of this play's performance, see "New Year Private Theatricals at Prof. Leacock's 'Old Brewery Players' Present 'Beauty and the Boss' Before a Select Audience," *Orillia Packet and Times*, 9 January 1930, p. 1; five plays ("The Raft: Danger & Love in One Act," "College Quartet," "The Dionne Quintublets," "The Return of Chaplain," and "Lady Godiva Rides by"), 3 August 1938; and "Blackout" (written by Michael O'Mara and James I. Armstrong) and "Cast Up by the Sea: An Old-Time Melodrama of the Year 1890," 12 August 1939. The latter programme (320 × 177 mm., stiff blue paper) was issued on the occasion of the Second Annual Mid-Summer Entertainment of the Old Brewery Players. Leacock undoubtedly had a hand in the printing of the programme. "Cast Up by the Sea" was a dramatic rendition of his sketch which first appeared in *Harper's Magazine* (C23.7) and then in *Over the Footlights and Other Follies* (A39). The performances were reported in the *Orillia Packet and Times*, 14 August 1939, p. 8 ("Dramatic Sketches Presented on Shores of Lake Couchiching Thrill Many Summer Residents"). According to the newspaper report, the plays were organized and directed by Peggy Shaw with the assistance of Barbara Nimmo, Leacock's niece. Approximately 200 people were in attendance.

Since most of these programmes, with the exception of the last one described above, were intended for distribution to the participants in the plays and not the public, they are mentioned here only but not described bibliographically. The programme for the Third Annual Mid-Summer Entertainment of the Brewery Players, however, was disseminated to a larger public and contains the text of one of Leacock's plays on that occasion.

The story of Leacock's play *The Babes in the Woods* concerns two children from England who are seeking shelter from the bombing of England during wartime. They grope in the darkness of the woods and discover that they are at Old Brewery Bay "in that wonderful place of Mrs. Shaw's where they hold the Brewery Bay Entertainment every year." The two young actors playing the part of the Babes are Miss Barbara Brown and Master Martin Brown from Gloucester, England. Leacock's other play, "Courage," is set in a village pub on the South coast of England, and has three characters: Saery (played by Miss Patsy Macauley), Father (played by Mr. John Evans), and Oklahoma Pete (played by Mr. Paul Copeland). Leacock undoubtedly arranged for the printing of this play bill, but the number of copies printed is not known. On the copy examined at QMMRB, Leacock has written: "Written for a Red Cross | Entertainment in 1940 | Stephen Leacock." See also "Entertainment and Play at Dr. Leacock's a Success," *Orillia Packet and Times*, 22 August 1940, p. 8.

*The Babes in the Woods* was reprinted in *Saturday Night* 56, no. 6 (19 October 1940): 12. See also A120 which reproduces these play bills in facsimile.

COPIES EXAMINED: QMMRB; SLM (twenty-five copies).


## A91 LAUGH PARADE 1940

STEPHEN LEACOCK'S | [the next two lines in informal brush script] *Laugh | Parade* | [caricature of a drum major portrayed as a book] | DODD, MEAD & COMPANY | NEW YORK 1940

◆ $1-21^8$. *i–iv*, v–viii, *1–2*, *1–326* pp. (168 leaves). 196 × 142 mm.

CONTENTS: p. *i* half title; p. *ii* list of twenty-four books by Leacock, the first being *Literary Lapses* and the last *The British Empire*; p. *iii* title; p. *iv* [thirteen lines with copyright dates and reference to Dodd, Mead, The Century Company, Harper & Brothers, and the John Lane Company; three lines concerning copyright permission] | PRINTED IN THE U. S. A. BY | Quinn & Boden Company, Inc. | [rule] | BOOK MANUFACTURERS | RAHWAY, NEW JERSEY; pp. v–vi preface; pp. vii–viii table of contents; p. *1* fly title; p. *2* blank; pp. *1–326* text.

TEXT: What I Don't Know about the Drama; Frenzied Fiction; "We Have with Us To-night"; Why I Am Leaving My Farm; The Man in Asbestos: An Allegory of the Future; Getting by at College; The Errors of Santa Claus; With the Photographer; Eddie the Bartender: A Ghost of the Bygone Past; The Perfect Salesman; Homer and Humbug: An Academic Discussion; Back to the Bush; The Doctor and the Contraption; The Awful Fate of Melpomenus Jones; Number Fifty-Six; My Victorian Girlhood; The Hidden Secret of the City; The Mariposa Bank Mystery; The Sit-Down Strike in My Parlour; When Men Retire; This Strenuous Age; How I Succeeded in My Business; Winsome Winnie, or, Trial and Temptation; Abolishing the Heroine; The Reading Public: A Book Store Study; How to Lose Money (for Amateurs); My Fishing Pond (includes My Ladders: A Sequel to My Fishing Pond); While You're at It; The Wizard of Finance; The Arrested Philanthropy of Mr. Tomlinson; On the Need for a Quiet College; Turn Back the Clock, or, at Least Make It Slower; First Call for Spring, or, Oh, Listen to The Birds; Hand Me Down That Book; What I Read Then — What You Read Now: An Essay for the Young; L'Envoi: In Praise of Americans.

BINDING AND DUST JACKET: Bound in red cloth, top edge stained blue. A solid rectangle is blind-stamped on the upper board. Within this rectangle are two raised rectangles which contain the following in raised characters: [jester's stick] STEPHEN [jester's stick] | LEACOCK | LAUGH | PARADE. Stamped on the spine in gilt: STEPHEN | LEACOCK'S |

LAUGH | PARADE | DODD, MEAD | & COMPANY.

The front and spine panels of the jacket have an illustration in red, yellow, white, and greyish blue of Leacock's books in a parade with balloons. The books are caricatured in human form with party hats, and are led by a drum major. The rest of the jacket is white. The back panel has a bluish photograph of Leacock in the upper left hand corner. To the right of this photograph are three lines in red: *Books by* | Stephen | Leacock. Quotations from reviews are printed below the photograph in blue with the heading in red, LAUGH WITH LEACOCK. Eighteen other titles in two columns are also listed on the back panel. Lettering on the flaps is printed in blue. The front flap has a synopsis of the book. The back flap has a similar descriptive advertisement for *Laugh with Leacock*. The last line on the back flap: B 38C–10–40.

NOTES: On 8 April 1940, after completing *The British Empire* and contemplating several other major writing projects, Leacock suggested to Frank C. Dodd that his next book would be entitled: "More Laughs with Leacock: A New Anthology of Stephen Leacock with a Discourse on This Business of Growing Old." Although Dodd liked "This Business of Growing Old" (see C39.57) very much, he was against including the essay in an anthology of humour. Dodd advised Leacock on 17 April 1940: ". . . let us make up the list of selections and submit it to you. Meantime, we will both think about a good title, which we shall need very shortly for our autumn list." On 30 April 1940, Dodd proposed three titles: "The Leacock Funnybus," "The Leacock Merry-Go-Round," and the book's eventual title. "Personally, I like the last best," he told Leacock. "I hope you will support me!" The sketches for the book were selected by Raymond T. Bond, and were sent for Leacock's approval on 25 June 1940. To Bond's list of stories Leacock added four others for inclusion: "Getting by in College," "I'll Stay in Canada," "My Victorian Girlhood," and "How to Lose Money." Leacock was asked to write a short preface (three leaves, undated, at QMMRB). Proofs were sent to him in two batches on 19 and 21 August 1941.

The contract with Dodd, Mead is dated 27 August 1940. Leacock received 10% on all copies sold, including those in Canada. Published 15 October 1940. Price $2.50. Two copies were received by the Copyright Office at DLC on 17 October 1940; the copyright was registered on 18 October 1940 (A145913). The copyright was renewed by Stephen Lushington Leacock on 12 February 1968 (R429561).

There was no English edition, but Leacock requested that Dodd, Mead supply The Bodley Head with sheets on 10 January 1941. Number of copies printed not known. In their report to Leacock's niece, Barbara Nimmo, dated June 1, 1944, Dodd, Mead recorded that between 1 February 1941 and 1 February 1944, the book had earned a royalty of $784.80 in American and Canadian sales. The copyright page of the sixth printing records the following information: second printing, December 1940; third printing, September 1941; fourth printing, April 1943; fifth printing, January 1944; sixth printing, February 1946. There was also a reprint in Dodd, Mead's Apollo Editions (A–53), a paperback published in [1961?] at $1.95.

COPIES EXAMINED: CS (first and sixth printings in jacket; second printing without jacket; Apollo Editions reprint); QMMRB (first printing in jacket).

## A92 CANADA: THE FOUNDATIONS OF ITS FUTURE 1941

### A92a *first edition*:

[in brown] CANADA | THE FOUNDATIONS | OF ITS FUTURE | *by STEPHEN LEACOCK* | [illustration within a semi-circle in brown and black of smokestacks, a train, boat, car, airplane, skyscrapers, forests, farm land, and a hydroelectric power station; centered at the base of the semi-circle is a brown leaf within three circles, and below that a rule] | *Illustrated by Canadian Artists* | [brown rule] | PRIVATELY PRINTED IN MONTREAL, CANADA | MCMXLI

◆ $1^8$ $2^{10}$ $3^8$ $4^{10}$ $5^8$ $6^{10}$ $7^8$ $8$–$10^{10}$ $11^8$ $12$–$16^{10}$. *i–xvi*, xvii–xix, *xx–xxi*, xxii–xxiii, *xxiv–xxvi*, xxvii–xxx, *1–3*, 4–10, *11–12*, 13–20, *21–22*, 23–27, *28–31*, 32–46, *47–48*, 49–52, *53–54*, 55–*58*, *59–60*, 61–66, *67–68*, 69–70, *71–73*, 74–78, *79–80*, 81–84, *85–86*, 87–95, *96–99*, 100–104, *105–106*, 107–112, *113–114*, 115–120, *121–123*, 124–128, *129–130*, 131–138, *139–140*, 141–147, *148–151*, 152–162, *163–164*, 165–170, *171–172*, 173–176, *177–179*, 180–186, *187–188*, 189–194, *195–196*, 197–199, *200–203*, 204–210, *211–212*, 213–216, *217–218*, 219–222, *223–225*, 226–228, *229–230*, 231–234, *235–236*, 237–240, *241–243*, 244–250, *251–252*, 253–257, *1–13* pp. (150 leaves). 257 × 179 mm.

CONTENTS: pp. *i–ii* blank; p. *iii* half title; p. *iv* blank; p. *v* title; p. *vi* A PRIVATE AND LIMITED EDITION | COPYRIGHT | ALL RIGHTS RESERVED; p. *vii* dedication by the House of Seagram with the House's coat of arms in brown; p. *viii* blank; pp. *ix–xv* introduction dated October 1941; p. *xvi* blank; pp. *xvii*, xviii–xix table of contents; p. *xx* blank; pp. *xxi*, xxii–xxiii list of illustrations; p. *xxiv* blank; p. *xxv* list of maps; p. *xxvi* blank; pp. xxvii–xxx author's foreword; p. *1* blank; p. *2* illustration; pp. *3–250* text (pp. *14*, 22, 29, 54, 60, 68, 71, 80, 86, 97, 106, 114, 121, 130, 140, 149, 164, 172, 177, 188, 196, 201, 212, 218, 223, 230, 236, and 241 blank); pp. *251–252* blank; pp. *253–257* index; p. *1* blank; p. *2* illustration of the House of Seagram; p. *3* blank; p. *4* biographical information about Leacock with a photo of him; p. *5* blank; p. *6* information on the artists who executed the illustrations; p. *7* blank; p. *8* information about the printer, the Gazette Printing Company; pp. *9–13* blank.

Colour illustrations (with tissue guards) on pp. *2, 30, 72, 98, 122, 150, 178, 202, 224,* and 242. Black-and-white illustrations on pp. *11, 21, 47, 53, 59, 67, 79, 85, 105, 113, 129, 139, 163, 171, 187, 195, 211, 217, 229, 235,* and 259. Maps on pp. 14, 44, 91, 108, 143, 157, 192, 208, and 237. There are also many other illustrations in brown for chapter headings and chapter endings by A. Sheriff Scott.

Artists represented: James Crockart (pp. *229, 235*); Charles W. Jefferys (pp. *30, 53, 59, 67, 79, 85*); Ernest Neumann (pp. *105, 259*); H.R. Perrigard (pp. *150, 171, 195, 224*); W.J. Phillips (pp. *163, 187, 217, 242*); Stanley Royce (pp. *21, 47, 72, 139*); A. Sherriff Scott (pp. *2, 11, 98, 178, 211*); T.M. Schintz (p. *202*); F.H. Varley (pp. *113, 122, 129*).

TEXT: chapter I The Empty Continent; chapter II The Colonial Era 1534–1713; chapter III British America and French Canada 1713–1763; chapter IV The Foundation of British Canada 1763–1815; chapter V The Middle Period: Ships, Colonies, Commerce 1815–1867; chapter VI The New Dominion Struggling into Life 1867–1878; chapter VII Bitter Times 1879–1896; chapter VIII The Opening of the Twentieth Century 1896–1914; chapter IX Canada as a Nation; chapter X Canada as a Future World Power.

BINDING: There are two binding variants: (1) the deluxe "edition" in red padded leather, gilt tooling on the inside edges of the boards, two signets, all edges gilt. Stamped on the upper board in gilt: [first line in tooled typed] CANADA | The | FOUNDATIONS | OF ITS FUTURE | [Canadian coat of arms with motto in colour mounted within a rectangle] | STEPHEN LEACOCK. Stamped in gilt down the spine: CANADA [illustration of leaf] LEACOCK. Within a plastic bag and enclosed within a red cardboard box; encased in a pictorial card box with flaps similar in design to the endpapers and finally within another plain cardboard box with flaps. (2) light blue buckram, quarter-bound in dark blue buckram, the latter with a vertical rule stamped in gilt on both boards. Enclosed within a blue cardboard box and apparently with a protective glassine wrapper. Stamping on the boards is the same as in (1) except the second, third, and fourth lines on the upper board are black. For this binding variant Samuel Bronfman's signature is reproduced in facsimile on p. *xv*; Leacock's signature in facsimile is on p. xxx.

Both binding variants have the same endpapers: a black-and-white illustration by Neumann of people at work — mining, fishing, farming, etc. Title-page decoration and cover design by Perrigard. Layout and typography by John W. Morrell.

NOTES: Acting on behalf of Samuel Bronfman of the Distillers Corporation — Seagrams Ltd., John Bassett, the president of the Gazette Printing Company and the *Montreal Gazette*, invited Leacock on 16 July 1940 to write a book on the historical development of Canada. "The idea sounds attractive and happens to be a thing that I have long wanted to do," Leacock replied by telegram on 18 July 1940. He was paid $5,000 to write the book. He met with Seagram's representatives during the late summer of 1940 at Old Brewery Bay, his home in Orillia, ON. On Leacock's instructions, an art advisor, A. Sheriff Scott, a muralist and landscape and portrait painter, was hired for the project in November 1940. Leacock apparently finished the writing of *Canada* in early February 1941. He corrected page proofs in July of that year. The Montreal poet, A.M. Klein, who worked for Bronfman as a public relations advisor and the principal writer of his speeches and correspondence, criticized Leacock's text in late September 1941. A number of Klein's suggested changes were incorporated into the text. Klein also wrote the introduction to the book, and he prepared elaborate inscriptions, which were transcribed by Bronfman in the deluxe copies for presentation to dignitaries and Bronfman's acquaintances. The book was printed by Gazette Printing Company, bound, and ready for distribution at the end of November 1941.

In view of the fact that the book was to be a "limited edition," Leacock hoped that Seagram's would quickly dispose of the copyright. He even offered Seagram's $1,000 in return for the copyright. In fact, Seagram's kept the book in print until 1967. It was given away free to anyone who asked for a copy. By 1955, 58,000 had been distributed, 73,000 by 1961, and 165,000 by 1967. In 1959 Seagram's was told to stop distribution of the book in British Columbia because its distribution contravened the anti-advertising section of the B.C. Liquor Act.

The first impression probably consisted of 8,000 copies. A92a was printed in 1941, 1943 (twice), 1945, and 1947. In all likelihood the deluxe "edition" consists of 300 to 400 copies. Between December 1942 and April 1943 Bronfman gave away approximately 120 of them.

The following information on the printing of the book occurs on p. *8* after the index:

The body matter, including head and tail pieces, is letterpress printed in two colours, the secondary colour [brown] being also used for the marginal notes. Black-and-white illustrations are reproduced in single-colour lithography, the same process in six colours being used for the full colour plates. The crest of the Dominion of Canada on the cover is in quadricolour letterpress.

For a complete publishing history of this book, see K87.1.

COPIES EXAMINED: CS (both variant bindings, two copies in red leather, one as issued in all boxes); LAT (red leather in red cardboard box); OORI (both binding variants); QMMRB (both variant bindings).

## A92a.1 *re-issue* (1951):

Transcription identical to A92a.

◆ $1-3^8$ $4-5^4$ $6-7^8$ $8-9^4$ $10-14^8$ $15-16^4$ $17-18^8$ $19-20^4$ $21-22^8$. *i–xvi*, xvii–xviii, *xix*, xx–xxi, *xxii–xxiii*, xxiv–xxvi, *1–3*, 4–10, *11–12*, 13–20, *21–22*, 23–27, *28–31*, 32–46, *47–48*, 49–52, *53–54*, 55–58, *59–60*, 61–66, *67–68*, 69–70, *71–73*, 74–78, *79–80*, 81–84, *85–86*, 87–95, *96–99*, 100–104, *105–106*, 107–112, *113–114*, 115–120, *121–123*, 124–128, *129–130*, 131–138, *139–140*, 141–147, *148–151*, 152–162, *163–164*, 165–170, *171–172*, 173–176, *177–179*, 180–186, *187–188*, 189–194, *195–196*, 197–199, *200–203*, 204–210, *211–212*, 213–216, *217–218*, 219–222, *223–225*, 226–228, *229–230*, 231–234, *235–236*, 237–240, *241–243*, 244–250, *251–253*, 254–257, *1–5* pp. (144 leaves). 254 × 177 mm.

CONTENTS: pp. *i–xv* identical to A92a; pp. *xvi*, xvii–xviii table of contents; pp. *xix*, xx–xxi list of illustrations; p. *xxiv* list of maps; pp. *xxiv*, xxviv–xxvi author's foreword; pp. *1–250* identical to A92a; p. *251* illustration of the House of Seagram; p. *252* blank; pp. *253*, *524–257* index; p. *1* information on the artists who executed the illustrations; p. *2* biographical information about Leacock with a photo of him; p. *3* information about the printer, the Gazette Printing Company; pp. *4–5* blank.

BINDING: The binding is almost the same as (2) of A92a, except the blue is a shade lighter. There are two signets. The binding has a protective glassine wrapper. The blue box is also of a smoother grain than the box of (2). The endpapers are the same, except they are yellower.

NOTES: According to Donald J. Deans, who worked for Seagram's in public relations, "The first 5 editions [i.e. impressions] were printed from the original type but to assure the continuance of high quality and fine printing, the entire book had to be re-set for later editions [i.e. impressions]" (letter to M.M. Schneckenburger, 5 September 1957, Seagram's Ltd. fonds, HAG). This would imply that a new setting of type occurred in 1951. There were further printings in 1953, 1955, 1958, 1961, 1964, and 1967.

In fact, the post-1951 impressions have not been re-set. In all probability they were photo-composed. The imposition has been altered. In addition, the preliminary pages and the pages after the text have been re-ordered primarily to eliminate blank pages. In reducing and re-ordering these pages of the book, the printers did not re-set the table of contents; as a result, errors occur in the table of contents with respect to the placement of these pages. In A92a each of the tissue guards for the colour illustrations has two lines in brown, indicating that the illustration in question is from an original painting and with the artist's signature in facsimile. In this re-issue the tissue guards have been eliminated, and the information on the tissue guards has been transferred onto the illustrations. This re-issue comes with a white card from the House of Seagram, informing the recipient that the copy is from "the private and limited edition."

COPIES EXAMINED: CS; OORI.

## A93 MY REMARKABLE UNCLE 1942

### A93a *first American edition*:

Stephen Leacock | [ornamental rule; the next line in open type] | My Remarkable Uncle | AND | [the next line in open type] Other Sketches | [publisher's device of Dodd, Mead: oval containing open book and portrait of classical figure with leaves and company name] | [ornamental rule; the next two lines in open type] | Dodd, Mead & Company | New York 1942

◆ $1$–$20^8$. *i–iv*, v–vi, *1–2*, 3–12, *13–14*, 15–21, *22–24*, 25–32, *33–34*, 35–44, *45–46*, 47–49, *50–52*, 53–60, *61–62*, 63–71, *72–74*, 75–82, *83–84*, 85–92, *93–94*, 95–100, *101–102*, 103–108, *109–110*, 111–117, *118–120*, 121–126, *127–128*, 129–137, *138–140*, 141–147, *148–150*, 151–161, *162–164*, 165–171, *172–174*, 175–180, *181–182*, 183–192, *193–194*, 195–199, *200–202*, 203–208, *209–210*, 211–217, *218–220*, 221–223, *224–226*, 227–232, *233–234*, 235–240, *241–242*, 243–263, *264–266*, 267–289, *290–292*, 293–301, *302–304*, 305–308, *309–310*, 311–313, *1* pp. (160 leaves). 196 × 140 mm.

CONTENTS: p. *i* half title; p. *ii* list of twenty-four other books by Leacock, the first *Literary Lapses* and the last *Stephen Leacock's Laugh Parade*; p. *iii* title; p. *iv* COPYRIGHT, 1942 | By DODD, MEAD AND COMPANY, INC. | ALL RIGHTS RESERVED | NO PART OF THIS BOOK MAY BE REPRODUCED | WITHOUT PERMISSION IN WRITING FROM THE PUBLISHER | PRINTED IN THE UNITED STATES OF AMERICA; pp. v–vi table of contents; pp. *1*–313 text (pp. 2, *14*, 22, *24*, 34, *46*, 50, *52*, 62, *72*, 74, *84*, 94, *102*, 110, *118*, *120*, 128, *138*, *140*, 148, *150*, 162, *164*, 172, *174*, 182, *194*, 200, *202*, 210, *218*, 220, *224*, 226, *234*, 242, *264*, 266, *290*, 292, *302*, 304, and *310* blank); p. *1* blank.

TEXT: There are six sections. The last five essays and sketches do not have a section heading.

The first section, Some Memories, consists of: My Remarkable Uncle: A Personal Document; The Old Farm and the New Frame; and The Struggle to Make Us Gentlemen (A Memory of My Old School).

The second section, Literary Studies, consists of: The British Soldier; The Mathematics of the Lost Chord; The Passing of the Kitchen; Come Back to School; What's in a Name?: Curiosities in Book Titles; Who Canonizes the Classics?; and Among the Antiques: An Adventure at Afternoon Tea.

The third section, Sporting Section, consists of: What Is a Sport?; Why Do We Fish?: The Complete Philosophy of the Angler; When Fellers Go Fishing; and Eating Air: A Discourse on the Magic of Eating Out of Doors.

The fourth section, Studies in Humour, consists of: The Saving Grace of Humour: Is There Any?; Laughing Off Our History; and War and Humour.

The fifth section, Memories of Christmas, consists of: Christmas Rapture: Pre-War; Christmas Shopping: Pre-War; War-Time Santa Claus; and War-Time Christmas.

The sixth section, Goodwill Stuff, consists of: Cricket for Americans; Our American Visitors: As Seen from Canada; A Welcome to a Visiting American: At the Canadian National Exhibition; Why Is the United States?

The last five essays and sketches are: The Transit of Venus: A College Story; Migration in English Literature: A Study of England and America; Three Score and Ten: The Business of Growing Old; Index: There Is No Index; and L'Envoi: A Salutation Across the Sea.

BINDING AND DUST JACKET: Bound in red cloth with a solid rectangle blind-stamped on the upper board. Within the rectangle is a raised thick-thin rectangle, also blind-stamped, and containing the following raised lines: MY REMARKABLE | UNCLE | [rule] | STEPHEN LEACOCK. Stamped on the spine in gilt: MY | REMARKABLE | UNCLE | [ornamental rule] | LEACOCK | DODD, MEAD | & COMPANY.

The front and spine panels of the jacket are primarily orange with a thick black border, extending from the bottom of the spine panel to the bottom of the front panel and to the right-hand side of the front panel. There is a concave, solid white rectangle (outlined in black) on the front panel which contains the title hand-written in orange and black. Under the concave rectangle are Leacock's name in capital letters and a photograph of his head. A similar configuration is on the spine panel with the addition of the publisher's name. Printed in orange and black, the back panel has a black-and-white photograph of Leacock, a list of books by him, and excerpts from reviews. The front flap has a synopsis of the book. The back flap has an advertisement for *Laugh Parade*. The last line on the back flap is: C–1–42–3M [oval with three lines, the first and last curved: PRINTED | IN | U.S.A.].

NOTES: On the suggestion of Jacques Chambrun who acted on behalf of *Reader's Digest*, Leacock wrote his essay entitled "My Remarkable Uncle" (entitled "The Most Unforgettable Character I've Met," see C41.11). In accepting the article for publication on 13 May 1941, DeWitt Wallace, the editor of *Reader's Digest*, remarked: "E.P. [Leacock] at the present moment undoubtedly is standing with one foot on some heavenly bar, bragging to his winged cronies about his nephew's latest triumph."

When Frank Dodd read Leacock's reminiscences of his uncle, he suggested on 16 August 1941 that they could be incorporated into "a new volume of published or about-to-be-published sketches." The contract for the book is dated 21 August 1941 (15% royalty with an advance on publication date equal to the accrued royalty earnings, rights including Canada).

Leacock sent Dodd the preface to the book on 18 September [1940]. He mailed manuscripts and other texts for the book shortly after 15 November 1941. "The Mathematics of the Lost Chord" was included in the book just before it was sent to the printer on 8 December 1941.

Published on 24 February 1942 at $2.50. Two days later, Leacock was sent a cheque for $290 as an advance on accrued royalties. Two copies were received by the Copyright Office at DLC on 19 February 1942; copyright registration occurred on 28 February 1942 (A161933). The copyright was renewed by Stephen Lushington Leacock on 17 February 1970 (R478970). By 1 February 1944 the book had earned a royalty of $1,810.77 in American sales (approximately 4,829 copies at $.375 royalty per copy) and $427.50 in Canadian sales (approximately 950 copies at $.45 royalty per copy).

Both Paramount Pictures Inc. (15 January 1942) and Twentieth Century-Fox Film Corporation (20 January 1942) inquired about the film rights to the book. Leacock informed these companies that the sketch, "My Remarkable Uncle," was only one of many in the book and probably not suitable as a result. Twentieth Century-Fox continued to be interested in the story as late as 20 February 1942; galleys were sent to their Coast Studio for their reaction.

According to the copyright pages of later impressions, the second printing occurred in March 1942, the third printing in May 1942, the fourth printing in February 1943, the fifth printing in November 1943, the sixth printing in October 1944, and the seventh printing in January 1946.

"War and Humour" reprinted in Ralph Gustafson, ed., *Canadian Accent* (London: Penguin, 1944), pp. 10–4.

COPIES EXAMINED: CS (first, second, sixth, and seventh printings, all in jacket); OTNY (first and sixth printings in jacket); QMMRB (two copies of the first printing, one in jacket).

**A93b** *English edition:*

MY | REMARKABLE | UNCLE | & *Other Sketches* | *by* | *Stephen Leacock* | London | JOHN LANE THE BODLEY HEAD

◆ $1^8$ $2$–$13^8$ $14^6$ [$1 signed]. 1–4, 5, 6, 7–96, 97, 98–218, 1–2 pp. (110 leaves). 183 × 122 m.

CONTENTS: p. *1* half title; p. *2* list of twenty-nine other books by Leacock published by The Bodley Head; p. *3* title; p. *4* First published 1942 | [the next four lines within an illustration of an open book which has a lion at the top of the book] | BOOK | PRODUCTION | WAR ECONOMY | STANDARD | THIS BOOK IS PRODUCED IN | COMPLETE CONFORMITY WITH THE | AUTHORIZED ECONOMY STANDARDS | Printed in Great Britain by | MORRISON AND GIBB LTD., LONDON AND EDINBURGH | for JOHN LANE THE BODLEY HEAD LIMITED | 8 Bury Place London W.C.1; pp. *5*–*6* table of contents; pp. *7*–*218* text; pp. *1*–*2* advertisements for *Our Heritage of Liberty* and *Our British Empire*.

TEXT: Identical to the American edition (A93a), except that the section "Goodwill Stuff" is entitled "Goodwill for America." Also, the titles of certain pieces have been slightly altered. For example, "The Mathematics of the Lost Chord" is entitled "The Mathematical Problem of the Lost Chord." "Why Is the United States?" is entitled "Uncle Sam: An Allegory." "Index: There Is No Index" is entitled "The Perfect Index: There Is No Index, and Why — ."

BINDING AND DUST JACKET: Bound in orange cloth with blue lettering on the spine as follows: [thick-thin rule] | MY | [at a diagonal] REMARKABLE | UNCLE | and | other | sketches | [thin-thick rule] | *Stephen* | *Leacock* | [rule] | The | Bodley | Head | [rule].

The front and spine panels of the jacket are blackish blue with lettering in white and orange and the title at a diagonal in ornamental type. The back panel of the jacket features advertisements for *Our Heritage of Liberty* and *Our British Empire*. The front flap briefly indicates the scope of *My Remarkable Uncle and Other Sketches* (price 7s 6d). The back flap is blank.

NOTES: On 11 November 1941, Leacock informed his English publisher that he was would be writing three books in the near future and that the manuscript of *My Remarkable Uncle and Other Sketches* would soon be in the mail. Leacock inquired whether it was possible to have proofs by 15 February 1941. C.J. Greenwood responded enthusiastically to Leacock's writing plans and sent him a contract for the book on 21 November 1941 (15% royalty with an advance on the day of publication equal to the amount earned by subscription sales). The manuscript arrived at The Bodley Head on 8 January 1942. It was sent to the printer soon thereafter. Leacock was requested to send a copy of "the American galleys, from which we can make the necessary corrections."

According to *The English Catalogue of Books*, publication occurred in July 1942. Number of copies printed not known.

COPIES EXAMINED: CS (in jacket); SLM (Leacock's copy in jacket).

**A93c** *second American edition* (abridged, [1946?]):

[all lines, except one, are within two rectangles in two columns separated by a vertical rule; to the right of the vertical rule, the first two lines in tooled type] My Remarkable | Uncle | *and Other Sketches* | by | STEPHEN LEACOCK | *Editions for the Armed Services, Inc.* | A NON-PROFIT ORGANIZATION ESTABLISHED BY | THE COUNCIL ON BOOKS IN WARTIME, NEW YORK | [remaining lines within the rectangles to the left of the vertical rule] PUBLISHED BY ARRANGEMENT WITH | DODD, MEAD AND COMPANY, INC., | NEW YORK | *All rights reserved. No part of* | *this book may be* *reproduced* | *in any form without permission* | *in writing from the publisher.* | COPYRIGHT, 1942, | BY DODD, MEAD AND COMPANY, INC. | [the next line, outside of the two rectangles, at the bottom left-hand corner] | 976

♦  $1^{64}$. 1–2, 3–127, 1 pp. (64 leaves). 97 × 139 m.

CONTENTS:  p. *1* title; p. 2 A few of the sketches in the | original printing of this book have | had to be eliminated in this edition. | *Manufactured in the United States of America*; pp. 3–4 table of contents; pp. 5–127 text.

TEXT:  This edition contains sixteen of the thirty essays and sketches that are found in the first edition (A93a). The text is in two columns. There are six sections with running heads at the bottom of the pages.

The first section, Some Memories, consists of: My Remarkable Uncle: A Personal Document; The Old Farm and the New Frame; and The Struggle to Make Us Gentlemen (A Memory of My Old School).

The second section, Literary Studies, consists of: The Mathematics of the Lost Chord; The Passing of the Kitchen; Come Back to School; and Among the Antiques: An Adventure at Afternoon Tea.

The third section, Sporting Section, consists of: What Is a Sport?; and When Fellers Go Fishing.

The fourth section, Studies in Humour, consists of: The Saving Grace of Humour: Is There Any?

The fifth section, Memories of Christmas, consists of: War–Time Christmas.

The sixth section, Goodwill Stuff, consists of: Cricket for Americans; Our American Visitors: As Seen from Canada; The Transit of Venus: A College Story; Three Score and Ten: The Business of Growing Old; and L'Envoi: A Salutation Across the Sea.

BINDING:  Bound in a multi-coloured wrapper, wire-stitched. The front of the wrapper is divided into two sections. The top section is light blue with a photograph of Leacock's book (as published by Dodd, Mead), the title of the book, Leacock's name, information on the Editions for the Armed Services, Inc., and a solid yellow circle (containing the lines: ARMED | SERVICES | EDITION). The circle overlaps with the bottom section of the front wrapper. The bottom section is a solid red band with the words SELECTED SKETCHES in yellow. The back of the wrapper has a solid yellow rectangle, outlined in white, with a red border having white stars. Within the rectangle, in two columns, is some information about the book, Leacock, and the Editions for Armed Services, Inc. The verso of the front wrapper has more information on the Armed Services Editions. The verso of the back wrapper has a list of other Armed Services Editions (authors and titles of numbers 975 to 1014 listed, Leacock's being 976).

NOTES: The Armed Services Editions were printed "in [a] small, convenient, and economical form," and were "intended for exclusive distribution to members of the American Armed Forces . . . not to be resold or made available to civilians." For general information on these editions, see *Editions for the Armed Services, Inc.: A History Together with the Complete List of 1324 Books Published for American Armed Forces Overseas* (New York: Editions for the Armed Services, Inc., [1948]); Leacock's book is found under the "CC" List (p. 73). At least 40,000 to 50,000 copies were printed of the Armed Services Edition of *My Remarkable Uncle and Other Sketches*.

COPIES EXAMINED: CS; DLC.

## A93d *first Canadian edition* (1965):

Stephen Leacock | [open swelled rule] | MY | REMARKABLE | UNCLE | AND OTHER | SKETCHES | Introduction: John Stevens | General Editor — Malcolm Ross | New Canadian Library No. 53 | [publisher's device: abstract design of a person on a horse-drawn chariot, taking aim with a bow and arrow] | MCCLELLAND AND STEWART LIMITED

◆ *i–v*, vi, *vii*, viii–xii, *13–14*, 15–29, *30–32*, 33–55, *56*, 57–65, *66–68*, 69–75, *76*, 77–85, *86–88*, 89–103, *104–106*, 107–109, *110*, 111–123, *124–126*, 127–139, *140–142*, 143–155, *156–158*, 159–172, *173–174*, 175–179, *180–182*, 183–184, *185–186*, 187, *188–191*,, 192 pp. (96 leaves). 183 × 111 mm.

CONTENTS: p. *i* half title; p. *ii* blank; p. *iii* title; p. *iv* Copyright 1942 by Dodd, Mead and Company Inc. | Introduction © 1965 by McClelland and Stewart Limited | [six lines concerning copyright] | *The Canadian Publishers* | McClelland and Stewart Limited | 25 Hollinger Road, Toronto 16 | PRINTED AND BOUND IN ENGLAND BY | HAZELL WATSON AND VINEY LTD | AYLESBURY, BUCKS; pp. *v–vi* table of contents; pp. *vii*–xii introduction by John Stevens, dated July 1965; pp. *13–187* text; p. *188* blank; p. *189* biographical information on Leacock; p. *190* blank; pp. *191–192* list of books in the New Canadian Library series, *My Remarkable Uncle and Other Sketches* being n 53.

TEXT: Identical to A93a.

BINDING: Perfect bound in stiff paper. The covers, designed by Frank Newfeld, are white with orange, red, and wine lettering and with a drawing of Leacock on the front cover.

NOTES: In September 1965 McClelland and Stewart arranged with Dodd, Mead to publish a paperback edition in the New Canadian Library (NCL) series. On 16 September 1965, Dodd, Mead informed McClelland and Stewart that the NCL edition would have to be limited to Canada only. John Stevens finished his introduction in July 1965. Production took place with Hazell Watson and Viney between 5 October and 10 November 1965. The Leacock estate received 5% royalty to 5,000 copies, 7% thereafter. The NCL edition was published on 6 December 1965. Price $1.25. By the end of 1966, 1,817 copies had sold. By the end of 1979, 15,391 had sold. There was a reprint in 1971 (with different covers and an increased price, $1.75) (information based on Dodd, Mead fonds; and file 14, "New Canadian Library," box 93, series A, and file 14, box Ca25, of the McClelland and Stewart fonds, OHM).

COPIES EXAMINED: CS (first and second impressions, including proof copy of first impression).

## A93e *second Canadian edition* (1989):

STEPHEN LEACOCK | My Remarkable Uncle | and Other Sketches | *With an Afterword by Barbara Nimmo* | [wavy, solid band, wavy rule] | M&S | [rule]

◆ *1–8, 9–30, 31–32, 33–76, 77–78, 79–102, 103–104, 105–125, 126–128, 129–151, 152–154, 155–173, 174–176, 177–194, 195–196, 197–215, 216–218, 219–225, 226–228, 229–232, 233–234, 235–237, 238, 239–243, 1–5* pp. (124 leaves). 177 × 109 mm.

CONTENTS: p. *1* biographical information on Leacock; p. *2* THE NEW CANADIAN LIBRARY | General Editor: David Staines | ADVISORY BOARD | Alice Munro | W.H. New | Guy Vanderhaeghe; p. *3* title; p. *4* Copyright © 1942 by Dodd, Mead and Company Inc. | Afterword copyright © 1989 by Barbara Nimmo | Reprinted 1989 | [five lines concerning copyright; nine lines Canadian Cataloguing Publication Data] | Typesetting by Pickwick | Printed and bound in Canada | McClelland & Stewart Inc. | *The Canadian Publishers* | 481 University Avenue | Toronto, Ontario | M5G 2E9; pp. *5–6* table of contents; pp. *7–237* text (pp. *8, 32, 78, 104, 126, 128, 152, 154, 174, 176, 196, 216, 218, 226, 228,* and *234* blank); p. *238* blank; pp. *239–243* afterword by Barbara Nimmo; p. *1* blank; pp. *2–4* list of books by Leacock; p. *5* titles by Leacock in the New Canadian Library series.

TEXT: Identical to A93a.

BINDING: Bound in glossy, stiff paper (grey, green, and white) with a reproduction of F.S. Challener's painting *Boy Fishing* on the front cover. Series design T.M. Craan. ISBN 0-7710-9965-7.

NOTES: Price $5.95. Published on 1 April 1989 in a print run of 7,755 copies. By the end of 1996 6,527 copies had sold.

COPIES EXAMINED: CS; SLM (many copies).


## A94 OUR HERITAGE OF LIBERTY 1942

### A94a *English edition*:

Stephen Leacock | OUR HERITAGE | OF LIBERTY | *Its Origin, Its Achievement, Its Crisis* | A BOOK FOR WAR TIME | [publisher's device of The Bodley Head (illustration of bust of Sir Thomas Bodley, with J and L to the left and right of the head and THE BODLEY HEAD in white at the bottom of the bust)] | John Lane The Bodley Head

◆ $1^8$ (−1A) $2$–$5^8$ [$1 signed (the rear pastedown is part of the last gathering)]. *1–6, 7–75, 1* pp. (38 leaves without the rear pastedown). 184 × 124 mm.

CONTENTS: p. *1* half title; p. *2* list of twenty-nine titles written by Leacock, the first being *Literary Lapses* and the last *My Remarkable Uncle and Other Sketches*; p. *3* title; p. *4* First published 1942 | COPYRIGHT IN U.S.A. | [illustration of a lion resting on top of an open book; the next four lines appearing on the pages of the book:] | BOOK | PRODUCTION | WAR ECONOMY | STANDARD | THIS BOOK IS PRODUCED IN | COMPLETE CONFORMITY WITH THE | AUTHORISED ECONOMY STANDARDS | Printed in Great Britain by | MORRISON AND GIBB LTD., LONDON AND EDINBURGH | for JOHN LANE THE BODLEY HEAD LIMITED | 8 Bury Place London W.C.1; p. *5* table of contents; p. *6* blank; pp. *7–75* text; p. *1* blank.

TEXT: Britain and America; The Good and the Bad Old Times; The March of Progress; Liberty in the Ancient World; The Shadow of the Dark and Middle Ages; National States; The Growth of Popular Rights; Reaction of America on Europe; Natural Liberty and Jean Jacques Rousseau; Age of Enlightenment; The Rights of Man and of the Citizen; The New Light Burns Dim; The Great Peace and Industrial Revolution; Enter Political Economy; John Stuart Mill; Anarchism and Wool-Gathering; The Vision of Socialism; National Liberty and Unity; The United States United; Individual Liberty and Mass Industry.

BINDING AND DUST JACKET: Bound in greenish yellow cloth with purple lettering down the spine as follows: OUR HERITAGE OF LIBERTY *Stephen Leacock*.

The dust jacket is beige with the lettering and illustrative designs in dark pink. There are dark pink, solid, vertical bands on either side of the front panel of the jacket with diamond-patterned, vertical rules on the insides of the bands. Between the bands is the following: *Our | Heritage | of | Liberty* | [ornamental diamond] | STEPHEN | LEACOCK. The band on the left side of the front panel also covers the spine panel of the jacket. Down the spine panel in white is the following: OUR HERITAGE OF LIBERTY *Stephen Leacock*. On the back panel within a ribbon rectangle (broken on the right-hand side) is an advertisement for Leacock's *Our British Empire*. On the front flap is a summary of *Our Heritage of Liberty* (priced at 3s 6d). The back flap features an illustration of the tower of London and concentric circles on top of a globe with the following words at slight angles: LONDON | CALLING | OVERSEAS. Below the illustration are several paragraphs which describe the services of the British Broadcasting Corporation during the war. The jacket was apparently issued with a glassine wrapper.

NOTES: On 13 February 1940, R.W. Bardwell of Row, Peterson & Company (Evanston, Illinois) asked Leacock to write a small book of forty-eight pages on "the common ties of people living in a democracy and what we need to preserve it." Leacock wrote a long, effusive letter in reply on 15 February 1940. He suggested a book of 15,000 words entitled "Liberty," a follow-up to the work of John Stuart Mill in view of the disappointments and developments in the last 100 years since the publication of Mill's classic, *On Liberty*. Leacock was to finish the pamphlet before the end of March 1940, once completing *The British Empire*. The contract is dated 4 March 1940 ($250 advance, 6% royalty on copies sold).

Leacock told Frank Dodd about the book on 28 March 1940, and Dodd stated on 1 April 1940: "Of course, there is no objection on our part to the short educational book, as no doubt it is out of our field." Leacock assured Bardwell on 5 April 1940 that barring illness or unforeseen circumstances, he would have the short book finished in a month's time. Bardwell inquired about the book on 17 September 1940: "I am glad that the manuscript for the little book 'Liberty' will soon be on the way." Bardwell received the manuscript on 8 October 1940, and he sent Leacock his advance.

Although pleased with the manuscript, Bardwell recommended "a revision in the process of editing." To this suggestion Leacock cabled on 15 October 1940: "DELIGHTED TO ACT ALONG THE LINES OF YOUR LETTER GO RIGHT AHEAD." But on 23 October 1940, Bardwell returned the manuscript with a number of criticisms: the book, particularly in the beginning section, was too "ephemeral"; the point of view was English, rather than American; the writing was beyond the comprehension of the average college student; at times Leacock had employed an oratorical style. On 21 March 1941, Bardwell asked Leacock to revise and reduce the manuscript so that it could be understood by "the young soldier." Ten days later, Bardwell suggested that the manuscript should be reduced to 14,000 words. On 11 June 1941, Bardwell inquired again on Leacock's ". . . progress on the *Liberty* manuscript." On 23 June 1941, however, Leacock told Bardwell that he could not revise the manuscript as suggested. In Leacock's opinion the manuscript was "first class, and only needs here and there the insertion of a lighter touch. . . . . . It is hard to touch a thing up after the fact; it is like putting paint on a finished picture." Leacock offered to return $100 of the advance and to take back his manuscript in anticipation of publication elsewhere. Although disappointed with Leacock's response, Bardwell stated on 7 July 1941 that "We will proceed with the editing of the manuscript under the original agreement, and send you copy before sending it to the press." Leacock made further additions at this point but to no avail. Bardwell informed Leacock on 1 August 1941 that the new introduction was too much like "a Rotary Club after-dinner speech" and that the other insertions ". . . allude to facts with which 99% of our boys are unfamiliar." Bardwell proposed to rework and edit the manuscript himself. Leacock gave his approval to this proposal on 5 August 1941 with the proviso his text would only be simplified here and there. The edited manuscript with an external editor's report was sent to Leacock on 25 September 1941. On 4 October 1941, Leacock asked Bardwell to return his original manuscript. The edited manuscript departed too much from Leacock's text: "I am afraid I cannot consent to sign my name to whole paragraphs which I did not write and do not approve." When Leacock received his original manuscript, he wrote to Bardwell on 12 October 1941, proposing to revise the manuscript along the lines of the external editor's report — providing a "*positive* statement of what free democracy has accomplished for the schools, etc. . ." and "discussing socialism" and doing more "justice to its *inspiration.*" He also had a new title in mind: "Our Heritage of Liberty: A Survey of Its Origins and History, Its Achievement, It Present Danger & Its Future Completion." But Leacock's revised manuscript was still "a treatise on Liberty for adult reading" and not suitable for "elementary and secondary schools," Bardwell told Leacock on 29 November 1941. Leacock requested the manuscript back as soon as possible. He offered $100 payment immediately and the remainder of the advance if the book took in over $1,000 royalties with another publishing company. Bardwell complied with this request on 4 December 1941.

Leacock submitted his manuscript to The Bodley Head on 8 December 1942. He explained his previous contract with Row, Peterson, and suggested a reduced royalty in view of the small book. The contract with The Bodley Head is undated (copy in the Nimmo collection at NAC). Leacock was to receive "Ten per cent (10%) of the published price on all copies sold with an advance on publication of the amount earned by the subscription sales." The contract gave The Bodley Head the right to consider for publication Leacock's next literary work. The book was published on 5 June 1942. The copyright in the English edition was registered with the Copyright Office at DLC on 30 July 1942 (Aint.27241). Number of copies printed not known.

COPIES EXAMINED: CS (two copies in jacket); QMMRB (in jacket).


## A94b *American edition* (1942):

*Stephen Leacock* | [swelled rule] | OUR HERITAGE | OF LIBERTY | Its Origin, Its Achievement, Its Crisis | *A Book for War Time* | [swelled rule] | *Dodd, Mead & Company* • *New York* | 1942

♦ *1–6*[8]. *1–8, 1–86, 1–2* pp. (48 leaves).

Contents: p. *1* half title; p. *2* blank; p. *3* title; p. *4* COPYRIGHT, 1942 | BY DODD, MEAD AND COMPANY, INC. | ALL RIGHTS RESERVED | NO PART OF THIS BOOK MAY BE REPRODUCED IN ANY FORM | WITHOUT PERMISSION IN WRITING FROM THE PUBLISHER | PRINTED IN THE UNITED STATES OF AMERICA | BY THE VAIL-BALLOU PRESS, INC., BINGHAMTON, N.Y.; p. *5* table of contents; p.*6* blank; p. *7* fly title; p. *8* blank; pp. *1–86* text; p. *1–2* blank.

TEXT: Identical to the English edition.

BINDING AND DUST JACKET: Bound in greenish beige cloth with the publisher's device of Dodd, Mead (oval with leaves enclosing a man reading a book) blind-stamped on the upper board. All lettering on the spine in brown as follows: [down the spine] OUR HERITAGE OF LIBERTY • STEPHEN LEACOCK | [the next two lines printed horizontally] DODD, MEAD | *&* COMPANY.

The dust jacket is white and dark red. The spine and front panels of the jacket are dark red with illustration and lettering in white. On the front panel: [leafy, vertical rule to the left of all lines] | *Our* | *Heritage* | *of* | *Liberty* | STEPHEN | LEACOCK. On the spine panel: LEACOCK | [the next line down the spine] OUR HERITAGE OF LIBERTY | DODD | MEAD. The back panel and the flaps are white with red lettering. The back panel features a photograph in red of Leacock in the upper left corner. To right of the photograph: *Books by* | Stephen | Leacock. The heading LAUGH WITH LEACOCK is under the photo, followed by excerpts from the *New York Times* and *The Spectator*. Seventeen other works *By the Same Author* are then listed in two columns. The front flap carries a description of *Our Heritage of Liberty* (priced at $1.25). The last line on the back flap (which advertises *Laugh with Leacock*) is: C–7–42–12C [oval with lines as follows: PRINTED | [ornament] IN [ornament] | U.S.A.].

NOTES: The manuscript was apparently received by Dodd, Mead sometime prior to 11 December 1941. E.H. Dodd, Jr. wrote a report declining it for publication. In his report Dodd stated that three-fourths of the manuscript was "extraordinarily good," but the last part focused on education and housing to the detriment of Leacock's general theme. He suggested a complete revision of the latter part. Dodd also felt that too much literature was available on this subject and that moreover, it would be difficult to market the book successfully in view of its expected low retail price.

On 8 April 1942, Dodd, Mead wrote to The Bodley Head about Leacock's short book. On 5 June 1942, the manager of the latter firm, C.J. Greenwood, offered Dodd, Mead two possibilities: that The Bodley Head would send Dodd, Mead "260/250 folded and collated sheets with your imprint at 17 cents per set"; or that Dodd, Mead could "photograph our typography . . . [at] a nominal fee of 20 dollars." Frank C. Dodd found both alternatives unsatisfactory. He wrote to Leacock on 2 July 1942, and told him that sales of the book would probably be "very limited in this market." He asked Leacock that if he would exempt his royalty on 500 copies, Dodd, Mead would manufacture "1000 copies as a minimum edition." On 6 July 1942, Leacock replied: "So glad you are making a U.S. edition of liberty and quite willing to meet you on the royalty exemption of 500 copies as in your of July 2." The American edition was published on 9 September 1942. Two copies were received by the Copyright Office at DLC on 27 August 1942; the copyright was registered on 12 September 1942 (A167014). The copyright was renewed by Stephen Lushington Leacock on 8 April 1970 (R482722). By 1 February 1943, 786 copies had sold (royalty of $35.94 earned). In a report of 1 June 1944 to Leacock's niece, Barbara Nimmo, Dodd, Mead recorded that by 1 February 1944, the book had earned $49.69 royalty in American sales.

COPIES EXAMINED: CS (in jacket); QMMRB (not in jacket).

## A95 MONTREAL, SEAPORT AND CITY 1942

A95a *advertising leaflet* (1942):

[caption title] STEPHEN LEACOCK | LOOKS AT | MONTREAL | [ornament] | [text]

◆ Leaflet folded once to form four unnumbered pages. 229 × 151 mm.

CONTENTS: An introductory paragraph and nine excerpts with headings. On the bottom of the last page is the following: MONTREAL, SEAPORT AND CITY | McClelland and Stewart, Limited, Publishers, Toronto. | Doubleday, Doran & Company, Inc. Publishers, New York. For sale at all Montreal Book Stores, Book Departments and Hotel | and Railway News Stands. | With end papers, 10 illustrations, more than 350 pages. | Canadian Retail Price $4.00.

BINDING: Issued on cream-coloured paper stock.

NOTES: On 12 August 1942, Leacock made numerous suggestions to T.B. Costain of Doubleday, Doran for the promotion of the book in Montreal. Costain informed him that promotional plans were already well underway by the book's Canadian distributor, McClelland and Stewart. Two weeks later on 26 August, Leacock told Costain that he wanted to print "a circular (four sheets, one fold) with a notice of the book and extracts specially selected to appeal in Montreal; in all 2400 words of type with headings." He proposed to arrange the printing himself: "5000 [2,000] copies for $26.00 — if I need so many. Postage $2.60 and envelopes about $4.00 — I propose to get Mrs. [May] Shaw to make out a social list and send the circular to them." Costain gave his blessing to Leacock's circular on 31 August, but he wanted McClelland and Stewart's involvement in this promotional scheme. On 2 September McClelland and Stewart agreed to Mrs. Shaw receiving $.10 on all copies sold in Montreal, but the firm requested to see Leacock's leaflet before it was printed.

Printing occurred on 12 September 1942; 200 copies were taken by Mrs. Shaw to Montreal. On 25 September Costain's secretary, Ethel M. Hulse, pointed out to Leacock that the leaflet seemed to imply that McClelland and Stewart was the book's principal publisher ("McClelland" was also misspelled "McLelland"). On 26 September Donald G. French of McClelland and Stewart returned the circular with corrections. Two days later Leacock arranged for the Orillia Packet-Times to print 2,000 copies. On the day that Leacock received his author copies in Montreal (6 November 1942), Mrs. Shaw mailed 1,000 leaflets to book stores, newspapers, and individuals. Henry Morgan and Co. of Montreal sent out 3,000 copies with their November advertising. These numbers would indicate that the leaflet was probably distributed both in its corrected and uncorrected states.

COPIES EXAMINED: CS (corrected state); SLM (more than thirty copies of the leaflet, including four "proof" copies).

**A95b** *American edition*:

[two wavy rules] | Montreal | SEAPORT AND CITY | By | STEPHEN LEACOCK | [rule] | [illustration of nautical theme — telescope, anchor, rope, ship's wheel, etc.] | [rule] | Doubleday, Doran & Company, Inc. | GARDEN CITY 1942 NEW YORK | [two wavy rules]

♦ 1–22$^8$. i–iv, v–vii, viii, ix–xi, 1–2, 2–331, 332, 333–340 pp. (176 leaves). 228 × 152 mm.

CONTENTS: p. *i* half title; p. *ii* list of twenty-nine other books by Leacock, the first being *My Remarkable Uncle and Other Sketches* and the last *Elements of Political Science*; p. *iii* title; p. *iv* PRINTED AT THE *Country Life Press*, GARDEN CITY, N. Y., U. S. A. | CL | COPYRIGHT, 1942 | BY STEPHEN LEACOCK | ALL RIGHTS RESERVED | FIRST EDITION; pp. v–vii preface, last two lines on p. vii: *McGill University* STEPHEN LEACOCK | 1942; p. *viii* blank; pp. ix–x table of contents; p. xi list of illustrations (illustrations include frontispiece and facing pp. 20, 100, 164, 180, 200, 212, 312); p. *1* blank; pp. 2, 2–328 text; p. 329 appendix no. 1 Population of Montreal; pp. 330–331 appendix no. 2 Chronological History of Montreal; p. 332 blank; pp. 333–340 index.

TEXT: chapter I Hochelega; chapter II Place Royale; chapter III Ville Marie de Montreal; chapter IV A Half Century of Struggle; chapter V The Old French Regime in Montreal 1713–63; chapter VI The Capitulation of Montreal 1760; chapter VII The American Occupation of Montreal; chapter VIII Lower Canada 1791–1841; chapter IX Montreal, Capital of United Canada 1841–1849–1867; chapter X Montreal, the Seaport of the New Dominion; chapter XI Montreal in the Twentieth Century; chapter XII The Port of Montreal; chapter XIII French and English; chapter XIV McGill University; chapter XV Come up on the Mountain; chapter XVI L'Envoi: The Problem of a Great City.

BINDING AND DUST JACKET: Bound in green buckram with an illustration of a ship and scroll blind-stamped on the upper board. Top edge stained yellowish blue. Stamped in brownish gold on the spine as follows: [rule, row of short, slanted, wavy lines, rule] | [illustration of crossed telescopes and a scroll] | [rule, row of short, slanted, wavy lines, rule] | MONTREAL | *Stephen* | *Leacock* | [rule] | DOUBLEDAY DORAN | [rule, row of short, slanted, wavy lines, rule] | [illustration of anchor] | [rule, row of short, slanted, wavy lines, rule] | [illustration of a sexton] | [rule, row of short, slanted, wavy lines, rule] | [ship's wheel] | [rule, row of short, slanted, wavy lines, rule].

The front and spine panels of the jacket are mainly green, resembling the buckram binding, with lettering in white and black. The lower section of the front panel has a colour reproduction of A View of Montreal from Helen's Island (identical to the black-and-white frontispiece). The centre section of this illustration is also found on the bottom of the spine panel. Other sections of the jacket are white with lettering primarily in black and, to a much lesser extent, in pink. The back panel has information on other books in the Doubleday, Doran Seaport Series. The front flap has a synopsis of the book with the price ($3.50), and states that *Montreal: Seaport and City* is the seventh volume of the Seaport Series. The last line on the front flap is 3609–42. An advertisement for United States War Savings Bonds Stamps and a plea to the reader to send the book to the Army Libraries (after reading) are on the back flap.

NOTES: On 8 December 1941, Costain of Doubleday, Doran brought to Leacock's attention his company's series on "Famous American Ports." Books in the series were wanted for port cities outside of the United States, and Costain suggested to Leacock that he might want to write a book on Quebec city. When Leacock opted for Montreal, Costain was delighted and offered him 15% royalty on all copies sold and an advance of $1,000 ($500 advance with the remainder on the day of publication). The contract, which is dated 2 January 1942, stipulates that Leacock would have the manuscript ready by 1 June 1942.

Leacock sent sections of his manuscript to various experts. He also obtained information from other individuals or government departments. Dr. Frank Adams of McGill University, for example, commented on the geological section of the book on 10 February 1942. John Murray Gibbon was consulted about maps on 13 March. Judge E.F. Surveyer sent Leacock information on Montreal's historical monuments on 16 and 23 March. On 31 March J.G. Macphail of Department of Transport gave Leacock information about the season of navigation. Leonard C. Marsh of the Committee on Reconstruction sent information on employment and housing in Montreal on 7 April. On 23 May 1942, Leacock asked John Culliton to check references in exchange for six presentation copies and a "handsome reference to your name in the preface herewith." The Dominion Bureau of Statistics supplied population statistics on 1 June.

By 7 February 1942, Leacock had written 3,000 to 4,000 words, and he sent Costain a portfolio of maps and illustrations. On 24 April he sent the table of contents, sample extracts of chapters, the entire final chapter, and illustrative suggestions. Delighted with what he had received, Costain informed Leacock on 28 April 1942: "All the chapters are interesting and I can see that you are throwing yourself into this work with a great deal of personal enjoyment. It is going to be an extremely fine thing in every way." By 7 May the jacket and endpapers were designed, and the frontispiece was chosen. Leacock's niece, Barbara Nimmo, typed most of the chapters in May and June. Leacock sent the complete manuscript on 13 June 1942. After reading it, Costain cabled on [22 June 1942]: "A COLORFUL WITTY THOROUGHLY CHARMING BOOK CONGRATULATIONS." A few days later, on 25 June, Leacock was sent the rest of his advance ($500). He prepared the index himself on 30 June, and the page proofs were sent to him on 3 August. Proofs of the index were mailed to Leacock on 9 September and proofs of the illustrations and the captions on 11 September.

Publication of book was postponed until 13 November 1942, although Leacock received his author copies in Montreal on 6 November and New York bookstores apparently had the book in stock before the end of October. Copies were received by the Copyright Office at DLC on 31 October and 1 November 1942; the copyright was registered on 27 November 1942 (A169211). The copyright was renewed by Stephen Lushington Leacock on 18 November 1969 (R474258). The print run of the first impression is not known. By 24 February 1943 just under 4,000 copies had sold. By 26 August 1943, 4,703 copies had sold. The book sold for $4.

For a greatly edited version of chapter XV, see "Come Up to the Mountain with Stephen Leacock," *Maclean's Magazine* 56, no. 3 (1 February 1943): 19–20, 24–5.

There are two notebooks at SLM (J66 and J75) which pertain to this book. J66 entitled "Montreal Port" has a few pages on the historical development of Canada. J75 is also fragmentary, consisting primarily of several pages in which Leacock has noted facts that need to be checked and verified.

COPIES EXAMINED: CS (two copies with FIRST EDITION on the copyright page; copy with FIRST EDITION missing from the copyright page; 1943 reprint. All in jacket); QMMRB (two copies of first edition, one in jacket).

**A95b.1** *Canadian issue* (1948):

[two wavy rules] | Montreal | SEAPORT AND CITY | By | STEPHEN LEACOCK | [rule] | [illustration of nautical theme — telescope, anchor, rope, ship's wheel, etc.] | [rule] | McCLELLAND *&* STEWART LIMITED | PUBLISHERS TORONTO | [two wavy rules]

Although the pagination for the Canadian issue is identical to the American edition, the collation of the Canadian issue is $1-11^{16}$ (229 × 151 mm.). The contents and text are identical to the American edition. The verso of the Canadian issue reads: Copyright in Canada, 1948 | by | McCLELLAND & STEWART LIMITED | Printed and Bound in Canada | by | The Hunter-Rose Co. Limited, Toronto. The paper stock is also thinner than that of the American edition.

BINDING AND DUST JACKET: Bound in green buckram. Stamping on the upper board and spine is the same as that of the American edition except for the following: the gold stamping on the spine is a brighter gold; DOUBLEDAY DORAN has been replaced by McCLEL-LAND [c raised] | *&* STEWART. The dust jacket is similar to its American counterpart. The front of both jackets are identical. The top portion of the Canadian jacket is solid black with the first five lines in white and with the publisher's name in black, the latter within a solid white rectangle. Other sections of the dust jacket are white with black lettering. The back panel has the publisher's device of McClelland and Stewart with a list of books *Now Available*. On the flaps is a synopsis of the book's contents.

NOTES: Hugh Kane of McClelland and Stewart arranged for the printing and binding of the Canadian issue (2,000 copies at $.84 per copy) with Hunter-Rose Co. Limited on 24 November 1947. The plates were supplied from Doubleday, Doran. Kane instructed Hunter-Rose "to match sample if possible," which suggests that he wanted the Canadian issue to resemble its American counterpart. On 23 March 1948, Kane cabled Joseph Marks of Doubleday, Doran: "CASE STAMPS LEACOCKS NOT RECEIVED WITH OTHER PLATES IF AVAILABLE RUSH BY MAIL IF NOT ADVISE." The book was apparently published shortly thereafter, selling at $4 per copy (information based on series Dk31 of the McClelland and Stewart fonds, OHM).

COPIES EXAMINED: CS.

**A95c** *Canadian edition* entitled *Leacock's Montreal*, revised edition (1963):

STEPHEN LEACOCK | [row of fleurs-de-lis] | [the next two lines in Fry's ornamented typeface] | LEACOCK'S | MONTREAL | [row of fleurs-de-lis] | EDITED BY JOHN CULLITON | [publisher's device: oval containing abstract figure, with bow and arrow, standing on a horse-drawn chariot] | PUBLISHERS | MCCLELLAND AND STEWART LIMITED | TORONTO-MONTREAL

◆ $1-11^{16}$. *i–iv*, v–xx, 1–332 pp. (176 leaves). 229 × 149 mm.

CONTENTS: p. *i* half title; p. *ii* blank; p. *iii* title; p. *iv* Copyright in Canada, 1948 by *McClelland and Stewart Limited* | REVISED EDITION; | © by McClelland and Stewart *Limited, 1963* | [four lines expressing thanks for assistance to Mrs. Nettie Harris, Mrs. A Godin, and Miss Florence Brennan in revising the text] | JOHN CULLITON | ALL RIGHTS RESERVED | [five lines concerning copyright and permission to quote] | *The Canadian Publishers* | McClelland and Stewart Limited | 25 Hollinger Road, Toronto 16 | PRINTED

AND BOUND IN CANADA BY | *The Hunter Rose Co. Limited, Toronto*; pp. v–xv introduction to the revised edition by John Culliton; pp. xvi–xviii Leacock's preface; pp. xix–xx table of contents; pp. 1–324 text (eight black-and-white photographs on four leaves between pp. 140 and 141); pp. 325–332 index.

TEXT: The titles of the chapters are the same as those of the American edition. In fact, up to chapter X, the text is practically identical, and has not been reset (statistical references are updated). Beginning at p. 219 of chapter XI, John Culliton has made a number insertions to update Leacock's history. Inserted passages are marked with a leaf symbol. In addition, a number of paragraphs from the American edition, including the appendices, are deleted by Culliton (e.g. pp. 227–229 and 233–226 of the American edition).

BINDING AND DUST JACKET: Bound in light blue cloth with a solid black, long oval on the spine. The oval is outlined in yellowish green; lettering and illustration within the oval is also in yellowish green. The title (*Leacock's Montreal*), the publisher's name, and Leacock's name are stamped within the oval; the former and the latter are printed vertically within patterns of fleurs-de-lis.

The front and back panels of the jacket are the same. They feature black-and-white illustrations of Montreal (a lithograph taken from Krieghoff's painting *Place D'Armes* and a contemporary photograph by Sam Lata of large buildings). The illustrations are separated by a light blue band with Leacock's name and the title in gold and a row of fleurs-de-lis in white. The spine panel is light blue with a rectangular section in black. On the flaps is a synopsis of the book with references to the illustrations on the jacket. Some printing on the flaps in light blue; two fleurs-de-lis on the front flap in gold. Jacket designed by Frank Newfeld.

NOTES: In the preface to the American edition of his book (A95b), Leacock acknowledged the assistance of "another old friend and former colleague, Professor John Culliton, who has very kindly checked over the economic material of this book, with a view to eliminating errors. Any left are his" (p. vii). Culliton completed his M.A. at McGill University in 1928 (see B17 which contains Leacock's preface to his master's thesis). He joined the Department of Economics and Political Science at McGill a few years later, and he shared Leacock's office. His reminiscences of Leacock are recorded in K44.10.

In 1960–1 J.G. McClelland discussed the possibility of a revised, updated edition of Leacock's book with several interested parties in Montreal, with Ralph L. Curry, then Director of the Stephen Leacock Memorial Home, and with Leacock's literary executor, Barbara Nimmo. Although he was recuperating from a series of cancer operations, Culliton agreed to take on the project (60% of the royalty to the Leacock estate, 40% to Culliton). Culliton and his assistants completed the introduction and revisions by May 1963; these were perused by Mrs. Nimmo. Several week prior to publication, however, Culliton lapsed into a coma. Agnes Culliton and Florence Brennan read and corrected the proofs of the book on 28 October 1963. Culliton died on 31 October 1963. The book was published a few days prior to 29 November 1963. Number of copies printed not known, although 167 copies sold in the last six months of 1965 (information based on file 17, box 22, series A, part I, and TR1 of the McClelland and Stewart fonds, OHM).

See also the interview with Culliton in Larry Grainger, " 'Montreal, Seaport and City' Leacock's Favorite Book Revised by Confrere," *Montreal Star*, 28 May 1963, p. 25.

COPIES EXAMINED: CS (in jacket); QMMRB (in jacket).

## A96 HOW TO WRITE 1943

### A96a *American edition*:

Stephen Leacock | [ornamental rule; the next line in open type] | How To Write | [publisher's device of Dodd, Mead: oval containing open book and portrait of classical figure with leaves and company name] | [ornamental rule; the next two lines in open type] | Dodd, Mead & Company | New York 1943

◆ $1$–$17^8$ $18^2$. i–iv, v–vii, $1$–$5$, $1$–$261$, $1$–$3$ pp. (138 leaves). 185 × 130 mm.

CONTENTS: p. *i* half title; p. *ii* list of twenty-five books by Leacock, the first being *Literary Lapses* and the last *My Remarkable Uncle*; p. *iii* title; p. *iv* COPYRIGHT, 1943, | BY DODD, MEAD AND COMPANY, INC. | ALL RIGHTS RESERVED | NO PART OF THIS BOOK MAY BE REPRODUCED IN ANY FORM | WITHOUT PERMISSION IN WRITING FROM THE PUBLISHER | PRINTED IN THE UNITED STATES OF AMERICA; pp. v–vii preface dated October 1942; p. *1* blank; p. *2* table of contents; p. *3* blank; p. *4* fly title; p. *5* blank; pp. 1–258 text; pp. 259–261 index; pp. 1–3 blank.

TEXT: chapter I The Desire to Write; chapter II The Laws of Grammar and Free Speech; chapter III The Mystery and Magic of Words; chapter IV The Complete Thought Called a Sentence; chapter V The Art of Narration; chapter VI Good and Bad Language; chapter VII How to Write History; chapter VIII How to Write Historical Novels; chapter IX How Not to Write Poetry; chapter X How Not to Write More Poetry; chapter XI How to Write Humour; chapter XII How to Write More Humour.

BINDING AND DUST JACKET: Bound in bright red cloth. A solid rectangle is blind-stamped on the upper board. Within this rectangle are two raised rectangles. The following lines are in raised characters within the raised rectangles: HOW TO WRITE | [rule] | STEPHEN LEACOCK. Stamped in gilt on the spine: HOW | TO | WRITE | [ornamental rule] | LEACOCK | DODD, MEAD | & COMPANY.

The front and spine panels of the jacket are divided into three bands of green, dark green, and green (with dark green rules extending across the lower band). Printed on the front panel of the jacket in white: How | to | Write | STEPHEN | LEACOCK. Printed on the spine panel in white: How | to | Write | * | Leacock | DODD, MEAD | & COMPANY. The back panel and the flaps are white with green lettering. The back panel has a green photograph of Leacock in the upper left hand corner. To the right of this photograph are three lines: *Books by* | Stephen | Leacock. Quotations from reviews are printed below the photograph with the heading, LAUGH WITH LEACOCK. Seventeen other titles in two columns are also listed on the back panel. The front flap has a synopsis of the book with the price ($2.50). The back flap has a similar descriptive advertisement for *My Remarkable Uncle*. The last line on the back flap is: C–10–42 30C [oval with three lines, the first and last curved: PRINTED | IN | U.S.A.].

NOTES: On 28 March 1940, after having finished writing *The British Empire*, Leacock wrote to Frank C. Dodd with several proposals for books. One of these was entitled "How to Write English." Dodd told him on 1 April 1940:

> HOW TO WRITE ENGLISH: We are all enthusiastic over this idea and I do hope you will get to it soon. Doing it in your own way, I am sure it will be inimitable, and it ought to be very successful for young people. If you want our choice for the next book, that is it. . . .

Dodd hoped that Leacock would complete the manuscript in the fall in anticipation of publication early in 1941. The book was delayed, however, because Leacock took on several other writing commitments, in particular *Canada: The Foundations of Its Future*. He sent a copy of the latter to Dodd on 4 February 1941, and remarked: "I now propose to write a book How to Write." The contract with Dodd, Mead is dated 6 February 1941. Leacock received 15% royalty on all copies sold (including Canada), with an advance on publication date equal to the accrued royalties. Edward Dodd, Jr. was ready on 24 April 1941 to have a dust jacket prepared and to announce the book's publication, but on 27 April [1941], Leacock said that he could not possibly complete the book by the beginning of September.

In sending the manuscript to The Bodley Head on 11 September 1942, Leacock mentioned that the book would be published in New York in October 1942. Published 5 January 1943. Two copies were received by the Copyright Office at DLC on 5 January 1943; the copyright was registered on 8 January 1943 (A170169). The copyright was renewed by Stephen Lushington Leacock on 8 April 1970 (R482733).

By 1 February 1944 the book had accrued a royalty of $1,839.98 in American sales (approximately 4,907 copies at $.375 royalty per copy) and $412.65 in Canadian sales (917 copies at $.45 royalty per copy). Second printing, February 1943; third printing, April 1943; fourth printing, November 1943. There was also a reprinting in August 1948 of 500 copies.

A notebook at SLM (J105) entitled "How to Write English" contains 9 pp. of notes. On the first page of this notebook, Leacock stated: "Opening chapter based on Gregg *article*" (C39.50).

Leacock sent an autographed copy of the book to Lomer on 11 January 1943. He told Lomer that the book ". . . is like a favorite child to me because I wrote it purely to suit myself with no eye on editors or sales or the public." According to Lomer (p. 33), it was adopted in 1950 as a reference text in South Africa, and 1,500 copies were ordered for that purpose.

Excerpts from chapter I were reprinted as: "How to Tell a Story," *Senior Scholastic* 43, no. 16 (24–29 January 1944): 13–4; "How to Write" in George Sanderlin, *College Reading: A Collection of Prose, Plays, and Poetry* (Boston: D.C. Heath and Company, 1953), pp. 21–32; "Anybody Can Learn to Write" in Edward G. Linnehan and Paul W. Partridge, Jr., eds., *Readings in College Composition* (New York: Charles Scribner's Sons, 1954), vol. 1., p. 139; "Anybody Can Learn to Write" in Harrison Hayford and Howard P. Vincent, *Reader and Writer* (Boston: Houghton Mifflin Company, 1954), pp. 89–101 and (Boston: Houghton Mifflin Company, 1959), 2nd ed., pp. 109–13; "Good and Bad Language" in Leonard F. Dean and Kenneth G. Wilson, eds., *Essays on Language and Usage* (New York: Oxford University Press, 1959), pp. 309–19; and "Anybody Can Learn to Write," in C. Merton Babcock, *Ideas in Process* (Port Washington, N.Y.: Kennikat Press, 1971), pp. 28–37. Excerpts from chapters V and VIII appear in Douglas Daymond and Leslie Monkman, eds., *Canadian Novelists and the Novel* (Ottawa: Borealis Press, 1981), pp. 118–23.

COPIES EXAMINED: CS (first and fourth printings in jacket, price clipped); QMMRB (two copies, one in jacket).

### A96b *advertising leaflet for the Canadian market*:

[cover title] *Just Published* | [the next line in script] | *How To Write* | By STEPHEN LEACOCK | *Professor Emeritus, McGill University* | Author of NONSENSE NOVELS, MY REMARKABLE UNCLE, etc. | [text]

♦ Leaflet folded once to form four unnumbered pages. 229 × 152 mm.

CONTENTS: This leaflet consists of excerpts from Leacock's book preceded by introductory paragraphs or sentences to the excerpts. The excerpts have headings such as: TAKE A MONTH TO THINK; BURNING THE BOY ON THE DECK; and so on. The last lines on p. 4 are the following: [two rules] | *At all Booksellers, or from $3.00 per copy* | DODD, MEAD & COMPANY (LTD.) CANADA | 215 VICTORIA STREET, TORONTO | Printed in U. S. A.

BINDING. Light orange paper stock with watermark, *T&H Tru-Colour*.

NOTES: On 20 January 1943, R.T. Bond of Dodd, Mead wrote to Leacock: "In reply to your letter of January 16th, let us know what you want on the circular and we will be glad to make one up for you. I presume it could be used both in Canada and this country." The leaflet was apparently ready for distribution sometime before 29 March 1943.

COPIES EXAMINED: CS; SLM (many copies).

## A96c *English edition* (1944):

*HOW | TO WRITE | by | Stephen Leacock | London | JOHN LANE THE BODLEY HEAD*

♦ 1^8 2–14^8 [$1 signed]. 1–5, 6–48, 49, 50–223, 1 pp. (112 leaves). 184 × 121 mm.

CONTENTS: p. 1 half title; p. 2 list of thirty books by Leacock, the first being *Literary Lapses* and the last *My Remarkable Uncle*; p. 3 title; p. 4 *First published* 1944 | [illustration of a lion resting on top of an open book; the next four lines appearing on the pages of the book:] | BOOK | PRODUCTION | WAR ECONOMY | STANDARD | *This book is produced in* | *complete conformity with the* | *authorized economy standards* | Printed in Great Britain by | MORRISON AND GIBB LTD., LONDON AND EDINBURGH | for JOHN LANE THE BODLEY HEAD LIMITED | 8 BURY PLACE, LONDON W.C.I; p. 5 table of contents; pp. 6–8 preface dated "*October* 1942"; pp. 9–48, 49, 50–223 text; p. 1 blank.

TEXT: Identical to the American edition.

BINDING AND DUST JACKET: Bound in red cloth with stamping in black on the spine as follows: HOW | TO | WRITE | [remaining lines in script] *Stephen* | *Leacock* | *The* | *Bodley* | *Head*.

The dust jacket is light orange. The jacket was originally used for other books (original design for other books on the jacket's verso) and then re-used for *How to Write*. The front panel of the jacket is as follows: [the first three lines in shadowed typeface, outlined in black and red] HOW | TO | WRITE | [in red] ★ | [the next two lines similar to brush typeface] *STEPHEN | LEACOCK*. The spine of the jacket is similar to the book's spine, except that the first three lines are red. The back panel has an advertisement for *My Remarkable Uncle* within two red rectangles. On the front flap are three paragraphs about *How to Write* with the price on the last line in red: 8s. 6d. net. On the back flap are the lines: *Printed in Great Britain for* | *John Lane The Bodley Head Ltd.* The jacket was apparently issued with a glassine wrapper.

NOTES: C.J. Greenwood of The Bodley Head mailed the contract to Leacock on 21 November 1941 (15% royalty with an advance on the date of publication equal to the amount earned by subscription sales). Leacock sent the manuscript on 11 September 1942 with the proviso that The Bodley Head would not control Canadian rights or serial production, movie, television, and radio. According to Lomer (p. 33), the English edition was published on 14 September 1944. *The English Catalogue of Books* has a publication date of October 1944; the 4th impression of June 1940 is referred to as the "cheap edition." The copyright page of the 6th impression records reprints in 1945, 1946, 1950, 1951 (twice). Number of copies printed not known.

COPIES EXAMINED: CS (first and 1945 reprint in jacket; verso of jacket of the first printing is David Glass's *The Town*); EVANS (6th impression, 1951, in jacket); QMMRB (first impression in jacket, verso is Noel Carrington's *Design*).

## A96d *Indian edition* (1961):

HOW TO WRITE | STEPHEN LEACOCK | [publisher's device: wheel with spokes with J in the centre] | JAICO PUBLISHING HOUSE | BOMBAY — NEW DELHI — CALCUTTA — MADRAS

◆ F. N. 1–F. N. 3$^{16}$ F. N. 4$^{16}$ F. N. 5$^{16}$ F. N. 6$^{16}$ F. N. 7$^{16}$ [F. N. 4 and F. N. 6 $1 signed]. *1–7, 8–9, 10–11, 12–31, 32, 33–47, 48, 49–60, 61, 62–71, 72, 73–101, 102, 103–112, 113, 114–213, 1–11* pp. (112 leaves). 161 × 108 mm.

CONTENTS: p. *1* [three paragraphs which highlight the book's contents] | [rule] | JAICO [publisher's device] BOOKS | INDIA'S OWN POCKET EDITIONS; p. *2* PRICE (IN INDIA ONLY) Rs. 2.00 NET; p. *3* title; p. *4* *All rights reserved* | JAICO PUBLISHING HOUSE | [six lines concerning copyright] | Jaico Book Edition | February 1961 | Printed in India by | Rev. Theodore A. Pereira | The Examiner Press | Bombay 1 | Published by | Jaman H. Shah | Jaico Publishing House | 125, Mahatma Gandhi Road, Bombay 1; p. *5* table of contents; p. *6* blank; pp. *7, 8–9* Leacock's preface; p. *10* blank; pp. *11–213* text; pp. *1–10* description with press opinions of published books and a list of Jaico Books, J1 to J164; p. *11* large publisher's device with information within the device about Jaico Books.

TEXT: Identical to A96a.

BINDING: Stiff covers glued to sewn gatherings. The front cover has a colour illustration of a male student standing beside a blackboard with the title, author's name, and other words written on the blackboard. The spine and back panels of the covers are dark yellow. The first two lines on the back panel are: *Is Leacock a Humorist | or a Professor?* Also on the back panel are press opinions, the price, the publisher's device and name, and the name of the cover designer, Tanvir. The spine has the series number, J–156, along with the title, author's name, and that of the publisher.

COPIES EXAMINED: CS.

## A97 MY OLD COLLEGE, 1843–1943 1943

[the first line in red] "MY OLD COLLEGE" | [the next four lines in grey] 1843–1943 | BY STEPHEN LEACOCK | PRIVATELY PRINTED BY | THE AUTHOR ● 1943 | [two red bars]

◆ 1$^{8}$. *1, 2–16* pp. (8 leaves). 178 × 135 mm.

CONTENTS: p. *1* title; p. *2* blank except the running head in red at the bottom of the page (also found on all pages); p. *3* photograph in grey of Leacock with his signature in facsimile and some of his qualifications; p. 4 [all lines in grey] COPYRIGHT | Requests for permission to reprint | (free of charge) should be addressed | to The Graduates' Society, 3466 | University Street, Montreal, P.Q. | Printed in Canada; pp. 5–10 text; pp. 11–12 McGill University a Record; p. 13 Some Statistics on McGill University of Today; pp. 14–16 chronology related to the Graduates' Society of McGill University.

BINDING AND ENVELOPE: Bound in stiff white wrappers, wire-stitched. The front of the wrapper is mainly red (top and bottom white). Within the red section of the front wrapper: [the first two lines in white] MY | OLD COLLEGE | [illustration in grey and white of the top of McGill's Arts Building] | [to the right of the next three lines is an illustration of the shield and banner with motto of McGill University] | [next two lines in grey] 1843 | 1943 | [remaining lines in white] by | STEPHEN | LEACOCK. The back of the wrapper has a horizontal red band that extends down the right side. Inside the band is the McGill shield and below the band is a line in grey about the shield.

Issued in an envelope for mailing free to all McGill graduates. On the envelope printed in red: "MY OLD COLLEGE" [solid bar] | 1843 1943 | IF UNDELIVERED RETURN TO | STEPHEN LEACOCK | 3466 UNIVERSITY ST., MONTREAL | POSTAGE GUAR-ANTEED. In addition to Leacock's pamphlet, the envelope contains another envelope addressed to Leacock and two form letters: one from the president of the Graduates' Society of McGill University and the other addressed to Leacock, the latter with a perforated slip soliciting a donation of $3 from members of the Society.

NOTES: Leacock sent the manuscript (entitled "The Ungrateful Graduate") of his pamphlet to Gordon Glassco, the secretary of the Graduates' Society of McGill University, on 15 December 1942. He asked Glassco to make two copies and also to send him a proof in due course. He suggested to Glassco "that you arrange to have me make a *record* of this for broadcasting. You can then use it over the radio & at a function. The C.B.C. would charge nothing. I do not *broadcast* directly." The manuscript at QMMRB lacks pp. 11–16 of the pamphlet, which suggests that it was not compiled by Leacock.

See also "Leacock Aids McGill Drive Members Attracted to Graduates' Society," *Montreal Daily Star*, 20 March 1943, p. 3. This article discloses that "Hundreds of replies have come in following the sending out of the booklet...." See also A118 and I2. With an excerpt reprinted in K83.1, p. 70.

COPIES EXAMINED: CS (no envelope); OONL (no envelope); QMMRB (with envelope and enclosures); SLM (four copies, no envelope).


## A98  WHY STUDY ENGLISH?  1943

[cover title; three rules, each diminishing in length] | WHY STUDY ENGLISH? | [two rules] | STEPHEN LEACOCK | [insignia of the Canadian Legion; crown on top of a circular design with a maple leaf in the centre of the circle and the words BRITISH • EMPIRE • SERVICE • LEAGUE and the words CANADIAN LEGION] | CANADIAN LEGION EDUCATIONAL SERVICES | 27 GOULBURN AVE. | OTTAWA | June, 1943. | [three rules, each increasing in length]

◆ Leaflet folded once. 1, 2–4 pp. (2 leaves). 144 × 101 mm.

CONTENTS: p. *1* title; pp. 2–4 text. The last line on p. 4. is: STEPHEN LEACOCK.

BINDING: Printed on grey paper stock with black flecks.

NOTES: Reprinted from Leacock's article by the same name in the *Montreal Daily Star*, 20 April 1943, p. 10 (see C43.15). Number of copies printed not known.

COPIES EXAMINED: SLM (three copies).

## A99 HAPPY STORIES 1943

### A99a *first American edition*:

[ornamental rule] | HAPPY STORIES | JUST TO LAUGH AT | By | STEPHEN LEACOCK | NEW YORK | DODD, MEAD AND COMPANY | 1943 | [ornamental rule]

♦ $1$–$15^8$ $16^6$. *i–vi*, vii–viii, *1–2*, *1–240*, *1–2* pp. (126 leaves). 187 × 130 mm.

CONTENTS: p. *i* half title; p. *ii* list of fourteen books by Leacock, the first being *Literary Lapses* and the last *Our Heritage of Liberty*; p. *iii* title; p. *iv* COPYRIGHT, 1943 | BY DODD, MEAD AND COMPANY, INC. | ALL RIGHTS RESERVED | NO PART OF THIS BOOK MAY BE REPRODUCED IN ANY FORM | WITHOUT PERMISSION IN WRITING FROM THE PUBLISHER | PRINTED IN THE UNITED STATES OF AMERICA | BY THE CORNWALL PRESS, CORNWALL, N. Y.; p. *v* Leacock's preface; p. *vi* blank; pp. vii–viii table of contents; p. *1* fly title; p. *2* blank; pp. *1–240* text; pp. *1–2* blank.

TEXT: I Mr. McCoy Sails for Fiji; II Pawn to King's Four; III Impervious to Women; IV The Jones's Enchanted Castle; V Mr. Alcorn Improves Himself; VI Clouds That Rolled by: Mr. Alldone's Awful Day; VII Angel Pond, Lure of the North; VIII Cooking for Victory; IX Good News! A New Party!; X The Life of Lea and Perrins; XI A Morning Off; XII Mr. Plumter, B.A., Revisits the Old Shop; XIII Allegory Island; XIV Damon and Pythias, Barristers, Solicitors, etc.; XV Boom Times: The Mirage of a Better World, a Word of Preface.

XVI, which is entitled Mariposa Moves on, consists of the following: 1 The Happy Warrior; 2 National Debt, National Blessing; 3 The Sultan Speaks from the Grave; 4 Have You Got Even One Cent?; 5 The Righteous Indignation of Angus McCordell; 6 The Chairman's Walking Stick; 7 Going! Going! Gone!; 8 A New Heaven and a New Earth.

BINDING AND DUST JACKET: Two binding variants were examined: one in pale green cloth and the other in buff cloth, both with stamping in maroon. Stamped on the upper board as follows: [all lines in pale green within a solid rectangle, which itself is within two rectangles] | HAPPY STORIES | [rule] | STEPHEN LEACOCK. Stamped on the spine as follows: HAPPY | STORIES | [ornamental rule] | LEACOCK | DODD, MEAD | *&* COMPANY.

The front panel of the jacket has an illustration in red and white against a light blue background of Leacock's head encircled with books portrayed as people. Above the illustration in brown script: *Happy Stories | Just to Laugh at*. Below the illustration in brown: STEPHEN LEACOCK. Printed on the spine panel of the jacket: [the first four lines in brown, the first two lines in script] | *Happy* | *Stories* | STEPHEN | LEACOCK | [illustration in pale red of a book portrayed as a person] | [the next two lines in white] | DODD, MEAD | *&* COMPANY. The back panel has a blue photograph of Leacock in the upper left-hand corner. To the right of this photograph are three lines in red: *Books by* | Stephen | Leacock. Quotations from reviews are printed below the photograph in blue with the heading in red,

LAUGH WITH LEACOCK. Fourteen other titles in two columns are also listed on the back panel. Lettering on the flaps is printed in blue against a white background. The front flap reprints (with two new sentences at the end) the preface of the book with the price ($2.50). The back flap has an advertisement for *Laugh Parade*. The last line on the back flap is: C–9–43–69C [oval with three lines, the first and last curved: PRINTED | IN | U.S.A.].

NOTES: On 18 February 1943, Leacock wrote to Frank C. Dodd:

> I am chiefly interested in getting out a book of little stories, — not essays, but sketches each of which is a story; so much of the material is ready or half-ready. . . . I want to put the book out under a happy, catchy title with the word *Stories* in it . . . so it will mean *Stories* to make people glad, to take people out of themselves. . . . We could use the phrase *Happy Stories* as a stop-gap title.

He estimated that the book would be 60,000 words in length.

The contract with Dodd, Mead is dated 25 February 1943. Leacock agreed to deliver the manuscript by 1 August 1943, but due to serial publication of some of the stories, he wrote into the contract that publication was not to occur before 1 October 1943. He received a royalty of 15% on all copies sold, including those sold in Canada. By 9 March 1943 he had completed more than 40,000 words. The first section of the manuscript was received by Dodd, Mead on 7 July 1943, and the remainder was sent on 19 July 1943. Galleys were mailed to Leacock in August 1943, and an extra set of galleys was delivered at Leacock's request to Metro-Goldwyn Mayer Pictures on 19 August 1943.

For the promotion of the Canadian edition Leacock suggested that a circular of approximately 2,000 words with a print run of 4,000 copies would be prepared under his direction by his research secretary, Mrs. H.T. Shaw, for distribution to Montreal, Toronto and Ottawa. Dodd, Mead accepted his proposal of a special circular, and offered to print it for distribution in America as well. Leacock was to receive 10¢ extra royalty per book sold in the Canadian cities, and McClelland and Stewart was supposed to keep track of the Canadian sales. No copy of this circular is known to be extant. Lomer (p. 32) erroneously records an edition published by Dodd, Mead in Toronto.

The book was published on 12 November 1943. Leacock was sent his author's copies on 3 November 1943. Two copies were received by the Copyright Office at DLC on 12 November 1943; the copyright was registered on 17 November 1943 (A176845). The copyright was renewed by Stephen Lushington Leacock on 7 October 1971 (R514378). By 1 February 1944 the book had accrued a royalty of $2,176.50 in American sales (approximately 5,804 copies at $.375 royalty per copy) and $672.30 in Canadian sales (approximately 1,494 copies at $.45 royalty per copy).

The dates of other impressions are as follows: second printing December 1943; third printing January 1944; fourth February 1944; fifth printing May 1944; sixth printing August 1944; seventh printing March 1945; eight printing September 1945.

"Pawn to King's Four" reprinted in Jerome Salzmann, comp. *The Chess Reader* (New York: Greenburg, 1949), pp. 284–94.

COPIES EXAMINED: CS (first printing, both binding variants in jacket, with a second copy in pale green cloth without jacket; third and fifth printings in jacket); OTNY (first printing in jacket); QMMRB (first printing in jacket); SLM (eighth printing, no jacket).

**A99b** *second American edition* [1944?]

[all lines, except the last one, within two rectangles; a vertical rule separates the title-page section from copyright information; to the right of the rule:] HAPPY | STORIES | JUST TO LAUGH AT | *by Stephen Leacock* | *Editions for the Armed Services, Inc.* | A NON-PROFIT ORGANIZATION ESTABLISHED BY | THE COUNCIL ON BOOKS IN WARTIME. NEW YORK | [to the left of the vertical rule] PUBLISHED BY ARRANGEMENT WITH | DODD, MEAD AND COMPANY, INC. | NEW YORK | *All rights reserved. no part of* | *this book may be reproduced in* | *any form without permission* | *in writing from the publisher* | COPYRIGHT, 1943 | BY DODD, MEAD AND COMPANY, INC. | [outside of the rectangles] L-10

◆ 1–7, 2–279, 1–3 pp. (144 leaves). 89 × 140 mm.

CONTENTS: p. *1* title; p. *2 Manufactured in the United States of America*; p. *3* (designated as iii in table of contents) preface; p. *4* blank; p. *5–6* table of contents; pp. *1, 2–279, 1* text; p. *2–3* biographical information on Leacock.

TEXT: Identical to A99a.

BINDING: Bound in stiff paper, wire-stabbed. The front cover is mainly light blue with a yellow band at the bottom (these coloured sections extend to the spine). The blue section of the cover has a photograph of the Dodd, Mead edition and to the bottom left of the photo within a solid red circle is the following in white: ARMED | SERVICES | EDITION. To the right of the photo is the following: [the first four lines in white, the first three in script] *Happy Stories,* | *Just to Laugh at* | *by* | STEPHEN LEACOCK | [seven lines about the Editions for the Armed Services]. Printed on the yellow band: THIS IS THE COMPLETE BOOK — NOT A DIGEST. The verso of the front cover has information on the Armed Services Editions with their logo.

The title and Leacock's name are printed down the spine in the blue section. Printed at the bottom of the spine in the yellow band: L | 10. On the back of the wrapper is a red rectangular border, yellow inside the border, with white stars inside the border. Printed within the border is: Leacock's preface in two columns with a few new lines added at the end; and four lines about this edition. On the verso of the back cover is a list of thirty-two books published by the Editions for the Armed Services, Inc. (L–1 to L–32).

NOTES: In the biographical information on Leacock after the text, reference is made to his death in 1944. This edition was, therefore, published after 28 March 1944 during the Second World War for distribution to American soldiers overseas. For general information on these editions, see *Editions for the Armed Services, Inc.: A History Together with the Complete List of 1324 Books Published for American Armed Forces Overseas* (New York: Editions for the Armed Services, Inc., [1948]). At least 40,000 to 50,000 copies were printed of the Armed Services Edition of *Happy Stories Just to Laugh at.*

COPIES EXAMINED: DLC; OTUTF.

**A99c** *English edition* (1945):

*HAPPY* | *STORIES* | *— just to Laugh at* | *by* | *Stephen Leacock* | *London* | JOHN LANE THE BODLEY HEAD

◆ $1^8$ 2–13$^8$ [$1 signed]. *1*–4, 5–207, *1* pp. (108 leaves). 184 × 122 mm.

CONTENTS: p. *1* half title; p. *2* list of thirty-one books by Leacock published by The Bodley Head, the first being *Literary Lapses* the last *How to Write*; p. *3* title; p. *4* *First published 1945* | [the next four lines within an illustration of an open book which has a lion at the top of the book] | BOOK | PRODUCTION | WAR ECONOMY | STANDARD | *This book is produced in* | *complete conformity with the* | *authorized economy standards* | Printed in Great Britain by | MORRISON AND GIBB LTD., LONDON AND EDINBURGH | for JOHN LANE THE BODLEY HEAD LIMITED | 8 BURY PLACE LONDON W.C.1; p. *5* table of contents; p. *6* Leacock's preface dated "*October 1943*"; pp. 7–207 text; p. *1* blank.

TEXT: The English edition omits the sketch, "A Morning Off" but has an additional one entitled "L'Envoi: The England I Remember," placed at the end.

BINDING AND DUST JACKET: Bound in pale yellow cloth with stamping in red on the spine as follows: [the first two lines at an angle] | HAPPY | STORIES | ★ | *Stephen* | *Leacock* | THE | BODLEY | HEAD.

The jacket is tan coloured with lettering primarily in blue and to a lesser extent in red. Printed on the front panel, the first two lines and the last two at a slight angle: HAPPY | STORIES | [three red stars on a diagonal] | STEPHEN | LEACOCK. Printed on the spine of the jacket: [the first two lines down the spine, the second under the first] | STEPHEN | LEACOCK | ★ | [down the spine in red] HAPPY STORIES | ★ | THE | BODLEY | HEAD. The back panel of the jacket has an advertisement for *Our Heritage of Liberty*. The front flap has a synopsis of *Happy Stories*. Printed on the bottom part of the back flap: *Printed in Great Britain for* | *John Lane The Bodley Head.*

The jacket for *Happy Stories* was recycled. Two different versos of the jacket were examined: one for *An English Treasury of Religious Prose* selected and arranged by J. Lewis May; and the other concerning Ernst Toller's *I Was a German*.

NOTES: The contract in the Nimmo collection at NAC is undated; the contract at READ (The Bodley Head fonds) is dated 19 June 1943. Leacock was to receive "Fifteen per cent (15%) of the published price on all copies sold, with an advance on publication of the amount earned by the subscription sales." The book was priced at 7s 6d. The contract gave The Bodley Head the right to consider for publication Leacock's next literary work. Lomer (p. 32) has a publication date of 19 October 1945, which is confirmed by *The English Catalogue of Books*. Price 7s 6d. Number of copies printed not known.

COPY EXAMINED: CS (in jacket with May verso); OTNY (in jacket with Toller verso).


## A100  A LETTER FROM DR. LEACOCK ON "THE DUKE"  1943

[cover title: the first letter is a swash character] *A LETTER* | FROM | [black-and-white photograph of Leacock (circa 1910) within three brown squares] | DR. LEACOCK | ON | "*THE DUKE*" | BY | RICHARD ALDINGTON

◆ Leaflet folded once to form four unnumbered pages. 203 × 138 mm.

CONTENTS: p. *1* cover title; p. *2* engraving in brown of Wellington's head and upper torso; p. *3* Leacock's letter, dated *Montreal, November 11, 1943* and addressed to Mr. Burton, with Leacock's signature in facsimile; p. *4* "*THE DUKE*" | by | RICHARD ALDINGTON

| [brown ornament] | PRICE $4.75 | [brown ornament].

BINDING: Issued on off-white paper stock.

NOTES: Issued as a leaflet for promotional purposes by the bookseller, Harry Burton of Burton's Ltd. of Montreal. Number of copies printed not known. Aldington's book, which won the James Tait Memorial Prize, is entitled *The Duke: Being an Account of the Life & Achievements of Arthur Wellesley, 1st Duke of Wellington*. See C43.40 for the publication of Leacock's letter in the *Montreal Gazette*.

COPIES EXAMINED: QMMRB.

## A101 MEMORIES OF CHRISTMAS 1943

𝔐emories of 𝔠hristmas | BY | STEPHEN LEACOCK | [illustration within an oval of a pine tree and three stars] | 1943 | PRIVATELY PRINTED | CHARLES BUSH LIMITED | WINNIPEG TORONTO MONTREAL

◆ $1^2$ $2-6^4$ $7^2$. $1-12$, $1-29$, $1-3$ pp. (22 leaves). Actually 24 leaves since leaves at either end are glued to the free endpapers. $153 \times 145$ mm.

CONTENTS: pp. *1–4* blank; p. *5* half title 𝔐emories of 𝔠hristmas | [cluster of many different stars in the shape of a triangle]; p. 6 blank; p. 7 title; p. 8 COPYRIGHT BY | DODD MEAD & COMPANY INC. | ALL RIGHTS RESERVED | We appreciate the co-operation | of McClelland & Stewart Ltd., | Canadian representatives of the | United States' publishers.; p. 9 GREETINGS | ★ | [three paragraphs in italics on the war and the Christmas season] | WILFRID C. KETTLEWELL | DECEMBER | NINETEEN-FORTY-THREE | TORONTO; p. *10* blank; p. *11* THE AUTHOR | ★ | [three paragraphs, the first two on Leacock, the last on the two Christmas essays which have been selected from *My Remarkable Uncle*]; p. *12* blank; pp. *1–29* text; pp. *1–3* blank.

TEXT: Christmas Shopping; War-Time Santa Claus.

BINDING AND DUST JACKET: Bound in purple boards, quarter-bound with silver cloth. Lettering and illustration on upper board in silver identical to the half title. Covered in a tissue wrapper. Dark purple endpapers.

NOTES: On 4 June 1943, Frank C. Dodd informed Leacock that "a certain Mr. Wilfred [sic] Kettlewell has asked permission to print two chapters from MY REMARKABLE UNCLE. . . . He is willing, of course, to pay a small royalty; and wants to print 600 copies." The royalty was 15%. On 23 June 1943, George Stewart of Dodd, Mead & Company (Canada) Limited also sought Leacock's permission on Kettlewell's behalf. The booklet was to be issued for Kettlewell's "own personal use, to give away as Christmas gifts." Stewart asked Leacock "if at the same time we could print up an extra number and sell them for .50¢ or .75¢, on which we would naturally allow you the usual 15% royalty" (no copy of the latter is known to be extant). Charles Bush Limited made a similar entreaty to Leacock on 14 July 1943. To all these requests Leacock gave his permission to proceed. In his account book (J3) at SLM, Leacock recorded that he received $75 from Kettlewell on 22 December 1943.

COPIES EXAMINED: CS; OTNY; QMMRB.

## A102 WHILE THERE IS TIME 1945

*While There Is Time* | [heavy rule] | The Case Against Social Catastrophe | *by* | STEPHEN LEACOCK | [rule] | McCLELLAND & STEWART, Limited | Publishers Toronto

◆ $1-9^8$. $1-8$, $1-136$ pp. (72 leaves). $203 \times 131$ mm.

CONTENTS: p. *1* half title; p. *2* blank; p. *3* title; p. *4* Copyright, Canada, 1945 | McCLEL-LAND & STEWART, LIMITED | *Printed in Canada* | by | THE HUNTER-ROSE CO. LIMITED | Toronto; p. *5* preface; p. *6* blank; p. *7* table of contents; p. *8* blank; pp. *1–136* text.

TEXT: chapter I The Gathering Crisis; chapter II Private Enterprise; chapter III The Utopia of Socialism; chapter IV Socialism in the Concrete; chapter V Escape; chapter VI To Develop Canada; chapter VII Provinces and Races; chapter VIII Canada and the Outside World.

BINDING AND DUST JACKET: Bound in dark brown buckram with cream-coloured letter-ing. Stamped on the upper board: WHILE THERE IS TIME | [rule] | STEPHEN LEACOCK. Stamped on the spine: WHILE | THERE | IS | TIME | • | LEACOCK | McCLELLAND | & STEWART.

   The front and spine panels of the jacket are brown and cream-coloured with a solid, blue rectangular compartment. On the front panel of the jacket: [illustration of birds outside the compartment with the first three lines, cream coloured, and within the compartment] | WHILE | THERE IS | TIME | [the next line in blue] STEPHEN LEACOCK | [illustration of a sun dial]. On the spine panel: [the first six lines, cream-coloured, within the compartment] | WHILE | THERE | IS | TIME | ★ | LEACOCK | [the next two lines cream coloured] | McCLELLAND | & STEWART. The back panel and flaps of the jacket, which are cream-coloured with blue lettering, describe the contents of Leacock's book with excerpts.

NOTES: On 27 January 1944, Leacock informed F. Cleveland Morgan: ". . . I am a very sick man. . . . Meantime th[e] doctors say that it is good for me to keep up such work as interests me without fatigue. At present I am working to finish a small book on *The Case against Social Catastrophe* which may have a wide national influence" (letter at QMMRB). In the preface to this posthumous publication, Leacock credits some of his ideas taken from previous works — notably, *Afternoons in Utopia* and *The Unsolved Riddle of Social Justice*; he acknowledges that "the concluding chapters" make ". . . use also of articles recently contributed by me to the Toronto *Financial Post*" (see C43.42–5, C44.3–5, C44.7–9) which appeared in nine chapters between 4 December 1943 and 5 February 1944). The contract in the Barbara Nimmo collection at NAC between herself and McClelland and Stewart is dated 4 January 1945: 15% royalty, 10% on paper covered editions, 10% on reprints or cheaper editions. According to a statement of royalties owing to Leacock at the time of his death at SLM, Raymond T. Bond of Dodd, Mead arranged for the book with Leacock, and the manuscript was due on 16 February 1944. The Leacock estate received $500 for receipt of the manuscript in June 1944. A brief table of contents indicates that it contained 22,265 words. The book sold for $2. Exact date of publication and number of copies sold not known. There was no American edition.

COPIES EXAMINED: CS (two copies in jacket); OTNY (in jacket); QMMRB (in jacket).

## A103 LAST LEAVES 1945

### A103a *American edition*:

[row of leaves] | STEPHEN LEACOCK | [the next line in tool type and swash characters] | *LAST LEAVES* | NEW YORK | DODD, MEAD *&* COMPANY | 1945 | [row of leaves]

◆ 1–15⁸. i–vi, vii–xxi, 1–5, 3–31, 32–34, 35–75, 76–78, 79–107, 108–110, 111–130, 131–132, 133–162, 163–164, 165–213, 1–3 pp. (120 leaves). 202 × 139 mm.

CONTENTS: p. *i* half title; p. *ii* list of thirteen books written by Leacock, the first being *Literary Lapses* and the last *Last Leaves*; p. *iii* title; p. *iv* COPYRIGHT, 1945, | BY DODD, MEAD AND COMPANY, INC. | ALL RIGHTS RESERVED | NO PART OF THIS BOOK MAY BE REPRODUCED IN ANY FORM | WITHOUT PERMISSION IN WRITING FROM THE PUBLISHER | ★ ★ ★ | THIS BOOK IS COMPLETE AND UNABRIDGED. IT IS | MANUFACTURED UNDER WARTIME CONDITIONS IN CON- | FORMITY WITH GOVERNMENT REGULATIONS CONTROL- | LING THE USE OF PAPER AND OTHER MATERIALS | PRINTED IN THE UNITED STATES OF AMERICA; p. *v* acknowledgments; p. *vi* blank; pp. vii–xx preface by Barbara Nimmo, "Stephen Leacock (December 30, 1869 — March 28, 1944)"; p. xxi table of contents; p. *1* blank; p. *3* fly title; pp. 4–5, 3–213 text (pp. *5, 32, 34, 76, 78, 108, 110, 132,* and *164* blank); pp. *1–3* blank.

TEXT: The text consists of six parts. Part I: Are Witty Women Attractive to Men?; Living with Murder; What Can Izaak Walton Teach Us?; A Lecture on Walking; Good-bye, Motor Car! Part II: Common Sense and the Universe; An Apology for the British Empire; Britain and Canada: Old Phases and New; Generals I Have Trained. Part III: The Business of Prophecy; Rebuilding the Cities; Casting Out Animosity; Woman's Level; The School Is the Lever; To Every Child. Part IV: Gold; Can We Beat Inflation?. Part V: Uncle Sam, Good Neighbour: An Allegory; All Right, Mr. Roosevelt (Canada and the United States). Part VI: Alice Walks in Wonderland; Gilbert's "Bab" Ballads.

BINDING AND DUST JACKET: Bound in red cloth. Blind-stamped on the upper board as follows: [the first line in calligraphic-style type, the last two lines in stencil type] | Last Leaves | STEPHEN | LEACOCK. Stamped in gilt on the spine as follows: [the first line down the spine, the first two words in calligraphic-style type] | Last Leaves STEPHEN LEACOCK | DODD, MEAD | & COMPANY.

The dust jacket is off-white with brown lettering on the back of the jacket and the flaps. The front panel has a list of the sketches and essays in alternating, red and blue lines, a photograph of Leacock's face to the right of these lines, and the following three lines in brown over the lines of the list: [in calligraphic-style type] Last Leaves | [the next two lines in stencil type at an angle] | STEPHEN | LEACOCK. The spine panel of the jacket, in blue and brown words, is similar to the stamping on the spine of the cloth. The back panel has a photograph of Leacock in brown, two excerpts from reviews, and a list of other books by Leacock published by Dodd, Mead. The front flap provides a synopsis of *Last Leaves*, while the back flap features an advertisement (price included) for *Happy Stories Just to Laugh at*. The last line of the back flap is as follows: C 3–45 58C [oval with three lines, the first and last curved: PRINTED | IN | U.S.A.].

NOTES: Towards the end of his life (22 February 1944) when he tried to finish his autobiography, Leacock gathered together some manuscripts of sketches which he labelled

"Barbara's Book." His intention was that his niece, Barbara Nimmo, would oversee the publication of the book after his death.

The contract for this book between Dodd, Mead and Mrs. Nimmo, is dated 25 October 1944. The royalty was 10% on the first 2,500 copies, 12½% on the next 2,500 copies, and 15% thereafter. There also was an advance royalty of $250 payable to Mrs. Nimmo on demand. Dodd, Mead paid Doubleday, Doran and Co. $100 for the right to use "Alice Walks in Wonderland" and "Gilbert's *Bab Ballads*." Although the planned publication was April–May 1945, the book was published on 25 September 1945 (copyright registration number A190108 at DLC). The copyright was renewed by Dodd, Mead on 13 September 1973 (R558896). Reprinted January 1946. Mrs. Nimmo received a royalty cheque from Dodd, Mead for $93.50 in May 1952. Consequently, the book was still in print at that time. Number of copies printed not known.

The Bodley Head Ltd. inquired about a British issue on 18 March 1947. The Bodley Head apparently paid Dodd, Mead £30 for a photographic reprint of the book. No copy of this issue is known to be extant.

COPIES EXAMINED: CS (first and second printings in jacket); QMMRB (second printing, not in jacket).

## A103a.1 *Canadian issues*:

[row of leaves] | STEPHEN LEACOCK | [the next line in tool type and swash characters] | *LAST LEAVES* | McCLELLAND *&* STEWART LIMITED | TORONTO, CANADA | [row of leaves]

There are two Canadian issues. The leaves of both issues measure 202 × 133 mm. The issues can be differentiated in the following respects. (1) On the verso of the title leaf of the American edition, the last line reads: PRINTED IN THE UNITED STATES OF AMERICA. In the first Canadian issue this line has been omitted. In the second issue the last line in the American edition has been replaced by: PRINTED IN CANADA. | WRIGLEY PRINTING COMPANY LIMITED | 578 SEYMOUR STREET, VANCOUVER, B.C. (2) The paper stock of the issues is different. The sheets of the second issue are much thicker than those of the first issue.

BINDING AND DUST JACKET: The binding of the first Canadian issue is simulated, dark brown leather (i.e. paper boards), blind-stamped on the upper board as the American edition, with gilt lettering on the spine similar to the American edition except that DODD, MEAD | & COMPANY has been replaced by McClelland | & Stewart. The binding of the second issue is a lighter shade of brown, and the imprint on the spine reads McCLELLAND | & STEWART.

The dust jackets of both Canadian issues are identical. They are similar to their American counterpart, but the colour is a much brighter white. On the spine panel DODD, MEAD | & COMPANY is replaced by McCLELLAND | & STEWART. The back panel of the Canadian jacket does not have a photograph of Leacock, and the first three lines read: ★ [hand-written at an angle] *Books by* | [hand-written at an angle] *Stephen Leacock* | ★ |. Also the last line on the back panel is: McCLELLAND & STEWART LIMITED – TORONTO. In addition to McClelland and Stewart's name on the flaps of the Canadian jacket, the flaps bear certain differences in terms of typography and the omission of features such as the price of *Happy Stories Just to Laugh at*.

NOTES: There is a memorandum of agreement between Dodd, Mead and McClelland and Stewart dated 9 May 1945. On 26 July 1945, Dodd, Mead shipped a set of electrotype plates to McClelland and Stewart for the Canadian issue. McClelland and Stewart paid for one-half of the cost of the manufacture of the plates ($456.28), and were required to pay Dodd, Mead a royalty of 15% on all copies sold of the Canadian issue. McClelland and Stewart paid Dodd, Mead $799.62 on 19 February 1946. Number of copies printed not known.

COPIES EXAMINED: CS (both issues in jacket); OTNY (both issues in jacket); QMMRB (second issue in jacket).

A103a.2 *Canadian issue — photographic reprint* (1970):

[rule] | *Stephen Leacock* | [rule] | *Last Leaves* | [rule] | INTRODUCTION: J. M. ROBINSON | GENERAL EDITOR: MALCOLM ROSS | *New Canadian Library No. 69* | [publisher's device; abstract design of a person on a chariot, taking aim with a bow and arrow] | *McClelland and Stewart Limited* | TORONTO/MONTREAL

◆ i–iv, v–xxv, *1*, 3–31, *32–34*, 35–75, *76–78*, 79–107, *108–110*, 111–130, *131–132*, 133–162, *163–164*, 165–213, *1–3* pp. (120 leaves). 183 × 109 mm.

CONTENTS: p. *i* half title; p. *ii* blank; p. *iii* title; p. *iv* Copyright © McClelland and Stewart Limited, 1970 | Introduction © McClelland and Stewart Limited, 1970 | ALL RIGHT RESERVED | [six lines regarding copyright permission] | *The Canadian Publishers* | McClelland and Stewart Limited | 25 Hollinger Road, Toronto 374 | Printed and bound in Canada by | T. H. Best Printing Company Limited; p. v table of contents; pp. vi–xii introduction by J.M. Robinson, dated August 1969; pp. xiii–xxv, *1*, 3–213 identical to A103 photographically reprinted; pp. *1–2* list of titles in the New Canadian Library series; p. *3* biographical information about Leacock.

BINDING: Perfect bound, stiff paper covers, predominantly yellow but with orange, black, and white compartments. Cover design by Frank Loconte. Abstract design on the front cover.

NOTES: Published on 28 February 1970. New Canadian Library N 69. $1.95. By the end of 1970 2,077 copies had sold. By the end of 1979 9,900 copies had sold (information based on file 14, "New Canadian Library," box 93, series A, part I, McClelland and Stewart fonds, OHM).

COPIES EXAMINED: CS; SLM (reprint by Webcom Limited, [198?]).

## A104 THE BOY I LEFT BEHIND ME 1946

A104a *American edition*:

[illustration of leaves] | [all lines within two rectangles with illustrations of leaves at the bottom corners] *THE BOY I LEFT* | *BEHIND ME* | by | Stephen Leacock | DOUBLEDAY & COMPANY, INC. | *Garden City 1946 New York*

◆ 1–12^8. *1–12*, 9–43, *44–46*, 47–101, *102–104*, 105–148, *149–150*, 151–184, *1–4* pp. (96 leaves). 180 × 122 mm.

CONTENTS: pp. *1–2* blank; p. *3* half title; p. *4* list of thirty other books by Leacock, the first being *Montreal* and the last *Elements of Political Science*; p. *5* title; p. *6* COPYRIGHT, 1946, BY MAY SHAW | ALL RIGHTS RESERVED | PRINTED IN THE UNITED STATES | AT | THE COUNTRY LIFE PRESS, GARDEN CITY, N.Y. | FIRST EDITION; p. *7* publisher's note; p. *8* blank; p. *9* table of contents; p. *10* blank; pp. *11–12, 9–184* text (pp. *12, 44, 46, 102, 104,* and *150* blank); pp. *1–4* blank.

TEXT: There Will Always Be an England; Life on the Old Farm; My Education and What I Think of It Now; Teaching School.

BINDING AND DUST JACKET: Bound in wine cloth with lettering in gilt stamped on the spine as follows: STEPHEN | LEACOCK | [leafy rule] | THE BOY | I LEFT | BEHIND | ME | [leafy rule] | DOUBLEDAY.

The front and spine panels of the jacket are grey with pinkish brown and green illustrations. On the front panel: STEPHEN LEACOCK | [illustration of a farm] | [thick rule] | [the next six lines within a solid green rectangle, the first five lines in white] THE | BOY | I LEFT | BEHIND | ME | *The great humorist's own story of his early years* | [thick rule] | [on the left, illustration of a woman in a chair reading to three children; on the right, illustration of buildings and trees]. Printed on the spine panel: [rule] | [the next five lines in white within a solid green rectangle] THE | BOY | I LEFT | BEHIND | ME | [rule] | STEPHEN | LEACOCK | DOUBLEDAY. On the back panel is a photograph taken by Karsh of Leacock seated at his writing desk in his home at Orillia, ON. The flaps of the jacket are white. The front flap has a synopsis of Leacock's memoirs. The first two lines are: T.B.I.L.B. M. | *Price*, $2.00. The last line of the front flap is: 4767–45. On the back flap is an advertisement for Ernst Lothar's *The Door Opens*.

NOTES: As early as 30 August 1935, the British American Newspaper Services suggested that Leacock should write a series of autobiographical articles with titles such as "My Ghastly Youth," "My Rise to Dizzying Fame," and "The Inside Dope on the Professor Racket." A similar appeal came from Leacock's publisher, Frank C. Dodd. In a short-hand note written in September of that year, Leacock observed: "My life is I think uninteresting to other people but I think I can make it interesting. I would write the stuff in an imaginative way not exactly a funny book but an easy book to read. . . ." He planned to write a "humorous & wise book", "not *comic* not *celebrities*." He wanted to delay his autobiography, but nevertheless asked Dodd for 15% royalty up to 10,000 copies, 20% thereafter. On 31 October 1935, he told Dodd that he was not interested in writing "a comic life." Dodd replied on 20 November 1935, expressing the hope that Leacock's autobiography would ". . . develop in due course."

Leacock received further encouragement from Dodd on 15 August 1941, who told him: "I am enthusiastically of the opinion that your own autobiography, written now, is a book which you not only owe to the public but which would bring you worth while returns." Thomas B. Costain of Doubleday, Doran made a similar overture on 21 August 1941. On the same day that Costain attempted to gain Leacock's interest in the project, Leacock signed a contract with Dodd, Mead for "Recollections and Reflections: An Autobiography" (copy in Dodd, Mead fonds at OHM and at SLM): 15% royalty on all copies sold (including Canada) with an advance on publication date equal to the accrued royalty earnings up to the date of publication. In signing the contract, Leacock added: "I should not wish to publish this till the war is over as I think it would attract more attention in a quieter world."

Leacock did not start writing his autobiography until September 1943. He approached Jacques Chambrun, who had arranged for the publication of "My Remarkable Uncle" in *Reader's Digest*, to serialize "Recollections and Reflections" in the United States. Dodd asked Leacock on 10 November 1943: "Aren't we going to have the Autobiography for 1944?" By this time, however, Leacock was a very sick man. On 22 February 1944, a few weeks before he had an operation for throat cancer, he sent the first instalment, "There Will Always Be an England," to his agent, Paul R. Reynolds: "I am beginning a series of *My Memories* for use presently as a book," he told Reynolds. "For magazine use they could carry the subtitle *Fragments of Autobiography*. My advanced age & the condition of my health makes [sic] this uncertain." Reynolds offered Leacock's memoirs to the *Atlantic Monthly* and *Harper's*, but both magazines turned down publication (information based on the Reynolds fonds at COL).

The second contract for the book with Dodd, Mead (in the Nimmo collection at NAC) is dated 10 March 1944, less than three weeks before Leacock's death on 28 March 1944. The contract is for a book of not less than 50,00 words entitled "My Memories (My Earlier Life)." It covered the rights in the United States and Canada and gave Leacock a royalty of 15% and an advance of $500 against royalties on delivery of the completed manuscript. Leacock authorized Dodd, Mead to make all royalty payments to Mrs. H.T. (May) Shaw.

Given the commitments in these previous contracts, it is unclear why Dodd, Mead did not publish Leacock's autobiography. His death and the unfinished state of the work may have nullified the contract. On 12 December 1944, Costain informed Mrs. Shaw:

> We have decided definitely to publish MEMORIES separately first under the title "The Boy I Left Behind Me" and we will probably make an announcement to that effect shortly. Whether the book can be published next year or not is still undecided as we are not sure how much paper we are going to have. I think, however, that we will try to get it into our 1945 schedule.

The American edition was published on 24 January 1946. Copies were received by the Copyright Office at DLC on 4 and 26 January 1946; the copyright was registered by Mrs. Shaw (A774). The copyright was renewed by Stephen Lushington Leacock on 16 April 1973 (R547689). Number of copies printed not known.

Excerpts are contained in "Stephen Leacock" in Margaret J. Miller, *Seven Men of Wit* (London: Hutchinson, 1960), pp. 157–72; M.G. Hesse, *Childhood and Youth in Canadian Literature* (Toronto: Macmillan of Canada, 1979), pp. 17–8.

COPIES EXAMINED: CS (in jacket); QMMRB (not in jacket).

## A104b *English edition* (1947):

[swelled rule] | The Boy I Left | Behind Me | [swelled rule] | STEPHEN LEACOCK | THE BODLEY HEAD • LONDON

♦ A–G$^{16}$ [$1 signed, fifth leaf of A gathering signed A*]. 1–6, 7–15, 16, 17–224 pp. (112 leaves). 182 × 119 mm. Frontispiece photograph taken by Karsh of Leacock laughing with a straw hat in his hand.

CONTENTS: p. *1* half title; p. *2* list of thirty-one books by Leacock, the first being *Literary Lapses* and the last *Happy Stories*; p. *3* title; p. *4* *First published 1947* | [three lines concerning copyright] | *Printed in Great Britain by* | BUTLER AND TANNER LTD.,

FROME, SOMERSET | *for* JOHN LANE THE BODLEY HEAD LTD. | 8 BURY PLACE, LONDON, W.C.1; p. *5* table of contents; p. *6* blank; pp. *7–15* "Stephen Leacock (December 30, 1869 — March 28, 1944) A Personal Note" by Barbara Nimmo; p. *16* blank; pp. *17–224* text.

TEXT: Leacock's text consists of two parts and an epilogue. Part One, entitled Some Chapters of Autobiography, has the same four sections (numbered 1 through 4) of Leacock's unfinished autobiography that are published in the American edition. Part Two, entitled A Last Miscellany, is comprised of ten essays or sketches: 1 Are Witty Women Attractive to Men?; 2 Living with Murder; 3 What Can Izaak Walton Teach Us?; 4 Andrew Macphail; 5 Gilbert's "Bab" Ballads; 6 Common Sense and the Universe; 7 A Plea for Geographical Science; 8 An Apology for the British Empire; 9 Britain and Canada; 10 The Business of Prophecy. The Epilogue reprints an essay from *My Remarkable Uncle* entitled Three Score and Ten — the Business of Growing Old.

BINDING AND DUST JACKET: Bound in yellowish green cloth with lettering in gilt. Stamped on the upper board: THE BOY I LEFT BEHIND ME. Stamped on the spine: Stephen | Leacock | [down the spine] The Boy I Left Behind Me | The | Bodley | Head.

There are two variant dust jackets. (1) The earlier jacket is black and white with a photograph of Leacock on the front panel (identical to the frontispiece). There are ads on the back panel for E.M. Almedingen's *Tomorrow Will Come* and *The Almond Tree* and for Clifton Reynolds's *Autobiography*, a synopsis of the book on the front flap along with the price (8s 6d), and information on the National Book League on the back flap. (2) The second jacket (from the "cheap edition" issued in January 1952) is orange with black lettering, and has a protective glassine wrapper. On the front panel of the jacket: STEPHEN LEACOCK | [the next three lines in orange, slanted, and within a solid black ornamental oval] THE BOY | I LEFT | BEHIND ME | STEPHEN LEACOCK. Lines are printed down the spine except for the last three lines (the publisher's name): STEPHEN | [the next line under and to the right of the previous line] | LEACOCK | [the next line (the title) in orange within a solid black ornamental oval] | The Boy I Left Behind Me | The | Bodley | Head. The back panel lists cheap editions published by The Bodley Head. The front flap features a synopsis of the book. On the back flap is a list of other cheap editions written by Leacock, each priced at 6s net.

NOTES: There are two contracts with The Bodley Head. The terms are similar to those agreed by Dodd, Mead. The first contract (copy at SLM) for "Recollections and Reflections" was sent to Leacock by C.J. Greenwood on 21 November 1941 (15% royalty with an advance on the date of publication equal to the amount earned by subscription sales). The second contract between Leacock and The Bodley Head for a book entitled "My Memories — Fragments of Autobiography" is undated (probably 1944, copy in Nimmo's papers at NAC). The book was to consist of 50,000 words or thereabouts and to be priced at 8s 6d. Leacock agreed to a royalty of 15% with an advance against royalties of £50 on the delivery of the typescript. He assigned the copyright in the English edition to Mrs. Shaw. The contract gave The Bodley Head the right to consider for publication Leacock's next literary work. *The English Catalogue of Books* has November 1947 as the date of publication. Price 8s 6d. Number of copies printed not known.

COPIES EXAMINED: CS (two copies, each with a different jacket); EVANS ("cheap edition" in jacket).

## A105 THE LEACOCK ROUNDABOUT 1946

THE LEACOCK | ROUNDABOUT | A TREASURY OF | THE BEST WORKS |
OF | STEPHEN LEACOCK | NEW YORK | DODD, MEAD & COMPANY |
1946

◆ $1-12^{16}$ $13^8$ $14^{16}$. *i–iv*, v–vii, *1–3*, 1–8, *9–10*, 11–47, *48–50*, 51–83, *84–86*, 87–126, *127–128*,
*129–184*, *185–186*, 187–232, *233–234*, 235–276, *277–278*, 279–375, *376–378*, 379–422 pp. (216
leaves). 203 × 139 mm.

CONTENTS: p. *i* half title; p. *ii* list of twenty-nine books by Leacock, the first being *Literary
Lapses* and the last *Last Leaves*; p. *iii* title; p. *iv* COPYRIGHT, 1913, 1915, | BY DODD,
MEAD & COMPANY | COPYRIGHT, 1916, 1917, 1920, 1922, 1923, 1924, 1925, 1926,
1928, 1929, | 1930, 1931, 1932, 1936, 1937, 1938, 1939, 1940, 1942, 1945 | BY DODD,
MEAD & COMPANY, INC. | COPYRIGHT, 1913, | BY THE CENTURY COMPANY |
COPYRIGHT, 1913, 1914, | BY THE CROWELL PUBLISHING COMPANY | COPYRIGHT,
1920, | BY HARPER & BROTHERS | COPYRIGHT, 1914, 1915, | BY JOHN LANE
COMPANY | [three lines pertaining to copyright] | PRINTED IN THE UNITED STATES
OF AMERICA; pp. v–vii table of contents; p. *1* blank; p. *2* fly title; p. *3* blank; pp. 1–422
text (pp. *10, 48, 50, 84, 86, 128, 186, 234, 278, 376,* and *378* blank).

TEXT: With the exception of the first essay ("Humour as I See It") which stands by itself,
the text is arranged into nine sections, each with a heading and containing a selection of
stories and sketches taken from Leacock's previously published books.

Personal Experiences and Stories — My Financial Career; The Marine Excursions of the
Knights of Pythias; How We Kept Mother's Day; Why I Am Leaving My Farm; With the
Photographer; First Call for Spring.

Nonsense Novels and Model Memoirs — Buggam Grange: A Good Old Ghost Story;
Gertrude the Governess; or, Simple Seventeen; My Victorian Childhood by Lady Nearleigh
Slopover; Guido the Gimlet of Ghent: A Romance of Chivalry.

Detective Stories — The Great Detective; My Revelations As a Spy; Maddened by
Mystery; or, the Defective Detective; Living with Murder; Shorter Stories Still.

Fishing and Other Madness — The Old, Old Story of How Five Men Went Fishing; Cricket
for Americans; My Fishing Pond; My Ladders: A Sequel to My Fishing Pond; When Fellers
Go Fishing; The Familiar Magic of Fishing; A Lecture on Walking; Personal Experiments
with the Black Bass; Back to the Bush; Come Out into the Garden; A Mediaeval Hole in
One.

Friends and Relatives — My Remarkable Uncle; The Hallucination of Mr. Butt; The
Retroactive Existence of Mr. Juggins; Eddie the Bartender; The Awful Fate of Melpomenus
Jones; Number Fifty-Six; My Lost Dollar; Simple Stories of Success; When Men Retire; My
Tailor.

Drama — Cast Up by the Sea; Historical Drama; The Faded Actor.

Homer and Humbug — Homer and Humbug: An Academic Discussion; Education Eating
Up Life; Softening the Stories for the Children; Oxford as I See It; The Reading Public; On
the Need for a Quiet College; What I Read Then — What I Read Now.

Lectures — The Give and Take of Travel; "We Have With Us To-Night"; So This Is the
United States; The Hidden Secret of the City.

Foibles and Follies — Are Witty Women Attractive to Men?; Old Junk and New Money;
The Errors of Santa Claus; The Doctor and the Contraption; The Dissolution of Our Dinner

Club; Uncle Sam, Good Neighbour: An Allegory; Three Score and Ten; Index: There Is No Index.

BINDING AND DUST JACKET: Bound in beige cloth, top edge stained light green. Stamped in gilt on the upper board: THE | LEACOCK | ROUNDABOUT | [wavy rule]. Stamped in gilt down the spine: [wavy rules on each side] THE LEACOCK ROUNDABOUT DODD, MEAD [under Dodd, Mead] & COMPANY.

The front and spine panels of the jacket are dark green. The front panel has an illustration in yellow, white, green, and pink of books attached to a merry-go-round. Beneath the illustration is the following: [first two lines in yellow] The LEACOCK | ROUNDABOUT | [in white] A treasury of the best works of | [in pink] STEPHEN LEACOCK. The jacket's spine has the title down the spine in yellow with the publisher's name printed horizontally in white. The back panel and flaps are printed in blue. The back panel has a photograph of Leacock's head and shoulders, tributes by Will Cuppy and Christopher Morley, and a list of ten other books by Leacock. On the front flap is a paragraph on *The Leacock Roundabout*; the back flap carries an advertisement for *Last Leaves*.

NOTES: The contract for this book, which is dated 25 October 1944, was signed by Leacock's older brother, George Leacock, his niece, Barbara Nimmo, and Frank Chauvin, legal counsel of the Leacock estate. The working title was "Time for Laughter: Stephen Leacock Anthology." Royalty on the book was 10% on all copies sold; one-fifth of the royalties were to be paid to the book's editor, Raymond T. Bond. Although the planned publication was autumn 1945, the "press copy" at DEL is dated 29 October 1946. Number of copies printed not known.

In 1957 there was a printing of 1,000 copies. The Leacock estate received $80 prepayment royalty instead of the contractual royalty. Bond received $20 (information based on Dodd, Mead fonds at OHM).

In addition to the first printing, the following impressions were examined: 1947, 1949, 1957, 1959, 1962, 1963, 1965, 1966, and 1972.

COPIES EXAMINED: CS (all impressions, except 1947, all in jacket); OTNY (first printing in jacket); QMMRB (first printing in jacket; 1947 impression, not in jacket).

## A106 OTHER PEOPLE'S MONEY 1947

[ornamental rule; the first line in script] | *Other People's* | MONEY | *An Outside View of* | *Trusts and Investments* | *by* | STEPHEN LEACOCK | [ornament] | *Published by* | THE ROYAL TRUST | COMPANY | [ornamental rule]

◆ $1^{12}$. *1–6, 7–21, 1–3* pp. (12 leaves). 204 × 129 mm.

CONTENTS: p. *1* half title; p. *2* blank; p. *3* title; p. *4* *Canadian rights reserved*; p. *5* foreword signed in facsimile by Paget Hett, the last line being: *October 1947* President, The Royal Trust Company; p. *6* blank; pp. *7–21* text; pp. *1–3*.

TEXT: Leacock's essay consists of various sections. Section headings are as follows: Trust, Spend, or Lose?; Ignorance of Money Is No Excuse?; Rainbow's End; Diminishing Returns; Easy — When You Know; Beware the Name without the Nature.

BINDING: Bound in beige paper boards, quarter-bound in dull gold cloth, with beige endpapers. A rectangular compartment is blind-stamped on the upper board. A cream-coloured paper label is affixed to the upper board within the compartment. Printed on the label in brown: [ the first line in script] *Other People's* | MONEY | STEPHEN LEACOCK. Issued without a dust jacket.

Also examined was the second printing of 1963 and the third printing of 1969. Copies of these printings are wire-stitched. The second printing has a new foreword by John M. Wells, President of the Royal Trust Company. Pasted to the page with the foreword is a paper slip, *Note to the reader*, signed in facsimile by C.F. Harrington, also President of the company (and a former student of Leacock). The second printing is bound in black-and-white, stiff paper with photographs by Karsh on the covers. The foreword is re-written in the third printing by Harrington, dated October 1969. The type in the third printing is brown. The title page has been altered slightly with printing information on the verso of the title leaf. The third printing is bound in brown-and-white stiff paper with the same photographs by Karsh used in the second printing.

NOTES: Exact date of publication and number of copies printed not known. "Other People's Money" was written in the first days of 1940. Leacock sent a copy to Curtis Brown on 3 January 1940 for serial publication in England. See C40.3.

COPIES EXAMINED: CS (three copies of the first printing plus copies of the second and third printings); OONL (four copies of the first printing); QMMRB (three copies of the first printing; one copy of second printing).

## A107 THE BODLEY HEAD LEACOCK 1957

### A107a *English edition*:

[the first two lines in open type] THE BODLEY HEAD | LEACOCK | EDITED AND INTRODUCED BY | J. B. PRIESTLEY | ★ | THE BODLEY HEAD • LONDON

◆ $A^{16}$ B–$N^{16}$ $O^8$ $P^{16}$ [$1 signed]. *i–iv*, v–vii, 1, 9–13, 14, 15–464 pp. (232 leaves). 191 × 115 mm.

CONTENTS: pp. *i* half title; p. *ii* blank; p. *iii* title; p. *iv First published in 1957* | © | THE BODLEY HEAD | 1957 | [six lines concerning copyright] | *Set in Plantin and printed in Great Britain by* | *Purnell and Sons, Ltd., Paulton (Somerset) and London* | *for The Bodley Head Limited* | *10 Earlham Street, London, W.C.2*; pp. v–vii table of contents; p. *1* blank; pp. 9–13 editor's introduction; p. *14* blank; pp. 15–22 Barbara Nimmo's essay, "Stephen Leacock (December 30, 1869 — March 28, 1944): A Personal Note"; pp. 23–464 text.

TEXT: The text is divided into twenty numbered chapters, each containing a selection of stories and sketches taken from Leacock's previously published books.
1 from *Literary Lapses* — My Financial Career; Boarding-House Geometry; The Awful Fate of Melpomenus Jones; A,B, and C: The Human Element in Mathematics.
2 from *Nonsense Novels* — Sorrows of a Super Soul; The Man in Asbestos: An Allegory of the Future.
3 from *Behind the Beyond* — Homer and Humbug: An Academic Discussion
4 from *Moonbeams from the Larger Lunacy* — The Reading Public: A Book-Store Study.
5 from *Further Foolishness* — Are the Rich Happy?
6 from *Sunshine Sketches of a Little Town* — chapter 1 The Hostelry of Mr. Smith; chapter 3 The Marine Excursions of the Knights of Pythias; chapter 9 The Mariposa Bank

Mystery; chapter 11 The Candidacy of Mr. Smith.

7 from *My Discovery of England* — Impressions of London; Oxford As I See It; We Have with Us To-night.

8 from *The Hohenzollerns in America* — How to Introduce Two People to One Another.

9 from *Over the Footlights* — Cast Up by the Sea; Roughing it in the Bush; L'Envoi: To a Faded Actor.

10 from *The Iron Man and the Tin Woman* — Further Progress in Specialization; Eddie the Bar-tender: A Ghost of the By-gone Past.

11 from *The Dry Pickwick* — The Dry Pickwick; Ho for Happiness: A Plea for Lighter and Brighter Literature.

12 from *Winnowed Wisdom* — Our Summer Convention As Described by One of Its Members; At the Ladies' Culture Club.

13 from *Short Circuits* — Old Junk and New Money: A Little Study in the Latest Antiques; How to Borrow Money; Save Me from My Friends; The Old Men's Page.

14 from *Model Memoirs* — My Victorian Childhood by Lady Nearleigh Slopover; Over-working the Alphabet.

15 from *Essays and Literary Studies* — Fiction and Reality: A Study of the Art of Charles Dickens.

16 from *Frenzied Fiction* — The New Education.

17 from *Too Much College* — Bass Fishing on Lake Simcoe with Jake Gaudaur.

18 from *The Boy I Left Behind Me* — Andrew Macphail.

19 from *My Remarkable Uncle and Other Sketches* — My Remarkable Uncle; The Transit of Venus: A College Story.

20 from *Arcadian Adventures with the Idle Rich* — chapter 4 The Yahi-Bahi Oriental Society of Mrs. Rasselyer-Brown; chapter 6 The Rival Churches of St. Asaph and St. Osoph; chapter 7 The Ministrations of the Reverend Uttermust Dumfarthing; chapter 8 The Great Fight for Clean Government.

BINDING AND DUST JACKET: Bound in orange paper boards with the following stamped in gilt on the spine: [the first four lines within two rectangles] THE | BODLEY | HEAD | LEACOCK | BODLEY HEAD.

The jacket is white with the following printed on the front panel: [all lines within two rectangles] THE | BODLEY HEAD | [in red] LEACOCK | *edited and introduced by* | J. B. PRIESTLEY | [in red] ★. Printed on the jacket's spine panel: THE | [in red] ★ | BODLEY | [in red] ★ | HEAD | [in red] ★ | LEACOCK | [in red] ★ | THE | BODLEY HEAD. The back panel is blank. The front flap discusses Leacock as a humorist and quotes from Priestley's introdcution. The price on the front flap is 20s net. To the left of the price: 3/2059. The back flap is blank.

NOTES: On 31 May 1957, J.B. Blackley of The Bodley Head informed McClelland and Stewart that in the autumn of that year they were planning to publish an anthology of Leacock's works edited by J.B. Priestley. The English edition was at the proof stage in June and July 1957. Priestley received 5% on the sales of the English edition. The first printing consisted of 6,000 copies. According to *The English Catalogue of Books*, publication occurred on 4 November 1957, although copies were apparently available by the end of September. More than 5,000 copies had sold by 11 December 1957, necessitating a reprint in January 1958 (information based on file 41, box 10, series A, part I, of the McClelland and Stewart fonds, OHM).

COPIES EXAMINED: CS (first and third impressions (1965), both in jacket, plus a proof copy of the first printing); QMMRB (first printing in jacket).

**A107a.1** *Canadian issue* entitled *The Best of Leacock*:

[the first two lines in open type] THE BEST OF | LEACOCK | EDITED AND INTRODUCED BY | J. B. PRIESTLEY | ★ | McCLELLAND AND STEWART LIMITED | TORONTO | 1957

The Canadian issue is identical to A107a with the exceptions of the title leaf, the spine imprint (McCLELLAND | AND | STEWART), and various sections of the jacket. The verso of the title leaf reads: *Copyright Canada* | 1957 | McCLELLAND AND STEWART LIMITED | [five lines regarding copyright] | *Set in Plantin and printed in Great Britain by* | *Purnell and Sons, Ltd., Paulton (Somerset) and London.* The Canadian jacket has the change of title on the front panel, the appropriate publisher on the spine, and the lack of price and number on the lower portion of the front flap.

NOTES: On 5 June 1957, J.G. McClelland expressed his interest in The Bodley Head's proposal to publish an anthology of Leacock's works edited by J.B. Priestley. The Bodley Head agreed to supply 1,000 copies of the Canadian issue at $1 apiece. McClelland and Stewart paid Priestley a royalty of 15¢ per copy (1/3 of the royalty paid to Priestley, the other 2/3 to the Leacock estate). Priestley signed and returned the contract on 17 September. McClelland sent Priestley several copies of the Canadian issue on 20 November. By 4 December 1957 McClelland informed Max Reinhardt that little stock remained of the first printing. He ordered 1,500 copies from The Bodley Head on 24 December 1957. The second printing of the Canadian issue was available in February 1958. There was another reprinting of 1,500 copies on 9 April 1959 (information based on file 41, box 10, series A, part I, of the McClelland and Stewart fonds, OHM).

COPIES EXAMINED: CS (first impression plus 1958, 1960, 1965, and 1969 reprints, all in jacket; the latter three printed by Lowe and Brydone (Printers) Limited); QMMRB (1958 reprint in jacket).

**A107a.2** *Australian issue* (1966 in two volumes):

[volume 1] MY FINANCIAL | CAREER | *and other stories* | [rule] | BEING THE FIRST OF TWO PARTS OF | *The Best of Stephen Leacock* | EDITED BY J. B. PRIESTLEY | HUMORBOOKS

Although the Australian issue appears in two volumes, it is from the same setting of type as A107a. 184 × 115 mm. Vol. 1 contains the editor's introduction, Nimmo's essay, and the first nine chapters up p. 226. Preliminary pages of volume 1 are as follows: p. *1* information about vol. 1; p. 2 blank; p. *3* title; p. *4* [abstract illustration within a square of the sun and an individual on a reclining chair] | *First published in Humorbooks 1966* | *by Ure Smith Pty Ltd, 166 Phillip Street, Sydney* | *This international edition printed by* | The Continental Printing Co. Ltd, Hong Kong | [rule] | [three lines about the first publication of the book by The Bodley Head] | [rule] | [five lines about copyright].

BINDING: Perfect bound. Glossy, stiff paper covers in white, yellow, green, black, and orange. On the front cover is an illustration of a man lying down with £ and $ signs above him. On the back cover is a photo of Leacock with a quotation from Priestley. On the versos of the covers is a list of titles published by Humorbooks. This volume is H 28 in the series. Cover design by Wally Jex. Price: Australia 80¢, 8/–; New Zealand 6/6. Vol. 2 not seen.

COPIES EXAMINED: CS (vol. 1); EVANS (vol. 1).

## A108 LAUGH WITH LEACOCK 1959

STEPHEN LEACOCK | [rule] | LAUGH WITH | LEACOCK | [rule] | [publisher's device: circle containing illustration a dog (corgi) with a book in its mouth and the words CORGI BOOKS curved] | TRANSWORLD PUBLISHERS | LONDON

♦ $LWL-1^8$ $LWL-2-18^8$ [$1 signed]. 1–10, 11–288 pp. (144 leaves). 161 × 108 mm.

CONTENTS: p. 1 three paragraphs with headings: *Who is Leacock?*; *What did Leacock write?*; *What is | LAUGH WITH LEACOCK?*; p. 2 blank; p. 3 title; p. 4 LAUGH WITH LEACOCK | A CORGI BOOK | PRINTING HISTORY | Corgi Edition published 1959 | All Stephen Leacock's books are published by | The Bodley Head Limited, by arrangement | with whom this selection has been made. | [four lines about copyright and required permission from The Bodley Head] | Corgi Books are published by Transworld Publishers Ltd., | Park Royal Road, London, N.W.10. | Made and printed in Great Britain by | Hunt, Barnard & Co., Ltd., Aylesbury, Bucks.; p. 5 fly title; p. 6 blank; pp. 7–10 table of contents; pp. 11–288 text.

TEXT: The sketches in this anthology were selected from Leacock's previously published books of humour. The arrangement of the selected sketches is as follows:

From *Literary Lapses* — My Financial Career; Boarding-House Geometry; The New Food; Men Who Have Shaved Me; Number Fifty-Six; The Conjuror's Revenge; A Manual of Education; Insurance Up to Date; Borrowing a Match; A Lesson in Fiction; A Model Dialogue; Back to the Bush; Reflections on Riding; A, B, and C: The Human Element in Mathematics.

From *Nonsense Novels* — Maddened by Mystery, or, The Defective Detective; Guido the Gimlet: A Romance of Chivalry; Gertrude the Governess, or, Simple Seventeen; Soaked in Seaweed, or, Upset in the Ocean; The Man in Asbestos: An Allegory of the Future.

From *My Discovery of England* — Impressions of London; "We Have with Us To-night."

From *The Hohenzollerns in America* — How to Introduce Two People to One Another.

From *Over the Footlights* — "Cast Up by the Sea"; My Lost Dollar; Personal Experiments with the Black Bass; My Affair with My Landlord; The Give and Take of Travel; How My Wife and I Built Our Home for $4.90; How We Kept Mother's Day; The Laundry Problem.

From *Short Circuits* — Old Junk and New Money: How to Borrow Money; Save Me from My Friends; The Old Men's Page.

From *Frenzied Fiction* — The New Education; The Old, Old Story of How Five Men Went Fishing; Simple Stories of Success, or, How to Succeed in Life.

From *Moonbeams from the Larger Lunacy* — The Reading Public: A Book-Store Study.

From *Further Foolishness* — Are the Rich Happy?; The Snoopopaths, or, Fifty Stories of Success; Humour As I See It.

BINDING: Paperback, perfect bound with red, black, yellow, and white card covers. Five horizontal bands on the front and back covers are separated by four white horizontal bars.

The bands contain black-and-white photographs of the heads of laughing men. Opposite the photographs are the series name (Corgi Giant) and price (3s 6d), the title, and lines about the book and Leacock. The series number on the spine is GH736.

NOTES: Published on 2 October 1959 according to *The English Catalogue of Books*. Number of copies printed not known. Although this book has the same title as the anthology published by Dodd, Mead in 1930 (A56), the contents of the two books are not the same.

COPIES EXAMINED: CS.

## A109 THE UNICORN LEACOCK 1960

EDITED BY JAMES REEVES | The Unicorn | Leacock | *Illustrated by* | FRANCISZA THEMERSON | [publisher's device of bull within a modified circle] | HUTCHINSON EDUCATIONAL

◆ A$^{16}$ B–F$^{16}$ [$1 signed; also with initials T.U.L. at each signature]. *1–6, 7–191, 1* pp. (96 leaves). 183 × 118 mm.

CONTENTS: p. *1* half title with series title and paragraph about Leacock; p. *2* UNICORN BOOKS | General Editor: JAMES REEVES | ★ | [list of ten titles and authors]; p. *3* title; p. *4* HUTCHINSON EDUCATIONAL LTD | *178–202 Great Portland Street, London, W.1* | London Melbourne Sydney | Auckland Bombay Toronto | Johannesburg New York | ★ | *This selection first published in Unicorn Books 1960* | *This book has been set in Baskerville type face. It has* | *been printed in Great Britain by The Anchor Press,* | *Ltd., in Tiptree, Essex, on Smooth Wove paper and* | *bound by Taylor Garnett Evans & Co., Ltd., in* | *Watford, Herts*; pp. *5–6* table of contents; pp. *7–191* text with the final line on the last page as follows: Illustrations © Hutchinson & Co. *(Publishers)* Ltd. 1960 | Text © James Reeves 1960.

TEXT: My Financial Career; Reflections on Riding; My Lost Dollar; The New Attaboy Language: A Little Study in Culture from Below Up; How to Make a Million Dollars; Truthful Oratory; or, What Our Speakers Ought to Say; The Perfect Lover's Guide; or, How to Select a Mate, on Sea or on Shore; Boarding-House Geometry; The Approach of the Comet: Do You Really Care If It Hits You; How to Be a Doctor; The Blue and the Grey: A Pre-War Story; Heroes and Heroines; The Christmas Ghost: Unemployment in One of Our Oldest Industries; My Memories and Miseries As a Schoolmaster; My Unknown Friend; The Art of Conversation; Gertrude the Governess; or, Simple Seventeen; Maddened by Mystery; or, The Defective Detective; The Candidacy of Mr. Smith; Cast Up by the Sea: A Seacoast Melodrama; Have the English Any Sense of Humour?.

BINDING: Bound in purple and turquoise paper boards with an illustration of the head of a unicorn and an ornamental design on both boards. On the spine in turquoise: ★ ★ | [down the spine:] The Unicorn Leacock *Editor* JAMES REEVES | Hutchinson.

NOTES: According to *The English Catalogue of Books*, *The Unicorn Leacock* was published on 2 May 1960. It is described as "Cr. 8vo," selling for 6s. Number of copies printed not known.

COPIES EXAMINED: OONL.

## A110 SELECTED WRITINGS OF STEPHEN LEACOCK 1960

*Selected Writings of* | STEPHEN LEACOCK | *Education* AND *Living* | THE IMAGE OF AMERICA | *Published by* TYREX INC. | 350 FIFTH AVENUE, NEW YORK

◆ 1–2⁸. *1–6, 7–8, 9–12, 13–18, 19–20, 21–31, 1* pp. (16 leaves). 215 × 138 mm.

CONTENTS: p. *1* series statement; p. *2* caption for the woodcut on the next page; p. *3* woodcut portrait of Leacock by Jacob Landau; p. *4* blank; p. *5* title; p. *6* © *1960 by Tyrex Inc.* | TRADE MARK REGISTERED | PRINTED IN THE U. S. A.; pp. *7–8* foreword by William Dalton; p. *9* table of contents; p. *10* blank; pp. *11–31* text; p. *1* blank.

TEXT: The text consists of two parts: 1 Education; and 2 Living. Part 1 is comprised of the following sections: Education in the Tissue of Every Day (from "Education Eating Up Life"); The Dormitory (from "Oxford As I See It"); The College with a Difference (from "On the Need for a Quiet College"); Fund Raising (from *The Pursuit of Knowledge*, pp. 25–26); and The Inner Compulsion (from *The Pursuit of Knowledge*, pp. 47–48). Part 2 has the following sections: The Nature of Humour (from "Humour as I See It"); Going Fishing (from "When Fellers Go Fishing"); Retirement (from "When Men Retire"); The Great City (from "The Hidden Secret of the City"); My Tailor (from "My Tailor"); Non Omnis Moriar (from "Three Score and Ten").

BINDING: Bound in off-white linen with Leacock's signature in facsimile stamped in scarlet on the upper board. A solid scarlet rectangle is stamped down the spine, containing the following in gold: Selected Writings of Stephen Leacock. The book was apparently issued with a glassine wrapper. Scarlet endpapers.

NOTES: This is volume 4 of the Image of America Series published by Tyrex Inc. The book consists of excerpts from Leacock's writings, primarily essays and sketches in *The Leacock Roundabout*. Published on 16 November 1960 (copyright registration number at DLC, A5113159). Number of copies printed and price not known.

COPIES EXAMINED: CS; QMMRB.

## A111 PERFECT LOVER'S GUIDE AND OTHER STORIES 1960

**a111a** *second edition*:

[hand-written] STEPHEN | [black-and-white photograph of Leacock in his later years] | [the next three lines hand-written] LEACOCK | PERFECT LOVER'S GUIDE | and other stories | FOREIGN LANGUAGES PUBLISHING HOUSE | Moscow *1960*

◆ 1 — 3499⁸ 2 — 3499–22 — 3499⁸ [$2 signed; second leaf of each gathering signed *, e.g. 13*]. *1–4, 5–19, 20–22, 23, 24, 25–58, 59, 60–100, 101, 102–110, 111, 112–125, 126, 127–151, 152, 153–208, 209, 210–227, 228, 229–265, 266, 267–270, 271, 272–283, 284, 285–310, 311, 312–320, 321–324, 325–350, 1–2* pp. (176 leaves). 199 × 127 mm.

CONTENTS: p. *1* blank; p. *2* abstract illustrations of people as found in Leacock's sketches — a photographer, a detective, etc.; p. *3* title; p. *4* [four lines in Russian] | *Second edition*; pp. *5–20* introduction by N. Mikhaĺskoi; p. *21* fly title; p. *22* blank; pp. *23–24* table of contents; pp. *25–321* text; p. *322* blank; pp. *323–350, 1* annotations in Russian by

l. Manenok to English words in the text (p. 324 blank); p. 2 copyright information.

TEXT: The text consists of the following sketches selected from Leacock's previously published books.

From *Literary Lapses* — The Awful Fate of Melpomenus Jones; The Conjurer's Revenge; How to Avoid Getting Married; How to Be a Doctor; How to Live to Be 200; A Manual of Education; My Financial Career; A New Pathology; Number Fifty-Six.

From *Nonsense Novels* — Gertrude the Governess: or, Simple Seventeen; Guido the Gimlet of Ghent: A Romance of Chivalry; Maddened by Mystery: or, the Defective Detective; The Man in Abestos: An Allegory of the Future.

From *Behind the Beyond* — My Unknown Friend; With the Photographer.

From *Moonbeams from the Larger Lunacy* — Afternoon Adventures at My Club: The Hallucination of Mr. Butt; The Reading Public: A Book Store Study.

From *Further Foolishness* — Every Man and His Friends: His Little Son; Humor As I See It; Madeline of the Movies: A Photoplay Done Back into the Words; A Study in Still Life — My Tailor.

From *Frenzied Fiction* — Ideal Interviews: With Our Greatest Actor, With Our Typical Novelists; The Cave-Man As He Is; The Errors of Santa Claus; To Nature and Back Again; Personal Adventures in the Spirit World; The Sorrows of a Summer Guest.

From *Over the Footlights* — First Call for Spring; or, oh, Listen to the Birds; How I Succeeded in My Business: Secrets of Success Related in the Best Current Literature; My Lost Dollar; Roughing It in the Bush: My Plans for Moose Hunting in the Canadian Wilderness.

From *The Garden of Folly* — The Perfect Lover's Guide; or, How to Select a Mate, on Sea or on Shore; Romances of Business, no. I Alfred of the Advertisements, no. II Tom Lachford Promoter, no. III Our Business Benefactors.

From *Winnowed Wisdom* — How We Kept Mother's Day As Related by a Member of the Family.

From *Here Are My Lectures* — Frenzied Fiction: First Lecture, Murder at $2.50 a Crime.

From *Model Memoirs* — Mrs. Easy Has Her Fortune Told; Mrs. Newrich Buys Antiques; My Victorian Childhood by Lady Nearleigh Slopover.

From *Last Leaves* — A Lecture on Walking; Living with Murder.

BINDING: Bound in pictorial green and white paper boards, quarter-bound in greyish white buckram. The illustrations on both boards are abstract in character, and consist chiefly of a couple and flowers. Stamped up the spine: [flower] [handwritten] STEPHEN LEACOCK [flower].

NOTES: This selection of Leacock's stories was used as a school edition primarily for the use of students learning English in the Soviet Union. First edition not seen. Price on lower board, 7 rubles, 15 kopecs.

COPIES EXAMINED: QMMRB.

## A111b *third edition* (1963):

[hand-written] STEPHEN | [black-and-white photograph of Leacock in his later years] | [the next three lines hand-written] LEACOCK | PERFECT LOVER'S GUIDE | and other stories | FOREIGN LANGUAGES PUBLISHING HOUSE | Moscow, 1963

◆ *1 — 1837*[8] *2 — 1837–20 — 1837*[8] *21 — 1837*[4] *22 — 1837*[8] [$2 signed; second leaf of each gathering signed *, e.g. 13*]. *1–4, 5–20, 21–24, 25, 26, 27–59, 60, 61–70, 71, 72–99, 100, 101–109, 110, 111–123, 124, 125–149, 150, 151–155, 156, 157–205, 206, 207–224, 224, 225–260, 261, 262–265, 266, 267–278, 279, 280–304, 305, 306–314, 315–318, 319–342, 1–2* pp. (172 leaves). 201 × 128 mm.

CONTENTS: p. *1* blank; p. *2* abstract illustrations of people as found in Leacock's sketches — a photographer, a detective, etc.; p. *3* title; p. *4* [five lines in Russian]; pp. *5–21* introduction by N. Mikhaĭskoi; p. *22* blank; *23* fly title; p. *24* blank; pp. *25–26* table of contents; pp. *27–315* text; p. *316* blank; pp. *317–342, 1* annotations in Russian by I. Manenok to English words in the text (p. *318* blank); p. *2* copyright information.

TEXT: Identical to A111a.

BINDING: Identical to A111a except for the price on the lower board, 66 kopecs.

COPIES EXAMINED: CS; OWTU.


## A112 ON THE CONTINUED PROGRESS OF MCGILL UNIVERSITY [1961]

[cover title, all lines in brown] ON THE | CONTINUED | PROGRESS OF | McGILL | UNIVERSITY [to the right of these lines is a black-and-white photograph of Leacock with his signature in facsimile]

◆ Leaflet folded once at the top with the text on the inside. 185 × 83 mm. On the back of the leaflet is a paragraph in italics, McGill University's shield in brown, and the following line: THE McGILL ALMA MATER FUND *3618 University St., Montreal 2, Que.*

BINDING: Cream-coloured simulated laid paper.

NOTES: The back section of this leaflet notes that "On the Continued Progress of McGill University" was first published in the *Old McGill Annual 1926* (see C25.1) "thirty-five years ago" and that Leacock was appointed to McGill University as a Special Lecturer on Political Science "sixty years ago" (i.e. 1901). Leacock's little essay is a message to graduates that McGill University always needs financial support. The McGill Alma Mater Fund issued this leaflet for this purpose to alumni. Exact date of publication and number of copies printed not known.

COPIES EXAMINED: QMMRB.


## A113 CAROLINE'S CHRISTMAS 1961

A113a *American edition*:

[the first two lines in Fry's ornamented typeface] CAROLINE'S | CHRISTMAS | or | The Inexplicable Infant | *by* | *Stephen Leacock* | [illustration of an evergreen tree with house in the background] | *1961* | *The Fireside Press* | *Portland, Maine*

◆ *1*[16]. *1–8, 1–21, 1–3* pp. (16 leaves). 176 × 118 mm.

CONTENTS: pp. *1–2* blank; p. *3* title; p. *4 This booklet has been | hand set, printed, and bound | by | Marybelle and Royal Boston | as a | Christmas Greeting | to their friends | December 1961 | This is | Number . . . . . | of one hundred ten copies*; pp. *5–6* preface (one paragraph, extracted from Leacock's *Nonsense Novels*); p. *7* fly title; p. *8* blank; pp. *1–21* text; pp. *1–3* blank.

BINDING: Bound in a light green wrapper with the following in red on the front of the wrapper: [the first two lines in Fry's ornamented typeface] CAROLINE'S | CHRISTMAS | [ornament] | STEPHEN LEACOCK.

NOTES: 110 copies printed. See also C10.41.

Copy Examined: QMMRB (no. 81).

## A113b *Canadian edition* (1969):

[all lines and illustrations within a rectangle] | [red C within a green and black leafy illustration] | Caroline's Christmas | [red C within a green and black leafy illustration] | by Stephen Leacock

◆ *1–6, 1–11, 1–3* leaves (20 leaves). 285 × 119 mm. This booklet consists of five oblong 4to sheets, each unopened at the top. The gatherings are not sequential. The sheets have been stacked together, and are wire-stitched. Printing, when it occurs, is on the recto of the first conjugate leaf (verso blank) and on the verso of the second conjugate leaf (recto blank).

CONTENTS: folios *1–2* blank; folio *3* half title; folio *4* blank; folio *5* title; folio *6 Caroline's Christmas* is from *Nonsense Novels* by Stephen Leacock and is | reproduced by special arrangement with McClelland and Stewart; folios *1–11* text; folio *1* This keepsake | has been designed | for the friends of | Cooper & Beatty, Limited | [illustration in red and green] | Christmas, 1969; folios *2–3* blank. The text is contained within ruled frames with colour illustrations on folios 1, 3, 5, 7, 9, and 11.

DUST JACKET AND ENVELOPE: The wrapper consists of stiff white paper with flaps, not stitched to the booklet. The front of the wrapper is identical to the title page. The back of the wrapper and the flaps are blank. The envelope which accompanies this pamphlet has the following on its front: [all lines except the last one within the left side of a split rectangle; red C within a green and black leafy illustration] | A Christmas Book | [red B within a green and black leafy illustration] | From Cooper & Beatty, Limited 401 Wellington Street West, Toronto 135, Canada.

NOTES: The Toronto typesetting company, Cooper & Beatty, Limited, was established in 1921 using the name Trade Composition Company. The company issued Christmas cards as early as the 1930s. Beginning in 1956 with the publication of F. Scott Fitzgerald's *Turkey Remains and How to Inter Them with Numerous Scarce Recipes from the Note-Books*, the company issued Christmas keepsakes to be sent to colleagues and friends. This edition of *Caroline's Christmas* won a New York Type Directors award for its art nouveau style. The LOCIS database at DLC states that this edition was designed and illustrated by Jim Donoahue. Number of copies printed not known. For more information on Cooper & Beatty, see Edna Hajnal and Richard Landon, *Cooper & Beatty: Designers with Type, An Exhibition* (Toronto: Thomas Fisher Rare Book Library, University of Toronto, 1996). See also 122a and A128a.

COPIES EXAMINED: CS (in envelope); LAT (three copies in envelope); OHM (file 11, box 36, series A, part I, McClelland Stewart fonds); QMMRB (in envelope).

## A114 LAUS VARSITATIS 1962

[caption title; all printing in blue] THE VARSITY MAGAZINE SUPPLEMENT |
Laus Varsitatis [hand-written by J.C. Evans] (1916) | A Song in Praise of the
University of Toronto | BY STEPHEN LEACOCK | [rule]

♦ Broadside, white paper stock. 279 × 214 mm.

CONTENTS: Leacock's poem on both sides, photographically reduced and reprinted from
the *Varsity Magazine* Supplement (see C16.24 for its original appearance) with page
number, 115, centered on the bottom of the recto; on the verso after the poem is a letter
printed in facsimile, dated December 1962, signed by J.C. Evans, Director of Alumni Affairs,
the University of Toronto.

NOTES: The *Varsity Magazine* Supplement (360 × 270 mm.) was published in December
1916 by the Students Administrative Council of the University of Toronto as a tribute to
the students, staff, and faculty of the university who served in the armed forces during the
First World War. It contains photographs of more than 2,000 soldiers, articles on the war
by writers such as Ralph Connor and Winston Churchill, and advertisements from companies and businesses. According to his notebook of recorded publications at QMMRB,
Leacock wrote his contribution to the supplement on 11 September 1916 (see C16.24).

See Joe Evans, "The Bulldozers Are at My Door," *Varsity News* (University of Toronto)
5, no. 2 (December 1962): 14. In this article Evans talks about the University of Toronto's
Alumni archives, which at that time were in the process of moving to new quarters in New
College. Evans came across a copy of the *Varsity Supplement*, which contained Leacock's poem.
Four stanzas are reprinted in this issue of *Varsity News* with the following editorial note:

> It is our guess that many readers of these Random Notes from the Man in the Alumni
> House will want the entire song. Joe says he is having some copies run off that a note
> or postcard addressed to him at Alumni House, University of Toronto, will get results
> by return mail.

Number of copies printed not known.

COPIES EXAMINED: CS.

## A115 STEPHEN LEACOCK ON BANKING [1967]

[caption title] Stephen Leacock | on Banking | [within a rectangle a bluish
black-and-white photograph of Leacock by Karsh] | My Financial Career

♦ Leaflet folded twice to form six unnumbered pages. 217 × 96 mm. folded; 217 × 285 mm. unfolded.

CONTENTS: Leacock's story, "My Financial Career," takes up three pages. At the bottom
of the third page of the text is: *Reprinted by The Bank of Nova Scotia | from Stephen
Leacock's "Literary Lapses" | with permission of McClelland & Stewart Limited*. One page
is an illustration: a black drawing against a blue background of the main character in
Leacock's story, who is seated and in discussion with the Bank manager. The caption reads:
We both sat down and looked at each other. I found | no voice to speak. | "You are one of
Pinkerton's men, I presume," he said.

Of the remaining two pages one concerns the Personal Security Program Account and

Scotia Plans Loans. The address given on this page is: THE BANK OF NOVA SCOTIA | 56 Mississaga Street East, Orillia | Telephone 325–1341. The other page has the following within a blue border: an invitation to the public to attend the opening of this branch on 21 January [1967], coinciding with Orillia's one hundredth birthday; a paragraph about Leacock's story, which was reprinted by The Bank of Nova Scotia in December 1908 in its first staff magazine; and a photograph of the branch's manager, P.J. Beseau.

NOTES: Printed and distributed as a promotional leaflet by The Bank of Nova Scotia in January 1967 on the occasion of the opening of this branch in Orillia. Also examined was an apparent second printing of this leaflet. The text and illustration are the same, but the remaining two pages concern the Scotiabank Cheque Guarantee Card and various accounts offered by the Bank. The latter printing occurred in September 1969 or thereabouts since the expiry date on the credit card is 09–69. Number of copies printed not known. The Bank of Nova Scotia paid McClelland and Stewart $100 on 31 January 1967 for the use of Leacock's text (information based on TR1, McClelland and Stewart fonds, OHM). See also C95.1.

COPIES CS (both printings); LAT (both printings); OORI (six copies of later printing); SLM (three copies of later printing, J.A. "Pete" McGarvey collection).

## A116 GERTRUDE THE GOVERNESS 1967

[cover title] 30093 | ES/3 | [triangle] | [the next two lines in orange; the next three lines in biform type] GERTRUDE THE GOVERNESS: | OR, SIMPLE SEVENTEEN | STEPHEN LEACOCK | PAPERTEXTS | Associated Educational Services Corporation | a subsidiary of SIMON & SCHUSTER, INC. | [publisher's device in orange to the left of the three previous lines; P within an oval] | [rule] | [illustration in orange and black of a man and woman sitting in a horse-drawn carriage, flanked by a man on a rearing horse, all people in nineteenth-century dress]

◆ 1⁸. 1–2, 3–16 p. (8 leaves). 229 × 158 mm.

CONTENTS: p. 1 title; p. 2 sections containing biographical notes, background, troublesome words, and theme question — the last five lines are: "Gertrude the Governess: or, Simple Seventeen" from *Laugh with Leacock* by Stephen | Leacock. Copyright 1930 by Dodd, Mead & Company, Inc. Reprinted by permission of | Dodd, Mead & Company, Inc. Illustration by Harry Bennett. Supplementary material copy- | right © by Associated Educational Services Corporation. All rights reserved. Printed | in the U.S.A.; pp. 3–11 text; pp. 12–16 supplementary material with titles: I Ideas Worth Considering; II Vocabulary Review; III Writing Features; and IV Suggested Composition Activities.

BINDING: White paper stock, no wrapper, wire-stitched.

NOTES: The Papertexts Series is a series of educational pamphlets. The texts are primarily by contemporary writers such as Stephen Crane, Bret Harte, H.G. Wells, F. Scott Fitzgerald, and a host of others. Each pamphlet is organized in the same way: a text with supplementary information intended for students to appreciate a certain text while developing their own writing skills. Published on 15 December 1967 (copyright registration number A13173 at DLC). Number of copies printed not known. See also C10.39.

COPIES EXAMINED: QMMED.

## AII7 LITERATURE AND EDUCATION IN AMERICA [1967?]

[transcription taken from p. 4] LITERATURE AND EDUCATION IN | AMERICA

◆ *I–4, 4–17, I–2* pp. (10 leaves). 238 × 179 mm.

CONTENTS: pp. *I–3* blank; pp. *4, 4–17* text; pp. *I–2* blank.

BINDING: Bound in a stiff, flecked grey wrapper with a dark brown strip glued over the spine area; the leaves glued together at the spine.

NOTES: This pamphlet lacks a title page, copyright information, and a cover title. It is a photographic reprint in brown type of Leacock's article originally published in the *University Magazine* 8, no. 1 (February 1909). See C9.3. Although neither a publisher nor a date of publication is stated, the pamphlet was issued by the Canadiana House in Toronto, a second hand bookseller owned and operated by William J. Noxon and his son, David B. Noxon. In 1963 the Canadiana House published and arranged for the printing with the University of Toronto Press of some 2,000 copies of Mrs. F.E.O. Monck's *My Canadian Leaves*, originally published in 1893 for private circulation. The republication of scarce or unusual items of Canadiana recommenced in 1967 on a much more modest scale using a duplicating machine which the Canadiana House employed to produce its monthly catalogues. No more than 200 copies of the pamphlet were printed. Price and exact date of publication not known (information based on a letter from David B. Noxon to Carl Spadoni, 21 August 1997).

COPIES EXAMINED: CS; OWA.

## AII8 LAUGHTER BY LEACOCK 1969

[cover title; brown floral ornament, brown thin-thick rule] | Laughter | by Leacock | [brown thick-thin rule, brown floral ornament upside down] | A tribute to Stephen Leacock, | humorist and humanist, | on the centennial of his | birth in 1869

◆ Leaflet folded once with flaps folded inward. 231 × 100 mm. (231 × 392 mm. unfolded).

CONTENTS: Cover title; front flap has a photograph of Leacock by Karsh and biographical information about Leacock in brown type; the text is printed on the inside front flap, the connected two pages, and the inside back flap; back flap has two paragraphs in brown type, noting the centennial of Leacock's birth, the issuing of a Canadian stamp of Leacock, and the preparation of a biography of Leacock (by Ralph Curry); on the back of the leaflet: "While there is time, | let us be up and doing. . ." | [paragraph extracted from Leacock's "The Oldest Living Graduate", *McGill Annual* (1922)] | [shield of McGill University in brown] | [remaining lines in brown] | THE [raised c] McGILL FUND COUNCIL | 3618 University Street | Montreal 112, Que., Canada | Printed in Canada.

TEXT: The text consists of twenty-one excerpts from Leacock's works. Each excerpt has a heading (for example, MEDICAL MIRACLES, GOLF HAZARDS, etc.) with the source of the excerpt identified.

BINDING: Printed on brown paper stock.

NOTES: On 5 September 1969, Bruce N. Jones of the McGill Alma Mater Fund sought copyright clearance from McClelland and Stewart to produce a leaflet of 2,500 words of quotations from Leacock's works. The leaflet was to be distributed to 50,000 people associated with McGill University in order to capitalize on the commemorative Leacock stamp issued on 13 November 1969. Copyright clearance for this apparent non-commercial leaflet was obtained on 8 September. On 1 December 1969 Jones reported that the Fund intended to sell five to ten thousand copies to the National Library of Canada for a Leacock exhibition scheduled for January to April 1970 (necessitating a reprint). 5,000 copies, enclosed in an unaddressed envelope with the Leacock stamp, were also sold to stamp collectors at $1 (information based on file 11, box 36, series A, part I, McClelland Stewart fonds).

COPIES EXAMINED: CS; OTNY (with envelope); SLM ("Pete" McGarvey collection).

## A119  CAN WE BELIEVE IN SANTA CLAUS?  1969

[cover title; the first line in red, and the next six lines handwritten in white with the endings of various swash letters tipped red] " | Can | We | Believe | In | Santa Claus | [quotation marks in red] ?" | Stephen Leacock | answers his own question

◆  Leaflet folded once to form four unnumbered pages. 217 × 95 mm.

CONTENTS: p. 1 cover title; p. 2 explanation of the text with illustration of a sock hanging by a nail on a fireplace; p. 3 text with the first letter handwritten in white and swash within a solid red rectangle; p. 4 [the first two lines handwritten in white with various swash letters tipped red] Seasons | Greetings | [shield of McGill University] | The McGill Fund Council | 3618 University Street | Montreal 112, Que., Canada. | Printed in Canada.

BINDING: Printed on green stiff paper stock. The copy examined contained within it a bookmark issued by McGill University which has a portrait of Leacock and a quotation by him about his appointment to McGill.

NOTES: Issued on the centenary anniversary of Leacock's birth by the McGill Alma Mater Fund to "some 30,000 graduates, parents and other friends of McGill." Copies were printed and available by 1 December 1969. The Associate Director of the Fund, Bruce N. Jones, obtained copyright clearance from the Leacock estate and McClelland and Stewart on 21 November 1969. The text reprints the last six paragraphs from "War-Time Santa Claus" (reproduced from *My Remarkable Uncle and Other Sketches*). Information based on file 11, box 36, series A, part I, McClelland Stewart fonds.

COPIES EXAMINED: OHM (file 11, box 36, series A, part I, McClelland Stewart fonds).

## A120  LEACOCK JACKDAW NO.C24  1970

[transcription taken from the front of the portfolio which has a background black-and-white photograph by Karsh of Leacock seated in a boat; all lines except the last one on the front flap:] Jackdaw No.C24 | Written and compiled | by Stephen Franklin | Clarke Irwin [publisher's device; a bird standing on an urn within an oval] | [in green outlined in black] LEACOCK | Centennial 1970

◆ Portfolio, stapled at the edges, with a folded front flap and a pocket. 226 × 349 mm. The back of the portfolio is black with printing in white. It has a list of the titles in the Canadian Series of Jackdaws, a list of the contents of the portfolio, and information about Leacock and the compiler, Stephen Franklin. Printed on the bottom part of the back of the portfolio: Published by | CLARKE, IRWIN & COMPANY LTD, | 791 St. Clair Avenue West, | Toronto 10, Canada, | [to the left of these lines is an illustration within a rounded square of a person seated at a word bench; to the left of the above lines is the following:] in association with | JACKDAW PUBLICATIONS LTD, | 30 Bedford Square, London WC1, England, | and GROSSMAN PUBLISHERS, INC., | 125A East 19th Street, New York 10003, U.S.A.

CONTENTS: Inside the portfolio are a series of eleven numbered exhibits. They include: colour facsimiles of letters, manuscripts, and printed documents; and a flexdisc record (exhibit 11) which has Leacock reading "My Old College" (see A97) on side 1 and two readings by John Drainie of "Helping the Armenians" and "Five Dollars, Right Now" on side 2.

The facsimiles are as follows: 1 letter from Leacock to his father, Peter Leacock, 28 June 1884; 2 "The Awful Fate of Melpomenus Jones from *Truth* (see C96.2); 3 advertising placard for *Nonsense Novels*; 4 the first four pages of the manuscript of chapter I of *Sunshine Sketches of a Little Town*; 5 letter from F. Scott Fitzgerald to Leacock, [1915]; 6 leaflet advertising Leacock's 1921 lecture tour of England and Scotland (see A30b); 7 poster for the Old Brewery Players, New Year's Eve 1929 (see A90); 8 draft of a day lettergram from Leacock to Hon. George Henry, [1932]; 9 "Leacock Reviews the Canadian Scene as Set for 1938: King, Rowell, Hepburn, and Aberhart in Leading Roles," *Montreal Daily Star*, 22 January 1938, p. 11 (see C38.5).

In addition to these exhibits the portfolio contains: an introductory sheet in green with notes on the exhibits and a section on "More Reading"; four posters with text by Franklin — "Stephen Leacock," "A Great and Contagious Humorist," "Professor and Pundit," and "Baron of Brewery Bay"; and a poster photograph of Leacock by Karsh with the heading "I am a great believer in luck, and I find the harder I work the more I have of it."

NOTES: The Canadian Series of Jackdaws consists of portfolios of facsimiles of original documents with commentary. These documents were intended for educational purposes to convey a sense of Canada's history and its culture.

Leacock was born on 30 December 1869. Stephen Franklin, the Executive Director of the Stephen Leacock Centennial Committee, organized the publication of this portfolio to celebrate the centenary of Leacock's birth. One of the objectives of the committee was to prepare "A multi-purpose booklet" (from Franklin's report, 27 January 1970). "The booklet will be used by the Leacock associates, the Leacock Memorial Home, the Centennial Committee, the Department of Tourism and Information and others," Franklin opined. He conjectured: "Depending on cost per unit of the booklet (approx. 24 pages to fit a no. 10 envelope) initial demand is in the neighborhood of 75,000 copies."

On 14 January 1970, Richard Howard, the editor of the Jackdaw Series, confirmed his agreement with Franklin that if a suitable sponsor could be found, Clarke Irwin would publish a Jackdaw on Leacock at 5% royalty (price $2.95). The designer Helmut Weystrahs discussed the cover design of the portfolio with Franklin and Howard on 12 February 1970. On 5 March 1970, L.A.D. Stephens of the Department of External Affairs committed the Department to taking 2,000 copies at $1.25 for free distribution.

Franklin received an advance royalty of $150 on 13 March 1970. 8,200 flexdisc records were manufactured by Park Lane Recordings on 22 March 1970 at a cost of $735. 8,000 Leacock personality posters were ordered from Downset Offset Printing Co. on 13 March 1970. Photographic work was done through the Manuscript Division of the Public Archives of Canada, which was microfilming the Leacock papers from the Leacock Museum at the time. 8,000 copies of the portfolio were produced by General Printers Limited at a cost $4,936. Publication occurred in June 1970. Jackdaw Publications Ltd. handled English sales; Grossman Publishers, Inc. took care of American orders. By the end of January 1971 5,700 were still in stock (information based on files 3 and 10, box 27 and file 13, box 28 of the Clarke Irwin archives, OHM).

COPIES EXAMINED: CS (three copies); OHM.

## A121 FEAST OF STEPHEN 1970

### A121a *first edition*:

Feast | of | Stephen | [the next four lines to the right of the second line] An anthology of some of the less | familiar writings of Stephen Leacock, | with a critical introduction | by Robertson Davies | McClelland and Stewart Limited | Toronto/Montreal | [publisher's device within an oval to the left of the previous two lines: abstract sketch of a man standing on a horse-drawn chariot, taking aim with a bow and arrow]

◆ $1-5^{16}$. $1-6$, $1-49$, $50$, $51-154$ pp. (80 leaves). $215 \times 136$ mm.

CONTENTS: p. *1* half title; p. 2 blank; p. 3 title; p. 4 Copyright © 1970 by McClelland and Stewart Limited | Introduction copyright © 1970 by Robertson Davies | All rights reserved | 07710-2578-5 | The selections in this edition have been taken from a variety | of editions, Canadian, British, and American. | Spelling and style of the source editions have been retained. | [nine lines of acknowledgment for permission from Doubleday Inc., Dodd, Mead and Co. and the Stephen Leacock Estate] | The introduction is available in a slightly different version in | a paperback entitled *Stephen Leacock*, by Robertson Davies | McClelland and Stewart Limited | *The Canadian Publishers*; pp. *5* table of contents; p. 6 blank; pp. 1–45 Davies's introduction in four chapters; pp. 46–49 selected bibliography; p. *50* fly title; pp. 51–154 text.

TEXT: Life on the Old Farm; The Mathematics of the Lost Chord; Hoodoo McFiggin's Christmas; The Hero of Home Week; Mr. Chairman, I Beg to Move — ; Love Me, Love My Letters; Saloonio: A Study in Shakespearean Criticism; Telling His Faults; Impervious to Women; The Apology of a Professor: An Essay on Modern Learning; My Memories and Miseries As a Schoolmaster; Education Eating Up Life; Humour As I See It; When Men Retire; L'Envoi. The Train to Mariposa.

BINDING AND DUST JACKET: Bound in green paper boards with the following stamped in gilt down the spine: Robertson Davies Feast of Stephen [publisher's device] McClelland & Stewart.

The dust jacket is multi-coloured. The front panel has an illustration of Leacock's home in Orillia, ON. Printing on the spine panel of the jacket is in black and white and is the same as the stamping on the book's spine. The back panel has an illustration of Leacock's head and shoulders within a series of coloured diamonds. The flaps, which are white, summarize

Davies's introduction and provide biographical information about him. The price of the book is found on the front flap ($5.95). Jacket design by David John Shaw.

NOTES: *Feast of Stephen* is an anthology of sketches and essays taken from *The Boy I Left Behind Me, Happy Stories Just to Laugh at, Too Much College,* and *The Iron Man and the Tin Woman.*

The novelist, playwright, and critic, Robertson Davies, spoke on CBC Radio about Leacock in 1956. He also wrote the introductions to the New Canadian Library editions of *Literary Lapses* (1957, see A5e) and *Moonbeams from the Larger Lunacy* (1964, see A21c). On 30–31 October 1970 at Massey College in the University of Toronto, he partook in a seminar on "The Other Leacock." Davies's presentation on that occasion, "Leacock as a Literary Artist," was published with other contributions to the symposium in the *University of Toronto Graduate* 3, no. 4 (Winter 1970–71): 78–87. Even more interesting in terms of Davies's association with Leacock is *The McFiggin Fragment*, a pamphlet which purports to be Leacock's diary of his life in a Toronto student boarding-house. Written by Davies, *The McFiggin Fragment* was specially printed for members of the symposium by the Massey College Press.

The exact date of publication of *Feast of Stephen* is not known. Number of copies printed not known.

On 14 February 1970, McClelland and Stewart published Davies's *Stephen Leacock*, no. w7 of the New Canadian Library subseries, Canadian Writers. This consists of Davies's introduction to *The Feast of Stephen*. However, Davies was much displeased by it:

> . . . I am ashamed to speak of it to my friends and could not dream of recommending it to students. . . . I feel compelled, therefore, to say that I will not sign a contract for *Feast of Stephen*, or do any further work on its preparation, until I have a letter from McClelland and Stewart guaranteeing that the whole of the material contained in *Stephen Leacock* will be printed as an introduction, that the text will be what I have written and not what your anonymous editor prefers. . . , and that corrections which I will make in the proof will be heeded. (quoted by Judith Skelton Grant, *Robertson Davies: Man of Myth* (Toronto: Viking, 1994), p. 441.

Reprinted as a "trade paperback for the first time in 1990." The front cover of the latter has a caricature by Graham Pilsworth of Davies and Leacock shaking hands.

COPIES EXAMINED: CS (first edition in jacket and 1990 reprint); QMMRB (first edition in jacket).

## A121a.1 *New Canadian Library issue* (1974):

Feast | of | Stephen | An anthology of some of the less | familiar writings of Stephen | Leacock, with a critical introduction by Robertson Davies | General Editor: Malcolm Ross | New Canadian Library No. 95 | [publisher's device within an oval: abstract sketch of a man standing on a horse-drawn chariot, taking aim with a bow and arrow] | McClelland and Stewart Limited | *The Canadian Publishers*

This is a photographic reprint (180 × 111 mm.) of A121a published in 1974 in the New Canadian Library series at $1.95. Perfect bound in multi-coloured stiff paper (primarily in orange and green). 2,228 copies sold in 1974. Up to the end of 1979, 4,986 copies sold (information based on file 14, "New Canadian Library," box 93, series A, McClelland and Stewart fonds, OHM).

COPIES EXAMINED: CS.

## A122 HOODOO MCFIGGIN'S CHRISTMAS 1970

### A122a *Canadian edition*:

[all lines within three rectangles, the second one thick] HOODOO | McFIGGIN'S [the c is raised] | CHRISTMAS | [rule touching both sides of the inner rectangle; illustration of sleigh; rule touching both sides of the inner rectangle] | BY STEPHEN LEACOCK

◆ $1^6$. *1–12* pp. (6 leaves). 301 × 233 mm.

CONTENTS: p. *1* title; p. *2* Hoodoo McFiggin's Christmas is from Nonsense Novels by Stephen Leacock and is reproduced by special arrangement with McClelland and Stewart Limited. | The reproductions of the 1910–1911 Fall & Winter catalogue pages appear through the kind permission of the archives of The T. Eaton Company Limited.; pp. *3, 5, 7, 9* and *11* text of Leacock's short story, with the text on each page within three rectangles, the second one thick; pp. *4, 6, 8* and *10* illustrations from The T. Eaton catalogue; p. *12* colophon within three rectangles, the second one thick: This keepsake has been designed | for the friends of Cooper & Beatty, Limited | Christmas, 1970 | [rule touching both sides of the inner rectangle; illustration of children's building blocks].

BINDING: Beige flecked paper wire-stitched in a dark brown wrapper with the front of the wrapper as on the title page.

NOTES: This is the second story by Leacock issued by Cooper & Beatty, Limited as a Christmas keepsake. See also A113b and A128. Number of copies printed not known. See C99.1 for the original publication of this story.

COPIES EXAMINED: CS (two copies).

### A122b *English edition* (1985):

HOODOO McFIGGIN'S | CHRISTMAS | *A Story by* | STEPHEN LEACOCK | [illustration in blue of a child in bed with a Christmas stocking and wrapped presents at the foot of the bed; the next three lines within the illustration:] | Illustrated by | PHILLIDA | GILI | CHRISTOPHER SKELTON | 1985

◆ $1–5^8$. *1–4, 5–8, 9–10,* 11, 12, 13, 14, 15, *16,* 17, *18,* 19, 20, 21, 22, 23, 24, 25, 26, 27, 28, 29, *30, 31, 32, 33, 34, 35, 36, 37, 1–3* leaves. 140 × 102 mm. Leaves are unopened at the top. For each pair of conjugate leaves printing is on the recto of the first leaf and the verso of the second leaf.

CONTENTS: folio *1* half title; folio 2 blank; folio *3* title; folio 4 [all lines in blue] *Published by* | Christopher Skelton | at the September Press | Bridge Approach, Mill Road | Wellingborough, England | NN8 1QN | ISBN 0 9503226 7 9 (Wrappered) | ISBN 0 9503326 8 7 (Hard–back) | Foreword © Bernard Braden 1985 | This story was first published in *Literary Lapses* | (The Bodley Head, 1910) and is reproduced | here with the permission of The Bodley Head | Limited, London, and Dodd, Mead and | Company, New York. | Printed in England; folios 5–9 Braden's foreword dated October 1985; folios 11, 13, 15, 17, 19,

21, 23, 25, 27, 29, 31, 33, 35, and 37 text; folios *10, 12, 14, 16, 18, 20, 22, 24, 26, 28, 30, 32, 34, 36,* and *1* illustrations of Christmas gifts and Hoodoo McFiggin; p. 2 colophon in blue; p. 3 blank.

BINDING AND DUST JACKET: There are three binding variants:

1. purple wrappers glued to the sewn gatherings with a rectangular illustration (boots, 'collars, shorts, suspenders, a toothbrush, and a book) in blue on the front of the wrapper and the title in red on the front and spine. 400 copies.

2. red buckram with a circular paper label affixed to the upper board and the title stamped in gilt on the spine. The paper label has an illustration in blue similar to the title page with the title on the label in red. The dust jacket is white with the same illustration and lettering as the wrapper of 1. 250 copies.

3. red cloth, with head and tail pieces, covered with batik-pattered paper. The title is printed in red on a paper label affixed to the spine. The dust jacket is the same as 2. Twenty-five numbered copies "specially bound" by Clare Skelton.

The endpapers for each variant are the same, and consist of the following: the same illustration used for the wrapper of 1 and the dust jacket of 2 and 3; rectangular illustration in blue of a drum, rifle, sled, watch, dog, pen, skates, and a boathouse.

NOTES: This edition of *Hoodoo McFiggin's Christmas* was the first of two imprints published by the September Press, the other being John Dryden's *Alexander's Feast.* According to the colophon, the book was printed by Christopher Skelton and Alan Bultitude in Monotype Modern No. 7 on Amatruda Amalfi hand-made paper in an edition of 675 copies. Variant 1 sold for £8, 2 for £12, and 3 for £37.

See also GAS [Geoffrey Spencer], "Christmas Perspective," *Amphora* 74 (December 1988): 8–16. Spencer relates that he acquired ". . . the printed sheets, printed one side only, from Christopher Skelton at the September Press in Wellingborough, and bound them in full chocolate-brown morocco. The decorations are yet to come. . . ." (at pp. 15–6).

COPIES EXAMINED: CS (all three variant bindings; no. 22 of variant 3).


## A123 THE PRIZE FIGHT OF THE FUTURE [1973]

[cover title; the first line in outline type] THE PRIZE FIGHT OF THE FUTURE. | A FORECAST. | BY STEPHEN LEACOCK. | [text of Leacock's story in two columns with two illustrations] | reproduced by offset lithography from the original printing in Our Monthly | magazine, exactly as it appeared in 1896.

◆ Leaflet folded once to form four pages. *1, 24–25, 1* pp. 278 × 215 mm.

CONTENTS: p. *1* as described in the quasi-facsimile; pp. 24–25 text; p. *1* Our Literary Discovery at ManuLife (article in two columns which explains how "The Prize Fight of the Future" was first published in *Our Monthly*, with photograph of the Leacock Memorial Medal).

BINDING: Printed by offset lithography on light yellow paper stock.

NOTES: *Our Monthly*, the house organ of the Manufacturers Life Insurance Company of Toronto, began in 1891, four years after the company was established. The magazine was a literary journal for a brief period. Leacock's story, "The Prize Fight of the Future. A Forecast," was first published in the May 1896 issue (see C96.6). According to the explanation on the last page of this leaflet, Leacock was paid $5 for his story.

A script writer for ManuLife's audio-visual department, Jack Blackman, rediscovered the story in September 1972 while browsing through the company's early publications. The story was brought to the attention of Ralph Curry, the curator of the Stephen Leacock Museum. Copies of the story were sent to several newspapers, "and several availed themselves of the opportunity to reprint it." On June 16 1973 at the Leacock Dinner, ManuLife presented a cheque for $500 to Don Bell, the Leacock Medal winner and author of *Saturday Night at the Bagel Factory*. A copy of *Our Monthly* containing Leacock's story was also presented to the Leacock Museum at that time. This leaflet was apparently published shortly after the rediscovery of the story in November 1972.

COPIES EXAMINED: CS; LAT; SLM (three copies).

## A124 THE SOCIAL CRITICISM OF STEPHEN LEACOCK 1973

The social criticism of Stephen Leacock | EDITED AND INTRODUCED BY ALAN BOWKER | UNIVERSITY OF TORONTO PRESS

◆ $1-5^{16} \; 6^{18}$. *i–viii*, ix–xlviii, *1–3*, 4–11, *12–13*, 14–26, *27*, 28–39, *40–41*, 42–50, *51*, 52–60, *61*, 62–69, *70–73*, 74–83, *84–85*, 86–92, *93*, 94–101, *102–103*, 104–113, *114–115*, 116–121, *122–123*, 124–132, *133*, 134–145, *1–3* pp. (98 leaves). 215 × 138 mm.

CONTENTS: p. *i* The social history of Canada | MICHAEL BLISS, EDITOR; p. *ii* sub-title: THE UNSOLVED RIDDLE OF SOCIAL JUSTICE | AND OTHER ESSAYS; p. *iii* title; p. *iv* © University of Toronto Press 1973 | Toronto and Buffalo | Printed in Canada | ISBN (casebound) 0-8020-1997-8 | ISBN (paperback) 0-8020-6201-6 | LC 73-79860 | Dates of original publication | [seven lines listing the title of each publication and the year first published]; p. *v* table of contents; p. *vi* blank; p. *vii* An introduction | BY ALAN BOWKER; p. *viii* blank; pp. ix–xlviii Bowker's introduction, including notes and a selected bibliography; p. *1* fly title; p. 2 blank; pp. 3, 4–145 text (pp. *12, 40, 70, 84, 102, 114,* and *122* blank); pp. *1–3* blank.

TEXT: Greater Canada: An Appeal; Literature and Education in America; The Apology of a Professor: An Essay on Modern Learning; The Devil and Deep Sea: A Discussion of Modern Morality; The Woman Question; The Tyranny of Prohibition; *The Unsolved Riddle of Social Justice* (text identical to A31).

BINDING AND JACKET: There are two binding variants: black paper boards with black endpapers; and white glossy stiff paper, perfect bound. Stamped down the spine of the former in silver: Social criticism Leacock Toronto.

Copies in paper boards have a glossy white dust jacket. Printed on the front panel of the jacket: The | social | criticism | of | Stephen | Leacock | [to the right of these lines is a solid red circle with a zig-zag circumference; the next three lines are in blue at an angle within the circle] | The unsolved riddle | of social justice | and other essays | [the next line in red] Edited and introduced by Alan Bowker. Printed down the jacket's spine: [in red] Social criticism [in blue] Leacock [in black] Toronto. On the back panel of the jacket, printed in two columns, is a list of titles in The Social History of Canada series, general editor Michael Bliss. *The Social Criticism of Stephen Leacock: The Unsolved Riddle of Justice and Other Essays* is listed in the right-hand column, "$3.95 paper / $12.50 cloth [i.e. paper boards]".

The front flap has a synopsis of the book's contents along with the price; the back flap has biographical information on Leacock and Bowker and the ISBN and LC numbers.

Printing on the binding in stiff paper is similar to that on the dust jacket. The front cover and spine are identical. Information on the back of the jacket is printed on the inside of the back cover. Information on the flaps of the jacket is printed on the back cover.

NOTES: Alan Bowker was a graduate student in history at the University of Toronto in 1973. His supervisor was the historian, Michael Bliss. Bowker joined the Department of External Affairs without completing his doctorate. For his edition of Leacock's political writings, he was paid a flat fee. He recalls proofreading the galleys of the book in September and October 1973. Publication apparently occurred the following month in an edition of 2,000 copies. On 22 March 1973, the University of Toronto Press paid McClelland and Stewart $250 (half to Barbara Nimmo) for the use of Leacock's texts (information based on TP1, McClelland and Stewart fonds, OHM).

Also examined was the 1996 photographic reprint with the title: *Social Criticism: The Unsolved Riddle of Social Justice and Other Essays*. The preliminary pages (i.e. prior p. *viii*) have been reset. Bowker has added a postscript and supplementary bibliography (pp. *xlix–lix*). Price $14.95, perfect binding (215 × 138 mm.), with a black-and-white photograph of Leacock (1914) on the front cover.

COPIES EXAMINED: CS (both binding variants and 1996 reprint).


## A125 THE PENGUIN STEPHEN LEACOCK 1981

**A125a** *first edition*:

THE PENGUIN | STEPHEN LEACOCK | *Selected and Introduced by* | ROBERTSON DAVIES | [Penguin Book's publisher's device: illustration of a penguin within an oval] | PENGUIN BOOKS

◆ *i–ix*, x–xii, 1–527, 1–5 pp. (272 leaves). 196 × 125 mm.

CONTENTS: p. *i* half title; p. *ii* blank; p. *iii* title; p. *iv* [five lines which list addresses of Penguin Books Ltd. and its branches in England, the United States, Australia, Canada, and New Zealand] | First published 1981 | This collection copyright © Penguin Books Canada Limited, 1981 | Introduction copyright © Robertson Davies, 1981 | All rights reserved | Permission to use the stories in this collection was | kindly granted by McClelland and Stewart Limited and The Bodley Head | Manufactured in Canada by Webcom Limited | [nine lines pertaining to copyright]; pp. *v–vii* table of contents; p. *viii* blank; pp. *ix*–xii Robertson Davies's introduction, dated 5 February 1981; pp. *1–527* text; pp. *1–5* advertisements for *Peguinews*, books published by Penguin, Wayne Grady's *The Penguin Book of Canadian Short Stories*, books by Davies, and Hugh MacLennan's *Voices in Time*.

TEXT: The text is divided into twenty-one numbered chapters, each containing a selection of stories and sketches taken from Leacock's previously published books.
1 from *Literary Lapses* — My Financial Career; Boarding-House Geometry; The Awful Fate of Melpomenus Jones; A, B, and C: The Human Element in Mathematics.
2 from *Nonsense Novels* — Gertrude the Governess: or Simple Seventeen; Guido the Gimlet of Ghent: A Romance of Chivalry; Hannah of the Highlands: or The Laird of Loch Aucherlocherty.

3 from *Behind the Beyond* — Homer and Humbug: An Academic Discussion.

4 from *Moonbeams from the Larger Lunacy* — The Spiritual Outlook of Mr. Doomer.

5 from *Arcadian Adventures with the Idle Rich* — chapter 6 The Rival Churches of St. Asaph and St. Osoph; chapter 7 The Ministrations of the Reverend Uttermust Dumfarthing; chapter 8 The Great Fight for Clean Government.

6 from *Further Foolishness* — Are the Rich Happy?

7 from *Sunshine Sketches of a Little Town* — chapter 1 The Hostelry of Mr. Smith; chapter 3 The Marine Excursions of the Knights of Pythias; chapter 9 The Mariposa Bank Mystery; chapter 11 The Candidacy of Mr. Smith.

8 from *My Discovery of England* — Oxford as I See It; We Have with Us To-night.

9 from *The Hohenzollerns in America* — How to Introduce Two People to One Another.

10 from *Over the Footlights* — Oroastus — A Greek Tragedy.

11 from *The Iron Man and the Tin Woman* — Further Progress in Specialization; Eddie the Bar-tender.

12 from *The Dry Pickwick* — The Perfect Optimist; Ho for Happiness: A Plea for Lighter and Brighter Literature.

13 from *Winnowed Wisdom* — Our Summer Convention As Described by One of Its Members; At the Ladies' Culture Club: A Lecture on the Fourth Dimension.

14 from *Short Circuits* — Old Junk and New Money: A Little Study in the Latest Antiques; How to Borrow Money; Save Me from My Friends; The Old Men's Page.

15 from *Model Memoirs* — My Victorian Childhood by Lady Nearleigh Slopover; Overworking the Alphabet.

16 from *Essays and Literary Studies* — Fiction and Reality: A Study of the Art of Charles Dickens.

17 from *Frenzied Fiction* — The New Education.

18 from *Too Much College* — Bass Fishing on Lake Simcoe with Jake Gaudaur.

19 *The Boy I Left Behind Me* (the entire book except the epilogue, see A104b).

20 from *My Remarkable Uncle and Other Sketches* — My Remarkable Uncle.

21 from *Last Leaves* — Three Score and Ten: The Business of Growing Old.

BINDING: Perfect binding in stiff paper. On the front cover is the following: The Penguin [Penguin Book's publisher's device] | [rule] | [the next two lines in purple] Stephen | Leacock | [partial rule] | *Selected* | *and* | *Introduced by* | *Robertson* | *Davies* | [to the right of the previous five lines is a colour illustration of a Leacock's head and shoulders]. Printed down the spine: The Penguin [next two words in purple] STEPHEN LEACOCK ISBN 0 14 [rest of ISBN number under the first part of the number] 00.5890 7 [Penguin Book's publisher's device]. The back cover has two paragraphs about Leacock and the collection of stories in *The Penguin Stephen Leacock*, the ISBN number, and the recommended price (blacked out).

NOTES: Number of copies printed and publication date not known.

COPIES EXAMINED: CS.

## A125b *second edition* (1985):

[transcription identical to A125a]

◆ *1–5*, 6–447, *1* pp. (224 leaves). 210 × 142 mm.

CONTENTS: p. *1* half title with biographical information about Leacock; p. *2* blank; p. *3* title; p. *4* [five lines which list addresses of Penguin Books Ltd. and its branches in England, the United States, Australia, Canada, and New Zealand] | First published 1981 | Reprinted 1982, 1985 | This collection copyright © Penguin Books Canada Limited, 1981 | Introduction copyright © Robertson Davies, 1981 | All rights reserved | Permission to use the stories in this collection was | kindly granted by McClelland and Stewart Limited and The Bodley Head | Typeset, printed and bound in Great Britain by | Hazell Watson & Viney Limited, | Member of the BPCC Group, | Aylesbury, Bucks | Set in VIP Times | [nine lines pertaining to copyright]; pp. 5–6 table of contents; pp. 7–10 Robertson Davies's introduction, dated 5 February 1981; pp. 11–447 text; pp. 1 blank.

TEXT: Identical to A125a.

BINDING: Perfect binding in stiff, goldish brown paper with lettering in black and illustrations in metallic green, black, white, and orange. The front cover features a round, abstract portrait of Leacock; beneath the portrait in the left-hand corner is Penguin Book's publisher's device, and above the portrait within a rectangle is: A COMPENDIUM OF COMIC GEMS | THE PENGUIN | STEPHEN LEACOCK. The spine has the title within a rectangle, the ISBN number, and the publisher's device. On the back cover within a rectangle is the following: [publisher's device] | DELICIOUS STORIES AND OCCASIONAL PIECES | BY THE GREAT CANADIAN HUMOURIST [sic] | STEPHEN LEACOCK. Beneath the rectangle is a paragraph on the contents of the book, a quotation from Davies's introduction, the prices in various countries ($9.95 Canadian), and the ISBN number. Cover illustration by Leslie Howell.

NOTES: Although the verso of the title leaf states that this is a reprint of A125a, it is in fact a new setting of type.

COPIES EXAMINED: CS.

## A126 CHRISTMAS WITH STEPHEN LEACOCK 1988

[all lines within a rectangle; the first four lines in open type] CHRISTMAS | WITH | STEPHEN | LEACOCK | REFLECTIONS | ON THE | YULETIDE | SEASON | NATURAL HERITAGE/NATURAL HISTORY INC. | TORONTO, ONTARIO

◆ 1–7, 8–111, [1] pp. (56 leaves). 250 × 201 mm.

CONTENTS: p. 1 black-and-white photograph (extending from the inside of the front cover) taken from the back of the Stephen Leacock Museum, arches and an alcove looking out to trees and land covered with snow; p. 2 blank; p. 3 title; p. 4 blank; p. 5 paragraph extracted from Leacock's essay "War-Time Santa Claus"; p. 6 copyright page in two columns — the right-hand column, titled A SELECTED BIBLIOGRAPHY, lists published stories (name of publication where the stories appeared) and unpublished stories — the left-hand column consists of: [Canadian Cataloguing in Publication Data, source of the cover photo] | Christmas with Stephen Leacock | Published by Natural Heritage/Natural History Inc. | P.O. Box 69, Postal Station H | Toronto, Ontario | M4C 5H7 | Copyright © November 1988 | [four lines about copyright] | Design: Derek Chung Tiam Fook | Text Production: Robin Brass Studio | Printed and bound in Canada by | T.H. Best Printing Company Limited; p. 7 table of contents; p. 8 information about the author; pp. 9–11 introduction by Ralph L. Curry; p. 12 four short paragraphs by Gary Lautens; pp. 13–107 text; pp. 108–109

"Afterword: A Christmas in Contemporary Mariposa" by Jay Cody; p. 110 acknow-ledgements; p. 111 publisher's comments from Barry L. Penhale; p. 1 black-and-white photograph (extending from the inside of the back cover) of Leacock's writing desk, windows, and snow on the land outside of the Stephen Leacock Museum. Black-and-white photographs on pp. 107 (mementos and documents on Leacock's desk), 109 (Jay Cody and his secretary at the Leacock Museum), and 110 (Don Standfield, photographer).

TEXT: Christmas Rapture; Merry Christmas; Let Us Be Thankful: A Few Thoughts for Christmas; First Aid to the Christmas Tourist: An Attempt to Lighten His Burden of Information; Merry Christmas, Mars: An Optimist Sends Greetings across Space; This Merry Christmas: A Christmas Star Shines Through the Mists; Christmas Fiction and National Friction: An Application of the Dear Old Christmas Stories to National Harmony and World Peace; Hoodoo McFiggin's Christmas; A Christmas Examination; A Christmas Letter; Caroline's Christmas: or, The Inexplicable Infant; The Errors of Santa Claus; A Blighted Christmas; The Discoloured Christmas; The Christmas Ghost: Unemployment in One of Our Oldest Industries; War-Time Santa Claus; War-Time Christmas; Scenes from a Renovated Christmas.

BINDING: Perfect bound, stiff paper covers. The front cover has a blurry photograph of a winter scene — Leacock, circa 1928, attired in his racoon-skin coat with his hat and walking stick (courtesy of the National Archives of Canada). The photograph is framed within a gold rectangle, and to the right of Leacock, within a solid wine-coloured rectangle, is the title. The spine is gilt with words vertically displayed: CHRISTMAS WITH STEPHEN LEACOCK [remaining words in white] NATURAL HERITAGE. The back cover is wine-coloured with lettering in white. A gold rectangle contains a black-and-white photograph of the Leacock Museum during winter and several paragraphs by John Robert Colombo. Outside the rectangle is the ISBN number (0-920474-47-0).

NOTES: This book, which gathers together Leacock's sketches about Christmas from magazines and Leacock's books, was initiated by Jay Cody, the Director of the Stephen Leacock Museum. Five apparently unpublished sketches are contained in the book: Let Us Be Thankful: A Few Thoughts for Christmas (see C20.27, however); First Aid to the Christmas Tourist: An Attempt to Lighten His Burden of Information; Merry Christmas, Mars: An Optimist Sends Greetings Across Space; A Blighted Christmas (see C21.43, however); and The Discoloured Christmas (see C20.29, however). Although the book was advertised in *Quill & Quire* in September 1987 with a projected publication date of October 1987, it was still at the printers in April 1988. Published in November 1988 in an edition of 3,225 copies. Price. $14.95.

COPIES EXAMINED: CS; OHM.

## A127  WANTED – MORE PROFITEERS  1988

[cover title; the first two lines in white against a solid black, rectangular background] WANTED – MORE PROFITEERS | STEPHEN LEACOCK | [to the right of the first two lines and attached to the black background is a black rectangle containing the following logo, the letters joined and the L resembling a V on its side:] LA

♦ Broadside, plain white paper stock. 297 × 211 mm.

CONTENTS: Leacock's essay, "Wanted – No More Profiteers," printed in two columns on both sides. At the bottom left-hand corner of the recto, within a rectangle, is the following: Libertarian Reprints No. 10 | ISSN 0267 6796 ISBN 1 870614 09 7 | An occasional publication of the Libertarian Alliance, | [two lines with the address of the Alliance in London, England] | © 1988, Libertarian Alliance. | [to the right of the last three lines, the letters joined and the L resembling a V on its side:] LA | This piece of writing was first published as | Chapter VII of *My Discovery of England*, | (John Lane, The Bodley Head, London, 1922 second edition [i.e. printing]). | Humorous author Professor Stephen Leacock's best known | books were *Literary Lapses*, *Nonsense Novels*, *Sunshine Sketches* | *of a Little Town*, and *Arcadian Adventures with the Idle Rich*. | The views expressed in this publication are those of its author, | and not necessarily those of the Libertarian Alliance, its | Committee, Advisory Council or subscribers, and that applies | with particular force to Leacock's abysmal final paragraph. | LA Secretary and Editorial Director: Chris R. Tame | Executive Editor: Brian Micklethwait | FOR LIFE, LIBERTY AND PROPERTY.

NOTES: Leacock's essay, "Wanted – No More Profiteers," originally appeared in *Collier's* under the title, "Wanted — More Profiteers: The World Is to the Strong: Let's Demand Better Prices" (see C22.17). Publication subsequently occurred in book form in A37 with the title, "Business in England. Wanted — More Profiteers."

The Libertarian Alliance is an international organization devoted to libertarian principles. The Alliance publishes a journal, *Free Life*, and also publishes a variety of series in leaflet and pamphlet format. Leacock's essay appeared as no. 10 of the Libertarian Reprints series. Price 20p. According to the Director of the Alliance, Chris R. Tame, no records are kept ". . . of how many copies we print, but, like all our 550 plus (and growing) publications, it is kept constantly in print" (e-mail to Carl Spadoni, 8 January 1998). The Alliance objected to the last paragraph of Leacock's essay, which reads as follows: "And incidentally, when the profiteer has finished his work, we can always put him back into the penitentiary if we like. But we need him just now."

In the copies examined, the address of the Alliance was crossed out in pen and a more current address was stamped above the cover title. For further information on the Alliance and its publishing programme, see the Web site at: http://www.digiweb.com/igeldard/LA.

COPIES EXAMINED: CS (two copies).


## A128 THE ERRORS OF SANTA CLAUS 1989

[all lines within two rectangles, the outer rectangle thick and green; the first two lines in script with swash capitals] *The Errors of* | *Santa Claus* | STEPHEN LEACOCK | [green ornament] | Toronto | COOPER & BEATTY | 1989

♦ $1^8$. *1-16* pp. (8 leaves). 230 X 153 mm.

CONTENTS: pp. *1-2* blank; p. *3* [in script with swash capitals] *A Christmas Keepsake*; p. *4* blank; p. *5* title; p. *6* Reprinted by permission of Dodd, Mead & Company, Inc. from WEST WISDOM [sic] AND DRY HUMOR by Stephen Leacock. | Copyright 1931 by Dodd, Mead & Company, Inc. Copyright renewed 1959 by Stephen L. Leacock.; pp. *7-13* text of Leacock's short story, with the text on each page within two rectangles, the outer one thick and green; p. *14* [logo of Cooper & Beatty] This keepsake | is sent with | best wishes from Cooper & Beatty | for Christmas | 1989; pp. *15-16* blank.

BINDING: Stiff white paper, wire-stitched. Dark red paper covers (with flaps) are glued to the white paper. Printed in white on the front cover in script with swash capitals: *The Errors of | Santa Claus.*

NOTES: This is the third story by Leacock issued by Cooper & Beatty, Limited as a Christmas keepsake. See also A113b and A122a. Number of copies printed not known. Designed by Tony Mann. The reference on the copyright page to *West Wisdom and Dry Humor* is wrong. The book is entitled *Wet Wit & Dry Humour* (A57). See C16.26 for the original publication of this story.

COPIES EXAMINED: CS (with letters from Tony [Mann] indicating that he designed the keepsake).

# A129 THE MAN IN ASBESTOS 1990

THE MAN IN | [the next line in grey inline type] ASBESTOS | An Allegory of the Future | by | Stephen B. Leacock | 1990 | Foolscap Press | Berkeley / Santa Cruz

◆ *1-6⁴. 1-13, 2-3, 4, 5, 6, 7, 8, 9, 10, 11, 12, 13-15, 16, 17, 18, 19-21, 22, 23, 24, 25, 26, 27-28, 1-8* pp. (24 leaves). 166 × 228 mm.

CONTENTS: pp. *1-4* blank; p. *5* half title; p. *6* geometric illustration; p. *7* title; p. *8* Copyright © 1990 Foolscap Press | Illustrations by Jan Vredeman de Vries, | first published in PERSPECTIVE (1604-05) | and re-published by Dover Publications, Inc. 1968. | Additional illustrations © 1990 by Peggy Gotthold.; p. *9* introduction by the publishers; p. *10* blank; p. *11* fly title; p. *12* geometric illustration; pp. *13, 2-28* text (geometric illustrations on pp. *4, 6, 8, 10, 12, 16, 18, 22, 24,* and *26*); pp. *1-2* blank; p. *3* colophon; pp. *4-8* blank.

BINDING: Bound in dark blackish blue cloth, with a large, irregularly shaped, greyish white paper label affixed to the boards and spine. Printed on the label on the upper board in grey: THE MAN IN | ASBESTOS. The endpapers are comprised of grey geometric illustrations.

NOTES: According to the colophon and a prospectus, this book is "the premiere edition of the Foolscap Press." It was designed, printed, and bound by Peggy Gotthold and Lawrence G. Van Velzer in a limited edition of 150 copies. The book is "printed letterpress on Mohawk Superfine paper on a Hacker Hand Press. The type is set in Monotype Sans Serif and the books are bound in Japanese cloth over boards." The majority of illustrations are "photo-engravings of drawings by Jan Vredeman de Vries, the Dutch architect, painter, and engraver of the 16th century." His illustrations are found on the endpapers, on separate pages, and in the outer margins of the text. Additional photo-engravings of drawings depicting the character of the Man in Asbestos are by Gotthold. Price $50 ($5 for shipping and handling).

Leacock's essay "The Man in Asbestos: An Allegory of the Future" was first published in *Saturday Night* (see C11.13) under the title, "The Man in Asbestos; or, An Allegory of the Future."

COPIES EXAMINED: CS (with prospectus); QMMRB (with prospectus).

## A130 SELECTED READINGS FROM STEPHEN LEACOCK 1992

Selected Readings | From Stephen Leacock | [six lines in Chinese: title (Li-k̓e-ke yu mo tso p̓in hsuan tu); names of the editors (Li Chi-chi, Sheng Chih, Cheng Li, and Cheng Chien-hua); place of publication (Changsha); publisher (Chung-nan kung yeh ta hsueh ch pan she); and apparent date of publication (July 1991)]

◆ 1–6, 1–161, 1 pp. (84 leaves). 185 × 130 mm.

CONTENTS: p. 1 title; p. 2 copyright page in Chinese; p. 3 drawing of Leacock; p. 4 blank; p. 5 table of contents; p. 6 blank; pp. 1–7 introduction in Chinese; pp. 8–161 text with annotations in Chinese following each story; p. 1 blank.

TEXT: 1 My Financial Career; 2 The Awful Fate of Melpomenus Jones; 3 A Christmas Letter; 4 How to Make a Million Dollars; 5 How to Live to Be 200; 6 Saloonio; 7 Soaked in Seaweed; 8 The Raft: An Interlude; 9 The Mariposa Bank Mystery; 10 A Brief Account of Myself; 11 How We Kept Mother's Day; 12 The Hallucination of Mr. Butt; 13 My Affair with My Landlord; 14 The Retroactive Existence of Mr. Juggins; 15 Humour as I See It; 16 The Survival of the Fittest; 17 My Remarkable Uncle.

BINDING: Perfect bound in a light bluish green wrapper. On the front wrapper is an abstract drawing of a smiling face wearing a hat, the title in English and Chinese, the names of the editors, and the abstract drawing upside down. The back wrapper has the title in English and Chinese, the ISBN number, and price ($2.50).

NOTES: According to the copyright page, this selection of Leacock's stories, intended for Chinese students studying English, was published in an edition of 1,200 copies in March 1992.

COPIES EXAMINED: OONL.

## A131 MY FINANCIAL CAREER AND OTHER FOLLIES 1993

Stephen Leacock | MY FINANCIAL | CAREER | and Other Follies | *Selected and* | *with an Afterword by David Staines* | [publisher's device: thick, wavy band; wavy rule] | M&S | [thick rule]

◆ 1–8, 9–197, 198, 199–203, 1–5 pp. (104 leaves). 177 × 108 mm.

CONTENTS: p. 1 biographical information about Leacock; p. 2 THE NEW CANADIAN LIBRARY | General Editor: David Staines | ADVISORY BOARD | Alice Munro | W.H. New | Guy Vanderhaeghe; p. 3 title; p. 4 Copyright © 1993 by McClelland & Stewart Inc. | Afterword copyright © 1993 by David Staines | [seven lines concerning copyright; nine lines of Canadian Cataloguing in Publication Data, including ISBN 0-7710-9892-8] | Series design by T.M. Craan | Cover design by Andrew Skuja | Typesetting by M&S, Toronto | The support of the Government of Ontario through the Ministry of | Culture and Communications is acknowledged. | Printed and bound by Webcom Ltd. | [five lines giving the address of McClelland & Stewart Inc.]; pp. 5–6 table of contents; pp. 7–8 acknowledgements, providing the source where the stories and essays first appeared in book form; pp. 9–197 text; p. 198 blank; pp. 199–203 afterword by David Staines; pp. 1–3 list of Leacock's books, divided into categories such as autobiography, biography, etc.; p. 4 blank; p. 5 list of five of Leacock's books published by McClelland & Stewart in the New Canadian Library series.

TEXT: My Financial Career; The Awful Fate of Melpomenus Jones; Gertrude the Governess: or, Simple Seventeen; The Marine Excursion of the Knights of Pythias; The Dentist and the Gas; The Love Story of Mr. Peter Spillikins; The Reading Public: A Book Store Study; The Snoopopaths or Fifty Stories in One; My Revelations as a Spy; Personal Adventures in the Spirit World; War and Peace at the Galaxy Club; Buggam Grange: A Good Old Ghost Story; How We Kept Mother's Day As Related by a Member of the Family; Old Junk and New Money: A Little Study in the Latest Antiques; A Lesson on the Links: The Application of Mathematics to Golf; Fifty Cents' Worth; The Perfect Optimist or Day-Dreams in a Dental Chair; Ho for Happiness: A Plea for Lighter and Brighter Literature; My Remarkable Uncle: A Personal Document; Good News! A New Party!; Humour As I See It; The Saving Grace of Humour: Is There Any?.

BINDING: Paperback. Perfect binding with glossy exterior covers. The covers are multi-coloured: light pinkish brown, blue, black, and white. On the front cover is a reproduction of David Milne's *Columbus Monument*. The back cover features three paragraphs on the book's contents and significance, a citation to Milne's painting, the ISBN number and bar code, and the publisher's name and logo. The ISBN number and bar code are also found on the verso of the front cover.

NOTES: David Staines is a professor of English at the University of Ottawa, author, translator, and editor of many books (e.g. *Tennyson's Camelot*, *The Canadian Imagination: Dimensions of a Literary Culture*, etc.), and the general editor of the New Canadian Library series. In 1986 he edited *Stephen Leacock: A Reappraisal* (Ottawa: University of Ottawa Press). Staines's afterword provides some biographical information on Leacock and comments on his conception of humour. The afterword quotes from an unpublished letter written by Leacock to his son, Stevie, in 1934 on religious belief.

The back cover states that *My Financial Career and Other Follies* ". . . is an original New Canadian Library collection." Staines's anthology gathers together a number of Leacock's vintage pieces of humour from a number of his books. The collection also has two of Leacock's essays on the nature of humour. Published on 1 July 1993 at $5.95. 10,812 copies were printed. By the end of 1996 3,059 copies had sold (1,405 copies sold in 1993, 381 copies in 1994, 753 copies in 1995, and 520 copies in 1996). See also Staines, "Confessions of a Leacock Anthologist," *Newspacket* (Orillia, newsletter of the Stephen Leacock Associates) 21, no. 1 (April 1994): 1, 3.

COPIES EXAMINED: CS (two copies, one sent by Staines on 1 September 1993); OHM; SLM (many copies).

## A132 A LESSON ON THE LINKS 1994

[the first line is a red, swash character drawn in a calligraphic hand] A | LESSON | ON | THE | LINKS | [in red] STEPHEN LEACOCK | AFTERWORD BY | [in red] PETER GZOWSKI | SUPERIOR PROPANE INC. | 1 JUNE 1994

◆ 1$^8$. 1–6, 7–11, 12, 13–14, 1–2 pp. (8 leaves). 216 × 139 mm.

CONTENTS: p. 1 half title; p. 2 frontispiece sketch of Leacock (graphite on paper) by Garth Armstrong; p. 3 title; p. 4 [in red] A LESSON ON THE LINKS | Printed in Canada | Published by Superior Propane Inc. | 75 Tiverton Court | Unionville | L3R 9S3 | Canada |

[in red] AFTERWORD | Copyright © 1994 | Peter Gzowski | [in red] FRONTISPIECE | Sketch | Copyright © 1993 | The Hedge Road Press; p. 5 [the line in red with square brackets] | [x/1 + x2/1 . . . xn/1]; p. 6 blank; pp. 7–11 text of Leacock's sketch; p. 12 blank; pp. 13–14 Gzowski's afterword; p. 1 blank; p. 2 colophon.

BINDING: Bound in white stiff paper stock, somewhat thicker than the paper of the pamphlet's contents, wire-stitched. On the front of the wrapper: [the first word is a red, swash character drawn in a calligraphic hand] A LESSON ON THE LINKS | BY STEPHEN LEACOCK | WITH AN AFTERWORD | by PETER GZOWSKI | IS PUBLISHED IN SUPPORT | OF NATIONAL LITERACY | by SUPERIOR PROPANE INC. | ON THE OCCASION OF | THE FIFTH ANNUAL | PGIs PLAY THE BARN | AT LAKE SIMCOE | CANADA.

According to the designer of this pamphlet, Peter Sibbald Brown, there was also a limited boxed edition of ten copies (not seen).

NOTES: In 1986 Peter Gzowski and other volunteers began raising money for a national adult-literacy programme, Frontier College, by hosting amateur golf tournaments throughout Canada. The Peter Gzowski Invitational (PGI) was first held at the Briars Resort in Jackson's Point, ON, on Lake Simcoe in June 1989. The reference to PLAY THE BARN is to the barbecue-and-show event held at the Red Barn Theatre in Jackson's Point the night before the golf tournament. In his afterword Gzowski muses whether Leacock played golf at the Briars, which was established in 1924: "As a boy, Leacock would have gazed down from the garden of his family farm on the lands from which the course was to be built."

According to the colophon this pamphlet was designed and set into Bembo type by Peter Sibbald Brown. It was printed with vegetable inks at Proving Graphics on 100% recycled paper.

The print run was 1,000 copies. Distributed to the public at no charge. Copies were sold at the gift shop of SLM for $1.99.

The first known appearance of *A Lesson on the Links* occurred on 15 October 1927 (see C27.53). The article was syndicated by the Metropolitan Newspaper Service, New York. It was anthologized in *Short Circuits* (A52) as "A Lesson on the Links: The Application of Mathematics to Golf."

COPIES EXAMINED: CS; SLM (numerous copies examined at the SLM's gift shop in July 1994).


## A133 THE STEPHEN LEACOCK QUOTE BOOK 1996

[dotted rule] | THE | STEPHEN LEACOCK | QUOTE BOOK | [dotted rule] | Compiled by John Robert Colombo | [dotted rule] | [dotted rule] | Colombo & Company | [dotted rule]

◆ *1–58* leaves. 217 × 140 mm. Printing on rectos only.

CONTENTS: folio *1* title; folio *2* [dotted rule] | Copyright © 1996 by J.R. Colombo | All Rights Reserved. | ISBN: 1-896308-79-1 | A QuasiBook | Colombo & Company | 42 Dell Park Avenue | Toronto M6B 2TC | Canada | [four lines in italics providing telephone number, FAX number, e-mail address, and Web address] | Printed in Canada. | [dotted rule]; folios *3–9* Colombo's preface; folios *10–11* Appreciations of Leacock; folios *12–57* text; folio *58* paragraph about the book and another about Colombo.

TEXT: The text consists of "one hundred or so 'quotable quotes'" selected by Colombo from Leacock's writings. The quotations are alphabetically arranged under headings from Achievement to Writing. The sources of the quotations are not identified.

BINDING: Cerlox bound with clear plastic covers. There is also a back cover in stiff white paper.

NOTES: Colombo & Company is the publishing imprint for books written, edited, and translated by the author and anthologist, John Robert Colombo. *The Stephen Leacock Quote Book* was advertised in the September 1996 issue of *Quill & Quire*. Colombo sent a copy of the book to Daphne Mainprize, the curator of the Stephen Leacock Museum, for her approval and comments in early September 1996. When asked about the date of publication and print run of the book, Colombo told Carl Spadoni in an e-mail message of 1 October 1996:

> I have created a publishing imprint for what is known in the book trade as "demand publishing." There is no "print run" per se. There is no inventory. Capital costs are infinitesimal. Copies are produced in small quantities to meet orders on hand.
>
> The imprint by necessity specializes in "QuasiBooks." I originated the term to refer to a specific format. A QuasiBook is the complete text of a book in photocopied form with its own covers and binding.
>
> Colombo and Company is a micropublisher. The idea is to make available to the general public, but specifically to the specialist market, works of marginal commercial but genuine cultural interest, in a speedy fashion.
>
> Price $15.

COPIES EXAMINED: CS; SLM.

## A134 MY RECOLLECTION OF CHICAGO AND THE DOCTRINE OF LAISSEZ FAIRE 1998

STEPHEN LEACOCK | My Recollection of Chicago | AND | The Doctrine of *Laissez Faire* | Edited and introduced by Carl Spadoni | UNIVERSITY OF TORONTO PRESS | Toronto Buffalo London

• $1\text{-}3^{16}$ $4\text{-}6^{8}$ $7^{16}$. *i-vii*, viii-xliv, *1-3*, 4-6, *7-11*, 12-13, *14-15*, 16, *17*, 18-19, *20*, 21-26, *27*, 28-34, *35*, 36-40, *41*, 42-46, *47*, 48-54, *55*, 56-64, *65*, 66-75, *76*, 77-82, *83*, 84-92, *93*, 94-101, *102*, 103-106, *107*, 108-116, *117*, 118-122, *123*, 124-126, *1-6* pp. (88 leaves). 212 × 139 mm.

CONTENTS: p. *i* half title with synopsis of the book and information about the editor; p. *ii* blank; p. *iii* title; p. *iv* © University of Toronto Press Incorporated 1998 | Toronto Buffalo London | Printed in Canada | ISBN 0-8020-4286-4 (cloth) | ISBN 0-8020-8121-5 (paper) | [infinity symbol within a circle] | Printed on acid-free paper | [rule] | [nine lines of Canadian Cataloguing in Publication Data] | [rule] | [six lines regarding the illustrations on p. 8 and the front cover; six lines acknowledging the financial assistance of publishing subsidies from governmental agencies]; p. *v* table of contents; p. *vi* blank; pp. *vii*-xxxix editor's introduction; p. *xxx* blank; pp. *xxxi*-xliv editorial note; pp. *1*-116 text (pp. 2 and 9 blank); pp. *117*-122 bibliography; pp. *123*-126 index; pp. *1-6* blank.

TEXT: My Recollection of Chicago; and Leacock's doctoral thesis, The Doctrine of *Laissez*

*Faire*. The latter consists of a preface and the following chapters: I The Physiocratic Doctrine of the State; II Adam Smith and Government; III The Classical Economists and the Development of Individualism; IV *Laissez Faire* and Legislation; V The Counter Current; VI The Climax of Individualism: Bastiat and Spencer; VII The Middle Century: The Turn of the Tide; VIII The Economists of the Close of the Century: England; IX English Legislative Policy: The New State Interference; X American Economists and American Legislative Policy; XI German Economists and the Kulturstaat; XII Summary and Conclusion.

Leacock's notes to "The Doctrine of *Laissez Faire*" appear after the text. The title page of the manuscript of the thesis is reproduced in facsimile on p. *8*.

BINDING: There are two binding variants. (1) The paperback is perfect bound and has glossy stiff paper covers in camel brown with printing, mainly in red and white, of the title, author and editor's names, and the University of Toronto Press logo. The front cover features a photograph, outlined in red, of a young Leacock (prior to 1910); on the back cover are quotations, printed in red, from the texts and the ISBN number. (2) Bound in red cloth with stamping in gilt on the upper board as follows: [the first twelve lines within a rectangular frame, the left side of the frame missing] My | Recollection | of | Chicago | AND | The Doctrine of | *Laissez* | *Faire* | STEPHEN | LEACOCK | EDITED AND INTRODUCED | BY CARL SPADONI. Stamped on the spine: [down the spine] LEACOCK My Recollection of Chicago AND The Doctrine of *Laissez Faire* | UTP | [logo of the University of Toronto Press: open book within a shield].

NOTES: Leacock pursued graduate studies in political economy and political science at the University of Chicago between 1899 and 1903. His Ph.D. was conferred on 16 June 1903. This book publishes his doctoral dissertation along with an essay of reminiscences (written in 1942 or 1943). The manuscripts of these two pieces of writing were acquired by the Department of Special Collections, University of Chicago Library, from Barbara Nimmo in 1964.

The editor of this book approached the University of Toronto Press about publication on 30 August 1996. The contract is dated 5 March 1997 (signed on 12 March 1997 by the editor). The editor received a royalty of 5% on all copies old. Two sets of page proofs and the edited typescript were sent to the editor on 29 January 1998. The book was published in paperback (800 copies) on 26 June 1998 at $17.95 and in cloth (300 copies) on 25 July 1998 at $40.

COPIES EXAMINED: CS (six copies in paperback, one being an advance copy in gatherings; five copies in cloth); OHM (cloth).

# B Section: CONTRIBUTIONS TO BOOKS

## B1 A HISTORY OF UPPER CANADA COLLEGE, 1829–1892 1893

A HISTORY | OF | Upper Canada College, | 1829 — 1892. | WITH CONTRIBUTIONS BY | Old Upper Canada College Boys, | LIST OF HEAD-BOYS, EXHIBITIONERS, UNIVERSITY | SCHOLARS AND MEDALLISTS, AND A | ROLL OF THE SCHOOL. | [rule] | COMPILED AND EDITED BY | GEORGE DICKSON, M.A., | AND | G. MERCER ADAM. | [rule] | *ILLUSTRATED.* | [rule] | TORONTO: | ROWSELL & HUTCHISON. | [rule] | 1893

◆ 1⁴ 2–41⁴ [$1 signed]. *1–3*, 4–5, *6–9*, 10–11, *12*, 13–22, *23*, 24–43, *44*, 45–49, *50*, 51–65, *66*, 67–75, *76*, 77–86, *87*, 88–96, *97*, 98–104, *105*, 106–112, *113*, 114–126, *127*, 128–135, *136*, 137–155, *156*, 157–176, *177*, 178–199, *200*, 201–217, *218*, 219–231, *232*, 233–262, *263*, 264–270, *271*, 272–327, *1* pp. (164 leaves). 248 × 186 mm.

TEXT: Probably chapter XVIII College Journalism by An Old College Boy, pp. 232, 233–262 (see the notes concerning Leacock's authorship).

BINDING: Two binding variants were examined: bright blue cloth and dark brown cloth, both with bevelled edges and top edge stained gilt. The former has dark brown endpapers and the latter brown and gold patterned marbled endpapers.

Stamping on both variants is identical. Stamped on the spine: [two rules] | HISTORY | OF | UPPER | CANADA | COLLEGE | [rule; ornament blind-stamped; two rules]. Stamped in gilt on the upper board within two blind-stamped rectangles is a crest, a crown, a scroll with the college motto (PALMAM QUI MERUIT FERAT), and the dates, 1829–1892. Blind-stamped on the lower board within two blind-stamped rectangles is a crest with the words UPPER CANADA | COLLEGE.

NOTES: This commemorative history was edited by the Principal of Upper Canada College, George Dickson (b. 1846) and by the author, editor, and publisher, Graeme Mercer Adam (1839–1912). In the preface the editors list eighteen individuals ". . . who have contributed to the volume or furnished materials for it. . . ." Although Leacock is listed, it is not clear what he wrote or furnished by way of information. The book contains twenty-one chapters plus four further chapters of appendices. Three chapters have pseudonymous contributors: chapter V The Régime of Rev. Walter Stennett, M.A., 1857–61 ("Head Boy"); chapter XII Through Upper Canada College ("Contributed"); and chapter XVIII College Journalism ("An Old College Boy").

Chapter XII is not by Leacock because the writer of that chapter states that he entered Upper Canada in 1868 (Leacock was a student at Upper Canada between 1882 and 1887). Leacock graduated from Upper Canada as head boy, and on that basis it is possible that he wrote chapter V. However, more likely is his authorship of chapter XVIII since he was the co-editor of thirteen issues of volume 6 of the *College Times* from 4 November 1886 to 9 June 1887. Leacock's editorial association with the *College Times* would have provided him a good background to write a chapter on college journalism. It is also entirely possible that Leacock did not write any of these chapters at all and that instead he contributed or furnished information to other chapters of the book.

Number of copies printed and date of publication not known.

COPIES EXAMINED: CS (dark brown cloth); OHM (bright blue cloth).

## B2 ADDRESSES DELIVERED BEFORE THE CANADIAN CLUB OF OTTAWA 1910

ADDRESSES | DELIVERED BEFORE | THE CANADIAN CLUB | OF OTTAWA | 1903 — 1909 | EDITED BY | GERALD H. BROWN, | *First Vice-President.* | [coat of arms of The Canadian Club (beaver, crown and banner) | OTTAWA: | THE MORTIMER PRESS | 1910

• $1^8$ $2$–$14^8$ $15^2$ [$1 signed]. *1*–3, 4, 5 6–227, *1* pp. (114 leaves). 225 × 150 mm.

TEXT: Leacock's address (pp. 161–164) entitled "The Political Achievement of Robert Baldwin," delivered on 23 January 1909.

BINDING: Issued in gold cloth, all lettering in black. Stamped on the upper board, within a black rectangle: ADDRESSES | DELIVERED BEFORE | THE CANADIAN CLUB | OF OTTAWA | 1903 — 1909. Stamped on spine: [double rule] | ADDRESSES | BEFORE THE | CANADIAN | CLUB | OTTAWA | 1903–1909 | [double rule].

NOTES: According to the "Introductory," the Canadian Club of Ottawa was established on 9 October 1903 for the purpose of fostering Canadian patriotism; the only qualification for membership was British citizenship either by birth or adoption. Initial membership in the Club totalled 237 members, and by 1910 it had increased to 1,100 members. On 27 April 1909, a resolution was adopted to publish the addresses delivered at the Club. Membership fees were increased from $1 to $1.50 to cover the cost of publication. The texts of the addresses were based on stenographic notes or reports published by the Ottawa press. See also D9.2 for a report of Leacock's speech.

COPIES EXAMINED: CS; OHM.

## B3 TRADE AND COMMERCE 1910

B3a *first issue*:

BUSINESS | ADMINISTRATION | *THEORY, PRACTICE AND APPLICATION* | [rule] | *Editor-In-Chief* | WALTER D. MOODY | GENERAL MANAGER, THE CHICAGO ASSOCIATION OF COMMERCE, | AUTHOR, "MEN WHO SELL THINGS." | *Managing Editor* | SAMUEL MacCLINTOCK, PH. D. | EDITORIAL AND EDUCATIONAL DIRECTOR, | . LA SALLE EXTENSION UNIVERSITY | [rule] | *This work is especially designed to meet the practical every-day needs of | the active business man, and contains the fundamental and basic | principles upon which a successful business is founded, con- | ducted and maintained. To those looking forward to | a business career, this work forms the basis | for a practical and systematic course in | "Business Administration" |* [rule] | PUBLISHED BY | LA SALLE EXTENSION UNIVERSITY | CHICAGO

◆ $\pi^{12}$ ($-\pi$11, $\pi$12) B–IV–1–14$^8$ B.IV–15$^8$ B–IV–16–18$^8$ B.IV–19–20$^8$ B–IV–21–22$^8$ Vol. V–23$^8$ B–IV–24–28$^8$ B.IV–29–31$^8$ [\$1 signed (i.e. rectos of the first leaf of each gathering signed B–IV–, B.IV–, or Vol. V–)]. *1–16, i–iii, 1–2, 2–459, 460, 461–485, 486, 487–492, 1–4* (258 leaves). 236 × 159 mm.

TEXT: Leacock's contribution (pp. 171–355) is entitled "Government and Industry." It consists of the following sections: pp. 171–184 Introduction; pp. 184–207 I Individualism and the Era of Free Trade; pp. 207–239 II Tariff Protection to Industry; pp. 239–276 III Railroad Regulation; pp. 276–305 IV The Government and the Trust; pp. 305–342 V The Government and the Working Class; pp. 342–355 VI Socialism and Its Program. The table of contents (pp. ii–iii) has a further analysis of each section. There are also twenty-one questions for students on Leacock's contribution at the back of the book in the section "Questions in Business Administration" (pp. 467–468).

BINDING: Bound in dull green buckram. There are three brown labels affixed to the spine with stamping on the labels in gilt. On the label on the top portion of the spine: [rule] | BUSINESS | ADMINISTRATION | [rule] | PRINCIPLES | AND | PRACTICE | [rule]. On the label in the centre of the spine: [rule] | TRADE | COMMERCE | [rule]. On the label on the lower portion of the spine: [rule] | LA SALLE EXTENSION | UNIVERSITY | [rule].

NOTES: La Salle Extension University was established in 1909 by the former Vice-President of the United States, General Adlai E. Stevenson. The university offered a three-year diploma course by correspondence in business administration. In addition to a series of special lectures that were mailed each month, students were expected to read twelve textbooks of reference. Samuel MacClintock was the Director and Editor in Chief of the university.

On p. 68 of his notebook of recorded publications and speeches at QMMRB, Leacock wrote: "On Thursday, May 27 [1909], arranged with LaSalle Extension University of Chicago to do a book of 55 to 60 thousand words on *Government and Industry*." He indicates that he finished the book on 27 June 1909, although elsewhere in his notebook he says the writing was finished a day later. There are three tables of contents for the book in his notebook. The first draft apparently had ten chapters, the second nine chapters, and the third, which he revised on 6 June 1909, had eight chapters. The remuneration Leacock received, the date of publication, and the number of copies printed of this textbook are not known.

This volume of *Business Administration* is entitled *Trade and Commerce* (see p. 7). The verso of the title leaf has the following: [rule] | Copyright, 1910, | LASALLE EXTENSION UNIVERSITY. | [rule].

In *Looking Back: An Autobiographical Sketch* ([Urbana, Illinois: s.n. 1959]), p. 36, Simon Litman recalled:

> Part of the time in 1909 was taken up by my writing a book for LaSalle Extension University on *Trade and Commerce*. . . . The work was bound in the same volume with Stephen Leacock's *Government and Industry*, a strange coincidence — a work of a political scientist bracketed with one who graduated from a school of political science before getting his doctor's degree in Zurich.

COPIES EXAMINED: SLM (Leacock's copy).

**B3a.1** *second issue* (1911)

[all lines within a rectangle] | *INTERSTATE COMMERCE* | TRADE AND COMMERCE | [rule] | SIMON LITMAN, PH.D. | University of Illinois | STEPHEN LEACOCK, PH.D. | McGill University | THEODORE H. BOGGS JOHN BOULTER | WILFRED H. SCHOFF JOHN BARRETT | LEWIS NIXON | *Managing Editor* | SAMUEL MACCLINTOCK, PH.D. | Editorial and Educational Director, | LaSalle Extension University | [rule] | This course is designed to meet the demand for efficient training in Inter- | state Commerce; to train men for industrial or railroad traffic | work; and also to prepare students to pass the Interstate | Commerce Commission Examination | for Government Service | [rule] | PUBLISHED BY | LaSALLE EXTENSION UNIVERSITY | CHICAGO

♦ $\pi^{16}$($-\pi$1)B–IV–1–14$^8$ B.IV–15$^8$ B–IV–16–18$^8$ B.IV–19–20$^8$ B–IV–21–22$^8$ Vol. V–23$^8$ B–IV–24–28$^8$ B.IV–29–31$^8$ [\$1 signed (i.e. rectos of the first leaf of each gathering signed B–IV–, B.IV–, or Vol. V–)]. *1–6, i–iii, 1, 1, 2–459, 460, 461–485, 486, 487–492, 1–4* (253 leaves). 232 × 156 mm.

TEXT: Identical to B3a.

BINDING: Bound in dark green buckram. In the two copies that were examined, there was no stamping on the upper and lower boards, but the labels on the spine differed. On one copy (MOSTJMW), there are two black labels with lettering stamped in gilt. On the label on the top portion of the spine: [rule] | INTERSTATE | COMMERCE | [rule]. On the label on the lower portion of the spine: [rule] | LA SALLE EXTENSION | UNIVERSITY | [rule]. The other copy (KKU) had three black labels present on the spine with gilt lettering. On the label on the top portion of the spine: [rule] | INTERSTATE | COMMERCE | [rule]. On the label in the middle of the spine: [rule] | TRADE | COMMERCE | [rule]. On the label on the lower portion: [rule] | LA SALLE | UNIVERSITY | [rule].

NOTES: The verso of the title leaf has the following: [rule] | Copyright, 1911, | LASALLE EXTENSION UNIVERSITY. | [rule]. Date of publication and number of copies printed not known.

COPIES EXAMINED: KKU; MOSTJMW.

## B3α GREAT DEBATES IN AMERICAN HISTORY 1913

[the first two lines in red] GREAT DEBATES IN | AMERICAN HISTORY | *From the Debates in the British Parliament on the* | *Colonial Stamp Act* *(1764–1765) to the Debates* | *in the Congress at the Close of the Taft* | *Administration (1912–1913)* | EDITED BY | MARION MILLS MILLER, LITT.D. (PRINCETON) | Editor of "The Life and Works of Abraham Lincoln," etc. | IN FOURTEEN VOLUMES | EACH DEALING WITH A SPECIFIC SUBJECT, AND CONTAINING A SPECIAL INTRODUC- | TION BY A DISTINGUISHED AMERICAN STATESMAN OR PUBLICIST | [the next four lines in red] VOLUME TWELVE | REVENUE: THE TARIFF AND TAXATION | With an introduction by IDA M. TARBELL, L.H.D. | Associate Editor of the *American Magazine* | CURRENT LITERATURE PUBLISHING COMPANY | NEW YORK

• $\pi^6$ XII—1–13$^8$ *XII*—14$^8$ XII—15–29$^8$ XII—30$^4$ [$1 signed]. *1*-4, iii-vii, *viii*, ix-x, 1-472 pp. (242 leaves). 231 × 157 mm.

TEXT: Excerpt from a speech by Leacock against reciprocity, delivered on 20 March 1911 at Windsor Hall in Montreal. Six paragraphs are quoted (pp. 453–4).

BINDING: Bound in dark brown buckram. The general title, the title of the specific volume, the volume number, rules, and compartments are blind-stamped on the spine.

NOTES: The chief issue that decided the 1911 federal election in Canada concerned free trade with the United States. An agreement in principle had been arranged between Sir Wilfrid Laurier's Liberal government and the American administration of William H. Taft, but the issue was divisive and a number of prominent Liberals, including the Minister of the Interior, the Hon. Clifford Sifton, broke ranks with the government. When Sifton toured the country during the election campaign and visited Montreal on 20 March 1911, Leacock and several others joined him and spoke out against the agreement. According to newspaper reports, thousands of citizens took to the streets in spite of the chilliness of the March night air. A vast crowd filled Windsor Hall and overflowed into Dominion Square. Leacock spoke twice — at the Strathcona Monument and then again inside Windsor Hall. Although the audience reacted positively to Sifton's visit and to Leacock's stirring address, a small minority of students from McGill University attacked Sifton's carriage, smashed windows, and tore down trolley wires. The students ejected Sifton and his friends from their carriage (Leacock presumably was in the carriage with Sifton), saturated it with coal oil, set it on fire, and then dragged it through the streets.

It is not known whether this excerpt from Leacock's address was taken from a newspaper source or was obtained directly from him. Number of copies printed and exact date of publication not known. See also E11.5 for newspaper reports.

COPIES: OTU.

## B4 BRITISH FRENCH ITALIAN BELGIAN RUSSIAN COOKERY 1916

### B4a *Canadian edition*:

[cover title: coloured illustration of the flags of the five allied countries, flying on flagpoles which have a white ribbon intertwined loosely between the poles; all lines in blue unless indicated otherwise] | BRITISH | FRENCH . . . . ITALIAN . . . . RUSSIAN | BELGIAN | [in red] COOKERY | ARRANGED BY | GRACE CLERGUE HARRISON | . . . AND . . . | GERTRUDE CLERGUE | [in red] *TO AID THE SUFFERERS IN THE DEVASTATED DISTRICTS OF FRANCE* | INTRODUCTION BY | HON. RAOUL DANDURAND | COMMANDEUR DE LA LÉGION D'HONNEUR | PREFACE BY | PROF. STEPHEN LEACOCK | McGILL UNIVERSITY, MONTREAL

• $1^{20}$. *1*-6, 7–38, *1*-2 pp. (20 leaves, plus an errata leaf before p. *1*). 215 × 148 mm.

TEXT: Leacock's preface entitled "Allied Food," pp. *3*-4, with his signature in facsimile.

BINDING: Bound in brown paper wrappers, wire-stitched. Front cover as described above in the quasi-facsimile. The back cover is blank. The versos of the wrappers are cream-coloured. Printed on the verso of the back cover: [rule] | CONSOLIDATED LITHOGRAPHING & MANUFACTURING CO., LIMITED, MONTREAL.

NOTES: During the First World War on behalf of the Belgium Relief Fund, Leacock gave readings of his humorous work to the public. In February 1916, for example, he spoke at six different Ontario cities for this cause. Although the sales from this cook book went specifically to Le Secours National of France, it was undoubtedly through Leacock's wartime initiatives for the Belgium Relief Fund that he was asked to write a preface to this cook book.

The text of Leacock's preface in the Canadian edition varies somewhat from that of the American edition. Beneath the title on p. 3 of the Canadian edition is the following statement, which does not appear in the American edition: *A Special Preface Written for this Volume and | Inserted only after Strong Protest from the Editors.* In the fourth paragraph of Leacock's preface, the second sentence in the Canadian edition reads: "One may judge, therefore, with what delight I received the news of the patriotic enterprise of Miss Clergue and Mrs. Harrison." In the American edition, the sentence ends with the word "enterprise." In the Canadian edition, the end of the eighth paragraph reads as follows: "The obvious conclusion is that while this book was in the press my recipes were stolen out of it. This may have been done by a German spy. I hope so." The last two sentences do not appear in the text of the American edition. In the ninth paragraph, the first sentence of the Canadian edition includes the typographical error (noted on the errata slip), "were of no distinctive a character." In the American edition this phrase reads, "were of so distinctive a character." That same paragraph in the Canadian edition ends as follows: "To say that there were dishes for a king is to understate the fact. There were certain of them which I should have liked to feed to the German Emperor." This last sentence does not appear in the American edition. Finally, the Canadian edition ends with the following sentences, which do not appear in the American edition.:

> It was only after my collaboration that I discovered that the proceeds of this book were to go to the Belgian and French Refugees. As soon as I knew this, I sent a cheque to the editors and begged them to put me down for a thousand copies. I am sorry to find that my cheque has come back to me, the bank having very generously refused to accept it.
>
> But my sympathy and cooperation in this good work are none the less sincere.

The Canadian edition also has a few spelling variants and a number of italicized words.

The errata slip states that the book went to press before ". . . the planting season of 1916. . . ." Other statements by the other contributors are dated 2 March 1916. Price 50¢. On the copy examined 4200 is stamped in red on the verso of the front cover. This suggests that at least that number of copies was printed.

COPIES EXAMINED: CS.

**B4b** *American edition* entitled *Allied Cookery: British French Italian Belgian Russian*:

[all lines within a rectangle] Allied | Cookery | [double, vertical rule to the right of the previous two lines; the next five lines to the right of this rule] | British | French | Italian | Belgian | Russian | Arranged by | Grace Clergue Harrison | and | Gertrude Clergue | *TO AID THE WAR SUFFERERS IN THE DEVASTATED DISTRICTS | OF FRANCE* | Introduction by | Hon. Raoul Dandurand |

Commandeur de la Légion d'Honneur | Prefaced by | Stephen Leacock AND Ella Wheeler Wilcox | G. P. Putnam's Sons | New York and London | 𝕿𝖍𝖊 𝕶𝖓𝖎𝖈𝖐𝖊𝖗𝖇𝖔𝖈𝖐𝖊𝖗 𝕻𝖗𝖊𝖘𝖘 | 1916

◆ 1–7⁸. $1$–2, 3–4, 1–4, 5–108 pp. (56 leaves). 204 × 136 mm. A blank leaf (not part of the gatherings but belonging to the endpapers) is found at the beginning and end of the book.

TEXTS: Leacock's preface ("Allied Food") on pp. 8–11 with his signature in facsimile on p. 11.

BINDING: Bound in brown stiff paper boards. On the upper board is a coloured illustration of the flags of the five allied countries (identical to the illustration on the cover of B4a). Beneath the illustration is the following: [the first line in red] ALLIED COOKERY | [the next six lines in blue] BRITISH. . . .BELGIAN | FRENCH. . . .ITALIAN. . . .RUSSIAN | ARRANGED BY | GRACE CLERGUE HARRISON | AND | GERTRUDE CLERGUE | [the next line in red] TO AID THE SUFFERERS IN THE DEVASTATED DISTRICTS OF FRANCE. The spine and lower board are blank.

NOTES: In addition to the preface by Ella Wheeler Wilcox, A4b contains more and different recipes than A4a. See the notes to A4a for omissions and differences with respect to Leacock's preface. The publication date and number of copies printed of A4b are not known.

COPIES EXAMINED: CS.

## B5 THE WORLD'S BEST LITERATURE 1917

B5a *first edition*:

[all lines within two rectangles] UNIVERSITY EDITION | [in red] THE WARNER LIBRARY | IN THIRTY VOLUMES | VOLUME 19 | [rule] | THE | WORLD'S BEST | LITERATURE | EDITORS | JOHN W. CUNLIFFE | ASHLEY H. THORNDIKE | PROFESSORS OF ENGLISH IN COLUMBIA UNIVERSITY | FOUNDED BY | CHARLES DUDLEY WARNER | [circular portrait of Warner] | [in red] NEW YORK | PRINTED AT THE KNICKERBOCKER | PRESS FOR THE WARNER LIBRARY COMPANY | TORONTO: GLASGOW, BROOK & COMPANY | [in red] 1917

◆ i–vi, vii–xiii, xiv, xv, 1, 11179–11408, 11408a–11408r, 11409–11700, 11700a–11700r, 11701–11756, 11756a–11756l, 11757–11804, $1$–2 pp. (346 leaves). 214 × 142 mm.

TEXT: "William Sydney Porter (O. Henry) (1862–1910)," pp. 11756a–11756f.

BINDING: Bound in pebbled-grain maroon cloth, top edge gilt. On the spine stamped in gilt is a rectangle containing a series of rectangles and leafy compartments specifying the Warner Library, the University edition, the range of authors (Patmore to Prescott), and the volume number.

NOTES: Each volume of *The World's Best Literature* contains selections from the works of various authors preceded by a critical essay. Leacock's notebook of recorded publications at QMMRB has the entry: "Dec 9 [1916] O. Henry (for World's Great Literature)." He mailed his manuscript to John W. Cunliffe at that time (Cunliffe fonds, COL). Date of publication and number of copies printed not known.

COPIES EXAMINED: CHAR.

**B5b** *second edition* (1929):

*The | Columbia University Course | in | Literature |* [leafy ornament] | *Writers of Modern America | New York* [illustration of a crown set above an illustration of a person with a book who is seated on a throne surrounded by three naked children, with mottos in Latin and Hebrew] *Mcmxxix | Columbia University Press*

◆ *i–iv*, v–xi, *1*, 1–648 pp. (330 leaves) 225 × 143 mm.

TEXT: "William Sydney Porter (O. Henry)," pp. 423–434.

BINDING: Bound in maroon cloth with a floral border embossed on the upper board. An illustration similar to the title page but within two circles is stamped in gilt on the upper board with COLVMBIA VNIVERSITY PRESS between the circles. Stamped in gilt on the spine: [rules and a scroll ] | COLUMBIA | UNIVERSITY | COURSE IN | LITERATURE | — 18 — | WRITERS | OF MODERN | AMERICA | [illustration of a woman holding an open book in a classical pose; logo of Columbia University Press similar to that on the upper board]. The endpapers, which are designed by Paul Laune, feature an illustration in brown and white of knights on horseback, a river, birds flying overhead, pyramids, castles, a woman and a child, etc.

COPIES EXAMINED: OTU.

**B5b.1** *second edition, issue* (1969):

*The | Columbia University Course | in | Literature |* [leafy ornament] | *XVII | Writers of Modern America | Essay Index Reprint Series |* [publisher's device to the left of the next two lines: abstract design of building with four columns] BOOKS FOR LIBRARIES PRESS | FREEPORT, NEW YORK

The verso of the title leaf reads as follows: Copyright 1928–29 | United States Publishers Association, Inc. | Reprinted 1969 by arrangement | STANDARD BOOK NUMBER: | 8369-0037-5 | LIBRARY OF CONGRESS CATALOG CARD NUMBER | 68-58779 | PRINTED IN THE UNITED STATES OF AMERICA. Pagination is the same as B5b, except that there are two blank leaves after p. 648. Leaves measure 228 × 150 mm. Bound in blue cloth with the publisher's device blind-stamped on the upper board. The spine has the title, subtitle, and volume number stamped in gilt within two solid maroon compartments. Stamped in gilt at the foot of the spine within an oval: B | *f* | L.

COPIES EXAMINED: OHM.

**B6** THE NEW ERA IN CANADA 1917

**B6a** *English edition*:

[all lines within a rectangle] THE | [in red] NEW ERA IN CANADA | ESSAYS DEALING | WITH THE UPBUILDING OF THE | CANADIAN COMMONWEALTH | [rule] | Edited By | J.O. MILLER | Principal of Ridley College | [rule] | LONDON | PARIS – TORONTO | [in red] J. M. DENT & SONS, LTD. | 1917

◆ *1–4*[8] *5–26*[8] *27*[4] [$1 signed]. *1–4, 5–10,11–12, 13–33, 34–36, 37–57, 58–60, 61–73, 74, 75–99, 100–102, 103–127, 128–130, 131–157, 158–160, 161–189, 190–192, 193–207, 208–210, 211–226,*

227–228, 229–259, 260–262, 263–275, 276–278, 279–299, 300–302, 303–330, 331–332, 333–345, 346–348, 349–380, 381–382, 383–406, 407–408, 409–421, 1–3 pp. (212 leaves, plus frontispiece photograph of drawing of a Canadian soldier, reproduced from *Punch*, and tissue guard inserted before the title leaf). 188 × 128 mm.

TEXT: Includes two essays by Leacock: "Democracy and Social Progress" (pp. 13–33); and "Our National Organization for the War" (pp. 409–21). Only the former appears for the first time. A note following the latter reads:

> This paper was written by Professor Leacock for the use of the Government, which has printed a quarter of a million copies. It has attracted considerable attention in England, and especially in the London *Times*. Professor Leacock has very kindly allowed me to use it here. — EDITOR.

BINDING AND DUST JACKET: Bound in dark olive green cloth. Stamped on the upper board within two blind-stamped rectangles: [two rules blind-stamped] | THE | NEW ERA | IN | CANADA | Edited by J. O. MILLER. Stamped on the spine: THE | NEW ERA | IN | CANADA | EDITED BY | J. O. MILLER | [ornament] | J. M. DENT | & SONS, LTD. | LONDON, PARIS AND | TORONTO | [two rules blind-stamped].

The dust jacket is white. The front and back panels are identical, and are as follows: [all lines within a green rectangle; the first four lines in red within a green garland] THE | NEW ERA | IN | CANADA | [the remaining lines in green] BY THE FOLLOWING WRITERS: | [list of 15 writers]. The spine panel is as follows: [two green rules] | [the next four lines in red] THE | NEW ERA | IN | CANADA | [green rule] | [in green] $1.50 | [green rule] | [the next four lines in red] J. M. DENT | & SONS | LONDON, PARIS AND | TORONTO | [two green rules]. The front and back flaps are identical with lines within a green rectangle as follows: [red ornament] | [the next two lines in red] ALL | PROFITS | [the next nine lines in green] | FROM | THE | SALE | OF | THIS | BOOK | ARE | TO GO | TO | [the next five lines in red] THE | CANADIAN | RED | CROSS | SOCIETY | [red ornament].

NOTES: According to Leacock's notebook of publications and speeches at QMMRB, "Democracy and Social Progress" was completed on 28 March 1917. With respect to "Our National Organization for the War," see A25. Date of publication and number of copies printed not known.

COPIES EXAMINED: CS (two copies, one in jacket).

## B6a.1 *American issue*:

The title page is identical to that of the English edition with two following exceptions: there are no rules; and J. M. DENT & SONS, LTD. has been replaced by NEW YORK: E.P. DUTTON & CO. The title leaf is a cancel. Otherwise, the only other difference concerns the spine where the imprint reads: E. P. DUTTON | & CO. Dust jacket of the American issue not seen.

COPIES EXAMINED: SUNY.

## B7 COMMEMORATION OF THE CENTENARY OF THE BIRTH OF JAMES RUSSELL LOWELL 1919

COMMEMORATION | OF THE CENTENARY OF THE BIRTH OF | JAMES RUSSELL LOWELL | POET, SCHOLAR, DIPLOMAT | BORN IN CAMBRIDGE, MASS., FEBRUARY 22, 1819 | DIED IN CAMBRIDGE, AUGUST 12, 1891 | HELD UNDER THE AUSPICES OF THE | AMERICAN ACADEMY OF ARTS AND LETTERS | IN NEW YORK, FEBRUARY 19-22, 1919 | [illustration of medal depicting Pegasus, with words AMERICAN ACADEMY OF ARTS [AND] LETTERS and the motto OPPORTUNITY INSPIRATION ACHIEVEMENT on the medal] | PUBLISHED FOR THE ACADEMY | NEW YORK: CHARLES SCRIBNER'S SONS | 1919

◆ $1$-$6^8$. $1$-$4$, v-vi, $1$-$6$, $5$-$31$, $32$, $33$-$75$, $76$, $77$-$80$, $81$-$82$, $83$-$84$, $85$-$86$, $87$-$88$ pp. (48 leaves, plus frontispiece photograph of Lowell and tissue guard inserted before the title leaf). 248 × 173 mm.

TEXT: Includes a speech by Leacock (pp. 64-67) in praise of Lowell that comments on American-Canadian relations. Leacock's address is preceded by a short introduction by Chancellor William M. Sloane. The speech is listed under the section, "Literary Exercises, Ritz-Carlton Hotel."

BINDING AND DUST JACKET: Issued in beige paper boards, quarter-bound with purple cloth with a gold vertical rule stamped on both boards along the edge of the cloth. Top edge stained gold. Stamped on upper board in purple: COMMEMORATION | OF THE CENTENARY OF THE BIRTH OF | JAMES RUSSELL LOWELL | FEBRUARY 22, 1819 | UNDER THE AUSPICES OF THE | AMERICAN ACADEMY OF ARTS AND LETTERS | HELD IN NEW YORK FEBRUARY 19-22, 1919. Stamped on the spine in gilt: JAMES | RUSSELL | LOWELL | 1819 | [wavy rule] | 1919.

The dust jacket is cream-coloured with purple lettering. The front panel is identical to the title page, except that the three lines giving the imprint and date do not appear, and the three lines of type above the medal on the title page appear below the illustration on the jacket. The other panels of the jacket are blank. A card (63 × 127 mm.) inserted in the book reads: [all lines in blue lettering] WITH THE COMPLIMENTS of | THE AMERICAN ACADEMY OF | ARTS AND LETTERS | ROBERT UNDERWOOD JOHNSON | Permanent Secretary | 347 Madison Avenue, New York.

NOTES: On 25 January 1919, Leacock initially told Murray Butler, the President of Columbia University, that he could not accept the invitation to attend the centenary celebration of James Lowell's birth in New York City. He accepted the invitation on 13 February (information based on Carnegie Endowment fonds, COL). Leacock was one of several speakers who were present at the Ritz-Carlton Hotel on 22 February 1919. Others included Barrett Wendell, Alfred Noyes, Edgar Lee Masters, and Samuel McChord Crothers. A number of prominent authors and statesmen from Great Britain and Canada were invited as guests of the American Academy of Arts and Letters. See D19.1.

In the Barbara Nimmo collection at NAC, there is a newsclipping from the *North American* (Philadelphia), dated 17 May 1919, which reports: "A commemorative volume on the Lowell Centenary celebration, held February 19 to 22, last, under the auspices of the American Academy of Arts and Letters, will be issued by the Scribners. The volume will include the addresses by . . . Stephen Leacock and many distinguished guests who attended the Centenary. . . ." In C33.11, Leacock wrote of the occasion:

> I remember . . . at the Lowell Centenary at Columbia University, ten or eleven years ago, meeting good old — no, I won't name him; the famous old Harvard professor of English who played such a large part at the gathering — all right, then — Barrett Wendell. He shook me warmly by the hand and said heartily: "I'm so glad to have the opportunity of meeting you; my children read your books." I answered, "Thank you! My mother reads yours!"

COPIES EXAMINED: CS (two copies, only one in jacket).

## B8 REQUIESCANT AND OTHER POEMS 1919

REQUIESCANT | AND | OTHER POEMS | *By* | WILLIAM QUINTARD KETCHUM

♦ $1^{18}$. $1$-$8$, $9$-$36$ pp. (18 leaves). 180 × 129 mm. Frontispiece photograph of Ketchum inserted before the title leaf.

TEXT: Leacock's preface dated McGill University, November 1919, pp. 7–8.

BINDING: Bound in dark greyish green wrappers. The front cover duplicates the text on the title page. On the bottom right corner of the back cover: THE MORTIMER CO. LIMITED. A matching string is threaded through three pin holes holding the leaves and wrappers together in a single gathering.

NOTES: William Quintard Ketchum served during the First World War in France with the Divisional Signal Company of the Canadian Engineers. He dedicated his book of verse to the memory of his cousin, James Carleton Ketchum, who died at Vimy Ridge. In his preface Leacock states that he remembered

> . . . James Ketchum only as a little boy, for I never had the pleasure of knowing him in the days of his early manhood as a student and a solder. But his father, Thomas Carleton Lee Ketchum, is one of my oldest friends, with whom I have ties of association and good fellowship that carry me back thirty years to the time when we were young men and house mates together in Toronto.

Leacock was apparently asked by the Ketchum family to write a preface to this book of verse. Number of copies printed not known.

COPIES EXAMINED: CS; EVANS.

## B9 THE LETTERS OF SI WHIFFLETREE — FRESHMAN 1921

*The Letters of* | *Si Whiffletree — Freshman* | EDITED BY | FRANK D. GENEST | *WITH A PREFACE BY* | STEPHEN LEACOCK | *AND* | *WITH ILLUSTRATIONS IN BLACK-AND-WHITE BY* | G. E. TREMBLE | MONTREAL | 1921

♦ $1$-$5^8$ $6^4$ (the last leaf is the rear paste-down). $1$-$13$, $2$, $3$, $4$-$8$, $9$, $10$-$14$, $15$, $16$-$20$,$21$, $22$-$33$, $34$, $35$-$39$, $40$, $41$-$44$, $45$ $46$-$55$, $56$, $57$-$61$, $62$, $63$-$66$, $67$, $68$-$69$, $1$-$7$ pp. (44 leaves, counting the rear end papers). 172 × 127 mm.

TEXT: Leacock's preface on pp. *9*-*11*.

BINDING AND DUST JACKET: Issued in beige paper boards. Stamped on upper board, the first three lines in red: The Letters of | Si Whiffletree-Freshman | Edited by FRANK D. GENEST | [illustration in red and black of freshman holding banner marked "McG," wearing sweater with the letter "M" on it] | [illustration signed in facsimile in black:] G.E. TREMBLE –. The spine and lower board are blank.

The dust jacket is off-white. The front panel of jacket repeats the type and illustration on the upper board, and adds the following beneath Tremble's signature: [in red] WITH A PREFACE BY | STEPHEN LEACOCK. A sticker affixed to the lower left corner reads: "Price 75c." The rest of the jacket is blank. The copy at QMMRB has a glassine wrapper over the jacket, but no price tag.

NOTES: Frank Genest (1896-1944) was a Montreal lawyer and short story writer. His humorous book, prefaced by Leacock, was written and published while he was a student at McGill University. Silas's letters about his curious experiences at McGill University, addressed to his parents, "Ma" and "Pa," appeared in previous McGill publications, primarily the *McGill Daily*. After completing degrees in arts and in law, Genest spent a year in Chicago as an editor of a monthly publication. He returned to Montreal and practised law for twenty-five years, first with the firm of Long and Harold and then as a partner in Genest and Savage. An active member of the Montreal Branch of the Canadian Authors' Association, he wrote many newspaper articles and other publications, some under the pen name of Frank D. Wrenton.

The reviewer of Genest's book in the *McGill Daily* (see "F.D. Genest to Publish Letters. . . .," 10, no. 125 (19 March 1921): 1-2) was ". . . permitted to have an advance peep into the pages of a real book published by a real undergraduate at McGill." Publication of Genest's book was also announced in the *Critic* (McGill University) 1, no. 7 (23 March 1921): 16. Copies were for sale at the University Book Store. Number of copies printed not known.

COPIES EXAMINED: CS (in jacket); OONL (two copies lacking jackets); QMMRB (in jacket).


## BIO OF ALL THINGS 1922

OF ALL THINGS | By ROBERT C. BENCHLEY | With an Introduction by STEPHEN LEACOCK | Illustrated by GLUYAS WILLIAMS | JOHN LANE THE BODLEY HEAD LIMITED | LONDON, VIGO ST. MCMXII

♦ A⁸ B-Q⁸ [$1 signed]. *i–viii*, ix–xi, *xii*, xiii–xvii, *1–3*, 3–15, *16*, 17–54, *55*, 56–65, *66*, 67–96, *97*, 98–111, *112*, 113–175, *176*, 177–198, *199*, 200–214, *215–216*, 217–238 pp. (128 leaves). 186 × 120 mm.

TEXT: Introduction, pp. ix–xi.

BINDING AND DUST JACKET: Bound in dark greenish grey cloth with white lettering, top edge stained yellow. Stamped on the upper board: [all lines within an ornamental, rectangular compartment] Of All Things | Robert C. Benchley. Stamped on the spine: [ornament and rules] | Of All | [dotted rule] | Things | [small, solid diamond] | Robert C. | Benchley | THE BODLEY HEAD | [different ornament and rules].

The jacket is white with black lettering and illustration. Printed on the front panel: OF ALL THINGS | BY ROBERT BENCHLEY | WITH AN INTRODUCTION | BY STEPHEN LEACOCK | [illustration of a restaurant scene with snobby waiters] | ILLUSTRATED BY

GLUYAS WILLIAMS | Six Shillings Net. Printed on the spine of the jacket: OF | ALL | THINGS | ROBERT | BENCHLEY | WITH AN | INTRODUCTION | BY STEPHEN | LEACOCK | 6/– | NET | THE | BODLEY | HEAD. On the back panel is an advertisement for Leacock's *My Discovery of England*. The front flap quotes a paragraph from Leacock's introduction. On the back flap is an advertisement for Ben Travers's *A Cuckoo in the Nest*.

NOTES: *Of All Things* was Robert Benchley's first book, and Leacock's introduction, apparently sent to B.W. Willett of John Lane The Bodley Head at the beginning of 1922, was intended to introduce Benchley to the British public. On 19 January 1922 Willett told Leacock:

> I have only to-day heard that Henry Holt & Co. have accepted our terms for the BENCHLEY book. Benchley is delighted with the idea of your writing an Introduction, and will accept your judgment in every way with regard to the arrangement. If, therefore, you could find a few minutes to write us an Introduction, I should be awfully grateful. . . .

The American edition of Benchley's book, which was published by Henry Holt in 1921, lacks Leacock's introduction (see Nathaniel Benchley, *Robert Benchley* (New York: McGraw-Hill, 1955), p. 138). Leacock's copy of the American edition at SLM is inscribed: "To Stephen Leacock who certainly *ought* to like most of the stuff in this book as he wrote it himself first. gratefully Bob Benchley 'so teach us to number our days that we may apply our hearts unto wisdom' New York February 22,* 1927 *no offense."

Printed by Butler & Tanner. Number of copies printed not known. See also K57.1.

COPIES EXAMINED: CS (no jacket); CUL (in jacket).

## BII A CONNECTICUT YANKEE IN KING ARTHUR'S COURT 1923

[the first four lines in red] A | CONNECTICUT YANKEE | IN | KING ARTHUR'S COURT | BY | MARK TWAIN | [illustration within a compartment of a steam boat on a river] | NEW YORK | [the next line in red] GABRIEL WELLS | MCMXXIII

◆ *i–iv*, v–vii, *viii*, ix–xiii, *xiv*, xv–xxii, *1–2*, 1–8, 9, 10–450 pp. (237 leaves). 216 × 139 mm. With frontispiece sketch of Twain dated 1884. Illustrations with tissue guards facing pp. 96, 178, 266, and 390.

TEXT: "An Appreciation," pp. ix–xiii, with Leacock's signature stamped in facsimile on p. xiii.

BINDING: The copy examined was rebound (preliminary and end leaves may be missing). However, DLC reports two binding variants: beige paper and royal blue cloth with paper labels pasted on the spine; matching half morocco. Spine title: The works of Mark Twain.

NOTES: The "definitive edition" of *The Writings of Mark Twain* in thirty-seven volumes, published between 1922–5, is comprised of 1,024 numbered sets. Tipped in vol. 1 is a manuscript leaf signed by Twain in 1906 in anticipation of the definitive edition of his works. The introductions to each volume, biography of Twain, and editing of his letters were done by Albert Bigelow Paine.

In his notebook of recorded publications and speeches at QMMRB, Leacock indicates that on 1 September 1922, he wrote an introduction to an edition of Twain's books published by Harper Bros. No edition published by Harper Bros. was located. *A Connecticut Yankee in King Arthur's Court* is vol. 14 of the "definitive edition."

COPIES EXAMINED: GPM.

## B12 THE TRANSPORTATION OF CANADIAN WHEAT TO THE SEA 1925

[all lines within three rectangles] McGill University Economic Studies | No. 1 No. 1 | NATIONAL PROBLEMS | OF | CANADA | [circular illustration of McGill University's insignia with shield and motto] | THE TRANSPORTATION OF | CANADIAN WHEAT TO THE SEA | [rule] | L. M. FAIR, M. A. | [rule] | Published at St. Martin's House, Toronto, by | The MacMillan [Macmillan] Company of Canada, Limited, | for the Department of Economics and | Political Science, McGill University, | Montreal. | *Price 40c.*

◆ $1-5^8$. *1–2*, III–IV, *5–76*, *1–4* pp. (40 leaves). 218 × 145 mm.

TEXT: Leacock's preface, dated "McGill University, May 1, 1925," on pp. III–IV.

BINDING: Issued in red wrappers, glued to wire-stitched gatherings. The title page is reproduced on the front cover. On one copy that was examined (OHM), the following is rubber-stamped on the front wrapper: McGILL UNIVERSITY PUBLICATIONS | Series XV. On the back of the wrapper within a rectangle is the following: McGill University Economic Studies | IN THE | NATIONAL PROBLEMS of CANADA | No. 1 *The Transportation of Canadian Wheat* | No. 2 *Ocean and Inland Water Transport* | No. 3 *The Taxation of Corporations in Canada* | No. 4 *Reciprocal and Preferential Tariffs* | IN PREPARATION FOR 1926 | [numbers 5 to 9 listed].

NOTES: Louisa Margaret Fair graduated from McGill University's Royal Victoria College with an Honours degree in Economics in 1923–4. Her M.A. thesis was the first monograph in the series, the McGill University Economic Studies in the National Problems of Canada (Series XV). In all, seventeen theses, written primarily by graduate students in the Department of Economics and Political Science at McGill University, were published in the series. Leacock wrote prefaces to six of them (numbers 1, 2, 4, 6, 9, and 14 — see B13, B14, B15, B17, and B19).

Although in his prefaces to numbers 2 and 4 Leacock expressed the Department's obligation to his colleague, W.W. Goforth, "under whose direction and editorship this booklet, and others, have been prepared," Leacock arranged for the publication of these theses. Numbers 1 to 8 and 10 to 13 were published by the Macmillan Company of Canada. Number 9 was published by the Federated Press Limited and distributed by the Macmillan Company of Canada. Numbers 14 to 17 were published by the Packet-Times Press Limited.

On 26 April 1926, Leacock drafted an agreement for the publication of the series with the Macmillan Company of Canada. Also extant is a formal memorandum of agreement dated 1 May 1928. McGill University originally paid the Macmillan Company $50 for each thesis published. The university received fifty complimentary copies of each thesis (twenty-five to the author, five for the library, and twenty for the Department). No royalties were paid to the authors unless sales exceeded 500 copies (in which case a royalty of 10% was applicable). The series, however, was a losing proposition from the outset. According Hugh Eayrs of the Macmillan Company, the Macmillans purchased 300 copies of numbers 1 to 4 from McGill University at 25¢ each. They were sold to the trade at a 25% discount, leaving a margin of 4¢ for profit. "That 4 cents doesn't even pay our overhead," he informed Leacock on 31 August 1926. "I am willing to take virtually no profit on the new books. All this preamble by way of letting you know that I don't care a rap whether there is any money in it for us or not. . . . I want to continue an association with you and your Department to the development of the idea." (information based on Leacock's fonds at SLM and Macmillan Company of Canada fonds at OHM).

For a discussion of the series, see K83.2.

COPIES EXAMINED: CS; OHM.

## B13 OCEAN AND INLAND WATER TRANSPORT 1925

[all lines within three rectangles] McGill University Economic Studies | No. 2 No. 2 | NATIONAL PROBLEMS | OF | CANADA | [circular illustration of McGill University's insignia with shield and motto] | OCEAN AND INLAND WATER | TRANSPORT | [rule] | THE 1925 GRADUATING CLASS IN COMMERCE | [rule] | Published at St. Martin's House, Toronto, by | The Macmillan Company of Canada, Limited, | for the Department of Economics and | Political Science, McGill University, | Montreal. | *Price 40c.*

◆ $1-2^8 \, 3^{10}$. *1*-2, III, 4, 5–52 pp. (26 leaves). 216 × 146 mm.

TEXT: Leacock's preface on p. III.

BINDING: Issued in red wrappers, glued to wire-stitched gatherings. The title page is reproduced on the front cover. Rubber-stamped above the rectangles on the front of the wrapper: McGILL UNIVERSITY PUBLICATIONS | Series XV. The back of the wrapper is identical to L.M. Fair's *The Transportation of Canadian Wheat to the Sea* (see B12).

NOTES: In his preface Leacock states that the "present monograph" is "written by Messrs. [John] Glassco, [Walter Locke] Johnston, [Alfred Cliff] Yerxa, [Frank Cyril] Murphy and [Edwin Manson] Milne and other members of the 1925 graduating class in Commerce. . . ." With the exception of the first sentence, the first paragraph is identical to the opening paragraph in Fair's thesis. See the notes to B12 for discussion of the series.

COPIES EXAMINED: CS; OHM.

## B14 RECIPROCAL AND PREFERENTIAL TARIFFS 1925

[all lines within three rectangles] McGill University Economic Studies | No. 4 No. 4 | NATIONAL PROBLEMS | OF | CANADA | [circular illustration of McGill University's insignia with shield and motto] | RECIPROCAL AND | PREFERENTIAL TARIFFS | [rule] | THE 1925 GRADUATING CLASS | IN COMMERCE | [rule] | Published at St. Martin's House Toronto, by | The Macmillan Company of Canada, Limited, | for the Department of Economics and | Political Science, McGill University, | Montreal. | *Price 40c.*

◆ $1-2^8 \, 3^4$. *1*-2, III, 4, 5–40 pp. (20 leaves). 218 × 145 mm.

TEXT: Leacock's preface on p. III.

BINDING: Issued in red wrappers, glued to wire-stitched gatherings. The title page is reproduced on the front cover. On one copy that was examined (OHM), the following is rubber-stamped on the front wrapper above the rectangles: McGILL UNIVERSITY PUBLICATIONS | Series XV. The back of the wrapper is identical to L.M. Fair's *The Transportation of Canadian Wheat to the Sea* (see B12).

NOTES: In his preface Leacock states that the "present monograph" is "written by Messrs. [John] Glassco, [Donald Rand] Patton, [Terence F.] Mitchell, [Walter Baden-Powell] Potter, [A. Wright] Case, [Frederick Chipman] Schofield, [Lovell Grant] Mickles [Jr.], [Philip Aylmer] Wait, [Frederick Williams] Fairman, [John J.D.] Quinlan, [Erwin Hughes] Elliott and [F. Cuthbert B.] Falls. . . ." The second paragraph is identical to a passage written by Leacock for numbers 1 and 2 of the series. See the notes to B12 for discussion of the series. The last page of the text is dated "May 1, 1925."

COPIES EXAMINED: CS; OHM.

## B15 THE PORT OF MONTREAL 1926

[all lines within three rectangles] McGill University Economic Studies | No. 6 No. 6 | NATIONAL PROBLEMS | OF | CANADA | [circular illustration of McGill University's insignia with shield and motto] | THE PORT OF MONTREAL. | [rule] | LAURENCE CHALMERS TOMBS, M.A. | [rule] | Published at St. Martin's House, Toronto, by | The Macmillan Company of Canada, Limited, | for the Department of Economics and | Political Science, McGill University, | Montreal. | *Price 75c.*

◆ $1^2$ $2$–$12^8$ $13^2$. 1–6, 3–171, 1, 172–174 (3 folded maps, versos not paginated or numbered), *1–2*, 175–178 pp. (92 leaves, excluding pp. 172–173 which are stapled to p. 174, the latter being integral). 206 × 142 mm.

TEXT: Leacock's preface dated "October 15, 1926" on pp. 5–6.

BINDING: Bound in stiff red wrappers, glued to wire-stitched gatherings. The title page is reproduced on the front cover. On the back of the wrapper within a rectangle is the following: McGill University Economic Studies | IN THE | NATIONAL PROBLEMS of CANADA | *PUBLISHED IN 1925* | [eight lines listing numbers 1 to 4 of the series] *PUBLISHED IN 1926* | [five lines listing numbers 5 to 8 of the series] | *TO BE PUBLISHED IN 1927* | [nine lines listing five titles].

Also examined were two copies in purple flexible calf (sewn gatherings). These are presentation copies. One copy has lettering in gilt on the upper board as follows: 𝔑𝔞𝔱𝔦𝔬𝔫𝔞𝔩 𝔓𝔯𝔬𝔟𝔩𝔢𝔪𝔰 | 𝔬𝔣 𝔔𝔞𝔫𝔞𝔡𝔞 | 𝔗𝔥𝔢 𝔓𝔬𝔯𝔱 𝔬𝔣 𝔐𝔬𝔫𝔱𝔯𝔢𝔞𝔩. The other copy is from Leacock's library, and is inscribed by Tombs and dated February 1927. It is stamped in gilt on the upper board as follows: *THE PORT OF MONTREAL* | BY LAURENCE CHALMERS TOMBS, M. A. | STEPHEN LEACOCK.

NOTES: Born in Quebec City on 23 July 1903, Laurence Chalmers Tombs graduated with a B.A. from McGill University in 1924. While at McGill, he was associate editor of the *Old McGill* annual and night editor of the *McGill Daily*. "I admired Leacock enormously," Tombs recollected. "I was an enthusiastic young man and a fairly good student, but I wasn't one of the most extraordinary students that Leacock ever had" (quoted in K83.1, p. 204).

When the price of numbers 5 to 8 of the McGill University Economic Studies was raised from 40¢ to 75¢, the Macmillan Company of Canada took 300 copies of each on consignment. These were sold to the trade at 60¢, 20% off the list price. Besides being listed in the Macmillan catalogues, the monographs were itemized and described on a separate order form. An interested buyer could check the desired monographs and mail the form to Leacock, care of the Macmillan address. See also the notes to B12 for fuller discussion of the series.

COPIES EXAMINED: CS (purple, flexible calf); OHM (stiff red wrappers, three copies); SLM (Leacock's copy).

## B16 THE FOREIGN TRADE OF CANADA [1930]

THE | FOREIGN TRADE OF | CANADA | *By* | HENRY LAUREYS | [three lines in italics listing Laureys's credentials] | TRANSLATED FROM THE FRENCH EDITION BY | H. A. INNIS, PH.D. | *Associate Professor at the Department of Political Science of the University of Toronto,* | AND | ALEXANDER H. SMITH, M.A. | *Head of the English Department at the School of Higher Commercial* | *Studies of Montreal.* | WITH A PREFACE BY | STEPHEN LEACOCK, Ph.D., Litt.D., LL.D. | *Professor of Political Economy at McGill University.* | [publisher's device of The Macmillans in Canada: leaves and books within rectangle with motto FOLIA INTER FOLIA] | TORONTO: THE MACMILLAN COMPANY OF | CANADA LIMITED, AT ST. MARTIN'S HOUSE | MCMXXIX

◆ 1–21⁸ 22⁴. 1–4, v–ix, $x$, xi–xvi, 1–325, 1–3 pp. (172 leaves). 210 × 136 mm.

TEXT: Preface, dated at McGill University, 1929, pp. vii–ix.

BINDING AND DUST JACKET: Bound in maroon, ribbed grain cloth with a rectangle blind-stamped on the upper board. Stamped on the spine in gold: THE | FOREIGN | TRADE | OF | CANADA | LAUREYS | MACMILLAN.

The dust jacket is beige with brown lettering. On the front panel of the jacket is the following: THE | FOREIGN TRADE OF | CANADA | *By* | HENRY LAUREYS | *Preface by* | STEPHEN LEACOCK | [within a thick-thin rectangle is a synopsis of the book]. The spine panel is identical to that of the spine, except that the word OF is in lower-case and in italics. On back panel within a thick-thin rectangle, is a list entitled *Canadian* | Macmillan Books | *1929*, listing fifteen titles. Following the list, hand-lettered: *The* MACMILLAN COMPANY *of* CANADA *Limited* | St. Martin's House Toronto 2. A synopsis of the book is printed on the front flap, while information about Laureys appears on the back flap.

NOTES: Although the title page has 1929 as the date of publication (in contrast to the 1930 copyright date), the production card at the Macmillan Company of Canada fonds at OHM indicates that printing by the Hunter-Rose Co., Ltd. began on 2 January 1930 and was finished on 20 January of the same year. 1,515 copies were printed, and the total cost of production was $1,198.81.

In his introduction, Leacock points out that Laureys accepted a professorship at Montreal's École des Hautes Études Commerciales in 1911 and was appointed director of that institution in 1916. *The Foreign Trade of Canada* is a translation of Laureys's *La conquête des marchés extérieurs* (Montréal: Bibliothèque de l'Action Française, 1927), which won the David prize.

COPIES EXAMINED: CS (in jacket); OTNY (in jacket); QMMRB (no jacket); SLM (Leacock's copy, no jacket).

## B17 ASSISTED EMIGRATION AND LAND SETTLEMENT [1930]

McGill University Economic Studies | No. 9 No. 9 | National Problems | of Canada | [circular illustration of McGill University's insignia with shield and motto] | Assisted Emigration and | Land Settlement | With Special Reference to Western Canada | [rule] | JOHN THOMAS CULLITON, M.A. | [rule] | Published by The Federated Press Limited, Montreal, | for the Department of Economics | and Political Science | McGill University, Montreal.

♦ $1-5^8$. $1-2$, $3-79$, $1$ pp. (40 leaves). $219 \times 147$ mm.

TEXT: Leacock's preface, dated "January 1st, 1928," on p. 3.

BINDING: Issued in red wrappers, glued to the gatherings. The title page is reproduced on the front cover within three rectangles. On the back of the wrapper within a rectangle is a list of titles in the series, McGill University Economic Studies in the National Problems of Canada. The last two lines on the back of the wrapper are: *Published in 1927* | No. 9 Assisted Settlement in the Canadian West.

NOTES: After completing his M.A. thesis in 1928, John Culliton taught in the Department of Economics and Political Science at McGill University. He shared Leacock's office until Leacock retired, and in 1963, he edited and revised *Montreal: Seaport and City* (see *Leacock's Montreal*, A95c). In spite of the fact that the back of the wrapper gives the publication date as 1927, Culliton's thesis was not published until the end of February 1930 in an edition of 250 copies (probably at 75¢ per copy). The thesis was published by The Federated Press Limited of Montreal and distributed by the Macmillan Company of Canada.

Manuscripts of numbers 9 to 13 of the series arrived at the Toronto office of the Macmillan Company in November 1928. Although in 1926 Leacock had arranged with Hugh Eayrs of the Macmillan Company (see B12) for the publication of a monographic series of theses written by McGill's graduate students, by early 1929 Eayrs was reluctant to proceed much further with publication of the McGill theses in view of the poor sales. Leacock approached corporations with the offer that they could buy advertising in the monographs at $25 a page. He arranged for the Macmillan Company to receive an extra $25 per monograph in addition to the $50 per monograph called for in the original contract. He was also willing to assume $200 of the deficit incurred in printing the monographs.

Primarily due to Eayrs's friendship with Leacock, the Macmillan Company agreed to distribute Culliton's thesis and to publish numbers 10 to 12 of the series. By 21 November 1929 the Macmillan Company had already invested between $650 and $700 towards the publication of numbers 9 to 13 of the series, and a month later, it cost the company another $700 to complete the work. Notwithstanding $425 secured from advertising, $300 from McGill, and $200 from individual orders and subscriptions, the Macmillan Company lost approximately $500 on the four monographs.

COPIES EXAMINED: CS.

## B18 MODERN WRITERS AT WORK 1930

MODERN WRITERS | AT WORK | *Edited* | BY | JOSEPHINE K. PIERCY | INSTRUCTOR IN ENGLISH, | INDIANA UNIVERSITY | New York | THE MACMILLAN COMPANY | 1930

◆ 1–64[8]. i–vi, vii–xix, 1–3, 3–9, 10, 11–71, 72, 73–137, 138, 139–175, 176, 177–197, 198, 199–204, 205, 206–238, 239, 240–305, 306–308, 309–384, 385, 386–420, 421, 422–439, 440–442, 443–475, 476–478, 479–488, 489, 490–597, 598, 599–675, 676–678, 679–693, 694, 695–747, 748–750, 751–794, 795, 796–929, 930, 931–941, 942, 943–988, 989–990, 991–993, 1–11 pp. (512 leaves). 195 × 132 mm.

TEXT: Untitled essay ["On Learning to Write"], pp. 448–449.

BINDING: Bound in purple cloth with stamping in silver. Stamped on the upper board: MODERN | [rule] | WRITERS | [rule] | AT WORK | [rule] | • | PIERCY | [vertical bar to the right of the previous lines] | [ornamental vertical rule]. Stamped on the spine as follows: MODERN | WRITERS | AT WORK | • | PIERCY | [vertical bar to the right of the previous lines] | [ornamental vertical rule] | MACMILLAN | . . . Dust jacket not seen.

NOTES: Piercy's anthology gathers together pieces of writing from contemporary authors (essayists, humorists, short-story writers, fantasy writers, and novelists). She wrote to most of these authors and asked questions such as "What is the use of composition?". Leacock's manuscript in Piercy's papers at LILLY is entitled "On Learning to Write" (3 pp.). He gave Piercy permission to publish it on 14 July 1926. Along with this piece the anthology reprints "The Drama as I See it" (pp. 450–461).

Piercy's preface is dated August 1930. According to the copyright page the book was published in September of that year. Number of copies printed not known.

COPIES EXAMINED: OHM (two copies).

## B19 THE ASBESTOS INDUSTRY OF CANADA 1930

McGill University Economic Studies | No. 14 No. 14 | NATIONAL PROBLEMS | OF | CANADA | [circular illustration of McGill University's insignia with shield and motto] | The Asbestos Industry of Canada | [rule] | By M. M. MENDELS | [rule] | Published by the Packet-Times Press, Limited, Orillia, | for the Department of Economics and Political | Science, McGill University, Montreal. | *Price 75c.*

◆ 1–5[8] 6[6]. 1–2, 3–79, I–VI, 1–7 pp. (46 leaves). 219 × 151 mm.

TEXT: Preface, dated "Dec. 1, 1930 McGill University," on p. 2.

BINDING: Issued in red wrappers, glued to the gatherings. The title page is reproduced on the front of the wrapper within three rectangles. On the back of the wrapper within a rectangle is the following: McGill University Economic Studies | IN THE | NATIONAL PROBLEMS OF CANADA | [rule] | ALREADY PUBLISHED | [twenty-two lines listing numbers 1 to 13 of the series] | PUBLISHED IN 1930 | [five lines listing numbers 14 to 17] | [rule] | *Any of these publications may be obtain-* | *ed through the Packet-Times Press Limited,* | *Orillia, Ontario; The Poole Bookstore, Mon-* | *treal; W. Tyrrell & Co., Booksellers, Toronto;* | *Russell-Lang's Book Shop, Winnipeg; James* | *Hope & Sons, Limited, Ottawa; The Book Room,* | *141 Granville St., Halifax, or by subscription* | *$2.00 (a year for four numbers) from Professor* | *Stephen Leacock, McGill University, Montreal.*

NOTES: Morton Mendels graduated with an undergraduate degree in Commerce from McGill University in 1928. His M.A. thesis, number 14 of the McGill University Economic

Studies, was the sixth of the series to which Leacock wrote a preface. When Leacock's colleague, John Percival Day, declined to write a preface to Mendels's thesis, Mendels asked Leacock to write the preface on 5 August 1930. Mendels had written previously to Leacock about the proofs to his thesis: "As I remarked then, Mr. [J.R.] Hale of the Orillia Packet & Times promised to interview you personally. I do not know whether he has done so, and look forward to hearing either from him or yourself as to the possibility of my receiving these in the near future." Leacock received proofs of Mendels's thesis on 4 October 1930.

When the Macmillan Company of Canada decided against continuing the publication of the series in 1929, Leacock obtained estimates in November and December of that year from six different printing firms (William Brendon & Son Ltd., Butler & Tanner Ltd., Anchor Press, Ltd., etc.). The estimates included the cost of composition, paper, printing, and binding. On 26 September 1930, Leacock arranged for the Packet-Times Press from his home town, Orillia, ON, to manufacture and distribute numbers 14 to 17 of the series. Each monograph cost $175 to produce in editions of 500 copies. For distributing the series, the Packet-Times Press received 10¢ per copy sold. Numbers 14 to 17 sold at 75¢ apiece, to the trade at 60¢, or at a subscription price of 50¢ each for all four numbers. 500 advertising circulars were also printed. Leacock agreed to pay postage and related costs, and he contacted various bookstores in major Canadian cities to sell the monographs. The students obtained the proofs from Leacock.

Numbers 14 to 17 of the series contain full-page advertisements (The Royal Bank of Canada, The Canadian Manufacturers' Association, the Bank of Montreal, the Canadian Pacific Railway, and the Sun Life Assurance Company of Canada). These were also arranged by Leacock. The ad for the Canadian Pacific Railway, entitled *The Spirit of Progress*, has excerpts written by Leacock for a publication of the Department of Immigration and Colonialization, *Agricultural and Industrial Progress* (see C28.36).

For further discussion of the McGill University Economic Studies, see the notes to B12.

COPIES EXAMINED: CS.

## B20 THE STORY OF MONEY 1932

THE STORY OF | MONEY | *By* | MARY DUNCAN | CARTER | [illustration of a coin with the number 1 in the centre and the letters HB (joined), E, M, N, and B around it] | *With a Preface by* | PROFESSOR STEPHEN LEACOCK and Illustrations by | ALLAN McNAB | FARRAR & RINEHART | INCORPORATED | *Publishers New York*

◆  $1-5^8$ $6^4$. 1–6, vii–xi, *xii*, xiii, *xiv*, xv, 1–3, 3–29, 30, 31–61, 62, 63–71, 1 pp. (44 leaves). 179 × 131 mm.

TEXT: "Preface for Grown-Ups," dated at McGill University, 1932, on pp. vii–xi.

BINDING AND DUST JACKET: Bound in green cloth. Stamped on the upper board: THE STORY OF | MONEY | [ornament] | MARY DUNCAN CARTER. Stamped down the spine: THE STORY OF MONEY [ornament] CARTER.

The dust jacket is light gold with brown lettering. The front panel is as follows: [the first two lines in ornamental type] THE STORY OF | MONEY | [illustration in green and brown within two green circles of two white men talking with four native indians in front of a

tepee] | [the next two lines in ornamental type] BY | MARY DUNCAN CARTER |
*Introduction by PROFESSOR LEACOCK.* Printed down the spine panel of the jacket:
THE STORY OF MONEY [publisher's device of Farrar & Rinehart in green]. On the back
panel is an excerpt from Leacock's preface, referred to as "Preface for Parents." On both
flaps is a synopsis of the book. The front flap includes the price: $1.25.

NOTES: In February 1932 Mary (Duncan) Carter sent Leacock her proposed book and
asked him to write a preface to it. Leacock replied on 22 February [1932] that he thought
the book excellent and that he was quite prepared to do a preface of 500 words for $50.
He added:

> But your letter leaves some doubt as to whether it is a *preface* that is wanted or an
> introductory chapt. as a part of the book. The latter I should not care to undertake
> as it implies a sort of joint authorship to which I would have no real claim and for
> which therefore I should not feel entitled to see my name used.

The publisher Farrar & Rinehart was very pleased that Leacock liked Carter's book and
agreed to his fee for the preface. On 23 March 1932, John Farrar asked Leacock to send
the preface by 10 April or thereabouts. On 6 April 1932, Farrar wrote to Leacock: "The
Preface arrived yesterday afternoon; I have just read it and am delighted at the way you
have handled the whole thing. It will do a great deal for the book."

In January 1937 Carter assumed the position of Director of the Library School of Southern
California. Prior to that time she was Assistant Director of the Library School and Assistant
Professor of Library Administration at McGill University.

Also examined was a copy lacking the publisher's device of Farrar & Rinehart on the
copyright page.

COPIES EXAMINED: CS (one in jacket, the second lacking the jacket and the publisher's
device on the copyright page).

## B21 A CHRISTMAS CAROL 1934

A Christmas Carol | IN PROSE | *Being a Ghost Story of Christmas* | BY |
CHARLES DICKENS | [illustration of leaf] | WITH ILLUSTRATIONS BY
GORDON ROSS | AND AN INTRODUCTION BY STEPHEN LEACOCK | Boston |
*Printed for the members of The Limited Editions Club at* | THE MERRYMOUNT
PRESS, CHRISTMAS, 1934

◆ 1–7⁸ 8⁴. 1–7, vi–xi,1–2, 2–23, 24, 25–44, 45, 46–72, 73, 74–91, 92, 93–100, 1–6 pp. (60 leaves,
illustrated with six water-colour drawings by Gordon Ross, hand-coloured). 255 × 178 mm.

TEXT: Introduction, pp. 7, vi–xi.

BINDING AND DUST JACKET: Bound in green paper boards, patterned with evergreen trees,
quarter-bound in green buckram, top edge rust coloured. The paper label affixed to the top
of the spine is cream-coloured, and reads as follows: [wavy rule] | A | Christmas | Carol | in
Prose | [fleuron] | Dickens | [wavy rule] | [the remaining lines in calligraphic style type] The
Limited | Editions Club. Protected in a glassine jacket and in a cream-coloured box with a
paper label affixed to the spine portion of the box. The label on the box is identical to the
label on the book's spine up to the second wavy rule. The label on the box has the following
additional lines: No. [number of the particular copy] | [wavy rule].

NOTES: On 19 July 1934, Grace Macy, the Director of The Limited Editions Club, wrote to Leacock, informing him that the Club wanted to publish "an edition of A Christmas Carol this Christmas." "We hope to make ours the loveliest of all editions," he told Leacock. He asked Leacock to write an introduction of approximately 2,000 words, for which "we will pay you a prompt hundred dollars for it." Gracy had, in fact, sent a cable several days earlier, and Leacock had cabled back, accepting the assignment on 17 July [1934]. Gracy acknowledged receiving Leacock's introduction on 20 August 1934: "I am rushing it to Mr. Updike [of the Merrymount Press] who is printing this edition, and I attach our check in payment." Published on 19 December 1934 (copyright registration number at DLC A84204). The copyright was renewed by the George Macy Companies on 2 January 1962 (R288067). Leacock received a copy of the book sometime prior to 1 February 1935.

A Christmas Carol was first published in 1843. This edition belongs to the Sixth Series published by The Limited Editions Club. The colophon is as follows: [illustration within a circle of three men in nightcaps] I THIS EDITION IS DESIGNED AND PRINTED I BY D. B. UPDIKE, THE MERRYMOUNT PRESS, I BOSTON, FIFTEEN HUNDRED COPIES BEING I PREPARED FOR ISSUE TO THE MEMBERS OF I THE LIMITED EDITIONS CLUB I CHRISTMAS 1934 I THE ILLUSTRATIONS ARE BY GORDON ROSS, I WHO HERE SIGNS: I [Ross's signature in red ink] I THIS COPY NUMBER I [hand-written number, in red]. See item 61 of Ralph Geoffrey Newman and Glen Norman Wiche, comps., *Great and Good Books: A Bibliographical Catalogue of The Limited Editions Club, 1929–1985* (Chicago: Ralph Geoffrey Newman, Inc., 1989).

COPIES EXAMINED: CS (no. 103).

## B22 LA LIBERTÉ D'OPINION [1934?]

PUBLICATIONS I GUY DRUMMOND I [circular illustration of McGill University's insignia with shield and motto] I LA LIBERTÉ D'OPINION I Une étude comparée des libertés publiques I en France et au Canada. I George R. W. Owen, M.A.

♦ $1-8^8$ $9^4$. *1–5, 6, 7, 8–13, 14–15, 16–27, 28–29, 30–67, 68–69, 70–95, 96–97, 98–123, 124–125, 126–131, 132–133, 134, 1–2* pp. (68 leaves). 229 × 152 mm.

TEXT: Preface in French, on pp. 5–6, dated: Université McGill, I 1er décembre 1934.

BINDING: Issued in light blue paper covers, sewn signatures, perfect bound. The title page is reproduced on the front cover within two rectangles. The spine and back cover are blank.

NOTES: George Robert Whitely Owen (1912–) entered McGill University in 1929. While at McGill, he partook in many extracurricular activities, including Class Vice-President in 1932–3. He graduated in 1934 with a master's degree in economics. In 1968 he served as a judge at the Court of Appeal in Montreal.

In his preface Leacock recounts that Guy Drummond graduated from McGill's Faculty of Arts, continued his studies at l'École Libre des Sciences Politiques in Paris, and was killed during the First World War at Ypres on 22 April 1915. In Leacock's opinion ". . . l'ouvrage de M. George Owen . . . est entièrement digne de la Fondation sous laquelle il est publié et du nom du Fondateur qu'il aide ainsi à commémorer." Number of copies printed, exact date of publication, and price not known. Printed by Librairie Beauchemin.

COPIES EXAMINED: SLM (Leacock's copy).

## B23 THE PREMIER SPEAKS TO THE PEOPLE 1935

[the first three lines are printed within an outline map of Canada; the first word of the first line in script] *The* PREMIER | SPEAKS [the next two words in script] *to the* | PEOPLE | [illustration of maple leaf] | The Prime Minister's | January Radio Broadcasts | issued in book form | [illustration of maple leaf] | THE FIRST ADDRESS | Delivered from Ottawa on Wednesday, | January 2nd, 1935, between | 9:00 and 9:30 p.m. | With a Foreword by Stephen Leacock. B.A., Ph.D., LL.D. | Head of the Department of Political Economy of McGill University | Published by the | DOMINION CONSERVATIVE HEADQUARTERS | 128 Queen Street, Ottawa, Ontario

◆  $1^{10}$. 1–2, 3, 4, 5–7, 8, 9–20 pp. (10 leaves). 224 × 152 mm.

TEXT: Foreword, pp. 5–7.

BINDING: Bound in wire-stitched, blue paper wrappers. The front cover duplicates the title page up to the second maple leaf, after which is: THE FIRST ADDRESS | With a Foreword by Professor Stephen Leacock, B.A., Ph.D., LL.D. | *Head of the Department of Political Economy* | *of McGill University.* On the bottom right-hand corner of the back cover is an oval with the following printed within it: [curved] PRINTED | IN | [curved] CANADA.

NOTES: On 8 January 1935, R.B. Bennett thanked Leacock for his "kind message of good-will," which was sent to Bennett following his first radio address. "I realize that my declaration involves me in much hard work and I am no longer young," Bennett explained. "Nevertheless I propose to go forward with my proposals to the fullest extent of my ability." J. Earl Lawson of the Conservative Dominion Headquarters wrote to Senator C.C. Ballantyne on 13 February 1935 in which he told the Senator that the Headquarters proposed to publish Bennett's five radio speeches, "each in a separate pamphlet, although the five pamphlets will be mailed at the same time in one envelope to 250,000 people across Canada." Senator Ballantyne was asked to approach Leacock in order to obtain a foreword from him of 1,000 words. Leacock consented on 21 February 1935. Proofs of the speeches were sent to him on 13 March 1935. He apparently completed and mailed his foreword on 26 March 1935, and Lawson informed him on 1 April 1935 that "the best expression of appreciation I can give you is to tell you that we decided to print your preface as the fore-word to the first radio speech so that it would have priority over all others." Bennett expressed his thanks to Leacock on 18 April 1935: "I have not had an opportunity before this to thank you for the foreword which contributed to my radio addresses, published in pamphlet form. Your reference to my personal efforts during the past few years touched me deeply, and I appreciate your remarks greatly."

COPY EXAMINED: CS; LAT; OTAR.

## B24 LE NATIONALISME ÉCONOMIQUE FRANÇAIS 1935

PUBLICATIONS GUY DRUMMOND | [circular illustration of McGill University's insignia with shield and motto] | HARRISON CLARK, M.A. | LE NATIONALISME ÉCONOMIQUE | FRANÇAIS | Une étude de l'autarchie économique | en France | Préface du Professeur Stephen Leacock

◆ $1-7^8$. $1-7$, $8-15$, $16-17$, $18-28$, $29$, $30-53$, $54-55$, $56-81$, $82-83$, $84-94$, $95$, $96-103$, $104-105$, $106-108$, $1-4$ pp. (56 leaves). 228 × 151 mm.

TEXT: Preface on p. 5, dated: *McGill University,* | *Oct. 1, 1935.*

BINDING: Issued in light blue paper covers, sewn signatures, perfect bound. The title page is reproduced on the front cover within two rectangles. The spine and back cover are blank.

NOTES: According to Leacock preface, "Mr. Edgar Harrison Clark, M.A., of McGill University, was the holder of the Guy Drummond Fellowship for the session 1934–35." During the tenure of his award Clark attended the École Libre des Sciences Politiques in Paris. In Leacock's papers at SLM, there is an unsigned typed letter (possibly from John Culliton), dated 1 October 1935, and addressed "Dear Stephen":

> About Mr. Clark's thesis: Everything including your preface is at the publisher's. They will publish as soon as you can give the order. Their name is [la Librairie] Beauchemin and the man in charge of the work is M. Adamar. As for the translation and typing it is understood that as soon as you can give the word a cheque for $35.00 should be sent to Mr. Michel Seymour.

Leacock's preface appears in English in contrast to Harrison Clark's text which is in French. Copies printed and price not known.

COPIES EXAMINED: QMG; SLM (two copies, Leacock's library).

## B25 MARK TWAIN WIT AND WISDOM 1935

### B25a *American edition*:

MARK TWAIN | WIT and WISDOM | Edited by | CYRIL CLEMENS | and with a preface by | STEPHEN LEACOCK | [illustration of house and trees] | FREDERICK A. STOKES COMPANY | NEW YORK | MCMXXXV

◆ $1-11^8$ $12^4$. $1-6$, vii–xi, $1-3$, $1-167$, $1-3$ pp. (92 leaves). 207 × 140 mm. Frontispiece (black-and-white photograph of Twain) with tissue guard inserted facing title.

TEXT: Preface, pp. vii–viii.

BINDING AND DUST JACKET: Issued in beige cloth, all lettering in red. On upper board: MARK TWAIN | WIT [the next word raised] AND WISDOM | [in script] *Cyril Clemens.* On spine: MARK | TWAIN | WIT | AND | WISDOM | [the next two lines in script] | *Cyril* | *Clemens* | STOKES.

The dust jacket is cream coloured. On the front panel of the jacket is a drawing of Twain, after which is: CHARLES E. PONT [signature of artist] | [the remaining lines in red] MARK TWAIN | WIT [the next word raised] AND WISDOM | [in script] *by Cyril Clemens.* On spine panel of the jacket, all lettering in red: MARK | TWAIN | WIT | AND | WISDOM | CLEMENS | [illustration of house, similar to that on title page, in black] | STOKES. On the back panel is an order form, printed in red and black, entitled BOOKS WORTH OWNING, which lists works by twenty-six authors with checkmark boxes beside them. At the bottom of the list are mailing instructions and blank lines for the buyer's name and address. The front flap includes the price ($1.75), a synopsis of the book, and information about Cyril Clemens. The back flap is an advertisement and blurb for *Coolidge:*

*Wit and Wisdom, 125 Short Stories about "Cal,"* compiled by John Hiram McKee.

NOTES: This book of Mark Twain's humorous anecdotes was published in the same year in which Leacock was awarded the Mark Twain Medal; he accepted the medal at a dinner at St. Louis, MI, on 16 January 1935. Date of publication and number of copies printed not known. Published prior to 31 July 1935 since reviews appeared at that time.

COPIES EXAMINED: CS (in jacket); SLM (two copies not in jacket, Leacock's library).

### B25a.1 *first issue*:

MARK TWAIN | WIT and WISDOM | Edited by | CYRIL CLEMENS | and with a preface by | STEPHEN LEACOCK | *FOLCROFT LIBRARY EDITIONS* | 1977

This is a photographic reprint of A25a. An extra title leaf has been added, and the photo frontispiece appears on an ordinary page without a tissue guard. The leaves measure 223 × 161 mm. Bound in blue plastic over paper boards. Price $20. Another photographic reprint was issued in 1978 by Norwood Editions of Norwood, Penn. Price $25. (copy at DLC).

COPIES EXAMINED: OWTU

### B26 THE FRENCH FRANC AND THE GOLD STANDARD 1936

GUY DRUMMOND PUBLICATIONS | [[circular illustration of McGill University's insignia with shield and motto] | THE FRENCH FRANC | AND THE GOLD STANDARD | 1926–1936 | PHILIP F. VINEBERG, M.A. | Preface by Professor Stephen Leacock

◆  $1-4^8 \ 5^{12} \ 6^4 \ 7^2$. 1–7, 8–13, 14, 15–31, 32, 33–49, 50, 51–55, 56, 57–64, 65, 66–75, 76, 77–83, 84, 85–95, 1–5 pp. (50 leaves). 227 × 152 mm.

TEXT: Preface on p. 5 dated: McGill University, | August, 1936.

BINDING: Issued in blue paper covers, sewn signatures, perfect bound. The title page is reproduced on the front cover within two rectangles. The spine and back cover are blank.

NOTES: When Philip F. Vineberg graduated from McGill University in 1935, he was awarded the Guy Drummond Fellowship. He studied in Paris at l'École Libre des Science Politiques. Leacock took an active interest in Vineberg's progress, and he suggested several topics for a suitable M.A. thesis, including "La Scandale de Stavisky." In his preface Leacock differed from Vineberg's point of view about the inevitable devaluation of the French franc. In fact, Vineberg's predictions and analysis proved to be accurate. His recollections of Leacock's involvement in the publication of his thesis are recorded in K83.1, pp. 176–7. Probably published in October 1936 since A.E. Morgan, the Principal of McGill University, thanked Vineberg for sending a copy of the book on 5 October [1936] (file 955, container 59, RG2, at QMM Archives). Printed at the Witness Press in Montreal. Number of copies printed and price not known.

COPIES EXAMINED: CS; QMM.

## B27 UNSOLVED MYSTERIES OF THE ARCTIC 1938

**B27a** *first American edition, first issue*:

UNSOLVED | MYSTERIES | [the next two words raised] OF THE ARCTIC | [the next word raised] BY VILHJALMUR | STEFANSSON | introduction by [slightly lower] STEPHEN | LEACOCK | telling how this book | came to be | written. | NEW YORK • 1938 | THE MACMILLAN COMPANY

◆ $1^{10}$ $2-25^8$. *1–6*, v–xi, *1–7*, *1–2*, 3, *4–36*, 37, 38–192, *193*, 194–369, *370*, 371–381, *1–3* pp. (202 leaves). 220 ×146 mm. Frontispiece (with tissue guard) signed by Rockwell Kent.

TEXT: "Introduction (Telling How This Book Came to Be Written)," dated September 1938, pp. v–viii.

BINDING: Bound in silver flecked blue boards, quarter-bound with blue buckram. There is a light blue label mounted on the spine. The label has a blue rectangle that is split into two connected compartments. The title and author's name are printed vertically in black in two lines within the top compartment; printed in black in the lower compartment: THE | EXPLORERS | CLUB. Endpapers in light blue. The dust jacket is blue with a simulated laid-paper pattern of chain and wire lines. Lettering on the spine panel is similar to the spine of the book.

NOTES: This issue was published before the trade edition. The following is on p. *1*: *This special edition of Vilhjalmur Stefansson's* | UNSOLVED MYSTERIES OF THE ARCTIC, *consisting of* | *two hundred numbered copies, has been printed* | *for the Explorers Club. Each copy contains a* | *frontispiece by Rockwell Kent and is autographed* | *by both Mr. Stefansson and Mr. Kent.* | This is copy No. . . . . . .

On 14 March 1936 Leacock sent Stefansson an outline for a book entitled "Unsolved Mysteries of the Arctic Regions." Leacock suggested to Stefansson that he should write seven chapters plus an appendix with maps. Leacock would contribute a preface. Stefansson replied a few days later on 23 March: "You cannot overestimate my pleasure at receiving your letter of March 14, prodding me once more towards working on a book we may appear as collaborators." Leacock sent his preface to Stefansson sometime after 3 September 1938. The manuscript of the preface is located in a copy of the book at the University of London Library London.

COPIES EXAMINED: OTNY (no jacket); OTUTF (in jacket).

**B27a.1** *second issue* (1939):

This is the regular trade edition published by the Macmillan Company in 1939. In contrast to B27a, it lacks the frontispiece, the preliminary leaf with regard to the Explorers Club, and the last leaf of the book. Bound in blue cloth with lettering primarily in silver or in raised blue letters against solid silver rectangles. Dust jacket not seen.

NOTES: Reprinted February 1939, April 1939, November 1942, December 1943, February 1945, and 1956.

COPIES EXAMINED: CS (first printing without jacket; ninth printing (1956) in jacket).

**B27a.2** *third issue* (1972):

UNSOLVED | MYSTERIES | [the next two words raised] OF THE ARCTIC |

[the next word raised] BY VILHJÁLMUR | STEFÁNSSON | introduction by [slightly lower] STEPHEN | LEACOCK | telling how this book | came to be | written. | *Essay Index Reprint Series* | [publisher's device, two lines in height, to the left of the next two lines: abstract design of building with four columns] | BOOKS FOR LIBRARIES PRESS | FREEPORT, NEW YORK

The first five lines of the copyright page read: Copyright 1938 by Vilhjalmur Stefansson. | Copyright © renewed 1966 by | Evalyn Stefansson Nes. | Reprinted 1972 with | The Macmillan Company.

With the exceptions of the binding, paper stock, and the versos of the half title and title leaves, this issue is identical to B27a.1. The leaves measure 215 × 138 mm. Photographically reprinted by New World Book Manufacturing Co., Inc. Bound in blue cloth with the publisher's device blind-stamped on the upper board. The title and author's last name are stamped down the spine in gilt within a solid maroon rectangle. Below the rectangle is an oval with the lines: B | *f* | L.

COPY EXAMINED: OPET.

## B27b *first English edition* (1939):

[three vertical rules, the middle one thick, run down the left-hand side of the page above and below the N of UNSOLVED and the publisher's device] UNSOLVED MYSTERIES | OF THE ARCTIC | *By* | VILHJALMUR STEFANSSON | *With a Foreword by* | STEPHEN LEACOCK | [to the left of the remaining lines is the publisher's device: illustration of a winged horse above H, the latter two lines in height] | GEORGE G. HARRAP *&* CO. LTD. | LONDON TORONTO BOMBAY SYDNEY

◆ A⁸ B–Y⁸. *1*–6, *7*–13, *14*, *15*, *16*, *17*–18, *19*, 20–102, *103*, 104–186, *187*, 188–351, *1* pp. (176 pp.) 217 × 140 mm.

TEXT: Leacock's foreword (Telling How This Book Came to Be Written), pp. 7–10.

BINDING AND DUST JACKET: Bound in turquoise cloth with a rectangle and other vertical and horizontal lines blind-stamped on the upper board. Stamped on the spine in white: UNSOLVED | MYSTERIES | OF THE | ARCTIC | VILHJALMUR | STEFANSSON | [publisher's device] | HARRAP.

The front and spine panels of the jacket have a background illustration in light blue and white of an Arctic scene with a sailing ship land-locked in the ice and snow. Printed on the front panel in red block letters: VILHJALMUR STEFANSSON | UNSOLVED | MYSTERIES | OF THE ARCTIC. Printed on the spine panel in red: STEFANSSON | ★ | UNSOLVED | MYSTERIES | OF THE | ARCTIC | HARRAP. The back panel and flaps are white with printing in red. The back panel, which has a synopsis of the book, has the heading: *This is the most important book | on Arctic exploration for many years!*. This synopsis is continued on the front flap (price 10s 6d). On the back flap is an advertisement for Louis Segal's *The Conquest of the Arctic*.

NOTES: Number of copies printed not known. According to *The English Catalogue of Books*, the English edition was published in October 1939.

COPIES EXAMINED: CS.

**B27c** *second American edition* (1962):

[title page consists of two pages; on left-hand page:] VILHJALMUR STEFANSSON | [the next two lines in outline type] UNSOLVED [on right-hand page:] MYSTERIES | [on left-hand page:] OF THE [on right-hand page:] ARCTIC | Introduction by | STEPHEN LEACOCK | COLLIER BOOKS | NEW YORK, N. Y. | [on left-hand page to the left of the previous two lines in an ornamented design] C

◆ *1–6, 7–9, 10, 11–13. 14–16, 17–308, 309–310, 311–320* pp. (160 leaves). 179 ×102 mm.

TEXT: Introduction, pp. 7–9, identical to B27a.

BINDING: Perfect bound in stiff paper. The front cover is dark blue with an illustration of a sailing ship stuck in the ice. Also on the front cover in white are the title, the author's name, a quotation from the *Geographical Review*, and the number AS 3 5 1X. On the back cover is information about the book and Stefansson, an excerpt from a review, and the publisher's name.

NOTES: Price $1.10 in Canada, 95¢ in the U.S.A.

COPIES EXAMINED: CS (first, third (1967), and fourth (1970) printings).

**B27c.1** *second American edition, photographic reprint* [1985]:

Vilhjalmur Stefansson | ■ | Unsolved | Mysteries | of the Arctic | INTRODUCTION BY | Stephen Leacock | PRESS NORTH | AMERICA | 835 Lakechime Dr. | Sunnyvale, CA 94089

Although the leaves of this issue measure 211 × 131 mm., it is photographically reprinted and enlarged from the same setting of type as B27c. The verso of the title leaf indicates that book was printed by Griffin Printing and Lithograph Co., Inc. Glendale, California. The page opposite the title page (p. 2) is blank. Perfect bound with a colour photograph of snow and ice on the front cover. The back cover has dates and narrative of significant events related to Arctic exploration with the heading: What Happened? Cover designed by Ann Flanagan Typography, Berkeley, California.

COPIES EXAMINED: PHOEN.

## B28 THIS IS MY BEST 1942

**B28a** *first issue*:

America's 93 Greatest Living Authors Present | [in script] *This Is My Best* | [leafy ornament] OVER 150 SELF-CHOSEN AND | COMPLETE MASTERPIECES, TOGETHER WITH | THEIR REASON FOR THEIR SELECTIONS | [illustration of a small angel astride a lion, both within an oval compartment] *Edited by Whit Burnett* | BURTON C. HOFFMAN THE DIAL PRESS NEW YORK, 1942.

◆ *1-75*[8]. *i-vi*, vii-xiv, *1-2, 3-119, 120-122, 123-227, 228-230, 231-425, 426-428, 429-593, 594-596, 597-653, 654-656, 657-723, 724-726, 727-817, 818-820, 821-885, 886-888, 889-1017, 1018-1020, 1021-1175, 1176, 1178-1180, 1-6* pp. (600 leaves). 215 × 144 mm.

TEXT: "Why He Selected My Remarkable Uncle," p. 77, dated July 1942. Includes reprinting of "My Remarkable Uncle" (C41.11) on pp. 77-84.

BINDING: Bound in greyish beige buckram. Stamped on the upper board in gilt is an angel-lion illustration similar to that on the title page. The spine has a crisscross pattern in green with a solid green rectangle, and stamped in gilt within the rectangle are the title, the names of the editor and publisher, an ornament, and rules. Dust jacket not seen.

NOTES: The contributors to this anthology were selected on the basis of a reader survey taken from the subscribers to the *Atlantic Monthly*, *Harper's Magazine*, and the *New Yorker*. The editor, Whit Burnett, wrote to Leacock on 10 July 1942. He asked Leacock to select his preferred essay for inclusion in the book and to explain why he had made the selection. The manuscript of Leacock's explanation (2 pp.) to "My Remarkable Uncle" has the same title as the essay itself. Leacock was paid $25 for reprinting the essay. Burnett sent Leacock biographical and bibliographical notes on 24 July 1942. Leacock corrected some of the errors in the notes, although he left others uncorrected. The book was apparently published in time for the Christmas market of 1942 (information based on the Leacock folder, Group 1, Burnett fonds, Department of Rare Books and Special Collections, Princeton University Libraries).

COPIES EXAMINED: CS.

## B28a.1 *second issue* (1945):

America's 93 Greatest Living Authors Present | [in script] *This Is My Best* | [leafy ornament] OVER 150 SELF-CHOSEN AND | COMPLETE MASTERPIECES, TOGETHER WITH | THEIR REASON FOR THEIR SELECTIONS | *Edited by* *Whit Burnett* | THE BLAKISTON COMPANY | *Philadelphia*

The leaves measure 208 × 138 mm. The table of contents, the acknowledgments, and the index to authors have been reset; the half title has been omitted. This issue has eight less leaves than B28a. Bound in maroon cloth, all edges stained maroon. Stamped in gilt on the spine: [thick-thin rule] | This Is | My Best | *Edited by* | *Whit Burnett* | [ornament] | [thin-thick rule] | BLAKISTON.

COPIES EXAMINED: CS.

## B29 HIGH PARK RIDING ELECT GEORGE DREW 1943

[cover title] HIGH PARK RIDING | ELECT | GEORGE DREW | [to the left of the first three lines is a black-and-white photo of Drew's head and shoulders; beneath the lines is a typed letter, signed by Drew in facsimile, addressed to his constituents]

◆ Leaflet folded once to form four unnumbered pages. 281 × 216 mm.

TEXT: On p. 3, three paragraphs in double columns beneath a photograph of Drew, "George Drew" with Leacock's signature in facsimile, dated Orillia, Ont., July, 1943.

BINDING. Issued on white glossy paper stock, without a wrapper.

NOTES: This campaign leaflet consists of a cover title (described in the quasi-facsimile), an article taken from the *Toronto Globe and Mail* ("Drew Offers 50 p.c. Cut in Ontario School

Tax"), quotations about Drew from other newspapers, photographs of him (leaving No. 10 Downing Street, with his family, and in military uniform), the address of his Committee Rooms, and the date of the Polling Day, 4 August 1943.

Leacock sent "*Colonel George Drew and Conservatism. — About* 1100 *words.*" to [G. Larratt?] Smith on 7 July 1943. The manuscript is at SLM.

COPIES EXAMINED: SLM.

## B30 A FORUM OF THE FUTURE 1944

A FORUM | OF THE | FUTURE | 1942 THROUGH 1943 | PRESENTED BY PAN AMERICAN AIRWAYS | [the next line in script] *The System of the Clippers* | *Copyright, 1944, by Pan American Airways System*

◆ $1^{18}$. *1*, 2–3, *4–5*, 6–7, *8–11*, 12–13, *14–19*, 20–21, *22–25*, 26–27, *1–9* pp. (18 leaves). 290 ×210 mm.

TEXT: Leacock's contribution (p. 25) is entitled "To Every Child We Must Give the Chance to Live, to Learn, to Love." His signature appears in facsimile on the same page.

BINDING: Wire-stitched. Bound in light blue stiff paper with lettering in white on the front of the cover as follows: A FORUM OF | THE FUTURE | 1942 through 1943 | Contributors: | JOHN DEWEY • DR. HU SHIH • ARCHBISHOP OF CANTERBURY • COUNT SFORZA • MASARYK | DR. CRILE • COMPTON • ARANHA • PADILLA • LEACOCK • ARCHBISHOP STRITCH • STEFANSSON.

NOTES: The verso of the title leaf states that Pan American World Airways published a series of announcements in national magazines from August 1942 to April 1944. Twelve statements were made by important individuals "on what the post-war world will, or might at least, be made *for the common man.*" The magazines in questions were *Life*, *Time*, *News-Week*, and so on. Although a search of these magazines turned up some of the statements from the other contributors, Leacock's statement was not located in any magazine.

Published sometime after April 1944. Number of copies printed not known.

COPIES EXAMINED: SLM.

## B31 CANADA'S WAR AT SEA 1944

[in script] *Canada's War at Sea* | IN TWO VOLUMES | • | Volume I | CANADA AND THE SEA | *by* | STEPHEN LEACOCK | • | Volume II | CANADA AND THE WAR AT SEA | *by* | LESLIE ROBERTS | • | [five lines in italics and within quotation marks from] | — RIGHT HONOURABLE WILLIAM LYON MACKENZIE KING

Volume I | [in script] *Canada and the Sea* | *by* | STEPHEN LEACOCK | [ornament] | ALVAH M. BEATTY | *Publisher* | PUBLICATIONS (1943) LIMITED | 1075 Beaver Hall Hill = Montreal | 1944

◆ $1–20^8$ $21^2$. *1–13*, 14–15, *16–17*, 18–19, *20–21*, 22–23, *24–25*, 26–27, *28–29*, 30–31, *32–33*, 34–35, *36–37*, 38–39, *40–41*, 42–44, *45–47*, 48–51, *52–53*, 54–57, *58–59*, 60–63, *1–12*, 10–18,

*19–21, 22–28, 29–31, 32–37, 38–39, 40–43, 44–45, 46–49, 50–51, 52–57, 58–59, 60–69, 70–71, 72–74, 75–85, 86–92, 93–95, 96–99, 100–101, 102–103, 104–113, 114–119, 120–121, 122–123, 124–125, 126–127, 128–129, 130–136, 137–147, 148–150, 151, 152–155, 1–3, 1–5, 6–9, 10, 11–12, 13–14, 15, 16–17, 18, 19–28, 29, 30, 31, 32–33, 34–35, 36–66, 67, 68–72, 73, 74–84, 85, 86–99, 1* pp. (162 leaves). 293 × 221 mm.

TEXT: Leacock's contribution, "Canada and the Sea," consists of the following chapters: chapter I The Seacoast of Canada; chapter II The Twilight of Our Early Sea History; chapter III Exploration and Discovery; chapter IV In the Days of New France; chapter V Peace and War on Hudson Bay; chapter VI Britannia Rules the Lakes; chapter VII By the St. Lawrence to the Sea; chapter VIII The Arctic Voyages; chapter IX The Calm Pacific; chapter X The Great Shipping Days of Quebec and the Maritimes; chapter XI The Twentieth Century.

Simplified pagination for Leacock's text is: *1–63, 1–3, 149–150*. Leacock's foreword with his signature in facsimile is dated January 1944. The index appears after the text up to the letter M, and is continued at the end of volume II. In addition, there is a foreword by Mackenzie King, colour illustrations, maps, and a photograph of Leacock (the latter opposite his foreword).

BINDING: Bound in dark blue cloth, the endpapers light blue. Stamped in gilt on the upper board: CANADA'S | WAR [the next word raised] AT SEA | [illustration of an anchor] | [wavy rule] | CANADA AND THE SEA *by Stephen Leacock* | CANADA AND THE WAR AT SEA *by Leslie Roberts*. The spine is also in gilt with lines stamped vertically beginning at the foot of the spine (names of authors, title, and Publications (1943) Limited).

NOTES: Leacock wrote "Canada and the Sea" in June and July 1943. During that period he sent parts of the manuscript to his niece, Barbara Nimmo, for typing. He sent the complete manuscript (presumably a typescript) to the publisher, Alvah M. Beatty, on 26 July 1943. Beatty complimented Leacock on "a fine job" on 1 August 1943. He informed Leacock: "I plan to have it typeset commencing early next week, and altho[ugh] I won't have it paged until labor day, I'll have the galleys clipped to page size. . . . I plan to print your book and the photographic section in September. . . ." Leacock received proofs before 15 September 1943. Printing was to commence on 1 October in anticipation of publication in December 1943.

Beatty issued a pamphlet of "Advance Information" on *Canada's War at Sea* (copy at SLM). The publisher describes the publication, slated for December 1943, as a history in four volumes bound between the same covers. Leacock's volume, "Canada and the Sea," was to be an outline of Canada's Maritime history up to the outbreak of the world war (1939). In his pamphlet Beatty states:

> The publisher of *Canada's War at Sea* considers himself singularly fortunate in receiving his collaboration. Professor Leacock's volume, historical in its nature but much more than that, is one of his outstanding efforts and well entitled to rank with anything his magic pen, his keen erudition, and peerless wit have ever produced.

Publication was postponed. On 13 January 1944, Beatty requested Leacock to write captions for the paintings that were to be used as illustrations to accompany his text. The plan for *Canada's War at Sea* to consist of four volumes was also abandoned. The book consists of two volumes in one. The second volume by Leslie Roberts has three parts with part three written by Wallace Ward and J. Alexander Morton.

Beatty was to pay Leacock 5¢ a word for his contribution (32,000 words). He had not been paid for the work at the time of his death. $1,600 was still owing to the estate. According to the book's copyright page, publication occurred in December 1944. Price and number of copies printed not known.

Roberts, a former student of Leacock, was the editor of the *Montrealer* (published twice a month by Beatty). In a reminiscence of Leacock (K61.2), he recalled (at p. 63):

> Midway through World War II, I asked Stephen if he would write a foreword for a book I had written on the Canadian Navy and its gallant role in convoy escort. He agreed. Some time later he handed me more than 20,000 words, in which he had told the whole fascinating background story of Canada's lifelong relationship to the sea. His research was staggering to a reporter who had simply described events and engagements to which he had been an eyewitness.
>
> "I got interested in the subject," he explained. "If you don't like it, throw it away and I'll write something shorter."
>
> Not a word was changed. To my joy, the book appeared under our joint by-lines. Soon after, throat cancer took Stephen from the thousands of Old McGillers who loved him.

COPIES EXAMINED: CS; OTNY; QMMRB (two copies).


## B32 UNUSUAL FACTS OF CANADIAN HISTORY 1947

Unusual Facts of Canadian | History | by | W. A. L. STYLES, M.D., | *Wtth [sic] an Introduction* | *by* | STEPHEN B. LEACOCK | McCLELLAND AND STEWART LIMITED | PUBLISHERS TORONTO

◆ 1–6⁸ 7¹⁰. 1–8, 9–42, 43, 44–113, 1–3 pp. (58 leaves). 172 × 126 mm.

TEXT: Introduction on pp. 5–6.

BINDING: Bound in dark grey buckram with a paper label mounted on the upper board. On the label, within a solid light blue rectangle, is the following printed in white: Unusual | Facts of | Canadian | History | *by* | *WILLIAM L. STYLES*. Outside of the blue rectangle is a black border decorated with historical scenes in white (a windmill, a woman baking bread, etc.). Stamped down the spine: UNUSUAL FACTS OF CANADIAN HISTORY — Styles McCLELLAND | [beneath the previous line] & STEWART. The book was issued without a dust jacket.

NOTES: The date when Leacock wrote this introduction to this book is not known. Hugh Kane of McClelland and Stewart arranged with the Thorn Press to print and bind Styles's book. 2,500 copies (at 31¢ per copy) were delivered to McClelland and Stewart on 7 February 1947. The book apparently sold at $1.25 with a royalty of 10% to the author. Kane's instructions specified that instead of a jacket there would be a printed sheet pasted on to the upper board, but the Thorn Press inquired about the absence of a jacket on 6 May 1947. It would appear that the book was published shortly thereafter (information based on series Dk32 of the McClelland and Stewart fonds, OHM).

COPIES EXAMINED: CS; OHM; QMMRB.

## B33 THE WHARF THAT CHARLIE BUILT 1966

[cover title: all lines hand-written; the first line in light blue] THE WHARF
THAT | [the next line in light blue shaded in black] CHARLIE | [letters, B, I and
T, in red; U and I in light blue] BUILT | [above the second line at an angle in light
blue] BY | [across the second line is a hammer at an angle with the following
inscribed on the handle] M.S. ..C.E.F. ..D.M. [D.N.] ..F.J.L.E.

♦ 8 unnumbered leaves, including the covers. 261 ×177 mm.

TEXT: Probably entitled "Epilogue to These Stanzas," on folios 7 (recto and verso) and 8
(recto only). Photograph of Leacock's typescript signed by him.

BINDING: All leaves are on cardboard paper, glued at the spine, of colour photographs of
illustrations and typescripts. On the back of the lower board is an illustration of lakefront
property with a notice posted on a tree; below the illustration is a Mechanic Liens Notice
dated at Orillia, ON, 9 August 1943, from Fairweather and Evans, General Contractors.
Accompanying this book are: an explanatory pamphlet in a cerlox binding (215 ×141 mm.)
signed by F.L.J. Evans and W.D. Nimmo and dated 1 April 1966; a camel-brown wrapper
with an envelope affixed to the verso of the front of the wrapper.

NOTES: *The Wharf That Charlie Built* concerns the rebuilding of May Shaw's dock situated
on Old Brewery Bay at Lake Couchiching, close to Leacock's home in Orillia, ON. Mrs.
Shaw (M.S. on the cover title) acted as Leacock's research assistant and confidante (see A51,
A95a, and A104). In August 1943 when Charles E. Fairweather (C.E.F.) vacationed with
his sister-in-law, Mrs. Shaw, he found her dock in a demolished state. He began to rebuild
it with the assistance of various friends — Donald Nimmo (Barbara Nimmo's husband,
D.N., mistakenly rendered as D.M. on the cover title) and F.L.J. Evans (a lawyer from
Hamilton, ON, who rented a cottage nearby). This book contains colour illustrations of
paintings by Peggy Shaw (May's daughter, later Mrs. Kenneth Smith, see A88a), photographs of the dock and surrounding area, and verse by those who had a hand in the dock's
reconstruction. Leacock's contribution comments on each verse and on the good time
experienced by the participants.

The original manuscripts and artifacts for this book belonged to Mrs. Shaw. Fairweather
died on Christmas day 1964. Evans and Nimmo arranged for publication of the book in a
limited edition of twelve copies, numbered I to XII, mainly for presentation to the offspring
of the various authors. The book is dedicated to Mrs. Shaw "through whose kindness the
several authors enjoyed many happy days at Old Brewery Bay."

COPIES EXAMINED: EVANS (no. X, some leaves stuck together, including folios 6 and 7
obscuring the first page of Leacock's typescript).

# C Section: CONTRIBUTIONS TO SERIALS

**C87.1** "The Vision of Mirza (New Edition)," *College Times* (Upper Canada College, Toronto) 6, no. 10 (7 April 1887): 75–6. Signed S.B.L. Leacock was joint editor with F.J. Davidson of this high school journal and chairman of the Publications Committee for the academic year 1886–7. Thirteen numbers were published. The editorial material is unsigned. The story is partially reproduced in facsimile in K70.3 (illustration no. 10).

**C87.2** "U.C.C.," *College Times* (Upper Canada College, Toronto), 6, no. 10 (7 April 1887): 101. Poem. Signed S.B.L.

**C90.1** "The Sanctum Philosopher," *Varsity* (University of Toronto) 10 (7 October 1890): 8–9; (14 October 1890): 20; (4 November 1890): 56; (11 November 1890): 68; (2 December 1890): 104. These articles are all unsigned. Lomer (p. 126) states: "A column contributed at irregular intervals by Leacock when he was an associate editor during the autumn of 1890."

**C90.2** "The Decay of Fiction," *Varsity* (University of Toronto) 10 (21 October 1890): 28–9.

**C90.3** "A Lost Work [by the Sanctum Philosopher.]," *Varsity* (University of Toronto) 10 (18 November 1890): 76–7. Unsigned. The square brackets appear in the text.

**C90.4** "The Philosophy of Love *Translated from the German of Immerschnaps*," *Varsity* (University of Toronto) 10 (9 December 1890): 112–3.

**C91.1** "Imogene: A Legend of the Days of Chivalry," *Varsity* (University of Toronto) 11 (6 October 1891): 2–3.

**C94.1** "ABC: or, The Human Element in Mathematics," *Grip* 41, no. 20, whole no. 1,068 (19 May 1894): 155–6; 41, no. 21, whole no. 1,069 (26 May 1894): 163–4. Reprinted as "Jazzing up Arithmetic: Putting 'Human Interest' into Mathematics: Weaving the Romances of A,B,C," *Montreal Standard*, 7 November 1925, final ed., p. 28. Illustrated by A.G. Racey. Syndicated by Metropolitan Newspaper Service, New York. As "A, B, and C — The Human Element in Mathematics," in Essie Chamberlain, ed., *Essays Old and New* (New York: Harcourt, Brace, 1926, 1934), pp. 103–7 and Robert U. Jameson, ed. (1957), pp. 157–62; in Rose Adelaide Witham, ed., *Essays of Today: Informal and Formal* (Boston: Houghton Mifflin, 1931), pp. 34–8; in G. Fred McNally, ed., *A Book of Good Stories* (Toronto: Macmillan, 1934) pp. 71–8; in Bertha Evans Ward, ed., *Essays of Our Day* (New York: Appleton-Century-Crofts, 1937), pp. 128–33; in John A. Lester, ed., *Essays of Yesterday and Today* (New York, Chicago: Harcourt, Brace, 1948), pp. 23–7; in John D. Robins and Margaret V. Ray, eds. *A Book of Canadian Humour* (Toronto: Ryerson, 1951), pp. 212–6; in Joseph T. Browne, ed., *The Pageant of Literature: A Book of Nonfiction* (New York:

Macmillan, 1960), pp. 245–9; in Hart Day Leavitt, ed., *The Looking Glass Book of Stories* (New York: Random House, 1960), pp. 196–202; in Clifton Fadiman, ed., *Mathematics for Golfers* (New York: Simon & Schuster, 1962), pp. 148–52; in Georgess McHargue, ed., *The Best of Both Worlds: An Anthology of Stories for All Ages* (Garden City, New York: Doubleday, 1968), pp. 369–73; in Alice C. Baum, ed., *Designs in Nonfiction* (New York: Macmillan, 1968), pp. 106–11; in Ethel M. Sealey, ed., *A Book of Good Essays* (Vancouver: Copp Clark, n.d.), pp. 22–7; in David Arnason, ed., *Nineteenth Century Canadian Stories* (Toronto: Macmillan, 1976), pp. 204–8; in Allan Gould, ed., *The Great Big Book of Canadian Humour* (Toronto: Macmillan Canada, 1992), pp. 5–8. See also C28.52.

Electronically available (12 October 1997) at the National Library of Canada's Leacock Web site: http://www.nlc-bnc.ca/leacock/abc.htm

**C94.2** "That Ridiculous War in the East: Latest Account of the Naval Engagement at Yalu," *Grip* 42, no. 14, whole no. 1,088 (6 October 1894): 107.

**C94.3** "I. — Mr. Wordsworth and the Little Cottage Girl," *Saturday Night* (Toronto) 7, no. 50, whole no. 362 (3 November 1894): 6. A humorous sketch published under a general column, "Half Hours with the Poets," with poetry from other contributors. Reprinted as "The Little Cottage Girl," *Answers* 61, no. 1,581 (14 September 1918): 206.

**C94.4** "II — How Tennyson Killed the May Queen," *Saturday Night* (Toronto) 7, no. 51, whole no. 363 (10 November 1894): 6. A humorous sketch published under a general column, "Half Hours with the Poets," with poetry from other contributors.

**C94.5** "III. — Old Mr. Longfellow on Board the Hesperus," *Saturday Night* (Toronto) 7, no. 52, whole no. 364 (17 November 1894): 6. A humorous sketch published under a general column, "Half Hours with the Poets," with poetry from other contributors.

**C94.6** "An Outline of a New Pathology: Diseases of the Clothes," *Saturday Night* (Toronto) 8, no. 3, whole no. 367 (8 December 1894): 7. Apparently also appeared in the *Lancet* (London) and translated by various German periodicals and newspapers. Reprinted as "Pathology of the Pantaloon: Science of Medicine Lags in Diagnosing How Much Clothes May Un-Make the Man," *Montreal Standard*, 17 January 1925, final ed., p. 28. Illustrated by A.G. Racey. Syndicated by Metropolitan Newspaper Service, New York.

**C95.1** "My Financial Career," *Life* 25, no. 641 (11 April 1895): 238–9. Condensed in *Orillia Packet and Times*, 10 December 1908, p. 6 which gives its source as the *Sovereign Visitor*; reprinted in *Answers* (London) 61, no. 1,576 or no. 11 in that vol. (10 August 1918): 128; as "Creating a Stir in Banking Circles," *Vancouver Sunday Sun*, 28 January 1923, ("Magazine"), p. 7 as part of a syndication by Metropolitan Newspaper Service, New York. Condensed as "Stephen Leacock's Prize Story," *Orillia News-Letter*, 4 December 1929, p. [3], with an editorial notation that this story won first prize in the United States in a competition over 25 years ago. Condensed from *Literary Lapses* in *Reader's Digest* 22, no. 129 (January 1933): 24–5; *Reader's Digest* 41, no. 244 (August 1942): 40–2; *Senior Scholastic* 46, no. 15, Teachers Edition (14 May 1935): 19; *This Month* 1, no. 8 (October 1945): 42–4; *Mirror: Monthly Illustrated Review* 3, no. 32 (February 1951): 11–3; *Reader's Digest* 77 (December 1960): 192; *Canadian Banker* 100, no. 3 (May–June 1993): 24–5.

Reprinted in Joel Chandler Harris, ed., *American Wit and Humor* (New York: Review of Reviews Co., 1909), pp. 160–3; in Donald Graham French, ed., *Standard Canadian Reciter* (Toronto: McClelland & Stewart, 1921), pp. 1–5; in Albert Durrant Watson and Lorne Albert Pierce, eds., *Our Canadian Literature* (Toronto: Ryerson, 1922), pp. 233–6; in

Thomas L. Masson, ed., *Masterpieces of American Wit and Humor* (Garden City, New York: Doubleday, Page, 1922), pp. 19–23; in R.N. Linscott, ed., *Omnibus of American Humor (Comic Relief)* (Montreal: Better Publications of Canada Ltd., 1932), pp. 124–6 (note: this book originally published as *Comic Relief*); in *Life and Literature, Book One Grade Seven (Fourth Form, Junior Grade)* (Toronto: Thomas Nelson & Sons; The Educational Book Company, 1937), pp. 222–5; in Elizabeth Frances Ansorge et al., eds., *Prose and Poetry for Appreciation* (Syracuse, New York: L.W. Singer Co., 1942),pp. 738–42; in Louis Untermeyer, ed., *A Treasury of Laughter* (New York: Simon and Schuster, 1946), pp. 416–8; in John D. Robins, ed., *A Pocketful of Canada* (Toronto: Collins, 1946), pp. 208–10 and (Toronto: Collins, 1948), pp. 235–7; May Lamberton Becker, ed., *The Home Book of Laughter* (New York: Dodd, Mead, 1948), pp. 11–3; in *Fun Fare: A Treasury of Reader's Digest Wit and Humor* (Pleasantville, New York: Reader's Digest, 1949), pp. 301–3; in W.F. Longford, ed., *Essays — Light and Serious* (Toronto: Longmans, Green, 1954), pp. 1–4; partially as "On Visiting a Bank," in Margaret J. Miller, ed., *Seven Men of Wit* (London: Hutchinson, 1960), pp. 155–6; in *Clifton Fadiman's Fireside Reader* (New York: Simon and Schuster, 1961), pp. 346–9; in Gunnar Horn, *A Cavalcade of World Writing* (Boston: Allyn and Bacon, Inc., 1961), pp. 455–8; in Philip Penner and Edna Baxter, eds., *The Canada Books of Prose and Verse 2: Life and Adventure* (Toronto: Ryerson Press and Macmillan, 1962), pp. 392–4; in Bert Case Diltz, ed., *Frontiers of Wonder Book II* (Toronto: McClelland and Stewart, 1968), pp. 33–7; in *Fun & Laughter; A Treasure House of Humor* (Pleasantville, New York: Reader's Digest, 1968), pp. 609–13; in Desmond Pacey, ed., *Selections from Major Canadian Writers* (Toronto: McGraw-Hill Ryerson, 1974), pp. 173–4; in Carl F. Klinck and Reginald E. Watters, eds., *Canadian Anthology* (Toronto: Gage, 1974), pp. 164–6. Plagiarized under the name of A.E. Nash in *Book-Keeper* 14th year, no. 5 (December 1901): 63–5; under the name of L.T. Blount, as "My Bank Account," *Standard News* (Standard Oil Company of England) (Feb. 1930) with an apology printed in the March issue, p. 82. Lomer lists a reprint in *Senior Scholastic* (H.S. Teachers, ed.) 25 (12 January 1935): 7. See also A14, A115, and E2.1.

Electronically available (12 October 1997) at the National Library of Canada's Leacock Web site: http://www.nlc-bnc.ca/leacock/fincial.htm

**C95.2** "An Experiment with Policeman Hogan," *Truth* 14 (29 June 1895): 10–1.

**C95.3** "The Puppet Show," *Truth* 14 (3 August 1895): 10–1.

**C95.4** "Home Again," *Truth* 14 (26 October 1895): 4.

**C95.5** "The Force of Statistics," *Truth* 14, no. 453 (21 December 1895): 14. Reprinted as "Wonderful Things, Sir. Statistics," *Reader's Digest* 81 (August 1962): 141.

**C95.6** "A Model Dialogue, in Which Is Shown How the Drawing-Room Juggler May Be Permanently Cured of His Card Trick," *Truth* 14, no. 453 (21 December 1895): 9. Reprinted as "A Model Dialogue," *Golden Book Magazine* 18, no. 105 (September 1933): 273–4; as "The Sleeve Trick," *Reader's Digest* 41, no. 247 (November 1942): 37–8; in R.N. Linscott, ed., *Omnibus of American Humor (Comic Relief)* (Montreal: Better Publications of Canada Ltd., 1932), pp. 87–8 (originally published as *Comic Relief*); in H. Allen Smith, ed., *Desert Island Decameron* (Garden City, New York: Doubleday, 1945), pp. 164–6.

**C95.7** "Telling His Faults," *Truth* 15, no. 454 (28 December 1895): 15.

**C96.1** "The New Food," *Truth* 14, no. 455 (4 January 1896): 7.

**C96.2** "The Awful Fate of Melpomenus Jones," *Truth* 15, no. 457 (18 January 1896): 10. Reprinted in Grenville Kleiser, ed., *Humorous Hits and How to Hold an Audience* (New York: Funk & Wagnallis, 1908) pp. 25–7; in *Golden Book Magazine* 16, no. 95 (November 1932): 413–4. Illustrated by Dorothy McKay. In Eric Duthie, ed., *Tall Short Stories* (New York: Simon and Schuster, 1959), pp. 256–8; in Kathleen Lines, ed., *The Faber Books of Stories* (London: Faber, 1960), pp. 207–9; in Carl F. Klinck and Reginald E. Watters, eds., *Canadian Anthology* (Toronto: Gage, 1974), pp. 166–8.

Electronically available (12 October 1997) at the National Library of Canada's Leacock Web site: http://www.nlc-bnc.ca/leacock/jones.htm

**C96.3** "The Conjurer's Revenge," *Truth* 15, no. 460 (8 February 1896): 10. Reprinted as "Tempting Revenge — The Conjuror's Revenge," *Vancouver Sunday Sun*, 22 July 1923, ("Magazine"), p. 7. Syndicated by Metropolitan Newspaper Service, New York. In Alan Walker, ed., *The Treasury of Great Canadian Humour* (Toronto: McGraw-Hill Ryerson, 1974), pp. 1–3.

**C96.4** "Hints to Travellers," *Truth* 15, no. 462 (22 February 1896): 10. Reprinted in *Vancouver Sunday Sun*, 11 March 1923, ("Magazine"), p. 7. Syndicated by Metropolitan Newspaper Service, New York.

**C96.5** "How Gorillas Talk," *Truth* 15 (18 April 1896): 17. Illustrated by Hy Mayer.

**C96.6** "The Prize Fight of the Future. A Forecast," *Our Monthly* (Manufacturers Life Insurance Co., Toronto) (May 1896): 23–5. Reprinted in *Toronto Globe and Mail*, 4 November 1972, p. 7; *Montreal Star*, 11 November 1972, p. C1; in facsimile in Zdeňka Vávrová-Rejšková, *Stephen Leacock and the Art of Humour* (Prague: Univerzita Karlova, 1987), pp. 43–5. See also A123.

**C96.7** "A Manual of Education," *Truth* 15, no. 499 (7 November 1896): 6. Reprinted in Werner Taylor, ed., *Types and Times in the Essay* (New York: Harper & Bros., 1932), pp. 523–5.

**C96.8** "Reflections on Riding," *Truth* 15, no. 500 (14 November 1896): 7. Reprinted in Carl F. Klinck and Reginald E. Watters, eds., *Canadian Anthology* (Toronto: Gage, 1974), pp. 163–4; in Theresa Ford, ed., *Canadian Humour and Satire* (Toronto: Macmillan, 1976), pp. 11–2.

**C96.9** "A Lesson in Fiction," *Truth* 15 (5 December 1896): 10–1. Reprinted in *Vancouver Sunday Sun*, 21 October 1923, ("Magazine"), p. [4]. Syndicated by Metropolitan Newspaper Service, New York.

**C96.10** "On the Old Homestead," *Truth* 15 (12 December 1896): 12. Illustrated by Henderson.

**C97.1** "Saloonio," *Truth* 16, no. 507 (1 January 1897): 10. Illustrated by Hy Mayer.

**C97.2** "Self-Made Men," *Truth* 16, no. 511 (28 January 1897): 11. Illustrated by Hy Mayer. Reprinted in *Vancouver Sunday Sun*, 26 August 1923, ("Magazine"), p. 4. Syndicated by Metropolitan Newspaper Service, New York. In Frank Muir, ed., *The Oxford Book of Humorous Prose from William Caxton to P. G. Wodehouse: A Conducted Tour* (Oxford University Press, 1990), pp. 435–7.

**C97.3** "Getting the Thread of It," *Truth* 16, no. 514 (18 February 1897): 11. Illustrated by Hy Mayer. Reprinted in *Answers* 61, no. 1,580 (7 September 1918): 192; *Vancouver*

*Sunday Sun*, 7 October 1923, ("Magazine"), p. 5. Syndicated by Metropolitan Newspaper Service, New York. Also as "Getting the Thread of It: How One Man Explains a Story He Is Reading to a Reluctant Companion," *Glasgow Sunday Mail*, 22 November 1925, p. 6.

C97.4 "A New Winter Game," *Truth* 16, no. 519 (25 March 1897): 11. Illustrated by Hy Mayer.

C97.5 "Boarding-House Geometry," *Truth* 16, no. 522 (15 April 1897): 3. Reprinted in *McGill Fortnightly* 6, no. 3 (November 1897): 66. Also in "Dr. Stephen Leacock As a Humorist," *Halifax Herald*, 29 April 1907, p. 7. The *Herald* notes that "through the courtesy of a citizen," it is publishing "a couple of humorous articles," "Boarding House Geometry" and "Postulates and Propositions." Apparently reprinted in *Queen's College Journal* 25, no. 4 (December 1897): 63–4. In John W. Cunliffe and Ashley H. Thorndike, eds., *Warner Library of the World's Best Literature* (New York: The Warner Library Company, 1917), vol. 15, pp. 8928 s-t; in Robert Thomas Allen, ed., *A Treasury of Canadian Humour* (Toronto: McClelland and Stewart, 1967), p. 39; in Frank Muir, ed., *The Oxford Book of Humorous Prose from William Caxton to P.G. Wodehouse: A Conducted Tour* (Oxford: Oxford University Press, 1990), p. 434.

Electronically available (12 October 1997) at the National Library of Canada's Leacock Web site: http://www.nlc-bnc.ca/leacock/board.htm

C97.6 "Borrowing a Match," *Truth* 16, no. 523 (22 April 1897): 6. Reprinted in Alan Walker, ed., *The Treasury of Great Canadian Humour* (Toronto: McGraw-Hill Ryerson, 1974), pp. 310–1.

C97.7 "Helping the Armenians," *Truth* 16, no. 526 (13 May 1897): 10.

C97.8 "On Collecting Things," *Truth* 16, no. 539 (14 August 1897): 3.

C98.1 "Insurance Up-to-Date," *Canadian Magazine of Politics, Science, Art and Literature* 12 (November 1898): 89.

C98.2 "The Poet Answered," *Canadian Magazine of Politics, Science, Art and Literature* 12 (December 1898): 187.

C99.1 "Hoodoo McFiggin's Christmas," *Canadian Magazine of Politics, Science, Art and Literature* 12 (January 1899): 285–6. Reprinted in *McGill Daily*, 16 December 1911, p. 2; *Homemaker's Magazine* 26, no. 8 (November/December 1991): 14, 16, 18–20; *Toronto Globe and Mail*, 24 December 1994, p. C5; in Grant Huffman, ed., *Canadiana: An Anthology of Nostalgic, Humorous and Satirical Writing for Secondary Schools* (Toronto: McClelland and Stewart, 1970), pp. 57–9; *Telling Tales: An Anthology of Shorter Stories*, Book 1 (Toronto: McClelland and Stewart, 1973), pp. 95–7; in Patrick Crean, *The Fitzhenry & Whiteside Fireside Book of Canadian Christmas* (Markham, Ont.: Fitzhenry & Whiteside, 1986), pp. 54–6. See also A122.

C99.2 "Timothy's Homecoming," *College Times* (Upper Canada College, Toronto) (midsummer 1899): 1–5.

C1.1 "Children's Corner," *University Magazine* (Montreal) 1 (December 1901): 80–4. See also C25.56 and C26.43.

C3.1 "The Philosophic Premier," *Montreal Herald*, 28 November 1903, p. 6. Poem. Reprinted in *McGill Outlook* 6, no. 8 (1 December 1903): 194–5.

C4.1 "Looking After Brown," *Old McGill 1905* 8 (1904): 226–8.

C4.2 "The Constant Reader," *Saturday Night* (Toronto) 18, no. 3, whole no. 887 (26 November 1904): 14. Poem. Reprinted in *McGill Outlook* 7, no. 9 (15 December 1904): 217-8.

C4.3 "The Bluff That Failed," *Montreal Herald*, 3 December 1904, p. 6. Poem.

C4.4 "A Combination of Drama," *McGill Outlook* 7, no. 9 (15 December 1904): 227-8. Signed "S.L." Although the other two pieces (C4.2 and C4.5) in this issue are signed in full by Leacock, it is more than probable that he wrote this item as well. It contains the outline of a humorous melodrama. With respect to the outline the author states: "I am convinced that any man who has once seen this play of mine, will never want to see another."

C4.5 "Humor Unappreciated," *McGill Outlook* 7, no. 9 (15 December 1904): 233-4. Leacock includes a letter supposedly written by an editor who has rejected one of his humorous contributions because the contribution was too dangerous for public consumption. The printers laughed so hard when they tried to put the article into type that it almost killed them.

C5.1 "American Secretaryship. (An Address Read by Dr. Leacock to the Literary Society)," *McGill Outlook* 7, no. 19 (16 March 1905): 473-7. The text of Leacock's speech entitled "Higher Education and the Present Tendencies of American Scholarship," delivered to the McGill Undergraduates' Literary Society on 10 March 1905. A report of the speech is found on p. 482. Leacock was also toast-master at the Society's banquet on 17 March 1905. See "The Literary Banquet," 7, no. 20 (6 April 1905): 505. See also E5.3.

C5.2 "Future of French Canada," *Morning Post* (London), 12 December 1905, p. 4. Signed: "From our correspondent. Montreal, November 30." Listed in Leacock's notebook of recorded publications and speeches at QMMRB. Three other articles appeared in the *Morning Post* under a similar designation — "Canadian Wheat Crop," *Morning Post* (London), 26 May 1905, p. 5 ("From our Canadian correspondent, May 25"); "Canadian Militia," *Morning Post* (London), 6 November 1905, p. 5 ("From our Canadian correspondent"); and "The Canadian Tariff," *Morning Post* (London), 8 November 1905, p. 8 ("From our Canadian correspondent, November 7"). In his notebook at QMMRB, Leacock records the latter article as having appeared in the *Guardian* (Manchester). See also E5.5.

C6.1 "University Extension Lectures by Professor Leacock of McGill," *Ottawa Evening Journal*, 20 January 1906, p. 19. The text of Leacock's first lecture, delivered on 12 January 1906, on "The Making of the Empire: The Lessons of Its History," delivered at Queen's Hall in Ottawa and sponsored by the May Court Club. He gave six lectures on this subject on alternating Friday evenings. Also as "Story of the British Empire First of the Series of Lectures to Be Delivered by Professor Leacock of McGill University Under the Auspices of the May Court Club," *Ottawa Citizen*, 20 January 1906, p. 13. The *Citizen* noted that the complete lecture is being published "with the exception of a few paragraphs which were missing from the manuscript." Also earlier, but with less text, as "The British Empire; A Phenomenon Unique in Political History of Mankind. Its Loss in America. Secession of the United States Deprived World of Great Peace-Making Power," *Montreal Gazette*, 18 January 1906, p. 9. The latter part of the lecture on the settlement of the Australasian colonies and the expansion into Africa is not included. This version was in turn condensed as "Dr. Leacock's Lecture; On the Making of the British Empire," *Orillia Packet*, 8 February 1906, p. [6]. The *Packet* notes "The lecture is reported at length in the *Montreal Gazette*, we give considerable extracts." See also A1, C6.2, C6.3, and D6.2-3.

**C6.2** "Developing Government; Second of Professor Leacock's Lectures on the British Empire — The Evolution of the Colonies," *Ottawa Citizen*, 3 February 1906, p. 16. An extended excerpt.

**C6.3** "Advocated Free Trade within the Empire and Tariff Barriers Against the World," *Ottawa Citizen*, 17 February 1906, p. 13.

**C6.4** "The Imperial Crisis," *Proceedings of the Canadian Club, Toronto for the Year 1905–1906* 3: 114–8. The text of Leacock's address on 2 April 1906 to the Canadian Club. Reported as "Britain Must Look to Colonies. Prof. Leacock Speaks on 'The Imperial Crisis.' Need for Federation. Tells Canadian Club This Country Could Not Hold Out as an Independent Nation," *Toronto Mail and Empire*, 3 April 1906, p. 7, six paragraphs quoted; as "Is an Imperial Crisis. Prof. Leacock of McGill Speaks upon the Empire; Advocates Colonial Representation in the British Parliament, and the Taxation of the Colonies for Imperial Defence," *Toronto Globe*, 3 April 1906, p. 11, with quotations; "The Imperial Crisis," *Orillia Packet*, 5 April 1906, p. [2], with quotations; "The Future of Canada: Prof. Leacock Speaks of an 'Imperial Crisis,' " *Saturday Night* (Toronto) 19, no. 22, whole no. 958 (7 April 1906): 9. Report (signed "Hal.") with quotations. See also E6.4 and E6.6.

**C6.5** "The Passing of the Poet," *Canadian Magazine of Politics, Science, Art and Literature* 27 (May 1906): 71–3. See also E5.4.

**C6.6** "The Rehabilitation of Charles II," *University Magazine* (Montreal) 5 (May 1906): 266–81. See also E4.2.

**C6.7** "Post-Graduate Study," *McGill Outlook* 9, no. 3 (25 October 1906): 59–63.

**C7.1** "What Protection Does for Canada," *Guardian* (Manchester), 4 January 1907, p. 8. Signed "From a Canadian Correspondent." Identified as Leacock from his notebook of recorded publications and speeches at QMMRB.

**C7.2** "Aristocratic Education," *Puck* 60, no. 1,560 (23 January 1907): [4–5].

**C7.3** "The Psychology of American Humour," *University Magazine* (Montreal) 6 (February 1907): 55–75.

**C7.4** "Education and Empire Unity," *Empire Club Speeches* (1907): 276–305. The text of Leacock's speech before the Empire Club and the Toronto Educationists on 19 March 1907 appears on pp. 280–96. The introduction by Dr. E. Clouse and J. P. Murray is on pp. 276–79; discussion with remarks by Alfred Baker, James L. Hughes and Murray is on pp. 296–303; Leacock's thank you is on pp. 303–4; Professor McGillivray of Glasgow concludes on pp. 304–05. Excerpt reprinted in George H. Locke, ed., *Builders of the Canadian Commonwealth* (Toronto: Ryerson Press, 1923), pp. 223–6. The speech was reported as "Dare to Be Partner. Prof. Leacock to Empire Club. Time for Canada to Realize She Is Grown Up and to Cease Mewling and Puking in the Nurse's Arms," *Toronto Telegram*, 20 March 1907, p. 18, several paragraphs quoted; "Prof. S. Leacock on Imperialism; Scholarly Address Before Empire Club Last Night. Canada No Longer a Colony; Speaker Hopes for the Time When There Will Exist an Indivisible Empire," *Toronto Mail and Empire*, 20 March 1907, p. 6, with three paragraphs quoted; "Fires of Imperialism. Prof Leacock of M'Gill University at Empire Club. Said Time for Canada to Assert Itself, and Petty Statecraft Could Only Be Burned Out by Imperialism," *Toronto Globe*, 20 March 1907, p. 14, a few sentences quoted. Some quotations appear in the *Canadian Annual Review of Public Affairs* (1907): 374. See also E7.6.

**C7.5** "Greater Canada: An Appeal," *University Magazine* (Montreal) 6 (April 1907): 132–41. Reprinted as "Imperialism as Anti-Colonialism," in Carl Berger, ed., *Imperialism and Nationalism, 1884–1914: A Conflict in Canadian Thought* (Toronto: Copp Clark, 1969), pp. 47–51; as "Greater Canada: An Appeal Let Us No Longer Be a Colony," in R. Douglas and Donald B. Smith, *Readings in Canadian History — Post-Confederation* (Toronto: Holt, Rinehart and Winston, 1982), pp. 108–13. In "The Imperial Conference," *Orillia Packet*, 28 March 1907, p. [2], it was noted that the pamphlet (see A3) had been issued and several sentences from it are quoted.

**C7.6** "Responsible Government in the British Colonial System," *American Political Science Review* 1 (May 1907): 355–92.

**C7.7** "After the Conference. John Bull and His Grown Up Sons," *Morning Post* (London), 17 May 1907, p. 7. Reprinted as "How Professor Leacock Stirs Them Up," *Montreal Herald*, 28 May 1907, p. 6. Also reprinted as "John Bull, Farmer. Dr. Leacock's Satire on the Colonial Conference," *Orillia Packet and Times*, 30 May 1907, p. 2. Leacock's article prompted a response, written in the same humorous tone, by A.E. Taylor, "Mr. Bull and the Friend of the Family," *Montreal Witness*, 6 June 1907, p. 6.

**C7.8** "Discussion" [of W.L. Griffith's paper "Some Phases of Canada's Development"], *Proceedings of the Royal Colonial Institute* 38 (1906–7): 304–6. Griffith, who was Secretary to the High Commissioner's Office, delivered his paper on 14 May 1907 in London at the Seventh Ordinary General Meeting of the Session. This volume appeared sometime after 22 July 1907 (the date on the verso of the title leaf).

**C7.9** "The Imperial Aspect. 'A Group of Mighty States,' " *Dominion* (Wellington, N.Z.), 26 September 1907, p. 8.

**C8.1** "The International Tax Conference and Canadian Public Finance," *University Monthly* (University of Toronto) 9, no. 1 (November 1908): 8–12.

**C8.2** "College Journalism," *Martlet* (McGill University) 1, no. 3 (5 November 1908): 36–7. See also C30.4.

**C8.3** "The Limitations of Federal Government," *Proceedings of the American Political Science Association* 5 (1908): 37–52. Text of speech that Leacock delivered during its 5th annual meeting that took place 28–31 December 1908 in Washington, D.C. and Richmond, Virginia. See also E8.7.

**C9.1** "Sir Wilfrid Laurier's Victory," *National Review* (London) 52 (January 1909): 826–33. Excerpts from Leacock's article are contained in "Stephen Leacock on Politics," *Saturday Night* (Toronto) 22, no. 14, whole no. 1,102 (16 January 1909): 4.

**C9.2** "The Yellow Peril A Very Real One Says Prof. Leacock; The Asiatic Wherever He Gets Hold Drives the White Man Out — False Political Economy Doctrine of 'Blind and Brutal Competition' Is the Only Argument in Their Favor," *Montreal Daily Herald*, 30 January 1909, p. 18. A report of Leacock's speech to the St. James' Literary Society on 27 January 1909. According to the *Herald* the report was a "statement of the case edited by himself." See also E9.7.

**C9.3** "Literature and Education in America," *University Magazine* (Montreal) 8 (February 1909): 3–17. See also A117 and E9.1.

**C9.4** "The Naval Crisis in the Empire," *Ottawa Citizen*, 12 April 1909, p. 4. The article drew a response from John S. Ewart. See "The Vortex," 14 April 1909, p. 9.

**C9.5** "Studies in Still Life. The Country Hotel," *Puck* 65, no. 1,684 (9 June 1909): [11]. See also E8.5.

**C9.6** "Canada and the Monroe Doctrine," *University Magazine* (Montreal) 8 (October 1909): 351–74. See also E6.11 and E7.2.

**C9.7** "The Dean's Dinner, the Faculty of Arts (Verses Written for Dean Moyse's Dinner to the Professors of the Faculty, October 29, 1909)," *Montreal Daily Star*, 13 November 1909, p. 2. See also C23.38 and E9.16.

**C10.1** "The Apology of a Professor," *University Magazine* (Montreal) 9 (April 1910): 176–91. Two lengthy paragraphs are reprinted in "The Professor," *Orillia Packet*, 28 April 1910, p. 4. Also as "Has the Professor Any Right to Exist?," *Montreal Daily Herald*, 16 April 1910, pp. [11], 24, with a preface added by the *Herald*, illustrated by Fitzmaurice. The article drew a response letter to the editor, "What A McGill Student Thinks About a Professor's Right to Exist," *Montreal Daily Herald*, 19 April 1910, p. 4. Leacock's article reprinted as "The Apology of a Professor: An Essay on Modern Learning," in Malcolm Ross, ed., *Our Sense of Identity: A Book of Canadian Essays* (Toronto: Ryerson Press, 1954), pp. 301–14. See also E10.4.

**C10.2** "Dr. Leacock on the Constitution Crisis, Death of King Occurs at a Most Difficult Moment and May Do Harm," *Montreal Herald*, 7 May 1910, p. 23.

**C10.3** " 'Great World Questions of the Present Day; Socialism and the Future' Article No. 1," *Montreal Standard*, 14 May 1910, late news ed., p. 5; reprinted 21 May, literary ed., p. 5.

**C10.4** " 'Great World Questions of the Present Day.' Germany as a World Power," *Montreal Standard*, 21 May 1910, late news ed., p. 5; reprinted 28 May, literary ed., p. 13. See also D10.2 and E9.15.

**C10.5** "The Birthday of Another British Dominion: Union of South Africa Takes Place on Tuesday," *Montreal Standard*, 28 May 1910, late news ed., pp. 5–6; reprinted 4 June, literary ed., pp. 5–6. This article is part of the series ("Great World Questions of the Present Day"), though it is not titled as such.

**C10.6** " 'Great World Questions of the Present Day.' The Outlook for Imperial Unity," *Montreal Standard*, 4 June 1910, late news ed., p. 10; reprinted 11 June, literary ed., p. 2. See also E10.1.

**C10.7** " 'Great World Questions of the Present Day.' The House of Lords Question," *Montreal Standard*, 11 June 1910, late news ed., p. 12; reprinted 18 June, literary ed., p. 12.

**C10.8** "Back Door of the Continent," *Canadian Century* (Montreal) (9 July 1910): 7–8.

**C10.9** "Vanitas: A Song for Summer Time," *Canadian Century* (Montreal) 2, no. 4 (30 July 1910): 9. Illustrated by George E. McElroy. Poem. Reprinted as "Idleness — A Song for a Long Vacation, Being a Joyous Canticle Upon the Superior Triumphs of Unperturbed Indolence," *Vanity Fair* 21, no. 2 (October 1923): 59.

**C10.10** "Today in History August 8, 1842. (The Annexation of Natal.)," *Ottawa Evening Journal*, 8 August 1910, p. 6. Poem. The first poem in a series on historical events, copyright, 1910, by Publishers' Press. Leacock's authorship of the two unsigned poems in the series is certain since they are reprinted in A40. See also C23.42 and C24.3.

C10.11 "Today in History August 9, 1902. (King Edward VII Crowned)," *Ottawa Evening Journal*, 9 August 1910, p. 6. Poem.

C10.12 "Today in History August 10, 1866. (The Straits Settlements Founded)," *Ottawa Evening Journal*, 10 August 1910, p. 6. Poem.

C10.13 "Today in History August 11, 1535. (Jacques-Cartier Discovered the St. Lawrence)," *Ottawa Evening Journal*, 12 August 1910, p. 6. Poem. Unsigned.

C10.14 "How to Make a Million Dollars," *Canadian Century* (Montreal) 2, no. 6 (13 August 1910): 7. Illustrated by George McElroy. Also in *Saturday Night* (Toronto) 23, no. 44, whole no. 1,184 (13 August 1910): 4. Illustrated with a portrait; *Ottawa Evening Journal*, 13 August 1910, p. 14; *Vancouver Sunday Sun*, 29 April 1923, p. 5. Syndicated by Metropolitan Newspaper Service, New York. See also A14.

C10.15 "Today in History August 12, 1905. (Anglo-Japanese Alliance)," *Ottawa Evening Journal*, 13 August 1910, p. 6. Poem. Reprinted in F.R. Scott and A.J.M. Smith, eds., *The Blasted Pine: An Anthology of Satire Invective and Disrespectful Verse Chiefly By Canadian Writers* (Toronto: Macmillan, 1957), pp. 106–7.

C10.16 "Today in History (August 15, 1870) Manitoba Becomes a Province," *Ottawa Evening Journal*, 15 August 1910, p. 6. Poem. Reprinted in F.R. Scott and A.J.M. Smith, eds., *The Blasted Pine: An Anthology of Satire Invective and Disrespectful Verse Chiefly By Canadian Writers* (Toronto: Macmillan, 1957), pp. 74–5.

C10.17 "Today in History August 16, 1713. New Brunswick Founded," *Ottawa Evening Journal*, 16 August 1910, p. 6. Poem.

C10.18 "Today in History August 17, 1896. Gold Discovered in the Yukon," *Ottawa Evening Journal*, 17 August 1910, p. 6. Poem. Unsigned.

C10.19 "Today in History Birth of Rubens. August 18, 1577," *Ottawa Evening Journal*, 18 August 1910, p. 6. Poem.

C10.20 "Today in History August 19, 1897. Introduction of the Horseless Cab," *Ottawa Evening Journal*, 19 August 1910, p. 6. Poem. Reprinted as "Introduction of the Horseless Cab," *Library Digest* 80, no. 4 (26 January 1924): 36. Poem.

C10.21 "Today in History August 20, 1896. Fridjof Nansen's Ship the Fram. Returns Safely to Skjervoe," *Ottawa Evening Journal*, 20 August 1910, p. 6. Poem.

C10.22 "Today in History August 22nd, 1903. Expedition of the Neptune, Under Commander Low, to Hudson Straits," *Ottawa Evening Journal*, 22 August 1910, p. 6. Poem.

C10.23 "Today in History August 23, 1839. Captain Eliot Captured Hong Kong," *Ottawa Evening Journal*, 23 August 1910, p. 6. Poem.

C10.24 "Today in History August 24th, 1890. Sarnia Tunnel Completed," *Ottawa Evening Journal*, 24 August 1910, p. 6. Poem.

C10.25 "Today in History August 25th, 1860. Opening of the Victoria Bridge, Montreal, by the Prince of Wales," *Ottawa Evening Journal*, 25 August 1910, p. 6. Poem.

C10.26 "Today in History August 26, 1346. Great Slaughter of the French by the English at Crecy," *Ottawa Evening Journal*, 26 August 1910, p. 6. Poem.

C10.27 "Men Who Have Shaved Me," *Canadian Century* (Montreal) (27 August 1910): 16. Illustrated by C. Thompson. Also in *Saturday Night* (Toronto) 23, no. 46, whole no.

1,186 (27 August 1910): 6. Illustrated by C. Thompson; *Ottawa Evening Journal*, 27 August 1910, p. 2; *Answers* 61, no. 1,575 (3 August 1918): 111.

C10.28 "Today in History August 27th, 1870. Invention of the Gramophone," *Ottawa Evening Journal*, 27 August 1910, p. 6. Poem.

C10.29 "How to Live to Be 200," *Canadian Century* (Montreal) (10 September 1910): 13. Illustrated by C. Thompson. Also in *Saturday Night* (Toronto) 23, no. 48, whole no. 1,188 (10 September 1910): 4. Illustrated by C. Thompson; *Answers* (London) 61, no. 1,574 (27 July 1918): 99. Reprinted as "How to Live to Be 200 Years," *Vancouver Sunday Sun*, 6 May 1923, ("Magazine"), 6 May 1923, p. 4. Syndicated by Metropolitan Newspaper Service, New York; as "How to Live to Be 200: Do Those Things You Should Not Have Done and Leave Undone Those You Should Do," *Sunday Mail* (Glasgow), 6 December 1925, p. 10. Illustrated by Kessler. In Robert Thomas Allen, ed., *A Treasury of Canadian Humour* (Toronto: McClelland and Stewart, 1967), pp. 41–2; in Ronald Conrad, *The Act of Writing: Canadian Essays for Composition*, 3rd ed. (Toronto: McGraw-Hill Ryerson, 1990), pp. 241–4.

C10.30 "How to Avoid Getting Married," *Canadian Century* (Montreal) 2, no. 12 (24 September 1910): 7. Illustrated by C. Thompson. Also in *Saturday Night* (Toronto) 23, no. 50, whole no. 1,190 (24 September 1910): 4. Illustrated by C. Thompson. Also as "How to Keep from Getting Married," *Ottawa Evening Journal*, 24 September 1910, p. 14. Reprinted as "How to Avoid Getting Married Heart Problems Solved for Flattering Young Men," *Montreal Standard*, 27 June 1925, final ed., p. [20]. Illustrated by A.G. Racey. Syndicated by Metropolitan Newspaper Service, New York.

C10.31 "How to Be a Doctor," *Canadian Century* (Montreal) 2, no. 14 (8 October 1910): 14. Also in *Saturday Night* (Toronto) 23, no. 52, whole no. 1,192 (8 October 1910): 4; *Ottawa Evening Journal*, 8 October 1910, p. 19. Illustrated by C. Thompson; *Answers* 61, no. 1,579 (31 August 1918): 174; as "How to Become a Doctor: An Easy Course in One Lesson on the Treatment of Disease," *Montreal Standard*, 14 February 1925, final ed., p. [36]. Syndicated by Metropolitan Newspaper Service, New York; *Syndrome* (McMaster University, Hamilton) 6, no. 2 (November/December 1981): 13–5.

C10.32 "Back to the Bush," *Saturday Night* (Toronto) 24, no. 2, whole no. 1,194 (22 October 1910): 4; *Ottawa Evening Journal*, 5 November 1910, p. 14; *Rod and Gun in Canada* 33, no. 7 (December 1931): 5–6, 28. Illustrated by A.M. Pattison.

C10.33 "The Union of South Africa," *American Political Science Review* 4 (November 1910): 498–507. See also E8.4.

C10.34 "[Practical Political Economy] 1. Theory of Value," *Saturday Night* (Toronto) 24, no. 5, whole no. 1,197 (12 November 1910): 15. First and second articles of the series together as "Political Economy (1) The Theory of Value (2) Monopoly Prices and the Trust Problem," *Ottawa Evening Journal*, 3 December 1910, p. 14. This series was syndicated in *Vancouver Province, Saskatoon Phoenix, Strathcona Plaindealer, Montreal Witness*, and other newspapers; as "Theory of Value," *Lethbridge* (AB) News, 3 December 1910. It began running as "Wealth and Value as Economic Terms," *Vancouver Province*, 17 November 1910, p. 4. See also A6.

C10.35 "[Practical Political Economy] II. Monopoly Prices and the Trust Problem," *Saturday Night* (Toronto) 24, no. 6, whole no. 1,198 (19 November 1910): 21. Reprinted as "Price Monopoly of Today; Intimately Connected with Expansion and Consolidation; Carries with It the Whole Question of Trust Legislation," *Strathcona* (AB) *Plaindealer*, 29 November 1910, pp. 6–7.

**C10.36** "[Practical Political Economy] III. Railroad Rates and Railroad Legislation," *Saturday Night* (Toronto) 24, no. 7, whole no. 1,199 (26 November 1910): 4, 22. Third and fourth articles of the series together as "Political Economy Practically Explained (3) Railway Rates and Highway Legislation (4) The Theory of Money," *Ottawa Evening Journal*, 10 December 1910, p. 12.

**C10.37** "The Devil and the Deep Sea," *University Magazine* (Montreal) 9 (December 1910): 616–26. Reprinted in J.W. Cunliffe and Gerhard R. Lomer, eds., *Writing of Today: Models of Journalistic Prose* (New York: Century, 1915), pp. 194–9 and (1921, 2nd and rev. ed.), pp. 211–6; in Thomas E. Rankin et al., eds., *Further Adventures in Essay Reading* (New York: Harcourt, Brace, 1928), pp. 501–13; in *The Columbia University Course in Literature VIII, The Great Literature of Small Nations* (New York: Columbia University Press, 1928–29; Freeport, New York: Books for Libraries Press, 1969), pp. 514–21; as "The Devil and the Deep Sea: A Discussion of Modern Morality," in Carl F. Klinck and Reginald E. Watters, eds., *Canadian Anthology* (Toronto: Gage, 1974), pp. 184–7; in Gerald Lynch and David Rampton, eds., *The Canadian Essay* (Toronto: Copp Clark Pitman, 1991), pp. 24–31.

Electronically available (12 October 1997) at the National Library of Canada's Leacock Web site: http://www.nlc-bnc.ca/leacock/sea.htm

**C10.38** "Practical Political Economy IV. — The Theory of Money," *Saturday Night* (Toronto) 24, no. 8, whole no. 1,200 (3 December 1910): 12.

**C10.39** "Novels in Nutshells 1. Gertrude the Governess; or, Simple Seventeen," *Saturday Night* (Toronto) 24, no. 9, whole no. 1,201 (10 December 1910): 4, 9; *Ottawa Evening Journal*, 17 December 1910, p. 15. In J.M. Parrish and John R. Crossland, eds., *The Great Book of Humour* (London: Odhams Press Ltd., 1935), pp. 336–43; as "Gertrude the Governess: or, Simple Seventeen," in Ellery Sedgwick and Harry A. Domincovich, eds., *Novel and Story: A Book of Modern Readings* (Boston: D.C. Heath and Company, 1939), pp. 180–9; as "Gertrude the Governess: or, Simple Seventeen," in Louis Untermeyer, ed., *A Treasury of Laughter* (New York: Simon and Schuster, 1946), pp. 408–16; as "Gertrude the Governess: or Simple Seventeen," in May Lamberton Becker, ed., *The Home Book of Laughter* (New York: Dodd, Mead, 1948), pp. 14–23; in Scott Meredith, ed., *The Fireside Treasury of Modern Humor* (New York: Simon & Schuster, 1963), pp. 568–75; as "Gertrude the Governess or Simple Seventeen," in Mordecai Richler, ed., *The Best of Modern Humor* (New York: Alfred A. Knopf, 1983; Toronto: McClelland and Stewart, 1983), pp. 1–8; as "Gertrude the Governess; or, Simple Seventeen," in Frank Muir, ed., *The Oxford Book of Humorous Prose from William Caxton to P. G. Wodehouse: A Conducted Tour* (Oxford: Oxford University Press, 1990), pp. 436–43; in Allan Gould, ed., *The Great Big Book of Canadian Humour* (Toronto: Macmillan Canada, 1992), pp. 172–9. See also A7 and A116.

**C10.40** "Practical Economy V. — Bi-Metallism," *Saturday Night* (Toronto) 24, no. 9, whole no. 1,201 (10 December 1910): 23. Fifth and sixth articles of the series together as "Political Economy Practically Explained (5) Bi-Metallism (6) Paper Money," *Ottawa Evening Journal*, 10 December 1910, p. 13.

C10.41 "Novels in Nutshells II. Caroline's Christmas; or, The Inexplicable Infant," *Saturday Night* (Toronto) 24, no. 10, whole no. 1,202 (17 December 1910): 4, 9; *Ottawa Evening Journal*, 24 December 1910, p. 16. Reprinted as "Caroline's Christmas," in *The Second Century of Humour* (London: Hutchinson & Co., n.d.), pp. 41–50; in *A Canadian Yuletide Treasury* (Toronto: Clarke, Irwin, 1982), pp. 143–52. See also A113.

C10.42 "Practical Political Economy VI. — Paper Money," *Saturday Night* (Toronto) 24, no. 10, whole no. 1,202 (17 December 1910): 21–2.

C10.43 "Novels in Nutshells Soaked in Seaweed; or, Upset in the Ocean. An Old-Fashioned Sea Story," *Ottawa Evening Journal*, 17 December 1910, p. 15; as "Novels in Nutshells III. Soaked in Seaweed; or, Lost in the Ocean (An Old-Fashioned Sea Story)," *Saturday Night* (Toronto) 24, no. 11, whole no. 1,203 (24 December 1910): 9. Reprinted as "Soaked in Seaweed or Upset in the Ocean" in C.A. Dawson Scott and Ernest Rhys, eds., *Twenty-Seven Humorous Tales*, vol. 4, The Short Story Series (London: Hutchinson & Co., [1926]), pp. 24–34; as "Soaked in Seaweed," in H. Douglas Thomson and C. Clark Ramsay, eds., *The Big Book of Great Short Stories* (London: Odhams Press, 1935), pp. 166–74; as "Soaked in Seaweed," in Morris Bishop, ed., *A Treasury of British Humor* (New York: Coward-McCann, 1942), pp. 460–8; as "Soaked in Seaweed; or, Upset in the Ocean (An Old-Fashioned Sea Story)," in J.E. Parsons, ed., *Quest for Greatness* (Toronto: Ginn and Co., 1966), pp. 123–34; as "Soaked in Seaweed or Upset in the Ocean (An Old-Fashioned Sea-story)," in P.G. Wodehouse, ed., *A Century of Humour* (London: Hutchinson & Co., n.d.), pp. 695–704.

C10.44 "A Bundle of Xmas Correspondence," *Saturday Night* (Toronto) 24, no. 11, whole no. 1,203 (24 December 1910): 4.

C10.45 "Practical Political Economy VII. — The Movement of Prices and the Rise in the Cost of Living," *Saturday Night* (Toronto) 24, no. 11, whole no. 1,203 (24 December 1910): 21–2. As "Political Economy Practically Explained (7) The Movement of Prices and the Rise in the Cost of Living," *Ottawa Evening Journal*, 24 December 1910, p. 13.

C10.46 "Novels in Nutshells IV. A Hero In Homespun; or, The Life Struggle of Hezekiah Hayloft," *Saturday Night* (Toronto) 24, no. 12, whole no. 1,204 (31 December 1910): 4, 13; *Ottawa Evening Journal*, 7 January 1911, p. 10. See also C21.27 and E10.9.

C10.47 "Practical Political Economy VIII. — The International Movement of Money and the Foreign Exchanges," *Saturday Night* (Toronto) 24, no. 12, whole no. 1,204 (31 December 1910): 10. As "Political Economy Practically Explained (8) The International Movement of Money and Foreign Exchanges," *Ottawa Evening Journal*, 31 December 1910, p. 15.

C11.1 "My College Days: A Retrospect," *Old McGill* 15 (1911): 28. See also C23.21, C23.26, C23.30, and C23.33.

C11.2 "Novels in Nutshells V. Maddened by Mystery; or, The Defective Detective," *Saturday Night* (Toronto) 24, no. 13, whole no. 1,205 (7 January 1911): 4, 13; *Ottawa Evening Journal*, 14 January 1911, p. 16. Apparently reprinted in *Book Digest*, November 1937; supposedly as "Maddened by Mystery: or, The Defective Detective," *Lilliput* 2 (January 1938): 73–6, 78–9. Illustrated by Joyce Dennys. Reprinted as "Maddened by Mystery or, the Defective Detective," in R. N. Linscott, *Omnibus of American Humor (Comic Relief)* (Toronto: Better Publications of Canada Ltd., 1932), pp. 101–8 (originally published as *Comic Relief*); as "The Great Detective," in E. C. Bentley, ed., *The Second Century of Detective Stories* (London: Hutchinson, [1938]), pp. 751–61; in Ellery Queen, ed., *The Misadventures of Sherlock Holmes* (Boston: Little, Brown, 1944), pp. 218–6; in E.A. Seaborne, ed., *The Detective in Fiction: A Posse of Eight* (Toronto: Clarke, Irwin; London: G. Bell & Sons, 1960), pp. 224–34; as "Maddened by Mystery," in Grant Huffman, ed., *12 Detective Stories* (Toronto: McClelland and Stewart, 1965), pp. 71–9; as "The Great Detective," in Alan Walker, ed., *The Treasury of Great Canadian Humour* (Toronto: McGraw-Hill Ryerson, 1974), pp. 68–82; as "Maddened by Mystery or the Defective Detective," in Alberto Manguel, ed., *Canadian Mystery Stories* (Toronto: Oxford University Press, 1991), pp. 25–32. See also C21.22.

C11.3 "Practical Political Economy IX. — The Theory of Free Trade," *Saturday Night* (Toronto) 24, no. 13, whole no. 1,205 (7 January 1911): 10. As "Political Economy Practically Explained (9) The Theory of Free Trade," *Ottawa Evening Journal*, 7 January 1910, p. 14.

C11.4 "Novels in Nutshells VI. Guido the Gimlet of Ghent; or, A Romance of Chivalry," *Saturday Night* (Toronto) 24, no. 14, whole no. 1,206 (14 January 1911): 4, 9. Reprinted as "Novels in Nutshells 6. — Guido the Gimlet of Ghent — A Romance of Chivalry," *Ottawa Evening Journal*, 21 January 1911, p. 10. See also C21.25.

C11.5 "Practical Political Economy X. — Free Trade in Great Britain," *Saturday Night* (Toronto) 24, no. 14, whole no. 1,206 (14 January 1911): 10, 21. As "Political Economy Practically Explained (10) Free Trade in Great Britain," *Ottawa Evening Journal*, 14 January 1911, p. 14.

C11.6 "Novels in Nutshells VII. Hannah of the Highlands; or, The Laird of Loch Aucherlocherty," *Saturday Night* (Toronto) 24, no. 15, whole no. 1,207 (21 January 1911): 4, 27; *Ottawa Evening Journal*, 28 January 1911, p. 10.

C11.7 "Practical Political Economy XI. — The Economic Basis of Protection," *Saturday Night* (Toronto) 24, no. 15, whole no. 1,207 (21 January 1911): 10, 21. As "Political Economy Practically Explained (11) The Economic Basis of Protection," *Ottawa Evening Journal*, 21 January 1910, p. 13.

C11.8 "Novels in Nutshells VIII. The Sorrows of a Super Soul; or, The Memoirs of Marie Mushenough," *Saturday Night* (Toronto) 24, no. 16, whole no. 1,208 (28 January 1911): 5, 9; *Ottawa Evening Journal*, 11 February 1911, p. 10.

C11.9 "Practical Political Economy XII. — The Tariff Policy of the German Empire," *Saturday Night* (Toronto) 24, no. 16, whole no. 1,208 (28 January 1911): 21. As "Political Economy Practically Explained (12) Tariff Policy of the German Empire," *Ottawa Evening Journal*, 28 January 1911, p. 13.

C11.10 "The Islanders: The Latest Development in the British Imperial Movement — The Organization of the Islanders, a Powerful Body — Its Programme and Its Aims," *Ottawa Evening Journal*, 4 February 1911, p. 3.

C11.11 "Novels in Nutshells IX. 'Q' a Psychic Story of Psupernatural," *Saturday Night* (Toronto) 24, no. 17, whole no. 1,209 (4 February 1911): 4, 9. Reprinted in John W. Cunliffe and Ashley H. Thorndike, eds., *Warner Library of the World's Best Literature* (New York: The Warner Library Company, 1917), vol. 15, pp. 8929 t-z, a. See also G1.

C11.12 "Practical Political Economy XIII. — Free Trade in Great Britain and Protection in Germany; A Comparison," *Saturday Night* (Toronto) 24, no. 17, whole no. 1,209 (4 February 1911): 10. As "Political Economy Practically Explained XIII — Free Trade in Great Britain, and Protection in Germany; A Comparison," *Ottawa Evening Journal*, 4 February 1911, p. 12.

C11.13 "Novels in Nutshells X. The Man in Asbestos; or, An Allegory of the Future," *Saturday Night* (Toronto) 24, no. 18, whole no. 1,210 (11 February 1911): 4, 31. As "Novels in Nutshells 9. — The Man in Asbestos — An Allegory of the Future," *Ottawa Evening Journal*, 18 February 1911, p. 10. See also A129.

Electronically available at: http://www.mtroyal.ab.ca/programs/arts/english/gaslight/asbestos.htm

C11.14 "Practical Political Economy XIV. — The Tariff System of the United States," *Saturday Night* (Toronto) 24, no. 18, whole no. 1,210 (11 February 1911): 10. As "Political Economy Practically Explained VI[sic] — The Tariff System of the United States," *Ottawa Evening Journal*, 11 February 1911, p. 13.

C11.15 "Practical Political Economy XV. — The Theory of Banking and the Bank of England," *Saturday Night* (Toronto) 24, no. 19, whole no. 1,211 (18 February 1911): 23. With same title under the general series "Political Economy Practically Explained," *Ottawa Evening Journal*, 18 February 1911, p. 13.

C11.16 "Practical Political Economy XVI. — The National Banking System of the United States," *Saturday Night* (Toronto) 24, no. 20, whole no. 1,212 (25 February 1911): 21. With same title under the general series "Political Economy Practically Explained," *Ottawa Evening Journal*, 25 February 1911, p. 14.

C11.17 "The Case Against Reciprocity," *Saturday Night* (Toronto) 24, no. 21, whole no. 1,213 (4 March 1911): 2.

C11.18 "Practical Political Economy XVII. — The Theory of Wages," *Saturday Night* (Toronto) 24, no. 21, whole no. 1,213 (4 March 1911): 21. With same title under the general series "Political Economy Practically Explained," *Ottawa Evening Journal*, 4 March 1911, p. 16.

C11.19 "Canadian Women and Their Work," *Canadian Century* (Montreal) 3, no. 10 (11 March 1911): 8–9. This speech was reported as "Are Machines Driving Women from Home Life? Such Is the Contention of Professor Stephen Leacock of McGill, Who Tells Women's Canadian Club That Sex Lines Are Being Obliterated," *Montreal Daily Star*, 8 March 1911, p. 10. The first three paragraphs of this article are a summary of Leacock's views in his speech to the Women's Canadian Club in Montreal. The remainder of the article appears to be verbatim extracts from Leacock's address. See also E11.4.

C11.20 "Practical Political Economy XVIII. — Industrial Legislation: Factory Acts," *Saturday Night* (Toronto) 24, no. 22, whole no. 1,214 (11 March 1911): 10. With same title under the general series "Political Economy Practically Explained," *Ottawa Evening Journal*, 11 March 1911, p. 10.

C11.21 "Practical Political Economy XIX. — State Insurance and Old Age Pensions," *Saturday Night* (Toronto) 24, no. 23, whole no. 1,215 (18 March 1911): 5, 23. With same title under the general series "Political Economy Practically Explained," *Ottawa Evening Journal*, 18 March 1911, p. 7.

C11.22 "Practical Political Economy XX. — State Arbitration of Industrial Disputes,"

*Saturday Night* (Toronto) 24, no. 24, whole no. 1,216 (25 March 1911): 5, 10. With same title under the general series "Political Economy Practically Explained," *Ottawa Evening Journal*, 25 March 1911.

C11.23 "Great Auction of Forest Assets," *Pulp and Paper Magazine of Canada* (April 1911): ?. News clipping at SLM.

C11.24 "Reciprocity between Canada and the United States," *Quarterly Review* (London) 214, no. 427 (April 1911): 491–508. Review of *Tariff Regulations between the United States and Canada* (Ottawa: Government Printing Bureau, 1911), *Canadian Reciprocity* (Washington: Government Printing Bureau, 1911), *Special Message of the President of the United States* (January 26, 1911). Not signed but identified as Leacock by his notebook of recorded publications and speeches at QMMRB.

C11.25 "Canada and the Immigration Problem," *National Review* (London) 57 (April 1911): 316–27. Excerpts from Leacock's article are contained in *Saturday Night* (Toronto) 24, no. 29, whole no. 1,221 (29 April 1911): 1–2.

C11.26 "Practical Political Economy XXI. — The General Theory of Taxation," *Saturday Night* (Toronto) 24, no. 25, whole no. 1,217 (1 April 1911): 9, 14. With same title under the general series "Political Economy Practically Explained," *Ottawa Evening Journal*, 1 April 1911, p. 13.

C11.27 "Practical Political Economy XXII. — Taxation in Great Britain," *Saturday Night* (Toronto) 24, no. 26, whole no. 1,218 (8 April 1911): 10. With same title under the general series "Political Economy Practically Explained," *Ottawa Evening Journal*, 8 April 1911, p. 13.

C11.28 "Practical Political Economy XXIII. — Taxation in the United States," *Saturday Night* (Toronto) 24, no. 27, whole no. 1,219 (15 April 1911): 9–10.

C11.29 "Political Economy Practically Explained XXIV — The Theory of Socialism," *Ottawa Evening Journal*, 15 April 1911, p. 11. With same title under the general series "Practical Political Economy," *Saturday Night* (Toronto) 24, no. 28, whole no. 1,220 (22 April 1911): 15, 20.

C11.30 "Practical Political Economy XXV. — Socialism as a Political Force," *Saturday Night* (Toronto) 24, no. 29, whole no. 1,221 (29 April 1911): 5, 23.

C11.31 "The Political Rights of Women — The Case Against the Suffrage; Women's Nature Unfits Her for Use of the Ballot — Suffragists Beg the Question — Nursing Constituencies and Nursing Babies Do Not Go Together — Women Not Really in Business," *Toronto Star Weekly*, 13 May 1911, p. 12.

C11.32 "McGill's New Departure; University School of Commerce to Be Established Shortly; Evening Classes. Important New Announcement Which Will Bring University to Town," *Montreal Witness*, 26 May 1911, p. 2. Unsigned announcement about the establishment of McGill's University School of Commerce. See A10 concerning his authorship of this article. See also "Experts' View on School of Commerce. . . . ," *Montreal Daily Star*, 3 June 1911, p. 31, which describes a meeting of teachers and professors at McGill University where Leacock submitted a scheme as a basis for the School's curriculum.

C11.33 "The Great Victory in Canada," *National Review* (London) 58 (November 1911): 381–92. See also A8.

C11.34 ["Canada and the Empire"], *Industrial Canada* (Toronto) 12, no. 4 (November 1911): 467c-g. The text of Leacock's speech at the banquet of the annual meeting of the Canadian Manufacturers Association, Toronto, King Edward Hotel, 12 October 1911. See also D11.4 and E11.11.

C11.35 "Epoch-Making Address Created Great Impression at Arts Society Meeting," *McGill Daily*, 9 November 1911, pp. 1, 2. The text of a speech, "First Steps in Politics," which Leacock delivered in Strathcona Hall the previous evening. He advocates that students should become politicians not as devout Liberals or staunch Conservatives but as Canadians. Reported, with quotations, as "Wants Students to Enter Politics, Professor Leacock Advises Students to Help the Broken Liberal Cause. . . . ," *Montreal Gazette*, 9 November 1911, p. 4. See also E11.14.

C11.36 "The Economic Position of Women," *Saturday Night* (Toronto) 25, no. 7, whole no. 1,251 (25 November 1911): 25, 27. See also Frederic Davidson's "Women and Economics: A Reply to Prof. Leacock," *Saturday Night* (Toronto) 25, no. 9, whole no. 1253 (9 December 1911): 25.

C11.37 "What Shall We Do about the Navy: The Policy of a United Fleet," *University Magazine* (Montreal) 10 (December 1911): 534–53. Many paragraphs appear in "The Navy Question. Prof. Leacock's Views," *Orillia Packet*, 22 February 1912, p. 2. See also A9.

C11.38 "Stephen Leacock: Professor and Humorist," *Canada: An Illustrated Weekly for All Interested in the Dominion* (London) 24, no. 311 (23 December 1911): 415. Reprinted as "Prof. Leacock on Prof. Leacock," *Montreal Star*, 4 January 1912, p. 2; "Stephen Leacock's Career. He Tells the Story of His Own Life," *Orillia Packet*, 11 January 1912, p. [2]. Also as "The Autobiography of a Humorist," *Saturday Night* (Toronto) 25, no. 14, whole no. 1,258 (13 January 1912): 3; "Who is Leacock: The McGill Professor Answers the Question Himself," *Montreal Standard*, 26 February 1921, final ed., p. 40; in Thomas L. Masson, *Our American Humorists* (Freeport, New York: Books for Libraries Press, 1931), pp. 221–4; as "Stephen Leacock's Own Story of His Early Life," *Orillia Packet and Times*, 30 March 1944, p. 1.

Electronically available (12 October 1997) at the National Library of Canada's Leacock Web site: http://www.nlc-bnc.ca/leacock/preface.htm

C12.1 "Great Problems of the British Empire I. Their Present Status and Origin," *Saturday Night* (Toronto) 25, no. 13, whole no. 1,257 (6 January 1912): 4, 10.

C12.2 "Great Problems of the British Empire II. Imperial Defence — The Riddle of the Sphinx," *Saturday Night* (Toronto) 25, no. 14, whole no. 1,258 (13 January 1912): 4, 27.

C12.3 "Great Problems of the British Empire III. Nationalism and Independence," *Saturday Night* (Toronto) 25, no. 15, whole no. 1,259 (20 January 1912): 4, 27.

C12.4 "Slates Students for 'Farming out' Their Subjects, Prof Leacock Sharply Criticizes Students Who Ask Others to Do Their Work," *Montreal Star*, 30 January 1912, p. 9. Leacock received a letter, dated 25 January 1912, from "John Smith" of Madison, Wisconsin. The correspondent requested Leacock to send "data on the character of the Canadian people, with reference to the possible success of co-operative credit associations." Leacock sent Mr. "Smith's" letter to the *Montreal Star*, with a letter to the editor in which he took the student to task for asking others to do his own work. Leacock's letter, dated "Jan. 29 1912," has the heading, "Silly Practice Must Stop."

**C12.5** "Prof. Leacock Moved to Boost the Horniman Co. Speaks as an Expert, for He Was an Actor Till the Police Interfered," *Montreal Herald*, 17 February 1912, p. 2. Letter to the editor, dated 16 February 1912, in which Leacock urges people "not to miss the exceptional opportunity offered by the visit to our city of the Horniman Repertory Company now playing at His Majesty's Theatre." Also as "Professor Leacock Makes Appeal for English Repertory Company," *McGill Daily*, 17 February 1912, p. 8.

**C12.6** "Sunshine Sketches of a Little Town 1. Mariposa and Its People," *Montreal Daily Star*, 17 February 1912, pp. 21, 23. Illustrated by A.G. Racey. Reprinted as "The Town of Mariposa" in J.G. Gordon and T.S. Roebuck, eds., *Twentieth Century Prose* (Toronto: Clarke, Irwin, 1962), pp. 73–7; as "Mariposa," *Ontario A Bicentennial Tribute* (Toronto: Key Porter, 1983), pp. 55–6; as "Small Town," in William Toye, ed., *A Book of Canada* (London: Fontana Books, 1968), pp. 232–7. This is first of twelve sketches in this series (see A11). See also C17.10, C27.30, C27.33, and C27.36–8.

**C12.7** "Sunshine Sketches of a Little Town 2. The Glorious Victory of Mr. Smith," *Montreal Daily Star*, 24 February 1912, p. 12. Illustrated by A.G. Racey.

**C12.8** "Sunshine Sketches of a Little Town 3. The Speculations of Jefferson Thorpe," *Montreal Daily Star*, 2 March 1912, p. 23. Illustrated by A.G. Racey. Reprinted as "The Speculations of Jefferson Thorpe," in Desmond Pacey, ed., *A Book of Canadian Stories* (Toronto: Ryerson Press, 1947), pp. 103–17; in George E. Nelson, ed., *Cavalcade of the North* (Garden City, New York: Doubleday, 1958), pp. 584–94; in L.H. Newell and J.W. MacDonald, eds., *Short Stories of Distinction* (Agincourt: Book Society of Canada, 1960), pp. 63–79.

**C12.9** "Sunshine Sketches of a Little Town 4. The Marine Excursion of the Knights of Pythias," *Montreal Daily Star*, 16 March 1912, p. 23. Illustrated by A.G. Racey. Reprinted as "The Marine Excursion of the Knight of Pythias," in Robert Weaver, ed., *Canadian Short Stories* (London: Oxford University Press, 1960), pp. 27–51 and (Toronto: Oxford University Press, 1966), pp. 27–51; as "The Sinking of the 'Mariposa Belle,'" in J.L. Gill and L.H. Newell, *Prose for Senior Students: An Anthology of Short Stories and Essays* (Toronto: Macmillan, 1951), pp. 15–26; as "The Sinking of the Mariposa Belle," in William K.F. Kendrick, ed., *Canadian Stories in Verse and Prose* (Toronto: Clarke, Irwin, 1932, 1936), pp. 132–147; as "The Marine Excursion of the Knights of Pythias," in May Lamberton Becker, ed., *Golden Tales of Canada* (Toronto: McClelland and Stewart; New York: Dodd Mead, 1938), pp. 4–28; as "An Excursion on the *Mariposa Belle*," in C.L. Bennet and Lorne Pierce, ed., *Argosy to Adventure* (Toronto: Ryerson and Macmillian, 1935, 1950), pp. 463–76; as "The Marine Excursion of the Knights of Pythias," in Muriel Whitaker, ed., *Great Canadian Adventure Stories* (Edmonton: Hurtig, 1979), pp. 195–213; in Peter Carver, ed., *Water* (Toronto: Peter Martin Associates, n.d.), pp. 44–52; in *Celebrating Ninety Years, McClelland & Stewart 1906–1996, 90 Years of Canadian Publishing: Selections from the New Canadian Library* (Toronto: McClelland and Stewart, 1996), pp. 12–7.

**12.10** "Sunshine Sketches of a Little Town 5. The Ministrations of Canon Drone," *Montreal Daily Star*, 23 March 1912, p. 23. Illustrated by A.G. Racey.

**C12.11** "Sunshine Sketches of a Little Town 6. Mariposa's Whirlwind Campaign," *Montreal Daily Star*, 30 March 1912, pp. 23, 42. Illustrated by A.G. Racey.

C12.12 "Sunshine Sketches of a Little Town 7. The Entanglement of Mr. Pupkin," *Montreal Daily Star*, 13 April 1912, p. 27. Illustrated by A.G. Racey.

C12.13 "Sunshine Sketches of a Little Town. The Fore-Ordained Attachment of Zena McGaw and Peter Papkin [Pupkin] VIII," *Montreal Daily Star*, 20 April 1912, p. 21. Illustrated by A.G. Racey.

C12.14 "Sunshine Sketches of a Little Town. The Great Mariposa Bank Mystery IX," *Montreal Daily Star*, 4 May 1912, p. 23. Illustrated by A.G. Racey. Reprinted as "The Mariposa Bank Mystery," in J.G. Gordon and T.S. Roebuck, eds., *Twentieth Century Prose* (Toronto: Clarke, Irwin, 1962), pp. 109–121.

C12.15 "Sunshine Sketches of a Little Town. The Great Election in Missinaba County [X]," *Montreal Daily Star*, 25 May 1912, p. 22. Illustrated by A.G. Racey. Condensed as "Missinaba County Saves the Empire," *Reader's Digest* 132, no. 794 (June 1988): 169–72, 175–80, 182, 184–6. Illustrated by Bruce Johnson. Reprinted as "The Great Election in Missinaba County," in Raymond Knister, ed., *Canadian Short Stories* (Toronto: Macmillan, 1928), pp. 87–118; as "The Great Election," in John M. Gray and Frank A. Upjohn, eds., *Prose of Our Day* (Toronto: Macmillan, 1940), pp. 220–33.

C12.16 "Sunshine Sketches of a Little Town. The Candidacy of Mr. Smith XI," *Montreal Daily Star*, 8 June 1912, p. 21. Illustrated by A.G. Racey. See also C18.20.

C12.17 "Sunshine Sketches of a Little Town. L'Envoi — The Train to Mariposa XII," *Montreal Daily Star*, 22 June 1912, p. 22. Illustrated by A.G. Racey. Reprinted in John W. Cunliffe and Ashley H. Thorndike, eds., *Warner Library of the World's Best Literature* (New York: The Warner Library Company, 1917), vol. 15, pp. 8929 a-e; in W.J. Alexander, ed., *Short Stories and Essays* (Toronto: Ryerson, 1928), pp. 385–91; in John D. Robins, ed., *A Pocketful of Canada* (Toronto: Collins, 1946), pp. 48–53 and (Toronto: Collins, 1948), pp. 50–55; in John Stevens, *The Ontario Experience* (Toronto: Macmillan of Canada, 1976), pp. 46–51; in Michael Ondaatje, ed., *From Ink Lake: Canadian Stories* (Toronto: Lester & Orpen Dennys, 1990), pp. 676–81.

C12.18 "A Humorist in Paris The Beautiful City — The World's Fair of the Nations — The Paris Season — Half a Million Visitors — The Invasion of the Americans — The Glories and the Tragedies of France," *Saturday Night* (Toronto) 25, no. 40, whole no. 1,284 (13 July 1912): 4–5.

C12.19 " 'A Humorist in Paris II. The Man from Kansas and the French Language — How to Talk French in Paris — An Adventure with a French Tailor," *Saturday Night* (Toronto) 25, no. 41, whole no. 1,285 (20 July 1912): 4–5. Reprinted as "Completes," in A.B. Harley, ed., *Character Sketches and Encores* (London: Oliver and Boyd, 1933, reprinted 1947), pp. 5–8.

C12.20 "Gazing on Gay Paree The Tipping System — The Joys of Philanthropy — The Gladsomeness of Carrying a Pocketful of Coppers — The Cost of Cleanliness — An Adventure with the British Ambassador," *Saturday Night* (Toronto) 25, no. 43, whole no. 1,287 (3 August 1912): 4–5.

C12.21 "Gazing on Gay Paree A Visit to Versailles — An Engine with a Skirt — The Grand Monarch and His Chateau — The Hall of Mirrors — The Gallery of Battles," *Saturday Night* (Toronto) 25, no. 44, whole no. 1,288 (10 August 1912): 4–5.

C12.22 "Gazing on Gay Paree Fashionable Paris — A Childless City — The Dog Craze

— Dog's Luncheon Parties — The Dog's Cemetery — An Oriental Fete," *Saturday Night* (Toronto) 25, no. 47, whole no. 1,291 (31 August 1912): 4–5.

C12.23 "Gazing on Gay Paree Paris at Night — 'Seeing Something Wicked' — The Gayeties of the Boulevard — Oriental Dancers — The Night Cafes of Montmartre," *Saturday Night* (Toronto), 25, no. 49, whole no. 1,293 (14 September 1912): 4–5.

C12.24 "A Xmas Examination," *McGill Daily* Christmas no., 1912, pp. 8, 9.

C13.1 "Familiar Incidents: IV. My Unknown Friend," *Saturday Mirror* (Montreal) 1, no. 6 (8 March 1913): 8, 12. Reprinted in *American Magazine* 76, no. 5 (November 1913): 71–2. Illustrated by J. Norman Lynd. Reprinted as "My Unknown Friend; A Delicate Gamble Between Knowing Too Little & Knowing Too Much," *Orillia News-Letter*, 29 September 1926, p. 11. Also as "My Unknown Friend," *Montreal Standard*, 2 October 1926, final ed., p. 31. Illustrated by A.G. Racey. Syndicated by Metropolitan Newspaper Service, New York. In Donald Graham French, ed., *Standard Canadian Reciter* (Toronto: McClelland & Stewart, 1921), pp. 196–202.

C13.2 "Familiar Incidents: V. Under the Barber's Knife," *Saturday Mirror* (Montreal) 1, no. 9 (29 March 1913): 8. Reprinted in *American Magazine* 76, no. 4 (October 1913): 84, 86. Illustrated by J. Norman Lynd. Reprinted as "Under the Barber's Knife," *Vancouver Sunday Sun*, 4 November 1923, ("Magazine"), p. 5. Syndicated by Metropolitan Newspaper Service, New York. As "Under the Barber's Knife," *Edmonton Bulletin*, 19 November 1938, p. 5. Syndicated by Miller Services Ltd. as part of series.

C13.3 "[*Arcadian Adventures with the Idle Rich*]," *Bookseller and Stationer* 29 (April 1913): 52. Letter to the editor regarding his future publishing plans.

C13.4 "The Hopeless Fight Against the High Cost of Living," *Saturday Night* (Toronto) 26, no. 28, whole no. 1,924 (19 April 1913): 4–5, 7. As "The High Cost of Living," *Addresses Delivered before the Canadian Club of Montreal* (season 1913–1914): 44–52. Read by Leacock on 3 November 1913. Reported as "The High Cost of Living. Dr. Stephen Leacock Believes Plethora of Gold Is the Cause," *Orillia Packet*, 6 November 1913, p. 5 [misnumbered for p. 7], with quotations. See also E13.7.

C13.5 "The Canadian Senate and the Naval Bill," *National Review* (London) 61 (July 1913): 986–98. Extracted in "The Senate and the Naval Bill. Dr. Stephen Leacock Outlines the Situation for English Readers," *Orillia Packet*, 2 October 1913, p. 6.

C13.6 "Familiar Incidents: The Dentist and the Gas," *American Magazine* 76, no. 1 (July 1913): 71–2. Illustrated by J. Norman Lynd. Reprinted as "The Dentist and the Gas," *Vancouver Sunday Sun*, 16 September 1923, ("Magazine"), p. 4. Syndicated by Metropolitan Newspaper Service, New York. In James A. MacNeill, ed., *Early September: An Anthology of Short Stories* (Toronto: Nelson, 1980), pp. 75–9; as "The Perfect Optimist or Daydreams in a Dental Chair," in Robert Thomas Allen, ed., *A Treasury of Canadian Humour* (Toronto: McClelland and Stewart, 1967), pp. 37–8.

C13.7 "Behind the Beyond: In Three Acts and Two Drinks," *American Magazine* 76, no. 2 (August 1913): 46–52. Illustrated by Lejaren à Hiller.

C13.8 "The Retroactive Existence of Mr. Juggins," *Popular Magazine* 29, no. 3 (15 August 1913): 205–7. Reprinted in H. Allen Smith, ed., *Desert Island Decameron* (Garden City, New York: Doubleday, 1945), pp. 384–8; in Giose Rimanelli and Roberto Ruberto, eds., *Modern Canadian Stories* (Toronto: Ryerson Press, 1966), pp. 28–31; in Carl F. Klinck and Reginald E. Watters, eds., *Canadian Anthology* (Toronto: Gage, 1974), pp. 168–70.

C13.9 "Familiar Incidents: With the Photographer," *American Magazine* 76, no. 3 (September 1913): 82–4. Illustrated by J. Norman Lynd. Reprinted as "With the Photographer," *Vancouver Sunday Sun*, 18 February 1923, ("Magazine"), p. 7. Syndicated by Metropolitan Newspaper Service, New York; as "I Am Photographed," *Lilliput* 1, no. 6 (December 1937): 63–4, 66 (reprinted in *Lilliput Annual* (London: Pocket Publications, 1937?) which bound together the first six numbers); in Morris Bishop, ed., *A Treasury of British Humor* (New York: Coward-McCann, 1942), pp. 469–72; in *125th Anniversary Anthology 1938–1965* (New York: Dodd, Mead, 1964), pp. 174–7. See also C25.30.

C13.10 "Homer and Humbug," *Century Magazine* 86 (October 1913): 952–5. Reprinted as "Homer and Humbug, an Academic Discussion," in John Milton Berdan, John Richie Schultz, and Hewette Elwell Joyce, eds., *Modern Essays* (New York: Macmillan, 1915, 1924), pp. 334–40; in Raymond M. Alden, ed., revised by Robert M. Smith *Essays English and American* (Chicago: Scott, Foresman, 1918, 1927), pp. 557–63; in Warner Taylor, ed., *Essays of the Past and Present* (New York: Harper & Brothers, 1927), pp. 413–8; as "Homer and Humbug," in Joseph M. Bachelor and Ralph L. Henry, *Challenging Essays in Modern Thought* (New York: Century, 1928), pp. 149–54; in John O. Beaty, Ernest E. Leisy, Mary Lamar, eds., *Facts and Ideas for Students of English Composition* (New York: F. S. Crofts, 1930), pp. 330–5; as "Homer and Humbug, an Academic Discussion," in Desmond Pacey, ed., *Our Literary Heritage* (Toronto: Ryerson and Macmillan, 1967), pp. 509–12; in William E. Brennan, comp., *Essays for College English* (New York: Century, 1930), pp. 421–6; in Robert Thomas Allen, ed., *A Treasury of Canadian Humour* (Toronto: McClelland and Stewart, 1967), pp. 47–8.

C13.11 "Prof. Leacock's Greetings," *Montreal Daily Mail*, 8 October 1913, p. 9. Letter to the editor dated 7 October. Leacock congratulates the *Mail* on its proposal "to conduct a newspaper that shall voice an honest independent opinion."

C13.12 "Canada and Home Rule," *Montreal Daily Mail*, 25 October 1913, p. 11. Six sentences are repeated under a separate heading, "Some Leacock Sayings," also on p. 11.

C13.13 "The Cry of the Consumer," *Montreal Daily Mail*, 1 November 1913, p. 9.

C13.14 "Temperance and Legislation; a Plea for Fair-Mindedness," *Montreal Daily Mail*, 15 November 1913, p. 7.

C13.15 "The Awfulness of Austria," *Montreal Daily Mail*, 22 November 1913, p. 3.

C13.16 "Social Reform in the Coming Century. A Wonderful Age — The Triumph of Machinery — Riches and Poverty. The Failure of Individualism," *Saturday Night* (Toronto) 27, no. 6, whole no. 1,354 (22 November 1913): 4–5.

C13.17 "Social Reform in the Coming Century. II. The Programme of Socialism — A Beautiful Impossibility — The Coming State — The Position of Women," *Saturday Night* (Toronto) 27, no. 7, whole no. 1,355 (29 November 1913): 4–5.

C13.18 "Making a Magazine: The Dream of a Contributor," *American Magazine* 76, no. 6 (December 1913): 69–70, 72. Illustrated by J. Norman Lynd.

C13.19 "The University and Business," *University Magazine* (Montreal) 12 (December 1913): 540–9.

C13.20 "Are Canadians Provincial," *Montreal Daily Mail*, 6 December 1913, p. 6.

C13.21  "The Asiatic and the Empire," *Montreal Daily Mail*, 13 December 1913, p. 10.

C13.22  "Egg-O-Mania; or, Young Canada at School," *Saturday Night* (Toronto) 27, no. 10, whole no. 1,358 (20 December 1913): 3.

C13.23  "Municipal Home Rule," *Montreal Daily Mail*, 20 December 1913, p. 9.

C13.24  "A Few Reflections for the New Year," *Montreal Daily Mail*, 27 December 1913, p. 9.

C14.1  "Aristocratic Anecdotes or Little Stories of Great People," *Century Magazine* 87 (March 1914): 803–5. Illustrated by Reginald Birch.

C14.2  "Education Made Agreeable," *American Magazine* 77, no. 3 (March 1914): 55–6. Illustrated by J. Norman Lynd. Reprinted in *Vancouver Sunday Sun*, 2 September 1923, ("Magazine"), p. 4. Syndicated by Metropolitan Newspaper Service, New York.

C14.3  "The First Newspaper: A Sort of Allegory," *Popular Magazine* 31, no. 4 (1 March 1914): 168–72. Reprinted as "The First Newspaper," *University Magazine* (Montreal) 13 (April 1914): 220–9. "Published under arrangement with The Popular Magazine Copyright."

C14.4  "An Every-Day Experience," *Century Magazine* 87 (April 1914): 968.

C14.5  "Truthful Oratory: What Our Speakers Ought to Say," *Puck* 75, no. 1, 936 (11 April 1914): [5] or [6]. Reprinted as "Truthful Oratory," *Saturday Night* (Toronto) 27, no. 29, whole no. 1,377 (2 May 1914): 4–5.

C14.6  "Who Is Also Who: A Companion Volume to Who's Who, Edited," *American Magazine* 77, no. 5 (May 1914): 64–5. See also C27.19.

C14.7  "Afternoon Adventures at My Club I. The Anecdote of Dr. So and So," *Vanity Fair* 2, no. 3 (May 1914): 54.

C14.8  "Afternoon Adventures at My Club; The Shattered Health of Mr. Podge," *Vanity Fair* 2, no. 4 (June 1914): 55. Illustrated by Louis Fancher.

C14.9  "Arcadian Adventures with the Idle Rich: A Little Dinner with Mr. Lucullus Fyshe," *American Magazine* 78, no. 1 (July 1914): 29–34. Illustrated by F. Strothmann. A five-part series, ending in November 1914. See also C14.13, C14.15, C14.17, C14.21, C27.50–2, and C27.54–6.

C14.10  "Spoof: Our Thousand-Guinea Novel," *Methuen's Annual* (London) (1914, first published 23 July 1914): 82–94. Reprinted in E. V. Lucas, ed. *Macmillan's Annual* (New York: Macmillan, 1914), pp. 111–27, note cover title: *Lucas' Annual*; as "Spoof. A Thousand-Guinea Novel. New! Fascinating! Perplexing!" in Joseph Lewis French, ed. *Sixty Years of American Humor* (Boston: Little, Brown, 1924), pp. 213–26; in Joseph Lewis French, ed. *The Best of American Humor from Mark Twain to Benchley a Prose Anthology* (Garden City, New York: Garden City Publishing, 1941), pp. 213–26. See also C21.30 and E14.2.

C14.11  "Afternoon Adventures at My Club; The Amazing Travels of Mr. Yarner," *Vanity Fair* 2, no. 6 (August 1914): 46–7. See also C25.32.

C14.12  "American Humour," *Nineteenth Century and After* 76 (August 1914): 444–57. Reprinted in *Living Age* 7th series, 65, no. 3,666, vol. 283 (10 October 1914): 92–102; in Werner Taylor, ed., *Types and Times in the Essay* (New York and London: Harper & Bros.,

1932), pp. 237–55. Excerpt in Carl F. Klinck and Reginald E. Watters, eds., *Canadian Anthology* (Toronto: Gage, 1974), pp. 188–9.

C14.13 "Arcadian Adventures with the Idle Rich: The Wizard of Finance," *American Magazine* 78, no. 2 (August 1914): 34–9. Illustrated by F. Strothmann.

C14.14 "Afternoon Adventures at My Club: The Spiritual Outlook of Mr. Doomer," *Vanity Fair* 3, no. 1 (September 1914): 45, 94. Reprinted as "The Spiritual Outlook of Mr. Doomer," *Golden Book Magazine* 22 (September 1935): 285–7. See also C26.18.

C14.15 "Arcadian Adventures with the Idle Rich: The Arrested Philanthropy of Mr. Tomlinson," *American Magazine* 78, no. 3 (September 1914): 32–8. Illustrated by F. Strothmann.

C14.16 "Vanity Fair Has a Party," *Vanity Fair* 3, no. 1 (September 1914): 23–6. Letters of congratulations on the magazine's first anniversary; Leacock's letter, with facsimile signature, appears on p. 26 and reads as follows: "A child that is so good-natured and entertaining during the period of teething certainly has a great future in front of it. It is a promising little chap, and all my good wishes go to it."

C14.17 "The Arcadian Adventures with the Idle Rich: The Yahi-Bahi Oriental Society of Mrs. Rasselyer-Brown," *American Magazine* 78, no. 4 (October 1914): 49–54. Illustrated by F. Strothmann. See also C27.52.

C14.18 "The Survival of the Fittest," *Vanity Fair* 3, no. 2 (October 1914): 29. Reprinted in Grant Huffman, ed., *Canadiana: An Anthology of Nostalgic, Humorous, and Satirical Writing for Secondary Schools* (Toronto: McClelland and Stewart, 1970), pp. 68–71.

C14.19 "Afternoon Adventures at My Club; The Last Man Out of Europe," *Vanity Fair* 3, no. 3 (November 1914): 41.

C14.20 "Our Literary Bureau: Novels Read to Order. First Aid for the Busy Millionaire: No Brains Needed. No Taste Required. Nothing but Money. Send It to Us," *Century Magazine* 89 (November 1914): 156–60. Illustrated by John Leach. See also C18.23.

C14.21 "Arcadian Adventures with the Idle Rich; The Love Story of Mr. Peter Spillikins," *American Magazine* 78, no. 5 (November 1914): 50–4, 81–2. Illustrated by F. Strothmann. See also C27.54–5.

C14.22 "Prof. Leacock Writes About German Papers," *Montreal Star*, 14 November 1914, p. 5. Letter to the editor. One paragraph is reprinted in "Postoffice is Lax Says Prof. Leacock; News Matter from Germany Allowed Free Circulation in Canada," *Toronto World*, 16 November 1914, p. 4.

C14.23 "The American Attitude," *University Magazine* (Montreal) 13 (December 1914): 595–7.

C15.1 "The Political Economy Club," *Old McGill 1916* 19 (1915): 216. The article on this subject is signed "A.O." (i.e. A. Oliver), the Club's President. To Oliver's description of the Club's activity, Leacock has appended the sentence: "The absolute accuracy of the above account of the Political Economy Club, and especially the unflinching truthfulness of the last paragraph [which refers to the fact that the Club's success is in large part due to Leacock's efforts], is hereby corroborated under oath by the Honorary President of the Club."

C15.1a "For Belgium's Sake," *Addresses Delivered Before the Canadian Club of Hamilton 1914–15*: 226–7. Remarks made by Leacock on 30 March 1915 to the Canadian Club of

Hamilton following a reading from his humorous works in aid of the Belgian Relief Fund. See also D15.4 and E15.7.

C15.2 "That School of Journalism," *McGill Daily*, 10 February 1915, pp. 1, 4. Letter to the editor dated 9 February 1915. Leacock felt that the establishment of a school of journalism at McGill was not necessary.

C15.3 "Side Lights on the Supermen: An Interview with General Bernhardi," *McGill Daily* Special War Contingent Supplement (March 1915): 10, 40. Reprinted as "An Interview with General Bernhardi," *Maclean's Magazine* 24, no. 1 (November 1915): 15–6, illustrated by H.W. Cooper; *A.M.C. Reveille* (Base Hospital, Toronto) 1, no. 5 (May 1918): 4–6; as "An Interview with Bernhardi," *Answers* 61, no. 1,584 (5 October 1918): 254.

C15.4 "Why People Should Own and Read Books," *North American Book Page*, 20 March 1915. News clipping at SLM.

C15.5 "Prof. Leacock Gave Readings to Aid the Belgian Relief Fund," *Montreal Herald*, 23 March 1915, p. 5. Letter to the editor in which Leacock complains about the interview (see F15.1) in the *Montreal Gazette* on 23 March 1915, following his reading of his works at Montreal's Windsor Hall. Leacock writes: "The interview consisted of a lot of vulgar egotistical trash. . . . The whole interview was fabricated. I never wrote a word of it."

C15.6 "Brief Studies in Idiocy; The Reminiscences of Mr. Apricot," *Vanity Fair* 4, no. 2 (April 1915): 53. Reprinted as "Mr. Apricot's Bigger and Better Past: When the Club's Oldest Member Gives His Reminiscences Their Head," *Montreal Standard*, 21 November 1925, final ed., p. [30]. Illustrated by A.G. Racey. Syndicated by Metropolitan Newspaper Service, New York.

C15.7 "The Canadian Balance of Trade," *Journal of the Canadian Bankers' Association* 12 [actually 22], no. 3 (April 1915): 165–77.

C15.8 "A Dickens Fireside Fantasy," *Bookman* 41, no. 2 (April 1915): 169–78.

C15.9 "Topics of the Day," *University Magazine* (Montreal) 14 (April 1915): 155–6. Re "the Made-in-Canada movement." Signed by S.L.

C15.10 "Studies in Idiocy; the War Mania of Mr. Jinks and Mr. Blinks," *Vanity Fair* 4, no. 3 (May 1915): 47. As "The War Mania of Mr. Jinks and Mr. Blinks," *Triad* [Australian journal?] (10 April 1916): 29–30.

C15.11 "The Ground Floor; A Little Lesson for Investors," *Vanity Fair* 4, no. 4 (June 1915): 49.

C15.12 "Speeding Up Business," *Puck* 77 (17 July 1915): 9, 13. Illustrated by N. I. Pernissen. Reprinted in *Answers* 61, no. 1,583 (28 September 1918): 241; *Vancouver Sunday Sun*, 4 March 1923, ("Magazine"), p. 7. Syndicated by Metropolitan Newspaper Service, New York.

C15.13 "The Hallucination of Mr. Butt," *Vanity Fair* 5, no. 1 (September 1915): 45. Reprinted as "Stephen Leacock Now Writes of Mr. Butt, Who Lives for His Friends," *Vancouver Sunday Sun*, 10 February 1924, ("Magazine"), p. 2. Syndicated by Metropolitan Newspaper Service, New York. In Giose Rimanelli and Roberto Ruberto, eds. *Modern Canadian Stories* (Toronto: Ryerson Press, 1966), pp. 23–7.

C15.14 "The Lot of the Schoolmaster," *Maclean's Magazine* 28, no. 11 (September 1915): 11–3, 101–2. Illustrated by H. W. Cooper.

C15.15 "The Two Stephen Leacocks," *Bodleian. A Journal of Books at the Bodley Head* 7, no. 78 (September 1915): 1,050. Contains extract from a letter from Leacock to John Lane announcing the birth of Leacock's son on 19 August 1915.

C15.16 "Topics of the Day," *University Magazine* (Montreal) 14 (October 1915): 292–4. Re the Royal Geographical Society and Sven Hedin, and Colonel [Theodore] Roosevelt's speech at Plattsburg. Signed by S.L.

C15.17 "War Scenes Across the Canadian Border," *Vanity Fair* 5, no. 2 (October 1915): 43.

C15.18 "The Woman Question," *Maclean's Magazine* 28, no. 12 (October 1915): 7–9.

C15.19 "The Inevitable Topic Reported, Verbatim from a Hundred Dinner Parties," *Vanity Fair* 5, no. 3 (November 1915): 55, 106.

C15.20 "Two Little Boys: An Allegory," *Collier's* 56, no. 11 (27 November 1915): 50.

C15.21 "Are the Rich Happy?" *Vanity Fair* 5, no. 4 (December 1915): 75. Reprinted in *Answers* 61, no. 1,588 (2 November 1918): 319; *Vancouver Sunday Sun*, 14 October 1923, ("Magazine"), p. 5. Syndicated by Metropolitan Newspaper Service, New York. In *Famous Story Magazine* 6 (January 1927): 19–21.

C15.22 "On the Joy of a New Book," *Bookseller and Stationer* 31, no. 12 (December 1915): 31. Possibly reprinted from *Christmas Bulletin*.

C15.23 "The Peace Makers," *Maclean's Magazine* 29, no. 2 (December 1915): 7–9, 104, 106–8.

C15.24 "Topics of the Day," *University Magazine* (Montreal) 14 (December 1915): 437–40. Re the Edith Cavell League and new labour legislation. Signed by S.L.

C15.25 [book review of Beatrice Redpath, *Dawn Shutters: A Volume of Poems* in] "Book Reviews and Literary Notes," *University Magazine* (Montreal) 14 (December 1915): 564–5. Unsigned. Authorship ascribed to Leacock based on his letters to John Lane of 12 October and 28 November 1915 at TEX.

C15.26 "Madeline of the Movies; A Photoplay Done Back into Words," *Puck* 78 (4 December 1915): 22, 30, 32, 34, 44. See C24.30.

C16.1 "After the War — Ruin or Prosperity?: A Fifteen Year Prophecy," *Maclean's Magazine* 29, no. 3 (January 1916): 11–3, 107–8.

C16.2 "[Letter in praise of *Puck*]," *Vanity Fair* 5, no. 5 (January 1916): 125. Leacock's letter appears along with those from Holworthy Hall, George Ethridge, the *New York Sun*, and C. Hilton Keith in an advertisement for the magazine.

C16.3 "What Are the Greatest Books in the English Language?" *Bookseller and Stationer* 32, no. 1 (January 1916): 32. Letter by Leacock in which he lists six books by Charles Dickens "that I like best."

C16.4 "Mr. Blinks and His Friends," *Puck* 78 (1 January 1916): 17, 23–4. See also C15.10.

C16.5 "Simple Stories of Success: or How to Succeed in Life," *Maclean's Magazine* 29, no. 4 (February 1916): 203. Illustrated by C.W. Jefferys.

C16.6 "The Snoopopaths or Fifty Stories in One," *Vanity Fair* 5, no. 6 (February 1916): 63, 112, 114. Reprinted as "Thrills in a Snoopopathic Yarn," *Vancouver Sunday Sun*, 25 November 1923, ("Magazine"), p. 4. Syndicated by Metropolitan Newspaper Service, New York.

C16.7 "English As She Is Taught," *Harper's Weekly* 62, no. 3088 (26 February 1916): 203.

C16.8 "Germany from within," *Maclean's Magazine* 29, no. 5 (March 1916): Illustrated by C.W. Jefferys. Reprinted in *Orillia Packet*, 2 March 1916, p. 3.

C16.9 "More Than Twice-Told Tales: or Every Man His Own Hero," *Maclean's Magazine* 29, no. 6 (April 1916): 39–41, 56. Illustrated by C.W. Jefferys. Reprinted as "Every Man His Own Hero: More than Twice-Told Tales Which Advance Solely upon the Best Foot," *Montreal Standard*, 30 January 1926, final ed., p. [36]. Illustrated by A.G. Racey. Syndicated by Metropolitan Newspaper Service, New York.

C16.10 "The Old, Old Trouble," *Puck* 79 (15 April 1916): 10. See also E16.3.

C16.11 "Humor As I See It: And Something About Humor in Canada," *Maclean's Magazine* 29, no. 7 (May 1916): 11–3, 111–3. Illustrated by C.W. Jefferys. Reprinted as "Humor As I See It," in Thomas R. Cook, ed., *Essays in Modern Thought* (Toronto: Copp Clark, 1940), pp. 35–44; in Homer C. Combs, ed., *A Book of the Essay: From Montaigne to E.B. White* (New York: Charles Scribner's Sons, 1950), pp. 355–60; in J.L. Gill and L.H. Newell, *Prose for Senior Students: An Anthology of Short Stories and Essays* (Toronto: Macmillan, 1951), pp. 233–41 and (Toronto: Macmillan, 1960, rev. ed.), pp. 217–24; as in Grant Huffman, ed., *Canadiana: An Anthology of Nostalgic, Humorous, and Satirical Writing for Secondary Schools* (Toronto: McClelland and Stewart, 1970), pp. 159–164. See also C16.13.

C16.12 "Mr. Grunch's Portrait Gallery; A Sort of Who's Who in Dyspepsia," *Vanity Fair* 6, no. 3 (May 1916): 57. Reprinted as "Those Things We Do Not Say: Every Man and His Friends; Mr. Grunch's Portrait Gallery," *Montreal Standard*, 19 July 1924, morning ed., p. 19. Illustrated by A.G. Racey. Also as "Things We Think About and Do Not Say Mr. Grunch's Secret Opinions About People; As Edited From His Private Thoughts — And Men Are Even Worse Than Women — Sidetracked with a Supreme Old Shriveled Prune of a Professor," *Toronto Star Weekly*, 2 August 1924, p. 24. Illustrated by Kessler. Syndicated by Metropolitan Newspaper Service, New York.

C16.13 "Address of Mr. Leacock" ["Humour as I Have Seen It, with Digressions"], *The Bankers Club of Cleveland, First Year Book 1916*: 30–47. The transcribed text of Leacock's address to the Bankers Club of Cleveland delivered at the Union Club on 18 May 1916. Much of Leacock's address was extemporaneous, but some passages were taken from "Humour As I See It." See also C16.11 and E16.10.

C16.14 "Our 'Shorter Still' Stories," *Century Magazine* 92 (June 1916): 318–9. Reprinted as "Stories That Are Shorter Still," *Vancouver Sunday Sun*, 19 August 1923, ("Magazine"), p. 4. Syndicated by Metropolitan Newspaper Service, New York.

C16.15 "These Troubled Times; Extracts from the Supposed Diary of a President. Arranged and Edited," *Vanity Fair* 6, no. 4 (June 1916): 53.

C16.16 "Our Perplexity Column; Instantaneous Answers to All Questions," *Puck* 79 (17 June 1916): 13. See also C23.16.

C16.17 "Light Housekeeping for Men with Sincere Apologies to Ladies' Periodicals," *Vanity Fair* 6, no. 5 (July 1916): 41. Reprinted as "The Grass Bachelor's Guide," *Vancouver Sunday Sun*, 15 July 1923, ("Magazine"), p. 4. Syndicated by Metropolitan Newspaper Service, New York. As "The Grass Bachelor's Guide: With Sincere Apologies to the Ladies'

Periodicals," *Montreal Standard*, 4 July 1925, final ed., p. 20. Illustrated by A.G. Racey. Also as "The Grass Bachelor's Guide," *Famous Story Magazine* 4 (September 1926): 335–7.

C16.18  "My Delusions," *Puck* 80 (29 July 1916): 10.

C16.19  "Is Permanent Peace Possible?" *Maclean's Magazine* 29, no. 10 (August 1916): 7–8, 77–9; 29, no. 12 (October 1916): 12–3, 92–3.

C16.20  "My Tailor: A Study in Still Life," *Century Magazine* 92 (August 1916): 637–8. See also C28.46.

C16.21  "Our Perplexity Column; All Questions Answered Instantaneously by Electricity," *Puck* 80 (19 August 1916): 10. See also C23.16.

C16.22  "Let Us Learn Russian," *Toronto Star*, 21 September 1916, p. [7].

C16.23  "Abdul Aziz Has His: The Adventures of a Canadian Professor in the Yildiz Kiosk," *Maclean's Magazine* 30, no. 2 (December 1916): 19–22, 77–81. Illustrated by C.W. Jefferys.

C16.24  "Laus Varsitatis: A Song in Praise of the University of Toronto," *Varsity Magazine Supplement* (December 1916): 115–6. Poem. Briefly extracted in *Varsity Magazine* (1917): 5 and *Varsity News* 5, no. 2 (December 1962): 14. See also A114.

C16.25  "Second-Hand Interviews with a European Prince — Any European Prince — Travelling in America," *Vanity Fair* 7, no. 4 (December 1916): 59.

C16.26  "The Errors of Santa Claus," *Puck* 81 (2 December 1916): 17, 48. Illustrated by Ralph Barton. Reprinted in *Sunday Dispatch* (London), 24 December 1939, p. 6; in May Lamberton Becker, ed., *The Home Book of Christmas* (New York: Dodd, Mead, 1941), pp. 479–82; in Eric Posselt, ed., *The World's Greatest Christmas Stories* (Englewood Cliffs, New Jersey: Prentice-Hall, 1950), pp. 89–93; in Frank Keating, ed., *Tiny Tim's Christmas Anthology 1955* (Montreal: Tiny Tim Christmas Fund of the Montreal Children's Hospital), pp. 39–44; in Eric Posselt, ed., *A Merry, Merry Christmas Book* (Englewood Cliffs, New Jersey: Prentice-Hall, 1956), pp. 146–52; in *A Canadian Yuletide Treasury* (Toronto: Clarke, Irwin, 1982), pp. 37–40. See also A128.

C16.27  "O. Henry and His Critics," *New Republic* 9 (2 December 1916): 120–2.

C17.1  "In Dry Toronto: As Told by a Montreal Man," *Maclean's Magazine* 30, no. 3 (January 1917): 13–5. Illustrated by C.W. Jefferys.

C17.2  "An Interview with a Great Actor That Is, with Any of the Sixteen World's Greatest Actors," *Vanity Fair* 7, no. 5 (January 1917): 67. See also C23.23.

C17.3  "Lost In New York; A Visitor's Soliloquy," *Puck* 81 (20 January 1917): 9, 24. Illustrated by Hess.

C17.4  "In Merry Mexico," *Maclean's Magazine* 30, no. 4 (February 1917): 16–8, 76–9. Illustrated by C.W. Jefferys. Reprinted in *The Book of Laughter* (Manchester: Allied Newspapers, n.d.), pp. 165–77.

C17.5  "Are School Boys Happy?" *Argus* (Appleby School Yearbook, Oakville, Ont.) 2, no. 1 (March 1917): [2–4].

C17.6  "Ten Million Dollars for the Asking: An Offer to the Government of Canada," *Maclean's Magazine* 30, no. 5 (March 1917): 9–12. Illustrated by C.W. Jefferys.

C17.7  "An Irreducible Detective Story: Hanged by a Hair or a Murder Mystery Minimized,"

*DAC News* (Detroit Athletic Club) 2, no. 4 (April 1917): 40, 42. This brief story is contained in an article, "You Will Enjoy Stephen Leacock, April 14," notifying members of Leacock's upcoming lecture. Reprinted in Charles R. Cecil, comp. and ed., *The Popular Reciter* (London: W. Foulsham & Co., n.d.), pp. 54–5. As "An Irreducible Detective Story," *Golden Book Magazine* 15 (May 1932): 419, illustrated by John Vassos; in Ellery Queen, ed., *The Misadventures of Sherlock Holmes* (Boston: Little, Brown, 1944), pp. 227–8; in *The Game Is Afoot: Parodies, Pastiches and Ponderings of Sherlock Holmes* (New York: St. Martin's Press, 1994), pp. 246–7.

C17.8 "This Strenuous Age; The Confessions of a Sinner," *Vanity Fair* 8, no. 2 (April 1917): 51.

C17.9 "Forty Years Ago," *Puck* 81 (14 April 1917): 10. Written for the fortieth anniversary of *Puck*.

C17.10 "Sunshine in Mariposa: A Play in Four Acts," *Maclean's Magazine* 30, no. 7 (May 1917): 18–21, 75–6, 78–82; 30, no. 8 (June 1917): 23–6, 83–4, 86–9; 30, no. 9 (July 1917): 51–3, 95–8, 100–2. Illustrated by C.W. Jefferys. Based on *Sunshine Sketches in a Small Town* (A11). See also C12.6–17.

C17.11 "Father Knickerbocker — A Fantasy," *Hearst's Magazine* 31, no. 6 (June 1917): 482–3, 497. Illustrated by F. Strothmann. There is an editorial note that Leacock will in future be a frequent contributor to *Hearst's*.

C17.12 "The Economic Aspect of War," *Journal of the Canadian Bankers' Association* 24 (July 1917): 302–15. See also C18.11.

C17.13 "Personal Adventures in the Spirit World," *Hearst's Magazine* 32, no. 1 (July 1917): 43, 52. Illustrated by F. Strothmann.

C17.14 "Frenzied Fiction for the Dog Days (Done by the Dipperful)," *Maclean's Magazine* 30, no. 10 (August 1917): 33–5. Illustrated by C.W. Jefferys. Apparently reprinted as "Frenzied Fiction," in *Sunday Dispatch* (London), after 15 June 1939.

C17.15 "The Sorrows of a Summer Guest," *Hearst's Magazine* 32, no. 2 (August 1917): 126–7, 136. Illustrated by F. Strothmann. See also C25.42.

C17.16 "Back to Nature and Return," *Hearst's Magazine* 32, no. 3 (September 1917): 204–5, 233. Illustrated by F. Strothmann. See also C23.29.

C17.17 "The New Education; Which Teaches Us How to Break Society Up into Its Elements," *Vanity Fair* 9, no. 1 (September 1917): 61, 98. Illustrated by Dorothy Ferriss. Reprinted as "The New Education," in Louis G. Locke, William M. Gibson, and George Arms, eds., *Toward Liberal Education* (New York: Rinehart & Co., 1948), pp. 63–7; in Robert Thomas Allen, ed., *A Treasury of Canadian Humour* (Toronto: McClelland and Stewart, 1967), pp. 44–6.

Electronically available (12 October 1997) at the National Library of Canada's Leacock Web site: http://www.nlc-bnc.ca/leacock/educat.htm

C17.18 "The Old, Old Story of How Five Men Went Fishing," *Maclean's Magazine* 30, no. 11 (September 1917): 21–3. Illustrated by F. Horsman Varley. Reprinted as "How Five Men Went Fishing: An Authentic Chronicle Which Would Strain No Tape Measure and Hold Good in Any Court of Law," *Montreal Standard*, 23 May 1925, final ed., p. 20. Illustrated by A.G. Racey. Syndicated by Metropolitan Newspaper Service, New York.

C17.19 "Back to the City!: This Is the End of a Perfect Growing Season," *Maclean's Magazine* 30, no. 12 (October 1917): 39–42. Illustrated by C.W. Jefferys.

C17.20 "My Revelations as a Spy," *Hearst's Magazine* 32, no. 5 (November 1917): 385, 428. Illustrated by F. Strothmann. Reprinted in *Golden Book Magazine* 19 (April 1934): 417–21; and Thomas B. Costain, *Read With Me* (Garden City, New York: Doubleday, 1965), pp. 335–43.

C17.21 "The Prophet in Our Midst; A Perfectly Lucid Reply to the Query of How Will the War End?" *Vanity Fair* 9, no. 3 (November 1917): 51, 100.

C17.22 "The Fine Art of Introduction; How to Introduce According to Recognized Formula," *Vanity Fair* 9, no. 4 (December 1917): 55.

C17.23 "Merry Christmas," *Hearst's Magazine* 32, no. 6 (December 1917): 478–9, 503. Illustrated by F. Strothmann. Reprinted as "Father Time and Father Christmas," *Ottawa Citizen*, 24 December 1993, p. B5. Illustrated by Paul Gilligan. See also A27.

C17.24 "Politics from within," *Maclean's Magazine* 31, no. 2 (December 1917): 23–5. Illustrated by C.W. Jefferys.

C17.25 "A Subscription and Some Reflections Therewith," *Rebel* (University of Toronto) 2, no. 3 (December 1917): 86–7.

C17.26 "Things We Hear About the Rebel," *Rebel* (University of Toronto) 2, no. 3 (December 1917): 128. Letter addressed to Pelham [Edgar] on the importance of the *Rebel*.

C17.27 "Preparing for Canada's War Pensions Problem: Annual Outlay on This Head May Reach Total of $25,000,000 Per Year — The Duty of Every Man to Comprehend the Subject," *Saturday Night* (Toronto) 31, no. 8, whole no. 1,295 (8 December 1917): 13. This was one of a series of four articles on pensions; the other articles have not been located.

C18.1 "Canning Columbus," *Hearst's Magazine* 33, no. 1 (January 1918): 43, 57–8. Illustrated by F. Strothmann.

C18.2 "Inside the Tank: An Allegory for the New Year," *Maclean's Magazine* 31, no. 3 (January 1918): 38–40. Illustrated by C.W. Jefferys.

C18.3 "The Art of Opening a Conversation; The Social Equivalent to Going Over the Top," *Vanity Fair* 9, no. 5 (January 1918): 61, 84. Condensed in *Reader's Digest* 31, no. 187 (November 1937): 90–1. Reprinted in *The Reader's Digest Treasury of American Humor* (A Reader's Digest Press Book published in conjunction with McGraw-Hill, 1972), pp. 521–2.

C18.4 "How Much Can Germany Pay?" *Montreal Daily Star*, 4 January 1918, p. 10.

C18.5 "My New Year's Resolutions," *Puck* 82 (20 January 1918): 9. Illustrated.

C18,6 "'Boots and Beef' Heroines and Others," *Hearst's Magazine* 33, no. 2 (February 1918): 116, 150. Illustrated by F. Strothmann.

C18.7 "War Heroes in Our Midst; A Portrait Gallery of the People Who Are Doing Their Bit to Lose the War at Home," *Vanity Fair* 9, no. 6 (February 1918): 35.

C18.8 "The War Efforts of an Average Club; A Record of Charity Relief — with a Moral," *Vanity Fair* 10, no. 1 (March 1918): 46.

C18.9 "The Death of John McCrae," *University Monthly* (University of Toronto) 18, no. 7 (April 1918): 245–8. See also C21.39 and C38.9.

C18.10  "War News I No Longer Read," *Vanity Fair* 10, no. 2 (April 1918): 49, 108.

C18.11  "The Economic Aspect of the War," *Montreal Daily Star*, 20 April 1918, p. 20. See also C17.12.

C18.12  "May Time in Mariposa," *Maclean's Magazine* 31, no. 7 (May 1918): 13–5. Illustrated by Lou Skuce.

C18.13  "The World As It May Be: If Germany and the German System Win," *Vanity Fair* 10, no. 3 (May 1918): 41.

C18.14  "How to Live in War Time; Hints for Patriotic Women Based on Information from the Latest Ladies Magazine," *Vanity Fair* 10, no. 4 (June 1918): 30, 84. Illustrated by Thelma Cudlipp.

C18.15  "Edwin Drood Is Alive," *Bellman* (Minneapolis) 24, no. 622 (15 June 1918): 655–62.

C18.16  "The War Sacrifices of Mr. Spugg; In Drafting One Must Draw the Line Some-where," *Vanity Fair* 10, no. 5 (July 1918): 37, 72. Reprinted as "The War Sacrifices of Mr. Spugg; In the Process of Drafting for Military Service, One Must Draw the Line Somewhere," *Vanity Fair* 21, no. 7 (March 1924): 41, 74; as "The Patriotic Sacrifices of Mr. Spugg," *Orillia News-Letter*, 30 June 1926, p. 3. Also in *Montreal Standard*, 3 July 1926, final ed., p. 34. Illustrated by A.G. Racey. Syndicated by Metropolitan Newspaper Service, New York.

C18.17  "The Boarders' War Pledge," *Puck* 83 (August 1918): 21. Illustrated.

C18.18  "War Finances for Beginners; Elementary Lessons in Getting the Financial System Under Control," *Vanity Fair* 10, no. 6 (August 1918): 25.

C18.19  "Those Dear Old Days," *Answers* 61, no. 1,577 (17 August 1918): 128.

C18.20  "The Life of John Smith," *Answers* 61, no. 1,578 (24 August 1918): 159.

C18.21  "The Upfall of Our Literature; One More Startling Side Effect of the War," *Vanity Fair* 10, no. 7 (September 1918): 37.

C18.22  "A Few Just Complaints about the War; Criticisms of the Way in Which It Is Being Conducted," *Vanity Fair* 10, no. 8 (October 1918): 52.

C18.23  "Our Literary Bureau," *Answers* 61, no. 1,585 (12 October 1918): 273. Reprinted in *Vancouver Sunday Sun*, 22 April 1923, ("Magazine"), p. 5. Syndicated by Metropolitan Newspaper Service, New York. See also C14.20.

C18.24  "Better Dead: The Silly World of the Spiritualists," *Maclean's Magazine* 31, no. 3 (November 1918): 24–6. Illustrated by C.W. Jefferys.

C18.25  "The Boy Who Came Back; An Incident of Everyday, Everywhere with or without a Moral," *Vanity Fair* 11, no. 3 (November 1918): 35, 94.

C18.26  "Old Theories and New Facts; The Economic World After the War," *Montreal Star*, 2 November 1918, pp. 14, 33. One of several articles under the heading "Canada in the Building."

C18.27  "Wet or Dry?" *Saturday Night* (Toronto) 32, no. 13, whole no. 1,351 (22 November 1918): 2. — Reprinted in *Montreal Daily Star*, 21 December 1918, p. 10. There was a series of letters to the editor, 21 December 1918, *Montreal Daily Star*, in response. See also A28.

C18.28 "The Hohenzollerns in America; Leaves from a Royal Diary, Dealing with Their Voyage Across the Atlantic," *Vanity Fair* 11, no. 4 (December 1918): 28, 86, 88. See also A29, C19.2, C19.4, and C23.12.

C18.29 "Is Monarchy Coming to an End?" *Montreal Daily Star*, 7 December 1918, p. [10]. Response came in the form of "Prof. Leacock Criticized Sir Charles Hibbert; Tupper Takes Exception to One of His Articles in the Star," *Montreal Daily Star*, 20 December 1918, p. 10.

C18.30 "Bolshevism and Common Sense," *Montreal Daily Star*, 14 December 1918, p. 10.

C19.1 "The Book Agent; or Why Do People Buy Books?" *Canadian Bookman* n.s. 1, no. 1 (January 1919): 17–9. Excerpts appear on the editorial page of the *Orillia Packet*, 1 January 1920, p. [7].

C19.2 "The Hohenzollerns in New York, Begun in the Preceding Issue of *Vanity Fair*," *Vanity Fair* 11, no. 5 (January 1919): 25, 70. See also C23.12.

C19.3 "More about Germany from Within," *Maclean's Magazine* 32, no. 2 (February 1919): 10–1, 65–7. Illustrated by C.W. Jefferys.

C19.4 "The Hohenzollerns in New York; Cousin Willie Behaves Like a Real German Prince," *Vanity Fair* 12, no. 1 (March 1919): 33, 80.

C19.5 "Common Sense and the Tariff Question," *Montreal Star*, 26 March 1919, p. [10].

C19.6 "Reconstruction in Turkey," *Maclean's Magazine* 32, no. 4 (April 1919): 20–1, 66. Illustrated by C.W. Jefferys.

C19.7 "Is New York Going Crazy? An Occasional Visitor's Account of Its Nightly Dinner and Supper Routine," *Vanity Fair* 12, no. 3 (May 1919): 45, 86.

C19.8 "The Warning of Prohibition in America," *National Review* (London) 73 (July 1919): 680–87.

C19.9 "What Shall We Do with Our Churches? An After-Dinner Symposium Among Big Business Men," *Vanity Fair* 12, no. 5 (July 1919): 25.

C19.10 "The Lecturer at Large: A Few Painful Reminiscences of the Platform," *Maclean's Magazine* 32, no. 8 (August 1919): 13–4, 61–2. Illustrated by C.W. Jefferys.

C19.11 "The Tyranny of Prohibition," *Living Age* 302 (2 August 1919): 301–6.

C19.12 "The Revival of the Tariff Issue," *Montreal Daily Star*, 16 August 1919, p. 14. One of two articles under the heading "Canada in the Building."

C19.13 "The New Tyranny That Threatens Us: How Prohibition Became the Law in America — a Warning to Britain," *Sunday Pictorial* (London), 24 August 1919, p. 5.

C19.14 "A World of Machinery That Wastes Human Energy: Social Unrest Made Acute by the War's Demonstration That the Huge Man Power Diverted to Destruction Cut Off Production Mainly from Glittering Superfluities of Peace, While What Was Left Sufficed to Keep Things Going: I. The Troubled Outlook for the Present Hour," *New York Times*, 31 August 1919, sec. 4, p. 1. Author's note titled "Possibilities of Social Reform" also appears on p. 1. According to Leacock's notes, this article and C19.15–8 and C19.21–2 from the *New York Times* were syndicated in the *Montreal Daily Star*, the *Toronto Star*, and the *Express* (London) as well as other newspapers. See also A31.

C19.15 "The Road to Freedom: Man's Intellectual Progress During the Age of Machinery Has Led Away from Individualism Toward Collectivism: II. Life, Liberty, and the Pursuit of Happiness," *New York Times*, 7 September 1919, sec. 4, p. 1.

C19.16 "Man's Work and His Wage: Theory That a Worker's Reward Is a Fair Measure of His Productive Value in the Face of Shattered Faith in Our Old Social System: The Road to Freedom — : III. The Failures and Fallacies of Natural Liberty," *New York Times*, 14 September 1919, sec. 4, p. 7.

C19.17 "Peril of Industrial Balance of Power: An Economic Force of Capital and Labor Varies, Scales Are Tipped Disastrously — Each Man Gets What He Can Extort, Not What He Produces: The Road to Freedom: IV. — Work and Wages," *New York Times*, 21 September 1919, sec. 3, p. 4.

C19.18 "Socialism: A Machine Which Won't Work: Born in the Bitter Discontent After the Napoleonic Wars, Utopian Dream Has Misled Thousands of Visionaries — A Tainted Creed Menacing the Social Structure: The Road to Freedom: V. — The Socialist Utopia," *New York Times*, 28 September 1919, sec. 9, p. 2.

C19.19 "The Present Outlook in Our Home Town; A Few Characteristic Signs of the General Social Unrest," *Vanity Fair* 13, no. 2 (October 1919): 39.

C19.20 "The Passing Wave," *Judge* 77, no. 1,981 (4 October 1919): 5. Illustrated by Lauren Scott. In the previous issue, 17 September 1919, p. [35], there was a full page notice with an autographed photograph stating that Stephen Leacock will become a regular contributor to *Judge*.

C19.21 "Socialism in Operation: A Prison: Edward Bellamy Pictured a State in Which Every Citizen Bade Farewell to Freedom and Surrendered to the Elected Boss — Required Population of Angels: The Road to Freedom: VI. — 'Looking Backward,' " *New York Times*, 5 October 1919, sec. 10, p. 3.

C19.22 "Social Control for Equal Opportunity: A Forecast of a Future Somewhere between the Iniquitous Conditions Brought about by Individualism and the Vagaries of Socialism. The Road to Freedom: — Vision of the Future: Seventh and Last Article," *New York Times*, 12 October 1919, sec. 9, pp. 2–3.

C19.23 "My Memories and Miseries as a Schoolmaster," *Maclean's Magazine* 32, no. 11 (November 1919): 18–9. Illustrated by C.W. Jefferys. Reprinted in Claude M. Fuess and Emory S. Basford, eds., *Unseen Harvests* (New York: Macmillan, 1974), pp. 424–9. See also A34 and C23.34.

C19.24 "This Bright New World; A Glance at Which Should Prove to Us That Sunshine Is Everywhere," *Vanity Fair* 13, no. 3 (November 1919): 39. Reprinted in *Orillia News-Letter*, 20 November 1929, p. [11]. Syndicated by Metropolitan Newspaper Service, New York.

C19.25 "Letters to the New Rulers of the World No. 1. To the Secretary of the League of Nations," *Judge* 77, no. 1,987 (15 November 1919): 5–6.

C19.26 "Letters to the New Rulers of the World II. To a Hotel Manager," *Judge* 77, no. 1,989 (29 November 1919): 5–6.

C19.27 "The Passing of the Christmas Ghost Story," *Bookman* 50, nos. 3–4 (November–December 1919): 257–61. See also C24.55.

C19.28 "Two Christmas Greetings; Specially Devised and Arranged for the Glad Season," *Vanity Fair* 13, no. 4 (December 1919): 55. The greetings are to a Bolshevik and a Profiteer.

C19.29 "Letters to the New Rulers of the World Number 3 — To a Plumber," *Judge* 77, no. 1,992 (20 December 1919): 5–6. Reprinted as "Letters to the New Rulers of the World: in Which the Sceptre Gives Way to the Monkey Wrench, and Courses of Lectures on Plumbing and the Kitchen Tap Are Given in National Universities," *Montreal Standard*, 7 June 1924, final ed., p. 21; illustrated by A.G. Racey. Also as "Every Man His Own Plumber Is Grim Possibility of the Future; Noted Humorist Says Plumbers Are Working Their Mystery to Death — Time for Universities to Explain Cause of Sizzling Taps," *Toronto Star Weekly*, 7 June 1924, p. 40; illustrated by Kessler. — Syndicated by Metropolitan Newspaper Service, New York.

C19.30 "Letters to the New Rulers of the World: IV. To a Disconsolate King," *Judge* 77, no. 1,993 (27 December 1919): 5–6.

C20.1 "The Teaching of French in Ontario," *Canadian Bookman* n.s. 2 (January 1920): 6–9.

C20.2 "Standardized Conversation; What They Are Saying at the Dinners and Dances of 1920," *Vanity Fair* 13, no. 5 (January 1920): 37.

C20.3 "To a Prohibitionist; Fifth Letter to the New Rulers of the World," *Judge* 79, no. 1,994 (3 January 1920): 5–7.

C20.4 "My Quarrel with the Spirits," *Leslie's Illustrated Weekly Newspaper* 131 (10 January 1920): 42–3. Leacock's article appears under the main title "Is Spiritualism a Fraud? Two Opinions from Hostile Camps." The rejoinder is by Hereward Cannington, "The 'Spirits' Quarrel with Mr. Leacock," p. 43.

C20.5 "Little Glimpses of the Future in America; or, Where Shall We Soon Be At?" *Vanity Fair* 13, no. 6 (February 1920): 39. Reprinted as "Little Glimpses of the Future of America; or, Where Shall We Soon Be At?" *Orillia News-Letter*, 16 October 1929, p. 12. Syndicated by Metropolitan Newspaper Service, New York. See also C20.10 and C24.46.

C20.6 "The Rectification of the American-Canadian Exchange," *Montreal Daily Star*, 7 February 1920, p. 1.

C20.7 "To a Spiritualist; Sixth of the Letters to the New Rulers of the World," *Judge* 78, no. 1,997 (7 February 1920): 5–7.

C20.8 "Prohibition at Work: The American Lesson to England," *Times* (London), 23 March 1920, p. 10. Letter to the editor.

C20.9 "The Restoration of Whiskers; Fibre of Our People Being Destroyed! Launching of Great Movement to Restore Whiskers," *Vanity Fair* 14, no. 2 (April 1920): 43. Reprinted as "The Restoration of Whiskers," *Passing Show* Christmas no. (December 1922): 20–1; as "The Restoration of Whiskers: Launching of a Great National Movement to Re-Whisker Citizens, As Their Fibre Is Being Destroyed, at the Root, by Clean Shaving," *Montreal Standard*, 3 May 1924, final ed., p. 21. Illustrated by A.G. Racey. Also as "The Restoration of Vanishing Whiskers. Fibre of Our People Being Destroyed, at the Root, by Clean Shaving — Launching of a Great National Movement to Re-Whisker the Citizenry," *Hamilton Spectator*, 3 May 1924, p. [17]. Syndicated by Metropolitan Newspaper Service, New York.

C20.10 "Little Glimpses of the Future; Prophetic Snap-Shots of the Fifty-Year Curriculum and the Growth of the Deportation Habit," *Vanity Fair* 14, no. 4 (June 1920): 53. See also C20.5 and C24.45.

C20.11 "New Nonsense Novels: Winsome Winnie, or Trial and Temptation," *Harper's Magazine* 141 (July 1920): 187–95. Reprinted as "Winsome Winnie (Narrated After the Best Models of 1875)," *Bystander* (London) 67 (7 July 1920): 47–8, 50, 52 (14 July 1920): 117–8, 121–2, with illustrations by Frank R. Grey; *Mountain Echo* (Hamilton, Ont.) 1, no. 9 (Oct. 1921): 8–12. See also C21.17.

C20.12 "A Guide to the Province of Quebec; For the Use of American Tourists," *Vanity Fair* 14, no. 3 (May 1920): 65. Reprinted as "New Guide to Province of Quebec: Compiled for the Benefit of Our Cousins from the United States Who Spend Their Vacation in Its Cities and Towns, and on Its Mountains, Lakes and Streams," *Montreal Standard*, 24 May 1924, final ed., p. 21. Illustrated by A.G. Racey. Syndicated by Metropolitan Newspaper Service, New York. As "The Humour of Serious Things. A Guide to Quebec. What Attracts Some Americans to the Canadian Province," *Times and Mirror* (Bristol), 20 December 1924, p. 14. Also as "The Humour of Serious Things (IV) A Guide to Quebec. What Attracts Some Americans to the Canadian Province," *Gazette* (West Sussex), 25 December 1924, p. 6; as "The Humour of Serious Things (4) A Guide Book for the 'Wets'. Why Quebec Attracts Americans," *Gazette* (Birmingham), 30 December 1924, p. 4.

C20.13 "My Lost Dollar," *DAC News* (Detroit Athletic Club) 5, no. 5 (May 1920): 61–2. Illustrated by Russell Legge. Apparently appeared also in *Sphere* (London). Reprinted in *Vancouver Sunday Sun*, 16 December 1923, ("Magazine"), p. 4. Syndicated by Metropolitan Newspaper Service, New York. Reprinted as "My Lost Dollar: One of the Little Things One May Forgive But Does Not Forget," *Montreal Standard*, 1 August 1925, final ed., p. 31. Illustrated by A.G. Racey.

C20.14 "The Comedies of Prohibition: How America Pretends to Be Convivial," *Sunday Pictorial* (London), 9 May 1920, p. 5.

C20.15 "John and I," *Bystander* (London) 67 (21 July 1920): 191–2, 194; (28 July 1920), 267–8, 270, with illustrations by Frank R. Grey. Reprinted as "New Nonsense Novels: John and I, or How I Nearly Lost My Husband," *Harper's Magazine* 141 (September 1920): 545–9. Reprinted as "John and I: or How I Nearly Lost My Husband: Narrated After the Approved Fashion of the Best Heart and Home Magazines," *Mountain Echo*, (Hamilton, Ont.) 1, no. 10 (Nov. 1921): 11–3; in *Golden Book Magazine* 10, no. 58 (October 1929): 73–6. As "John and I or How I Almost Lost My Husband," in Grant Huffman, ed., *15 Stories* (Toronto: McClelland and Stewart, 1960), pp. 149–57.

C20.16 "A Daily Paper — for Any Date; A Comprehensive Digest for the World's News, Good All the Year Round," *Vanity Fair* 14, no. 5 (July 1920): 69.

C20.17 "What I Read As a Child; Stephen Leacock Tells of his Earliest Adventures with Dickens and Jules Verne," *Toronto Public Library Book Bulletin* n.s. 10, no. 7–9 (July–September 1920): 1–2. Reprinted in H.P. Sawyer, ed., *The Library and Its Contents* (New York: The H.W. Wilson Company, 1925), pp. 143–4.

C20.18 "My Experience as a Political Speaker; A Personal Contribution to the Presidential Campaign," *Vanity Fair* 6, no. 14 (August 1920): 51, 100.

C20.19 "New Nonsense Novels: The Split in the Cabinet, or the Fate of England," *Harper's Magazine* 141 (August 1920): 305–11. Reprinted as "The Split in the Cabinet,"

*Bystander* (London) 67 (8 September 1920): 621–2, 624; (15 September 1920): 697–8, 700, 704, with illustrations by Frank R. Grey; as "The Split in the Cabinet; or the Fate of England: A Political Novel of the Days That Were," *Mountain Echo* (Hamilton, Ont.) 1, no. 11 (December 1921): 8–11. See also G5.

C20.20  "Who Do You Think Did It? (Done After the Very Latest Fashion in This Sort of Thing)," *Bystander* (London) 67 (11 August 1920): 389–90, 392; (18 August 1920): 451–2, 454; (25 August 1920): 513–4, 516; (1 September 1920): 559–60, 562, with illustrations by Frank R. Grey. Reprinted as "New Nonsense Novels: Who Do You Think Did It? Or the Mixed-up Murder Mystery," *Harper's Magazine* 141 (October 1920): 599–610.

C20.21  "Selecting a President — in the Future; National Convention Notes, Copied From a Forthcoming History of the United States," *Vanity Fair* 15, no. 1 (September 1920): 45, 122.

C20.22  "Broken Barriers, or Red Love on a Blue Island," *Judge* 79, no. 2,031 (2 October 1920): 5–8; no. 2,032 (9 October 1920): 5–10. Reprinted as "Broken Barriers. Red Love on a Blue Island (The Kind of Thing That Has Replaced the Good Old Sea Story)," *Bystander* (London) 68 (13 October 1920): 125–6, 130, 132; (20 October 1920), 217–8, 220, 222, with illustrations by Frank R. Grey.

C20.23  "The Need for Dormitories at McGill," *Montreal Daily Star*, 29 October 1920, p. 3. Reprinted as "How Leacock Would Go About Founding University," *McGill Daily*, 11 November 1920, p. 4; "What the College Really Needs," *New York Times*, 14 November 1920, sec. 3 ("Book Review and Magazine"), p. 16; as "McGill University," *Times* (London), "Educational Supplement," 18 November 1920, p. 607; as "Students' Residences," *Redcliff Review* 10, no. 49 (2 December 1920); as "College Dormitories," *Harvard Advocate* 107, no. 4 (17 December 1920): 109–10 and subsequently collected in Richard M. Smoley, ed. *First Flowering the Best of the Harvard Advocate* (Reading, Mass.: Addison-Wesley, 1977), pp. 88–90. See also A33.

C20.24  "The Kidnapped Plumber: A Tale of Tomorrow A Hitherto Suppressed Chapter from the Reminiscences of a Feed-Pipe Expert," *Leslie's Illustrated Weekly Newspaper* 131 (30 October 1920): 549, 565–6. Illustrated by Walter de Maris. Also as "The Kidnapped Plumber. A Tale of the New Time," *Bystander Annual of 1920*: 65–8, 70, 94, 98. An advertisement in the *Bystander* noted that the annual was due out on 29 November 1920. Reprinted in *World's Great Humorous Stories* (New York: Editions for the Armed Services, [1945]), pp. 205–17. See also C23.9.

C20.25  "Our Little Soviet — One of Its More Serious Members Explains How It Works in An Apartment House," *Vanity Fair* 15, no. 3 (November 1920): 58, 106. Illustrated by Dorothy Ferrics. Reprinted as "Our Little Soviet," *Vancouver Sunday Sun*, 5 August 1923, ("Magazine"), p. 4. Syndicated by Metropolitan Newspaper Service, New York.

C20.26  "Personal Experiments with the Black Bass," *Saturday Night* (Toronto) 36, no. 3, whole no. 1,448 (13 November 1920): 3, 11. Reprinted in *DAC News* (Detroit Athletic Club) 5, no. 12 (December 1920): 33–4, with illustrations by Russell Legge; *Bystander* (London) 68 (1 December 1920): 645–6, 648, with illustrations by Frank R. Grey. Reprinted as "Delving into Black Bass Studies Reveals Crafty Creature's Habits," *Vancouver Sunday Sun*, 2 March 1924, ("Magazine"), p. 2. Syndicated by Metropolitan Newspaper Service, New York.

C20.27 "Let Us Be Thankful; A Few Glad Thoughts Which Should Be of Comfort at Christmas Time," *Vanity Fair* 15, no. 4 (December 1920): 64.

C20.28 "[The Campaign to Raise Money for McGill University]," *McGill News* 2, no. 1 (December 1920): 10.

C20.29 "The Discolored Christmas," *Life* Special Christmas no. (2 December 1920): 1,037–8.

C21.1 "The D'Annunzio Touch; the Liberator of Fiume Is Finding his Imitators in America," *Vanity Fair* 15, no. 5 (January 1921): 43, 104.

C21.2 "'The Moral Wave of the New Year, and How to Duck Under It,'" *Montreal Standard*, 1 January 1921, final ed., p. 10. Illustrated by A.G. Racey. Syndicated by Metropolitan Newspaper Service, New York.

C21.3 "Tight Money," *Montreal Standard*, 8 January 1921, final ed., p. 11. Illustrated by A.G. Racey. Syndicated by Metropolitan Newspaper Service, New York. Reprinted in *Nash's and Pall Mall Magazine* 67 (July 1921): 377–9. Illustrated by W. Heath Robinson. Apparently also appeared in *Indianapolis Sunday Star*, 9 January 1921, p. 2.

C21.4 "That Vampire Woman: I Want to Meet Her," *Montreal Standard*, final ed., 15 January 1921, p. 11. Illustrated by A.G. Racey. Syndicated by Metropolitan Newspaper Service, New York. See also C24.8.

C21.5 "The Crime Wave," *Montreal Standard*, 22 January 1921, final ed., p. 11. Illustrated by A.G. Racey. Syndicated by Metropolitan Newspaper Service, New York.

C21.6 "Crossing the Frontier," *Montreal Standard*, 29 January 1921, final ed., p. 11. Illustrated by A.G. Racey. Syndicated by Metropolitan Newspaper Service, New York.

C21.7 "A Sermon on Humour," *Goblin* 1, no. 1 (February 1921): 9–10. Reprinted in *Graduate* (University of Toronto) (April 1970): 34–6; John N. Mappin, *The Goblin: A Brief History of Canada's Humour Magazine of the 1920s* (Montreal: printed for John N. Mappin by The Porcupine's Quill, 1988), pp. 19–22. With excerpts in K83.1, pp. 90–1.

C21.8 "Literary Successes of 1921; A Confidential Announcement of Some Coming Successes Among the New Books," *Vanity Fair* 15, no. 6 (February 1921): 39.

C21.9 "Is Dancing Immoral?" *Montreal Standard*, 5 February 1921, final ed., p. 11. Illustrated by A.G. Racey. Syndicated by Metropolitan Newspaper Service, New York.

C21.10 "This Blue Law Business," *Montreal Standard*, 12 February 1921, final ed., p. 11. Illustrated by A.G. Racey. Syndicated by Metropolitan Newspaper Service, New York.

C21.11 "Why I Murdered My Landlord," *Montreal Standard*, 19 February 1921, final ed., p. 11. Illustrated by A.G. Racey. Syndicated by Metropolitan Newspaper Service, New York. Reprinted as "Why I Murdered My Landlord. A Plain Statement by a Very Plain Tenant. The Rent Act," *Pall Mall Gazette* (London), 9 December 1922, p. 7; as "Why I Shot My Landlord," *Vancouver Sunday Sun*, 9 December 1923, ("Magazine"), p. 4; also as "Why I Murdered My Landlord: Deed Makes Me Eligible for Gold Medal," *Sunday Mail* (Glasgow), 27 December 1925, p. 8. Illustrated by Kessler.

C21.12 "The Drama As It Was and Is," *Montreal Standard*, 26 February 1921, final ed., p. 25. Illustrated by A.G. Racey. Syndicated by Metropolitan Newspaper Service, New York. Reprinted as "When the Drama Was Drama," *Strand Magazine* (London) 62 (21 August 1921): 132–4; as "The Decline of the Drama," in Christopher Morley, ed. *Modern Essays*

(New York: Harcourt, Brace, 1921), pp. 145–52; in Norris Hodgins, ed., *Some Canadian Essays* (London: Thomas Nelson, 1932), pp. 115–121.

C21.13 "The Approach of the Comet," *Montreal Standard*, 5 March 1921, final ed., p. 11. Illustrated by A.G. Racey. Syndicated by Metropolitan Newspaper Service, New York. Reprinted as "Approach of the Comet: Reacting to an Astronomical Imminence and How I Figured to Beat the Game," *Montreal Standard*, 8 November 1924, final ed., p. 23. Syndicated by Metropolitan Newspaper Service, New York.

C21.14 "Easy Marks," *Montreal Standard*, 12 March 1921, final ed., p. 17. Illustrated by A.G. Racey. Syndicated by Metropolitan Newspaper Service, New York.

C21.15 "Whose Move Is It?" *Montreal Standard*, 19 March 1921, final ed., p. 29. Illustrated by A.G. Racey. Syndicated by Metropolitan Newspaper Service, New York.

C21.16 "Are Moving Pictures Punk?" *Montreal Standard*, 26 March 1921, final ed., p. [19]. Illustrated by A.G. Racey. Syndicated by Metropolitan Newspaper Service, New York.

C21.17 "Leacock's Burlesque in 'Winsome Winnie,'" *Montreal Standard*, 26 March 1921, p. 33. Prints extracts from *Winsome Winnie* because of the huge and favourable response to the stories appearing since January. See also C20.11.

C21.18 "The Dry Banquet; Why I Want to Start A National Movement to Abolish It," *Vanity Fair* 16, no. 2 (April 1921): 39. Reprinted as "The Dry Banquet: If We Must Be Prohibitionists, Why Not Do the Thing Properly. If the Wine Is Out, Away with the Banquet," *Montreal Standard*, 15 March 1924, final ed., p. 23. Illustrated by A.G. Racey. Syndicated by Metropolitan Newspaper Service, New York.

C21.19 "First Call for Spring," *Montreal Standard*, 2 April 1921, final ed., p. 11. Illustrated by A.G. Racey. Syndicated by Metropolitan Newspaper Service, New York. Reprinted as "Oh Listen to the Birds Leacock's Spring Song," *Toronto Star Weekly*, 22 March 1924, p. 31. Illustrated by Kessler. Also as "First Call for Spring — or, Oh, Listen to the Birds," *Vancouver Sunday Sun*, 30 March 1923, ("Magazine"), p. 2; "First Call for Spring: Signs Begin to Multiply that Spring Is Approaching. The Birds and Flowers Are Beginning to Appear and There Are Many Evidences of Renewed Life," *Montreal Standard*, 22 March 1924, final ed., p. 21. Illustrated by A.G. Racey. Syndicated by Metropolitan Newspaper Service, New York. Reprinted in *Reader's Digest* 38, no. 227 (March 1941): 80; in *Reader's Digest* 78 (May 1961): 180; in *Peter Gzowski's Spring Tonic* (Edmonton: Hurtig, 1979), pp. 139–40.

C21.20 "Why I Refuse to Play Golf," *Montreal Standard*, 9 April 1921, final ed., p. 23. Illustrated by A.G. Racey. Syndicated by Metropolitan Newspaper Service, New York. Reprinted as "My Objections to Golf. The Sordid History of Three Scots, Three Crooked Sticks, and A Ball. A Nation Bunkered," *Pall Mall Gazette* (London), 6 January 1923, p. 7; as "My Objections to Golf," *Living Age* 317, no. 4,116 (26 May 1923): 477–80. According to *Living Age*, this is a reprint from *St. Martins-in the Fields Review* 386 (April 1923): 163–6. See also C24.29.

C21.21 "Should Bachelors Be Taxed to Extinction?" *Montreal Standard*, 16 April 1921, final ed., p. 17. Illustrated by A.G. Racey. Syndicated by Metropolitan Newspaper Service, New York.

C21.22 "The Great Detective and the Dog Catcher: Maddened by Mystery," *Montreal*

*Standard*, 30 April 1921, final ed., p. 29. Syndicated by Metropolitan Newspaper Service, New York. See also C11.2.

C21.23 "In the Wake of Mr. Chesterton; The Appalling Catastrophe Recently Occasioned in Our Quiet Home Town by a Public Lecture," *Vanity Fair* 16, no. 3 (May 1921): 50.

C21.24 "A Reckless Deal with the World of Spirits," *Montreal Standard*, 7 May 1921, final ed., p. 37. Syndicated by Metropolitan Newspaper Service, New York.

C21.25 "Guido the Gimlet of Ghent," *Montreal Standard*, 14 May 1921, final ed., p. 41. Syndicated by Metropolitan Newspaper Service, New York. See also C11.4.

C21.26 "On the Art of Taking a Vacation," *Outlook* (New York) 128 (25 May 1921): 160–2. Reprinted as "On Taking a Vacation; A Word of Caution Against Becoming Addicted to Habits of Industry That Will Not Halt," *Orillia News-Letter*, 20 April 1927, p. 9; as "On Taking a Vacation," *Montreal Standard*, 23 April 1927, final ed., p. 46. Illustrated by A.G. Racey. Syndicated by Metropolitan Newspaper Service, New York.

C21.27 "A Hero in Homespun," *Montreal Standard*, 28 May 1921, final ed., p. 23. Syndicated by Metropolitan Newspaper Service, New York. See also C10.46.

C21.28 "A Painless Task," *Collier's* 67, no. 25 (18 June 1921): 5–6, 17, 25–6. Illustrated by Herbert M. Stoops.

C21.29 "My Hotel Breakfast," *Judge* 81, no. 2,072 (16 July 1921): 5.

C21.30 "Spoof," *Montreal Standard*, 21 July 1921, p. 26. Syndicated by Metropolitan Newspaper Service, New York. See also C14.10.

C21.31 "How I Succeeded in My Business; Secrets of Success As Revealed by the Best Current Literature," *Vanity Fair* 16, no. 7 (September 1921): 46. See also C24.5.

C21.32 "Tom Lachford, Promoter," *Life* (London) 78, no. 2,027 (8 September 1921): 17, 26. Illustrated by Rea Irvin.

C21.33 "Disarmament and Common Sense," *Collier's* 68, no. 15 (8 October 1921): 5–6, 26.

C21.34 "A Great Humorist on Humour," *Daily Mail* (London), 12 October 1921, p. 8.

C21.35 "My Impressions of England: As Exported to America," *Illustrated Sunday Herald* (London), 16 October 1921, p. 5. See also C22.3.

C21.36 "A Staggering Blow," *Passing Show* (London) 14, no. 345 (22 October 1921): 113. Illustrated by A.C.B.

C21.37 "When Britain Goes Bone-Dry: Graphic Picture of Life under Prohibition," *Sunday Pictorial* (London), 30 October 1921, p. 7.

C21.38 "British-American Union," *Landmark: the Monthly Magazine of the English-Speaking Union* 3, no. 11 (November 1921): 703–4.

C21.39 "'In Flanders Fields.' Col. McCrae's Vision of the Poppies," *Times* (London), 11 November 1921, p. 13. See also C18.9 and C38.9.

C21.40 "Does Euclid Make Good Wives? Failure of Sex-Equality in the Class-Room; By Stephen Leacock Whose Experience of Co-education Prompts Him to Suggest a Separate Curriculum for Women," *Sunday Pictorial* (London), 20 November 1921, p. 7.

C21.41 "Stephen Interviews Leacock: The Art of Being Interviewed in England, Canada, and the United States," *Maclean's Magazine* 34, no. 21 (1 December 1921): 9. Illustrated by C.W. Jefferys. Apparently reprinted as "Stephen Leacock Interviews Himself," *Detroit Athletic Club News* 6 (December 1921): 33 and also in the *Sunday Herald* (London).

C21.42 "The Income Tax. Its Fallacy and Failure. Mr. Stephen Leacock's Alternative. A Measure of Painless Extraction. Relief for Industry and Thrift," *Morning Post* (London), 12 December 1921, pp. 7–8. There was a response, "The Income Tax. Mr. Harold Cox on Mr Leacock's Alternative. True Basis of Taxation. Views of Business Men," *Morning Post* (London), 14 December 1921, p. 4. The editorial introduction to this response noted that Leacock's proposal had created a great deal of interest throughout Britain. Cox's article is followed by four letters to the editor on the topic. There was also a response from Hartley Withers, "Income Tax," *Saturday Review Financial* Supplement, 132, no. 3451 (17 December 1921): 74.

C21.43 "My Blighted Christmas," *Sunday Express* (London), 25 December 1921, p. 6.

C21.44 "My Ideal Christmas: What I Plan — and What I Really Do," *Sunday Pictorial* (London), 25 December 1921, p. 5. Reprinted as "My Ideal Christmas," *Vancouver Sunday Sun*, 23 December 1923, ("Magazine"), p. 2. Syndicated by Metropolitan Newspaper Service, New York. Also in *Tit-Bits* no. 2, 252, Christmas number (13 December 1924): 452.

C21.45 "We Are Teaching Women All Wrong," *Collier's* 68, no. 27 (31 December 1921): 15, 26. *Collier's* invited women to reply to Leacock's article since he questioned the need for higher education for women and argued that marriage is a woman's career. The magazine offered $50 for the best reply and ten consolation prizes of $5 each. For the letters in reply to Leacock's article, see "Now, Listen, Professor Leacock!" *Collier's* 69, no. 7 (18 February 1922): 16, 26. See also Margaret Gillett, "Leacock and the Ladies of R.V.C.," *McGill Journal of Education* 16, no. 2 (Spring 1981): 121–9, which reprints extracts from Leacock's article (at p. 127). See also C22.5–6.

C22.1 "The Oldest Living Graduate," *McGill Year Book* 1 (1922): 60. Published by the class of 1922. Reprinted in *Old McGill 1930* 33 (1929?): 236; in *McGill Journal of Education* 6, no. 1 (Spring 1971): 77; in K83.1, pp. 212–3.

C22.2 "McGill in 2000 A.D.; A Fragment from a Future History as Foreseen," *Old McGill 1923* 25 (1922): 201. Published by the Junior Class in the year before their graduation.

C22.3 "Impressions of England; A Letter from London Attempting to Do for the English as We Have Been Done by Them," *Vanity Fair* 18, no. 5 (January 1922): 46. See also C21.35.

C22.4 "Prohibition Comes to London: A Letter to a Canadian Friend," *Maclean's Magazine* 35, no. 1 (1 January 1922): 16. Illustrated by C.W. Jefferys. A lengthy excerpt reprinted as "A Satirical Legend," *Maclean's Magazine* 108, no. 12 (20 March 1995): 61.

C22.5 "Leacock Roasts Co-education," *Maclean's Magazine*, 35, no. 2 (15 January 1922): 28. The article is reprinted from an unknown magazine in the "Review of Reviews." See also C21.45.

C22.6 "Co-Education Roasted," *McGill Daily*, 31 January 1922, p. 2. According to Lomer (p. 70), this is from *Collier's* (C21.45).

C22.7 "Stories and Story-Tellers," *Outlook* 130 (1 February 1922): 183–4.

C22.8 "Exporting Humor to England," *Harper's Magazine* 144 (March 1922): 433–40.

**C22.9** "My Discovery of England," *Harper's Magazine* 144 (April 1922): 560–8. Lengthy excerpts appear in "'Let's Discover England,' Exclaims Stephen Leacock," *Toronto Globe*, 24 March 1922, p. 12; a brief excerpt appears as "Beverage? Tut!" *Newspacket* (Orillia) 6, no. 2 (Summer 1978): [4]. Excerpted in John Fischer, Lucy Donaldson, eds., *Humor from Harper's* (New York: Harper & Brothers, 1961), pp. 94–101. Reprinted in Malcolm Ross and John Stevens, eds. *In Search of Ourselves* (Toronto: J.M. Dent, 1967), pp. 113–22.

**C22.10** "Why I Like Bad Music," *Fellowcrafter* (Detroit) 4, no. 1 (April 1922): 10–1. Illustrated by William O. Fitzgerald. Reprinted as "Bad Music; A Discussion of Why It is Better Than Good," *Orillia News-Letter*, 24 August 1927, p. 10. Also as "Bad Music," *Montreal Standard*, 27 August 1927, final ed., p. 36. Illustrated by A.G. Racey. Syndicated by Metropolitan Newspaper Service, New York. Apparently reprinted in Roberthaven Schauffer, ed., *The Magic of Music* (New York: Dodd, Mead, 1935).

**C22.11** "Is Prohibition Coming to England?" *Collier's* 69, no. 15 (15 April 1922): 9–10. Illustrated by Tony Sarg.

**C22.12** "Oxford As I See It. Medieval Horrors of Its Buildings," *Morning Post* (London), 29 April 1922, p. 7. C22.12 and C22.15–6 are reprinted as "Oxford As I See It," *Harper's Magazine* 144 (May 1922): 738–45; "The Horrors of Oxford," *Living Age* 313, no. 4,068 (24 June 1922): 779–81. Excerpts from the *Morning Post* were reprinted as "Soda Biscuits Here and a Whole Roast Ox There," *Toronto Star Weekly*, 10 June 1922, p. 22; the excerpts concern the differences between Oxford and the University of Toronto. Reprinted in Christopher Morley, ed., *Modern Essays (Second Series)* (New York: Harcourt, Brace, 1924, 1927), pp. 3–25; in Kenneth Allan Robinson, William Benfield Pressey, and James Dow McCallum, *Essays Toward Truth*, series 1 (New York: Henry Holt, 1924), pp. 72–93; Essie Chamberlain, ed., *Essays Old and New* (Harcourt, Brace, 1926, 1934), pp. 92–102; in F. H. Pritchard, ed., *Humour of To-Day* (London: George G. Harrop & Son, 1927), pp. 148–64; in Joseph M. Bachelor and Ralph L. Henry, eds., *Challenging Essays in Modern Thought* (New York: Century, 1928), pp. 18–34; partially as "Notes by Stephen Leacock," in R.A.H. Spiers, ed., *Round about the 'The Mitre' at Oxford (Episodes of the University, City and Hotel)*, 2nd ed. (Oxford: Published at "The Mitre", 1929), p. 149; in Kendall B. Taft, John Francis McDermott, and Dana O. Jensen, *College Readings in Contemporary Thought* (Boston: Houghton Mifflin, 1929), pp. 205–21, also published as *Contemporary Attitudes: Essays in Many Fields of Thought*; in Edward S. Noyes, ed., *Readings in the Modern Essay* (Boston: Houghton Mifflin, 1933), pp. 423–43; in Raymond Woodbury Pence, ed., *Readings by Present-Day Writers* (Macmillan: New York, 1933), pp. 257–70; in John Abbot Clark, ed., *The College Book of Essays* (New York: Henry Holt, 1939), pp. 137–55; in E.F. Kingston, ed., *Essays and Short Stories for Matriculation Classes* (Toronto: J.M. Dent, 1948), pp. 234–45; *Humorous Stories* (London: Octopus Books, 1986), pp. 226–240 (originally published in 1984, revised and expanded in 1985). Lomer (p. 118) also records reprints in: J.W. Cunliffe and Lomer, eds., *Writing of Today* (New York: Century, 1925), 4th ed.; L. Wann, ed., *Century Readings in the English Essay* (New York: 1926), pp. 509–17.

**C22.13** "Wild Chairman I Have Met; How Different Types of Presiding Officers Tend to Enliven the Meeting," *Vanity Fair* 18, no. 3 (May 1922): 48, 94.

**C22.14** "As I Saw Politics in England," *Maclean's Magazine* 35, no. 9 (1 May 1922): 20, 46–8. Illustrated by C.W. Jefferys. An excerpt appears as "King George in Orillia; As

Stephen Leacock Imagines the Event," *Orillia Packet*, 4 May 1922, p. 1. Probably reprinted as "A Clear View of the Government and Politics of England," in Raymond Woodbury Pence, ed., *Essays by Present-Day Writers* (New York: Macmillan, 1924), pp. 153–66; in N.R. Fallis, *A Miscellany of Tales and Essays* (Toronto: Clarke, Irwin, 1935), pp. 111–29; in Robert Thomas Allen, ed., *A Treasury of Canadian Humour* (Toronto: McClelland and Stewart, 1967), pp. 43–4.

C22.15 "Oxford As I See It. Where Salesmanship Is Still Untaught II," *Morning Post* (London), 1 May 1922, p. 6.

C22.16 "Oxford as I See It. What Are Women Doing There," *Morning Post* (London), 2 May 1922, p. 6.

C22.17 "Wanted — More Profiteers: The World Is to the Strong: Let's Demand Better Prices," *Collier's* 69, no. 18 (6 May 1922): 3–4, 29. Illustrated by Herbert M. Stoops. See also A127.

C22.18 "The British and the American Press," *Harper's Magazine* 145 (June 1922): 1–9. See also C23.32.

C22.19 "Roughing It in the Bush: My Plans for Moose Hunting in the Canadian Wilderness," *Maclean's Magazine* 35, no. 19 (1 October 1922): 18. Illustrated by Lou Skuce. Also as "My Plans for Moose Hunting in the Canadian Wilderness," *DAC News* (Detroit Athletic Club News) 7, no. 10 (October 1922): 21–3. Illustrated by Burt Thomas. Apparently also appeared in *Royal Magazine*, February 1923. Reprinted as "Roughing It in the Bush," *Vancouver Sunday Sun*, 27 January 1924, ("Magazine"), p. 2. Syndicated by Metropolitan Newspaper Service, New York; as "Roughing It in the Wilds: My Well-Laid Plans for Stag Hunting in His Highland Haunts," *Sunday Mail* (Glasgow), 10 January 1926, p. 14; in David McCord, *Once and for All* (New York: Coward-McCann, 1929), pp. 288–93; in Robert Thomas Allen, ed., *A Treasury of Canadian Humour* (Toronto: McClelland and Stewart, 1967), pp. 39–41; in Herbert Rosengarten and Jane Flick, eds., *The Broadview Reader* (Peterborough, Ont.: Broadview Press, 1987), pp. 219–23. See also C27.34.

C22.20 "Abolishing the Heroine: A Plea That Fewer Heroines and More Crimes Would Add Sprightliness to Our Fiction," *Vanity Fair* 19, no. 4 (December 1922): 49. Reprinted as "Abolishing the Heroine," *Vancouver Sunday Sun*, 30 December 1923, ("Magazine"), p. 3. Syndicated by Metropolitan Newspaper Service, New York.

C22.21 "Clementina Click and Mr. Sprott. A Film Not Four-Fifth Piffle and One-Fifth Poison. Moving Movie Drama," *Pall Mall Gazette* (London), 2 December 1922, p. 7.

C22.22 "Those Wicked New Dances. A Tale of Willie Entitled 'Whirled into Unhappiness.' The Bingo Peril," *Pall Mall Gazette* (London), 16 December 1922, p. 7.

C22.23 "Dry Prowler on the Frontier. A Tale of the Desperate Flask Gang and the Pussyfoot's Chosen. 'Groggy' Interludes," *Pall Mall Gazette* (London), 23 December 1922, p. 7.

C22.24 "The Truth about My Wife's Dog: Will It Ever Enter into My Life Again; By Stephen Leacock: the Canadian Humorist Describes the Mysterious Circumstances of Wee Jee's Disappearance," *Sunday Pictorial* (London), 24 December 1922, p. 7. See also C23.19.

C22.25 "My Unhappy New Year. Robbed of Its Brightness by Those Good Resolutions. Let's Be Wicked!" *Pall Mall Gazette* (London), 30 December 1922, p. 7.

C23.1 "'The Old College and the New University,'" *Old McGill 1924* 26 (1923): 21–2.

C23.2 "The Faded Actor: A Brief Discourse on Art and the True Artistic Temperament," *Goblin* 3, no. 1 (January 1923): 11, 25.

C23.3 "Balance of Trade in Traveler's Impressions Is Alarmingly Disturbed and Out of Gear; Noted Humanist Sets Out to Make Some Discoveries in Tight Little Isle; Clever Comeback to Overseas Critics Traffic Is Irregular and Much Too One-Sided to Be of Pecuniary Benefit," *Vancouver Sunday Sun*, 7 January 1923, p. 7. Syndicated by Metropolitan Newspaper Service, New York.

C23.4 "Being Interviewed on Possibilities of London Rare Sport for a Humorist; Finds Himself Prepared to Prophesy Bright Future for Metropolis; Reporters Harp on One Question Cut and Dried Quizzes Cannot Be Answered Like They Can at Home," *Vancouver Sunday Sun*, 14 January 1923, p. 24. Syndicated by Metropolitan Newspaper Service, New York.

C23.5 "Impressions of London as Viewed by Stephen Leacock," *Vancouver Sunday Sun*, 21 January 1923, ("Magazine"), p. 6. Syndicated by Metropolitan Newspaper Service, New York. See also "Impressions of London," in Sharon Brown, ed., *Essays of Our Times* (Chicago, Atlanta, New York: Scott, Foresman, 1928), pp. 239–46.

C23.6 "Stephen Leacock Wants a Henhouse; Told Forestry Men How Rise in Hemlock Thwarted His Ambition; Cheaper Lumber Needed: Prices and Wages All Round Must Come Down — Only Way of Salvation, Said Professor," *Montreal Gazette*, 24 January 1923, p. 5. Verbatim report of Leacock's speech to the Conference of the Quebec Forest Protective Association at the Mount Royal Hotel on 23 January 1923. Also, with only one sentence quoted, as "Leacock Wants a Hemlock Hen House," *Montreal Herald*, 24 January 1923, p. 3; in full as "Stephen Leacock Wants a Henhouse; also Declares Orillia Is the Intellectual Capital of Ontario," *Orillia Packet*, 1 February 1923, p. 2. Probably reprinted as "The Sad Story of Stephen Leacock's Hen House," *Orillia Packet and Times*, 20 April 1944, p. 1. The source for the latter reprint is the *Timber News*, the organ of the Canadian Lumberman's Association. See also E23.7.

C23.7 "The Drama As I See It: Studies in the Plays and Films of Yesterday and To-day: I. 'Cast Up by the Sea' (As Thrown Up for 30 Cents about the Year 1880 — A Sea-Coast Melodrama)," *Harper's Magazine* 146 (February 1923): 290–306. Illustrated by John Held, Jr. Also in *Maclean's Magazine* 36, no. 3 (1 February 1923): 15–6, 46, 48–51. The subtitle appears as "A Sea Coast Melodrama as Thrown Up for 30 Cents — Period, 1880". Illustrated by C.W. Jefferys. Reprinted in *Montreal Standard*, 16 February 1924, final ed., pp. 19, 40. Syndicated by Metropolitan Newspaper Service, New York.

C23.8 "The Organization of Prosperity in Canada," *Listening Post* (Montreal) 1, no. 1 (February 1923): 9.

C23.9 "The Kidnapped Plumber — A Tale of New Times," *Vancouver Sunday Sun*, 4 February 1923, ("Magazine"), p. 7. Syndicated by Metropolitan Newspaper Service, New York. See also C20.24.

C23.10 "The Discovery of America," *Vancouver Sunday Sun*, 11 February 1923, ("Magazine"), p. 7. Syndicated by Metropolitan Newspaper Service, New York.

C23.11 "The Drama As I See It: Studies in the Plays and Films of Yesterday and To-day: II. 'The Soul Call' An Up-to-Date Piffle-Play — Period 1923 (In Which a Woman and a Man,

Both Trying to Find Themselves, Find Each Other," *Harper's Magazine* 146 (March 1923): 430–9. Illustrated by John Held, Jr. Also in *Maclean's Magazine* 36, no. 5 (1 March 1923): 14–5, 65–7. The subtitle appears as "An Up-to-date Piffle Play. Period, 1923 in Which a Man and Woman, Both Trying to Find Themselves, Find One Another." Illustrated by C.W. Jefferys. See also C24.33.

C23.12  "Memoirs of a Certain Hohenzollern," *Vancouver Sunday Sun*, 18 March 1923, ("Magazine"), p. [5]. Syndicated by Metropolitan Newspaper Service, New York. See also C18.28.

C23.13  "The Cave Man As He Is," *Vancouver Sunday Sun*, 25 March 1923, ("Magazine"), p. 5. Syndicated by Metropolitan Newspaper Service, New York. Apparently appeared originally in *Hearst's Magazine*, possibly 9 August 1917 and was then reprinted in *Hearst's International Magazine* (? November 1922). Reprinted as "The Cave-Man As He Is," in Lancelot Oliphant, *Great Comic Scenes from English Literature* (London: Gregg, 1930), pp. 241–8. See also C25.52.

C23.14  "My Lost Opportunities; The Anguish of Discovering Too Late the Chances Which Were Let Go," *Toronto Star Weekly*, 31 March 1923, p. 26. Illustrated by Kessler. Syndicated by Metropolitan Newspaper Service, New York.

C23.15  "The Drama As I See It: Studies in the Plays and Films of Yesterday and To-day: III. 'Dead Men's Gold' A Film of the Great Nevada Desert," *Harper's Magazine* 146 (April 1923): 567–75. Illustrated by John Held, Jr. Also in *Maclean's Magazine* 36, no. 7 (1 April 1923): 18–9, 57–8. Illustrated by C.W. Jefferys. See also C24.13 and C25.4.

C23.16  "The Perplexity Column," *Vancouver Sunday Sun*, 15 April 1923, ("Magazine"), p. 5. Syndicated by Metropolitan Newspaper Service, New York. See also C16.16 and C16.21.

C23.17  "The Drama As I See It: Studies in the Plays and Films of Yesterday and To-day: IV. 'The Greek Drama' as Presented in Our Colleges," *Harper's Magazine* 146 (May 1923): 723–32. Illustrated by John Held, Jr. Also in *Maclean's Magazine* 36, no. 9 (1 May 1923): 22–3, 73–4. Illustrated by C.W. Jefferys.

C23.18  "My Unposted Correspondence: A Study Showing That Second Thoughts Are Generally But a Part of Cowardice," *Vanity Fair* 20, no. 3 (May 1923): 50, 100. Reprinted in *Vancouver Sunday Sun*, 10 June 1923 ("Magazine"), p. 5 with the permission of the Metropolitan Newspaper Service, New York; in *London Magazine* (December 1923): 751–3.

C23.19  "Life and Achievements of My Wife's Dog, Wee Wee," *Vancouver Sunday Sun*, 20 May 1923 ("Magazine"), p. 4. Syndicated by Metropolitan Newspaper Service, New York. See also C22.24.

C23.20  "The Drama As I See It: Studies in the Plays and Films of Yesterday and To-day: V. 'Masterpieces of Other Nations,'" *Harper's Magazine* 147 (June 1923): 7–16. Illustrated by John Held, Jr. Also as "The Drama As I See It: Masterpieces of Other Nations V. The Sub-Contractor An Ibsen Play Done Out of the Original Norwegian with an Axe," *Maclean's Magazine* 36, no. 11 (1 June 1923): 22–3, 48, 50. Illustrated by C.W. Jefferys. Reprinted as "'The Sub Contractor,' Original of the Norwegian with an Axe," *Vancouver Sunday Sun*, 17 February 1924, ("Magazine"), p. 2; as "The Sub-Contractor: An Ibsen Play. Done Out of the Original with an Axe," *Montreal Standard*, 23 February 1924, final ed.,

p. 19. Illustrated by A.G. Racey. Syndicated by Metropolitan Newspaper Service, New York. As "The Sub-Contractor," in John D. Robins and Margaret V. Ray, eds., *A Book of Canadian Humour* (Toronto: Ryerson Press, 1951), pp. 266–72.

**C23.21** "My College Days Part 1. Souvenirs of Those Hallowed, Mellow and Sainted Days at School," *Vanity Fair* 20, no. 4 (June 1923): 47, 98, 100. See also C11.1, C23.26, C23.30, and C23.33.

**C23.22** "With Anyone of Our 16 Greatest Actors," *Vancouver Sunday Sun*, 3 June 1923 ("Magazine"), p. 5. Syndicated by Metropolitan Newspaper Service, New York and Dodd and Mead. See also C17.2.

**C23.23** "With our Typical Novelists," *Vancouver Sunday Sun*, 17 June 1923 ("Magazine"), p. [4]. Syndicated by Metropolitan Newspaper Service, New York.

**C23.24** "Mr. Juggins Works Backward Through Life, Finishes Nothing, He's So Strong on Preparation," *Toronto Star Weekly*, 23 June 1923, p. 26. Illustrated by Kessler. Also as "Working Backwards Through a Life Career," *Vancouver Sunday Sun*, 24 June 1923 ("Magazine"), p. [4]. Syndicated by Metropolitan Newspaper Service, New York.

**C23.25** "Analyzing the Average Man," *Life* (London and New York) 81, no. 2,121, special Canadian no. (28 June 1923): 4. See also C25.39.

**C23.26** "My College Days: A Retrospect Part 2. Casual Reflections Upon the Oldest Living Graduate and Those Most Reluctant," *Vanity Fair* 20, no. 5 (July 1923): 53, 100. See also C11.11, C23.21, C23.30, and C23.33.

**C23.27** "The Drama As I See It: Studies in the Play and Films of Yesterday and To-day: VI. 'The Historical Drama,'" *Harper's Magazine* 147 (July 1923): 178–87. Illustrated by John Held, Jr. Also in *Maclean's Magazine* 36, no. 14 (15 July 1923): 14–5, 40–1, 44. Illustrated by C.W. Jefferys.

**C23.28** "Reading Greek Classic Headlines of Today," *Vancouver Sunday Sun*, 8 July 1923, ("Magazine"), p. 4. Syndicated by Metropolitan Newspaper Service, New York.

**C23.29** "To Nature and Back Again," *Vancouver Sunday Sun*, 29 July 1923, ("Magazine"), p. [4]. Syndicated by Metropolitan Newspaper Service, New York. Reprinted as "To Nature and Back Again: My Experiment in Living Without the Arts and Luxuries of Civilization; Why I Abandoned the Simple Life," *Sunday Mail* (Glasgow), 3 January 1926, p. 8. Syndicated. See also C17.16.

**C23.30** "My College Days: A Retrospect Part 3. Proposal for Our Children's Corner, with Divers Suggestions for Harmless Undergraduate Amusement," *Vanity Fair* 20, no. 6 (August 1923): 42. See also C11.1, C23.21, C23.26, and C23.33.

**C23.31** "My Interviewer," *Harper's Magazine* 147 (August 1923): 425–7. Illustrated by John Held, Jr.

**C23.32** "The British and the American Press," *Vancouver Sunday Sun*, 12 August 1923, ("Magazine"), p. 4. Syndicated by Metropolitan Newspaper Service, New York. See also C22.18.

**C23.33** "My College Days: A Retrospect; Conclusion. A Reflection Upon Traditions, with an Ideal Plan for Holiday Examinations," *Vanity Fair* 21, no. 1 (September 1923): 57, 102. See also C11.1, C23.21, C23.26, and C23.30.

**C23.34** "A Schoolmaster Known by His Lickings," *Vancouver Sunday Sun*, 9 September

1923, ("Magazine"), p. 4. Syndicated by Metropolitan Newspaper Service, New York. See also C19.23.

C23.35 "Gusto of Rounding up Rarities," *Vancouver Sunday Sun*, 23 September 1923, ("Magazine"), p. 4. Syndicated by Metropolitan Newspaper Service, New York.

C23.36 "Breaking the Social Ice," *Vancouver Sunday Sun*, 30 September 1923, ("Magazine"), p. [4]. Syndicated by Metropolitan Newspaper Service, New York.

C23.37 "Brain Power of the Sexes," *Vancouver Sunday Sun*, 28 October 1923, ("Magazine"), p. 4. Syndicated by Metropolitan Newspaper Service, New York.

C23.38 "The Dean's Dinner; Prexy Is Host, at a Lavish Commemorative Banquet, to the Faculty of Arts ," *Vanity Fair* 21, no. 3 (November 1923): 56, 96. Poem. See also C9.7.

C23.39 "Why They Drink in Scotland," *Vancouver Sunday Sun*, 11 November 1923, ("Magazine"), p. 4. Syndicated by Metropolitan Newspaper Service, New York. Reprinted as "Why They Drink in Scotland: Duty Provides an Impressive Variety of Reasons for Taking the National Liquid; on the Other Hand, England," *Sunday Mail* (Glasgow), 29 November 1925, p. 8.

C23.40 "Making Paris Understand You," *Vancouver Sunday Sun*, 18 November 1923, ("Magazine"), p. 4. Syndicated by Metropolitan Newspaper Service, New York.

C23.41 "Then and Now: The College News of Forty Years Ago and the College News of Today," *McGill News* 5, no. 1 (December 1923): 2–3. Syndicated by Metropolitan Newspaper Service, New York. Reprinted as "College News of Forty Years Ago and the College News of To-day; Instead of Wrecking Several Square Miles of the City the Meds on a Night Off Gather at the Y.W.C.A. Building to Sing Medical Hymns," *Toronto Star Weekly*, 19 January 1924, p. 36; as "College News of Then and College News Now," *Vancouver Sunday Sun*, 20 January 1924, ("Magazine"), p. 2. Illustrated by Kessler.

C23.42 "Today in History, Odes and Epodes Indited in Whimsical Commemoration of Famous and Infamous Historical Episodes," *Vanity Fair* 21, no. 4 (December 1923): 67. Poem. See also C10.10.

C23.43 "Business of Crowning a New Poet," *Vancouver Sunday Sun*, 2 December 1923, ("Magazine"), p. 4. Syndicated by Metropolitan Newspaper Service, New York.

C24.1 "The Proper Limitations of State Interference," *Empire Club Speeches* (1924): 109–23. The text of Leacock's speech in Toronto on 6 March 1924. The speech ends on p. 123; Sir Robert Falconer's thank you is on pp. 123–4. Reported as "World Must Return to Sane Capitalism; Prof. Leacock Warns of Drift Toward Abyss of Socialism. Meddling by State; Canada Suffering from Undue Repression, He Tells Empire Club," *Toronto Mail*, 7 March 1924, p. 5; "Men Should Speak Out; College Thought Subdued; Stephen Leacock Calls This 'Timid Age' — Veiled Reference to the O.T.A.," *Toronto Telegram*, 7 March 1924, p. 22; "Would Let Each Man Speak His Own Thoughts; Prof. Leacock Sees Safety-Valve in Freedom of Speech," *Toronto Globe*, 7 March 1924, p. 10. All reports have quotations. A critique of Leacock which includes quotations from the speech appears as "When Professor Leacock Is Serious," *Toronto Star*, 14 March 1924. See also E24.16.

C24.2 "Things Wanting at McGill; A Message to the Annual," *Old McGill 1925* 27 (1924): 30.

C24.3 "Today in History; Another Series of Heroic Addresses, Designed in Commemoration of Notable Events," *Vanity Fair* 21, no. 5 (January 1924): 47, 98. Poem. See also C10.10.

C24.4 "The Platter of Life," *Vancouver Sunday Sun*, 13 January 1924, ("Magazine"), p. 2. Syndicated by Metropolitan Newspaper Service, New York. Reprinted as "The Platter of Life: How Scenario-Makers Make Scenarios. First Thing Is to Get General Topic or Story. Take any Fairy Tale or Nursery Rhyme, Say Jack Spratt," *Montreal Standard*, 1 March 1924, final ed., p. 23. Illustrated by A.G. Racey.

C24.5 "The Secrets of Success," *Harper's Magazine* 148 (February 1924): 334–42. Illustrated by John Held, Jr. Apparently articles published in *Harper's* in 1924 appeared in *Gaiety* in England. See also C21.31.

C24.5a "Let Me Show You Our Town," *Vancouver Sunday Sun*, 3 February 1924, ("Magazine"), p. 2. Syndicated by Metropolitan Newspaper Service, New York.

C24.6 "A Manual of the New Mentality," *Harper's Magazine* 148 (March 1924): 471–80. Illustrated by John Held, Jr. Condensed as "Road Map of the New Mentality: Everybody's Mind Is Now Analyzed. Some of the Biggest Business Men Have Failed in the Intelligent Test and Have Been Ruined," *Montreal Standard*, 10 May 1924, final ed., p. 21; "A Road Map of the New Mentality. Progress of Human Mind Reduced to Decimals," *Hamilton Spectator*, 10 May 1924, p. [19]. Syndicated by Metropolitan Newspaper Service, New York.

C24.7 "Stephen Leacock Digs Up His Share of Little Glimpses of Great Lives. Has Discovered Some Obscure Stories Which Lift Curtain on Famous Personalities . . . ," *Toronto Star Weekly*, 1 March 1924, p. 22. Illustrated by Kessler. Reprinted as "Anecdotes Which Lift Curtain on Lives of Noted Personalities," *Vancouver Sunday Sun*, 16 March 1924, ("Magazine"), p. 2; as "Intimate Glimpses into Great Lives: Some Obscure Anecdotes Which Lift the Curtain from the Doings of Famous Personalities," *Montreal Standard*, 16 August 1924, morning ed., p. 35. Illustrated by A.G. Racey. Syndicated by Metropolitan Newspaper Service, New York.

C24.8 "People We Meet in Movies: Wherever One Sees the Pictured Vampire Woman It's Always the Lucky Nut Who Is With Her," *Montreal Standard*, 3 March 1924, final ed., p. 25. Illustrated by A.G. Racey. Syndicated by Metropolitan Newspaper Service, New York. See also C21.4.

C24.9 "Is Your Memory All Upside Down? Try Leacock's Fifty Cent System," *Toronto Star Weekly*, 8 March 1924, p. 28. Illustrated by Kessler.

C24.10 "Literature by the Pound: Snappy Book Selling," *Vancouver Sunday Sun*, 23 March 1924, ("Magazine"), p. 5. Syndicated by Metropolitan Newspaper Service, New York.

C24.11 "How to Be Your Own Napoleon: Vital Things Never Touched Upon by the Standard Histories Are to Be Found in Advertising Pages of Illustrated Weeklies," *Montreal Standard*, 29 March 1924, final ed., p. 21. Illustrated by A.G. Racey. Also as "How to Be Your Own Napoleon. Lessons in Life from the Advertising Column," *Hamilton Spectator*, 29 March 1924, p. [19]. Syndicated by Metropolitan Newspaper Service, New York. See also C24.15.

C24.12 "The Human Body — Its Care and Prevention," *Harper's Magazine* 148 (April 1924): 593–602. Illustrated by John Held, Jr.

C24.13 "Dead Men's Gold: Drama of Love and Adventure in a Desert in Which Love Triumphs and Twin Souls Join to Walk Life's Pathway Hand in Hand," *Montreal Standard*, 5 April 1924, final ed., p. 21. Illustrated by A.G. Racey. Syndicated by Metropolitan Newspaper Service, New York. See also C23.15 and C25.4.

C24.14 "On Winning the Championship in Woe. Oroastus, Greek Tragedy — As Presented in Our Colleges," *Hamilton Spectator*, 5 April 1924, p. [31]. Also as "Greek Drama Has Stomach Ache; King Howls While Chorus Groans; It's One Brick After Another — Until the King Moans, What's Going to Hit Me Next — Even His Doggies Sent to Hades," *Toronto Star Weekly*, 5 April 1924, p. 45. Both articles illustrated by Kessler. Syndicated by Metropolitan Newspaper Service, New York.

C24.15 "Historical Drama: About Once in Every Ten Years Some Actor, Intoxicated By Success, Decides That He Wants to Be Napoleon, and a New Napoleon Play is Produced," *Montreal Standard*, 12 April 1924, final ed., p. 27. Illustrated by A.G. Racey. Syndicated by Metropolitan Newspaper Service, New York. See also C24.11 and C24.22.

C24.16 "Wild Indian Life in the Canvas Woods. Where the Historical Drama Reaches Its Zenith, Out-Shakespearing Shakespeare," *Hamilton Spectator*, 12 April 1924, p. [15]. Syndicated by Metropolitan Newspaper Service, New York.

C24.17 "Over Hurdles to Success: Self-Taught Shoe-Magnate Demonstrates Vast Superiority of Business Character and Business Training to a College Education," *Montreal Standard*, 19 April 1924, final ed., p. 21. Illustrated by A.G. Racey. Also as "Over the Hurdles to Success. Self-Taught Shoe Magnate Demonstrates the Vast Superiority of Business Character to a College Education," *Hamilton Spectator*, 19 April 1924, p. [17]; "Squeeze Out the Shareholders and Marry the Boss' Daughter; Over the Hurdles to Success with a Self-Taught Shoe Merchant — Demonstration of Vast Superiority of Business Character to a College Education," *Toronto Star Weekly*, 19 April 1924, p. 41. Both the *Spectator* and the *Star Weekly* illustrated by Kessler. Syndicated by Metropolitan Newspaper Service, New York.

C24.18 "Life-Saving a la Mode: Dramatic Interlude Such as Is Presented Between Dances in Musical Revue Showing Hero and Heroine Adrift on a Raft," *Montreal Standard*, 26 April 1924, final ed., p. 21. Illustrated by A.G. Racey. Also as "Life-Saving a la Mode. Adrift on a Raft in the Middle of the Modern Stage," *Hamilton Spectator*, 26 April 1924, p. [28]. Syndicated by Metropolitan Newspaper Service, New York. Reprinted as "The Raft, an Interlude" in John Stevens, ed., *Ten Canadian Short Plays* (Toronto: Dell, 1975), pp. [13]-22.

C24.19 "Business As I See It," *Harper's Magazine* 148 (May 1924): 815–25. Illustrated by John Held, Jr.

C24.20 "Thoughtful Thinking of Animals: Mentality of the Hoopoo Scrutinized Like That of the Garden Worm and the Bengal Tiger," *Montreal Standard*, 17 May 1924, final ed., p. [21]. Illustrated by A.G. Racey; the drawing is of Leacock. Also as "Thoughtful Thinking of Some Animals. The Mentality of the Hoopoo Scrutinized Like That of the Garden Worm and the Bengal Tiger," *Hamilton Spectator*, 17 May 1924, p. [15]; "Thinking a Very Foolish Habit; Animals Gave It Up Long Ago; Mental Reactions and Complexes of the Hoopoo Scrutinized Like That of Those Garden Worms and the Bengal Tiger," *Toronto Star Weekly*, 17 May 1924, p. 22. Illustrated by Kessler. Syndicated by Metropolitan Newspaper Service, New York.

C24.21  "Putting Pep into One's Personality: Great New Movement to Increase One's Efficiency by Extending One's Self in All Directions and by Cultivating Cheerfulness," *Montreal Standard*, 31 May 1924, final ed., p. 21. Illustrated by A.G. Racey. Syndicated by Metropolitan Newspaper Service, New York. Also as "On Pepping Up Your Personality. The Great New Movement to Increase Your Efficiency in Mating and Money Making," *Hamilton Spectator*, 31 May 1924, p. [13].

C24.22  "The Personal Habits and Sayings of the Emperor Napoleon," *Harper's Magazine* 149 (June 1924): 126–7. See also C24.15 and C40.2.

C24.23  "Teaching the Unteachable," *Teacher's Magazine* (McGill University) 6 (June 1924): 13. Reprinted in *Monday Morning: Canada's Magazine for Professional Teachers* (Toronto) 4, no. 3 (November 1969): 26–7. This issue of *Monday Morning* also includes an article by Robertson Davies, "Leacock the Humorist, Leacock the Teacher," pp. 24–5 which contains one quotation by Leacock. The manuscript of Leacock's article is printed in facsimile in *McGill Journal of Education* 6, no. 1 (Spring 1971): [67–74].

C24.24  "Pruning a Promoter: Modern Method in a Business Study of Virtue Seasoned with Gumption and Common Sense," *Montreal Standard*, 14 June 1924, final ed., p. 19. Illustrated by A.G. Racey. Also as "Pruning a Promoter. The Modern Mode in a Business Story of Virtue Seasoned with Gumption," *Hamilton Spectator*, 14 June 1924, p. [11]. Syndicated by Metropolitan Newspaper Service, New York.

C24.25  "Foolishness of Feeding: In Relation to the Marvelous Achievement of Science in Discovering a Perfect Breakfast Food," *Montreal Standard*, 21 June 1924, final ed., p. 19. Illustrated by A.G. Racey. Also as "The Foodlessness of our Feeding. As Against the Latest Triumph of Science, Appetiteless Eating," *Hamilton Spectator*, 21 June 1924, p. [26]. Syndicated by Metropolitan Newspaper Service, New York.

C24.26  "The Urge of Exercise: What History Would Have Missed If the Modern Upkeep of the Body Had Been in Vogue," *Montreal Standard*, 28 June 1924, final ed., p. 19. Illustrated by A.G. Racey. Also as "Stephen Leacock Discovers Great Secrets of Endless Life and Perpetual Youth; The Urge of Exercise — What History Would Have Missed If the Modern Upkeep of Body Had Been in Vogue," *Toronto Star Weekly*, 28 June 1924, p. 28. Illustrated by Kessler. Syndicated by Metropolitan Newspaper Service, New York.

C24.27  "Alfred of the Advertisements — A Romance in the Manner of the Art and Heart Pages of the Magazine," *Montreal Standard*, 5 July 1924, final ed., p. 19. Illustrated by A.G. Racey. Syndicated by Metropolitan Newspaper Service, New York.

C24.28  "Methuselah's Fish Stories: A Reel of Those Tried and True Narrations Which Have Survived the Passing of Ages and the Fall of Empires," *Montreal Standard*, 12 July 1924, morning ed., p. 19. Illustrated by A.G. Racey. Syndicated by Metropolitan Newspaper Service, New York. Reprinted as "The Humour of Serious Things. Methuselah's Fish Stories. A Reel of Those Tried and True Narrations Which Have Survived the Passing of the Ages and the Fall of Empires," *Times and Mirror* (Bristol), 13 December 1924, p. 14. Also as "The Humour of Serious Things. Methuselah's Fish Stories. Tales That Never Wear Out," *Gazette* (Birmingham), 15 December 1924, p. 4; "The Humour of Serious Things (III) Methuseleh's Fish Stories. A Reel of Those Tried and True Narrations Which Have Survived the Passing of Ages and the Fall of Empires," *Gazette* (West Sussex), 18 December 1924, p. 6.

**C24.29** "More Respectable God-Fearing Citizens Fall Before Insidious Scotch Lure of Golf," *Toronto Star Weekly*, 19 July 1924, p. 29. Illustrated by Kessler. See also C21.20

**C24.30** "Following the Flicker: Madeline of the Movies Takes Part in a Thrilling Drama Played Back in the Woods," *Montreal Standard*, 26 July 1924, final ed., p. 19. Illustrated by A.G. Racey. Reprinted as " 'Shoot and Shoot to Kill,' Said the Inspector; 'Madeline of the Movies' Done into Words; Stephen Leacock Follows the Flicker — Thinks He Was Born Too Soon to Understand Moving Pictures — Remembers the Good Old Days When Magic Lantern Gave Robinson Crusoe Six Scenes," *Toronto Star Weekly*, 6 September 1924, Magazine Sec., Part 1, p. 23. Illustrated by Kessler. Syndicated by Metropolitan Newspaper Service, New York. See also C15.26.

**C24.31** "Taking Their Money and Making Them Like It," *Montreal Standard*, 2 August 1924, final ed., p. [35]. Illustrated by A.G. Racey. Also as "Salesmen — Gain the Figure of Venus DeMilo; Secrets for Charming Money from People," *Toronto Star Weekly*, 16 August 1924, p. 26. Illustrated by Kessler. Syndicated by Metropolitan Newspaper Service, New York.

**C24.32** "Peanut-Roasters in Convention," *Montreal Standard*, 9 August 1924, morning ed., p. 35. Illustrated by A.G. Racey. Syndicated by Metropolitan Newspaper Service, New York.

**C24.33** "Ultra-Ult of Modern Drama: an Up-to-Date Play (Period 1924) in Which a Man and Woman Both Trying to Find Themselves Find One Another," *Montreal Standard*, 23 August 1924, final ed., p. [34]. Syndicated by Metropolitan Newspaper Service, New York. See also C23.11.

**C24.34** "Putting Pep into Public Notices: Applying the Principles of Modern Punch to Poetry and Public Instruction," *Montreal Standard*, 30 August 1924, final ed., p. [25].

**C24.35** " 'State Salary,' " *Collier's* 74 (30 August 1924): 19.

**C24.36** "Pity the Poor Humorist: Audiences Pay Thirteen Cents Each to Hear Him, and They Don't Listen When They Don't Pay," *Montreal Standard*, 6 September 1924, final ed., p. 33. Illustrated by A.G. Racey. Syndicated by Metropolitan Newspaper Service, New York. Reprinted as "When the Lecturer's Emotions Fry," *Los Angeles Times*, Sunday Magazine, 16 November 1924, p. 19. Illustrated by Kessler.

**C24.37** "Perfect Lover's Guide: A New Manuel [sic] of Love for Beginners Based Upon Current Literature Dealing with Love, Courtship and Marriage," *Montreal Standard*, 13 September 1924, morning ed., p. [29]; final ed., p. 33. In the final edition, the spelling of "Manuel" was corrected to "Manual". Illustrated by A.G. Racey. Syndicated by Metropolitan Newspaper Service, New York.

**C24.38** "Etiquette of Courtship: A Guide for Lads and Lasses Who Desire to Master the Technique of Dealing with the Emotions," *Montreal Standard*, 20 September 1924, morning ed., p. [29]; final ed., p. 33. Illustrated by A.G. Racey. Syndicated by Metropolitan Newspaper Service, New York.

**C24.39** "Tangled Problems of Love: As Straightened Out in the Correspondence Department Manual on Courtship and Marriage," *Montreal Standard*, 27 September 1924, morning ed., p. [29]; final ed., p. 33. Illustrated by A.G. Racey. Syndicated by Metropolitan Newspaper Service, New York.

**C24.40** "Physiological Philip: Romance of an Ardent Young Man Revealed in Language of Our Latest Fiction Writers," *Montreal Standard*, 4 October 1924, final ed., p. 33. Illustrated by A.G. Racey. Syndicated by Metropolitan Newspaper Service, New York.

**C24.41** "The Rush to the Colleges," *McGill Daily*, literary supplement 1, no. 1 (8 October 1924): 1–2. Reprinted as "Why Students Are Crowding College; Today's Conception of College Training Is Utilitarian One. . . . ," *Montreal Daily Star*, 22? October 1924. See also C25.9.

**C24.42** "Mother's Birthday: Our Manner of Celebrating the Great Day, As Related by a Member of the Family," *Montreal Standard*, 11 October 1924, final ed., p. 33. Illustrated by A.G. Racey. Syndicated by Metropolitan Newspaper Service, New York. Reprinted as "The Humour of Serious Things. Article No. 2. How We Kept Mother's Birthday: As Related by One of the Family," *Times and Mirror* (Bristol), 6 December 1924, p. 14. Also in *Gazette* (Birmingham), 9 December 1924, p. 4; as "The Humour of Serious Things (II) How We Kept Mother's Birthday. As Related by a Member of the Family," *Gazette* (West Sussex), 11 December 1924, p. 16; as "All Up for Mother's Day," *Edmonton Bulletin*, 13 May 1939, p. 8. Syndicated by Miller Services Ltd. as part of series. Condensed as "How We Kept Mother's Day," in *The Bedside Book of Laughter* (London: Reader's Digest, n.d.), pp. 115–8; in *Reader's Digest* 56, no. 337 (May 1950): 99–100; in *Reader's Digest* 78 (May 1961): 216; in *Reader's Digest* (Canadian) 146, no. 877 (May 1995): 31–4, illustrated by Jean-François Vachon. Reprinted as "How We Kept Mother's Day As Related by a Member of the Family," in Helen Hoke, ed., *The Family Book of Humor* (Garden City, New York: Doubleday, 1957), pp. 2–5; as "How We Kept Mother's Day," in Thomas B. Costain and John Beecroft, selectors, *30 Stories to Remember* (Garden City, New York: Doubleday, 1962), pp. 216–8; in Florence A. Harris, ed., *A Packet of Prose* (Toronto: McClelland and Stewart, 1967), pp. 130–4; in Jack Hodgins and William H. New, eds., *Voice and Vision* (Toronto: McClelland and Stewart, 1972), pp. 90–2.

**C24.43** "Living in a Modern Hotel: Acting As if to the Menu Born in a Modern Victuals Emporium," *Montreal Standard*, 18 October 1924, final ed., p. 33. Illustrated by A.G. Racey. Syndicated by Metropolitan Newspaper Service, New York. Reprinted as "The Humour of Serious Things. Living in an Hotel: Acting As if to the Menu Born in a Modern Victuals Emporium," *Times and Mirror* (Bristol), 29 November 1924, p. 14. Also as "The Humour of Serious Things (1). Life in an Hotel. How to Treat the Head Waiter," *Gazette* (Birmingham), 1 December 1924, p. 1; "The Humour of Serious Things (I) Living in an Hotel," *Gazette* (West Sussex), 4 December 1924, p. 6.

**C24.44** "The National Menace of the Golf Ball: A Call to All Good Men and True to Make a Last Heroic Stand," *Hamilton Spectator*, 18 October 1924, p. [32]. Syndicated by Metropolitan Newspaper Service, New York.

**C24.45** "Little Glimpses of the Future: Where Things Will Eventually Head in Unless Headed Off," *Montreal Standard*, 25 October 1924, final ed., p. 33. Illustrated by A.G. Racey. Syndicated by Metropolitan Newspaper Service, New York. See also C20.5 and C20.10.

**C24.46** "Such Fine Murders We're Having!: 'What,' Asks This Moralist, 'Is the Effect on Our Minds and Characters of the Everlasting Dwelling Upon Crime?'" *Collier's* 74, no. 18 (1 November 1924): 16, 37. Illustrated by Stuart Hay.

C24.47 "Russian Drama, Old and New: Mellow Charm of Bewhiskered Foregrounds, with an Incidental Accompaniment of Gas and Gurgle," *Montreal Standard*, 1 November 1924, final ed., p. 23. Illustrated by A.G. Racey. Syndicated by Metropolitan Newspaper Service, New York. Reprinted as "The Humour of Serious Things (V) Russian Drama Old and New. Mellow Charm of Bewhiskered Foregrounds with the Incidental Accompaniment of Gasp and Gurgle,"*Gazette* (West Sussex), 1 January 1925, p. 6. Also in *Times and Mirror* (Bristol), 3 January 1925, p. 14; *Gazette* (Birmingham), 5 January 1925, p. 4.

C24.48 "The Give and Take of Travel: Experience of an Absent-Minded Traveller During His Railway Journeys and His Stay in Hotels," *Montreal Standard*, 15 November 1924, final ed., p. 23. Illustrated by A.G. Racey. Syndicated by Metropolitan Newspaper Service, New York. Reprinted as "The Give and Take of Travel," in Lawrence Lariar, ed., *Happy Holiday: A Traveler's Treasury of Humorous Writings and Cartoons* (New York: Dodd, Mead, 1956), pp. 88–92; as "Travel: A Study in Petty Larceny, Pro and Con," in Alex Wilson and Ralph L. Curry, eds., *The Leacock Festival of Humour Annual* (Orillia, Ont.: The Leacock Festival of Humour Foundation, 1975), vol. 1, pp. [1–3].

C24.49 "Randolph Ketchum Jones," *Financial Post* (Toronto) 18, no. 47 (21 November 1924): 10.

C24.50 "John Smith, You and Me: Lives of Great Men All Remind Us of the Great Unwritten Biography," *Montreal Standard*, 22 November 1924, p. 41. Illustrated by A.G. Racey. Syndicated by Metropolitan Newspaper Service, New York.

C24.51 "Frizzing Up the Indoor Game: Some Suggestions for Putting a Little Voltage into a Winter's Evening's Pastimes," *Montreal Standard*, 29 November 1924, final ed., p. 23. Illustrated by A.G. Racey. Syndicated by Metropolitan Newspaper Service, New York.

C24.52 "The Outlines of Everything: Designed for Busy People at Their Busiest and Especially Adapted for the Kansas Public Schools," *College Humor* 3, no. 5 (December 1924): 9–10. See also C25.7, C25.10, and C26.17.

C24.53 "Extracting the Pith from Poetry: Getting Down to Brass Tacks, Hard Pan, and Rock Bottom of Lyric Art," *Montreal Standard*, 6 December 1924, final ed., p. 23. Illustrated by A.G. Racey. Syndicated by Metropolitan Newspaper Service, New York.

C24.54 "Our Own Business Barometer: If You Want a Really Good Forecast Don't Bother With All the Statistics and the Index Numbers and Averages. Go Get Your Fortune Told in the Good Old-Fashioned Way," *Montreal Standard*, 13 December 1924, final ed., p. 23. Illustrated by A.G. Racey. Reprinted as "A Barometer of Our Own Business: An Accurate Foretaste for the Whole World," *Hamilton Spectator*, 27 December 1924, p. 12. Syndicated by Metropolitan Newspaper Service, New York.

C24.55 "The Christmas Ghost: How the Pinch of Unemployment Has Extended to One of the Most Venerable Institutions," *Montreal Standard*, 20 December 1924, final ed., p. [29]. Illustrated by A.G. Racey. Also as "The Christmas Ghost: How the Pinch of Unemployment Has Extended to One of the Most Venerable Holiday Institutions," *Hamilton Spectator*, 20 December 1924, p. 4. Syndicated by Metropolitan Newspaper Service, New York. Also as "The Humour of Serious Things. The Christmas Ghost. Is He to Be Crowded Out?" *Gazette* (Birmingham), 24 December 1924, p. 4; as "The Humour of Serious Things. The Christmas Ghost. How the Pinch of Unemployment Has Extended to One of the Most Venerable Holiday Institutions," *Times and Mirror* (Bristol), 27 December

1924, p. 12; in *Gazette* (West Sussex), 8 January 1925, p. 6. See also C19.27.

C24.56 "Round Our City: A Lecture on the Fourth Dimension at the Ladies' Culture Club," *Montreal Standard*, 27 December 1924, final ed., p. 27. Illustrated by A.G. Racey. Reprinted in *Hamilton Spectator*, 3 January 1925, p. 21. Syndicated by Metropolitan Newspaper Service, New York.

C25.1 "On the Continued Progress of McGill University," *Old McGill 1926* 28 (1925): 56. See also A112.

C25.2 "Bygone Education and Radio," *Radio, The Wireless Quarterly* 1 (1 January 1925): 6–7. Lengthy extracts of the article are reprinted in K51.2.

C25.3 "Cross-Word Conversation: What Is Happening to the Language Under Our Very Ears," *Montreal Standard*, 3 January 1925, final ed., p. 27. Illustrated by A.G. Racey. Syndicated by Metropolitan Newspaper Service, New York.

C25.4 "A Throbbing Thrill in the Screenland: 'Dead Men's Gold' — a Movie After the Fan's Own Heart," *Montreal Standard*, 10 January 1925, final ed., p. 27. Illustrated by A.G. Racey. Syndicated by Metropolitan Newspaper Service, New York. See also C23.15 and C24.13.

C25.5 "How My Wife and I Built Our Home for $4.90," *Maclean's Magazine* 38, no. 2 (15 January 1925): 7, 55. Illustrated by C.W. Jefferys. Reprinted in *Cosmopolitan* 78, no. 2 (February 1925): 38–9, illustrated by Tony Sarg; as "How We Built Our Home for $4.90: Related in the Manner of the Best Models in the Magazine," *Montreal Standard*, 11 April 1925, final ed., p. 23, illustrated by A.G. Racey. Syndicated by Metropolitan Newspaper Service, New York. Reprinted as "How My Wife and I Built Our Home for $4.90," *Harrowsmith* 14, no. 85 (May/June 1989): 88–93, illustrated by John Bianchi.

C25.6 "Last Words on Shakespeare: Mystery of Bard's Life Finally Cleared Up," *Sunday Pictorial* (London), 18 January 1925, p. 7.

C25.7 "Outline of Shakespeare: Designed for Busy Men at Their Busiest and for Students Who Wish to Memorize the Poet's Characteristics," *Montreal Standard*, 24 January 1925, final ed., p. 27. Illustrated by A.G. Racey. Syndicated by Metropolitan Newspaper Service, New York. Apparently in *College Humor* (December 1924). See also C24.52 and C25.6.

C25.8 "New Attaboy Language: Sparks from the Twentieth Century Tongue Contrasted with the English of Macaulay or Gibbon," *Montreal Standard*, 31 January 1925, final ed., p. 27. Illustrated by A.G. Racey. Syndicated by Metropolitan Newspaper Service, New York.

C25.9 "The Rush to the Colleges; Its 'Why' and — Which is More Important — Its 'Whither,'" *Vanity Fair* 23, no. 6 (February 1925): 29. See also C24.41.

C25.10 "The Outlines of Everything: Specially Revised to Suit Everybody. II. The Theory of Evolution," *College Humor* 4, no. 1 (February 1925): 41–2, 111. See also C24.52, C25.7, and C26.17.

C25.11 "Family Pride: The Unsolved Secret of Lord Oxhead," *Montreal Standard*, 7 February 1925, final ed., p. 36. Illustrated by A.G. Racey. Syndicated by Metropolitan Newspaper Service, New York.

C25.12 "The Laundry Problem: The Washerwoman Is Gone Now; but That Humble Woman Would Be Welcomed Back," *Montreal Standard*, 21 February 1925, final ed., p. 36. Syndicated by Metropolitan Newspaper Service, New York. Lomer (p. 98) records

"The Laundry Problem," in B.A. Hendrick, ed., *Familiar Essays of Today* (New York: 1930), pp. 235–42.

C25.13 "Œsophagus Islands and Elsewhere: A Discussion of Charles Darwin, as Set Forth in His Great Book," *Montreal Standard*, 28 February 1925, final ed., p. 36. Illustrated by A.G. Racey. Syndicated by Metropolitan Newspaper Service, New York.

C25.14 "Seventeen and a Half Million? — I'll Give it All," *McGill Daily*, 4 March 1925, p. 4. Undated letter to the University of Chicago regarding fund raising. Reprinted in K70.3, pp. 144–6.

C25.15 "The Questionnaire Nuisance: Only Remedy Is to Try to Form a League of Grown-Up People Who Refuse to Be Investigated," *Montreal Standard*, 7 March 1925, final ed., p. 36. Illustrated by A.G. Racey. Syndicated by Metropolitan Newspaper Service, New York.

C25.16 "This Expiring World: Everything Seems to Be Declining Even Statesman as a Class Are Done," *Montreal Standard*, 14 March 1925, final ed., p. 26. Illustrated by A.G. Racey. Syndicated by Metropolitan Newspaper Service, New York.

C25.17 "Spring Wedding Problems: Accident of Past Impels the Standard's Humorist to Write on Coming Bridal Season," *Montreal Standard*, 21 March 1925, final ed., p. 33. Illustrated by A.G. Racey. Syndicated by Metropolitan Newspaper Service, New York.

C25.18 "Delaying the Parting Guest: Sad Case of Young Curate Who Did Not Know When to Say 'Good-Night,'" *Montreal Standard*, 28 March 1925, final ed., p. 20. Illustrated by A.G. Racey. Syndicated by Metropolitan Newspaper Service, New York.

C25.19 "Describes First Lessons in Riding a Horse: An Important Essential Is to Keep One's Feet in the Pedals," *Montreal Standard*, 4 April 1925, final ed., p. 20. Syndicated by Metropolitan Newspaper Service, New York.

C25.20 "My Pink Georgette Suit: My Friends All Agreed That the Color Was Just Lovely and Said They Were Crazy to Get One Like Mine," *Montreal Standard*, 18 April 1925, final ed., p. 31. Syndicated by Metropolitan Newspaper Service, New York.

C25.21 "The Merry Month of May: A Modernized Version of the Old Style Almanac," *Montreal Standard*, 25 April 1925, final ed., p. 20. Illustrated by A.G. Racey. Syndicated by Metropolitan Newspaper Service, New York.

C25.22 "Words of Royal Wisdom: As Dropped from Continental Lips Which Can Speak English as Fluently as Chinese," *Montreal Standard*, 2 May 1925, final ed., p. 20. Syndicated by Metropolitan Newspaper Service, New York.

C25.23 "The Efficiency Epidemic: The Appalling Mania for Work and the Moot Problem of an Empty Stomach or an Empty Head," *Montreal Standard*, 9 May 1925, final ed., p. 20. Illustrated by A.G. Racey. Syndicated by Metropolitan Newspaper Service, New York.

C25.24 "What About a New Car? The Secret of Auto Contentment Is Sedulously to Know Nothing — but to Speak Fluently — of Innards," *Montreal Standard*, 16 May 1925, final ed., p. [20]. Illustrated by A.G. Racey. Syndicated by Metropolitan Newspaper Service, New York.

C25.25 "The Place of History in Canadian Education," *Canadian Historical Association* (report of the Annual Meeting held in the City of Montreal), 21–3 May 1925: 33–4.

C25.26 "— And Humors of War," *Collier's* 75, no. 22 (30 May 1925): 11, 38. Illustrated by Ray Rohn.

C25.27 "Plight of Over-Bidden Guest: From Toils of Summer Hospitality a Desperate Stroke for Freedom," *Montreal Standard*, 30 May 1925, final ed., p. 20. Illustrated by A.G. Racey. Syndicated by Metropolitan Newspaper Service, New York.

C25.28 "Why Men Leave Home: The Call of the Wild Pamphlet and Its Effect on Sedentary Knee-Caps," *Montreal Standard*, 6 June 1925, final ed., p. 20. Illustrated by A.G. Racey. Syndicated by Metropolitan Newspaper Service, New York.

C25.29 "My 24 Hour Visit to the South: Impressions of Southern Life, Character and Industry," *Montreal Standard*, 13 June 1925, final ed., p. 20. Syndicated by Metropolitan Newspaper Service, New York.

C25.30 "The Photographer Does His Best: And When He Had Done That Is Asked to Keep Picture for Himself and Friends," *Montreal Standard*, 20 June 1925, final ed., p. 20. Illustrated by A.G. Racey. Syndicated by Metropolitan Newspaper Service, New York. See also C13.9.

C25.31 "Painless Pedantry: New Wrinkles in the Education of the Bright Young Thing, et al.," *Montreal Standard*, 11 July 1925, final ed., p. 29. Illustrated by A.G. Racey. Syndicated by Metropolitan Newspaper Service, New York.

C25.32 "The Art of Un-Telling a Story: In the Flitful Footsteps of Mr. Yarner, as He Backs His Way Around the World," *Montreal Standard*, 18 July 1925, final ed., p. [31]. Illustrated by A.G. Racey. Syndicated by Metropolitan Newspaper Service, New York. See also C14.11.

C25.33 "Slams Across the Sea: 'The American Girl's Shortcomings,' Says Lady V., 'May Be Due to Her Habit of Chewing Tobacco.' And That's That," *Collier's* 76, no. 3 (18 July 1925): 16, 34. Illustrated by Ray Rohn. Reprinted as "Slams Across the Sea; 'The American Girl's Shortcomings,' Says Lady V, 'May Be Due to Her Habit of Chewing Tobacco,'" *Orillia News-Letter*, 4 September 1929, p. 12. Syndicated by Metropolitan Newspaper Service, New York.

C25.34 "The Everlasting Angler. A Reel of Fish Stories for Summer Use," *Humorist* 7, no. 125 (25 July 1925): 16–7. Apparently this story was syndicated on 25 May 1924.

C25.35 "First Call for Next War! Visiting Generals, Counts, Sea Dogs, and Chemists Show What Will Not Be Left of Us," *Montreal Standard*, 25 July 1925, final ed., p. 31.

C25.36 "All Aboard for Europe! Some Humble Advice to Travellers About the Ups and Downs of an Ocean Voyage," *Montreal Standard*, 8 August 1925, final ed., p. [26]. Illustrated by A.G. Racey. Syndicated by Metropolitan Newspaper Service, New York.

C25.37 "'Song of the Shirt; Applying the Latest Principles of Chinks — Analysis to the Venerable Theme of the Poet," *Montreal Standard*, 15 August 1925, final ed., p. [29]. Illustrated by A.G. Racey. Syndicated by Metropolitan Newspaper Service, New York.

C25.38 "When a Man Spreads Himself: The Exceedingly Active Ownership of a Proprietor Afflicted with 'Expanded Personality,'" *Montreal Standard*, 22 August 1925, final ed., p. 39. Illustrated by A.G. Racey. Syndicated by Metropolitan Newspaper Service, New York.

C25.39 "The Average Man — Can You Identify the Picture?" *Montreal Standard*, 29 August 1925, final ed., p. 30. Illustrated by A.G. Racey. Syndicated by Metropolitan Newspaper Service, New York. Reprinted as "The Average Man," *Lilliput* 1, no. 4 (October 1937): 7–8. Reprinted as "Stephen Leacock's 'Average Man,'" *Toronto Star Weekly*," 18 December 1937, p. 5.

C25.40  "As the Cat Jumps: A Lesson in French Politics for Beginners," *Collier's* 76, no. 9 (29 August 1925): 23. Illustrated by Ray Rohn. Reprinted as "As the Cat Jumps; A Lesson in French Politics in Paris," *Passing Show* 24, no. 624 (7 August 1926): 22–3.

C25.41  "The Mother of Parliaments: What's Wrong Lately with Mother?" *Harper's Magazine* 151 (September 1925): 418–9. Condensed as "Mother of Parliaments: And What's Wrong Lately with Mother," *Montreal Standard*, 14 November 1925, final ed., p. [30]. Illustrated by A.G. Racey. Syndicated by Metropolitan Newspaper Service, New York.

C25.42  "Summer Sorrows of Super-Rich: Those Desperate Problems Which Seem to Make a Life of Luxury Not Worth Living," *Montreal Standard*, 5 September 1925, final ed., p. 26. Illustrated by A.G. Racey. Syndicated by Metropolitan Newspaper Service, New York. Reprinted as "The Sorrows of a Summer Guest," *Famous Story Magazine* 1 (October 1925): 97–102. See also C17.15.

C25.43  "Tangled Lives: Model Novel Submitted for the Ten Thousand Dollar Prize Offered by Big Publishing House," *Montreal Standard*, 12 September 1925, final ed., p. 30. Illustrated by A.G. Racey. Syndicated by Metropolitan Newspaper Service, New York.

C25.44  "New Light from Light Minds: When You Want to Learn Something Ask Those Who Don't Know. The Idea Is Simple and Should Have Been Thought of Before," *Collier's* 76, no. 11 (12 September 1925): 15. See also C26.6

C25.45  "Back to Work: Everybody's Doing It — But This Is to Investigate — A Movement to the Contrary," *Montreal Standard*, 19 September 1925, final ed., p. 26.

C25.46  "As the Man with the Hoe: Looking Back Across a Summer of Agricultural Intensity," *Montreal Standard*, 26 September 1925, final ed., p. [30]. Illustrated by A.G. Racey. Syndicated by Metropolitan Newspaper Service, New York.

C25.47  "Information While You Eat; What Gets to Hard-Listening Members of Luncheon Club Through Static of Mid-Day Fellowship," *Montreal Standard*, 3 October 1925, final ed., p. 30. Illustrated by A.G. Racey. Syndicated by Metropolitan Newspaper Service, New York.

C25.48  "Stampede to the Colleges: A Few Words without Music on the Modern Educational System of Putting Fees in a Slot to Draw out a Salary," *Montreal Standard*, 10 October 1925, final ed., p. 30. Illustrated by A.G. Racey. Syndicated by Metropolitan Newspaper Service, New York.

C25.49  "Have We Got the Year Backwards? First Peep of Oyster from Half-Shell and First Bright Flush of Broiled Lobster Among Reasons Why Autumn Should Begin It," *Montreal Standard*, 17 October 1925, final ed., p. 31. Illustrated by A.G. Racey. Syndicated by Metropolitan Newspaper Service, New York.

C25.50  "Back from Europe: Does Travel Derange the Mind?" *Montreal Standard*, 24 October 1925, final ed., p. [35]. Illustrated by A.G. Racey. Syndicated by Metropolitan Newspaper Service, New York.

C25.51  "Vehicle for Literary Expression Is Needed at McGill," *McGill Daily*, 28 October 1925, p. 1.

C25.52  "When Cave Man Meets Cave Man; Solving a Problem That the Movies Like to Film in the Way the Rock-Throwers of the Old Days Would Have Done It," *Toronto Star Weekly*, 31 October 1925, p. 21. Syndicated by Metropolitan Newspaper Service, New York. See also C23.13.

C25.53  "Speaking of Insurance Agents: How I Became Initiated into the Charms of Legal Phraseology," *Sunday Mail* (Glasgow), 15 November 1925, p. 6.

C25.54  "The Flight of College Time," *McGill Fortnightly Review* 1, no. 1 (21 November 1925): 3.

C25.55  "If at First You Don't Succeed, Quit at Once," *Montreal Standard*, 28 November 1925, final ed., p. 30. Illustrated by A.G. Racey. Syndicated by Metropolitan Newspaper Service, New York.

C25.56  "The Children's Column: Up-to-Date, as Compared with That of the More or Less Good Old Days," *Montreal Standard*, 5 December 1925, final ed., p. 30. Illustrated by A.G. Racey. Syndicated by Metropolitan Newspaper Service, New York. Reprinted as "The Children's Column (Up-to-Date)," *Passing Show* 23, no. 608 (10 April 1926): 24–5. See also C1.1 and C26.43.

C25.57  "The Flip-Flops of Fate: The Little Knocks of Opportunity and the Little Nicks of the Needy," *Montreal Standard*, 12 December 1925, final ed., p. 32. Illustrated by A.G. Racey. Syndicated by Metropolitan Newspaper Service, New York.

C25.58  "Jazzing Up Education: Aids to Teaching Which Import a Charm to Dry-as-Dust Scholarship," *Sunday Mail* (Glasgow), 13 December 1925, p. 10.

C25.59  "A Concentrated Christmas: The Efficiency Touch Applied to the Glad Season," *Montreal Standard*, 19 December 1925, final ed., p. 36. Illustrated by A.G. Racey. Syndicated by Metropolitan Newspaper Service, New York.

C25.60  "The Gasoline Goodbye: And What Would Have Happened to the Big Moments of History if the Motor Had Taken a Hand in Them," *Montreal Standard*, 26 December 1925, final ed., p. 28. Illustrated by A.G. Racey. Syndicated by Metropolitan Newspaper Service, New York.

C26.1  "The Transit of Venus," *Good Housekeeping* 82 (January 1926): 78–81, 151–5. Illustrated by T. D. Skidmore. Reprinted in Malcolm Ross and John Stevens, eds., *Images of Man* (Toronto: J.M. Dent, 1966), pp. 237–54. According to Lomer (p. 138), this was reprinted in L.W. Smith, ed., *Short Stories for English Classics* (Philadelphia: [1929]), pp. 170–90.

C26.2  "An Advance Cable System: All the European Cables for the Next Three Weeks," *Montreal Standard*, 2 January 1926, final ed., p. 26. Illustrated by A.G. Racey. Syndicated by Metropolitan Newspaper Service, New York. Reprinted as "Our Advance Cable System; Why Worry About Newspapers? We Can Give You the World's News in Advance, and Put You Wise to All the Happenings Long Before They Happen," *Passing Show* 24, no. 630 (18 September 1926): 18–9.

C26.3  "Three Strikes and Out: Recent Pages Extracted from the Diary of a Consumer," *Montreal Standard*, 9 January 1926, final ed., p. 36. Illustrated by A.G. Racey. Syndicated by Metropolitan Newspaper Service, New York.

C26.4  "Throwing Down the Uplift: When Professional Beggars Lose Their Wooden Legs and Cyrian Camel Drivers Are Jobless Someone Has to Foot the Bill. Here's One Who Won't," *Collier's* 77, no. 2 (9 January 1926): 22, 45. Illustrated by Ray Rohn. Reprinted as "Throwing Down the Uplift: I Decide to Forego the Luxury of Being Pan-Handled De Luxe," *Montreal Standard*, 27 March 1926, final ed., p. 36. Illustrated by A.G. Racey. Syndicated by Metropolitan Newspaper Service, New York.

**C26.5** "French Politics for Beginners: Why Not Roll Your Own, Like This. My Personal Interpretation of Recent and Possible Developments," *Montreal Standard*, 16 January 1926, final ed., p. [36]. Illustrated by A.G. Racey. Syndicated by Metropolitan Newspaper Service, New York.

**C26.6** "New Light from New Minds: When You Want to Learn Something, Ask Those Who Don't Know," *Montreal Standard*, 23 January 1926, final ed., p. [30]. Illustrated by A.G. Racey. Syndicated by Metropolitan Newspaper Service, New York. Reprinted as "New Light from Light Minds; When You Want to Learn Something Ask Those Who Don't Know," *Passing Show* 24, no. 625 (14 August 1926): 12. See also C25.44.

**C26.7** "[Statement on the Death of His Wife,]" in "McGill Is at Work, But Not In Lead-Solution," *Toronto Telegram*, 23 January 1926, p. [21]. This newspaper report contains the text of a statement Leacock issued to the Canadian Press, clarifying that his wife did not receive treatment for cancer in Liverpool as had been previously reported. Also in "No Cancer Treatment Was Given to Mrs. Leacock; Patient Was Too Weak to Receive Treatment at Liverpool, Is Statement," *Toronto Globe*, 23 January 1926.

**C26.8** "First Aid to Conversation: A Simple Lesson in How to Shine as an Evening Star," *Montreal Standard*, 6 February 1926, final ed., p. [36]. Illustrated by A.G. Racey. Syndicated by Metropolitan Newspaper Service, New York.

**C26.9** "On Debates at Colleges," *McGill Daily*, 6 February 1926, p. 2. Apparently also in *McGill Fortnightly Review* 1 (16 February 1926): 47–8.

**C26.10** "Come Down the Taxes: But Who Gets Out from Under?" *Montreal Standard*, 13 February 1926, final ed., p. 36. Illustrated by A.G. Racey. Syndicated by Metropolitan Newspaper Service, New York.

**C26.11** "The Prophecy Business: Is a Useful Old Profession Falling into Neglect?" *Montreal Standard*, 20 February 1926, final ed., p. 36. Illustrated by A.G. Racey. Syndicated by Metropolitan Newspaper Service, New York.

**C26.12** "Drawing Room Pests: Man with Card Trick," *Montreal Standard*, 27 February 1926, final ed., p. [36]. Illustrated by A.G. Racey. Syndicated by Metropolitan Newspaper Service, New York.

**C26.13** "The Work of the Universities," *Institute Bulletin* (Ottawa) 4, no. 3 (March 1926): 2–8. The text of Leacock's address to a joint luncheon of the Professional Institute of the Civil Service of Canada and the Ottawa Valley Graduates Society of McGill University held at the Chateau Laurier in Ottawa on 23 February 1926. See also D26.1 and E26.1.

**C26.14** "How I Raised My Own Salary: Applying the Promulgated Principles of Hitting Your Work Like a Bullet and Out-Sprinting the Clock," *Montreal Standard*, 6 March 1926, final ed., p. 36. Illustrated by A.G. Racey. Syndicated by Metropolitan Newspaper Service, New York. Reprinted as "How I Raised My Own Salary; What to Do When Your Employer Does Not Appreciate Your Value to the Firm," *Passing Show* 24, no. 627 (28 August 1926): 18–9.

**C26.15** "How I Raised My Salary: A Further Application of the Promulgated Principles from Bring the Boss Across," *Montreal Standard*, 13 March 1926, final ed., p. 36. Illustrated by A.G. Racey. Syndicated by Metropolitan Newspaper Service, New York. Reprinted as

"How I Raised My Own Salary; Further Revelations on the Art of Mastering the Secrets of Success," *Passing Show* 24, no. 628 (4 September 1926): 18–9.

C26.16 "Turning on a Literary Light: A Magazine Editor in His Workshop Plying the Tools of His Trade," *Montreal Standard*, 20 March 1926, final ed., p. 36. Illustrated by A.G. Racey. Syndicated by Metropolitan Newspaper Service, New York.

C26.17 "Outlines of Everything: Designed for Busy People at Their Busiest, and Especially for Members of Women's Cultural Clubs," *Montreal Standard*, 3 April 1926, final ed., p. 36. Illustrated by A.G. Racey. Syndicated by Metropolitan Newspaper Service, New York. See also C24.52, C25.7, and C25.10.

C26.18 "Forecasting Doom of Mr. Doomer: What He and We Will Soon Be Coming to if Our Materialistic Outlook Is Not Diluted," *Montreal Standard*, 10 April 1926, final ed., p. 36. Illustrated by A.G. Racey. Syndicated by Metropolitan Newspaper Service, New York. See also C14.14.

C26.19 "The Ecstacy of Statistics: Our National Passion for Facts and Figures," *Montreal Standard*, 17 April 1926, final ed., p. 36. Illustrated by A.G. Racey. Syndicated by Metropolitan Newspaper Service, New York. Reprinted as "The Ecstasy of Statistics; Facts and Figures Are the Favourite Mental Food of the Average American, But His British Cousin Does Not Share His Thirst for Statistical Information," *Passing Show* 24, no. 626 (21 August 1926): 18–9.

C26.20 "Lo, the Poor Student: What Are They Doing to Him in the Effort to Test His Fitness to Get Fit for Anything?" *Montreal Standard*, 24 April 1926, p. [30]. Illustrated by A.G. Racey. Syndicated by Metropolitan Newspaper Service, New York.

C26.21 "How to Kill a Story: the Dangerous Art of Anecdote in Homicidal Hands," *Montreal Standard*, 1 May 1926, final ed., p. 38. Illustrated by A.G. Racey. Syndicated by Metropolitan Newspaper Service, New York.

C26.22 "Dr. Stephen Leacock Urges Overhead Bridge to Barnfield Park," *Orillia News-Letter*, 5 May 1926, p. 1. Text of Leacock's letter to the Orillia town council, n.d., but the article notes it was received on 3 May 1926. Leacock's property adjoined the park.

C26.23 "My Proposed Polar Flight: How the Interests of Science Impel Me to Join the Procession," *Montreal Standard*, 8 May 1926, final ed., p. 38. Illustrated by A.G. Racey. Syndicated by Metropolitan Newspaper Service, New York.

C26.24 "Pointed Politics; A Little Lesson In Prismatic Personalities for the Approaching Elections," *Orillia News-Letter*, 12 May 1926, p. 11. This is the first of Leacock's syndicated stories carried by the *Orillia News-Letter*. It was illustrated, as were all subsequent stories that had illustrations, by the illustrator hired by the Metropolitan Newspaper Service. The illustrator signed with an "S" inside a box. Also in *Montreal Standard*, 15 May 1926, final ed., p. 38. Illustrated by A.G. Racey. Syndicated by Metropolitan Newspaper Service, New York.

C26.25 "Spring Poetry Season: But When the Time of Year Comes to Consider the Spring Poet, Is There Any Spring Poet Left to Consider," *Montreal Standard*, 22 May 1926, final ed., p. 38. Illustrated by A.G. Racey. Syndicated by Metropolitan Newspaper Service, New York.

C26.26 "How I Made Myself Young at Seventy; How to Beat the Game Instead of Beating Yourself," *Orillia News-Letter*, 26 May 1926, p. 9. Also as "Young at Seventy: How to

Beat the Game Instead of Beating Yourself," *Montreal Standard*, 29 May 1926, final ed., p. 36. Illustrated by A.G. Racey. Syndicated by Metropolitan Newspaper Service, New York. Reprinted as "How I Made Myself Young at 70; an Outburst of Good Advice," *Nash's-Pall Mall* 78, no. 406 (March 1927): 14–5. Illustrated by Aubrey Hammond.

C26.27  "The Return of the Graduate: When Dear Old Alma Mater Does a Flop," *Orillia News-Letter*, 2 June 1926, p. 11. Also in *Montreal Standard*, 5 June 1926, final ed., p. 38, with "the" missing from the title. Illustrated by A.G. Racey. Syndicated by Metropolitan Newspaper Service, New York.

C26.28  "If Our Speakers Were Really Outspoken; A General Emancipation of What Is Really on the Chest," *Orillia News-Letter*, 9 June 1926, p. 11. Also as "If Our Speakers Were Outspoken: A General Emancipation of What Is Really on the Chest," *Montreal Standard*, 12 June 1926, final ed., p. 36. Illustrated by A.G. Racey. Syndicated by Metropolitan Newspaper Service, New York.

C26.29  "The Problems of the Plutocrats; How to Keep the Servants Serving," *Orillia News-Letter*, 16 June 1926, p. 11. Syndicated by Metropolitan Newspaper Service, New York. Also in *Montreal Standard*, 19 June 1926, final ed., p. 36. Illustrated by A.G. Racey. Syndicated by Metropolitan Newspaper Service, New York.

C26.30  "A Diary of the League of Nations from Our Special Correspondent at Geneva," *Saturday Evening Post* 198, no. 52 (26 June 1926): 11. Illustrated by Wyncie King.

C26.31  "My Fellow Club-Men; The Medical Member with the Anecdote and the Talkative Bridge Expert, the Deadliest of the Species," *Orillia News-Letter*, 23 June 1926, p. 11. Reprinted, with no hyphen in "Clubmen" in *Montreal Standard*, 26 June 1926, final ed., p. 34. Illustrated by A.G. Racey. Syndicated by Metropolitan Newspaper Service, New York.

C26.32  "What the Duce!: The Seer Looks into the Future or Something and Decides That Life Won't Be Monotonous If Mussolini Visits America," *Collier's* 78, no. 1 (3 July 1926): 15. Illustrated by Ray Rohn. Reprinted as "If Mussolini Comes; What One Would Be Entitled to Conclude Would Occur, If One Could Believe All That Is Said About Him," *Orillia News-Letter*, 25 August 1926, p. 9. Also as "If Mussolini Comes," *Montreal Standard*, 28 August 1926, final ed., p. 42. Illustrated by A.G. Racey. Syndicated by Metropolitan Newspaper Service, New York.

C26.33  "Our Pictured Personalities: The Present Passion for Pen Pictures of Prominent People," *Orillia News-Letter*, 7 July 1926, p. 11. Also in *Montreal Standard*, 10 July 1926, final ed., p. 34. Syndicated by Metropolitan Newspaper Service, New York.

C26.34  "The Twenty-Second General Strike in England as Reported in the Current Annuals of a Few Years Hence," *Orillia News-Letter*, 14 July 1926, p. 3. Also as "The Twenty-Second General Strike in England," *Montreal Standard*, 17 July 1926, final ed., p. 34. Illustrated by A.G. Racey. Syndicated by Metropolitan Newspaper Service, New York.

C26.35  "The Obliging Man and Why He Ought to Be Exterminated," *Orillia News-Letter*, 21 July 1926, p. 3. Also in *Montreal Standard*, 24 July 1926, final ed., p. 34. Illustrated by A.G. Racey. Syndicated by Metropolitan Newspaper Service, New York.

C26.36  "Joys of Philanthropy or 'Saying It with Francs' in Paris," *Orillia News-Letter*, 28 July 1926, p. 11. Also in *Montreal Standard*, 31 July 1926, final ed., p. 34. Illustrated by A.G. Racey. Syndicated by Metropolitan Newspaper Service, New York.

**C26.37** "How to Borrow Money; The Process Is Quite Easy, Provided You Borrow Enough," *Orillia News-Letter*, 4 August 1926, p. [9]. Also in *Montreal Standard*, 7 August 1926, final ed., p. 38. Illustrated by A.G. Racey. Syndicated by Metropolitan Newspaper Service, New York. Reprinted as "Borrowing Made Easy; the Less One Tries to Borrow the Harder It Becomes," *Passing Show* 24, no. 643 (18 December 1926): 22–3. Illustrated by Wilkinson. As "How to Borrow Money," *Lilliput* 1, no. 2 (August 1937): 3–8. Illustrated by Nicola Bentley. Reprinted in condensed form in *New Current Digest* 11, no. 5 (September 1937): 4–7; in *Lilliput Annual* (London: Pocket Publications 1937?) which contains the first six numbers. As "How to Borrow Money," in *Humorous Stories* (London: Octopus Books, 1986), pp. 245–9.
  Electronically available (12 October 1997) at the National Library of Canada's Leacock Web site: http://www.nlc-bnc.ca/leacock/money.htm

**C26.38** "Record Runs in Heroes and Heroines; Ether[e]al Madeline, Her Long-Winded Immaculate Suitor, and Lord de Viperous Noble Ned, Who Puts Cannibals in Their Places and History on Its Feet," *Orillia News-Letter*, 11 August 1926, p. 11. Also as "The Long-Winded Immaculate Hero," *Montreal Standard*, 14 August 1926, final ed., p. 38. Ends "to be continued." Illustrated, but not signed by A.G. Racey. Syndicated by Metropolitan Newspaper Service, New York.

**C26.39** "Record Runs in Heroes and Heroines; the Boots and Bed Heroines of the Nineties, the Air and Grass Men & Their Charlestonian Successors," *Orillia News-Letter*, 18 August 1926, p. 9. Also as "Record Runs in Heroes & Heroines. II," *Montreal Standard*, 21 August 1926, final ed., p. [42]. Illustrated by A.G. Racey. Syndicated by Metropolitan Newspaper Service, New York.

**C26.40** "The Valetudinarian; I Give Some Medical Advice to Mr. Podge, Which He More Than Takes to Heart," *Orillia News-Letter*, 1 September 1926, p. 11. Also as "The Valetudinarian," *Montreal Standard*, 4 September 1926, final ed., p. 30. Illustrated, but not signed by A.G. Racey. Syndicated by Metropolitan Newspaper Service, New York.

**C26.41** "Come Back to School and Let Us See What the Dear Old Days Felt Like," *Orillia News-Letter*, 8 September 1926, p. 11. Also as "Come Back to School," *Montreal Standard*, 11 September 1926, final ed., p. 30. Illustrated, but not signed by A.G. Racey. Syndicated by Metropolitan Newspaper Service, New York. As "Come Back to School; Let's Hear No More of This Nonsense from Grown-Ups About School-Days Being the Happiest Days of Their Lives," *Passing Show* 24, no. 641 (4 December 1926): 18–9.

**C26.42** "Pets in Season as Presented by Our Enthusiastic Nature Writers," *Orillia News-Letter*, 15 September 1926, p. 9. Also as "Pets in Season," *Montreal Standard*, 18 September 1926, final ed., p. 30. Illustrated by A.G. Racey. Syndicated by Metropolitan Newspaper Service, New York.

**C26.43** "A Children's Corner for College Boys and Girls; Lines from Little Letters Culled Little Friends of the Days When Cheek Meets Greek," *Orillia News-Letter*, 22 September 1926, p. 11. Also as "A Children's Corner for College Boys and Girls," *Montreal Standard*, 25 September 1926, final ed., p. 31. Illustrated, but not signed by A.G. Racey. Syndicated by Metropolitan Newspaper Service, New York. See C1.1 and C25.56.

**C26.44** "The Quebec Liquor Law: II," *American Review of Reviews* 74 (October 1926): 370. Part I is by William Wallace Goforth, pp. 369–70.

C26.45 "The Stock Exchange from without in; or, Where Does Its Language Leave You? — A Modern Version of the Lady & the Porker," *Orillia News-Letter*, 6 October 1926, p. 11. Also as "The Stock Exchange from without in," *Montreal Standard*, 9 October 1926, final ed., p. [45]. Illustrated by A.G. Racey. Syndicated by Metropolitan Newspaper Service, New York.

C26.46 "Life's Minor Contradictions; The Difference Between Things As They Are and As They Seem," *Orillia News-Letter*, 13 October 1926, p. 11. Also as "Life's Minor Contradictions," *Montreal Standard*, 16 October 1926, final ed., p. [50]. Illustrated by A.G. Racey. Syndicated by Metropolitan Newspaper Service, New York; *Passing Show* 25, no. 646 (8 January 1927): 18–9.

C26.47 "The Old Men's Page; A Brand New Feature in Journalism," *Orillia News-Letter*, 20 October 1926, p. 11. Also as "The Old Men's Page," *Montreal Standard*, 23 October 1926, final ed., p. 50. Illustrated by A.G. Racey. Syndicated by Metropolitan Newspaper Service, New York.

C26.48 "The Fall Fair and the Autumn Exposition; A Comparison of Midgeville in 1880 and Midge City in 1926," *Orillia News-Letter*, 27 October 1927, p. 9. Also as "The Fall Fair and the Autumn Exposition," *Montreal Standard*, 30 October 1926, final ed., p. 54. Illustrated. Syndicated by Metropolitan Newspaper Service, New York.

C26.49 "Old Junk and New Bunk: Here's a Simple Rule for Collectors: If It Isn't Useless, It Isn't a Real Antique," *Collier's* 78, no. 18 (30 October 1926): 20. Illustrated by Harry Haenigsen. Reprinted as "Old Junk and New Money," *Montreal Standard*, 18 December 1926, final ed., p. 42. Illustrated by A.G. Racey. Syndicated by Metropolitan Newspaper Service, New York. As "Old Junk and New Bunk; Here's a Simple Rule for Collectors: If It Isn't Useless, It Isn't a Real Antique," *Passing Show* 25, no. 651 (12 February 1927): 18–9. Illustrated by Wilkinson. Reprinted as "Old Junk and New Money," *Humorous Stories* (London: Octopus Books, 1986), pp. 241–4.

C26.50 "The Value of Criticism," *Bookman* (London) 71 (November 1926): 105–07 (at 105). Leacock's brief contribution is followed by A. A. Milne, John Hassall, Gerald Gould, Mary Borden, Norman O'Neill, O. Douglas, and Cecil Roberts.

C26.51 "How to Use a Telephone; the Latest Technical Improvement in Conversation or Saying It with Silence," *Orillia News-Letter*, 3 November 1926, p. 11. Also as "How to Use a Telephone," *Montreal Standard*, 6 November 1926, final ed., p. [48]. Illustrated. Syndicated by Metropolitan Newspaper Service, New York.

C26.52 "A Year at College as Revealed by the Newer Journalism," *Orillia News-Letter*, 10 November 1926, p. 11. Also as "A Year at College," *Montreal Standard*, 13 November 1926, final ed., p. 48. Illustrated by A.G. Racey. Syndicated by Metropolitan Newspaper Service, New York. Reprinted as "A Year at College; What It Is Like if Comic Papers Are to Be Believed," *Passing Show* 25, no. 653 (26 February 1927): 22–3. Illustrated by Wilkinson.

C26.53 "The European Situation; Polite Prandial Parley in Which I Find Myself Snnk [sic]," *Orillia News-Letter*, 17 November 1926, p. 11. Also as "The European Situation," *Montreal Standard*, 20 November 1926, final ed., p. [48]. Illustrated by A.G. Racey. Syndicated by Metropolitan Newspaper Service, New York. See also C27.4.

C26.54 "This World Championship Stuff; The Present Radius of Competition in Everything Is Taking All the Privacy Out of War and Peace," *Orillia News-Letter*, 24 November 1926, p. 9. Reprinted as "This World Championship Stuff," *Montreal Standard*, 27 November 1926, final ed., p. 47. Illustrated by A.G. Racey. Syndicated by Metropolitan Newspaper Service, New York. Also as "This World Championship Stuff; Competition in Everything Is Taking All the Privacy out of War and Peace," *Passing Show* 25, no. 654 (5 March 1927): 18–9. Illustrated by Wilkinson.

**C26.55** "Ancient Custom, Gown Greatest Dust Protector and Clothes Saver Yet Invented," *McGill Daily*, [early December 1926]. Unsigned, undated clipping at SLM. Date is inferred from D26.3.

**C26.56** "A Guide to the Underworld," *Montreal Standard*, 4 December 1926, final ed., p. 47. Illustrated by A.G. Racey. Syndicated by Metropolitan Newspaper Service, New York. Reprinted as "The Underworld; A Little Unsocial Register for the Use of Readers of Up-to-Date Fiction," *Passing Show* 25, no. 649 (29 January 1927): 18–9. Illustrated by Wilkinson.

**C26.57** "The Family at Football," *Montreal Standard*, 11 December 1926, final ed., p. 42. Illustrated by A.G. Racey. Syndicated by Metropolitan Newspaper Service, New York.

**C26.58** "The Haunted Grange," *Montreal Standard*, 25 December 1926, p. [32]. Illustrated by A.G. Racey. Syndicated by Metropolitan Newspaper Service, New York. Apparently a condensation of "Buggam Grange: A Good Old Ghost Story" (see A32). See also C39.49.

**C27.1** "With the Authors," *Montreal Standard*, 1 January 1927, final ed., p. 33. Illustrated by A.G. Racey. Syndicated by Metropolitan Newspaper Service, New York. See also C27.9 and C27.11.

**C27.2** "Taking a Shot at Radio; A Little Target Practice at Examination Questions Which Any Modern Schoolboy Eats Out of the Shell," *Orillia News-Letter*, 5 January 1927, p. 1. Also as "Taking a Shot at Radio," *Montreal Standard*, 8 January 1927, final ed., p. 47. Illustrated by A.G. Racey. Syndicated by Metropolitan Newspaper Service, New York.

**C27.3** "More Queens Coming But Even Then Will There Be Enough?" *Orillia News-Letter*, 12 January 1927, p. 11. Also as "More Queens Coming," *Montreal Standard*, 15 January 1927, final ed., p. 51. Illustrated by A.G. Racey. Syndicated by Metropolitan Newspaper Service, New York.

**C27.4** "The European Situation; What with the Litts and the Letts and the Checko-Slovakians, the Man Who Would Keep au Fait with the European Situation Is Doomed to Intensive Study," *Passing Show* 25, no. 648 (22 January 1927): 18–9. See also C26.53.

**C27.5** "Love Me Love My Letters," *Montreal Standard*, 22 January 1927, final ed., p. [45]. Illustrated by A.G. Racey. Syndicated by Metropolitan Newspaper Service, New York.

**C27.6** "Extinct Monsters; All That Will be Left of Our Household Pets in 1000 Years," *Orillia News-Letter*, 26 January 1927, p. 1. Also as "Extinct Monsters," *Montreal Standard*, 29 January 1927, final ed., p. 47. Illustrated by A.G. Racey. Syndicated by Metropolitan Newspaper Service, New York. In *Nash's Magazine* 79, no. 411 (August 1927): 16–7.

**C27.7** "Easy Ways to Success; A Letter to a Parlor Bolshevik Just Out of College," *Orillia News-Letter*, 2 February 1927, p. [9]. Reprinted as "Easy Ways to Success," *Montreal Standard*, 5 February 1927, final ed., p. 44. Illustrated by A.G. Racey. Syndicated by

Metropolitan Newspaper Service, New York. Also as "Easy Ways to Success," *Nash's Magazine* 79 (June 1927): 14–5.

C27.8 "The Stamp-Album World; The Habitable Globe as Seen Through Optics of Juvenile Collector," *Orillia News-Letter*, 9 February 1927, p. 11. Also as "The Stamp Album World," *Montreal Standard*, 12 February 1927, final ed., p. 44. Illustrated by A.G. Racey. Syndicated by Metropolitan Newspaper Service, New York.

C27.9 "More Great Authorities at Home; Further Glimpses of Those Who Do Big Things," *Orillia News-Letter*, 16 February 1927, p. 14. Also as "More Great Authors at Home," *Montreal Standard*, 19 February 1927, final ed., p. 44. Illustrated by A.G. Racey. Syndicated by Metropolitan Newspaper Service, New York. Leacock writes that this article has been written because of the response he has received to C27.1. See also C27.11.

C27.10 "Things I Hardly Dare Whisper; More Revelations of Another Unknown European Diplomat. By an Undisclosed Author of European Disreputation. Two Volumes. Ten Dollars Each, or the Two for Seven Fifty," *Orillia News-Letter*, 23 February 1927, p. 11. Also as "Things I Hardly Dare Whisper," *Montreal Standard*, 26 February 1927, final ed., p. 44. Illustrated by A.G. Racey. Syndicated by Metropolitan Newspaper Service, New York.

C27.11 "More Great Authorities at Home; Some Further Intimate Studies of the Truly Great," *Orillia News-Letter*, 2 March 1927, p. [3]. Also as "More Great Authorities at Home," *Montreal Standard*, 5 March 1927, final ed., p. 44. Illustrated by A.G. Racey. Syndicated by Metropolitan Newspaper Service, New York. See also C27.1 and C27.9.

C27.12 "What the Radio Overheard; An Evening at the Home of the Uptown Browns," *Orillia News-Letter*, 9 March 1927, p. 11. Also as "What the Radio Overheard," *Montreal Standard*, 12 March 1927, final ed., p. 44. Illustrated by A.G. Racey. Syndicated by Metropolitan Newspaper Service, New York. See also C27.14.

C27.13 "Not According to Hoyle; Home Life with the Experts as It Might Have Happened," *Passing Show* 25, no. 655 (12 March 1927): 18–9. Illustrated by Wilkinson.

C27.14 "What the Radio Overheard; An Evening at the Home of the Uptown Browns. Part 2," *Orillia News-Letter*, 16 March 1927, p. 9. Also as "What the Radio Overheard II," *Montreal Standard*, 19 March 1927, final ed., p. 49. Illustrated by A.G. Racey. Syndicated by Metropolitan Newspaper Service, New York. See also C27.12.

C27.15 "A Run On Royalties; In Democratic America the Demand for Crowned Heads Bids Fair to Exceed the Supply," *Passing Show* 25, no. 656 (19 March 1927): 18–9. Illustrated by Wilkinson.

C27.16 "The Perfect Gift; a Little Study in the Art of Tactful Giving," *Orillia News-Letter*, 23 March 1927, p. 11. Also as "The Perfect Gift," *Montreal Standard*, 26 March 1927, final ed., p. 44. Illustrated by A.G. Racey. Syndicated by Metropolitan Newspaper Service, New York.

C27.17 "The Passing of the Back Yard; Another Social Revolution Coming Straight at Us," *Orillia News-Letter*, 30 March 1927, p. [9]. Also as "The Passing of the Back Yard," *Montreal Standard*, 2 April 1927, final ed., p. 44. Illustrated by A.G. Racey. Syndicated by Metropolitan Newspaper Service, New York. In *Nash's Magazine* 79, no. 410 (July 1927): 22–3.

C27.18  "One Crowded Quarter Second; How They Make Life Move in the Movies," *Orillia News-Letter*, 6 April 1927, p. 9. Reprinted as "One Crowded Quarter Second," *Montreal Standard*, 9 April 1927, final ed., p. 40. Illustrated by A.G. Racey. Syndicated by Metropolitan Newspaper Service, New York. Also as "One Crowded Quarter Second. On How They Make Life Move in the Movies," *Nash's Magazine* 79, no. 412 (September 1927): 24–5.

C27.19  "Who Is Also Who; A Brief Account of Some Important — and Typical — People of Today Who Get Out of the Guide Books," *Orillia News-Letter*, 13 April 1927, p. 9. Also as "Who Is Also Who," *Montreal Standard*, 16 April 1927, final ed., p. 44. Illustrated by A.G. Racey. Syndicated by Metropolitan Newspaper Service, New York. See also C14.6.

C27.20  "Great Moments in Fiction; How They Find 'The Body' in a Detective Story," *Orillia News-Letter*, 27 April 1927, p. [9]. Also as "Great Moments in Fiction," *Montreal Standard*, 30 April 1927, final ed., p. 44. Illustrated by A.G. Racey. Syndicated by Metropolitan Newspaper Service, New York. Article ends "to be continued."

C27.21  "The Detective Sleuth Hound on the Trail; Another One of Those Great Moments in Fiction. When the Reader's Breath Takes a Vacation. II," *Orillia News-Letter*, 4 May 1927, p. [9]. Also as "The Detective Sleuth Hound on the Trail," *Montreal Standard*, 7 May 1927, final ed., p. 45. Illustrated by A.G. Racey. Syndicated by Metropolitan Newspaper Service, New York. Article ends "to be continued."

C27.22  "How the Murder Mystery Is Mastered; The Greatest of All Great Moments in Fiction, When the Reader Gets a Tumble. III," *Orillia News-Letter*, 11 May 1927, p. [9]. Also as "How the Murder Mystery Is Mastered," *Montreal Standard*, 14 May 1927, final ed., p. 44. Illustrated by A.G. Racey. Syndicated by Metropolitan Newspaper Service, New York. Article ends "to be continued."

C27.23  "The Riddle Unravelled — and Then What? A Great Moment in Fiction, Which Has Been Built Up into Literature's Flattest Note. IV," *Orillia News-Letter*, 18 May 1927, p. [9]. Also as "The Riddle Unravelled and Then What?" *Montreal Standard*, 21 May 1927, final ed., p. 44. Illustrated by A.G. Racey. Syndicated by Metropolitan Newspaper Service, New York.

C27.24  "If They Go On Swimming; A Forecast of the End of a New Hobby — What We Shall Be Reading Hence," *Orillia News-Letter*, 25 May 1927, p. [9]. Reprinted as "If They Go On Swimming," *Montreal Standard*, 28 May 1927, final ed., p. 44. Illustrated by A.G. Racey. Syndicated by Metropolitan Newspaper Service, New York. Also as "If They Go On Swimming; What May Happen When Channel Swimmers Seek Fresh Seas to Conquer," *Passing Show* 26, no. 692 (26 November 1927): 22–3.

C27.25  "A Moving Day for Literature. A Suggestion to Novelists Who Find That Prohibition Interferes with Literary Flavour," *Vanity Fair* 28, no. 4 (June 1927): 67, 114. Reprinted as "A Moving Day for Literature; Why Not Shift the Scene to Montreal and Escape the Eighteenth Amendment," *Orillia News-Letter*, 21 September 1927, p. 10. Also as "A Moving Day for Literature," *Montreal Standard*, 24 September 1927, final ed., p. [48]. Illustrated by A.G. Racey. Syndicated by Metropolitan Newspaper Service, New York.

C27.26  "The Truth About the College Girl; Now That It Can Be Told — A Few Reflections Suitable to the Approach of Graduation Day," *Orillia News-Letter*, 1 June 1927, p. [9]. Also as "The Truth About the College Girl," *Montreal Standard*, 4 June 1927, final ed.,

p. 44. Illustrated by A.G. Racey. Syndicated by Metropolitan Newspaper Service, New York.

C27.27 "When the College Course Runs Amuck; A Close-Up of Graduation Day in 1950," *Orillia News-Letter*, 8 June 1927, p. [9]. Also as "When the College Course Runs Amuck," *Montreal Standard*, 11 June 1927, final ed., p. 44. Illustrated by A.G. Racey. Syndicated by Metropolitan Newspaper Service, New York.

C27.28 "Illustrations I Can Do Without; Some Gentle Suggestions for the Contemporary Illustrated Magazines," *Orillia News-Letter*, 15 June 1927, p. [9]. Also as "Illustrations I Can Do Without," *Montreal Standard*, 18 June 1927, final ed., p. 44. Illustrated by A.G. Racey. Syndicated by Metropolitan Newspaper Service, New York. In *Passing Show* 26, no. 677 (13 August 1927): 18–9. Illustrated by "S," the illustrator hired by Metropolitan Newspaper Service.

C27.29 "The Little Town in the Sunshine; Some Summer Sketches of a Place Dear to Most of Us — Life as Lived When We Were Young," *Orillia News-Letter*, 22 June 1927, p. [11]. Also as "The Little Town in the Sunshine," *Montreal Standard*, 25 June 1927, final ed., p. 64. Illustrated by A.G. Racey. Syndicated by Metropolitan Newspaper Service, New York. Both articles end "to be continued." See also C12.6–17, C17.10, C27.30, C27.33, and C27.36–8.

C27.30 "Jefferson Thorpe Magnate of Finance; an Episode in the Chronicle of the Little Town in the Sunshine — More of Life as Lived When We Were Young," *Orillia News-Letter*, 29 June 1927, p. [9]. Also as "Jefferson Thorpe: Magnate of Finance," *Montreal Standard*, 2 July 1927, final ed., p. 44. Illustrated by A.G. Racey. Syndicated by Metropolitan Newspaper Service, New York. Articles end "to be continued."

C27.31 "Children's Poetry Revised: How the Dear Old Poems of Our Childhood Need to Be Brought Up to Date," *Harper's Magazine* 155 (July 1927): 252–4. This is one of several articles by different authors in the sec. "The Lion's Mouth." Reprinted as "Children's Poetry Revised," in Grant Huffman, ed., *Canadiana: An Anthology of Nostalgic, Humorous, and Satirical Writing for Secondary Schools* (Toronto: McClelland and Stewart, 1970), pp. 89–92.

C27.32 "The Environment of Letters: Culture of the Mind: A Call to Youth," *Times* (London), Canada no., 1 July 1927, p. xxi. The Canada number is an occasional supplement to the *Times*.

C27.33 "The Fall of a Northern Star; An Episode in the Chronicle of the Little Town in the Sunshine — More of Life as Lived When We Were Young," *Orillia News-Letter*, 6 July 1927, p. [3]. Also as "The Fall of a Northern Star," *Montreal Standard*, 9 July 1927, final ed., p. 44. Illustrated by A.G. Racey. Syndicated by Metropolitan Newspaper Service, New York.

C27.34 "Roughing It: Maybe You Think Your Annual Return to the Simple Life Isn't So Complicated, But — Be Honest Now!" *Collier's* 80, no. 2 (9 July 1927): 27. Illustrated by Ray Rohn. See also C22.19.

C27.35 "Save Me from My Friend the Guide," *New Yorker* 3, no. 21 (9 July 1927): 14–5. Reprinted as "Save Me From the Guibe [sic] of the Woods; the Friend Who Warmly Takes Everything You've Got," *Orillia News-Letter*, 7 March 1928, p. [12]. Also as "Save Me From the Guide of the Woods," *Montreal Standard*, 16 March 1928, final ed., p. 48.

Illustrated by A.G. Racey. Syndicated by Metropolitan Newspaper Service, New York. As "The Guide of the Woods; Sometimes You Meet a Guide Who Does Not Know His Way . . . ," *Passing Show* 27, no. 716 (12 May 1928): 16.

**C27.36** "The Height of the Season in Mariposa; The Great Steamboat Excursion of the Knights of Pythias — As It Was in the Years Gone By," *Orillia News-Letter*, 13 July 1927, p. [9]. Also as "The Height of the Season in Mariposa," *Montreal Standard*, 16 July 1927, final ed., p. 42. Illustrated by A.G. Racey. Syndicated by Metropolitan Newspaper Service, New York. Article ends "to be continued."

**C27.37** "The Great Excursion in the Sunshine; How the Steamer Threatened to Sink with All Hands — A Record from an Earlier Age," *Orillia News-Letter*, 20 July 1927, p. 11. Also as "The Great Excursion in the Sunshine," *Montreal Standard*, 23 July 1927, final ed., p. 42. Illustrated by A.G. Racey. Syndicated by Metropolitan Newspaper Service, New York. Article ends "to be continued."

**C27.38** "When a Steamer Has a Sinking Spell; The Gallant Rescue They Still Tell About in the Little Town in the Sunshine," *Orillia News-Letter*, 27 July 1927, p. 13. Also as "When a Steamer Has a Sinking Spell," *Montreal Standard*, 30 July 1927, final ed., p. 44. Illustrated by A.G. Racey. Syndicated by Metropolitan Newspaper Service, New York.

**C27.39** "Scenery and Signboards," *Harper's Magazine* 155 (August 1927): 382–3. This is one of several articles by different authors in the sec. "The Lion's Mouth." Reprinted as "Scenery and Signboards; A Vision of Travel from New York to Washington," *Orillia News-Letter*, 9 November 1927, p. 12. Also as "Scenery and Signboards," *Montreal Standard*, 12 November 1927, final ed., p. [46]. Illustrated by A.G. Racey. Syndicated by Metropolitan Newspaper Service, New York. As "Scenery and Signboards; From New York to Washington by Way of the Outdoor Publicity Route," *Passing Show* 27, no. 701 (28 January 1928): 18–9.

**C27.40** "Inference as an Art; How Even an Amateur May Forge a Chain of Logic," *Orillia News-Letter*, 3 August 1927, p. 4. Also as "Inference As An Art," *Montreal Standard*, 6 August 1927, p. 36. Illustrated by A.G. Racey. Syndicated by Metropolitan Newspaper Service, New York. As "The Art of Inference; It's Elementary, My Dear Watson, Positively Elementary," *Passing Show* 26, no. 678 (20 August 1927): 18–9. Illustrated by "S".

**C27.41** "Where Do We Go from Here? How Various Types of People Help You Find Your Way in the Country," *Orillia News-Letter*, 10 August 1927, p. 11. Also as "Where Do We Go From Here?" *Montreal Standard*, 13 August 1927, p. 24. Illustrated by A.G. Racey. Syndicated by Metropolitan Newspaper Service, New York.

**C27.42** "Where Do We Go from Here? Some Timely Cautions for the Vacation Season," *Orillia News-Letter*, 17 August 1927, p. 10. Reprinted as "Safety First Last and Always," *Montreal Standard*, 20 August 1927, p. 36. Illustrated by A.G. Racey. Syndicated by Metropolitan Newspaper Service, New York. Also as "Where Do We Go From Here? How Various Types of People Help You to Find Your Way in the Country," *Passing Show* 26, no. 692 (29 October 1927): 18–9. Illustrated by Wilkinson.

**C27.43** "If We Had to Do the Summer Over Again; Second-Guessing on Where and How One Would Have Spent It," *Orillia News-Letter*, 31 August 1927, p. 2. Also as "If We Had to Do the Summer Over Again," *Montreal Standard*, 3 September 1927, final ed., p. [38]. Illustrated by A.G. Racey. Syndicated by Metropolitan Newspaper Service, New York.

C27.44 "Save Me from the Man Who Has a Speech to Make," *Harper's Magazine* 155 (September 1927): 516–7. Also in *Orillia News-Letter*, 22 February 1928, p. [4]; *Montreal Standard*, 3 March 1928, final ed., p. 48. Illustrated by A.G. Racey. Syndicated by Metropolitan Newspaper Service, New York. The article was also sold to *London Opinion*.

C27.45 "Save Me from My Friend the Deadbeat," *New Yorker* 3, no. 29 (3 September 1927): 14–5. Reprinted as "Save Me from My Friends. A Little Story that Will Draw Tears from Your Eyes," *Nash's Magazine* 80, no. 416 (January 1928): 28–9. Also as "Another Friend to Save Me from; The Deadbeat," *Orillia News-Letter*, 15 February 1928, p. [14]. As "Another Friend to Save Me From," *Montreal Standard*, 25 February 1928, final ed., p. 49. Illustrated by A.G. Racey. Syndicated by Metropolitan Newspaper Service, New York.

C27.46 "The More Than Complete Letter-Writer; A New Manual for Up-to-Date Occasions," *Orillia News-Letter*, 7 September 1927, p. 11. Reprinted as "The More Than Complete Letter Writer," *Montreal Standard*, 10 September 1927, final ed., p. 44. Illustrated by A.G. Racey. Syndicated by Metropolitan Newspaper Service, New York. Also as "The More-than-Complete Letter-Writer; Correspondence Guides of Old Are Out-of-Date, We Need New Ideas to Keep Pace With a Changing World," *Passing Show* 26, no. 693 (3 December 1927): 18–9.

C27.47 "Children's Poetry Revised; How the Dear Old Poems of Childhood Need to Be Brought Up to Date," *Orillia News-Letter*, 14 September 1927, p. 12. Also as "Poetry Revised," *Montreal Standard*, 17 September 1927, final ed., p. [46]. Illustrated by A.G. Racey. Syndicated by Metropolitan Newspaper Service, New York. The article was also sold to *London Opinion*.

C27.48 "A Moving Day for Literature; Why Not Shift the Scene to Montreal and Escape the Eighteenth Amendment," *Orillia News-Letter*, 21 September 1927, p. 10. Also as "A Moving Day for Literature," *Montreal Standard*, 24 September 1927, final ed., p. [48]. Illustrated by A.G. Racey. Syndicated by Metropolitan Newspaper Service, New York.

C27.49 "My Friend the Reporter," *Harper's Magazine* 155 (October 1927): 647–8. This is one of several articles by different authors in the sec. "The Lion's Mouth." The article was also sold to *London Opinion*.

C27.50 "Afternoon Adventures with the Idle Rich; The Preferred Stock of the Mausoleum Club," *Orillia News-Letter*, 28 September 1927, p. 10. Also as "Afternoon Adventures with the Idle Rich," *Montreal Standard*, 1 October 1927, final ed., p. 50. Illustrated by A.G. Racey. Syndicated by Metropolitan Newspaper Service, New York. See also A16, C14.9, C14.13, C14.15, C14.17, C14.21, C27.51–2, C27.54–6.

C27.51 "Hunting Big Game at the Mausoleum Club; The Kind of Pelt in Which the Members Really Take an Interest," *Orillia News-Letter*, 5 October 1927, p. 10. Also as "Hunting Big Game at the Mausoleum Club II," *Montreal Standard*, 8 October 1927, final ed., p. 47. Illustrated by A.G. Racey. Syndicated by Metropolitan Newspaper Service, New York.

C27.52 "Mrs. Rasselyer-Brown Entertains; One of the Most Adventurous Adventures with the Idle Rich," *Orillia News-Letter*, 12 October 1927, p. 12. Also as "Mrs. Rasselyer-Brown Entertains III," *Montreal Standard*, 15 October 1927, final ed., p. 46. Illustrated by A.G. Racey. Syndicated by Metropolitan Newspaper Service, New York. See also C14.17.

C27.53 "Lessons on the Links; The Application of Mathamatics [sic] to Golf Yields Some Surprising Results," *Passing Show* 26, no. 686 (15 October 1927): 18–9. Reprinted as

"Lessons on the Links; The Application of Mathematics to Golf," *Orillia News-Letter*, 18 April 1928, p. [12]. Also as "Lessons on the Links," *Montreal Standard*, 28 April 1928, final ed., p. [50]. Illustrated by A.G. Racey. Syndicated by Metropolitan Newspaper Service, New York. As "Mathematics for Golfers," *Harper's Magazine* 156 (April 1928): 647–9. This is one of several articles by different authors in the sec. "The Lion's Mouth." Reprinted in James R. Newman, ed., *The World of Mathematics*, vol. 4 (New York: Simon and Schuster, 1956), pp. 2456–9. See also A132.

Electronically available at: http://duke.usask.ca/~buydens/leacock/golfer.html

C27.54 "Romance on Plutoria Avenue; The Love Story of Mr. Peter Spillikins," *Orillia News-Letter*, 19 October 1927, p. 10. Also as "Romance on Plutoria Avenue," *Montreal Standard*, 29 October 1927, final ed., p. 46. Illustrated by A.G. Racey. Syndicated by Metropolitan Newspaper Service, New York. Article ends "to be continued." See also C14.21.

C27.55 "The Love Story of Mr. Peter Spillikins; What Happens When an Irresistable [sic] Force Meets a Movable Object," *Orillia News-Letter*, 26 October 1927, p. [12].

C27.56 "How We Cleared Up the City; Plutoria Avenue Leads an Elevating Crusade," *Orillia News-Letter*, 2 November 1927, p. 12. Also as "How We Cleared Up the City VI," *Montreal Standard*, 5 November 1927, final ed., p. 46. Illustrated by A.G. Racey. Syndicated by Metropolitan Newspaper Service, New York.

C27.57 "Life in the Open; Reflections Vouchsafed to [M]e By My Hostess in the Wilderness," *Orillia News-Letter*, 16 November 1927, p. 12. Also as "Life in the Open," *Montreal Standard*, 19 November 1927, final ed., p. 46. Illustrated by A.G. Racey. Syndicated by Metropolitan Newspaper Service, New York.

C27.58 "The Love-Life of John Mutation Smith; A Typical Citizen of Today and His Typical Heart-Throbs," *Orillia News-Letter*, 30 November 1927, p. 11. Also as "The Life of John Mutation Smith," *Montreal Standard*, 26 November 1927, final ed., p. 48. Illustrated by A.G. Racey. Syndicated by Metropolitan Newspaper Service, New York. Article ends "to be continued."

C27.59 "The Love Life of John Mutation Smith," *Montreal Standard*, 3 December 1927, final ed., p. 48. Illustrated by A.G. Racey. Syndicated by Metropolitan Newspaper Service, New York.

C27.60 "The 'Funny Stuff' in Business; Is a Sense of Humor a Financial Asset?" *Orillia News-Letter*, 7 December 1927, p. [10]. Also as "The 'Funny Stuff' in Business," *Montreal Standard*, 10 December 1927, final ed., p. 52. Illustrated by A.G. Racey. Syndicated by Metropolitan Newspaper Service, New York.

C27.61 "Get Off the Earth; Now That This Globe Is Used Up, Let's Look for Another," *Orillia News-Letter*, 14 December 1927, p. [14]. Also as "Get Off the Earth," *Montreal Standard*, 17 December 1927, final ed., p. 48. Illustrated by A.G. Racey. Syndicated by Metropolitan Newspaper Service, New York. This article was also sold to *London Opinion*.

C27.62 "Interviewing a Great Man of Today; Joe Brown, Champion Pie-Eater," *Orillia News-Letter*, 21 December 1927, p. [12]. Also as "Interviewing a Great Man of Today," *Montreal Standard*, 24 December 1927, final ed., p. 42. Illustrated by A.G. Racey. Syndicated by Metropolitan Newspaper Service, New York. Also as "A Great Man of To-Day . . . Here Is Recorded an Interview With, Perhaps, the Greatest Champion of Them All," *Passing Show* 27, no. 715 (5 May 1928): 16.

C27.63 "Conviviality and Literature; How Prohibition Has Hit the Poor American Author," *Passing Show* (Christmas no. 1927): 68, 70.

C27.64 "Continuing to Be Back from Europe; Talking All Winter About Being There All Summer — But Why Go There At All?" *Orillia News-Letter*, 28 December 1927, p. [7]. Also as "Continuing to Be Back from Europe," *Montreal Standard*, 7 January 1928, final ed., p. 46. Illustrated by A.G. Racey. Syndicated by Metropolitan Newspaper Service, New York.

C28.1 "Annual Events," *Old McGill 1929* 31 (1928): 24

C28.2 "People We Know; The Man in the Pullman Car," *Orillia News-Letter*, 4 January 1928, p. [12]. Also as "People We Know," *Montreal Standard*, 14 January 1928, final ed., p. 36. Illustrated by A.G. Racey. Syndicated by Metropolitan Newspaper Service, New York.

C28.3 "The Lost World of Yesterday; A Pen Picture of the Vanished Past — The Horse and Buggy," *Orillia News-Letter*, 11 January 1928, p. [4]. Also as "The Lost World of Yesterday," *Montreal Standard*, 21 January 1928, final ed., p. 36. Illustrated by A.G. Racey. Syndicated by Metropolitan Newspaper Service, New York.

C28.4 "More People We Know; The Criminal by Proxy Who Gloats Over the Crime," *Orillia News-Letter*, 18 January 1928, p. [4]. Also as "More People We Know," *Montreal Standard*, 28 January 1928, final ed., p. 36. Illustrated by A.G. Racey. Syndicated by Metropolitan Newspaper Service, New York. Also as "The Criminal by Proxy; Many of Us Are Interested in Criminology Because It Is a Subject Which Possesses a Certain Fascination . . . ," *Passing Show* 27, no. 713 (21 April 1928): 16.

C28.5 "The Literary Sensations of 1929; A Confidential Guide to New Books," *Orillia News-Letter*, 25 January 1928, p. [4]. Also as "The Literary Sensations of 1929," *Montreal Standard*, 4 February 1928, final ed., p. 46. Illustrated by A.G. Racey. Syndicated by Metropolitan Newspaper Service, New York. Reprinted as "The Literary Sensations of 1929. A Confidential Guide to the New Books," *Gallant Adventure: TOC H Annual 1928* (London: The Saint Catherine Press), pp. 58–62.

C28.6 "Save Me from My Friends; The College President," *Orillia News-Letter*, 1 February 1928, p. [4]. Also as "Save Me from My Friends," *Montreal Standard*, 11 February 1928, final ed., p. 38. Illustrated by A.G. Racey. Syndicated by Metropolitan Newspaper Service, New York.

C28.7 "Done into Movies," *New Yorker* 3, no. 51 (4 February 1928): 59–61. Reprinted as "Done into Movies; But Can You Recognize the Good Old Stories When They Get Them Done?" *Orillia News-Letter*, 28 March 1928, p. [10]. Also as "Done into Movies," *Montreal Standard*, 7 April 1928, final ed., p. 50. Illustrated by A.G. Racey. Syndicated by Metropolitan Newspaper Service, New York.

C28.8 "Our Get-Together Movement; The Way We Have Organized to 'Get Together' In Our Town," *Orillia News-Letter*, 8 February 1928, p. [4]. Also as "Our Get-Together Movement," *Montreal Standard*, 18 February 1928, final ed., p. 52. Illustrated by A.G. Racey. Syndicated by Metropolitan Newspaper Service, New York.

C28.9 " 'Speaking of India —,' " *New Yorker* 3, no. 53 (18 February 1928): 19–20. Reprinted as " 'Speaking of India —' What to Do in Company When Your Husband Tells in Company His Same Old Story," *Orillia News-Letter*, 11 April 1928, p. [10]. Also as

" 'Speaking of India —,' " *Montreal Standard*, 21 April 1928, final ed., p. 46. Illustrated by A.G. Racey. Syndicated by Metropolitan Newspaper Service, New York.

C28.10  "Home from Home; Verily, There is Nothing Like Travel for Narrowing Anyone's Mind. Ask Any American Tourist," *Passing Show* 27, no. 705 (25 February 1928): 18–9.

C28.11  "If Only We Had the Radio Sooner; The Man Who Has a Speech to Make," *Orillia News-Letter*, 29 February 1928, p. [10]. Also as "If Only We Had the Radio Sooner," *Montreal Standard*, 10 March 1928, final ed., p. 48. Illustrated by A.G. Racey. Syndicated by Metropolitan Newspaper Service, New York. Reprinted as "1066 on the Air," *Lilliput* 1, no. 3 (September 1937): 86–8, 90; in *Lilliput Annual* (London: Pocket Publications, 1937?) which bound together the first six numbers.

C28.12  "Mother Goose-Step for Children," *Forum* 79 (March 1928): 365–9. Illustrated by Johan Bull. Also as "Mother Goose-Step for Children; A Modern Idea — Unknown to Our Grandfathers — Is That Children Should Not Be Allowed to Sup on the Horrors of Red Riding Hood . . . ," *Passing Show* 27, no. 714 (28 April 1928): 16. Reprinted in Phyllis Fenner, ed., *Something Shared: Children and Books* (New York: John Day, 1959), pp. 87–92.

C28.13  "See the Conquering Aero Comes! With Apologies to Colonel Lindbergh, to the American Press, to the League of Nations, to Everybody," *Goblin* [8?] (March 1928): 9.

C28.14  "The Unintelligence Test; What a Well-Equipped Man Ought Not to Know in This Year of 1928," *Passing Show* 27, no. 707 (10 March 1928): 18–9.

C28.15  "Home Was Never Like This; Putting the Suite In Home, Sweet Home," *Orillia News-Letter*, 14 March 1928, p. [10]. Also as "Home Was Never Like This," *Montreal Standard*, 24 March 1928, final ed., p. 48. Illustrated by A.G. Racey. Syndicated by Metropolitan Newspaper Service, New York.

C28.16  "Startling Events of 1928; An Advance View of Some of the Exceptional Happenings of the Current Year," *Orillia News-Letter*, 21 March 1928, p. [10]. Also as "Startling Events of 1928," *Montreal Standard*, 31 March 1928, final ed., p. 48. Illustrated by A.G. Racey. Syndicated by Metropolitan Newspaper Service, New York.

C28.17  "Roughing It in the Rockies; Read Here of the Simple Life, Plain Living and High Thinking as Practised in the USA," *Passing Show* 27, no. 710 (31 March 1928): 18–9.

C28.18  "Softening the Stories for the Children; But Don't Do It — They Prefer Them Rough," *Orillia News-Letter*, 4 April 1928, p. [18]. Also as "Softening the Stories for the Children," *Montreal Standard*, 14 April 1928, final ed., p. 50. Illustrated by A.G. Racey. Syndicated by Metropolitan Newspaper Service, New York. It was sold to the *Forum* in December 1927 and may have made its first appearance there. Reprinted in Grant Huffman, ed., *Canadiana: An Anthology of Nostalgic, Humorous, and Satirical Writing for Secondary Schools* (Toronto: McClelland and Stewart, 1970), pp. 43–6. See also C40.15.

C28.19  "High Standing for McGill Students. . . . ," *Montreal Gazette*, 5 April 1928, p. 4. Leacock issued a statement on the occasion of the graduate fellowship competition sponsored by the Royal Bank of Canada. He congratulated the winner, stated that the winner had accepted an invitation to take his graduate year as a fellow at McGill University, and noted the excellent showing of McGill's own students in the competition.

C28.20  "Hands Across the Sea; What Will Happen When America Has Removed All the

European Art," *Orillia News-Letter*, 25 April 1928, p. 10. Also as "Hands Across the Sea," *Montreal Standard*, 5 May 1928, final ed., p. 44. Illustrated by A.G. Racey. Syndicated by Metropolitan Newspaper Service, New York.

C28.21 "Good-Night, Dear," *New Yorker* 4, no. 10 (28 April 1928): 23–4.

C28.22 "Control of Liquor in Canada," *Plain Talk* 2 (May 1928): 535–9.

C28.23 "The Economic Aspect of Aviation," *Transactions of the Royal Society of Canada* series 3, 22, sec. 2 (May 1928): 213–32.

C28.24 "An Elegy Written near a City Freight Yard," *Forum* 79 (May 1928): 690–3. Illustrated by Johan Bull. Poem.

C28.25 "Ghost of the Bygone Past; Eddie the Bartender," *Orillia News-Letter*, 2 May 1928, p. 10. Also as "Ghosts of the Bygone Past," *Montreal Standard*, 12 May 1928, final ed., p. 49. Illustrated by A.G. Racey. Syndicated by Metropolitan Newspaper Service, New York.

C28.26 "The Man with the Adventure Story; and How He Thrills Those Who Hear Him," *Orillia News-Letter*, 9 May 1928, p. 10. Also as "The Man with the Adventure Story," *Montreal Standard*, 19 May 1928, final ed., p. 40. Illustrated by A.G. Racey. Syndicated by Metropolitan Newspaper Service, New York.

C28.27 "The Typical Business Man As Seen in Type; One of the People You Meet Only in the Books," *Orillia News-Letter*, 16 May 1928, p. [10]. Also as "The Typical Businessman Seen in Type," *Montreal Standard*, 26 May 1928, final ed., p. 46. Illustrated by A.G. Racey. Syndicated by Metropolitan Newspaper Service, New York.

C28.28 "The Gentleman of the Old School and What He Didn't Learn There; One of the People You Meet in the Books," *Orillia News-Letter*, 23 May 1928, p. [12]. Also as "The Gentleman of the Old School and What He Didn't Learn There," *Montreal Standard*, 2 June 1928, final ed., p. 46. Illustrated by A.G. Racey. Syndicated by Metropolitan Newspaper Service, New York.

C28.29 "Rural Urbanity; Showing How the Country Is Now Certified Citified," *Orillia News-Letter*, 30 May 1928, p. 10. Also as "Rural Urbanity," *Montreal Standard*, 9 June 1928, final ed., p. 47. Illustrated by A.G. Racey. Syndicated by Metropolitan Newspaper Service, New York.

C28.30 "Life's Little Inconsistencies; Why Things Never Are What They Would Be If They Were," *Orillia News-Letter*, 6 June 1928, p. 10. Reprinted as "Life's Little Inconsistencies," *Montreal Standard*, 16 June 1928, final ed., p. [47]. Illustrated by A.G. Racey. Syndicated by Metropolitan Newspaper Service, New York. Also as "Life's Little Inconsistencies; Why Things Never Are What They Would Be If They Were," *Passing Show* 29, no. 751 (12 January 1929): 18–9.

C28.31 "Conversations I Can Do without; Enough of Some People's Talk to Explain Why," *Orillia News-Letter*, 13 June 1928, p. 8. Also as "Conversations I Can Do without," *Montreal Standard*, 23 June 1928, final ed., p. 46. Illustrated by A.G. Racey. Syndicated by Metropolitan Newspaper Service, New York.

C28.32 "Fuzzy the Burglar and His Cute Little Automatic; A Bed-time Story for Grown-ups — With Apologies to Our Children's Writers," *Orillia News-Letter*, 20 June 1928, p. [12]. Also as "Fuzzy the Burglar and His Cute Little Automatic," *Montreal Standard*,

30 June 1928, final ed., p. 46. Illustrated by A.G. Racey. Syndicated by Metropolitan Newspaper Service, New York. See also C28.34.

C28.33  "The Janitor Who Fell Heir to a Fortune; or How Daniel J. Edwards Stuck to the Job," *Orillia News-Letter*, 27 June 1928, p. [12]. Also as "The Janitor Who Fell Heir to a Fortune," *Montreal Standard*, 7 July 1928, final ed., p. 46. Illustrated by A.G. Racey. Syndicated by Metropolitan Newspaper Service, New York.

C28.34  "Bed-Time Stories for Grown-Up People; with Apologies to Our Best Children's Writers," *Passing Show* (Summer Annual 1928): 22–3. Illustrated by Harry Rowntree. According to Lomer (p. 65), this appeared originally as "Bed-Time Stories for Grown-Up People," *Forum* 79 (30 May 1925): 11. See also C28.32.

C28.35  "Heroines," *Forum* 80 (July 1928): 45–8. Illustrated by Johan Bull. Reprinted as "Why is a Heroine and What? How the Fiction Writer Struggles to Make an Attractive Woman," *Orillia News-Letter*, 17 September 1928, p. 4. Also as "Why is a Heroine and What?" *Montreal Standard*, 15 September 1928, final ed., p. 48. Illustrated by A.G. Racey. Syndicated by Metropolitan Newspaper Service, New York.

C28.36  "[Statement about Canadian prosperity]," *Agricultural and Industrial Progress in Canada* (Montreal) 10, no. 7 (July 1928): 123. The statement reads as follows: "It is not possible to doubt that Canada is destined to go forward economically at least as fast in the future as in the past. The measure of what we are going to do is what we have already done.... In my opinion there is every economic indication of an era of prosperity in Canada unrivalled even in the past. Those who come may share it." Reprinted but with three extra sentences added in M.M. Mendels's *The Asbestos Industry in Canada* (see B19), p. 5 of the advertisements. Also reprinted in the advertisements of nos. 15–17 of the McGill University Economic Studies series.

C28.37  "The Hero of Home Week; How Ed Smith Came Back to Our Home Town," *Orillia News-Letter*, 4 July 1928, p. 4. Also as "The Hero of the Home Week," *Montreal Standard*, 14 July 1928, final ed., p. 44. Illustrated by A.G. Racey. Syndicated by Metropolitan Newspaper Service, New York.

C28.38  "A Midsummer Detective Mystery; Showing the Effect of Hot Weather on Cold Criminality," *Orillia News-Letter*, 11 July 1928, p. [12]. Also as "A Midsummer Detective Mystery," *Montreal Standard*, 21 July 1928, final ed., p. 46. Illustrated by A.G. Racey. Syndicated by Metropolitan Newspaper Service, New York.

C28.39  "Putting the College to the People; How the Graduating Class Line Up at the Barbers' College," *Orillia News-Letter*, 18 July 1928, p. [12]. Also as "Putting the College to the People," *Montreal Standard*, 28 July 1928, final ed., p. 44. Illustrated by A.G. Racey. Syndicated by Metropolitan Newspaper Service, New York.

C28.40  "One Glorious Day's Fishing; Just a Plain Statement of What Happened — No Exaggeration," *Orillia News-Letter*, 25 July 1928, p. [12]. Also as "One Glorious Day's Fishing," *Montreal Standard*, 4 August 1928, final ed., p. 36. Illustrated by A.G. Racey. Syndicated by Metropolitan Newspaper Service, New York.

C28.41  "The Day After Tomorrow; The Athletic News of 1950," *Orillia News-Letter*, 1 August 1928, p. [12]. Reprinted as "The Day After Tomorrow," *Montreal Standard*, 11 August 1928, final ed., p. 38. Illustrated by A.G. Racey. Syndicated by Metropolitan Newspaper Service, New York. Also as "The Day After To-Morrow; If We Go On As We

Seem to Be Going . . . the Athletic News of 1950 . . . ," *Passing Show* (Christmas Annual 1928): 18–9.

**C28.42** "The Golfmaniac; One of the People We Know Because We Can't Help It," *Orillia News-Letter*, 15 August 1928, p. [12]. As "The Golfmaniac," *Montreal Standard*, 18 August 1928, final ed., p. 36. Illustrated by A.G. Racey. Syndicated by Metropolitan Newspaper Service, New York. Also as "The Golfmaniac; Surely You've Met Someone Exactly Like Him!" *Passing Show* 28, no. 743 (17 November 1928): 18–9. Reprinted in Herbert Warren Wind, ed., *The Complete Golfer* (New York: Simon and Schuster, 1954), pp. 130–1; as "The Golf Maniac; for Most People, It's Just a Sport. But for a Fanatic Few, It Becomes an Obsession," *Reader's Digest* (Canadian) 128, no. 770 (June 1986): 39–40, 42 with illustration by Norman Cousineau; as "Golfomaniac" in *Golf Tales: Classic Stories from the Nineteenth Hole* (New York: Viking Studio Books, 1991), pp. 9–10, 12–4; as "Golfomaniac" in Paul D. Staudohar, ed., *Golf's Best Short Stories* (Chicago: Chicago Review Press, 1997), pp. 123–6.

**C28.43** "The Newer Truthfullness; How the Up-to-Date Biographer Slates His Hero," *Orillia News-Letter*, 22 August 1928, p. [12]. Also as "The Newer Truthfulness," *Montreal Standard*, 25 August 1928, final ed., p. 38. Illustrated by A.G. Racey. Syndicated by Metropolitan Newspaper Service, New York.

**C28.44** "The Golfer's Pocket Guide; A Manual to Help Him Recover His Game," *Orillia News-Letter*, 29 August 1928, p. [4]. Also as "The Golfer's Pocket Guide," *Montreal Standard*, 1 September 1928, final ed., p. 54. Illustrated by A.G. Racey. Syndicated by Metropolitan Newspaper Service, New York.

**C28.45** "The Case Against Prohibition: An Address by Stephen Leacock," *Fellowship* (London) 8, no. 9 (September 1928): 194–5.

**C28.46** "A Study in Still Life; The Tailor Who Smiled a Welcome for Thirty Years," *Orillia News-Letter*, 5 September 1928, p. 4. Also as "A Study in Still Life," *Montreal Standard*, 8 September 1928, final ed., p. 50. Illustrated by A.G. Racey. Syndicated by Metropolitan Newspaper Service, New York. See also C16.20.

**C28.47** "My Lost Walking-Stick; An Intimate Talk to My Friends," *Orillia News-Letter*, 19 September 1928, p. [12]. Also as "My Lost Walking Stick," *Montreal Standard*, 22 September 1928, final ed., p. 48. Illustrated by A.G. Racey. Syndicated by Metropolitan Newspaper Service, New York.

**C28.48** "New Words — New Things; When a Gentleman of 1901 Tries to Talk to a Youth of Today," *Orillia News-Letter*, 24 September 1928, p. [12]. Also as "New Words — New Things," *Montreal Standard*, 29 September 1928, final ed., p. 50. Illustrated by A.G. Racey. Syndicated by Metropolitan Newspaper Service, New York.

**C28.49** "Train That Goes Back to Yesterday; 'The Five O'Clock' That You're Always Going to Take Some Day," *Orillia News-Letter*, 3 October 1928, p. [12]. Also as "Train That Goes Back to Yesterday," *Montreal Standard*, 6 October 1928, final ed., p. 50. Syndicated by Metropolitan Newspaper Service, New York.

**C28.50** "The Repatriation of the Minstrel," *New Yorker* 4, no. 33 (6 October 1928): 28. Reprinted in *Montreal Standard*, final ed., 17 November 1928, final ed., p. 50. Illustrated by A.G. Racey. Also as "The Repatriation of the Minstrel; Organization To Be Formed to Put All Singers Back Where They Want to Go," *Orillia News-Letter*, 28 November 1928,

p. [18]. Syndicated by Metropolitan Newspaper Service, New York. As "The Repatriation of the Minstrel; It Is High Time That Something Should Be Done About All the Home-Sick Singers of This Earth," *Passing Show* 29, no. 755 (9 February 1929): 18–9.

C28.51 "The Flying Carpet," *Montreal Standard*, 13 October 1928, final ed., p. 50. Illustrated by A.G. Racey. Also as "The Flying Carpet; And What If It Flew Now?" *Orillia News-Letter*, 17 October 1928, p. 4. Syndicated by Metropolitan Newspaper Service, New York.

C28.52 "Arithmetic Heroes — 1928 Model," *Montreal Standard*, 20 October 1928, final ed., p. 44. Illustrated by A.G. Racey. Also as "Arithmetic Heroes — 1928 Model; An Up-to-Date View of A, B, and C, the Famous Textbook Characters," *Orillia News-Letter*, 24 October 1928, p. 10. Syndicated by Metropolitan Newspaper Service, New York. See also C94.1.

C28.53 "Willie Nut Tries to Enter College," *Montreal Standard*, 27 October 1928, final ed., p. [50]. Illustrated by A.G. Racey. Syndicated by Metropolitan Newspaper Service, New York.

C28.54 "The Last of the Rubber Necks," *Montreal Standard*, 3 November 1928, final ed., p. 52. Illustrated by A.G. Racey. Also as "The Last of the Rubber Necks; Around the World in a Sight-Seeing Air Bus in 1950," *Orillia News-Letter*, 7 November 1928, p. [11]. Syndicated by Metropolitan Newspaper Service, New York.

C28.55 "The Golf Season in Retrospect," *Montreal Standard*, 10 November 1928, final ed., p. 48. Illustrated by A.G. Racey. Also as "The Golf Season in Retrospect; A Personal Review of the Big Games of the Year," *Orillia News-Letter*, 21 November 1928, p. 11. Syndicated by Metropolitan Newspaper Service, New York.

C28.56 "The Startling Disclosures of a Wronged Woman," *Montreal Standard*, 24 November 1928, final ed., p. 44. Illustrated by A.G. Racey. Also as "The Startling Disclosures of a Wronged Woman; Is Turned Upside Down and Then Right Side Up; A Palpitating Story in Which a Woman's Soul [sic]," *Orillia News-Letter*, 5 December 1928, p. 10. Syndicated by Metropolitan Newspaper Service, New York.

C28.57 "The National Literature Problem in Canada," *Canadian Mercury* 1 (December 1928): 8–9.

C28.58 "More Startling Disclosures of a Wronged Woman," *Montreal Standard*, 1 December 1928, final ed., p. 50. Illustrated by A.G. Racey. Also as "More Startling Disclosures of a Wronged Woman; The First Awakening of Love — Lilac Time and the Summer Boarder," *Orillia News-Letter*, 12 December 1928, p. [12]. Syndicated by Metropolitan Newspaper Service, New York.

C28.59 "More and More Startling Disclosures of a Wronged Woman," *Montreal Standard*, 8 December 1928, final ed., p. 52. Illustrated by A.G. Racey. Syndicated by Metropolitan Newspaper Service, New York.

C28.60 "The Future of American Humor," *St. Louis Post Dispatch*, 9 December 1928, American sec. of the 50th anniversary issue supp., pp. 4–5. This edition has 232 pages divided in sections with pagination beginning again for each section. On p. 1 of the American section, there is a notice that this section contains an article by Stephen Leacock. The microfilm edition filmed by the Recordak Corp. of St. Louis is missing pp. 4 and 5 of the section, and there is no article by Leacock on the other pages. Pagination confirmed by

Lomer (p. 83). Reprinted in *The Drift of Civilization* (New York: Simon and Schuster, 1929), pp. 227–34; (London: Allen and Unwin, 1930), pp. 243–54.

**C28.61** "Astronomical Alarms," *Montreal Standard*, 15 December 1928, final ed., p. 54. Illustrated by A.G. Racey. Reprinted as "Astronomical Alarms; Terrifying Reports from the Observatories," *Orillia News-Letter*, 19 December 1928, p. [11]. Syndicated by Metropolitan Newspaper Service, New York. Also as "Astronomical Alarms; But They Should Trouble Posterity Rather Than Ourselves," *Passing Show* 29, no. 763 (6 April 1929): 14.

**C28.62** "Back at School," *Montreal Standard*, 22 December 1928, final ed., p. 52. Illustrated by A.G. Racey. Syndicated by Metropolitan Newspaper Service, New York. Also as "Back at School; It's Hard on Parents but the Children's Homework Must Be Done," *Passing Show* 29, no. 757 (23 February 1929): 18–9. See also C29.38.

**C28.63** "More Literary Scandals," *Montreal Standard*, 29 December 1928, final ed., p. 46. Illustrated by A.G. Racey. Reprinted as "More Literary Scandals; Reputations of Adam, Noah, and Tut-ankh-Amen Shaken to the Very Base," *Orillia News-Letter*, 9 January 1929, p. 9. Syndicated by Metropolitan Newspaper Service, New York. Also as "More Literary Scandals; Making Free With the Reputations of Noah, Adam and Tut-Ankh-Amen," *Passing Show* 29, no. 764 (13 April 1929): 14.

**C29.1** "In the Bright Time to Come," *Montreal Standard*, 5 January 1929, final ed., p. 48. Illustrated by A.G. Racey. Syndicated by Metropolitan Newspaper Service, New York.

**C29.2** "More Messages from Mars," *Montreal Standard*, 12 January 1929, final ed., p. 54. Illustrated by A.G. Racey. Also as "More Messages from Mars; A Personal Encounter with the First Martian Across," *Orillia News-Letter*, 23 January 1929, p. [11]. Syndicated by Metropolitan Newspaper Service, New York.

**C29.3** "The Iron Man Proposes to the Tin Woman," *Montreal Standard*, 19 January 1929, final ed., p. 44. Illustrated by A.G. Racey. Also as "The Iron Man Proposes to the Tin Woman; Some Further Light on the Future Significance of the Newly Invented Iron Man," *Orillia News-Letter*, 30 January 1929, p. 11. Syndicated by Metropolitan Newspaper Service, New York.

**C29.4** "Memoirs of an Iceman," *Montreal Standard*, 26 January 1929, final ed., p. 50. Illustrated by A.G. Racey. Also as "Memoirs of an Iceman; Another Splendid Volume Added to the Growing List of Memoirs," *Orillia News-Letter*, 6 February 1929, p. 11. Syndicated by Metropolitan Newspaper Service, New York.

**C29.5** "Further Progress in Specialization," *Montreal Standard*, 2 February 1929, final ed., p. 48. Illustrated by A.G. Racey. Also as "Further Progress in Specialization; What Is Going to Happen When All the Professions Follow the Lead of the Doctors," *Orillia News-Letter*, 13 February 1929, p. 13. Syndicated by Metropolitan Newspaper Service, New York.

Electronically available (12 October 1997) at the National Library of Canada's Leacock Web site: http://www.nlc-bnc.ca/leacock/special.htm

**C29.6** "The Criminal Face," *Montreal Standard*, 9 February 1929, final ed., p. [50]. Illustrated by A.G. Racey. Also as "The Criminal Face: If You Have It, Apply at Once for a Room in the Penitentiary," *Orillia News-Letter*, 27 February 1929, p. 13. Syndicated by Metropolitan Newspaper Service, New York.

**C29.7** "Naval Disagreement for the Current Year," *Montreal Standard*, 16 February 1929, final ed., p. 50. Illustrated by A.G. Racey. Also as "Naval Disagreement for the Current Year; A Retrospect as Reported in the Press of 1930," *Orillia News-Letter*, 6 March 1929, p. [12]. Syndicated by Metropolitan Newspaper Service, New York.

C29.8   "Isn't It Just Wonderful?" *Montreal Standard*, 23 February 1929, final ed., p. 48. Illustrated by A.G. Racey. Also as "Isn't It Just Wonderful; Some of the New Marvels of Long-Distance Messages Over the Radio," *Orillia News-Letter*, 13 March 1929, p. [10]. Syndicated by Metropolitan Newspaper Service, New York.

C29.9   "Conversations of the Hour," *Montreal Standard*, 2 March 1929, final ed., p. 50. Illustrated by A.G. Racey. Also as "Conversations of the Hour; to Illustrate Life at the Close of the Third Decade of the Twentieth Century," *Orillia News-Letter*, 20 March 1929, p. 13. Syndicated by Metropolitan Newspaper Service, New York.

C29.10   "Other People's Lives," *Montreal Standard*, 9 March 1929, final ed., p. 52. Illustrated by A.G. Racey. Also as "Other People's Lives; the Memoirs of a Night Watchman," *Orillia News-Letter*, 27 March 1929, p. [13]. Syndicated by Metropolitan Newspaper Service, New York.

C29.11   "This Heart-to-Heart Stuff," *Montreal Standard*, 16 March 1929, final ed., p. 50. Illustrated by A.G. Racey. Also as "This Heart-to-Heart Stuff; Some 'Birdie-Birdie' Shot for the 'Kiddy-Kiddy' Writers," *Orillia News-Letter*, 3 April 1929, p. 13. Syndicated by Metropolitan Newspaper Service, New York.

C29.12   " 'Mr. Chairman, I Beg to Move — ,' " *Montreal Standard*, 23 March 1929, final ed., p. 52. Illustrated by A.G. Racey. Also as "Mr. Chairman I Beg to Move — Showing the Wonderful Effectiveness of What Is Called Legislative Procedure," *Orillia News-Letter*, 10 April 1929, p. 10. Syndicated by Metropolitan Newspaper Service, New York.

C29.13   "Long After Bedtime," *Montreal Standard*, 30 March 1929, final ed., p. 48. Illustrated by A.G. Racey. Also as "Long After Bedtime; A Night Mystery Story in the Mysterious Style," *Orillia News-Letter*, 17 April 1929, p. [12]. Syndicated by Metropolitan Newspaper Service, New York.

C29.14   "Tributes of Mark Twain," *Overland Monthly and Out West Magazine* 87, no. 4 (April 1929): 107–8, 123. Leacock's tribute, one of several, appears on p. 108. Reprinted in *Tributes to Mark Twain by Members of the Society* (Paris: Mark Twain Society, 1930), p. 12.

C29.15   "The Life of J. Correspondence Smith," *New Yorker* 5, no. 7 (6 April 1929): 33–4, 36. Reprinted as "Typical Lives of the Future," *Montreal Standard*, 18 May 1929, final ed. p. 54. Illustrated by A.G. Racey. Also as "Typical Lives of the Future; the Life of J. Correspondence Smith," *Orillia News-Letter*, 5 June 1929, p. 10. Syndicated by Metropolitan Newspaper Service, New York.

C29.16   "Overhauling the Encyclopedia," *Toronto Star Weekly*, 6 April 1929, p. 7. Also in *Montreal Standard*, 6 April 1929, final ed., p. 50, illustrated by A.G. Racey; *Boston Sunday Advertiser*, 7 April 1929, p. 7; as "Making Encyclopedia," *Chicago Herald and Examiner*, 14 April 1929, p. 8; as "Overhauling the Encyclopedia; How to Make It Bigger, Brighter, Brainier," *Orillia News-Letter*, 24 April 1929, p. [12]. Syndicated by Metropolitan Newspaper Service, New York. Also in *Passing Show* 30, no. 779 (27 July 1929): 18–9.

C29.17   "Portents of the Future," *Montreal Standard*, 13 April 1929, final ed., p. 50. Illustrated by A.G. Racey. Also as "Portents of the Future; a Few Extraordinary Cases of

Second, and Even Third Sight," *Orillia News-Letter*, 1 May 1929, p. [10]. Syndicated by Metropolitan Newspaper Service, New York. In *Passing Show*, 30, no. 777 (13 July 1929): 18–9.

C29.18   "All Up!" *Montreal Standard*, 20 April 1929, p. 32. Illustrated by A.G. Racey. Also as "All Up! Average Life at the Average College, As Gathered from the Pages of Any College Daily at Any Alma Mater," *Orillia News-Letter*, 8 May 1929, p. [12]. Syndicated by Metropolitan Newspaper Service, New York.

C29.19   "Confessions of a Super-Criminal," *Montreal Standard*, 27 April 1929, p. 34. Illustrated by A.G. Racey. Reprinted as "Confessions of a Super-Criminal; Revelations of the Underworld," *Orillia News-Letter*, 15 May 1929, p. 12. Syndicated by Metropolitan Newspaper Service, New York. Also as "Confessions of a Super Criminal; Dreadful Disclosures of the City Underworld," *Passing Show* 30, no. 783 (24 August 1929): 18–9.

C29.20   "Human Interest Put into Mathematics," *Mathematics Teacher* 22, no. 5 (May 1929): 302–4.

C29.21   "Legislative Language," *Montreal Standard*, 4 May 1929, final ed., p. 54. Illustrated by A.G. Racey. Also as "Legislative Language; Showing the Simplicity of Our Statues," *Orillia News-Letter*, 22 May 1929, p. [10]. Syndicated by Metropolitan Newspaper Service, New York.

C29.22   "Speculative Credit," *Montreal Standard*, 11 May 1929, final ed., p. 56. Illustrated by A.G. Racey. Also as "Speculative Credit; the Complaint of One of the Millions," *Orillia News-Letter*, 29 May 1929, p. 10. Syndicated by Metropolitan Newspaper Service, New York.

C29.23   "Forty Years of Billiards," *Montreal Standard*, 25 May 1929, final ed., p. 52. Illustrated by A.G. Racey. Also as "Forty Years of Billiards; Hints From an Old Hand to Youngsters at the Game," *Ottawa Citizen*, 25 May 1929. (There are no page numbers visible on the microfilm of the *Ottawa Citizen* held at the Toronto Reference Library.) Also in *Orillia News-Letter*, 12 June 1929, p. [2]. Syndicated by Metropolitan Newspaper Service, New York. Reprinted in Robert Byrne, ed., *Byrne's Book of Great Pool Stories* (San Diego: Harcourt Brace & Co., 1995), pp. 59–64.

C29.24   "Who Reads What; Tell Me Who You Are and I'll Tell You What You Read," *Orillia News-Letter*, 19 June 1929, p. [2]. Syndicated by Metropolitan Newspaper Service, New York.

C29.25   "My Amusing Friends: a Few Samples of Their Endless Fun," *Orillia News-Letter*, 26 June 1929, p. 10. Syndicated by Metropolitan Newspaper Service, New York.

C29.26   "The Days That Were," *College Times* (Upper Canada College, Toronto) (Summer 1929): 60–1.

C29.27   "A Backward Look at the College Year; With a Forward Look to More Like It," *Orillia News-Letter*, 3 July 1929, p. 12. Syndicated by Metropolitan Newspaper Service, New York.

C29.28   "Breakfast at the Smiths; a Little Study in the Beauty of Cheerfulness," *Orillia News-Letter*, [10 July 1929], p. 12. Syndicated by Metropolitan Newspaper Service, New York.

C29.29   "Come and See Our Town; How the Visitor Feels When Shown Around," *Orillia News-Letter*, 24 July 1929, p. 12. Syndicated by Metropolitan Newspaper Service, New York.

C29.30 "Correspondence Manual Number One: a Foundation Guide-Book for All the Others," *Orillia News-Letter*, 14 August 1929, p. 13. Syndicated by Metropolitan Newspaper Service, New York. Also in *Passing Show* 30, no. 801 (28 December 1929): 18–9.

C29.31 "The Conquest of Peru; A Story of the Eleventh of August," *Orillia News-Letter*, 28 August 1929, p. 12. Syndicated by Metropolitan Newspaper Service, New York.

C29.32 "Fifty Cents Worth; The Thin Veil Between Humor and Tragedy," *Orillia News-Letter*, 18 September 1929, p. [10]. Syndicated by Metropolitan Newspaper Service, New York.

C29.33 "Potter's Corners; and Why They Never Sleep There," *Orillia News-Letter*, 25 September 1929, p. 10. Syndicated by Metropolitan Newspaper Service, New York.

C29.34 "Good-By, Summer; a Regret and a Resolution," *Orillia News-Letter*, 23 October 1929, p. 9. Syndicated by Metropolitan Newspaper Service, New York.

C29.35 "Uninvented Inventions; a Big Chance for Big Money," *Orillia News-Letter*, 30 October 1929, p. 10. Syndicated by Metropolitan Newspaper Service, New York.

C29.36 "How to Listen to Golf; or Won't you Tell Me All About It," *Orillia News-Letter*, 6 November 1929, p. 10. Syndicated by Metropolitan Newspaper Service, New York.

C29.37 "Back at College; Notes on the Opening at Any Alma Mater," *Orillia News-Letter*, 13 November 1929, p. 11. Syndicated by Metropolitan Newspaper Service, New York. See also C28.62.

C29.38 "One Hundred Per Cent; a Suggestion for Keeping Our School Histories Thoroughly American," *Orillia News-Letter*, 27 November 1929, p. 9. Syndicated by Metropolitan Newspaper Service, New York.

C30.1 "A Convenient Calendar for Future Years," *Old McGill 1931* 34 (1930): 62. Reprinted as "A Calendar for Future Years," *McGill News* 50, no. 6 (November 1969): 13; as "The Calendar According to Stephen Leacock," *McGill Reporter*, 21 November 1979, p. 3.

C30.2 "A Medieval Hole-in-One," *Harper's Magazine* 160 (January 1930): 249–52. This is one of several articles by different authors in the sec. "Lion's Mouth." Reprinted in Paul D. Staudohar, ed., *Golf's Best Short Stories* (Chicago: Chicago Review Press, 1997), pp. 215–23.

C30.3 "Sault Ste. Marie Will Turn Green With Envy When It Reads This One. Swiss Paper Crowns Orillia with the Prize for Animal Stories," *Orillia Packet and Times*, 9 January 1930, p. 1. The story reports that the extract printed is translated from a recent issue of the *Swiss Journal of Geneva*, and that the quotation was given to the paper by Stephen Leacock. The extract concerns Orillia being taken over by squirrels, mud turtles, skunks, muskrats, and a porcupine. Leacock is also reported as sending the paper a Canadian Press story which he will be sending on to Geneva titled "Kangaroo Outbreak in Geneva."

C30.4 "The Perils and Pitfalls of College Journalism," *McGilliad* 1, no. 1 (March 1930): 3. See also C8.2.

C30.5 "In Praise of Petroleum," *Imperial Oil Review* 14, no. 4 (August–September 1930): 8–9. Reprinted in *Imperial Oil Review* (February 1955): 10–1.

C30.6 "In Praise of the Brook Trout," *Holiday* 1, no. 1 (October 1930): 31, 67.

**C30.7** "What Next?" *Spectator* no. 5,343 (22 November 1930): 776–7.

**C30.8** "Once to Every Man," *Sportsman Pilot* (December 1930): 17, 46.

**C30.9** "Walking Out on the Guide-Book," *Holiday* 1, no. 3 (December 1930): 15, 50. Illustrated by Bruce Bairnsfather.

**C30.10** "Brighter Breakfasts; A Domestic Possibility," *Passing Show* ([1930]) (Christmas Holiday Annual): 20–1.

**C31.1** "Why Graduate? A Last Appeal to the Class of 1932," *Old McGill 1932* 35 (1931): 60.

**C31.2** "Our Class: Advice and Warning from 1891 to 1931," *Cornell Widow* (1931, special issue): 20. The issue also contains a tribute to Leacock, "Stephen Leacock As I See Him" (p. 21) by K.N. Cameron, a McGill student.

**C31.3** "Charles Thompson Noble," *McGill News* 12, no. 2 (March 1931): 53–5.

**C31.4** "Writes on Debt Problem; Canadian Economist Would Have Us Cancel but Not Reduce," *New York Times*, 8 March 1931, sec. 3, p. 6. Report of a letter by Leacock to the press on whether the United States should reduce the war-debt owned by Britain by up to one-half. Two sentences from the letter are quoted in the article, dateline Ottawa, 4 March. Despite the headline, the article states that Leacock would favour reduction but not on the grounds that it would be an act of justice by the United States.

**C31.5** "Stephen Leacock Mourns Mates Caught in Varsity Editorial Clutches," *Varsity* (University of Toronto) (20 March 1931): 7. Leacock's reminiscences of editing the *Varsity* during his undergraduate years at the University of Toronto, sent to the *Varsity* on its fiftieth anniversary of publication.

**C31.6** "Back at School (from a Parent's Point of View)," *Elevator* (published by the students of Belleville Collegiate and Vocational School) (Easter 1931): 22.

**C31.7** "Americans Are Queer," *Forum* 85 (April 1931): 224–5. Illustrated by Julian de Miskey. Reprinted as "A Neighbor Looks at America," in Fred J. Ringel, ed., *America as Americans See It* (New York: Harcourt Brace/Literary Guild, 1932), pp. 362–5, Leacock's text begins on p. 363; in Joseph M. Bachelor and Ralph L. Henry, eds., *Challenging Essays in Modern Thought (Second Series)* (New York: D. Appleton-Century Co., 1933), pp. 104–6; in Kendall B. Taft, John Francis McDermott, and Dana O. Jensen, eds., *Contemporary Opinion* (Boston: Houghton Mifflin, 1933), pp. 73–5; in Raymond Woodbury Pence, ed., *Essays of Today* (New York: Macmillan, 1935), pp. 380–2; in R.W. Pence and Fred L. Bergmann, eds., *Writing Craftsmanship* (New York: W.W. Norton, 1956), pp. 67–9; excerpted in "As Others See Us," *Reader's Digest* 30, no. 179 (March 1937): 93–4 (Lomer, p. 63) says this is the last paragraph); condensed in *Reader's Digest* 33, no. 197 (September 1938): 33–4.

**C31.8** "The Fall of the Pound Sterling," *Montreal Daily Star*, 10 October 1931, pp. 1, 7; 13 October 1931, pp. 1, 21.

**C31.9** "Professor Leacock Declares Shadow of Brother Stiggins Still Falls on Our Hotels," *Montreal Herald*, 6 November 1931, pp. 1, 3. Reprint of letter from *New York Herald Tribune*. The *Tribune* quotes a letter from the *St. Louis Post-Dispatch* in which Leacock defended the Canadian system of liquor control. The quotation of the first letter occasioned a second letter by Leacock.

C31.10  "Pax Vobiscum: Let There Be Peace in Saskatchewan," *Sheaf* (University of Saskatchewan) 20, no. 6 (12 November 1931): 1.

C31.11  "Leacock Calls for Many-Sided Empire Preference Plan; British Tariff First Step to Flowing Trade; Professor of Economics at McGill Points Way to Greater Market. Asks Mutual Pool; Asserts Imperial Parley Has Chance to Start Interchange," *Toronto Mail and Empire*, 16 November 1931, pp. 1, 3. This article, dateline Montreal 15 November, is on the upcoming Imperial Economic Conference at Ottawa. The editor commented in "Triangular Preferences One Need of the Empire," *Toronto Mail and Empire*, 16 November 1931, p. 8. Also as "The Coming Imperial Conference . . . . ," *Montreal Herald*, 16 November 1931, p. 4.

C31.12  "Inflation and Deflation," *Spectator* no. 5,395 (21 November 1931): 697–8. According to Lomer (p. 95), this was reprinted in *World Wide* 31 (12 December 1931): 1,977–8. Excerpted as "Inflation and Deflation: Orillia Humorist Gets a Laugh Even Out of the Depression," *Orillia Packet and Times*, 21 January 1932, p. 7.

C31.13  "Beating Back to Prosperity," *Toronto Mail and Empire*, 28 November 1931, p. 3. The article is signed by Leacock in facsimile. Reprinted in *Imperial Oil Review* 15, no. 3 (December 1931): 2–4.

C31.14  "Needed — A Happy New Year," *New York Herald Tribune*, 27 December 1931, sec. 12, pp. 1–2. Reprinted in *World Wide* 32, no. 2 (9 January 1932): 47–8.

C32.1  "War Stuff! . . . A Few Words of Comfort," *Rotarian* 40 (January 1932): 9–10, 49. Illustrated by Tony Sarg.

C32.2  "Colonies for War Debts? Give America the Rich Congo Basin Instead of Cash — That Is the Suggestion of This Economist," *New York Herald Tribune*, 17 January 1932, sec. 12 ("Magazine"), pp. 1, 2.

C32.3  "Novel Idea Proposed Recommending a Weekly Literary Issue," *McGill Daily*, 22 January 1932, p. 1. Letter to the editor from Leacock. See also C32.4. Responses to his proposal appeared on 23 January 1932, p. 2 and 25 January 1932, p. 1.

C32.4  "More Suggestion on the 'Friday Daily,' " *McGill Daily*, 28 January 1932, p. 2. Letter to the editor.

C32.5  "Brook Trout . . . As a National Asset; Hours of Pleasure and Dollars of Revenue Are Lying Idle in Hundreds of Farmland Creeks for Want of Re-Stocking and Improvement," *Rod and Gun in Canada* 33, no. 10 (March 1932): 5–7. The magazine notes the article was "written especially for Rod and Gun." A lengthy extract appears as "Stephen Leacock Suggests How Farmers Can Make Money; Creeks Are a Source of Potential Wealth If Turned into Trout Streams," *Orillia Packet and Times*, 17 March 1932, pp. 1, 4.

C32.6  "This Business of Prophecy," *New York Times*, 21 March 1932, sec. 6 ("Magazine"), p. 12. Illustrated by Carl Rose.

C32.7  "Baron de Lahontan, Explorer," *Canadian Geographical Journal* 4 (May 1932): 281–94. See also D33.9.

C32.8  "Professor Leacock Practises Precepts," *Montreal Daily Star*, 27 May 1932, p. 18. Dateline 26 May 1932, Ottawa. This short article contains the following text written by Leacock: "As a matter of personal economy, I wish to resign as a member of the Royal Society of Canada." Action on Leacock's resignation was deferred until a later meeting of the Society, but Pelham Edgar inquired whether the Society should take up a subscription to pay for Leacock's membership fee.

**C32.9** "If Gold Should Cease to Be 'Gold,'" *Canadian Institute of Mining and Metallurgy Bulletin* no. 224 (August 1932): 430–6. The text of Leacock's address delivered at the Annual General Meeting of the Institute in Montreal at the Windsor Hotel on 5 April 1932. Discussion following Leacock's address with his replies to comments and questions is found on pp. 436–9. Reported as "Grave Possibility of Catastrophic Gold Decline Seen If Gold Standard Goes, Then Gold Goes, Dr. Leacock Tells Mining Men. . . . ," *Montreal Gazette*, 6 April 1932, p. 5; "Two Graduates Speak on the Gold Standard," *University Monthly* (University of Toronto) 27, no. 8 (May 1932): 296–7. See also E32.7.

**C32.10** "Christmas Fiction and National Friction: An Application of the Dear Old Christmas Stories to National Harmony and World Peace," *Spectator* no. 5,447 (18 November 1932): 730, 732. Reprinted in Peter Fleming and Derek Verschoyle, eds., *Spectator's Gallery: Essays, Sketches, Short Stories & Poems* (London: Jonathan Cape, 1933), pp. 243–57.

**C32.11** "Mr. Gandhi and Uncle Sam," *Spectator* no. 5,452 (23 December 1932): 888–9.

**C33.1** "The Riddle of the Depression," *Empire Club of Canada Addresses Delivered to the Members during the Year 1933–34*: 70–83. An address read to the Empire Club of Canada in Toronto on 16 February 1933 (see E33.8). Reported as "Leacock Suggests Devaluating Dollar; Would Reduce Gold Basis of Canadian Currency. Relief in Six Days," *Toronto Mail and Empire*, 17 February 1933, p. 5; one paragraph is quoted on the C.C.F. Party, among other quotations. The speech was broadcast over the radio and heard in Orillia on CPRY. Also reported, with lengthy quotations, as "Devalued Dollar Urged by Leacock; Hopes Canada and U.S. Will Co-operate in Move," *Toronto Globe*, 17 February 1933, p. 10; "Cheap Dollar Urged for Halting Slump; Professor Leacock Wonders If C.C.F. Will 'Socialize Their Pants,'" *Toronto Star*, 17 February 1933, p. 3 (three paragraphs quoted); "Stephen Leacock Declares Depression Can Be Cured; Outlines Plan Which He Says Will Give Relief in Six Days. Relief Would Be Temporary, But Would Give A Chance for Readjustment," *Orillia Packet and Times*, 23 February 1933, p. 1.

**C33.2** "Happy New Year, Mars!" *New York Herald Tribune*, 1 January 1933, sec. 11 ("Magazine"), pp. 1–2. Illustrated by C.R. Twelvetrees.

**C33.3** "Ourselves and the Communists; Professor Leacock Discusses Our Relations with Russia," *Ottawa Journal*, 2 January 1933, pp. 1–2. Letter to the editor in which Leacock conveys his reaction to a report of a speech on Russia given at an Ottawa luncheon club and his revulsion to communism. The letter was reprinted on 4 January 1933, p. 6. An editorial titled "Professor Leacock Spanks," 4 January 1933, p. 6, praised Leacock's analysis of the political situation in Russia. Also reprinted as "Stephen Leacock in Russia," *Toronto Mail and Empire*, 11 January 1933, p. 8.

**C33.4** "Canadians Hopeful But Not Predicting; Men See the Country Ready for Upturn but Won't Discuss Dates," *New York Times*, 8 January 1933, sec. 4, p. 8. In a story by V.M. Kipp, four paragraphs from Leacock's New Year's Message are quoted. The quotations condemn Russia while finding hope for Canada, despite the bleakness in both countries.

**C33.5** "Finding a Formula: A Diplomatic Episode," *Harper's Magazine* 166 (March 1933): 490–2.

**C33.6** "The Economic Analysis of Industrial Depression," *Papers and Proceedings of the Fifth Annual Meeting of the Canadian Political Science Association* 5 (May 1933): 5–24. Delivered 22 May 1933 in Ottawa.

**C33.7** "Stephen Leacock Wants Rule for Shooting Chicken Thieves. Appeals to Deputy Attorney-General After Visits of Thieves to His Hen Roosts," *Orillia Packet and Times*, 17 August 1933, p. 1. Extract from Leacock's letter to the Deputy Attorney-General after the theft of 40 Rhode Island Reds and 20 Plymouth Rocks. Leacock asks if he could shoot the thieves in the legs or did he have to wrestle them in the grass. The article notes that Leacock has also sent a letter to Premier Henry but it is not quoted. See K83.1 (p. 142) which prints, in facsimile, Leacock's day letter telegram to Henry. Article apparently reprinted as "Stephen Leacock Wants to Know," *Orillia Packet and Times*, July 1939. See also K93.1.

**C33.8** "A Plain Man at the Play," *Rotarian* 43 (October 1933): 20–1, 55–6. Illustrated by John Fulton.

**C33.9** "A Rare Traveller's Account," *Canadian Historical Review* 14 (December 1933): 409–11. Book review of [Thomas Sibbald], *A Few Days in the United States and Canada with Some Hints to Settlers*, 1842 or 1843.

**C33.10** "General Currie," *Montreal Herald*, 6 December 1933, p. 6. Reprinted in *London (Ont.) Advertiser*, 11 December 1933; *Halifax Chronicle*, 12 December 1933; *Charlottetown Guardian*, 13 December 1933; *St. Catharines Standard*, 14 December 1933; *Nanaimo Free Press*, 15 December 1933; *Glace Bay (N.S.) Gazette*, 18 December 1933; *Sackville (N.B.) Tribune*, 18 December 1933; *Edmonton Journal*, 20 December 1933; partial reprintings in other Canadian newspapers. Reprinted in R.C. Fetherstonhaugh, *McGill University at War: 1914–1918, 1939–1945* (Montreal: McGill University, 1947), pp. 110–1; Daniel G. Dancocks, *Sir Arthur Currie: A Biography* (Toronto: Methuen, 1985), pp. 284–5. See also A66.

**C33.11** "Who's Who in Humor. 'I'll Make 'Em Blush Yet,' Stephen Leacock Tells Himself in This Autobiographical Interview, the Fifth of a Series by Noted Humorists," *New York Herald Tribune*, 10 December 1933, pp. 9–10. Illustrated by Everett Shinn.

**C34.1** "Ars Examinandi," *Old McGill 1935* 38 (1934): 98, 299. Reprinted as "How to Pass Exams without Trying," in K83.1, pp. 215–6.

**C34.2** "Recovery After Graduation; Thoughts for the Class of 1935," *Old McGill 1935* 38 (1934): 110, 293. Reprinted as "Recovery After Graduation," *Golden Book Magazine* 21 (February 1935): 114–6. Also as "Looking Back on College," *McGill News* 17, no. 3 (Summer 1936): 7–8. Two paragraphs are reprinted under the title, "Leacock Recalls Old Experiences. . . . ," *Montreal Daily Star*, 13 June 1936, p. 3. As "Laugh with Leacock," *McGill News* 50, no. 6 (November 1969): 13–4; with original title in K83.1, pp. 216–8.

**C34.3** "The Advancement of Learning: A Talk to Graduate Students," *McGill Daily*, 16 March 1934, pp. 2, 4. The text of a speech given on 15 March 1934 (E34.8). Reprinted in *Montreal Daily Herald*, 20 March 1934, p. 5; as "Stephen Leacock Looses His Harpoons on Commercialized Educational System," *Detroit Free Press*, 8 April 1934; in *McGill Daily*, 20 April 1934, pp. 2–3. See also E34.8.

**C34.4** "The Last Five Years in Canada: How the Country Reacted in a Period of Depression," *World Today: Encyclopaedia Britannica* 1 (April 1934): 22–5.

C34.5 "Why Do We Laugh?" *Christian Science Monitor*, 18 April 1934, ("Weekly Magazine Sec."), pp. 1–2. Illustrated by C.H. Rinks.

C34.6 "The Humorist Who Made Lincoln Laugh: Artemus Ward, Born A Century Ago, Gave to the Nation in His Time 'the Bright Happiness of Childish Merriment,'" *New York Times*, 22 April 1934, sec. 6 ("Magazine"), pp. 8–9.

C34.7 "Resuscitation After Apparent Graduation," *English Journal* (Chicago College Edition) 33 (May 1934): 412–3. The title is footnoted "Dr. Leacock's own summary of his address before the Detroit meeting of the National Council of Teachers of English, December 2, 1933." See E33.27.

C34.8 "The Revision of Democracy," *Papers and Proceedings of the Sixth Annual Meeting of the Canadian Political Science Association* 6 (May 1934): 5–16. Presidential address delivered on 21 May 1934 in Montreal. See also D34.5 and E34.14.

C34.9 "The Gospel According to Charles Dickens," *Saturday Review of Literature* 10 (19 May 1934): [697]–8. Book review of Charles Dickens, *The Life of Our Lord*, written in 1849 but just published by Simon and Schuster of New York. Leacock's remarks follow those by John Haynes Holmes, William Lyon Phelps and Alexander Woollcott, and precede those by Louis I. Newman, George N. Schuster and Alfred H. Holt.

C34.10 "Stirring Pageant of Canadian History: In Four Vivid Centuries a Wilderness Has Been Transformed into the Great Commonwealth of Today," *New York Times*, 19 August 1934, sec. 6, ("Magazine"), pp. 6–7, 17. Illustrated by C.W. Jefferys.

C34.11 "Two Humorists: Charles Dickens and Mark Twain," *Yale Review* n.s. 24 (September 1934): 118–29.

C34.12 "Graham Towers," *McGill Daily*, 5 December 1934, p. 2. Also as "New Bank Governor Praised by Leacock; Towers' Days at McGill Recalled," *Montreal Daily Star*, 5 December 1934, p. 11.

C34.13 "Leacock Asks: 'Is Canada Breaking Up?'; To 'Federate' All This Might Seem Impossible"; Provinces Are Demanding — and Getting — More and More Self-Rule — Leading Men Half Century Ago Ignored Provinces for Ottawa but Ottawa No Longer Has Monopoly of Best Political Brains of Country," *Montreal Daily Star*, 15 December 1934, p. 19. Reprinted as "Is Canada Breaking Up? Will America Eventually Have a Group of 'Balkans' on the North? Perhaps, Says This Noted Canadian. For While Our Government Is Being Centralized, Dominion Provinces Are Demanding and Getting — More and More Self-Rule," *New York Herald Tribune*, 16 December 1934, sec. 8 ("Magazine"), pp. 12–3, 20.

C34.15 "Our Lost Anatomist," *Montreal Herald*, 17 December 1934, p. 4. A poem read by Leacock at Col. and Mrs. Cape's house on Redpath Crescent, 12 December 1934, at the farewell party for Professor Samuel Whitnall ("Tingle") who was leaving McGill for the School of Anatomy in Bristol, Somerset. Reprinted in S.E. Whitnall, *Jokings Apart* (Oxford: Alden Press, 1950), pp. 136–43.

C35.1 "What Is Left of Adam Smith?" *Canadian Journal of Economics and Political Science* 1 (February 1935): 41–51.

C35.2 "Bankers Are Farmers at Heart, Talk Beans, Hens, Leacock Finds; New York Money Barons Dispel Humorist's Awe with Nostalgic Debates on Barred Rock vs. Leghorn and Hog Feed vs. Straw for Bed Ticks," *New York Herald Tribune*, 11 February 1935, pp. 1, 13. Leacock spoke to the bankers on 9 February 1935 (see D35.3 and E35.8). In an article, "Stephen Leacock Declares His Hens Are Paying; Hobnobs with the Big Wigs of Wall Street and Finds Them Interested in Hogs and Hens," *Orillia Packet and Times*, 7 March 1935, p. 5, the *Packet and Times* notes that Leacock "gave his impressions to the *New York Herald Tribune* and the article has come to us courtesy of the *St. Thomas Times Journal*." Apparently reprinted as "How Bankers Talk," *Banker's Magazine* 130 (April 1935): 512–3.

**C35.3** "A Correction," *Montreal Daily Star*, 12 March 1935, p. 10. Letter to the editor correcting the report carried by the Canadian Press of his speech at Windsor, Ont. See also C63.1, D35.6, and E35.16.

**C35.4** "Mr. Bennett's National Policy," *McGill News* 16, no. 2 (Spring 1935): 7. A contribution to a general discussion entitled "Premier Bennett's Reform Program — Three Attitudes." The two other contributors are F.R. Scott and G. Miller Hyde.

**C35.5** "Mark Twain and Canada," *Queen's Quarterly* 42 (Spring 1935): 68–81.

**C35.6** "Stephen Leacock and De Puisaye," *Toronto Mail and Empire*, 18 April 1935, p. 8. Letter to the editor asking for information on the De Puisaye colony in Aurora in 1795 for his colleague, Professor D'Hauteserve, who was writing a monograph. The letter is dated 17 April 193[5?] at Toronto.

**C35.7** "Club of Ignoramuses Just Dotes on Brains," *Buffalo Evening News*, ("Saturday Magazine"), 4 May 1935, p. 1. Also as "The Rogues' Gallery: Our Ignoramus Club, What It Is, What a Hit It Makes," *Chattanooga Times*, 5 May 1935, p. 6. Reprinted as "The Ignoramus Club," *Column Review* 1, no. 6 (August 1935): 73–5. Illustrated by Abner Dean. According to Curry in Staines's *Stephen Leacock: A Reappraisal* (p. 151), the article appeared as "Our Ignoramus Club," *Washington (D.C.) Star*, 2 June 1935. Apparently this was the first of a series of Rogues' Gallery articles which perhaps lasted for a month and may have recommenced in mid-July 1935. Syndicated by Bell Syndicated Inc.

**C35.8** "Good Times Can Come Again," *Current History* 42 (June 1935): 233–9.

**C35.9** "Economic Separatism in the British Empire," *Quarterly Review* (London) 265, no. 525 (July 1935): 1–11.

**C35.10** "The Everlasting Woman Question," *Rotarian* 47, no. 2 (August 1935): 13–4, 56. A reply, "These Men!" by Nina Wilcox Putnam, follows Leacock's article.

**C35.11** "The Lake Simcoe County," *Canadian Geographical Journal* 11 (September 1935): 109–16. Illustrated by several photographs, including an autographed one of Leacock at Lake Couchiching and one of his summer home.

**C35.12** "Social Credit Is Doomed Claims Stephen Leacock; Only Possible in Perfect Community and Therefore Not Needed, Urges McGill Economist," *Toronto Telegram*, 9 September 1935, p. 14. Copyright by the *Telegram* and the North American Newspaper Alliance.

**C35.13** "Canada's Crossroad; Canada Holds a General Election Tomorrow — with Conservatives Fighting Liberals and Socialist Groups Joining the Fray. Who'll Be the Winners? Upon the Answer May Depend the Whole Future of the Dominion," *New York Herald Tribune*, 13 October 1935, sec. 8 ("This Week Magazine"), pp. 2, 24–5.

C35.14 "Leacock Talks, Reports Speech, Pens Headline," *New York Herald Tribune*, 9 November 1935. Interview with Leacock before he was scheduled to deliver a speech to the New York alumni banquet of Acadia University, Nova Scotia. The interview contains Leacock's replies to queries and also the text of his own description of his speech: "Turn Back the College Clock; More Dreams Needed on the Campus and Fewer Diagrams; Stephen Leacock Looks Round in Vain for Men Like Himself." Also as "Leacock Writes Story of His New York Speech; Humorist Deplores Inability to Find Universities Producing More Professor Stephen Leacocks," *Montreal Daily Star*, 9 November 1935, pp. 1–2.

C35.15 "Mark Twain," *Evening Standard* (London), 18 November 1935, pp. 7, 10; illustrated by "E". Reprinted as "Mark Twain: Frustration of Would-Be Minstrel," *Montreal Daily Star*, 30 November 1935, sec. 2, p. 17.

C35.16 "Memorandum Read by Dr. Leacock at the Meeting of the Political Economy Club Last Night," *McGill Daily*, 22 November 1935, p. 1. See also E35.46.

C35.17 "Scenes from a Renovated Xmas," *National Home Monthly* (Winnipeg, MB) 36 (December 1935): 21, 46–7.

C35.18 "McGill's Loss Will Be Gain for Wild Tribes of Himalayas," *Montreal Daily Star*, 28 December 1935, p. 3. Upon receiving a fan letter from Private P. Fitzharris of the 2nd Argyll Sutherland Highlanders who was stationed in India at Rawalpindi, Leacock sent the following cable in reply: "Stop raiding that tribe and ask if they can use a first class economist, prophesy included." Reprinted as "Political Economist to Frontier Tribes; Prof. Leacock Applies for Post," *Times India*, 25 January 1936 (dateline 17 January 1936, London).

C36.1 "What Price Victory?" *Veteran Review* (Toronto) (1936): 21–4.

C36.2 "Tattered Guides," *Atlantic Monthly* 157 (February 1936): 179–81.

C36.3 "The Tide Turns in Canada: The Recent Election and What It Means," *World Today: Encyclopaedia Britannica* 3, no. 3 (February 1936): 7–10.

C36.4 "Stephen Leacock on 'Academic Freedom,'" *Maclean's Magazine* 49, no. 3 (1 February 1936): 14–5, 38–9. See also B. Spears, "Academic Freedom: A Reply to Professor Leacock," *Maclean's Magazine* 49, no. 7 (1 April 1936): 47–8.

C36.5 "No, I Shall Not Come 'Home' by S.L., Litt.D, LL.D.," *Evening News* (London), 4 February 1936, p. 8. Reprinted as "'I'll Stay in Canada,'" *Ottawa Evening Citizen*, 7 March 1936, p. [26 or 28]. Also in *New York Herald Tribune*, 8 March 1936, sec. 8, ("This Week"), pp. 6, 21. As "'So I'll Stay in Canada' Declares Stephen Leacock. . . . ," *Toronto Daily Star*, 7 March 1936. Condensed in *Reader's Digest* 28, no. 169 (May 1936): 19–21.

C36.6 "Return of Old Spelling Bee Welcomed by Prof. Leacock," *Montreal Daily Star*, 8 February 1936, p. 3. A letter written by Leacock in which he congratulates the *Star* for reviving the tradition of having spelling bees. He recalls winning a spelling bee at his school in the Township of Georgina.

C36.7 "Private Honesty in Public Affairs," *Financial Post* 30, no. 8 (22 February 1936): [11]. This is one of several contributions in this issue to the first appearance of the series "Canada — and the Next Five Years: Prominent Canadian Business and Professional Leaders Outline Main National Issues and Offer Solutions." Other contributors were C.H. Carlisle, E.J. Young, James J. Warren, and Robert Falconer.

C36.8 "Edward VIII and Canada," *Review of Reviews* 93, no. 3 (March 1936): 29–30.

Reprinted as "Stephen Leacock Views the King and the Empire," *Toronto Star Weekly*, 21 March 1936, General Sec. No. 2, p. 12. Also as "Stephen Leacock's Interview with King: Humorist Claims He Did All the Talking," *Orillia Packet and Times*, 2 April 1936, p. 5.

C36.9 "Diplomatic Detours," *New York Herald Tribune*, 8 March 1936, sec. 8 ("This Week"), p. 7.

C36.10 "The Past Quarter Century: We've Found a Soul but Need Dreamers, Says Stephen Leacock," *Maclean's Magazine* 49, no. 6 (15 March 1936): 36, 38.

C36.11 "Alberta's Financial Experiments: The Story of the Social Dividend of $25.00 a Month for Adults," *The World Today: Encyclopaedia Britannica* 4 (June 1937): 17–18.

C36.12 "The International Stuff," *Rotarian* 49, no. 1 (July 1936): 6–8. Illustrated by Ray Inman.

C36.13 "Through a Glass Darkly," *Atlantic Monthly* 158 (July 1936): 94–8.

C36.14 "What the Reviewers Missed," *American Mercury* 38 (July 1936): 368–71.

C36.15 "The Financial Condition of Canada No. I The Dominion: A Survey of the Present Critical Situation," *Morning Post* (London), 6 July 1936, p. 10. Reprinted (with 7 July 1936 article) as "Our Gathering Financial Crisis; National Extravagance Piling up Debt to Staggering Total — Nearly 40 % of Canadian Income Required for Interest Payments I The Dominion," *Financial Post* (Toronto) 30 (26 September 1936): 3.

C36.16 "The Financial Condition of Canada No. II Plight of the Provinces of Municipalities: The Piling Up of Colossal Debts," *Morning Post* (London), 7 July 1936, p. 10.

C36.17 "The Financial Condition of Canada No. III A Survey of the Railway Systems: Aftermath of the Pre-War Boom," *Morning Post* (London), 8 July 1936, p. 10. Reprinted as "Our Gathering Financial Crisis; Railway Losses Menace Solvency; Public Ownership Experiment with Old Inter-Colonial Grows to Mammoth Proportions and Staggering Deficits," *Financial Post* (Toronto) 30 (3 October 1936): 3.

C36.18 "The Financial Condition of Canada No. IV Summing Up: The Dominion's Salvation Lies in Her Vitality and Her Resources," *Morning Post* (London), 9 July 1936, p. 10. Reprinted as "Our Gathering Financial Crisis; Canada's Salvation Is In Rising Prices; Sane Policies for Railways and Taxation Will Help Mines to Aid," *Financial Post* (Toronto) 30 (10 October 1936): 3.

C36.19 "[Letter to the editor in reply to Geo. E. Cole's query about Leacock's first lectures on Political Economy at McGill University]," *McGill News* 17, no. 4 (Autumn 1936): 53. Coles's letter appears on pp. 52–3.

C36.20 "Canada Won't Go Yankee," *American Mercury* 39 (September 1936): 37–40. Condensed in *Reader's Digest* 29, no. 174 (October 1936): 8–10. According to Lomer (p. 68), the article also appeared in *Congressional Digest* 17 (August 1938): 219–21.

C36.21 "Too Much Alphabet," *Parade* 1, no. 12 (September 1936): 113–5. This a condensed version of the article. Apparently appeared originally as "Overworking the Alphabet," *Better English* (New York), possibly in September 1936. Probably condensed as "Initial Complaint," *Reader's Digest* 33, no. 199 (November 1938): 22. Lomer (p. 96) also lists another reprint: "Initial Complaint," *Scholastic* 30 (6 February 1937): 7–8.

C36.22 "Imaginary Persons," *Atlantic Monthly* 158 (October 1936): 490–3. Reprinted as "Who's Who in Never-Never Land: Are John Doe, Jack Robinson and Mr. Punch

Creatures of Our Imagination?" *Scholastic* 30, no. 1 (6 February 1937): 7–8, 21.

**C36.23** "Social and Other Credit in Alberta," *Fortnightly Review* (London) 146, n.s. 140 (November 1936): 525–35. Condensed as "Social Credit: A Criticism of the Alberta Experiment," *Review of Reviews* 95 (January 1937): 65–6. Condensed in *Magazine Digest* (Toronto) 14, no. 1 (January 1937): 92–6. Leacock wrote to the magazine to protest this unauthorized publication. See also C36.27.

**C36.24** "Roosevelt Win Is Daylight In Wood for All Democracy, Stephen Leacock Rejoices; Happy Sage of McGill Hopes All Dictators Will Emulate Landon in Defeat by Going 'Duck Hunting' — Regulation Is in the Cards," *Winnipeg Evening Tribune*, 11 November 1936, pp. 1, 15. — Syndicated by the North American Newspaper Alliance, Inc. in eighteen newspapers including the *Cleveland News*, *Buffalo News*, and *Boston Globe*.

**C36.25** "Stephen Leacock Becomes 'Daily' Staff Correspondent," *McGill Daily*, 2 December 1936, pp. 1, 4.

**C36.26** "Dr. Leacock Tours Western Canada," *McGill News* 18, no. 1 (Winter 1936): 54. This article publishes a letter from Leacock, dated 28 November 1936, addressed to Gordon Glassco, executive secretary of McGill University's Graduates' Society. In his letter Leacock discusses the reception given to him the previous evening at a meeting of the Graduates' Society in Port Arthur, ON where he gave his first lecture during his tour of western Canada. Reprinted as "Leacock at the Lakehead," *Fort William Daily Times-Journal*, 5 November [actually December] 1936, p. 4. The entire issue of 5 December is misdated November but it is found in the correct chronological sequence in the microfilm held at the OONL.

**C36.27** "The 'Social Credit' Warning," *New York Herald Tribune*, 13 December 1936, sec. 11 ("This Week Magazine"), pp. 4, 29.

**C36.28** "How Soon Can We Start the Next War?" *Amherst Alumni Council News* 10, no. 2, supplement 2 (December 1936): 51–65. Text of speech to the Alumni Council on 14 November 1936 (E36.26). A partial copy with holograph emendations is contained in Leacock's lecture notebooks at NAC. Reported as "Leacock Hits Nationalism; He Tells Amherst Alumni That the World Needs New Spirit," *New York Times*, sec. 2, 15 November 1936, p. 8; one sentence is quoted.

**C36.29** "My Fishpond," *Atlantic Monthly* 158 (December 1936): 720–2. Reprinted in *Evening Standard* (London), 1 February 1937, p. 7; illustrated by "Mendoza". Condensed in *Atlantic Digest* 1, no. 3 (January 1937): [8–10]; *Reader's Digest* 30, no. 178 (February 1937): 30–2; *Reader's Digest 40th Anniversary Treasury* (Montreal: Reader's Digest, 1961), pp. 409–11. Reprinted in *Le Parc National des Laurentides* (Ottawa: Department of Mines, 1939), p. [18]; in Theodore J. Gates and Austin Wright, eds., *College Prose* (Boston: D.C. Heath and Company, 1942), pp. 490–4; in Homer Andrew Watt, Oscar Cargill and William Charvat, eds., *New Highways in College Composition* (New York: Prentice Hall, 1946), pp. 520–2 (also in 2nd edition (1955), pp. 343–5 according Curry); *Reader's Digest* 86 (April 1965): 244. Apparently in *Unified English Composition* (New York: F.S. Crofts & Co., 1942). See also C38.10.

**C36.30** "Reflections on the North," *Beaver* 267, no. 3 (December 1936): 9–12. Illustrated by D'Egville. Reprinted in *Beaver* 301 (Summer 1970): 48–51; in *Beaver* 75, no. 2 (April–May 1995): 35–9; in Clifford Wilson, ed., *Northern Treasury* (Toronto: Thomas Nelson & Sons, n.d.), pp. 56–64.

**C36.31** "What Leacock Thinks," *Vancouver Sun*, 22 December 1936, p. 22. This article, which Leacock wrote and handed to interviewers he met in Vancouver on 21 December 1936, outlines his views on British Columbia, Social Credit, and his book on the West.

**C37.1** "Stephen Leacock Replies," *Argosy Weekly* (Mount Allison University) 63, no. 11 (9 January 1937): 1. Letter, written in Saskatoon, 11 December 1936, in response to a letter sent by the *Argosy* which said that the writer had enjoyed Leacock's *Nonsense Novels*. Reprinted as "Forgotten Leacockiana," *Mount Allison Record* 37, no. 4 (Winter 1954): 140; "His Mother Was Just Crazy Over Them," *Montreal Gazette*, 24 July 1954, p. 6.

**C37.2** "Leacock Gives Some Advice to Victoria," *Victoria Times*, 13 January 1937, p. 1.

**C37.3** "Pay for Defense in Wheat Prof. Leacock Thus Would Also Avoid Canada's Carryover Problem," *Toronto Globe and Mail*, 16 February 1937, p. 6. Letter to the editor.

**C37.4** "McGill in the West: Notes on a Personally Conducted Tour," *McGill Graduates' Bulletin* 1, no. 1 (March 1937): 3–6. Reprinted in *McGill News* 37, no. 1 (Winter 1955): 15, 25.

**C37.5** "My Discovery of the West: Article I," *Toronto Globe and Mail*, 6 March 1937, pp. 1, 10. The introduction to this article in the *Globe and Mail* states that it is "The first installment of Dr. Stephen Leacock's latest book, 'My Discovery of the West,' which The Globe and Mail has obtained the exclusive privilege of publishing in this form . . . ." The articles were syndicated by the Miller Services Ltd. in *Montreal Daily Star*, *Lethbridge Herald*, *Ottawa Citizen*, *Regina Daily Star*, *Vancouver Province*, *Edmonton Journal*, *Ottawa Citizen*, *Moncton Transcript*, and *Saskatoon Star*. See A82.

**C37.6** "My Discovery of the West: Article I. Why I Left Home — Travel Impressions and How to Avoid Them — At the Head of the Lakes — The City of Giants," *Montreal Daily Star*, 6 March 1937, p. 11. The introduction in the *Montreal Daily Star* states that it is "the first of 12 weekly articles" concerning "Dr. Leacock's recent visit to the Western provinces." The *Star* condensed the text as published in the *Globe and Mail*.

**C37.7** "My Discovery of the West: Article II," *Toronto Globe and Mail*, 8 March 1937, pp. 1, 11.

**C37.8** "My Discovery of the West: Article II, Fort William and the Waterway," *Montreal Daily Star*, 13 March 1937, p. 11.

**C37.9** "My Discovery of the West: Article III," *Toronto Globe and Mail*, 13 March 1937, pp. 1, 9.

**C37.10** "My Discovery of the West: Article IV," *Toronto Globe and Mail*, 15 March 1937, pp. 1, 12.

**C37.11** "My Discovery of the West: Article V," *Toronto Globe and Mail*, 16 March 1937, pp. 1, 12.

**C37.12** "My Discovery of the West: Article VI," *Toronto Globe and Mail*, 20 March 1937, pp. 1, 10.

**C37.13** "My Discovery of the West: Article III, So This Is Winnipeg," *Montreal Daily Star*, 20 March 1937, p. 11.

**C37.14** "My Discovery of the West: Article VII," *Toronto Globe and Mail*, 22 March 1937, pp. 1, 11.

C37.15 "My Discovery of the West: Article IV, Winnipeg and the East," *Montreal Daily Star*, 27 March 1937, p. 14.

C37.16 "My Discovery of the West: Article VIII," *Toronto Globe and Mail*, 27 March 1937, pp. 1, 11.

C37.17 "My Discovery of the West: Article IX," *Toronto Globe and Mail*, 29 March 1937, pp. 1, 13.

C37.18 "My Discovery of the West: Article V, Saskatchewan and Wheat," *Montreal Daily Star*, 3 April 1937, p. 11; 5 April 1937, p. 5.

C37.19 "My Discovery of the West: Article X," *Toronto Globe and Mail*, 3 April 1937, pp. 1, 8.

C37.20 "I Think We Are in for a Spell of Good Times; There Will Be No War; Rising Prices Easing Burdensome Debt; Unemployment Declining; Signs of Genuine Recovery Unmistakable," *Barron's* 17, no. 14 (5 April 1937): 17.

C37.21 "My Discovery of the West: Article VI, Our Eldorado in the Wilderness," *Montreal Daily Star*, 10 April 1937, p. 11.

C37.22 "My Discovery of the West: Article XII," *Toronto Globe and Mail*, 10 April 1937, pp. 1, 5.

C37.23 "My Discovery of the West: Article XIII," *Toronto Globe and Mail*, 12 April 1937, pp. 2, 12.

C37.24 "My Discovery of the West: Article XIV," *Toronto Globe and Mail*, 13 April 1937, p. 5.

C37.25 "My Discovery of the West: Article VII, Debit and Credit in Alberta," *Montreal Daily Star*, 17 April 1937, p. 11; 19 April 1937, p. 11.

C37.26 "My Discovery of the West: Article XV," *Toronto Globe and Mail*, 17 April 1937, p. 11.

C37.27 "My Discovery of the West: Article XVI," *Toronto Globe and Mail*, 19 April 1937, p. 3.

C37.28 "My Discovery of the West: Article VIII, The Pure Theory of Social Credit," *Montreal Daily Star*, 24 April 1937, p. 11; 26 April 1937, p 11.

C37.29 "My Discovery of the West: Article XVII," *Toronto Globe and Mail*, 24 April 1937, p. 5.

C37.30 "My Discovery of the West: Article XVIII," *Toronto Globe and Mail*, 26 April 1937, p. 9.

C37.31 "Disown Your Own Home; Expert Advice on Knocking Your House into Shape," *Commentator* 1, no. 4 (May 1937): 14–6.

C37.32 "The Two Milords; or, the Blow of Thunder: An Internationally Air-Conditioned Play, for the Coronation-Exposition Theatres of 1937," *Atlantic Monthly* 159 (May 1937): 597–9. Reprinted as "The Two Milords: Or the Blow of Thunder," *Fiction Parade and Golden Book Magazine* 5 (July 1937): 296–8; in *John O' London's Weekly* 38 (Christmas 1937): 389, 394.

C37.33 "Labor Should Organize But Do It the Right Way or Suffer Stiff Setback; Stephen Leacock Points Out Lessons to Be Learned as a Result of Oshawa Strike; Praises Hepburn,

Slaps the Law; Federal Laws in Need of a Good Over-Hauling — Courage and Right the Winners," *Toronto Telegram*, 1 May 1937, p. 29. Apparently also as "Labor and Law in Canada: An Interpretation of the Oshawa Strike," *Montreal Standard*, 1 May 1937, p. 1. Syndicated in *Winnipeg Tribune*, *Regina Leader-Post*, *Moose Jaw Times*, and *Saint John Telegraph-Journal*.

C37.34 "My Discovery of the West: Article XIX," *Toronto Globe and Mail*, 1 May 1937, p. 11.

C37.35 "My Discovery of the West: Article IX, Monarchy in the West," *Montreal Daily Star*, 1 May 1937, p. 11.

C37.36 "My Discovery of the West: Article XX," *Toronto Globe and Mail*, 3 May 1937, p. 11.

C37.37 "Leacock Bewildered by Law's Possibilities. Fined for Allowing Truck to Be without Flares, Professor Wonders If Green Paint All Right," *Toronto Globe and Mail*, 5 May 1937, p. 1. Three paragraphs are quoted from Leacock's letter to the magistrate in Brockville, ON as well as three answers to questions posed on the summons. Leacock paid $19 in fines and costs for truck infractions. Also reported as "Stephen Leacock Pays $19 Fine But Declares the Law Is an Ass," *Montreal Gazette*, 5 May 1937, p. 1; "Leacock Tells Ontario Court He Prefers Quebec Justice," *Montreal Daily Star*, p. 11; "Stephen Leacock Protests Against Fine for Infraction of Truck Regulations; Says Nobody Told Him It Had to Carry Flares," *Orillia Packet and Times*, 6 May 1937, p. 5. The *Packet and Times* quotes two paragraphs from Leacock's letter. One paragraph appears in K83.1, p. 180.

C37.38 "My Discovery of the West: Article XXI," *Toronto Globe and Mail*, 8 May 1937, p. 11.

C37.39 "My Discovery of the West: Article X, British Columbia: Empire Province," *Montreal Daily Star*, 8 May 1937, p. 11; 10 May 1937, p. 11.

C37.40 "My Discovery of the West: Article XXII," *Toronto Globe and Mail*, 10 May 1937, p. 10.

C37.41 "My Discovery of the West: Article XXIII," *Toronto Globe and Mail*, 11 May 1937, p. 9.

C37.42 "My Discovery of the West: Article XXIV," *Toronto Globe and Mail*, 15 May 1937, p. 5.

C37.43 "My Discovery of the West: Article XI, The Island of the Blest," *Montreal Daily Star*, 15 May 1937, p. 11.

C37.44 "My Discovery of the West: Article XXV," *Toronto Globe and Mail*, 17 May 1937, p. 13.

C37.45 "My Discovery of the West: Article XXVI," *Toronto Globe and Mail*, 22 May 1937, p. 5.

C37.46 "My Discovery of the West: Article XII, Provinces and Dominion," *Montreal Daily Star*, 22 May 1937, p. 11.

C37.47 "My Discovery of the West: Article XXVII," *Toronto Globe and Mail*, 24 May 1937, p. 10.

C37.48 "Alberta's Fairy Story; The Moral Seems to Be That Even If You Flunk in

Economics, You Won't Be Deprived of Your Dinner," *Commentator* 1, no. 5 (June 1937): 67–72.

**C37.49** "Gold Mines as Investments; Nine Different Kinds of Mining Ventures. Four General Conclusions on the Problem of Yellow Metal. Currency Management a Dream," *Barron's* 17, no. 24 (June 1937): 3, 4.

**C37.50** "When Mr. Richardson Went Fishing," *Lilliput* 1, no. 1 (July 1937): 34–6. Reprinted in *Lilliput Annual* (London: Pocket Publications, 1937?) which bound together the first six numbers.

**C37.51** "Farewell to Farms; The Highfalutin Language the Farmers Eat by the Paragraph These Days Is Too Much for a Mere Retired University Professor," *Commentator* 2, no. 1 (August 1937): 9–11.

**C37.52** "Barrie and O. Henry," *Mark Twain Quarterly* 2, no. 1 (Fall 1937): 3. Barrie was James Matthew Barrie.

**C37.53** "Free, but a Bit Forlorn; Our Most Famous Humorist, Having Retired After Years of Hard Work, Finds It's Not All It's Cracked Up to Be," *Commentator* 2, no. 2 (September 1937): 19–22. Apparently condensed as "Think Before You Stop," *Reader's Digest* 56, no. 334 (February 1950): 112.

**C37.54** "Foggy Finance; Be a Fiscal Expert and Learn Less Than You Know," *Commentator* 2, no. 4 (November 1937): 17–21. Reprinted in Stewart Morgan and William Thomas, eds., *Opinions and Attitudes in the Twentieth Century* (New York: Thomas Nelson and Sons, 1938), rev. ed., pp. 444–9. See also A85.

**C37.55** "History Revised: 1. Columbus and the Egg; II. Wolfe and Gray's Elegy; III. King Alfred and the Cakes," *Lilliput* 1, no. 5 (November 1937): 40–4. Reprinted in the *Lilliput Annual* (London: Pocket Publications, 1937?) in which the first six numbers were bound together.

**C37.56** "Stephen Leacock Writes of One-Man Rule; Cites Hepburn Victory in Ontario to Point a Moral and Adorn A Tale," *Barron's* 17, no. 45 (8 November 1937): 11.

**C37.57** "Why I Am Leaving My Farm: I Can't Live Up to It!" *John O'London's Weekly* 38, no. 971 (19 November 1937): 300. As "I'm Leaving My Farm," *Edmonton Bulletin*, 3 December 1938, p. 24. Syndicated by Miller Services Ltd. as part of series.

**C37.58** "What's Next in Alberta; Checked by the Dominion Government, Aberhart Pushes Battle in the Courts," *Barron's* 17, no. 47 (22 November 1937): 11–2.

**C37.59** "Another Year," *Atlantic Monthly* 160 (December 1937): 799–800.

**C37.60** "Can Professors Teach Bankers?" *Banking* 30 (December 1937): 20–1.

**C37.61** "The Nine Sovereignties of Canada: How a Royal Commission Keeps Trouble Asleep," *Barron's* 17, no. 50 (13 December 1937): 12.

**C38.1** "The Lot of the Soldier: A Discussion with a Moral," *Veterans' Annual Commentator* (Toronto) (1938): 11–4.

**C38.2** "The World's Muddle over Gold; World Trade Is Stifled Because of the Lack of a Real Monetary Standard," *Nation's Business* 26 (January 1938): 18–20, 103. Illustrated by Charles Dunn. The *Nation's Business* was the official magazine of the U.S. Chamber of Commerce.

**C38.3** "Congratulations," *Saturday Night* 53, no. 9 (1 January 1938): 4b. One of several letters to the editor on the publication's 50th birthday. Leacock sends thanks for "early and kind recognition of my first attempts at writing humor."

**C38.4** "The Happy Horoscope of 1938; Such 'Normal Things as War in Spain, Revolutions in South America and Volcanic Eruptions in Fiji Will Not Mar a Pleasantly Uneventful Year," *Barron's* 18, no. 2 (10 January 1938): 11–2.

**C38.5** "Leacock Reviews the Canadian Scene as Set for 1938: King, Rowell, Hepburn, and Aberhart in Leading Roles," *Montreal Daily Star*, 22 January 1938, p. 11. Also as "Leacock Views Dominion as Beautiful Stage Setting with Actors Sound Asleep; Hepburn Just Beginning Comic Curtain-Raiser in Setting of Very Latest Assets; Mysteries of '38 Very Much Like 1937; Provinces Seen Eating Federal Government as Latter Rehearses 'Sleeping Beauty,'" *Toronto Telegram*, 22 January 1938, p. 13.

**C38.6** "The Anglo-American Trade Pact — So Far; Daylight? Or Just Another Day Dream That Never Can Come True," *Barron's* 18, no. 5 (31 January 1938): 11.

**C38.7** "I Want to Build a College; And If I Do It Will Be a Place in Which Students May Be Able to Get an Education," *Commentator* 3, no. 1 (February 1938): 78–82. Reprinted as "On the Need for a Quiet College," *McGill Daily* 3 February 1938, pp. 2, 4; in Louis S. Locke, William M. Gibson and George Arms, eds., *Toward Liberal Education* (New York: Rinehart & Co., 1952), rev. ed., pp. 68–72.

**C38.8** "Mr. Peabody's Portrait Gallery: What He Thinks of His Fellow Men," *Lilliput* 2, no. 2 (February 1938): 193–7.

**C38.9** "John McCrae (Letter on the Death of)," *McGill Daily*, 2 February 1938, p. 1. See also C18.9 and C21.39.

**C38.10** "My Ladders," *Atlantic Monthly* 161 (March 1938): 410. Re C36.29. Preceding story, "More Than to Read, More Than to Hold," might be by Leacock as well.

**C38.11** "Emigration in English Literature," *Quarterly Review* 270, no. 536 (April 1938): 204–20.

**C38.12** "Hoe, Hoe! Spring Is Here; And It's Time to Do That Heavy Work in the Garden," *Commentator* 3, no. 3 (April 1938): 141–5.

**C38.13** "The Man Who Lived to Do Good," *Lilliput* 2, no. 4 (April 1938): 369–72, 374.

**C38.14** "What Happened Next? The Sequel to Some Famous World-Famous Stories," *Lilliput* 2, no. 6 (June 1938): 605–8.

**C38.15** "The Outbreak of Peace in Europe; World Cannot Face War Monster It Has Created. 'Attack' Again Has Ascendancy," *Barron's* 18, no. 23 (6 June 1938): 13.

**C38.16** "Comes the Comic College: Can We Believe What We See — Or Are We Too Close At Hand to Find the Truth Behind the Spoofing?" *Commentator* 3, no. 6 (July 1938): 86–9.

**C38.17** "Conversation Pieces: Stephen Leacock in Answers," *Reader's Digest* 33, no. 195 (July 1938): 68. A condensation of various articles written for *Answers*.

**C38.18** "All Is Not Lost! The Sun Still Shines!: 'It's a Good World,' Says Leacock, 'If We Can Only Cast Aside the Evil Spirit of Fear,'" *New York Times*, 7 August 1938, sec. 7 ("Magazine"), pp. 1–2, 14. Abridged as "All Is Not Lost!" *Reader's Digest* 33, no. 198 (October 1938): 33–5.

C38.19 "Hand Me Down That Book," *Answers* (Chicago) 1, no. 15 (1 September 1938): 4–5.

C38.20 "Who? When? Where? What? — The Questions Fly," *New York Times*, 11 September 1938, sec. 7 ("Book Review"), pp. 3, 26.

C38.21 "Is Education Eating Up Life?: A Plain Man's Grievance: Too Many Years in School," *New York Times*, 23 October 1938, sec. 7 ("Magazine"), pp. 1–2, 19. Reprinted in Andrew T. Smithberger, ed., *Essays British and American* (New York: Greenwood Press, 1953), pp. 449–59. Condensed in Leonard F. Dean, ed., *Perspectives* (New York: Harcourt, Brace, 1954), pp. 33–7. See also C38.22.

C38.22 "How to Keep Education from Eating Up Life: Stephen Leacock Proposes to Slay a Few Dragons," *New York Times*, 30 October 1938, sec. 7 ("Magazine"), pp. 3, 20.

C38.23 "What's Next in Europe: Behind the Whirling Wheel of Armament Permanent Peace Is Discernible," *Barron's* 18, no. 45 (7 November 1938): 3.

C38.24 "Model Memoirs: My Victorian Girlhood by Lady Nearleigh Slopover," *Saturday Evening Post* 211, no. 20 (12 November 1938): 32, 129–30, 132. Illustrated by George Shanks.

C38.25 "Thrown Out," *Edmonton Bulletin*, 12 November 1938, p. 4. This is the first article in the series "Stories Here and There from His Books, Lectures and Conversations." Many of these stories are extracted, sometimes rewritten, from previous publications. Syndicated by Miller Services Ltd. in *Ottawa Citizen*, *Winnipeg Free Press*, *Saint John Telegraph-Journal*, *Vegreville Observer*, *Halifax Chronicle* and *Simcoe Reformer*.

C38.26 "Auto Waves Magic Wand: Under Its Spell, Old Order of World Has Given Place to New," *New York Times*, 13 November 1938, sec. 11, pp. 1, 10.

C38.27 "How Teachers Swim," *Edmonton Bulletin*, 26 November 1938, p. 9. Syndicated by Miller Services Ltd. as part of series.

C38.28 "Andrew Macphail," *Queen's Quarterly* 45, no. 5 (Winter 1938–39): 445–52.

C38.29 "A Capsule for the Utopians," *Banking* 31 (December 1938): 22–3.

C38.30 "How I Read My Newspaper," *Rotarian* 53, no. 6 (December 1938): 16–7. Illustrated by Don Herold.

C38.31 "My Resurrected Friend," *Edmonton Bulletin*, 10 December 1938, p. 5. Syndicated by Miller Services Ltd. as part of series.

C38.32 "Feeding Time," *Edmonton Bulletin*, 17 December 1938, p. 6. Syndicated by Miller Services Ltd. as part of series.

C38.33 "Dickens: A Self-Portrait," *Saturday Review of Literature* 19, no. 9 (24 December 1938): 3–4, 16. Book review of Walter Dexter, ed., *The Letters of Charles Dickens*. This article drew a response from Edward Wagenknecht in the letter to the editor's column, *Saturday Review of Literature* 19, no. 12 (14 January 1939): 4.

C38.34 "All Nice People," *Edmonton Bulletin*, 24 December 1938, p. 11. Syndicated by Miller Services Ltd. as part of series.

C38.35 "A Christmas Star Shines Through the Mists: The World, Says Stephen Leacock, May Be Nearer Peace and Happiness Than We Think," *New York Times*, 25 December 1938, sec. 7 ("Magazine"), pp. 3, 12.

C38.36 "Attention, Psychologists," *Edmonton Bulletin*, 31 December 1938, p. 15. Syndicated by Miller Services Ltd. as part of series.

C39.1 "The Art of Carving; or, Hints for the Hapless: Leacock Gives Advice and A Timely Warning," *New York Times*, 1 January 1939, sec. 7 ("Magazine"), pp. 7, 11. Illustrated by Gide Zayas.

C39.2 "Truck Problem Solved," *Edmonton Bulletin*, 7 January 1939, p. 10. Syndicated by Miller Services Ltd. as part of series.

C39.3 "Canada's Horoscope of 1939; Wheat Surplus and Railroad Problem Evil Omens, but Capital Immigration a Favorable Factor," *Barron's* 19, no. 2 (9 January 1939): 12.

C39.4 "Quality Does It," *Edmonton Bulletin*, 14 January 1939, p. 19. Syndicated by Miller Services Ltd. as part of series.

C39.5 "How Much Does Language Change?" *John O'London's Weekly* 40 (20 January 1939): 621–2, 630, 632.

C39.6 "The Way of the Professor," *Edmonton Bulletin*, 21 January 1939, p. 5. Syndicated by Miller Services Ltd. as part of series.

C39.7 "For Puzzle Men Only," *Edmonton Bulletin*, 28 January 1939, p. 12. Syndicated by Miller Services Ltd. as part of series.

C39.8 "A Note on Latin," *Classical Outlook* 16, no. 5 (February 1939): 45.

C39.9 "No . . . Go to Mother!" *Winnipeg Free Press*, 4 February 1939, magazine sec., p. 8. Written specially for the *Free Press* because the editor objected to the syndicated article, "A Laugh on the Law Books" (C39.10). In the *Free Press* the series was called "Stephen Leacock Chuckles."

C39.10 "A Laugh on the Law Books," *Ottawa Citizen*, 4 February 1939, p. [26]. This was the regular article for Leacock's syndicated column. The *Edmonton Bulletin* did not publish a Leacock story this week. The series column was called "Stephen Leacock Stories."

C39.11 "Meet the College President," *Winnipeg Free Press*, 11 February 1939, magazine sec., p. 3. Syndicated by Miller Services Ltd. as part of series.

C39.12 "Five Dollars, Right Now," *Edmonton Bulletin*, 18 February 1939, p. 24. Syndicated by Miller Services Ltd. as part of series.

C39.13 "Are Professors Absent-Minded?" *Edmonton Bulletin*, 25 February 1939, p. 9. Syndicated by Miller Services Ltd. as part of series.

C39.14 "Our 'Living Language': A Defense," *New York Times*, 26 February 1939, sec. 7 ("Magazine"), pp. 9, 14. Reprinted in Howard W. Hintz and Bernard D.N. Grebanier, *Modern American Vistas* (New York: The Dryden Press, 1940), pp. 428–32; in Warren Bower, ed., *New Directions; Second Series* (New York: J. B. Lippincott, 1941), pp. 263–7.

C39.15 "Canada and National Unity," *Journal of the Canadian Dental Association* 5 (March 1939): 147–9.

C39.16 "Our Dinner Club and How It Died," *Rotarian* 54, no. 3 (March 1939): 11–3. Illustrated by Gene Thornton.

C39.17 "Wanted: A Gold Fish," *Edmonton Bulletin*, 4 March 1939, p. 12. Syndicated by Miller Services Ltd. as part of series. Reprinted in *Lilliput* 6 [?], no. 6 (June 1940): 539.

C39.18 "As History Grows Dim (All That Will Be Left of Our Forgotten Worthies in a

Future Dictionary)," *New Yorker* 15, no. 4 (11 March 1939): 34. Apparently reprinted in *Lilliput*, ca. June 1939.

**C39.19** "Couldn't Sleep a Wink," *Edmonton Bulletin*, 11 March 1939, p. 12. Syndicated by Miller Services Ltd. as part of series.

**C39.20** "Three on Each," *Edmonton Bulletin*, 18 March 1939, p. 23. Syndicated by Miller Services Ltd. as part of series.

**C39.21** "Nothing Missing," *Edmonton Bulletin*, 25 March 1939, p. 12. Syndicated by Miller Services Ltd. as part of series.

**C39.22** "Charles Dickens and Canada," *Queen's Quarterly* 46 (Spring 1939): 28–37.

**C39.23** "Thinking of Tomorrow," *Edmonton Bulletin*, 1 April 1939, p. 15. Syndicated by Miller Services Ltd. as part of series.

**C39.24** "Information While You Drink," *Edmonton Bulletin*, 8 April 1939, p. 27. Syndicated by Miller Services Ltd. as part of series.

**C39.25** "No Place for Gentleman," *Edmonton Bulletin*, 15 April 1939, p. 23. Syndicated by Miller Services Ltd. as part of series.

**C39.26** "Hurry, King and Queen We're Waiting," *Vogue* (London) 90, no. 47, whole no. 1,617 (19 April 1939): 55–6. This was part of a special "Royal Tour and World's Fairs Features"; p. 54 contains a full-page photo of George VI and Queen Elizabeth, p. 57 has a full-page photo of Lord and Lady Tweedsmuir. Mistakenly published as a new discovery in "An Essay Unveiled; Leacock Looks at Royal Visits," *Montreal Daily Star*, 28 February 1959, pp. 1–2. At the time this was thought to be the first publication of the essay "Hurry King and Queen," released by the trustees of the Stephen Leacock Memorial Home, originally written by Leacock in early 1939 shortly before the visit of George VI and the Queen Elizabeth to Canada. Also as "Leacock Manuscript Discovered! 'Hurry King and Queen; We're Waiting' Is Timely Again 20 Years After," *Toronto Telegram*, 28 February 1959, p. 5. Reprinted as "Long-Lost Leacock Article Bids Royal Visit Welcome in 1939," *Orillia Packet and Times*, [25?] July 1959.

**C39.27** "We Have with Us Tonight," *Edmonton Bulletin*, 22 April 1939, p. 12. Syndicated by Miller Services Ltd. as part of series. This is a condensation of Leacock's essay that appeared in A37. Reprinted in full in H.R. Leaver, ed., *Modern Literature for Schools* (Toronto: Copp Clark, 1937, 1950), pp. 474–82; in L.H. Newell, ed., *Essays to Enjoy* (Toronto: McGraw-Hill, 1967), pp. 11–16. See also C22.13 and C24.36.

**C39.28** "Oh, Sleep! Oh, Gentle Sleep!" *Edmonton Bulletin*, 29 April 1939, p. 5. Syndicated by Miller Services Ltd. as part of series.

**C39.29** "A Humble Lover," *Edmonton Bulletin*, 6 May 1939, p. 27. Syndicated by Miller Services Ltd. as part of series.

**C39.30** "Come out to Canada: Living On and Off a 'Little Place,'" *Times* (London), Canada no., 15 May 1939, p. xvii. Reprinted in *Canada* (London: Times Publishing Co., 1939): 110–4. Apparently reprinted in *Synopsis* (London). Condensed in *Reader's Digest* (Pleasantville, N.Y. and London) 35, no. 209 (September 1939): 11–3.

**C39.31** "Let's Be Very Careful," *Saturday Night* 54, no. 29 (20 May 1939): 36.

**C39.32** "The Magic of Finance," *Edmonton Bulletin*, 20 May 1939, p. 17. Syndicated by Miller Services Ltd. as part of series.

C39.33 "A Golfer Tells All," *New York Times*, 21 May 1939, sec. 8 ("Magazine"), pp. 9, 21. Apparently reprinted in *Strand* in June 1939 or later, although the *Strand* index does not list it.

C39.34 "He Guessed Right," *Edmonton Bulletin*, 27 May 1939, p. 12. Syndicated by Miller Services Ltd. as part of series.

C39.35 "Canada and the Monarchy," *Atlantic Monthly* 163 (June 1939): 735–43.

C39.36 "Who Canonizes the Classics?" *Answers* (Chicago) 1, no. 18 (June 1939): 3–5; also in *John O'London's Weekly*, 42, no. 1,076 (24 November 1939): 205–6, 212.

C39.37 "Electric Service," *Edmonton Bulletin*, 3 June 1939, p. 12. Syndicated by Miller Services Ltd. as part of series.

C39.38 "The Writers of Quebec," *Saturday Review of Literature* 20, no. 6 (3 June 1939): 10. Book review of Ian Forbes Fraser's *The Spirit of French Canada*.

C39.39 "Our Vanished Industries," *Edmonton Bulletin*, 10 June 1939, p. 6. Syndicated by Miller Services Ltd. as part of series.

C39.40 "Mushrooms," *Edmonton Bulletin*, 17 June 1939, p. 10. Syndicated by Miller Services Ltd. as part of series. See also C43.20.

C39.41 "Help Wanted," *Edmonton Bulletin*, 24 June 1939, p. 7. Syndicated by Miller Services Ltd. as part of series.

C39.42 "His Better Self," *Edmonton Bulletin*, 8 July 1939, p. 5. Syndicated by Miller Services Ltd. as part of series.

C39.43 "Twenty Cents' Worth of Murder," *Saturday Review of Literature* 20, no. 11 (8 July 1939): 10–1.

C39.44 "Atmosphere," *Edmonton Bulletin*, 15 July 1939, p. 11. Syndicated by Miller Services Ltd. as part of series.

C39.45 "Investing in Canada; U. S. Dollar Would Be Safer in Case of War Involving England," *Barron's* 19, no. 29 (17 July 1939): 7.

C39.46 "Let's Go Fishing," *Edmonton Bulletin*, 22 July 1939, p. 23. Syndicated by Miller Services Ltd. as part of series.

C39.47 "With Women or without," *Rotarian* 55, no. 2 (August 1939): 28–30. Illustrated by John Norment.

C39.48 "Lost in the Jungle of Economics," *New York Times*, 20 August 1939, sec. 7 ("Magazine"), pp. 1, 16, 18. Reprinted in A. Wigfall Green et al., *Complete College Composition* (New York: F.S. Crofts & Co., 1940), pp. 535–43.

C39.49 "Buggam Grange," *Picture Post* 4, no. 8 (26 August 1939): 69, 71, 73–4. There is a subtitle: "A Good Old Ghost Story." Also, there is a discrepancy for this item; the cover carries a different number than the table of contents. Reprinted as "Buggam Grange: A Good Old Ghost Story," in Ted Stone, ed., *13 Canadian Ghost Stories* (Saskatoon, Saskatchewan: Western Producer Prairie Books, 1988), pp. 44–52; in *The Oxford Book of Canadian Ghost Stories* (Toronto: Oxford University Press, 1990), pp. 63–9; in Alan Maitland, ed., *Favourite Winter Stories from Fireside Al* (Toronto: Viking, 1994), pp. 2–9. See also C26.58.

C39.50 "Can I Learn to Be a Writer?" *Gregg Writer* 42 (September 1939): 11–4. This may have originally appeared in *Good Housekeeping* (London), April 1939 or later. Apparently reprinted in *Synopsis* (London), August 1939 and in *English Digest*.

**C39.51** "Come into the Kitchen: A Study in Evolution," *Canadian Home Journal* 36, no. 5 (September 1939): 46–7.

**C39.52** "We Are What We Joke About," *New York Times*, 3 September 1939, sec. 7 ("Magazine"), pp. 4–5, 14.

**C39.53** "Charles Dickens and the World He Lived in: Part One," *Answers* (Chicago) 1, no. 20 (December 1939): 3–4.

**C39.54** "Christmas Shopping," *C-I-L Oval: The Magazine of Canadian Industries Limited* (Montreal) 8, no. 6 (December 1939): 2, 4, 20. Illustrated by Peggy Shaw. Reprinted as "19 Days to Christmas," *C-I-L Oval* 18, no. 6 (December 1949): 6. Apparently reprinted in *John O'London's Weekly*, December 1939.

**C39.55** "Leacock Sees Good Times Ahead; Predicts that War Boom Which Is Coming in Canada Will Spill Over into the United States," *Barron's* 19, no. 49 (4 December 1939): 9.

**C39.56** "We Need a Santa," *New York Times*, 24 December 1939, sec. 7 ("Magazine"), pp. 5, 15.

**C39.57** "This Business of Growing Old: Stephen Leacock, Looking Out from the Pinnacle of Seventy Years, Gives Us the Modern Version of a Classical Theme," *New York Times*, 31 December 1939, sec. 7 ("Magazine"), pp. 4, 15. Reprinted in *Reader's Digest* 36, no. 215 (March 1940): 78–80. See also C40.11.

**C40.1** "In Memory of René du Roure," *Old McGill 1941* 44 (1940): 11–3. Reprinted in *McGill News* 23, no. 1 (Autumn 1941): 18, 20.

**C40.2** "Napoleon at St. Helena," *Men Only* 13, no. 50 (January 1940): 57–60. See also C24.22.

**C40.3** "Other People's Money: An Outside View of Trusts and Investments," *Trusts and Estates* 79 (January 1940): 11–6. Also in *Cleveland Trust Magazine* 21, nos. 3–4 (March–April 1940): 3, 10. See also A106.

**C40.4** "Three Score and Ten," *Spectator* 164, no. 5,821 (19 January 1940): 72–3. Apparently condensed in *English Digest*, February 1940.

**C40.5** "Of Georgina Township and Its First Church," *Montreal Gazette*, 10 February 1940, p. 5. Book review of Francis Paget Hett's *Georgina: A Type Study of Early Settlement and Church Building in Upper Canada*. Also as "The Fly Leaf," *Toronto Globe and Mail*, 10 February 1940, p. 11; as "County Chronicle Recaptures Past," *Winnipeg Free Press*, 9 March 1940, p. 11.

**C40.6** "Charles Dickens and the World He Lived in: Part Two," *Answers* (Chicago) 1, no. 21 (March 1940): 3–5.

**C40.7** "The Nine Arts Of Living," *Saturday Review of Literature* 22, no. 25 (13 April 1940): 5, 17. Book review of André Maurois, *The Art of Living*.

**C40.8** "School — and Real Learning — for Oldsters: Stephen Leacock Has Discovered That We All Want to Go Back, So That There Is a Solid Backing for Adult Education," *New York Times*, 19 May 1940, sec. 7 ("Magazine"), pp. 8, 19.

**C40.9** "The Perfect Index," *Saturday Review of Literature* 22, no. 5 (25 May 1940): 9.

Reprinted as "Index: There Is No Index," in Norman D. Stevens, ed., *Library Humor: A Bibliothecal Miscellany to 1970* (Metuchen, N.J.: Scarecrow Press, 1971), pp. 419–21; in Allan Gould, ed., *The Great Big Book of Canadian Humour* (Toronto: Macmillan Canada, 1992), pp. 271–2.

C40.10   "Cricket for Americans," *Atlantic Monthly* 165 (June 1940): 766–9. Reprinted in Theodore J. Gates and Austin Wright, eds., *College Prose* (Boston: D.C. Heath and Company, 1942), pp. 495–500.

C40.11   "On Growing Old," *New World Illustrated* (Toronto) (August 1940): 41–3, 52. See also C39.57.

C40.12   "What Is . . . a Sport?" *Hunting and Fishing* 17, no. 8 (August 1940): 6–7. Illustrated by Norman Daly.

C40.13   "Leacock Bids U.S. Welcome," *Montreal Gazette*, 31 August 1940, p. 8. Reprinted from the *New York Daily News*.

C40.14   "The Bath Through the Ages," *Canadian Home Journal* 37, no. 5 (September 1940): 54–5.

C40.15   "Soft Stuff for Children," *Rotarian* 57, no. 4 (October 1940): 16–7. Illustrated by Gene Thornton. See also C28.18.

C40.16   "[book review of James Truslow Adams, *Empire on the Seven Seas: The British Empire 1784 — 1939*]," *Thought: Fordham University Quarterly*, 15 (December 1940): 690–2. Earlier that year Adams had reviewed Leacock's *The British Empire: Its Structure, Its Unity, Its Strength* (A89d). See "Stephen Leacock on the British Empire," *Thought* 15, no. 58 (September 1940): 389–91.

C41.1   "The Rowell-Sirois Report — Destination Unknown," *Quarterly Review of Commerce* (University of Western Ontario) 8, no. 2 (Winter 1940–1): 72. The editors of the journal asked several leaders of Canadian business and political thought to comment on the Royal Commission on Dominion-Provincial Relations. Leacock's reply consists of the following: "While the war lasts, the Federal Government has the power to do anything necessary for the prosecution of the war. Everything else can sleep. Much of it, like Marlowe's Edward the Second, will never wake. See also under Sleeping Beauty, Rip Van Winkle, Ephesus, Morpheus, etc., etc., etc."

C41.2   "A Memory of the Old School: The Struggle to Make Us Gentlemen," *Old Times* (supp. to the *College Times*, Upper Canada College, Toronto, ON) first no. (January 1941): 6–7. Reprinted as "A Memory of the Old School on King Street: The Struggle to Make Us Gentlemen," in Carolyn Gossage, *A Question of Privilege: Canada's Independent Schools* (Toronto: Peter Martin Associates, 1977), pp. 44–6.

C41.3   "The Whole Duty of a Citizen," *Canadian Spokesman*, 1, no. 1 (January 1941): 1–4. Reprinted in *Educational Courier* (Montreal): 5–6, 16.

C41.4   "The Stability of Canada; Unexpected Capacity for War Effort Being Shown," *Barron's* 21, no. 2 (13 January 1941): 42.

C41.5   "Minority Report," *Reader's Digest* 38, no. 228 (April 1941): 143. Taken from A91.

C41.6   "Our Politics: From Jest to Earnest," *Canadian Spokesman* (April 1941): 5–9.

C41.7   "How to Swear in Print," *Saturday Review of Literature* 23, no. 24 (5 April 1941): 7–8.

**C41.8** "Our American Visitors; 'Nothing Too Good for Them,' Says Stephen Leacock; Interchange of Ideas By Visits to Canada Better Than All Treaties," *Montreal Daily Star*, 23 April 1941, p. 17. Reprinted as "C'Mon Up, Country's Yours Leacock Bids Americans; 'I Wave My Round 1,000 Miles of Scenery, Give It to Them'; True Hospitality," *Toronto Star*, 24 April 1941 (news clipping at University of Toronto Archives). Also as "Canada Depicted As an Eager Host: Stephen Leacock Looks to Us to Satisfy the Dominion's Desire for Guests: Hospitality Is Assured: That Old-Fashioned-Inn Flavor, He Suggests, Will Enhance North American Unity," *New York Times*, 27 April 1941, p. 13; "Come Up to Canada," *Glamour* (June 1941): 44–5, 92–3; as "Come on Up," *McGill News* 22, no. 4 (Summer 1941): 20.

**C41.9** "The Difference of Degree," *Reader's Digest* 38, no. 229 (May 1941): 70.

**C41.10** "America: An Allegory," *New World Illustrated* (Toronto) 2, no. 5 (July 1941): 5.

**C41.11** "The Most Unforgettable Character I've Met," *Reader's Digest*, 39, no. 231 (July 1941): 18–22. This is Leacock's portrait of his uncle, E.P. Leacock. Reprinted as "My Uncle Was a Quaint Character," *Winnipeg Free Press*, 18 October 1941, magazine sec., p. 5; as "My Remarkable Uncle" in Howard Mumford Jones, Richard M. Ludwig and Marvin B. Perry, Jr., eds., *Modern Minds: an Anthology of Ideas* (Boston: D.C. Heath, 1949), pp. 495–500; in John D. Robins and Margaret V. Ray, eds., *A Book of Canadian Humour* (Toronto: Ryerson, 1951), pp. 26–33; as "My Remarkable Uncle," in Russell Nye, ed., *Modern Essays* (Chicago: Scott, Foresman, 1953), pp. 155–61; in Malcolm Ross and John Stevens, eds., *Man and His World: Studies in Prose* (Toronto: J.M. Dent, 1961), pp. 167–74; in Giose Rimanelli and Roberto Ruberto, eds., *Modern Canadian Stories* (Toronto: Ryerson, 1966), pp. 16–22; in Margaret L. Ford and Brian Meeson, *Writers' Workshop* (Agincourt, Ont.: The Book Society of Canada, 1966), pp. 189–95; in Grant Huffman, ed., *Canadiana: An Anthology of Nostalgic, Humorous, and Satirical Writing for Secondary Schools* (Toronto: McClelland and Stewart, 1970), pp. 131–6; as "My Remarkable Uncle: A Personal Document," in William H. New, ed., *Modern Canadian Essays* (Toronto: Macmillan, 1976), pp. 1–8. See also B28

**C41.12** "The Question Nobody Answers," *Canadian Banker* 48 (July 1941): 459–65. Apparently reprinted from *Banking, Journal of the American Bankers Association*.

**C41.13** [Letter to J.J. Carrick] in J.J. Carrick, "Books for the Boys: Sailors, Soldiers and Airman," *Toronto Globe and Mail*, 11 August 1941, p. 5. In his column Carrrick quotes an extract from a letter that he received from Leacock on the previous Saturday: "I like to think that even books such as mine are of some service to soldiers. I remember how a veteran of the last war said to me: 'Your books were a god-send to us in hospital,' then he added, 'You see, in the shape we were in, we could only read rot.'" Reprinted in Carrick, *Hall of Fame* (Toronto: Institution of Financial Education Ltd., 1943), p. 9; Carrick, *Carrick-atures* ([sn.: sl., 1946?]), p. 96.

**C41.14** "A Welcome to an American," *Think: A Survey of New Things and Thoughts in the World of Affairs* 7, no. 9 (Canadian National Exhibition no.) (September 1941): 19, 83–4.

**C41.15** "The Ceiling's the Limit," *Banking* 34 (December 1941): 11–9, 22.

**C42.1** "The Magic of Eating Outdoors: It Isn't the Food You Eat; It's the Air You Eat It with," *Hunting and Fishing* (Boston, Mass.) 19, no. 1 (January 1942): 14–5, 29. Illustrated by Dahl.

**C42.2**  "We Canadians," *Rotarian* 60, no. 1 (January 1942): 21–4.

**C42.3**  "Was Hochelaga a Myth?" *Montreal Standard*, 28 February 1942, ("Magazine"), pp. 10–11.

**C42.4**  "Common Sense and the Universe," *Atlantic Monthly* 169 (May 1942): 627–34. Reprinted in Robert E. Knoll, ed., *Contrasts: Idea and Technique* (New York: Harcourt Brace, 1955), pp. 186–197; in James R. Newman, ed., *The World of Mathematics*, vol. 4 (New York: Simon and Schuster, 1956), pp. 2460–9; in Isabel S. Gordon and Sophie Sorkin, eds., *The Armchair Science Reader* (New York: Simon and Schuster, 1959), pp. 515–520; in Gerald Lynch and David Rampton, eds., *The Canadian Essay* (Toronto: Copp Clark Pitman, 1991), pp. 32–42.

**C42.5**  "I Squirm to Recall," *Saturday Review of Literature* 25, no. 22 (30 May 1942): 13. Reprinted in *Saturday Review Reader: Articles of Enduring Interest Selected from The Saturday Review of Literature* (New York: Bantam, 1951), pp. 78–81. Also in *Reader's Digest* 41, no. 243 (July 1942): 43–4.

**C42.6**  "High Opinion of Major Murray Expressed by His Former Teacher," *Toronto Globe and Mail*, 5 August 1942, p. 6. Reprinted in Jack Kapica, ed., *Shocked and Appalled: A Century of Letters to the Globe and Mail* (Toronto: Lester & Orpen Dennys, 1985), pp. 153–4. Gladstone Murray resigned from the CBC in November 1942.

**C42.7**  "Blacking out the Consumer," *Woman's Day* fifth year, twelfth issue (September 1942): 9, 44–6. Illustrated by Will B. Johnstone.

**C42.8**  "The England I Remember," *New World Illustrated* (Toronto) 3, no. 8 (October 1942): 6–7, 9.

**C42.9**  "Good Bye Motor Car!" *Outdoors* 10, no. 8 (October 1942): 372–3. Illustrated by Harvey W. Kidder.

**C42.10**  "Do Men Like Witty Women? Few Men Willingly Keep Wits About Them," *Vogue* 100 (15 November 1942): 32, 74. Reprinted in *Vogue's First Reader* (New York: Julian Messner, 1942) pp. 275–80.

**C42.11**  "A New Program for Canada," *Saturday Night* (Toronto) 58, no. 12 (28 November 1942): 14.

**C42.12**  "Rebuilding the Cities: A Broad View of Reconstruction," *Journal Royal Architectural Institute of Canada* 19, no. 12 (December 1942): 229–30.

**C42.13**  "Gold Will Be Money; Its Future Held Assured Regardless of Just What Form a Future Gold Standard May Take," *Barron's* 22, no. 52 (28 December 1942): 3.

**C43.1**  "Optimism in War-time: I. — The Dentist," *Saturday Night* 58, no. 21 (30 January 1943): 8.

**C43.2**  "To Many Women Knitting," *Good Housekeeping* 116 (February 1943): 48. Poem.

**C43.3**  "Wartime Optimism: Cooking for Victory," *Saturday Night* 58, no. 23 (13 February 1943): 10.

**C43.4**  "Wartime Optimism: The Jones's Enchanted Castle," *Saturday Night* 58, no. 25 (27 February 1943): 17.

**C43.5**  "What Can Walton Teach Us?" *Outdoors* 11, no. 2 (March 1943): 16–7, 27–8. Illustrations from the Bettman Archive. About Isaac Walton.

**C43.6** "'A Tale of Two Cities,'" *Maclean's Magazine* 56, no. 5 (1 March 1943): 7–8, 40–2.

**C43.7** "Wartime Optimism: Mr. Alcorn Improves Himself," *Saturday Night* 58, no. 26 (6 March 1943): 10–1.

**C43.8** "Optimism for Wartime: Good News! A New Party!" *Saturday Night* 58, no. 28 (20 March 1943): 16–7. Reprinted in Claude Bissell, ed., *Great Canadian Writing: A Century of Imagination* (Toronto: Canadian Centennial Publishing Co., 1966), pp. 87–9.

**C43.9** "This Business of Prophecy: Stephen Leacock, Who Used to Be A Prophet Himself, Takes a Shot at Those Who Know What Will Happen After the War," *New York Times*, 21 March 1943, sec. 6 ("Magazine"), p. 12. Apparently reprinted in *Everybody's Digest*, 30 March 1943.

**C43.10** "Wartime Optimism: The Life of Lea and Perrins," *Saturday Night* 58, no. 29 (27 March 1943): 16.

**C43.11** "A Plea for Geographical Science," *Queen's Quarterly* 50 (Spring 1943): 1–13.

**C43.12** "Clouds That Rolled by: Mr. Alldone's Awful Day," *Saturday Night* 58, no. 30 (3 April 1943): 16.

**C43.13** "Angel Pond, Lure of the North," *Saturday Night* 58, no. 32 (17 April 1943): 18–9.

**C43.14** "Dickens Distilled: How to Lose Size without Losing Stature," *Saturday Review of Literature* 26, no. 16 (17 April 1943): 16–8. Review of M.L. Aswell, ed., *Dickens Digest*.

**C43.15** "Why Study English?" *Montreal Daily Star*, 20 April 1943, p. 10. See also A98.

**C43.16** "Leacock Tells How Sultan Abdul Raised Loans by Head-Chopping," *Montreal Gazette*, 29 April 1943, p. 13. This is the first of a series of articles to raise money for the 4th Victory Loan Campaign which began on 26 April and ended on 15 May. Also as "Leaflets on the Loan; the Sultan Speaks from the Grave," *Sarnia Canadian Observer*, 3 May 1943, p. 8.

**C43.17** "Leacock Writes Off Boob Smith; He's Made All Sacrifices He Can," *Montreal Gazette*, 30 April 1943, p. 13. Also as "Leaflets on the Loan; the Case of Boob Smith," *Sarnia Canadian Observer* 4 May 1943, p. 14.

**C43.18** "Gold," *Canadian Banker* 50 ([May] 1943): 39–51.

**C43.19** "Leacock Finds Loan Won't Bust Us; Call to Isley Found Unnecessary," *Montreal Gazette*, 1 May 1943, p. 13. Hon. J.L. Isley was the Minister of Finance.

**43.20** "Stephen Leacock's Mushroom Days," *Saturday Review of Literature* 26, no. 18 (1 May 1943): 13. Letter to the Editor. Condensed as "Are the Darned Things Mushrooms?" *Reader's Digest* 42, no. 254 (June 1943): 53–4; *Reader's Digest* 85 (October 1964): 188. See also 39.40.

**C43.21** "What's Ahead for Canada?" *Maclean's Magazine* 56 (1 May 1943): 12, 22, 24. Illustrated by Fred Finley. Not to be confused with a series of articles in the *Financial Post* between 4 December 1943 and 5 February 1944 (see C43.42–5, C44.3–5, C44.7–9).

**C43.22** "Piscatorial Perspicacities Make War Loan Publicity Substitute," *Montreal Gazette*, 3 May 1943, p. 17.

**C43.23** "Barber Shop Psychology Lesson Aids War Loan Certificate Sale," *Montreal Gazette*, 4 May 1943, p. 15.

**C43.24** "Leaflets on the Loan; the Happy Warrior," *Sarnia Canadian Observer*, 5 May

1943, p. 7. Reprinted in "Leacock VL Series Sells Bonds Again," *Toronto Telegram*, 6 August 1958, p. 18. This article notes that Leacock's World War II propaganda has been discovered at the Bank of Canada. In May 1943 Leacock agreed to write a series of ten articles from Mariposa, each article to include a sales message on behalf of the Victory Loan campaign. Some of the articles are now being re-published to help with a $6 billion conversion loan. "The Happy Warrior," one of the ten follows.

C43.25  "Leaflets on the Loan; the Righteous Indignation of Angus McCordell," *Sarnia Canadian Observer*, 6 May 1943, p. 11.

C43.26  "Fiery Scot to Wreck Mariposa if Leacock's Town Fails in Loan," *Montreal Gazette*, 6 May 1943, pp. 15–6.

C43.27  "Case of Whisky Too Sacrificial, Mariposa Loan Head Gets Cane," *Montreal Gazette*, 7 May 1943, pp. 13–4.

C43.28  "Leaflets on the Loan; the Chairman's Walking Stick," *Sarnia Canadian Observer*, 7 May 1943, p. 10.

C43.29  "Economic Paradise Is Uncovered in Wake of Farm Auction Sale," *Montreal Gazette*, 8 May 1943, p. 21.

C43.30  "Leaflets on the Loan; Going, Going Gone," *Sarnia Canadian Observer*, 8 May 1943, p. 11.

C43.31  "Leaflets on the Loan; National Debt National Blessing," *Sarnia Canadian Observer*, 10 May 1943, p. 8.

C43.32  "Leaflets on the Loan; Have You Got Even One Cent," *Sarnia Canadian Observer*, 11 May 1943, p. 9.

C43.33  "Leacock's Mariposa Out of Joint As Loan Drive Cuts Social Lines," *Montreal Gazette*, 15 May 1943, p. 23.

C43.34  "Loan Leaflets; A New Heaven and a New Earth," *Sarnia Canadian Observer*, 15 May 1943, p. 10. See also K61.1.

C43.35  "Some Anecdotes of McGill," *McGill News* 24, no. 4 (Summer 1943): 31–2. Reprinted in K83.1, pp. 213–5.

C43.36  "Statements on the Four Freedoms," *Biosphical Review* 6, no. 4 (June 1943): [?] A brief statement of approximately 100 words. In the introduction to this column the editor states that he wrote to "a number of prominent men inviting them to express their thoughts on this subject."

C43.37  "Britain and America," *Thought: Fordham University Quarterly* 18 (June 1943): 204–07.

C43.38  "Can We Beat Inflation?" *Woman's Day* (August 1943): 16, 54–5.

C43.39  "Stephen Leacock Debates Women's Level in Post-War Canada," *Chatelaine* 16, no. 10 (October 1943): 9, 45–6, 50–1. Illustrated by Grassick.

C43.40  "Leacock Likes Aldington's Book on Life of the Duke of Wellington," *Montreal Gazette*, 13 November 1943, p. 7. Letter to the Book Review Editor dated 11 November 1943. See also A100.

C43.41  "A Lecture on Walking," *Outdoors* 11, no. 10 (December 1943): 16, 43. Illustrated by Dahl.

**C43.42** "What's Ahead for Canada Chapter I — The Link with the Past," *Financial Post* (Toronto) 37, no. 49 (4 December 1943): 9, 16.

**C43.43** "What's Ahead for Canada Chapter 2 — The Astounding Resources of the Dominion," *Financial Post* (Toronto) 37, no. 50 (11 December 1943): 11, 19.

**C43.44** "What's Ahead for Canada Chapter III — The People of Canada — Past, Present and Future," *Financial Post* (Toronto) 37, no. 51 (18 December 1943): 11, 17.

**C43.45** "What's Ahead for Canada Chapter 4 — The Dominion and the Provinces," *Financial Post* (Toronto) 37, no. 52 (25 December 1943): 3.

**C44.1** "Generals I Have Trained," *B.M.A. Blitz* (Officers' Training Centre, Brockville, Ontario) 1 (January 1944): 7, 26. Special to the *Blitz*.

**C44.2** "Our Wild Game as Food," *Rod and Gun in Canada* 45, no. 8 (January 1944): 6–7, 15–6. Illustrated by Tom Hall.

**C44.3** "What's Ahead for Canada Chapter 5 — The Provinces Grow Rich," *Financial Post* (Toronto) 38, no. 1 (1 January 1944): 3.

**C44.4** "What's Ahead for Canada Chapter 6 — British and French Canada," *Financial Post* (Toronto) 38, no. 2 (8 January 1944): 9.

**C44.5** "What's Ahead for Canada? Chapter 7 [continuation of Chapter 6]: Stephen Leacock Tells Why French Canadians Do Not Share the Dominion's Growing Pride in Empire War Prowess," *Financial Post* (Toronto) 38, no. 3 (15 January 1944): 1, 8.

**C44.6** "Ready for Murder? This Famous Humorist Says He Has Read So Many Detective Tales That He's Always Expecting the Worst!" *New York Herald Tribune*, 16 January 1944, sec. 7 ("This Week Magazine"), p. 35. Reprinted as "Living with Murder," *Reader's Digest* (January 1952, year 31): 30; in *Laughter, the Best Medicine* (New York: Reader's Digest/ Berkley Book, 1981), pp. 152–3.

**C44.7** "What's Ahead for Canada? Chapter 7: Stephen Leacock Sketches for Canadians the Bold Task of Developing Half a Continent. 'Up and at It!' He Cries," *Financial Post* (Toronto) 38, no. 4 (22 January 1944): 12.

**C44.8** "What's Ahead for Canada? Chapter 8: Stephen Leacock Foresees Upsurge of Isolationism in Canada After the War and Closer Ties with Empire and U.S.," *Financial Post* (Toronto) 38, no. 5 (29 January 1944): 22.

**C44.9** "What's Ahead for Canada? Chapter 9: Socialism 'Wonderful but Impossible' Stephen Leacock Says 'in Reality It Is Just a Dream — a Soapbubble,'" *Financial Post* (Toronto) 38, no. 6 (5 February 1944): 11, 15.

**C44.10** "The School Is the Lever," *Saturday Night* 59, no. 22 (5 February 1944): 19.

**C44.11** "A Message to the Graduating Class of 1944," *McGill News* 25, no. 4 (15 May 1944, Summer): 7–8. Contains a letter (19 February 1944), printed in facsimile, from Leacock to Fraser Keith, President of the Graduates' Society at McGill University. Reprinted as "Dr. Leacock's Last Message," *Montreal Daily Star*, 23 May 1944, pp. 3, 5.

**C44.12** "I'm Going to Be a New Man," *Good Housekeeping* 119 (July 1944): 72. Condensed in *Reader's Digest* 45, no. 269 (September 1944): 99–100.

**C44.13** "Canada Can Support 100,000,000 People," *Rotarian* 65, no. 4 (October 1944): 16, 18. Oliver C. McIntyre responds, p. 17.

**C44.14** "My Particular Aversions," *American Bookman* 1, no. 1 (Winter 1944): 39–40. Reprinted in A. Wigfall Green, et al., *Complete College Composition* (New York: F.S. Crofts, 2nd ed., 1947), pp. 474–6.

**C63.1** [Report of Leacock's address, "The Colleges and the Public," delivered to the McGill Graduates' Society in Windsor, ON on 9 March 1935] in Sara Bowser, "About Canada," *Canadian Weekly* (15–21 June 1963): 6. One of Leacock's former students, Robert W. Jones, who worked as a reporter for the *Montreal Gazette*, attended this alumni dinner at the Prince Edward Hotel in Windsor. Jones asked Leacock if he could have a copy of his address. Leacock said that he did not have one, but he promised to write a summary of his speech for the *Montreal Gazette*. When Jones picked up Leacock's summary, it was addressed to the editor of the *Gazette* with a note asking to print the summary as written or none of it at all. It was not printed at that time, however. Leacock's report is written in the third person. A page of Leacock's report is reproduced in facsimile. See also E35.16.

# D Section: REPORTS OF SPEECHES AND LECTURES

**D6.1** "Prof. Leacock on Empire Tariff, Some Startling Arguments Advanced to Which Some Hearers Dissented," *Montreal Herald*, 19 February 1906, p. 4. Report with quotations from Leacock's address, "The Empire and the Tariff," given to the Canadian Club in Montreal.

**D6.2** "Canada and the British Empire; Lecture Before the May Court Club. By Prof. Leacock. Dominion Well Treated at Minimum Cost to Canadians," *Ottawa Citizen*, 24 February 1906, p. 9. Report with extensive quotations from Leacock's fourth lecture "Imperial Defence" and the following discussion, part of his lecture series on the British Empire under the auspices of the May Court Club. See also A1.

**D6.3** "Imperial Federation Prof. Leacock Talks on Great Question. Powerful Lecture. He Believes in Supreme Council of the Empire," *Ottawa Citizen*, 10 March 1906, p. 20. Report with quotations from Leacock's fifth lecture, "Imperial Federation," part of his lecture series on the British Empire under the auspices of the May Court Club. The few sentences that are quoted are mainly from the discussion that followed. Also reported as "Development of Federation Colonials in the British Parliament. Lecture by Prof. Leacock of M'Gill. . . . ," *Ottawa Evening Journal*, 10 March 1906, p. 7.

**D6.4** "Canada Must Assist. Was a Duty to Help Bear Burden of Imperial Defence. Should Lead Way in Solving Problem of Imperial Unity, Said Dr. Leacock — A Part in Council Was Ready When We Ask for It," *Toronto Globe*, 29 May 1906, p. 12; many paragraphs quoted. Report of speech on "Imperial Unity and Defence" on 28 May 1906 sponsored by the Daughters of the Empire. Also reported as "Be a Real Part of the Empire; Dr. Leacock's Address on Imperial Defence and Unity; On Imperial Councils; Canada Should Be Represented — Is Great Britain Willing? — Contributing to Imperial Defence," *Toronto News*, 29 May 1906, p. 4 with many paragraphs quoted; briefly as "Advocated Imperial Unity. Dr. Leacock Declares That Time for Action Has Arrived," *Toronto Telegram*, 29 May 1906, p. 15, with one sentence quoted.

**D6.5** "Canadian Club. Dr. Stephen B. Leacock on Imperial Tariff Reform," *Orillia Times*, 30 May 1906, p. 5. Report of speech on "The Imperial Tariff Problem" in Orillia on 29 May 1906; many paragraphs paraphrased containing a few quotations. The page of the *Orillia Packet* edition of 31 May 1906 which contained a report is missing from the microfilm held by OONL. J. Peace Derrington's letter to the editor appeared as "Criticism of Dr. Leacock's Address," *Orillia Packet*, 9 August 1906, p. [4]. It was dated 10 July 1906 from Birmingham, England. The letter quotes several remarks of Leacock's as reported by the *Packet*.

**D7.1** "Nations' Destinies on Opposite Roads; Prof. Leacock Says Canada and United States Can Never Be One; Monroe Doctrine's Masterful Handling; Eloquent Address in Which Call Is for Larger, National Canada," *London Free Press*, 18 January 1907, p. 3. Report of Leacock's mid-day luncheon speech to the Canadian Club on "The Monroe Doctrine and Its Application." Two sentences are quoted, several paragraphs are paraphrased.

**D7.2** "Canada Predominant to Head Empire, Remarkable Speech Delivered by Prof. Leacock. Doctrine of Progress. . . . ," *Montreal Star*, 26 February 1907, p. 12. Report with extensive quotations from Leacock's address "on the subject of a Greater Canada," delivered the previous evening at the fifth annual dinner of the Insurance Institute of Montreal. Extracts from the *Star* report appear as "Dr. Leacock Creates Great Enthusiasm. By an Unpremeditated Speech in Montreal," *Orillia Packet*, 7 March 1907, p. [1].

**D7.3** "Prof. Leacock's Inspiring Appeal for Imperialism; First Lecture in Empire Circling Tour of Rhodes Trust Missionary Delivered Before Large Audience of Canadian Club Members — Prof. Leacock an Eloquent and Magnetic Speaker," *St. John Sun*, 26 April 1907, p. 3. Report of speech on "The Imperial Movement" to the Canadian Club in Saint John, 25 April 1907; several sentences are quoted. Also reported as "Prof. Leacock's Address Before Canadian Club; the Imperial Movement Was the Theme of Able Address," *Saint John Globe*, 26 April 1907, p. 5, with one phrase quoted. Leacock agrees to address the club again at the conclusion of his tour.

**D7.4** "To Make Us the Brothers Not the Children of the People England; Dr. Stephen Leacock Tells the Halifax Canadian Club That There Must Be Advance Within Our Empire, That There Must Be a New Kind of Imperial Unity, or Otherwise There Shall Follow Disintegration. — He Believes in Imperialism as a Guarantee of the Peace of the World and the Well-Being of the Anglo-Saxon Race," *Halifax Herald*, 27 April 1907, pp. 1, 2. Report of speech to the Canadian Club in Halifax, 26 April 1907, with a few quotations; many remarks are paraphrased. Both the Saint John and Halifax speeches are reported as "Dr. Leacock's Mission. His Speeches at St. John and Halifax," *Orillia Packet*, 16 May 1907, p. 1.

**D7.5** "Canada and the Empire," *Times* (London), 16 May 1907, p. 4. Report of speech on "The Question of Canada" in the Portman Rooms, London, to the Victoria League on 15 May 1907.

**D7.6** "The Empire. Professor Leacock's Lecture. Some Common Sense," *Evening Post* (Wellington, N.Z.), 15 August 1907, p. 2. Report of lecture on "The British Empire of the Twentieth Century" in the Town Hall, Wellington, New Zealand, 14 August 1907; a few sentences quoted, many more paraphrased.

**D7.7** "Professor Leacock in West Australia," *Orillia Packet*, 5 September 1907, p. 1. Report of Leacock's lecture in Perth on "Imperial Unity" "on Friday evening at St. George's Hall."

**D7.8** " 'The Empire in the Twentieth Century," *Chronicle* (Wanganui, N.Z.), 12 September 1907, p. 7. Report of lecture in the Opera House, Wanganui, New Zealand, 11 September 1907; a few words quoted, many sentences paraphrased.

**D7.9** "Prof. Leacock in Australia, Address at Melbourne on 'Imperialism Versus Democracy.'. . . . ," *Montreal Star*, 14 December 1907, p. 7. Report with long quotations of Leacock's address.

D8.1 "The Asiatic Problem in the British Empire. Dr. Leacock's Instructive Address to the Canadian Club," *Orillia Packet*, 21 May 1908, p. 6. Report of Leacock's lecture to the Orillia Canadian Club on 15 May 1908. This was his first public lecture since his return from the Rhodes sponsored Empire tour. The article states: "Mr. C.J. Miller has kindly furnished the *Packet* with the subjoined report of Dr. Leacock's address, from his shorthand notes." Also reported, with quotations, as "Canadian Club. The Asiatic Problem in the British Empire," *Orillia Times*, 21 May 1908, p. 3.

D9.1 "Canada and British Diplomacy," *Times* (London), 5 January 1909, p. 6. Report of speech to the Commercial Travellers' Association in Montreal on 21 December 1908 with quotations.

D9.2 "Life Work of Robert Baldwin; Patriotic Address Before Canadian Club. Professor Leacock, McGill, Guest of Honor. Joint Organic Development of Two Races," *Ottawa Citizen*, 25 January 1909, p. [3]. Report of speech to the Canadian Club on Saturday, 23 January; many paragraphs quoted on Baldwin, responsible government, the future of Canada and the solution of the racial question. See also B2.

D9.3 "Canada Should Contribute to Navy's Support; Prof. Leacock Heard Here; Fine Address; Declares Canada Is Too Much Occupied with Internal Affairs," *Saint John Sun*, 3 February 1909, pp. 1, 2. Report of speech on the "External Relations of Canada" to the Canadian Club in Saint John, New Brunswick on 2 February 1909; several paragraphs are quoted. Despite the headline, the text quotes Leacock as saying he was not there to answer the question as to whether Canada should contribute to the British Navy or build one of its own.

D9.4 "Canada Should Contribute to Imperial Defence, Says Prof. Leacock," *Moncton Daily Times*, 5 February 1909, pp. 1, 4. Report of speech to the Canadian Club on 4 February 1909 on "The Future of Canada." Many paragraphs are paraphrased on Canada's defences, foreign trade, and Canada's relation to Britain; although quotation remarks are not used in the articles, many comments appear to be quotations. About Canada, Leacock says that we must not regard this as a country of a single tongue or a country of a single people.

D10.1 "[Speech at Quebec City on imperial unity, 20 January 1910.]" Three sentences on the navy are quoted in *Canadian Annual Report* (1910): 178

D10.2 "[Report of 'a recent lecture delivered before the St. James Literary Society, Montreal']," *Saturday Night* (Toronto) 23, no. 26, whole no. 1,166 (9 April 1910): 1–2. Quotes extensively from Leacock's speech in defence of protective tariffs. According to Leacock's record of publications, this speech took place on 16 March and was titled "Germany As a World Power"; according to the St. James Literary Society it took place on 10 March as was called "World Policy of the German Empire." See also C10.4.

D11.1 "Address at Queen's by Prof. Stephen Leacock of Montreal; He Dealt in an Admirable Way with the Question 'What the Universities Can Do for Canada,' " *Kingston Daily British Whig*, 9 February 1911, p. 2. Report of speech on 8 February 1911 to the Queen's University Arts Society; many paragraphs are quoted although the newspaper uses no quotation marks.

D11.2 "[Speech on reciprocity in Quebec City, 4 March 1911.]" One sentence is quoted in *Canadian Annual Review* (1911): 42.

**D11.3** "The Conservative Meeting. Strong Speeches by Mr. Bennett and Prof. Leacock," *Orillia Packet*, 7 September 1911, p. 6. Only one sentence is reported from Leacock's speech against reciprocity in the Opera House in Orillia on 1 September 1911 but the report is followed by "Dr. Leacock's Epigrams. Striking Sentences from His Speech on Friday Last," which quotes twenty-five of his remarks. W.H. Bennet was the Conservative candidate for East Simcoe in the federal election. Also reported as "Leacockian Logic," *Orillia Times*, 7 September 1911, p. 4, with one paragraph quoted.

**D11.4** "End Convention with a Banquet; Canadian Manufacturers Hear Able Addressees ... Professor Leacock Pleads for Imperialism," *Toronto Globe*, 13 October 1911, pp. 1, 8. Report of speech to the Canadian Manufacturers convention, 12 October 1911, with quotations (p. 8). Also reported as "In Peace or War We Are (Colonial Neutrality Thing of the Past Says Prof. Leacock) with Mother Country. Strong Utterances of Imperialism at Canadian Manufacturers' Banquet," *Toronto News*, 13 October 1911, p. 17, with quotations; as "They Had a Merry Time," *Toronto Telegram* under sub-heading "All for Imperialism", 13 October 1911, p. 21, with one paragraph quoted; as "Annual Banquet a Merry Affair," *Toronto Mail and Empire*, 13 October 1911, p. 4, one sentence quoted.

**D11.5** "Dominion Needs Public Opinion, Too Much Divorce between Ordinary Life and Polities [sic], Says Prof. Leacock. . . . ," *Montreal Gazette*, 23 October 1911, p. 5. Report with extensive quotations from Leacock's address, "Education and Politics," delivered before the Provincial Association of Protestant Teachers on Saturday morning. See also "Divorced from Politics, Prof. Leacock Says It Does Not Enter into Ordinary Life of Citizen. . . . ," *Montreal Witness*, 23 October 1911.

**D12.1** "Special Function of Universities. Should Aim to Produce Country's Best Citizens, Said Dr. Leacock," *Toronto Mail and Empire*, 15 January 1912, p. 7. Report of Leacock's address with quotations, "Universities and Citizenship," delivered at University Convocation Hall before the University Literary Society on 13 January 1912. President R.A. Falconer of the University of Toronto served as chairman.

**D12.2** "Fairy Stories Are Good for Children Says Prof. Leacock. . . . ," *Montreal Herald*, 21 February 1912, p. 6. Report of a speech, with quotations, given by Leacock to the Women's Art Society the previous day.

**D12.3** "Races That Never Fuse; Prof. Leacock on the Asiatic Problem in the British Dominions," *Montreal Witness*, 15 March 1912, p. 5. Report with one sentences quoted, many paragraphs paraphrased, from Leacock's speech, "Asiatic Problem in the Colonies," given at the St. James Literary Society the previous evening. The one quotation reads: "If you do not bring them in as equals should you bring them in [at] all?"

**D12.4** "Lift Public by Hair. Prof. Leacock Speaks of Newspaper's Mission," *Montreal Gazette*, 16 December 1912, p. 4. Brief report with quotations of Leacock's address, "College Education and Journalism," delivered before the Montreal Branch of the Journalists' Institute the previous Saturday, 14 December 1912.

**D12.5** "The Annual Meeting of the Toronto Branch of the Alumni Association," *University Monthly* (University of Toronto) 13, no. 8 (June 1913): 383–5. Report of a speech on "Social Reform and the New Century," with quotations, given by Leacock to an Alumni gathering in May 1913. According to Leacock's record of publications it took place on 16 May.

**D13.1** "Not Injustice of Sex Against Sex Says Prof. Leacock, Touching on Suffragettes' Cry of Man Injustice. . . . ," *Montreal Gazette*, 4 November 1913, p. 3. Report of Leacock's speech with a few quotations entitled "Social Reform in the Coming Century," given before the Women's Guild of Christ Church Cathedral the previous day.

**D13.2** "Prof. Leacock Spoke to the Kingston Women's Club on Friday; on the Participation of Women in the Work of the World — Their Reward Is Altogether Too Small," *Kingston British Whig*, 29 November 1913, p. 3. Report of speech to the Women's Canadian Club on 28 November 1913; several paragraphs quoted. There is a photograph of Leacock on p. 1. Also reported as "Competition Among Women Cause of Their Small Reward; Prof. Leacock Says They Are Not Allowed Entrance into Enough Employments. — No Women Lawyers in Quebec," *McGill Daily*, 2 December 1913, p. 4; one sentence is quoted.

**D15.1** "Patriotism and Humor Mixed: Prof. Leacock Draws Picture of House of Commons Meeting Which Stirs Audience; Irish in War; No Conflict over Home Rule Possible after Munsters and Fellows Have Died to Advance British Flag Is His Conception — Some Satirical Humor from Recent Works — Aiding Belgians a Worthy Cause," *St. John Daily Telegraph*, 16 February 1915, p. 5. Report of speech in St. John under the auspices of the Women's Canadian Club on 15 February 1915. One sentence is quoted from the imaginary House of Commons speeches by Sir Edward Carson and John Redmond; one sentence is quoted about the Belgians.

**D15.2** "A Happy Mixture of Humor and Patriotism; Prof. Stephen Leacock Gives Readings and Draws a Picture That Amuses and Stirs Large Audience. Satirical Humor From His Recent Works Easily Keeps the Audience in a Merry Mood. No Conflict Over Home Rule Is Possible After the Munsters and Fellows Have Died to Advance British Flag," *Halifax Herald*, 17 February 1915, pp. 1–2. Report of speech under the auspices of the Daughters of the Empire in Halifax on 16 February 1915. Leacock read from "Spoof," "Behind the Beyond" (his play), then on the Belgians (one sentence quoted), and then "a travesty purporting to be a London *Times* report of a British House of Commons session in 1916." These four elements formed the basis of all his speeches he gave on behalf of the Belgians.

**D15.3** "Leacock's Lecture. Large Audience Delighted with Humor of Montreal Man," *Toronto Evening Telegram*, 30 March 1915, p. [9]. Report of Leacock reading ("Spoof" and a parody of an English parliamentary report from the London *Times*) to an audience on behalf of the Franco-British Aid Society on 29 March. Several paragraphs are quoted from the parody.

**D15.4** "Leacock Draws Big Audience; Canadian Humorist Provides Evening of Fun; Readings Given Entirely From His Own Works; Handsome Sum Realized for Belgian Relief," *Hamilton Spectator*, 31 March 1915, p. 5. Lengthy report of Leacock's lecture of 30 March 1915 in Hamilton on behalf of the Belgian Relief Fund; one sentence quoted from "Spoof." See also C15.1a.

**D15.5** "Belgium's Stand Glorious, Says Prof. Leacock; McGill Professor Lauds Little Nation and Its Kindly Leader in the Struggle," *London Free Press*, 28 May 1915, p. [16]. Report of speech in London, ON, at the Masonic Temple on 27 May 1915 in aid of the Red Cross and Belgian relief funds, with quotations. Leacock is quoted as saying that his written material had been composed before the sinking of the *Luisitania*. He had placed the German Kaiser (Wilhelm II, Emperor of Germany) in a cage in one of his sketches; now he thought he should be hanged.

**D15.6** "An Evening with Leacock," *Guelph Evening Mercury*, 2 June 1915, p. 5. Report of speech at the Opera House in Guelph on 1 June 1915 under the auspices of the Red Cross Society, with quotations. The quotations concern two fictitious telegrams, one from the King of the Belgians, the other from Leacock's physician.

**D15.7** "Prof. Leacock Kept Audience in Good Humor; Noted Author and Humorist Provided Delightful Evening's Entertainment. A Worthy Cause; Proceeds Will Go to Belgian Relief and Red Cross Funds — Large Audience," *Brantford Expositor*, 4 June 1915, p. 9. Report of speech at the Victoria Hall in Brantford on 3 June 1915 with several quotations.

**D15.8** "Leacock Lecture Attracted a Large Crowd Last Night; Those Who Attended Laughed All the Way Home," *Sault Daily Star*, 12 June 1915, p. [3]. Report of speech "Laughing with Leacock" for the Belgian Relief Fund on 11 June 1915; one phrase is quoted from the House of Commons parody. The report notes that Leacock said that Canada and the other dominions should insist on the German Kaiser being hanged.

**D15.9** "Shakespeare Couldn't Pass English Exam. 'Silly Pursuit' Prof. Leacock Terms the Study of English Literature. Modern System Scored; Rudyard Kipling and Sir James Barrie Would Fail Hopelessly in the Matric," *McGill Daily*, 18 October 1915, pp. 1–2. Report of Leacock's speech to the convention of Protestant teachers of Quebec on 16 October 1915; several sentences quoted. See also K44.8.

**D16.1** "Professor Leacock Canadas [sic] Mark Twain," *Berlin News Record*, 21 February 1916, p. 1. Report of speech on 19 February 1916 in the Khaki Club in Berlin, Ont. [now Kitchener] on "Germany from within" and "Behind the Beyond." "Germany from Within" was about an imaginary trip through Germany. One sentence is quoted about helping the children in need because of the war.

**D16.2** "Unstinted Bounty for Returning Soldiers. Prof. Stephen Leacock Describes Great Problem," *Toronto Globe*, 3 June 1916, p. 8. Report of a speech with extensive quotations entitled "The Economic Problem Presented by the Treatment and Disposition of Returned Soldiers," given by Leacock at the closing session of the thirty-sixth annual conference of the Ontario Medical Association at the University of Toronto Mining Building on 2 June 1916. Also reported as "Stephen Leacock Lectures Doctors," *Toronto Daily News*, 3 June 1916, p. 6.

**D16.3** "Would Have All Silver Replaced by Nickle [sic] Coins Stephen Leacock, Professor of Political Economy at McGill, Makes Suggestion A Christmas Present of About Ten Millions to the Govt.," *Montreal Daily Star*, 11 December 1916, p. 3. Remarks made by Leacock to his Political Science class at McGill that the Canadian government should recall ". . . all its silver currency, and replace it by coins exactly similar, but made of nickel." Also reported as "Dr. S. Leacock Presents Novel Scheme to Government," *McGill Daily*, 12 December 1916, p. 4.

**D17.1** " 'Valueless,' Says Dr. Leacock of Note Dictation," *McGill Daily*, 17 January 1917, p. 1. Remarks Leacock made to his Political Science class on 16 January 1917. Extracts appeared as "Stephen Leacock Says Dictated Notes are Perfectly Valueless," *Varsity* (University of Toronto) 36, no. 41 (19 January 1917): 1.

**D17.2** "Great Famine Near, Says Prof. Leacock; Disaster Can Be Averted by Increased Production Only," *Toronto World*, 23 February 1917, p. 2. Report of speech to Montreal Housewives' League, at the Royal Victoria College, 22 February 1917; three paragraphs quoted.

**D17.3** "Prof. Leacock Popular at Windsor Hall [Hotel]," *McGill Daily*, 1 December 1917, pp. 1, 3. Report of Leacock's speech at a Win the War Meeting at the Windsor Hotel, Montreal, with a few quotations, including "too bad that women do not vote."

**D18.1** "Prof. Leacock on Frenzied Fiction; Witty Address Pleases Large Audience — How Fashions Change," *Montreal Daily Star*, 9 January 1918, p. 21. Brief report with a few quotations from Leacock's lecture, "Frenzied Fiction, a Talk on Books of Today," delivered to the members and friends of the Royal Victoria Alumnae Society at Royal Victoria College of McGill University on 8 January 1918. According to the report, "Prof. Leacock Spoke Before R.V.C. Society," *McGill Daily News*, 9 January 1918, p. 3. Proceeds from the gathering were for the purchase of books and magazines for convalescent homes for soldiers.

**D18.2** "Prof. Leacock on New War Poetry; Told I.O.D.E. Audience of Flood of Doggerel, Followed by Work of Bitter Calibre. . . . ," *Montreal Gazette*, 7 February 1918, p. 12. A report with only a couple of quotations from Leacock's lecture the previous evening at the Ritz-Carlton Hotel in Montreal. Leacock also commented on the increase in moving picture theatres. The lecture was organized by the Rupert Brooke Chapter of the Imperial Order of the Daughters of the Empire in Montreal.

**D19.1** "Common Speech Unites British and Americans; Lesson Emphasized by Speakers at Lowell Centenary Celebrations; Prof. Leacock's Address," *Montreal Gazette*, 24 February 1919, p. 9. A report of the various speeches given on 22 February 1919 at the close of James Russell Lowell Centenary Celebrations in New York. A paragraph from Leacock's address is quoted pertaining to the "common history and literature" of Great Britain and the United States. Also reported as "Leacock's Gay Vein at Lotos Dinner: Montreal Professor Forgets Seriousness and Makes an After-Dinner Speech of the Old-Time Sort," *New York Times*, 2 March 1919, sec. 4, p. 10. Ten paragraphs are quoted from the speech. See also B7.

**D19.2** "Cry of Child Must Reach Society; Social Reformation Must Begin with Young, Said Professor Leacock," *Montreal Gazette*, 12 March 1919, p. 11. Brief report with several quotations from Leacock's address delivered the previous afternoon to the Baby Welfare Committee at Almy's, Limited, in Montreal.

**D19.3** " 'Ned' Lashed by Leacock; Canada's Premier Humorist Airs the Frenzy in Fiction," *Toronto Globe*, 3 May 1919, p. 8. Report of speech on "Frenzied Fiction" at Convocation Hall, University of Toronto, 2 May 1919; several quotations. Also reported as "Stephen Leacock Vivisects Novel," *Toronto World*, 3 May 1919, p. 4, with quotations. Ned is a boy hero. See D21.7.

**D19.4** "The Worst Is Yet to Come, Says Leacock Heroes and Heroines of Novel of Tomorrow May Become Even Sillier Than at Present. Humorist Warmly Received," *Harvard Crimson*, 29 November 1919, p. 1. Report with quotations from Leacock's lecture, "Literature of Today and Tomorrow," given at Harvard University the previous evening. The lecture was announced as "A Great Humorist Stephen Leacock; First University Tea to Be Held This Afternoon," *Harvard Crimson*, 28 November 1919, p. 1.

**D20.1** "Stephen Leacock in Merry Mood; Delighted Large Audience at Convocation Hall Last Evening; On 'Frenzied Fiction'; Lecturer Also Turned His Attention to Creation of a Movie," *Toronto Mail*, 3 April 1920, p. 4. Report of speech to the Veteran Society at Convocation Hall, University of Toronto, 2 April 1920, with quotations.

**D21.1** "Prof. Leacock Gives Bank Men Economic View; Delivers First of Series on the Theory of Money; Supply and Demand; an Absolute Regulator in the End of Price — Analysis of Cost — the Gold Standard," *Financial Post* 15 (14 January 1921): 9. Report of Leacock's lecture, the first of series of six lectures on the theory of money, in connection with the bankers' course at McGill University; several sentences are quoted. Reprinted as "The Theory of Money; Explained to the Bankers by Stephen Leacock," *Orillia Packet*, 20 January 1921, p. 9. See also A35.

**D21.2** "U.S. Friendship Is Great Asset; Prof. Leacock Warns of Evil Influences to Create Trouble," *Montreal Daily Star*, 9 February 1921, p. 1. Short report of an address to the Sons of Brown in Boston the previous evening. One sentence is quoted: "The one great thing that we can look upon as an asset in the future is continued friendship of the American people."

**D21.3** "Says Prohibition Is a Lie and a Sham; Professor Leacock Finds It a Bad and Immoral Statute; Caused Crime Wave; Are Getting Back to Days of Bigotry, the Whip and the Scourge," *Toronto Mail and Empire*, 4 April 1921, p. 5. Lengthy report with many quotations from speech, "The Case Against Prohibition," to the Citizens Liberty League on 2 April 1921 at the Foresters' Hall, College Street. Also reported as "Liberty League Open Campaign; Professor Leacock Pours Imprecation on Prohibitionists and O.T.A.," [Ontario Temperance Act] *Toronto Globe*, 4 April 1921, p. 12; as "An Unjust Immoral Thing; Opinion Gagged and Stifled; Leacock Denounces Prohibition and Wishes He Had Shares in Brewery — O.T.A. a Criminal Statute," *Toronto Telegram*, 4 April 1921, p. 15; as "Case for Prohibition and Liberty League Given at Meetings; Professor Leacock Is Opposed to Prohibition as Matter of Principle. Liberty at Stake; Claims a Fanatical Minority Has Captured the Public and Legislature," *Toronto World*, 4 April 1921, pp. 1, 2; as "Leacock Scores 'Drys' in Address Defending 'Wets': Says Fanatical Minority Has Captured Public's Ear and Legislatures," *Montreal Daily Star*, 4 April 1921 p. 2. Large sections of the speech appear in *Canadian Annual Review* (1921): 554. The speech was criticized in an editorial "Professor Leacock's Speech," *Christian Guardian* 92, no. 15 (13 April 1921): 8 with quotations from the speech. See also A36a.

**D21.4** "Professor Leacock. Recipes for Fiction," *Daily Mail* (London), 18 October 1921, p. 5. Report of lecture on "Frenzied Fiction" at the Aeolian Hall in London on 17 October 1921. The report, with quotations, only concerns the section on modern magazine fiction. Also reported as "Trials of a Humorist. Mr. Stephen Leacock's Lecture," *Daily Telegraph* (London), 18 October 1921, p. 5. The report includes quotations on his experiences with various chairmen, as well as Victorian heroines. See also A30b.

**D21.5** "A British-U.S.A. Union Idea Voiced by Stephen Leacock; Canada's Humorist, Speaking at Oxford, Advocates Interchange of Ideas Between Britain and U.S.A.," *Toronto Telegram*, 29 October 1921, p. 25. Report of speech to the British-American Union, 28 October 1921, with quotations.

**D21.6** "Mr. Stephen Leacock's Lecture on the Drama," *Spectator* (London), 5 November 1921, pp. 589–91. Description with verbatim extracts of Leacock's lecture in which he relates his experience in working in theatre and in writing plays.

**D21.7** "Leacock in the Flesh. A Lecturer As Funny as His Books. His Biting Criticism of Our Fiction and Films," *Guardian* (Manchester), 17 November 1921, p. 9. Report of two lectures given on the same day by Leacock. The first was to an assembly of boys and girls at the Central High School where he spoke on "Moonbeams from the Larger Lunacy." This lecture was about an "educational film" titled "The Discovery of America"; the quotations concern Christopher Columbus and scenes from *Uncle Tom's Cabin*. The evening lecture was on "Frenzied Fiction" to a Y.M.C.A. gathering in Houldsworth Hall. The lecture was an examination of four types of fiction, with examples: 1. boys' adventure books, with the character "Ned" from the George Alfred Henty novels 2. Madeleine, the true Victorian heroine, from Scott 3. Miss Middleton, who has more "pep" than Madeleine, a type popularized by Marion Crawford and A.C. Gunter 4. modern magazine fiction where the man and woman are married to other people. This is an excellent summary of a lecture that Leacock was to give many times over the next two decades.

**D21.8** "Popular Fiction; Mr. Leacock's Satire," *Herald* (Glasgow), 22 November 1921, p. 8. Report of Leacock's lecture to the Palette Club on types of popular fiction. Several sentences are paraphrased on modern magazine fiction.

**D21.9** "Mr. Stephen Leacock in Glasgow: The Right to Individual Development," *Herald* (Glasgow), 29 November 1921, p. 8. Report of lecture on "Equality" to the Glasgow University Students' Union on the afternoon of 28 November 1921; several sentences paraphrased.

**D21.10** "Literature at Its Lightest," *Herald* (Glasgow), 29 November 1921, p. 8. Report of evening lecture to members of the Trinity Literary Society in Trinity Church, Glasgow. The report concerns the "educational" film "The Discovery of America" as well as audiences in the prairies. Several phrases are quoted.

**D21.11** "Modern Cervantes; Mr. Stephen Leacock on Literary Types," *Herald* (Glasgow), 30 November 1921, p. 10. Report of lecture at Y.M.C.A. Lyric Buildings on the four types of fiction; a few sentences are quoted, others paraphrased.

**D21.12** "Mr. Stephen Leacock on London. A Monument to Admire," *Times* (London), 10 December 1921, p. 12. Report of Leacock's lecture to the London Society at the Hotel Cecil, 9 December 1921, with many remarks paraphrased. Also reported, with several quotations, as "Humours of London. Mr. Leacock on Parliament," *Daily Telegraph* (London), 10 December 1921, p. 10. The report concerns London monuments and the financial district ("The City") in addition to Parliament.

**D21.13** "Old-Time Politics. Professor Leacock's Humour," *Daily Telegraph* (London), 13 December 1921, p. 14. Report of Leacock's lecture to the inaugural meeting of the London Canadian Club; several paragraphs are quoted. The names of some of those in attendance are also given. Also reported as "A Canadian Club in London. Mr. Leacock Entertained," *Times* (London), 13 December 1921, p. 5, with remarks on the Canadian election paraphrased; with several quotations, including remarks on his tour, as "Mr. Stephen Leacock. Advice to 'Honest Canadians in Dishonest London,'" *Daily Mail* (London), 13 December 1921, p. 12; as "Modest Mr. Leacock Sorry He Left Canada; Blames Himself for Meighen's Defeat — Tells How He Boosts Dominion," *Toronto Star*, 14 December 1921, p. [13]. The report, by Windermere, has two quotations. Windermere notes that Leacock's speeches are quoted in all the daily papers, especially those he makes on London and prohibition. Arthur Meighen was the Prime Minister of Canada at the time. Also as "When Leacock Was a Politician," *Montreal Daily Star*, 11 January 1922. The quotations concern the nature of political oratory in former years and his amusing incidents as a lecturer. Also as "Leacock's Can-Opener," *Toronto Star Weekly*, 25 February 1922, p. 14. This report is reprinted from the *Daily News* (London) and quotes three sentences.

**D22.1** "Dr. Leacock Addresses Westerners," *McGill Daily*, 9 February 1922, pp. 1, 4. Report of speech to the Western Club in the Union Cafeteria on his recent trip to England with quotations on English University chairmen and the Scottish sense of humour.

**D22.2** "Dr. Leacock Before Med. Undergrads," *McGill Daily*, 14 March 1922, p. 1. Report of speech to the McGill Medical Undergraduate Society on "The Lighter Side of Life," 13 March 1922, with quotations.

**D22.3** "Leacock Praises Quebec Liquor Law System May Shortly Be Universal in Dominion," *Montreal Daily Star*, 6 November 1922, p. 2. Brief report, with quotations from Leacock's lecture in Portland, Maine on prohibition.

**D23.1** "Montreal Cold? No! Says Leacock Professor; Discusses Weather, Liquor, Education and Civics in One," *Montreal Daily Star*, 26 January 1923, p. 8. Brief report with quotations from Leacock's address given the previous day before members of the Canadian Club on "The Future of Montreal." See also "No Love for Ontario; Prof. Leacock Resents Supposed Attitude Toward French Language," *Toronto Telegram*, 26 January 1923, p. 13. Brief report with quotations, deploring the attempts to stamp out the French language in Ontario.

**D23.2** "Ridicules Literary Bar: Leacock Favors a Bond of Letters Between Canada and U.S.," *New York Times*, 9 March 1923, p. 14. Two sentences paraphrased from remarks by Leacock on 8 March. Leacock was against a proposed tax on American books and magazines entering Canada.

**D23.3** "Leacock Pleads Capitalist's Case: Once 'Empire Builder,' but Now Called 'Profiteer,' Declares McGill Professor. Says Canada Needs Him. Describes Canadian National Railways as 'Conceived in Ignorance and Fashioned in Graft,' " *New York Times*, 11 March 1923, p. 8. Report of speech on 10 March to the Canadian Club of New York at the Hotel Belmont on "Empire Settlement and the Organization of Prosperity." Six paragraphs are quoted. Also briefly reported as "Leacock's Solution for C.N.R. Problem; Would Give the Railway Away and He Understands China Badly Needs One," *Montreal Gazette*, 12 March 1923, p. 2.

**D23.4** "Over Four Hundred McGill Graduates Are Given Degrees. . . . ," *Montreal Daily Star*, 29 May 1923, p. 3. Report, with quotations, from Leacock's convocation address on modern education. He began his address by saying that he was a stranger to convocations for twenty years owing to the coinciding of convocation with the "opening of the trout fishing season in Ontario."

**D23.5** "Dr. Leacock Would Omit All Women Characters from Crime Stories," *Montreal Daily Star*, 29 December 1923, p. 4. Brief report with snippets of quotation from Leacock's address at the annual meeting of the New Jersey State Teachers' Association on 28 December.

**D24.1** "French Cabinet Need Course in Economics? Stephen Leacock Would Like to Have Ministers as Sophomores; A Gold Standard; Restoration of World's Currency Is Most Urgent and Vital," *Toronto Star*, 1 February 1924, p. 1. Report of morning speech on "The Gold Standard" to the Life Underwriters' Educational Congress, 1 February 1924, with quotations. Also reported as "Uncle Sam World's Miser; French Policy 'Folly'; Stephen Leacock Declares Gold Standard Alone is Honest — Currency Restoration World's Need," *Toronto Telegram*, 1 February 1924, p. [21]; as "Stabilize Currency by Gold Standard, Says

Prof. Leacock; Thinks Outlook from Commercial Prosperity Depends Upon This," *Toronto Globe*, 2 February 1924, p. [13]; as "Return to Gold Basis Should be Clear Aim; Prof. Leacock Says That Obstacles in Path Are Exaggerated. Confusion in Europe; French Ministry Seems to Need a Lesson in Economics," *Toronto Mail*, 2 February 1924, p. 5. All reports have quotations. See also A42.

D24.2 "Protests Over-Organisation in Universities and Schools. Prof. Leacock Makes Plea for Education for Cultural Purposes Rather Than Gain, at McGill Alumnae Meet," *Hamilton Herald*, 12 February 1924, section 2, p. 5. Report by Clyde Corrigall who quotes extensively from Leacock's speech to the McGill Alumnae Association of Hamilton and Southern Ontario held at the Royal Connaught Hotel in Hamilton, ON. Also reported as "University Growth Not Unmixed Good; Ideals Apt to Be Crushed Under Overpowering Weight of Organization," *Toronto Globe*, 12 February 1924, p. 3. The *Globe* report says the speech was given to the McGill Alumni on 11 February.

D24.3 "Stephen Leacock Was 'Chunk of Ice'; Creates Amusement at St. Lambert with Recital of 'Stage Career'," *Montreal Daily Star*, 18 February 1924, p. 9. Report with quotations from Leacock's address, "The Lighter Side of Literature and Drama," delivered in St. Lambert, Quebec under the auspices of the St. Lambert's Women's Club on 16 February 1924. Also briefly reported as, "In Aid of Library Dr. Stephen Leacock Addresses St. Lambert Women's Club," *Montreal Gazette*, 18 February 1924, p. 3.

D24.4 "Restore Dominion to Gold Standard Professor Leacock's Remedy for Economic Ills Now Prevailing in Canada. . . . ," *Montreal Gazette*, 26 February 1924, p. 5. Report with quotations from Leacock's address, "The Reorganization of Canada for Prosperity," delivered the previous evening before members of the Liberal-Conservative Association in the ball room of Mount Royal Hotel in Montreal.

D24.5 " 'News to Me' Says Leacock As He Is Told of Subject; Literature, Drama Instead of England Discussed by Humorist; Talks Satirically on Modern Crime Stories," *Michigan Daily*, 6 March 1924, p. 1. Report of speech at the University of Michigan in Ann Arbor, 5 March 1924, on "New Matters in Literature and Drama" with brief quotations. Also reported as "Stephen Leacock on Novels," *McGill Daily*, 15 March 1924, p. 4 with quotations. See also F24.1.

D24.6 "Historic and Politic Economy Clubs of McGill Meet Jointly," *Montreal Herald*, 2 April 1924. News clipping held at QMM Archives; not located in microfilm edition of the newspaper. Brief report of several speeches at the first joint meeting of the Historical and Political Economy Clubs at McGill. Leacock is quoted as saying: "Any sane notion of international politics has to start from things as they are and not as they may be some day."

D24.7 "Usefulness Not Aim of Education; Dr. Stephen Leacock Scores Utilitarian Idea in Addressing Students. . . . ," *Montreal Gazette*, 26 April 1924, p. 10. Report of a lecture with quotations delivered to students at McGill University in which he discounts the importance of practical instruction in education.

D24.8 "Stephen Leacock on Education," *Toronto Mail*, 10 May 1924, p. 18. Report of a lecture "the other day" in Montreal on "True and False Education"; six paragraphs quoted.

D24.9 "Stephen Leacock Suggests Montreal as Future Athens. . . . ," *Montreal Gazette*, 2 December 1924, p. 5. Report with extensive quotations from Leacock's address, "The Place of Letters in National Life," delivered to the Canadian Club in Montreal on 1 December

1924. He supports the idea of a Canadian Book Week, but questions the restriction to Canadian books only. Also reported as "Wants Ideal in Canadian Literature," *McGill Daily*, 2 December 1924, pp. 1, 4.

**D24.10** "Noted Canadian Humorist Would Ignore Statistics," *Toronto Globe*, 18 December 1924, p. 2. Very brief report of speech in Montreal, 17 December 1924. No quotations but some remarks are paraphrased on the Canadian economy.

**D24.11** "Professor Leacock Sails: Canadian Writer Resents Rule Regarding Income Tax Proof for Voyagers," *New York Times*, 20 December 1924, p. 15. Remarks made to reporters on the ship he was taking to Nassau, Bahamas, on 19 December. Three sentences quoted on the fact he had to prove he had no earned income in the U.S. before his departure.

**D25.1** "Crowded House Greeted Humorist; Professor Leacock on Popular Novels at the Majestic," *Halifax Morning Herald*, 17 January 1925, p. 2. Report of speech on 16 January on "Frenzied Fiction"; one phrase is quoted about heroines.

**D25.2** "Defined Maximum of State Direction; Dr. Stephen Leacock Deals with Private and Public Enterprise," *Toronto Mail*, 21 February 1925, p. 12. Report of speech at a dinner of the Life Underwriters' Association of Canada, 19 February, with quotations. His topic is given as "private enterprise versus the state."

**D25.3** "Prof. Leacock Pleads for Cheaper Books; Says Restrictions Are Attempt to Overstimulate Small Market; Judge by Quality; Onslaught on Licensing Clauses Launched by Humorist at Ottawa," *Toronto Star*, 11 March 1925, p. 3. Report of speech to a special committee to consider the amendments to the Canadian copyright act in Ottawa, 10 March 1925, with quotations.

**D25.4** "Value of Local History Stressed; Oldest Country to Geologist, Canada Is Newest to Historian, Says Prof. Leacock. . . . ," *Montreal Gazette*, 23 May 1925, p. 4. Report with extensive quotations from Leacock's address, "Local History in Canada," delivered to the Canadian Historical Association at Royal Victoria College of McGill University. He encourages the preservation of historical records of a local character, and reminisces about his childhood in the township of Georgina. Also reported, but to a lesser extent, as "Children Need Historic Sense; Stories of Events Liable to Be Lost If Care Is Not Taken. . . . ," *Montreal Daily Star*, 23 May 1925, p. 35.

**D25.5** "Stephen Leacock Turns Guns on Factory-Type Colleges; Declares Undergraduates Now Even Wear Same Kind of Coats and Write Down Same Notes — Professors Often No More Individual Than Standardized Toys," *Toronto Star*, 16 October 1925, p. 44. Report of speech to the Alumnae of Queen's University in Kingston "on the subject of The Work of the Canadian Universities," 15 October 1925, with quotations.

**D26.1** "Leacock Describes Colleges of Past and Present Day. . . . ," *Montreal Gazette*, 24 February 1926, p. 10. Report, with quotations, from Leacock's address, "The Work of the Universities," given in Ottawa under the joint auspices of the Ottawa Valley McGill Graduates' Society and the Professional Institute of the Civil Service.

**D26.2** "Leacock Denounces Quacks: We Must Choke Them Out, He Says, at Dinner of Cancer Experts," *New York Times*, 25 September 1926, p. 20. Report of speech made at a dinner of the American Society for the Control of Cancer at the Hotel Astor, 24 September; four paragraphs quoted. The dinner closed a five-day international symposium at Lake Mohonk, N.Y. An editorial titled "The Warfare on Cancer," 26 September 1926, sec. 2,

p. 8 commented on the symposium and Leacock's speech. Also reported as "Prof. Leacock Assails Fake Cancer Cures," *Toronto Telegram*, 25 September 1925; two sentences quoted. News clipping of the *Telegram* in University of Toronto Archives could not be located on microfilm edition.

**D26.3** "Leacock Satirizes College Gown As McGill Controversy Develops," *Toronto Star*, 3 December 1926, p. 1. Dateline 4 December. Several quoted paragraphs on academic dress; no source is given for Leacock's remarks.

**D27.1** "Dominion's Need of Immigration Strongly Urged; Prof. Stephen Leacock Says Those Who Oppose More Migration to Canada Are Lacking in Larger Vision," *Ottawa Citizen*, 11 January 1927, p. 5. Report of Leacock's speech on "Some Aspects of Political Economy in Especial Relation to Public Policy in Canada," to the Professional Institute of the Civil Service; several paragraphs quoted. Also reported as "Must Solve Distribution of Wealth Says Leacock, or World Will Explode," *Toronto Star*, 11 January 1927, p. 1 with quotations; as "Present Distribution of Wealth Is Unfair; Dr. Stephen Leacock Declares There is a Need for Change," *Orillia News-Letter*, 2 February 1927, p. 1, five sentences are quoted. The *News-Letter* also notes that Leacock's speech was "one of a series of twelve lectures which are to be delivered by prominent persons of the country to members of Canada's Civil Service."

**D27.2** "Gold Standard Upheld by Professor Leacock Would Not Abandon Comfortable Vehicle," *Ottawa Citizen*, 8 February 1927, p. 12. Report with quotations from Leacock's address on 7 February 1927 to the Professional Institute of the Civil Service. Also reported as "Gold Standard Is Upheld by Leacock; Abolition As Basis of World Finance Would Wreck Commerce," *Montreal Gazette*, 8 February 1927, p. 1; "Stephen Leacock Speaks in Ottawa," *McGill Daily*, 9 February 1927, p. 1.

**D27.3** "Tommyrot, Leacock Calls Censorship Audience Should Walk out When Offensive Plays Are Shown. . . . ," *Montreal Gazette*, 9 March 1927, p. 9. Report with quotations from Leacock's address, "Education of Children," delivered under the auspices of the Women's Guild of St. George's Church in Montreal on 8 March. With respect to the books that children read, he defends old-fashioned dime novels and boys' literature as represented by G.A. Henty. Also reported as "Tommyrot, Leacock Calls Censorship," *McGill Daily*, 9 March 1927, p. 4.

**D27.4** "U.S. 'Blue Law' on Classics Riles Canada College Dons; Sir Arthur Currie and Stephen Leacock Condemn Trend Towards 'Thou-Shalt Not' Legislation — Want Decameron Shakespeare and Arabian Nights Unexpurgated for Adults," *Toronto Star*, 9 May 1927, p. 7. Report of speech to the McGill Society in the King Edward Hotel in Toronto on 8 May 1927. Several paragraphs are quoted on censorship from Leacock's speech. Rather interestingly, the report of the speech in the *Toronto Globe*, 9 May 1927, p. [13] says that Leacock spoke only about his chicken farm in Orillia; no quotations are given.

**D27.5** "Says Canadians Copy Us Too Much: Prof. Leacock, Criticising Our Immigration Theories, Contrasts Turks and Scots," *New York Times*, 18 August 1927, p. 6. Report of speech to a party of British journalists touring Canada; remarks were made 17 August 1927 at Macdonald Agricultural College at McGill. Two paragraphs are quoted. Leacock recommended that Canada not follow U.S. immigration policies.

**D27.6** "Advice on Books by Dr. Leacock; Patriotism Doesn't Mean Hostility Toward

Others," *Montreal Daily Star*, 11 November 1927, p. 13. Report, with quotations, from Leacock's address to the Junior League at the Ritz-Carlton Hotel in Montreal the previous day. Although he encourages the reading of books by Canadian authors, he tells his audience to remember the importance of "the republic of letters" outside of Canada.

**D28.1** "Plan Association to Probe Cause and Seek Cancer Cure. Discussion Held at McGill University Indicates That New Organization Will Be Started Here — to Inform Public on Danger — Research Work; Dr. Stephen Leacock Outlined Nature of Plans to Wage Fight Against Disease," *Montreal Daily Star*, 26 January 1928, p. 21. Report of meeting chaired by Leacock at McGill University, 25 January 1928. Many paragraphs are quoted from Leacock's speech. Dr. John Gerster, chairman of the New York committee for the American Society for the Control of Cancer, was the principal speaker. Dr. A.B. Macallum, Professor of Biochemistry, and Sir Arthur Currie, Principal of McGill University, also spoke. Two sentences by Leacock, thanking Dr. Macallum are also reported. See also F28.1.

**D28.2** "Dickens Would Not Kill Edwin Drood," *McGill Daily*, 7 February 1928, pp. 1, 3. Report of speech to the Women's Guild of Christ Church Cathedral on 6 February 1928 with quotations.

**D28.3** "Leacock Flays Movie History; Too Much Americanism and Lack of Facts, He Claims; War Pictures; Declares Canada's National History Is Wonderful Unused Epic," *Montreal Star*, 22 February 1928, p. 7. Report of speech to the Westmount Association of Protestant Teachers at Westmount High School on 21 February 1928; several paragraphs are quoted. Also reported, with quotations, as "Historic Sense of Children Spoiled Professor Stephen Leacock Takes Tilt at Influence of American Pictures," *Montreal Gazette*, 22 February 1928, p. 5; as "Leacock Deplores Effect of U.S. Films on Canada's Youth; Spread Strange and Distorted Ideas About the War, He Declares; Wilson versus Europe," *Toronto Globe*, 22 February 1928, p. 2. Woodrow Wilson was the President of the United States. Reaction to this speech by movie people in Toronto was reported in "Differ with Leacock on 'Yankee' Pictures," *Toronto Star*, 23 February 1928; news clipping in University of Toronto Archives, article not located on microfilm edition. The speech was also reported as "History in the U.S. Film. Dr. Leacock Sees Its Humour," *Daily Mail* (London), 7 March 1928, p. 6; six paragraphs are quoted.

**D28.4** "Leacock Praises McGill to Union; Says University Never Accepted Money Stipulating Restrictions," *Montreal Star*, 7 March 1928, p. 13. Report of speech on 6 March 1928 to the McGill Women's Union; four sentences are quoted on McGill's academic freedom. Also reported as "Claims Freedom of Opinion at McGill Stephen Leacock Points out Contrast with Most U.S. Universities. . . . ," *Montreal Gazette*, 7 March 1928, p. 9; as "Great Freedom of Opinion at McGill," *McGill Daily*, 7 March 1928, p. 1.

**D29.1** "Lauds Generosity of Sir V. Meredith and F.W. Molson; Prof. Leacock Voices Gratitude of McGill to Late Benefactors. . . . ," *Montreal Gazette*, 20 March 1929, p. 9. Report, with quotations, from Leacock's address on the function of a university delivered to the Women's Canadian Club in Montreal at the Windsor Hotel on 18 March 1929.

**D29.2** "Leacock Advises Canada to Throw Off U.S. Dominance, Says Time Has Come to Give Republic Friendliest of Jolts, Empire Co-operation," *Montreal Gazette*, 6 November 1929, p. 4. Report with quotations of Leacock's address to the Rotary Club of Montreal on 5 November 1929.

D30.1 "Medical Dinner Is Notable Meeting . . . Professor Stephen Leacock Gives Humorous Address as Chief Speaker," *Montreal Star*, 10 February 1930, p. 5. Report of Leacock's speech on Saturday evening. Only one line of his speech is quoted. See also "Medical Banquet Is Held at McGill University, Dr. Stephen Leacock, Economist and Humorist, Entertained as Guest of Honor," *Montreal Gazette*, 10 February 1930, p. 4.

D30.2 "Prof. Leacock Suggests Plan [for] Empire Unity; Noted Economist Says Credit Consolidation, Reciprocal Tariff, Controlled Migration Would Stimulate Growth," *Toronto Telegram*, 10 April 1930, p. 3. Report of speech to a special meeting of the Board of Trade, also attended by the Chamber of Commerce and Canadian Manufacturing Association in Montreal, 9 April 1930, with paraphrased remarks only. Also reported as "Economic Unity Urged in Empire by Leacock; McGill Professor in Address Advocates Debt Consolidation and Reciprocal Tariff," *New York Times*, 11 April 1930, p. 30, with one phrase quoted; also as "Responsible Government and Empire Trade: Professor's Leacock View," *Times* (London), 12 April 1930, p. 11. The speech is critiqued in "Prof. Leacock and Empire Finance," *Saturday Night*, 3 May 1930, p. 1.

D31.1 "Leacock Confident Russia Will Fall: Communism Doomed to Destruction, Declares McGill Economist," *Montreal Daily Star*, 21 March 1931, pp. 1, 3. Report and most of the text of Leacock's address to the Montreal Junior Board of Trade, which met at the Windsor Hotel in Montreal on 20 March 1931. For a similar report but with fewer quotations from Leacock's address, see also "Soviet Five-Year Plan Doomed, Says Stephen Leacock. Bound to Crack and Worst Despotism of History Will Fail," *Montreal Gazette*, 21 March 1931, p. 15. Also reported, with quotations, as "Dr. Stephen Leacock Sees Russian Break; Communism Will Prove Unavailing, Declares McGill Economist. 5–Year Plan Fails," *Toronto Mail*, 21 March 1931, p. 3; as "Russian 5 Year Plan Cannot Be Success in Opinion of Dr. Stephen Leacock," *Orillia Packet and Times*, 26 March 1931, p. 11, with five paragraphs quoted.

D31.2 "Sincerity Needed Judging Books Library Convention Is Told; Dr. Stephen Leacock Delivers Interesting Address at Annual Meeting of District Librarians," *Orillia News-Letter*, 15 July 1931, p. 1; several sentences quoted. Report of speech to the Library Institute, consisting of more than fifty librarians and trustees between Toronto and Midland, on 14 July 1931. Also reported as "Be Honest With Yourself in Choosing Your Reading Is the Advice Given by Dr. Leacock at Library Institute," *Orillia Packet and Times*, 16 July 1931, pp. 1, 2; several paragraphs paraphrased with brief quotations. Reprinted as "Be Honest with Yourself in Choosing Your Reading," *Ontario Library Review* 16, no. 1 (August 1931): 15–6.

D31.3 "Note and Comment," *Orillia Packet and Times*, 29 October 1931, p. 5. Editorial by C.H. Hale of Leacock's recent speech to the Protestant Teachers' Association of Quebec. Hale quotes a phrase from the speech and also notes Sir Arthur Currie's reaction to the speech — that Leacock not be taken seriously when he suggests that education standards are higher in Ontario than in Quebec.

D31.4 "Leacock Advises Trade Exchanges upon Quota Basis. . . . ," *Montreal Gazette*, 10 December 1931, p. 10. Report, with quotations, from Leacock's address to members of the Builders Exchange in Montreal the previous day. His remarks pertain to tariffs within the British Empire, the cancellation of war debts, Communism, and the quota system.

D32.1 "Advocates Return to Gold Standard Necessary to Economic Equilibrium, Says Professor Leacock," *Montreal Daily Star*, 5 February 1932, p. 20. Report of a speech with a few quotations on the gold standard given by Leacock to the McGill Alumnae Society at Royal Victoria College on 4 February 1932. Also reported as "Leacock Predicts Blue Ruin If Gold Standard Dropped," *McGill Daily News*, 5 February 1932, pp. 1, 4; one quotation.

**D32.2** "Noted Humorist Serious, When Discussing Canada," *Cincinnati Times-Star*, 19 February 1932. Report with quotations from Leacock's address, "The National Problems of Canada," which he gave to the Business and Professional Men's Group at the University of Cincinnati.

**D32.3** "Peace Goal 'Is Drawing Nearer,' Stephen Leacock Asserts in Queen City Club Address," *Cincinnati Enquirer*, 28 February 1932. Report with quotations from Leacock's speech, "Some Glimpses of the Future," delivered at the Queen City Club in Cincinnati before members of the Commercial and Commonwealth Clubs.

**D32.4** "Canada Great Export Country; Must Buy in Order to Sell; Prof. Leacock Outlines the Difficulties That Face Ottawa Conference in Address to Kiwanis Club," *Orillia Packet and Times*, 30 June 1932, p. 1. Report of Leacock's speech to a joint meeting of the Toronto Downtown Kiwanis Club and the Orillia Kiwanis Club at the Kiwanis Boys' Camp on Lake Simcoe on 29 June 1932; several sentence quoted, others paraphrased.

**D33.1** "Leacock Sarcastic about Education Riddles Overburdened Curricula and Length of Graduation Period," *Montreal Gazette*, 10 January 1933, p. 11. Report with quotations from Leacock's address, "The Waste Spaces in Modern Education," given at the annual banquet of the American College of Physicians.

**D33.2** "Dr. Leacock on Russia," *Orillia Packet and Times*, 26 January 1933, p. 9. Report of speech on New Year's Day in Montreal on the Russian Five-Year Plan. Six paragraphs are quoted from press reports.

**D33.3** "Leacock Offers Cure for Crisis; Pegging of Gold Standard One-Third Lower, Is Proposal. . . . ," *Montreal Daily Star*, 27 January 1933. News clipping at QMM Archives; report not located on microfilm edition. Report, with quotations, from Leacock's address, "The Riddle of the Depression," delivered the previous day at a meeting of the Women's Canadian Club at the Mount Royal Hotel in Montreal. Also reported, with a few quotations, as "Leacock Presents a Scheme for Halting of Depression," *Toronto Mail and Empire*, 27 January 1933, p. 13.

**D33.4** "Leacock Speaks at Cincinnati; Urges Gold Value Be Decreased as Possible Means of Recovery," *Montreal Gazette*, 4 February 1933, p. 2. Report, with quotations, from Leacock's address the previous day to an audience of business and professional men assembled at the University of Cincinnati.

**D33.5** "Leacock Teases Doctors in After-Dinner Address," *Montreal Herald*, 10 February 1933, p. 6. Report, with quotations, from Leacock's address delivered the previous evening to members of the American College of Physicians at their annual banquet in Montreal's Windsor Hotel. Leacock states that he originally had intended to deliver a serious discussion of "The Waste Spaces of Modern Education." Also reported as "Ills of Present System of Education Deplored," *McGill Daily*, 10 February 1933, pp. 1, 4. One humorous sentence is quoted.

**D33.6** "Au Circle des Femmes Canadiennes. La causerie de M. Stephen Leacock," *L'évenément* (Quebec), 29 March 1933, p. 5. Report with quotations of Leacock's speech to the Circle des Femmes Canadiennes entitled "L'instruction à la verge " ("Education by the Yard") which he gave at the Chateau Frontenac in Quebec City on 28 March 1933. Also as "Prof. S. Leacock Says Democracy Has Ended Study for Study's Sake," *Quebec Chronicle-Telegraph*, 29 March 1933, p. 3. Report with quotations of Leacock's speech "Education by the Yard."

**D33.7** "Education System Defeating Own End; Modern Mechanism of Tests and Examinations Condemned by Prof. Leacock. . . . ," *Montreal Gazette*, 31 March 1933, p. 5. Report, with many quotations, from Leacock's address to the McGill Commercial Society in the McGill Union on the previous afternoon.

**D33.8** "Inflation in Canada Is Urged by Leacock; Asks Premier to Save Nation's Buying Power," *New York Times*, 12 August 1933, p. 4. Four sentences paraphrased from speech on "Ways Out of the Depression" to the Canadian Institute on Economics and Politics, 10 August 1933, at Geneva Park, Lake Couchiching. The premier referred to in the title is Prime Minister R.B. Bennett. C.H. Hale in an editorial in *Orillia Packet and Times*, 17 August 1933, p. 5, quotes briefly from the speech.

**D33.9** "Lahontan in Minnesota," *Minnesota History* 14, no. 4 (December 1933): 367–77. An abstract of an address delivered before the Minnesota Historical Society on 18 October 1933. See also C32.7.

**D34.1** "Stephen Leacock at His Best in Lecture. Everything from Love Stories of the 'Decline and Fall of the Roman Empire' Is Given the Acid Test of Laughter," *Burlington* (VT) *Free Press and Times*, 2 February 1934. News clipping seen at SLM.

**D34.2** "Two Female Types Found in Dickens; Women Were Either Angels or Freaks, Dr. Stephen Leacock States. . . . ," *Montreal Gazette*, 28 February 1934, p. 11. Report, with quotations, from Leacock's address, "Dickens and Women," delivered before the Montreal branch of the Dickens Fellowship in Victoria Hall the previous evening. See also K44.3.

**D34.3** "Stephen Leacock Charges Starving of Scholarships; 'Disservice of Organized Athletics' Asserted to McGill Group; Old Days Contrasted," *Toronto Globe*, 7 March 1934, pp. 4–5. Report of speech on "The Relations of the Present-Day University to the Public Body" to McGill Society of Toronto at the Royal York Hotel, 6 March 1934; several paragraphs quoted. Also reported as "Leacock Condemns Stress on University Athletics; Scholarship Frozen Out by 'Hysteria', Says Professor; Lean on Rich," *Toronto Star*, 7 March 1934, p. 30 with several paragraphs quoted; as "Universities Strangled by Wealthy, Stephen Leacock Charges; Big Business Dominance Plus Athletic Influence Said Universities' Bane," *Toronto Telegram*, 7 March 1934, p. [19] with several quotations. Additional quotations are in "Fiery Phrases from Speech by Prof. Stephen Leacock," *Toronto Telegram*, 7 March 1934, p. [19].

**D34.4** "Real Advertising a Social Service, States Leacock; Regrets Way Liquor Ads. Forced Upon People in Quebec — U.S. and Canadian Clubs in Convention," *Toronto Globe*, 19 May 1934, p. 4. Report of speech to a convention of Advertising Affiliated at the Royal York in Toronto on 18 May 1934; several paragraphs quoted. Also reported as "Leacock Condemns Scenic Advertising; Professor-Humorist Gives Frank Opinions to Convention. Onlooker at Game; Countryside Desecrated by Miles of Signboards, He Says," *Toronto Mail and Empire*, 19 May 1934, p. 4, with two paragraphs quoted; as "Billboard Advertiser Not Liked by Leacock; He Says Their Background Blots Out Beauty of Countryside," *Toronto Star*, 19 May 1934, p. 22, with a few sentences quoted.

**D34.5** "Leacock Has Contempt for Modern Democracy; McGill University Professor Delivers Presidential Address to Political Science Association," *Montreal Daily Star*, 22 May 1934, pp. 1, 16. Report with extensive quotations from Leacock's presidential address delivered the previous evening at a joint banquet with the Canadian Historical Association in Montreal's Windsor Hotel. See also C34.8.

**D34.6** "Sweepstakes Bill Killed at Ottawa," *New York Times*, 27 May 1934, sec. 4, p. 7. In an article by John MacCormac about the Canadian Parliament, two sentences from a speech by Leacock on democracy are quoted. The speech was given during the week of 20 May before a joint meeting of the Canadian Historical Association and the Political Science Association. Presumably it is the speech in D34.5.

**D34.7** "Civilization Faces Possible Cataclysm States Dr. Leacock," *McGill Daily*, 2 November 1934, pp. 1–2. Report of speech on "The United States" to McGill Undergraduates Commercial Society at the McGill Union on 1 November 1934; one quotation, remainder paraphrased.

**D35.1** "Canadian Humorist Pays Tribute to Mark Twain: Stephen B. Leacock, Here to Receive Medal of Honor, Eulogizes Missouri Writer and Discusses His Works," *St. Louis Post-Dispatch*, 16 January 1935, p. 10A. Report with quotations of Leacock's acceptance speech on receiving the Mark Twain Medal under the auspices of the International Mark Twain Society at the Jefferson Memorial on 15 January in St. Louis, Missouri. Also as "Mark Twain Medal Is Presented Here to Stephen Leacock: Honor Bestowed on Economist, Lecturer and Humorist from Toronto," *St. Louis Globe-Democrat*, 16 January 1935, and as "Leacock Says Humor Badly Needed Today," *Columbia Missourian*, 16 January 1935, pp. 1–2.

**D35.2** "Leacock Attacks Democratic Rule; If a Country Has a Good Dictator, Keep Him, He Urges," *Toronto Mail and Empire*, 31 January 1935, p. 4. Report of Hart House debate on democracy in which Leacock participated on 31 January 1935. The vote was 109–71 against democracy. Also reported as "Say Democracy Fails; Students Vote with Leacock for Political Change," *Toronto Star*, 31 January 1935, p. 42. Both newspapers quote the same sentences on democracy; the *Mail and Empire* includes some additional sentences on the lack of honesty in government in Ottawa.

**D35.3** "Leacock Sees World In Life-Death Race; Greatest Problem Is Social He Says After Humorous Talk About Avoiding War," *New York Times*, 10 February 1935, sec. 2, p. 2. Two sentences paraphrased from speech before the New York Chapter of the American Institute of Banking on 9 February 1935. The audience at the Waldorf-Astoria hotel numbered 1,200. See also C35.2.

**D35.4** "Clearance of Slums May Be Investment; Economic Aspect Shown by Dr. Leacock," *Montreal Daily Star*, 15 February 1935, p. 22. Report of the annual dinner of the University Settlement in Montreal. Leacock seconded the adoption of the reports made by the officers and board members of the Settlement, and then commented on the existence of slums as an "unnatural growth."

**D35.5** "War in World Today Shown as Absurdity; Prof. Leacock Satirizes National Disputes," *Montreal Daily Star*, 8 March 1935, p. 22. Report with quotations from Leacock's address, "How Soon Can We Start the Next War?," delivered the previous afternoon at a luncheon of the Notre Dame de Grace Women's Club in Montreal's Mount

Royal Hotel. Also as "Leacock Sees Unity Coming; Blind World Wards It Off with Talk and Thoughts of War," *Toronto Telegram*, 8 March 1935, p. 3; several paragraphs quoted.

**D35.6** "Leacock Says Colleges Becoming Machine Shops. . . . ," *Montreal Daily Star*, 11 March 1935, p. 1. Report with quotations from Leacock's address given at Windsor, Ont. to the Essex-Kent branch of the McGill Society on 9 March 1935. Prior to his address Leacock gave an interview in which he answered questions about world trade, Huey Long, and Father Coughlin. Also reported as "Education System of 13th Century Is Leacock's Ideal; Noted Economist Hints of Needed Reconstruction at McGill; Flay Gold Tax," *Toronto Globe*, 12 March 1935, p. 3. This report says the speech took place on 11 March 1935 which is incorrect. Several sentences are quoted as well as some sentences from an interview prior to the speech on gold and the Canadian dollar, Huey Long, and Father Coughlin. Also reported as "Leacock Says Colleges Becoming Machine Shops; Would Like to See a Return to System of 13th Century," *Orillia Packet and Times*, 14 March 1935, p. 7. Several sentences are quoted from the speech as well as an interview prior to the speech. In addition extracts from Leacock's letter to the *Montreal Star* are quoted in which Leacock states that reports of his speech carried by the Canadian Press were misleading and were based on the interview (see C35.3). Also reported as "Graduates Society Branch Activities," *McGill News* 16, no. 3 (Summer 1935):48–9. Section title "Essex-Kent Branch." This report confirms the date of the speech as 9 March.

**D35.7** "Barbaric Normans Enriched English; Purged Language of Complexities, Prof. Stephen Leacock Claims," *Montreal Gazette*, 13 March 1935, p. 7. Report with quotations from Leacock's address, "The English Languaage as an Instrument of Expression," delivered to the Quebec Library Association at the Mechanics' Institute in Montreal. Also reported as "Leacock Draws Applause; McGill Professor in Rare Form Lecturing on and in Praise of English Language," *Montreal Daily Star*, 13 March 1935, p. 8.

**D35.8** "More Humor Asked in Cheerless Day; Grow Fat and Laugh, Leacock Advises Audience in Lachine," *Montreal Gazette*, 27 March 1935, p. 3. Report of speech on the theory of humour to the Teachers' Association of the Lachine Protestant Schools, 26 March 1935, with quotations. Also reported more briefly as "Prof. Leacock Points out Need for Humor; World Suffering from Over-Strain," *Montreal Daily Star*, 27 March 1935, p. 5.

**D35.9** "Comic Verse Theory Expounded by Leacock," *Montreal Daily Star*, 3 April 1935, p. 8. Report with quotations from Leacock's speech, "The Theory of Comic Verse," which he delivered to the Alumnae Society of McGill University at Royal Victoria College on 2 April 1935.

**D35.10** "Leacock Makes Bitter Attack on Cancer 'Quack'," *Montreal Daily Star*, 16 May 1935, pp. 1–2. Report with quotations from Leacock's address at the opening of an exhibit mounted by the New York City Cancer Committee in New York on 15 May 1935.

**D35.11** "Social Changes Coming Manufacturers are Told; But Professor Leacock Lashes Out at Communism in Economic Address Last Night," *Orillia News-Letter*, 12 June 1935, p. 1; several sentences are quoted. Report of Leacock's speech to the Board of Trade "Manufacturers Night", 11 June 1935 in Orillia on "The Outlook of the World at Large, the Outlook for Canada, and the Outlook for Our Own Town." Also reported as "War in Europe Unlikely Control of Industry Coming Stephen Leacock's Opinion; World Stumbles within Step of Millennium. Communism Denounced; Economist Claims All Classes Are Suffering Together, and Urges Cooperation in Finding Way Out," *Orillia Packet and Times*,

13 June 1935, pp. 1, 7. Two sentences are quoted; many paragraphs are paraphrased.

**D35.12** "Leacock Backs Capitalism; No Substitute for System, He Says at Midland," *Toronto Globe and Mail*, 23 September 1935, p. 9. Report of speech to the Conservatives' opening campaign meeting on 21 September 1935; one paragraph quoted. The Conservative candidate was John Drinkwater. Also reported as "Leacock Assails King's 'Erroneous Doctrines'. . . . ," *Montreal Daily Star*, 23 September 1935, p. 4.

**D36.1** "Leacock Raps Practical Trend in Curriculums, Sees Changes: Renaissance of Imagination Soon," *McGill Daily*, 31 January 1936, pp. 1, 4. Report of Leacock's address to the Juniors of Royal Victoria College at McGill University delivered on 30 January 1936; extensive quotations. Also reported as "Leacock Deplores Practical Trend of Modern College; Disciplinary Curriculum Trains Students to Learn More Aptly; Older System Cited; Balance in Curriculum Wisest State Authorities of College," *Varsity* (University of Toronto), 55, no. 73 (4 February 1936): 1, 4; as "Leacock Looks at Future Training; Humorist Also Compares Education Ideas of Present with Past," *Orillia Packet and Times*, 6 February 1936, p. 2; seven paragraphs quoted.

**D36.2** "Immigration Seen As Duty of Empire; Leacock Condemns Closed Door Policy as Selfish, Shortsighted," *Montreal Gazette*, 4 February 1936, p. 6. Report of Leacock's speech, 3 February 1936, to the Twentieth Century Institute of National Affairs, with quotations.

**D36.3** "Dickens Lauded as Great Speaker; Prof. Leacock Heard at Annual Banquet of Local Society," *Montreal Daily Star*, 8 February 1936, p. 3. Report with quotations from Leacock's address delivered the previous evening to the Montreal branch of the Dickens Fellowship on the occasion of the "Pickwick" Centenary.

**D36.4** "Stephen Leacock Addresses His Last Montreal Audience," *McGill Daily*, 12 February 1936, pp. 1, 4. Report of Leacock's speech, "The Art and Mystery of Language," given before the Alumni and Alumnae of the University of Toronto at the Windsor Hotel in Montreal, 12 February 1936. Also reported as "Nothing to Say, Leacock States; Well-Known Writer Makes His Montreal Farewell," *Toronto Globe and Mail*, 12 February 1936, p. 2, with a few sentences quoted; as "Dr Leacock Makes Last Appearance; Tells Audience He Will Stay on the Shelf and Reflect; Lectures on Language; Slang Is Upheld in Address to University of Toronto Societies — New Poem Read," *Montreal Daily Star*, 12 February 1936, p. 8, with quotations; "Prof Leacock Makes Last Montreal Speech; Declares He Is Going to 'Remain on the Shelf', " *Orillia Packet and Times*, 20 February 1936, p. 4. The *Packet* report is reprinted from the *Montreal Star*. "Stephen Leacock, '91 C, Addresses Montreal Meeting," *University Monthly* (University of Toronto) 36, no. 6 (March 1936): 193, with several quotations. On Leacock's death in 1944, the *Orillia Packet and Times*, 13 April 1944, p. 7, reprinted an undated article, "Stephen Leacock Humanitarian," from the *Montreal Gazette* which quotes two sentences from this retirement speech.

**D36.5** " 'Senility Gang Execution' Described by Leacock," *Montreal Star*, 25 March 1936, p. 35. Report of Leacock's speech on his forced retirement from McGill University at a dinner in his honour at Montreal's Berkeley Hotel on 24 March 1936, sponsored by the McGill Political Economy Club; several paragraphs quoted. Also reported as "Dr. Leacock Feted by Student Group; Retiring Economics Professor Honored by Political Economy Club," *Montreal Gazette*, 25 March 1936, p. 11. In this report Leacock states that his first lecture at McGill on 7 January 1901 was "The Monarch of England."

**D36.6** "Language Seen Factor in Amity of U.S., Canada; Responsible for Friendly Feeling on Both Sides of Border, Noted Author Avers," *Buffalo-Courier-Express*, 23 April 1936, p. 14. Report, by Bennett Davis, on Leacock's speech on "The Art and Mystery of Language," in the Buffalo Public Library on 22 April 1936, the first of a series of events to celebrate the centennial of the Buffalo Public Library; a few sentences are quoted. Also reported as "Place of Library as Force for Intelligence Stressed; Leacock and O'Brian Speak as 600 Note 100th Anniversary of Buffalo Institution," *Buffalo Evening News*, 23 April 1936, p. 6; several sentences quoted.

**D36.7** "Prof. 'Stevie' Leacock Gives 'Last Lecture': Speaks to Large Gathering of Former Pupils at Testimonial Dinner," *Montreal Daily Star*, 5 May 1936, p. 19. Quotes extensively from Leacock's address (entitled "Paradise Lost") at a banquet held in his honour at the Ritz-Carlton Hotel in Montreal on 4 May 1936 on the occasion of his retirement from McGill University. The *Star* report is reprinted as "Stephen Leacock's Last Lecture to Old Pupils at McGill; Retiring Professor Is Honoured by Banquet at the Ritz-Carlton," *Orillia Packet and Times*, 14 May 1936, p. 5. Also reported as "Leacock Delivers Farewell Address. Is Honored Guest of 150 Old Students at Hilarious Gathering," *Montreal Gazette*, 5 May 1936, p. 15; as "Leacock: For the Last Time He Says, 'That'll Be All for Today'," *News-Week* 7, no. 20 (16 May 1936): 44. This last report also appears to be an interview since it quotes Leacock poking fun at his colleagues and also he talks about breaking the ice in his wash basin at 5 o'clock in the morning.

**D36.8** "Latin is 'Phoney' Asserts Leacock," *Montreal Daily Star*, 10 November 1936, p. 2. The dateline is Memphis, Tenn., 23 October 1936. On that day Leacock gave two speeches in Memphis. The quotation about Latin in this article is presumably from one of those speeches.

**D36.9** "Leacock Greeted at Alumnae Fete in Neighbor City; Celebrated Author and Humorist Begins Series of Lectures Here — On Way to West," *Fort William Daily Times-Journal*, 28 November 1936, p. 3. Report with quotations from Leacock's address, "Our Colleges and What They Stand for," delivered under the auspices of the McGill Alumni at the Prince Arthur Hotel in Prince Arthur, in the evening of 27 November. Also as "Says Lakehead Cities Are Dominion Centre; Leacock Turns Barrage of Sarcastic Humor on Sectional Differences Which Threaten the Confederation of Canada," *Port Arthur News Chronicle*, 28 November 1936, pp. 1, 12 with two paragraphs quoted; as "Re-Confederation Urged for Canada Professor Leacock Points to Short-Sighted Separatism Spirit Now Apparent," *Montreal Gazette*, 28 November 1936, p. 18. The latter report focuses primarily on Leacock's plea for "the re-union and re-confederation of Canada."

**D36.10** "Leacock Urges Canada Take Passive Stand; Courage Will Never Die But War Will, Keynote of Address Today," *Port Arthur News Chronicle*, 28 November 1936, p. 3. Report of Leacock's noon-hour speech in Fort William to the joint Canadian clubs; three paragraphs are quoted.

**D36.11** "'When I Pay $2 for Book I Want Murder in It' — Says Stephen Leacock in Stories," *Winnipeg Tribune*, 1 December 1936, p. 8. Report of speech to the Women's Canadian Club on Monday night, 30 November, at the Fort Garry Hotel on "Literature at Its Lightest and Most Foolish"; several paragraphs are quoted. Also reported as "Canada's No 1. Humorist Is Accorded Rousing Welcome at Women's Canadian Club," *Winnipeg Free Press*, 2 December 1926, p. 1; one sentence is quoted.

**D36.12** "Leacock Deplores Education by the Yard, Which Does Not Teach Students to Think; Advises Philosophy Students to Quote From Writers Professor Has Not Heard of in Language He Cannot Understand," *Winnipeg Tribune*, 3 December 1936, p. 3. Report of speech to students at the University of Manitoba on 1 December 1936; several sentences are quoted.

**D36.13** "Cheerful Tail Wagging Is Proof Dogs More Sensible Than Humans, Says Leacock," *Winnipeg Tribune*, 5 December 1936, p. 6. Report of speech on "When Can We Start Another War" to the Canadian Club on Friday, 4 December 1936 in the Fort Garry Hotel; several paragraphs quoted.

**D36.14** "University Women's Club Hears Noted Humorist on 'An Analysis of Humor'," *Winnipeg Tribune*, 7 December 1936, p. 8. Report of speech on 5 December 1936 at the Fort Garry Hotel; a few paragraphs are quoted.

**D36.15** "Leacock Burlesques Love Literature to Joy of Women's Club," *Regina Leader-Post*, 8 December 1936, p. 6. Report of speech to the Women's Canadian Club on 7 December 1936 at the Hotel Kitchener; many paragraphs quoted. Reprinted as "Stephen Leacock Talks About Love Past and Present," *Orillia Packet and Times*, 31 December 1936, p. [10].

**D36.16** "Education Must Keep Desire to Know, Says Dr. Leacock; Humorist, Economist Speaks to 1,000 in Varsity Address; Was in Merry Mood," *Edmonton Journal*, 15 December 1936, pp. 13, 15. Report of speech at the University of Alberta on 14 December 1936 on "Recovery after Graduation." Many paragraphs are quoted. Also, additional remarks from the speech are given separately under the title "Audience Pleased by Leacock-ism," p. 13.

**D36.17** "Warns Against Idealism Ban in Education; Humorist-Economist Sees Excessive Sweep to 'Practicality'; Address to Alumni; Believes There Can Be Too Much 'Student Activity,'" *Edmonton Journal*, 16 December 1936, pp. 13, 15. Report of speech on "College As It Was and As It Is," to the Edmonton Branch of the University of Toronto Alumni at the Macdonald Hotel on 15 December 1936. Many paragraphs are quoted. Also reported as "Dr. Stephen Leacock in Confidential Mood; Noted Canadian Humorist Drops Gems of Wisdom," *Edmonton Bulletin*, 16 December 1936, p. 3, also with many paragraphs quoted. Additional quotations are contained in "Facts about Professor Leacock" also on p. 3.

**D36.18** "Stephen Leacock Recalls Election Campaigning in E. Simcoe and N. Ontario; Keeps Audience at Regina in Roars of Laughter," *Orillia Packet and Times*, 17 December 1936, p. [9]. Report taken from the *Regina Leader-Post* of Leacock's speech to the Canadian Club at the Hotel Saskatchewan, 8 December 1936, on Canadian and international politics. Many paragraphs are quoted from the humorous speech in which Leacock recollects, among many other things, the 1911 election campaign.

**D36.19** "Evolution of Humor Traced by Leacock in Speech Here; Edmonton Authors Enjoy Humorist in Happy Mood; Last Address Here," *Edmonton Journal*, 17 December 1936, p. 14. Report of speech to the Women's Press Club of Edmonton and the Edmonton Branch of the Canadian Authors Association on "The Theory of Comic Verse" at the Macdonald Hotel; a few paragraphs are quoted. Also reported as "Dr. Leacock Gives An Analysis of Humor in Clever Talk to Writers," *Edmonton Bulletin*, 17 December 1936, p. 8; a few quotations are given.

**D36.20** "Murder Committed in Pen and Ink Discussed by Dr. Stephen Leacock at Canadian Club, Rouses Laughter; Beloved Humorist Talks Nonsense on Fiction," *Calgary*

*Herald,* 19 December 1936, pp. 20, 17. Report of Leacock's address, "Frenzied Fiction," delivered to the Women's Canadian Club at the Palliser Hotel in Calgary on 18 December 1936; many paragraphs quoted.

D36.21 "Stephen Leacock Proved a Most Delightful and Instructive Entertainer," *Medicine Hat News,* 21 December 1936, pp. 1, 10. Report of Leacock's lecture to the Quota Club at the Hotel Cecil on "Hard Money, or Daniel in the Lion's Den"; one sentence is quoted on Aberhart and Social Credit, many paragraphs are paraphrased.

D36.22 "'Shotgun Only Answer to Communism'; Prof. Leacock Before Canadian Club," *Vancouver Sun,* 22 December 1936, pp. 1, 4. Report of speech at noon at the Hotel Vancouver on 22 December 1936 on "The New Economic World Order." Many paragraphs are quoted. Also reported as "Socialism Is a System for Angels — Leacock; Humorist, Economist Talks of New Trends," *Vancouver Daily Province,* 23 December 1936, p. 5 with several paragraphs quoted. In a separate column, "Leacock Lapses" under the same main heading are thirteen quotations from the speech, varying in length from one to three sentences.

D36.23 Jack Boothe, "Bits of Stephen Leacock," *Vancouver Province,* 23 December 1936, p. 4. Six different sketches of Leacock lecturing showing various parts of him, e.g., head, arms, hands, accompanied by written comments about him. One example: "During his talk [Leacock] mentioned 'the impossible clothes of the French.' Mr. Leacock wore a coat two sizes too big."

D36.24 "Leacock Tilts at Economists; Never Lose Grip on Lighter Side of Life," *Vancouver Sun,* 29 December 1936, p. 7. Report of speech on "Social Credit and Social Progress" to the annual dinner of the Foreign Trade Bureau, Vancouver Board of Trade in the Hotel Vancouver on 28 December 1936 with several paragraphs quoted. Also reported as "'Buy and Buy and Buy,' Says Leacock 'Enjoy the Fruits of Your Labor,' Is Address Theme," *Vancouver News-Herald,* 29 December 1936, p. 2, with extensive quotations; also as "Immigrant the Greatest of Canada's Assets — Leacock Says Ban on Settlers Would Lead to Ruin," *Vancouver Daily Province,* 29 December 1936, p. 6, with several paragraphs quoted. In a separate column on the same page, "Leacock Chuckles," under the same main heading are thirteen quotations from the speech, varying in length from one to six sentences.

D36.25 "Women Hear Stephen Leacock Talk on 'Frenzied Fiction'," *Vancouver Sun,* 29 December 1936, p. 9. Report with several sentences quoted from "Getting on with Frenzied Fiction," Leacock's humorous discussion of the detective story and the love story, which he gave to the Vancouver Women's Canadian Club on 28 December 1936. Five additional quotations also appear under the title "Leacock . . . . 'isms'" on the same page. Also reported as "Stephen Leacock Entertains Women's Club," *Vancouver Daily Province,* 29 December 1936, p. 9; two paragraphs quoted.

D37.1 "Leacock Wants Britons Here; Economist Calls for Immigration in Address Before Canadian Club," *Victoria Times,* 4 January 1937, p. 13. Report with quotations of Leacock's speech, "Economic Separatism in the British Empire," at the Men's Canadian Club at the Empress Hotel luncheon on the 4 January in Victoria, British Columbia; several paragraphs quoted. Also reported as "More United Stand Is Advocated by Dr. Stephen Leacock; Canada in Particular and British Empire As a Whole Needs New Ideals, But Speaker Says He Cannot Offer Details for More," *Victoria Daily Colonist,* 5 January 1937, p. 3. Several sentences quoted; many more paraphrased.

**D37.2** "Noted Canadian Humorist Entertains Big Audience," *Victoria Daily Colonist*, 6 January 1937, p. 8. Report with several quotations from Leacock's address, "Humor, a Serious Matter," delivered to the Women's Canadian Club at the Empress Hotel on 5 January. Also reported as "Over 700 Laugh with Dr. Stephen Leacock; Noted Canadian Humorist Regales Women's Canadian Club Gather with Characteristic Talk," *Victoria Times*, 6 January 1937, p. 7; two sentences quoted.

**D37.3** "Dr. Stephen Leacock Urges Preserving College Traditions," *Victoria Daily Colonist*, 7 January 1937, p. 2. Report of Leacock's humorous speech on "Preserving College Traditions" to the McGill Graduates' Association of Victoria on 6 January at the Empress Hotel in which he stressed "the value of lectures and traditional ceremonies in Canadian universities"; several sentences quoted. Also reported as "Leacock Talks to McGill Men," *Victoria Daily Times*, 7 January 1937, p. 5; several sentences quoted.

**D37.4** "Uses Satire in Plea for Peace; Dr. Stephen B. Leacock Addresses Rotarians at Luncheon Meeting," *Victoria Daily Colonist*, 9 January 1937, p. 3. A report of Leacock's speech on 7 January to the Rotary Club at the Empress Hotel, "How Soon Do We Start the Next War?" Several sentences quoted; others paraphrased.

**D37.5** "Stephen Leacock Makes Last Lecture in Canada Retiring from Platform Soon He Tells U.B.C. Students," *Vancouver Sun*, 14 January 1937, p. 2. Report of Leacock's speech "Looking Back on College." Several paragraphs are quoted. Based on C34.2. Also reported as "Stephen Leacock Retires from Lecture Platform," *Orillia Packet and Times*, 21 January 1937, p. 1. The article notes that Leacock told the audience of 1,500 students at the University of British Columbia that he still had some American lecture commitments to fulfil; one sentence is quoted.

**D37.6** "Civic Club Smiles at Leacock Wit. Author and Humorist Jibes at Detective and Love Stories," *Harrisburg* (PA) *Patriot*, 16 February 1937, p. 8. Report which quotes extensively from Leacock's address, "Murder at $2.50 a Volume, and Love at $1.25," delivered to the Civic Club on 15 February 1937.

**D39.1** "Humorist Heard by McGill Men; Stephen Leacock Talks at Westmount Dinner," *Kitchener Record*, 17 June 1939, p. 3. Report of Leacock's speech in praise of McGill University, delivered the previous evening to the McGill Association of Ontario at the Westmount Golf Club. Leacock's opening remark: "I live in repentance for the speeches I have made" is quoted as well as a paragraph. Leacock was followed by his long-time friend René Du Roure who spoke affectionately about him.

# Section E: LECTURES GIVEN

This list of Leacock's lectures is based chiefly on his lecture notebooks in the Barbara Nimmo collection at NAC (vol. 4, MG 30, D40). The notebooks record the date, place, and title of lectures, and are often accompanied by comments, notes, news clippings, and other ephemera. The first date in the notebooks is 7 January 1915, although there is an anomalous earlier date of 12 January 1912. The last date in the notebooks is 9 March 1937. When two dates are given, both appear in the notebooks. Extracts from the lecture notebooks are given in quotation marks at the end of entries following the designation, LEACOCK'S NOTES, usually when no report of the lecture has been located. References to newspaper reports and cross references to other sections of the bibliography have also been supplied. Inferred comments, titles, and other information are enclosed in square brackets. Most abbreviations have been silently expanded; a few are enclosed in square brackets. The page count refers to the number of pages in the notebooks that Leacock wrote in preparation for a particular lecture. When no page count is given, the notebook entry is brief. Additional entries have been taken from Leacock's correspondence, his notebook of his recorded publications and speeches at QMMRB, and other pertinent archival documents. All published reports cited contain no quotations. See references to D items contain quotations.

## 1886

E86.1  9 December. Upper Canada College, Toronto, Ontario. Debate: "Was the Execution of Mary, Queen of Scots Justifiable?" Leacock argued in the negative. Reported as "U.C.C. Literary and Debating Society," *College Times* (Upper Canada College, Toronto) 6, no. 4 (2 January 1887): 26–7.

## 1890

E90.1  4 December. Toronto, Ontario. University of Toronto Meds' Banquet. Rossin House. Reported in the *Varsity* (University of Toronto) 10, no. 10 (9 December 1890): 115.

## 1891

E91.1  9 March. Toronto, Ontario. University of Toronto. Modern Language Club. "*Stummenliebe* of Musäus." Reported in *Varsity* (University of Toronto) 10, no. 19 (10 March 1891): 223.

## 1899

E99.1  after September. Chicago, Illinois. University of Chicago, Political Science Club. "China, Her Past and Her Future." Moderated by Professor Harry Pratt Judson.

## 1901

E1.1  25 November. Montreal, Quebec. Royal Victoria College. Delta Sigma Society annual lecture. "Anarchism." Reported in *Orilla Packet*, 5 December 1901, p. 3. The *Packet* took its report from the *Montreal Witness* but that report could not be located.

## 1902

E2.1  1 February. Montreal, Quebec. Pen and Pencil Club. "Opening a Bank Account." Probably "My Financial Career" (see C95.1).

E2.2  15 March. Montreal, Quebec. Pen and Pencil Club. "Things That I Do Not Want to Read Anymore."

## 1903

E3.1  December. [Montreal, Quebec]. MacKenzie Club. "Free Trade."

E3.2  12 December. Montreal, Quebec. Pen and Pencil Club. "We Are Seventeen." Poem.

## 1904

E4.1  12 November. Montreal, Quebec. Pen and Pencil Club. "Nothing." Poem.

E4.2  10 December. Montreal, Quebec. Pen and Pencil Club. "The Rehabilitation of Charles II." See C6.6.

## 1905

E5.1  18 February. Montreal, Quebec. Pen and Pencil Club. "The Malthusian Theory."

E5.2  23 February. Montreal, Quebec. St. James' Literary Society. "Malthusian." Reported as "Professor Leacock on 'Problems of Poverty'," *Montreal Daily Star*, 24 February 1905.

E5.3  10 March. Montreal, Quebec. McGill Undergraduates' Literary Society. "Higher Education and the Present Tendencies of American Scholarship." See C5.1.

E5.4  25 November. Montreal, Quebec. Pen and Pencil Club. "The Passing of the Poet." See C6.5.

E5.5  9 December. Montreal, Quebec. Pen and Pencil Club. "The Future of the French Canadian." See C5.2.

E5.6  23 December. Montreal, Quebec. Pen and Pencil Club. "Merry Xmas."

## 1906

E6.1  12 January–23 March. Ottawa, Ontario. Queen's Hall. "Six Lectures on the British Empire." This lecture series, given on alternate Friday evenings, was sponsored by the May Court Club under the auspices of McGill University. The third lecture was reported as "The British Empire Free Trade Within But Tariff Wall Against Rest of World, Says Prof. Leacock," *Ottawa Citizen*, 10 February 1906, p. 2. The sixth lecture was reported as "May Court Lectures. An Excellent Course Concluded. Prof. Leacock Spoke Last Night on Extension of British Empire," *Ottawa Citizen*, 24 March 1906, p. 10, no quotations. According to the *Orillia Packet*, 31 May 1906, Leacock was supposed to repeat his course of lectures on the British Empire in Toronto. See A1, C6.1–3, and D6.2–3.

E6.2  17 February. Montreal, Quebec. Canadian Club. "The Tariff." See D6.1.

E6.3  23 February. Ottawa, Ontario. "Naval Defence." Prime Minister Borden disagrees with Leacock's remark on the Monroe Doctrine.

E6.4  2 April. Toronto, Ontario. Canadian Club. "The Imperial Crisis." See C6.4.

E6.5  11 May. Brockville, Ontario. United Counties Teachers Association. "Imperial Crisis."

E6.6  28 May. Toronto, Ontario. Massey Music Hall. "Imperial Unity and Defence." See D6.4

E6.7  29 May. Orillia, Ontario. Canadian Club. "The Imperial Tariff Problem." See D6.5.

E6.8  October. Montreal, Quebec. Canadian Club. "Education."

E6.9  November. Montreal, Quebec. Royal Victoria College. "Foreign Policy."

E6.10  November. Montreal, Quebec. The Association. "American Humor."

E6.11  1 December. Montreal, Quebec. Pen and Pencil Club. "The Monroe Doctrine and Canada." See C9.6.

## 1907

E7.1  12 January. Montreal, Quebec. Pen and Pencil Club. "A Sitting of the House of Lords in 1912."

E7.2  18 January. London, Ontario. Canadian Club. "The Monroe Doctrine and Its Application to Canada." See D7.1.

E7.3  February. Westmount. [Montreal, Quebec]. Two Addresses. "Education Question in England." "Evolution and Socialism."

E7.4  25 February. Montreal, Quebec. Windsor Hotel. Insurance Institute of Montreal Banquet. "Empire." See D7.2.

E7.5  9 March. Montreal, Quebec. Pen and Pencil Club. "Greater Canada."

E7.6  19 March. Toronto, Ontario. Empire Club. "Education and Empire Unity." See C7.4.

E7.7  23 April — 5 March 1908. Tour of the British Empire under the auspices of the Cecil Rhodes Trust. Leacock sailed for England on 27 April from Halifax. He was scheduled to go to New Zealand, Australia, Tasmania, and then on to South Africa. During August up to 12 September, he was in New Zealand; from 16 September to 1 November, in Sydney; from 1 to 15 November in Melbourne; from 15 November to 15 December at sea; and from 15 December to 1 February 1908 in South Africa; from 1 to 21 February at sea; 21 February to 4 March in England; and 4 to 10 March at sea on the way back to Canada. The schedule originally called for Leacock to arrive in Vancouver on 1 February 1908 and begin a cross-country tour, but this part of the schedule was not carried out.

E7.8  23 April. Ottawa, Ontario.

E7.9  25 April. Saint John, New Brunswick. Canadian Club. "The Imperial Movement." See D7.3.

E7.10  26 April. Halifax, Nova Scotia. Canadian Club. "The Imperial Movement." See D7.4.

E7.11  15 May. London, England. Victoria League. "The Question of Canada." See D7.5.

E7.12  May. Oxford, England. Examinations Schools.

E7.13  14 August. Wellington, New Zealand. "The British Empire of the Twentieth Century." See D7.6. The *Times* (London), 16 Aug. 1907, p. 3, also briefly records this speech.

E7.14  11 September. Wanganui, New Zealand. Speech. In "Empire in the Twentieth Century," *Wanganui Chronicle*, 10 September 1907, p. 5, it is noted that Leacock has already spoken in Christchurch, and Dunedin. See D7.8.

E7.15  12 September. Auckland, New Zealand.

E7.16  September. Perth, Australia. "Imperial Unity." See D7.7.

E7.17  November. Melbourne, Australia. "Imperialism Versus Democracy." See D7.9.

## 1908

E8.1  15 May. Orillia, Ontario. Canadian Club. "The Asiatic Problem in the British Empire." See D8.1.

E8.2  24 October. Montreal, Quebec. Pen and Pencil Club. "The Visitation of Sir Wilfrid."

E8.3  1 November. Montreal, Quebec. Pen and Pencil Club. "Anthropological Inquiry with the Material Constituents of Latent Evolution."

E8.4  November. Montreal, Quebec. Canadian Club. "Union of South Africa." See C10.33.

E8.5  19 December. Montreal, Quebec. Pen and Pencil Club. "Studies in Simple Life." See C9.5.

E8.6  21 December. Montreal, Quebec. Windsor Hotel. Commercial Travellers' Association banquet. On Canada and British Diplomacy. See D9.1.

E8.7  December. Washington, D.C. Political Science Association. "Limitations of Federal Government." See C8.3.

## 1909

E9.1  2 January. Montreal, Quebec. Pen and Pencil Club. "Literature and Education in America." See C9.3.

E9.2  6 January. Kingston, Ontario. Queen's University. "Asiatic Question."

E9.3  15 January. Montreal, Quebec. "Is Graduation the Grave of Education?" Reported as "Literary Society," *Martlet* (McGill University) 1, no. 12 (22 January 1909): 267.

E9.4  20 January. [Montreal, Quebec]. Literary and Historical Society of Quebec.

E9.5  23 January. Ottawa, Ontario. Canadian Club. "Robert Baldwin." See B2 and D9.2.

E9.6  25 January. Montreal, Quebec. Jewish Society. "Disraeli."

E9.7  27 January. Montreal, Quebec. Nomad's Club. St. James' Literary Society. "The Asiatic Question in the British Empire." See C9.2.

E9.8  January. [Montreal?, Quebec]. University Club Dinner. "Anthropological Enquiry."

E9.9  1 — 5 February. Tour of the Maritime Provinces. Addresses relating to Canada's relations and its future, in Woodstock and Saint John, New Brunswick, Amherst, Nova Scotia, and Moncton, New Brunswick. See D9.3–4.

E9.10  18 February. Baltimore, Maryland. Johns Hopkins University. "Federal Government in Canada."

E9.11  27 February. Montreal, Quebec. Pen and Pencil Club. "Manichean Philosophy in a Novel Light."

E9.12  1 March. Montreal, Quebec. McGill University. Royal Victoria College. Public Lecture. "Development in Modern Democracy." Reported as "Modern Democracy Prof. Leacock Speaks of Its Development Since the Protestant Reformation. . . . ," *Montreal Gazette*, 2 March 1909, p. 7. His address drew a long letter to the editor from C.D. Sheldon, "Prof. Leacock's Lecture. A Critic of His Views," *Montreal Gazette*, 6 March 1909, p. 5.

E9.13  15 March. [Montreal?, Quebec]. Political Economy Club. On Federal Government. See E8.7.

E9.14  30 March. Montreal, Quebec. Erskine Church Young Men's League. "Some Current Problems in Canadian Development." Reported as "Canadian Development. Prof. Leacock Delivers Address on Some of Its Current Problems," *Montreal Gazette*, 1 April 1909, p. 9.

E9.15  15 April. [Montreal?, Quebec]. Literary and Historical Society of Quebec. "The World Policy of Germany." See C10.4 and D10.2.

E9.16  6 November. Montreal, Quebec. Pen and Pencil Club. "The Faculty of Arts — a Melody." See C9.7.

E9.17  2 December. [Montreal, Quebec]. Canadian Manufacturers Association. "Education and National Life."

## 1910

E10.1  20 January. Quebec City, Quebec. Literary and Historical Society of Quebec. "Outlook for Imperial Unity." See C10.6 and D10.1.

E10.2  31 January. Political Economy Club. "Economics and Immigration."

E10.3  11 February. Ste. Anne de Bellevue. McGill University. Macdonald College. "Citizenship."

E10.4  19 February. Montreal, Quebec. Pen and Pencil Club. "The Apology of a Professor." See C10.1.

E10.5  10 or 16 March. Montreal, Quebec. St. James' Literary Society. "Germany as a World Power." See D10.2.

E10.6  16 March. Montreal, Quebec. St. James' Cathedral Women's Guild. "Germany as a World Power."

E10.7  17 March. [Montreal, Quebec.] Crescent Presbyterian Church Banquet. "The Citizen and the State."

E10.8  18 March. [Montreal?, Quebec]. Literary and Historical Society of Quebec. "Socialism."

E10.9  17 December. Montreal, Quebec. Pen and Pencil Club. "A Hero in Homespun." See C10.46.

## 1911

E11.1  8 February. Kingston, Ontario. Queen's University Arts Society. "The Influence of the University on the National Life of Canada." Reported as "Prof. Leacock Lectures. Influence of University Discussed by McGill Man," *Montreal Daily Star*, 10 February 1911, p. 5. See D11.1.

E11.2   March. [Montreal?, Quebec]. Literary and Historical Society of Quebec. "Canada as a Nation."

E11.3   5 March. Quebec City, Quebec. Public Meeting. Speech against reciprocity. Reported as "Prof. Leacock on Reciprocity, Declares It Would Undo at One Stroke All the Work of Confederation. . . . ," *Montreal Gazette*, 6 March 1911, p. 1; also as "Professor Leacock's Trade Agreement, Addresses Meeting at Quebec in Opposition to Reciprocity Agreement," *Toronto Globe*, 6 March 1911, p. 1.

E11.4   8? March. Montreal, Quebec. Women's Canadian Club. "Economic Position of Women." See C11.19.

E11.5   20 March. Montreal, Quebec. Windsor Hall. Speech against reciprocity. Leacock was one of a series of speakers following an address by the Hon. Clifford Sifton. See "Montreal Protest" and "Speakers Appeal to Crown at Strathcona Monument," *Montreal Daily Star*, pp. 3, 9. See also B3α.

E11.6   24 April. [Montreal?, Quebec]. St. George's Dinner. Speech.

E11.7   28 April. Saint John, New Brunswick. Keith's Theatre. Women's Canadian Club. Afternoon speech. Reported as "The Course at University; Prof Leacock's Ideas in Regard to What Is Needed; A Possible Danger; Would Have University Practical to a Certain Degree, But Would Hesitate About Excluding Ancient History, Foreign Language and the Higher Sciences," *St. John Daily Telegraph*, 29 April 1911, p. 11. Several paragraphs are paraphrased.

E11.8   28 April. Saint John, New Brunswick. St. Andrew's Curling rink. Evening speech against reciprocity. Reported as " 'Rubbish,' Says Feminine Hearers; Women Couldn't Agree with Arguments of Messrs. Daniel, Ames and Leacock Last Night," *St. John Daily Telegraph*, 29 April 1911, p. 10. Leacock is not mentioned in the text of this article.

E11.9   1 September. Orillia, Ontario. Opera House. Conservative Party election meeting. See D11.3.

E11.10   September. Election Speeches in support of Conservative Party candidates in East Simcoe and northern Ontario. Compton. Stanstead. Brome. See D11.3.

E11.11   12 October. Toronto, Ontario. Canadian Manufacturers Convention. ["Canada and the Empire"]. See C11.34 and D11.4.

E11.12   20 October. Montreal, Quebec. Provincial Association of Protestant Teachers. "Education and Politics." See D11.5.

E11.13   24 October. Montreal, Quebec. McGill University. Remarks at a Debate. Reported as "Speeches of Good Quality Marked First Trial Debate," *McGill Daily*, 31 October 1911, pp. 2, 3.

E11.14   8 November. Montreal, Quebec. Strathcona Hall. "First Steps in Politics." See C11.35.

E11.15   2 December. Montreal, Quebec. Pen and Pencil Club. Portions of "The Voyages of Jacques Cartier." See A18.


1912

E12.1   12 January. Grand Rapids, Michigan. "How Cheerful . . . Some of the Sillier Sides of [the] Lit[erature] of Today."

LEACOCK'S NOTES: 1 page.

E12.2  13 January. Toronto, Ontario. University of Toronto Literary Society. "Universities and Citizenship." See D12.1.

E12.3  27 January. Montreal, Quebec. Pen and Pencil Club. "The Transformation of Mr. Smith," beginning part of the series: Town Life in Canada. See also A11.

E12.4  January. [Montreal?, Quebec]. Knights of Columbus. "The New Democracy."

E12.5  20 February. Montreal, Quebec. Women's Art Society. "Education of Children." See D12.2.

E12.6  24 February. Montreal, Quebec. Pen and Pencil Club. One of his "Sunlight [Sunshine] Sketches."

E12.7  27 February. Montreal, Quebec. Mount Royal Literary Society. "Poverty and Riches." Reported as "Poverty Not Necessary; Prof. Leacock Predicts a Better Age in Lecture on Poverty and Riches," *Montreal Witness*, 28 February 1912.

E12.8  14 March. Montreal, Quebec. St. James' Literary Society. "Asiatic Problem in the Colonies." See D12.3.

E12.9  15? March. Burlington, Vermont. University of Vermont. Vermont educationalists. "Democracy and Progress." Leacock's forthcoming appearance was reported in "Famous McGill Professor Receives Another Honour," *McGill Daily*, 4 March, 1912, p. 1.

E12.10  6 April. Montreal, Quebec. Pen and Pencil Club. Another of his "Sunlight [Sunshine] Sketches of Maraposa [Mariposa]."

E12.11  22 October. Montreal, Quebec. McGill Arts Undergraduates Society. "British and American Humour." Reported as "Arts Undergraduate Society Holds Successful Meeting," *McGill Daily*, 23 October 1912, p. 1. Leacock read some passages of Mark Twain.

E12.12  23 November. Montreal, Quebec. McGill University. Union Building. Reported as "Successful Smoker Was Held Last Saturday Night. Dr. Leacock's Address on Tobacco Brought Down the House," *McGill Daily*, 25 November 1912, p. 3.

E12.13  14 December. Montreal, Quebec. Montreal Branch, Journalists' Institute. "College Education and Journalism." See D12.4.

### 1913

E13.1  10 January. [Montreal?, Quebec]. Junior Staff Association. "High Cost of Living." See C13.4.

E13.2  13 February. Boston, Massachusetts. Westminster Hotel. Victorian Club. "Imperial Unity." Notice that the speech is going to be delivered is found in "Popular Professor the Guest of Honor at Boston Banquet," *McGill Daily*, 13 February 1913, p. 1.

E13.3  3 March. Montreal, Quebec. Western Club. McGill University Dining Hall. Reported as "Prof. Leacock Gives Interesting Talk at Western Club; Traces History of Western Movement from Earliest Times," *McGill Daily*, 4 March 1913, p. 1.

E13.4  16 May. Toronto, Ontario. Royal Alexandra Theatre. University of Toronto Alumni. "Social Reform in the New Century." See C13.16–7 and D13.1.

E13.5  18 October. Montreal, Quebec. "Toronto and McGill." Poem.

E13.6  28 October. Montreal, Quebec. McGill Literary and Debating Society. "How to

Pass Examinations." Reported as "Dr. Leacock on Examinations," *McGill Daily*, 29 October 1913, p. 4.

E13.7  3 November. Montreal, Quebec. Canadian Club. "Rise [in the] Cost [of] Living." See C13.4.

E13.8  3 November. Montreal, Quebec. Women's Guild of Christ Church Cathedral. "Social Reform in the Coming Century." See D13.1.

E13.9  20 November. Montreal, Quebec. McGill University. Reported as "Economists Form Club," *McGill Daily*, 21 November 1913, pp. 1, 2. Brief words of advice by Leacock are summarized.

E13.10  28 November. Kingston, Ontario. Women's Canadian Club. See D13.2.

## 1914

E14.1  19 January. Montreal, Quebec. Victoria Hall. Dickens Fellowship. "The Mind of the Master." Reported as "Dr. Leacock Had Them Summoned Before Himself in the Court of Opinion," *McGill Daily*, 22 January 1914, p. 4.

E14.2  24 January. Montreal, Quebec. Pen and Pencil Club. "Spoof."
LEACOCK'S NOTES: "A satire on the methods employed by modern magazine publishers to advertise their wares." See C14.10.

E14.3  30 November. Montreal, Quebec. McGill Political Economy Club. Reported as "Financial Side of Big Conflict Was Discussed," *McGill Daily*, 1 December 1914, pp. 1, 3.

E14.4  12 December. Montreal, Quebec. Pen and Pencil Club. Reading on the contributions by A. Campbell Geddes and René du Roure.

## 1915

E15.1  7 January. Philadelphia, Pennsylvania. Philadelphia Browning Society.
LEACOCK'S NOTES: "Readings from My Works. No programme kept. Included Behind the Beyond, Mr. Roosevelt."

E15.2  15 February. Saint John, New Brunswick. Women's Canadian Club. Reported as "Prof. Leacock Pleased a Large Audience with Readings in Aid of the Belgian Fund," *Saint John Globe*, 16 February 1915, p. 6. See D15.1.

E15.3  16 February. Halifax, Nova Scotia. Belgian Relief Fund. See D15.2

E15.4  8 March. Quebec City, Quebec.
LEACOCK'S NOTES: "For the Belgian Fund. In all these, Behind the Beyond, The Good Time, After the War, Spoof?"

E15.5  22 March. Montreal, Quebec. Windsor Hall. Belgian Fund. Reported as "Professor Leacock Delights a Large Audience of Montrealers," *McGill Daily*, 30 March 1915, p. 1

E15.6  29 March. Toronto, Ontario. Royal Alexandra Theatre. On behalf of the Franco-British Aid Society. Same programme as E15.4. See D15.3.

E15.7  30 March. Hamilton, Ontario.
LEACOCK'S NOTES: "[For the Belgian Fund.]" See also C15.1a and D15.4.

E15.8  24 May — 11 June. Welland, Galt [now Cambridge], London, St.Catharines, Guelph, Brantford, Fort William, Sault Ste. Marie, Ontario.
LEACOCK'S NOTES: "[For the Belgian Fund.]" See D15.5–8.

E15.9   28 September. Montreal, Quebec. Montreal Protestant Teachers. "Is Our Education Too Mechanical?"
LEACOCK'S NOTES: 4 pages. This speech may have been deferred until 16 October.

E15.10   16 October. Montreal, Quebec. Protestant Teachers. English Literature. See D15.9.

E15.11   18 October. Montreal, Quebec. McGill Literary Society. Reported as "Good Start Is Given to Literary Society," *McGill Daily*, 19 October 1915, p. 1.

E15.12   20 November. Montreal, Quebec. Royal Victoria College. Fourth University Overseas Company. Reported as "Professor Leacock Before Soldiers," *McGill Daily*, 22 November 1915, weekly alumni ed., p. 3. Leacock read a satire on a peace convention.

## 1916

E16.1   February. Brockville, Cobourg, Kingston, Peterborough, Woodstock, Berlin [now Kitchener], Ontario. The Kingston speech was on 16 February; Berlin speech was on 19 February. The Kingston and Brockville speeches were reported as "Prof. Leacock on Pacifists," *McGill Daily*, 17 February 1916, p. 4 and "Dr. Leacock, the McGill Humorist," *McGill Daily*, 21 February 1916, p. 4. See D16.1 for the speech in Berlin.
LEACOCK'S NOTES: For the Belgian Fund.

E16.2   21 February. New York. Astor Hotel. Canadian Camp dinner. Reported as "Professor Leacock Made a Big Hit with N.Y. Audience," *Montreal Herald*, 22 February 1916, p. 2. The report states that the 500 assembled guests experienced "paroxysms of laughter," but Leacock also raised ". . . them to their feet to express their sympathy for the Canadian nation achieving manhood through the stress of war. . . ."

E16.3   11 March. Buffalo, New York. University Club. "These Troubled Times." See C16.15.

E16.4   8 — 16 April. Tour. [Cities are listed in the order Leacock has them in his record of publications.]

E16.5   April. Pittsburgh, Pennsylvania. The Contemporary Club. "The Outlook for Literature in the 20th Century."

E16.6   April. Cleveland, Ohio. University Club.
LEACOCK'S NOTES: "Readings [from my works]."

E16.7   April. Baltimore, Maryland.
LEACOCK'S NOTES: "For the Belgian Fund. Behind the Beyond."

E16.8   April. Wellesley, Massachusetts. Wellesley College.
LEACOCK'S NOTES: "For the Belgian Fund. Readings [from my works]."

E16.9   26 April. [Ithaca, New York]. Cornell University. Book & Bowl Club. "Education As I See It."

E16.10   18 May. Cleveland, Ohio. Bankers' Club Dinner. "Humour As I See It." See C16.13.

E16.11   2 June. Toronto, Ontario. University of Toronto Mining Building. Ontario Medical Association Conference. "The Economic Problem Presented by the Treatment and Disposition of Returned Soldiers." See D16.2.

E16.12   20 or 26 November. Baltimore, Maryland. The Phoenix Club. "A Discourse on Humour with Some Samples of My Own."

LEACOCK'S NOTES: 4 pages.

E16.13   9 December. Indianapolis, Indiana. Contemporary Club.
LEACOCK'S NOTES: "Readings [from my works]."

E16.14   10 December. Chicago, Illinois. The Book and Play Club.

## 1917

E17.1   21 or 31 January. Rochester, New York. The Contemporary Club. He was paid in March for the Rochester Century Club, Middletown lecture, and Hartford College W. Club. There are many Middletowns in the U.S.; there is one in New York.
LEACOCK'S NOTES: "Readings [from my works]."

E17.2   13 February. Montreal, Quebec. McGill University. Royal Victoria College. Reported as "Prof. Leacock in Lecture on Mark Twain, Very Fine," *Montreal Daily Star*, 14 February 1917, p. 13; "A Lecture on 'Mark Twain' by S. Leacock," *McGill Daily*, 14 February 1917, p. 2.

E17.3   22 February. Montreal, Quebec. Royal Victoria College. Montreal Housewives' League. ["Great Famine Near . . ."]. See D17.2.

E17.4   31 March. [New Haven, Connecticut]. Yale University. Dramatic Club.

E17.5   April. Brooklyn, New York. Brooklyn Academy.

E17.6   2 April. New York, New York. Princess Theatre. "Literary Tendencies of Today." The programme is extant. Leacock's was the last of six Literary Afternoons organized by the J.B. Pond Lyceum Bureau.

E17.7   14 April. Detroit, Michigan. Athletic Club. "How to Keep Cheerful."

E17.8   19 April. Chicago, Illinois. University of Chicago. Moody Lecture. "The Mutability of Literature." His financial records indicate he also gave a lecture in Philadephia.

E17.9   1 May. Duluth, Minnesota.
LEACOCK'S NOTES: "Readings [from my works].

E17.10   2 May. Lowell, Massachusetts.
LEACOCK'S NOTES: "Readings [from my works]."

E17.11   28 May. Collingwood, Ontario.
LEACOCK'S NOTES: "[For the] Belgian Fund."

E17.12   30 May. Meaford, Ontario.
LEACOCK'S NOTES: "[For the] Belgian Fund."

E17.13   20 June. Providence, Rhode Island. Brown University. Leacock's notes are written over the commencement programme but his name is not printed in it as a speaker. According to his record of publications he received a Litt.D. degree.

E17.14   30 November. Montreal, Quebec. Windsor Hotel. Win-the-War Meeting. See D17.3.

E17.15   7 December. Quebec. Morrin College. Douglas Lecture. "Literature in the 20th Century."

E17.16   17 December. Philadelphia, Pennsylvania. Philadelphic . . . Society. "Literature in the 20th Century."

E17.17   28 December. Detroit, Michigan. Athletic Club.

## 1918

E18.1  8 January. Montreal, Quebec. Royal Victoria College Alumnae Society. McGill University. "Frenzied Fiction." See D18.1.

E18.2  12 January. Grand Rapids, [Michigan].

E18.3  15 January. St. Louis, Missouri.

E18.4  16 January. Cincinnati, Ohio. The Womans Club. "Literary Tendencies of Today." LEACOCK'S NOTES: 2 pages.

E18.5  17 January. Erie, Pennsylvania.

E18.6  19 January. Buffalo, New York.

E18.7  6 February. Montreal, Quebec. Ritz-Carlton Hotel. I.O.D.E. See D18.2.

E18.8  1 March. Philadelphia, Pennsylvania.

E18.9  2 March. New York, New York. Carnegie Hall. "Canada and the War." LEACOCK'S NOTES: 1 page.

E18.10  4 March. Providence, Rhode Island.

E18.11  19 March. Bridgeport, Connecticut. The Contemporary Club. "Frenzied Fiction."

E18.12  3 May. Rochester, New York LEACOCK'S NOTES: "Hospital Fund and Fatherless Children in France."

E18.13  11 May. Oshawa, Ontario. LEACOCK'S NOTES: "[For the] Belgian Fund."

## 1919

E19.1  14 January. Springfield, Ohio. "Frenzied Fiction."

E19.2  20 January. Bronxville, New York. "Frenzied Fiction."

E19.3  22 January. Springfield, Massachusetts. "Frenzied Fiction."

E19.4  15 February. Springfield, Massachusetts. Colony Club. "Literary Follies of Today."

E19.5  22 February. New York, New York. Lotus Club. James Russell Lowell Centennial. See B7 and D19.1.

E19.6  2 March. New York, New York. Pilgrims Banquet. Date not clear in record of publications but could also be 23 March.

E19.7  11 March. Montreal, Quebec. Almy's Limited. Baby Welfare Committee. See D19.2.

E19.8  8 April. New York, New York. Authors League Banquet.

E19.9  15 or 16 April. Minneapolis, Minnesota. Womans Club. "Frenzied Fiction." LEACOCK'S NOTES: 1 page.

E19.10  17 April. Farragut, Minnesota [?]. Shattuck School. "Literary Follies." There is no Farragut in Minnesota but there is such a place in Iowa.

E19.11  19 April. St. Louis, Missouri. "Literary Follies."

E19.12  20 April. Iowa City, Iowa. "Frenzied Fiction."

E19.13  21 April. South Bend, Indiana. "Frenzied Fiction."

E19.14  2 May. Toronto, Ontario. University [of Toronto] Convocation Hall. "Frenzied

Fiction." See D19.3.

E19.15  20 June. Norfolk, Connecticut. Litchfield County University Club. "Frenzied Fiction."

E19.16  16 or 17 October. [Montreal, McGill University]. Speech at the installation of Edward Wentworth Beatty and Robert Bruce Taylor.

E19.17  28 November. [Cambridge, Massachusetts]. Harvard University. Harvard Union. "Literature of Today and Tomorrow." See D19.4.

E19.18  17 December. Auburndale [Auburn], New York. Lasell Seminary.

E19.19  19 December. Pittsburgh, Pennsylvania. Chamber of Commerce. A printed announcement is extant which gives the date as 19 December; the lecture notebook lists 17 December as the date.

E19.20  19 December. Pittsburgh, Pennsylvania. Art Society. "What I Don't Know About Literature."
LEACOCK'S NOTES: 1 page.

E19.21  20 December. New York, New York. New England Society Dinner.

## 1920

E20.1  11 January. Ann Arbor, Michigan. University of Michigan. "Frenzied Fiction."

E20.2  12 January. St. Paul, Minnesota. St. Paul Institute. "Frenzied Fiction or What I Don't Know about Literature."
LEACOCK'S NOTES: 2 pages.

E20.3  13 January. [Minneapolis, Minnesota]. University of Minnesota. "Problem of Social Justice."
LEACOCK'S NOTES: 2 pages.

E20.4  14 January. Milwaukee, Wisconsin. December Club. "Frenzied Fiction."

E20.5  14 January. Chicago, Illinois. Young Fortnightly Club. Temple Sholom. "Frenzied Fiction."
LEACOCK'S NOTES: 1 page.

E20.6  15 January. Chicago, Illinois. Elizabeth Kirkland School.
LEACOCK'S NOTES: "Teaching of English, Spoof."

E20.7  15 January. Chicago, Illinois. Quadrangle Club.
LEACOCK'S NOTES: "Politics."

E20.8  17 January. Milwaukee, Wisconsin. The City Club. "The Problem of Social Justice."
LEACOCK'S NOTES: 1 page.

E20.9  16 February. New York, New York. GlenRidge.
LEACOCK'S NOTES: "Frenzied Fiction, Snoop."

E20.10  17 February. New York, New York. Dutch Treat Club. Lunch. "Whiskers."

E20.11  17? February. White Plains, [New York]. "Frenzied Fiction." This entry is before Holyoke in Leacock's record of publications.

E20.12  17 February. Holyoke, Massachusetts.
LEACOCK'S NOTES: "Frenzied Fiction, Pol[itics] & Sn[oops]."

E20.13   18 February. Buffalo, New York. The Garret Club.
LEACOCK'S NOTES: "Chair, Pol[itics], Snoop."

E20.14   18 or 28 February. New York, New York. The Coffee House.
LEACOCK'S NOTES: "Politics." The date of 18 February comes from his record of publications.

E20.15   26 February. New York, New York. Columbia University. "Literature & Progress."
LEACOCK'S NOTES: 1 page.

E20.16   6 March. Detroit, Michigan. Athletic Club.
LEACOCK'S NOTES: "Shakespeare, Politics, Whiskers, Poetry."

E20.17   11 March. Buffalo, New York. Saturn Club. "Drama As I See It."
LEACOCK'S NOTES: 2 pages.

E20.18   2 April. Toronto, Ontario. University of Toronto. Convocation Hall. Veteran Society.
LEACOCK'S NOTES: "Frenzied Fiction, Politics, Whiskers, Moving Pictures, Snoops"; 1 page. See D20.1.

E20.19   6 April. Montreal, Quebec. Windsor Hall.
LEACOCK'S NOTES: "For Women's Directory. See Toronto Ap[ril] 6 [sic, 2]."

E20.20   19 April. Cleveland, Ohio. Jewish Women's Club.
LEACOCK'S NOTES: "Politics, Pictures, Snoop."

E20.21   20 April. Wooster, Ohio.
LEACOCK'S NOTES: "Politics, Pictures, Snoop."

E20.22   21 April. Cincinnati, Ohio. Glendale. "Frenzied Fiction."
LEACOCK'S NOTES: 1 page.

E20.23   27 April. Waterbury, Connecticut. Teachers.
LEACOCK'S NOTES: "Politics, Pictures, Snoop."

E20.24   28 April. Brockton, Massachusetts. Teachers. "Frenzied Fiction."
LEACOCK'S NOTES: 1 page.

E20.25   29 April. New London, Connecticut. Women's Club.
LEACOCK'S NOTES: "Politics, Pictures, Snoop."

E20.26   18 May. South Bend, Indiana. Knife & Fork Club.
LEACOCK'S NOTES: "Politics, Pictures, Snoop"; 1 page.

E20.27   16 June. Cleveland, Ohio. [Case] West[ern Reserve] University. Med[ical] Alumni.
LEACOCK'S NOTES: "Politics, Heroes, Snoops."

E20.28   18 June. Chazy, New York. Central Rural School. "The New Social Outlook."

E20.29   23 June. [Hanover, New Hampshire]. Dartmouth College. Alumni Lunch. This speech is reported very briefly in *Dartmouth Alumni Magazine* 12, no. 8 (July, August 1920): 872. Leacock received an honorary Litt.D.

E20.30   9 July. Chicago, Illinois. University of Chicago.
LEACOCK'S NOTES: "Frenzied Fiction (Heroes), Snoops."

E20.31   3 August. Montreal, Quebec. Imperial Press Conference Banquet.

E20.32  5 November. Montreal, Quebec. McGill Economics Club.

E20.33  1 December. Montreal, Quebec. Lady Davis Charity. "The Drama As I Know It."

E20.34  15 December. Middlebury, Vermont. Middlebury College. "Frenzied Fiction."
LEACOCK'S NOTES: 1 page.

E20.35  30 December. Boston, Massachusetts. Boston City Club. "Frenzied Fiction."
LEACOCK'S NOTES: 1 page.

## 1921

E21.1  17 January. Brooklyn, New York. Brooklyn Institute.
LEACOCK'S NOTES: "Heroes, Snoops, Taft, Ned"; 1 page.

E21.2  18 January. Naugatuck, Connecticut
LEACOCK'S NOTES: "Heroes, Snoops, Taft, Ned." This entry written above a crossed-out entry for Terre Haute, Indiana.

E21.3  19 or 20 January. Richmond, Indiana.
LEACOCK'S NOTES: "Literary Follies of the Day, Behind Beyond I Act, Moving Pictures, Snoops"; 1 page.

E21.4  20 or 21 January. Terre Haute, Indiana. State Normal School.
LEACOCK'S NOTES: "Frenzied Fiction, Farmers, Taft, Heroes, Snoops"; 1 page.

E21.5  22 January. Ann Arbor, Michigan. University of Michigan.
LEACOCK'S NOTES: "Light House, Behind Beyond, Moving Pictures, Spoof"; 1 page.

E21.6  8 February. Boston, Massachusetts. Sons of Brown. See D21.2.

E21.7  [Financial records show he was paid on 28 Feb. for DePauw lectures; this could be a university in Indiana.]

E21.8  2? March. Montreal, Quebec. McGill University. Reported as "Question Is Can Germany Pay Indemnity an Annual Open meeting of Economics Club. D. Leacock Presided. . . . ," *McGill Daily*, 3 March 1921, p. 4. Leacock chaired the meeting and outlined the discussion in which one of his students explained the importance of J.M. Keynes's *The Economic Consequences of the Peace.*

E21.9  12 March. Buffalo, New York. Saturn Club.
LEACOCK'S NOTES: "Drama, Pol[itics], Snoop."

E21.10  2 April. Toronto, Ontario. Foresters Hall. Citizens Liberty League. "The Case Against Prohibition." See A36a and D21.3.

E21.11  18 April. Andover, [Massachusetts]. Phillips Academy.
LEACOCK'S NOTES: "Drama, Politics"; 1 page.

E21.12  18 April. Andover, Massachusetts. November Club.

E21.13  19 April. Philadelphia, Pennsylvania. University of Pennsylvania.

E21.14  20 April. Cleveland, Ohio. Statler Hotel. The Ad Club. "The High Brow Drama and the Low Brow Movie."
LEACOCK'S NOTES: 6 pages, including "The Drama As I Know It."

E21.15  21 April. Milwaukee, Wisconsin. Women's Club.
LEACOCK'S NOTES: "Drama, Heroes, Snoops"; 1 page.

E21.16  22 April. Burlington, Iowa. High School Building.

LEACOCK'S NOTES: "Heroes, Heroines, Snoops"; 1 page.

E21.17   23 April. Louisville, Kentucky. The Auditorium. "Frenzied Fiction."

E21.18   24 April. Toledo, Ohio. Jewish Men's Club.

E21.19   25 April. Evanston, Illinois.

E21.20   26 April. Youngstown, Ohio.

E21.21   12 May. Lancaster, New Hampshire. American Veterans.

E21.22   22 May. Mishawaka, Indiana.

E21.23   4 October. Thirsk, Yorkshire, England. Thirsk Institute. "Frenzied Fiction."

E21.24   11 October. Liverpool, England. Playhouse, Williamson Square. "Frenzied Fiction."

E21.25   12 October. Bristol, England. Clifton College. "Frenzied Fiction."

E21.26   17 and 19 October. London, England. Aeolian Hall. "Frenzied Fiction." See A30b for the programme for all four Aeolian Hall lectures and D21.4.

E21.27   18 October. Devonshire Park, Winter Garden, Eastbourne, Sussex, England. "Frenzied Fiction."

E21.28   19 October. Southend-on-Sea, Essex, England. Cliff Town Congregational Church. "Literature at Its Lightest."

E21.29   20 and 21 October. London, England. Aeolian Hall. "The Drama As I See It." See E21.26.

E21.30   25 October. Shrewsbury, Shropshire, England. Shrewsbury School. "Frenzied Fiction."

E21.31   26 October. Wokingham, Berkshire, England. Wokingham Lecture Society. "Frenzied Fiction."

E21.32   28 October. Oxford, England. British-American Union. See D21.5.

E21.33   31 October. London?, England. Blinded Soldiers and Sailors Hostel. According to Curry's biography (p. 360), Leacock was in Litchfield.

E21.34   1 November. Folkstone, Kent, England. Bouverie Literary Society. "Frenzied Fiction."

E21.35   2 November. Ipswich, Suffolk, England. The Institute. "Frenzied Fiction."

E21.36   3 November. Bristol, England. The Public Hall. "Laughing with Leacock." According to Curry's biography (p. 360), Leacock was in Carshalton, Surrey.

E21.37   4? November. London, England. ["Drama"].

E21.38   7 November. Cardiff, Wales. Central YMCA. "Frenzied Fiction."

E21.39   9 November. Bristol, England. Young People Institute.

E21.40   10 November. Wolverhampton, West Midlands, England. Literary and Scientific Society. "Literature at Its Lightest."

E21.41   12 November. Malvern, Worcester, England. Malvern College.

E21.42   14 November. Birmingham, England. Birmingham and Midland Institute. "Literature at Its Lightest."

E21.43  15 November. Harrogate, Yorkshire, England. The College. "Literature at Its Lightest."

E21.44  16 November. Manchester, England. Central High School. "Moonbeams from the Larger Lunacy." See D21.7.

E21.45  16 November. Manchester, England. YMCA. "Frenzied Fiction."

E21.46  17 November. Moseley, England. Birmingham, Moseley & Balsall Heath Institute. "Frenzied Fiction."

E21.47  18 November. Bristol, England.

E21.48  21 November. Glasgow, Scotland. The Palette Club Ltd. "Laughing with Leacock." See D21.8.

E21.49  22 November. Edinburgh, Scotland. Philosophical Institution. "Literature at Its Lightest."

E21.50  23 November. Aberdeen, Scotland. Aberdeen Chamber of Commerce.

E21.51  24 November. Falkirk, Scotland. Erskine Church Guild. "Laughter with Leacock."

E21.52  25 November. Greenock, Scotland. Philosophical Society. "The Drama as I See It."

E21.53  26 November. Bridge of Allan, Scotland. "Frenzied Fiction."

E21.54  28 November. Glasgow, Scotland. Glasgow University Students' Union. "Equality." See D21.9.

E21.55  28 November. Glasgow, Scotland. Trinity Literary Society. "Literature at Its Lightest." See D21.10.

E21.56  29 November. Glasgow, Scotland. YMCA. "Laughing with Leacock." See D21.11.

E21.57  30 November. Leeds, England. Leeds Institute. "Frenzied Fiction."

E21.58  2 December. Rotherham, Yorkshire, England. Rotherham School Lectures. "Literature at Its Lightest."

E21.59  3 December. Barrow-in-Furness, Cumbria, England. Technical School Popular Lectures. "Literature at Its Lightest."

E21.60  5 December. Tunbridge Wells, Kent, England. Afternoon, 3 p.m. "Frenzied Fiction."

E21.61  5 December. Eltham, S.E., London suburb, England. Everard Hesketh. "Laughing at [sic] Leacock."

E21.62  6 December. Hampstead, London suburb, England.

E21.63  7 December. Westbourne Park Institute, Wales. Undoubtedly Westbourne Park, a suburb of London rather than in Wales. "An Evening with Stephen Leacock or Frenzied Fiction."

E21.64  7 December. Brighton, Sussex, England. Theatre Royal.

E21.65  8 December. London, England. City Temple Literary Society. "Frenzied Fiction." Reported as "Professor Leacock's Humour," *Daily Telegraph* (London), 9 December 1921, p. 6.

E21.66  9 December. London, England. London Society. "Impressions of London." See D21.12.

E21.67  10 December. Goudhurst, Kent, England. Bedgebury Park School. Speech suitable for girls, 10–17.

E21.68  12 December. London, England. Canadian Club inaugural meeting. See D21.13.

E21.69  13 December. Ossett, Yorkshire, England. Ossett & Hornsbury Literary Society. "Frenzied Fiction."

E21.70  14 December. Dewsbury, Yorkshire, England. Dewsbury Adult Education Association. "The Drama as I See It."

E21.71  15 December. Dumfries, Scotland. Mechanics' Institute. "Frenzied Fiction."

E21.72  16 December. Dundee, Scotland. The Armistead Trust. "Literature at Its Lightest."

E21.73  18 December. Newcastle-on-Tyne, England. Tyneside Sunday Lecture Society. "The Drama As I See It."

E21.74  19 December. Blundellsands, Lancashire, England. St. Nicholas Lectures and Entertainment. "Frenzied Fiction."

E21.75  20 December. Northwich, Cheshire, England. Crescent Literary and Scientific Society. "Laughing with Leacock."

E21.76  21 December. Kingston-on-Thames, England. Kingston Congregation[al] Church Guild. "Frenzied Fiction."

E21.77  23 December. Bournemouth, Hampshire, England. Winter Gardens. See F21.11.

1922

E22.1  February. Groveton, New Hampshire. He was paid on 23 February for this speech.

E22.2  8 February. Montreal, Quebec. Union Cafeteria. Students Western Club. See D22.1.

E22.3  21 February. Albany, New York.
LEACOCK'S NOTES: "Frenzied Fiction, Raft."

E22.4  6 March. [Brunswick, Maine]. Bowdoin College. "Drama As I See It."

E22.5  9 March. Nfd's [Newfoundland's?] Students Club.
LEACOCK'S NOTES: "Culture & War"; 1 page.

E22.6  13 March. Montreal, Quebec. McGill Medical Undergraduate Society. "The Lighter Side of Life." See D22.2.

E22.7  16 March. Montreal, Quebec. Ritz Grill room. McGill Arts Undergraduate dinner. Reported as "Arts Dinner Proved Very Interesting," *McGill Daily*, 17 March 1922, p. 4.

E22.8  18 March. Syracuse, New York. Syracuse University.
LEACOCK'S NOTES: "Criminals not here, Ossett, U[ncle] Tom, Light House, Moving Picture, Spoof"; 2 pages.

E22.9  1 April. Schenectady, New York.

E22.10  8 April. Boston, Massachusetts. Jordan Hall.
LEACOCK'S NOTES: "Criminals, Ossett, Frenzied Fiction, Madeleine, Snoops"; 1 page.

E22.11  15 April. Philadelphia, Pennsylvania. Academy of Music.
LEACOCK'S NOTES: "Since England, Literary Criminals, Ossett, Behind Beyond Act I, Drama, Moving Pictures"; 1 page.

E22.12  18 May. Evansville, Indiana.

LEACOCK'S NOTES: "Criminals, Ossett, Drama, Snoops"; 1 page.

E22.13   19 May. Jamestown, New York.

E22.14   May. Delaware, Ohio.

E22.15   11 or 21 or 24 or 25 September. Detroit, Michigan. Knights of Columbus.
LEACOCK'S NOTES: "Eng[land], Drama, Radio, Heroines, Light House, Raft, Snoops"; 6 pages.

E22.16   11 October. St. Johnsbury, Vermont. Vermont State Teachers Association. "Education as I See It."
LEACOCK'S NOTES: 3 pages.

E22.17   27 October. Cincinnati, Ohio. Teachers Association of Ohio. "Education as I See It."
LEACOCK'S NOTES: "Radio."

E22.18   28 October. Columbus, Ohio. Memorial Hall. Women's Lecture Club.
LEACOCK'S NOTES: "Drama, Madeleine, Raft, Radio, Snoops, Criminals, Ossett"; 2 pages.

E22.19   4 November. Portland, Maine. Wellsley? College Alumni.
LEACOCK'S NOTES: "Same as Columbus"; 2 pages. See E22.18.

E22.20   12 December. Montreal, Quebec. Cercle Français. "Study of Languages."

E22.21   29 December. Charleston, West Virginia.
LEACOCK'S NOTES: "Drama, Radio, Madeleine, Snoops."

## 1923

E23.1   1 January. Montreal, Quebec. St. James' Club. New Year's Luncheon.
LEACOCK'S NOTES: "Some of our Troubles"; 2 pages.

E23.2   3 January. Montreal, Quebec. St. Paul's Church Society.
LEACOCK'S NOTES: "Same as Detroit." See E22.15.

E23.3   3 January. Laconia, New Hampshire. American Legion.
LEACOCK'S NOTES: "Same as Detroit K[nights] of Col[umbus] Sept." See E22.15. "Crim[inals], Ossett, Drama, Radio, Raft, Mad[eleine], Snoop with Whiskers"; 1 page. See also previous entry of same date.

E23.4   16 January. Elmira, New York. Free Academy.
LEACOCK'S NOTES: "Same as K[nights] of C[olumbus] Detroit + New Raft." 1 page. See E22.15. Reported as "Leacock Makes Elmira Feel Happier," *Elmira Star Gazette*, 17 January 1923.

E23.5   17 January. Elyria, Ohio. City Teachers Club. At the High School. "My Discovery of England and Other Things."
LEACOCK'S NOTES: "Same as Det[roit]." See E22.15. "Radio, Drama, Moving Pictures, British and American Press, Raft, Snoops"; 2 pages.

E23.6   18 January. Toledo, Ohio.
LEACOCK'S NOTES: "Detroit Prog[ramme]." See E22.15.

E23.7   23 January. Montreal, Quebec. Mount Royal Hotel. Conference of the Quebec Forest Protection Association. See C23.6.

E23.8   25 January. [Montreal, Quebec]. Club Canadien. "Future of Montreal."

LEACOCK'S NOTES: 2 pages. See D23.1.

**E23.9** 10 February. Providence, Rhode Island.
LEACOCK'S NOTES: "Drama, Radio, Abolish, Snoops."

**E23.10** 13 February. Pittsburgh, Pennsylvania.
LEACOCK'S NOTES: "Detroit Prog[ramme]." See E22.15.

**E23.11** 14 February. Oxford, Ohio. Miami University.
LEACOCK'S NOTES: "Frenzied Fiction, Radio."

**E23.12** 3 March. Lowell, Massachusetts. Parker Lectures: Muncipal?.
LEACOCK'S NOTES: "Criminals, Ossett, Drama, Action, Radio, Angelina, Heroine, General Melod[rama], Modern Play"; 2 pages.

**E23.13** 10 March. Plainfield, New Jersey. The Plainfield Lectures (written afterwards).
LEACOCK'S NOTES: "Criminals, Ossett, Radio, Curbstone, Snoops. See Lowell [see E23.12]." 1 page.

**E23.14** 10 March. New York, New York. Canadian Club. "Organization and Prosperity in Can[ada]."
LEACOCK'S NOTES: 1 page. See D23.2.

**E23.15** 24 March. New Rochelle, New York. High School. "Frenzied Fiction."
LEACOCK'S NOTES: "Criminals, Ossett, Frenzied Fiction, Snoops"; 1 page.

**E23.16** 2–6 April. Richmond, Virginia. University of Richmond. "The Evolution of Democracy." An announcement regarding these lectures is entitled: "Announcement of the Forty-sixth Course of Lectures on the James Thomas Jr., Foundation." The lectures themselves are subsequently listed as follows: "Monday, April 2nd: The Origins of Modern Democracy; Wednesday, April 4th: The American and French Revolutions; Thursday, April 5th: Democracy and Laissez-Faire in the XIX Century; Friday, April 6th: Democracy of Today."
LEACOCK'S NOTES: For the fourth lecture include "T[om] Paine, Democracy & Corruption, Direct Government, Commission Government, Democracy & Culture, Education, Literature under Democracy"; 2 pages.

**E23.17** 4 April. Richmond, Virginia. University of Richmond.
LEACOCK'S NOTES: "Frenzied Fiction, Criminals, Ossett"; 1 page.

**E23.18** 26 April. Raleigh, North Carolina. Meredith College.
LEACOCK'S NOTES: "See Richmond" [E23.17].

**E23.19** 28 April. [Iowa City]. State University of Iowa. "The Lighter Side of Literature, Moving Pictures, and Drama."
LEACOCK'S NOTES: 1 page. According to his correspondence he spoke on "Education and Democracy."

**E23.20** 15 May. Bowling Green, Ohio.
LEACOCK'S NOTES: "Criminals, Ossett, Frenzied Fiction, Madeleine, Kate, Radio, Abolish, Snoop"; 1 page.

**E23.21** 16 May. Fort Wayne, Indiana.

**E23.22** 22 May. Ottawa, Ontario. Royal Society. "Pop[ular] Econ[omic] Fallacies."

**E23.23** 26 May. Waterloo? Ames? Iowa. Iowa Federation Women's Club. "Education and

Democ[racy]." Leacock's notes indicate some doubt about the location of this lecture. Both Waterloo and Ames are listed and followed by question marks, in the manner noted above. See E23.34. His financial records refer to two Iowa lectures and one in Scranton, which is also in Iowa.

E23.24  29 May. Montreal, Quebec.  McGill University Convocation. "Education and Democracy." See D23.4.

E23.25  9 June. Wilkes Barre, Pennsylvania.
LEACOCK'S NOTES: "Criminals, Ossett, Drama, Mad[eleine], Kate."

E23.26  22 June. Chicago, Illinois. University of Chicago.
LEACOCK'S NOTES: "Criminals, Ossett, Drama, Ibsen, Napoleon, Radio, Curbstone, Snoops"; 2 pages.

E23.27  13 October. Varsity Dinner.
LEACOCK'S NOTES: 1 page.

E23.28  18 October. Trenton, New Jersey. "Frenzied Fiction."
LEACOCK'S NOTES: 1 page.

E23.29  19 October. Altoona, Pennsylvania.
LEACOCK'S NOTES: "Criminal, Ossett, Mad[eleine], Mark, Abolish, Radio, Snoops. See Trenton" [E23.28]. 1 page.

E23.30  20 October. Meadville, Pennsylvania. Allegheny College. "Frenzied Fiction."
LEACOCK'S NOTES: "See Trenton" [E23.28]. 1 page.

E23.31  27 October. Providence, Rhode Island. Rhode Island Institute of Instruction. Central High School. "Frenzied Fiction."
LEACOCK'S NOTES: "See Trenton" [E23.28]. 1 page.

E23.32  28 October. Portland, Maine.
LEACOCK'S NOTES: "See Trenton" [E23.28].

E23.33  29 October. Cooperstown, New York.
LEACOCK'S NOTES: "See Trenton" [E23.18].

E23.34  1 November. Des Moines, Iowa. State Teachers' Association. "Education and Democracy."

E23.35  2 November. Normal (Bloomington) In[diana]. Normal University. "Frenzied Fiction."

E23.36  3 November. Piqua, Ohio. "Frenzied Fiction."

E23.37  10 November. Cleveland, Ohio. Principal Teachers Association.
LEACOCK'S NOTES: "Criminals, Ossett, Latest Things in Literature, Drama, Abolish, Lighthouse, Ibsen, Radio, Raft, Snoops"; 1 page.

E23.38  12 November. Kalamazoo, Michigan. Teachers Association.
LEACOCK'S NOTES: "Frenzied Fiction, Criminals, Ossett, Madeleine, Kate, Snoops"; 1 page.

E23.39  21? November. Montreal, Quebec. McGill University. Political Economy Club. "Immigration." Reported as "Where Do Immigrants Go? Leacock Inquires," *Montreal Daily Star*, 22 November 1923, p. 2; "Economists Discussed Immigration," *McGill Daily*, 22 November 1923, pp. 1, 3.

E23.40   29 November. Concord, [Massachusetts]. St. Paul's School.
LEACOCK'S NOTES: "Criminals, Ossett, Ned, Madeleine, Kate, Curbstone, Snoops";
1 page.

E23.41   2 December. Springfield, Massachusetts. "Frenzied Fiction."
LEACOCK'S NOTES: "Criminals, Ossett, Drama, Madeleine, Curbstone, Snoops"; 1 page.

E23.42   27 December. Newark, New Jersey. New Jersey Teachers' [Association].
LEACOCK'S NOTES: "Criminals, Ossett, Drama, Uncle Tom, Radio, Abolish, Snoops."

E23.43   28 December. Bayonne, New Jersey. New Jersey Teachers' Association. See D23.5.

## 1924

E24.1   3 January. Norfolk, Virginia. Jewish Women's Society.

E24.2   4 January. Lynchburg, Virginia. "Frenzied Fiction."
LEACOCK'S NOTES: "Ned, Madeleine, Kate, Radio, Curbstone, Snoops"; 1 page.

E24.3   4 January. Goldsborough, North Carolina.

E24.4   5 January. Greensboro, North Carolina. State College for Women. "Frenzied
Fiction."
LEACOCK'S NOTES: "Drama, Ibsen, Radio, Heroine, Snoops, Full Whiskers"; 1 page.

E24.5   14 January. Haverhill, Massachusetts. High School.
LEACOCK'S NOTES: "Frenzied Fiction (straight), Criminals, Ossett, Ned, Kate, Curbstone,
Snoops"; 1 page.

E24.6   15 January. Boston, Massachusetts. McGill [University] Alumni. Vendome Hotel.
LEACOCK'S NOTES: "Personal, Currie, Harkness, Cosmopolitan"; 1 page.

E24.7   15 January. Quincy (Boston), Massachusetts. "Straight Frenzied Fiction."

E24.8   16 January. North Adams, Massachusetts. "Frenzied Fiction."

E24.9   1 February. Toronto, Ontario. Life Underwriters Convention. "Restoration of the
Gold Standard."
LEACOCK'S NOTES: 1 page. See A42.

E24.10   11 February. Hamilton, Ontario. McGill Alumni of Hamilton and Southern
Ontario. The programme is extant with some notes written on it. See D24.2.

E24.11   16 February. St. Lambert, Quebec. St. Lambert's Women's Club. "The Lighter Side
of Literature and Drama." See D24.3.

E24.12   19 February. Plattsburg, New York. Normal School Teachers. "Frenzied Fiction."
LEACOCK'S NOTES: 1 page.

E24.13   25 February. Montreal, Quebec. Liberal-Conservative Association. Mount Royal
Hotel. "The Reorganization of Canada for Prosperity." See D24.4.

E24.14   4 March. Williamsport, Pennsylvania.

E24.15   5 March. Ann Arbor, Michigan. University of Michigan. "New Matters in Literature and Drama." According to the *Michigan Daily*, the speech was supposed to be
"Rediscovering England." See D24.5.

E24.16   6 March. Toronto, Ontario. Empire Club, K[ing] E[dward] Hotel. "Proper Limits
of State Interference."
LEACOCK'S NOTES: 2 pages. See C24.1.

E24.17  8 March. New Haven, Connecticut. Yale University.
LEACOCK'S NOTES: "Drama, [Uncle] Tom, Ibsen, Sub Contractor, Curbstone, Snoops, Whiskers"; 1 page.

E24.18  13 March. Rome, New York. The Free Academy.
LEACOCK'S NOTES: "Frenzied Fiction, Madeleine, Kate, Snoops, Curbstone, Whiskers"; 1 page.

E24.19  ?1 April. Montreal, Quebec. McGill University. Joint meeting of the Historical and Political Economy Clubs. See D24.6.

E24.20  9 April. Montreal, Quebec. Catholic Women Teachers. "Random Thoughts on Education."
LEACOCK'S NOTES: 4 pages.

E24.21  ?25 April. Montreal, Quebec. McGill University.
LEACOCK'S NOTES: "On Education." See D24.7.

E24.22  3 May. Buckhannon, West Virginia.

E24.23  4 May. Portsmouth, Ohio. High School.

E24.24  5 or 7 May. Muncie, Indiana. High School. "Frenzied Fiction."
LEACOCK'S NOTES: "Thread, Kate, Ned, Curbstone, Snoops, Whiskers"; 1 page.

E24.25  22 May. Toronto, Ontario. Upper Canada College dinner. Not confirmed that he spoke.

E24.26  10 June. Pittsfield, Massachusetts. Teachers' Association. "Frenzied Fiction."
LEACOCK'S NOTES: "Madeleine, Kate, Radio, Snoops"; 1 page.

E24.27  15 July. [University Park, Pennsylvania]. State College, Pennsylvania. "Frenzied Fiction."

E24.28  September.
LEACOCK'S NOTES: "Lecture Tour Virginia, etc Sep[tember] 1924; Schedule of Material; Subjects; at the High School Roanoke; The Wreck of My Education (use Iowa Cath[olic] Teachers etc); elsewhere: The Lighter Side of Literature; or else; What I Don't Know About the Drama"; 2 pages of subject material follow.

E24.29  September. Richmond, Virginia. "Charles Dickens."
LEACOCK'S NOTES: 3 pages.

E24.30  18 September. Roanoke, Virginia. The University Club, held at Jefferson High School. "Frenzied Fiction."
LEACOCK'S NOTES: 1 page.

E24.31  18 September. Roanoke, Virginia. Jefferson High School. "What I Don't Know."
LEACOCK'S NOTES: 1 page.

E24.32  19 September. Rock Hill, South Carolina. Winthrop College. "Frenzied Fiction."
LEACOCK'S NOTES: 1 page. Date also given in notebook as 18 September but this seems unlikely.

E24.33  23 September. Charlotte, North Carolina. Davidson College. "Frenzied Fiction."
LEACOCK'S NOTES: 2 pages.

E24.34  24 September. Atlanta, Georgia. Agnes Scott College. "Modern Drama: What I Don't Know about the Drama."

LEACOCK'S NOTES: 1 page.

E24.35  Johnson City, Tennessee. This undated entry follows Atlanta in Leacock's list of lectures.

E24.36  9 October. Potsdam, New York. New York State Teachers. "The Lighter Side of the Study of Literature."
LEACOCK'S NOTES: 1 page.

E24.37  16 October. Syracuse, New York. University of Syracuse. Faculty Club. "Frenzied Fiction."
LEACOCK'S NOTES: 1 page.

E24.38  17 October. Cortland, New York.

E24.39  18 October. Cooperstown, New York.
LEACOCK'S NOTES: "Kingston [on Thames], Ibsen, Shakespeare"; 1 page.

E24.40  23 October. Utica, New York. "Lighter Side of the Study of Literature."
LEACOCK'S NOTES: 1 page.

E24.41  30 October. Troy, New York. Teachers Convention. "Lighter Side of the Drama and Literature."
LEACOCK'S NOTES: 2 pages.

E24.42  1 November. New York, New York. Washington Irving School. "Lighter Side of the Study of Literature."
LEACOCK'S NOTES: 3 pages.

E24.43  10 November. Northampton, Massachusetts. Smith College.
LEACOCK'S NOTES: "Frenzied Fiction."

E24.44  13 November. Buffalo, New York. Teachers. "The Lighter Side of the Study of Lit[erature]."
LEACOCK'S NOTES: 1 page.

E24.45  15 November. Rochester, New York. Chamber of Commerce. "The Making of a University."

E24.46  15 November. Rochester, New York. Teachers. "Frenzied Fiction."

E24.47  1 December. Montreal, Quebec. Canadian Club. "The Place of Letters in National Life." See D24.9.

E24.48  8 December. Montreal, Quebec. McGill Cercle Français. Announced as "Cercle Français to Hold Debate," *McGill Daily*, 6 December 1924, p. 3. The announcement notes that Leacock will "have some words" on the debate that the pen is mightier than the sword.

E24.49  13 December. Danbury, [Connecticut]. Womens Club.
LEACOCK'S NOTES: "Straight Frenzied Fiction, Criminals, Ossett, Madeleine, Kate, Curb[stone], Snoops"; 1 page.

E24.50  14 December. Springfield, Massachusetts. Young Men's Christian Association.
LEACOCK'S NOTES: "Latest Things in Love Stories, Radio, Raft, Philip, Spoof"; 2 pages, programme is also extant.

E24.51  14 December. Westfield, [Massachusetts].
LEACOCK'S NOTES: "Love Stories, Curbstone, Radio, Kate, Snoops"; 1 page.

E24.52  16 December. Montreal, Quebec. McGill Commerce Society. Reported as "Value of the Classics in an Education Very Great Is Claim of Dr. Leacock; Favours Organized Athletics But Is Against Playoffs on Neutral Ground — Described His Life at College — Scored Materialism and Co-education — Regrets Passing of Cap and Gown," *McGill Daily*, 17 December 1924, pp. 1, 3.

E24.53  17 December. Montreal, Quebec. ["The Canadian Economy"]. See D24.10.

*E24.54 30 December. Nassau, Bahamas. "Frenzied Fiction."

## 1925

E25.1  13 January. Saint John, New Brunswick. Canadian Club. Reported as "Gleam of Light Seen by Leacock; Believes Canada Can Be Saved if Dominion Follows His Advice; Immigration Essential," *Toronto Globe*, 14 January 1925, p. 3.

E25.2  14 January. Kentville, Nova Scotia. "Frenzied Fiction."

E25.3  15 January. Yarmouth, [Nova Scotia]. "Frenzied Fiction."

E25.4  15 January. Halifax, Nova Scotia. McGill [University] Graduates. "Frenzied Fiction."

E25.5  16 January. Halifax, Nova Scotia. Majesty Theatre. In support of Halifax Infants Home. "Frenzied Fiction." Reported as "Record Audience Enjoy Humorist," *Halifax Herald*, 17 January 1925, p. 2. The report states that this is the fourth time Leacock has appeared in Halifax. See also D25.1.

E25.6  17 January. Moncton, New Brunswick. City Hall. Reported as "Frenzied Fiction Discussed by Leacock. Noted Canadian Humorist Lectured to Large Audience Here Saturday Night," *Moncton Daily Times*, 19 January 1925, p. 8.

E25.7  c. 27 January. Kingston, [Ontario?]. "Frenzied Fiction."

E25.8  19 February. Toronto, Ontario. Life Underwriters' Association of Canada. "Private Enterprise Versus the State." See D25.2.

E25.9  23 or 24 February. Pittsburgh, Pennsylvania. Bellevue High School.

E25.10  24 or 25 February. Philadelphia, Pennsylvania. Philadelphia Forum at Academy of Music.

E25.11  3 March. Montreal, Quebec. Presbyterian College. "Political, Economic and Social Betterment." Reported as "Dr. Leacock on Economics and the Problems of Society," *McGill Daily*, 4 March 1925, p. 1.

E25.12  10 March. Ottawa, Ontario. Special Committee to Consider the Amendments to the Canadian Copyright Act. See D25.3.

E25.13  2 April. St. Louis, [Missouri]. Teachers. "Education As a Personal Asset."
LEACOCK'S NOTES: "Radio, Curbstone, Ronald, Snoops."

E25.14  3 April. Indianapolis, [Indiana]. Contem[porary] Club.
LEACOCK'S NOTES: "Phila[delphia] Program" [see E25.10].

E25.15  4 April. Indiana Sta[te] College.
LEACOCK'S NOTES: Phila[delphia] Program" [see E25.10].

E25.16  4 May. New Concord, Ohio. Muskingum College.

E25.17  4, 5 May. [Granville, Ohio]. Denison College.

E25.18  21–3 May. Montreal, Quebec. McGill University. Canadian Historical Association. "Local History in Canada." See D25.4.

E25.19  1 July. Orillia, Ontario. Speech in honour of Samuel de Champlain.

E25.20  10 July. Chicago, Illinois. University of Chicago. "Literature & Progress."
LEACOCK'S NOTES: "Radio, Philip, Curbstone, Attaboy, Raft"; 1 page.

E25.21  14 October. New York, New York. [illegible] Club. "Frenzied Fiction."

E25.22  15 October. Kingston, Ontario. Queen's University Alumnae. "The Work of Canadian Universities." See C26.13 and D25.5.

E25.23  17 October. Worcester, Massachusetts. Clark University. "Frenzied Fiction."


## 1926

E26.1  ?23 February. Ottawa, Ontario. Ottawa Valley McGill Graduates and the Professional Institute of the Civil Service. "The Work of the Universities." Reported as "Cannot Legislate a College Curriculum; Dr. S. Leacock in Interesting Luncheon Talk", *Ottawa Citizen*, 24 February 1926, p. 2. See C26.13 and D26.1.

E26.2  16 June. Orillia, Ontario. Liberal-Conservative Association picnic at Couchiching Beach Park. Leacock acted as chairman, introducing the Premier of Ontario, G. Howard Ferguson, and gave a short address afterward. Leacock's remarks were not quoted or summarized in the report, "Premier Ferguson Speaks to East Simcoe Electors Following Opening of Bridge at Narrows," *Orillia News-Letter*, 23 June 1926, p. 13.

E26.3  3 August. Orillia, Ontario. Opera House. Leacock entertained Prime Minister Arthur Meighen and Meighen's wife at his home, then accompanied them to the political rally where he acted as chairman. Two sentences from his introduction of Meighen and two sentences from his introduction of local candidate, A.B. Thompson, are paraphrased in "Premier Meighen Addressed Two Large Audiences Last Night," *Orillia News-Letter*, 4 August 1926, p. 4.

E26.4  10 September. Orillia, Ontario. Opera House. Leacock chaired a meeting of Conservatives where candidate A.B. Thompson spoke.

E26.5  24 September. New York, New York. Hotel Astor. American Society for the Control of Cancer. See D26.2.

E26.6  1 November. Orillia, Ontario. Opera House. Reported as "Premier Ferguson Loudly Acclaimed by Large Audience as He Outlines His Policy; William Finlayson Chosen as Standard Bearer for East Simcoe — Mr. Finlayson and Prof. Leacock Also Deliver Stirring Addresses", *Orillia News-Letter*, 3 November 1926, p. 3; two paragraphs of Leacock's speech are paraphrased.

E26.7  11 November. Montreal, Quebec. McGill Commercial Society. McGill Union. "Business and Bunk."
LEACOCK'S NOTES: "Purpose to Discuss the Business man and how he is made"; 2 pages.

E26.8  22 November. [Montreal, Quebec]. University Club. "Fighting the Liquor Fiend in Ontario."
LEACOCK'S NOTES: 5 pages.

## 1927

**E27.1**  10 January. Ottawa, Ontario. Professional Institute of the Civil Service. "Some Aspects of Political Economy in Especial Relation to Public Policy in Canada."
LEACOCK'S NOTES: "University Extension Course." See D27.1.

**E27.2**  7 February. Ottawa, Ontario. Professional Institute of the Civil Service. ["Gold"].
LEACOCK'S NOTES: "University Extension Course." See D27.2.

**E27.3**  10 February. Montreal, Quebec. Delta Sigma Society. "Literature and Progress." Reported as "The Slip of a Girl Overdone in Fiction," *McGill Daily*, 11 February 1917, p. 1.

**E27.4**  8 March. Montreal, Quebec. Women's Guild. St. George's Church. "Education of Children." See D27.3.

**E27.5**  7 May. Toronto, Ontario. McGill Society of Toronto. See D27.4.

**E27.6**  17 August. [Ste. Anne de Bellevue]. McGill University. Macdonald Agricultural College. Group of British Journalists Touring Canada. See D27.5.

**E27.7**  22 October. Montreal, Quebec. Women's Press Club. "The Art of Bad Language."
LEACOCK'S NOTES: 3 pages.

**E27.8**  10 November. Montreal, Quebec. Junior League. Ritz-Carlton Hotel. ["Books"]. See D27.6.

**E27.9**  23 November. Montreal, Quebec. McGill Literary and Debating Society. Reported as "Thompson Has No Influence on Relations," *McGill Daily*, 24 November 1927, p. 1. Bill Thompson was an Illinois mayor.

**E27.10**  25 November. Chicago, Illinois. Fortnightly Club. "Literature & Press."
LEACOCK'S NOTES: 1 page.

## 1928

**E28.1**  19 January. Providence, Rhode Island. The British Empire Club. "This Present Age, Up to Right Now."
LEACOCK'S NOTES: 1 page.

**E28.2**  Note: Leacock was to lecture on "Railway Rates in Canada" and "Economic Conditions in the Maritimes and Their Causes," for the Department of Extra-Mural Relations in Quebec. This is reported in "Taschereau Enrolls Economics Course," *McGill Daily*, 20 January 1928, pp. 1, 4. The dates of the lectures are not given.

**E28.3**  25 January. Montreal, Quebec. McGill University. Anti-Cancer Speech. See D28.1.

**E28.4**  1 February. Lachine, Quebec. "The Present Moment in Journalism & Literature."

**E28.5**  3 February. Quebec City, Quebec. "Investment of American Capital in Canada."
LEACOCK'S NOTES: 4 pages.

**E28.6**  6 February. Montreal, Quebec. Women's Guild. Christ Church Cathedral. See D28.2.

**E28.7**  11 February. Pawling, New York. Pawling School. "The Present Moment."
LEACOCK'S NOTES: "Press Pictures and Fiction Up to Date"; 1 page.

**E28.8**  21 February. Montreal, Quebec. Westmount Association of Protestant Teachers. On American Movies. See D28.3.

**E28.9**  1 March. Montreal, Quebec. McGill University. Economics Club. Reported as

"Problems of Waterways Elucidated," *McGill Daily*, 2 March 1928, p. 1. Leacock's remarks came at the end of the meeting, following the formal speeches.

E28.10   6 March. Montreal, Quebec. McGill Women's Union. Strathcona Hall.
LEACOCK'S NOTES: "Our Academic Freedom, Our Freedom from Legislative Control"; 1 page. See D28.4.

E28.11   13 March. [Montreal, Quebec]. University Club.
LEACOCK'S NOTES: "Dinner to Lord Willingdon, [Governor General of Canada]"; 1 page.

E28.12   23 March. Carbondale, Illinois. Southern Illinois Teachers Association. "Education & Democ[racy]."
LEACOCK'S NOTES: 3 talks.

E28.13   18 April. Pittsburgh, Pennsylvania. University of Pittsburgh. "Frenzied Fiction." The programme is extant.

E28.14   25 April. Rochester, New York. City Club. "My Discovery of England."
LEACOCK'S NOTES: 2 pages.

E28.15   14 May. Detroit, Michigan. Teachers Association. "Literature at Its Lightest and Latest."
LEACOCK'S NOTES: 1 page.

E28.16   19 June. Hamilton, Ohio. Hamilton High School Graduation.
LEACOCK'S NOTES: "Address change to Attaboy, etc."

E28.17   19 June. Dayton, Ohio. Women's Press Club.
LEACOCK'S NOTES: "6 o'clock. Dayton Business College Grad."

E28.18   2 July. Kalamazoo, Michigan. State College. Summer Session. "On the Teaching & Writing of English."
LEACOCK'S NOTES: 1 page.

E28.19   8 October. Columbus, Ohio. Women's Club. Memorial Hall. "Frenzied Fiction."
LEACOCK'S NOTES: 1 page.

E28.20   16 October. South Bend, Indiana. Knife And Fork Club. "Literature and Progress (Are we moving forward, backward or sideways?)"
LEACOCK'S NOTES: 1 page. The programme is also extant.

E28.21   30 October. Syracuse, New York. Faculty Club. Baptist Auditorium. "Drama."
LEACOCK'S NOTES: 1 page.

E28.22   10 November. Canton, Ohio. Women's Club.

E28.23   11 November. Hamilton, Ohio. Women's Club.
LEACOCK'S NOTES: "Adventure Stories, Ned, Miss Middleton, Croyden, Detective, Curbstone"; 2 pages.

E28.24   15 November. Hartford, Connecticut. "Literature at its Lightest and Latest."
LEACOCK'S NOTES: 1 page.

E28.25   22 November. Buffalo, New York. Rotary Club. "Frenzied Fiction."
LEACOCK'S NOTES: 1 page.

E28.26   22 November. Rochester, New York. "Further Foolishness."
LEACOCK'S NOTES: 1 page.

E28.27   27 November. Manchester, New Hampshire. The Institute.

LEACOCK'S NOTES: "Detective, Curbstone, Ronald, Middleton, Snoops."

E28.28  3 December. Cleveland, Ohio. Alber's Lecture Course. New Music Hall. "Further Foolishness."
LEACOCK'S NOTES: 2 pages.

E28.29  8 December. Cleveland, Ohio. City Club or Commercial Club. "Things of Today."
LEACOCK'S NOTES: "International Situation, Next War, Our Language, Attaboy, The Language of Love, Moving Pictures"; 1 page. Two different sponsoring groups are recorded in two entries in different Leacock lecture notebooks.

E28.30  13 December. Montreal, Quebec. Delta Sigma Society. Royal Victoria College. Reported as "Leacock Speaks at Delta Sig Amid Uproar," *McGill Daily*, 14 December 1928, p. 1. The speech covered a variety of topics, including the dangers of the press regarding attacks made by it on women, the next war, literature and love stories.

## 1929

E29.1  16 January. Washington, D.C. Trinity College.
LEACOCK'S NOTES: "Detective, Physiological Stuff, Curbstone, Poetry, Attaboy, Love Stories, Ronald, Snoops"; 1 page. See also E29.2, also dated 16 January in Leacock's lecture notebooks.

E29.2  16 January. Akron, Ohio. Women's Club.
LEACOCK'S NOTES: "Detective, Margaret, Curbstone, Attaboy, Poetry, Snoops"; 1 page. See also E29.1, also dated 16 January in Leacock's lecture notebooks.

E29.3  17 January. Pittsburgh, Pennsylvania.
LEACOCK'S NOTES: "Detective, Heroine, Curbstone, Poetry, Attaboy, Love, Ronald, Middleton, Snoops"; 1 page.

E29.4  12 February. Ann Arbor, Michigan. University of Michigan. "Frenzied Fiction."
LEACOCK'S NOTES: 1 page.

E29.5  19 February. Newton (Boston), Massachusetts. "Frenzied Fiction."
LEACOCK'S NOTES: 1 page.

E29.6  2 March. Cooperstown, New York. The Knox School.
LEACOCK'S NOTES: "Dickens, Pickwick, Oliver Twist, Nicholas N[ickleby], Bleak House, Hard Times, M[ark] Twain, Huck Finn, Yankee"; 1 page.

E29.7  18 March. Montreal, Quebec. Women's Canadian Club. "Function of a University."
See D29.1.

E29.8  28 April. Philadelphia, Pennsylvania. Young Men's & Young Women's Hebrew Association. "Frenzied Fiction."
LEACOCK'S NOTES: 1 page.

E29.9  29 April. Morgantown, West Virginia. University of West Virginia.
LEACOCK'S NOTES: "Detective, Curbstone, Poetry, Love Stories, Ronald, Kate M[iddleton], Snoops"; 1 page.

E29.10  30 April. Delaware, Ohio. Wesleyan University. See E29.9 for notes.

E29.11  [1 May]. Sandusky, Ohio. High School. See E29.9 for notes.

E29.12  22 May. Ottawa, Ontario. Economic Association.
LEACOCK'S NOTES: "Study of Political Econ[omy] in Canada"; 2 pages.

**E29.13** 9 July. Kalamazoo, Michigan. "Writing and Teaching English."
LEACOCK'S NOTES: 1 page.

**E29.14** 11 July. Columbia, Missouri. University of Missouri. "Writing and Teaching English."
LEACOCK'S NOTES: "See Kalamazoo 1928." He lectured on 12 July 1928 on this topic and it appears from his notebooks that he did again on 9 July 1929. See E28.18 and E29.13.

**E29.15** 12 July. Kirksville, Missouri. University of Missouri.
LEACOCK'S NOTES: "See Kalamazoo" (E29.13). The university is in Columbia; perhaps this lecture may have been to an alumni group.

**E29.16** 5 November. Montreal, Quebec. Rotary Club. See D29.2.

**E29.17** 21 November. [Montreal?, Quebec]. Medical Societies. "Standardisation of Education."

## 1930

**E30.1** 8 February. Montreal, Quebec. Medical Banquet. See D30.1.

**E30.2** 9 April. [Montreal, Quebec]. Board of Trade Address.
LEACOCK'S NOTES: 2 pages. See D30.2.

**E30.3** 26 September. Midland, [Ontario]. Church of England Guild.
LEACOCK'S NOTES: "Detective, John Curbstone, Poetry, Love Stories, Lord Ronald, The Rough Stuff, Miss Croyden on the Raft"; 1 page.

## 1931

**E31.1** 20 March. Montreal, Quebec. Windsor Hotel. Montreal Junior Board of Trade. ["The Soviet Union"]. See D31.1.

**E31.2** 16 May. Lewiston, Maine. Bates College. Federated Women's Club. "Literature at its Lightest and Latest."
LEACOCK'S NOTES: There are three different sets of notes; 3 pages.

**E31.3** 30 June. Kalamazoo, Michigan. Western State Teachers' College.
LEACOCK'S NOTES: "Next War, Radio, Hastings & Rubberneck, College Stuff"; 1 page.

**E31.4** 14 July. Orillia, Ontario. Library Institute. See D31.2.

**E31.5** October. Quebec. Protestant Teachers' Association. See D31.3.

**E31.6** 9 November. Geneva, New York. Teachers' Association. "Literature at its Lightest."
LEACOCK'S NOTES: 1 page.

**E31.7** 10 November. Syracuse, New York. Kiwanis Club Lunch. "Peace and Prosperity."
LEACOCK'S NOTES: 1 page.

**E31.8** 10 November. Syracuse, New York. Monarch Club. "This New World We Live in."
LEACOCK'S NOTES: 1 page.

**E31.9** 9 December. Montreal, Quebec. Builders Exchange. See D31.4.

## 1932

**E32.1** 26 January. Montreal, Quebec. Mount Royal Hotel. Women's Canadian Club. ["Gold Standard"].

E32.2  4 February. Montreal, Quebec. Royal Victoria College. McGill University Alumnae Society. ["Gold Standard"]. See D32.1.

E32.3  19 February. Cincinnati, Ohio. University of Cincinnati. Business & Professional Men's Group Lectures. "The National Problems of Canada."
LEACOCK'S NOTES:  1 page. See D32.2.

E32.4  26 February. Cleveland, Ohio. Advertising Club. "Glimpses of the Future."
LEACOCK'S NOTES:  3 pages. According to Leacock's correspondence, this was broadcast over the NBC-WEAF network.

E32.5  27 February. Cincinnati, Ohio. Commercial Club. "The Future".
LEACOCK'S NOTES:  1 page. See D32.3.

E32.6  23 March. Westmount [Montreal, Quebec]. Victoria Hall. Dickens Fellowship. "Is Edwin Drood Alive?" Reported as "Mystery of Edwin Drood Worked out; Leacock Offers Solution and Analyzes Dickens' First and Last Novels," *Montreal Gazette*, 23 March 1932, p. 14.

E32.7  5 April. Montreal, Quebec. Canadian Institute of Mining and Metallurgy.
LEACOCK'S NOTES:  "Gold — Danger of collapse of value if not used as money." See C32.9.

E32.8  7 April. Montreal, Quebec. Graduates' Club.
LEACOCK'S NOTES:  "College Stuff, the College Band"; 1 page.

E32.9  21 May. Bridgeport, Connecticut. "Teaching & Writing English."
LEACOCK'S NOTES:  1 page.

E32.10  29 June. Orillia, Ontario. Kiwanis Club Boys' Camp. Joint meeting of the Toronto Downtown Kiwanis Club and the Orillia Kiwanis Club. On the Ottawa Economic Conference. See D32.4.

E32.11  11 November. Montreal, Quebec. University Club.
LEACOCK'S NOTES:  "28th Ann[iversary]."

E32.12  14 November. Utica, New York. St. Francis de Sales Auditorium. University Club. This entry appears on the same page and above the 11 November lecture; the 14 November date comes from Leacock's correspondence.

## 1933

E33.1  1 January. Montreal, Quebec. Russian Five-Year Plan. See D33.2.

E33.2  9 January. Montreal, Quebec. American College of Physicians. "The Waste Spaces in Modern Education."
LEACOCK'S NOTES:  2 pages. Leacock's notebook gives the date of this lecture as 9 February. See D33.1.

E33.3  26 January. Montreal, Quebec. Women's Canadian Club. ["The Riddle of the Depression"]. See D33.3.

E33.4  3 February. Cincinnati, Ohio. University of Cincinnati. Business & Professional Men's Group. See D33.4.

E33.5  6 February. Montreal, Quebec. Christ Church Women's Guild. "The Ancient Victorians."
LEACOCK'S NOTES:  1 page.

E33.6  9 February. Montreal, Quebec. Windsor Hotel. American College of Physicians. See D33.5.

E33.7  11 February. Buffalo, New York. Buffalo Athletic Club. Lincoln Day Dinner. "Lincoln and American Humor."
LEACOCK'S NOTES: 2 pages. The programme is extant.

E33.8  16 February. Toronto, Ontario. Empire Club. "The Riddle of the Depression." See C33.1.

E33.9  28 February. Minneapolis, Minnesota. Kappa Delta Pi. "Freedom & Compulsion in Education."
LEACOCK'S NOTES: 1 page.

E33.10  28 March. Quebec City, Quebec. Women's Canadian Club. "Education by the Yard."
LEACOCK'S NOTES: "Much the same as Minneapolis." See E33.9 and D33.6.

E33.11  30 March. Montreal, Quebec. McGill Commercial Society. "Redemption after Graduation." See D33.7.

E33.12  late April. Chicago, Illinois. English-Speaking Union. The lecture was a few days before 28 April.

E33.12a  May. Ottawa. Canadian Political Science Association. "The Economic Analysis of the Depression." See C33.6.

E33.13  9 June. Toronto, Ontario. University College Alumni Association dinner. University of Toronto. Hart House. "On Recovery from Graduation." Reported as "University Alumni Gather Once Again at Dinner Reunion; Stephen Leacock Doubts Tendencies of Modern Universities," *Toronto Globe*, 10 June 1933, p. 3, and as "Conferred First Degree in '83 Sir William Mulock Recalls," *Toronto Mail and Empire*, p. 4. The report in the *Globe* has one paragraph of paraphrased remarks.

E33.14  Ottawa, Ontario. Although undated and with no other information provided, this entry appears between E33.13 and E33.15 in Leacock's lecture notebooks.

E33.15  17 June. Lake Forest, Illinois. Academy. Seventy-Fifth Year Celebration. "Ideals in Education."
LEACOCK'S NOTES: "Minneapolis program + add & insert Shakespeare Criticism & Tennyson 'Crossing the Bar.'" See E33.9.

E33.16  17 June (evening). Lake Forest, Illinois. Mrs. Laplin's [Laflin's] House. "Literature at its Latest and Lightest."
LEACOCK'S NOTES: 1 page.

E33.17  27 June. Kalamazoo, Michigan. Western State Teachers College. "Education by the Yard."

E33.18  10 August. Lake Couchiching, Ontario. Canadian Institute on Economics and Politics. "Ways Out of the Depression." See D33.8.

E33.19  9 October. [Montreal?, Quebec]. Protestant Teachers of Quebec.

E33.20  16 October. Sioux City, Iowa. Association of University Women. "Recovery after Graduation." According to Leacock's correspondence the lecture took place on 16 October, but according to the notebooks he was lecturing in Minneapolis that day.

E33.21  17 October. Minneapolis, Minnesota. Women's Club. Lunch. "Literature at its Lightest."
LEACOCK'S NOTES: 1 page.

E33.22  16–7 October. Minneapolis, Minnesota. English Teachers Club. Evening. "Teaching and Writing English."
LEACOCK'S NOTES: 1 page written on post card.

E33.23  St. Paul, [Minnesota]. This undated entry appears between the above entry and E33.27 in Leacock's lecture notebooks.

E33.24  18 October. Minneapolis, Minnesota. Minneapolis College Women's Club. "Education by the Yard."

E33.25  18 October. Minnesota Historical Society. "Lahontan in Minnesota." See D33.9.

E33.26  19 October. Minneapolis, [Minnesota]. University of Minnesota Convocation. "Technique of Humor."

E33.27  2 December. Detroit, Michigan. National Council of Teachers of English. "Resuscitation After Apparent Graduation." See C34.7.

## 1934

E34.1  1 February. Burlington, Vermont. Women's Club. "Literature at Its Lightest and Latest."
LEACOCK'S NOTES: 1 page. See D34.1.

E34.2  3 February. Boston, Massachusetts. The Beacon Society. (Dinner at the Algonquin Club.) "The Technique of Humour or How to Be Funny When You Try."
LEACOCK'S NOTES: 1 page.

E34.3  4 February. Boston, Massachusetts. Algonquin Club. "A Conversation: Literature at Its Lightest."
LEACOCK'S NOTES: "In this talk I kept going for 3/4 of an hour without any other material than the Detective & Curbstone by putting in all sorts of side issues & excursions."

E34.4  27 February. Westmount [Montreal, Quebec]. Dickens Fellowship. Victoria Hall. "Charles Dickens & Women." See D34.2.

E34.5  2 March. Detroit, Michigan. Detroit Town Hall Friday Morning Series. Cass Theatre. "Frenzied Fiction."
LEACOCK'S NOTES: 3 pages.

E34.6  5 March. Detroit, Michigan. Highland Park Senior? College. "Brotherly Love Among the Nations."
LEACOCK'S NOTES: "(first time [this lecture was] given)"; 1 page.

E34.7  6 March. Toronto, Ontario. McGill Society of Toronto. On Athletic Scholarships. See D34.3.

E34.8  15 March. Montreal, Quebec. Strathcona Hall. McGill Graduate Students. "The Advancement of Learning."
LEACOCK'S NOTES: "As at Toronto." Reported as "Leacock Raps Rise of Spectatorial Collegiate Sports," McGill Daily, 16 March 1934, p. 1. See C34.7.

E34.9  20 March. Boston, Massachusetts. Tavern Club.
LEACOCK'S NOTES: "The Intellectually [sic] Tyranny of the Lower Class, Attaboy, Lincoln,

My Discovery, The Moving Picture, Our Colleges, 'Sex Appeal' "; 1 page.

**E34.10**  29 March. Buffalo, New York. Rotary Club. "Slams Across the Sea or Why We Love Everybody."
LEACOCK'S NOTES: 1 page.

**E34.11**  12 April. Plattsburg, New York. "This Rapid Age."

**E34.12**  5 May. East Northfield, [Massachusetts].

**E34.13**  18 May. Toronto, Ontario. International Advertising Club. "The Philosophy of Publicity." See D34.4.

**E34.14**  21 May. Montreal, Quebec. Canadian Political Science Association and Canadian Historical Association. Presidential Address. "The Revision of Democracy." See C34.8 and D34.5.

**E34.15**  8 June. Midland, Ontario. Political speech for Hon. William Finlayson, the provincial Conservative candidate for East Simcoe.

**E34.16**  13 June. Washago, Ontario. Political speech for Hon. William Finlayson.

**E34.17**  21 June. Lennoxville, Quebec. Bishop's University. Convocation Address on Receiving the degree D.C.L. Honoris Causa.

**E34.18**  20 July. Grand Rapids, Michigan. International Lions' Convention. "How Soon Can We Start the Next War."
LEACOCK'S NOTES: 1 page.

**E34.19**  6 October. Toronto, Ontario. McGill Society of Ontario. Reported as "New McGill Society Organized Saturday for Ontario Section," *McGill Daily*, 9 October 1934, p. 1.

**E34.20**  19 October. Indianapolis, Indiana. Luncheon given by the University of Indiana. "Humour as a College Curriculum."
LEACOCK'S NOTES: 1 page.

**E34.21**  19 October. Indianapolis, Indiana. Indiana State Teachers' Convention. "Education by the Yard."
LEACOCK'S NOTES: 1 page.

**E34.22**  29 October. Chicago (Evanston), Illinois. Illinois State Teachers. "Education & Democracy."
LEACOCK'S NOTES: 1 page.

**E34.23**  29 October. Chicago (Oak Park), Illinois. "Social Teaching of the Greater Humorists."
LEACOCK'S NOTES: 1 page.

**E34.24**  30 October. Chicago, Illinois. Council of Foreign Relations. Palmer House House Lunch. "How Soon Can We Start the Next War?"
LEACOCK'S NOTES: 1 page.

**E34.25**  31? October. Chicago, Illinois. Northwestern University. "How Soon Can We Start the Next War?"

**E34.26**  1 November. [Montreal, Quebec]. McGill University. Commerce Students. "The United States." See D34.7.

**E34.27**  5 November. Pittsburgh, Pennsylvania. Twentieth Century Club. "Frenzied Fiction."
LEACOCK'S NOTES: 1 page.

E34.28  5 November. Pittsburgh, Pennsylvania. Dickens Fellowship. "An Estimate of Charles Dickens."
LEACOCK'S NOTES: "Informal Talk at Mrs. F[illegible]'s house"; 1 page.

E34.29  6 November. Pittsburgh, Pennsylvania. Carnegie Tech. "How Soon Can We Start the Next War."
LEACOCK'S NOTES: "Same as Chicago but shorter"; 2 pages. See E34.24.

E34.30  15 December. Montreal, Quebec. Bishop's College School Old Boys' Dinner. Mount Royal Hotel. Reported as "Professor Leacock Addresses Old Boys; Gives Talk to Graduates of Bishop's College," *Montreal Daily Star*, 17 December 1934, p. 8; as "Ideals of School Years Binding; Tie Precious Qualities Often Not Early Realized, Says Stephen Leacock. . . . ," *Montreal Gazette*, 17 December 1934, p. 5. Leacock speech touched on memories of schooldays and the friendships formed during that period.

E34.31  17 December. Montreal, Quebec. Dinner of Class of 1932 at the Samovar. "The Theory of Comic & Super Comic Verse."
LEACOCK'S NOTES: 1 page.

## 1935

E35.1  14 January. Charleston, Illinois. State Teachers' College. "How Soon Can We Start the Next War."
LEACOCK'S NOTES: "See Chicago & Pittsburgh" [E34.24 and E34.29]; 1 page.

E35.2  15 January. St. Louis, Missouri. International Mark Twain Society.
LEACOCK'S NOTES: "Speech on Mark Twain in acknowledging award of medal by International Mark Twain Society." See D35.1.

E35.3  16 January. Columbia, Missouri. University of Missouri. Mark Twain Centennial Meeting. "Mark Twain & American Humour."
LEACOCK'S NOTES: 1 page.

E35.4  17 January. Cedar Rapids, Iowa. Town Hall Lecture Series. "Education by the Yard."
LEACOCK'S NOTES: 1 page.

E35.5  18 January. Des Moines, Iowa. University Club. "Education by the Yard."
LEACOCK'S NOTES: "Same as Cedar Rapids [E35.4] but with Augustus as a tale piece."

E35.6  30 January. Toronto, Ontario. University of Toronto. Hart House Debate. "Democracy." The programmme is extant. The question for debate was "That in the opinion of this House representative democratic government as understood in the nineteenth century no longer fits the age in which we live." See D35.2.

E35.7  5 February. St. Lambert, Quebec. "Frenzied Fiction."
LEACOCK'S NOTES: 1 page.

E35.8  9 February. New York, New York. American Institute of Bankers. Waldorf Astoria Hotel. "How Soon Can We Start the Next War."
LEACOCK'S NOTES: 1 page. See D35.3.

E35.9  14 February. Montreal, Quebec. University Settlement Annual Dinner.
LEACOCK'S NOTES: 1 page on slum clearance. See D35.4.

E35.10  18 February. Green Bay, Wisconsin. "Frenzied Fiction."

LEACOCK'S NOTES: 1 page.

E35.11   18 February. Green Bay, Wisconsin. "Literature & Progress."
LEACOCK'S NOTES: 1 page.

E35.12   18 February. Appleton, Wisconsin. "How Soon Can We Start the Next War?"
LEACOCK'S NOTES: 1 page.

E35.13   1 March. Annapolis, Maryland. United States Naval Academy. "The New World We Live in."
LEACOCK'S NOTES: 1 page.

E35.14   7 March. Montreal, Quebec. Mount Royal Hotel. Notre Dame de Grace Women's Club. "How Soon Can We Start the Next War?" See D35.5.

E35.15   9 March. Detroit, Michigan. Detroit Schoolmen's Club Luncheon. "Waste Spaces in Mod[ern] Educ[ation]."
LEACOCK'S NOTES: 1 page.

E35.16   9 March. Windsor, Ontario. The McGill Society Graduates' Dinner. Prince Ed[ward] Hotel. "The Colleges & the Public."
LEACOCK'S NOTES: 1 page. See D35.6 and C63.1.

E35.17   12 March. Westmount [Montreal, Quebec]. Mechanics' Institute. Quebec Library Association. "English as an Instrument of Expression." See D35.7.

E35.18   20 March. Glens Falls, New York. [Public School] Teachers Association. "Social Teaching of the Greater Humorists."
LEACOCK'S NOTES: 1 page.

E35.19   21 March. Glens Falls, New York. Rotary [Club]. "How Soon Can We Start the Next War?"
LEACOCK'S NOTES: 1 page.

E35.20   26 March. Lachine, Quebec. [Lachine Protestant] Teachers Association. See D35.8.

E35.21   2 April. Montreal, Quebec. McGill Alumnae R[oyal] V[ictoria] C[ollege]. See D35.9.

E35.22   9 April. Beauharnois, Quebec. Parents and Teachers Association.

E35.23   13 May. Lafayette, Indiana. Purdue University. Annual Literary Banquet. "This College Stuff."
LEACOCK'S NOTES: 1 page.

E35.24   15 May. New York, New York. Cancer Control Committee. Plaza Hotel. "The Conquest of Disease." See D35.10.

E35.25   23 May. New York, New York. Iron & Steel Institute.
LEACOCK'S NOTES: "Things Round the Corner, Peace & War, Specialisation, Education"; 1 page.

E35.26   4 June. Baltimore, Maryland. Goucher College Commencement. "Humor as a Serious Matter."
LEACOCK'S NOTES: 1 page. The commencement programme is extant.

E35.27   11 June. Orillia, Ontario. Board of Trade Supper. "The Outlook of the World at Large, the Outlook for Canada, and the Outlook for Our Own Town." See D35.11.

**E35.28**  23 August. Brantford, Ontario. McGill Society Dinner.
LEACOCK'S NOTES: 1 page.

**E35.29**  21 September. Midland, Ontario.
LEACOCK'S NOTES: "Elections Speech in support of John Drinkwater, the Conservative candidate in East Simcoe"; 2 pages. See D35.12.

**E35.30**  23 September. Coldwater, Ontario.
LEACOCK'S NOTES: "Repeat with variations" [E35.29].

**E35.31**  24 September. Orillia, Ontario. West Ward.
LEACOCK'S NOTES: "Repeat with variations" [E35.29].

**E35.32**  26 September. Montreal, Quebec. Mount Royal Club Dinner. Dinner of Sir Edward Beatty to His Excellency Lord Bessborough.
LEACOCK'S NOTES: 1 page.

**E35.33**  1 October. Montreal, Quebec. United Service Club Lunch. "What I Don't Know About Abyssinia and What You Don't."
LEACOCK'S NOTES: 2 pages.

**E35.34**  3 October. Coaticook, Quebec. Elections Speech.
LEACOCK'S NOTES: 1 page. Pasted on the page of Leacock's notebook is an unidentified, untitled fragment of a newsclipping quoting Leacock on the C.C.F. and the Liberal Party.

**E35.35**  12 October. Montreal, Quebec. Elections Speech. Mount Royal Riding.
LEACOCK'S NOTES: 1 page.

**E35.36**  15 October. Iowa City, Iowa. State University of Iowa. "How Soon Can We Start the Next War?"
LEACOCK'S NOTES: 1 page.

**E35.37**  16 October. Mason City, Iowa. Women's Club. "Education by the Yard."
LEACOCK'S NOTES: "See Cedar Rapids Jan. 1935" [E35.4]; 2 pages.

**E35.38**  17 October. Warrensburg, Missouri. District Teachers Convention. "Education & Democracy."
LEACOCK'S NOTES: "Practically same as yesterday."

**E35.39**  October. Warrensburg, Missouri. "Social Teachings of the Greater Humorists."
LEACOCK'S NOTES: 1 page.

**E35.40**  18 October. Kirksville, Missouri. "Social Teaching of the Greater Humorists."
LEACOCK'S NOTES: A.M.

**E35.41**  18 October. Kirksville, Missouri. "Literature at its Lightest & Latest."
LEACOCK'S NOTES: P.M.; 1 page.

**E35.42**  1 November. Boston, Massachusetts. Essex Co[unty] Teachers Association. Tremont Hall/Temple. "Education and Democracy."
LEACOCK'S NOTES: 1 page. The programme is also extant.

**E35.43**  1 November. Worcester, Massachusetts. Teachers' Convention.
LEACOCK'S NOTES: "Literature Lightest etc." Includes a newspaper photograph of the event from *Worcester Daily Telegraph*.

**E35.44**  8 November. New York, New York. Acadia [University] Alumni Banquet. Midston House.

LEACOCK'S NOTES: "Radio, Hastings, Detective, Attaboy, Detective." The advertising flyer is extant.

E35.45  11 November. Chicago, Illinois. Northwestern University Series. "How Soon Can We Start the Next War?"
LEACOCK'S NOTES: "Same as Iowa City" [see E35.36].

E35.46  21 November. Montreal, Quebec. Economics Club. Reported as "Stephen Leacock Speaks on Female Question at Economics Club," *McGill Daily*, 22 November 1935, p. 1. See C35.16.

E35.47  7 December. Boston, Massachusetts. Beacons' Club Dinner. "Aspects of Mark Twain."
LEACOCK'S NOTES: 1 page.

E35.48  8 December. Boston, Massachusetts. Algonquin Club. "Frenzied Fiction Up to Date."
LEACOCK'S NOTES: 1 page. The programme, indicating this was a luncheon speech, is extant.

E35.49  9 December. Boston, Massachusetts. New England Women's Luncheon Club. "Mark Twain."
LEACOCK'S NOTES: "Follow Missouri lecture of January 1935."

E35.50  14 December. Montreal, Quebec. Thistle Curling Club Lunch. "Hellements of Hickonomics." Reported as "Prof. Leacock Tells Curler of His Book," *Montreal Standard*, 14 December, Sports Extra section, p. [3]. This report states that Leacock read portions of his new book but does not quote or paraphrase his speech.

## 1936

E36.1  13 January. Philadelphia (Jenkintown Suburb), Pennsylvania. Beaver College. "Literature Lightest & Latest."
LEACOCK'S NOTES: 1 page.

E36.2  30 January. Montreal, Quebec. Royal Victoria College Juniors. See D36.1.

E36.3  3 February. Montreal, Quebec. Twentieth Century Institute [of National Affairs]. Windsor Hotel. "Redistribution of the Undeveloped Territory of the World." See D36.2.

E36.4  7 February. Montreal, Quebec. The Dickens Fellowship Dinner, commemorating the Centenary of "Pickwick." "The Immortal Genius of Charles Dickens." See D36.3. The advertising flyer for this event is extant.

E36.5  11 February. Montreal, Quebec. University of Toronto Alumnae and Alumni. "The Art & Mystery of Language." See D36.4.

E36.6  26 February. Syracuse, New York. [Syracuse] University Department of English. "Frenzied Fiction."
LEACOCK'S NOTES: 1 page.

E36.7  12 March. Aurora, New York. Wells College. "Frenzied Fiction."
LEACOCK'S NOTES: 1 page.

E36.8  25 March. Montreal, Quebec. Berkeley Hotel. McGill University Political Economy Club. Retirement Dinner. See D36.5.

E36.9  2? April. Chicago, Illinois. Wayfarers' Dinner Club.

E36.10   22 April. Buffalo, New York. Buffalo Public Library. Centennial Celebration. "The Art and Mystery of Language." See D36.6.

E36.11   27 April. Chicago, Illinois. The University Club. Dinner Group.
LEACOCK'S NOTES: "Ordinary Curriculum, Mathematics, Method"; 1 page.

E36.12   28 April. Chicago, Illinois. North Shore Congregation. "Is Literature [illegible]."
LEACOCK'S NOTES: "Detective, Sherlock Holmes Saga, Ronald, Love Stories, Love Letters, Croyden, Farmer"; 1 page.

E36.13   April. Chicago (Glencoe), Illinois.

E36.14   4 May. Montreal, Quebec. Dinner at Ritz Carlton
LEACOCK'S NOTES: "given for me by my old students." See D36.7.

E36.15   23 May. Detroit, Michigan. Alumni of Wayne University. "Looking Back on College."
LEACOCK'S NOTES: 4 pages.

E36.16   28 May. Montreal, Quebec. Sir Ed.[ward] Beatty's Lunch.
LEACOCK'S NOTES: "My thanks for LL.D."

E36.17   5 June. Detroit, Michigan. Liggett School Commencement. "Looking Back on College."
LEACOCK'S NOTES: 4 pages.

E36.18   6 June. Greenwich, Connecticut. Greenwich Academy Commencement. "Looking Back on College."
LEACOCK'S NOTES: "Practically same as Detroit" [see E36.17].

E36.19   22 October. Memphis, Tennessee. Western Tennessee Teachers' Association. "Looking Back on College."
LEACOCK'S NOTES: 1 page.

E36.20   23 October. Memphis, Tennessee. English Section Teachers Association. "The Literary Technique of Humour."
LEACOCK'S NOTES: 2 pages.

E36.21   23 October. [Memphis, Tennessee]. Lunch Meeting. "Canada and the United States."
LEACOCK'S NOTES: "See Springfield, Mass. Oct. 30 [E36.23]." "A Little Farewell to Economics" was the original speech scheduled. See D36.8.

E36.22   23 October. Memphis, Tennessee. Southwestern College. Dinner Speech. "How Soon Can We Start the Next War?"
LEACOCK'S NOTES: "Follow Iowa" [see E35.36]. 1 page.

E36.23   30 October. Springfield, Massachusetts. Hampden Co[unty] Teachers. "Literature [at its] Lightest."
LEACOCK'S NOTES: 1 page.

E36.24   30 October. [Springfield, Massachusetts]. Rotary Club Lunch. "United States and Canada."
LEACOCK'S NOTES: 1 page.

E36.25   12 November. Middletown, New York. University Women's Club.
LEACOCK'S NOTES: "Looking Back, Experience, Shakespeare, Poetry, Tennyson"; 1 page.

E36.26   14 November. Amherst, Massachusetts. Amherst College Alumni Council. "How

Soon Can We Start the Next War?"
LEACOCK'S NOTES: 1 page. See C36.28.

E36.27  25 November. Leacock leaves Montreal on a tour of western Canada, sponsored by the Canadian Bankers Association. Unbeknownst to Leacock, ten banks contributed $15,000 to Cockfield, Brown & Co., the tour organizer. Leacock was paid $10,000. Cockfield, Brown had a clipping file of 250 items at the end of the tour; unfortunately, it is no longer extant.

E36.28  27 November. Port Arthur, Ontario. Prince Arthur Hotel. McGill Graduate Society Dinner. "Confederation of Canada." Alternative title, "Our Colleges and What They Stand for." See D36.9.

E36.29  28 November. Fort William, Ontario. Royal Edward Hotel. Mens' & Women's Canadian Club. Royal Edward Hotel Lunch. "Canada and the United States." See D36.10.

E36.30  30 November. Winnipeg, Manitoba. Women's Canadian Club. "Literature at Its Lightest, Latest and Most Foolish." See D36.11.

E36.31  1 December. Winnipeg, Manitoba. University of Manitoba. "Education by the Yard." See D36.12.

E36.32  3 December. Winnipeg, Manitoba. Winnipeg Press Club Dinner. "The Written Word." Reported as "Dr. Leacock Makes Informal Speech at Press Club Dinner," *Winnipeg Tribune*, 4 December 1936, p. 26. This report notes that the speech was off the record but does paraphrase one remark about the importance of the human brain and personality over machines in the delivery of the news.

E36.33  4 December. Winnipeg, Manitoba. Men's Canadian Club. Fort Garry Hotel. "When Can We Start the Next War?" See D36.13.

E36.34  5 December. Winnipeg, Manitoba. Women's University Club. Fort Garry Hotel. "An Analysis of Humor." See D36.14.

E36.35  7 December. Regina, Saskatchewan. Women's Canadian Club. "Literature and Progress."
LEACOCK'S NOTES: 2 pages. See D36.15.

E36.36  8 December. Regina, Saskatchewan. Men's Canadian Club. Hotel Saskatchewan. "Brotherly Love Among the Nations."
LEACOCK'S NOTES: 2 pages. See D36.18.

E36.37  8 December. Regina, Saskatchewan. McGill Graduate Society. "The Value of Imbecility in Education." See also "Speaking in Saskatchewan," *Newspacket* (Orillia, newsletter of the Stephen Leacock Associates) 11, no. 1 (May 1984): [4].

E36.38  10 December. Saskatoon, Saskatchewan. University of Saskatchewan. "Education by the Yard (Standardized Education)."
LEACOCK'S NOTES: 1 page.

E36.39  10 or 11 December. Saskatoon, Saskatchewan. Mens' & Women's Canadian Club and McGill Grad[uates]. Bessborough Hotel & Broadcast. "Murder at $2.50 a Volume and Love at $1.25."
LEACOCK'S NOTES: "Detective, Ronald, Red Love, Blue Island"; 1 page. See also D37.6.

E36.40  14 December. Edmonton, Alberta. University of Alberta. "Recovery after Graduation." See D36.16.

E36.41 15 December. Edmonton, Alberta. Macdonald Hotel. University of Toronto Alumni Dinner. "College as It Was and As It Is." See D36.17.

E36.42 15 December. Edmonton, Alberta. Political Science Club Students. "Is Adam Smith Dead?"
LEACOCK'S NOTES: 1 page.

E36.43 16 December. Edmonton, Alberta. Men's & Womens' Canadian Club and McGill Graduates. Hotel MacDonald. "Debit and Credit." See K92.1.

E36.44 16 December. Edmonton, Alberta. Women's Press Club and Canadian Authors Dinner. MacDonald Hotel. "The Theory of Comic Verse."
LEACOCK'S NOTES: "Same as Winnipeg but Insurance" [E36.32–4]. See D36.19.

E36.45 18 December. Calgary, Alberta. Canadian Club and Board of Trade. Hudson's Bay Dining Room. "Social Credit."
LEACOCK'S NOTES: "Broadcast: S. Alberta"; 1 page. See F36.8.

E36.46 18 December. Calgary, Alberta. Women's Canadian Club. Palliser Hotel. "Frenzied Fiction." See D36.20.

E36.47 18 December. Calgary, Alberta. McGill & Varsity Graduates. Palliser Hotel. Reported as "Leacock Recalls Years at College," *Calgary Daily Herald*, 19 December 1936, p. 14.

E36.48 19 December. Medicine Hat, Alberta. Quota Club Dinner. Hotel Cecil. "Hard Money, or Daniel in the Lion's Den." See D36.21.

E36.49 22 December. Vancouver, British Columbia. Men's Canadian Club. Hotel Vancouver. "The New Economic World."
LEACOCK'S NOTES: 1 page. See D36.22.

E36.50 28 December. Vancouver, British Columbia. Women's Canadian Club, Hotel Vancouver. "Frenzied Fiction: or Murder at Two Fifty a Volume and Love at One Twenty Five."
LEACOCK'S NOTES: "Intro[duction] and then same as Regina" [E36.37]. See D36.25.

E36.51 28 December. Vancouver, British Columbia. Foreign Trade Bureau, Vancouver Board of Trade Dinner. Hotel Vancouver. "Social Credit & Social Progress."
LEACOCK'S NOTES: 1 page. See D36.24.

E36.52 28 December. Vancouver, British Columbia. Board of Trade. "Enjoy the Fruits of Your Labour."

## 1937

E37.1 4 January. Victoria, British Columbia. Canadian Club. Empress Hotel. "Economic Separatism in the British Empire." See D37.1.

E37.2 5 January. Victoria, British Columbia. Women's Canadian Club. Empress Hotel. "Humour As a Serious Manner."
LEACOCK'S NOTES: 1 page. See D37.2.

E37.3 6 January. Victoria, British Columbia. McGill Graduates Association Dinner. Empress Hotel. "Preserving College Traditions." See D37.3.

E37.4 7 January. Victoria, British Columbia. Rotary Club, Empress Hotel. "How Soon Can We Start the Next War?" See D37.4.

**E37.5**  7 January. Victoria, British Columbia. Union Club. Upper Canada College Grads Dinner. "History of Upper Canada College." Reported as "Former Pupils Fete Leacock," *Victoria Daily Times*, 8 January 1937, p. 9

**E37.6**  8 January. Victoria, British Columbia. Victoria Teachers Association. Empress Hotel. "What I Don't Know About Education." Reported as "Leacock Talks to Teachers," *Victoria Daily Times*, 9 January 1937, p. 13.

**E37.7**  13 January. Vancouver, British Columbia. University of British Columbia. "Looking Back on College." See D37.5.

**E37.8**  22 January. Philadelphia, Pennsylvania. Teachers' Association. "Frenzied Fiction." LEACOCK'S NOTES: "Much as before."

**E37.9**  2 February. Watertown, New York. College Women's Club. "Frenzied Fiction."

**E37.10**  15 February. Harrisburg, Pennsylvania. Civic Club. "Frenzied Fiction." LEACOCK'S NOTES: 1 page. See D37.6.

**E37.11**  9 March. Buffalo, New York. Buffalo Ad. Club Lunch. Hotel Statler. "Humour's Commercial [illegible] Value." LEACOCK'S NOTES: "Hot Air & Gas, Politics, Business"; 1 page.

**E37.12**  9 March. Buffalo, New York. Buffalo Teachers' Association. Girls' Vocational High School. "Looking Back on Fifty Years of Teaching."

**1939**

**E39.1**  16 June. Kitchener, Ontario. McGill Association of Ontario. See D39.1.

# F Section: INTERVIEWS

F7.1 [British Empire Tour], *New Zealand Free Lance* (Wellington, N.Z.), 24 August 1907, p. 5. Several sentences are quoted in an untitled column about the interest in the Empire concerning imperial concerns.

F11.1 Anne E. Nias, "Interviews with Authors," *Saturday Night* (Toronto) 25, no. 1, whole no. 1,245 (14 October 1911): 27. Leacock replies to a number of questions — whether he is primarily a professor of political economy or a humorist, whether he has read a review comparing him to Lewis Carroll, etc.

F12.1 Ella May, " 'Never Made a Joke in My Life,' Stephen Leacock Tells . . . ," *Montreal Daily Star*, 2 November 1912. News clipping held at QMM Archives but not located in microfilm edition of the newspaper. Leacock comments on the nature of humour, on writing stories for the press, etc. When asked about his next book, he remarks: "Yes. Put down: 'They say that it is going to deal with the idle rich. It has been whispered on the Stock Exchange that people are avoiding him in the Club.' "

F13.1 "Dr. Leacock and the Naval Bill. No Foundation for the Statement He Is Opposed to It," *Orillia Packet*, 22 May 1913, p. 1. Interview concerning Prime Minister Borden's naval policy during Leacock's "recent" visit to Orillia.

F13.2 "Nominates Prof. Mavor. Prof. Leacock Says He Should Direct Cost of Living Inquiry," *Toronto Evening Telegram*, 2 December 1913, p. 10. An interview in Montreal in which Leacock suggests James Mavor should chair a royal commission on the cost of living; two paragraphs quoted. Leacock said he would serve on the commission under Mavor but only as an unpaid member.

F14.1 "The European War; Dr. Leacock's Views on the Conflict and Its Outcome", *Orillia News Letter*, 12 August 1914, p. 1. An interview upon Leacock's return from a three-month vacation in Europe; many paragraphs are quoted on the French, Germans, British, and the outcome of the war. Leacock predicted "utter ruin" for Germany.

F15.1 "Big Audience Rocks in One Long Laugh; Prof. Stephen Leacock Reads from His Own Work at Windsor Hall for Belgian Relief Problems; of Bergsonian Illusionism and the Relationship to Tea to Problem Plays Explained," *Montreal Gazette*, 23 March 1915, p. 5. Report of Leacock's reading of his works ("Spoof" among others) on 22 March 1915. The report includes an interview in which he comments on the audience's reaction to his humour and to the plight of the Belgians. An editorial that appeared on 24 March 1915 in the *Gazette* apologized to Leacock for the report. See also C15.5, in which Leacock complained about the truthfulness of the interview.

F17.1 "Democracy of the Joke and Lack of German Humor Discussed by Leacock: Famous Canadian Wit Also Gives His Views on the Perversity of the Russian Verb," *New York*

*Times*, 8 April 1917, sec. 6 ("Magazine"), p. 7. Contains several quotations from a recent interview in New York City on subjects in addition to those listed in the title: differences and similarities between the U.S. and Canada, the future of democracy in general and in Russia in particular, and the universality of humour.

F20.1 "Spiritism Is Absurd, Says Leacock; Canadian Humorist Discusses 'Tommyrot' While Sir Oliver Lodge Speaks on the After-Life," *New York Evening Post*, 19 February 1920, pp. 1–2. An interview with Leacock in the Biltmore hotel on the morning of 19 February. At the same time Lodge was speaking in Carnegie Hall. There are quotations about Conan Doyle, Lodge, Sir Ernest Rutherford and Professor Jastrow. With respect to the hereafter he remarks: "And I don't think I'm going to like it. . . . Being snowbound on earth is bad enough, but think of what is in store for us when we pass into the great beyond that Conan Doyle has prepared for us." Reprinted as "Leacock Would 'Lay' All Spirits with Ridicule; Gives an Entertaining Rehearsal Before Interviewer in New York; Hits Lodge and Doyle. . . . ," *Montreal Gazette*, 20 February 1920, p. 6.

F21.1 "Only Two Parties Now; Prof. Leacock's Viewpoint; Liberalism Remains Only as a Name — Forces of Stability Must Merge to Withstand Radical Wave," *Toronto Telegram*, 12 March 1921, p. 23. Brief interview, with quotations, with Leacock at the Prince George hotel; he was on his way to Buffalo.

F21.2 "Here for 'Anti-Drys,' Leacock Praises Laws. Praises Mothers' Pensions and Minimum Wage Legislation — Criticizes Methodist Plans," *Toronto Daily Star*, 2 April 1921, p. 2. Interview, with quotations, mainly about prohibition. There is no discussion of the minimum wage despite the headline. Leacock was in Toronto to speak "that evening." It is noted that his speech is going to be printed in pamphlet form and circulated as "wet" propaganda. See A36a.

F21.3 "Mr. Leacock and Prohibition," *Daily Telegraph* (London), 27 September 1921, p. 7. Interview by the paper's Liverpool correspondent upon Leacock's arrival. There is one quotation on prohibition; the rest concern his upcoming lecture tour of England and Scotland. Leacock left Liverpool for London at the conclusion of the interview.

F21.4 "A Master of Satire. Mr. Stephen Leacock in London. The Secret of Humorous Writing," *Times* (London), 27 September 1921, p. 12. Lengthy interview, containing several quotations, with Leacock on his arrival in London. Reprinted as "Stephen Leacock in England," in *Orillia Packet*, 10 November 1921, p. 4.

F21.5 "Literary Humorist. Mr. Stephen Leacock Comes to Town," *Daily Express* (London), 27 September 1921, p. [5]. Interview, with several paraphrased remarks. Leacock is reported as thinking that *Nonsense Novels* (A7) is his best work, stating it is now used in American classrooms as an example of how not to write. In addition to the four lectures, "Frenzied Fiction," "Literature at Its Lightest," "Drama As I See It," and "Laughing with Leacock," that he was scheduled to give, he said he hoped to talk and write against prohibition about and his scheme for currency reform.

F21.6 "Man Who Enjoys His Own Jokes. Mr. Stephen Leacock in England. Some Stories," *Daily Mail* (London), 27 September 1921, p. 5. Interview, with quotations, which took place at a West End London hotel. A Canadian reporter was also present. That reporter's interview (see F21.8) appeared on 13 October 1921.

F21.7 "Leacock Lurking in the Limelight; In England to Make People Laugh — Yorkshire

Gets It First," *Toronto Star*, 29 September 1921, p. [13]. Interview, by Windermere, dateline London, 29 September, with quotations. Leacock states his tour will begin in Thirsk, Yorkshire, on October 4.

**F21.8** "Stephen Leacock in England, Man Who Enjoys Own Jokes; Montreal Professor and Humorist Says He Does His Brightest Work Early in the Day — His Methods as School Teacher," *Toronto Star*, 13 October 1921. News clipping in University of Toronto Archives; not located on microfilm of the newspaper at OHM. Interview, with quotations, date line London, Sept. 26, in a West End hotel. The interviewer notes that Leacock was with a reporter from the *Daily Mail* (see F21.6). Also reported as "Stephen Leacock Tells How He Writes Humor, Early Rising and Sleeping Outside Essentials; Secure Funny Ideas and Just Write Them Down on Bits of Paper — How He Broke into Print — Stories of the Canadian Humorist," *Toronto Star Weekly*, 22 October 1921. Covers same subjects as the *Toronto Star* but in greater detail.

**F21.9** "A Humorist Abroad," *New York Times*, 22 October 1921, p. 12. An editorial which quotes from an unidentified interview given by Leacock on his arrival in Liverpool for a lecture tour. Leacock's answer to the question, "How many jokes are needed for a comic lecture?" is quoted.

**F21.10** "How Leacock Suffers When He Entertains Country Audiences with Humor," *Montreal Herald*, 25 October 1921, p. 4. An interview conducted on 15 October 1921 in London. He discusses the appreciation of humour in different countries and the Canadian emigration policy.

**F21.11** "Mr. Stephen Leacock's Tour Ended. Tribute to British Sense of Humour," *Times* (London), 24 December 1921, p. 7. Interview with the *Times* Bournemouth correspondent. Leacock gave his last lecture in Bournemouth. Curry's *Stephen Leacock: Humorist and Humanist* reprints Leacock's remarks, p. 155, but incorrectly states they are from the lecture.

**F21.12** "S. Leacock Broadens out; Finds English and Scottish Understand Him, Now for the French People," *Montreal Herald*, 27 December 1921. An interview, dateline 27 December from London, in which Leacock comments on his appreciative audiences in England and Scotland and reviews the industrial situation and the threat of Bolshevism.

**F22.1** "Leacock Finds Voyage No Joke; Arrives in New York on Ice-Encrusted Liner," *Montreal Daily Star*, 22? January 1922. News clipping at QMM Archives could not be located in the microfilm edition of the newspaper. Leacock is interviewed on his return from his lecture tour of Great Britain. Only one sentence from Leacock is quoted regarding unemployment in Britain.

**F22.2** "Dr. Leacock Returns to Old McGill," *McGill Daily*, 26 January 1922, p. 1. Two quotations about McGill after his return from his lecture tour of Great Britain.

**F22.3** "Leacock's Success in Britain," *Saturday Night* (Toronto) 37, no. 16, whole no. 1,512 (18 February 1922): 2. Quotation from an interview with a reporter following his lecture at the Bournemouth Winter Gardens in which Leacock expresses his gratitude to the British public for their kindness and appreciation.

**F22.4** "Dr. Leacock Advocates U.S. Rugby," *McGill Daily*, 31 October 1922, p. 1. Leacock attended a rugby game at the State University in Columbus, Ohio. Quotations in this article pertain to the game and also how impressed he was with public support for the University. Reprinted in the *McGill Daily*, 19 March 1936, p. 3.

**F23.1** "Leacock Makes Elmira Feel Happier," *Elmira* (NY) *Star Gazette*, 17 January 1923. Report of Leacock's speech sponsored by the Community Lyceum committee along with an interview in which Leacock states: "My only regret is that I didn't arrive early enough this afternoon to visit Mark Twain's home at Quarry Farm . . . Some day I want surely to do that. How proud you Elmirans must be that you can claim Mark Twain as your fellow citizen."

**F24.1** "Leacock Raps Co-Education," *Michigan Daily* (University of Michigan), 6 March 1924, p. 1. Report of interview in a taxi with Leacock after his lecture at the University of Michigan in Ann Arbor on 5 March 1924; several sentences quoted. See also D24.5.

**F24.2** "Professor Leacock Sails: Canadian Writer Resents Rule Regarding Income Tax Proof for Voyagers," *New York Times*, 20 December 1924, p. 15. Remarks made to reporters on the ship he was taking to Nassau, Bahamas, on 19 December. Three sentences are quoted on the fact he had to prove he had no earned income in the U.S. before his departure.

**F25.1** "Do Universities Attempt Too Much; Prof. Leacock Advises Attention to Essentials of Education," *Montreal Daily Star*, 19 January 1925. Report of an interview with Leacock that occurred after a lecture in Moncton, New Brunswick. A similar interview appears as "Stephen Leacock Spoke at Moncton; Deprecates Expansion of Universities and Teaching of Irrelevant Subjects," *Montreal Gazette*, 20 January 1925, p. 6. The interview apparently appeared first in a Moncton newspaper.

**F25.2** "'Gown Should Be, But Should Be Cheap.' — Leacock," *McGill Daily*, 31 January 1925, p. 1. An interview on 30 January 1925; Leacock is in favour of gowns for undergraduates.

**F26.1** "Industry Needs to Be Overhauled Top to Bottom; Dr. Stephen Leacock, Discussing Coal Strike, Thinks Shareholders Right as Miner; Baldwin Only Hope; New Coal Fields of Greater Wealth and Easier Access Now Worked," *Toronto Star*, 7 May 1926. News clipping in University of Toronto Archives; not located in the microfilm edition of the newspaper. Interview in Toronto, on 7 May 1926, where Leacock had arrived for a week, with quotations, on the General Strike in England.

**F26.2** "Gown Favored by Dr. Leacock," *McGill Daily*, 2 December 1926, p. 1. This interview contains many quotations.

**F27.1** "Leacock Recalls College Days with Prime Minister; University Then College and 'Horrible Red Brick Buildings' Housing School of Science — Premier Graduated Two Minutes Before Humorist; McGill Professor to Receive LL.D. [sic] Degree," *Toronto Star*, 6 October 1927, p. [39]. Breakfast interview, with several quotations, about Leacock's days at the University of Toronto, in Toronto, 6 December 1927, where he stopped en route from Montreal to Orillia. The premier referred to was Howard Ferguson. The interviewer notes that Leacock will be returning later to Toronto to accept the degree. He actually received a D.Litt.

**F27.2** "May Persuade Ferguson Believes Prof. Leacock. Possibility Still Seen That Ontario Premier Will Accept Conservative Leadership," *Toronto Telegram*, 8 October 1927, p. 27. Interview, with quotations, the day after he received his honorary degree at the University of Toronto.

**F28.1** "Meeting Called to Plan Drive for Cancer Cure; Prof. Leacock Backs Proposal to Establish Research Centre; Public Invited; Noted Expert on Disease Will Address Meeting at McGill," *Montreal Daily Star*, 24 January 1928, pp. [3], 34. Remarks made by Leacock with regard to a meeting scheduled for 25 January 1928 which he had helped to organize and was going to chair. Many paragraphs are quoted on the need for public support for cancer research. See also D28.1.

**F28.2** "Humorist-Economist Talks Immigration; Prof. Stephen Leacock Thinks Canada Can Absorb 500,000 a Year," *Toronto Globe*, 18 October 1928, p. 14. Interview, with quotations, on immigration, 17 October 1928. Leacock was in Toronto for a few hours en route to Montreal after completing a lecture tour in the United States. A similar interview appears as "Leacock Urges No Immigration Bars. . . . ," *Montreal Daily Star*, 18 October 1928, p. 23.

**F32.1** M.H. Halton, "He Can't Help Being Funny Professor Leacock Admits; What's a Man to Do When His Audience Starts to Laugh? Humor Overflow," *Toronto Star*, 25 May 1932, p. 10. Interview about listening to other people's speeches, looking like a farmer, and humour, with many quotations. Halton shared a taxi with Leacock en route from the Canadian Political Science Association meeting, where Leacock had lectured, to the train station.

**F33.1** R.E. Knowles, "Leacock Says Sir A. Currie Most Distinguished Pupil; Humorist, Author and Economist Here to Speak at Empire Club; Teacher 44 Years," *Toronto Star*, 16 February 1933, pp. 1–2. Interview on the pronunciation of his name, teaching, Mark Twain, newspapers in general, and the *Star* in particular, with many quotations.

**F35.1** "Stephen Leacock Here, Praises NRA and Mark Twain," *St. Louis Star-Times*, 16 January 1935. Interview with Leacock on his arrival in St. Louis, Missouri to receive the Mark Twain Medal. Re his views on prohibition, the gold standard, and Twain.

**F35.2** "Leacock Foresees End of New Deal; Professor of Economics Returns from Trip to United States," *Montreal Daily Star*, 21 October 1935, pp. [3], 13. Interview about life in the U.S. Middle West (Missouri and Iowa) in general and the New Deal specifically after Leacock's return from a lecture tour. He also comments on the Canadian elections: "I was asked again and again about the Canadian elections. I always gave the same answer: The people voted Liberal to show how Conservative they are."

**F35.3** "Leacock Retired by McGill," *New York Times*, 19 December 1935, p. 23. Two sentences quoted from remarks made on 18 December about his retirement. The same sentences appear in "Leacock Retires in 1936; Will Tell McGill 'Plenty', 'I Have All Eternity to Say It — I Shall Shout It Down to Them,'" *Toronto Mail and Empire*, 19 December 1935, p. 1.

**F36.1** "Leacock Will Write Book Following Trip; Plans Work After Lecture Tour of West," *Montreal Daily Star*, 10 November 1936, p. 4. Interview with a *Star* representative that morning in which Leacock gives details about his proposed western tour of Canada. Some of his comments are directed especially to McGill alumni societies in the West.

**F36.2** "Leacock Sees Era of Great Prosperity; Declares Canada Will Share in Benefits if Alive to her Chances," *Winnipeg Free Press*, 30 November 1936, pp. 1, 5. Lengthy interview with Leacock upon his arrival in Winnipeg on 29 November, at the Royal Alexandra Hotel, during his tour of western Canada. He prophesies prosperity for the North American continent, discusses the differences between Canada and the United States, and laments the rivalries among the provinces and regions of Canada. A similar interview appeared as

" 'Provincialism' Will Wreck Canada's Opportunities for Prosperity, Warns Leacock; Lack of Unity and Petty Differences Leave Country Unprepared for Coming Wave of Prosperity, Says Noted Economist and Humorist," *Winnipeg Tribune*, 30 November 1936, pp. 1, 10.

F36.3   J.E. Thompson, "Stephen Leacock Too Busy Writing and Lecturing to Start Enjoying Retirement; Dean of Canadian Humorists, on First Visit Here, Makes It Plain He Finds Greater Pleasure in Reputation as Humorist," *Winnipeg Tribune*, 30 November 1936, p. 3. Interview in which Leacock says that he is too busy to enjoy retirement. He also comments on the beauty of the Lake Superior shore line and Winnipeg, and refers to his first lecture at McGill University in 1901, "The Monarchy of England."

F36.4   "Aberhart Leaves for East As He Comes West, Says Leacock," *Regina Leader-Post*, 7 December 1936, p. 3. Interview in Regina on the morning of 7 December about his time in Winnipeg, and his next destination, Edmonton; a few sentences are quoted. William Aberhart was the Premier of Saskatchewan.

F36.5   "Says Conservative Party Outlook in West Is Excellent: 'You Can't Kill It' Declares Noted Economist," *Regina Star*, c.7 December 1936. News clipping seen at SLM.

F36.6   "Stephen Leacock Asks, What's Perjury? He'll Sign S[ocial] C[redit] Covenants," unidentified Saskatoon newspaper, c.10 December 1936. Interview with Leacock on his arrival in Saskatoon on Wednesday, 9 December. According to this article both of Leacock's speeches were supposed to be on the following day. New clipping seen at SLM.

F36.7   "Dr. S. Leacock Making First Visit to West; Noted Canadian Humorist Pays Tribute to Edmonton War Hero," *Edmonton Bulletin*, 14 December 1936, pp. 9, 11. Interview upon his arrival in Edmonton. Leacock is quoted on the adventures of his father, uncles, and brothers in the West, the abdication crisis, mosquitos in East Simcoe, and his upcoming lectures scheduled for Edmonton. The hero mentioned in the headline was Allan Oliver, a former student of his at McGill University.

F36.8   "Leacock Sees Nothing New in S[ocial] C[redit] Ideas; Will Be No Dividend in Literal Sense, Says Humorist," *Calgary Daily Herald*, 19 December 1936, p. 2. Interview with the *Herald* in the morning about his noon speech to a joint luncheon meeting of the Canadian Club and the Board of Trade in the Hudson's Bay Elizabeth Room. Most of the quotations come from the interview rather than the speech itself. Leacock noted that the speech was supposed to be about Peace and War but was changed to Social Credit by request.

F36.9   " 'Consolidate Debts,' Says Leacock; Noted Writer Says Troubles Easily Adjusted," *Vancouver Sun*, 22 December 1936, p. 22. An interview at the Hotel Vancouver on 21 December 1936 upon his arrival in Vancouver. Many quotations are given by reporter Bob Bouchette, mostly on economic matters. A number of reporters were present. Bouchette explains that Leacock handed out a prepared interview to all of them that he had composed himself. He still allowed himself to be questioned, however. See also C36.31.

F36.10   "Humorist in Happy Mood on Birthday; Professor Leacock Forgets Economics as He Moralizes on Life's Voyage; Visitor Charmed with Pacific Coast," *Victoria Daily Colonist*, 31 December 1936, p. 6. An interview with Leacock on 30 December at the Empress Hotel in which he makes observations about life and old age, and makes quips about his "dead" friends who appear regularly in clubs and hotels.

F37.1   "Leacock Made Aberhart Laugh: Well Known Humorist Makes Some Observations on Social Credit," *Lethbridge Herald*, 19 January 1937, p. [12]. Interview with Leacock about Social Credit conducted in Winnipeg CP station during his return trip from his lecture tour of western Canada. Among other things he recounts lecturing to Aberhart in Vancouver and quoting from the second book of Kings, chapter 13, verse 27: "And he said saddle me the ass, and they saddled him."

**F37.2** "Leacock Refuses B.C. Post; Press of Literary Work Bars Acceptance of Attractive Offer," *Montreal Gazette*, 13 December 1937, p. 13. Leacock was offered a position in the Department of Economics at the University of British Columbia. When questioned by the press about his telegram in reply to the offer, Leacock stated that ". . . he had too much literary work on hand, although he would like very much to go there."

**F38.1** "Leacock Favors Canada and U.S. Economic Entity; Hepburn Vision True and Inspiring, Economist States; Ottawa Doubtful," *Toronto Star*, 6 October 1938, p. [25]. Special to the *Star* from Montreal contains two paragraphs of quotations.

**F39.1** "Dr. Leacock Goes to Rescue Then Tries to Prove Youth Saved Self From Drowning," *Toronto Telegram*, 10 July 1939, p. 1. Re the rescue of Peter Bartleman from his upturned canoe by Leacock and his caretaker, John Kelly, on 9 July; includes several quotations. Also as "Leacock Life-Saver 'Twaddle' He Replies; 'Youth Saved Himself,' He Declares After Helping to Rescue Canoeist; Disclaims Heroism," *Toronto Star*, 10 July 1939, p. 3; as "Stephen Leacock Aids Rescue of Canoeist in Stormy Lake; Humorist and Couple in Launch Are Turned Back Twice Before Reaching Youth Clinging to Craft," *Toronto Globe and Mail*, 10 July 1939, pp. 1, 5. Only two sentences are quoted in this report, both on p. 1.

**F39.2** "Leacock Says London Editors Persuading Him He's Hero; Humorist About to Revise His Role in Rescue After Insistent Transatlantic Telephone Calls," *Toronto Globe and Mail*, 13 July 1939, p. 5. Re London, England newspapers calling him to interview him about the rescue. Similar quotations appear in "Leacock Fed Up On 'This Hero Business'; Never Rescue Anyone in Future, Not Even Women, He Vows," *Toronto Star*, 13 July 1939, p. 3.

**F39.3** "Call From McGill News to Leacock; But Rumor Persists Noted Humorist Sought as Economics Head," *Toronto Telegram*, 16 November 1939. News clipping at the University of Toronto Archives. Special to the *Telegram* from Montreal about the rumor that Leacock would be made the Head of McGill's Department of Commerce. A few sentences are quoted in a humorous vein about Leacock not being able to answer hypothetical questions. The microfilm (Home edition) held at OONL has only a condensed version, with no quotations, as "Hint Prof. Leacock Called by McGill," p. 2. More quotations appear in "Back to College? Professor Leacock Has the Answer; It's 3 Questions," *Montreal Herald*, 17 November 1939.

# G Section: AUTHORIZED ADAPTATIONS, SEPARATELY PUBLISHED

### G1 "Q": A FARCE IN ONE ACT 1915

Stephen Leacock and Basil Macdonald Hastings. *"Q": A Farce in One Act*. London; New York: Samuel French, Ltd., 1915. French's Acting Edition. No. 2459. $1^{10}$. 1–2, 7, 8, 9–23, 1 pp. (10 leaves). 184 × 123 mm. Bound in a tan wrapper with lettering in blue. On the front of the wrapper within a rectangle is the title, the names of the authors, the revised price, and publisher's name; the series is printed outside of the rectangle. On the back of the wrapper within a rectangle is a list of some London productions published in French's Acting Edition series. Printed by Butler & Tanner, Ltd. Price 1s 6d; 50¢.

NOTES: This play, written by Basil Macdonald Hastings, is based on Leacock's short story, "'Q' A Psychic Pstory of the Psupernatural," first published in *Saturday Night* (see C11.11) and then anthologized in *Nonsense Novels* (A7).

At READ and SLM is a contract dated 31 August 1915 between Leacock and Basil Macdonald Hastings of the one part and Charles H. Hawtrey of the other part for a performance of the plan on or before 26 November 1915, one guinea per performance with a guarantee of thirty performances. Hawtrey obtained exclusive rights for one year in Great Britain with an option to purchase rights in United States and Canada. A programme of plays performed at the London Coliseum has survived in Leacock's papers at SLM. "Q" premiered on 29 November 1915.

"Q" was published on 30 December 1915. The copyright was claimed and registered at the Copyright Office of DLC by Samuel French on 14 January 1915 (Entry Cl. D, XXc No. D42753). The copyright was renewed by the widow of Basil Macdonald Hastings on 26 January 1943.

There were many performances of the plan well into the 1930s. On 2 December 1921, for example, The Bodley Head sent Leacock a cheque for £67s 6d for fifteen performances.

COPIES EXAMINED: CS (possibly a reprint, with label of Samuel French (Canada) Limited affixed to the copyright page).

### G2 WINSOME WINNIE: A ROMANTIC DRAMA IN THREE ACTS 1932

V.C. Clinton-Baddeley. *Winsome Winnie: A Romantic Drama in Three Acts*. Adapted from the story by Stephen Leacock. London and Glasgow: Gowans & Gray, Ltd.; Boston: The Baker International Play Bureau, 1932. Repertory Plays, No. 123. $R330–R331^{8}$ [$1 signed].

1–9, 10–16, 17, 18–24, 25, 26–31, 1 pp. (16 leaves). 148 × 102 mm. Bound in an off-white wrapper with a cream-coloured, pictorial jacket folded over the wrapper. On the front of the jacket within an ornamental rectangle is a colour caricature of a young woman by Joyce Dennys. The name of the series is printed above the rectangle, and the imprint is printed below the rectangle. The title and author's name are printed down the spine. Printed by Turnbull & Spears. Price 1s.

NOTES: V.C. Clinton-Baddeley, a history don at Jesus College, Cambridge University, first contacted Leacock on 10 October 1926. He informed him that some three or four years ago he had adapted "Behind the Beyond: A Modern Problem Play" (see A12) for the stage at a private smoking concert of the Cambridge University Amateur Dramatic Society. He asked Leacock's permission to publish the play and to have it played to the public. Leacock cabled his permission to let Clinton-Baddeley stage "Behind the Beyond" as part of a Christmas revue at Cambridge. Clinton-Baddeley expressed his thanks on 11 December 1926 and enclosed a programme of the revue.

Clinton-Baddeley pressed Leacock to consent to a "dramatised version of it to the commercial theatre. But to that I have had no answer." He cited Macdonald Hastings's *Q* (G1), and requested a similar kind of collaboration and arrangement of royalties:

> The idea is yours, and the plot, and most of the dialogue. I, on the other hand, have (1) had to add to it and fill out the dialogue for stage purposes and in places to re-shuffle it (2) have had to "*produce*" it, to make it "*work*" on the stage, to invent the business, and the movements etc; and (3) should finally have the work of trading it to a London Producer.

Clinton-Baddeley wrote again on 24 December 1926. He told Leacock that

> "Behind the Beyond" is definitely billed to be put on at the St. Martin's Theatre as a curtain-raiser to "Berkeley Square" by Baldertson and J.C. Squire. The St. Martin's management (Alec Rea) is undoubtedly the best in London: it is to be produced by Frank Birch who produced "Berkeley Square"; and he is to play Sir John, which part (he being also a Cambridge Don) he originally played at the A.D.C. The first night is to be on Dec 31st & has been definitely announced in all the London papers.

On 31 December 1926, Leacock gave Clinton-Baddeley *carte-blanche* to proceed: "You have done more for Behind the Beyond than it has done for you. Go ahead and use it in any way you like and pay me whenever you like." The royalty arrangement was 50% to Clinton-Baddeley and 50% to Leacock and The Bodley Head.

Clinton-Baddeley's adaptation enjoyed a good run at the St. Martin's Theatre (eighty-four performances up to 5 March 1927). Leacock received a royalty of £61. At that time Clinton-Baddeley again inquired about dramatic rights and publication. Leacock reiterated his cooperation on 27 March 1927: "I am quite safe in your hands. Any arrangement you make suits me." He invited Clinton-Baddeley to adapt his other short stories for the stage. Clinton-Baddeley returned to the subject of publication on 16 October [1927]. He expressed his concern about American copyright problems. "Behind the Beyond" had earned a profit of £130. He had written other skits ("The Split in the Cabinet," "Winsome Winnie," and "The Billiard Room Mystery") based on Leacock's stories, and had deposited them with the Society of Authors. He also mentioned Margaret Yarde, "the best burlesque actress in London," who had read the skits and loved them.

Clinton-Baddeley sent Leacock "the first of my adaptations" on 20 April [1932].

> It is, I hope you will agree, exceedingly well done by Gowans & Gray (& God knows they've taken long enough doing it). The other 3 are to follow rapidly (so he says).
>
> Joyce Dennys who had done the cover is a great friend of mine, & a very well-known English comic artist.

Presumably what he sent to Leacock was *Winsome Winnnie: A Romantic Drama in Three Acts*. The only other mention of *Winsome Winnie* in the correspondence of Leacock and Clinton-Baddeley occurs in the context of a royalty payment sent to Leacock on 13 September 1936. Clinton-Baddeley stated most of the royalty concerned *Winsome Winnie* which had been performed in the United States. The fee for a performance of the play was one guinea within the British Empire (except Canada) or $5 for Canada and the United States. According to *The English Catalogue of Books*, this adaptation was published in May 1932.

COPIES EXAMINED: CS; QMMRB.

## G3 BEHIND THE BEYOND: A PLAY IN THREE ACTS 1932

V.C. Clinton-Baddeley. *Behind the Beyond: A Play in Three Acts*. Adapted from the original by Stephen Leacock. London and Glasgow: Gowans & Gray, Ltd.; Boston: The Baker International Play Bureau, 1932. Repertory Plays, No. 124. R340–R341$^8$ R342$^4$ R343$^4$ [$1 signed]. *1–9, 10–18, 19, 20–29, 30, 31–36, 1–12* pp. (24 leaves). Photograph from the production between pp. 6–7. 148 × 101 mm. Bound in an off-white wrapper with a cream-coloured, pictorial jacket folded over the wrapper. Printed on the front of the jacket: REPERTORY PLAYS No 124 | BEHIND THE BEYOND : [colour caricature by Joyce Dennys of a man and woman in formal evening attire, the man holding a knife and looking menacingly at another man] | BY | V.C. CLINTON-BADDELEY | AND | STEPHEN LEACOCK | LONDON & GLASGOW GOWANS & GRAY LTD. The title and Clinton-Baddeley's name are printed down the spine. Printed by Turnbull & Spears. Price 1s.

NOTES: According to *The English Catalogue of Books*, this adaptation was published in November 1932. See also the notes to G2 for the publishing history of this adaptation. A dispute arose in October 1937 when the BBC did a "television adaptation" of "Behind the Beyond." Clinton-Baddeley complained on 7 October 1937 that Leacock had given him sole dramatic rights over this and other plays. However, Leacock told Clinton-Baddeley on 17 October that to the best of his recollection, his permission to stage the play gave no such absolute control.

Several copies that were examined had a paper label on the title page pasted over the original imprint. The label is dated 1943 with the imprint of Thomas Nelson and Sons Ltd. This would indicate that by that date, if not earlier, the rights were transferred to Thomas Nelson.

COPIES EXAMINED: CS (two copies, one with the paper label); EVANS; QMMRB; SLM (two copies, both with the paper label).

## G4 THE BILLIARD-ROOM MYSTERY 1932

V.C. Clinton-Baddeley. *The Billiard-Room Mystery; or, Who D'You Think Did It?: A Murder Mystery in Two Acts.* Adapted from the original by Stephen Leacock. London and Glasgow: Gowans & Gray, Ltd.; Boston: The Baker International Play Bureau, 1934. Repertory Plays, No. 125. R386–R388[8] [$1 signed]. *1–9, 10–24, 25, 26–35, 1–13* pp. (24 leaves). 146 × 101 mm. Bound in an off-white wrapper with a cream-coloured, pictorial jacket folded over the wrapper. On the front of the jacket within an ornamental rectangle is a caricature in pink and black by Joyce Dennys of a man in a tuxedo who is lying on the floor with his feet raised and resting on the corner of a billiard table. The name of the series is printed above the rectangle, and the imprint is printed below the rectangle. The title and Clinton-Baddeley's name are printed down the spine. Printed by Turnbull & Spears. Price 1s.

NOTES: *The Billiard-Room Mystery* was first performed on stage on 13 April 1931 at the Festival Theatre, Cambridge. The play is based on "Who You Think Did It? (Done After the Very Latest Fashion in This Sort of Thing" (see C20.20). The play was also broadcast by the BBC in London on 22 March 1934 at five guineas per broadcast (Clinton-Baddeley to Leacock, 7 March [1934], The Bodley Head fonds, READ).

One copy that was examined had a paper label pasted over the imprint on the title page and another label pasted on to the verso of the half title. The labels are undated but transfer the rights to Thomas Nelson and Sons Ltd.

COPIES EXAMINED: CS (with paper labels); QMMRB.

## G5 THE SPLIT IN THE CABINET 1938

V.C. Clinton-Baddeley. *The Split in the Cabinet: A Play in Two Acts.* Adapted from the story by Stephen Leacock. London and Glasgow: Gowans & Gray, Ltd.; Boston: The Baker International Play Bureau, 1938. Repertory Plays, No. 126. R398–R400[8] [$1 signed]. *1–9, 10–20, 21, 22–36, 1–12* pp. (24 leaves). 150 × 100 mm. Bound in an off-white wrapper with a cream-coloured, pictorial jacket folded over the wrapper. On the front of the jacket within an ornamental rectangle is a caricature in pink and black by Joyce Dennys of a man in a tuxedo and a woman in an evening dress (the woman is facing the man and has her hands on his chest). The name of the series is printed above the rectangle, and the imprint is printed below the rectangle. The title and Clinton-Baddeley's name are printed down the spine. Printed by Turnbull & Spears. Price 1s.

NOTES: According to *The English Catalogue of Books*, this adaptation, based on C20.19, was published in September 1938. The play was first performed on 12 October 1930 at the Everyman Theatre, Hampstead. On 3 March [1935], when he sent Leacock royalties for *Behind the Beyond*, Clinton-Baddely told Leacock:

> The fact is that Gowans & Gray, who produce these things remarkably well, are run by a doddering old gentleman, who has not yet discovered the use of typewriters or secretaries, and persists in conducting the whole of an extensive business entirely on his own — which results in endless postponements & apologies. He has taken all this time to produce the 3rd of these plays *"The Billiard Room Mystery"* — & the 4th & last, *The Split in the Cabinet* is not yet in proof.

On one copy that was examined, there is a paper label on the title page pasted over the original imprint. The label is undated, but indicates that Thomas Nelson and Sons Ltd. took over the publication of the play from Gowans & Gray, Ltd.

COPIES EXAMINED: QMMRB; UWO (with paper label).

# H Section: TRANSLATIONS

## Armenian

**H1** *Jumorističeskie rasskazy.* (*Humorous Stories*). Trans H.T. Gračjan and B.G. Barsegjan. Erevan: Ajastan, [1972?]. 119 pp.
SOURCE: *Index Translatonium* 26 (1973): 823.

**H2** *Ošibka deda Moroza.* (*The Errors of Santa Claus*). Erevan: Sovetakan groh., 1981. 106 pp.
SOURCE: *Index Translatonium* 34 (1981): 787; Paul Aubin and Louis-Marie Côté, *Bibliographie de l'histoire du Québec et Canada / Bibliography of the History of Quebec and Canada: 1981–1985* (Québec: Institut québécois de recherche sur la culture, 1981), item 15426.

## Bulgarian

**H3** *Pregrešenija na peroto.* (*Perfect Lover's Guide and Other Stories*). Trans. Veselin Laptev. Plovdiv: Hristo G. Danov, 1986. 229 pp.
SOURCE: *Index Translatonium* 39 (1986): 253.

## Chinese

**H4** *Hsiao chen yen yang lu.* (*Sunshine Sketches of a Little Town*). Trans. Chung-wen Hunag. [Nan-ching shih]: Chiang-su jen min chú pan she, 1982. 1–6, 207, 1 pp.
SOURCE: CS (two copies); OCLC WorldCat database; RLIN database.

**H5** *Li-kè-kè yu mo shui pi hseuch.* Trans. Lan Jen-che pien hsuan and Chia-na-ta yen chiu shuo ho i. Chung-chíng: Chung-chíng chú pen she, 1984. Title on back cover: *Stephen Leacock's Selected Humorous Essays.* 1–4, 262 pp.
SOURCE: CS (two copies); QMMRB.

**H6** *Le-k'e-ke yu mo hsiao p'in hsuan.* Trans. Xiao Qian. Pei-ching: Tso chia ch'u pan she, 1990. 1–10, 1–2, 1–194 pp. Text in Chinese; foreword in Chinese, English and French by Earl Drake of the Canadian Embassy.
SOURCE: OONL; RLIN database.

**H7** *Mo shu shih te pao fu.* (Selections. Chinese). Lan-chou: Tun-huang wen ich'u pan she, 1991. 295, [3] pp.
SOURCE: OONL; OCLC WorldCat database.

## Czech

**H8** *Arkadská dobrodružství horních deseti tisíc.* (*Arcadian Adventures with the Idle Rich*). Trans. Vojtěch Zamarovksy. Praha: Snklhu, 1959. 224 pp.
SOURCE: *Index Translatonium* 12 (1959): 502; National Library, Czech Republic.

H9  *Kanadske žertíky*. Trans. Alois Vinař. Praha: Práce, 1979. 302 pp.
SOURCE: OONL; National Library, Czech Republic.

H10  *Liternární poklesky*. (*Literary Lapses*). Trans. František Vrba, Libuše Vrbová, Tomás Vrba, and Helena Beguivinová. Praha: Mladá fronta, 1963. 156 pp.; 1966 — 166 pp.; 1971 — 192, 1–4 pp.; 1986 — 245, 1–3 pp.
SOURCE: CS (1971 and 1986 editions); OONL (1963 edition); OTMCL (1986 edition); *Index Translatonium* 16 (1963): 593; 19 (1966): 636; 25 (1972): 680; 39 (1986): 979; National Library, Czech Republic (1966, 1971, and 1986 editions); RLIN database (1963 edition).

H11  *Pochybné podniky*. Trans. Vojtěch Zamarovsky. Praha: Nakladatelství Josefa Šimona, 1995. 188 pp.
SOURCE: National Library, Czech Republic.

## Danish

H12  *Hvem var morderen?*. (*Winsome Winnie and Other New Nonsense Novels*). Trans. Timme Rosenkrantz. Ill. Herluf Bidstrup. København: Thaning & Appels Forlag, 1947. 122 pp.
SOURCE: SLM.

H13  *John Smith og andre fortællinger*. (*Literary Glimpses* [*Literary Lapses?*] and *Non-sense Novels*). Trans. Iver Gudme. København: Thaning & Appel, [1960?]. 109 pp.
SOURCE: *Index Translatonium* 14 (1961): 164.

H14  *Blandt millionærer*. (*Arcadian Adventures with the Idle Rich*). Trans. Iver Gudme. København: Thaning & Appel, 1963. 147, 1 pp.
SOURCE: OONL; *Index Translatonium* 16 (1963): 180.

## Dutch

H15  *Nonsens-verhalen*. (*Nonsense Novels*). Trans. J.P. Wesselink van Rossum. Rijswijk (Z.-H.): Blankwaardt & Schoonhoven, [1915]. 204 pp.
SOURCE: OONL; University Library, Katholieke Universiteit Nijmegen, Erasmuslaan, The Netherlands.

H16  *Dwaze invallen*. Trans. Frederika Quanjer. Rijswijk (Z.-H.): Blankwaardt & Schoon-hoven, [1916]. 245, [1] pp.
SOURCE: University Library, Katholieke Universiteit Nijmegen, Erasmuslaan, The Netherlands.

## Estonian

H17  *Defektiive detektiiv*. (*Perfect Lover's Guide and Other Stories*). Trans. H. Kross. Tallin: Gaz.-Žurn. 54 p.
SOURCE: *Index Translatonium* 13 (1960): 605.

## Finnish

H18  *Aurinkoisia piirteitä pienestä kauppalasta*. (*Sunshine Sketches of a Little Town*). Trans. W. Eklund. Sudbury, ON: Vapaus Publishing Company Limited, 1951. 189, 1 pp.
SOURCE: CS; OONL; OTMCL; SLM; *Index Translatonium* 4 (1951): 96. Published on 3 September 1951 in an edition of 1,200 copies. The first Finnish translation of a Canadian author published in Canada.

## French

**H19**  *L'humour américain.* Traduit et édités par Cecil Georges-Bazile. Paris: C. Georges-Bazile, Éditeur, 1918. Les Cahiers Britanniques et Américains, no. 3 2e Année, 15 février 1918. 32, iv pp. Translation of "American Humour," part I of "Shorter Stories Still" ("An Irreducible Detective Story: Hanged by a Hair or a Murder Mystery Minimized"), and "Weejee, the Pet Dog: An Idyll of the Summer." With a frontispiece photograph of Leacock sitting at a writing desk and his signature in facsimile.
SOURCE: Leacock fonds, NAC.

**H20**  *Anthologie des meilleurs humoristes anglaises et américains. Le rire dans le brouillard.* Trans. Maurice Debroka. Paris: Flammarion, [1927]. 286 pp. Includes translations of extracts of "Gertrude the Governess," "Guido the Gimlet of Ghent: A Romance of Chivalry," "Memoirs of Marie Mushenough," and "Soaked in Seaweed; or, Upset in the Ocean."
SOURCE: Lomer, p. 53.

**H21**  *Histoires humoristiques. (Literary Lapses).* Traduites de l'anglais et présentées par Michel Chrestien. Paris: Laffont, 1963. 222, 1–2 pp.
SOURCE: CS; RLIN database; *Index Translatonium* 26 (1973): 394, lists a reprint: Paris: Le Livre de poche, 1972. 222 pp. See also H24.

**H22**  *Mémoires d'une jeune fille victorienne. (My Victorian Girlhood).* Présentation et traduction de Jean Gattégno. Passeport 8. Paris: Lettres modernes, 1964. 61, 1–3 pp., 4 ill.
SOURCE: CS; *Index Translatonium* 18 (1965): 283. Text in English and French.

**H23**  *Textes choisis.* Traduit de l'américain par Francine Sternberg. Humour secret [9]. Paris: Julliard [1966]. 245 p.
SOURCE: *Index Translatonium* 19 (1966): 303.

**H24**  *Ne perdez pas le fil: histoires humoristiques. (Literary Lapses).* Trans. Michel Chrestien. Paris: Union générale des éditions, 1981. 270 pp.
SOURCE: OONL; *Index Translatonium* 34 (1981): 399; RLIN database.

**H25**  *Un grain de sel . . ..* Textes choisis et traduits de l'anglais par Suzanne Saint-Jacques Mineau. Collection des deux solitudes. Montréal: Pierre Tisseyre, 1985. xvi, 142 pp. Translations of the following: the preface to *Sunshine Sketches of a Little Town.* "Familiar Incidents" 1. "With the Photographer"; 2. "The Dentist and the Gas"; 3. "My Lost Opportunities"; 4. "My Unknown Friend"; 5. "Under the Barber's Knife." Selected passages from *Arcadian Adventures with the Idle Rich.* "How We Kept Mother's Day." "Back from the Land." "We Have with Us Tonight." "Parisian Pastimes" 1. "The Advantages of a Polite Education"; 2. "The Joys of Philanthropy"; 3. "The Simple Life in Paris"; 4. "A Visit to Versailles"; 5. "Paris at Night." "Three Score and Ten."
SOURCE: CS; *Index Translatonium* 39 (1986): 268; RLIN database.

**H26**  *Un été à Mariposa. (Sunshine Sketches of a Little Town).* Traduit par Élise de Bellefeuille et Michel St-Germain. Collection Littérature d'Amérique. Montréal: Québec/Amérique, 1986. 173, 1–3 pp.
SOURCE: CS; QMMRB.

**H27**  *Leacock-à-l'âne.* Texte choisi et adaptés de l'anglais par Élise de Bellefeuille et Michel Saint-Germain. Montréal: Guérin littérature, 1992. 415, 1 pp. Translations of "Guido the Gimlet of Ghent," "Caroline's Christmas," "Historical Drama," "Behind the Beyond,"

"Winsome Winnie," "The Great Detective," "Broken Barriers," "My Affair with My Landlord," "The Laundry Problem," "Further Progress in Specialization," "The Merry Month of May," "Softening the Stories for Children," "The Retroactive Existence of Mr. Juggins," "Simple Stories of Success," "How My Wife and I Built Our Home for $4.90," "The Human Body — Its Care," "Letters to the New Rulers of the World," "My Revelations as a Spy," "French Politics for Beginners," and "The Next War."
SOURCE: CS; OONL; OTMCL.

## Georgian

**H28** *Rukovodstvo dlja ideal'nogo vljublennogo i drugie rasskazy. (Perfect Lover's Guide and Other Stories)*. Tibilsi: Merani, 1986. 159 pp.
SOURCE: *Index Translatonium* 39 (1986): 1113.

## German

**H29** *Die Abenteuer der armen Reichen. (Arcadian Adventures with the Idle Rich)*. Trans. E.L. Schiffer-Williams. Charlottenburg: Williams & Co., 1925. 1–4, 243, 1 pp.
SOURCE: CS; QMMRB (three copies); Walter E. Riedel, *Das literarische Kanadabild* (Bonn: Bouvier Verlag Herbert Grundmann, 1980), p. 128; Lomer, p. 53. See also H31.

**H30** *Humor und Humbug*. Trans. E.L. Schiffer-Williams. Charlottenburg: Williams & Co., 1925. vii, 1, 231, 1 pp. Trans. of the following: "With the Photographer"; "The Dentist and the Gas"; "My Tailor: A Study in Still Life"; "Under the Barber's Knife"; "Boarding-House Geometry"; "Everyman and His Friends"; "Insurance Up to Date"; "The Two Sexes in Five or Sixes: A Dinner Party Study"; "First Call for Spring"; "The Radio: A New Form of Trouble"; "The Grass Bachelor's Guide"; "Roughing It in the Bush"; "Personal Experiments with the Black Bass"; "The Joys of Philanthropy"; "Hoodoo McFiggins's Christmas"; "Are the Rich Happy?"; "My Lost Opportunity"; "How I Succeeded in My Business"; "My Financial Career"; "Stories Shorter Still"; "Making a Magazine"; "The Vampire Woman As Met in the Movies"; "The Platter of Life"; "The Raft"; "Homer and Humbug."
SOURCE: CS; OONL; QMMRB; Walter E. Riedel, *Das literarische Kanadabild* (Bonn: Bouvier Vrelag Herbert Grundmann, 1980), p. 128; Lomer, p. 53.

**H31** *Die Abenteuer der armen Reichen. (Arcadian Adventures with the Idle Rich)*. Trans. E.L. Schiffer-Williams. Heinz Seydel, ed. Berlin: Eulenspiegel Verlag, 1955. 208 pp.
SOURCE: OONL; Harmut Froeschle and Lothar Zimmerman, *German Canadiana: A Bibliography / Deutschkanadische Bibliographie* (Toronto: Historical Society of Mecklenburg Upper Canada, 1990), 340; Walter E. Riedel, *Das literarische Kanadabild* (Bonn: Bouvier Verlag Herbert Grundmann, 1980), p. 128.

**H32** "Das füerchterlich Schicksal des Melpomenus Jones." ("The Awful Fate of Melpomenus Jones"). Trans. Armin Arnold. In Armin Arnold and Walter Riedel, eds., *Kanadische Erzaehler der Gegenwart* (Zuerich: Manesse, 1967). Pagination not given.
SOURCE: Harmut Froeschle and Lothar Zimmerman, *German Canadiana: A Bibliography / Deutschkanadische Bibliographie* (Toronto: Historical Society of Mecklenburg Upper Canada, 1990), p. 340.

**H33** "Die Wasserfahrt der Pythia-Ritter." ("The Marine Excursions of the Knights of Pythias"). Trans. Angela Uthe-Spencker. In Angela Uthe-Spencker, ed., *Stories from Canada* (Ebenhausen: Langenwiese-Brandt, 1969; Muenchen: Dtv, 1969). Pagination not given.

SOURCE: Harmut Froeschle and Lothar Zimmerman, *German Canadiana: A Bibliography / Deutschkanadische Bibliographie* (Toronto: Historical Society of Mecklenburg Upper Canada, 1990), p. 340.

**H34** *Der Asbestmann und andere Nonsens-Novellen* (*Nonsense Novels*). Trans. Manfred Bartz. Hannover: Fackelträger, 1987. 151, 1 pp.
SOURCE: CS (two copies).

**H35** *Die liebreizende Winnie: Neue Nonsens-Novellen.* (*Winsome Winnie and Other New Nonsense Novels*). Trans. Manfred Bartz. Hannover: Fackelträger, 1988. 172 pp.
SOURCE: CS (two copies).

**H36** *Die Hohenzollern in Amerika und andere Satiren.* (*The Hohenzollerns in America and Other Impossibilities*). Trans. Beate Blatz. Hannover: Fackelträger, 1989. 136 pp.
SOURCE: CS (two copies); OONL.

## Gujerati

**H37** ["With the Photographer"] in *Wismi suttee* (June 1918): 220–3; lubnar, Rao Iusan; chitrakar, Uflatun. Bombay: Hajimohamed Ularbia Shwaji, 1918.
SOURCE: Lomer, p. 53; Leacock fonds, NAC (MG 30, D40, vol. 3, file 34).

## Hebrew

**H38** *T'hi ima.* Trans. J. Zvi. Tel-Aviv: Y'diot Aharonot, 1948. 63 pp.
SOURCE: *Index Translatonium* 4 (1951): 222.

**H39** ["My Financial Career"] in Marion Richmond and Robert Weaver, eds., *25 Top Canadian Prose Writers: An Anthology*. Trans. Arie Hashavia. (Tel-Aviv: "Yachdav" United Publishers Co. Ltd., 1982), pp. 201–4.
SOURCE: CS.

## Hungarian

**H40** *Humoreszkek.* (*Short Stories*). Trans. Karinthy Frigyes. Budapest: Athenauem Irodalmi és Nyomdai R.-T. kiadàsa, [192?]. 147, 1 pp. Translations of: "Gertrude the Governess"; "Soaked in Seaweed"; "Guido the Gimlet of Ghent"; "Caroline's Christmas; A Hero in Homespun"; "'Q': A Psychic Pstory of the Psupernatural"; "Sorrows of a Supersoul"; "Maddened by Mystery"; "The Man in Asbestos"; and "Behind the Beyond."
SOURCE: QMMRB; Lomer, p. 53.

**H41** *Humoreszkek.* Trans. Karinthy Frigyes and Tivadar Szinnai. Budapest: Szépirodalmi Kiadó, [1955]. 231 pp.
SOURCE: *Index Translatonium* 8 (1955): 215.

**H42** *A Mauzóleum Klub.* Trans. Antal Szerb. Budapest: Magvetö, [1955]. 271 pp.
SOURCE: *Index Translatonium* 8 (1955): 215.

**H43** *A rejtély titka.* (*Nonsense Novels* and selected stories from *Literary Lapses*). Trans. Frigyes Karinthy, Tivadar Szinnai, and János Aczél. Budapest: Szépirodalmi Könyvkiadó, 1969. 199, [5] pp.
SOURCE: *Index Translatonium* 22 (1969): 367.

H44 *Rosszcirkeff Mária és társai.* (*Stephen Leacock's Laugh Parade, The Bodley Head Leacock, The Leacock Roundabout*). Trans. János Aczél. Bratislava, Slovakia: Madách, 1985. 344 pp.
SOURCE: *Index Translatonium* 39 (1986): 979.

H45 *Rosszcirkeff Mária és társai.* Trans. János Aczélet. Budapest: Európa, 1985. 343 pp.
SOURCE: *Index Translatonium* 38 (1985).

## Japanese

H46 *Watakushi no eikuku hakken.* (*My Discovery of England*). Trans. Shintaro Ishida. Tokyo: Kei-o Gijuku Shuppan Kyoku, 1924. 5, 207 pp.
SOURCE: QMMRB; Lomer, p. 54.

## Kazahskij

H47 *Š'ajyr'al sözder.* Trans. Müqaš Särsekeev. Alma-Ata: Žazušy. 133 pp. A translation of the Russian *Jumorističeskie rasskazy.*
SOURCE: *Index Translatonium* 22 (1969): 758.

## Latvian

H48 *Izgērbtie džentlmeņi.* Trans. Ojārs Sarma. Riga: Liesma, 1986. 205 pp.
SOURCE: *Index Translatonium* 39 (1986): 1113.

## Malayalam

H49 *Sahityakkirukkukal.* (*Literary Lapses* and *Laugh with Leacock*). Trans. P. Somarajan. Kottaytam: D.C. Books, 1982. 104 pp.
SOURCE: *Index Translatonium* 36 (1983): 539.

## Moldavian

H50 *Povestir' umorističe.* Trans. Naum Bernštejn. Kišinev: Literatura artisikė, 1984. 287 pp.
SOURCE: *Index Translatonium* 37 (1984): 918.

## Romanian

H51 *Povestiri umoristice.* (*Short Stories*). Trans. Tudor Măinescu and Micaela Ghițescu. București: Editura pentru literatuă universală, 1965. 445, [1] pp. Translation of selections from *The Bodley Head Leacock, The Unicorn Leacock,* and *Perfect Lover's Guide.* Complete translation of *The Boy I Left Behind Me* and *Arcadian Adventures with the Idle Rich.*
SOURCE: QMMRB; *Index Translatonium* 18 (1965): 555.

## Russian

H52 *Smeshynye rasskazy.* (*Amusing Stories*) Mikhail Koltoz, ed. Trans. G. Landau. Moskva: Pravda, [1937]. 63 pp. Biblioteka Krokodila series. Includes "The Great Sleuth," "My Financial Career," "The Problems of a Washerwoman," "A Romance of the Middle Ages," and "My Affair with the Landlord."
SOURCE: QMMRB; SLM.

**H53** *Jumorističeskie rasskazy.* (*Humorous Stories*). Trans. D. Livšic *et al.* Moskva; Leningrad: Goslitizdat, 1962. 470 pp. Moskva: Hudož, [1967], 454, *1–2* pp.
SOURCE: CS (1967 edition); *Index Translatonium* 16 (1963): 686; 20 (1967): 763.

**H54** *Yumoristycheskie rasskazy.* (*Humorous Stories*). Trans. Perevod s angleeskovo. [Redaktor E. Velikanova. Predisl. B. Smirnova]. Moskva: Gos. izd-vo khudozh. lit-ry, 1962. 469, *1–3* pp. Translation of stories from several of Leacock's books (*Literary Lapses, Nonsense Novels, Behind the Beyond,* etc.).
SOURCE: OONL; RLIN database.

**H55** *Rudovodstvo Dlia Ideal 'Nogo Vliu Blennogo.* (*Perfect Lover's Guide and Other Stories*). Moskva: Lit. Za Inostr. Iazyki, 1963.
SOURCE: Paul Aubin and Louis-Marie Côté, *Bibliographie de l'histoire du Québec et Canada / Bibliography of the History of Quebec and Canada: 1981–1985* (Québec: Institut québécois de recherche sur la culture, 1981), item 15427.

**H56** *Iumoristicheskie rasskazy.* (*Humorous Stories*). Moskva, Leningrad: Khudozh. lit-ra, 1967. 454 pp.
SOURCE: OCLC WorldCat database.

**H57** "Vodnoe stranst vie kavalerov pifeĩa" ("The Marine Excursion of the Knights of Pythias.") In *Rasskazy kanadskikh pisaelei.* Trans. Perevod A. Sherbakova. Leningrad: Khudozhestvennaĩaliterartura, Lenningradskoe otdelenie, 1985, pp. 65–84.
SOURCE: OTMCL.

**H58** *Kat stat millionerom.* Moskva: "Politicheskaia literature," 1991. 508 pp.
SOURCE: OCLC WorldCat database.

## Serbo-Croatian (Roman)

**H59** *Junak u pelengirima.* Trans. Ljuba Popović and Mirko Dimitrijević. Beogard: Novinsko izdavačko preduzeće Saveza novinara FNRJ, 1948. 104 pp.
SOURCE: *Index Translatonium* 3 (1950): 344.

**H60** "Moja finansijka kaijera." ("My Financial Career.") In *Antologija kratke price Kanade,* priredio. Trans. V. Kostov. Kruševac: Bagdala, 1986. 179 pp. (at pp. 24–32). Savremena svetska prica.
SOURCE: OTMCL.

**H61** *U svim pravcima.* (selections from *Literary Lapses, Nonsense Novels, Moonbeams from the Larger Lunacy, Short Circuits,* and *Model Memoirs*). Trans. Vlada Stojiljković. Beograd: Nolit, 1986. Biblioteka raspat series 43. 197, *1–5* pp.
SOURCE: OONL; OCLC WorldCat database; RLIN database.

## Spanish

**H62** *Elementos de cienca politica.* (*Elements of Political Science*). Mexico City: Imprenta Victoria, 1924. 370 pp.
SOURCE: OCLC WorldCat database.

**H63** *Cuentecitos risuenos.* Trans. Liliana Ventura. New York: Ventura, 1987. Pagination not given.
SOURCE: RLIN database.

**H64** "El terrible destino de Melpomenus Jones" ("The Awful Fate of Melpomenus Jones"), *Zurgai* (Bilbao) (June 1990): 96–8. Trans. Juan José Lanz.
SOURCE: GZM; OCLC WorldCat database under the title *Poesia anglosajona*.

## Swedish

**H65** *Konstiga romaner.* (*Nonsense Novels*). Trans. C. Christiansson. Stockholm: Fahl-crantz, 1914. 203 pp.
SOURCE: QMMRB; Lomer, p. 54.

**H66** *Bakom forlaten och andra bidrag till Manniskokannedom.* (*Behind the Beyond and Other Contributions to Human Knowledge*). Trans. C. Christiansson. Stockholm: Fahl-crantz, 1915. 167 pp.
SOURCE: Lomer, p. 54.

**H67** *Millionarer i Arkadien.* (*Arcadian Adventures with the Idle Rich*). Trans. Elisabeth Krey-Lange. Stockholm: Svenska andelsforl, 1920. 248 pp.
SOURCE: Lomer, p. 54.

# Section I: RECORDINGS BY LEACOCK, BRAILLE, TALKING BOOKS, AND FILMS

## Recordings by Leacock

I1  *Professors; or, My Fifty Years Among the Chalk Dust* and *What I Don't Know About the Drama*. [Toronto?]: Canadian Broadcasting Corporation, 3 and 5 February 1938. Aluminum acetate transcription, 33 1/3 rpm, 16 inches. With an audio cassette transcribed from the original by John Stratton on 18 October 1994. "Professors; or, My Fifty Years Among the Chalk Dust" was re-broadcast on CBC, Morningside with Peter Gzowski, on 10 October 1994.
SOURCE: CS. See "Leacock Recording Acquired by Museum," *Toronto Globe and Mail*, 10 September 1994, p. C3.

I2  "My Old College." 3 reel-to-reel tape recordings, 7.5 speed, 1943, nos. AT1266, AT1267, and AT7084 (recorded by the Canadian Broadcasting Corporation, 8 December 1969), and AT7070.
SOURCE: QMM Archives. See also A97 and A120.

I3  *The Voice of Stephen Leacock*. Orillia, ON: The Stephen Leacock Museum, 1995. Introduced by Peter Gzowski. Audio cassette, RDRC–1826. Includes "Professors; or, My Fifty Years Among the Chalk Dust," "What I Don't Know About the Drama," and "My Old College." Also the following read by John Drainie: "The Difficulties with Public Speaking," "A Study in Still Life," "The Country Hotel," "He Guessed Right," and "While You're at It."
SOURCE: CS (2 copies); SLM (many copies for sale).

## Braille

I4  *Mark Twain*. [New York?]: SBH sponsor, Amercan Red Cross, New York Chapter, transcribing agency, 1934. 2 vols., 29 × 28 cm. handcopied, grade 2. BR.
SOURCE: LOCIS DATABASE.

I5  *Charles Dickens*. 1934. [s.n.]: DBPH, sponsor. CPH, transcribing agency, 1934. 3 vols., 28 × 28 cm. press, grade 2. BR.
SOURCE: LOCIS DATABASE. According to Curry ("Stephen Butler Leacock: A Check-List," *Bulletin of Bibliography* 22, no. 5 (January–April 1958): 106–9), this transcription was published in Cincinnati by Clovernook Printing House.

I6  *How to Write*. Louisville, KY: American Printing House for the Blind, 1943. 3 vols.
SOURCE: SLM; Curry (see I5).

I7 *Happy Stories Just to Laugh at.* Louisville, KY: American Printing House for the Blind, 1944. 2 vols.
SOURCE: Curry (see I5).

I8 *My Discovery of England.* Toronto: CNIB, 1962. 3 vols.
SOURCE: LOCIS DATABASE. Another entry in this database has the date [197?], and notes that this Braille edition was transcribed from the 1961 M&S edition (A37c).

I9 *The Boy I Left Behind Me.* Toronto: CNIB, [197?]. 4 vols.
SOURCE: LOCIS DATABASE (transcribed from the English edition, A104b).

I10 *Moonbeams from the Larger Lunacy.* Toronto: CNIB, [197?]. 4 vols.
SOURCE: LOCIS DATABASE (transcribed from the 1969 reprint of the 1964 M&S edition, A21c).

I11 *Winnowed Wisdom.* London: Royal National Institute for the Blind, [197?]. 2 vols.
SOURCE: LOCIS DATABASE.

I12 *Arcadian Adventures with the Idle Rich.* Toronto: CNIB, 1980. 4 vols.
SOURCE: CNIB; LOCIS DATABASE.

I13 *Feast of Stephen: An Anthology of the Less Familiar Writings of Stephen Leacock, with a Critical Introduction by Robertson Davies.* Toronto: CNIB, 1980. 4 vols.
SOURCE: CNIB; SLM; LOCIS DATABASE.

I14 *Further Foolishness: Sketches and Satires on the Follies of the Day.* Toronto: CNIB, 1980. 4 vols.
SOURCE: CNIB; LOCIS DATABASE.

I15 *Nonsense Novels.* Toronto: CNIB, 1980. 3 vols.
SOURCE: CNIB; LOCIS DATABASE.

I16 *Sunshine Sketches of a Little Town.* Toronto: CNIB, 1980. 4 vols.
SOURCE: CNIB; LOCIS DATABASE.

I17 *Literary Lapses.* With an afterword by Robertson Davies. Toronto: CNIB, 1984. 3 vols.
SOURCE: CNIB; LOCIS DATABASE.

### Talking Books

I18 *Laugh with Leacock: An Anthology of the Best Work of Stephen Leacock.* [s.n.]: DBPH, sponsor. APH, recording agency. APH, distributor, n.d. 14 sides, 10 inches, 16 rpm TB.
SOURCE: LOCIS DATABASE.

I19 *My Discovery of England.* Louisville, KY: American Printing House for the Blind, 1941. 8 records.
SOURCE: Curry (see I5).

I20 *My Remarkable Uncle and Other Sketches.* Louisville, KY: American Printing House for the Blind, 1943. 3 records.
SOURCE: Curry (see I5).

I21 *Happy Stories Just to Laugh at.* Louisville, KY: American Printing House for the Blind, 1943. 14 records.
SOURCE: Curry (see I5).

**I22** *Sunshine Sketches of a Little Town.* [s.n.]: CBC/Radio-Canada, 1963. Expiry: June 30/[19]63. 13 phonodiscs, 33 1/3 rpm, 12 inches. Programme E–161. Thirteen instalments read by John Drainie for the Canadian Broadcasting Corporation.
SOURCE: CS.

**I23** *The World of Stephen Leacock a 13–part Anthology.* Montreal: Radio Canada International, [197?]. 7 sound discs (391 minutes), 33 1/3 rpm, stereo, 12 inches, E–675–687, E–102. Narrator: John Drainie. Includes excerpts from *Literary Lapses, Nonsense Novels, Behind the Beyond, Frenzied Fiction, My Discovery of England, Winnowed Wisdom, Short Circuits, The Iron Man and the Tin Woman, Model Memoirs, Too Much College,* and *My Remarkable Uncle.* Also contains "The Wizard of Finance," "The Arrested Philanthropy of Edward Tomlinson," "The Rival Churches of St. Asaph and St. Osoph," and "Cast Up by the Sea." With "Stephen Leacock, a Portrait from Memory: Recollections of Family and Friends."
SOURCE: RLIN database.

**I24** *Bernard Braden Reads Stephen Leacock.* [London?]: Capitol, [1970?]. 33 1/3 rpm, microgroove, stereo, 12 inches, ST 6335. Recorded in England, at the Oxford Union Society before undergraduates, on the occasion of the centenary of Leacock's birth. Includes "Insurance Up to Date," "We Have with Us Tonight," "The Conjurer's Revenge," "Impressions of London," "My Financial Career," "A Model Dialogue," "Oxford As I See It," and "Save Me from My Friends."
SOURCE: OONL.

**I25** *John Drainie Reads Stephen Leacock.* Waterloo, ON: Melbourne, SMLP 4015, 1970. 33 1/3 stereo, 12 inches, phonodisc. Includes "My Financial Career," "We Have with Us Tonight," "My Lost Dollar," "Borrowing a Match," "My Friend the Reporter," "Mother's Day," "How to Borrow Money," "While You're at It," "Boarding House Geometry," and "Familiar Magic of Fishing."
SOURCE: CS; OH.

**I26** *Laugh with Leacock: An Anthology of the Best Work of Stephen Leacock.* Louisville, KY: American Printing House for the Blind, 1971. Narrator, Barry Bernson. 7 audio cassettes, 10:30 hours.
SOURCE: OTNY.
  Also issued in Toronto: CNIB, 1980. 2 audio cassettes, 2.5 cm., 4 track, mono.
SOURCE: CNIB.

**I27** *The Art of the Essay: from Francis Bacon to Stephen Leacock.* New York: Caedmon Records, 1974. Narrator: Ian Richardson.
SOURCE: DLC.

**I28** *College Days.* Vancouver: Charles Crane Memorial Library, 1974. 2 audio cassettes, 3 hours, 4.75 cm., 2 track, mono. Narrator: Catherine Crowell.
SOURCE: LOCIS DATABASE.

**I29** *Sunshine Sketches of a Little Town.* Vancouver: Charles Crane Memorial Library, 1976. Narrator: Barbara-Anne Eddy.
SOURCE: LOCIS DATABASE.

**I30** *Gertrude the Governess and Other Works.* New York: Caedmon Records, 1977. 1 audio cassette, 48 minutes; 1 7/8 mon. Dolby processed disc., CDL 51559. Also issued as a

phonodisc 33 1/3 rpm, TC 1559. Adapted and read by Christopher Plummer. Includes "I Wish I Could Remember," "It Is a Very Great Pleasure," "My Financial Career," "Gertrude the Governess." "Let Me Sing to You the Nothingness," "The Business of Growing Old," "Shakespeare," "The Life of Lea and Perrins," "The Awful Fate of Melpomenus Jones," and "Idleness."
SOURCE: CS (record); OH (cassette); OTNY (cassette); LOCIS DATABASE (cassette).

131 *Nonsense Novels.* Chicago: Illinois Regional Library, sponsor. Johanna Bureau for the Blind and Visually Handicapped, recording agency, 1977. 2 audio cassettes, C–90, 15/16 ips, 2 track.
SOURCE: LOCIS DATABASE.

131a *The Hallmark Playhouse.* Houston: Pastime Products, 1977. 1 audio cassette, 2 track, mono. Includes "My Financial Career," broadcast on 18 November 1948, ". . . stars Jack Benny in a comedy about a man who has an irrational fear of banks."
SOURCE: OCLC WorldCat database.

132 *Laugh with Leacock: An Anthology of the Best Work of Stephen Leacock.* Vancouver: Charles Crane Memorial Library, 1978. 7 audio cassettes, 1 7/8 ips, 2 track, mono.
SOURCE: LOCIS DATABASE.

133 *Stories for Christmas.* Toronto: Canadian Broadcasting Corporation, 1980. 1 sound disc recording, 33 1/3 rpm, mono, PR-15 WRC-1364. A selection of Christmas stories read by Alan Maitland, including Leacock's "Hoodoo McFiggin's Christmas" and "The Errors of Santa Claus."
SOURCE: OONL.

134 *Sunshine Sketches of a Little Town.* Toronto: CNIB, 1980. 5 audio cassettes, 2 track, mono, 7:30 hours. Narrator, John Drainie.
SOURCE: OTNY.
Also issued in 2 audio cassettes, 2.5 cm., 4 track, mono, 6:15 hours.
SOURCE: CNIB; LOCIS DATABASE (dated [197?]).

135 *An Evening with Stephen Leacock.* Toronto: Tapestry Records & Tapes Ltd., 1981. 1 sound disc recording, 33 1/3 rpm, stereo, 12 inches, GD 7376. Also issued as an audio cassette, 4.75 cm., 2 track, mono. Recorded live at the National Arts Centre, Ottawa, 28–9 November 1980. Read by John Stark, introduction narrated by Gordon Pinsent. Includes "Ladies & Gentlemen Stephen Leacock," "Insurance As I See It," "With the Photographer," "The New Food," "The Card Trick," "The Conjurer's Revenge," "My Financial Career," "Speaking Patois," "In Dry Toronto," and "Save Me from My Friends." Leacock's stories adapted by Stark and Jovanka Bach.
SOURCE: CS (2 copies, disc); OH (disc); LOCIS DATABASE (cassette).

136 *Arcadian Adventures with the Idle Rich.* Toronto: CNIB, 1982. 2 tape reels, 18 cm., master 9.5 cm., 4 track, mono.
SOURCE: LOCIS DATABASE (recorded from the 1969 reprint of the 1959 M&S edition, A16d).

137 *Literary Lapses.* With an afterword by Robertson Davies. Toronto: CNIB, 1982. 1 audio cassette, 2.5 cm., 4 track, mono, 6 hours. Narrator, Steve Dalton.
SOURCE: CNIB.
Also issued in 4 cassettes, 2 track mono, with introduction by Davies and publication date of 1983.

SOURCE: OTNY; LOCIS DATABASE (1982 date, 5:05 hours, recorded from 1957 M&S edition, A5e).

**138** *My Remarkable Uncle and Other Sketches.* With an afterword by Barbara Nimmo. Toronto: CNIB, 1982. 2 audio cassettes, 2.5 cm., 4 track, mono, 6:30 hours. Narrator, Pete McGarvey.
SOURCE: CNIB.
  Also issued in 5 cassettes, 2 track, mono, with publication date of 1983.
SOURCE: OTNY; LOCIS DATABASE (1982 date, 7 hours, recorded from 1965 M&S edition, A93d). Another recording, dated 1982, consists of 2 tape reels, 18 cm., master 9.5 cm., 4 track, mono.
SOURCE: LOCIS DATABASE.

**139** *Un été à Mariposa: croquis en clin d'oeil.* Montreal: INCA, 1986. 1 audio cassette, 3:25 hours, matrice 15/16 po/s. 4 pistes, mono. Narrator, Roger Gagnon.
SOURCE: LOCIS DATABASE.
  Also issued Montreal: CNIB, 1987. 2 audio cassettes, 6:30 hours, 2.5 cm., 4 pistes, mono. Narrator, Gisèle Trepanier.
SOURCE: LOCIS DATABASE.

**140** *Un grain de sel.* [Montreal]: CNIB, 1986. 1 cassette, C–90, 15/16 ips., 4 track. Narrator: Roger Gagnon.
SOURCE: LOCIS DATABASE.
  Also issued in Montreal: INCA, 1987. 2 audio cassettes, 6:30 hours, matrice 2.5 cm., 4 pistes, mono. Narrator, Gisèle Trepanier.
SOURCE: LOCIS DATABASE.

**141** *Laugh with Leacock: An Anthology of the Best Work of Stephen Leacock.* [s.n.]: NLS, sponsor. Talking Book Publishers, recording agency, EVA, distributor, 1987. 2 audio cassettes, C–90, 15/16 ips, 4 track. Narrator, Harry Elders.
SOURCE: LOCIS DATABASE.

**142** *Leacock Collection.* Toronto: CBC Radio Works, 1994. RW 9417, 1 audio cassette, stereo. Narrator, Alan Maitland. Includes "My Financial Career," "How to Live to Be 200," "The Great Election of Missinaba County," "The Old, Old Story of How Five Men Went Fishing," "Buggam Grange: A Good Old Ghost Story."
SOURCE: CS; OH; OTNY; SLM (many copies).

**143** *Spirited Yarns: Classic Humorous Ghost Stories.* Vol. 1. Vancouver: Stuffed Moose, 1996. 1 audio cassette. Contains selections from Charles Dickens, Arthur Conan Doyle, Mark Twain, and Leacock. Includes "Buggam Grange: A Good Old Ghost Story." Audio of this story avaliable at hhtp.//www.scifi/pulp/set/Leacock.
SOURCE: hhtp.//www.amazon.com.

**144** *The Prose and Poetry Series.* Album 1. [s.l.]: Enrichment Teaching Materials, n.d. 12 inch 33 1/3 rpm record, 4 sides, mono. Includes a selection of literary pieces, including "How We Kept Mother's Day."
SOURCE: A-V Online.

**145** *Canadian Writers and Their Themes Series.* Toronto: CBC, n.d. 1 track, one 7/8 cassette, mono. Includes a dramatization of "My Financial Career."
SOURCE: A-V Online.

## Films

**146**  *My Financial Career.* New York: National Film Board of Canada, 1962. Distributed by Sterling Educational Films. 16 mm film optical sound, 6 minutes, 30 seconds, colour, animated version. Directed by Gerald Potterton; animated by Gerald Potterton and Grant Munro; voice and narration by Stanley Jackson.
SOURCE: A-V ONLINE.

**147**  *The Awful Fate of Melpomenus Jones.* [Ottawa]: National Film Board of Canada, 1983. 7 minutes, 48 seconds, colour, animated version. Directed and animated by Gerald Potterton; voice and narration by Mavor Moore.
SOURCE: NATIONAL FILM BOARD OF CANADA WEB SITE (http://www.nfb.ca).

**148**  *How We Kept Mother's Day.* [Ottawa]: National Film Board of Canada, 1994. 9 minutes, 53 seconds, colour, animated version. Directed and animated by Eva Szasz; voice and narration by Brian Richardson.
SOURCE: NATIONAL FILM BOARD OF CANADA WEB SITE (http://www.nfb.ca).

**149**  *Hoodoo McFiggin's Christmas.* [Ottawa]: National Film Board of Canada, 1995. 8 minutes, 38 seconds, colour, animated version. Director Eva Szasz. Voice and narration by Alan Maitland.
SOURCE: NATIONAL FILM BOARD OF CANADA WEB SITE (http://www.nfb.ca).

# Section J: DICTIONARY AND ENCYLOPEDIA ARTICLES

**J6.1** "#12 Local Government," in Frederick Converse, ed., *The Americana: A Universal Reference Library* (New York: Scientific American Compiling Department, 1906), vol. 3, not paged. Article within the section of Department of Canadian History and Development. Reprinted in vol. 4 of the 1911 ed.

**J6.2** "#14 Imperial Federation," in Frederick Converse, ed., *The Americana: A Universal Reference Library* (New York: Scientific American Compiling Department, 1906), vol. 3, not paged. Article within the section of Department of Canadian History and Development. Reprinted in vol. 4 of the 1911 ed.

**J6.3** "#19 Public Education," in Frederick Converse, ed., *The Americana: A Universal Reference Library* (New York: Scientific American Compiling Department, 1906), vol. 3, not paged. Article within the section of Department of Canadian History and Development. Reprinted in vol. 4 of the 1911 ed.

**J6.4** "#29 The Ashburton Treaty," in Frederick Converse, ed., *The Americana: A Universal Reference Library* (New York: Scientific American Compiling Department, 1906), vol. 3, not paged. Article within the section of Department of Canadian History and Development. Reprinted in vol. 4 of the 1911 ed.

**J6.5** "#30 Clergy Reserves," in Frederick Converse, ed., *The Americana: A Universal Reference Library* (New York: Scientific American Compiling Department, 1906), vol. 3, not paged. Article within the section of Department of Canadian History and Development. Reprinted in vol. 4 of the 1911 ed.

**J6.6** "#33 The Washington Treaty," in Frederick Converse, ed., *The Americana: A Universal Reference Library* (New York: Scientific American Compiling Department, 1906), vol. 3, not paged. Article within the section of Department of Canadian History and Development. Reprinted in vol. 4 of the 1911 ed.

**J6.7** "#45 Granger Movement," in Frederick Converse, ed., *The Americana: A Universal Reference Library* (New York: Scientific American Compiling Department, 1906), vol. 3, not paged. Article within the section of Department of Canadian History and Development. Reprinted in vol. 4 of the 1911 ed.

**J6.8** "#48 Reciprocity Between Canada and the United States," in Frederick Converse, ed., *The Americana: A Universal Reference Library* (New York: Scientific American Compiling Department, 1906), vol. 3, not paged. Article within the section of Department of Canadian History and Development. Reprinted in vol. 4 of the 1911 ed.

**J6.9** "Canadian Universities," in Frederick Converse, ed., *The Americana: A Universal*

*Reference Library* (New York: Scientific American Compiling Department, 1906), vol. 3, not paged. Reprinted in vol. 4 of the 1911 ed.

J6.10  "Riel's Rebellion," in Frederick Converse, ed., *The Americana: A Universal Reference Library* (New York: Scientific American Compiling Department, 1906), vol. 13, not paged. Reprinted in vol. 16 of the 1911 ed.

J20.1  "#13 Local Government," *The Encyclopaedia Americana*, vol. 5 (1920): 348–9. In the Canada section. Reprinted in the 1923, 1924, 1929, and 1937 eds. As "#11 Local Government," vol. 5 (1945): 350–1.

J20.2  "#14 Imperial Federation," *The Encyclopaedia Americana*, vol. 5 (1920): 350–2. In the Canada section. Reprinted in the 1923, 1924, 1929, and 1937 eds. As "#9 Imperial Federation," vol. 5 (1945): 343–7.

J20.3  "#20 Public Education," *The Encyclopaedia Americana*, vol. 5 (1920): 374–7. In the Canada section. Reprinted in the 1923, 1924, and 1929 eds. In the 1937 ed., the entry appears in vol. 23, "Revised by M. Edmund Speare, Editorial Staff of The Americana."

J20.4  "#33 The Ashburton Treaty," *The Encyclopaedia Americana*, vol. 5 (1920): 418–9. In the Canada section. Reprinted in the 1923, 1924, 1929, and 1937 eds. As "#13 The Ashburton Treaty," vol. 5 (1945): 353–4.

J20.5  "#34 Clergy Reserves," *the Encyclopaedia Americana*, vol. 5 (1920): 419–20. In the Canada section. Reprinted in the 1923, 1929, and 1937 eds. As "#14 Clergy Reserves," vol. 5 (1945): 354–5.

J20.6  "#37 The Washington Treaty," *The Encyclopaedia Americana*, vol. 5 (1920): 425–6. In the Canada section. Reprinted in the 1923, 1924, 1929, and 1937 eds. As "#41 Location Government," vol. 5 (1945): 464–5.

J20.7  "#50 Granger Movement," *The Encyclopaedia Americana*, vol. 5 (1920): 473–4. In the Canada section. In the Canada section. Reprinted in the 1924 ed.

J20.8  "Riel's Rebellion," *The Encyclopaedia Americana*, vol. 23 (1920): 514–5. In the Canada section. Reprinted in the 1923, 1929, 1937, and 1945 eds.

J26.1  "New Brunswick," *Encyclopaedia Britannica*, 13th ed., supp. vol. 2 (1926): 1043. Signed "S. Lea."

J26.2  "Nova Scotia," *Encyclopaedia Britannica*, 13th ed., supp. vol. 2 (1926): 1091. Signed "S. Lea."

J26.3  "Ontario," *Encyclopaedia Britannica*, 13th ed., supp. vol. 2 (1926): 1116–7. Signed "S. Lea."

J26.4  "Prince Edward Island," *Encyclopaedia Britannica*, 13th ed., supp. vol. 3 (1926): 218. Signed "S. Lea."

J26.5  "Quebec," *Encyclopaedia Britannica*, 13th ed., supp. vol. 3 (1926): 271. Signed "S. Lea."

J29.1  "Humour," *The Encyclopaedia Britannica*, 14th ed., 11 (1929): 885. Signed "S. Lea." The first part of the article is signed "G. K. C." (i.e. Gilbert Keith Chesterton). Leacock wrote the section entitled "American Humour."

J29.2  "Browne, Charles Farrar," in Allen Johnson, ed., *Dictionary of American Biography* (New York: Charles Scribner's Sons, 1929), vol. 3, 162–4. Signed "S.L."

**J34.1** "Newell, Robert Henry," in Dumas Malone, ed., *Dictionary of American Biography* (New York: Charles Scribner's Sons, 1934), vol. 13, 448–9. Signed "S.L."

**J34.2** "Nye, Edgar Wilson," Dumas Malone, ed., *Dictionary of American Biography* (New York: Charles Scribner's Sons, 1934), vol. 13, 598–699. Signed "S.L."

**J38.1** "Canada," *Encyclopaedia Britannica Book of the Year* (1938 [for 1937]): 131–4. Signed "S. Lea." The volumes of the *Britannica Book of the Year* for 1937 to 1941 were also published cumulatively in 1942 under the title *Britannica Book of the Year Omnibus*.

**J39.1** "Canada," *Encyclopaedia Britannica Book of the Year* (1939 [for 1938]): 139–42. Signed "S. Lea."

**J40.1** "Canada," *Britannica Book of the Year* (1940 [for 1939]): 127–8, 130–1. Signed "S. Lea." All sections written by Leacock except "War Finance and Industry. " English issue entitled *Supplement to 1940 Britannica Book of the Year*.

**J41.1** "Humour," *Encyclopaedia Britannica* 11 (1941): 883–5. Signed "S. Lea." Identified as the author of this article in reprintings up to 1959.

**J41.2** "Canada," *Supplement to 1941 Britannica Book of the Year* (1941 [for 1940]): 127–30. Signed "S. Lea." All sections written by Leacock except the final section, "War Finance and Industry. "

**J42.1** "Canada, Dominion of," *Britannica Book of the Year* (1942 [for 1941]): 138–40, 142. Signed "S. Lea." All sections written by Leacock except the final section, "Canada at War."

**J42.2** "Meighen, Robert," *Britannica Book of the Year* (1942 [for 1941]): 424–5. Unsigned. Leacock sent his "little biography" of Meighen to *Britannica*'s editor, Walter Yust, on 8 January 1942.

**J43.1** "Canada, Dominion of," *Britannica Book of the Year* (1943 [for 1942]): 148–53. Signed "S. Lea." On p. xviii Leacock is recorded as having written only a part of this article for the yearbook. It would appear that he wrote the entire article, however, and that the editors carried over the listing of authorship from the previous year. In the section of the article on "Canada at War," the reader is informed that the Canadian government withheld all information in regard to the war. The section is based on the monthly publication, *Canada at War*, and the *Canada Year Book*, both of which are found in Leacock s library at SLM.

**J43.2** "Conant, Gordon," *Britannica Book of the Year* (1943 [for 1942]): 202. Unsigned.

**J43.3** "Acadia," *Encylopaedia Britannica* 1 (1943): 89. Unsigned. Trivial revision or mere inspection.

**J43.4** "Alberta," *Encylopaedia Britannica* 1 (1943): 525–7. Signed "S. Lea." Serious revision (1,000 words). Identified as the author of this article in reprintings up to 1952, as a co-contributor up to 1963.

**J43.5** "Brandon," *Encyclopaedia Britannica* 4 (1943): 34. Unsigned. Trivial revision or mere inspection.

**J43.6** "Charlottetown," *Encylopaedia Britannica* 5 (1943): 296. Unsigned. Trivial revision or mere inspection.

**J43.7** "Chatham or Miramichi," *Encylopaedia Britannica* 5 (1943): 320. Unsigned. Trivial revision or mere inspection.

J43.8 "Chatham [Ontario]," *Encylopaedia Britannica* 5 (1943): 320–1. Unsigned. Trivial revision or mere inspection.

J43.9 "Chicoutimi," *Encylopaedia Britannica* 5 (1943): 462. Unsigned. Trivial revision or mere inspection.

J43.10 "Cobalt," *Encylopaedia Britannica* 5 (1943): 929. Unsigned. Trivial revision or mere inspection.

J43.11 "Cobourg," *Encylopaedia Britannica* 5 (1943): 936. Unsigned. Trivial revision or mere inspection.

J43.12 "Collingwood," *Encylopaedia Britannica* 6 (1943): 19. Unsigned. Trivial revision or mere inspection.

J43.13 "Cornwall," *Encylopaedia Britannica* 6 (1943): 454. Unsigned. Trivial revision or mere inspection.

J43.14 "Dartmouth," *Encylopaedia Britannica* 7 (1943): 64. Unsigned. Trivial revision or mere inspection.

J43.15 "Dawson," *Encylopaedia Britannica* 7 (1943): 91. Unsigned. Trivial revision or mere inspection.

J43.16 "Edmonton," *Encylopaedia Britannica* 7 (1943): 961. Unsigned. Trivial revision or mere inspection.

J43.17 "Esquimault or Esquimalt," *Encylopaedia Britannica* 8 (1943): 715. Unsigned. Trivial revision or mere inspection.

J43.18 "Fernie," *Encylopaedia Britannica* 9 (1943): 180. Unsigned. Trivial revision or mere inspection.

J43.19 "Fort William," *Encylopaedia Britannica* 9 (1943): 547. Unsigned. Trivial revision or mere inspection.

J43.20 "Fredericton," *Encylopaedia Britannica* 9 (1943): 728. Unsigned. Trivial revision or mere inspection.

J43.21 "Glace Bay," *Encylopaedia Britannica* 10 (1943): 374. Unsigned. Trivial revision or mere inspection.

J43.22 "Grand Banks," *Encylopaedia Britannica* 10 (1943): 631. Unsigned. Trivial revision or mere inspection.

J43.23 "Grand Forks," *Encylopaedia Britannica* 10 (1943): 634. Unsigned. Trivial revision or mere inspection.

J43.24 "Grand'mere," *Encylopaedia Britannica* 10 (1943): 635. Unsigned. Trivial revision or mere inspection.

J43.25 "Guelph," *Encylopaedia Britannica* 10 (1943): 947. Unsigned. Minor revision (150 words).

J43.26 "Halifax," *Encyclopaedia Britannica* 11 (1943): 94. Unsigned. Trivial revision or mere inspection.

J43.27 "Hamilton," *Encylopaedia Britannica* 11 (1943): 128–9. Unsigned. Minor revision (150 words).

J43.28 "Hull," *Encylopaedia Britannica* 11 (1943): 874. Unsigned. Trivial revision or mere inspection.

J43.29 "Ingersoll," *Encylopaedia Britannica* 12 (1943): 351. Unsigned. Trivial revision or mere inspection.

J43.30 "Kamloops," *Encylopaedia Britannica* 13 (1943): 251. Unsigned. Trivial revision or mere inspection.

J43.31 "Kenora," *Encylopaedia Britannica* 13 (1943): 326. Unsigned. Trivial revision or mere inspection.

J43.32 "Kingston," *Encylopaedia Britannica* 13 (1943): 401. Unsigned. Trivial revision or mere inspection.

J43.33 "Kitchener," *Encylopaedia Britannica* 13 (1943): 420. Unsigned. Trivial revision or mere inspection.

J43.34 "Lachine," *Encylopaedia Britannica* 13 (1943): 572 Unsigned. Trivial revision or mere inspection.

J43.35 "Lévis," *Encylopaedia Britannica* 13 (1943): 979. Unsigned. Trivial revision or mere inspection.

J43.36 "Lindsay," *Encylopaedia Britannica* 14 (1943): 151. Unsigned. Trivial revision or mere inspection.

J43.37 "London [Ontario]," *Encylopaedia Britannica* 14 (1943): 346. Unsigned. Trivial revision or mere inspection.

J43.38 "Louisburg," *Encylopaedia Britannica* 14 (1943): 423 Unsigned. Trivial revision or mere inspection.

J43.39 "Manitoba," *Encylopaedia Britannica* 14 (1943): 812–3. Signed "S. LEA". Serious revision (1,000 words). Identified as the author of this article in reprintings up to 1951 and as a co-author up to 1960.

J43.40 "Moncton," *Encylopaedia Britannica* 15 (1943): 690. Unsigned. Trivial revision or mere inspection.

J43.41 "Montreal," *Encylopaedia Britannica* 15 (1943): 770–2. Signed "S. LEA." Identified as the author of this article in reprintings up to 1952 and as a co-author up to 1960.

J43.42 "Moose Jaw," *Encylopaedia Britannica* 15 (1943): 786. Unsigned. Trivial revision or mere inspection.

J43.43 "Nanaimo," *Encylopaedia Britannica* 16 (1943): 65. Unsigned. Trivial revision or mere inspection.

J43.44 "Nelson," *Encylopaedia Britannica* 16 (1943): 206. Unsigned. Trivial revision or mere inspection.

J43.45 "New Brunswick," *Encylopaedia Britannica* 16 (1943): 277–8. Signed "S. LEA." Serious revision (1,000 words). Identified as the author of this article in reprintings up to 1952 and as a co-author up to 1960.

J43.46 "New Glasgow," *Encylopaedia Britannica* 16 (1943): 296. Unsigned. Trivial revision or mere inspection.

**J43.47** "New Westminster," *Encylopaedia Britannica* 16 (1943): 365. Unsigned. Trivial revision or mere inspection.

**J43.48** "Newfoundland," *Encylopaedia Britannica* 16 (1943): 287–95. Signed "B.W.; X." By Beckles Willson but revised by Leacock. "X" is the initial used for anonymous contributors.

**J43.49** "Niagara Falls," *Encylopaedia Britannica* 16 (1943): 406. Unsigned. Trivial revision or mere inspection.

**J43.50** "North Bay," *Encylopaedia Britannica* 16 (1943): 519. Unsigned. Trivial revision or mere inspection.

**J43.51** "Northwest Territories," *Encylopaedia Britannica* 16 (1943): 542, 542A–8. Signed "S. LEA." Identified as the author of this article in reprintings up to 1952 and as a co-author up to 1959.

**J43.52** "Nova Scotia," *Encylopaedia Britannica* 16 (1943): 569–71. Signed "S. LEA." Serious revision (800 words). Identified as the author of this article in reprintings up to 1952 and as a co-author up to 1960.

**J43.53** "Ontario — History," *Encylopaedia Britannica* 16 (1943): 796–7. Signed "G.M.W.; X." By George Mackinnon Wrong but revised by Leacock. "X" is the initial used for anonymous contributors. Serious revision (1,500 words).

**J43.54** "Orillia," *Encylopaedia Britannica* 16 (1943): 903. Unsigned. Trivial revision or mere inspection.

**J43.55** "Oshawa," *Encylopaedia Britannica* 16 (1943): 949. Unsigned. Trivial revision or mere inspection.

**J43.56** "Ottawa," *Encylopaedia Britannica* 16 (1943): 963–4. Signed "L.J.B.; X." By Lawrence J. Burpee but revised by Leacock. "X" is the initial used for anonymous contributors. Minor revision (150 words).

**J43.57** "Owen Sound," *Encylopaedia Britannica* 16 (1943): 981. Unsigned. Trivial revision or mere inspection.

**J43.58** "Pembroke," *Encylopaedia Britannica* 17 (1943): 458. Unsigned. Trivial revision or mere inspection.

**J43.59** "Peterborough," *Encylopaedia Britannica* 17 (1943): 647. Unsigned. Trivial revision or mere inspection.

**J43.60** "Pictou," *Encylopaedia Britannica* 17 (1943): 914. Unsigned. Trivial revision or mere inspection.

**J43.61** "Portage La Prairie," *Encylopaedia Britannica* 18 (1943): 245. Unsigned. Trivial revision or mere inspection.

**J43.62** "Port Arthur," *Encylopaedia Britannica* 18 (1943): 246. Unsigned. Trivial revision or mere inspection.

**J43.63** "Prince Edward Island," *Encylopaedia Britannica* 18 (1943): 495–6. Signed "S. LEA."

**J43.64** "Prince Rupert," *Encylopaedia Britannica* 18 (1943): 496. Unsigned. Trivial revision or mere inspection.

**J43.65** "Quebec [province]," *Encylopaedia Britannica* 18 (1943): 836–8. Signed "W. BY." Written by Wilfrid Bovey but according to Leacock, he made serious revisions (1,000 words) to the entry.

**J43.66** "Quebec [city]," *Encylopaedia Britannica* 18 (1943): 838–40. The first part signed "A. P. CO.; W. S. WA" (Arthur Philemon Coleman and W.S. Wallace). The section part, "Wolfe's Quebec Expedition," signed "B.H.L.H.; X." (Captain B.H. Liddell Hart and anonymous contributor). According to Leacock, he made minor revisions to this entry (200 words).

**J43.67** "Red River Settlement," *Encyclopaedia Britannica* 19 (1943): 26. Unsigned. Trivial revision or mere inspection.

**J43.68** "Regina," *Encyclopaedia Britannica* 19 (1943): 71. Unsigned. Trivial revision or mere inspection.

**J43.69** "Revelstoke," *Encyclopaedia Britannica* 19 (1943): 239. Unsigned. Trivial revision or mere inspection.

**J43.70** "Rivière du Loup," *Encyclopaedia Britannica* 19 (1943): 338. Unsigned. Trivial revision or mere inspection.

**J43.71** "Rouyn," *Encyclopaedia Britannica* 19 (1943): 588. Unsigned. Trivial revision or mere inspection.

**J43.72** "Sarnia," *Encyclopaedia Britannica* 19 (1943): 1001. Unsigned. Trivial revision or mere inspection.

**J43.73** "St. Catharines," *Encyclopaedia Britannica* 19 (1943): 824. Unsigned. Trivial revision or mere inspection.

**J43.74** "Ste. Anne de Beaupré," *Encyclopaedia Britannica* 19 (1943): 827. Unsigned. Trivial revision or mere inspection.

**J43.75** "St. Hyacinthe," *Encyclopaedia Britannica* 19 (1943): 834. Unsigned. Trivial revision or mere inspection.

**J43.76** "Saint John," *Encyclopaedia Britannica* 19 (1943): 835. Unsigned. Trivial revision or mere inspection.

**J43.77** "St. John's," *Encyclopaedia Britannica* 19 (1943): 838. Unsigned. Trivial revision or mere inspection.

**J43.78** "St. Thomas," *Encyclopaedia Britannica* 19 (1943): 859. Unsigned. Trivial revision or mere inspection.

**J43.79** "Saskatchewan," *Encylopaedia Britannica* 20 (1943): 2A–B, 3. Signed "S. LEA." Serious revision (1,000 words). Identified as the author of this article in reprintings up to 1952 and as a co-author up to 1960.

**J43.80** "Saskatoon," *Encylopaedia Britannica* 20 (1943): 3. Unsigned. Trivial revision or mere inspection.

**J43.81** "Shawinigan Falls," *Encylopaedia Britannica* 20 (1943): 471–2. Unsigned. Trivial revision or mere inspection.

**J43.82** "Sherbrooke," *Encylopaedia Britannica* 20 (1943): 495. Unsigned. Trivial revision or mere inspection.

**J43.83** "Smith's Falls," *Encylopaedia Britannica* 20 (1943): 836. Unsigned. Trivial revision or mere inspection.

**J43.84** "Sorel," *Encyclopaedia Britannica* 21 (1943): 2. Unsigned. Trivial revision or mere inspection.

**J43.85** "Stratford," *Encyclopaedia Britannica* 21 (1943): 459. Unsigned. Trivial revision or mere inspection.

**J43.86** "Three Rivers or Trois Rivières," *Encyclopaedia Britannica* 22 (1943): 161. Unsigned. Trivial revision or mere inspection.

**J43.87** "Timmins," *Encyclopaedia Britannica* 22 (1943): 229. Unsigned. Trivial revision or mere inspection.

**J43.88** "Toronto," *Encyclopaedia Britannica* 22 (1943): 300. Unsigned. Trivial revision or mere inspection.

**J43.89** "Truro," *Encyclopaedia Britannica* 22 (1943): 510. Unsigned. Trivial revision or mere inspection.

**J83.90** "Ungava," *Encyclopaedia Britannica* 22 (1943): 699. Unsigned. Trivial revision or mere inspection.

**J83.91** "Valleyfield," *Encyclopaedia Britannica* 22 (1943): 956. Unsigned. Trivial revision or mere inspection.

**J83.92** "Vancouver," *Encyclopaedia Britannica* 22 (1943): 970. Unsigned. Trivial revision or mere inspection.

**J43.93** "Victoria," *Encyclopaedia Britannica* 23 (1943): 137. Unsigned. Trivial revision or mere inspection.

**J43.94** "Windsor," *Encyclopaedia Britannica* 23 (1943): 650. Unsigned. Trivial revision or mere inspection.

**J43.95** "Winnipeg," *Encyclopaedia Britannica* 23 (1943): 658. Unsigned. Trivial revision or mere inspection.

**J43.96** "Woodstock," *Encyclopaedia Britannica* 23 (1943): 725. Unsigned. Trivial revision or mere inspection.

**J43.97** "Yarmouth," *Encyclopaedia Britannica* 23 (1943): 878. Unsigned. Trivial revision or mere inspection.

**J43.98** "Yukon Territory," *Encyclopaedia Britannica* 25 (1943): 925. Unsigned. Trivial revision or mere inspection.

**J44.1** "Amherst," *Encyclopaedia Britannica* 1 (1944): 808. Unsigned. Trivial revision or mere inspection.

**J44.2** "Annapolis Royal," *Encylopaedia Britannica* 1 (1944): 982. Unsigned. Trivial revision or mere inspection.

**J44.3** "Banff," *Encyclopaedia Britannica* 3 (1944): 29. Unsigned. Trivial revision or mere inspection.

**J44.4** "Barrie," *Encyclopaedia Britannica* 3 (1944): 141. Unsigned. Trivial revision or mere inspection.

**J44.5**  "Belleville," *Encylopaedia Britannica* 3 (1944): 380. Unsigned. Trivial revision or mere inspection.

**J44.6**  "Brantford," *Encylopaedia Britannica* 4 (1944): 38. Unsigned. Trivial revision or mere inspection.

**J44.7**  "British Columbia," *Encylopaedia Britannica* 4 (1944): 170–3. Signed. Signed "S. Lea." Serious revision (1,000 words). Identified as the author of this article in reprintings up to 1952 and as a co-contributor from 1953–63.

**J44.8**  "Brockville," *Encylopaedia Britannica* 4 (1944): 227. Unsigned. Trivial revision or mere inspection.

**J44.9**  "Calgary," *Encylopaedia Britannica* 4 (1944): 584. Unsigned. Trivial revision or mere inspection.

**J44.10**  "Canada," *Encylopaedia Britannica* 4 (1944): 690–714. Sections written by several contributors: A. P. Co. (Arthur Philemon Coleman), E. M. W. (E.M. Walker), etc. "Area and Population" signed "S. Lea.," but by his own reckoning, Leacock seriously revised the entire article (5,000 words). Leacock's name appears as a co-author of this article in reprintings up to 1958.

**J44.11**  "Cape Breton Island," *Encylopaedia Britannica* 4 (1944): 776–7. Unsigned. Minor revision (150 words).

**J44.12**  "Carleton Place," *Encylopaedia Britannica* 4 (1944): 874. Unsigned. Trivial revision or mere inspection.

**J44.13**  "Franklin," *Encylopaedia Britannica* 9 (1943): 696. Unsigned. Trivial revision or mere inspection.

**J44.14**  "Kirkland Lake," *Encylopaedia Britannica* 13 (1944): 414–5. Unsigned. Minor revision (150 words).

**J44.15**  "Klondike," *Encylopaedia Britannica* 13 (1944): 427. Unsigned. Trivial revision or mere inspection.

**J44.16**  "Mackenzie [river]," *Encylopaedia Britannica* 14 (1944): 589. Unsigned. Article sent to the *Encyclopaedia*'s Walter Yust on 4 June 1943.

**J44.17**  "Sudbury," *Encylopaedia Britannica* 21 (1944): 514. Unsigned. Trivial revision or mere inspection.

**J44.18**  "Sydney," *Encylopaedia Britannica* 21 (1944): 698. Unsigned. Trivial revision or mere inspection.

**J44.19**  "Breadner, Lloyd Samuel," *Britannica Book of the Year* (1944 [for 1943]): 123–4. Signed "J. I. C.; S. Lea." Co-authored with John I. Cooper.

**J44.20**  "Canada, Dominion," *Britannica Book of the Year* (1944 [for 1943]): 150–1. Signed "J. I. C.; S. Lea." Co-authored with John I. Cooper.

**J44.21**  "Drew, George Alexander," *Britannica Book of the Year* (1944 [for 1943]): 240. Signed "J. I. C.; S. Lea." Co-authored with John I. Cooper.

**J44.22**  "McGill, Frank Scholes," *Britannica Book of the Year* (1944 [for 1943]): 414. Signed "S. Lea."

**J44.23**  "McNaughton, Andrew George Latta," *Britannica Book of the Year* (1944 [for 1943]): 416. Signed "J. I. C.; S. Lea." Co-authored with John I. Cooper.

# K Section: CONTRIBUTIONS IN SERIAL ARTICLES AND BOOKS BY OTHERS

**K3.1** Macfarlane Davidson, "Undergraduates," *University Magazine* (Montreal) 2 (April 1903): 138. Davidson reports that Leacock acted as adjudicator of the Freshman-Sophomore debate at McGill University. Leacock declared the sophomores winners because of "the energy of Mr. Edwards, the exactness of Mr. Adams, and the vociferous positiveness of Mr. Jenkins." See also "Literary Society," *McGill Outlook* 5, no. 14 (10 February 1903): 319.

**K22.1** William Caldwell, "Impressions of Ontario V. A Visit to a Canadian Author," *Canadian Magazine of Politics, Science, Art and Literature* 59, no. 1 (May 1922): 55–60, at p. 56. One sentence by Leacock to the desk clerk at the hotel where Caldwell was staying in Orillia is quoted; reprinted as "A Visit to Stephen Leacock in His Orillia Home; Professor William Caldwell, in the 'Canadian Magazine' for May," *Orillia Packet*, 11 May 1922, p. 12.

**K22.2** G.B. Burgin, *More Memoirs (And Some Travels)* (London: Hutchinson, 1922), pp. 33–5. Burgin quotes Leacock's remark, as the guest of a literary club, declining burial near Lord Strathcona at Highgate cemetery because he already had made arrangements for Westminster Abbey. Reprinted as "Stephen Leacock Will Not Be Buried in Orillia," *Orillia Packet*, 30 November 1922, p. 1; in O.J. Stevenson, "The Inimitable Leacock," in *Through the Years* (Toronto: Ryerson, 1952), p. 20. The book is a compilation of contributions that Stevenson made to the *Ontario Agricultural College Review* between 1927 to 1939.

**K23.1** G.B. Burgin, *Many Memories* (New York: E.P. Dutton, 1923), p. 207. Recollected remark of Leacock's, from conversation, about the number of good short speeches given in England.

**K24.4** Rosamond Boultbee, *Pilgrimages and Personalties* (London: Hutchinson & Co., 1924), p. 206. A letter from Leacock to Boultbee, dated 30 October 1916, is printed.

**K26.1** H.M. Ridley, "Leacock, as Master, Made Boys Kiss Each Other Each Minute for Forty-Five Minutes," *Toronto Star Weekly*, 18 December 1926, p. 52. Ridley quotes from a conversation about smoking between Leacock and George R. Parkin, the principal at Upper Canada College. He also quotes a remark of Leacock's recollected by Pelham Edgar concerning a practical joke played on Leacock.

**K34.1** Joseph Dorfman, *Thorstein Veblen and His America* (New York: Viking Press, 1934), pp. 250–1, 506. At the University of Chicago Leacock was a student of Veblen. Dorfman quotes Leacock about Veblen's character and lecturing style.

**K34.2** E.V. Lucas, *Post-Bag Versions* (London: Methuen, 1934). Lucas prints two letters from Leacock, 9 February 1915, p. 43, on satire and 11 May 1917, p. 61.

**K35.1** D.S.R. [Douglas S. Robertson], "Stephen Leacock's Letter to a Writer Recalls a Caning," *Toronto Telegram*, 6 September 1935, p. 6. Leacock wrote a circular letter to a number of his acquaintances. One of the recipients of the letter, D.S.R., who also happened to be one of Leacock's former students at Upper Canada College, quoted part of the letter in his column, "In the Spotlight": "I want you to vote for him [Douglas Gooderham Ross, the Conservative candidate for the Dominion Parliament in St. Paul's riding, Toronto] not because you and I are Conservatives, but because I think that Douglas Ross is the kind of man needed in our Parliament now. We do not want outsiders, cranks and crooks. We need people of our own stock and inheritance on whose character we can rely." After quoting from the letter, D.S.R. recollects his various encounters with Leacock at Upper Canada College. See also K44.2.

**K44.1** *Orillia Packet and Times*, 30 March 1944, p. 5. Unidentified quotations by Leacock about gardening, his great-grandfather John Leacock, and literary composition appear under photographs by Karsh.

**D44.2** D.S.R. [Douglas S. Robertson], "Caned by Leacock — Famous Humorist as Pedagogue," *Toronto Telegram*, 1 April 1944, p. 6, "In the Spotlight" column. Recollections of Leacock as a teacher at Upper Canada College with a brief quotation from conversation.

**K44.3** J.R. Hale, "Local Aspects of the World," *Orillia Packet and Times*, 6 April 1944, p. 1. Hale prints a recent letter to him from Henry Mainer. Mainer quotes some of Leacock's remarks at a lecture to the Dickens Fellowship in Montreal. Although Mainer does not give the date of the lecture, he gives the topic as "Dickens and Women." Leacock gave this talk on 27 February 1934 (see D34.2). Curiously, Mainer says that Leacock at the time was refusing to give speeches. Mainer also quotes Leacock in an anecdote about hat buying.

**K44.4** *Orillia Packet and Times*, 6 April 1944, p. 16, reprints a story from the *Winnipeg Free Press* with quotations about a confrontation between Irvin Cobb and Leacock at the Canadian Club in New York where both were speaking.

**K44.5** Robert M. Bingay, "The Angels Laughing," *Orillia Packet and Times*, 6 April 1944, p. 6. This story, reprinted from the *Detroit Free Press*, quotes from recollected conversations of Leacock.

**K44.6** F.D.L. Smith, "As Stephen Leacock Saw Toronto 70 Years Ago," *Toronto Globe and Mail*, 6 April 1944, p. [6]. One sentence is quoted from a letter to Smith concerning *Canada: the Foundations of Its Future* (A92).

**K44.7** "Good Night — Forever," *Time* 53, no. 15 (10 April 1944): 8. Obituary notice which includes Leacock's comment when he was forced to retire from McGill University: "When I was lecturing at McGill on winter afternoons . . . I must say 'Good night, gentlemen — forever.' " Also includes his quip about the Americanization of Canadian newspapers.

**K44.8** Percy Ghent, "Leacock Manuscript Sent to Collector with a Jovial Note," *Toronto Telegram*, 11 April 1944, p. 6, "In the Spotlight" column. Reprinted as "Stephen Leacock's Opinions on Teaching English," *Toronto Telegram*, 23 August 1949, p. [6]. Ghent includes the text of a letter from Leacock to Mr. Saunders on 31 January 1920 concerning Saunders's request for one of Leacock's manuscripts ("English As She Is Taught in College"). Ghent also quotes from Leacock's manuscript that Rudyard Kipling and Sir James Barrie would have failed entrance examinations to any Canadian University and also includes a quotation on grammar. He notes that both the letter and manuscript are in "our own collection" (i.e.

McGill University); he does not know where or when the manuscript was published (see D15.9). Ghent also quotes the last sentence that Leacock spoke just before his death after Ghent and a fellow technician took radiographs of his chest: "Was I a good boy?"

**K44.9**  J.R. Hale, "Local Aspects of the World," *Orillia Packet and Times*, 27 April 1944, p. 1. Hale quotes Adelphi, the English correspondent of the *Financial Post* relating a story of Leacock giving directions. Since Hale says that Adelphi made these remarks last week, presumably Hale saw them in the *Financial Post*.

**K44.10**  John Culliton, "Stephen Leacock," *McGill News* 25, no. 1 (15 May 1944, Summer): 24–5. Culliton recounts a number of stories about Leacock as a colleague and friend. Several quotations are attributed to Leacock — for example, "If all men were decent and reasonable there would be no need for all the trouble in this world."

**K44.11**  J.P.D. [J.P. Day], "Professor Leacock at McGill," *Canadian Journal of Economics and Political Science* 10 (May 1944): 226–8. On p. 228, Day quotes a letter Leacock sent a colleague at McGill in thanks for a photograph.

**K44.12**  Cyril Clemens, "An Evening with Stephen Leacock," *Catholic World* 951 (June 1944): 236–41. This is presented as a conversation between Leacock and Clemens the year that Leacock retired from McGill University, although it is quite possible that Clemens is using published material without acknowledgement. Many paragraphs are quoted on Lytton Strachey, lecturing, Bismarck, R. Amundsen, Sir Ernest Shackleton, Leacock's early days, Ralph Connor, Louis Hémon, *Literary Lapses* (A5) as possibly his favourite book, *Huckleberry Finn*, Bret Harte, and British and American humour.

**K44.13**  "Leacock Not Ashamed of His Ignorance of Church Titles," *Orillia Packet and Times*, 8 June 1944, p. 6. P.D. Knowles wrote to Leacock on 25 January [1944]. In *Montreal, Seaport and City* (A95) Leacock had referred to the Archbishop of Canterbury as the "Right Rev." The correct appellation should have been "Most Rev." Leacock replied to Knowles: "I did not know that an English Archbishop was Most Rev. and I'm not ashamed of it."

**K45.1**  G.G. Sedgewick, "Stephen Leacock as Man of Letters," *University of Toronto Quarterly* 15 (October 1945): 17–26. On p. 21, Sedgewick notes that he met Leacock only once at a small luncheon party where he believes that Leacock kept saying "ain't." On p. 25, he quotes Leacock as saying: "Her aunt had carefully instructed her in Christian principles. She had also taught her Mohammedanism to make sure."

**K46.1**  Pelham Edgar, "Stephen Leacock," *Queen's Quarterly* 53, no. 2 (Summer 1946): 173–84. Reprinted in *Across My Path* (Toronto: Ryerson, 1952), pp. 90–8. Recollections from conversations appear on pp. 92–4; reprinted in Malcolm Ross, ed., *Our Sense of Identity: A Book of Canadian Essays* (Toronto: Ryerson, 1954), pp. 134–46.

**K49.1**  "A Glance at the Past," *Quill and Quire* 15, no. 7 (July 1949): 6–7. This article reprints a letter from Leacock to the publisher, W.C. ("Billy") Bell, 22 June 1932, in facsimile. Brief extracts from the letter are reprinted in "Traveller's Tales," 60th anniversary supp., *Quill and Quire* 61, no. 4 (April 1995): 9.

**K50.1**  Frederick B. Taylor, "I Painted Stephen Leacock," *McGill News* 31, no. 4 (Summer 1950): 48–50. Taylor quotes a number of comments made by Leacock in 1939–40 when he painted his portrait in Montreal. The comments concern Taylor's progress, Leacock's appreciation of the portrait, and Leacock's ability to make people laugh (almost to the point of death).

**K50.2** William Dudley Woodhead, "Stephen Leacock — 'a Fellow of Infinite Jest,' Canadian Personalities No. 3," *Sun Life Review* (Montreal) 7, no. 4 (October 1950): 2–4. Woodhead, who was the chairman of the Department of Classics at McGill University, recounts his reminiscences of Leacock. Several quotations are attributed to Leacock, including an anecdote about leaving behind an honorary degree from McGill at the Mount Royal Club. The article reproduces in facsimile Leacock's inscriptions in two books from the Norman H. Friedman collection at McGill. In addition, there is a tribute from one of Leacock's students, E.R. Alexander.

**K51.1** B.K. Sandwell, "How the 'Sketches' Started," *Saturday Night* (August 1951): 7. Reprints a letter concerning Leacock's friend, George Rapley. Leacock tells Bunting, Rapley's nephew, that Rapley was one of his best friends, that Rapley appeared as George Popley in the serialization of *Sunshine Sketches of A Little Town* (A11) in the *Montreal Daily Star*, and that the name Popley was changed to Mullins when the book was finally published. The letter apparently first appeared in July 1951 in the *Orillia Packet and Times* in reply to an article in the *Toronto Telegram* that doubted the identification of Mariposa with Orillia. Leacock's letter to Bunting is reproduced in facsimile in a programme that was prepared for the awarding of the Leacock Memorial Medal for Humour in 1953: *Leacock Memorial Dinner and Presentation of Leacock Memorial Medal for 1952 to Mr. Lawrence Earl Author of "The Battle of Baltinglass"*, 26 June 1953, p. [4].

**K51.2** Gladstone Murray, "Stephen Leacock and His Humour," *Montreal Gazette*, 20 September 1951, p. [9]. This is the text of Murray's address in Orillia on the unveiling of the Stephen Leacock memorial. Murray quotes recollected remarks from conversation as well as the text of a letter Leacock sent him in 1925 on humour. He also quotes extracts from an article Leacock wrote for the journal he founded, *Radio, The Wireless Quarterly*. See C25.2.

**K53.1** Trent Frayne, "The Erudite Jester of McGill," *Maclean's Magazine* 66 (1 January 1953): 18–9, 37–39. Frayne quotes a number of reminiscences by acquaintances, particularly those of John Culliton related to his work on *Montreal, Seaport and City* (A95). There is a photograph of Leacock on p. 18; the text begins on p. 19

**K54.1** Gerhard R. Lomer, comp., *Stephen Leacock: A Check-List and Index of His Writings* (Ottawa: National Library, 1954). Lomer prints Leacock's inscriptions found in books in Norman H. Friedman's Leacock collection at QMMRB (see pp. 22, 26–7, 32–5, 38–9, and 44–5.

**K55.1** Victor C. Wansborough, "Stephen Leacock," *McGill News* 37, no. 1 (Winter 1955): 13–14, 51–55. Wansborough quotes the text of a letter written by Leacock, [Easter 1935], to the Headmaster of Lower Canada College concerning Stephen Leacock, Jr.'s attendance at that school. He also quotes Leacock's remarks about Stephen, Jr. and his conversation with Wansborough circa 1940 with respect to his refusal to give lectures and the extent of his writing after leaving McGill.

**K57.1** Ralph L. Curry, "Robert Benchley and Stephen Leacock: An Acknowledged Literary Debt," *American Book Collector* 7, no. 7 (March 1957): 11–15. In discussing the relationship between these two humorists, Curry prints their entire correspondence.

**K58.1** Thomas B. Costain, introduction to George E. Nelson, ed., *Cavalcade of the North* (Garden City, New York: Doubleday, 1958), pp. 7–10. Costain's introduction includes, on

p. 9, a recollected conversation with Leacock in Orillia; Leacock had received a letter without a return address.

**K58.2**   Dora Hood, *The Side Door: Twenty-Six Years in My Book Room* (Toronto: Ryerson Press, 1958). Hood prints two letters she received from Leacock: p. 78, an undated letter ordering a book; and one of 3 April 1953, p. 81, about Upper Canada College days. She also prints a book inscription on p. 81. See also A60.

**K59.1**   Ralph L. Curry, *Stephen Leacock: Humorist and Humanist* (Garden City, New York: Doubleday, 1959), passim. The first biography of Leacock with extensive quotations from unpublished material.

**K59.2**   Loring Holmes Dodd, "Stephen Leacock, Wit and Political Scientist," *Worcester* (Mass.) *Telegram*, 5 July 1959. (news clipping in OTUTF, University of Toronto Archives). Recollected conversation from a meeting on 17 October 1925 before and after a lecture Leacock gave at Clark University. Re the pronunciation of his name, writing a preface for a new edition of Mark Twain's *Connecticut Yankee in Court* (B11), teaching English, and lecturing in Boston while being very ill.

**K61.1**   Howard O'Hagan, " 'Stephie'," *Queen's Quarterly* 68 (Spring 1961): 135–46. O'Hagan's reminiscences of Leacock from the time O'Hagan attended Leacock's class in Political Science 1 in the early 1920s to the spring of 1943. O'Hagan recollects several comments made by Leacock: John Dwiggins's essay on Sir Ernest Shackleton; Leacock's salary and teaching; the idea of starting a literary magazine; the Mount Logan expedition; farming; and Sir Edward Beatty. O'Hagan's article was reprinted in two installments: part 1 as "Howard O'Hagan's Fond Recollections of 'Stephie'," *McGill News* 42, no. 34 (Summer 1961): 20–2 (but without quotations of Leacock's conversations); part 2, as "Recollections of 'Stephie'," *McGill News* 42, no. 4 (Fall 1961): 22–4 with the addition of the first page of Leacock's manuscript in facsimile entitled "Leaflets on the Loan: A New Heaven and a New Earth" (see C43.34). Leacock's manuscript in facsimile also appears in E.A. Corbett's "McGill Men and the Start of the Western Universities," *McGill News* 39, no. 4 (Autumn 1958): 24–8 (at p. 27). According to the latter article, Leacock's manuscript was found in the vault of the Bank of Canada.

**K61.2**   Leslie Roberts, "The Most Unforgettable Character I've Ever Met," *Reader's Digest* 78, no. 470 (June 1961): 59–64. Reprinted as "Unforgettable Stephen Leacock," in *Salute to Canada* (Montreal: Reader's Digest, 1967), pp. 22–7. Recollected remarks from lectures and conversations on humorous topics as well as their joint book on the navy. See also B31.

**K63.1**   Gary Lautens, "The Sketches Weren't All Sunshine," *Toronto Star*, 3 July 1963, p. 19. Lautens quotes three remarks that Leacock made to his son, Stephen, Jr., as recollected by Stephen, Jr.: (1)"People who die don't go anywhere. They're just dead. But the good that they do lives on." (2) On billiards: "You may win but your strategy is all wrong." (3) "You may keep up with my pace until 40 but after that . . . ."

**K65.1**   "A Leavening of Leacock," *Douglas Library Notes* (Queen's University) 14, no. 3 (Summer 1965): 6–10. This article quotes from archival documents written by Leacock at Queen's University Archives: correspondence with Bruce Taylor, Lorne Pierce, Peter McArthur, and B.K. Sandwell. A manuscript of a poem by Leacock, "A Valentine Wish for Messrs Allcock, Laight & Westwood (Manufacturers of Fishing Tackle)," is reproduced in facsimile.

**K66.1** John Archer Carter, "When Leacock Interviewed Himself," *Montreal Star*, 15 January 1966, p. 2. Carter recalls meeting Leacock "some forty years ago" in Richmond, Virginia, when Leacock was lecturing at the University of Richmond. At the time Carter was a reporter for the *Richmond News Leader*, and he was asked to interview Leacock. Leacock, however, wrote his own interview, and gave the manuscript of it to Carter. The text of Leacock's manuscript is published here for the first time along with a facsimile of the last page of the manuscript. Carter also quotes a long conversation with Leacock about O. Henry.

**K66.2** Stanley Cohen, " 'Sunshine Sketches' Outline More Original Leacock Found," *Montreal Star*, 31 August 1966, p. 5. This article reproduces the following in facsimile: an outline in Leacock's hand, dated 7 January 1912, for *Sunshine Sketches of a Little Town* (A11); an undated letter from Leacock to Colonel J.J. Creelman; and an autograph inscription found in Creelman's copy of the book. Creelman was Leacock's pupil at Upper Canada College. He also took a BLC degree at McGill. These documents were revealed to the press by Creelman's daughter, Mrs. Peter M. McEntyre, one week after the original manuscript of the book was acquired by the Leacock Museum.

**K67.1** Watson Kirkconnell, *A Slice of Canada* (Toronto: University of Toronto Press, 1967), p. 265. Kirkconnell prints a letter to him from Leacock written in 1943, declining an invitation to be the banquet speaker at the Canadian Authors Association convention.

**K68.1** Edgar Andrew Collard, "Laurier's Horror," *Montreal Gazette*, 17 February 1968. Column entitled "Of Many Things." Collard quotes a remark apparently made by Leacock about the grim relics in the Tower of London: "You'd think they'd want to throw the horrid things away. . . . But oh, no, not in the least. They're delighted to have them!"

**K69.1** Grace Crooks, "A Taste for Humour," *Canadian Library Journal* 26, no. 3 (May–June 1969): 222–8. Quotes the text of a letter written by Leacock to his mother, 30 May 1907. There are also extracts from another letter, September 1907, to his sister, Margaret Burrowes.

**K70.1** Carl Berger, *The Sense of Power: Studies in the Ideas of Canadian Imperialism 1867–1914* (Toronto: University of Toronto Press, 1970), p. 39. William Grant, who taught history and geography at Upper Canada College between 1898 and 1902, asked Leacock about the principal of the college, Sir George Parkin: "Has he no friends below the rank of Viscount?" Leacock replied: "Plenty — back on the farm."

**K70.2** Elizabeth Kimball, *The Man in the Panama Hat: Reminiscences of My Uncle, Stephen Leacock* (Toronto: McClelland and Stewart, 1970), pp. 94, 96–8, 108–9. Recollected conversations of Leacock are quoted. In addition, Kimball prints extracts from a journal, "House, Garden & Fish Book Vol. 2," that Leacock kept in 1943 at Old Brewery Bay. Photographically reprinted as *My Uncle, Stephen Leacock* (Halifax, NS: Goodread Biographies, 1983).

**K70.3** David M. Legate, *Stephen Leacock: A Biography* (Toronto: Doubleday Canada, 1970), passim. Photographically reprinted in the Laurentian Library series, (Toronto: Macmillan of Canada, 1978). The second biography of Leacock with extensive quotations from unpublished documents.

**K74.1** Edgar Andrew Collard, "Voices from the Past," *McGill News* 55, no. 4 (Winter 1974): 32. Collard gathers together the recollections of several of Leacock's students:

William H. Pugsley, S. Boyd Millen, Fred V. Stone, Eugene A. Forsey, and Col. H. Wyatt Johnston. Pugsley, Millen, and Forsey quote statements apparently made by Leacock. See also K75.2.

**K75.1** Vishnu R.K. Chopra, ed., "Stephen Leacock: An Edition of Selected Letters." (Ph.D. thesis, McGill University, 1975). Seventy letters written by Leacock are edited by Chopra. Excerpts from other letters written by Leacock are quoted in the critical introduction and in the notes.

**K75.2** Edgar Andrew Collard, *The McGill You Knew: An Anthology of Memories 1920–1960* (Don Mills, ON: Longman Canada, 1975). The following stories contain snippets of Leacock's conversation as recollected by his students and colleagues: H. Carl Goldenberg, "Senator Goldenberg's Leacock Memories," pp. 47–50; Eugene A. Forsey, "Senator Forsey's Leacock Memories," pp. 50–2; William H. Pugsley, "Professor Pugsley's Leacock Memories," pp. 52–4; Fred V. Stone, "Fred Stone's Leacock Memories," pp. 54–6; Mrs. H. Wyatt Johnston (Beatrice Lyman), "If He Didn't Know the Answer," p. 57; W.I. Nelson Crutchfield, "Last Word to Commerce Students," p. 57; G.B. Puddicombe, "He Left Us Jubilant," pp. 57–8; David C. Munroe, "What He Thought of McGill," p. 58; S. Boyd Millen, "An Amazing Feat of Memory," pp. 58–9; Norman H. Friedman, "Leacock's $500 Story," pp. 59–60; David M. Legate, "Authors Exchange Their Books," p. 61; Percy E. Corbett, "He Put It in the Barn at Orillia," p. 61.

**K76.1** Ralph Curry and Janet Lewis, "Stephen Leacock: An Early Influence on F. Scott Fitzgerald," *Canadian Review of American Studies* 7 (Spring 1976): 5–15. Prints a brief letter, on p. 5, from Leacock to Fitzgerald, dated 16 March 1917, in reply to Fitzgerald's query about his own writing.

**K76.2** Alec Lucas, "Leacock Writes for *Truth*," *Studies in Canadian Literature*, 1, no. 2 (Summer 1976): 254–8. Prints extracts from letters to Peter McArthur, 16 July 1923, and Lorne Pierce, January 1923, both on p. 254.

**K76.3** Ralph L. Curry, "A Note to Leacock Collectors," *Newspacket* (Orillia, newsletter of the Stephen Leacock Associates) 4, no. 1 (Summer 1976): 3. Curry quotes from a letter, written by Leacock on 7 February 1931, to Frank Paget Hett, concerning a book plate designed by Miss V. Talbot.

**K78.1** J.E. McDougall, "Meeting Stephen Leacock," *Montreal Star*, 15 February 1978, p. A8. McDougall recounts meeting Leacock in the early winter of 1933 when he worked for an advertising agency and attempted to get Leacock to do a series of radio broadcasts. McDougall's reminiscences quote a number of Leacock's remarks. See also K83.1.

**K78.2** "A Leacock Letter on French at McGill," *McGilliana* (The History of McGill Project) no. 6 (September 1978): 2. Letter dated 21 November 1934 to Sir Edward Beatty in which Leacock asks if the university's Board of Governors can give $500 for the establishment of a French Club.

**K80.1** David Savage, "Dr. Stephen Leacock," *McGill News* 61, no. 1 (Spring 1980): 28. In 1934 Savage took Leacock's introductory course in political science and the following year Leacock's course on the British Empire. He attributes several quotes to Leacock, one concerning honesty in the everyday citizen: "Would he cheat his wife? No! Would he cheat his butcher? Never! Would he cheat the paper boy? Unthinkable! Would he cheat the government on his income tax? Ah, that's quite different!"

**K80.2** John E. Peckitt, "Famous Pen Profiles," *Portico* (Sheridan College, Oakville, ON) 4, no. 4 (1980): 8–[18]. On p. [16] a letter from Leacock to Helen, dated 6 December 1937, is reproduced in facsimile with numbers added by the author. The author's purpose in reproducing the letter is to analyze Leacock's handwriting; Helen is not identified.

**K81.1** Allan Anderson, "A Memorable Man: One of His Students Recalls Mr. Leacock," *Review* no. 5 (Imperial Oil Ltd., Toronto) (1981): 8–9, 11. Anderson prints a recommendation letter that Leacock wrote for him, dated 9 March 1936. He also outlines Leacock's behaviour at the Political Economy Club meetings. "Stop," he would shout, and then talk for ten minutes or so about problems with the speaker that particular night. Anderson also repeats a story concerning Leacock at the American border and a telegram that he sent to the Buffalo sponsors of a speech: "No hooch, no spooch." This event, if it did take place, dates from before Anderson knew Leacock. See also K83.1.

**K81.2** Bruce Whiteman, comp. "The Raymond Knister Papers," in *Library Research News* (McMaster University) 5, no. 3 (December 1981). At p. 36, a letter from Knister to Leacock dated 3 February 1928 is reproduced in facsimile. Leacock's reply, "Most certainly. Pleasure," is written across the bottom in response to Knister's request to reprint stories from *Sunshine Sketches of a Little Town* (A11).

**K83.1** Allan Anderson, *Remembering Leacock: an Oral History* (Ottawa: Deneau, 1983). This book contains reminiscences of ninety people — family, friends, employees, students, and colleagues who knew Leacock. About eighty per cent of the stories contain recollected quotations from conversation with Leacock. In addition, Anderson prints the following: p. 9, Anderson quotes from a telegram about liquor; p. 10, Philip Vineberg quotes a note he saw on a questionnaire; p. 23, letter to Joe McDougall, 12 January 1926; pp. 44–5, Grace Reynolds quotes a shorthand note she saw; p. 64, letter to Eve, in facsimile; p. 65, note on a letter as remembered by Anderson in "Ask and Ye Shall Be Told"; p. 72, letter to Philip Vineberg; p. 79, telegram as remembered by Fred Stone in "How, How!"; pp. 98, letter to Leacock's mother, 30 May 1907; p. 142, telegram to Premier Henry of Ontario, 1932, in facsimile; p. 142, reward for theft of chickens in facsimile (see also K93.1); p. 156, letter to E.V. Lucas, 9 Feb. 1915; p. 161, letter to H. Outridge, 1938; p. 169, poem, n.d., no title; p. 178, letter to Dr. Marvin, Royal Bank, 22 September 1932; p. 182, excerpt from article on preparing speeches; p. 187, letter to Mr. Kon, 15 September 1936; p. 200, facsimile of post card, showing photo of Brewery Bay house with note underneath to H. Carl Goldenberg, c. 1928.

**K83.2** Carl Spadoni, "Leacock and the Macmillan Company of Canada," *Papers of the Bibliographical Society of Canada* 22 (1983): 56–80. Extracts from Leacock's letters to the publisher, Hugh Eayrs, are quoted.

**K85.1** Albert and Theresa Moritz, *Leacock: A Biography* (Toronto: Stoddart Publishing, 1995), passim. The third comprehensive biography of Leacock with numerous quotations from previously unpublished documents.

**K86.1** F. Wesley Thompson, "My Encounters with Stephen Leacock," *Newspacket* (Orillia, newsletter of the Stephen Leacock Associates) 13, no. 1 (April 1986): [3]. Thompson was the manager of Bell Telephone in Orillia in the 1930s. His article quotes a letter written by Leacock to install a telephone at Old Brewery Bay.

**K86.2** Elizabeth Kimball, "Sunshine Sketch," *Toronto Life* (August 1986): H37–41.

Kimball recounts her uncle's intentions in building a house at Old Brewery Bay. Leacock's letters to his mother are quoted.

**K86.3** Ralph L. Curry, "Leacock and the Media," in David Staines, ed., *Stephen Leacock: A Reappraisal* (Ottawa: University of Ottawa, 1986), pp. 23–31. Curry quotes from Leacock's letters concerning his involvement in film, radio, and television.

**K87.1** Carl Spadoni, "Leacock's *Canada*: The Book That Booze Bought," *Papers of the Bibliographical Society of Canada* 26 (1987): 88–105. Leacock's letters to representatives of the Distillers Corporation — Seagrams Ltd. and a letter to Dorothy Duncan (15 February 1943) are quoted. See also A92.

**K89.1** Vishnu R. Chopra, "From Manuscript to Print: Stephen Leacock's 'The Transit of Venus,'" *Canadian Literature* no. 121 (Summer 1989): 42–53. Chopra traces the origins of Leacock's story, "The Transit of Venus," from its publication in *Good Housekeeping* in 1926 (C26.1) to its beginnings in September 1914 as part of a series of connected stories on college life entitled "The Annals of Concordia College." He quotes from a letter (7 May 1925) written by Leacock to his agent, Paul Reynolds. Excerpts from related unpublished manuscripts (at QMMRB) are also quoted.

**K92.1** Robert M. MacIntosh, "Leacock's Expedition," *Canadian Banker* 99, no. 1 (January–February 1992): 21. Prints an excerpt from MacIntosh's (a former Canadian Banking Association president) book, *Different Drummers — Banking and Politics in Canada*, in which MacIntosh quotes an extract from a speech that Leacock gave in Edmonton. The speech is presumably the one given on 16 December 1936 on "Debit and Credit" (E36.43).

**K92.2** James Doyle, *Stephen Leacock: The Sage of Orillia* (Toronto: ECW Press, 1992), passim. Quotations from Leacock's letters are sprinkled throughout this short biography.

**K93.1** Robert M. Robinson's untitled article in David Helwig, ed., *Back Then: Voices of Memory 1915–45* (Ottawa: Oberon Press, 1993), pp. 29–32. Robinson's grandfather owned the drugstore in Orillia in the 1930s. His article contains recollected conversations between Leacock and his grandfather from 1933. It also prints the text of a leaflet issued by Leacock offering a reward for information about the theft of chickens from his property as well as extracts from Leacock's letter to Attorney General. This letter also appears in the *Orillia Packet*, 17 August 1933 (see C33.7) where the recipient is given as the Deputy Attorney General.

**K94.1** James A. "Pete" McGarvey, *The Old Brewery Bay: A Leacockian Tale* (Toronto: Dundurn Press, 1994), p. 9. McGarvey quotes from a letter dated 1 September 1928 from Leacock to Kenneth Noxon of the architectural firm, Wright and Noxon.

**K94.2** Bruce Whiteman, "Leacock Remains at McGill: Some Notes on the Stephen Leacock Collection," *Fontanus* 7 (1994): 11–4. Whiteman quotes an inscription written by Leacock in Norman H. Friedman's guest book concerning Friedman's Leacock collection (apparently first printed in the *Montreal Gazette*, 6 April 1970). In addition, entries from Leacock's notebook of recorded speeches and publications (acquired by QMMRB in 1984 from J. Robert Janes) are printed.

**K94.3** Marcel Caya, "Leacock Enters McGill," *Fontanus* 7 (1994): 149–52. Caya's article publishes four letters written by Leacock in 1900 to William Peterson, McGill University's Principal. At the time Leacock was a graduate student at the University of Chicago. He wrote to Peterson and applied for the position of lecturer in political economy.

# L Section: LOST LEADS

**L90.1** "University of Moon College," *Varsity* (University of Toronto) 10 (1890).
SOURCE: Lomer, p. 140. The issue of 2 December 1890 carries a notice that Leacock was resigning as an editor on staff but would still contribute as a writer. Not found in microfilm ed. held at the University of Toronto.

**L3.1** "We are Seven," *Montreal Herald*, November 1903. Poem.
SOURCE: notebook of recorded publications and speeches at QMMRB. Presumably written in response to "Three Are French Seven Are English," *Montreal Herald*, 13 November 1903, p. 1. Re the language division in Canada. The poem could not be located on the microfilm edition. However, the issue of 24 November 1903 was not microfilmed.

**L4.1** "Nothing," *Montreal Herald*, December 1904. Poem.
SOURCE: notebook of recorded publications and speeches at QMMRB.

**L5.1** "Canadian Tariff," *Guardian* (Manchester), November 1905.
SOURCE: notebook of recorded publications and speeches at QMMRB. An article with the same title, however, was found in the *Morning Post* (London), 8 November 1905.

**L9.1** "The Case Against Woman Suffrage," *Women's Witness*, 12 May 1909.
SOURCE: notebook of recorded publications and speeches at QMMRB.

**L10.1** "Number Fifty-Six," *Detroit Free Press*, pre-1910.
SOURCE: preface to A5a.

**L10.2** articles on Hudson's Bay, Canada and the World's Wheat Supply, Canadian Women in the World of Art. Publisher Press Syndicate, June 1910.
SOURCE: notebook of recorded publications and speeches at QMMRB.

**L10.3** "Fragoletta. A Vaudeville Sketch," 19 June 1910.
SOURCE: notebook of recorded publications and speeches at QMMRB.

**L10.4** "Life of Strathcona," Publisher Press Syndicate, 15 July 1910.
SOURCE: J84 notebook at SLM.

**L10.5** article for *Canadian Educational Institute* (?), August 1910.
SOURCE: J84 notebook at SLM.

**L10.6** articles on "Georgian Bay Ship Canal," "Power Development in Canada," and "Conservation of Canadian Resources," August 1910.
SOURCE: J84 notebook at SLM.

**L10.7** "Vanitas" poem series, [December 1910]. Only one article apparently published (see C10.9).
SOURCE: J84 notebook at SLM.

L10.8   Christmas poem, syndicated, December 1910.
SOURCE: J84 notebook at SLM.

L10.9   three articles for *Trail* magazine, late 1910.
SOURCE: J84 notebook at SLM.

L11.1   "Casey at the Bat (A New Version)," *Parks and Playgrounds* ([1910–11?]): 29.
SOURCE: news clipping at QMMRB. Not signed by Leacock but the introduction to the poem states: "The following poem was forwarded to us by a certain university professor. We do not whether he wrote it or stole it. It is certainly not the version known from the recitations of Mr. De Wolf Hopper. The style suggests the work of the late Lord Tennyson, with perhaps a little assistance here and there from Robert Browning. We understand that the professor in question has been reciting this poem during the winter at various dinners and functions, where the civility of the occasion rendered protest impossible. We publish it, therefore, with a view to prevent further trouble of this sort." The newspaper clipping may be from a Montreal newspaper containing a section titled "Parks and Playgrounds."

L11.2   Twelve, possibly fourteen, syndicated articles against reciprocity, February–March 1911.
SOURCE: notebook of recorded publications and speeches at QMMRB.

L11.3   "Who Pays the Taxes," three articles, November 1911.
SOURCE: notebook of recorded publications and speeches at QMMRB.

L12.1   encyclopedia article on Jacques Cartier. 1912.
SOURCE: J84 notebook at SLM. It is possible that the article may have been written for Appleton's Encyclopaedia. Leacock indicates in his notebook "Appleton & Co (balance)."

L12.2   article, *Boston American*. 1912.
SOURCE: J84 notebook at SLM.

L13.1   two pamphlets, United Editors. 1913. Leacock was paid $48.50 for both.
SOURCE: J84 notebook at SLM.

L13.2   articles reprinted from *Literary Lapses*, *New York Evening Post*, 11 January 1913.
SOURCE: notebook of recorded publications and speeches at QMMRB; J84 notebook at SLM.

L13.3   "Familiar Incidents," I–III, *American Magazine* and *Saturday Mirror* (Montreal).
SOURCE: notebook of recorded publications and speeches at QMMRB.
Only incidents IV–V (C13.1–2) have been verified as numbered incidents. There are two later unnumbered verified incidents as well (C13.6 and C13.9).

L13.4   "An Illiad of Orillia. From the Toronto 'Telegram',", *Orillia Packet*, 17 July 1913, p. 4. Re Leacock telling the town council about explosive powder being stored near his house. In "Town Council," *Orillia Packet*, 10 July 1913, it was reported that Leacock had written the council protesting the blasting powder on C.P.R. property near the ice house. The original article in the *Toronto Telegram* was not located.

L13.5   "Passionate Paragraphs," *Life*, December 1913.
SOURCE: notebook of recorded publications and speeches at QMMRB.

L14.1   "The Mind of the Master," *Bookman* (New York), 20 January 1914.
SOURCE: notebook of recorded publications and speeches at QMMRB.

L14.2   "Ram Spudd: The New World Singer," *Life*, April 1914.
SOURCE: notebook of recorded publications and speeches at QMMRB.

**L14.3** "Barbara Plynlimmon," *Century Magazine*, 8 April 1914.
SOURCE: notebook of recorded publications and speeches at QMMRB.

**L14.4** article, Appleton's Encyclopaedia. 23 May 1914.
SOURCE: J84 notebook at SLM.

**L14.5** "Our Debt to the United States," Montreal, ? 22 November 1914.
SOURCE: notebook of recorded publications and speeches at QMMRB.

**L15.1** "Weejee the Pet Dog," *Life*, 12 July 1915.
SOURCE: notebook of recorded publications and speeches at QMMRB.

**L15.2** "Sergius Ivanovitch," (Complete Novels II) *Harper's Bazaar*, August 1915.
SOURCE: notebook of recorded publications and speeches at QMMRB.

**L17.1** "Fetching the Doctor," *American Home Journal*, 31 January 1917.
SOURCE: notebook of recorded publications and speeches at QMMRB.

**L17.2** "The Present Crisis," *Canada Weekly*, 2 December 1917.
SOURCE: notebook of recorded publications and speeches at QMMRB.

**L20.1** *Liberty Laws of the Province of Quebec*. 4 May 1921.
SOURCE: notebook of recorded publications and speeches at QMMRB. Leacock records having written a "500 Word Circular."

**L20.2** "Xmas from a Writer's Point of View," *Echoes* (Daughters of the Empire), 21 November 1920.
SOURCE: notebook of recorded publications and speeches at QMMRB.

**L21.1** "Noise," *Noiseless Typewriter Magazine* and *Whispers*, 2 May 1921.
SOURCE: notebook of recorded publications and speeches at QMMRB.

**L21.2** "The Fall of the German Mark," *Passing Show* (London), 4 October 1921.
SOURCE: notebook of recorded publications and speeches at QMMRB.

**L21.3** "Stories and Story Tellers," *London Magazine*, 30 October 1921.
SOURCE: notebook of recorded publications and speeches at QMMRB.

**L21.4** "A Perfectly Simple View of Relativity," *Gaiety* (London), 21 December 1921.
SOURCE: notebook of recorded publications and speeches at QMMRB.

**L22.1** "Living in a Hotel," 4 January 1922.
SOURCE: notebook of recorded publications and speeches at QMMRB.

**L22.2** "Sack the Lot," *Vaudeville Burlesque Junior League*, journal of the society?, 24 February 1922.
SOURCE: notebook of recorded publications and speeches at QMMRB.

**L22.3** article in the *Times* (London) in which Leacock advocates that British parents send their sons to McGill.
SOURCE: reference in *Montreal Daily Star*, 20 March 1922, to Leacock's article. A letter to the *Times* from a father in search of a career for his son was published on 16 March 1922, p. 8. This letter engendered many replies, beginning 20 March 1922, p. 12. Issues were searched until 30 March 1922 but nothing was found by Leacock.

**L22.4** "If I Were Designing a Car," Packard Motor Company, 5 August 1922.
SOURCE: notebook of recorded publications and speeches at QMMRB.

**L22.5** "Radio," *Ladies Home Journal*, 15 September 1922; apparently reprinted in *Gaiety*,

January 1923.
SOURCE: notebook of recorded publications and speeches at QMMRB.

L22.6  "Population of Canada," *Maclean's*, 17 October 1922.
SOURCE: notebook of recorded publications and speeches at QMMRB.

L23.1  "Physiology and Fiction," Metropolitan Newspapers Service, New York. February 1923.
SOURCE: Copyright Office at DLC.

L23.2  *Pearson* published material from *College Days*, May and June 1923.
SOURCE: Leacock fonds, SLM.

L23.3  "Call of the Carburetor," *Washington Sunday Star*, 16 September 1923. Syndicated.
SOURCE: Copyright Office at DLC.

L23.4  Christmas article, *Lower Canada Magazine*, December? 1923.
SOURCE: Leacock fonds, SLM (letter, 31 March 1924, from Max Elser, Jr. of the Metropolitan Newspaper Service).

L24.1  *Gaiety*, articles from *Harpers*, 1924.
SOURCE: Leacock fonds, SLM.

L24.2  "Stephen Leacock and His Will," *Washington Sunday Star*, 6 January 1924. Syndicated.
SOURCE: Copyright Office at DLC.

L24.3  "Physiology and Education," *Leslie's* and *Judge*, May 1924.
SOURCE: Leacock fonds, SLM.

L24.4  "Our Summer Convention," 2 June 1924. Syndicated.
SOURCE: notebook of recorded publications and speeches at QMMRB.

L24.5  "How I Made Myself Young," *Hearst's International*, 21 June 1924.
SOURCE: notebook of recorded publications and speeches at QMMRB.

L24.6  article for *Morning Post* (London), June 1924.
SOURCE: Leacock fonds, SLM.

L24.7  "Are We Fascinated with Crime?" 10 August 1924.
SOURCE: notebook of recorded publications and speeches at QMMRB.

L24.8  "What College Did for Me," 5 September 1924, *Co-Ed* (November 1924?); *College Humour* (after July 1925).
SOURCE: notebook of recorded publications and speeches at QMMRB.

L24.9  "Bringing the Message to the Consumer," *Washington Sunday Star*, 14 September 1924.
SOURCE: Copyright Office at DLC.

L24.10  "Prosperity," *McGill Annual*, 5 February 1925.
SOURCE: notebook of recorded publications and speeches at QMMRB.

L25.1  "International Amenities," *Collier's*, 22 February 1925. Syndicated.
SOURCE: notebook of recorded publications and speeches at QMMRB.

L25.2  "How to Propose Marriage," syndicated 26 March 1925.
SOURCE: Copyright Office at DLC.

L25.3  "Vacation Time Is Coming," *Outlook*, 30 March 1925. Syndicated.

SOURCE: Leacock fonds, SLM.

**L25.4** "The New Imperial Unity," *Morning Post* (London), May 1925.
SOURCE: notebook of recorded publications and speeches at QMMRB.

**L25.5** "Nothing for It Now But to Burn My Office," *Philadelphia Record*, 14 June 1925.
Syndicated.
SOURCE: Copyright Office at DLC.

**L25.6** "Old Proverbs Reexamined," 17 August 1925. Syndicated.
SOURCE: notebook of recorded publications and speeches at QMMRB.

**L25.7** "Why I Left Our Workers Social Guild," *Collier's*, 13 September 1925.
SOURCE: notebook of recorded publications and speeches at QMMRB.

**L25.8** "The Detective Story," 22 September 1925.
SOURCE: notebook of recorded publications and speeches at QMMRB.

**L25.9** "Bull Hyde and Little Peewee," *College Humor*, October 1925.
SOURCE: Leacock fonds, SLM.

**L25.10** "My Approaching Demise," *London Opinion*, November 1925.
SOURCE: Leacock fonds, SLM.

**L25.11** "Thankful Thoughts for Thanksgiving," *Philadelphia Record*, 22 November 1925. Syndicated.
SOURCE: Copyright Office at DLC.

**L25.12** "1926 Revised Edition of Old Proverbs with Amendments," *Philadelphia Record*, 27 December 1926.
SOURCE: Copyright Office at DLC.

**L27.1** "The Colleges and Humour," *Martlet* (McGill University) 1 (March 1927): 7–8, 32–3.
SOURCE: Lomer, p. 70.

**L28.1** *A Proposal for a Montreal Association for Cancer Control and Cancer Research.* McGill University, 1928.
SOURCE: Ralph L. Curry, "Stephen Butler Leacock: A Check-list," p. 108.

**L29.1** "The Memoirs of a Night-Watchman," Metropolitan Newspaper Service, New York (10 March 1929).
SOURCE: Copyright Office at DLC.

**L29.2** "Great Modern Adventures," "Great Modern Doings," *Boston Sunday Advertiser* and *New York American*, 26 May 1929, 2 June 1929, 9 June 1929, 16 June 1929, 23 June 1929, 30 June 1929, 7 July 1929, 14 July 1929, 21 July 1929, 28 July 1929, 4 August 1929, 11 August 1929, 25 August 1929, 8 September 1929, 15 September 1929, 22 September 1929, 6 October 1929. Syndicated. Apparently generic series title with specific titles.
SOURCE: Copyright Office at DLC.

**L29.3** "Tennis at the Smiths," Metropolitan Newspaper Service, New York (4 August 1929).
SOURCE: Copyright Office at DLC.

**L29.4** "Campus Life on Again," *Boston Sunday Advertiser*, 20 October 1929. Syndicated.
SOURCE: Copyright Office at DLC.

L29.5 "America for Us All," *Boston Sunday Advertiser*, 3 November 1929. Syndicated.
SOURCE: Copyright Office at DLC.

L29.6 "Visit to the Old Farm," *Boston Sunday Advertiser*, 10 November 1929. Syndicated.
SOURCE: Copyright Office at DLC.

L29.7 "Sequels to Old Tales," *Boston Sunday Advertiser*, 17 November 1929. Syndicated.
SOURCE: Copyright Office at DLC.

L29.8 "Before a Big Game," *Boston Sunday Advertiser*, 1 December 1929. Syndicated.
SOURCE: Copyright Office at DLC.

L29.9 "Beware of All Signs," *Boston Sunday Advertiser*, 8 December 1929. Syndicated.
SOURCE: Copyright Office at DLC.

L30.1 "In Best of Humor. At It Again," *Fort Worth Star-Telegram*, 19 January 1930. Syndicated.
SOURCE: Copyright Office at DLC.

L31.1 reminiscences, *Cap and Gown Magazine* (Wycliffe College Literary Society, Toronto), September 1931.
SOURCE: Leacock fonds, SLM. A page of ms. is extant.

L31.2 "Correspondence, the Tangent and the Ten Cent Plug," *McGill Daily*, 28 November 1931, p. 2.
SOURCE: Curry, "Stephen Leacock: The Writer and His Writings," p. 148.

L32.1 "Mythical Men," Rogue's Gallery, syndicated, 1932. Lomer, p. 112.

L32.2 "Ominous News," Rogue's Gallery, syndicated, 1932. Lomer, p. 115.

L33.1 article on wine, *New York Herald Tribune*, c. 28 March 1933.

L33.2 "Dr. Leacock's Protest," *London (Ontario) Advertiser*, 2 June 1933.
SOURCE: Curry, "Stephen Leacock: The Writer and His Writings," p. 150.

L35.1 "Sex, Sex, Sex," *Rotarian*, 11 September 1934. Rogue's Gallery, syndicated by the Bell Syndicated Inc. and appeared as "Sex, Sex, Sex — I'm Sick of It," *Chattanooga Times*, 5 May 1935, p. 6.
SOURCE: Lomer, p. 128; Leacock fonds, SLM.

L35.2 "Opening Day at College," *Liberty*, after September 1934.
SOURCE: Leacock fonds, SLM.

L35.3 article on examinations, *Daily Princetonian*, February 1935.
SOURCE: Leacock fonds, SLM.

L35.4 "Crisis Held Rising on the Rhine Zone," *New York Times*, 21 May 1935, p. 9. Curry, "Stephen Leacock: The Writer and His Writings," p. 151.

L35.5 Commencement address at Goucher College, *Quarterly* (college magazine, Batimore, Maryland), after 15 June 1935.
SOURCE: Leacock fonds, SLM.

L35.6 "Will Prices Rise?" or "Will There Be a Rise in Prices?" *Current Controversy* (New York), September or October 1935.
SOURCE: Leacock fonds, SLM.

L36.1 Message of encouragement to young writers written in June 1936 for *Interlude*, a

Canadian journal, possibly published in Winnipeg.
SOURCE: Leacock fonds, SLM.

**L36.2** "His Parse Perch," *Montreal Herald*, 14 September? 1936, p. 4. Possibly a letter to the editor.
SOURCE: Leacock fonds, SLM.

**L37.1** "Notes on a Continental Trip," 4 January 1937, Bell Syndicate pays Leacock for the article.
SOURCE: Leacock fonds, SLM.

**L37.2** introduction to *Canada and Its History*, *Encyclopaedia Britannica*, March–April 1937.
SOURCE: Leacock fonds, SLM.

**L37.3** "How to Lose Money Like a Gentleman," *New York Herald Tribune*, "This Week" magazine, April 1937.
SOURCE: Leacock fonds, SLM.

**L37.4** biographical article on Charles Dickens, *Compton's Pictured Encyclopedia*, written July 1937.
SOURCE: Leacock fonds, SLM. See also K59.1 (pp. 345, 376) which refers to an unsigned entry in the 1941 ed.

**L37.5** "Parlez-vous français?" received by the Bell Syndicate on 17 September 1937, to be published in the Rogues Gallery column; fourteen sketches were received by 27 October 1937.
SOURCE: Leacock fonds, SLM.

**L37.6** *Chatter* (Ottawa), payment for an article was sent to Leacock on 26 October 1937.
SOURCE: Leacock fonds, SLM.

**L38.1** article on French Canada, *Globe: The International Magazine* (St. Paul, Minnesota), after January 1938.
SOURCE: Leacock fonds, SLM.

**L38.2** "If I Had My Life Again," *World Horizons*, after January 1938.
SOURCE: Leacock fonds, SLM.

**L38.3** article, *Murray Quarterly*, after 23 April 1938.
SOURCE: Leacock fonds, SLM.

**L38.4** article, *Regina Daily Star*, ca. 15 June 1938.
SOURCE: Leacock fonds, SLM.

**L38.5** preface to Mrs. Angus S. Cassils's *Crossword Puzzle Dictionary*, November 1938.
SOURCE: Leacock fonds, SLM. Leacock sent the manuscript of this little book on crossword puzzles to Frank Dodd on 30 November 1938. See also D. Cassils, "Stephen Leacock Memorabilia [letter to the editor]," *Montreal Gazette*, 27 January 1970. "In the late thirties, my mother, Mrs. Angus S. Cassils, was compiling what must have been one of the early conceptions of a Crossword Puzzle Dictionary. She mentioned her project to Mr. Leacock, and the idea seemed to strike his funny bone. He delightedly dubbed the proposed dictionary: 'Double Crossing The Crosswords,' and subsequently provided her with a several-page Preface, all in his own handwriting, that wittily illustrated the pure fun of his title." D. Cassils goes on to say that after his mother's death in 1960, Leacock's manuscript disappeared.

**L39.1** "When Men Retire," *Good Housekeeping* (London), after April 1939.

SOURCE: Leacock fonds, SLM.

L39.2 contribution to the Dominion of Canada supp., *Daily Telegraph* (London), May 1939.
SOURCE: Leacock fonds, SLM.

L39.3 "Education and Child Upbringing," and "Education and Child Expression," *John O'London's Weekly*, autumn 1939.
SOURCE: Leacock fonds, SLM.

L39.4 Seven articles in *Regina Daily Star*, December 1939, placed by the Associated Newspapers.
SOURCE: Leacock fonds, SLM.

L40.1 article on college life in eastern Canada, *Beaut Magazine* (Montreal), August 1940.
SOURCE: Leacock fonds, SLM.

L40.2 "Functions of a Teacher," *John O'London's Weekly*, ca. July 1940.
SOURCE: Leacock fonds, SLM.

L40.3 article on war activities in Canada, *Vogue* (London), after July 1940.
SOURCE: Leacock fonds, SLM.

L40.4 "What the Public Wants," *Pocket Sketch* (Minneapolis), sent in July 1940 and possibly published in September 1940. After it was published, another article was requested for November or December.
SOURCE: Leacock fonds, SLM.

L40.5 "Courage: An Interlude on the South Coast of England," *Montreal Standard*, 26 October 1940, p. 11.
SOURCE: Curry, "Stephen Leacock: The Writer and His Writings," p. 157.

L41.1 article about health and happiness, *Beauty and Health*, after 21 March 1941.
SOURCE: Leacock fonds, SLM.

L42.1 "Christmas, 1941," *New World* (Montreal) 2 (January 1942): 122, 169.
SOURCE: Lomer, p. 69.

L42.2 "Knowing Your Fishing Lore Pays Dividends (in Scotch) When Canvassing Leacock," *Toronto Globe and Mail*, ca. 1941–2.
SOURCE: Leacock fonds, SLM.

L42.3 article, *Canadian Heroes* (Montreal), June 1942.
SOURCE: Leacock fonds, SLM.

L42.4 article, *Philadelphia Record*, ca. 20 August 1942.
SOURCE: Leacock fonds, SLM.

L42.5 "Blacking Out the Consumer," *Woman's Day*, autumn 1942.
SOURCE: Leacock fonds, SLM.

L42.6 "A Letter on Conscription," privately printed by Leacock and sent to editors, 1942.
SOURCE: Ralph L. Curry, "Stephen Butler Leacock: A Check-list," p. 107.

L43.1 article, *Northern Miner* (Toronto), accepted on 2 November 1943.
SOURCE: Leacock fonds, SLM.

L44.1 article, *Crow's Nest* (Montreal or Halifax), a Navy newspaper, appeared by 14 February 1944.
SOURCE: Leacock fonds, SLM.

# INDEX

"With the Photographer" A12, A55, A91, A105, A111, C13.9, H30 (German), H37 (Gujerati), I35

"With Women or without" C39.47

"The Wizard of Finance" A16, A55, A91, C14.13

Wm. Collins Sons & Co. Ltd. A5c.1, A11d

"The Woman Question" A22, A47, A55, A124, C15.18

"Woman's Level" A103

Women A22, A47, A103, A124, C11.19, C11.31, C11.36, C13.17, C15.18, C18.14, C21.40, C21.45, C22.16, C35.10, C39.47, C42.10, C43.39, D13.2, D34.2, E11.4, E34.4, E35.46, L9.1, L10.2

"Wonderful Things, Sir. Statistics" C95.5

Woodhead, William Dudley K50.2

"Woodstock" J43.96

"Words and How to Use Them: A Wise-Crack About the Beans of Most Guys" A80

"Words of Royal Wisdom: As Dropped from Continental Lips Which Can Speak English As Fluently as Chinese" C25.22

Wordsworth, William C94.3

"Work and Wages" A31

"The Work of Canadian Universities" E25.22

"The Work of the Universities" C26.13, E26.1

"Working Backwards Through a Life Career" C23.24

"The World As It May Be: If Germany and the German System Win" C18.13

"A World of Machinery That Wastes Human Energy: Social Unrest Made Acute by the War's Demonstration That the Huge Man Power Diverted to Destruction Cut Off Production Mainly from Glittering Superfluities of Peace, While What Was Left Sufficed to Keep Things Going: I. The Troubled Outlook for the Present Hour" C19.14

*The World of Stephen Leacock a 13-part Anthology* I23

"The World Policy of Germany" E9.15

*The World's Best Literature* B5

"The World's Muddle over Gold; World Trade Is Stifled Because of the Lack of a Real Monetary Standard" C38.2

"The Writers of Quebec" C39.38

"Writes on Debt Problem; Canadian Economist Would Have Us Cancel but Not Reduce" C31.4

Writing A96, B18, C39.50, E29.13–5, E32.9, E33.22, E36.32

"Writing and Teaching English" E29.13–5

*The Writings of Mark Twain* B11

"The Written Word" E36.32

*Xmas Convivial and Pleasant at No. 19 Redpath Crescent* A51

"A Xmas Examination" C12.24

"Xmas from a Writer's Point of View" L20.2

"The Yahi-Bahi Oriental Society of Mrs. Rasselyer-Brown" A16, A21, A55, A107, C14.17

"Yarmouth" J43.97

"A Year at College As Revealed by the Newer Journalism" C26.52

"A Year at College As Revealed in the Newer Comic Journalism" A52, A76

"The Yellow Peril A Very Real One Says Prof. Leacock" C9.2

"Young at Seventy: How to Beat the Game Instead of Beating Yourself" C26.26

Yukon C10.18, J43.98

"Yukon Territory" J43.98

*Yumoristycheskie rasskazy* H54

Zamarovksy, Vojtěch H8, H11

Zvi, J. H38